From Van Eyck to Bruegel

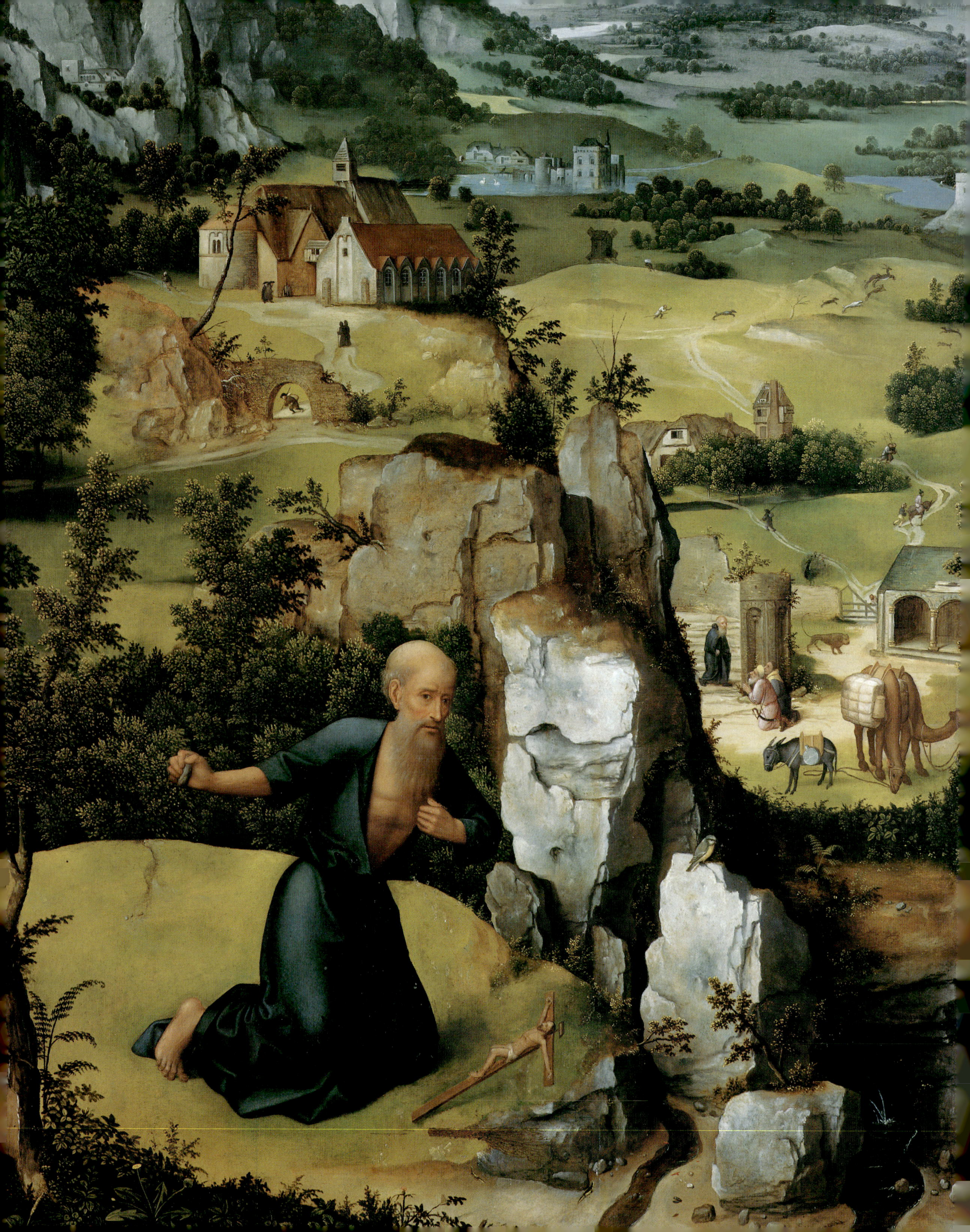

From Van Eyck to Bruegel

Early Netherlandish Painting in The Metropolitan Museum of Art

Edited by Maryan W. Ainsworth and Keith Christiansen

with contributions by Maryan W. Ainsworth, Julien Chapuis, Keith Christiansen, Everett Fahy, Nadine M. Orenstein, Véronique Sintobin, Della C. Sperling, and Mary Sprinson de Jesus

The Metropolitan Museum of Art, New York

Distributed by Harry N. Abrams Inc., New York

This volume has been published as a catalogue of key works in the collection of early Netherlandish paintings in The Metropolitan Museum of Art, New York. Other paintings in this collection are treated in a less complete way in a section at the back of the book, where they are illustrated and captioned. The book also serves to accompany "From Van Eyck to Bruegel: Early Netherlandish Painting in The Metropolitan Museum of Art," the exhibition of those works shown at the Museum (together with the loans listed on page x) from September 22, 1998, to January 3, 1999.

The exhibition is made possible in part by The Kossak Family Foundation.

This publication is made possible in part by The Andrew W. Mellon Foundation.

Published by The Metropolitan Museum of Art, New York

John P. O'Neill, Editor in Chief
Carol Fuerstein, Editor
Bruce Campbell, Designer
Gwen Roginsky and Hsiao-ning Tu, Production

New photography at The Metropolitan Museum of Art by Bruce Schwarz, Juan Trujillo, and Susanne Cardone, the Photograph Studio, The Metropolitan Museum of Art, New York

Set in Adobe Garamond and Centaur by Professional Graphics, Rockford, Illinois

Separations by Professional Graphics, Rockford, Illinois

Printed and bound by Arnoldo Mondadori, S.p.A.

Jacket/cover illustration: Hans Memling, detail, *The Annunciation*, cat. no. 12

Frontispiece: Joachim Patinir, detail, *The Penitence of Saint Jerome*, cat. no. 88

Library of Congress Cataloging-in-Publication Data

Metropolitan Museum of Art (New York, N.Y.)
From Van Eyck to Bruegel: early Netherlandish painting in the Metropolitan Museum of Art / edited by Maryan W. Ainsworth and Keith Christiansen; with contributions by Maryan W. Ainsworth . . . [et al.].
p. cm.
Catalog of an exhibition held at the Metropolitan Museum of Art, Sept. 22, 1998–Jan. 3, 1999.
Includes bibliographical references and index.
ISBN 0-87099-870-6 (hc.) — ISBN 0-87099-871-4 (pbk.). — ISBN 0-8109-6528-3 (Abrams)
1. Panel painting, Flemish—Exhibitions. 2. Panel painting—15th century—Flanders—Exhibitions. 3. Panel painting—16th century—Flanders—Exhibitions. 4. Panel painting—New York (State)—New York—Exhibitions. 5. Metropolitan Museum of Art (New York, N.Y.)—Exhibitions. I. Ainsworth, Maryan Wynn. II. Christiansen, Keith. III. Title
ND669.F5M47 1998
759.9493'074'7471—dc21 98-22196
CIP

Contents

Director's Foreword

This exhibition has two principal objectives: to put the Metropolitan Museum's extraordinary collection of early Netherlandish painting at center stage and, in so doing, to reexamine the qualities that make the period from Van Eyck to Bruegel one of the pivotal moments in the history of Western art. An in-house exhibition of this sort could only be attempted at the Metropolitan, which possesses a collection of early Netherlandish paintings that is the most comprehensive in this hemisphere and among the most distinguished in the world. It includes one hundred and forty works representing almost every major painter—the most conspicuous exceptions are perhaps those of Hieronymus Bosch, Lucas van Leyden, Pieter Coeck van Aelst, Jan van Scorel, and Pieter Aertsen. The Museum has four, six, and even sixteen panels by some masters, offering a rare overview of their production; there are four panels by Petrus Christus, six by Hans Memling, sixteen plus one miniature by Gerard David, and seven by Joos van Cleve. Just as notably, the collection comprises virtually every type of painting carried out during this century and a half of achievement, revealing the variety of functions that those works served: folding altarpieces for public display, portraits intended to stand in isolation or as parts of diptychs and triptychs, small panels for private devotion, and several works that reflect the rising taste for secular painting in the fifteenth and sixteenth centuries.

That the Museum's holdings should be so rich is all the more remarkable when we recall how few early Netherlandish paintings of the first order were available at the late date the Metropolitan began collecting them. It is worth noting that when, in 1929, a "Loan Exhibition of Flemish Primitives" was held at Kleinberger Galleries in New York, the eminent scholar Max J. Friedländer observed that "private collections in the United States are richer than the public ones." And, indeed, the Metropolitan owes much of its strength in this area to the generosity of New York collectors: Henry G. Marquand, Benjamin Altman, Michael Friedsam, Jules Bache, Mary Stillman Harkness, Robert Lehman, and Jack and Belle Linsky, among others. Without them the holdings would lack the depth and scope that are the marks of a truly great collection. Marquand set the stage with his gift in 1891 of Petrus Christus's jewel-like *Lamentation*, while it is to Altman's bequest in 1913 that we owe the extraordinary selection of paintings by Memling—easily the most popular early Netherlandish painter in the nineteenth and early twentieth centuries. Altman's donation included Memling's extraordinary *Tommaso Portinari* and *Maria Baroncelli*—among the masterpieces of early Netherlandish portraiture—as well as the the same artist's beautiful *Virgin and Child with Saints Catherine of Alexandria and Barbara.* Friedsam's name is perhaps most commonly associated with the magical *Annunciation* by an artist from the circle of Van Eyck (possibly Petrus Christus), but in fact he bequeathed no fewer than twenty-four early Netherlandish paintings to the Metropolitan—the largest gift of works of the period bestowed by any single donor. These included Rogier van der Weyden's haunting portrait of Francesco d'Este and Quentin Massys's stern *Portrait of a Woman.* The pattern established between 1891 and 1932 continued in the ensuing years, the most splendid recent gifts being those of Robert Lehman, in 1975, and Jack and Belle Linsky, in 1982.

Curators were not idle. During the same period they succeeded in purchasing an astonishing group of masterpieces: Bruegel's unforgettable *Harvesters*, obtained in 1919 from the heirs of a Brussels collector on a hunch that what was called a school piece might be a lost original by Bruegel himself; the miraculously detailed diptych by Jan van Eyck, acquired through Knoedler from the Soviet government in 1933; and the dazzling triptych by Patinir, sold to the Museum in 1936 by the monastery of Kremsmünster to which it had been given by Emperor Leopold I of Austria. In 1956 the keystone to the collection, Robert Campin's *Merode Altarpiece*, was purchased for The Cloisters. Through these outstanding acquisitions the topography of the Metropolitan's expanding collection, which is particularly strong in paintings from the southern Netherlands of the period 1425 to 1520, gained clarity and relief.

Remarkably, the early Netherlandish collection has never been shown together, with the result that its full range and depth have not been fully appreciated. It is, in fact, necessary to visit three collections in the main building and to make a pilgrimage to The Cloisters in Fort Tryon Park to gain an idea of the extraordinary richness of the Metropolitan's holdings in this area. And while a catalogue of the Linsky Collection appeared in 1982 and another devoted to the early Netherlandish paintings in the Robert Lehman Collection was published this year, the main collection was last catalogued in 1947, before some of our most remarkable pieces were acquired. The publication of the present volume, which includes a generous selection of over a hundred of the most important paintings from the various collections, is, therefore, a landmark event.

Like the exhibition, this catalogue is divided along thematic lines that have been chosen with a view to the strengths of the Metropolitan's holdings as well as to key areas of artistic endeavor. There are sections on religious painting, portraiture, workshop practice, Gerard David, and Bruegel's *Harvesters*—an organization that will allow visitors to encounter the collection in a fashion not possible in the installations in the permanent galleries. There are times when the permanent holdings of museums seem to play second fiddle to loan exhibitions. Here the permanent collection has become the subject of an exhibition, and loans have been rigorously restricted to works that complete or enhance our understanding of paintings in the Metropolitan. Among these loans are the lateral wings of altarpieces in the collection or pendants to portraits owned by the Museum. Others are drawings or manuscript illuminations that enlarge upon or clarify the creative process of an artist. And there is a group of devotional books and objects chosen to underscore the way some of the pictures were perceived by contemporary viewers. We would like to express our deep gratitude to all lenders for affording rare opportunities to see pictures in the permanent collection in a fuller context.

On behalf of the Museum, I extend my sincere thanks to The Kossak Family Foundation for its generous support of the exhibition. The Museum is extremely grateful for the assistance provided by The Andrew W. Mellon Foundation in support of this publication. The catalogue has been written exclusively by staff members, who have worked with Hubert von Sonnenburg and the Department of Paintings Conservation. Every early Netherlandish painting in the collection has been examined by the conservators, and some pictures that have languished in the storerooms have been transformed through cleaning and restoration and will now find a place on permanent display. The result of all this work is a re-presentation as well as a scholarly reassessment of the Museum's holdings, and it is our hope that, like the fabled early Netherlandish exhibition held in Bruges in 1902, this show will excite the imagination of visitors and ignite new interest in this fascinating school of European painting.

Philippe de Montebello
Director

Acknowledgments

The authors would like especially to recognize the close collaboration of Hubert von Sonnenburg and his staff in the Department of Paintings Conservation: George Bisacca, Nicholas Dorman, Charlotte Hale, Christopher McGlinchey, Dorothy Mahon, Kirsten Younger, and Katherine Blaney-Miller. Research would have been far more difficult without the work of Lisa M. Murphy, Victoria Reed, and Aileen Wang. Alison Gilchrest assisted with several of the illustrations. The aid and support of William D. Wixom, Barabara Drake Boehm, and Timothy B. Husband of the Department of Medieval Art and The Cloisters were indispensable. Among the many others who provided help or information of one kind or another, the authors would like to thank: Elizabeth A. R. Brown, Edwin Buijsen, Lorne Campbell, Katria Czerwoniak, Alphonse L. Dierick, Clario di Fabio, George Fletcher, John Hand, Egbert Haverkamp-Begemann, Lynn Jacobs, Michael Jonker, Laurence B. Kanter, Ronda Kasl, Thomas Kren, Deidre Larkin, Donald J. LaRocca, Walter Liedtke, Philippe Lorentz, Katherine C. Luber, Jessie McNab, M. Giuseppina Malfatti, Susan T. Moody, Hélène Mund, Michael Pächt, Wolfgang Prohaska, Erich Schleier, Margaret Scott, Ron Spronck, Carl Brandon Strehlke, Cyriel Stroo, Pascale Syfer-d'Olne, Mark Tucker, William Voelkle, Roger Wieck, and Martha Wolff.

For the work on the catalogue, our gratitude is extended to: John P. O'Neill, Editor in Chief; Carol Fuerstein, Editor; Jean Wagner, bibliographer; Gwen Roginsky, Chief Production Manager; Hsiao-ning Tu, Production Associate; Bruce Campbell, designer; Robert Weisberg, Computer Specialist; and Bruce Schwarz, Juan Trujillo, and Susanne Cardone, Photographers. For assistance with the exhibition we thank: Daniel Kershaw, Exhibition Designer; Sue Koch, Senior Graphic Designer; Zack Zanolli, Lighting Designer; Linda M. Sylling, Associate Manager for Operations and Special Exhibitions; Herbert M. Moskowitz, Chief Registrar; and Aileen K. Chuk, Registrar.

Lenders to the Exhibition

GERMANY
Hamburg, Hamburger Kunsthalle fig. 92

THE NETHERLANDS
Amsterdam, Rijksmuseum (*The Hague*, Mauritshuis) fig. 97
Rotterdam, Museum Boijmans Van Beuningen fig. 64

UNITED STATES
Cambridge, Massachusetts, Harvard College, Harvard University Art Museums fig. 50
Houston, Museum of Fine Arts fig. 63
New York, The Pierpont Morgan Library figs. 42, 90; Morgan M.649, M.421
Philadelphia, Philadelphia Museum of Art fig. 95
Washington, D.C., National Gallery of Art fig. 99
Williamstown, Massachusetts, Sterling and Francine Clark Art Institute fig. 67

Private collections figs. 66, 79, 88, 100

Notes to the Reader

Abbreviated references are used throughout. For full listings, see the bibliography. The references listed in each catalogue entry are selected. Suggested readings are listed at the front of the bibliography. Within each section works are arranged chronologically. For reproductions of details of works not included in the relevant catalogue entries, see the index. Paintings in the collection that are not catalogued appear in the Additional Works section.

Unless otherwise noted, when the pictures are reproduced framed the frames are original. Wherever possible, paintings are reproduced cropped to their original edges. In all entries height precedes width. Diameter is signified by d. Measurements are given in centimeters and to the nearest eighth of an inch. Unless otherwise noted, artists listed in the headings of catalogue entries are Netherlandish. **Attributed to** indicates a certain amount of caution in ascribing the work to a particular artist. **Workshop of** indicates that the picture was executed in the artist's studio and therefore probably within his lifetime. **Assistant** and **collaborator** indicate participation by another artist: in the first case in the workshop, in the second by an independent painter. **Follower of** indicates similarity of style to the work of the artist cited but may imply execution at a significant distance in time or place of origin from that artist's oeuvre. **Copy after** indicates that the work is based on a known or presumed prototype.

Entries are signed with authors' initials, which are listed in the following key.

MWA Maryan W. Ainsworth
VS Véronique Sintobin
DCS Della C. Sperling
MSdJ Mary Sprinson de Jesus

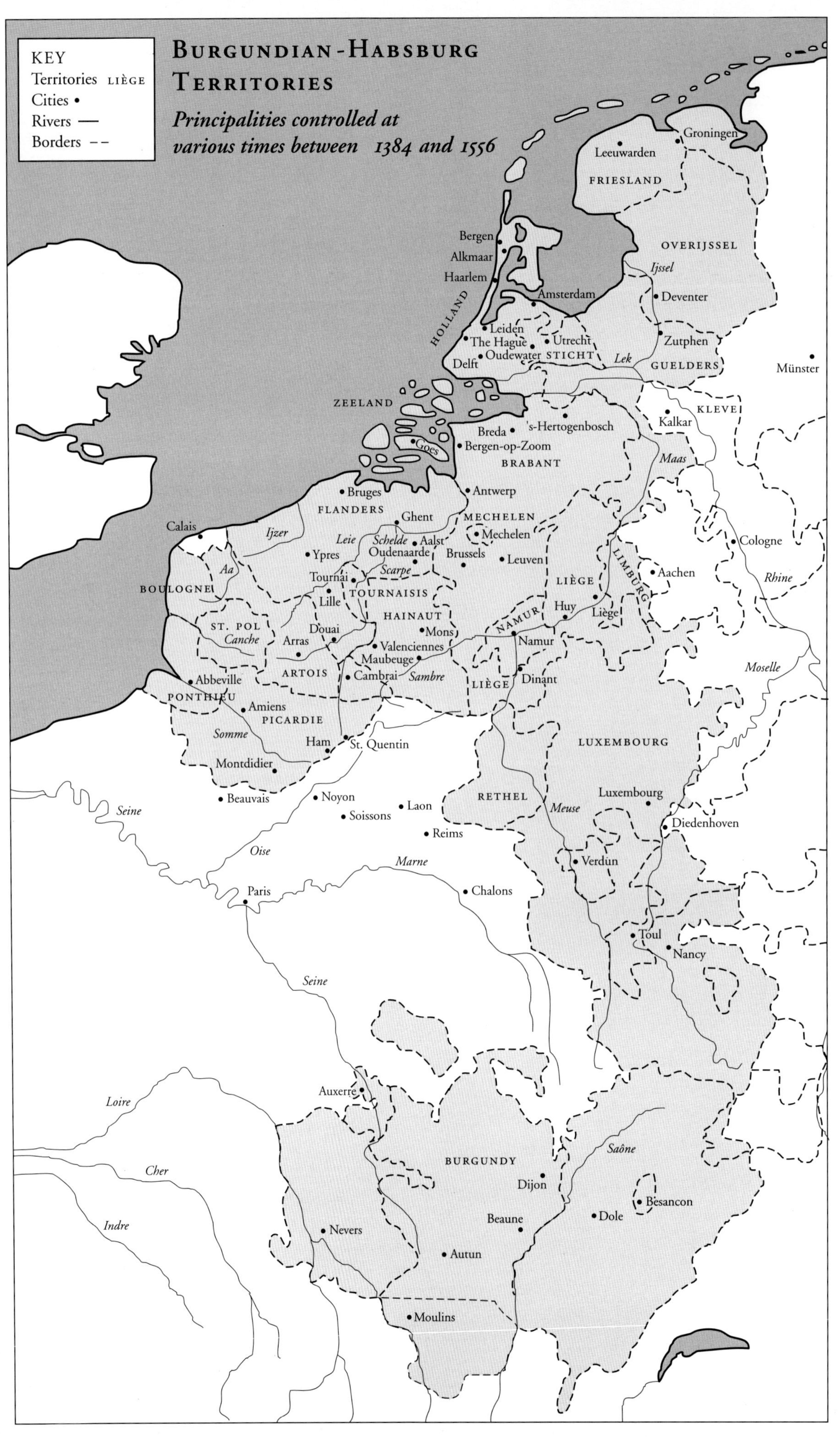

BURGUNDIAN-HABSBURG TERRITORIES
Principalities controlled at various times between 1384 and 1556
KEY
Territories LIÈGE
Cities •
Rivers —
Borders --
Groningen
Leeuwarden
FRIESLAND
OVERIJSSEL
Bergen
Alkmaar
Haarlem
Ijssel
Amsterdam
Deventer
HOLLAND
Leiden
The Hague
Utrecht
Zutphen
Oudewater
STICHT
Delft
Lek
GUELDERS
Münster
ZEELAND
KLEVE
Kalkar
Breda
's-Hertogenbosch
Goes
Bergen-op-Zoom
BRABANT
Maas
Bruges
Antwerp
FLANDERS
Ghent
MECHELEN
Calais
Ijzer
Mechelen
Cologne
Leie
Schelde
Aalst
Ypres
Oudenaarde
Brussels
Leuven
Aa
Scarpe
LIMBURG
Aachen
Tournai
Rhine
BOULOGNE
LIÈGE
TOURNAISIS
Lille
Huy
Liège
HAINAUT
ST. POL
Douai
NAMUR
Canche
Mons
Arras
Namur
Valenciennes
Moselle
Maubeuge
ARTOIS
Cambrai
Sambre
Dinant
Abbeville
LIÈGE
PONTHIEU
Amiens
PICARDIE
LUXEMBOURG
Somme
Ham
St. Quentin
Montdidier
RETHEL
Luxembourg
Noyon
Beauvais
Laon
Meuse
Seine
Soissons
Diedenhoven
Reims
Oise
Verdun
Marne
Paris
Chalons
Toul
Nancy
Seine
Auxerre
Loire
Saône
BURGUNDY
Cher
Dijon
Besancon
Dole
Indre
Beaune
Nevers
Autun
Moulins

From Van Eyck to Bruegel

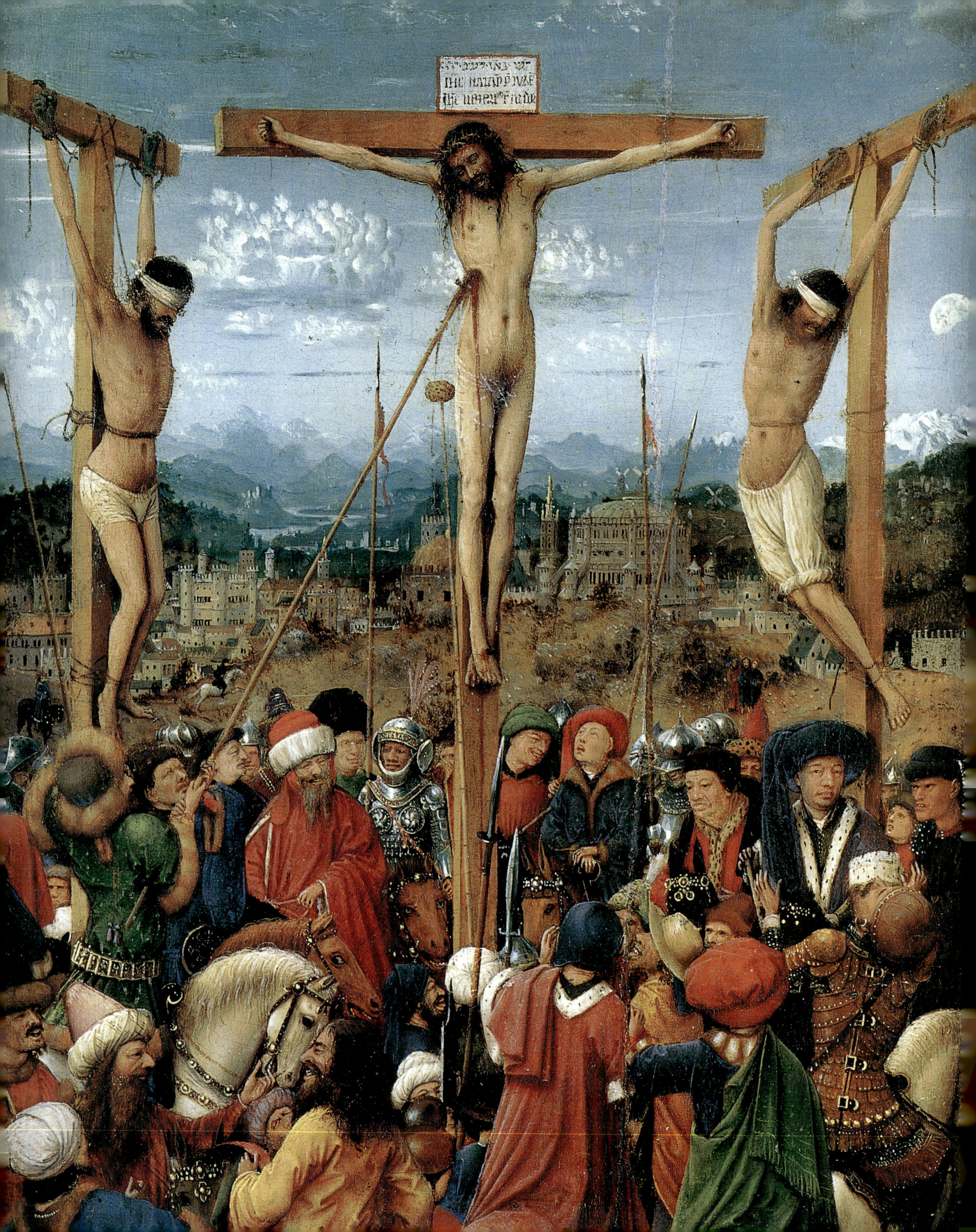

Early Netherlandish Painting: Shifting Perspectives

JULIEN CHAPUIS

In the summer months of 1902, over 35,000 visitors crowded through the halls of the Neo-Gothic Palais Provincial in Bruges to view an exhibition titled "Les Primitifs flamands et l'art ancien" (fig. 1). While the show included sculptures, tapestries, metalwork, and illuminated manuscripts, its emphasis lay on easel paintings. The title suggested that the presentation would survey the flowering of painting that occurred throughout the southern Lowlands in the fifteenth century. However, despite the loan of many pictures from public and private collections in Belgium and elsewhere, the exhibition clearly championed three painters from Bruges itself whose works were found in local collections. The towering figure of Jan van Eyck was represented, among others, by half a dozen pictures, including his stern and astonishingly uncompromising portrayals of Adam and Eve, then separated from the Ghent Altarpiece (fig. 2),[1] his monumental *Virgin with Canon George van der Paele* (fig. 4), and a severe portrait of his wife, Margaret, both from the Groeningemuseum in Bruges, as well as the two jewel-like paintings from the Koninklijk Museum voor Schone Kunsten in Antwerp, the *Saint Barbara* and the *Virgin and Child at the Fountain* (fig. 10), and the *Portrait of a Man*, now in Bucharest.[2] Some twenty works, among them the harrowing *Justice of Cambyses* panels (fig. 16), gave ample illustration of the genius of a newly rediscovered painter, Gerard David. Nonetheless, the star of the exhibition was unquestionably Hans Memling: thirty-eight panels attributed to him (see figs. 1, 3) displayed the devout, calm nature of his art, which had caused him to become the most popular of all Netherlandish painters; his superb portraits of Tommaso Portinari and Maria Baroncelli (cat. no. 27) were lent by Léopold Goldschmidt of Paris.[3] The accidents of securing loans, combined with an undeniable local chauvinism, worked to the detriment of artistic centers other than Bruges. Rogier van der Weyden, whose activity centered in Brussels and who was praised in fifteenth-century accounts as the equal of Van Eyck, was not represented by major works. Although the *Death of the Virgin*, a masterpiece by Hugo van der Goes, the visionary genius from Ghent, hung in the Groeningemuseum in Bruges, a critic described him as unworthy of attention.[4]

Looking back from a vantage point of almost a century, the Bruges exhibition still stands as a milestone. The show acts as a temporal hinge in the study and display of early Netherlandish painting, midway between its rediscovery in the early nineteenth century and the present exhibition at the Metropolitan Museum at the end of the twentieth. That first exhibition would not have been possible without the considerable advances in connoisseurship and archival research of the nineteenth century,

Opposite: Jan van Eyck, enlarged detail, upper half, *The Crucifixion* (cat. no. 1)

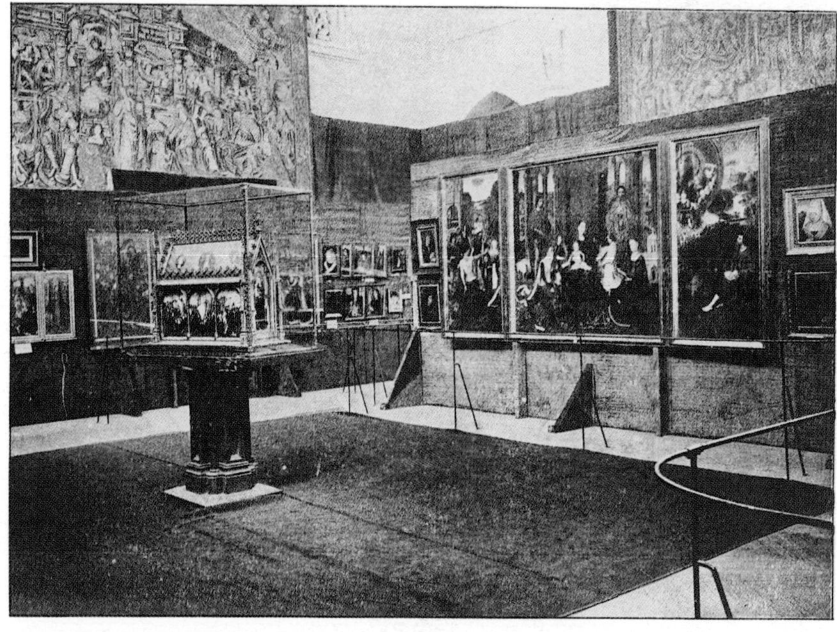

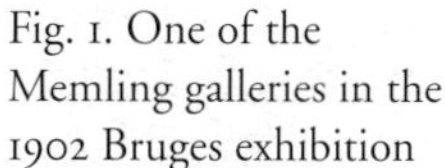

Fig. 1. One of the Memling galleries in the 1902 Bruges exhibition

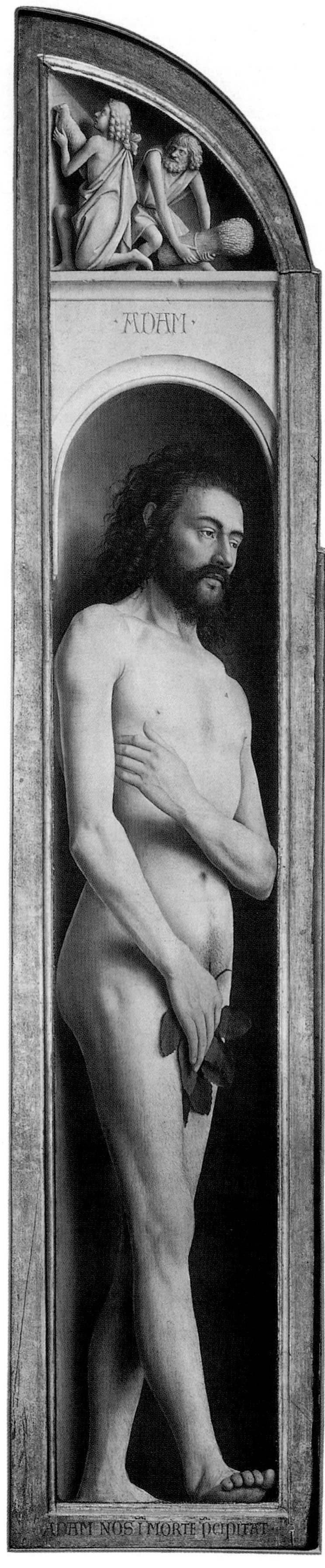

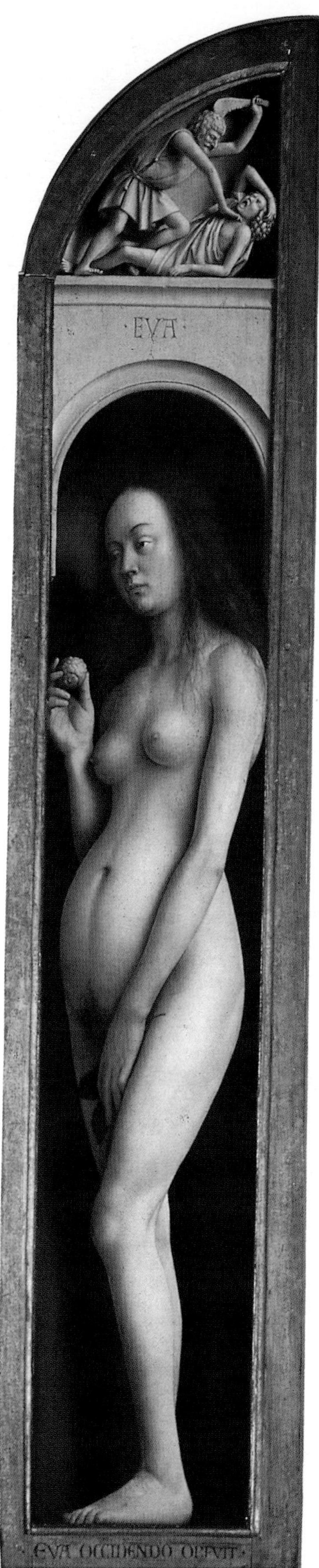

and it clearly reflected the strong nationalism that flavored much art-historical writing until World War I. In addition, the show was of paramount importance to scholars whose influence is still felt today. To use a simile favored by Netherlandish painters themselves, the Bruges exhibition functioned like a convex mirror, reflecting the past and pointing toward the future. In order to provide a historical perspective for the present exhibition, this essay traces the changing critical fortunes of early Netherlandish painting from its rediscovery in the early nineteenth century to the 1902 Bruges exhibition. It then examines the contribution of a few scholars influenced by it and reviews avenues of study that have been favored in recent decades. And finally it proposes that an investigation of how early Netherlandish painting engages the viewer might prove yet another rewarding approach to this art.

Connoisseurship, Archival Research, and Early Netherlandish Painting (1800–1902)

While the admiration for Italian art, especially the works of Leonardo da Vinci, Raphael, and Correggio, was widespread throughout Europe, the rediscovery of early Netherlandish painting is inextricably linked to issues of emerging nationalism. As such, it is an indirect consequence of the great upheavals that swept the Continent after the French Revolution. Although in the fifteenth century the southern Lowlands belonged to the duchy of Burgundy, a powerful state stretching from Dijon, in eastern France, to the North Sea, in the nineteenth century the painted production of that region was appropriated by both Germans and Belgians as an embodiment of their respective national cultures.

The Louvre, the first national museum, played an important role in the rediscovery of early Netherlandish painting. The king's former residence in Paris was opened to the public as a museum of

Fig. 2. Hubert and Jan van Eyck, *Adam* and *Eve*, lateral interior wings, Ghent Altarpiece, completed 1432. Oil on wood, Sint-Baafs (Saint Bavo's), Ghent

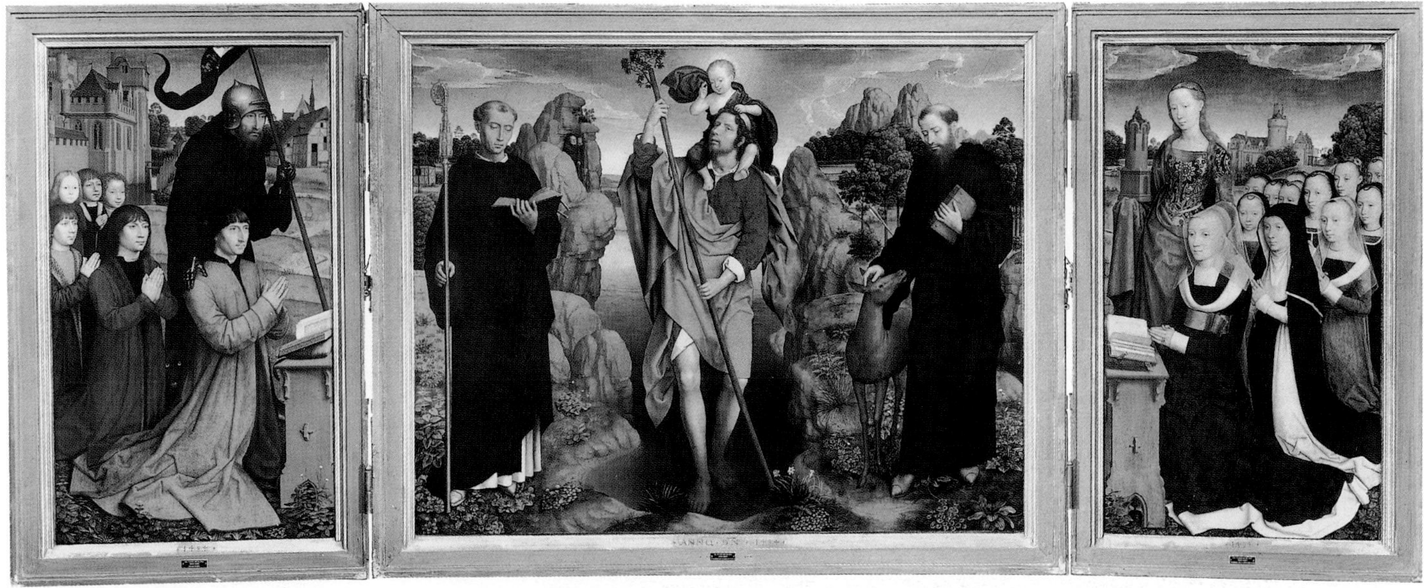

Fig. 3. Hans Memling, Saint Christopher Triptych (Moreel Triptych), dated 1484. Oil on wood, Groeningemuseum, Bruges

paintings in 1793, the fourth year of the Revolution.[5] The French royal collection, which had been moved from Versailles, reflected the then conventional taste, with its emphasis on such High Renaissance and Baroque masters as Leonardo, Raphael, Correggio, Titian, Rubens, Van Dyck, and Poussin. Only one early Netherlandish painting had found its way into royal possession: David's *Marriage at Cana*, then ascribed to Van Eyck, one of the few fifteenth-century northern artists whose name had not fallen into oblivion. In an effort to educate the people through exposure to art, the revolutionaries established the Commission Temporaire des Arts to select works in occupied territories for shipment to the Louvre.[6] After the conquest of the southern Lowlands by revolutionary troops in 1794, the exodus of numerous altarpieces by Rubens, Van Dyck, and Jacob Jordaens from Antwerp and other Flemish cities began. Although they did not fit in the accepted canon, a number of fifteenth-century paintings were sent to Paris as well; the criterion for their selection seems to have been their relatively large scale, which would ensure their visibility by crowds in the Grande Galerie of the Louvre. The central panels of Van Eyck's Ghent Altarpiece (fig. 18) left Sint-Baafs (Saint Bavo's) cathedral in that city, while his *Virgin with Canon George van der Paele* was removed from the Sint-Donaaskerk (the church of Saint Donatian) in Bruges. Two works by other Bruges masters were taken from that city: Memling's Moreel Triptych (fig. 3), which stood in the Sint-Juliaanshospitaal, and the *Justice of Cambyses* panels, which David had painted for the Town Hall. Paintings in the Grande Galerie were installed didactically according to *écoles*, a novel arrangement that had the merit of bringing the characteristics of each school to the fore.[7]

Among the many foreigners who traveled to Paris to admire the treasures gathered at the Louvre after the Treaty of Amiens was signed in 1802,[8] the German philosopher Friedrich Schlegel was to play a seminal role in reviving the appreciation of early Netherlandish painting.[9] Before arriving in Paris, in the summer of 1802, Schlegel had spent four months in Dresden. There he had become an enthusiastic admirer of Raphael and Correggio, both represented by masterpieces in that city's Gemäldegalerie. In Dresden Schlegel had befriended Ludwig Tieck, an ardent defender of early German painting.[10] In 1797, together with Wilhelm Wackenroder, Tieck had published the *Herzensergiessungen eines kunstliebenden Klosterbruders*, a short but influential essay that contributed

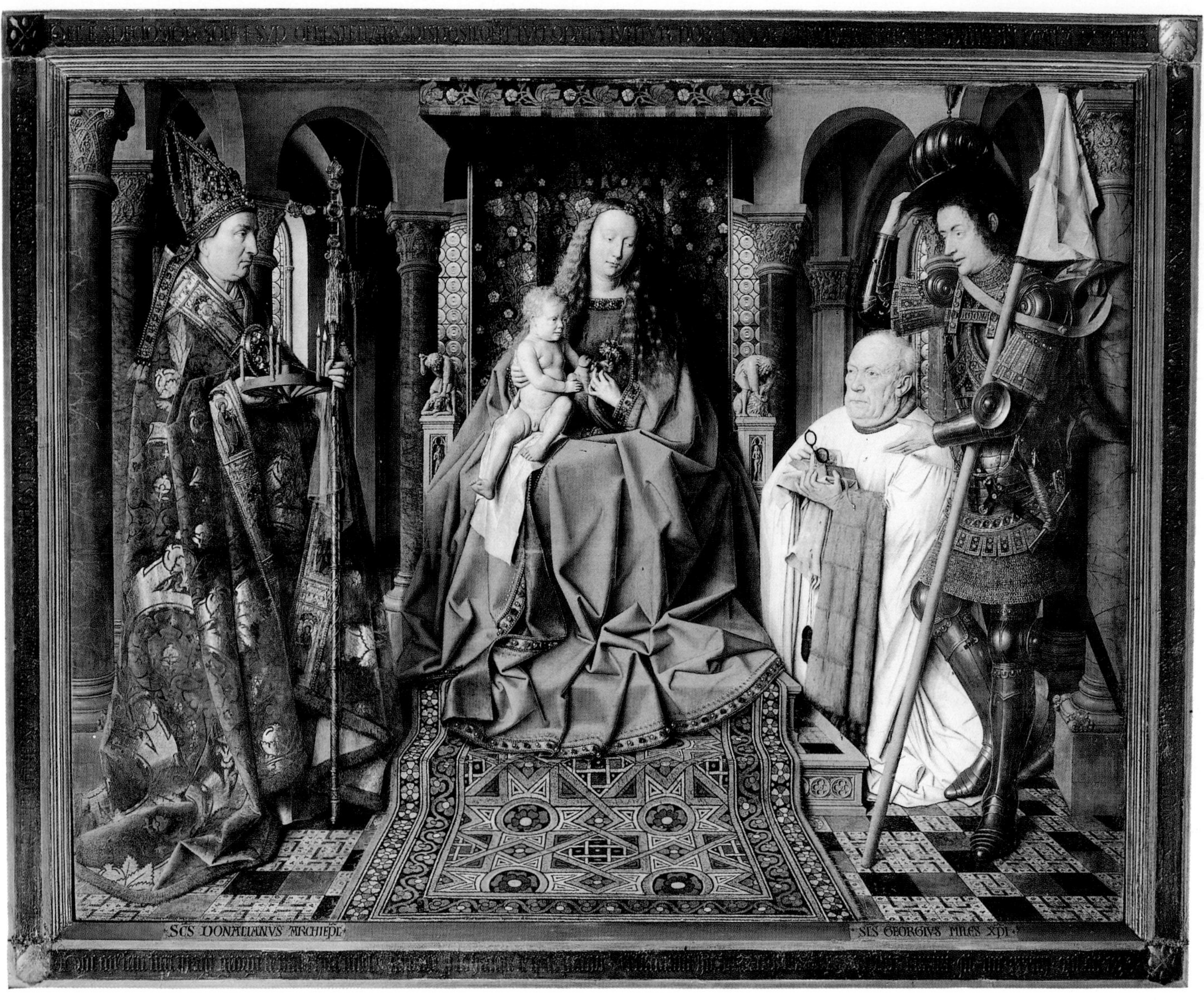

Fig. 4. Jan van Eyck, *Virgin with Canon George van der Paele*, dated 1436. Oil on wood, Groeningemuseum, Bruges

much to a revivified appreciation of northern painting. The text tells of an art-loving monk who visits a castle with a rich art collection, with as many works by Albrecht Dürer as by Raphael.[11] During the night, which he spends at the castle, the monk dreams that the painters are present in flesh and blood in front of their works. To his amazement, he notices that Dürer and Raphael are joining hands.[12] The message of this juxtaposition—that German painting is not inferior to Italian art—was not lost on his contemporaries, and certainly not on Schlegel.[13] Amid the Raphaels and Correggios at the Louvre, Schlegel was struck by the paintings gathered under the heading *École flamande:* not only the fifteenth-century works taken from the southern Lowlands but also a few Dürers and Hans Holbeins. His observations on the paintings, addressed to Tieck and published in 1803 and 1805, mark a new point in the appreciation of this art. In sharp contrast to conventional taste, Schlegel found the works of Van Eyck and Memling superior to those of Italian artists, even to Raphael's Sistine Madonna in Dresden, in their religious content, their spirituality, and their expression of Christian truth. Schlegel considered early Netherlandish painting to be German, hailing Van Eyck as the founder of the German school, because he seemed to have been a model for both Holbein and Dürer.[14]

This kind of emotional response, which combines devout piety and nationalist feeling, characterizes much Romantic writing on northern art at the beginning of the nineteenth century. It can be felt, for instance, in Goethe's works as well as in the correspondence of Melchior and Sulpiz Boisserée, two brothers from Cologne who assembled one of the earliest and finest collections of fifteenth-century painting (their prized holding was Rogier van der Weyden's altarpiece from the Pfarrkirche Sankt Columba (church of Saint Columba) in Cologne (fig. 5).[15] It also informs a book titled *Johann van Eyck und seine Nachfolger* (1822) by Johanna Schopenhauer, the philosopher's mother, whose main intent was to show that German culture flourished at an early date, and that Van Eyck's art is one of its most glorious manifestations.[16]

A second book on Van Eyck, which also appeared in 1822, broke new ground. Considered one of the first art-historical monographs, Gustav Waagen's *Hubert und Jan van Eyck* was published when the author, a nephew of Ludwig Tieck, was only twenty-eight years old. Waagen was indebted to the tradition of Schlegel and Schopenhauer—he states, for instance, that the Virgin in the central portion of the Ghent Altarpiece is in no way inferior to Virgins by Leonardo and Raphael;[17] however, he broke with his predecessors, who had often repeated untested legends, by combining his exceptionally sharp visual analyses of the paintings with a study of the historical sources that had survived.[18] Instead of calling Van Eyck a German, Waagen emphasized that the artist should be seen in a Netherlandish context, and further, that his works should be shown not in isolation but against the background of a continuous artistic development.[19]

The monograph did much to establish Waagen's reputation as a connoisseur—and it is connoisseurs and archivists above all who provided the building blocks of our knowledge of early Netherlandish painting. While the names of some northern artists were known, most were not, and many paintings in museums, churches, and private collections were too generously attributed to Van Eyck, Memling, Dürer, or Jan van Scorel. Since many works do not bear signatures—none of the panels ascribed to Robert Campin, Van der Weyden, or Van der Goes is signed—it is thanks to the discerning eyes of such men as Waagen that artistic oeuvres were made coherent through a process of constant revision. Much of the groundwork was laid in the early 1800s, before the advent of photography, when connoisseurs, who traveled from collection to collection, were required to combine a sharp eye with great visual memory. By applying classification methods derived from the natural sciences, they developed ways to define a painter's characteristics and to distinguish his individual style. By comparing works with a painting bearing a reliable signature—such as the *Virgin with Canon George van der Paele* by Van Eyck—they could assemble an oeuvre and ascribe it to a specific artist.[20]

Connoisseurship, the ability to assess quality and to make attributions based on style, is a prerequisite for museum curatorship since it is integral to acquiring and collecting artworks. The year after the publication of his Van Eyck monograph, Waagen was appointed to the governing body of the Gemäldegalerie in Berlin, of which he became the director in 1830.[21] During his long tenure he built the Berlin collection, which at the beginning of the century comprised mostly Italian Baroque and French Rococo pictures from the holdings of the Prussian king Frederick the Great, into one of the strongest repositories of early Netherlandish painting. At the end of his directorship, the Gemäldegalerie owned the wings of the Ghent Altarpiece—with the exception of the *Adam* and *Eve*, which remained in Brussels—two panels from Dieric Bouts's Sacrament Altarpiece, as well as three triptychs by Van der Weyden.[22] Connoisseurs were actively building the collections of other museums, and Charles Eastlake, director of the National Gallery in London, competed with his friend Waagen for acquisitions;[23] the Netherlandish paintings Eastlake purchased for London included two portraits by Van Eyck, two portraits by Campin, the *Magdalene Reading* by Van der Weyden, and a canvas showing the Entombment by Bouts; the most famous Flemish picture in the National Gallery, Van Eyck's Arnolfini portrait

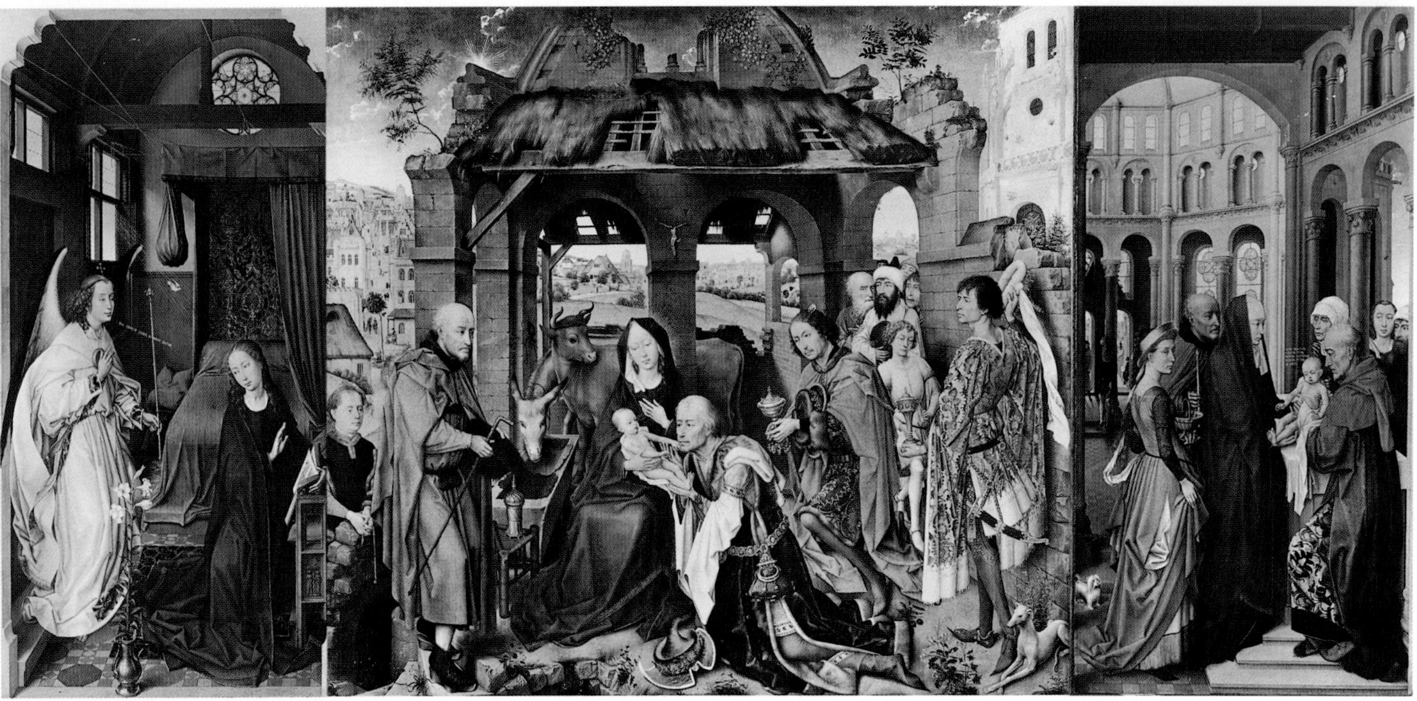

Fig. 5. Rogier van der Weyden, Columba Altarpiece, about 1450–55. Oil on wood, Alte Pinakothek, Bayerische Staatsgemäldesammlungen, Munich

(fig. 8), had been acquired before Eastlake's appointment.[24] In the same period Johann David Passavant, as keeper of the Städelsches Kunstinstitut in Frankfurt, secured four panels by Campin, the Medici Madonna by Van der Weyden, the Lucca Madonna by Van Eyck (fig. 26), and the *Virgin with Saints Jerome and Francis* by Petrus Christus.[25]

While connoisseurs traveled through Europe to compare paintings, assemble artistic oeuvres, and build collections, archivists were transcribing documents that told of forgotten artists or shed new light on the lives of known masters. Alphonse Wauters, for instance, demonstrated in 1846 that Vasari's mention of two artists named Roger—Roger of Bruges and Roger of Brussels—which had caused great confusion, actually referred to the same person, Rogier van der Weyden. Passavant ascribed a group of works to Rogier, including one of his masterpieces, the Columba Altarpiece, which earlier historians had given to Van Eyck. Gradually, scholars came to realize that Van der Weyden had not been an apprentice of Van Eyck in Bruges, as Vasari had reported, but of Campin in Tournai, as Alexandre Pinchart discovered in the 1870s.[26]

The most important of all archivists in the field of early Netherlandish painting was the Englishman James Weale.[27] A convert to Catholicism at seventeen, Weale was interested as much in Christian symbolism and liturgy as in Belgian churches. In 1855 he moved to Bruges, where he stayed for twenty-three years, and then moved back to London, returning to Bruges annually for visits. About 1860 he began his systematic researches in the Bruges archives, which have contributed enormously to our knowledge of the lives of the artists of this city. In 1861 he published a catalogue of the paintings in the Bruges Academy, which contains the first biography of Memling based on archival work. Weale's publications of the following years presented his findings on the lives of Petrus Christus, Jan Provost, and Adriaen Isenbrant. And in 1895 he published a monograph on David, whom he rediscovered. His book on Hubert and Jan van Eyck, published in 1908, remains an essential research tool because of the original documents it contains.[28]

Weale was also one of the leading forces behind the Bruges exhibition of 1902. In 1900 Paul Wytsman, a Belgian art critic, formulated the idea for an exhibition of early Netherlandish painting to be held in Brussels; he had recently visited shows with nationalistic undertones in Antwerp and Amsterdam that were devoted to Rubens and Rembrandt.[29] Because authorities in Ghent and Bruges refused to lend, for fear of damage both to the paintings and to tourism in their own cities, the organizing committee decided to move the venue to Bruges itself, where a number of great local artists, including Van Eyck, Memling, and David, were well represented in public collections. The major museums in London, Paris, Berlin, and Madrid sent only photographs of their paintings, and many works were borrowed from private owners. Weale, then regarded by many as the leading authority in the field of early Netherlandish painting, was invited to write the catalogue.[30] While the organizers, hailing works by Van Eyck and Memling as symbols of national identity, clearly intended the exhibition to be a celebration of Belgian culture, Weale was interested in promoting Flemish painting primarily because its "Christian feeling could help to rescue modern art from the pit of realism into which it had sunk."[31] Indeed, he singled out the devotional element as an essential characteristic of Flemish painting when he wrote in 1901, "John van Eyck saw with his eyes, Memlinc with his soul."[32] His enthusiasm for the pious quality of Memling's art calls to mind the writings of such German Romantics as Schlegel, who a century earlier had praised Memling's Moreel Triptych, then in the Louvre, for its sentiment.[33] Weale's championing of Memling was widely applauded, and with thirty-eight paintings in the exhibition, the artist occupied the *place d'honneur*.

The Bruges Exhibition and Its Influence

The exhibition made an impact on a number of scholars who were to exert a lasting influence on the study of early Netherlandish painting. One of them was the forty-year-old Belgian Georges Hulin de Loo, who published a *catalogue critique* of the pictures in the show in August 1902, while they were still on view. Weale's hands had been tied in writing the official catalogue because the organizing committee could accept no attributions but those provided by the owners of the works, most of them private collectors. Hulin, who did not have to spare their feelings, showed, for instance, that the *Enthronement of Saint Thomas à Becket*, a painting with a spurious Van Eyck signature lent by the duke of Devonshire (now National Gallery of Ireland, Dublin), was overpainted and had little to do with the artist responsible for the *Adam* and *Eve* and the *Virgin with Canon George van der Paele* hanging in the same gallery. Hulin's rejection of many of the official attributions established him as a leading connoisseur, a reputation he would maintain throughout the first half of the twentieth century.[34]

Another visitor to the Bruges exhibition was Max J. Friedländer, then curator at the Gemäldegalerie in Berlin, where he stayed until the Nazis forced him out of office in 1933. It was while working under Wilhelm von Bode in Berlin, with the collection gathered by Waagen, that he trained his exceptional eye. Like Waagen a century earlier, Friedländer became the best connoisseur of his time, and, again like Waagen, he saw several major works acquired for Berlin during his tenure: *Portrait of a Fat Man* and *Virgin and Child on a Grassy Bench* by Campin; *Portrait of Baudoin de Lannoy* by Van Eyck; *Portrait of a Lady* by Van der Weyden; *Christ in the House of Simon* by Bouts; and, most important, three masterpieces by that rarest of painters, Van der Goes, the *Adoration of the Shepherds*, the *Adoration of the Magi*, and the *Mourning Women*.[35] While the organizers of the Bruges exhibition were motivated primarily by a nationalistic impulse, and while Weale saw the Christian message of Netherlandish painting as its most important characteristic, Friedländer, like Hulin de Loo, was above all interested in matters of attribution. Before he saw the Bruges exhibition, he had devoted most of his efforts to the study of the graphic arts in Germany; after his visit, however, and until his death in 1957, he worked increasingly on issues of connoisseurship in early Netherlandish painting. His fourteen-volume *Die altniederländische Malerei*, published between 1924 and 1937, stands even today as the single most important piece of scholarship on Flemish painting of the fifteenth and sixteenth centuries.[36] Indeed, the justness of

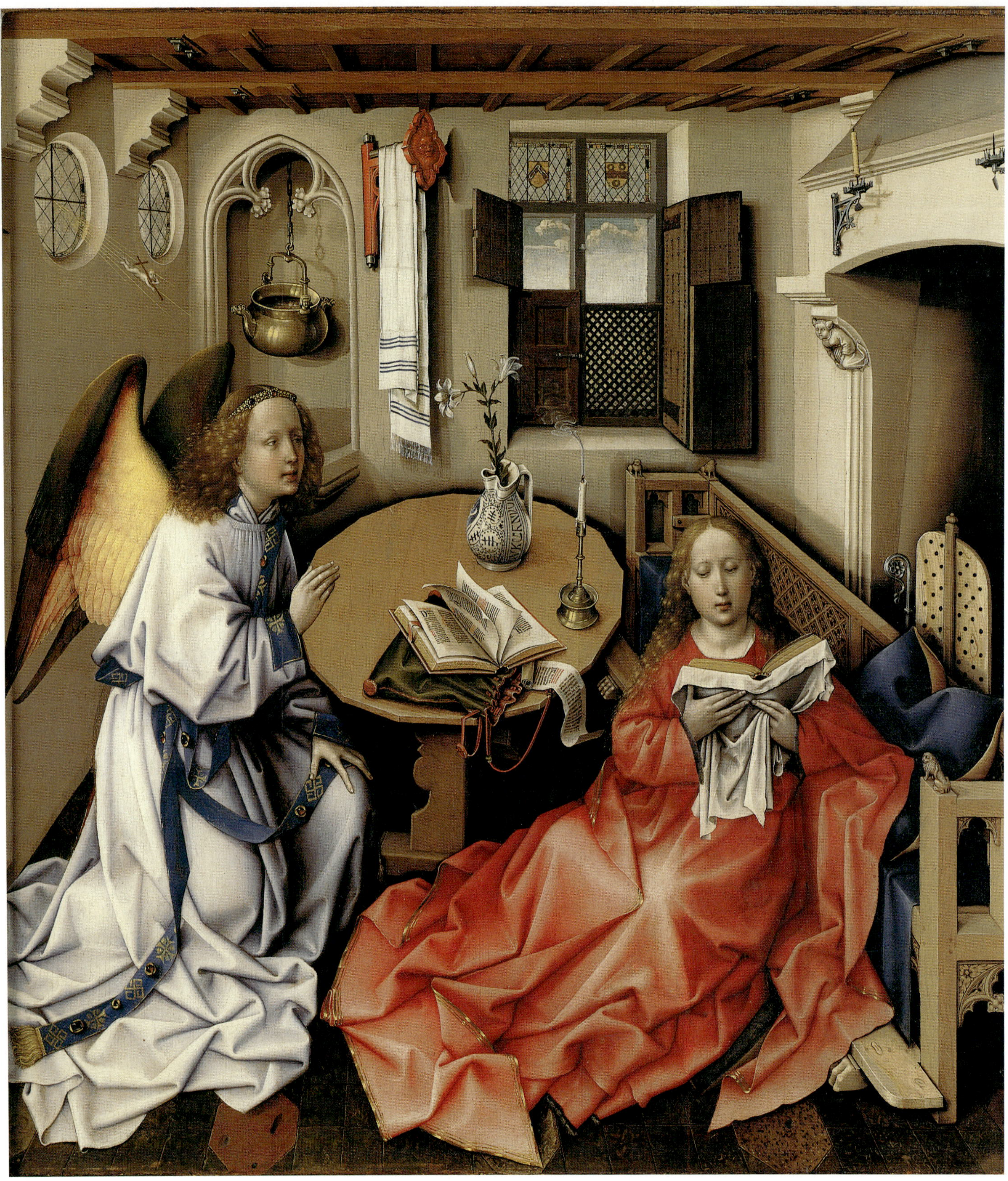

Fig. 6. Robert Campin, central panel, *The Annunciation Triptych (Merode Triptych)* (cat. no. 2)

his attributions has often been confirmed in recent years by scientific means of investigation.[37]

Dissent on the official line of the exhibition was voiced by the Belgian Hippolyte Fierens-Gevaert, who attacked its great star, Memling. Whereas Weale and the organizers had praised Memling for his calm and devout art, which they saw as the epitome of the Christian spirit, Fierens-Gevaert found Memling derivative, lacking in vigor, and mawkish, compared with Van Eyck, Van der Weyden, or Bouts. He termed Memling the Flemish Benozzo Gozzoli, who, although charming, did not measure up to Fra Angelico, Piero della Francesca, or Mantegna.[38] Until recent years this judgment has found acceptance;[39] indeed, a particularly condemning voice was that of the most influential art historian of the twentieth century, Erwin Panofsky, who referred to Memling as "that very model of a major minor master, . . . [who like the composer] Felix Mendelssohn . . . occasionally enchants, never offends and never overwhelms."[40]

Panofsky's immigration to the United States in 1934 marked the beginning of scholarly studies on fifteenth-century Flemish painting in this country, and his *Early Netherlandish Painting* (1953) defined the field well into the 1980s.[41] *Early Netherlandish Painting* was enormously appealing, especially in anglophone countries, because it was the first survey of the subject in English, and a survey of such weight that it suddenly shifted the center of Netherlandish studies from Europe to the East Coast of the United States. Moreover, judging from those fortunate enough to attend his lectures, Panofsky was a born teacher, and every page of the book bears witness to his formidable erudition, which, being a brilliant rhetorician, he wove effortlessly into compelling arguments. The enthusiasm for early Netherlandish painting awakened in America by the publication of Panofsky's survey was greatly increased three years later by the purchase of the *Merode Triptych* (cat. no. 2) for The Cloisters. The picture, which occupies a central position in Panofsky's book, had been jealously guarded in a private collection; it suddenly became accessible to numerous students of Flemish painting.

Although *Early Netherlandish Painting* is a multifaceted work that traces the roots of Van Eyck's naturalism to early-fifteenth-century manuscript illumination and analyzes the stylistic development of the major painters, its most influential aspect was the concept of disguised symbolism, to which Panofsky devoted an entire chapter.[42] The premise underlying this idea is that fifteenth-century painters struggled to reconcile the symbolic content of medieval art, often made explicit through inscriptions, with their conquest of the visible world.[43] According to Panofsky, they invested every detail of their paintings with symbolic meaning, which the beholder must decipher. Whereas in an earlier monument of scholarship, *The Autumn of the Middle Ages* (1919), the Dutch cultural historian Johan Huizinga had described the naturalistic rendering of reality in Flemish painting as "an immediate affection for the miracle of all things,"[44] Panofsky and his students saw it as a vehicle for complex theological programs. Noting that the portal in the Friedsam *Annunciation* (cat. no. 5) has both a Romanesque and a Gothic buttress, Panofsky interpreted this difference in architectural style as a reference to the antithesis between Judaism and Christianity.[45] Unraveling disguised symbolism in early Netherlandish painting became the focus of two generations of scholars. Yet there are problems with Panofsky's concept, among which is the term itself: if an object or a detail is commonly known as a reference to something else, why speak of *disguised* symbolism? The Virgin in the *Annunciation* of the *Merode Triptych* (fig. 6) is not sitting on the bench but on the ground in front of it; this is a rather obvious reference to her humility, all the more so since in Latin *humus*, ground, and *humilitas* derive from the same root.[46] Another difficulty arises from the fact that objects often carry more than one connotation. Thus, one interpretation states that the hearth in the *Merode Triptych* is a reference to the Jewish burnt offering soon to be replaced by the Christian Eucharist,[47] while another describes it as a reference to the chaste marriage of Mary and Joseph because the fire in it is extinguished.[48] How, then, is the viewer to establish which meaning is intended?

Not surprisingly the notion of disguised symbolism has come under attack in recent years. It has been argued, for example, that fifteenth-century sources offer no evidence that the patrons of these paintings engaged in the complex readings proposed by Panofsky and his followers.[49] On the contrary, Craig Harbison maintains that a more historically accurate approach to these paintings would examine their use as devotional objects.[50] The prevalent form of spirituality in fifteenth-century Flanders among the nobility and the wealthy burghers who commissioned paintings was what Harbison terms the prayer-book mentality.[51] Devotional literature encouraged the reader to meditate on aspects of the Scriptures, often episodes from Christ's Passion, and to mentally reenact them or visualize them. Although the monastic ideal was one of imageless meditation, images were tolerated, and eventually encouraged, as an aid to devotion and a necessary step that would ultimately be transcended when a higher form of spirituality was attained.[52] (This dependence on images also led to the fear of idolatry, which resulted in violent outbursts of iconoclasm in the northern Netherlands in the second half of the sixteenth century.[53]) Many paintings that include the donor witnessing an event from the Scriptures, Harbison argues, are depictions of visions, the experience of which was a primary religious goal for contemporary viewers.[54] The naturalism of Netherlandish painting can be interpreted as a means to enhance the efficacy of such images for private devotion. The patrons of the *Merode Triptych* (cat. no. 2; frontis., p. 138) are depicted without children, and it is attractive to think that witnessing Christ's conception in an interior not unlike the one in which they lived would have helped them visualize their hope for offspring. (They clearly are aware of what is happening on the middle panel, for the door at the top of the stairs is open and the key is on their side.)

The most cogent criticism of disguised symbolism is that presented by James Marrow in 1986. Questioning whether the conveying of symbolic meaning was really the central concern of, say, Van Eyck, Van der Weyden, or Van der Goes, Marrow points out that contemporary texts place greater emphasis on how works of art are to be experienced than on what they should represent. He posits that artists accordingly concentrated their attention on eliciting certain types of responses in their audience, on exploring "how art works," that is, "how it structures experience and interpretation" in the viewer.[55] Certainly, in devotional literature there was a shift away from focus on subject matter—for example, a particular event from the Passion—and toward the reaction expected of the reader.[56] Thus, the account of the Passion by the fourteenth-century author Ludolph of Saxony contains admonitions to the reader to empathize with the suffering of Christ. He interrupts his narrative of the Mocking of Christ to ask: "What would you do if you saw this? Would you not cast yourself upon our Lord, saying, 'Do not harm him so; behold, here am I, strike me instead?' . . . Compassionate [is] our Lord, for he is bearing all this torment for you; shed abundant tears and wash reverently away with them the spittle with which those profane wretches have besmeared his face. For who, hearing or considering this in his mind, . . . could refrain himself from tears?"[57]

Concurrently, fifteenth-century Netherlandish painters introduced in their works elements that direct the type of response expected of the viewer. A picture such as Christus's *Lamentation* (cat. no. 4) does just that.[58] The characters display a gamut of emotions, which the viewer is encouraged to duplicate: from the compassion of the Virgin for Christ's suffering, which is expressed through her fainting, to the concern of Mary Magdalene and Saint John for Mary, to the gentle consideration of Nicodemus and Joseph of Arimathea, who tender care to Christ's dead body, which seems to paraphrase Ludolph of Saxony's admonition to readers to wipe the spittle from Christ's face with their tears. Early Netherlandish paintings structure experience in different ways; some are clearly self-referential and make the viewer aware of standing in front of the picture. An important consequence of Marrow's argument is that a precise definition of meaning is necessarily elusive, since meaning is as much constructed by the beholder as by the creator of a painting. Each viewer's response is conditioned by personal beliefs, superstitions, experience of the world, knowledge of the past, and hope for the future. Investigating the diverse ways in which Netherlandish paintings engage the viewer is therefore one of the most promising new directions in the scholarship of the field.[59]

On a different level, our knowledge of early Netherlandish painting has been greatly increased in recent decades by advances in the scientific examination of works of art. While X-radiography of paintings had been carried out since the beginning of the twentieth century by scholars such as Christian Wolters in Vienna and Alan Burroughs at Harvard, it was the conservation treatment of the Ghent Altarpiece in the early 1950s that prompted the development of a methodology and the gradual recognition by scholars of Netherlandish painting that the results of technical studies often have a bearing on art-historical questions. Like many other major artworks, the Ghent Altarpiece suffered from the tribulations it was subjected to during World War II: its move in 1940 to Pau in France for safekeeping, its confiscation by the Germans in 1942, and its sojourns at Neuschwanstein and the Alt Aussee salt mine—where it was discovered by the Third American Army in 1945—had caused the paint in several areas to lift up.[60] In 1950, five years after its return to Sint-Baafs (Saint Bavo's) cathedral, the altarpiece was sent to the central laboratory of the Belgian museums, where its restoration was supervised by an international committee composed of conservators and art historians, including Panofsky. The ensuing report by the laboratory director, Paul Coremans, and his collaborators was published in 1953, the same year that Panofsky's *Early Netherlandish Painting* appeared.[61] The report acquainted a wide scholarly public with the physical construction of fifteenth-century Flemish paintings and with technical documents, such as paint cross sections, X-radiographs (which give a superimposed image of all the layers of a painting), and infrared photographs (which reveal the first layout on the prepared panel, known as the underdrawing, beneath the paint surface).

The contributions of technical studies to art history were spelled out in a groundbreaking dissertation of 1956 by Johannes Taubert, a German art historian and conservator who had studied with Coremans in Brussels.[62] One of the numerous discoveries was that aspects of a painter's technique, such as his underdrawing style or his buildup of paint layers, can be as individual as his treatment of light or his conception of space in the finished picture; technical studies, therefore, offer new tools with which to tackle questions of attribution.[63] Equally important, they offer insight into the sometimes complex creative processes that led to the final painted images. This information can, in turn, be compared to the results of archival research into workshop organization or patronage, whose findings they may support. For example, when infrared reflectography—a method of investigation that has a greater power of penetration than infrared photography and that also reveals underdrawing[64]—was used in a systematic study of the paintings ascribed to Rogier van der Weyden, it revealed variations in underdrawing style; these variations suggest a number of hands at work, confirming the image gleaned from the archives of Rogier as the head of a busy workshop with many assistants.[65]

Reflectography, X-radiography, and dendrochronology (the dating of wood panels) allow a better understanding of the production of copies in the fifteenth century; the information they yield is in accordance with archival evidence that over a third of the contracts between patrons and painters refer to an existing picture that the work to be executed must follow—revealing that our present-day emphasis on originality had little currency in the fifteenth century.[66]

Technical studies also throw light on the issue of artistic training in the lives of, say, Christus and Memling. Although Christus was long believed to be a pupil of Van Eyck's, reflectography of his paintings revealed that he had no knowledge of that master's underdrawing style, thereby confirming the evidence from documents that he arrived in Bruges only after the older artist's death.[67] Because of his direct borrowings from Van der Weyden, Memling is assumed to have been trained in Rogier's workshop in Brussels, despite the absence of documentary evidence. The relationship has been corroborated by the underdrawings of Memling's early works, which show the same mannerisms as Rogier's; since this aspect of Rogier's work was visible only in his workshop, it now seems certain that Memling was apprenticed to him[68] (see entry for cat. no. 10).

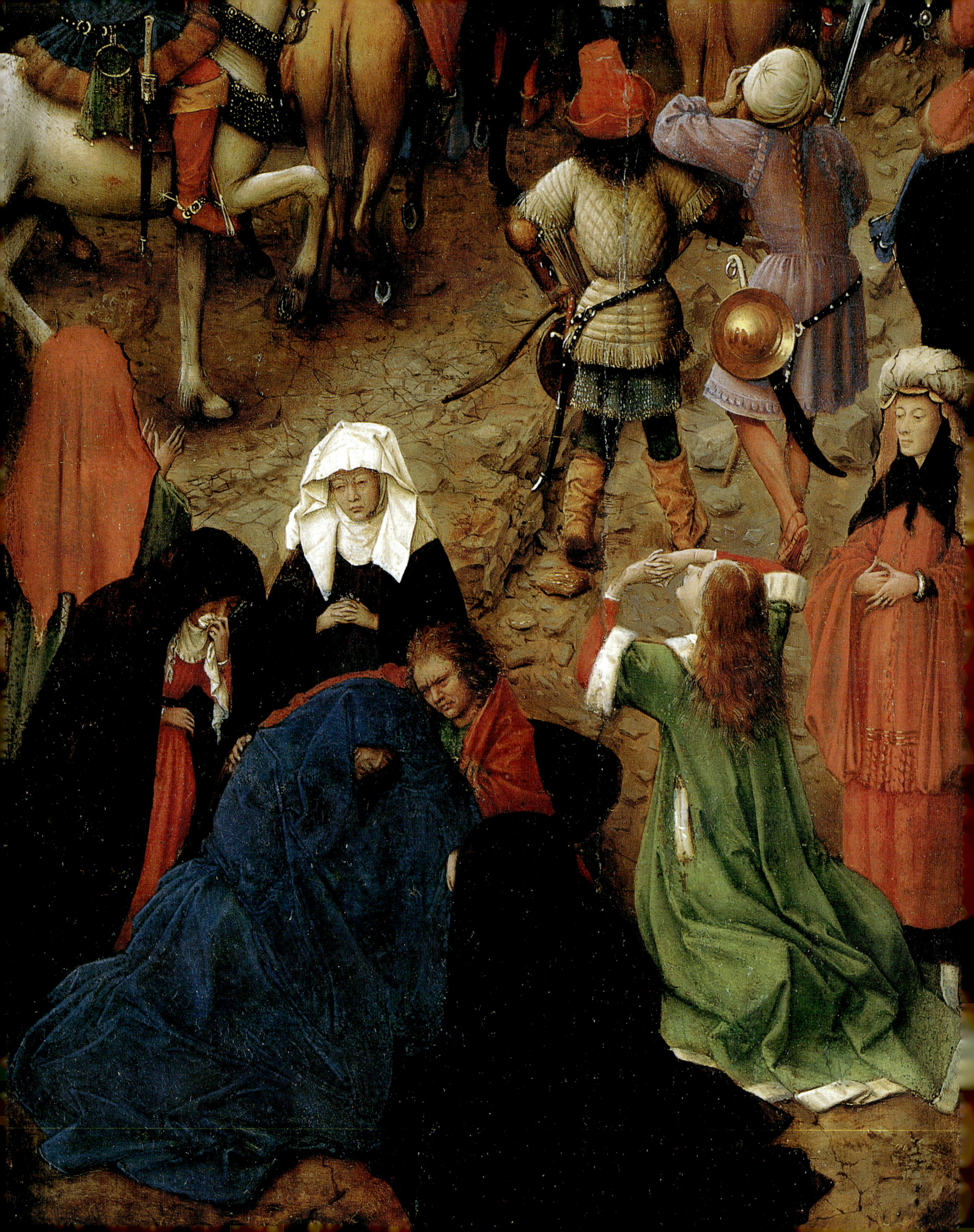

Visual Strategies of Flemish Painters

Like the Bruges show of 1902, the Metropolitan Museum exhibition offers a unique opportunity to take stock of our knowledge of early Netherlandish painting. It presents the sum of new researches that have led to fresh insights into how these works of art were commissioned and created, their original functions, and the way they were used. Several paintings underwent conservation treatment in preparation for our exhibition; rid of yellow varnish and discolored retouches, their original color schemes can now be fully appreciated. Many others were the subject of scientific examination, which yielded new information even on some of the Museum's most studied—and most popular—works by Campin, Van Eyck, and David.

While visitors cannot study the works on view with, say, infrared reflectography or X-radiography, they are encouraged to scrutinize the paintings carefully, as they were originally intended to be. In doing so, we might consider some visual strategies that Netherlandish painters used to engage the viewer in an active dialogue with their works. Most important is their use of naturalism, praised in contemporary writings, most of which are by Italians (see "The View from Italy" in this publication).[69] To humanist critics, Flemish paintings presented images that seemed so close to the real world as to be mistaken for it. Writing in 1449, Cyriac of Ancona described a painting, now lost, that he had admired in the collection of Prince Leonello d'Este in Ferrara. The picture was

> a most pious image [of the Descent from the Cross], with a large crowd of men and women about in deep mourning. All this is admirably depicted with what I would call divine rather than human art. There you could see those faces come alive and breathe which [the painter] wanted to show as living, and likewise the deceased as dead, and in particular, many garments, multicolored soldiers' cloaks, clothes prodigiously enhanced by purple and gold, blooming meadows, flowers, trees, leafy and shady hills, as well as ornate porticoes and halls, gold really resembling gold, pearls, precious stones, and everything else you would think to have been produced not by the artifice of human hands but by all-bearing nature itself.

Cyriac reports that the artist, Rogier van der Weyden, was considered "the outstanding painter of our time," second only to Jan van Eyck, "that famous man from Bruges, . . . the glory of painting."[70] Cyriac's enthusiasm for Netherlandish painting was shared by Bartolomeo Fazio, who, as a humanist at the court of Alfonso V of Aragon at Naples, knew firsthand the works of Van Eyck in the king's collection.[71]

A particular mark of appreciation for a Netherlandish painter appears in a complaint by Philip the Good, duke of Burgundy, addressed to his accountants in Lille in 1435. The accountants did not promptly pay the life pension that Philip had granted his court painter, Jan van Eyck, causing the artist to threaten to leave the duke's service. This, the duke writes, "would cause us great displeasure, for we would retain him for certain great works with which we intend henceforth to occupy him and we would not find his like more to our taste, one so excellent in his art and science."[72]

Looking at Van Eyck's *Crucifixion* (cat. no. 1; frontis., p. 2; fig. 7), we can appreciate Philip's description of the artist as unequaled in his "art and science," a judgment that seems to characterize Jan both as a virtuoso painter and as a brilliant intellect. The small painting is a tour-de-force achievement that creates a coherent narrative from dozens of figures, several on horseback, in front of a seemingly endless landscape. The bustling scene on Calvary occupies two-thirds of the narrow vertical field. Along the immediate lower edge of the picture the holy women and Saint John comfort Mary, who is crushed in despair. The crosses of Christ and the thieves tower over the crowd gathered in the middle ground. Behind the hill lies a fantastic view of Jerusalem, which juxtaposes domed buildings—perhaps references to the Dome of the Rock—with Western-style gabled

Opposite: Fig. 7. Jan van Eyck, enlarged detail, lower half, *The Crucifixion* (cat. no. 1)

houses, castles, and windmills. Farther back a river leads the eye into an infinite vista of hills and mountains covered with snow—which seems to reflect Jan's firsthand experience of the Alps, probably gained in 1426 on a diplomatic mission for Philip the Good that took him to Italy and the Holy Land.[73]

Like other paintings by Van Eyck, the *Crucifixion* reveals the complexity of human sight by offering an image that appears to duplicate our sensorial perception of the world, both close to us and at a distance. Its very size and its wealth of detail invite close scrutiny, which reveals the astonishing exactness of Van Eyck's observation: we recognize the stones in the foreground, a pair of boots made of soft leather, and the glistening spurs of a horseman as objects familiar from our world, and we forget for an instant that they are the products of the artist's brush. Onlookers ride magnificent horses, accurately rendered from different viewpoints, hitting the rocky terrain with their shining hooves. The costumes display the painter's unrivaled ability to render materials as diverse as velvet, fur, and the shining metal of armor. The clouds, both woolly and flat, are immediately recognizable from everyday experience. After looking for a few minutes, we realize that the thieves' hands, constricted by the ropes that bind them to their crosses, have turned black, as have the lips of the dead Christ. Using a technique known as atmospheric perspective, in which objects are painted in ever cooler greens and blues as they recede farther and farther, until their color becomes that of the sky, the artist has convinced us that the mountains are miles away, their contours blurred on the horizon. Thus, Van Eyck's powers of observation have been aptly compared to the combined effect of a microscope and a telescope.[74]

This acuity of vision is not an end in itself but a means toward a definite goal: by using terms borrowed from everyday life, the painter transposed the narrative of the Passion into the viewer's immediate realm of experience, thereby eliciting a strong emotional response. With its companion piece, the *Last Judgment*, the *Crucifixion* was either part of a diptych or a triptych, commissioned as an image for private devotion.[75] The original owner of the painting, presumably an individual of some learning, must have knelt regularly in front of it, reflecting on the events depicted while reciting prayers.

Van Eyck has succeeded in engaging us not only by presenting a world that seems borrowed from everyday experience but also by introducing figures that are metaphors for ourselves. A woman in green in the lower right foreground, perhaps Mary Magdalene, wrings her hands in despair while looking up at the crosses; like her, a woman with a red veil, on the left, watches the scene, her back turned to us. We are unable to see their faces, but our gaze follows theirs and is directed at Christ and the thieves, with whom we are meant to empathize. The two soldiers in the middle ground offer an obvious parallel to the viewer: the one in purple on the right looks up while resting his elbow on the shoulder of his companion, standing in front of Golgotha as we stand in front of the painting. A round copper shield hanging from the belt of the purple-robed soldier reflects the scene behind him, that is, the foreground with the mourning figures, and suggests our own space beyond it.

In his treatise *On Painting* the Italian Leon Battista Alberti describes the framed picture as "an open window in a wall," a much-quoted phrase that implies a movement into depth in the direction of the viewer's gaze.[76] Although no Netherlandish artists verbalized the concept of the picture in this way, a study of the works of art themselves reveals that the most useful metaphor for Netherlandish painting is probably a mirror. While vistas into seemingly endless space are not uncommon in the panels of Van Eyck, Van der Weyden, and Memling—the *Crucifixion* is a case in point—most Netherlandish paintings create a zone of tension between the picture plane and the viewer, in a direction contrary to his gaze, making him aware of his own position. This manipulation of space is achieved by various means, the most obvious being the inclusion of a painted mirror that reflects both the composition and, notionally, what is in front of it, thereby linking the space of the painting and that of the viewer. The round shield in the *Crucifixion* is an early example of this device: while it shows the foreground figures from the back, it also implies our presence before the painting.

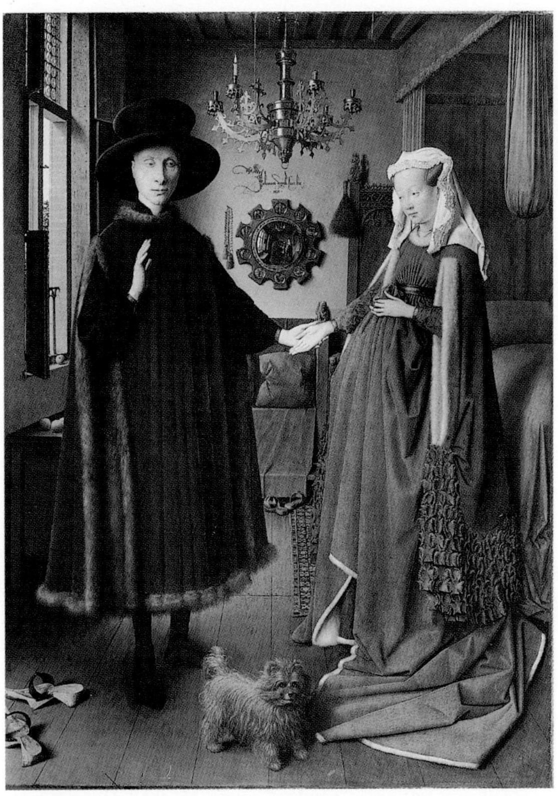

Fig. 8. Jan van Eyck, *Portrait of Giovanni (?) Arnolfini and His Wife*, dated 1434. Oil on wood, National Gallery, London

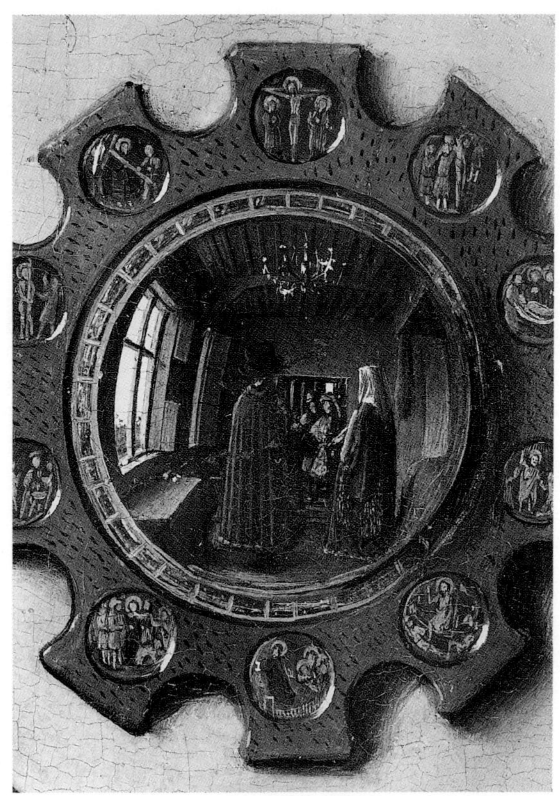

Fig. 9. Jan van Eyck, detail, mirror, *Portrait of Giovanni (?) Arnolfini and His Wife*, dated 1434. Oil on wood, National Gallery, London

The most famous example of such external inclusion is certainly that effected by the mirror in the back of Van Eyck's 1434 portrait of a member of the Lucchese Arnolfini family and his betrothed (figs. 8, 9).[77] The mirror reflects not only the couple, the entire room, and its furnishings but also the door in front of them, which is logically in our space. In the doorway are two figures who can be interpreted both as substitutes for the viewer and as the painter himself and a companion, since the inscription on the wall above the mirror reads in translation "Jan van Eyck was here." As the reflection in the mirror is so small, the faces of the figures cannot be distinguished; and thus the viewer and the painter collapse into one person.

Christus also included a mirror in *A Goldsmith in His Shop, Possibly Saint Eligius* (cat. no. 22), where it stands to the right of the counter. A convex surface, it reflects the saint's red sleeve, the stall's shutter, the street outside the shop, and two figures that, once again, are metaphors for the viewers in front of the painting. Christus teases our sense of space with the mirror: while we expect to be indoors when seeing pictures, the reflection suggests that we are standing in a street, under a pale blue sky. That convex mirrors were often used in goldsmiths' shops as security devices that protected against approaching thieves only enhances the pictorial wit involved.[78]

The reflection of the space in front of the work of art remained a motif much employed in Netherlandish painting well into the seventeenth century.[79] In Juan de Flandes's *Marriage Feast at Cana* of about 1500 (cat. no. 85), part of an extensive narrative altarpiece made for Queen Isabella the Catholic, a convex mirror hangs behind the bride and groom, reflecting the backs of their heads as well as a colonnade parallel to the picture plane, which

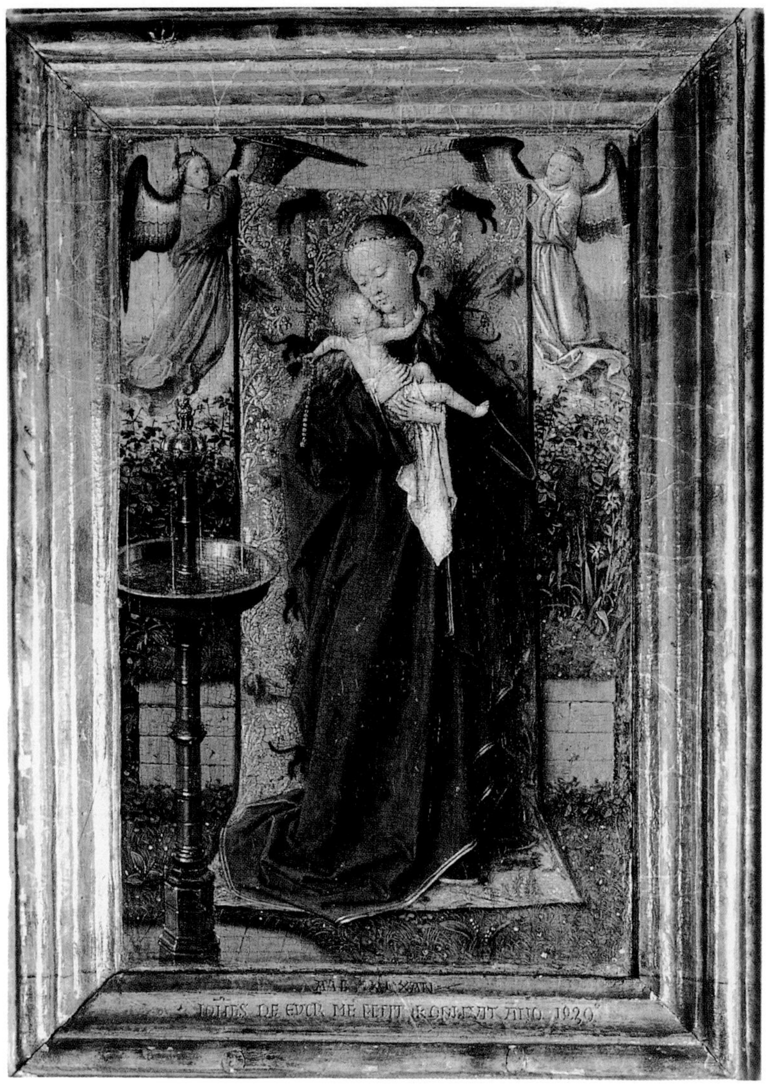

Fig. 10. Jan van Eyck, *Virgin and Child at the Fountain*, dated 1439. Oil on wood, Koninklijk Museum voor Schone Kunsten, Antwerp

is necessarily in our space. The impression is not unlike that in Van Eyck's Arnolfini portrait: the space of the picture continues into our space and we are made to think that we stand in the room itself, in the presence of Christ and the Virgin. The movement out of Juan's picture is accomplished by both the mirror, which returns our gaze, and by the figure on the left, who looks out of the picture directly at us, echoing the mirror's reflective character.

Another device Netherlanders used to activate the space between the painting and the viewer is the frame inside the picture. The frame is an essential element that negotiates the relationship of every painting to the surrounding world: it establishes a boundary between the image and everything that is nonimage. The frame defines that which is framed as a representation and separates it from the everyday world. Although the frame belongs to the realm of existence, it exists only because of its relationship to the image.[80] Several of Van Eyck's paintings have retained their original frames and demonstrate the artist's manipulations in this realm. The original frame of the *Virgin and Child at the Fountain* (fig. 10), for example, is painted to imitate marble, and an inscription with the artist's motto and signature is made to look as though it had been chiseled into the simulated stone. The frame in this case emphasizes both the preciousness and the physicality of the painted image, while separating it from the world in which it functions.

A frame inside the painting, by contrast, blurs the boundary between the image and the world,[81] as demonstrated by *Christ Appearing to His Mother* (cat. no. 46). This panel was originally the right wing of a nonfolding triptych donated by Queen Isabella the Catholic to the Capilla Real in Granada. Long considered an original by Van der Weyden, it is now thought to be an accurate copy made in Spain about 1496 by one of Isabella's court painters, after a portion of the triptych by Van der Weyden (fig. 81) that Isabella's father, King Juan II of Castile, gave to the Carthusian monastery at Miraflores, near Burgos, in 1445.[82] The quality of the pictorial execution is extremely high, and the painting reproduces Van der Weyden's invention faithfully. Christ's visit to Mary after the Resurrection takes place within an archway with archivolts depicting scenes from the life of the Virgin and statues of Saints Mark and Paul. Instead of serving as a conventional framing device, which would stand in front of the scene, the arch is shown behind the picture plane, while the action takes place in front of it, almost in the space of the beholder. The hem of Christ's red cloak at the level of his elbow falls over the frame on the left; a fold of Mary's cloak touches the edge of the step at the bottom, which appears to be in our space; and the bench on which her book rests casts a shadow on the column with Saint Paul. The movement forward accomplished by these strategies is not only spatial but also temporal: a road winds through the landscape, linking the mountains and the city in the background to the room behind the main figures; yet in addition it connects an earlier moment in the narrative of the Passion—the Resurrection on Easter morning—to Christ's appearance to the Virgin. The Resurrection is clearly the better known of the two events, and its position in the background ensures that the viewer will scrutinize the painting to decipher it and will mentally make the journey on the road, through space and through time. By juxtaposing the two events, Rogier brings to the viewer's mind the entire narrative of the Passion.[83]

In Christus's *Portrait of a Carthusian* of 1446 (cat. no. 21), the frame within the painting also unifies the space of the image with that of the viewer. The monk looks at us from the corner of a shallow boxlike space, behind a frame made to imitate marble and porphyry, reminiscent of Van Eyck's simulated stone frames. The lower ledge bears an inscription with the artist's name and the year of the painting's creation; a fly is depicted on the stone, exactly above the space separating the artist's first and last names. The fly carries various connotations.[84] A short-lived insect, it is, for example, a traditional symbol of the transience of life, and may have been intended as a reminder that this portrait would survive the death of both the sitter and the painter; it would, then, constitute a visualization of the saying "ars longa, vita brevis." The fly also serves to heighten the masterly illusionism of the portrait and to abolish the barrier of the picture plane; it is as though a fly from our world has landed in the space where the Carthusian sits and breathes.

In his portraits of the Florentine banker Tommaso Portinari and his wife, Maria Baroncelli (cat. no. 27), Memling went one step further than his predecessors and positioned his sitters in the space of the viewer. The dark background behind the subjects is framed with a profile of grayish stone, creating an ambiguity in our reading of the images. On the one hand, it seems as though we have in front of us two living individuals standing before the blank panels on which their likenesses will be painted. On the other, Tommaso Portinari and Maria Baroncelli appear to have just stepped out of their portraits and taken their places in our space.[85] Memling's consummate talent as a portraitist serves to heighten the illusion; the likenesses are such miracles of observation that we can apply to them Fazio's characterization of Van Eyck's portraits: they are distinguishable from their sitters only by their lack of speech.[86] From Memling on, portraiture constantly strove to break the picture plane, Marten van Heemskerck's painting of his father of 1532 (cat. no. 42) being a case in point. In the same period Jan Gossart used Memling's invention in a devotional painting and placed his *Virgin and Child* (cat. no. 40) in front of a frame to allow the original owner the impression that the object of his prayers was a tangible being in his space.

Netherlandish painters developed various strategies to draw the attention of the viewer and direct his interpretation. Most used naturalism to transpose biblical stories into the immediate realm of the beholder's experience, or to convey the impression that the sitters in portraits are alive in front of us. Their paintings often present a range of emotional responses that the beholder must emulate. Some devices are clearly self-referential: Van Eyck, Van der Weyden, Christus, and Memling, for instance, used metaphors for the viewer in the form of figures who look at the main scene, they depicted mirrors that reflect the space of the beholder, and they experimented with the frame inside the picture. From the start, these painters developed a rhetoric of the image that draws attention to itself; the paintings acknowledge their power to direct and shape our perception. Of equal, if not greater, importance, early Netherlandish paintings make the claim that the beholder "must engage works of art in terms that implicate him experimentally, not just conceptually, in the world of the image and its meaning."[87] Living in a world in which we take in hundreds of images daily, via television, films, newsprint, and advertisements, we find it hard to imagine a time when images were rare. The emergence of easel paintings in the southern Lowlands is one of the most remarkable events of the fifteenth century. It is hoped that we can be open to their freshness of vision. The works of Campin, Van Eyck, Memling, and David invite us to a rewarding dialogue.

I am most grateful to Maryan Ainsworth, Till Borchert, Keith Christiansen, Everett Fahy, Timothy Husband, and William D. Wixom for their critical reading of several drafts of the text. This essay is dedicated to Molly Faries, who taught me much of what is in it.

1. The Ghent Altarpiece was dismantled in the late eighteenth century and remained in that state until 1920. In 1794 the four central panels were selected for shipment to the Louvre during the occupation of the southern Lowlands by French revolutionary troops, but were returned to Sint-Baafs (Saint Bavo's) cathedral in Ghent in 1816. Also in 1816 the cathedral chapter sold the wings—except for the *Adam* and *Eve* panels, which had long been hidden away because their nudity was considered offensive—to the Brussels dealer Nieuwenhuys. The wings were acquired by James Solly of Aachen in the following year, and in 1821 they went to Berlin when Frederick William III of Prussia purchased the Solly collection. The wings remained in the Berlin museum until 1920, when they were returned to Belgium as a condition of the Versailles Treaty. The *Adam* and *Eve* panels were acquired by the Belgian state in 1861 and exhibited at the Musées Royaux des Beaux-Arts de Belgique in Brussels. See Coremans et al. 1953, pp. 21–32, and Nicholas 1994, p. 123. See also Dean 1998, which discusses the Ghent Altarpiece and scholarship on early Netherlandish painting in the context of emerging nationalism in the nineteenth and early twentieth centuries.
2. Bruges 1902, pp. 4–8.
3. Ibid., p. 26.
4. Haskell 1993, pp. 445–61.
5. On the creation of the Louvre, see McClellan 1994.
6. On the notion of the museum in revolutionary thought, see Poulot 1997, pp. 133–36.
7. Borchert 1995, pp. 144–52.
8. The Treaty of Amiens, signed by France, Britain, Spain, and the Netherlands, achieved peace in Europe for fourteen months during the Napoleonic Wars.
9. Borchert 1995, p. 150.
10. Haskell 1993, pp. 432–33.
11. As Till Borchert pointed out to me, the model for Wackenroder's art collection in a castle was probably the Schönborn collection at Pommersfelden.
12. Ridderbos 1995b, pp. 190–91.
13. It also greatly influenced a colony of German artists in Rome known as the Nazarenes, among whom was Johann David Passavant, whose role in building the collection of the Städelsches Kunstinstitut in Frankfurt and in ascribing an oeuvre to Van der Weyden is discussed below.
14. Haskell 1993, p. 433; Borchert 1995, pp. 152–53.
15. On the Boisserée brothers, see Firmenich-Richartz 1916.
16. Ridderbos 1995b, p. 196. It is interesting to note that Johanna Schopenhauer and other early critics often categorized sixteenth-century artists such as Dürer and Scorel with Van Eyck and Memling in their discussions of early Netherlandish painting.
17. Waagen 1822, p. 214.
18. Haskell 1993, p. 436.
19. Ridderbos 1995b, p. 196.
20. They also assembled groups of works around artistic personalities, that is, painters with individual styles whose identities cannot be recovered.
21. Borchert 1995, p. 160.
22. Ibid., p. 164. Like those from the Ghent Altarpiece, the panels from Bouts's Sacrament Altarpiece were returned to Belgium as a condition of the Versailles Treaty. On the restitution of the paintings, see Geismeier 1990 and Bode 1997, pp. 466–67; I thank Florian Illies for this reference.
23. See the excellent master's thesis by Illies (1997) on Waagen, which stresses the impact of his work on English scholarship and on Eastlake in particular.
24. Borchert 1995, pp. 177–80.
25. Ibid., pp. 165–66.
26. For a more detailed discussion of the rediscovery of Van der Weyden, see Ridderbos 1995b, pp. 207–10.
27. On Weale, see Van Biervliet 1991.
28. Ridderbos 1995b, pp. 214–16, with complete bibliographical references.
29. Haskell 1993, pp. 445–46.
30. Bruges 1902.
31. Haskell 1993, p. 453.
32. Weale 1901, p. 79.
33. Krul 1995, p. 262; Haskell 1993, p. 434.
34. Haskell 1993, pp. 461–62.
35. Gemäldegalerie 1975, pp. 62, 78, 148, 176–77, 473.
36. Haskell 1993, pp. 462–63; Ridderbos 1995b, pp. 225–31.
37. The *Portrait of a Man* by Van Eyck in Bucharest is a case in point; Van Asperen de Boer, Ridderbos, and Zeldenrust 1991.
38. Haskell 1993, p. 464.
39. Recent scholarship has reevaluated Memling's art, drawing attention to his innovations in narrative and portraits; see McFarlane 1971, Borchert 1993, De Vos 1994a, De Vos 1994b.
40. Panofsky 1953, p. 347.
41. It is beyond the scope of this essay to attempt a discussion of Panofsky's immensely rich oeuvre, which ranges from the theoretical writings of his Hamburg years, when he was working with the philosophers Ernst Cassirer and Fritz Saxl and with the cultural historian Aby Warburg, to books published after he came to America, on such subjects as Dürer, scholasticism and Gothic architecture, and the concept of the Renaissance. For two extremely useful discussions of Panofsky's works and his position in twentieth-century thought, see Podro 1982, pp. 178–217; and Holly 1984.
42. Panofsky 1953, pp. 131–48.
43. Ibid., pp. 140–41.
44. Harbison 1995c, p. 397, quoting Huizinga.
45. Panofsky 1953, p. 133.
46. Ridderbos 1995a, pp. 27–28.
47. O'Meara 1981, pp. 85–86.
48. Hahn 1986; Thürlemann 1997, pp. 23–26.
49. Hall 1994, chap. 4; Harbison 1995c.
50. Harbison 1985. Other important publications devoted to art as an aid to private devotion include Panofsky 1927, Ringbom 1965, Belting 1981, Falkenburg 1988, and Van Os 1995.
51. Harbison 1985, p. 87.
52. Ibid., pp. 112–14.

53. See in particular Freedberg 1986.
54. Harbison 1985, p. 95.
55. Marrow 1986, pp. 151–52; the second formulation is by Joseph Koerner, as cited in ibid.
56. Ibid., p. 155.
57. As cited in ibid.
58. See also Ainsworth 1994b, pp. 106–11.
59. See in that regard Acres n.d., an important forthcoming article that introduces the concept of pictorial time.
60. On the odyssey of the Ghent Altarpiece during World War II, see Nicholas 1994, pp. 85, 143–45, 313–14, 332, 346–47, 407–8.
61. Coremans et al. 1953.
62. Taubert 1956 and Taubert 1975; there are several publications illustrating the relevance of technical study to art history; see, among others, Ainsworth 1989a, Dijkstra 1995, and Faries 1998 (forthcoming).
63. See, for instance, Maryan Ainsworth's convincing attribution of the Friedsam *Annunciation* (cat. no. 5) to Christus, based on the picture's underdrawing, among other considerations; Ainsworth 1994b, pp. 117–25.
64. Van Asperen de Boer 1970.
65. Van Asperen de Boer et al. 1992; Campbell 1993.
66. Dijkstra 1990, especially p. 13; see also the entry for cat. no. 46.
67. Ainsworth 1994b, pp. 15, 53–55.
68. Faries 1993; Ainsworth 1994a, pp. 78–79; Faries 1997; see also De Vos 1994b, pp. 361–64.
69. See also Rohlmann 1994, pp. 119–24.
70. Quoted in Stechow 1966, pp. 8–9.
71. Ibid., p. 4.
72. Ibid.
73. Sterling 1976, pp. 28–29; see also Paviot 1990, p. 86.
74. Panofsky 1953, p. 182.
75. For two thorough studies on the *Crucifixion* and its companion, the *Last Judgment*, see Belting and Eichberger 1983 and Eichberger 1987.
76. Alberti 1966, p. 56.
77. Although traditionally referred to as a wedding portrait since a 1934 article by Panofsky, the painting actually depicts a betrothal, as Hall (1994) demonstrated. On mirrors in early Netherlandish painting, see, among others, Marrow 1983, Marrow 1986, pp. 161–65, and Borchert 1998, pp. 73–74.
78. Madou 1988, pp. 57–61; I would like to thank Till Borchert for this reference.
79. See Brusati 1990–91.
80. Stoichita 1993, p. 43.
81. Ibid., p. 72.
82. Dijkstra 1990, pp. 106–9; Ainsworth 1992b, pp. 59–68.
83. This point is convincingly articulated in Acres n.d.
84. For a discussion of the motif of the fly, see Panofsky 1953, pp. 310, 488–89; and Chastel 1984, pp. 14–20; see also Ainsworth 1994b, p. 94.
85. Stoichita 1993, p. 72.
86. As cited in Baxandall 1971, p. 106.
87. Marrow 1986, p. 163.

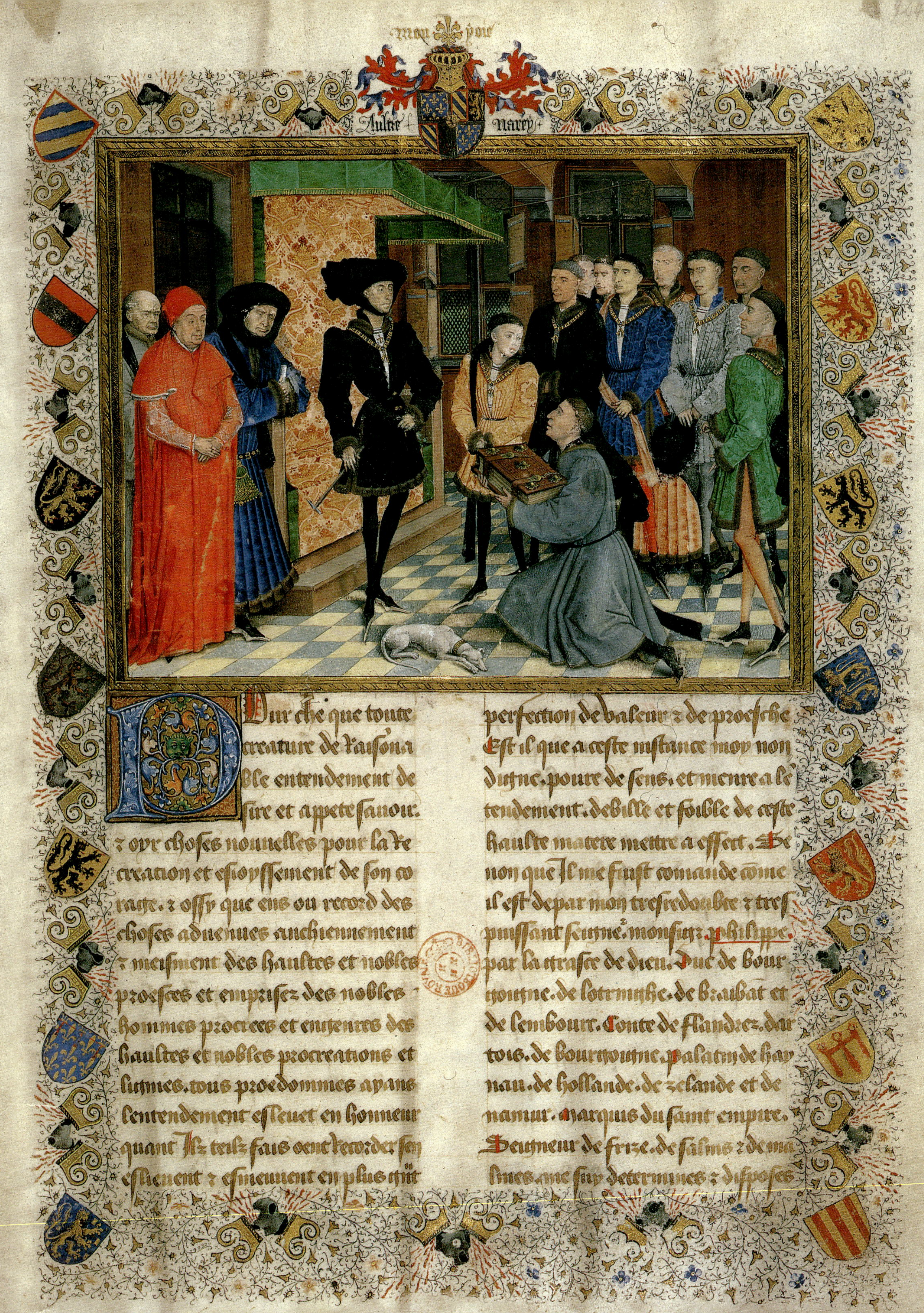
Pour che que toute
creature de raisona
ble entendement de
sire et appete savoir.
& oyr choses nouvelles pour la re
creation et esjoyssement de son co
rage. & ossy que eus ou record des
choses advenues anchiennement
& meismement des haultes et nobles
proesses et emprisez des nobles
hommes preceurs et ententes des
haultes et nobles procreations et
lignies. tous preudommes ayans
sentendement esleuet en honneur
quant ilz teulz fais oent recorder sen
esjoiessent & esmeuvent en plus gut

perfection de valeur & de proesche
Est il que a ceste instance moy non
digne. povre de sens. et menre a le
tendement. debille et foible de ceste
haulte matere mettre a effect. Se
non que il me fust commande comme
il est de par mon tresredoubte & tres
puissant seignr. monsigr. Philippe.
par la grasce de dieu. Duc de bour
goingne. de lotrijche. de brabat et
de lembourc. Conte de flandrez. dar
tois. de bourgoingne. palatin de hay
nau. de hollande. de zelande et de
namur. Marquis du saint empire.
Seigneur de frize. de salins & de ma
lines. me suy determines & disposes

The Business of Art: Patrons, Clients, and Art Markets

MARYAN W. AINSWORTH

Employment by the Dukes of Burgundy and at Foreign Courts

The most magnificent and certainly the most extravagant event that took place in fifteenth-century Bruges was the wedding of Duke Charles the Bold and the English princess Margaret of York on July 3, 1468.[1] The marriage ceremony itself was preceded by Charles's triumphal entry into the city on April 19 and by the meeting of the Order of the Golden Fleece at the church of Onze-Lieve-Vrouw (Our Lady). Together with the May fair, which included the annual procession of the Holy Blood, Bruges's most famous relic, these events totally consumed the energies of the Corporation of Imagemakers (*beeldemakers*), to which the painters belonged.

The pageantry of these events was only a prelude to the festivities surrounding the wedding. Olivier de la Marche, court chronicler, maître d'hôtel, and *capitaine des gardes* of Charles the Bold, has left the most complete description of the town transformed by the wedding festivities, which took place over a period of ten days, and of the entremets and plays for the banquets, which he had planned. Lining the route for the triumphal entry of Margaret of York were tableaux vivants with actors performing scenes from the Bible and ancient history—Adam and Eve in the Garden of Eden, the Marriage at Cana, Alexander and Cleopatra, and so forth. The Prinsenhof was decorated with the armorial insignia of the duke supported by two lions, as well as with newly built fountains—one surmounted by archers and another by a pelican pricking its breast—spouting wine of various types. A banquet hall, especially built for the occasion and attached to the Prinsenhof, had been prefabricated in Brussels and shipped to Bruges for reassembly. The hall was equipped with platforms for dancers, musicians, and actors and had walls hung with banners and tapestries and two giant mobile mechanical chandeliers suspended from its ceiling.

The wedding expenses were duly recorded by Fastre Hollet, who served as the accountant for the ducal household.[2] Hollet cites over 150 artists who were employed to decorate the city in advance of the arrival of Charles and Margaret, provide the props for tableaux vivants, and make heraldic banners and banquet decorations. (His list does not include the local painters, presumably because they had been involved in events of the preceding months that were paid for by the city magistrates.) Among those who came from outside Bruges were the most highly esteemed painters of the day: artists such as Hugo van der Goes and Lieven van Letham from Ghent and Jacques Daret from Tournai. Their efforts, and those of sculptors, embroiderers, and other artisans, were coordinated by Jean Hennecart and Pierre Coustain, court painters and *varlets de chambre* of the duke. The detailed records of payments throw surprising light on the relative importance of painters—the now little-known Daniel de Rycke, for example, was paid considerably more than Hugo van der Goes. Total expenses for the occasion surpassed the equivalent of the daily wages of 52,000 skilled craftsmen.[3]

Painters employed by the court spent a considerable part of their time preparing events like those surrounding the duke's wedding. But there were also long-term projects on a grand scale, such as the family mausoleum at the Carthusian monastery at Champmol, near Dijon, executed after a plan initiated in 1385 by Duke Philip the Bold and

Opposite: Netherlandish, *Presentation by Jean Wanquelin to Philip the Good of the Chroniques de Hainaut*, showing Nicolas Rolin and Jean Chevrot at left and the young Charles the Bold at right, frontispiece, *Chroniques de Hainaut*, 1448. Tempera on parchment. Bibliothèque Royale Albert Ier, Brussels (MS 9242, fol. 1)

the construction of a burial site at Brou for Margaret of Austria, planned in 1509.[4] Otherwise, as patrons the dukes of Burgundy favored tapestries, manuscript illuminations, and precious metalwork objects depicting themes that served as political propaganda for the legitimization of their military campaigns and territorial expansion. Paintings do not seem to have been commissioned routinely, except for those ordered for the obligatory decoration of chapels in various official residences: relatively few paintings as compared with more portable objects are recorded in inventories. This is partly explained by the fact that the court was an itinerant one, traveling often to Arras, Bruges, Brussels, Lille, and Dijon, and the dukes and their entourages required objects that could be transported easily. Occasionally, individual portraits were commissioned in particular circumstances, although few can be directly linked to ducal inventories.[5] During his diplomatic mission to Portugal for Philip the Good in 1428, for example, Jan van Eyck was asked to render the likeness of the infanta Isabella so that the duke could have it at hand as he negotiated his marriage to her.

However, an abundance of portraits by Rogier van der Weyden and his followers of Duke Philip the Good and of his son and successor, Charles the Bold, addressed sustained issues of genealogy and the line of succession at court. Given as gifts, hung in the various residences of the dukes or in municipal buildings and religious institutions patronized by them, these pictures provided a reminder of power, status, and hegemony in a world of shifting political alliances. Certain likenesses record fleeting and temporary associations: one example is Jean Hey's splendid *Portrait of Margaret of Austria* (cat. no. 35), which shows the aristocratic sitter as a young girl at the time she served briefly as "queen of France," before her betrothed, Charles VIII, the future king of France, rejected her in favor of Anne of Brittany.

The pattern of ducal and royal commissions was imitated by the members of the nobility. They, too, preferred precious and costly objects, such as illuminated manuscripts, metalwork, tapestries, and jewelry, to paintings. An indication of the importance of these arts in comparison with that of painting is conveyed by the 1460 will of Marguerite de Lannoy, dame de Santes. To her own family members Marguerite bequeathed her most valuable items—jewelry, silver objects, and relics—while the limited number of paintings she owned—three scenes of the Passion, three of the Virgin Mary, and two of the Annunciation—were given to the wives of her household staff.[6] Preoccupied with their own lineages and relationships to the ruling duke, the members of the nobility commissioned portraiture that constituted a statement about status and court affiliation. There is a singular lack of good documentation for such commissions, and clues to ownership have disappeared, frames that might have borne inscriptions have been lost, and the paintings themselves have been altered in various ways. Nevertheless, we can appreciate the marked formality of court portraiture, which is readily identifiable with the aims of the nobility. These images are manifestly elegant, presenting their subjects in terms of their prestige and stations in life. Thus, Van der Weyden's portrait of Francesco d'Este (cat. no. 23), the illegitimate son of the marquis of Ferrara, Leonello d'Este, shows the sitter, who was sent to be educated alongside the young Charles the Bold at the Burgundian court, with his attributes of position—a hammer, possibly a symbol of authority, and a ring, perhaps a prize won in a courtly amusement such as a tournament.

Certain artists, for example Jan van Eyck and the lesser-known Coustain and Hennecart, were fortunate enough to be salaried employees of the court, serving as *varlets de chambre* to the duke. This position guaranteed an annual pension as well as commissions from court functionaries who, following the taste of their sires, favored the officially appointed painter. Van Eyck served two successive rulers: in The Hague from 1422 to 1424 he worked for John of Bavaria, count of Holland, and mainly in Bruges from 1425 he was employed by Philip the Good, duke of Burgundy; moreover, an early tradition associates the Museum's Van Eyck diptych showing the Crucifixion and the Last Judgment (cat. no. 1) with Philip's great uncle, Jean, duc de Berry (1340–1416). Although Jean's inventory lists "uns grans tableaux en deux pièces, de painture, l'un de la Passion Nostre Seigneur et l'autre du Jugement," our diptych was painted at least a decade after his death. It nevertheless fits the profile of a ducal commission: the panels form a precious object that is painted in miniaturist style like the favored court art of manuscript illumination, and it was made by the preeminent court artist of the day.

The association between Charles the Bold and Simon Marmion—whom Jean LeMaire described as the "very prince of illumination"—likely began with commissions of illuminations for a breviary initiated by Philip the Good in 1467 and completed in 1470 under the patronage of Charles the Bold and Margaret of York (fig. 11).[7] Subsequently, the newly married Charles and Margaret commissioned a panel painting from Marmion; this was our *Lamentation* (cat. no. 9), which is decorated on its reverse with the couple's intertwined initials, C and M.

In the sixteenth century Jan Gossart and Bernaert van Orley also enjoyed the patronage of the court. Gossart entered the service of Philip of Burgundy, an illegitimate son of Philip the Good, by 1508, traveling with him to Rome, where he made drawings after antique sculpture and architecture. After Philip's death in 1524 he was employed by Philip's half brother, Adolf of Burgundy, marquis of Veere, at which time he reportedly painted a *Virgin and Child* modeled after the wife of the marquis, Anna van Bergen, and their son (see entry for cat. no. 40). The portraits Van Orley made in 1515 for Margaret of Austria, regent of the Netherlands, so impressed her that she appointed him official court painter in 1518. Not surprisingly, a number of his works of this period, notably the *Virgin and Child with Angels* (cat. no. 89), which features an elaborate fountain and a Renaissance palace, have a distinctly courtly flavor.

The famed court of the dukes of Burgundy, with its lavish lifestyle and illustrious painters, was envied by the ruling houses of the Italian and Spanish territories. Aspiring to emulate Burgundian magnificence, the southerners sought the services of Netherlandish artists, who worked in the painstaking and brilliant technique of oil painting, with its remarkable illusion of reality and precious jewel-like surfaces. The call from these foreign kingdoms attracted certain northerners, who, for whatever personal reasons, ventured south to seek their fortunes.

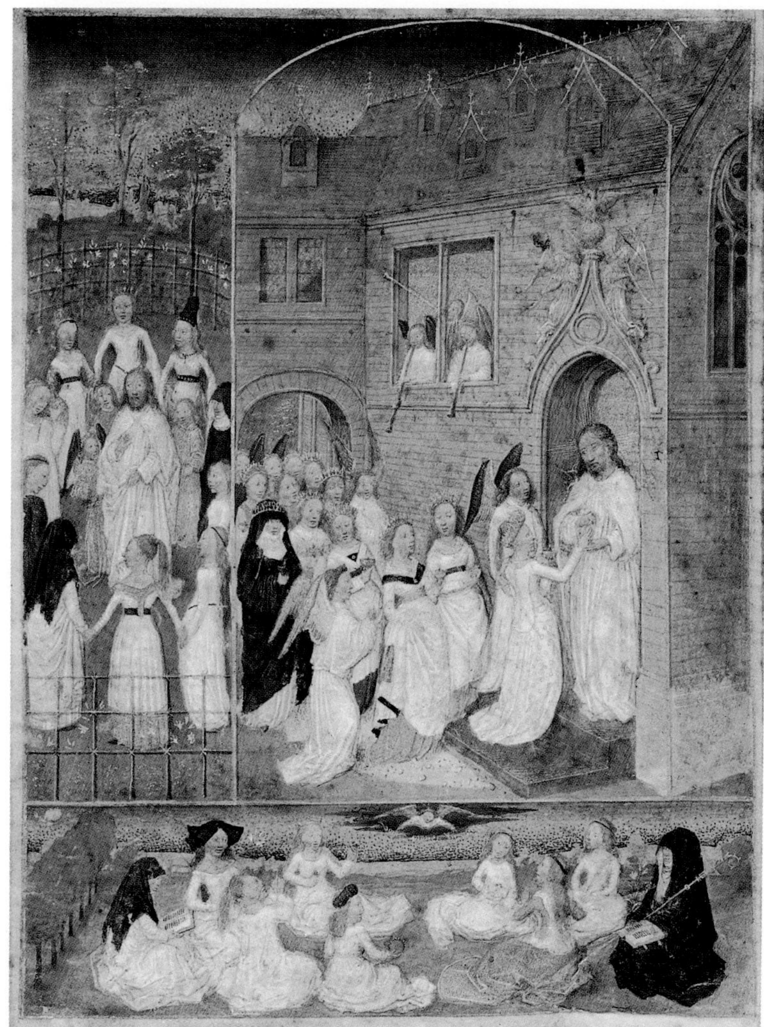

Fig. 11. Simon Marmion, *The Holy Virgins Greeted by Christ as They Enter the Gates of Paradise*, from *Breviary of Charles the Bold and Margaret of York*, about 1467–70. Robert Lehman Collection, The Metropolitan Museum of Art, New York

Joos van Gent is last known to have been in his native town in 1467, about the time he must have painted our *Adoration of the Magi* (cat. no. 7). Shortly thereafter, he departed for Italy, where he was employed by Federigo da Montefeltro, duke of Urbino, who, according to the nobleman's friend Vespasiano da Bisticci of Florence, was unable to find an artist in all of Italy who met his aesthetic standards. Joos's first major commission from Federigo was the *Communion of the Apostles* executed for the Confraternity of Corpus Domini in 1473–74. Once Joos successfully completed this important work, he assisted in the decoration of the *studioli* of the duke's palaces at Urbino and Gubbio with paintings representing Famous Men and the Liberal Arts.

Isabella of Castile, another important patron of the arts, had assembled at her Spanish court a collection of over three hundred paintings. She was particularly enamored of Netherlandish pictures and favored Bruges artists, in part because of the strong trade links between Bruges and Castile. Isabella hired two painters trained in Bruges, Michel Sittow, who entered her service in 1492 as a young man of twenty-five, and Juan de Flandes, who joined him at her court in 1496. Together the two collaborated on works for Isabella, including the Oratorio of Queen Isabella the Catholic, an extraordinary assembly of forty-seven small panels on the theme of the Life of Christ. Among the extant pictures from the series is the enchanting *Marriage Feast at Cana* in the Linsky Collection (cat. no. 85), which embodies the characteristics of Netherlandish painting so admired by Isabella: the meticulous rendering of realistic settings, abundant narrative detail, and an appealingly intimate devotional subject rendered in a style and perfected finish that recall book illumination.

Isabella's court artists were called upon to make copies of works in her collection, and Sittow is listed in her inventories as having assumed this task from time to time. It may have been Sittow or Juan de Flandes who produced an exceptionally careful copy after the portable Miraflores Altarpiece by Rogier van der Weyden, a triptych Isabella's father, Juan II, had donated to the Carthusian monastery of Miraflores in 1445. Isabella likely had a number of reasons for commissioning the replica, which consists of the *Christ Appearing to His Mother* in the Metropolitan (cat. no. 46) and the *Nativity* and the *Lamentation* now in the Capilla Real in Granada. Above all, she may have wanted the faithful copies to serve as a constant reminder of the devotional practices of her father and his first wife, Maria of Aragon, and of the Netherlandish masterpiece honoring their burial site, the monastery at Miraflores. The peripatetic queen's replica also could have provided some solace as she traveled from castle to castle in her far-flung territories.

Although Sittow left Spain in 1502 for the north and eventually returned to his hometown of Reval, Juan de Flandes remained in Spain until his death in 1519. Over the course of his long foreign residence, Juan made adjustments to his Flemish style and painting technique, assimilating the modes of his adopted home and accommodating the taste of his Spanish clients, as his *Saints Michael and Francis* (cat. no. 86) shows. In this panel, which was probably part of a large retable commissioned in 1505 for the chapel of the University of Salamanca, archaic gold backgrounds replace the illusionistic spaces and extensive landscapes of northern painting; the broad execution in thick, opaque applications of paint here bears little resemblance to the meticulous perfection of handling in the miniaturist style Juan employed in the earlier Oratorio of Queen Isabella the Catholic.

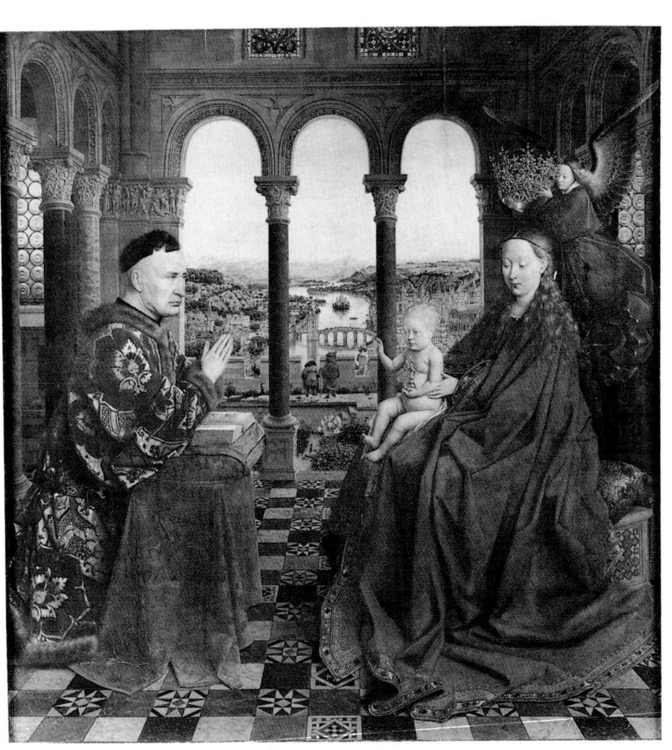

Fig. 12. Jan van Eyck, *The Virgin and Child with Chancellor Rolin*, about 1436. Oil on wood. Musée du Louvre, Paris

In Emulation of the Dukes: Commissions from Court Functionaries

The dukes of Burgundy are credited with centralizing Netherlandish political institutions and with reforms in the judicial and financial realms. The consolidation of power and guaranteeing of loyalties achieved under Philip the Good and Charles the Bold were to a significant degree affected by means of political appointments and considerable nepotism. As a result, growing numbers of court functionaries, such as financiers, lawyers, musicians,

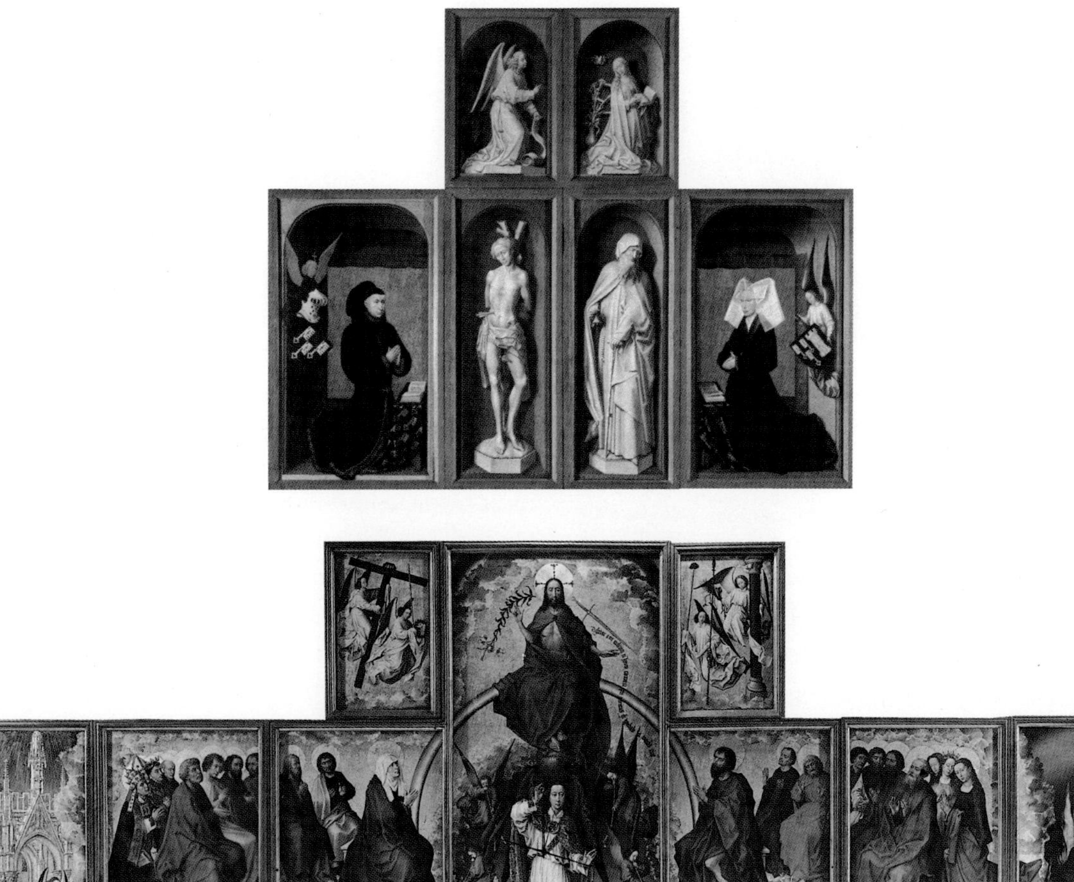

Fig. 13. Rogier van der Weyden, Last Judgment Altarpiece, 1446–50. Oil on wood. Hôtel Dieu, Beaune

chaplains, and secretaries to the dukes, moved into high positions, and their professional activities brought them increasing wealth, providing disposable income for luxury goods. Unlike the nobility, these court functionaries regularly commissioned paintings.[8] Thus we have Van Eyck's splendid *Virgin and Child with Chancellor Rolin* (fig. 12) and Van der Weyden's remarkable Last Judgment Altarpiece (fig. 13), both commissioned by the same Nicolas Rolin, the latter for the Hôtel Dieu in Beaune, which he founded with his third wife, Guigonne de Salins, in 1443. Certainly a sign of Rolin's religious devotion and desire for salvation, these works also served as an obvious display of wealth and power. His choice of the official court painter, Van Eyck, and one who often worked for the dukes, Van der Weyden, speaks not of mere expediency but rather of self-promotion. The *Virgin and Child*, in particular, refers to its patron's status and accomplishments. Rolin, initially a lawyer, later knighted, and made chancellor at the court of Philip the Good by 1422, was especially generous in his patronage of his parish church at Autun, Notre-Dame-du-Chastel (destroyed during the French Revolution), situated in the shadow of the cathedral of Autun. Whether the parish church or the cathedral (where Rolin's son, Jean, was appointed bishop in 1436) is depicted, a reference to the chancellor's beneficence was intended, and the painting is replete with other indications of his wealth and position: the rich vestments, crown of gold, and precious gems he gave to the parish church, and, if they are his own, the mansion and productive vineyards viewed at the left in the background.[9]

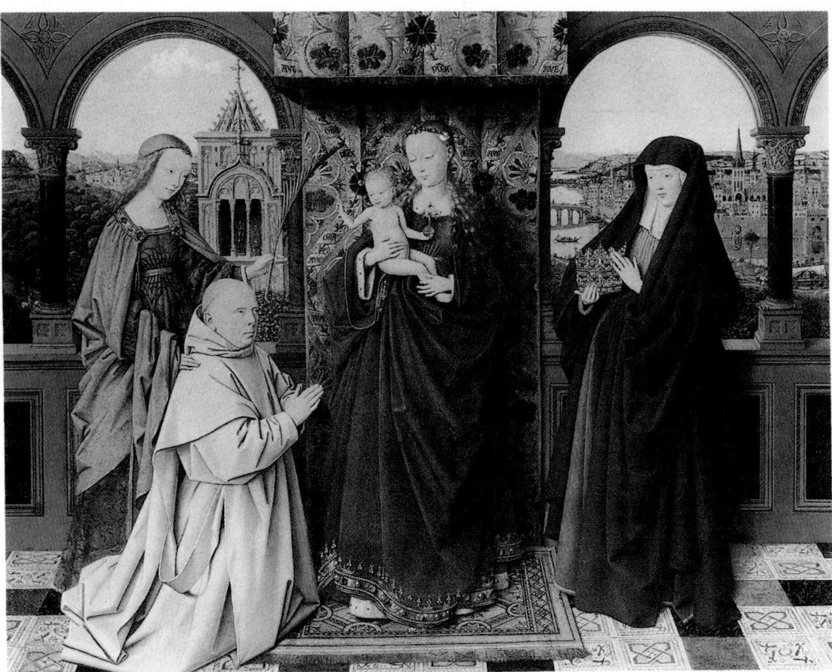

Fig. 14. Jan van Eyck and Workshop, *Virgin and Child with Saints Barbara and Elizabeth and Jan Vos*, about 1441–43. Oil on Masonite, transferred from canvas, transferred from wood, with oak veneer and cradled. The Frick Collection, New York

Was it in competition with Rolin's magnanimous but calculated patronage that Ferry or Willem de Clugny commissioned one of the largest extant Netherlandish paintings of the Annunciation, a panel produced in the workshop of Rogier van der Weyden (cat. no. 10)? We know the patron was a Clugny, for the coat of arms of the family (two keys united) can be identified on the window and in the pattern of the rug in this impressive painting, which may be the left wing of an even grander triptych. Both Ferry de Clugny and his brother, Willem, were distinguished jurists and members of the Grand Council of the Dukes. Ferry was appointed chancellor of the Order of the Golden Fleece in 1473 by Charles the Bold, and in 1474 was consecrated bishop of Tournai, while his brother became bishop of Poitiers in 1477. A picture as large as the *Annunciation* was surely not intended for private devotions but rather for a public space, such as Ferry's Chapelle Dorée, founded at the cathedral of Autun in 1465. By commissioning a monumental panel from the workshop of Van der Weyden, official city painter of Brussels and favored artist of Duke Philip the Good, Ferry or Willem demonstrated the wealth and influence of the Clugny family, keeping pace with the extravagant patronage of other court functionaries, Nicolas Rolin prominent among them.

Religious Institutions, Corporations, and Civic Commissions

Certain religious orders and monasteries were especially favored by the dukes of Burgundy and became the beneficiaries of their largesse.[10] One of these was the Carthusian monastery at Champmol, near Dijon, which Philip the Bold established early on and heavily endowed for the purpose of developing a mausoleum for the Burgundian dukes.[11] Partial to the Carthusians because of their strict adherence to their order's rule, the dukes were also generous to the Carthusian monastery at Genadedal, just outside the city walls of Bruges.[12] This institution housed many major artworks and was particularly renowned for its collection of manuscripts, now lost. Quite by coincidence, three paintings most likely associated with this eminent monastery have come to New York: the *Virgin and Child with Saints Barbara and Elizabeth and Jan Vos* from the workshop of Jan van Eyck (fig. 14), now in the Frick Collection, and the Metropolitan Museum's *Portrait of a Carthusian* by Petrus Christus (cat. no. 21) and *Virgin and Child with Four Angels* by Gerard David (cat. no. 81). The considerable importance of this monastery is indicated by the fact that Bishop Martinus of Mayo visited it in 1443, at which time he consecrated and attached indulgences to three paintings that the prior, Jan Vos, had given to the establishment. One of these was undoubtedly the Frick panel.[13] Although the details surrounding the commission of the Metropolitan's two paintings are not known, we can perhaps surmise that the *Virgin and Child with Four Angels* represents a venerated icon or cult object housed at the monastery, because the Virgin and Child motif featured is of a type that was frequently repeated in Bruges.[14] Like certain works carried out for particular orders, David's panel may have been made for the propagandistic purpose of expressing religious doctrine, as it clearly demonstrates the

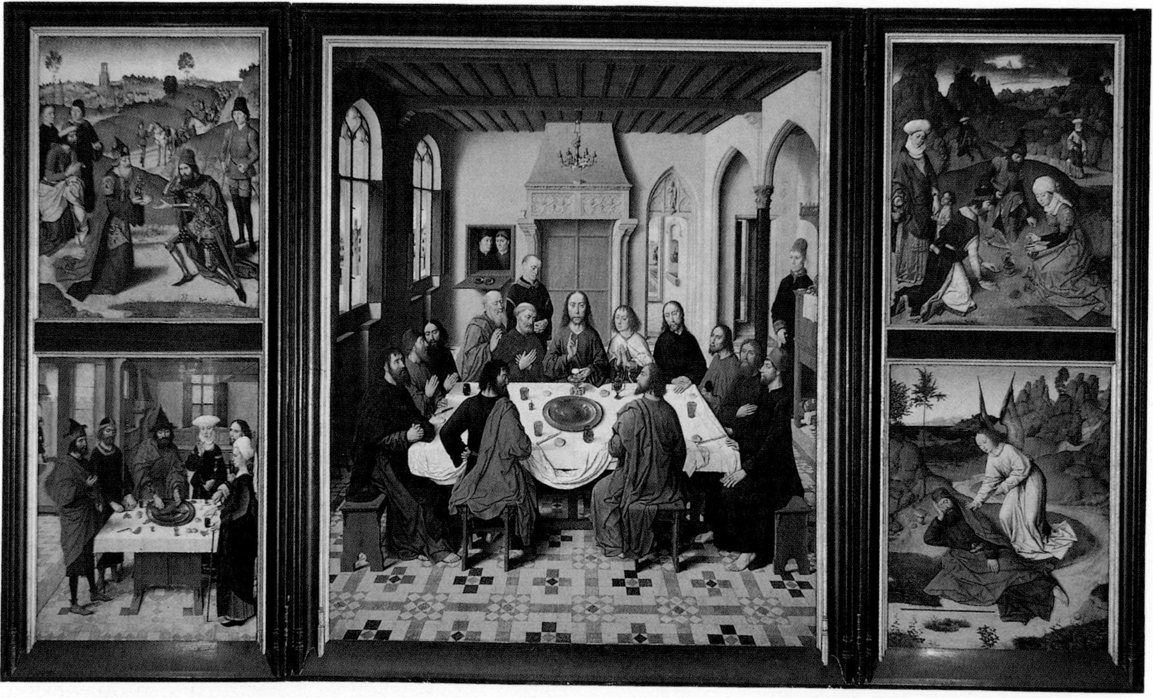

Fig. 15. Dieric Bouts, Holy Sacrament Triptych, about 1468. Central panel, oil on canvas, transferred from wood; wings, oil on wood. Sint-Pieterskerk, Leuven

concept of the Virgin as co-Redemptrix with Christ, an idea extensively discussed by Carthusian writers.

Orders for altarpieces to decorate the chapels of other types of religious institutions, confraternities, guilds, and charitable institutions were as important as the commissions initiated by major monasteries.[15] Such ensembles are sometimes identifiable by virtue of their subject matter, as well as by their large size and complexity, which indicate that they were placed in public as opposed to private, domestic locations. The *Life and Miracles of Saint Godelieve* (cat. no. 15) and *Scenes from the Life of Saint Augustine* (cat. no. 16), for example, are altarpieces that would have adorned the chapels of confraternities or religious institutions devoted to the saints depicted. *Abner's Messenger before David(?)* and the *Queen of Sheba Bringing Gifts to Solomon* (cat. no. 13), wings that once flanked a central panel portraying the Adoration of the Kings (Casa Colonna, Rome), show four donors dressed similarly, suggesting that the men were officers of a confraternity. The original function of the altarpiece was changed when crosses were added above the praying hands of the donors, indicating that they had died and transforming the work into a memorial to the deceased.

Surviving contracts for such commissions are rare. The oldest one known for a Netherlandish painting is dated 1464 and provides details concerning a triptych of the Holy Sacrament (fig. 15), commissioned from Dieric Bouts by the Brotherhood of the Holy Sacrament for the Sint-Pieterskerk in Leuven.[16] It specifies the themes of the inner and outer portions of the altarpiece, the participation of two professors of theology from the University of Leuven as counselors for the iconographic program, and the schedule of payments, and requires that Bouts devote all of his attention to this work during the course of its execution.

A series of accounts from the Brussels shoemakers' corporation provides further details of how works were ordered and executed. These documents relate to a polyptych commissioned from Aert van de Bossche that probably shows Saints Crispin and Crispinian (parts are now in Warsaw, Moscow, and Brussels).[17] The painter, who was to produce the panels between 1490 and 1494, was provided a significant advance and subsequently

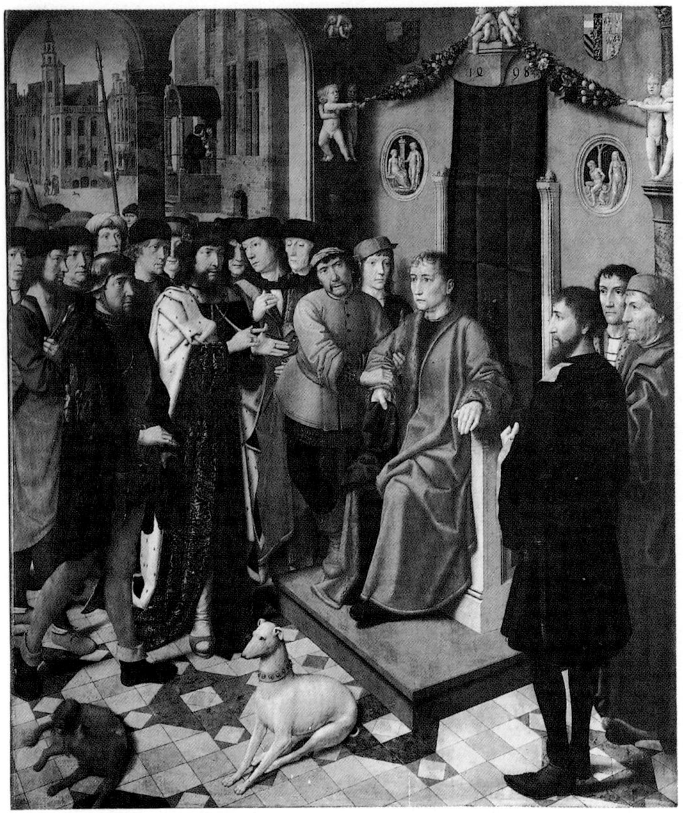

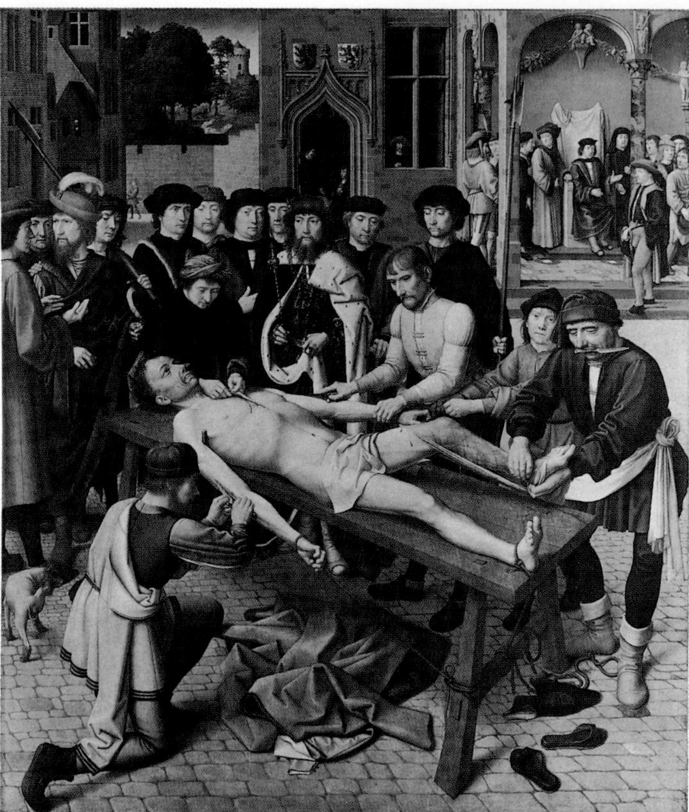

Fig. 16. Gerard David, *Justice of Cambyses: The Arrest of Sisamnes; The Flaying of Sisamnes*, 1498. Oil on wood. Groeningemuseum, Bruges

executed a design for a second payment. Only after his design was approved by the shoemakers was a contract prepared and a copy of the original design made for an additional small sum. The copy was probably retained by the corporation as a guarantee of the agreed-upon design; the original would have remained with the painter in his workshop, where it could have served a further purpose as the model for later productions based on the preliminary design. We know that the Cloisters Nativity Altarpiece (cat. no. 45), painted in the workshop of Rogier van der Weyden, is an example of an ensemble made in this manner, for it shows certain details that appear only in the underdrawing of Rogier's related Nativity Triptych in Berlin. This clearly indicates that the artist responsible for the Cloisters altarpiece based his picture on the set of drawings initially made for Rogier's picture, whose finished version he need not have seen.[18]

Official art of another kind, that is, of a secular nature, was required by local administrations for public areas, particularly for town halls and their justice chambers. Such commissions were often awarded to the officially appointed city painters, who in return received only small annual sums that were not nearly sufficient for their support. Only a small number of these commissions have remained: notable examples include the *Justice of Emperor Otto III*, painted by Bouts for the Leuven Town Hall (now in the Musées Royaux des Beaux-Arts de Belgique, Brussels), the *Justice of Cambyses* (fig. 16), produced by David for Bruges's justice chambers, and Van der Weyden's *Justice of Trajan and Herkinbald*, executed for the Brussels Town Hall (a work that survives only in a tapestry version). Evidently, projects of this nature took several years to complete, during which time the original commission was sometimes modified, due either to the painter's circumstances or the client's demands. Only two of the four intended Justice scenes were completed by Bouts and his workshop before Bouts's death in 1475, when the project was abandoned. And David made significant alterations to the first version of his panels, probably in response to changes in the taste of his patrons over time and perhaps because it was necessary for him to add portrait heads of newly elected members of the judicial body to the updated and final version of the work completed in 1498.

The Economic Power of the New Bourgeoisie

The growth of the middle class in the fifteenth and sixteenth centuries created a new group with the economic power to acquire paintings. The most spectacular extant work produced for a bourgeois patron is Hubert and Jan van Eyck's Ghent Altarpiece (figs. 17, 18), ordered by Jodocus Vijd. Destined for the Vijd family chapel in Sint-Baafs (Saint Bavo's) in Ghent, the altarpiece remains in the church, although not in its designated chapel. Altarpieces and smaller devotional panels commissioned for family chapels and burial sites, as well as for private display in the home, constituted a considerable percentage of the paintings made for middle-class patrons. Often produced in response to special concerns of the patrons, these works were frequently altered to reflect the changing circumstances of the client's life. Thus, the *Merode Triptych* (cat. no. 2) evolved with a symbolic emphasis on marriage and the family and details that referred specifically to the patron: initially the *Annunciation* centerpiece was customized by the addition of the left wing representing the donor, a man named Ymbrechts (Imbrecht, Imbrechts, Inghelbrechts, Engelbrecht, Ingelbrects, or Engelbrechts), and of the right wing showing Joseph; later, presumably when Ymbrechts married, the female donor and a figure at the gate of the garden enclosure were introduced over the completed painting on the left wing.

For commissions such as the *Merode Triptych*, artists kept on hand patterns and designs for frequently requested devotional images to which they added particular donor figures, patron saints, or the client's coat of arms to designate ownership. The *Virgin and Child* by the Master of the Saint Ursula Legend (cat. no. 49) is one of these standard devotional images, or best-sellers, itself adapted from one of the most famous images of the day, Van der Weyden's *Saint Luke Drawing the Virgin* (fig. 19). Our painting now exists as an individual panel, but other versions of the same Virgin and Child image (for example, one in the Fogg Art Museum, Cambridge, Massachusetts) form the left half of a diptych whose right half, representing the donor and his patron saint, is the customized portion of the commission.

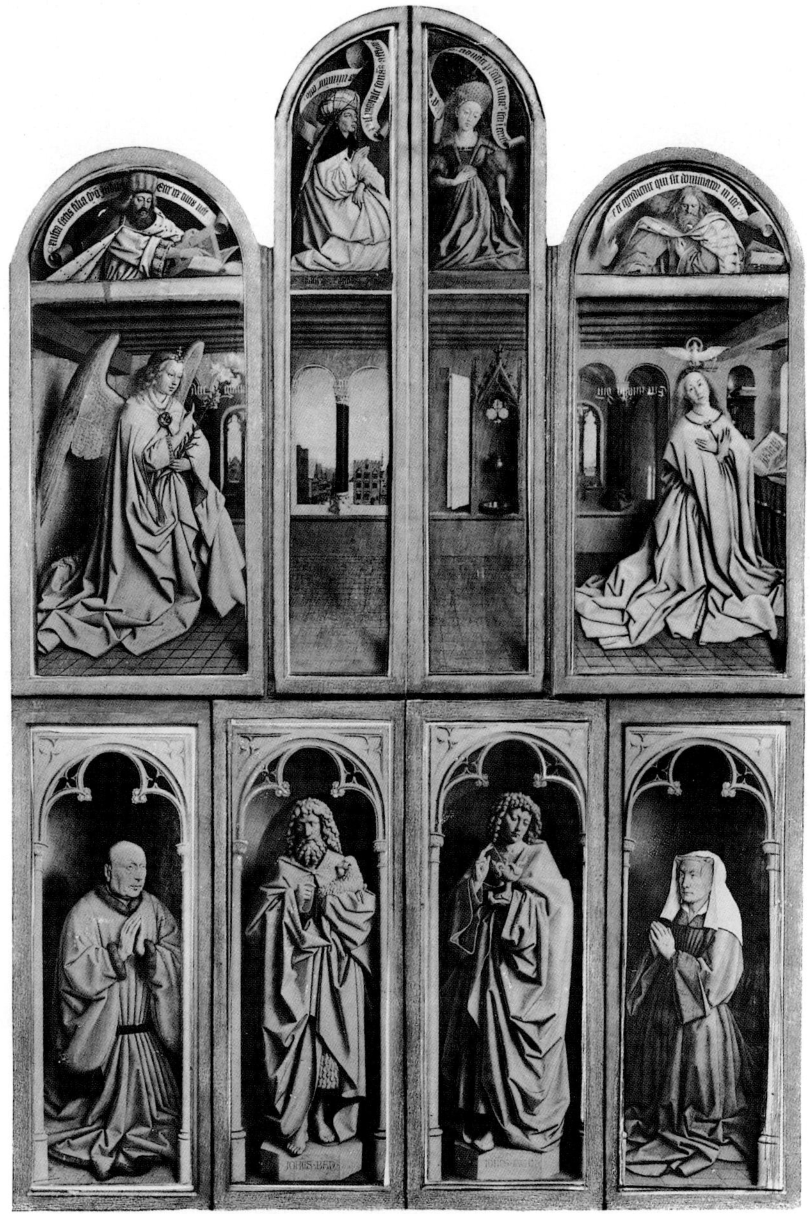

Fig. 17. Hubert and Jan van Eyck, Ghent Altarpiece (closed), completed 1432. Oil on wood, Sint-Baafs (Saint Bavo's), Ghent

Workshop inventories and wills of artists indicate that painters kept not only a supply of patterns but also a group of finished or partially completed works—a stock from which bourgeois clients

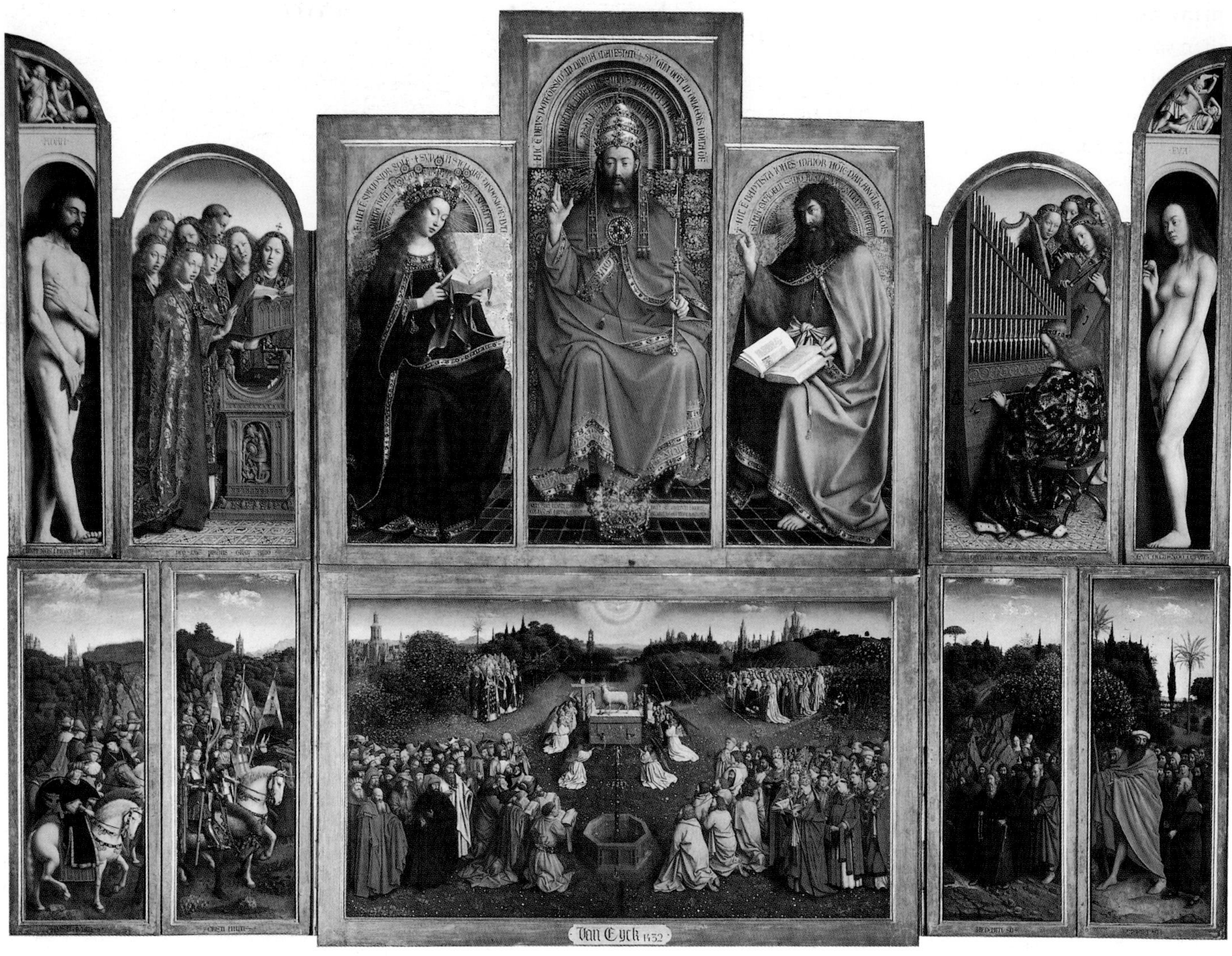

Fig. 18. Hubert and Jan van Eyck, Ghent Altarpiece (open), completed 1432. Oil on wood. Sint-Baafs (Saint Bavo's), Ghent

could buy outright. Following a practice that likely was standard, Bouts, in 1475, and Vrancke van der Stockt, in 1489, left unfinished pictures, patterns, and drawings to their sons to supply the ongoing needs of their clients; the finished paintings were bequeathed to the painters' wives, presumably as an inheritance they could sell.[19]

Their imposing size indicates that David's splendid Nativity Altarpiece (cat. no. 72), made for as-yet-unidentified donors, and Joos van Cleve's Crucifixion Triptych (cat. no. 95), produced for a certain Paul, were likely commissioned to adorn a family chapel in a church. These pictures, like others ordered for chapels, may have served a memorial function at the family burial site. However, when no inscriptions to this effect have been preserved, as is the case with our two works, this purpose cannot be confirmed. One example of a painted epitaph appears in a picture attributed to the Master of the Saint Ursula Legend: the *Virgin and Child with Saint Anne Presenting Anna van Nieuwenhove* (cat. no. 33), which was originally the right half of a diptych. This diptych was probably made to hang at Anna's burial site in the church of Onze-Lieve-Vrouw in Bruges, where the prominent Nieuwenhove family had its tomb. The painting's inscription provides the details of Anna's familial connections and the date of her death, the exact circumstances of which can only be surmised.

Well into the sixteenth century the wealthy bourgeoisie commissioned works not only to serve their devotional practices but also to decorate their residences. Some, like the prosperous banker Niclaes Jongelinck, began to form collections of many works by a single artist: he owned no fewer than sixteen paintings by Pieter Bruegel the Elder. Bruegel's Months series, which included our *Harvesters* (cat. no. 102), was part of a grand program that Jongelinck developed for Ter Beken, his suburban house outside the city walls of Antwerp. In an arrangement that included sculpture as well as paintings, Jongelinck endeavored to create a humanist, Renaissance vision of the universe and man's place in it. Considered a showplace by Antwerp society, Ter Beken expressed Jongelinck's status and prestige, much as the court functionaries' grand commissions of religious paintings had announced their own position and power in the fifteenth century.

The Evolution of Demand and Supply: Artists and Their Marketing Strategies

Over half the collection of early Netherlandish paintings at the Metropolitan Museum originated in either Bruges or Antwerp, the two principal centers of commerce and art of the Netherlands in the fifteenth and sixteenth centuries. Furthermore, the major artists of these cities are well represented in our holdings. Thus the Museum collection provides numerous and key examples of works that reflect the changing relationships of clients, art markets, and artists in a period of transition. A brief look at the relationship of these artists to their clients and an examination of marketing strategies illuminate the development from a privileged ducal patronage to mass-market sales.

Bruges and the Accommodation of Local and Foreign Clients

One of the largest cities in northwestern Europe and the most prominent commercial center of its day, Bruges by 1470 had some forty thousand inhabitants.[20] Not only the active court life and the wealthy entourages of the dukes contributed to the city's economic health; it was nourished as well by the exceptionally prosperous and broad commercial middle class of Bruges together with an unusually large group of resident foreign merchants.[21] The foreign community was extremely well established, with its own corporate buildings, chapels for regular religious services, and private living quarters. Its members were concentrated in three marketplaces north of the Groote Markt: the Italians lived around Beurze Square, the Iberians at Biscay Square, the Scots and the English in nearby streets, and the Hanse, or Germans, just beyond them. The clustering of these closely knit groups in one general area facilitated both trade and artistic exchange.

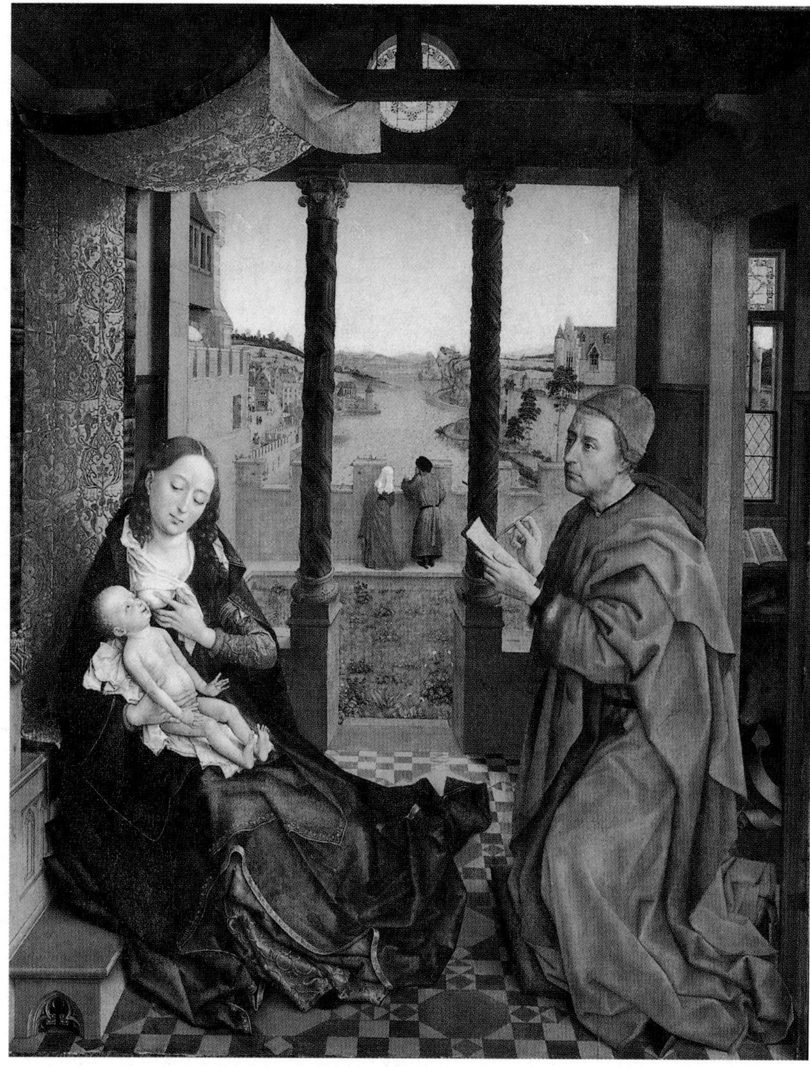

Fig. 19. Rogier van der Weyden, *Saint Luke Drawing the Virgin*, about 1435–40. Oil on wood. Museum of Fine Arts, Boston

It is no wonder, then, that the city attracted artists from other regions. None of the succession of leading Bruges painters of the fifteenth and early sixteenth centuries—Jan van Eyck, Petrus Christus, Hans Memling, and Gerard David—was a native of the town. Except for Van Eyck, these émigré artists were not attached to the court or provided with a steady pension from the city, and, as a consequence, commissions from the growing and newly wealthy bourgeoisie were key to their economic success.

To a significant degree the regulations for the Corporation of Imagemakers provided protective measures to help ensure the livelihoods of panel painters. It was necessary to have citizenship by birth or long residence or to purchase it to become a member of the guild, a requirement instituted for the purpose of controlling production. Bruges masters were allowed to exhibit and sell works only at the city's annual art fairs and one other place, usually their shops.[22] Further restrictions were put in place to eliminate competition. For example, the cloth painters, or *cleederscrivers*, were ranked as separate from and inferior to the class of panel painters, or *schilders*. (This held true even though painting on canvas was a major industry in Bruges, the chief center for its production until about 1530, where it was practiced by roughly 40 percent of artists in the fifteenth century.)[23] In lawsuits between the two groups, the standing regulations that were challenged clearly favored the panel painters: cloth painters were not allowed to exhibit openly for sale, nor were they permitted to paint in oil.[24] Another branch of painters, the illuminators, were also subject to restraints imposed in the interest of the panel painters and agreed upon by the city magistrates. At various points during the fifteenth century, the import and sale of single-leaf miniatures within the city walls of Bruges were prohibited. Miniaturists not only had to be citizens of Bruges but also were required to file their individual marks with the painters' corporation, presumably to facilitate the guild's exercise of control over their activities. Like the cloth painters, illuminators were not permitted to paint in oil.[25]

Within this tightly controlled guild system, how did individual artists secure their own share of the business of painting? A close look at the stylistic development of artists in Bruges and Antwerp reveals an important strategy, which has been little discussed: they catered to the clients whose patronage they sought by accommodating their presumed or stated aesthetic concerns and expectations. In Bruges the prominence of foreign businessmen—especially Italians and Spaniards—who had a considerable amount of disposable income was a determining factor in the evolution of this strategy and, by extension, the style of panel painting.

The leading painter in Bruges in the mid-fifteenth century, after Jan van Eyck died and before Hans Memling arrived in the city, was Petrus Christus. Significantly, nearly half of his small oeuvre was commissioned by Italians, has an Italian or Spanish provenance, or was early on copied by southern painters and sculptors.[26] It is not surprising to find that Christus appears to have appealed to the taste of his potential clients by adjusting his style to suit them. He moved toward implementing a one-point perspective scheme, a feature already fully in use in Italy and perhaps one that his Italian clients expected to see in his work. Christus also echoed Italian modes by employing the *sacra conversazione* format in at least one picture, the *Virgin Enthroned with Saints Jerome and Francis* (Städelsches Kunstinstitut, Frankfurt), and attempting to reduce and monumentalize form in certain of his Virgin and Child paintings. In what could well have been an astute business move, Christus joined the Confraternity of Our Lady of the Snow by 1467–68 and the Confraternity of the Dry Tree by 1469. The former counted among its many members Charles the Bold and Isabella of Portugal, as well as numerous aristocrats; all the Burgundian dukes were honorary members of the latter, which also included individuals from Bruges's most important upper-class families and in particular a large group of notable foreign merchants (the Portinari, Tani, Altoviti, Ricasoli, Villani, Cavalcanti, Arnolfini, and Cenami from the Italian community and the Gonsales, Loupes, de Castro, and Pardo families among the Spaniards).[27]

Hans Memling received most of his commissions from native and Italian residents of Bruges, fewer from the Spanish community, and still fewer from the English and Germans who lived in the city.[28] He effectively cornered the market in portraiture, which constituted a significant portion of the trade in paintings (see "Portraiture: A Meeting of the Sacred and Secular Worlds" in this publication). His ability to combine a striking verisimilitude with a certain idealization that conformed to the expectations of his sitters guaranteed Memling a prosperous business in this genre. This is an approach epitomized in his portraits of Tommaso Portinari and Maria Baroncelli (cat. no. 27), which convey the elegance of the courtly lifestyle to which his clients aspired. He seems to have attempted a pleasing conflation of northern and Italian modes of presentation in his portraits—juxtaposing an Italianate monumentality and simplification of form with a northern sense of atmosphere and light in a format that often placed his subjects before a charming, locally inspired landscape background. Perhaps in a further nod to Italian taste, Memling introduced decorative embellishments consisting of swags and putti to a number of his paintings of the Virgin and Child Enthroned. Commissions executed for major local patrons, in particular the altarpiece *Saint John the Baptist and Saint John the Evangelist* of 1479, made for the main altar of the Sint-Janshospitaal in Bruges, encouraged orders from other customers. Impressed by the grandeur of Memling's conception for the picture and by its prestigious location, they requested more modest variations, with the addition of their images as donors (cat. no. 11).

By the time Gerard David was a full-fledged guild member in 1484, economic circumstances were about to shift in Bruges. Maximilian banished the foreign merchants of the city to Antwerp, as punishment for Bruges's rebellious attempts to unseat him as regent of the northern territories and its imprisonment of him for three months in 1488. In consequence, a large segment of Bruges's prosperous trade was cut off; although some merchants returned after the peace of 1493, the damage had been done. At the same time the Zwin River, Bruges's main artery to the Atlantic Ocean, started to silt up and become unnavigable. As a result Bruges's position as the chief economic center of northwestern Europe was challenged and eventually usurped by Antwerp.

Although David enjoyed significant local business, he cannot have been unaffected by the new economic realities and, like other artists in Bruges, had to adopt new methods of attracting clients. He was perhaps the most enterprising of the Bruges artists of the period. On the death of Memling in 1494, he moved to Sint-Jorisstraat, the street where his successful predecessor had had his shop, most likely to garner the share of the local business the older painter had left behind. David advanced at a regular pace into successively more senior positions in the Corporation of Imagemakers, of which he was appointed dean in 1501. In 1507, like Christus before him, he joined the prestigious Confraternity of the Dry Tree, and in 1509 he very generously donated to the convent of Sion a large panel from his hand that was prominently placed on the high altar of the church. The painting depicted the Virgin among Virgins and included David's self-portrait and the likeness of his wife represented as donors. Perhaps uncertain that these shrewd business moves were sufficient to guarantee his livelihood in changing times, David joined the Painters' Guild in Antwerp in 1515, thus ensuring that he would be established in two major centers of art production at once.[29]

David's various strategies seem to have served his purpose, for in this period he received one of the most important commissions of the day, an order for a polyptych of seven separate panels devoted to the Virgin and Child for the abbey church of San Gerolamo della Cervara. The Metropolitan Museum's *Annunciation* panels (cat. no. 79) belonged to the second tier of this large ensemble, whose other elements are preserved in the Palazzo Bianco, Genoa, which houses four panels, and the Louvre, where the lunette, showing God the Father, is located. Unfortunately, the contract for the altarpiece no longer remains, and all that survives to provide information about the origins of this major work is the transcription of words said to have been inscribed on the now-lost original frame: "Vincenzo Sauli had this work made in 1506 on the seventh day of September."

Working in the vein of his immediate predecessors, David effected a conflation of Italian and northern modes of presentation in his altarpiece, as our *Annunciation* panels make clear. Here, the swirling draperies of Gabriel's ancient Greek-style peplos, a garment surely inspired by southern models, establish a type of urgent movement new in northern figures but already standard in Italian representations. Among the latter, Vincenzo Foppa's Gabriel in an *Annunciation* fresco, executed for the Portinari chapel at Sant' Eustorgio in Milan, may have served as a prototype for David, who could have seen it on a trip he likely took to Liguria and Lombardy. David's Virgin Annunciate, a direct descendant of the Virgin from the Ghent Altarpiece (fig. 17), however, remains true to her northern roots.

Antwerp: Market Center of the North

The number of paintings commissioned declined continuously in the late fifteenth and early sixteenth centuries, while more and more works were sold on the open market. These trends led to the development of ever greater specialization and collaboration on the part of artists, as an examination of the pictures produced at this time, especially in Antwerp, makes readily apparent.[30] The highly individual worldview landscapes of the Antwerp painter Joachim Patinir inspired a sudden demand for his work, especially for examples for export, as well as a surge of imitators. Patinir, whose career lasted only from 1515 to 1524, could not accommodate the market for landscapes of this kind, and many followers who specialized in the genre stepped in. These artists were not always adept at rendering the figures that appeared within their landscapes; as a consequence, they increasingly collaborated with specialists in figure painting, a practice Patinir and his contemporaries had to a certain extent already employed. Division of labor according to the different specialties of artists from the same or neighboring workshops was already well developed when Joos van Cleve produced his Crucifixion Triptych and *Virgin and Child* in the Linsky Collection (cat. nos. 95, 96), which evidence the procedure. In each picture Joos executed the figures and relied upon a specialist for the landscape.

The eccentric, mystical, and even macabre landscapes of Hieronymus Bosch were as much in vogue as the worldview landscapes of Patinir and his followers. Pictures by Bosch and his imitators were commissioned by members of the northern aristocracy, for example, Hendrik III of Nassau in Brussels. They were also acquired by Italian prelates, such as Cardinal Domenico Grimani in Venice, and obtained by Spanish royalty, especially Philip II, through trade or confiscation. Although Bosch died in 1516, paintings in his style continued to be produced far into the sixteenth century and constituted a significant part of the Antwerp art market. The quality of such works varies widely, and there were complaints about countless forgeries of Bosch's pictures, notably by Felipe de Guevara, writing in his *Commentarios de la pintura* of about 1560. It is in this context that the *Adoration of the Magi* (cat. no. 66), a mid-sixteenth-century pastiche of Boschian motifs set in a grand perspectival scheme, and Boschian paintings such as *Christ's Descent into Hell* (cat. no. 64) should be considered.

The Rest on the Flight into Egypt, the Holy Family, the Adoration of the Magi, and certainly the worldview landscapes introduced by Patinir were especially popular themes in Antwerp. Judging by the stylistic evidence, it would seem that the workshops of particular artists specialized in the production of given subjects: that of Joos van Cleve in representations of the Holy Family, David's in the Rest on the Flight into Egypt, the Antwerp Mannerists in general in the Adoration of the Magi, for example. It would appear as well that some of these themes derived their appeal from their focus on travel, and thus their connection with the contemporary concerns of Antwerp's merchants and tradesmen, who were dependent upon worldwide trade connections and expanding markets for their livelihoods.

Although many artists sold directly from their shops, displaying available works in their windows, others took advantage of the Pand, the fair held at regular intervals in Bruges and Antwerp.[31] Most of the stalls set up for the Bruges fairs were used by artists who had ready-made goods to sell and operated outside the city limits or in the less-desirable parts of town. The fact that David and other major artists did not rent stalls at the fairs indicates that they had well-established shops that provided them with adequate income. The Pand in Antwerp was already in operation by 1465 and steadily expanded until 1540, reflecting the increase in artistic trade that occurred during the period.

The six-week duration of the fair provided an excellent opportunity for artists to see how buyers responded to the various works on display. By observing which themes and types of representations were popular and which were no longer salable, a painter might choose to take up or increase production of certain kinds of works and abandon others. He might also attempt to create new demand by gauging the taste of buyers for artistic innovations and catering to it.[32] The sudden and intense popular interest in Italian art encouraged Netherlandish artists to adopt Italian motifs and stylistic modes, initially those influenced by Leonardo da Vinci and subsequently by Raphael. The artists ready and willing to implement the new style, Joos van Cleve (cat. no. 98) and Quentin Massys (cat. no. 99) among them, were able to attract new clients and retain old customers as well.

The shift away from commissions and toward sales on the open market had a long-lasting effect not only on methods of selling art but also on methods of making it. Procedures for streamlining production, such as the use of cartoons and patterns for the transfer of best-selling compositions, came to the fore. Artists began to rely more on assistants to increase their inventories and thus their incomes. Many paintings that issued from shops with numerous assistants were the product of the master in only the loosest sense (see cat. nos. 50, 58, 62, 65). Bruges artists such as Adriaen Isenbrant, to whom some five hundred paintings are attributed, and Ambrosius Benson, whose name is also attached to a large number of pictures, must be considered the heads of busy and productive shops rather than the authors of every work made in their establishments. It is in this connection that they are the precursors of Rubens and Van Dyck. This was the beginning of a new age in the business of art.

1. Martens 1992a, pp. 79–85.
2. Published by L. de Laborde, *Les Ducs de Bourgogne: Études sur les lettres, les arts et l'industrie pendant le XVe siècle, Preuves* (Paris, 1851), vol. 2, pp. 293–381, nos. 4410–4899, as cited in Martens 1992a, p. 80.
3. Martens 1992a, p. 84.
4. For patronage of the dukes and helpful bibliography, see Martens 1994a.
5. Campbell 1976, p. 189.
6. Ibid.
7. See Hindman 1992.
8. For a helpful bibliography on this subject, see Martens 1994a, pp. 632–33.
9. For these and further suggestions about reflections of Rolin's status in the painting, see Harbison 1991, pp. 100–118.
10. Further discussion and summary bibliography are found in Martens 1994a, p. 633.
11. See Morand 1991.
12. A summary of the patronage at Genadedal appears in Martens 1992a, pp. 331–42.
13. Scholtens 1938, p. 51; Ainsworth 1994b, pp. 72–78.
14. See Ainsworth 1998a.
15. For recent bibliography, see Martens 1994a, p. 633.
16. Comblen-Sonkes 1996, pp. 41–45, 73–76.
17. See Bonenfant-Feytmans 1991.
18. Discussed by Campbell 1995b, p. 6.
19. Campbell 1976, pp. 194–95.
20. On the status of Bruges, see Vermeersch 1992.
21. See Blockmans 1992.
22. See Weale 1911, especially pp. 28–29.
23. See Wolfthal 1989.
24. Ibid., pp. 6–12.
25. Van den Haute 1913, p. 49; Weale 1864–65, p. 299.
26. Ainsworth 1994b, pp. 60–62.
27. Martens 1992a, pp. 308–11.
28. Martens 1997.
29. Further information on David's entrepreneurial strategies is found in Ainsworth 1998a.
30. A review of the impact of economic factors on art markets of this period is found in Montias 1990.
31. See Wilson 1983 and Ewing 1990.
32. See Wilson 1986 and Wilson 1998.

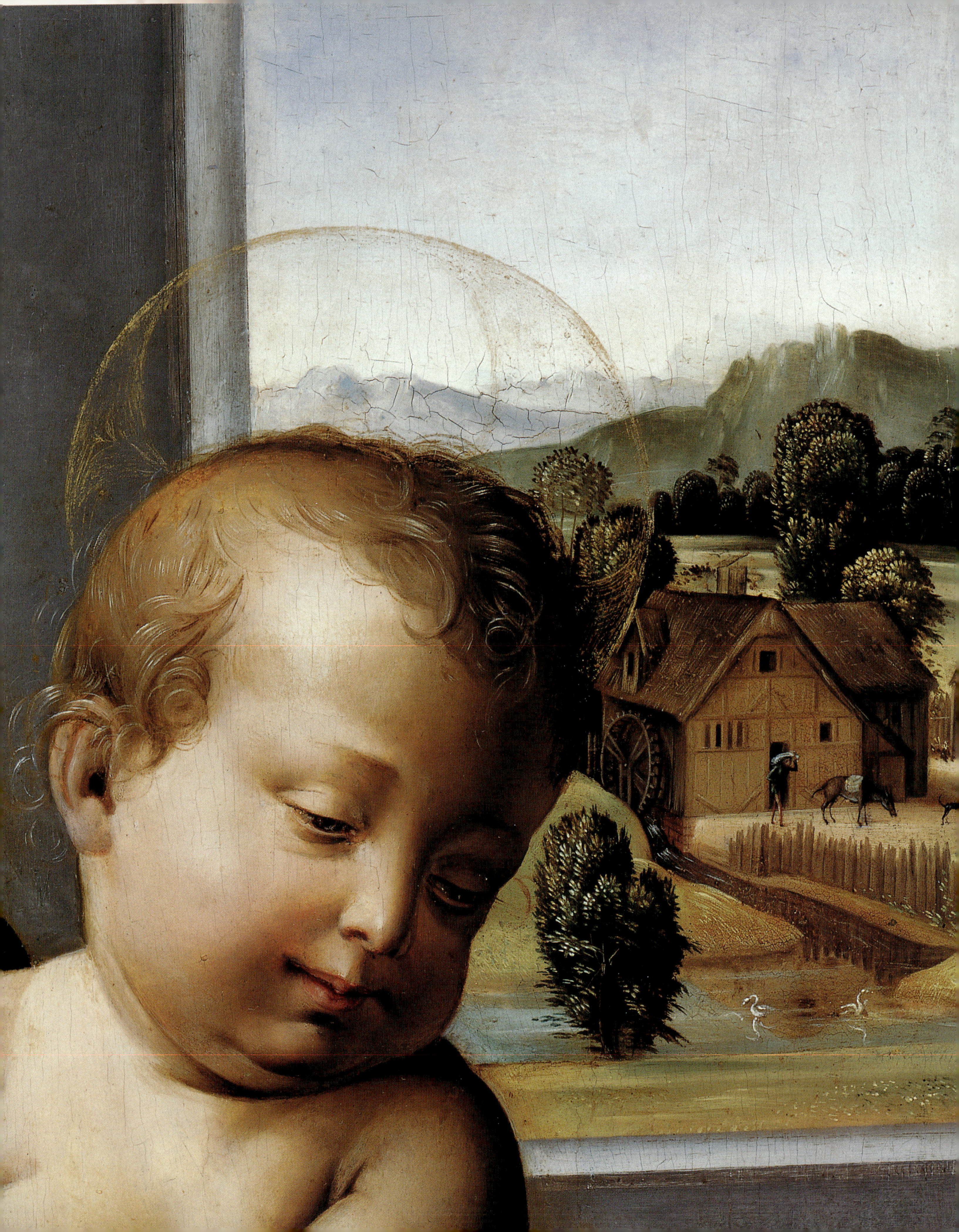

The View from Italy

KEITH CHRISTIANSEN

Opposite: Fra Bartolomeo, detail, *Madonna and Child with the Young Saint John the Baptist*, about 1490–93. Oil on wood. The Metropolitan Museum of Art, New York

In 1459 Pierre van der Meulen, dean of the church of Saint Paul at Liège, died, leaving to the treasury of his church a painting of the Tower of Babel. It was, his will reads, a small work, but painted with beauty and mastery.[1] The reference is interesting on a number of grounds, not least because the picture's unusual subject forecasts in such a striking fashion that of one of Bruegel's most haunting paintings carried out a hundred years later. But what is truly astonishing is the fact that this incidental and cryptic description is the nearest thing we possess to a critical appraisal of a Netherlandish painting by a compatriot of Jan van Eyck's and Rogier van der Weyden's. Contrast this to the situation in Italy, where, in 1449, the widely traveled antiquarian Cyriac of Ancona stopped at the Este court at Ferrara and was shown the duke's collection of paintings. The work that most impressed Cyriac was a triptych of the Descent from the Cross by Rogier—"after Jan [van Eyck] . . . the outstanding painter of our time." Of the triptych he has left an evocative and admiring account enumerating its outstanding qualities (the work itself, alas, does not survive). There were the expressions of the men and women about Christ, who "cry with great grief"; the pointed contrast between the faces of the living, who "seem to breathe as though they were alive," and the dead Christ, "in every way like a dead person"; and the depiction of fabrics, flowers, and landscape, which seemed "not of human artifice, but the products of Nature herself, who generates all things." It was, he wrote, a "most devout image"—*pientissima agalma*.[2] In a reversal of our expectations, Cyriac judged the Italian pictures he saw by the yardstick of Rogier's work.

Cyriac was not alone among fifteenth-century Italian humanists and writers in expressing admiration for the work of Netherlandish painters. There are the occasional mentions by writers such as the Florentine architect-sculptor-theorist Antonio Filarete and the more conspicuous treatment by Bartolomeo Fazio, the historian and secretary of King Alfonso V of Naples. In 1456 Fazio composed a book on the famous men of his day that includes thumbnail biographies of four outstanding painters: two Italians, Gentile da Fabriano and Pisanello, and two Netherlanders, Jan van Eyck and Rogier van der Weyden. Rogier's triptych at Ferrara is again mentioned, but so also is "a most notable painting in Genoa [by Rogier] in which there is a woman sweating in her bath, with a puppy near her and two youths on the other side secretly peering in at her through a chink, remarkable for their grins."[3] No less notable in Fazio's eyes was a painting by Van Eyck belonging to the nephew of the duke of Urbino showing "women of uncommon beauty emerging from the bath, the more intimate parts of the body being with excellent modesty veiled in fine linen, and of one of them he has shown only the face and breast but has then represented the hind parts of her body in a mirror painted on the wall opposite, so that you may see her back as well as her breast. In the same picture there is a lantern in the bath chamber, just like one lit, and an old woman seemingly sweating, a puppy lapping up water, and also horses, minute figures of men, mountains, groves, hamlets, and castles, carried out with such skill you would believe one was fifty miles distant from another."[4] (Again, neither work survives.)

These notices remind us of three things. First, that the taste for Netherlandish painting was a European, not a local, phenomenon—that it was, indeed, Netherlandish painting, not Italian, that held center stage for much of the fifteenth century. Second, that this taste was based on a far greater variety of works of art than we might imagine from what survives: not only religious paintings but also pictures with the kind of secular subjects more familiar today from printmaking. And third, that, paradoxical as it may seem, it was in Italy, with its flourishing humanist culture, that a critical lens for articulating an appreciation for Netherlandish painting was crafted. Paradoxically again, this same lens, when fully polished with the pumice of classical learning, was by the end of the fifteenth century to make Netherlandish art appear deficient to an informed public and, in so doing, contributed to its transformation. Far from being of peripheral interest, then, the view from Italy is in fact crucial to any history of Netherlandish painting.[5]

To speak of one view from Italy, however, is perhaps misleading. Depending on when and where we are—Ferrara, Florence, Venice, Milan, or Naples—and whose opinions we are analyzing—court humanist, collector, or artist—the attitude shifts. Attitudes, not attitude, are the subject of this essay, which attempts to give only a very impressionistic and necessarily fragmented survey of the various ways Italians reacted to the phenomenon of Netherlandish painting.

Collecting Netherlandish Painting

As we have seen, the Este dukes in Ferrara—particularly the brilliant, humanist-educated Leonello—had a pronounced taste for Netherlandish painting, which was ordered through a Lucchese merchant in Bruges, Paolo Poggi. In 1446 Leonello acquired a "very beautiful painting" of Saint George, and the following year he spent 120 ducats for a "most noble picture"—perhaps the triptych by Rogier van der Weyden that Cyriac and Fazio admired. Rogier is sometimes thought to have stopped in Ferrara on the occasion of a pilgrimage to Rome during the jubilee year of 1450, and that same year he was paid in Bruges through Paolo Poggi for further works ordered by Leonello. Leonello's illegitimate son Francesco sat to Rogier for a portrait after he moved to Brussels in 1444 (cat. no. 23).[6]

Leonello's taste for Netherlandish painting was perhaps inspired by his father-in-law, Alfonso of Aragon, king of Naples. Alfonso's collection included two works by Van Eyck—a triptych with the Annunciation that he acquired from the Genoese merchant Battista Lomellini and a *Saint George* purchased in Valencia in 1444 (both lost)—as well as an impressive set of canvases showing the Passion of Christ painted by Rogier van der Weyden.[7] Alfonso's predilection for Netherlandish art, which predated his transfer to Naples, created the conditions for a hybrid school of painting that, through the person of the great Sicilian master Antonello da Messina, was to have an enormous impact throughout the Italian peninsula. But it was Alfonso's predecessor, René of Anjou—ruler of Naples from 1438 until 1442—who laid the groundwork for these developments. René was himself a painter and an avid patron, and when he moved from Provence to Naples he seems to have brought with him a remarkable artist. This painter, who until recently was known variously as the Master of the Annunciation of Aix, the René Master, or the Master of the Coeur d'Amour Espris, has now been plausibly identified with the Netherlander Barthélemy d'Eyck (or van Eyck).[8] D'Eyck painted in a style that drew on the art of Robert Campin and Jan van Eyck, and it may have been through him that the secrets of Netherlandish oil painting were first taught to artists of the Neapolitan area, and in particular to Antonello's teacher, Niccolò Colantonio. Colantonio's own altarpiece for Alfonso, depicting Saint Jerome in his study removing a thorn from a lion's paw (fig. 20), certainly derived from the king's altarpiece by Jan van Eyck, which showed Saint Jerome in one of its wings; Colantonio also made a copy of Van Eyck's *Saint George* (like the original, the picture is lost).

The vogue for Franco-Burgundian culture was a pervasive factor in Italian court life. Although Leonello and Alfonso surrounded themselves with humanist writers, this does not mean they renounced the chivalric culture of France and Burgundy. French courtly literature found a place on their library shelves alongside works by Greek and Roman authors, and French tapestries decorated the walls of their castles. Yet this fascination with things Franco-Burgundian does not entirely account for the taste for Netherlandish painting in Italy, and it does not fully explain the decision of

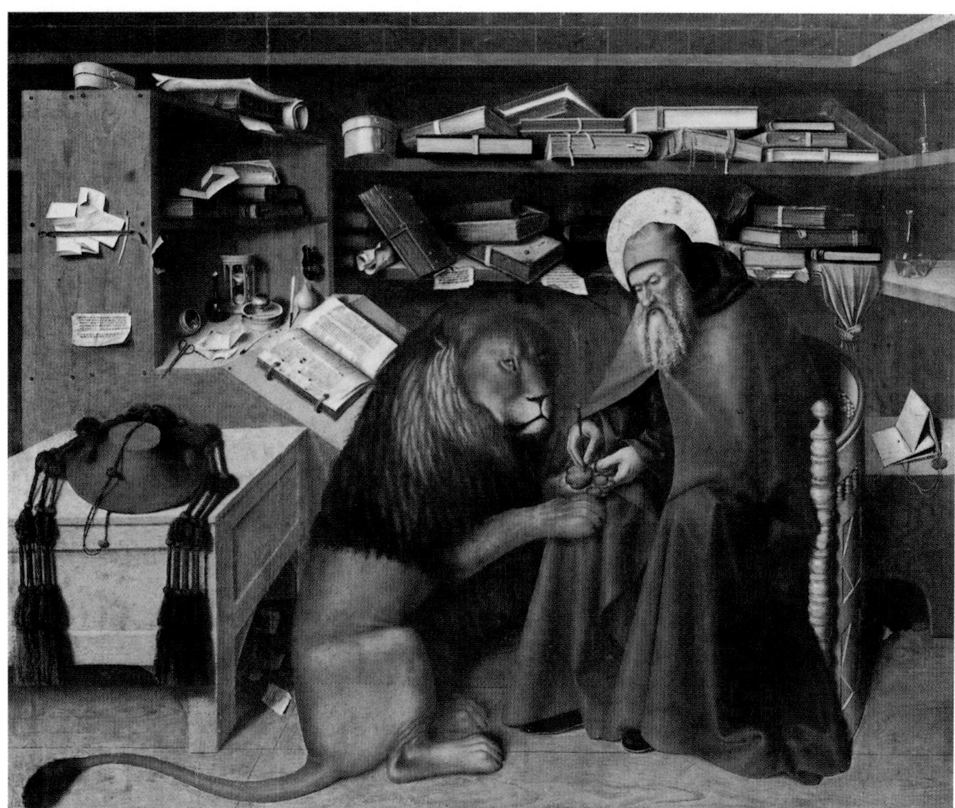

Fig. 20. Niccolò Colantonio, *Saint Jerome in His Study Removing a Thorn from the Lion's Paw*, about 1445. Oil on wood. Museo e Gallerie Nazionale di Capodimonte, Naples

the duke of Milan, Francesco Maria Sforza, to send a local painter, Zanetto Bugatto, to Brussels in 1460 to study with Rogier van der Weyden.[9] The duke's immediate objective seems to have been to raise the level of portraiture in Milan to the standards set by Netherlandish painting. Indicatively, after Zanetto's death in 1476 Francesco made an effort to secure the services of Antonello da Messina. Francesco's example established a pattern: Alfonso of Aragon's illegitimate son, Ferrante, sent Giovanni di Giusto to Bruges in 1469 so that he could learn the secrets of Netherlandish painting, and not much later Federigo da Montefeltro—that paragon of Renaissance princes and a key figure in any history of humanist culture—invited Joos van Gent to his court in Urbino (see cat. no. 7). Although today we tend to associate Federigo's name with that of Piero della Francesca, his well-informed bookseller-biographer, Vespasiano da Bisticci, has this to say: "[Federigo] was much interested in painting, and because he could not find in Italy painters in oil to suit his taste he sent to Flanders and brought thence a master who did at Urbino many very stately pictures, especially [for] Federigo's study. . . . He painted from life a portrait of the Duke which only wanted breath."[10] The likeness Vespasiano mentions and some of the pictures made for the study can still be seen in the Palazzo Ducale, and although the portrait is probably not by Joos but from the hand of the Spaniard Pedro Berruguete, its style is utterly Netherlandish.

Federigo's brother-in-law, Alessandro Sforza, duke of Pesaro, made a trip to the Netherlands in 1458, at which time he sat to Rogier van der Weyden for a portrait, procured another portrait, of the duke of Burgundy, and commissioned an altarpiece depicting the Crucifixion. The portraits were destroyed in a fire, but the altarpiece (fig. 21) survives. Although painted by workshop assistants rather than by Rogier himself, the *Crucifixion* was clearly important for a number of Italian artists: Perugino's altarpiece painted for Bartolomeo Bartoli (fig. 22), for example, must, to some degree, have been inspired by it. Alessandro Sforza brings the taste for Netherlandish painting in Italian courts full circle: Sforza, the brother of Francesco

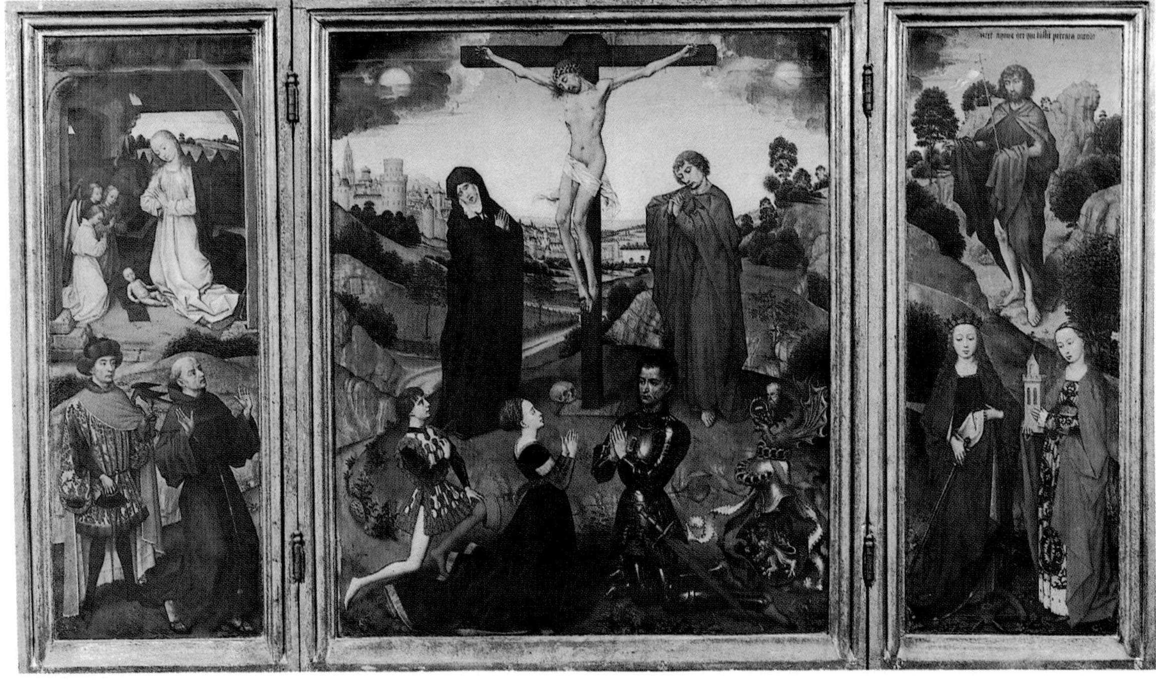

Fig. 21. Workshop of Rogier van der Weyden, *The Crucifixion* (Sforza Triptych), about 1460. Oil on wood. Musées Royaux des Beaux-Arts de Belgique, Brussels

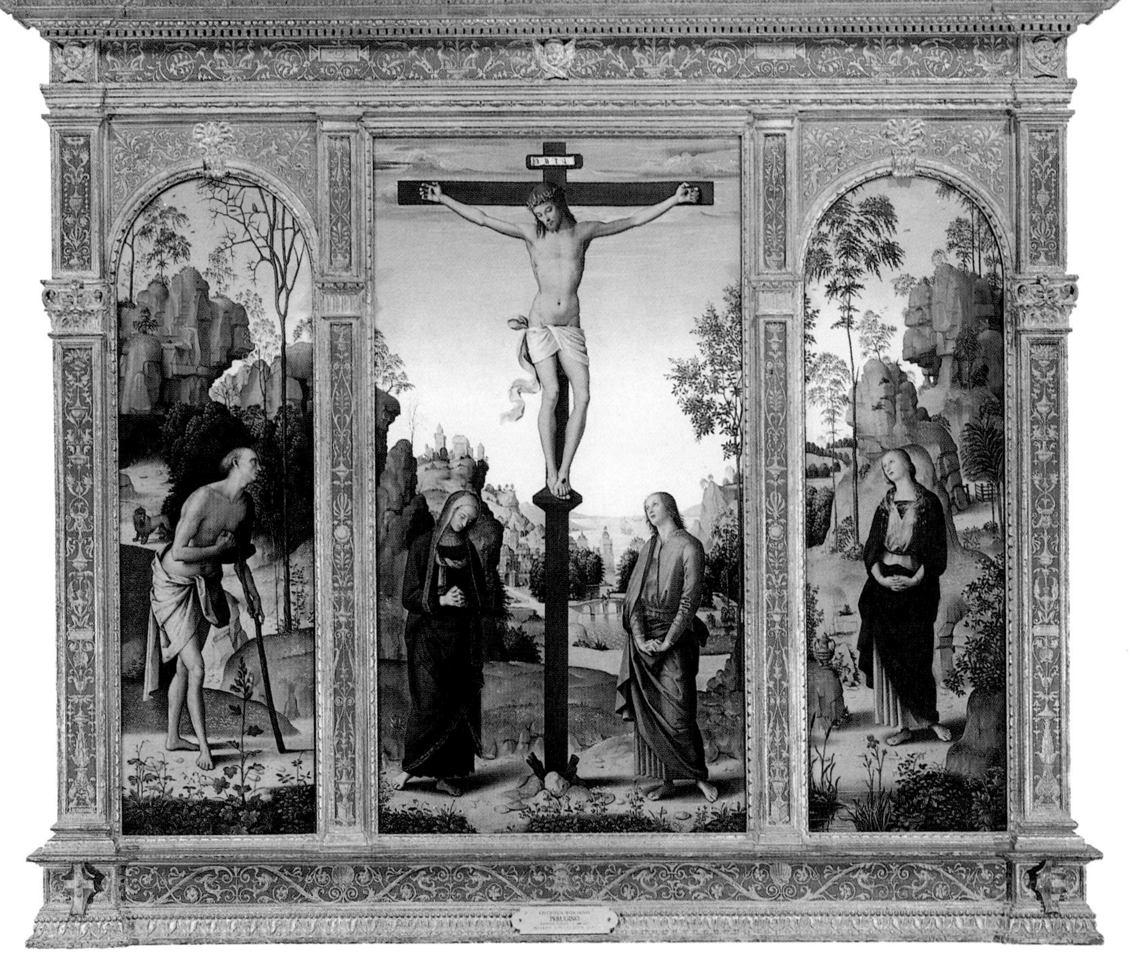

Fig. 22. Pietro Perugino, *The Crucifixion with the Virgin, Saint John, and Saints Jerome and Mary Magdalene*, about 1485. Oil on canvas, transferred from wood. Andrew W. Mellon Collection, The National Gallery of Art, Washington, D.C. 1937 1937.1.27

Maria, had been educated at Ferrara alongside Leonello d'Este.[11]

Significant as aristocratic patronage was, the taste for Netherlandish painting was not simply a court phenomenon. Commercial as well as political ties linked the various Italian cities and the north. In Bruges there were colonies of Italian merchants and bankers from Genoa, Lucca, Venice, and Florence, and these provided a primary conduit for large numbers of Netherlandish paintings. It was through commercial connections that the Villa family of Chieri, southeast of Turin, ordered at least two altarpieces from the workshop of Rogier van der Weyden—the *Annunciation* in the Louvre and a *Crucifixion* in Riggisberg.[12] Just possibly a member of the Villa family also owned Robert Campin's remarkable *Virgin and Child before a Firescreen* (National Gallery, London).[13]

Bruges had particularly close economic ties to Genoa, where there must have been numerous Netherlandish pictures. Battista Lomellino commissioned the Van Eyck triptych with the Annunciation that Alfonso acquired when Battista was part of a Genoese delegation to Naples, and the Lomellino family also seems to have owned a portable triptych by Petrus Christus (the wings are in the National Gallery of Art, Washington, D.C.). We know, too, of a small triptych by Van Eyck (Gemäldegalerie, Dresden) that was bought by Michele Giustiniani. Among the commissions ordered by Genoese in the first decades of the sixteenth century were Vincenzo Sauli's imposing altarpiece painted by Gerard David (cat. no. 79) and several works by Joos van Cleve.[14] Such was the prestige of Bruges painting in the region that Andrea della Costa proudly had his altarpiece inscribed "This [I] had made in Bruges in 1499."

The importance of the Medici bank in Bruges is well known, but it is still surprising to learn, from an inventory drawn up in 1492, that of the 142 paintings owned by the Medici and distributed among their Florentine palace and villas an astonishing 42 were Netherlandish.[15] The two most valuable were a painting of Saint Jerome in his study by Jan van Eyck and a portrait of a lady by Petrus Christus (neither certainly identifiable with surviving works, although the former may be a picture now in the Detroit Institute of Arts and the latter a work in the Gemäldegalerie, Berlin).[16] Additionally, there were numerous paintings on canvas—a more portable but less expensive and less durable support than wood.[17] These canvases were usually carried out in distemper rather than oil, and the largest may have served as inexpensive substitutes for tapestries, of which the Medici were as fond as the Este, Gonzaga, Sforza, and Montefeltro.[18] However, other canvases were framed and were clearly considered pictures (cat. nos. 7, 63). The subjects treated varied enormously. Some were religious scenes—the Virgin and Child, the Adoration of the Magi (possibly the canvas by Gerard David in the Uffizi, Florence),[19] the Entombment, the Crossing of the Red Sea. Others were distinctly profane and even erotic: dancers performing a moresca, a carnival scene, "a peacock in a basin on a sideboard," "a man playing the lute," "a half-length figure with books over his head and a pike biting his finger," "four women and three men giving each other pleasure," "two naked women bathing with other figures," and so on. A number of these were displayed in the Medici villa at Careggi, where they hung above the doors of the principal room. Lest we draw the conclusion that works of this sort were oddities, it is well to recall that the great Flemish composer in Cambrai, Guillaume Dufay, owned a picture of dancers; that one of the Netherlandish canvases purchased in 1460 by Alessandra Strozzi through her son in Bruges portrayed a peacock with foliage (the other two showed an Adoration of the Magi and a Holy Face), and that the Paduan humanist Leonico Tomeo owned a painting on canvas, said to be by Van Eyck, of trappers capturing an otter.[20] It may well have been paintings of this sort that are listed as "canvases with Flemish figures" in a 1497 inventory of the possessions of the Tornabuoni family in Florence.[21] Many of these pictures—obviously of key importance to the history of genre painting—were destroyed in Savonarola's bonfires of vanities, which, we are told, consumed "precious foreign canvases painted with most beautiful figures of great immodesty."[22]

The directors of the Medici bank in Bruges, Angelo Tani and Tommaso Portinari, were avid patrons of Hans Memling and Hugo van der

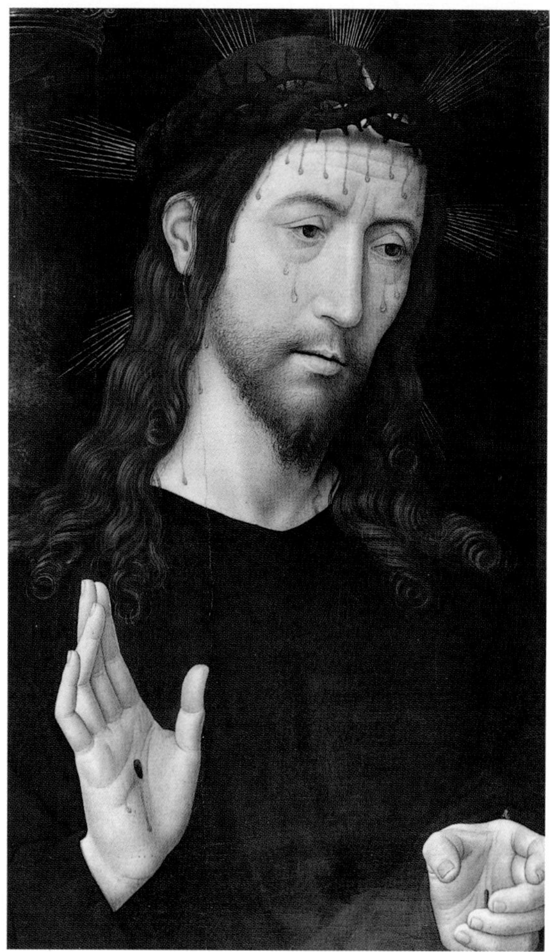

Fig. 23. Italian (Workshop of Ghirlandaio?), *Christ as the Man of Sorrows*, about 1485–90. Tempera and oil on wood. John G. Johnson Collection, Philadelphia Museum of Art

Goes—Portinari famously commissioned Van der Goes's Portinari Altarpiece (fig. 29) for the family chapel in Sant' Egidio, as well as a series of portraits and devotional works from Memling (see entry for cat. no. 27). Portinari's successor, Pierantonio Baroncelli, preferred the timid talents of an anonymous Netherlandish master. However, many of the pictures in the Medici collections were bought at the annual fair in Antwerp with a view to decorating the newly completed family palace: acquisitive desire, not geographical convenience, motivated their purchases. Two works by Rogier van der Weyden—an *Entombment* (Uffizi, Florence) and a *Virgin and Child with Saints* (Städelsches Kunstinstitut, Frankfurt)—can also be connected to the Medici, and an altarpiece by Nicolas Froment (Uffizi, Florence) was given to Cosimo de' Medici by Francesco Coppini, bishop of Terni, who commissioned the painting when he was on a mission to the Netherlands and England.[23]

The acquisitions of the Medici and their immediate circle account for a large percentage of the Netherlandish paintings that are known to have been in Florence, but not for all of them.[24] Apart from the paintings owned by the Pagagnotti (among which is cat. no. 14), there was a *Holy Face* by the Master of the Saint Ursula Legend (Pinacoteca Manfrediniana, Venice) for which Francesco del Pugliese, who was anti-Medici and pro-Savonarola, had Filippino Lippi paint wings. Another, similar image (private collection, New York), also by the Master of the Saint Ursula Legend, is known to have come from Florence,[25] and a devotional diptych by Memling showing Christ as the Man of Sorrows on one wing (Palazzo Bianco, Genoa) and the Grieving Virgin on the other (art market) achieved such popularity in the city that one panel was copied by an artist from the circle of Ghirlandaio (fig. 23).[26]

Netherlandish paintings were no less conspicuous in Venice and the Veneto, although the Venetian painters' guild tried to restrict the importation of foreign art.[27] In 1451 notice was made of an altarpiece by a Piero de Fiandro—Petrus Christus?—acquired for the church of the Carità, Venice. The future doge, Marco Barbarigo, was painted by a follower of Van Eyck in 1449 (National Gallery, London), during a diplomatic mission to London, and it may have been while he was ambassador to the Burgundian court, between 1471 and 1474, that Bernardo Bembo, father of the great poet Pietro Bembo, purchased a diptych from Memling (Alte Pinakothek, Munich, and possibly National Gallery of Art, Washington, D.C.).[28] We can also establish the presence in Padua prior to the mid-fifteenth century of a panel showing the Crucifixion by a follower of Van Eyck (Ca' d'Oro, Venice). Fifteenth-century Venetian inventories are, unfortunately, rare, and our best indication of the widespread popularity of Netherlandish painting in Venice and the Veneto comes from notes made by the collector-connoisseur Marcantonio Michiel on his visits to Venetian and north Italian collections in the 1520s and early 1530s. Michiel had a special interest in Netherlandish painting and records twenty-seven pictures, of which only a few can be traced today. He was a perceptive connoisseur but cannot be taken at his word.[29] For example, he describes two works, one by an anonymous Netherlander, the other by Rogier van der Weyden, that turn out to be a diptych by Jan Gossart (Galleria Doria Pamphili, Rome), one wing of which is copied from Van Eyck's *Virgin in the Church* in Berlin.[30]

Perhaps the Venetian collection richest in Netherlandish art was that of Cardinal Domenico Grimani, which Michiel went to see in 1521. Grimani owned a celebrated breviary illuminated by Simon Bening, but the centerpiece of his collection was a group of works by Memling: a supposed self-portrait; portraits of a husband and wife; and what Michiel calls "many other small panels with saints, all with shutters." Additionally, there was a portrait of Isabella "d'Aragona," ascribed to Memling but more likely a replica of Rogier van der Weyden's painting of Isabella of Portugal. In all, Grimani owned at least sixteen Netherlandish portraits, some of which must have been painted for Italian patrons in the fifteenth century. He also possessed an extensive group of landscapes, including three Michiel ascribed to Joachim Patinir and three he gave to Hieronymus Bosch (according to Michiel, they were on canvas, but he may have been wrong); the altarpieces by Bosch now in the Palazzo Ducale in Venice may have belonged to Grimani.[31] Boschian landscapes enjoyed enormous popularity in Venice, and we learn from later sources of a number of works in the city by Herri met de Bles (known in Italy as Civetta for the owl he was supposed to have introduced into his paintings as a sort of signature). Michiel writes of a portrait by Rogier van der Weyden owned by the Venetian Giovanni Ram and of the Van Eyck painting of trappers capturing an otter that we have noted in the collection of Leonico Tomeo in Padua. Mention should also be made of the 1581 notice by Francesco Sansovino of an otherwise undocumented altarpiece showing the Nativity ascribed to Jan van Eyck. We can infer some idea of the prestige such works enjoyed from Isabella d'Este's strenuous efforts to acquire what must have been a celebrated interpretation of the Drowning of Pharaoh in the Red Sea ascribed to Van Eyck: following the death in 1506 of its owner, the Venetian Michele Vianello, she was unsuccessful at auction but eventually struck a deal with its purchaser, Andrea Loredano, and bought from him as well what Michiel terms "a portrait of the same Jan of Bruges."

No survey, however sketchy, of the collecting of Netherlandish painting in Italy can omit mention of Cardinal Niccolò Albergati, from Bologna, who owned the *Saint Jerome in His Study* now in the Detroit Institute of Arts (possibly the same picture the Medici later owned and listed in their inventory).[32] The coat of arms of the Bolognese Loiano family appears on no fewer than three Netherlandish paintings, including one of Memling's rare secular works, a folding triptych with an allegory of Vanity (Musée des Beaux-Arts, Strasbourg).[33]

It is with the very considerable number of devotional images and portraits by Memling that show sitters in Italian dress or have an Italian provenance that we confront the limits of our ability to document the character and breadth of Italian patronage of fifteenth-century Netherlandish painting. Of the surviving pictures by Memling with some indication of provenance, over 20 percent are estimated to have been commissioned by Italians.[34] However, establishing their original owners is another matter. For example, is Memling's double portrait (fig. 24), now divided between the Louvre, Paris, and the Gemäldegalerie, Berlin, the same picture Michiel saw in the Grimani collection in Venice?[35] And what of Memling's triptych showing the Resurrection (Louvre, Paris), which a nineteenth-century sale catalogue says belonged to Count Tiepolo in Venice? The same is true of works by artists other than Memling, such as the impressive canvas altarpiece by Dieric Bouts now divided among the National Gallery, London; the Norton Simon Museum, Pasadena; the J. Paul Getty Museum, Los Angeles; a private collection; and, possibly, the Musées Royaux des Beaux-Arts de Belgique, Brussels, which is said to have come from the Foscari collection, Venice. Although Jan van Eyck's Lucca Madonna (fig. 26) was owned by the Marquis Cittadella of Lucca in the nineteenth century and may have been commissioned by one of the Lucchese merchants resident in Bruges, this

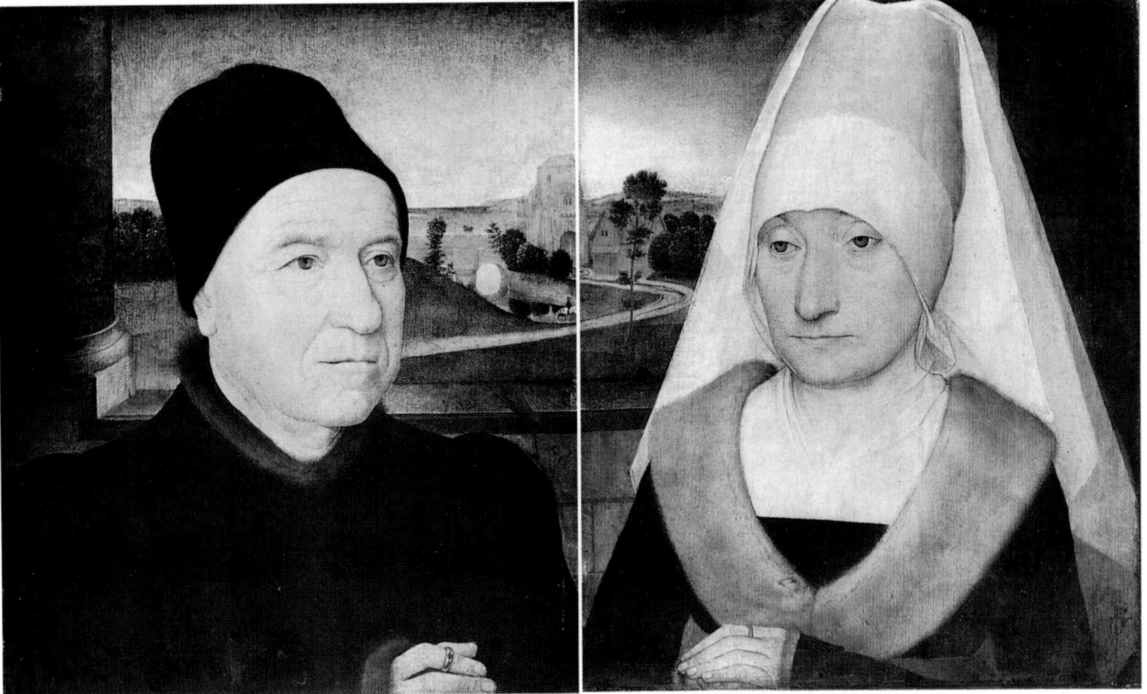

Fig. 24. Hans Memling, *Portrait of a Man and a Woman*, about 1470. Oil on wood. Gemäldegalerie, SMPK, Berlin, and Musée du Louvre, Paris

provenance cannot be taken at face value. Nor can that of the fragmentary *Deposition* on canvas by Hugo van der Goes (Christ Church Picture Gallery, Oxford), which has a putative provenance from the Durazzo collection in Genoa, or of a devotional diptych by the same artist, a wing of which (Gemäldegalerie, Berlin) comes from the Panciatichi collection in Florence. One of Dieric Bouts's most affecting small paintings of the Virgin and Child bears an inscription in Italian on the reverse ascribing it to Albrecht Dürer (cat. no. 6), while a fine replica is still to be seen in the Bargello, Florence: may we assume that their first owners were Italian?

Documented patronage is not necessarily a reliable guide either. The most celebrated painting commissioned by a Lucchese merchant from Van Eyck, a portrait of a member of the Arnolfini family and his betrothed (fig. 8), remained in the Netherlands until 1556, after which time it was taken to Spain. And Memling's great Last Judgment Triptych (Muzeum Narodowe, Gdansk), commissioned by the Medici's agent, Angelo Tani, was stolen en route to Florence in 1473 by the privateer Paul Benecke and installed in the church of Our Lady in Gdansk. Yet, even with these uncertainties, it is clear that Netherlandish painting had a wide audience in the heartland of the Renaissance and, as we shall see, held an irresistible fascination for Italian painters. Moreover, the taste continued unabated into the sixteenth century: we are told that 300 Netherlandish paintings were offered to the Gonzaga in Mantua in 1535 and that the duke bought 120.[36] However, by then the situation had changed dramatically, and northern artists were making regular trips to Italy to imbibe Renaissance norms at their source.

Critical Views

What about the critical lens through which these paintings were seen? We have already touched briefly on the views of Cyriac and Fazio, but it is important here to emphasize that, far from representing a parochial, courtly taste, as is sometimes maintained, their critical categories are informed by humanist criteria and can be taken to exemplify sophisticated opinion. Their tendency to linger over highly detailed pictures reflects the vogue for

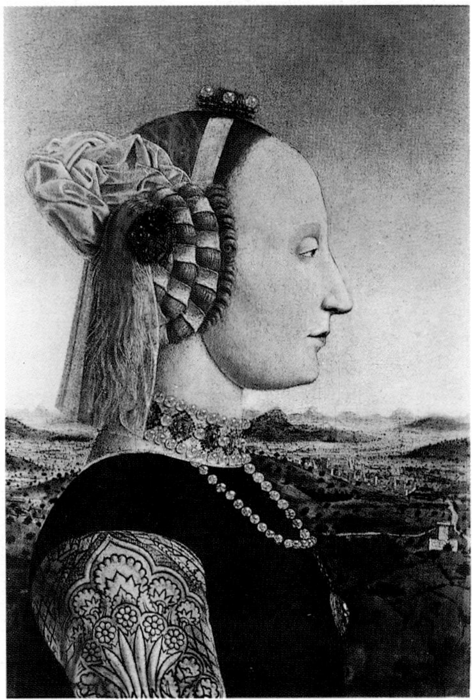
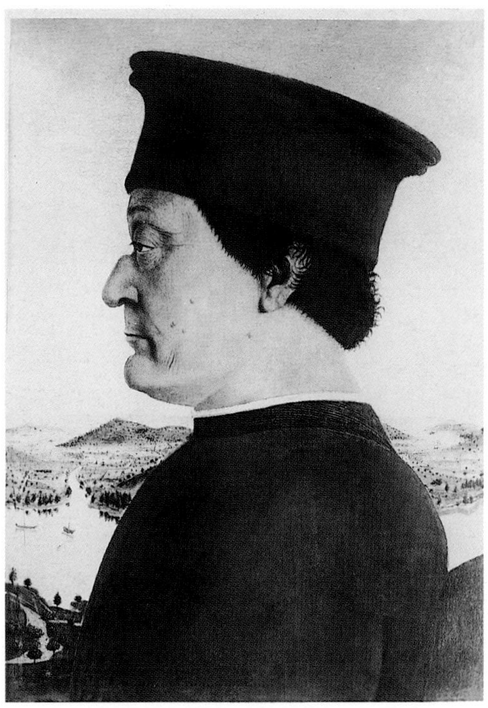

Fig. 25. Piero della Francesca, *Battista Sforza* and *Federico da Montefeltro*, about 1470. Oil on wood. Galleria degli Uffizi, Florence

a type of critical writing—the *ekphrasis*—that emphasized literary adeptness in description. Both men had also read Leon Battista Alberti's 1435 treatise on painting, in which the principles of Renaissance art were first and most authoritatively articulated, and with great adeptness they applied its ideas to the pictures they described. At the heart of Alberti's treatise lay his concept of painting as a poetic language that employed a naturalistic vocabulary grounded in geometry as well as in observation and that sought to give pleasure and moral instruction and to move viewers. His notions of affective gesture, expression, and decorum were largely derived from the treatises on rhetoric by Cicero and Quintilian, while Horace's *Ars Poetica* provided him with an analogy for poetic invention. Fazio and Cyriac embraced Alberti's view, albeit with a less idealistic and less theoretical frame of mind, and without Alberti's intimate knowledge of Florentine art.

The biographies by Fazio are remarkable for the distinction he makes between the art of Van Eyck and that of Van der Weyden, revealing that he saw more in their paintings than their foreignness and a detailed naturalism. Van Eyck's work is praised above all for its mimetic properties: "hair surpassing reality," "a ray of sun that you would take to be real sunlight," and so forth. At the same time the artist (whose use of colors is ascribed to a reading of Pliny) is lauded as a learned painter, "particularly in geometry," and as an innovator. Fazio follows up these observations with examples demonstrating Jan's use of the science of painting, noting about Alfonso of Aragon's altarpiece wing showing Jerome in his study, "If you move away from it a little it seems that it recedes inwards and that it has complete books laid open in it, while if you go near, it is evident that just their main features are there"—that is, the books are shown foreshortened so that only the front edges are visible. (In the 1492 inventory of Lorenzo the Magnificent's collection, Van Eyck's small panel with Saint Jerome in his study was also singled out for the perspective of its books.) In the category of decorum, so important in classical theory, a painting of the Virgin Mary is admired for its grace and modesty. And Fazio surely had the classical category of invention in mind when he described Van Eyck's painting of bathing women with a mirror reflecting those anatomical parts otherwise hidden from the viewer's eyes—a device Giorgione was later to resort to with enormous success—and the tour-de-force treatment of an artificial light source.

By contrast, the keynote of his biography of Rogier is expressivity[37]—which is also the focus of Cyriac's praise. The artist's panel showing a bathing woman is admirable not so much for the visual tricks it contains as for the grinning faces of youths peering through a chink. In a canvas representing Christ tormented, "you may distinguish a variety of feelings and passions in keeping with the variety of the action"—an echo of Alberti's thesis that "a *historia* will move spectators when the men painted in the picture outwardly demonstrate their own feelings as clearly as possible." Cyriac's contrasting of the spectators in the *Descent from the Cross* to the dead Christ recalls Alberti's description of a painting of the dead Meleager in which "there is no member [of the body] that does not seem completely lifeless . . . for to represent the limbs of the body entirely at rest is as much the sign of an excellent artist as to render them all alive and in action."[38] And Fazio's approbation of Rogier's conception of beauty as exemplified in the naked figures of Adam and Eve in the same altarpiece again casts the artist in Renaissance terms. Indeed, using the criteria provided by Fazio and Cyriac it is easy to see why, until his death, Rogier was the most admired Netherlandish painter in Italy.

A favorite strategy of humanist criticism was to compare a living artist with a figure of classical antiquity. Pisanello was conventionally—and rather inappropriately—likened to Zeuxis and Apelles, but the truth is that before about 1440 or 1450 few Italian painters exhibited the qualities Pliny ascribes to various ancient artists as dazzlingly as did Van Eyck and Van der Weyden. To a greater degree than their Italian contemporaries, Netherlandish artists possessed the mastery of the "realistic presentation of objects" that Pliny attributes to Apollodorus; the expressivity of the work of Polygnotus, who "introduced showing the mouth wide open and displaying the teeth and giving expression to the countenance"; Antiphilus's ability to show an apartment as though "lit by the reflection from the fire"; and the trompe-l'oeil effects of Zeuxis, "who produced a picture of grapes so successfully represented that birds flew up to the easel."[39] It has been noted that Van Eyck's royal patron, Philip the Good, was often likened to Alexander the Great and that, by implication, Van Eyck was his Apelles. That this analogy can be extended to suggest that Van Eyck actually studied optics and geometry or read classical authors such as Pliny—as Fazio would have it—seems doubtful, however; certainly he had not read Alberti's treatise.[40] Yet, ultimately, this is beside the point. Although neither Van Eyck nor Van der Weyden employed single-point perspective and neither was concerned with the critical language of humanism, they both played with illusionism in a self-conscious, masterly fashion, and the interior spaces described in their pictures are as compellingly real as any in Italian art. It was the way Netherlandish painting replaced the mere representation of time-honored subjects with a rich descriptive language that fascinated Fazio and his contemporaries; for them it was the act of describing, not some esoteric code of symbolism, that raised Netherlandish painting to the status of art.

The Responses of Italian Artists

Italian artists were well aware that as part of the visual frame of reference of collectors and critics Netherlandish painting posed a challenge to them. We have seen how, in the Ferrara of Leonello d'Este, Rogier's art was taken as a paradigm. Cyriac actually described the resident court artist, Angelo da Siena (known as Parrasio, after the celebrated ancient painter Parrhasias), who was busy painting a series of Muses for Leonello's study, as an imitator of Rogier; in fact, technical analysis of the surviving panels demonstrates that an attempt was made to follow the Netherlandish example and employ oil rather than tempera as the medium. The terms of criticism Cyriac used for Angelo's Muses are virtually identical to those he applied to Rogier's paintings. He admired the "calm joy in [the Muse's] living face" and the "gleaming pearls and gems" that seemed to be real and stand up in relief when viewed from one angle but which "from another position appear like areas of flat, smooth color." In the backgrounds of the surviving panels appear distant vistas traversed by minuscule figures that are patently inspired by those in Rogier's work. (An emphasis on detailed description became a primary ingredient in the paintings of Ferrarese artists such as Cosimo Tura and Ercole dei Roberti.)

When he worked for Federigo da Montefeltro at Urbino, Piero della Francesca knew that, inevitably, his efforts would be compared to Netherlandish art. (The duke did not hesitate to have the clasped hands Piero gave him in the great altarpiece now in the Brera, Milan, repainted in a Flemish style by Pedro Berruguete.) Whether Piero had a Netherlandish prototype in mind when, about 1470–72, he painted Federigo da Montefeltro and Battista Sforza (in oil) against a minutely described landscape (fig. 25) cannot be said, but it is certain that the ambition was to rival the descriptive powers of Netherlandish painting while retaining the Italian preference for princely portraits in profile.

In Florence the response to Netherlandish painting was no less notable, although more varied. Sometimes it was the still-life details or landscapes that impressed Florentine artists, and sometimes it was the technique or the representational solutions. In emulation of Netherlandish art, Filippo Lippi painted the Madonna in his *Virgin and Child* of 1437 (fig. 27) as a bourgeois mother in a domestic interior illuminated by a natural-seeming light with a view of a landscape out a shuttered window. Similarly, in his *Annunciation* of a few years later (San Lorenzo, Florence), he ostentatiously placed in the foreground a glass vase filled with water on whose surface we see the reflection of light and through which we view the vase distorted.[41] At precisely the same time Fra Angelico began to give the details of his paintings—the brass surface of a vase of flowers set before the Virgin in his altarpiece in Perugia and the pearls on an ecclesiastical vestment in the altarpiece commissioned by Cosimo de' Medici for San Marco, for example—a reflective brilliance and luster that lend his work a new dimension. As Meiss suggested years ago in a seminal article, Van Eyck's so-called Lucca Madonna (fig. 26) was perhaps the point of reference for both Lippi and Angelico.[42] (Was it this work or Van Eyck's triptych in Genoa that served as the model for Antonio da Fabriano's astonishing painting of Saint Jerome in his study, dated 1451 [fig. 28]?)[43]

In spite of what might be expected from Fazio's richly shaded terms of praise, Florentine artists tended to see in Netherlandish painting mostly a paradigm of verisimilitude and rich color (by the sixteenth century color, or *coloritio*, was more or less synonymous with naturalism). It is not difficult to see in their attitude a prefiguration of the later Italian complaint that northern artists were lacking in a sense of compositional structure and ideality—the province of drawing, or *disegno*, the foundation of Florentine painting. Only occasionally do we get a sense of Florentine artists responding to something more than the details of Netherlandish painting, even when the work in question was as impressive as Hugo van der Goes's Portinari Altarpiece (fig. 29), which arrived in Florence in 1483. That same year Filippino Lippi painted two circular panels portraying the Annunciation (fig. 30) in which he emulated the realism of Hugo's masterpiece through the inclusion of both domestic still-life details and narrative vignettes in the landscape backgrounds. He did this without sacrificing Italian ideals of beauty and grace. Ghirlandaio too saw in the Portinari Altarpiece only another Netherlandish source for arresting details: just as in his fresco of Saint Jerome in his study (church of the Ognissanti, Florence) he freely quoted from the Medici's little painting of the same subject by Van Eyck, so in his *Nativity* (Santa Trinita, Florence) he adapted the faces of the shepherds from those in the Portinari Altarpiece. Only Botticelli responded to the combination of realism, highly charged emotion, and sheer physical density of Van der Goes's figures, and it is this aspect of the Portinari Altarpiece he pays homage to in his great San Barnaba Altarpiece (Uffizi, Florence).

The landscape backgrounds of Netherlandish painting evoked varied reactions from Florentine artists. Occasionally, an artist such as Lorenzo di Credi tried to imitate their crystalline atmosphere and gentle hills as well as to emulate the subtle use of oil glazes. But just as frequently the vistas in the paintings of Van Eyck and Rogier van der Weyden,

Fig. 26. Jan van Eyck, *The Virgin and Child* (Lucca Madonna), about 1435. Oil on wood. Städelsches Kunstinstitut und Städtische Galerie, Frankfurt

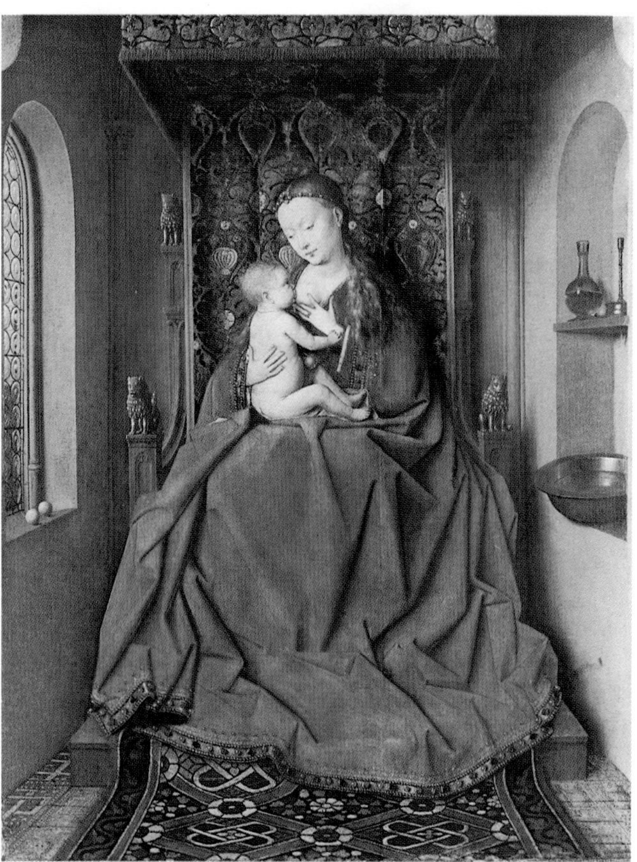

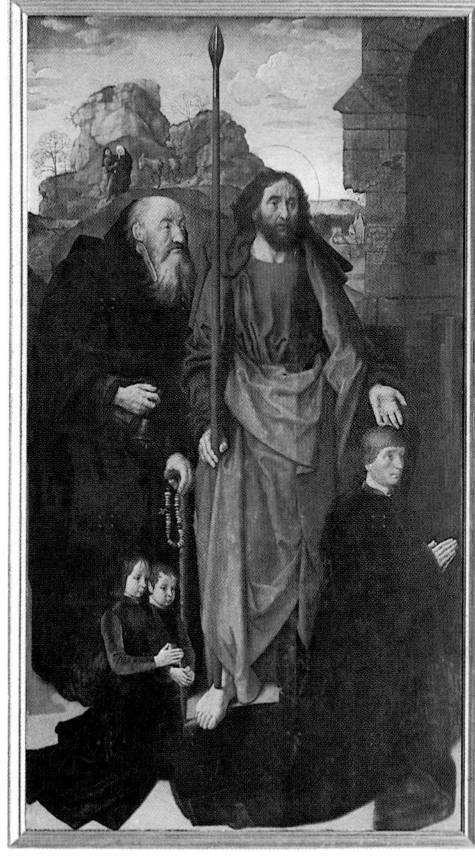

Left: Fig. 27. Filippo Lippi, *Virgin and Child* (Tarquinia Madonna), 1437. Tempera on wood. Galleria Nazionale, Palazzo Barberini, Rome

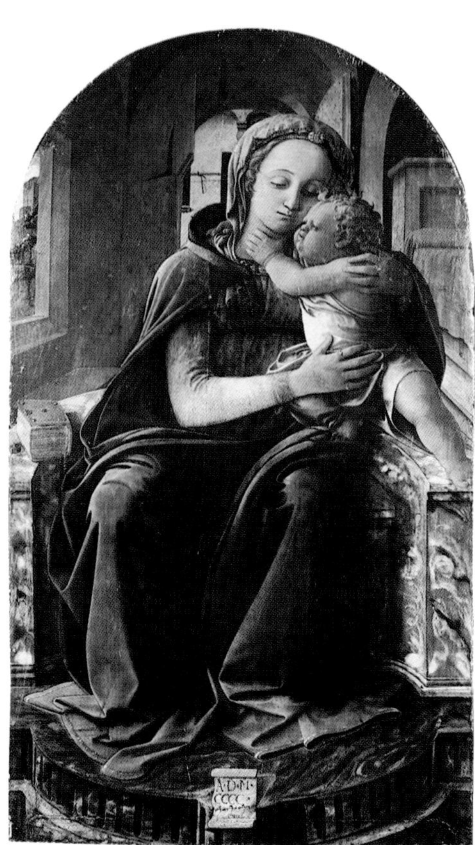

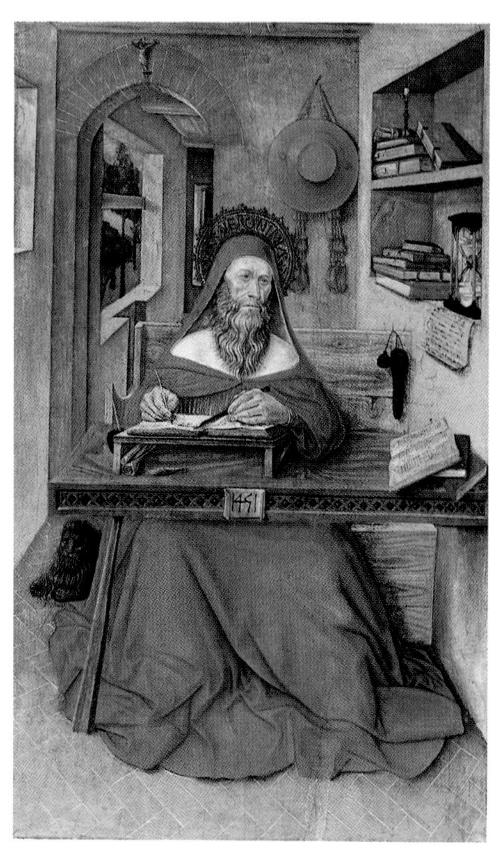

Right: Fig. 28. Antonio da Fabriano, *Saint Jerome in His Study*, 1451. Tempera on wood. Walters Art Gallery, Baltimore

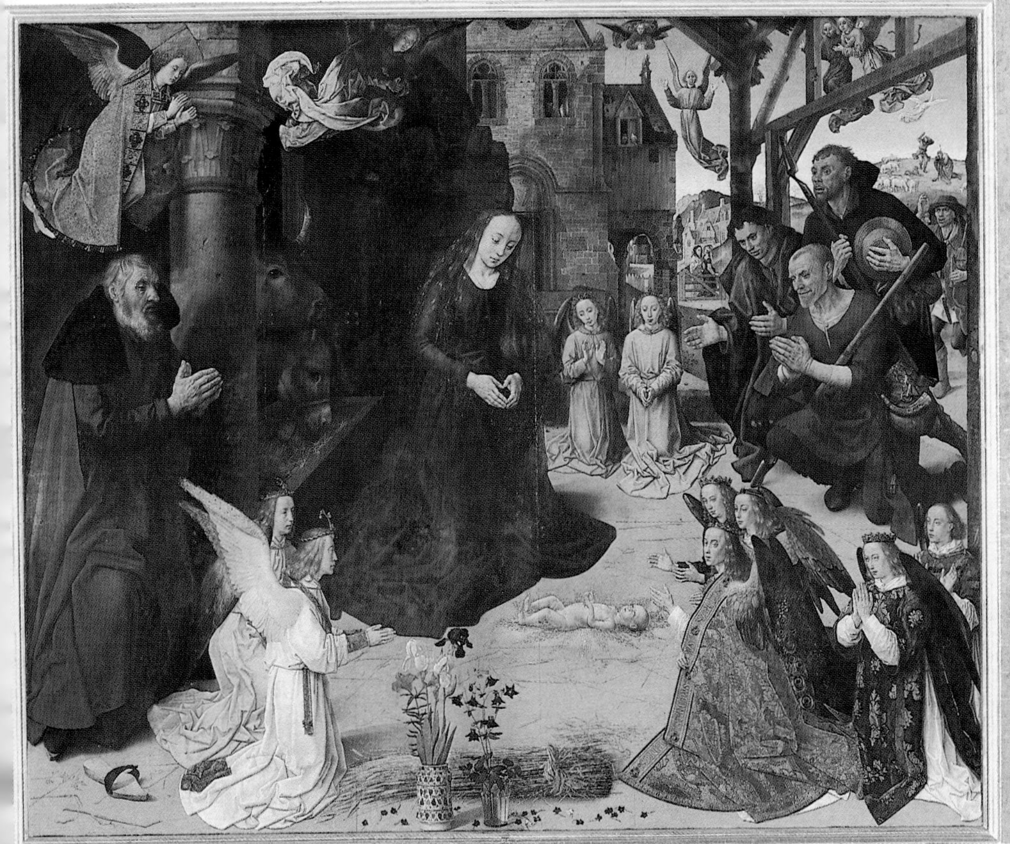

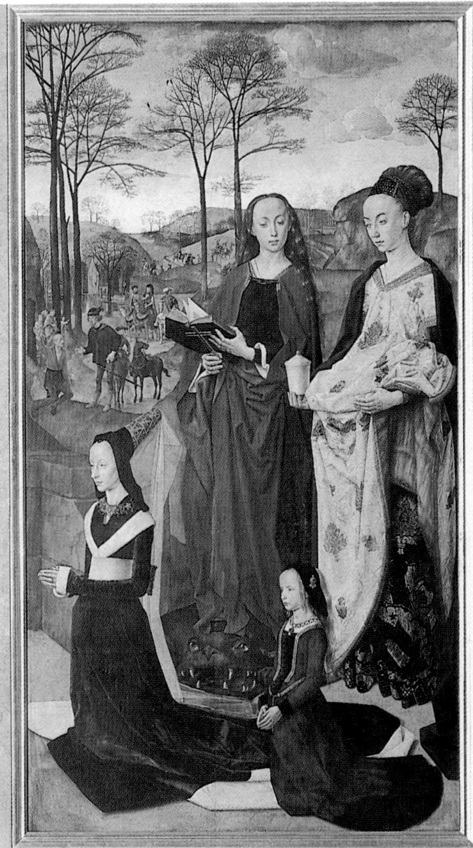

Fig. 29. Hugo van der Goes, Portinari Altarpiece, 1473–78. Oil on wood. Galleria degli Uffizi, Florence

with their rocky outcroppings and turreted castles, were mined for picturesque details, with a resulting disjunction between foreground and background. Botticelli, for example, staged the Annunciation in a Renaissance interior with a view, through an open door, of northern Gothic castles in the distance. It comes as something of a shock to realize that in his early *Adoration of the Magi* (fig. 32), Botticelli inserted behind a Renaissance stable a clifflike rock formation and a body of water with a small boat copied from Jan van Eyck's *Stigmatization of Saint Francis* (two versions are known: Galleria Sabauda, Turin, and Philadelphia Museum of Art [fig. 31]).[44] Other, similarly direct quotations can be found in a variety of Florentine paintings of the late fifteenth century as well as in some Venetian works.[45] Bellini had certainly seen something similar to Van Eyck's *Saint Francis* before he painted his three versions of *Saint Jerome in the Wilderness* (National Gallery, London; Contini Bonacossi collection, Florence; and National Gallery of Art, Washington, D.C. [fig. 33]); his *Sacred Allegory*

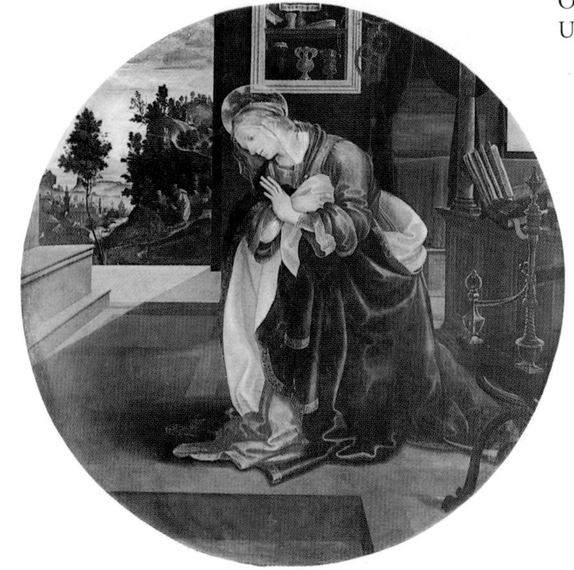

Fig. 30. Filippino Lippi, *Virgin of the Annunciation*, 1483. Tempera on wood. Museo Civico, San Gimignano

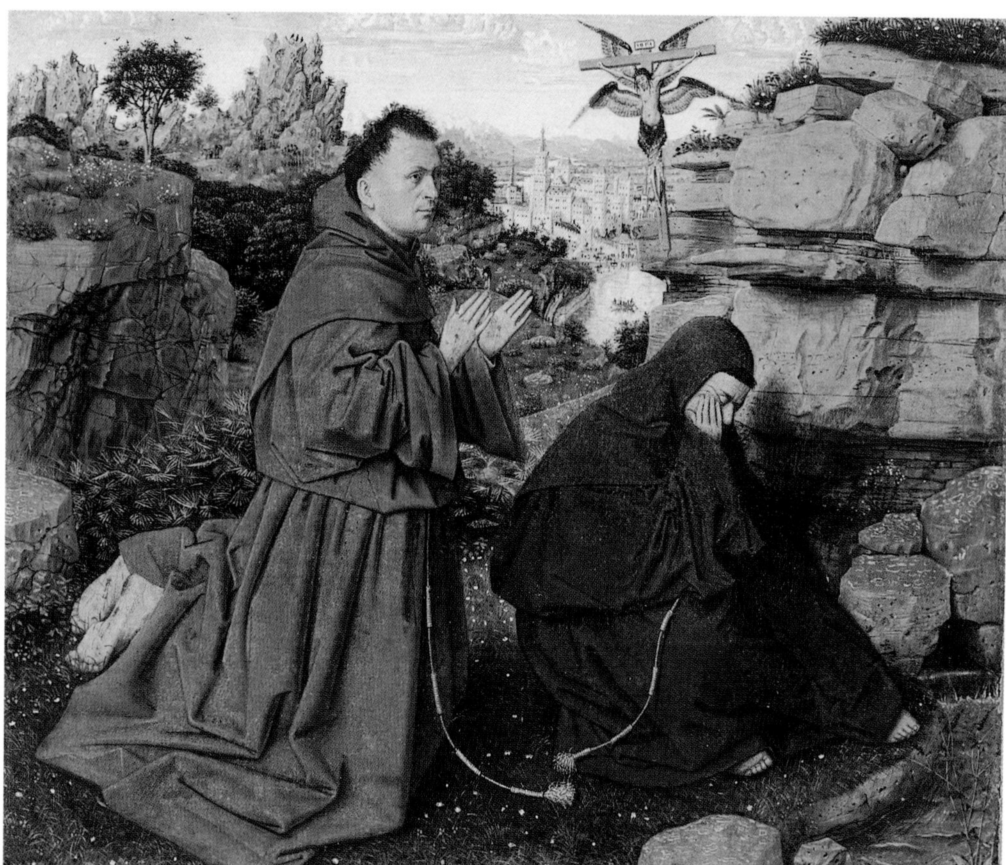

Fig. 31. Jan van Eyck?, *Stigmatization of Saint Francis*, about 1430. Oil on wood. John G. Johnson Collection, Philadelphia Museum of Art

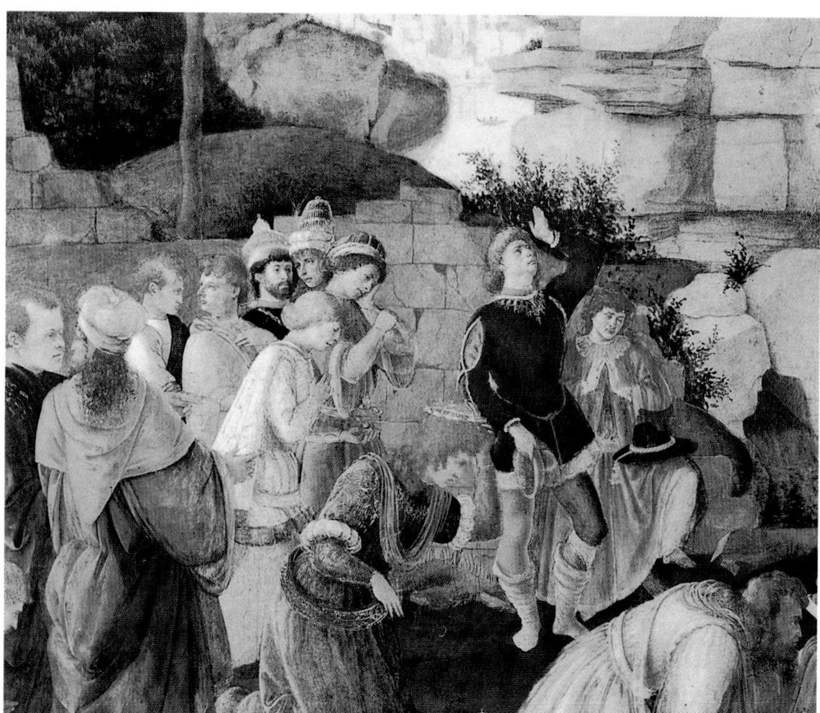

Fig. 32. Sandro Botticelli, detail, *Adoration of the Magi*, about 1470–75. Tempera on wood. National Gallery, London

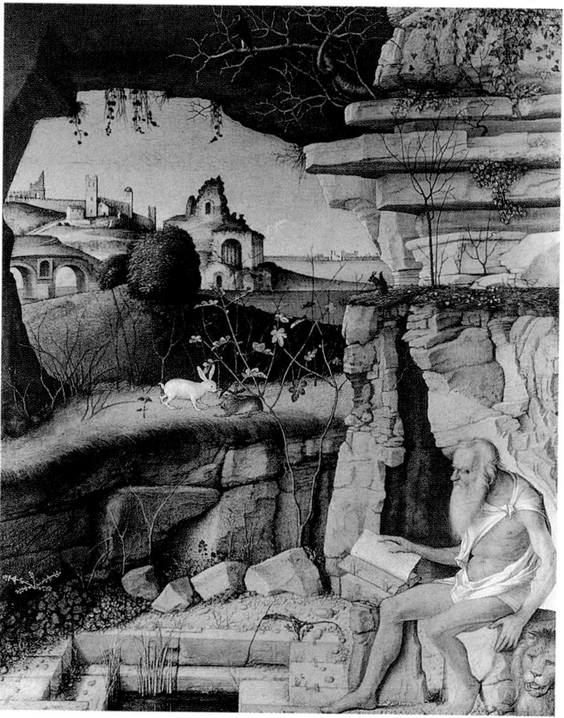

Fig. 33. Giovanni Bellini, *Saint Jerome in the Wilderness*, 1505. Oil on wood. Samuel H. Kress Collection, The National Gallery of Art, Washington, D.C.

(Uffizi, Florence) is set in a landscape that can only be described as in the Netherlandish style—or, in the critical terminology of the day, *alla ponentina*. But nowhere in Bellini's work do these northern vistas or buildings have the disjunctive effect they produce in Botticelli's pictures. Was the Florentine simply attempting to satisfy a Medici-sanctioned taste for northern landscapes or to suggest, through the inclusion of Gothic castles, the exotic flavor of the Orient? Or did he, perhaps, wish to exploit the foreignness of Netherlandish landscape details as an emblem of artistic genius and fantasy (*ingenio* and *fantasia* being two of the reigning terms in contemporary critical language)? It is, in any event, Botticelli's picture that alerts us to the way the stylized backgrounds of Late Gothic Florentine practice could be transformed, through the example of Netherlandish painting, into those mysterious landscapes of the imagination that appear in Leonardo da Vinci's *Madonna of the Rocks* in the Louvre and the *Mona Lisa* (fig. 39).[46] The transition seems to have been effected by Filippo Lippi—who was, after all, trained as a Gothic artist—in two landmark compositions with the Virgin and Child dating from the 1460s (Uffizi, Florence, and Alte Pinakothek, Munich).

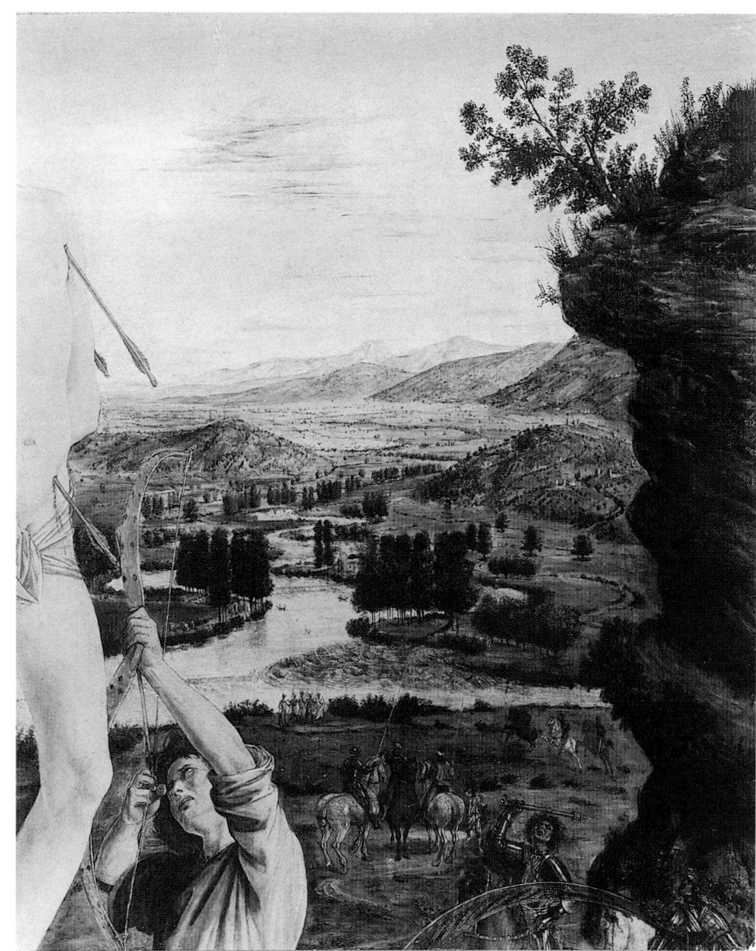

Fig. 34. Antonio Pollaiuolo, *The Martyrdom of Saint Sebastian*, 1475. Oil on wood. The National Gallery, London

The disjunctive relationship of background to foreground and figures to setting that Botticelli introduced into his work foreshadowed a feature that became widespread in the sixteenth century, when we find the truly fantasy landscapes of Patinir and his imitators—especially Herri met de Bles—reappearing first in the work of the Ferrarese court artist Dosso Dossi and then in the paintings of Mannerists throughout the Italian peninsula. Northern landscapes were understood by these artists as examples of *parerga*, a term employed by Pliny to describe the idiosyncratic backgrounds of the Greek painter Protogenes and evocatively explained by Paolo Giovio in the 1520s as consisting of "rocky hollows, green forests, shadowy riverbanks . . . and distant land and sea views."[47] Of Bosch's work the sixteenth-century Lombard painter-theorist Gian Paolo Lomazzo wrote, "In showing strange and terrifying apparitions and horrible dreams he was singular and truly divine."[48] The Brescian painter Savoldo was plainly catering to this taste for the extravagance and strangeness of northern landscapes when, about 1515–20, he divided the background of a depiction of the Temptation of Saint Anthony (Timken Art Gallery, San Diego) between a pastoral landscape derived from Patinir and an infernal one evocative of the paintings by Bosch he had seen in Venice.

The reasons for the change in attitude signaled by Botticelli's work are not difficult to understand, for by about 1460 Italian painting had begun to move beyond the example of Netherlandish painting and to redefine naturalism in terms of artistic theory. In that manifesto in miniature of humanist style, the *Saint Sebastian* in the Kunsthistorisches Museum, Vienna, Mantegna gave to the descriptive language of Netherlandish painting a Latin accent and used that language to revive the glories of a Roman past rather than to suggest a window onto the everyday world. Remarkably, he did this without abandoning the chisel-like precision of a native tempera technique.[49] Antonio Pollaiuolo, by contrast, coaxed out of the infinitely subtle glazes of Flemish oil painting a thick, viscous medium expressive of his Florentine, tactile vision.[50] His astonishing bird's-eye views of the Arno Valley—unquestionably inspired by those of Netherlandish practice—were used as a foil for figures shown in a type of violent action no Netherlander could match (fig. 34). Even Piero della Francesca, who deeply admired Netherlandish painting and, in his late *Nativity* (National Gallery, London), embraced the poetry of stillness that is one of its chief beauties, nonetheless found the empirical approach to space of Van Eyck and Van der Weyden deficient and their compositions lacking in geometric structure. In his hands Netherlandish descriptive techniques acquired an elevated, mathematical certitude. And by the mid-1470s Bellini had transformed the dispersed, northern light of Netherlandish practice into densely atmospheric skies of incomparable expressive subtlety.

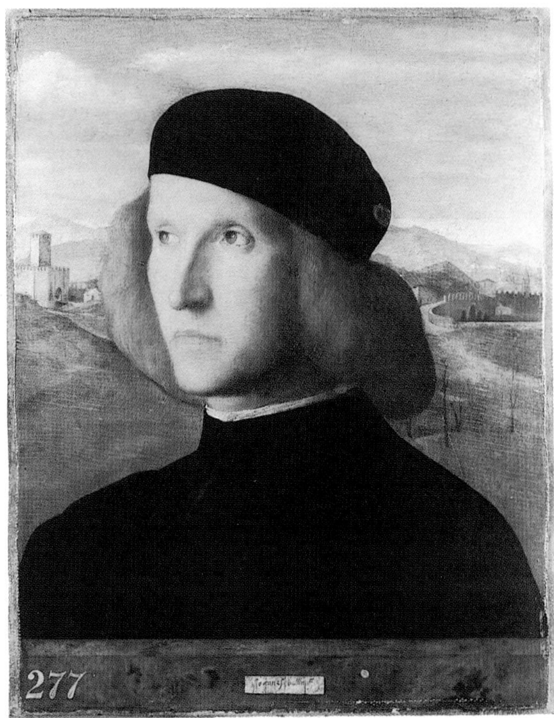

Fig. 35. Giovanni Bellini, *Portrait of a Young Man*, about 1505. Oil on wood. The Royal Collection, Her Majesty Queen Elizabeth II

To maintain that Netherlandish painting was entirely eclipsed by the work of these Italians would, nonetheless, be wide of the mark. We must remember that despite Fazio's tendency to see it through the lens of Albertian precepts, Netherlandish painting was not, in actuality, inspired by Alberti. It was unconcerned with the classical principles of eloquence and decorum, and it was innocent of the Renaissance notion of compositional harmony—what Alberti termed *concinnitas*—whereby part was related to part, and the whole expressed "that elegant harmony and grace . . . which is called beauty."[51] The closer Italian painting drew to these abstracting principles and the more it took ancient art as its guide, the less compelling the example of Netherlandish painting seemed. We may say that once Mantegna's engraving of the Entombment—the embodiment of the Albertian *historia*—and Pollaiuolo's engraving of the Battle of the Nudes were circulated, in the 1470s, Rogier van der Weyden's triptych in Ferrara could no longer be viewed as a paradigm of humanist values. In comparison to what we see in Mantegna's engraving, the gestures of Rogier's figures appeared forced or merely naturalistic and lacking in eloquence; their poses wooden and without grace; their drapery angular and heavy, weighing them down rather than sustaining an effect of movement; the figure types devoid of a sense of ideal beauty. In short, Netherlandish paintings began to look like the product of a foreign, Gothic culture, and increasingly their style is referred to by critics and compilers of inventories as *alla ponentina*, as though to emphasize their foreignness and geographical dislocation.

The Prestige of Memling

In written criticism the names of Jan van Eyck and Rogier van der Weyden retained their prestige into the sixteenth century, and Van Eyck came to be considered the mythic father of oil painting. The Italian canon Antonio De Beatis unhesitatingly declared Van Eyck's Ghent Altarpiece (figs. 17, 18) the finest painting in Christendom when he saw it in 1517.[52] But it was the contribution of Memling

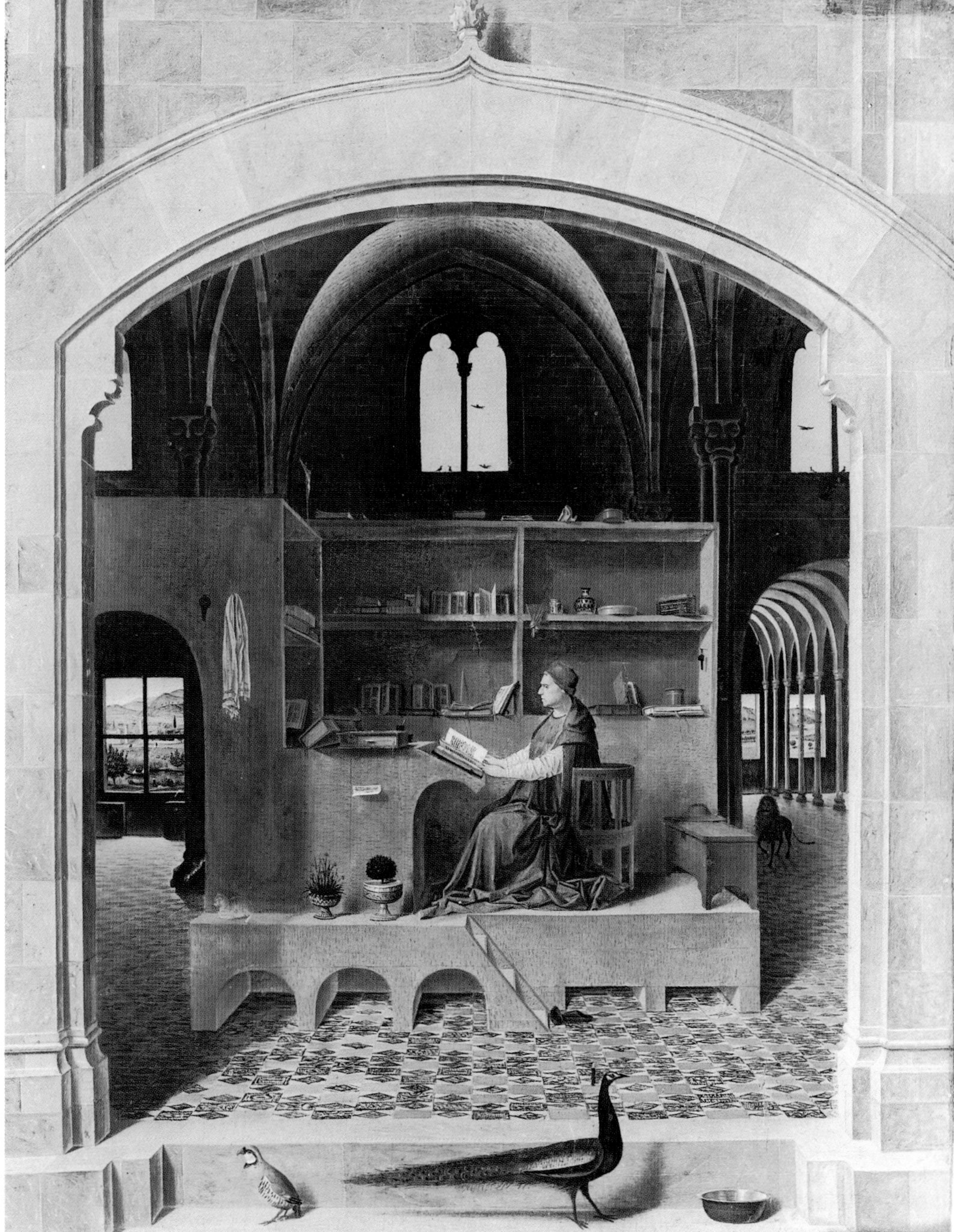

Fig. 36. Antonello da Messina, *Saint Jerome in His Study*, about 1475. Oil on wood. The National Gallery, London

that came to exert a widespread and vital influence on Italian painters. Scholars of Netherlandish art tend to pass over or to minimize Memling's achievement, perhaps in part because it is in his paintings that we first sense an effort to accommodate the tastes of Italian patrons. He must, at times, have worked from portrait drawings sent to him from Italy, and drawings and, possibly, bronze plaquettes may have provided him with the repertory of putti and swags of fruit he occasionally introduced in his portable altarpieces.[53] No less important, however, must have been his awareness of Italian aesthetic issues: the foreshortened positions of the soldiers in his *Resurrection* in the Louvre claim a mastery of precisely those *difficoltà* that Italians felt were an inherent part of art. Certainly, from the Italian point of view he was a figure to be reckoned with, and the chapter clerk of the Sint-Donaaskerk (Saint Donatian's) in Bruges was not exaggerating when he recorded, on the death of

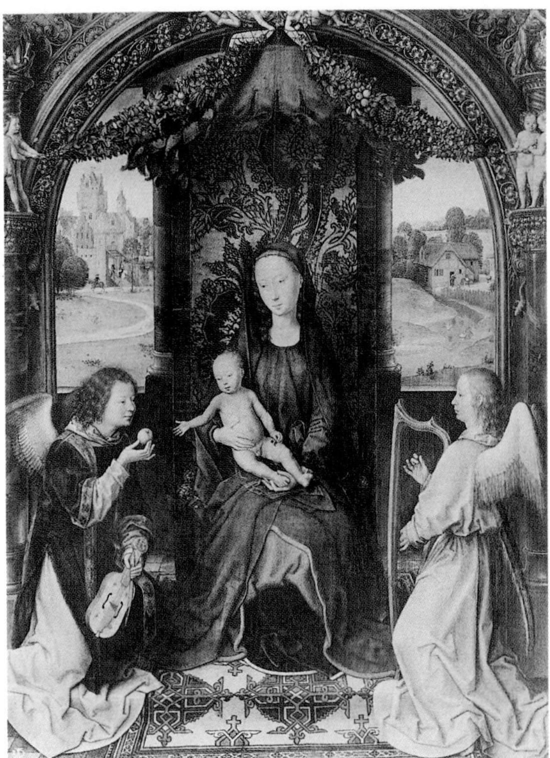

Fig. 37. Hans Memling, *Virgin and Child and Two Angels*, about 1490. Oil on wood. Galleria degli Uffizi, Florence

Memling in 1494, that the artist was "held to have been the most skillful and excellent painter in all of Christendom." Indicatively, at the very moment Florentine artists were reinterpreting the backgrounds in Van Eyck's and Van der Weyden's works in terms of artistic fantasy, they were eagerly examining those in Memling's for their atmospheric unity and sweet, uncomplicated naturalism. And not only Florentines fell under the spell of his paintings: the landscape backgrounds of Lorenzo Costa in Bologna are no less indebted to those of Memling, and the settings of Raphael's early paintings of the Virgin and Child would be inconceivable without the Netherlander. His early pendant paintings of Saint George and the Dragon and Saint Michael battling Satan (Louvre, Paris) contrast a Memling-like landscape with a Boschian one replete with monsters and a flaming castle.

It was, above all, Memling's portraits that impressed Italians, and, indeed, no one before Holbein could match them for their variety, inventiveness, and mobility of expression: sitters shown, sculpturelike, in three-quarter view against plain, dark backgrounds; in interior settings; or placed notionally out of doors before expansive landscapes. Without such works as Memling's *Portrait of a Man and a Woman* (fig. 24) and his *Portrait of a Man* (Accademia, Venice), Bellini is unlikely to have realized the poetic possibilities of the kind of landscape background he employed in his male portrait whose sitter sometimes is identified as Pietro Bembo (fig. 35). So accustomed are we to relating Bellini's portrait style to Antonello da Messina's presence in Venice in 1476 that we easily overlook how distant Bellini's later work is from the more archaic, Eyckian formulas Antonello introduced. It is, in any event, probably in Venice that Antonello himself first saw and was influenced by Memling's paintings, and we can well understand the perplexity of Marcantonio Michiel when he examined the Sicilian's *Saint Jerome in His Study* (fig. 36) in the house of Antonio Pasqualino in Venice. "Some believe it is from the hand of Antonello," Marcantonio writes, "but more, with justice, ascribe it to Jan [van Eyck] or to Memling. . . . And it displays that [Netherlandish] manner, although the face is finished in an Italian fashion, so that it seems the work of [the Venetian portraitist-illuminator] Jacometto. The buildings are *alla ponentina*; the landscape views naturalistic, detailed, and finished . . . and the whole work, for subtlety, colors, design, strength, and relief, is perfect."[54] There could be no finer analysis of the synthesis of Netherlandish and Italian styles in Antonello's work or clearer indication of the prestige Netherlandish painting continued to enjoy in Venice in the age of Giorgione and the young Titian.

The portraits and devotional paintings of Memling were no less fervently studied in Florence. Thus, the background of the Verrocchiesque *Virgin and Child* in the Louvre, sometimes ascribed to Ghirlandaio, was inspired by that of Memling's *Portrait of a Young Man* (cat. no. 28).[55] And although the setting of Fra Bartolomeo's early *Madonna and Child with the Young Saint John the Baptist* (frontis., p. 38), in which the figures are placed against the corner of a room pierced at each side by a window, seems to derive from a portrait by the Master of the Saint Ursula Legend (Philadelphia Museum of Art), the landscape views are quoted directly from the center panel of a triptych Memling painted for the Dominican Benedetto Pagagnotti (fig. 37), which Fra Bartolomeo, who was to take the Dominican habit himself, probably studied in Benedetto's lavish quarters at Santa Maria Novella.[56] But it was more than Memling's landscape backgrounds and domestic interiors that impressed Fra Bartolomeo and his contemporaries; it was also the lighting that creates a mood of serenity and binds the composition together.

Memling's paintings were crucial to the creation of a style that emerged in Italy in the 1480s and was particularly suited to devotional practice. This new, devout style, or *maniera devota*, as it was to become known, depended for its effectiveness on the harmonious combination of rich colors, tranquil landscapes bathed in a soft light, and figures with quietly pensive or reflective expressions.[57] Its masters were Francesco Francia, Perugino, and the young Raphael. (Raphael, it should be recalled, grew up in Urbino, where, as has been pointed out, a taste for Netherlandish painting had been cultivated by Federigo da Montefeltro.) According to Vasari, "people ran like madmen to see this new and more lifelike beauty," and if we think of a work such as Perugino's *Vision of Saint Bernard* (Alte Pinakothek, Munich), with its quality of ineffable grace and harmony and its use of soft, diaphanous light, it is easy to see why. We have already seen how prized Memling's devotional pictures were throughout Italy at the end of the fifteenth century, and we have noted the wide diffusion in Florence of those hypnotic images of the Veronica veil or head of Christ—some by Memling, some by the Master of the Saint Ursula Legend or other Netherlanders. The quality of contemplative calm that pervades these works is a far cry from the expressive urgency of Rogier's *Descent from the Cross* that had so impressed Cyriac of Ancona at midcentury; without the example of Memling's work, the emerging High Renaissance style of Raphael would have taken a very different turn.

In the art of Fra Bartolomeo, there is, moreover, an analogy between the new style and the religious thought of the day. "Thus we say of the painter who wants to proceed with too much artifice, that is, when he wants to show too much art, that he does not really imitate nature," declared Savonarola in 1496.[58] Fra Bartolomeo was a disciple of Savonarola's, and his interest in Memling's paintings must be ascribed, in part, to a desire to emulate their effect of artless simplicity and naturalism to achieve a Savonarolan ideal of devotional painting.

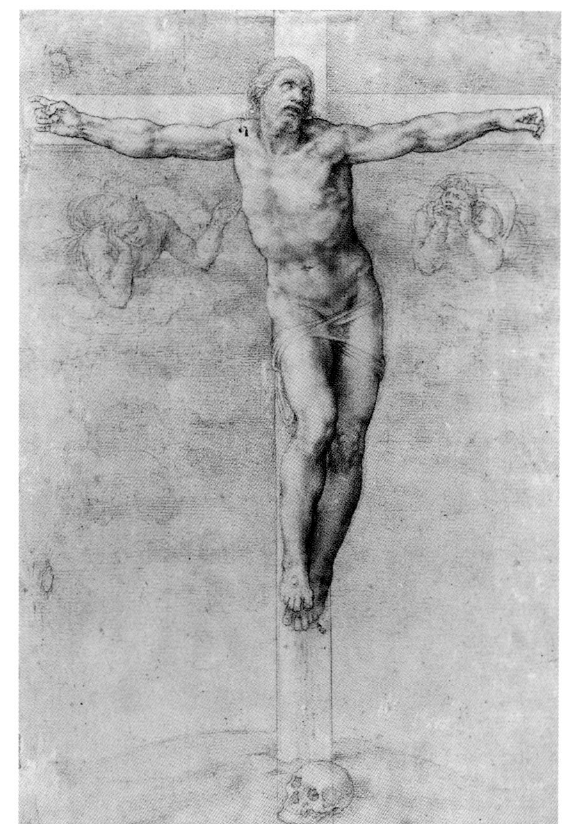

Fig. 38. Michelangelo, *The Crucifixion*, about 1538–40. Black chalk on paper. The British Museum, London

The Sixteenth-Century Reversal of Taste

As a youth in the workshop of Ghirlandaio, Michelangelo had been exposed to the vogue for Netherlandish painting and had made a copy of Martin Schongauer's engraving of the Temptation of Saint Anthony. He had doubtless been fascinated by the expressive angularity of the draped figure and the audacious poses of the flying monsters in Schongauer's print. However, he had no patience for the timid, devout style of Francia, Perugino, and, by extension, Memling. In a conversation published by the Portuguese artist Francisco d'Ollanda, Michelangelo famously dismissed Netherlandish painters as lacking in any real conception of art, deeming their work suitable only for monks and friars, and for very young or very old women. Michelangelo's comments gain special resonance in light of the fact that at the time he made them—about 1538—he was himself deeply interested in the matter of devotional painting. For the brilliant and intensely pious Vittoria Colonna, who had solicited his view on Netherlandish painting, he made several highly finished drawings, including one of the Crucifixion (fig. 38) and another of the Pietà. These are works that truly merit Cyriac's term *pientissima*. They are almost medieval in their spare vocabulary and repudiation of all anecdotal detail, yet the figures possess a tightly compressed physicality, and the eloquent poses and gestures are at once deeply expressive and self-consciously graceful and beautiful. ("I saw your Crucifix, which certainly has crucified in my memory every other picture I ever saw," Vittoria wrote him.) When we see these drawings, we sense why Netherlandish painting seemed to him—and to most other Italian painters and critics of the sixteenth century—little more than accumulations of details: "of stuffs, bricks and mortar, the grass of the fields, the shadows of trees, and bridges and rivers, which they call landscapes, and little figures here and there; and all this . . . is in truth done without reasonableness or art."[59]

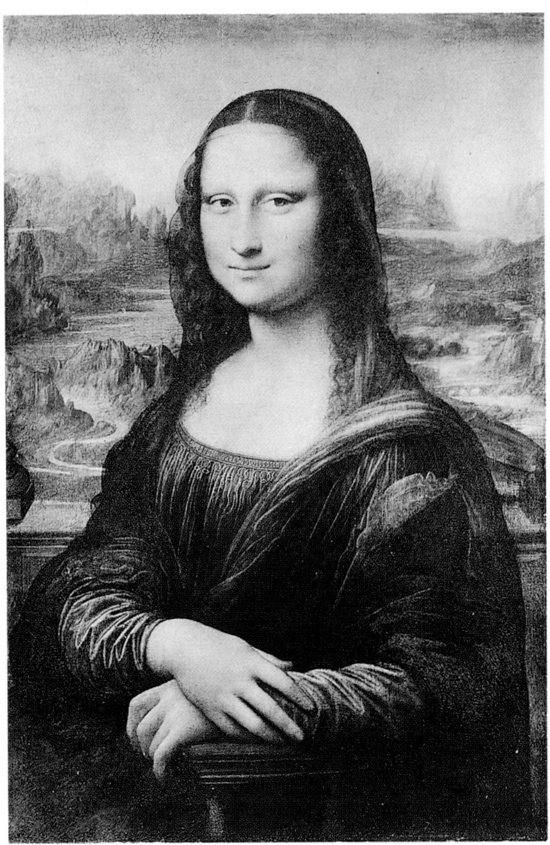

Fig. 39. Leonardo da Vinci, *Mona Lisa*, about 1503–5. Oil on wood. Musée du Louvre, Paris

The more Netherlandish artists came in touch with Italian ideas about art and the nature of artistic genius, the more they were moved to reconsider their native traditions. The impact of Italian art on Dürer is well known, but we can see that the new ideals of beauty, harmony, grace, and movement wrought a similar transformation on Netherlandish painting as well. The effect is, perhaps, most evident in the prints of Lucas van Leyden, which can stand beside those of Dürer. But it is also apparent in the airborne, swirling cloak of Gerard David's angel of the Annunciation (cat. no. 79), in the elegantly gesturing figures of Joos van Cleve's *Crucifixion with Saints and a Donor* (cat. no. 95) or the fluently posed nudes of his *Last Judgment* (cat. no. 98), in the deliberate, Leonardesque contrast Quentin Massys drew between the ideally ugly and grotesque and the ideally pretty in his *Adoration of the Magi* (cat. no. 99), and, most signally, in a new approach to portraiture adopted by a number of Netherlandish artists.

Alberti considered portraiture an index of the divine power of painting, for, "through painting, the faces of the dead go on living for a very long time." However, a tenet of humanist criticism also held that only the written word could truly convey the soul or life of a person, and that a painted portrait was able to represent merely the sitter's appearance and constituted little more than a faithful physical record—or *leal souvenir* (to stretch somewhat the admittedly ambiguous meaning of the motto Van Eyck inscribed on the stony ledge of one of his most arresting portraits). Various devices had been adopted in Italy to challenge this prejudice and to suggest a quality of inner life in portraits. The taut smile Antonello da Messina invariably gave his sitters was an attempt to break through the reticence of Eyckian portraiture. In the hands of Leonardo, the smile can express a sense of both the animation and the ambiguity of personality (fig. 39), which is further enhanced by his use of muted shadows, or sfumato. But there was another, more rhetorical strategy for suggesting life in a portrait, and that was to show the sitter as though caught in a momentary action or actively addressing the viewer.

Quentin Massys was fully aware of the humanist-defined poetic dilemma of portraiture, and he put on his bronze medal of Erasmus an inscription reading, "a portrait from life; [but] the better image will his writings show." In his magnificent series of male portraits—the *Portrait of a Canon* (fig. 40), the *Portrait of a Notary* (National Gallery of Scotland, Edinburgh), and the *Portrait of a Scholar* (Städelisches Kunstinstitut, Frankfurt)—no such apology was made, for in these works Massys resolved the problem in the same way as (and on the model of) his Italian contemporaries: through an eloquent use of gesture and gaze. What had been the neutral frame or parapet of Netherlandish portrait convention is transformed into a desk, behind which the sitter interrupts his scholarly activity, turns his head, and raises his hand in address. Massys showed a keen instinct for subordinating details to overall design, but his Netherlander's feeling for specificity is everywhere apparent. His *Portrait of a Woman* (cat. no. 38) is less eloquent and elaborate in its means but no less effective an example of the new, northern "speaking" portrait (mercifully, we are spared the caustic tones of the sitter's voice).

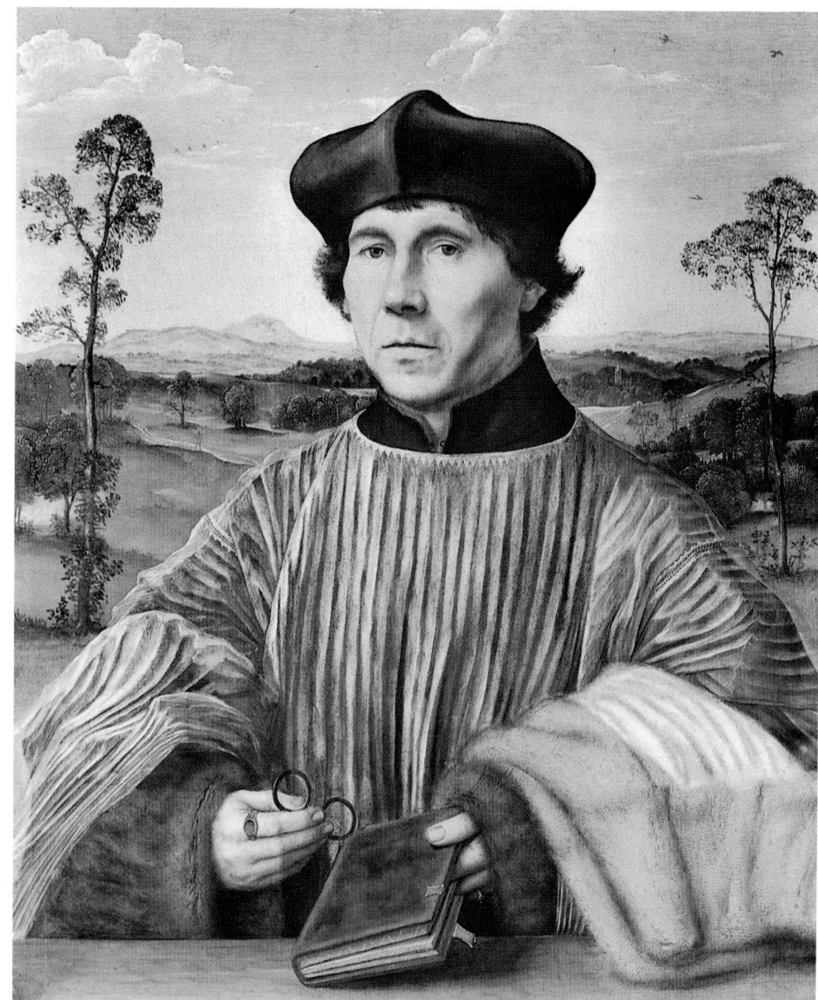

Fig. 40. Quentin Massys, *Portrait of a Canon*, about 1520–25. Oil on wood. The Collections of the Prince of Liechtenstein, Vaduz

Over the course of the sixteenth century, Netherlandish artists were to sacrifice many of their native traditions in their effort to emulate the ideals of Italian painting; some abandoned their homeland altogether and became Italian in all but name. There were attempts in Bruges—by then on its way to becoming a cultural backwater—to revive the halcyon era of Van Eyck by copying or updating his compositions for a public reluctant to abandon images and a style with which it had grown familiar. But the winds of change from the south eventually carried all before them. Sometimes we feel an almost schizophrenic tension between a native tradition for descriptive naturalism and the abstracting premise of Italian art. In Joos van Cleve's monumentally conceived but minutely executed *Virgin and Child* (cat. no. 96), the tension is strangely compelling. The almost surreal effect is enhanced by the overly precise, detailed landscape, which was painted by a specialist and competes for attention with the still life on the parapet. In Massys's portraits, by contrast, we sense the ways Italian theory could nourish, and not simply derail, the native traditions of one of the great schools of European painting.

1. "Tabulam parvam in qua pulchre et magistraliter depicta est turris Babel, quam caram habeo." See Campbell (1976, p. 189), who notes that this is a unique instance of a Netherlander expressing his opinion of a picture.
2. For Cyriac's text, see A. di Lorenzo in Mottola Molfino and Natale 1991, vol. 2, pp. 326–27.

3. All quotes from Fazio are from Baxandall 1986.
4. Ibid., p. 107.
5. The point of departure for all discussions on Italian responses to Netherlandish painting is Warburg 1932, vol. 1, pp. 287–312, and Weiss 1956–57. The literature has grown enormously in the last three decades. In the interest of brevity, I shall refer to recent sources, to which the reader is directed for earlier bibliography. For succinct surveys of what we know about the Italian communities in Bruges and Italian patronage of Netherlandish painting, see the essays of De Vos and Vandewalle and Geirnaert in Vermeersch 1992; De Vos also discusses Spanish, Portuguese, and German commissions. See also Castelnuovo 1987, pp. 514–23.
6. Here it ought to be mentioned that there is no evidence whatever that the portrait of Francesco was ever in the Este collections in Italy.
7. It has sometimes been supposed that Van der Weyden's canvases were tapestries, simply because of a reluctance to acknowledge the widespread use of canvas as a support in Netherlandish painting. On this, see Wolfthal 1989, p. 15.
8. For a somewhat different view of the presence of Barthélemy d'Eyck in Naples, see König (1996), who, however, does not discuss the apparent reflections of D'Eyck's work in Neapolitan paintings. For this, see Sricchia Santoro 1986, pp. 17–45.
9. Note should be made here of a document mentioning the presence of a "Piero di Burges," Zanetto Bugatto, and Antonello da Sicilia at the Sforza court in 1456 (actually 1453). Wherever he was from—Bruges, Borgo San Sepolcro, or elsewhere—the Piero cited was apparently a bowman, not Petrus Christus, as has sometimes been argued, and the Antonello is unlikely to have been Antonello da Messina: see Sricchia Santoro 1986, p. 41.
10. Vespasiano (1963) 1997, p. 101.
11. See Mulazzani 1971.
12. See Passoni 1988. The key figures were Oberto, Pietro, and Claudio Villa. By midcentury there were branches of the Villa businesses in Brussels, Douai, Bruges, and other northern cities, and in 1462 Pietro was among those invited to the annual banquet of the exclusive Confraternity of the Holy Cross in Brussels, where he would have found himself in the company of both Philip the Good and Rogier van der Weyden. Not surprisingly, the Villas commissioned other Netherlandish works, including a carved altarpiece and a missal that includes an illumination by Simon Marmion (Biblioteca Reale, Turin).
13. See Bomford, Campbell et al. 1996, p. 37.
14. For Joos van Cleve's work at Genoa, see Scailliérez 1991, pp. 77–83.
15. For these statistics, see especially Nuttall 1995, p. 135, with previous bibliography.
16. See Ainsworth 1994b, nos. 1, 19, for an analysis of the *Saint Jerome* in the Detroit Institute of Arts and the *Portrait of a Woman* in the Gemäldegalerie, Berlin.
17. Artists specializing in canvas paintings constituted a separate, clearly inferior, division of the painters' guild in Bruges. However, Jan van Eyck and Rogier van der Weyden are both known to have painted on canvas and there are surviving works on canvas by Dieric Bouts, Hugo van der Goes, Joos van Gent (cat. no. 7), Gerard David, Quentin Massys, Lucas van Leyden, and Bruegel: see Wolfthal 1989, pp. 6–12, 14–16. It is worth emphasizing that fifteenth-century Italian artists also painted on canvas and that the Medici inventory lists an allegorical canvas by Domenico Veneziano—a seminude woman holding a skull—that is not unrelated to the kinds of northern examples they collected in abundance (see Wohl 1980, pp. 196–97). Works on canvas remain by Fra Angelico, Paolo Uccello, Antonio Vivarini, Jacopo and Giovanni Bellini, Benozzo Gozzoli, Alesso Baldovinetti, Francesco del Cossa, Francesco Francia, Lorenzo Costa, Perugino, Luca Signorelli, Andrea Mantegna, inter alios. One of the most celebrated mythological paintings of the Renaissance, Botticelli's *Birth of Venus* (Uffizi, Florence), is executed in distemper on canvas. Both north and south of the Alps canvas was particularly popular for organ shutters, of which Cosimo Tura's *Annunciation* and *Saint George and the Dragon* (Museo del Duomo, Ferrara) are perhaps the most celebrated fifteenth-century examples.
18. See Rohlmann 1993a, pp. 181–82, for a convenient summary of known tapestry commissions and a list of the literature on them.
19. See Wolfthal 1989, p. 50, no. 20.
20. For the critical literature on Van Eyck's canvas paintings as well as canvas painting in general, see ibid., pp. 10–12.
21. I would like to thank Jean Cadogan for kindly making her transcription of the unpublished Tornabuoni inventory available to me.
22. Nuttall 1995, pp. 139–43.
23. For the works by Rogier, see ibid., pp. 144–49; on the Froment, see Grayson 1976.
24. For a convenient survey of commissions from the Medici circle, see Rohlmann 1993a.
25. See De Vos 1994a, p. 206, no. 72.
26. Memling's painting was formerly in the collection of the Marchesi Tempi, Florence: see De Vos 1994b, p. 226, and Galassi 1997.
27. The best summary of what we know about early Netherlandish painting in Venice is Campbell 1981b.
28. The diptych is mentioned in a letter of 1502 to Isabella d'Este. Marcantonio Michiel presumably saw the same diptych in the 1520s, although his description of the subject differs from that in the letter. Whether we are dealing with one or two diptychs remains uncertain: see Campbell 1981b, p. 471, and Hand and Wolff 1986, pp. 193–99.
29. See Frizzoni 1884. Campbell (1981b) has established the identities and authorship of some of the pictures Michiel saw. On Michiel, see Fletcher 1981.
30. That the panels seemed disparate to Michiel and that the copy after Van Eyck appeared to him to be a work of the first half of the century speak strongly for his critical eye.
31. On this, see Campbell 1981b, pp. 472–73.
32. Albergati is traditionally thought to have sat to Van Eyck for the portrait now in the Kunsthistorisches Museum, Vienna, but this notion has been challenged: see Hunter 1993.
33. See Lorentz 1995, pp. 47–56.
34. See ibid., p. 100 n. 15. The statistics are those of Martens 1997, pp. 35–36.

35. Although Michiel's text appears to describe a double portrait, the matter is not certain: see, most recently, Lorentz 1995, p. 71.
36. See Luzio 1913, p. 30; cited in Campbell 1976, p. 197.
37. Panofsky (1953, p. 458, n. 1 to p. 249) remarked that Fazio patterned his lives of Van Eyck and Van der Weyden on those of Apelles and Aristides in Pliny (*Natural History* 35. 79–100), but this should not blind us to the quality and justice of Fazio's observations.
38. All quotes are from Alberti 1972.
39. All quotes from Pliny are from vol. 9 of the 1952 translation of *Historia Naturalis*.
40. For the suggestion that Van Eyck did read classical texts, see Preimesberger 1991. I would grant that it is possible to interpret Van Eyck's paintings in terms of classical texts—which is what Fazio does—and that the artist could have had some knowledge of Pliny and Quintilian, but I reject the idea that he intended to establish a sort of *paragone* with ancient art and sculpture, such as we find later in the work of Mantegna (for which, see Christiansen 1992). To my mind, a precondition to this kind of conscious manipulation of classical sources was a humanist environment, which existed at Ferrara and Mantua but not at the court of Philip the Good. Indicatively, in his paintings Van Eyck never employed humanist lettering, which is the clearest emblem of humanist culture.
41. Ames-Lewis (1979) went so far as to propose that Lippi made a trip to the Netherlands. There is no basis for this conjecture, and indeed, that such a journey took place is in the highest degree unlikely. Ruda (1993, pp. 126–32) has discounted the impact of Netherlandish painting in these works—wrongly, I think.
42. Meiss 1956, pp. 62–63. I have argued these points elsewhere: see Christiansen 1990, p. 739.
43. The question cannot be answered definitively: the most recent discussion is that of De Marchi 1994. One of the key points of interest in any argument on the subject is the similarity of the compositional layout of Antonio's painting to that of Filippo Lippi's *Virgin and Child* of 1437.
44. The *Stigmatization* was owned by Anselmo Adorno, a Genoese resident of Bruges, and it was probably seen by Botticelli when Adorno stopped in Florence in February 1471. See Panhans 1974 and Spantigati and Rishel 1997, pp. 38, 81.
45. See Rohlmann (1992, 1993b), who discusses Botticelli's quotation of Van Eyck and numerous other Netherlandish derivations in Florentine painting.
46. Hills (1980) has attempted to trace the influence of Netherlandish painting in Leonardo's work. I find the impact less marked than does Hills.
47. Giovio quoted in Barocchi 1971–77, vol. 1, p. 18. A fine summary of the relationship of Ferrarese landscape backgrounds to Netherlandish painting is found in Turner 1966, pp. 133–52. Giovio used the term *parerga* in describing Dosso Dossi's work in 1527.
48. Lomazzo 1584, vol. 6, chap. 26, p. 350.
49. Here I feel obliged to record the articles of Ames-Lewis (1993a, 1993b), which I find somewhat diffuse.
50. On the relationship of Pollaiuolo's paintings to Netherlandish traditions, see Nuttall 1993.
51. Alberti 1972, paragraph 35. In his later treatise on architecture, the *De re aedificatoria* (9.5), Alberti refined and elaborated upon the notion of *concinnitas* in an important, indeed fundamental, way: "The three principal components of that whole theory [of beauty] into which we inquire are number, what we might call outline, and position. But arising from the composition and connection of these three is a further quality in which beauty shines full face: our term for this is *concinnitas*; which we say is nourished with every grace and splendor. It is the task and aim of *concinnitas* to compose parts that are quite separate from each other by their nature, according to some precise rule, so that they correspond to one another in appearance. . . . Beauty is a form of a sympathy and consonance of the parts within a body, according to definite number, outline, and position, as dictated by *concinnitas*, the absolute and fundamental rule in Nature" (Alberti 1988, pp. 302–3). It is not difficult to recognize in Alberti's conception of harmony the basis of the classical ideal of painting down to the mid-nineteenth century.
52. See Torresan 1981, p. 46.
53. The portrait of Angelo Tani's wife, Caterina Tanagli, on the exterior wing of Memling's *Last Judgment* in Gdansk must be based on a drawing sent to the artist from Florence. This would explain the generalized treatment of the sitter as well as the strongly three-dimensional character of the head, which makes it appear rather like a portrait bust. One Italian sitter (for the *Portrait of a Man* in Antwerp) supplied Memling with a Roman coin, and the gracefully twisting scroll and branch on the reverse of the portrait of Benedetto Portinari (Uffizi, Florence)—as exquisite as the device Leonardo painted on the reverse of his portrait of Ginevra de' Benci (National Gallery of Art, Washington, D.C.)—must also have been based on a Florentine drawing. I remain unconvinced that Memling made a trip to Italy, which has recently been suggested: see Angelantoni Malfatti 1997.
54. Quoted in Frizzoni 1884, pp. 188–89.
55. See Campbell 1983.
56. See Rohlmann 1995, p. 441; for a general survey of Memling's portraits of Florentines, see Castelfranchi 1997.
57. On the notion of a *maniera devota*, see especially Previtali 1964, pp. 16–21, and Dempsey 1987. Nuttall (1992, pp. 74–75) discusses the use of the word *devoto* by fifteenth-century writers.
58. *The Simplicity of Christian Life*, as excerpted in Gilbert 1992, p. 156.
59. Francisco d'Ollanda's *Dialogues* of 1548, as translated in Holroyd 1903, p. 280.

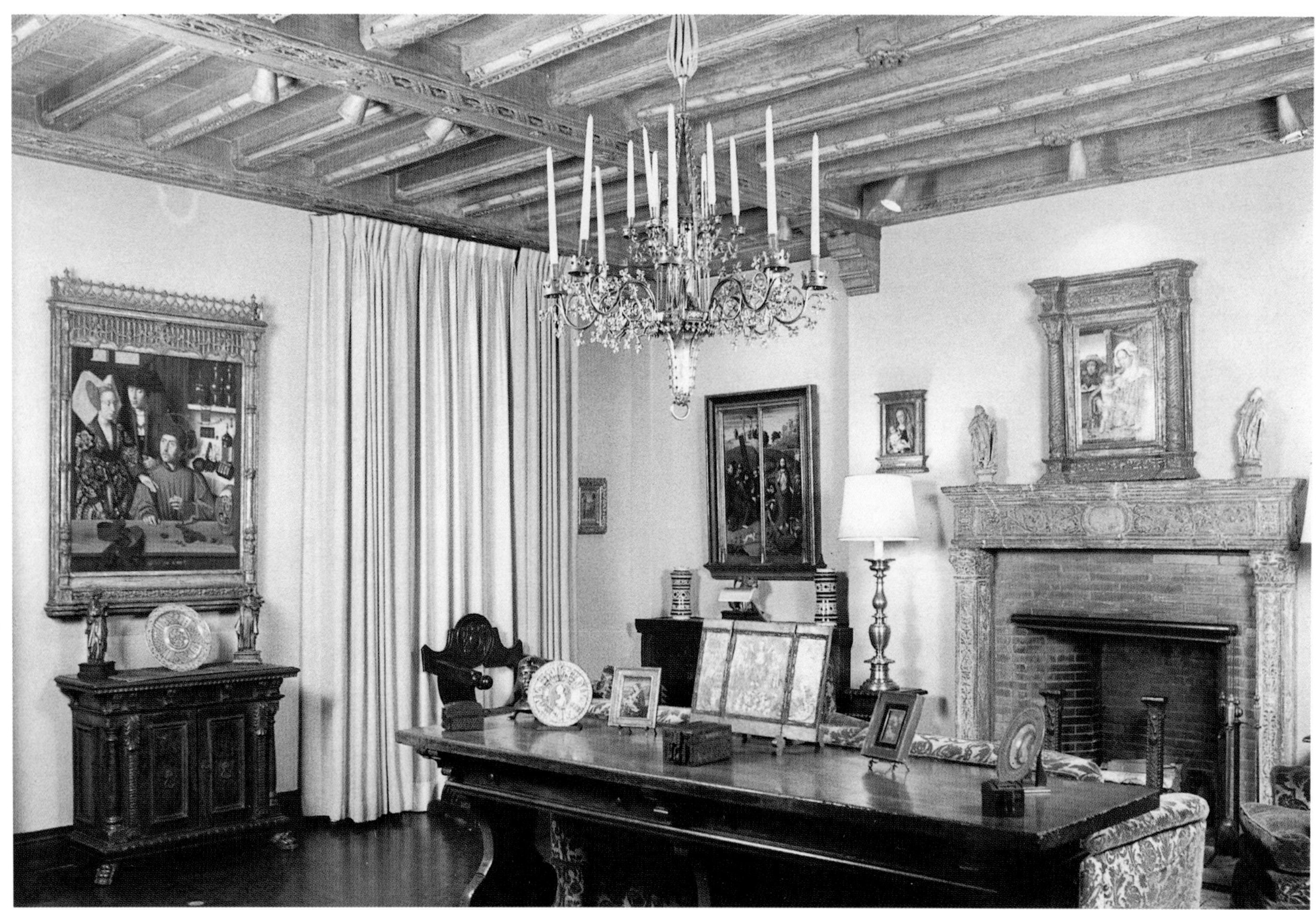

View of the coffee room of the Robert Lehman residence at 7 West 54 Street, New York, about 1960

How the Pictures Got Here

EVERETT FAHY

There are over 140 Netherlandish paintings in the Metropolitan Museum. They easily constitute the most comprehensive collection in America, encompassing works by most of the major painters from Robert Campin to Pieter Bruegel the Elder. These pictures have been assembled in the course of the 128-year history of the Museum, the first entering the collection in 1871 (cat. nos. 42, 58) and the most recent in 1987 (cat. no. 91). However, the period of greatest activity was unquestionably the years between 1905 and 1930, when several factors conspired to generate an unprecedented interest in Netherlandish painting, both among museum curators in America and, more especially, private collectors. By 1900 Netherlandish painting was no longer the recherché field it had been in previous centuries. Van Eyck, Van der Weyden, and Memling had assumed their places in the pantheon of European painting: Van Eyck figured prominently in Paul Delaroche's enormous mural of 1841 in the École des Beaux-Arts in Paris, which celebrated the greatest artists of the past, and twenty-two years later he appeared again, with his brother, Hubert, on the monument erected in memory of the British prince consort, the Albert Memorial, in London's Kensington Gardens. Moreover, Netherlandish works could be found prominently displayed in the National Gallery, London, the Musée du Louvre, Paris, and the Kaiser Friedrich Museum, Berlin.

Americans were seldom adventurous when it came to collecting old master paintings—they wanted blue chip rather than penny stocks—and the fact that these artists had recognized stature was certainly a precondition of their desirability. Benjamin Altman installed his Netherlandish paintings, which included superlative Memlings, in the same spacious gallery that housed his canvases by Rembrandt, Frans Hals, Ruisdael, and Van Dyck. Works by Netherlandish artists especially appealed to patrons with a taste for Gothic and Renaissance decorative arts, and in many American collections they found their place alongside dark-toned period furniture, precious goldsmith work, and tapestries. J. Pierpont Morgan's study in the Morgan Library gives us an idea of the opulent settings in which Netherlandish paintings were hung in the early decades of this century, as do the galleries of the Robert Lehman Collection at the Metropolitan, which re-create interiors of the Lehman town house on West 54th Street (frontis., p. 62).

Collecting has always been dependent on scholarship. The key figure in the first half of the twentieth century was unquestionably Max J. Friedländer, curator of the Gemäldegalerie of the Kaiser Friedrich Museum. His writings achieved for Netherlandish painting what Bernard Berenson's accomplished for early Italian art, and his advice was sought by both dealers and collectors. Another influential voice was that of William R. Valentiner. Like Friedländer, Valentiner had worked with the brilliant director at Berlin, Wilhelm von Bode, and in 1908 he moved to America to assume the newly created post of curator of decorative arts at the Metropolitan Museum. He remained at the Metropolitan until 1914, after which time he served as director at, successively, the Detroit Institute of Arts, the Los Angeles County Museum of Art, and the North Carolina Museum of Art, Raleigh.[1] Valentiner advised collectors and helped to shape the character of American museum collections. (He encouraged John G. Johnson in Philadelphia, writing two of the three volumes of the catalogue for his collection,[2] and it was while he was director at Detroit that the Institute of Arts acquired the *Saint Jerome in His Study* attributed to Jan van Eyck and Bruegel's *Peasant Wedding Dance*).

The core collections of Netherlandish paintings in the National Gallery, London, and the Kaiser Friedrich Museum, Berlin, had been formed in the nineteenth century, but there were still outstanding paintings available. It comes as a surprise to learn that masterpieces such as the two extraordinary altarpieces by Hugo van der Goes now in Berlin and Van der Weyden's Braque Triptych in the Louvre were obtained between 1903 and 1914. Although it was the exception rather than the rule to find works of this importance on the market, prior to 1930 it was still possible to make outstanding acquisitions. No single dealer specialized in Netherlandish painting, but in New York the Kleinberger gallery stands out in the field. Altman, who was a regular client of Duveen, purchased most of his Netherlandish paintings from Kleinberger, usually on the advice of Friedländer. And it was for Kleinberger that, in 1929, Friedländer organized "A Loan Exhibition of Flemish Primitives." In many ways this exhibition marked the end rather than the climax of this remarkable period in the history of American collecting. The show included pictures from most of the major American collectors of old master paintings, among them a number of future donors to the Metropolitan: Michael Friedsam, Jules Bache, and Florence and George Blumenthal (Benjamin Altman had bequeathed his collection in 1913). Friedländer had especially close ties with Friedsam, writing entries for his Netherlandish paintings, while Berenson supplied those for his Italian pictures (the catalogue was never published). The paintings these collectors sought were, on the whole, small in scale and precious in execution. Portraits were popular, but there was also a place for the occasional altarpiece. Friedsam showed no hesitation in acquiring Jean Bellegambe's *Le Cellier Altarpiece* (cat. no. 87)—after all, he also owned a full-scale Gothic polyptych by the fifteenth-century Sienese painter Giovanni di Paolo.

The exhibition at Kleinberger's took place during the year of the great Wall Street crash, which had a devastating effect on collecting. The story of Jules Bache's losses, recounted below, is typical—except that Bache, unlike many others, was able to recover his assets and his collection, which he bequeathed to the Metropolitan in 1949. As apartment houses replaced the cavernous mansions of the Gilded Age, and the taste for dimly lit Gothic and Renaissance interiors of Morgan's day was succeeded by one for airier eighteenth-century French rooms, Netherlandish painting no longer commanded the attention it had once attracted. Quite apart from the fact that it was no longer possible to find examples of the quality available earlier in the century, collectors were increasingly drawn to Impressionist rather than old master painting.

This essay touches upon the subject of the donors of the Metropolitan's Netherlandish paintings and the circumstances surrounding their acquisition. It also makes note of the Museum's purchases that did not simply fill in the inevitable gaps but rather gave the collection its marking posts. Wherever possible, prices paid for pictures have been included to give the reader an idea of the values that were attached to them. Much of this information, which often allows us to say precisely when and for how much paintings were sold, comes from the Kleinberger archives.[3] Although many of the Metropolitan's benefactors were buying works at the same time and from the same sources, discussions of them are ordered according to the years their collections entered the Museum.

In 1871, the year after the Metropolitan was founded and during the upheavals of the Franco-Prussian War, the trustees spent $116,180.27 ($1,555,000 in 1997 terms) from funds raised by public subscription to buy two collections of European paintings, one in Brussels, the other in Paris.[4] Overnight the Museum acquired 174 paintings dating from the sixteenth to the nineteenth century. Apart from some distinguished seventeenth-century Dutch paintings, an early Poussin, a fine *modello* by Giambattista Tiepolo, and two Guardis, they proved to be less than they might have been. Feeble copies, poorly preserved originals, and worthless daubs were subsequently sold off, with the proceeds going to the Fund for the Purchase of Objects of Art; today 66 pictures from the 1871 Purchase, as it is called, remain in the Museum, and of them only two, an early-sixteenth-century copy of a lost diptych by Dieric Bouts (cat. no. 58) and Marten van Heemskerck's portrait of his father (cat. no. 42), appear in the present exhibition.

The first benefactor to give truly outstanding pictures to the Museum was Henry G. Marquand (1819–1902), a railroad financier descended from a family of silversmiths. Early on he showed an interest in the visual arts. His legendary residence at the northwest corner of Madison Avenue and 68th Street in New York City was an opulent town house in the French Renaissance style, commissioned from Richard Morris Hunt, the architect who later designed the Great Hall and the Fifth Avenue facade of the Metropolitan. John La Farge, Louis C. Tiffany, Frederic Leighton, and Lawrence Alma-Tadema provided rich interiors in Pompeian, Moorish, Japanese, and Spanish styles. Marquand filled this exotic setting with Oriental and European objets d'art and contemporary American and French paintings. When the young Berenson visited Marquand in 1894, he wrote that the mansion was "tremendously luxurious and beautiful, a feast for the eyes."[5] None of the contents of the house came to the Museum because Marquand suffered financial setbacks late in life; his estate was sold off in a five-day auction in 1903 (the vagaries of taste are reflected in the highest price of the sale, $30,000 for Alma-Tadema's *A Reading of Homer*, now in the Philadelphia Museum of Art).

When Marquand became the Museum's second president in 1889, he turned his back on the kind of anecdotal nineteenth-century paintings he had in his house and bought no fewer than fifty old masters, which he presented outright to the Metropolitan in 1889 and 1891. Not all of them have withstood the test of time, but five or six of the best, including Vermeer's *Young Woman with a Water Jug* and Fra Filippo Lippi's *Portrait of a Man and Woman at a Casement* (then believed to be by Masaccio), rank with the finest works of art in the Museum. In the first group of paintings in Marquand's gift was a fine variant (cat. no. 48) of Van Eyck's *Virgin and Child at the Fountain*. No one knows how much Marquand paid for it, but three years before he acquired the picture from the Sedelmeyer gallery in Paris, it fetched £315 (about $1,500) at Christie's as an original work by Van Eyck. Included in the gift of 1891 was Petrus Christus's *Lamentation* (cat. no. 4), a small, highly expressive, perfectly preserved panel. It was sold by Sir John Charles Robinson, the first keeper of the South Kensington Museum, London (now the Victoria and Albert). Robinson also owned the so-called *Virgin of Salamanca* mentioned below.

The new century started auspiciously with a bequest of $5,000,000 from Jacob S. Rogers (died 1901), a locomotive manufacturer; suddenly the Museum was receiving an annual income of $200,000 restricted for the purchase of works of art. To obtain professional advice, the trustees employed Roger Fry, the English art critic and painter who served as the Museum's buying agent in Europe from 1905 to 1910 and as curator of paintings for eleven months in 1906. After his first visit to the Museum, Fry wrote his wife, "The pictures are a nightmare."[6] But he quickly took the situation in hand by making some excellent acquisitions. Among them were Robinson's *Virgin of Salamanca* (cat. no. 47), then believed to be by the Master of Flémalle, and a Crucifixion with Saint Jerome (cat. no. 75) by Gerard David. The *Virgin of Salamanca* proved to be a late-fifteenth-century copy of the lost *Virgin and Child in an Apse* by the Master of Flémalle (who meanwhile has been identified as Robert Campin). It was acquired in 1906 from the London firm of Dowdeswell and Dowdeswell for $14,793.40. Before shipping it to New York, Fry, who often worked as a restorer, took the liberty of having the picture transferred to canvas from the panel on which it had been painted. The David, bought for $4,875 in 1909, was the first of a number of paintings by the artist to come to the Museum, which now houses the largest group of his works in the world.

John Stewart Kennedy (1830–1909), "several times a millionaire" according to one of his obituaries,[7] vice president of the Museum, and donor of Emanuel Leutze's *Washington Crossing the Delaware*, enlarged the Museum's acquisitions funds with an unconditional bequest worth $2,600,000. Notable purchases made with money from the Kennedy Fund were two Netherlandish paintings of the

Adoration of the Magi. The first, by Quentin Massys (cat. no. 99), cost £7,000 in 1911—a price comparable to that paid for one of the greatest Italian paintings in the Museum, Veronese's *Mars and Venus United by Love*, obtained with Kennedy Fund money in 1910 for £8,000. The second (cat. no. 66), bought in 1913 for $14,430, was long believed to be by Hieronymus Bosch but in 1990 was recatalogued by the Museum as a pastiche in Bosch's style.

A turning point in the formation of the Metropolitan's Netherlandish holdings came in 1913 with the bequest of Benjamin Altman (1840–1913). The son of Bavarian immigrants who settled in New York about 1853, Altman made a fortune in the dry goods business. A bachelor who shunned publicity, he began as a collector by buying Chinese porcelain and Renaissance crystals for record prices. He discovered old masters after 1905, the year he moved into a new town house at 626 Fifth Avenue, fifteen blocks north of his massive limestone department store, B. Altman and Co., at Fifth Avenue and 34th Street. Much has been written about Duveen's role in forming Altman's collection; indeed, through Duveen he acquired magnificent seventeenth-century Dutch and Flemish paintings—by Rembrandt, Hals, Vermeer, and Van Dyck—and a dozen marvelous Italian Renaissance pictures. However, like so many other collectors, he obtained his Netherlandish works from Kleinberger: Memling's portraits of Tommaso Portinari and his wife (cat. no. 27) for $426,500 in February 1910, then a staggering sum but reflective of the artist's stature at the time; Memling's *Virgin and Child with Saints Catherine of Alexandria and Barbara* (cat. no. 11) for $200,000 in December 1911; Dieric Bouts's portrait of a man wearing a tall cap (cat. no. 26) for $110,000 in November 1912; and Memling's sympathetic portrait of an old man (cat. no. 29) for $82,000 in March 1913. He clearly knew what he liked and had the means to pay for it.

Like many collectors of his generation, Altman disposed of some of his earliest acquisitions, largely nineteenth-century English pictures and paintings of the Barbizon and Hague schools. Once he hit his stride, he was quite discriminating about his old masters. For example, in November 1912 he returned to Kleinberger the portrait of Jean de Gros by Van der Weyden that he had purchased for $47,000 only six months earlier. (In June 1913 Kleinberger sold it for $33,785 to Martin Ryerson, the Chicago collector of old masters, and it now belongs to the Art Institute of Chicago.) Alas, Altman never was offered Van der Weyden's triptych of Jean de Braque, which Kleinberger sold to the Louvre for $155,000 ($2,500,000 in 1997 terms) in August 1913, exactly two months before the great collector died. Altman toyed with the idea of establishing an Altman Museum of Art (his town house had a picture gallery like the West Gallery of the mansion that Henry Clay Frick would build in 1913 on Fifth Avenue between 70th and 71st Streets) but ultimately chose to give his works of art to the Metropolitan.

His decision was brokered by his slightly older contemporary, J. Pierpont Morgan (1837–1913), fourth president of the Museum. Morgan himself, however, did not directly enrich the Metropolitan but left his vast collections to his son with instructions "to make some suitable disposition of them or of such portions of them . . . which would render them permanently available for the instruction and pleasure of the American people."[8] As a result of the extraordinary liberality of J. P. Morgan Jr., the Museum received the bulk of his father's works of art, including five important Netherlandish paintings. How many millions of schoolchildren on their first visits to the Metropolitan have sat on the floor in awed silence before one of those pictures, the large Annunciation Altarpiece (cat. no. 10)? For decades considered a masterpiece by Van der Weyden and now thought to be possibly by the very young Memling, it was commissioned by a member of the Clugny family and must have decorated an important altar in the patron's native Autun.

A year after World War I ended, the Museum acquired one of the cornerstones of its collection, Bruegel's *Harvesters* (cat. no. 102). It belonged to Paul Jean Cels (died 1917), a Belgian artist who had come to America in his mid-twenties to improve his health. On his way back to Paris from Colorado in the spring of 1917, Cels called on Bryson Burroughs, Fry's successor as curator of paintings and an aspirant painter himself. He showed Burroughs photographs of some old pictures he wished to sell as a group for $10,000. That summer he returned from a bellicose Europe with four pictures and left two of them, the *Harvesters* and an Adriaen Brouwer (which the Museum did not acquire), with Burroughs; Cels consigned the other two to a New York restorer and set off for Adelaide, in South Australia. He traveled across the United States by train, making stops at New Orleans, El Paso, and San Francisco, and mailing letters to Burroughs in which he discussed his pictures.

Cels believed the *Harvesters* to be a work of the school of Pieter Bruegel the Elder, perhaps by his son Jan Brueghel the Elder. All that Cels could tell Burroughs about its history was that he had bought it from Jacques Doucet in Paris.[9] The *Harvesters* thus landed in New York without a word about its illustrious European lineage, which can be traced from 1566, the year after it was painted, until 1816, when it vanished after appearing at auction in Paris.

We now know that the *Harvesters* belongs to a set of six landscapes representing the extended Times of the Year or the Twelve Months, of which four other panels are known: *Hunters in the Snow*, the *Gloomy Day*, and the *Return of the Herd*, all signed and dated 1565, in the Kunsthistorisches Museum, Vienna, and *Haymaking*, now in the Roudnice Lobkowicz collection at Nelahozeves, near Prague. The series reportedly formed a frieze decorating a room in Niclaes Jongelinck's newly built villa outside the walls of Antwerp. In February 1566 Jongelinck pledged them, along with other paintings, to the city of Antwerp as collateral for a debt. The landscapes entered the Habsburg family collections in July 1594, when the city presented them to the stadtholder, Ernst (1553–1595), archduke of Austria and governor of the Spanish Netherlands. When Ernst died the next year, they passed to his brother, Holy Roman Emperor Rudolf II (1552–1612), who lived in Prague and Vienna. They are next recorded in 1659, in an inventory of works of art in Vienna belonging to Leopold Wilhelm (1614–1662), archduke of Austria. Leopold Wilhelm bequeathed them to his young nephew, future Holy Roman Emperor Leopold I (1640–1705), under whose reign the dispersed imperial collections were consolidated in the Hofburg, Vienna. In 1784 the *Harvesters* and the *Return of the Herd* were hanging in the Belvedere, Vienna, along with Bruegel's *Children's Games* and *Massacre of the Innocents* in a grouping intended to represent the Four Seasons (the *Gloomy Day* and *Hunters in the Snow* were kept in storage). In 1809 the *Harvesters* was part of the plunder seized by Napoleon's troops and carried off to Paris. The French restituted most of the paintings, but Count Antoine-François Andréossy retained the *Harvesters*, which was listed as an anonymous German work of 1546 in the 1816 sale of his possessions.

In November 1917, when Burroughs recommended the *Harvesters* to the trustees' Committee on Purchases, he cautiously wrote that it might be "one of the famous series of the Months in the Vienna Gallery, which it approaches in subject, in size, and in scale of figures." Writing separately to Robert de Forest, secretary of the board of trustees, Burroughs observed, "even if it should turn out to be by Jan [Brueghel the Elder], it would still be an advantageous purchase at $10,000." De Forest, on the other hand, questioned Cels's title to the picture: "We certainly would not wish to buy at any price from a possible thief," he wrote. So the trustees delayed until the Belgian consul in New York could report that Cels, the son of the retired librarian of the University of Brussels, was an upstanding citizen, who "seems to be a collector of pictures and possesses a fairly large fortune." On December 11 Burroughs offered Cels $6,000 in a letter addressed to him in Australia, which was returned in May 1918, stamped "Unclaimed." Three months later Burroughs learned that Cels had died at Adelaide. The Museum then negotiated with Cels's heirs through the Belgian Ministry of Foreign Affairs, and in November 1919 Cels's parents accepted $3,370.79 for the painting.[10]

Such a low sum is astonishing, especially when we consider the prices commanded a decade earlier by Duveen and Kleinberger. But the art market had virtually ceased to exist during the war, and the picture was obscured by dirt, discolored varnish, and strips of restoration along cracks in the panel where original paint had fallen off. Burroughs, however, knew how important the painting would be if it was found to be a Bruegel, and he understood its possible monetary value; he was aware of another Bruegel that Fry had tried to buy for the Museum, *Peasant Wedding Dance in the Open Air*. In 1908 Fry had written Burroughs about that work, "You, who know what Breughel [*sic*] is and how soon his reputation is likely to rank with the very highest names, will realize that we ought to make great efforts to secure this." Fry proposed offering the owner £400 (about $2,000) but urged Burroughs to be prepared to "impress upon individual members of the Committee the extreme desirability of such a splendid thing, say up to £4,000 [about $20,000]."[11] The Museum did not acquire the *Peasant Wedding Dance*, but the Detroit Institute of Arts purchased it in 1930 with a city appropriation for $35,075 ($340,000 in 1997 terms).

Burroughs's hunch about the authorship of the *Harvesters* proved to be right: when the picture was cleaned in 1920, the signature B R V E G E L and the date L X V came to light. In the Museum's *Bulletin* of May 1921, he published it as part of the set of landscapes now in Vienna and the Czech Republic. His identification was supported unexpectedly by the director of the Kunsthistorisches Museum when he visited the Metropolitan in 1950 on the occasion of the exhibition "Art Treasures from Vienna Collections"; he noticed the picture still retained its Viennese *Galerie-Rahmen*—a narrow, hand-carved gilt molding that was used on all the paintings in the imperial picture gallery of the Upper Belvedere in the eighteenth century. The three Vienna panels have since been put in reproduction mid-sixteenth-century frames, much like the one that was made for the *Harvesters* for the present exhibition.

For decades *Christ Appearing to His Mother* (cat. no. 46) has been one of the most admired Netherlandish pictures in the Museum. This small painting was left to the Museum by Michael Dreicer (1868–1921), a Fifth Avenue jeweler who had purchased it from Duveen in 1917, no doubt for a large sum. It is the right compartment of a triptych bequeathed in 1504 by Isabella the Catholic to the Capilla Real in the cathedral at Granada, which still houses the central and left compartments. A variant of the triptych, from the Carthusian monastery at Miraflores, near Burgos in northern Spain, belongs to the Gemäldegalerie, Berlin. The panels at Granada and in New York were long regarded as the work of Van der Weyden, and those in Berlin fine replicas, but technical evidence has now established the Miraflores triptych as the primary version. Dreicer's panel and its former companions at Granada are so beautifully painted that they must have been copied by an incredibly gifted artist—possibly Juan de Flandes, a court painter who was working at Miraflores in the late 1490s.

A more startling change of attribution involves Van der Goes's portrait of a man (cat. no. 30). Henry Osborne Havemeyer (1847–1907) purchased this panel for Fr 50,000 at auction in Paris in 1904, the same year he and his wife, Louisine, acquired El Greco's portrait of a cardinal and Goya's *Majas on a Balcony*. Ever since the 1870s, when it first appeared on the Paris art market, Van der Goes's portrait had been considered to be an Antonello da Messina. In her posthumously published book, Mrs. Havemeyer twice mentions that the picture hung in the library, or "the Rembrandt room" as the Havemeyers called it, of their town house at 1 East 66th Street; in the first codicil to her will, she calls it "One painting by Antonello da Messina, viz: Portrait of a Man (small)."[12] When the Museum received the picture as part of the Havemeyer Collection, the hands and window were not visible because they had been covered with black paint, evidently to hide the fact that the oval panel had been cut down from a larger rectangular piece of wood. Once free of overpaint, the portrait was immediately recognized to be a fragment of a larger work by the great Netherlandish painter.

The superb Bouts *Virgin and Child* (cat. no. 6) also came to the Museum misattributed, in this instance to Memling. A painting of the highest quality, it is the original version of a composition that exists in at least two workshop variants. It was bequeathed to the Museum, along with forty-nine other pictures (of which thirty-three remain in the collection), by Theodore M. Davis (1838–1915). A millionaire Egyptologist and notorious bargain hunter, Davis was Berenson's first important client—he began employing him regularly in 1893. "The blind confidence I have in your judgment and taste gives me great hope. . . . If you see any VERY fine picture which can be bought very cheap, please advise me," Davis wrote Berenson in 1894.[13] The Bouts came onto the market in Milan the following year, and Berenson must have brought it to his attention.

When Michael Friedsam (1858–1931) died, it was front-page news. "CITY MOURNS LEADER IN BUSINESS AND ART / OWNED FAMOUS PAINTINGS / Collection, Called One of the Finest in Private Hands, is Valued at $10,000,000," the headlines read.[14] A protégé of Altman's, Friedsam lacked his mentor's sense of quality and willingness to spend top dollar; as a consequence he acquired some good and some disappointing pictures. Friedsam started working for Altman at the age of seventeen and eventually became manager of B. Altman and Co. According to an obituary notice, Friedsam and Altman became close personal friends: "they usually dined together and spent their evenings discussing those things in which their interests lay"; they even went together "on many vacations in Europe and at home."[15] When Altman died, Friedsam succeeded him as president of the department store, and he inherited his friend's library, some of his paintings (we do not know which), and his residuary estate. Like Altman, Friedsam never married, but, in contrast to him, he carried on an active public life, working to repeal federal Prohibition and to improve public schools throughout the State of New York.

Friedsam is reported to have begun collecting in 1905—about the same time as Altman—with the purchase of some Barbizon and contemporary American paintings. He soon acquired a taste for European painting and sculpture, ceramics, tapestries, Chinese porcelains, Japanese arms and armor, and Near Eastern decorative arts. Eventually he allowed interested people to see his collection in the unusually large town house he built in 1922 at 44 East 68th Street. Friedsam gave more Netherlandish paintings to the Museum—thirty panels in all—than any other donor.

We do not know how much Friedsam paid for his two paintings of the Annunciation, the beautifully preserved and highly stylish one by Joos van Cleve (cat. no. 97) and the haunting fragment by an artist close to Van Eyck, possibly Petrus Christus (cat. no. 5). They were purchased in 1925 and 1926, respectively, from Kleinberger, who supplied most of his pictures. Nor do we have prices for the *Nativity*, an early David (cat. no. 72) acquired in March 1923, or for two upright panels by the same artist (cat. no. 73) bought seven months later in the belief that they came from the same triptych to which the first panel belonged. Records survive for most of his other purchases, beginning with the roundel of the Virgin and Child by Memling (cat. no. 55), which cost $23,400 in 1916. Compared with the sums Altman paid for his Memlings, this is quite a low figure, but it may reflect Kleinberger's awareness that the paint surface was badly abraded. In January 1918 Friedsam acquired the star of his Netherlandish holdings, Van der Weyden's portrait of Francesco d'Este (cat. no. 23), for $80,000. By contrast he paid only $7,500 in January 1924 for two mediocre panels by the Master of the Saint Ursula Legend (cat. no. 14). Friedsam acquired Gossart's strong likeness of an unknown man holding a scroll (cat. no. 39) as the artist's self-portrait for $17,500 in November 1926; Massys's portrait of a stern middle-aged woman (cat. no. 38), purchased for $34,000, followed in 1928 (the Museum of Fine Arts, Boston, had recently turned it down at $60,000). The undeniable beauty of Van Cleve's *Holy Family* (cat. no. 61) must account for the $70,000 Friedsam was willing to spend for it, in March 1930, after the stock market crash.

On May 13, 1931, the *New York Times* reported that "about $2,000,000 worth of old masters have disappeared from the Hermitage," the enormous Saint Petersburg museum filled with the art collections of the Russian czars, and that Andrew Mellon (1855–1937), United States secretary of the treasury, was rumored to be the principal buyer. Mellon publicly denied the allegations, but the truth emerged in 1935 during the federal investigation of his income-tax returns for 1931. The Soviet government was indeed selling prodigious masterpieces to obtain foreign currency for industrial imports. Its early sales of Russian art and antiques to Armand Hammer and a series of auctions in Berlin and Leipzig of nationalized property that had belonged to former Russian citizens, such as the entire contents of the Stroganov palace, had had poor results. So in the summer of 1929 the commissars turned to Calouste Gulbenkian, head of the Iraq Petroleum Company, and allowed him to select paintings and sculpture from the Hermitage for his own collection, now in the Museu Calouste Gulbenkian in Lisbon. The Soviets next approached Mellon. As an earnest of their commitment to sell, they sold him a Van Dyck in New York in March 1930 for $250,000. Over the next twelve months Mellon bought twenty-one paintings for almost $7,000,000 ($74,000,000 in 1997 terms). His most expensive purchase was Raphael's *Alba Madonna*, which cost $1,166,400, plus a 25-percent commission to the New York dealer Knoedler.[16]

For Van Eyck's *Annunciation* (fig. 44), now in the National Gallery of Art, Washington, D.C., Mellon paid $503,010 in May 1930, again plus a 25-percent commission to Knoedler. The Metropolitan Museum was interested in the other Van Eyck in the Hermitage, a diptych showing the Crucifixion and Last Judgment (cat. no. 1). In April 1931 Burroughs spoke with Charles Henschel, president of Knoedler, and inquired about the diptych, Raphael's *Alba Madonna*, and Titian's *Toilet of Venus*. The last two, Henschel said, had gone to "a foreign museum"—which turned out to be the Corcoran Gallery of Art in Washington, D.C., where Mellon stored his Soviet purchases until the National Gallery of Art opened—but the Van Eyck was available for $600,000, a price the Museum deemed too high. In the autumn, when Burroughs asked again about the diptych, the price had fallen to $400,000. Henschel wrote the president of the Museum that with the Great Depression deepening throughout the world, "nobody would pay any such price" and suggested it offer $200,000 in the hope of bringing the figure down to $250,000. In February 1933 the price stood at $300,000. In March the Museum's purchasing committee refused to spend more than $150,000. But, finally, in May both sides came to terms, and the Museum agreed to pay the Soviets $185,000, plus a 10-percent commission to Knoedler. The diptych was shipped from Leningrad to the Matthiesen gallery in Berlin, where William Ivins, assistant director of the Museum, inspected it; the money was paid in Swiss francs to the Matthiesen account in Zurich, and the diptych reached New York in June. Burroughs published it in the November 1933 issue of the Museum's *Bulletin* as the work of Hubert van Eyck, in his view a far greater artist than his younger brother, Jan, but that is another story.

Despite the Depression, the Metropolitan continued to acquire European paintings of major importance throughout the 1930s. After the Van Eyck, the most remarkable picture of the Netherlandish school to enter the collection during the decade was the triptych of Saint Jerome by Patinir (cat. no. 88), a perfectly intact altarpiece in pristine condition and arguably the artist's masterpiece. The identity of the triptych's patron remains a mystery, but we know that in 1674, almost 160 years after it was painted, Leopold I, one of the former owners of Bruegel's *Harvesters*, presented it to the Benedictine monastery at Kremsmünster, near Linz, in Austria. The altarpiece remained there undisturbed until 1936, when the Museum purchased it for $65,000 through Knoedler.

With the bequest of George Blumenthal (1858–1941), the Museum received the famous *Adoration of the Magi* by Joos van Gent (cat. no. 7). Blumenthal, a partner in the New York branch of Lazard Frères, was born in Frankfurt-am-Main, came to America at the age of twenty-four, and was president of the Museum from 1934 until he died. His interest in art was kindled by his first and by all accounts quite remarkable wife, Florence. After their only child, a boy, died at age nine, she followed the example of Isabella Stewart Gardner, befriending Berenson and devoting herself to the study of the history of art. Like Mrs. Gardner, she oversaw the construction of a grandiose palace that came to house the collection she assembled. Hers was situated at the southwest corner of 70th Street and Park Avenue, and in its center was the two-story patio from Velez Blanco that now graces the Museum. Germain Seligman wrote in his memoirs that when his father, Jacques, called on Blumenthal in 1913, he was "still living then on West 53rd Street and there is little to say about his collection at that time, except that it contained excellent examples of Barbizon painting." However, Mrs. Blumenthal soon filled their lavish new house with Italian gold grounds and a few Netherlandish paintings. Sometime after 1923 Germain Seligman sold Blumenthal the Joos van Gent. As Seligman later recounted, "It hung in the patio on the ground floor, which was not an ideal place for it, and Florence always promised to move it; but unfortunately failing health in her later years prevented her from giving her usual assiduous attention to details."[17]

Another benefactor of the Metropolitan was Jules Bache (1862–1944), a stockbroker who spent more than $6,000,000 ($56,600,000 in 1997 terms) on old masters from Duveen. He started collecting while living in Paris at the turn of the century. In his book on Duveen Brothers, Edward Fowles wrote that "in 1929, Bache's fortune, like that of many others, vanished into thin air. He owed us approximately $4,000,000—which he was unable to pay. . . . [Duveen] removed the unpaid articles—with the consent of Bache—to avoid their being impounded by another creditor. In spite of this temporary reversal of fortune, Bache refused to accept defeat. . . . Late in the 1930s, when the worst was over, he telephoned to say that he had an important business meeting and wanted his pictures back in the house. We delivered them, and in time he liquidated the debt."[18]

Bache opened the first three floors of his five-story limestone town house at 814 Fifth Avenue as a private museum in 1937. The venture was not a success, and two months before he died Bache announced his gift of sixty-nine old masters to the Metropolitan. Of his seven Netherlandish pictures, the finest are the allegorical painting of a young woman holding a pink attributed to Memling (cat. no. 32), purchased in 1926 from Kleinberger for $55,000, the portrait of a youthful Carthusian lay brother by Petrus Christus (cat. no. 21), acquired in 1927 from Knoedler for $80,000, and two Davids, both obtained from Duveen in 1928—the *Rest on the Flight into Egypt* (cat. no. 82) for $300,000 and a damaged but important triptych (cat. no. 80) for $400,000. Three further acquisitions from Duveen, all made in 1928, are less fine in quality: a portrait now somewhat dubiously attributed to Van der Weyden and deemed unworthy of inclusion in the present exibition cost $160,000; a Madonna from the Bouts workshop (cat. no. 52) $200,000; and a Madonna from the Memling workshop (cat. no. 54) $150,000.

In 1950 the Museum received handsome bequests from Mary Stillman Harkness (1874–1950) and her husband, Edward (1874–1940), son of one of the founders of the Standard Oil Company. A trustee from 1912 until his death, he favored Egyptian and eighteenth-century English art, whereas she preferred rare embroideries and Oriental objects. Their elegant town house on the north corner of 75th Street and Fifth Avenue contained marvelous paintings by Constable and Gainsborough, Pesellino and Antonio Pollaiuolo, and Holbein and Vigée Le Brun, all of them now in the Museum. Their Netherlandish pictures included the *Annunciation* by David (cat. no. 79), which they purchased in Munich in 1929, and a beguiling little portrait of a man holding a heart-shaped book by the Master of the View of Sainte Gudule (cat. no. 34), acquired from Knoedler in 1928.

The Metropolitan's collection of Netherlandish paintings was now the finest in the Western Hemisphere. It included works by the most highly esteemed painters, with one conspicuous exception. There was no autograph painting by the artist who, together with Van Eyck, founded the Netherlandish school: Robert Campin. This situation was rectified in 1956, when the Museum bought the *Merode Altarpiece* (cat. no. 2). According to family tradition, the work was acquired about 1820 at Bruges by Prince Pierre d'Arenberg (1790–1877). He gave it to his daughter Marie-Nicolette (1830–1905) when she married Charles, count de Merode in 1849, although there is some uncertainty about when she actually received it, for it may have passed to her upon her father's death. In any event, she gave the altarpiece to her daughter, Countess Jeanne de Merode, who owned it in 1923 and years later bequeathed it to her niece, Countess Jeanne de Grunne. The painting was well known from photographs but had been exhibited in public only twice, in 1907 at Bruges and in 1923 in Paris. James Rorimer, director of the Metropolitan, Theodore Rousseau Jr., curator of paintings, and Margaret Freeman, curator of The Cloisters, inspected the altarpiece in Basel on April 16, 1956, and decided that the Museum would purchase it. This transaction—unusually swift for a museum—was completed when the painting arrived in New York on April 22. It then was cleaned and restored by William Suhr and put in a new frame, which some "experts" have mistaken for the original.

The announcement of the purchase came in a long press release of December 11, 1957, stating that the altarpiece had been "obtained through income from the fund generously given by John D. Rockefeller, Jr., for the further enrichment of The Cloisters." In making the purchase, the Museum promised the New York dealers Rosenberg and Stiebel not to disclose the price. But *Life* magazine soon reported the painting cost "more than $750,000," and, two years later, John Canaday observed that "it was a bargain at a rumored price of $800,000."[19]

The Museum's holdings of Netherlandish paintings were further enriched by the bequest of Robert Lehman (1891–1969), senior partner of Lehman Brothers, one of the world's leading investment banking firms, and both a vice president of the Museum and a chairman of the board of trustees. As a young man in his twenties he helped his father, Philip Lehman (1861–1947), and his mother build an outstanding collection of old masters; after his father's death Robert continued to add works, notably drawings and nineteenth- and twentieth-century French paintings. Philip Lehman had made his first purchases of serious works of art about 1910. When Robert graduated from Yale in 1913, he did not immediately go into business but instead concentrated on his parents' art collection for several years and then served as an artillery captain in France during World War I. He was, in fact, almost thirty when he joined his father's firm. The elder Lehman paid the bills for the family's art collection through the mid-1920s; from 1928 onward the son, who had initiated most of the purchases, paid them. Their most significant acquisitions were made during the second and third decades of the century, at the same time Altman, Friedsam, Bache, and Blumenthal were amassing their collections. So even though the Lehman pictures entered the Metropolitan in the mid-1970s, the taste they exemplify belongs to an earlier era. The Lehmans thus differ from other two-generational collectors, such as the Mellons, the Thyssens, and William T. Walters of Baltimore and his son, Henry, who indulged their quite disparate personal tastes over a span of ninety years.

The earliest recorded Lehman acquisitions of Netherlandish paintings, the charming portrayal of the Virgin and Child with a dragonfly (cat. no. 51) and an epitaph panel (cat. no. 33), are by anonymous artists: the first, by the Master of Saint Giles, who worked in Paris, came from the Paris branch of Kleinberger in 1911; the second, by the Master of the Saint Ursula Legend, was purchased from Kleinberger in New York on February 20, 1912. These were soon followed by more important pictures, such as the exterior and interior wings of a folding triptych by David (cat. no. 78) acquired from Duveen by 1913 and two Memlings: a superb male portrait (cat. no. 28) bought from Knoedler in 1915 and a deeply poetic painting of the Annunciation (cat. no. 12) acquired from Princess Marie Branicka Radziwill through Duveen in 1920. The pièce de résistance of the Lehman holdings, Christus's large-scale depiction of an expensively dressed couple visiting a goldsmith (cat. no. 22), belonged to Philip Lehman by 1921. The painting had appeared at a widely publicized auction in Berlin shortly before the end of World War I, but how and when the Lehmans took possession of it are not known. In Kleinberger's stock records, Philip Lehman is recorded as the purchaser of Jean Hey's rare portrait of Margaret of Austria (cat. no. 35) on March 8, 1926.

In 1928 Robert Lehman published the monumental folio catalogue *The Philip Lehman Collection, New York: Paintings*, an unparalleled example of scholarly and filial dedication. By 1961 the collection—not only of old masters but also of drawings, modern French paintings, sculpture, majolica, and a wide range of other decorative arts—had grown to such an extent that he converted into a museum with a curator and guards the five-story town house at 7 West 54th Street that his parents had built in 1900. Unlike the Frick Collection and the short-lived Bache Museum, it was not open to the public, but students with a bona fide interest in art could apply for appointments, much as they had a generation earlier to view the Friedsam collection. Shortly before he died in the summer of 1969, Lehman decided to give most of his collection to the Metropolitan. The Robert Lehman Collection, housed in a modern glass pyramid overlooking Central Park, opened to the public in 1975, and its riches have enthralled visitors to the Museum ever since.

The most recent donor of Netherlandish paintings to the Metropolitan, Belle Linsky (1906–1987), also considered establishing a private museum for the remarkable collection she and her husband, Jack (1897–1980), had formed with unabashed enthusiasm over four decades. They acquired spectacular French eighteenth-century furniture, amazing porcelain, goldsmiths' work, Renaissance and Baroque bronzes, and rather small paintings that would fit comfortably into a New York apartment. After her husband's death, Mrs. Linsky explored the possibility of installing their holdings in 11 East 70th Street, a then-vacant town house overlooking the garden of the Frick Collection. The idea was for the Frick to administer a satellite museum of decorative arts to complement its own grand works; there were, however, no funds to endow it. In due time, in 1982, she gave her treasures to the Metropolitan and lived to see them installed in a suite of small galleries, not unlike the fourteen rooms of the Linskys' apartment at 927 Fifth Avenue, but much less cluttered.

Jack and Belle Linsky had been born in Russia and met each other in America. Their fortune came from "our little stationery business," as she liked to call it, the Swingline staple company in Brooklyn, where both worked until 1970. Collecting art was the Linskys' hobby. They were particularly proud of the painting by Joos van Cleve of the Virgin with a prayer book (cat. no. 96) that they acquired at the famous Julia Berwind estate sale in 1962 for only $40,000. Occasionally they bought from dealers, but they thrived on the fierce competition of the auction room, where they seldom were disappointed. Once they made up their minds, nothing could stop them, as John Walker, a former director of the National Gallery of Art in Washington, D.C., learned. In his memoirs Walker explained that the National Gallery had been prepared to pay $360,000 for two panels by Juan de Flandes that came up at Christie's in 1967. "The first painting to my delight went for just over $120,000, thus leaving us approximately $240,000 for the second, which I thought somewhat less beautiful," he wrote. "I had a false sense of security, for I did not know that Mrs. Jack Linsky, a most discerning collector, had decided that she wanted number two."[20] She got it for $244,020.

There was no question in Belle's mind about which of the two panels at Christie's was the more beautiful—it was without doubt the one showing the Marriage Feast at Cana (cat. no. 85). One of a series of forty-seven exquisite scenes from the lives of Christ and Mary, it had been painted for Isabella the Catholic. In the first record of the series, the pictures are said to be "en un armario" (in a cupboard), so Mrs. Linsky kept her panel in a cupboard and took great delight in bringing it out to show visitors. Now, thanks to her bountiful spirit, it is on display at the Museum for all to admire.

The Linskys were the last New Yorkers to acquire more than the occasional great Netherlandish painting. As has already been noted, this is due in part to the fact that it has become increasingly difficult to find pictures of the quality of those bought by Altman, Friedsam, and the Lehmans. There were exceptions, however, the most notable being a lovely painting by Van Eyck and his workshop acquired by the Frick Collection in 1954 and, of course, the *Merode Altarpiece*, purchased for The Cloisters in 1956. The trustees of the Frick also bought a handsome Memling from Kleinberger in 1968. And, more recently, two wonderful pictures by Bouts, executed in distemper on linen for the same large altarpiece, appeared on the art market: a *Resurrection*, purchased by Norton Simon at Sotheby's in 1980 for £1,700,000 ($7,735,000 in 1997 terms), and an *Annunciation*, bought three years later by the Getty Museum from the New York dealer E. V. Thaw.

It is difficult, however, to escape the conclusion that, so far as New York collectors are concerned, the moment for buying Netherlandish painting has passed, and this impression is not altered by Jayne and Charles Wrightsman's exceptional purchase in 1962 of an extremely fine work by David (cat. no. 81). As a result of the shift of interest away from Netherlandish "primitives" on the part of collectors, the Metropolitan's holdings, in important respects, have not kept pace with recent scholarship. Whereas the Museum is rich in works by artists from Bruges and Antwerp, the Romanist school of Brussels is poorly represented, and major figures such as Lucas van Leyden, Jan van Scorel, and Pieter Aertsen, to name just a few, have not found the place they deserve. It is to be hoped that a new generation of collectors will be inspired by the example of the public-spirited men and women mentioned in these pages.

PRICES PAID FOR NETHERLANDISH PAINTINGS AND THEIR 1997 VALUES

The following inflation-adjusted prices are based on statistics kindly provided by Sally Nuttall of Standard & Poor's.

1904 Van der Goes, *Portrait of a Man* (cat. no. 30): Fr 50,000 ($180,000)

1906 Campin, Copy after, *Virgin and Child in an Apse* (cat. no. 47): $14,793.40 ($265,000)

1909 David, *The Crucifixion* (cat. no. 75): $4,875 ($87,000)

1910 Memling, *Tommaso Portinari* and *Maria Maddalena Baroncelli* (cat. no. 27): $426,500 ($7,365,000)

1911 Massys, *The Adoration of the Magi* (cat. no. 99): £7,000 ($590,000)
Memling, *Virgin and Child with Saints Catherine of Alexandria and Barbara* (cat. no. 11): $200,000 ($3,455,000)

1912 Bouts, *Portrait of a Man* (cat. no. 26): $110,000 ($1,825,000)

1913 Bosch, Style of, *The Adoration of the Magi* (cat. no. 66): $14,430 ($235,000)
Memling, *Portrait of an Old Man* (cat. no. 29): $82,000 ($1,330,000)

1916 Memling, *Virgin and Child* (cat. no. 55): $23,400 ($345,000)

1918 Van der Weyden, *Francesco d'Este* (cat. no. 23): $80,000 ($850,000)

1919 Bruegel, *The Harvesters* (cat. no. 102): $3,370.79 ($31,300)

1924 Master of the Saint Ursula Legend, *Saint Paul with Paolo Pagagnotti*; *Christ Appearing to His Mother* (cat. no. 14): $7,500 ($70,500)

1926 Gossart, *Portrait of a Man* (cat. no. 39): $17,500 ($160,000)
Memling, Attributed to, *Young Woman with a Pink* (cat. no. 32): $55,000 ($500,000)

1927 Christus, *Portrait of a Carthusian* (cat. no. 21): $80,000 ($740,000)

1928 Bouts, Workshop of, *Virgin and Child* (cat. no. 52): $200,000 ($1,870,000)
David, *The Nativity with Donors and Saints Jerome and Leonard* (cat. no. 80): $400,000 ($3,735,000)
David, *The Rest on the Flight into Egypt* (cat. no. 82): $300,000 ($2,800,000)
Massys, *Portrait of a Woman* (cat. no. 38): $34,000 ($320,000)
Memling, Workshop of, *Virgin and Child* (cat. no. 54): $150,000 ($1,400,000)

1930 Van Cleve, *The Holy Family* (cat. no. 61): $70,000 ($675,000)

1933 Van Eyck, *The Crucifixion*; *The Last Judgment* (cat. no. 1): $203,500 ($2,535,000)

1936 Patinir, *The Penitence of Saint Jerome* (triptych) (cat. no. 88): $65,000 ($750,000)

1956 Campin, *The Annunciation Triptych* (cat. no. 2): $800,000 ($4,725,000)

1962 Van Cleve, *Virgin and Child* (cat. no. 96): $40,000 ($212,000)

1967 Juan de Flandes, *The Marriage Feast at Cana* (cat. no. 85): $244,020 ($1,175,000)

For help in preparing this essay, my thanks go to many colleagues, especially Maryan W. Ainsworth, Betsy Baldwin, Virginia Budny, Sharon Cott, Carol Fuerstein, Jeanie James—and Walter Liedtke, coeditor of the basic survey of the Flemish paintings in America (Bauman and Liedtke 1992). Keith Christiansen encouraged me to write this essay and helped give my text its final form. I also received useful advice from Paul Guth, Ed Weisl, and Gerald G. Stiebel.

1. For an excellent biography of Valentiner, see Sterne 1980.
2. Johnson collection 1913–14. The first volume, on Johnson's Italian paintings, was compiled by Berenson.
3. Kleinberger's papers were bequeathed to the Museum by Harry Sperling in 1972 and are housed in the Department of European Paintings. This essay also draws from records in the Museum's Archives.
4. For the current value of the sums paid for paintings in the Metropolitan cited in this essay, see the list preceding these notes.
5. Samuels 1979, p. 204.
6. Sutton 1972, vol. 1, p. 228.
7. *New York Times*, November 1, 1909.
8. Hoyt 1966, p. 337.
9. Doucet, an internationally known couturier and a remarkable connoisseur, had spent decades amassing a superb collection of eighteenth-century French art. In 1912 he startled the art world by selling off all his possessions—the Bruegel was not among them—reputedly making a profit of $2,000,000 ($33,000,000 in 1997 terms). He then proceeded to buy wonderful Postimpressionist and Cubist paintings, including Picasso's *Demoiselles d'Avignon*. For Doucet's first collection, see Chapon 1996, pp. 146–55, and the catalogue of his sale at Galerie Georges Petit, Paris, on June 6, 1912. The authority for Doucet's ownership of the *Harvesters* is Burroughs 1921, p. 96 n. 1. The *Harvesters* has been identified as a painting sold in Brussels before 1907 (Virch 1969, p. 224); however, the description of the painting said to have been sold then—"près d'eux des chevaux et au milieu de l'arrière-plan des bâtiments avec tour"—is at odds with the composition of the *Harvesters*.
10. Department of European Paintings archives, file for Pieter Bruegel the Elder, *The Harvesters* (19.164).
11. Sutton 1972, vol. 1, p. 297.
12. Havemeyer 1931, pp. 20, 310 n. 38; Gretchen Wold in Frelinghuysen et al. 1993, p. 343, no. 290.
13. Samuels 1979, p. 182.
14. *New York Times*, April 8, 1931.
15. Ibid., p. 16.
16. For the Soviet sales, see Walker 1969, pp. 108–22, 243, and Williams 1980, pp. 147–90.
17. Seligman 1961, pp. 142–47.
18. Fowles 1976, p. 156.
19. "A Medieval Masterwork of Hidden Symbols: Metropolitan Museum Buys World-Famous Flemish Altarpiece," *Life*, April 7, 1958; John Canaday, "8 Paintings: $4,532,000," *New York Times Magazine*, April 10, 1960, p. 17.
20. Walker 1969, pp. 42–44.

CATALOGUE

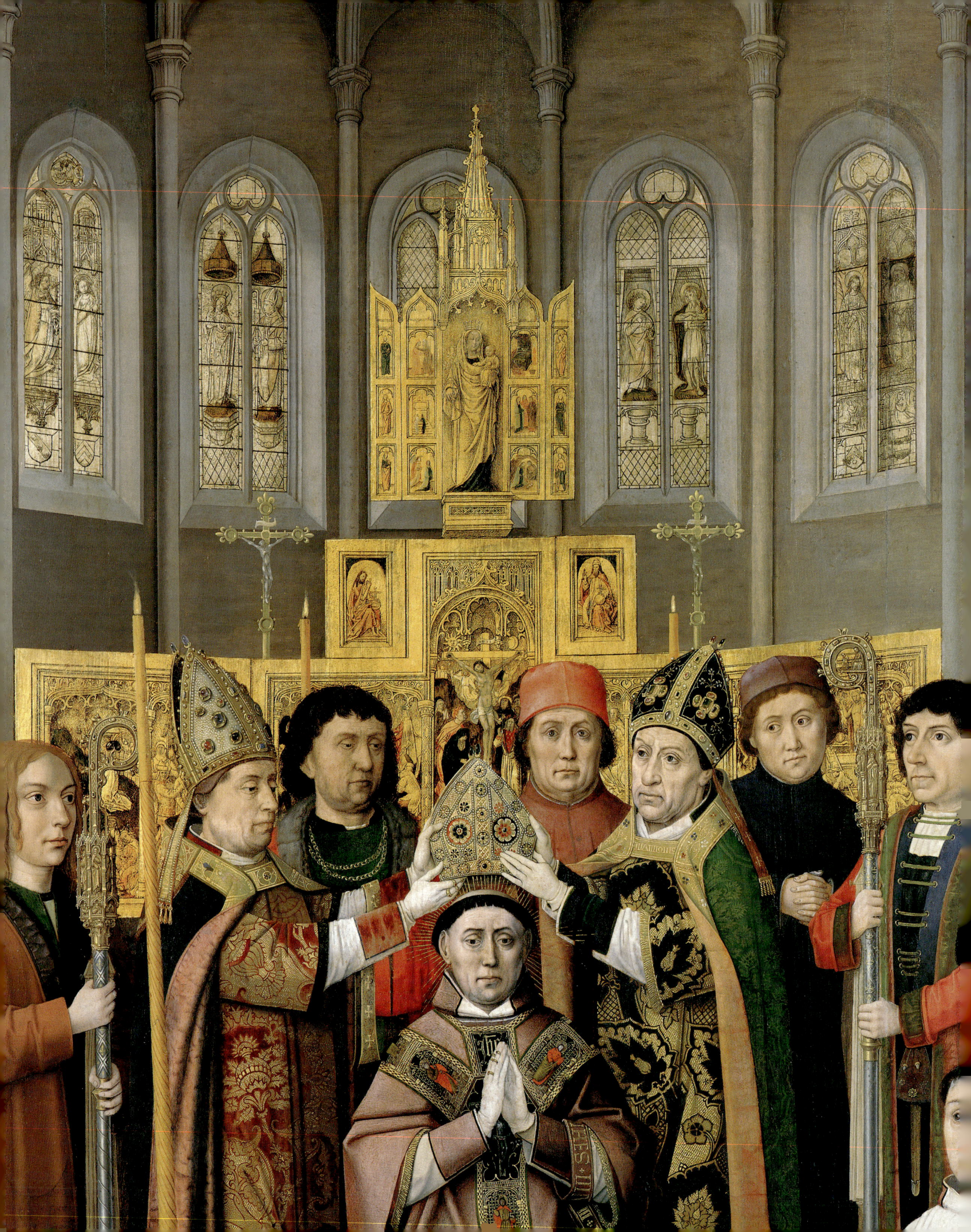

Religious Painting from about 1420 to 1500: In the Eye of the Beholder

Even taking into account large altarpieces intended for liturgical use (cat. no. 16; frontis., p. 78), early Netherlandish painting is primarily a matter of small scale and meticulous detail rather than monumentality and physical grandeur. Its diminutive features entice the viewer to encounter the world as a microcosm that is a personal realm for meditation and the experience of miraculous visions. These characteristics are shared by manuscript illumination, which, along with sculpture and architecture, had been one of the predominant art forms of the late Middle Ages. The aesthetic concerns of panel painting were at first closely allied with those of manuscript illumination and sculpture, but gradually, over the course of the fifteenth and early sixteenth centuries, a new mode was substituted for the old. This shift had to do not only with the evolution of artistic expression but also with subtle changes in devotional practice.

Precious illuminated books (for example, fig. 41) had provided one of the principal means of edification and devotional practice for religious orders and the wealthy, their intricately painted illustrations offering a visual counterpart to the written word. However, the *Biblia Pauperum*, or *Bible of the Poor* (fig. 42), was more widely popular and accessible to the masses. Initially the *Biblia Pauperum* was produced as an educational tool for clerics whose Latin was less than proficient. It supplied illustrations of biblical events alongside explanatory texts, aiming at a didactic presentation of Church doctrine by relating Old to New Testament scriptures. Each New Testament subject was enframed by its prefigurations from the Old Testament and accompanied by four Old Testament prophets who announced the theme. Another commonly used text, the *Speculum Humanae Salvationis*, or *Mirror of the Salvation of Man*, was not always illustrated but in similar fashion provided typological parallels of Old and New Testament themes.

Early Netherlandish painters adopted this late medieval convention of juxtaposing text and image and Old and New Testament themes. In his *Annunciation* (fig. 44) Jan van Eyck surrounded Gabriel and the Virgin with narrative episodes from the Old Testament that prefigure or augment the New Testament subject that is presented. Depicted unobtrusively in subordinate areas of the painting, these symbolic references include scenes from the life of Moses on the top of the back wall, as well as signs of the zodiac and other Old Testament stories, mostly relating to Samson, on the foreground floor tiles. In the Metropolitan Museum's diptych by Van Eyck (cat. no. 1) the themes of the Crucifixion and Last Judgment are augmented

Opposite: Master of Saint Augustine, detail, *Scenes from the Life of Saint Augustine* (cat. no. 16)

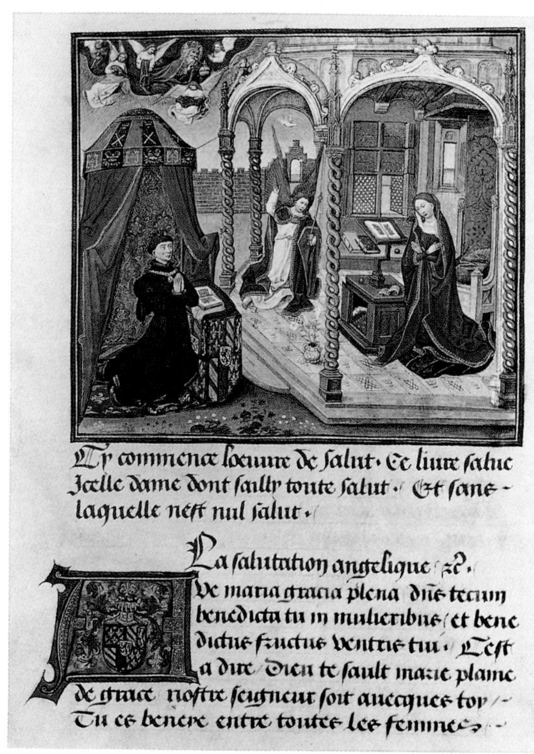

Cy commence loeuure de salut. Ce liure salue
Icelle dame dont saillit toute salut. Et sans
laquelle nest nul salut.

La salutation angelique &c.
Ave maria gracia plena dñs tecum
benedicta tu in mulieribus et bene
dictus fructus ventris tui. Cest
a dire Dieu te sault marie plaine
de grace nostre seigneur soit avecques toy
Tu es benete entre toutes les femmes

Fig. 41. Willem Vrelant, *Philip the Good Kneeling in Front of an Annunciation*, from Jean Miélot, *Traité sur la salutation angélique*, 1461. Tempera on vellum. Bibliothèque Royale Albert Ier, Brussels (MS 9270, fol. 2v)

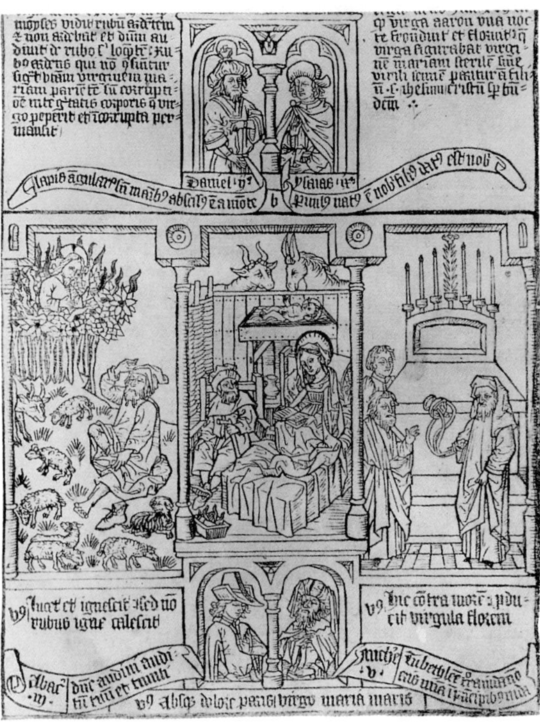

Fig. 42. Netherlandish, *The Nativity with Old Testament Prefigurations*, from *Biblia Pauperum*, about 1460. Woodcut on paper. The Pierpont Morgan Library, New York (PML 3193)

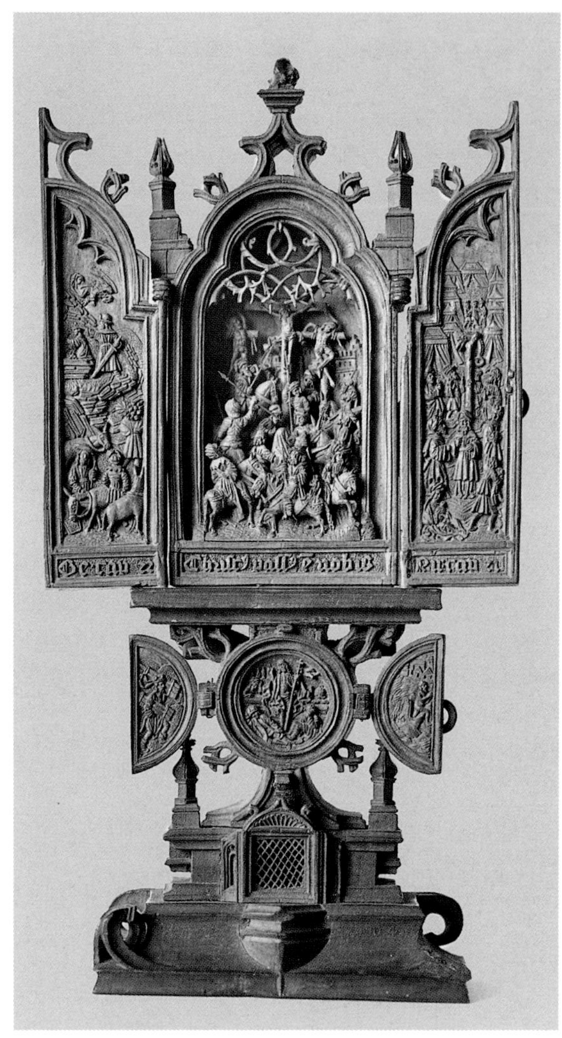

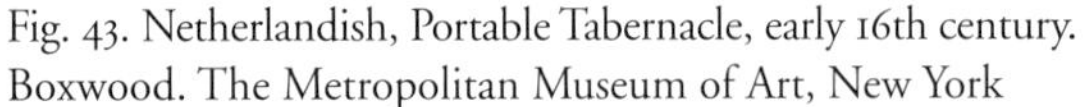

Fig. 43. Netherlandish, Portable Tabernacle, early 16th century. Boxwood. The Metropolitan Museum of Art, New York

by Latin inscriptions on the frames referring to Old and New Testament texts that clearly derive from similar juxtapositions in early illustrated Bibles. The inscriptions add an erudite, exegetical dimension to the compelling visual terms of the paintings.

In the last quarter of the fifteenth century what had been a typological subtext or footnote in earlier paintings sometimes acquired status equal to the primary subject. For example, in the triptych by the Master of the Saint Barbara Legend (cat. no. 13), the Old Testament scenes of King David receiving Abner's messenger and the Queen of Sheba presenting gifts to Solomon are shown on the wings and are given the same attention lavished on the Adoration of the Magi, the narrative on the central panel. And, somewhat later, in the sixteenth century, the Old Testament stories of Abraham and Melchizedek and the Gathering of Manna are given similar treatment in an altarpiece by an Antwerp Mannerist, where they are presented on the wings as precursors to the central scene of the Last Supper (cat. no. 68).

Texts such as the *Biblia Pauperum* inspired not only large panels and ensembles of paintings but also small devotional objects that could be carried by the owners on their travels. The intricately carved upper portion of the Museum's remarkable boxwood triptych (fig. 43) shows the typological pairings of Old and New Testament themes most common in medieval art: the Crucifixion with the Sacrifice of Isaac and Moses and the Brazen Serpent, and the Resurrection with Samson Carrying the Gates of Gaza (a reference to Christ Carrying the Cross) and Jonah Emerging from the Whale. Relics stored in compartments in the triptych's upper and lower divisions gave a tangible presence to the object of veneration. The miraculous properties of the relics were enhanced by a miracle of craftsmanship, and the miniature triptych asserts itself as both devotional object and work of art.

The influence of relief and architectural sculpture on fifteenth-century devotional painting can be recognized in the tipped-up space and vertical arrangement of objects in the domestic interior of the *Annunciation* panel of Robert Campin's *Merode Triptych* (cat. no. 2), as well as in the niche-like compartment for the figures in the Campin-inspired *Virgin and Child in an Apse* (cat. no. 47). Architectural features, together with inscriptions, play an important part in the painting of the Virgin and Child standing in a porch or niche (cat. no. 48), where texts from the Book of Genesis on the canopy over Mary and on the step below relate the story of Jacob and Rebekah and the tale of Jacob's dream of a ladder to heaven: contemporary devotional guides and sermons—Saint Bernard's sermon "De beata Maria Virgine," among others—refer variously to spiritual meditations as a ladder by which the believer ascends to union with God. Here the Virgin is the means of that access to God, for she is the intercessor for the faithful in their quest for eternal salvation in paradise. Reinforcing the continuity of the Old and the New Testament are portrayals of the prophets Moses and Isaiah, shown in niches at the top of the porch and, below, figures symbolizing the Synagogue, or Old Testament Law, and Ecclesia (the Church), or the New Testament Dispensation.

The archway that defines the foreground plane of *Christ Appearing to His Mother* (cat. no. 46) not only provides, quite literally, visual entry into the sacred realm of the scene that is depicted but also amplifies the main subject of the painting through the themes sculpted on it: the Three Marys at the Tomb, the Ascension of Christ, Pentecost, the Annunciation of the Death of Mary, the Dormition of the Virgin, and the Coronation of the Virgin. In the room beyond are traditional Old Testament prototypes of the Resurrection and Christ's conquest of evil in the form of capitals of columns decorated with carvings representing David and Goliath, Daniel in the Lion's Den, and Samson at the Gates of Gaza.

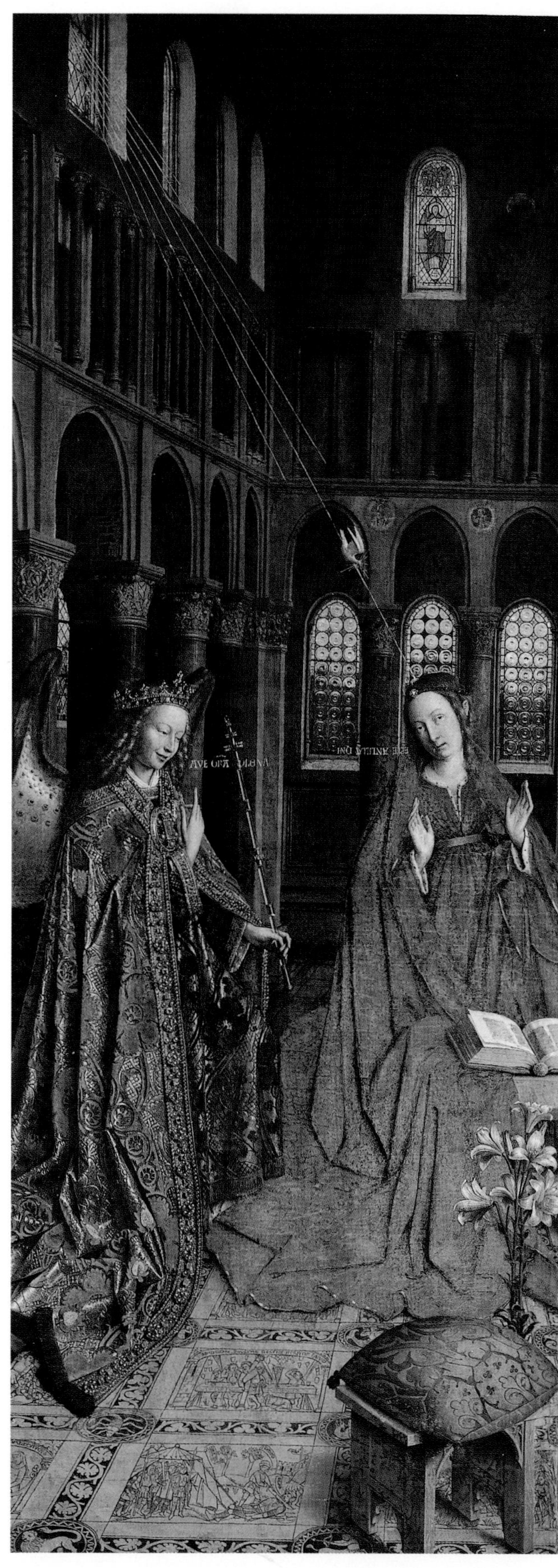

Fig. 44. Jan van Eyck, *The Annunciation*, about 1434–36. Oil on canvas, transferred from wood. Andrew W. Mellon Collection, National Gallery of Art, Washington, D.C.

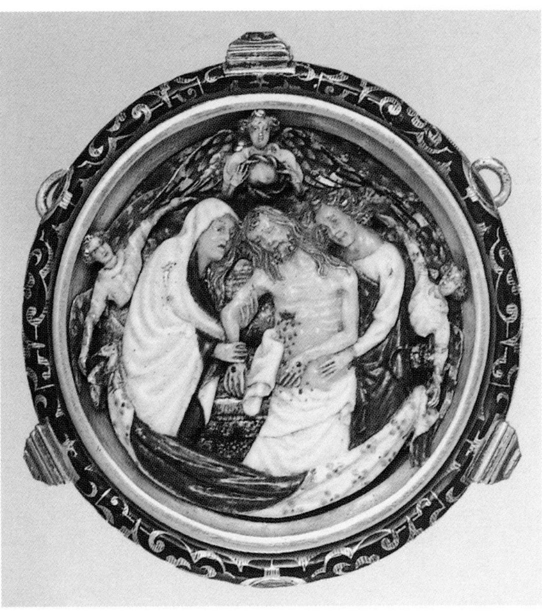

Fig. 45. French (Paris?), Pendant with *The Lamentation*, about 1400. *Ronde bosse* enamel, gold, and diamonds. The Metropolitan Museum of Art, New York

At the same time they employed these primarily symbolic depictions, artists were developing more purely visual strategies to draw the viewer into the scene. By placing the subject of his *Annunciation* from the *Merode Triptych* in a domestic setting instead of in a portico or church interior, Campin provided the spectator with an accessible and familiar devotional experience. Indeed, the sort of intentional naturalism seen here is a key feature of early Netherlandish painting, by means of which artists represented age-old biblical themes as if they were current events. Even symbolic motifs are integrated into compositions as genrelike details. Thus, a vase of lilies, a sign of the Virgin's purity, is prominently placed on the table at the center of Campin's picture, even though these flowers do not bloom in March, the presumed time of the Annunciation. But what of the other objects in his painting—the open book, the candle, the water basin? According to Panofsky, all such naturalistic details are disguised symbols—that is, every object masks or hides a symbolic meaning—for otherwise they would introduce a profane element at odds with the sacred idealism of late medieval art.

Recently some scholars have rejected Panofsky's notion and maintain, more convincingly, that artists introduced certain details in an attempt to use naturalism to create visually accessible images, and that they intended to encourage the viewer to identify with them individually as real, three-dimensional objects and experience their deliberate placement as part of an illusionistic construction of pictorial space. These objectives would be in keeping with the sweeping spiritual movements of the day, such as the Modern Devotion, whose proponents encouraged the faithful to meditate on sacred scenes as if they were actually taking part in them.

Although the fundamental source for the subject matter of most devotional painting was the Bible, the traditional accounts it provided were augmented by apocryphal Gospels that offered further narrative details, particularly relating to the lives of Christ and the Virgin Mary. Among these texts is a *Pseudo-Matthew* penned by Jacobus de Voragine, a Genoese bishop of the thirteenth century, to supply explications for the feast days of the liturgical calendar relating to the Virgin and to Christ. Another is Voragine's famous *Golden Legend*, which describes the details of the lives of the saints and special events associated with each day of the year. The *Golden Legend* had a significant influence on the iconography of the saints and was used by artists as a source for their own interpretations. The details in the extended narrative of the *Scenes from the Life of Saint Augustine* (cat. no. 16), for example, came from this book's discussions of the saint's life, and the Cloisters *Nativity* from the workshop of Rogier van der Weyden (cat. no. 45) follows its texts on the feasts of the Nativity and the Epiphany.

Netherlandish artists frequently relied on a variety of texts for inspiration, and sometimes theologians were made available for learned advice regarding content—as happened when Dieric Bouts was granted the important commission for an altarpiece showing the Last Supper for the Sint-Pieterskerk in Leuven. Quite often individual paintings evolved from a conflation of numerous sources that were not strictly tied to biblical accounts. This material, which very much enhanced the narrative or emotional appeal of the themes depicted, could be as varied as official Church doctrine found in papal bulls, synod pronouncements, and liturgical texts; hymns; and passages from mystery plays or mystical literature, such as the *Revelations* of Saint Bridget of Sweden, the *Meditations on the Life of Christ* of the Pseudo-Bonaventure, or the *Life of Christ* by Ludolph of Saxony.

The principal devotional theme of early Netherlandish painting was the suffering of Christ for man's redemption. Narrative representations centered on this subject most often drew from two great liturgical cycles, the Infancy of Christ and the Passion of Christ. Both were equally popular in other art forms of vastly different scales—ranging from enamel pendants and exquisitely wrought rosary beads that might show scenes of the Passion of Christ (figs. 45, 102) to monumental tapestries (fig. 46), which in the fifteenth century assumed the character of woven paintings in their formal and iconographic features. Individual episodes from one or the other of these two cycles were also featured as single devotional panels or as the centerpieces of triptychs, such as the Merode *Annunciation*. Treatments of these standard subjects vary considerably depending upon the specific text that informs them. Thus, the charming details of an early *Nativity* by Gerard David (cat. no. 72)—the Christ Child lying on the ground, the young Virgin with long, flowing hair, the particular way Joseph holds his hand as he shields his candle—were directly inspired by the account of Saint Bridget of Sweden's mystical vision. David's later rendition of the theme (cat. no. 80), however, equates Christ's Incarnation

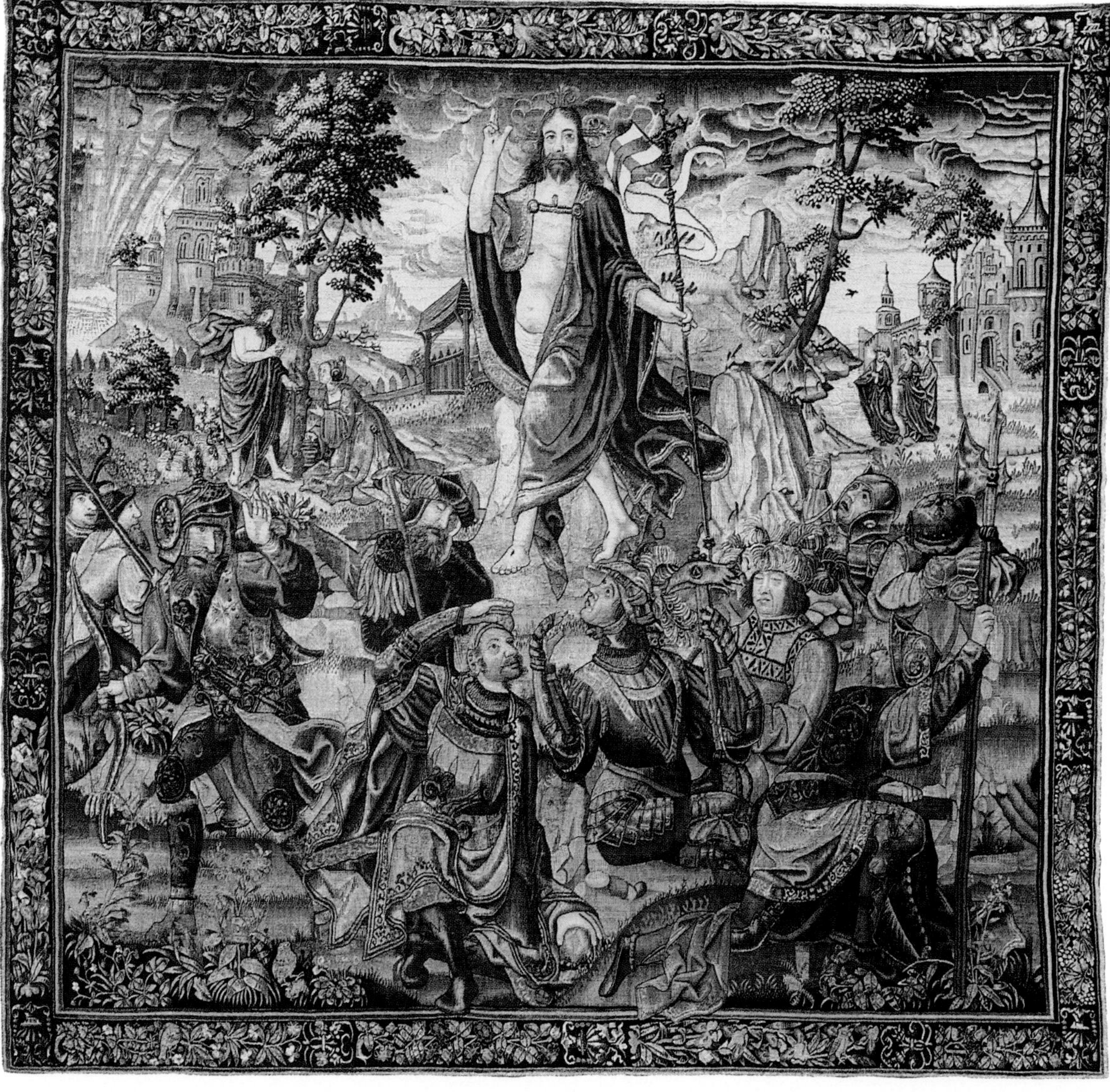

Fig. 46. South Netherlandish, *The Resurrection*, 1515–25. Tapestry. The Metropolitan Museum of Art, New York

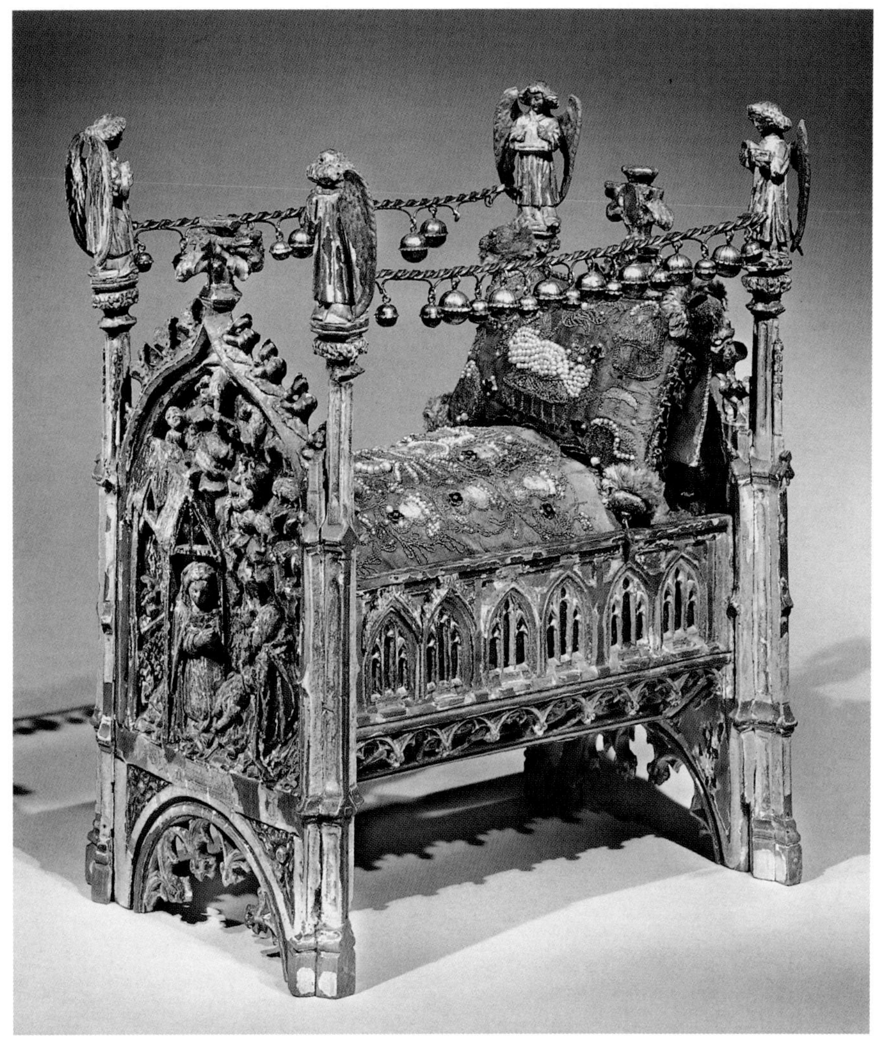

Fig. 47. South Netherlandish, *Crib of the Infant Jesus*, Brabant, 15th century. Carved and polychromed oak, copper gilt, silver gilt, painted parchment, and silk embroidered with gold seed pearls and translucent enamels. The Metropolitan Museum of Art, New York

and his sacrifice for mankind with liturgical practice, specifically the celebration of the Eucharist. And entirely different associations are called to mind by Joos van Gent's *Adoration of the Magi* (cat. no. 7), which in its setting and costumes and the theatrical gestures of its figures most closely evokes contemporary mystery plays performed in churches on the occasion of the Feast of the Epiphany.

Another type of picture demanded a devotional attitude linked with mystical thought and writings. These paintings almost invariably concern the suffering of Christ, shown as the Imago Pietatis (Christ of Pity), the Man of Sorrows, or the Holy Face. Essentially timeless private devotional images, such portrayals were not intended as parts of more extensive narrative treatments of Christ's life but rather were devised solely to evoke an empathic response. Some were attached to indulgences that required payments to the clergy and guaranteed spiritual rewards for the patron. The recitation of standard prayers before these images promised a number of years of release from the uncertainty of purgatory.

The subject in Petrus Christus's *Head of Christ* (cat. no. 3) maintains the direct eye contact with the viewer that is of paramount importance in works of this kind; it was perhaps inspired by the discussion about the nature of devotional images in the *Vision of God* of 1453 by Nicholas of Cusa, who declared that it was necessary to "see through" the portrayal to experience the actual physical presence of Christ. The workshop of Dieric Bouts specialized in a variation on the image of the suffering Christ that unites the Mourning Virgin with Christ as the

Man of Sorrows (cat. no. 58). The worshiper confronting this image was to emulate the Virgin in order to achieve the longed-for spiritual union with Christ. Changing tastes and evolving devotional practices apparently did not affect the popularity of this type of representation, which artists, especially those in Bouts's workshop, continued to execute in multiple copies from about 1460 to as late as 1530.

A new devotional fervor that developed during this period gave rise to an increase in the production of images of the Virgin and Child, many of which were derived from revered Byzantine icons. Although these portrayals may at first appear identical, they are in fact distinguished in pose, gesture, and/or type of symbolic attribute displayed, which encouraged the observer to meditate in different ways upon the Incarnation of Christ and his salvation of man. Thus the touching embrace of Christ and his mother depicted by Dieric Bouts (cat. no. 6) refers to the extremely popular Song of Solomon, passionate poetry that was interpreted in contemporary exegeses as an allegory of God's love. Other examples, in which the Virgin nurses the Child (cat. nos. 49, 61, 82), reads to him, or offers him a piece of fruit (cat. nos. 54, 70), convey shifting emphases and meanings. Consistent in all, however, is the solemn or sorrowful expression of the Virgin as she tends to the needs of her child, an indication of her prescience of man's rejection of Christ, which was prophesied to her by the aged priest Simeon at the Presentation in the Temple (Luke 2:33–35).

Ardent worship of cult images of this type involved the repeated recitation of certain prayers aimed at achieving a miraculous vision of the Virgin and Child. Sometimes these prayers are included in the picture, as in the *Virgin Suckling the Child* of about 1520 attributed to an Antwerp master (cat. no. 63), where the text surrounds the image on all four sides. Found both in breviaries and Books of Hours, the prayer "Ave regina celorum," starting at the lower left side, would have been recited daily or sung as a hymn at the close of Compline (the final office of the liturgical day), while the "Beata es Maria," at the base, was a response after the second lesson at Matins.

Personal devotions were also facilitated by small, tangible objects used for meditation, among them cradle reliquaries such as the Museum's splendid *Crib of the Infant Jesus* from the Begijnhof of Leuven (fig. 47). Cradle reliquaries, which include a small sculpture of the Christ Child (an element missing from our example), were often presented to noblewomen when they entered convents, in affirmation of the spiritual and sacrificial life they were about to undertake. Meditation on the cradle and contemplation of the narrative scenes on either end (depicting the Nativity and the Adoration of the Magi) encouraged the viewer to relive the events of Christ's life and sacrifice. Spiritual exercises of this sort allowed the observer to assume the role of the Virgin, lovingly caring for her child, and empathically sharing in his life.

The empathic response of the viewer confronting the image was considered key to the achievement of salvation. Toward this end, the suppliant appealed through prayer to the Virgin Mary to serve as an intercessor on his or her behalf. One of the most common of such prayers, frequently inscribed in full on the frames of paintings or in part on the hem of the Virgin's dress (cat. nos. 79, 89), is a humble entreaty:

Mary, Mother of Grace, Mother of Mercy
Protect us from the enemy and
At the hour of death receive me
O Mother of God, remember me.

MARYAN W. AINSWORTH

References: Panofsky 1953; Toussaert 1963; Ringbom 1969; Ozment 1980; Lane 1984; Harbison 1985; Mundy 1985; Lane 1986; Marrow 1986; Lane 1988; Lievens-de Waegh 1994 (with additional bibliography); Van Os et al. 1994

Jan van Eyck, active by 1422, died 1441, and Assistant

1. The Crucifixion; The Last Judgment, about 1430

Oil on canvas, transferred from wood; each panel 22¼ x 7⅔ in. (56.5 x 19.7 cm)
Inscribed: (on cross in Hebrew, Greek, and Latin) IHC • NAZAR[ENVS] • REX • IVDE[ORVM]; (twice, below Christ's hands) Venite benedi[c]ti p[at]ris mei (Come, ye blessed of my Father [Matthew 25:34]); (on Saint Michael's shield and armor) [illegible]; (twice, below Saint Michael's wings) . . . vos maledi[ct]i i[n] ignem [aeternum?] (. . . ye cursed, into everlasting fire [Matthew 25:41]); (on Death's wings) CHAOS MAGNV[M] / VMBRA MORTIS (great chaos / shadow of death); (in Hell) [illegible]; (on original gilt frame of Crucifixion*) DOMINVS POSVIT I EO INIQVITATE OMNIVM NRM OBLATVS E QVIA IPE VOLVIT + NON APERVIT OS SVV SIC OVIS AD OCCASIONE DVCET+QI[?] AGNVS CORAM TONDETE SE OBMVTESCET PPT SCEL PPLI MEI PERPERCVSSI EV ET DABIT IMPIOS PRO SEPVLTVRA ET DICITES PRO MORTE SVA VSAE[?] [T]R[ADI]DT I MORTE AIAM SVA + CV SCELERATIS REPV[T]ATVS E ET IPE PCCM MVLTORV TVLIT + PRO TRANSGRESSORIBVS ORAVIT (And the Lord hath laid on him the iniquity of us all. He was oppressed, and he was afflicted, yet he opened not his mouth: he is brought as a lamb to the slaughter, and as a sheep before her shearers is dumb, so he openeth not his mouth. . . . For the transgression of*

The quintessence of early Netherlandish painting is captured in these two diminutive panels, which juxtapose an astonishing depiction of the natural world with a hieratically organized vision of heaven and hell. Eichberger (1987) has insightfully noted that in an extraordinary pairing and a most daring design for its time Jan van Eyck portrayed the Crucifixion and Last Judgment as two peaks of Christ's existence, events that represent his deepest humiliation and his greatest triumph. The tall thin shape of the pictures (transferred from panels to canvas in 1867, while they were in the Hermitage) and the fact that when they were in the collection of Ambassador Tatistcheff they were mounted as the wings of a triptych whose centerpiece was an Adoration of the Magi have led to considerable speculation about their original context: whether they were meant as a diptych or parts of a triptych is still a matter of debate. Because Tatistcheff's central panel (thought to echo an Eyckian drawing of the Adoration of the Magi in the Kupferstichkabinett, Berlin) was stolen before 1841 and traces of grisaille figures on pedestals (known to Passavant in 1841) on the reverses of the *Crucifixion* and *Last Judgment* are no longer preserved, it is not possible to determine whether the ambassador's grouping represented Van Eyck's original concept or an altered one. Some scholars believe our panels were indeed elements of a triptych but have proposed different centerpieces: for example, Kern suggests it was a Way to Calvary, while Philip thinks it may have been a Resurrection scene reflected in an engraving after Pieter Bruegel the Elder, which, along with our works, formed a tabernacle for the Host.

However, our paintings could have formed a diptych. A 1416 inventory of the collection of Jean, duc de Berry, lists a two-part painting comprising a Passion and a Last Judgment, indicating that these subjects were sometimes paired. And as Eichberger (1987) has pointed out, this type of iconographic confrontation was not unusual: diptychs treating the two themes were in use for private devotion, especially in court circles. Further support for the diptych theory is found in the frames of the pictures, which are original. The upper portions of these frames show the marks of routed-out wood on the inside edges that are closely aligned for the placement of hinges, while the exterior edges preserve traces of an old clasp for closing a diptych.

No information about the commission for the panels has survived, but, given their remarkable quality, their production by a court artist, their intimate presentation in a manner resembling that of manuscript illumination, and, above all, the Latin texts inscribed on the frames in a protohumanist script, the patron was likely a highly educated member of the court. The idea that the person who ordered the panels was connected to the court is supported by the depiction of an unusual gathering of worldly kings and court figures in the realm of the elect in the *Last Judgment.* Some writers have supposed that the patron is the man elegantly dressed in an ermine-trimmed coat and extravagant chaperon who is shown at the right beneath the cross in the *Crucifixion.* They may well be correct, for the figure has the carefully described physiognomy of a portrait and directly confronts the viewer in the manner of many representations of donors. However, it has not yet been possible to identify him.

Despite their restricted format, both the *Crucifixion* and the *Last Judgment* are filled with an extraordinary amount of detail, which demands close scrutiny and yields exceptional rewards. The *Crucifixion* is shown as though seen from a considerable distance and height, so that the vertical arrangement of figures that fill the space below the high horizon line encourages the viewer to experience a sense of mounting Golgotha to its three crosses. These crosses, seen against a remarkably detailed vista of the city and landscape, anchor the upper portion of the composition, while at the bottom of the scene the Virgin, collapsed in grief, and Saint John

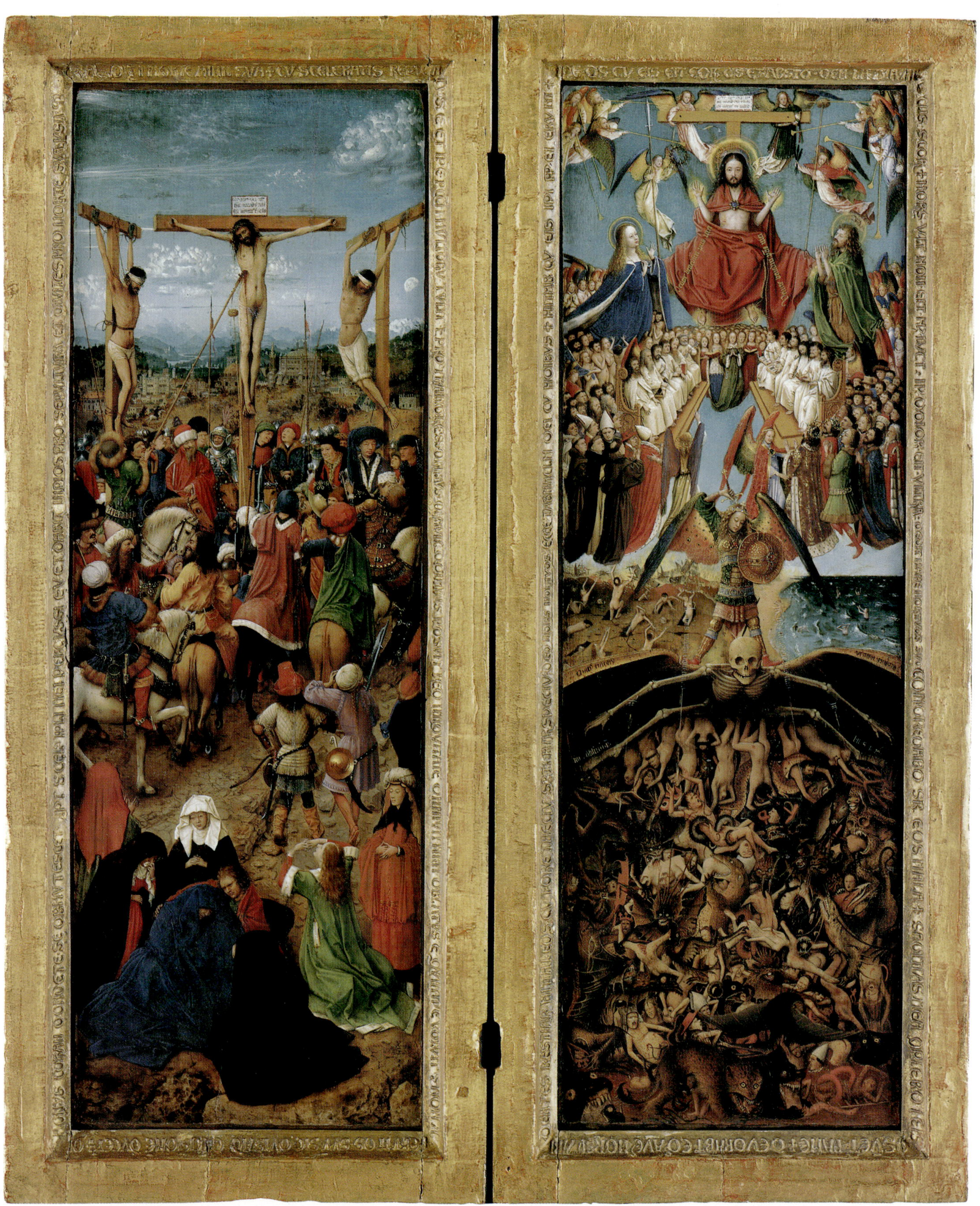

my people was he stricken. And he made his grave with the wicked, and with the rich in his death . . . and he was numbered with the transgressors; and he bare the sin of many, and made intercession for the transgressors [Isaiah 53:6–9,12].); (on original gilt frame of Last Judgment*) DED MORS MORTVOS ECCE TABNACLM DEI CV HOIBVS + HITAB CV EIS IPI PP EI ERVNT + IPE DS CV EIS EIT EOR [D]S ET ABSTG OEM LA[G]A AB OCLIS SCOR + MORS VLT NON EIT N[Q]LVC NQDOLOR EIT VLTRA DEDIT MARE MORTVOS SVO CONGREGABO SR EOS MALA SAGITTAS MEA OPLEBO I EIS OSVET FAME + DEVORABT EO AVE MORSV A[?] DESTES BESTIAR MITTA I EOS CV FORE THECIV SR T[?]A AQ SPECIV (And death and hell delivered up the dead which were in them [Revelation 20:13]; Behold, the tabernacle of God is with men, and he will dwell with them, and they shall be his people, and God himself shall be with them, and be their God. And God shall wipe away all tears from their eyes; and there shall be no more death, neither sorrow, nor crying, neither shall there be any more pain [Revelation 21:3,4]; And the sea gave up the dead which were in it [Revelation 20:13]; I will heap mischiefs upon them; I will spend mine arrows upon them. They shall be burnt with hunger, and devoured with burning heat, and with bitter destruction: I will also send the teeth of beasts upon them, with the poison of serpents of the dust [Deuteronomy 32:23,24].) Fletcher Fund, 1933 33.92ab*

and other despairing companions provide the models for the viewer's empathic response. An inescapable visual path is forged by means of the rhythmic flow of interconnected figures from the anguished Mary Magdalene in green, through two exotically dressed onlookers (one with a shield that seems to reflect our space, thus suggesting the viewer's presence at the event), and the horsemen in red and green, to Christ's cross surrounded by a dense gathering of Jews and soldiers.

Van Eyck was here attempting to record with historical accuracy the specific time of Christ's death as described in Matthew 27:39–48: Longinus (assisted by a servant because he is blind) pierces Christ's side with a spear, the vinegar-filled sponge offered to quench Christ's thirst is just being lowered, and the Roman centurion in armor at the right looks up with his head thrown back in astonishment, at that instant recognizing Christ as the Son of God. The sky begins to darken over the fantastic landscape, signaling the exact moment of death. The Virgin is shown in the extremity of her grief, for, as both the Pseudo-Bonaventure and Ludolph of Saxony note in their narrative expositions of the event, it is precisely at this point that she collapses, overwhelmed by compassion for her son.

The woman in red standing in the right foreground resolutely observing the grief-stricken Virgin has often been identified as the Erythraean Sibyl, who foresaw the end of the world and is, therefore, associated with the Last Judgment. Eichberger (1987), however, has argued that she is the Cumaean Sibyl, who predicted not only the Passion of Christ but also his return to earth; if she is correct, the figure to the far left in the red headdress, with her back turned to the viewer, is perhaps the Erythraean Sibyl. As Labuda notes, the depiction of the two would extend the theme of prophecy even into the panel of the *Last Judgment.*

In contrast to the panoramic vista of the natural world offered in the *Crucifixion*, with its bird's-eye view, atmospheric sky, and deep space, the *Last Judgment* is presented vertically, compressed into the flat foreground plane of the painting and divided into three layers corresponding to the realms of heaven—shown as an unmodulated, timeless blue sky—earth, and hell. In a novel formulation for its time, the damned and the saved are not segregated and placed to the right and left of Christ but are organized in groups above and below him. The significant numbers of the elect are assembled around the Twelve Apostles seated in glory, and the Virgin Mary and Saint John appear above them. Instead of blessing the saved and condemning the damned with the gestures more traditional for such depictions (see entry for cat. no. 98), Christ shows his stigmata in a reference to the scene of the *Crucifixion.* He is surrounded by the instruments of the Passion; featured in particular are the spear of Longinus at the left and the sponge with vinegar at the right—the same instruments that accompanied Christ in the last moments of his earthly existence as depicted in the *Crucifixion.*

Below the sword-brandishing Saint Michael is one of the more inventive representations of the punishments of hell, a portrayal not outdone by even that great painter of hell scenes Hieronymus Bosch. The wretched appear to be born from the figure of Death and fall into a swirling mass of horrifying monsters and fiends, who tear their bodies apart in especially graphic ways. As Pächt has noted, there are no fires here, only a sinister red glow in a ghastly environment that engulfs clergy and laity alike. The words on Death's wings, CHAOS MAGNVM (great chaos) and VMBRA MORTIS (shadow of death), as well as the menacing judgments falling as arrows on the damned, aptly describe this underworld from which there is no escape. Between the realms of the damned and the saved the earth and sea are shown splitting apart, surrendering their dead, as told in Revelation 20:13. The spectacular turmoil of that moment is indicated by the fires that destroy the cities of the earth and the rocky seas, whose waves engulf the resurrected bodies struggling toward judgment and salvation.

The highly imaginative scenes of the diptych are augmented by the written word in the form of inscriptions on the frames. These inscriptions are placed next to the visual representations they most closely describe, so that the viewer can simultaneously experience text and image. The strategy is one commonly found in illuminated manuscripts as well as in the *Biblia Pauperum*; however, unlike those books, our works, executed just as panel painting was emerging as an art form, are not entirely dependent upon the written word for their context.

Despite their many visual innovations, the *Crucifixion* and the *Last Judgment* show obvious links with miniaturist style; in fact, the diptych has often been compared to the Turin-Milan Hours, the famous illuminated book to which Jan van Eyck perhaps contributed images, in particular those attributed to Hand G. The panels of our diptych have indeed been given to Hand G, as well as to Hubert and to Jan van Eyck. Panofsky (1935) was the first to mention that the quality of execution in the two panels is not the same, and recent technical examination by Ainsworth and Buck (1995) indeed indicates that while the compositions of the two works seem to be underdrawn by the same artist (undoubtedly Jan van Eyck), portions of the *Last Judgment* were executed by an assistant. This assistant, who most likely was trained as a manuscript illuminator, apparently was responsible for the upper section of the *Last Judgment*, except for the more skillfully painted figure of Christ. His handling and execution present the opaque, additive strokes typical of an illuminator, rather than the carefully blended applications and sensitive modeling in light and shadow visible in the lower part of the *Last Judgment* (including Saint Michael) and in the entire *Crucifixion*. Eichberger (1987) has proposed that the iconography of the *Last Judgment* is related to that of manuscript illuminations by the so-called Bedford Master, who was active in Paris from about 1410 to 1435, and König (in Buck 1995, n. 31) identified a painter of the Bedford workshop as the minor Hand F in the Turin-Milan Hours. Given the lively connections between French and Netherlandish workshops that existed throughout the fifteenth century, it is not improbable that an illuminator from the Bedford workshop came to Bruges to participate in the activities in Jan van Eyck's atelier and contributed elements to the *Last Judgment*.

Scholars have long disagreed about the dating of the diptych, offering opinions that range from Durrieu's suggestion of 1413 to proposals by Peters, Snyder, Philip, Baldass, Eichberger, Buck, and others who place it in the 1430s, that is, close to the time the renowned Ghent Altarpiece (figs. 17, 18) was painted. Supporting a date in the 1430s is the style of the underdrawing, which is consistent with that of other paintings Van Eyck produced in the period, such as the *Saint Barbara* (Koninklijk Museum voor Schone Kunsten, Antwerp) and the Dresden Triptych (Staatliche Kunstsammlungen, Dresden), both dated 1437. Van Buren (personal communication), however, notes that, except for the garb of the possible patron depicted in the *Crucifixion*, which represents the fashions of about 1430, the costumes shown appear to date from the 1420s. These various factors argue that a date in the early 1430s would seem most likely for these two splendid paintings. If this date is correct, they would be among Van Eyck's earliest surviving works.

MWA

Provenance: Spanish convent; Russian ambassador D. Tatistcheff, Vienna (by 1841); The Hermitage, Saint Petersburg (by 1845–1933); [Knoedler, New York (1933)].

References: Durrieu 1920; Kern 1927, pp. 12–17; Panofsky 1935, pp. 433–34, 468, 471–72; Wehle and Salinger 1947, pp. 2–12 (with earlier bibliography); Baldass 1952, no. 62; Panofsky 1953, pp. 237–40, 242, 269, 309, 456; Peters 1968; Philip 1971, pp. 140–64; Fuchs 1977, pp. 15–17; Belting and Eichberger 1983 (with recent literature review and update); Snyder 1985, pp. 117–18; Eichberger 1987, pp. 13–35; Labuda 1993; Pächt 1994, pp. 190–95; Buck 1995.

Robert Campin, about 1375–1444, and Assistant (possibly Rogier van der Weyden)

2. *The Annunciation Triptych (Merode Triptych)*, about 1425–30

A keystone of Netherlandish painting, this triptych is the most celebrated of the not altogether homogeneous group of works ascribed to Campin, the so-called Master of Flémalle. It has been the focus of intense scrutiny, and questions continue to be raised about its manufacture, dating, authorship, commission, and meaning.

In a striking innovation for its time, the Annunciation takes place not in a church interior or portal but in a domestic setting that confers a sense of

Oil on wood; central panel 25¼ x 24⅞ in. (64.1 x 63.2 cm); each wing 25⅜ x 10¾ in. (64.5 x 27.3 cm)
Arms (central panel, left window): of the Ymbrechts

(also spelled Imbrecht, Imbrechts) or Ingelbrechts (also spelled Engelbrecht, Inghelbrechts, Engelbrechts) family of Mechelen; (central panel, right window) uncertain; (left wing, on messenger's badge) possibly of the city of Mechelen
The Cloisters Collection, 1956 56.70

Provenance: Acquired by Prince Pierre d'Arenberg (1790–1877) in Bruges (ca. 1820); his daughter Marie-Nicolette (1830–1905) upon her marriage to Charles, count de Merode (1849); by descent to Countess Jeanne de Grunne; [bought from Rosenberg and Stiebel, New York, April 10, 1956].

References: Bode 1887, p. 218; Tschudi 1893, p. 103; Tschudi 1898, pp. 9–12; Firmenich-Richartz 1899, pp. 131–34; Hymans 1907, pp. 204–7; Fierens-Gevaert 1908, pp. 64–65; Winkler 1913c, pp. 27–31; Conway 1921, pp. 118–19; Friedländer 1924–37, vol. 2 (1924), pp. 61–63; Verlant 1924; Hocquet 1925, pp. 6–11; Destrée 1928–29, pp. 84–92, 132–35; Pächt 1933, pp. 82–90; Robb 1936, pp. 504–8; De Tolnay 1939, pp. 24–26; Schapiro 1945; Baldass 1952, pp. 19–21; Panofsky 1953, pp. 142–43, 164–67, pl. 91; Freeman 1957; Rorimer 1957; Rousseau 1957; Suhr 1957; Schapiro 1959; De Tolnay 1959; De Tolnay 1960; Bruin 1966; Frinta 1966, pp. 13–28; Nickel 1966; Friedländer 1967–76, vol. 1 (1967), pp. 36–38, 70; Frinta 1968; Heckscher 1968; Blum 1969, pp. 9–11; Minott 1969;

actuality on the work. The angel Gabriel and, above him, the tiny Christ Child descending on seven rays of light enter from the left, the effect of their sudden arrival seeming to snuff out the flame of the candle on the table, ruffle the pages of a devotional book, and unfurl the scroll lying next to it. The Virgin sits on the footrest of the bench, signifying her humility, and remains undistracted from her devotional readings; as Falkenburg suggests, she thus spiritually receives the message of the Incarnation of Christ. There are references to Christ's sacrifice for mankind and to its liturgical celebration: the tiny Child already bears the cross, Gabriel is dressed as a deacon or assistant in the celebration of Communion, as Gottlieb pointed out, and a basin and towel like those used for the ritual cleansing before the Mass stand ready. The last two objects may also symbolize Mary's purity and chastity, which are certainly suggested by the lilies in the majolica pitcher on the table. Although various motifs here clearly have symbolic meaning, Panofsky's theory that most elements in the picture, and in early Netherlandish painting in general, are disguised symbols (see "Early Netherlandish Painting: Shifting Perspectives" in this publication) has been called into question repeatedly; for example, De Coo (1981a) emphasized that although the bench has lion finials and a blue pillow and cloth that may well allude to the throne of the Queen of Heaven, its value also rests on its appeal as a carefully observed piece of contemporary furniture (with the reversible backrest for sitting next to the fire in winter or close to the table in warmer seasons).

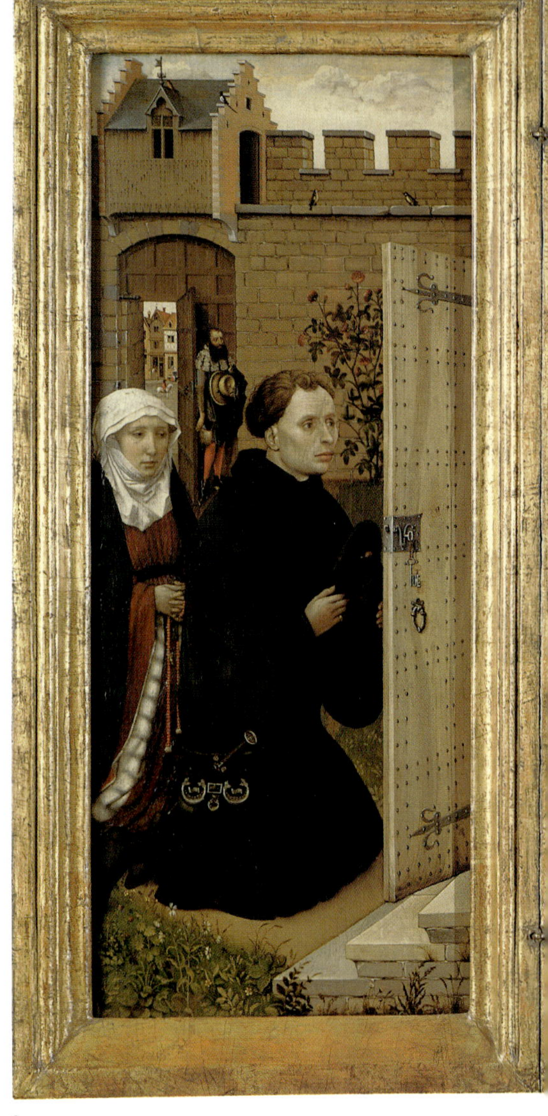
2

The unusual prominence given to Joseph, who occupies a wing of his own, is an indication of the growing popularity of his cult, which was encouraged in part by Jean Gerson's teachings that the saint was an equal participant with the Virgin in the physical and spiritual upbringing of the Christ Child (see entry for cat. no. 61). In connection with the Annunciation of the centerpiece, which presents Mary's heavenly union with the Holy Spirit, Joseph stands for the Virgin's earthly and chaste marriage. Hecksher, Arasse, and Hahn have variously described Joseph as making the top of a bait box (to catch the Devil), a strainer for a winepress (an allusion to the Eucharist), or a fire screen (to shield the Virgin from the flames of passion). If the object is a bait box, its significance would be related to Joseph's role in tricking the Devil, so that he does not discover that Mary's true bridegroom is the Holy Spirit. Schapiro (1945) called attention to the unfinished mousetrap that appears on Joseph's workbench and the finished one shown ready on the window ledge, noting that Saint Augustine linked the mousetrap to Christ's sacrifice and Crucifixion: according to Augustine, the cross was the Devil's mousetrap upon which the mortal Christ served as bait. As such, the mousetraps here resonate with the Christ Child bearing the cross in the central panel. In the scene of the city

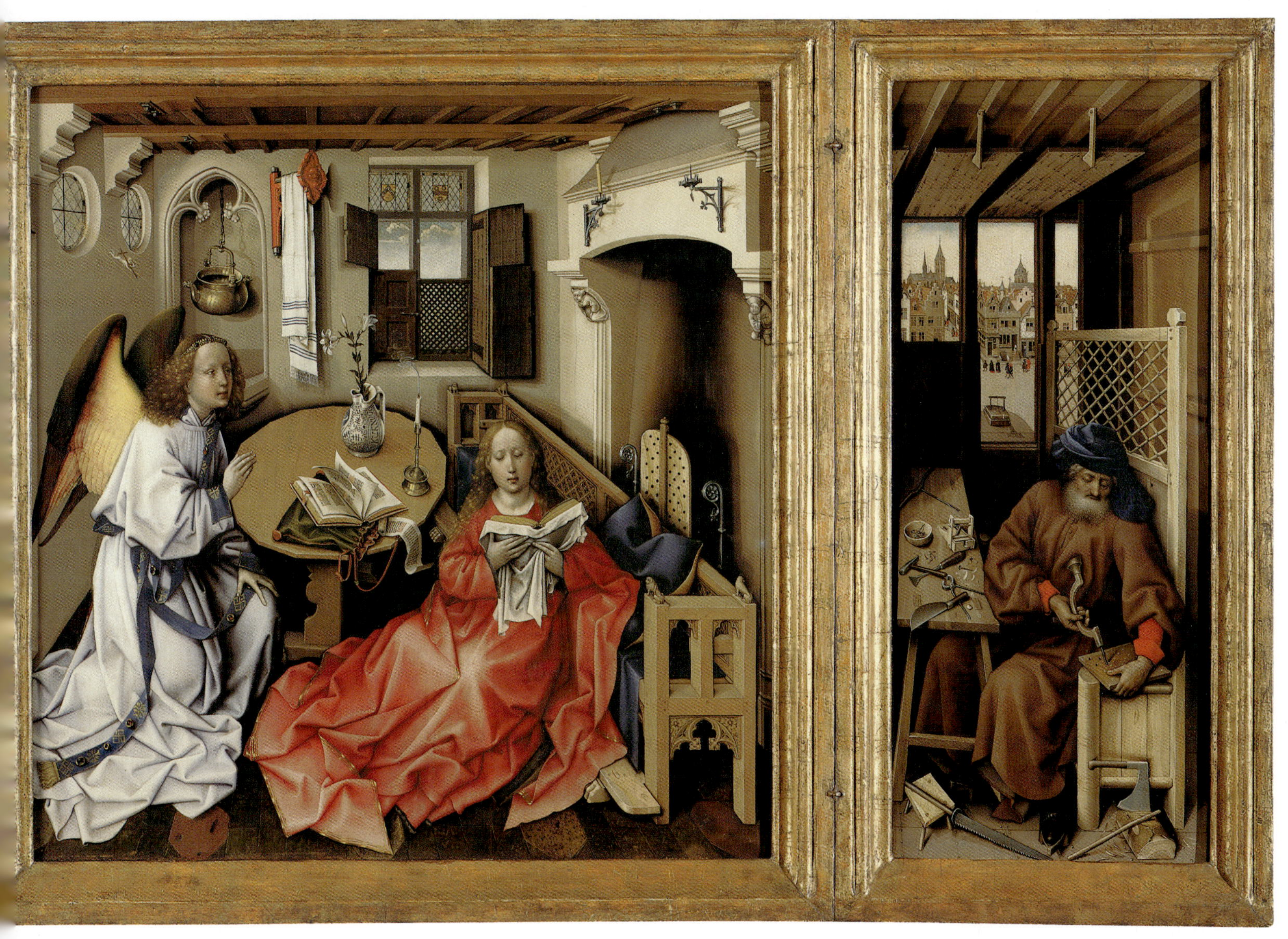

square visible through Joseph's window, snowflakes fall against the dark clothes of the tiny figures—marking winter, perhaps in reference to the season of Christ's birth—while in the left wing, by contrast, verdant spring, the time of his conception, may be intended.

The male donor on the left wing appears to observe through an open door the miraculous event of the Annunciation in the center panel; his wife, kneeling behind him, her view blocked, contemplates the event in her mind's eye while devoutly holding her rosary embellished with a pendant showing Saint Christopher, who, in his role as the Christ bearer, possibly serves as a metaphor for the woman's desire to bear her own child. Nickel identified the figure who stands patiently by the doorway in the back wall as a messenger (echoing Gabriel's function) from the city of Mechelen. Hahn has stressed the importance of the theme of the nuclear family in the triptych, noting that it is perhaps addressed to a newly married couple hoping for progeny and may even have served as an ex-voto in this regard. This theory is supported by the private devotional character of the ensemble; the triptych's relatively small size and very personal content suggest that it was made for home display and use—

Gottlieb 1970; Davies 1972, pp. 258–60; Campbell 1974, pp. 643–45; Arasse 1976; Duchesne-Guillemin 1976; Châtelet 1981b; De Coo 1981; Callmann 1982; Lane 1984, pp. 42–50; Hahn 1986; Williamson 1986; De Coo 1991, pp. 90–105; Falkenburg 1991; Klein 1991b; Van Asperen de Boer et al. 1992, pp. 13–14, 103–16; Blum in Bauman and Liedtke 1992, pp. 30–35; Botvinick 1992; Installé 1992; Belting and Kruse 1994, pp. 79–82, 166–67; Dijkstra 1994, p. 326; D. Martens 1994, pp. 256–58; Pächt 1994, pp. 54–63, 88–89; Thürlemann 1995; Châtelet 1996a, pp. 93–113, 291–95; Kemperdick 1997, pp. 77–99.

perhaps as the type of makeshift house altar depicted in Joos van Cleve's *Annunciation* (cat. no. 97). There is no trace of what may have been shown on the reverses of the wings, if indeed they were painted.

Although the three panels at first seem relatively coherent in program and presentation, several authors have noted anomalies and disparities in their treatment of space, background, figures, and light. (The frame is not original, as has been supposed, but of modern manufacture.) Pächt provided the most lucid account of the varied approaches to space, explaining that Gabriel is encountered at eye level and the Virgin from above, and that they inhabit a tipped-up room with a rapidly receding perspective of the type seen in contemporary relief sculpture, which, in fact, may have provided the source for the scene. (Campbell has cited a sculpted Annunciation installed in the Town Hall of Tournai in 1424 that was perhaps based on a design by Campin.) The left wing exhibits a more logical recession of space from the foreground to the town square in the background, but this view is discontinuous with the one shown from Joseph's window, which appears to be observed from an upper floor. Furthermore, the doorway of the house in the left wing, which opens outward into the viewer's space, is not properly aligned with the door opening behind Gabriel, and the round windows above him illogically show blue sky, whereas we might expect them to reveal a portion of the crenellated brick wall of the enclosed garden in the left panel. Finally, the perspective scheme of Joseph's atelier does not conform to that of either of the two other panels.

The illumination is similarly inconsistent. The figures in the central panel are shown in a diffuse golden light, while details of the room are accented by two sources of light from windows that cast double shadows. Although double shadows also appear in the panel with Joseph, his room is more dimly lit than the space in the central panel and displays stronger chiaroscuro effects. The figures in the left panel, like Gabriel and Mary, are presented in an overall uniform light, but there are no shadows. These disparities in the handling of light, as well as the variable treatment of space, raise questions about the triptych that bear on its authorship and production.

Essential to the study of these questions is a consideration of a version of the Annunciation in the Musées Royaux des Beaux-Arts de Belgique, Brussels, to which our central panel has always been compared. The underdrawings of the two pictures reveal that, despite differences in the details of the two compositions, both pictures appear to have originated from a similar workshop pattern; it is clear, however, that they were painted by different artists. The variant in the Musées Royaux and several other later versions (see Châtelet 1996a) are individual panels without wings, implying that the Merode *Annunciation* may also have been conceived initially as an independent work. Supporting this hypothesis is a fact noted by Suhr: the windows in our picture, originally painted gold (like those in the Brussels version), were at some point painted over with blue sky, cumulus clouds, and the donor's coats of arms, presumably to effect a connection with the left panel.

This evidence suggests that both wings could have been added to the *Annunciation* at the request of the client to personalize a picture based on a standardized workshop pattern. Indeed, Klein has shown that the wood of the central panel may have been cut as many as twenty-five years earlier than that used for the wings, suggesting—but not proving—that the elements were painted at different points. Moreover, infrared reflectography and X-radiography show that the left panel was first painted without the female donor and the messenger figure in the background. Thus, the physical examination of the paintings indicates that the triptych came together and that the sections assumed their final form as part of an evolving process: it seems that the center panel was most likely made first (and may even have remained in the artist's studio for a time) and that the wings were added at a slightly later point in response to the client's wishes. As Kemperdick points out, this would help to explain the somewhat awkward junctures between the wings and the central panel and the disparities that prompted the author or authors of the wings to fit the parts together by placing the donors at the same level as Gabriel and Joseph at the level of the seated Virgin. An organic development of this kind may also explain why the underdrawings in the three elements are different in character.

Opposite: Detail, cat. no. 2

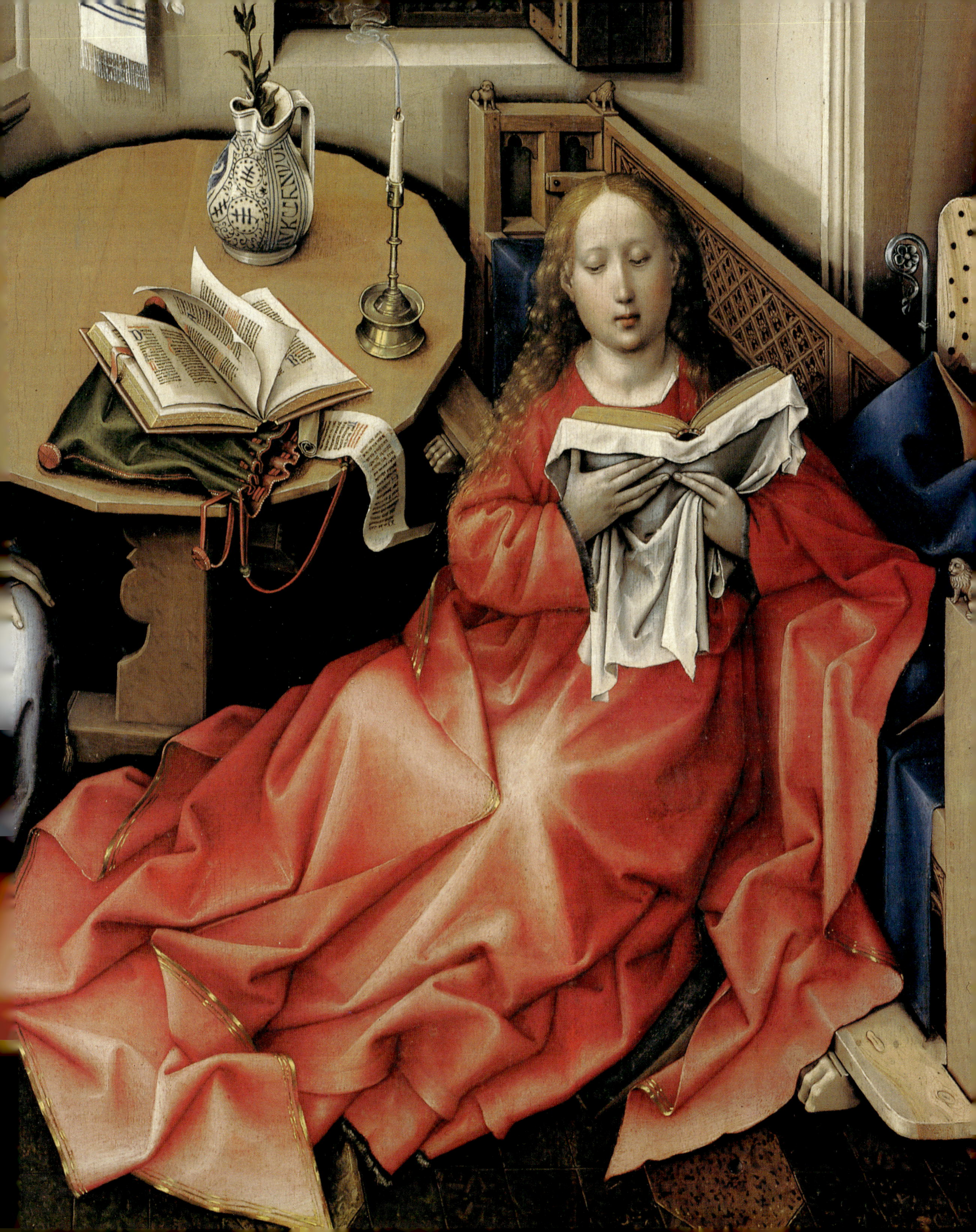

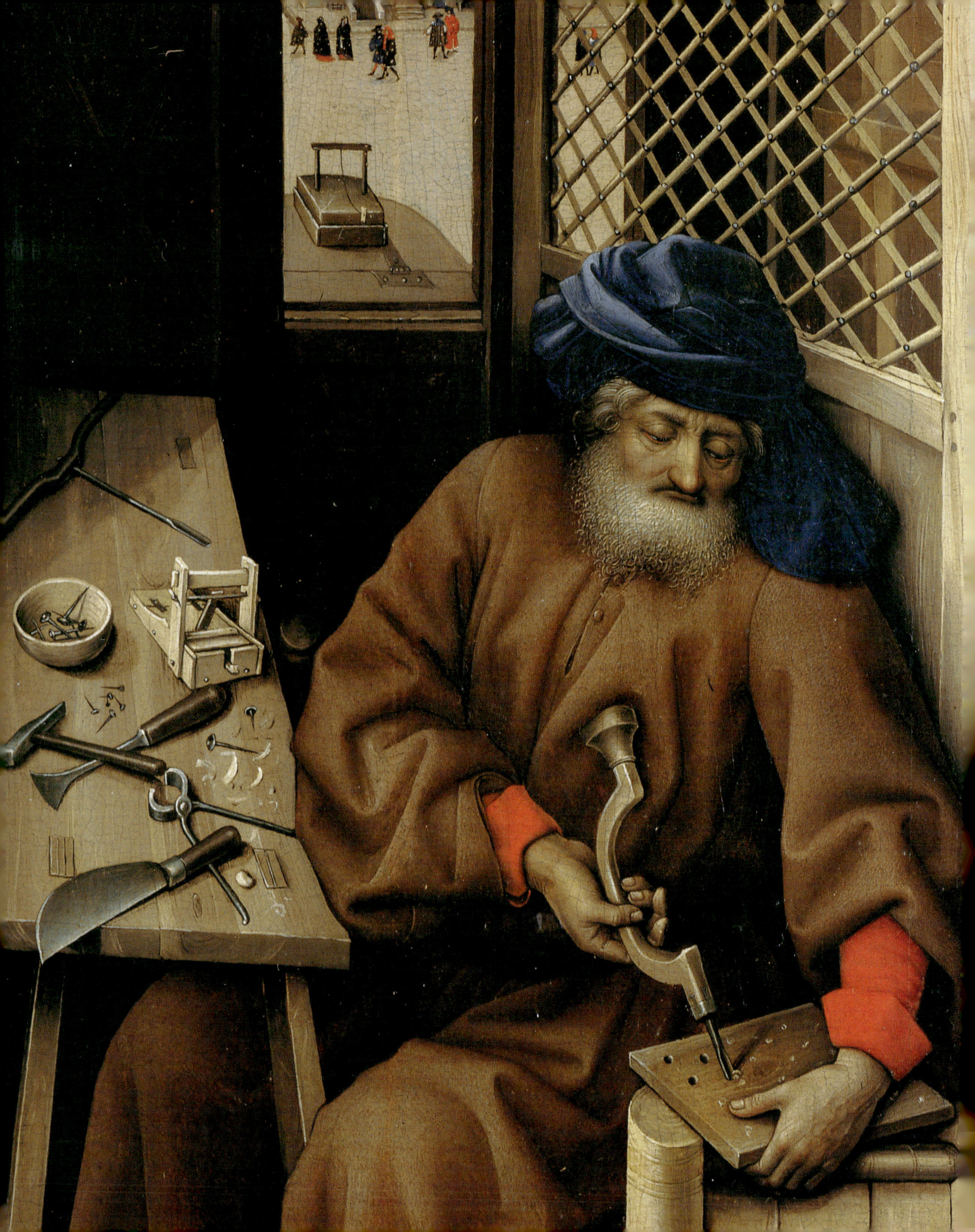

Tschudi (1898) discovered that the coat of arms on the left window on the back wall in the *Annunciation* belonged to a Mechelen family variously identified as Ymbrechts, Imbrecht, Imbrechts, Inghelbrechts, Engelbrecht, Ingelbrechts, or Engelbrechts; the shield on the window at the right has been less convincingly linked with the Calcum family, also called Lohausen, from Düsseldorf (Verlant 1924). De Coo (1981a) posited that Engelbrechts, meaning "the angel brings," in a reference to the theme of the Annunciation, might constitute a canting name, that is, a name that alludes to the subject of the painting. And Châtelet (1996a) suggested that the donors on the left wing are a certain Jan Ymbrechts and Elisabeth Spithoens, also known as Van Berg or De Cudseghem, whose shield was not passed down. The latter theory is problematic, as Elisabeth Spithoens had died by 1421–22, before the altarpiece was probably completed; the addition of her figure would have given the triptych a memorial function that seems quite out of keeping with its emphasis on family and progeny. Recent archival research by Installé and its analysis by Thürlemann have led to the development of an elaborate theory involving a Peter Engelbrechts of Cologne and Mechelen who was married three times: to Gretgin Schrinmechers of Cologne, between 1425 and 1428, to Heylwich Bille about 1456, and finally to Aleyde de Kempenere after about 1466. According to this argument, the name of the first wife, Schrinmechers, meaning "cabinetmaker," constituted a second canting name, in this case representing the theme of the right wing, Joseph as cabinetmaker. Thürlemann's theory holds that the woman shown on the left wing is Heylwich Bille, added after the death of the first wife, as companion to the male figure; he maintains it is Bille's coat of arms that appears on the right window on the back wall. The suggestion regarding canting names is appealing, although there is no known precedent in early Netherlandish art for their use in reference to subjects (examples involving associations of saints and their namesakes abound, however, but this is a different matter). More difficult to accept is the idea that the figure of Bille was introduced when she was married, which was about 1456, for the woman on the left wing is dressed in the style of the early 1420s. That her image would have been added to the panel that balances the cabinetmaker theme on the right wing evoking the canting name of her predecessor also seems questionable.

Basing his analysis on the evidence currently available, Kemperdick has drawn reasonable conclusions about the evolution of our triptych that can be summarized here. In the first stage the *Annunciation* panel, with its gold windows, was created from a workshop pattern in the atelier of Robert Campin, either to stand alone or as part of a projected triptych. Somewhat later the wings were added, at which point the blue sky with clouds was painted over the gold-leaf windows. At this stage the left panel would have shown only the kneeling male figure. The disjointed effects of space, backgrounds, and figure scale can be explained as a product of this second stage of work. Finally, in a third stage, the female figure and the messenger from Mechelen were added to the completed left wing, probably after the woman who is portrayed had married the donor.

Recent research on the paintings associated with Robert Campin has raised questions that have a direct bearing on the *Merode Triptych* (see also cat. no. 47). Which products of his workshop in Tournai can be considered to have been painted by Campin alone and which show evidence of the participation of his assistants, most notably Rogier van der Weyden, is still in dispute. Rogier, who was certainly in Brussels by 1435, is known to have worked in Campin's shop from 1427 to 1432, and it has been proposed that he contributed to our triptych. Frinta was the first to question the attribution of the left wing of the *Merode Triptych* to Campin; according to his theory, recently taken up by Thürlemann, that wing was painted by Rogier, while Campin was responsible for the center and right panels, a collaboration that explains the ensemble's stylistic discrepancies. It is certainly possible that Rogier played a part in the second stage of the triptych's execution: the cooperation of two artists on the same altarpiece was not unusual, and Rogier can surely be placed in Campin's shop at the time the donor wing was probably produced. Furthermore, an attribution of the left wing to Rogier is supported by stylistic evidence. The male donor figure shows similarities to the figure of Heinrich Werl in the *Saint John the Baptist and the Donor Heinrich Werl*, dated

Opposite: Detail, cat. no. 2

1438 (Prado, Madrid), which some attribute to Rogier instead of to Campin. And the treatment of the underdrawing for the figures, as well as the underdrawing and painting of the architecture in our left panel, is extremely close to that of other early works that are clearly by Rogier, especially the *Visitation* (Museum der Bildenden Künste, Leipzig).

The authorship not only of the left wing but also that of the central and right panels has been disputed, although study reveals that our *Annunciation* is closely connected to the *Virgin and Child before a Firescreen* in the National Gallery, London, and the *Nativity* in the Musées des Beaux-Arts, Dijon, which are almost always considered to be by Campin. Continued research on the subject of the extraordinary but still enigmatic Campin is required to further refine the still vexing questions of the authorship and precise chronology of his works. MWA

Petrus Christus, active by 1444, died 1475/76

3. Head of Christ, about 1445

Oil on parchment, laid down on wood; overall 5⅞ x 4¼ in. (14.9 x 10.8 cm); parchment 5¾ x 4⅛ in. (14.6 x 10.5 cm)
Inscribed (bottom, on simulated frame): Petr...
Bequest of Lillian S. Timken, 1959 60.71.1

Provenance: Private collection, Spain; [Moreno, Paris, until 1910]; [Kleinberger, Paris, 1910–31]; Mr. and Mrs. William R. Timken, New York (1931–49); Mrs. William R. Timken, New York (1949–59).

References: Friedländer 1916, pp. 21, 174; Friedländer 1924–37, vol. 1 (1924), p. 149, pl. 57; Bruyn 1957, p. 115; Upton 1972,

This image derives from a lost picture of the Holy Face by Jan van Eyck, now known only through copies, one dated 1438 (Gemäldegalerie, Berlin) and two dated 1440 (Groeningemuseum, Bruges, and formerly J. C. Swinburne collection, Newcastle-upon-Tyne). It is similar to Van Eyck's work in its fictive frame, lettering, staring frontal face, and floriated nimbus. Our painting differs from the serene Eyckian type, however, in presenting Christ with furrowed brow and drops of blood running down his forehead and onto his chest, details that refer not only to the Holy Face but also to Christ as the Man of Sorrows and to the Ecce Homo (Christ Presented to the People). A close textual source for the composition is John 19:5, which states, "Then came Jesus forth, wearing the crown of thorns, and the purple robe. And Pilate saith unto them, Behold the man!" The head is given its special character by means of its treatment as a portrait, with the marbleized molding used to emphasize the subject's closeness to the picture plane and thus its physical presence—features that relate the picture to Christus's *Portrait of a Carthusian* (cat. no. 21).

The *Head of Christ* may have been created for private devotional use and should be understood in the context of the rise in devotional piety that occurred in the Netherlands during the fourteenth and fifteenth centuries. This development resulted in the production of paintings whose specific purpose was, according to Ainsworth, "to stimulate emotional and compassionate responses by evoking the empathy of the viewer." Devotional painting of this type traces its origin to images of the living Christ believed to have been miraculously created; chief among these was the Holy Face or Veil of Veronica, the imprint left on a cloth Veronica used to wipe Christ's face while he was bearing the cross to Calvary. The cult of Veronica was extremely popular, and the recital of certain prayers before the relic of her veil or an image of it, such as our painting, earned an indulgence that swelled from ten days in the twelfth century to ten thousand or more days in the fifteenth. Other examples in our collection that represent the Veil of Veronica are *Emperor Vespasian Cured by the Veil of Veronica*, a Flemish tapestry dated about 1510, and Gerard David's *Holy Face* (cat. no. 74).

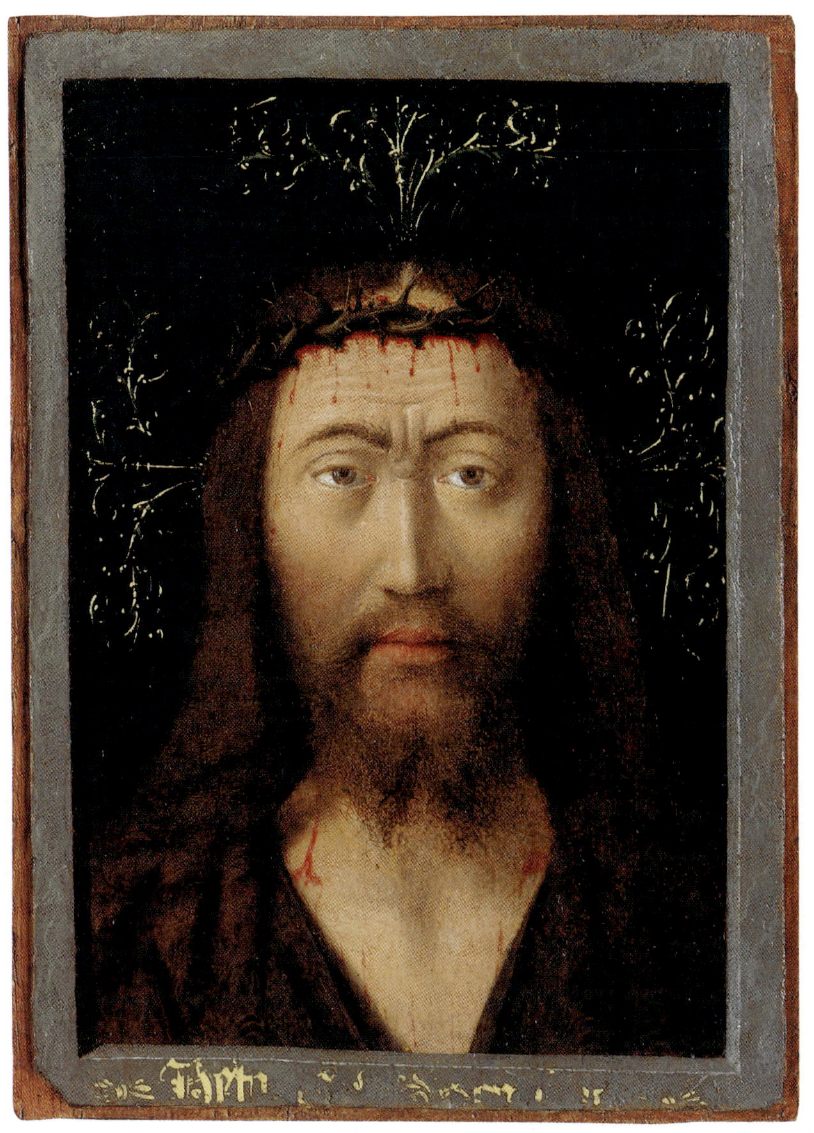

The parchment support of the *Head of Christ* was originally laid down onto an oak panel, which was shaved to a sliver when it was remounted on the painting's present mahogany support. The regularly spaced filled holes around the perimeter of the parchment suggest that it once may have been tacked to a panel, like the Holy Face depicted in the background of Christus's *Portrait of a Young Man* of about 1450 (National Gallery, London). Over the course of time, our painting has suffered major damage from abrasion. The largely illegible inscription on the bottom of the painted frame has been read as "Petrus Christus."

Ringbom shows that the influence of our *Head of Christ* reached Lombardy, citing a Milanese painting from the end of the fifteenth century (private collection, Milan) that reflects our picture's specific northern imagery and compelling emotional appeal.

DCS

pp. 139–40, 142–43, 152, 154, 179–80 n. 20, 368–72, no. 21, fig. 21; Schabacker 1974, pp. 17, 42–43, 46, 73, 80–81, 129–30, no. 2, fig. 2; Panhans-Bühler 1978, pp. 11–16, fig. 1; Ringbom 1984, p. 148; Upton 1990, pp. 1 n. 4, 56 n. 1, 57–59, 64–65, 70, fig. 58; Hand 1992, pp. 7, 10, 16, 17, nn. 1, 2, fig. 1; Ainsworth 1994b, pp. 32, 34, 53, 71, 80, 86–91, 105, 115, 178–79, no. 4, colorpl. p. 87, figs. 19, 105–6.

Petrus Christus, active by 1444, died 1475/76

4. The Lamentation, about 1450

Oil on wood; overall 10⅛ x 14 in. (25.7 x 35.6 cm); painted surface 10 x 13¾ in. (25.4 x 34.9 cm)
Marquand Collection, Gift of Henry G. Marquand, 1890 91.26.12

Provenance: Albert John Hamborough, Steephill Castle, Ventnor, Isle of Wight (until 1887); Sir John Charles Robinson, Newton Manor, Swanage, Dorset (from 1887); Henry G. Marquand, New York (by 1889–90).

References: Bode 1895, p. 17; Friedländer 1924–37, vol. 1 (1924), pp. 151–52, 157, 170, pl. 60; Pächt 1926, pp. 158–60, fig. 10; Post 1933, p. 29; Wehle and Salinger 1947, pp. 19–20, ill.; Panofsky 1953, pp. 235, 309, 488 n. 4, pl. 251; Marlier 1955, p. 12; Gellman 1970, pp. 205–9, 231–34, 248, 273, 347 nn. 107–8, 402, 407, 429, 431–33, 445, 485, no. 15, fig. 51; Sterling 1971, pp. 9, 21, 24, figs. 22, 24, 40; Upton 1972, pp. 20–21, 104–6, 109, 284, 295, 303–5, 311, 366, 373–78, 389, no. 22, fig. 22; Schabacker 1974, pp. 32, 35 n. 27, 38, 40, 46–50, 58–59, 72, 75, 101–2, 105–6, 120, no. 11, fig. 11; Ainsworth 1994b, pp. 35–36, 41, 83–84, 106–11, 115, 123, 192, no. 8, colorpl. p. 107, figs. 31, 32, 34, 102, 118, 119; Klein 1994a, p. 215; Ainsworth 1995, pp. 7, 215; Klein, Verougstraete, and Van Schoute in Ainsworth 1995, pp. 154, 162, 202.

A compact, tightly organized, and meticulously painted picture charged with intense emotion, the *Lamentation* was probably made as an independent panel intended for private devotion. The Gospel of John (19:33–41) is the primary source for the image and the only account of the Lamentation that includes references to both Joseph of Arimathea and Nicodemus. John is also the only apostolic narrative that cites the crucified Christ's words to his mother, "Woman, behold thy son!" and to his disciple John, "Behold thy mother!" (John 19:26–27). The latter admonition has profound meaning for our picture, as John is shown actively beginning his stewardship of the Virgin by supporting her in the embrace of his arms. Mary's pose, a sympathetic response to that of her dead son, illustrates the themes of *compassio* and *co-redemptio*; with her posture echoing Christ's, she shares his suffering and his role as Redeemer. Christus's choice of this subject would have been encouraged by the fact that the twelfth-century writings of Bernard of Clairvaux on the compassion of the Virgin had become doctrine by the fifteenth century; it was influenced as well by Denis the Carthusian, the main contemporary proponent of these ideas.

The presentation of this scene as a tableau vivant before a landscape backdrop reflects its association with a familiar episode from contemporary Passion plays that prominently featured Joseph of Arimathea and Nicodemus, who humbly says to his companion, "Take thou the head. I shall take the feet." Ainsworth (1994b) notes that the iconography is related to the Deposition scene in the Passion play series of about 1425 by the York Realist.

A *Lamentation* in the Louvre and another in the Musées Royaux des Beaux-Arts de Belgique, Brussels, are related to our work. The painting in the Louvre, a vertical composition, is by Christus and a follower; it likely dates to about 1445–50 and shows the influence of a miniature of the Pietà from the Turin-Milan Hours usually ascribed to Hand H (now destroyed). The *Lamentation* in Brussels is clearly by Christus (indeed, it bears an inscription that Verougstraete and Van Schoute [1995] have interpreted as a signature). The Brussels example, which possibly dates to the mid-1450s, is probably later than our panel but shares with it the inspiration of Rogier van der Weyden's *Deposition* of about 1435–40 (Prado, Madrid). Our picture is datable to about 1450, as supported by dendrochronological analysis.

The present panel appears to have been cut down at the top soon after it was painted. Two early-sixteenth-century copies (the centerpiece of a triptych in San Esteban, Hormaza, west of Burgos, and a picture sold at Sotheby's, London [April 8, 1981, no. 57, as Isenbrant]), similar in size to our painting, show the composition as it is now. A marble relief by Antonello Gagini in the cathedral at Palermo seems to derive from our *Lamentation* and may indicate that it was exported to Italy. DCS

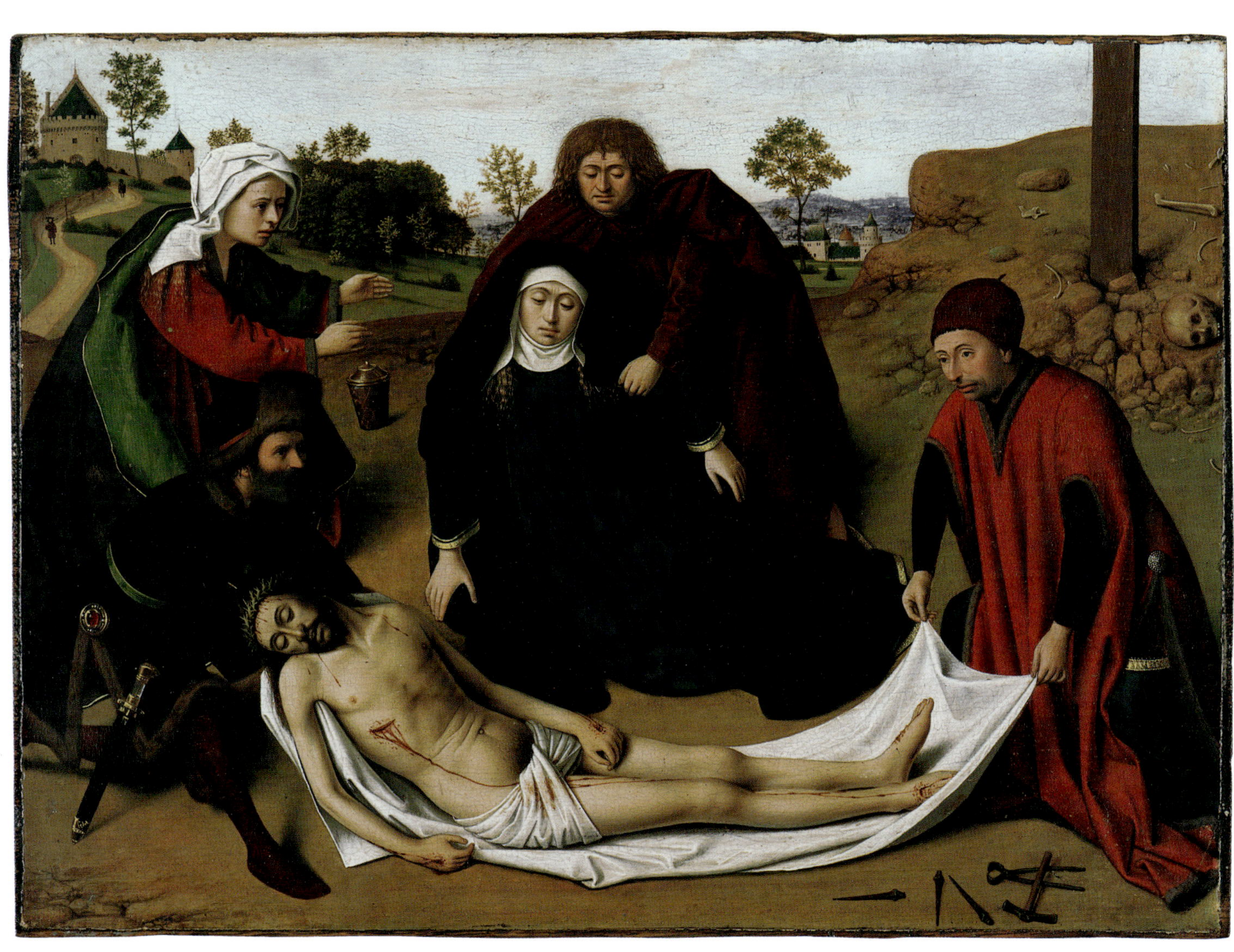

Attributed to Petrus Christus, active by 1444, died 1475/76

5. The Annunciation, about 1450

Oil on wood; overall 31 x 25⅞ in. (78.7 x 65.7 cm); painted surface 30½ x 25¼ in. (77.5 x 64.1 cm)
Inscribed (on step): REGINA C[O]ELI L[A]ET[ARE] (Queen of Heaven, rejoice [Easter antiphon of the Virgin].)
The Friedsam Collection, Bequest of Michael Friedsam, 1931 32.100.35

Provenance: Prince of Charleroi [prince of Charolais]; J. J. van Hal, Antwerp (his sale, Snyers, Antwerp, August 23, 1836, no. 80, as Jan van Eyck; to Nieuwenhuys for Fr 2,800); C. J. Nieuwenhuys, Brussels (1836–after 1847); M. Parent, Paris (by 1860); his granddaughter, Countess O'Gorman, Paris (until 1925); [Kleinberger, New York, 1925]; Philip Lehman, New York (1925–26); [Kleinberger, New York, 1926]; Michael Friedsam, New York (1926–31).

References: Waagen 1847, p. 163; Friedländer 1916, p. 21; Friedländer 1924–37, vol. 1 (1924), p. 158; Burroughs and Wehle 1932, pp. 14–16, fig. 14; Panofsky 1935, pp. 433–73, figs. 1, 5, 8; Robb 1936, pp. 505–7, 513, 519, fig. 30; Beenken 1937, pp. 220–41, figs. 1, 3; Friedländer 1924–37, vol. 14 (1937), pp. 77–78, 80; Panofsky 1938, pp. 419–24, fig. 5; Wehle and Salinger 1947, pp. 13–16, ill.;

In this work of haunting poetic beauty the miracle of the Annunciation is communicated as much by the rapturous depiction of a verdant nature as by the diminutive figures of the angel Gabriel and the Virgin. The panel is a fragment of what may have been a much larger horizontal composition: Ainsworth has noted that only the right edge is intact and that the horizontal wood grain indicates that the support may have been cut down. She suggests that the original oblong panel may have included the horizon and additional architecture at the top, as well as other, earlier scenes from the life of the Virgin. Repainting covers some areas of significant abrasion, especially in the now masklike faces of the Virgin and the angel Gabriel.

The outdoor setting and multiple points of view of the *Annunciation* are two of its most unusual features. No less notable is the placement of the standing Virgin in the doorway, a scheme that seems more Italianate than northern and contrasts with the better-known Flemish type of a unified interior, as seen in the *Merode Triptych* by Robert Campin (cat. no. 2). Ward notes that the poses, immobility, and solidity of the figures, as well as the nichelike space around the Virgin, suggest the influence of sculpture, or paintings that represent sculpture, specifically Jan van Eyck's two late grisaille Annunciations, datable to the mid-1430s, one in the Museo Thyssen-Bornemisza, Madrid, the other on the exterior wings of the Dresden Triptych at the Gemäldegalerie Alte Meister, Dresden.

Numerous iconographic references amplify the intent of the composition. The architectural elements of the ecclesiastical portal in which the Virgin stands contrast the outmoded Romanesque style to her left—representing Old Testament Judaism—with the newer, Gothic style to her right—symbolizing New Testament Christianity. An empty niche above the Virgin's head presumably awaits the figure of the unborn Christ, who will link these worlds. Mary's role as the spiritual doorway to heaven is, literally, spelled out on the tiles of the step. The placement of the Virgin Mary within the doorway, between the old and new worlds, refers not only to her part in the Annunciation but also to her larger roles as the personification of the Church and as intercessor for the salvation of humankind.

The plants represented (see fig. 48 and list at end of entry) are commonly found in fields, woodlands, and wetlands, with the exception of the lily, which in the mid-fifteenth century was grown solely for medicinal purposes. The particular flowering plants shown would not be in bloom on March 25, the date of the Annunciation, yet their detailed portrayal is based on sound botanical observation. These ordinary plants, which carpet almost a third of the painted surface here, serve as a foil for the formality of the Annunciation scene; the symbolism of some of them may serve to reinforce the picture's religious iconography. The most prominent flower is the lily, its blossom-laden stalks rising from a tin-glazed vase in the alcove between the figures of Gabriel and the Virgin.

The most persistent problem associated with the *Annunciation* is that of attribution. Because Petrus Christus, Jan van Eyck, and Hubert van Eyck have all been proposed as authors, the painting is often referred to as the Friedsam *Annunciation*, after the name of its last owner. Ainsworth has recently provided an X-radiograph of the painting, infrared reflectography of its underdrawing, and dendrochronological analysis of its panels, as well as comparisons with authenticated works by Christus, that eliminate both Van Eyck brothers as candidates and support a mid-fifteenth-century date, or at least one after the mid-1440s.

One picture certainly by the same artist is a small *Saint John the Baptist in a Landscape* in the Cleveland Museum of Art (15¾ x 4⅞ in.), which Ainsworth has argued is an early work by Christus. Both the Cleveland panel and our own are painted with a similar Eyckian attention to detail, particularly

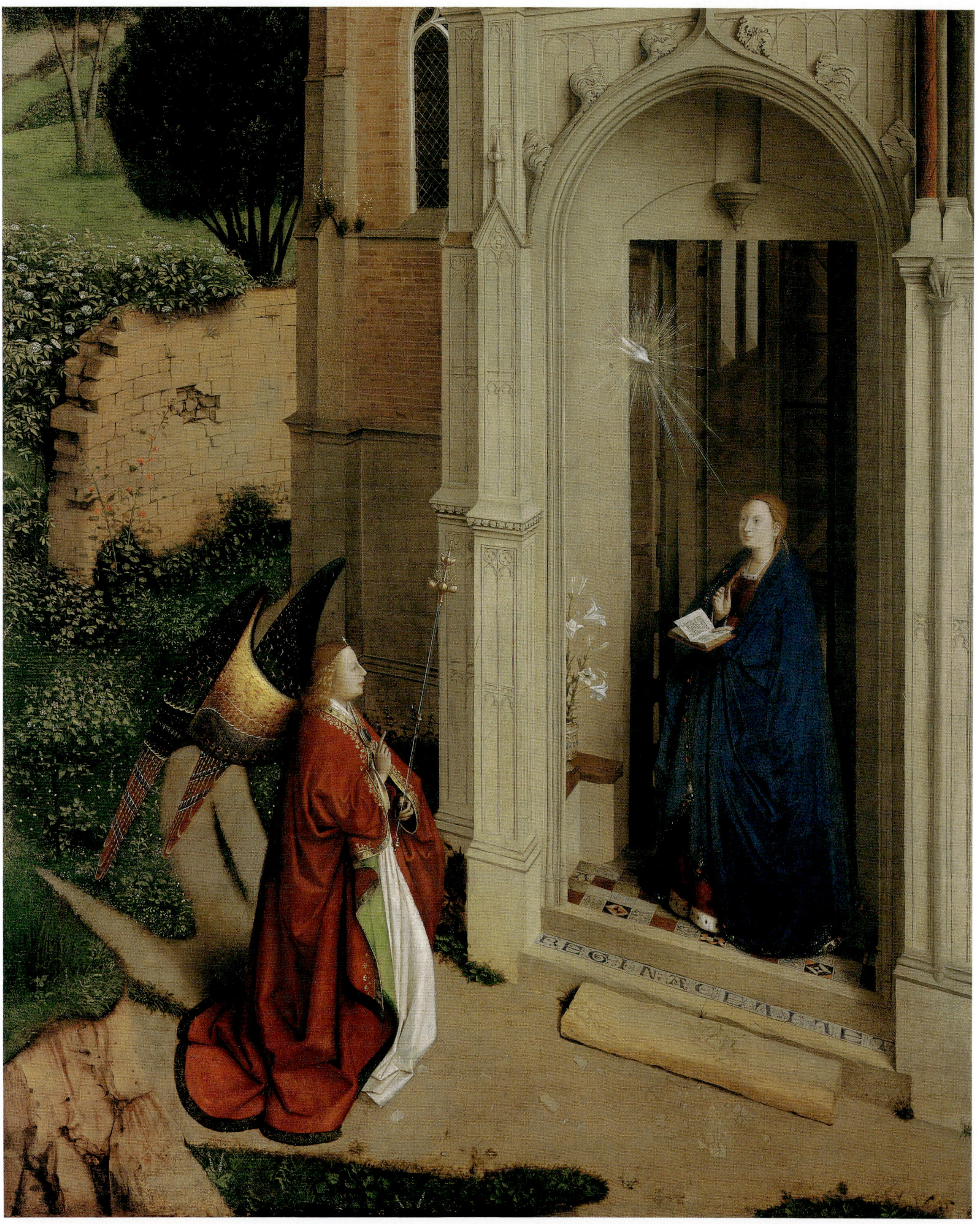

Panofsky 1953, pp. 133–34, 226, 230–32, 278, 305, 412 n. 2, 451 n. 2, pl. 152; Ward 1968, pp. 184–87, fig. 1; Russell 1978, pp. 23–27, fig. 1; Upton 1990, pp. 45, 65–66, 76 n. 70, 77–79, 81, 95 n. 21, 102 n. 42, fig. 69; Ainsworth 1994b, pp. 80, 117, 119, 122–25, 179, 182, no. 10, colorpl. p. 118, figs. 128–32; Klein 1994a, p. 215.

noticeable in the botanical exactitude of the plants represented. The greatest obstacle to assigning these works to Christus is the poetry of their exalted vision of nature; this quality is part of the powerful legacy of Jan van Eyck that Christus encountered in Bruges upon his arrival there in 1444, but it is not characteristic of the younger artist's oeuvre.

The plants in the painting are:

1. Madonna lily (*Lilium candidum*), symbol of purity associated with the Virgin and especially with the Annunciation

2. English daisy (*Bellis perennis*), representing sweet innocence, especially that of the Christ Child

3. wild strawberry (*Fragaria vesca*), white flowers of innocence and leaves in the sacred trefoil form of the Trinity, symbol of perfect righteousness and the virtues of Mary, bearing the perfect fruit, with neither thorn nor pit

4. early purple orchid (*Orchis mascula*), symbol of fertility

5. common plantain (probably *Plantago major* or *Plantago lanceolata*), thrives even on trodden paths and therefore symbolic of the multitude that seeks the path of Christ

6. stonecrop (possibly *Sedum album*), symbol of tenderness of heart, full of God-given virtue

7. hollyhock (*Althea*), symbol of salvation

8. sweet woodruff (*Galium odoratum*), lady's bedstraw or a similar plant of the genus *Galium* (bedstraw), representing the bedstraw said to have been mixed with the hay that lined the bed in which Mary gave birth to Christ

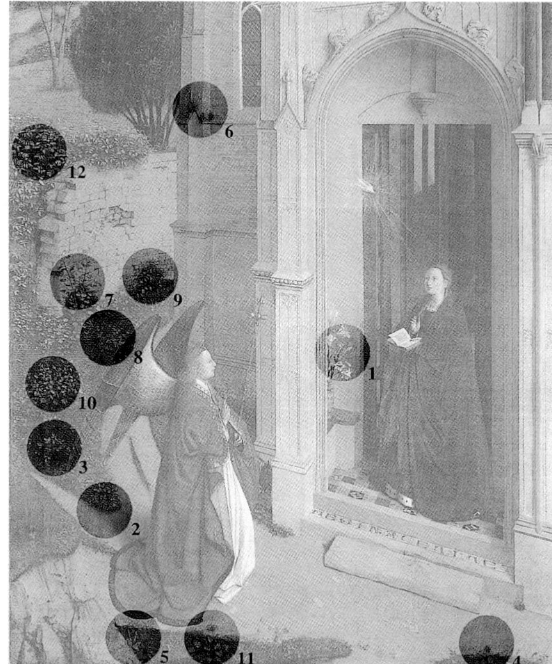

Fig. 48. Key to plants

9. mint (*Mentha*), the herb of the Virgin Mary

10. mallow (*Malva*), with its characteristic straight stems, opposing leaves, and tiered flowers, symbol of fertility and salvation

11. water avens or a similar plant (*Geum* family)

12. a climbing vine, such as a variety of clematis (*Clematis*), or a shrub or bush, such as hydrangea (*Viburnum*) or elderberry (possibly *Sambucus nigra*) DCS

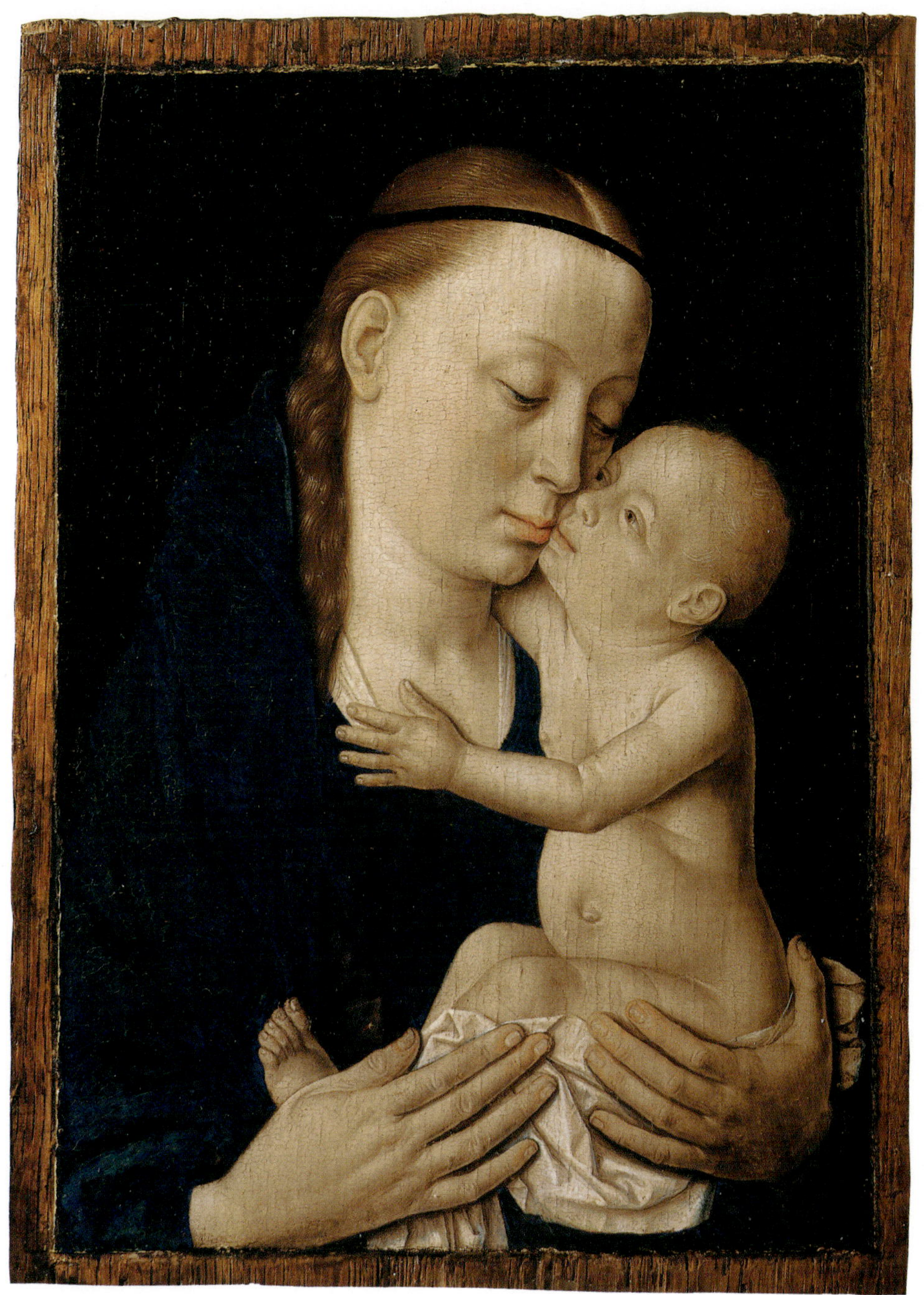

Dieric Bouts, active by 1457, died 1475

6. Virgin and Child, about 1455–60

A work from Bouts's early period, this small, exquisitely tender representation of the embracing Virgin and Child reveals the artist's roots in the school of Haarlem and, more particularly, the influence of Aelbert van Ouwater, who, Van Mander tells us, was the founder of this school. The relatively short, plump fingers and plain features of the Virgin—stressing her simplicity rather than her elegance—and the illusion of human flesh that creases, dimples, and yields to the touch are all consistent with Bouts's

Oil on wood, 8½ x 6½ in. (21.6 x 16.5 cm)
Theodore M. Davis Collection, Bequest of Theodore M. Davis, 1915
30.95.280

Provenance: Luigi Bonomi, Milan?; Signora Cereda-Rovelli, Milan; Bonomi-Cereda, Milan (by 1872–95); Theodore M. Davis, Newport (1895-1915).

References: Mantz 1872, p. 459; Hulin de Loo 1924, pp. 59–60; Friedländer 1924–37, vol. 3 (1925), pp. 47, 107, no. 9a; Schöne 1938, pp. 5, 7, 26, 30, 77–78, 133, 139, pl. 7; Wehle and Salinger 1947, pp. 44–45, ill.; Panofsky 1953, pp. 317, 492 n. 2 (for p. 317), pl. 268; Friedländer 1967–76, vol. 3 (1968), pp. 29, 60, no. 9, pl. 17; Veronée-Verhaegen 1968, pp. 5–10, fig. 1; De Vos 1971, pp. 146–47, 159, 161, fig. 82; Van Miegroet in Bauman and Liedtke 1992, pp. 67–69, color ill.; Ainsworth 1993–95, pp. 1–19, ills.

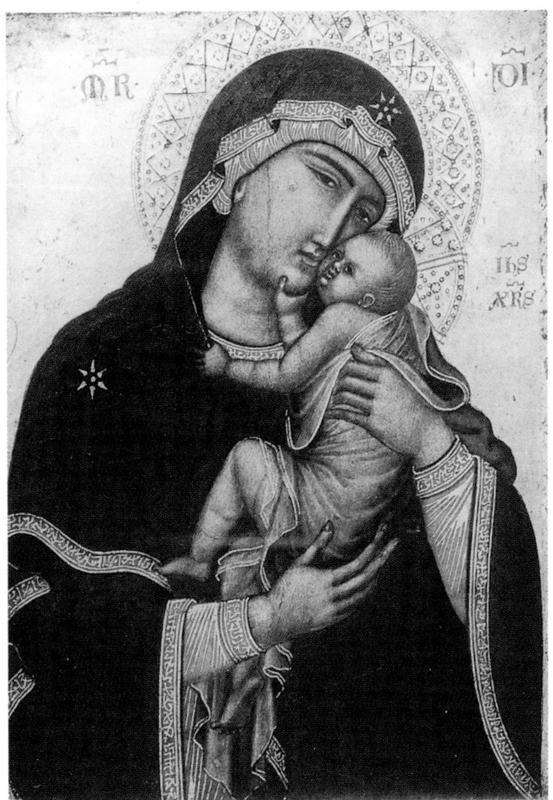

Fig. 49. Sienese, *Notre-Dame de Grâce* (Cambrai Madonna), about 1340. Oil on wood. Cathedral, Cambrai

youthful sensibility. By about 1465, in his *Virgin and Child* in the National Gallery, London, the influence of Rogier van der Weyden's more attenuated aristocratic ideal became evident in his work.

The composition was repeated in at least two surviving variants that Ainsworth has shown were produced in Bouts's workshop. In the somewhat larger version in the Fine Arts Museums of San Francisco a gold brocade background has been added and the Virgin wears a red robe over her blue dress, while the one in the Carrand collection at the Bargello, Florence, which is almost identical to our panel in its dimensions, introduces a deep red for Mary's undergarment; the muted palette of the latter painting is otherwise similar to that of ours. Although the three works are extremely close superficially, a careful visual comparison and recent examination with X-radiography and infrared reflectography by Ainsworth confirm that the panels in San Francisco and Florence were produced by two different workshop assistants. Our picture can be confidently attributed to Bouts himself, working between about 1455 and 1460. The extraordinary correspondence of the three panels and the merely cursory underdrawing present in each make it clear that they were produced through the use of pattern drawings, a common practice in artists' workshops of the fifteenth-century Netherlands.

The composition of these panels is loosely based on a fourteenth-century Italian portrayal of the Virgin and Child known as the Cambrai Madonna (fig. 49), itself a replica of an earlier Italo-Byzantine icon. This picture, installed in 1452 in the cathedral of Cambrai, was a highly popular model for private devotional works, as numerous miracles were attributed to it. During the fifteenth century it was believed to have been painted by Saint Luke. Documents record the commission of three copies of the Cambrai Madonna from Petrus Christus in 1454 and twelve from Hayne de Bruxelles in the following year. Rogier van der Weyden must also have produced a composition inspired by the painting, as an excellent replica of one from his workshop survives in the Museum of Fine Arts, Houston.

In the Cambrai Madonna, a copy of it ascribed to Hayne de Bruxelles (Nelson-Atkins Museum of Art, Kansas City), and the Rogierian painting in Houston, Christ clutches or reaches for his mother's chin with his right hand, while in the panels by Bouts and his workshop, he has put his arm around her neck, a more human gesture, suggesting a closer bond. In the last three pictures Christ and the Virgin look directly into each other's eyes, rather than abstractedly down, or out at the viewer, creating an unusual effect of spiritual intimacy. As Ainsworth notes, this altered pose corresponds to passages in the Song of Solomon in the Old Testament: "His left hand should be under my head, and his right hand should embrace me" (8:3), and "Let him kiss me with the kisses of his mouth" (1:2). The love poetry in this text was understood during the fifteenth century as an allegory of the relationship of Christ with the Church and with the Virgin Mary.

MSdJ

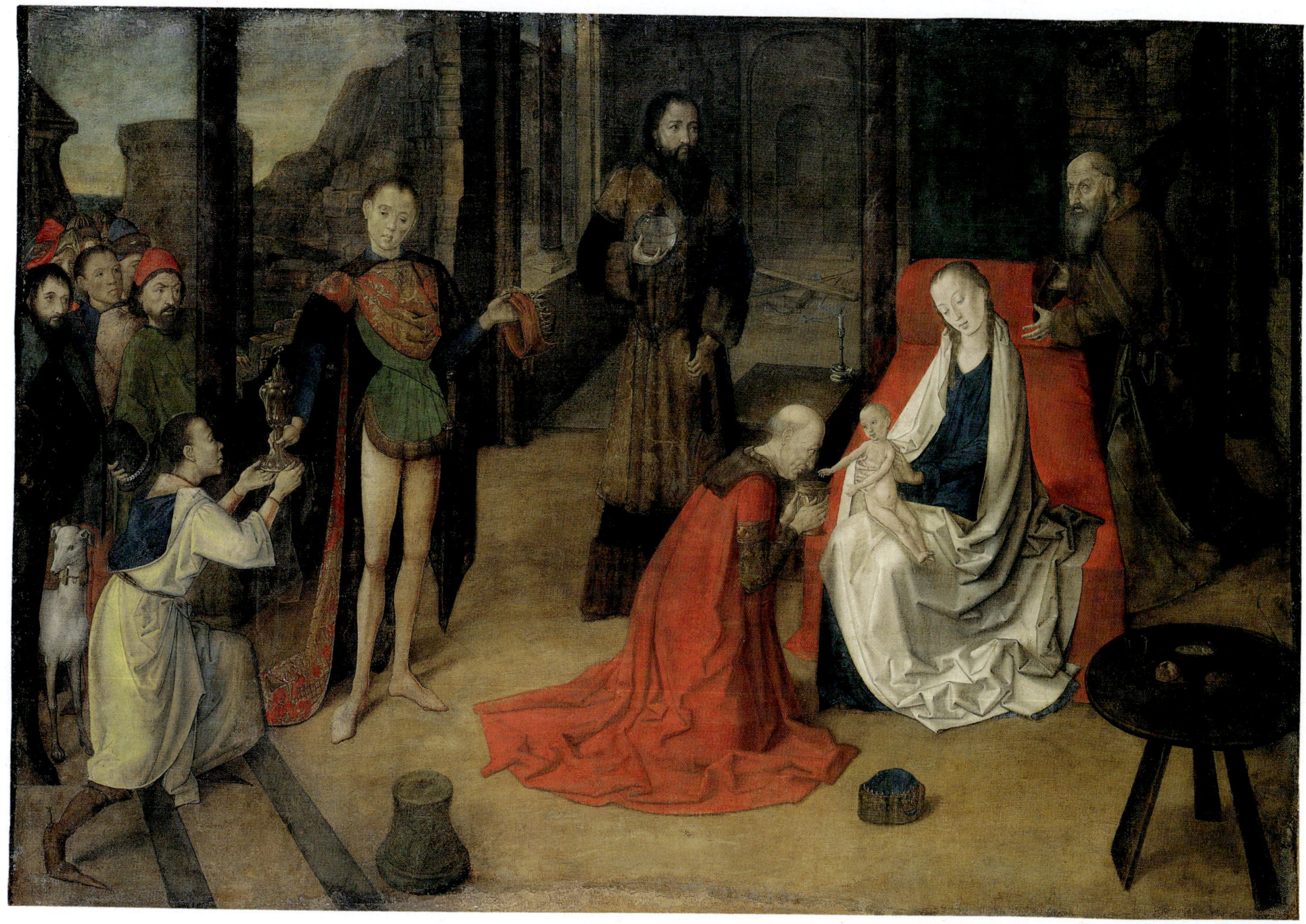

Joos van Gent, active by 1460, died about 1480

7. *The Adoration of the Magi,* about 1465

This austere but lyrical *Adoration* is one of only two works generally attributed to Joos van Gent before he left the Netherlands for Italy in or after 1469. The narrative has been cast in symbolic terms centering on themes of the Epiphany and the Eucharist. Instead of a stable, the Adoration takes place in a more formal building in a state of ruin, and the usual manger has been replaced with the *thalamus virginis*, or wedding bed of the Virgin as Bride of Christ. Joseph's carpenter's tools can be seen in a room in the middle background, and at the far right, in an adjoining stable, are an ox and ass. In addition to the bowl of milk soup, the Christ Child's standard meal in early Netherlandish art, the still life on the table in the foreground includes two small loaves of bread and a glass of wine, drawing attention to the painting's eucharistic theme. This theme is reiterated in the ornament surmounting the youngest magus's gift, a pelican piercing its breast to feed its young with its own blood—a symbol of Christ's sacrifice for the salvation of mankind. A fifteenth-century viewer would have recognized the mysterious object in the left foreground as the relic of the column to which Christ was bound during the Flagellation. The main figures are dispersed across the spare stage in two parallel diagonal rows,

Distemper on canvas, 43 x 63 in. (109.2 x 160 cm)
Bequest of George Blumenthal, 1941 41.190.21

Provenance: ?Don Pedro Fernández de Velasco, count of Haro and constable of Castile (d. 1492), convent of Santa Clara, Medina de Pomar, near Burgos; his

heirs, dukes of Frias, convent of Santa Clara; [Jacques Seligmann, Paris and New York (by 1923)]; [Germain Seligman, New York (1923–24/25)]; George and Florence Blumenthal, New York (by 1925–41).

References: Demonts 1925, pp. 56–62, 65–69, 72–74, pl. 1; Friedländer 1924–37, vol. 3 (1925), pp. 84–86, 129, no. 101, pl. 83; Lavalleye 1936, pp. 79–81, pl. 6; Wehle 1943, pp. 133–37, ill.; Wehle and Salinger 1947, pp. 54–56, ill.; Panofsky 1953, pp. 341–42, 503 (n. 2 for p. 341), fig. 450; Nilgen 1967, pp. 311–16, fig. 15; Friedländer 1967–76, vol. 3 (1968), pp. 47–49, 74, no. 101, pl. 105; McNamee 1976, pp. 109–10; Wolfthal 1987, pp. 86–87; Wolfthal 1989, pp. 33, 41–42, no. 5, figs. 19, 23, 26, 39, 45, 62–63; Belting and Kruse 1994, pp. 222–23, colorpls. 162, 163; Eeckhout 1994, p. 422.

with the Virgin seated at the foot of the crimson-covered bed and the Christ Child perched on her knees. A curious and admiring throng gather at the far left; over their heads and through the columns of the porch we can see rocky cliffs, a patch of blue sea, and the towers of two exotic-looking buildings. The stagelike space of the setting, distinctive costumes, and careful arrangement of the figures across the space—as in a tableau vivant—suggest that the artist was inspired by the mystery plays enacted during the Middle Ages in large churches and cathedrals on the Feast of the Epiphany.

Certain figures, particularly those of Saint Joseph and the two older magi, are reminiscent of types in the work of Hugo van der Goes, a close friend of Joos's, and Joseph's gesture recalls the attitudes of the awestruck shepherds who admire the Holy Infant from the boundaries of Hugo's Adoration scenes. At the same time, the predilection we see in the Museum's canvas for somewhat stiff, elongated figures, judiciously spaced across the picture plane and in depth, is a hallmark of the style of Dieric Bouts, in whose workshop Joos may have been active. Notwithstanding the close ties we can discern here with these important masters of the Netherlandish school, the composition, color sensibility, and feeling for narrative are strikingly original and inventive. On the basis of their stylistic similarities, the Museum's canvas and the Crucifixion Altarpiece in Sint-Baafs (Saint Bavo's) cathedral in Ghent—the only other surviving work by Joos that predates his Italian journey—are usually dated about 1465 or shortly thereafter. The figure of the youngest magus in the Ghent triptych bears a striking resemblance to its counterpart in our picture.

A rare example of canvas, or *tüchlein*, painting, the *Adoration of the Magi* was carried out in an aqueous medium on a fine linen support. Although perhaps 40 percent of the paintings produced in the Netherlands during the fifteenth century and early sixteenth century had canvas supports, due to their extraordinary fragility and vulnerability to the damp local climate, fewer than one hundred of these works have survived. Contemporary artists' manuals recommended the lightest possible sizing of the linen, which allowed much of the medium to soak into the fabric. The result, as in our *Adoration*, is a subdued, matte surface, in which the texture of the linen is evident—conveying an effect conspicuously different from that of the deeply saturated colors, crisp drawing, and smooth, luminous surfaces of the more familiar fifteenth-century media of tempera and oil applied to a well-primed panel.

The present picture was probably a commissioned altarpiece. The convent of Santa Clara, near Burgos, from which it came, was built in the second half of the fifteenth century as the pantheon for the Fernández de Velasco family and functions as a convent to this day. Our *Adoration* may have been one of the many works of art imported from the Netherlands for the convent's decoration and perhaps hung in its chapel of the Immaculate Conception. The painting could by itself have served as an altarpiece or it may originally have had wings. As so few works on linen have survived, it is difficult to hypothesize about the original context of this important picture.

MSdJ

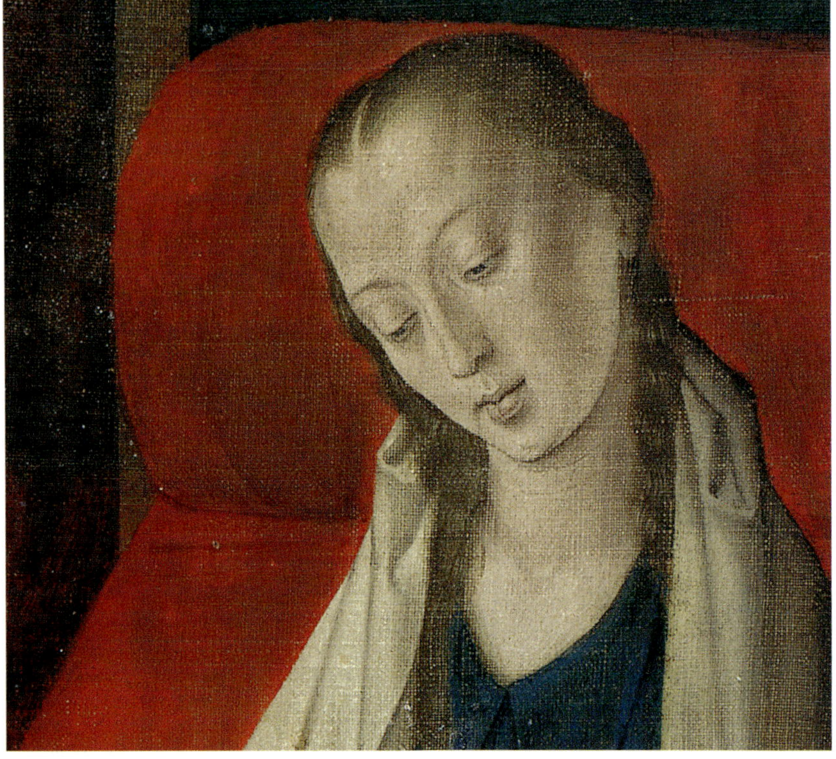

Detail, cat. no. 7

North Netherlandish (possibly Utrecht) Painter

8. Christ Bearing the Cross, about 1470

In a procession originating from a contemporary Flemish town transformed into the holy city of Jerusalem by the insertion of the church of the Dome of the Rock at its center, Christ slowly makes his way on the path that climbs to the rocky plateau of Golgotha. There the crosses are raised in preparation for the crucifixion of the Son of God and two common thieves. In keeping with the precepts of the *Modern Devotion,* which became increasingly popular during the fifteenth century, this Bearing of the Cross is embellished with details intended to elicit the viewer's compassion for Christ's suffering. Totally despairing and weighed down by his cross, Christ is tormented by soldiers who beat him, drag him by a rope encircling his waist, and pull his hair—thus fulfilling the Old Testament prophecies that tell of the lamb willingly led to slaughter (Isaiah 53:7 and Jeremiah 11:19). The viewer is meant to identify with the prominently placed and sympathetic Simon of Cyrene, who helps to bear the burden of the cross, and with Veronica, who, according to legend, holds her veil ready to wipe Christ's brow, thereby miraculously imprinting his image on the cloth. Some of the bystanders appear in exotic costumes—for example, the man at the lower left wearing the conical yellow hat with a red upturned brim—meant to suggest the Jews and underscore their responsibility for the Crucifixion of Christ (Luke 23:25: "but [Pilate] delivered Jesus to their will"). The portrayal is inspired by the minimal account of the Bearing of the Cross in the Gospels and also by the Pseudo-Bonaventure's augmented treatment in his *Meditations on the Life of Christ,* which relates how the Virgin took a shorter route in order to meet her son at the joining of two paths: this episode is depicted in the middle ground, where the Virgin prays, accompanied by the grief-stricken Saint John and the other Marys.

A partially legible inscription on the red robe and hat of the horseman viewed from the back in the middle ground at the left appears to be in Dutch; as transcribed by Sosson (in Urbach) it reads: EL BEEF GHELOVTE E.P. OMAGAME SALIAT EEN SC. DAET SAT DI BLOET M. . . . Urbach wondered whether the phrase might refer to the cult of the Holy Blood of Christ, a subject that warrants further consideration. The words *omagame* (procession) and *bloet* (blood) may indeed have some connection with the procession held annually since 1281 in Bruges, where the renowned relic of the Holy Blood is housed in the Basiliek van het Heilig Bloed (basilica of the Holy Blood) in the southwest corner of the Burg square. The Noble Brotherhood of the Holy Blood, long responsible for overseeing the chapel, its relic, and the procession, was formed as early as 1405 and has traditionally included thirty-one men appointed from the nobility of the city as well as the dukes of Flanders, who were honorary members. It is possible that some of this elite group are pictured in the vignette of five horsemen with sensitively rendered, portraitlike heads who follow the cross at the right in what may well be the Bruges procession. The man in armor bearing an indecipherable inscription across the chest carries a staff with an elaborate finial surmounted by a bird (possibly a pelican pricking its breast, a symbol of Christ's sacrifice and Resurrection), which perhaps represents one of the many processional reliquaries made to house the Holy Blood. The man to his left in an extravagant ermine-trimmed costume and accompanied by two youthful grooms appears to be a royal personage. And the nobleman shown in profile behind him has been identified, albeit controversially, on the basis of a likeness in the Arras Codex, as Duke John of Bavaria, count of Holland and prince-elector of Liège. If the painting does indeed represent the procession of the Holy Blood in Bruges, this might account for the detailed portrayal of the Flemish townscape and distinguished members of the nobility who traditionally took part in this famous religious observance; it would explain as well the theatrical presentation of the subject, with lavish costumes, and a dramatic

Oil on wood, 42⅜ x 32⅜ in. (107.6 x 82.2 cm)
Inscribed (on red robe of horseman in middle ground at left and on armor of man on white horse in right foreground): [fragmentary and mostly illegible]
Bequest of George D. Pratt, 1935 43.95

Provenance: Count Wilczek, Schloss Kreutzenstein, near Vienna (until 1907); [Kleinberger, Paris (1907–10)]; George D. Pratt, New York, as Dieric Bouts (by 1910).

References: Grisebach 1912, p. 265, n. 2; Winkler 1916, pp. 292ff.; Zimmermann 1917, cols. 15ff.; Baldass 1920–21a, p. 32; Friedländer 1924–37, vol. 1 (1924), p. 121; Hoogewerff 1936–47, vol. 1 (1936), pp. 505–8; Schöne 1937, pp. 154ff.; Priest 1940, p. 237; Wehle and Salinger 1947, pp. 23–25; Musper 1948, pp. 87–88, 94–96, 102–3; Panofsky 1953, pp. 236–37, 453 n. 2 (for p. 237); Garas 1954, pp. 257–58; Larsen 1960, pp. 39–40, 110; Carter 1962, pp. 14–21, 24; Scillia 1975, pp. 78–97, 100–101, 103–7, 109, 110, 134–35, 257–58; Smeyers and Cardon 1991, pp. 89–104; Urbach 1991, pp. 83–86.

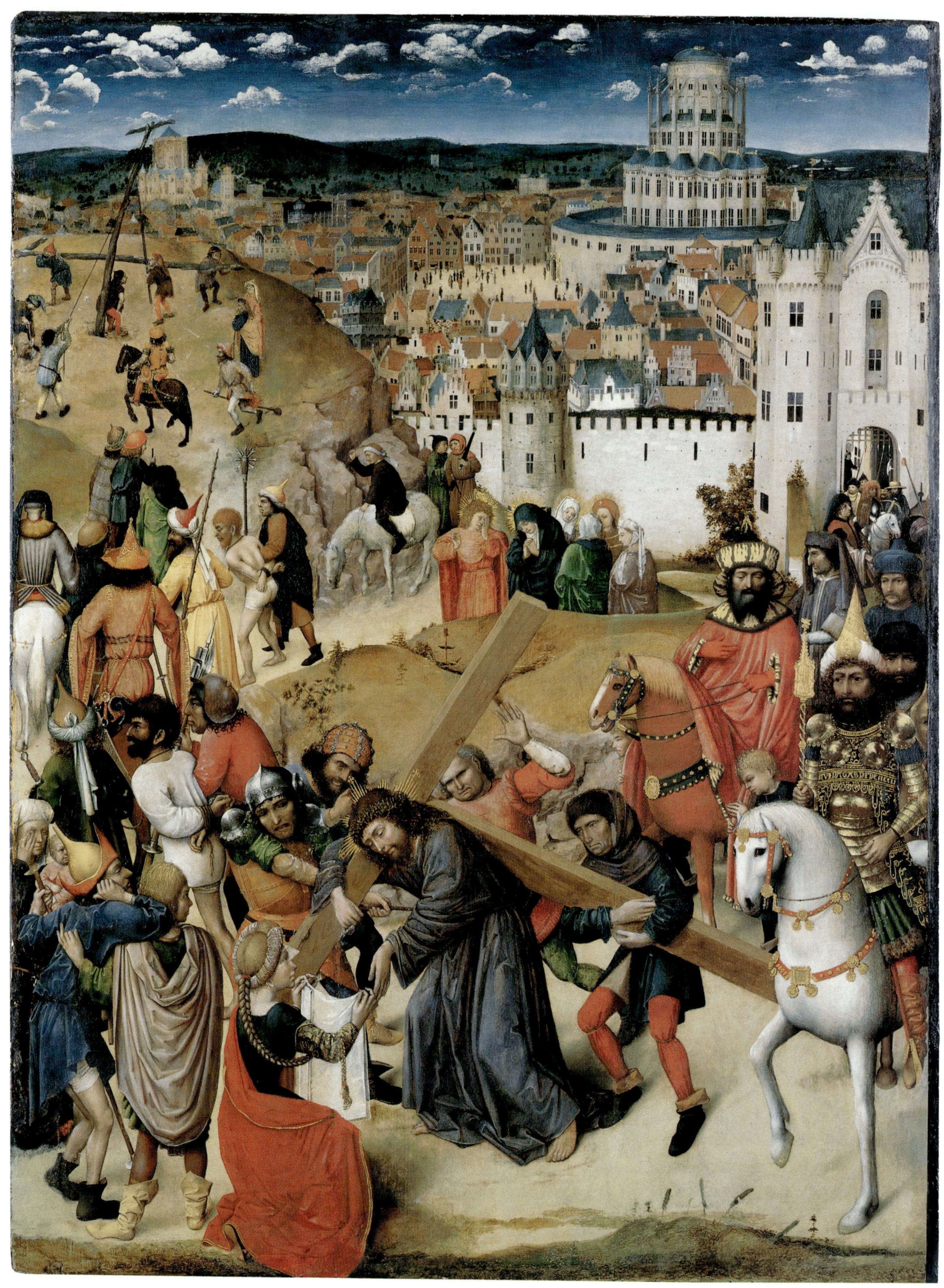

8

development of the narrative that shows pivotal events, such as the encounter between Christ and Veronica, as if they were occurring during pauses along the way.

This panel joins a number of other images—paintings, manuscript illuminations, and drawings—that completely or partially record a lost Christ Bearing the Cross attributed to Jan van Eyck. Our painting is most often related to a mid-sixteenth-century version of horizontal format in the Szépmüvészeti Múzeum, Budapest; both show motifs and groupings of figures that refer to Eyckian workshop models, some of which are known from extant drawings after Jan's designs, notably one of a group of the horsemen in the Herzog Anton Ulrich-Museum, Braunschweig, and a more or less complete composition in the Graphische Sammlung Albertina, Vienna.

In style, however, the present work is more closely connected to manuscript illuminations associated with the Master of Evert Zoudenbalch, an illuminator and panel painter who was strongly influenced by the early works of Jan van Eyck. In a number of illuminations linked to this master, for example the *Entombment* and the *Arrest of Christ* from the Book of Hours of Jan van Amerongen/Mary of Vronensteyn (Bibliothèque Royale Albert I, Brussels, Ms. II 7619) and the *Arrest of Christ* from the Book of Hours of Gijsbrecht van Brederode (Bibliothèque de l'Université, Liège, Ms. Wittert 13), just as in our painting, the predominant event occurs in the foreground, rocky masses define the middle ground where subsidiary scenes can take place, and a cityscape fills the background to a high horizon line set below a narrow strip of sky filled with feathery clouds. As Scillia has pointed out, the works of the Master of Evert Zoudenbalch also share with our picture certain facial types and similar figural proportions, costumes, and decorative motifs. These parallels indicate that although the identity of the artist who produced the Metropolitan painting remains unknown, he can probably be associated with the panel painters and illuminators in the circle of the Master of Evert Zoudenbalch, who worked during the third quarter of the fifteenth century in Utrecht. Close connections existed between illuminators in Utrecht and in Bruges at that time, and in light of this fact, which has been noted by Smeyers and Cardon, it is not unlikely that an artist from Utrecht came for a period to Bruges, where he produced our *Christ Bearing the Cross* and perhaps other, similar paintings.

The damaged condition of our panel does not diminish its charm and theatrical appeal or its significance as a possible visual record of events in fifteenth-century Bruges. MWA

Simon Marmion, active by 1449, died 1489

9. The Lamentation, early 1470s

Oil and tempera? on wood, 20⅜ x 12⅞ in. (51.8 x 32.7 cm)
Arms (verso) of Charles the Bold and Margaret of York, surrounded by four pairs of entwined initials (CM)
Robert Lehman Collection, 1975 1975.1.128

In his own time Marmion was as highly regarded as Jan van Eyck and Jean Fouquet, as Jean Lemaire's *Plainte du désiré* testifies, and was called the "very prince of book illumination" in the contemporary poem "La couronne margaritique." Marmion's involvement with manuscript illumination can be inferred from the cool pastel colors and the matte finish of the disengaged rather than fully blended brushstrokes of the *Lamentation.* In fact, he may have employed tempera, which was commonly used in manuscript illumination, as well as oil paints in this work.

Unlike the *Lamentation* by Petrus Christus (cat. no. 4), which depicts the moment after the body of Christ was lowered from the cross for burial preparations, Marmion's painting shows the corpse placed across the lap of the Virgin by Joseph of Arimathea and Nicodemus in what is essentially a Pietà. The change emphasizes the devotional aspect of the theme, turning it into an Adoration of the Dead

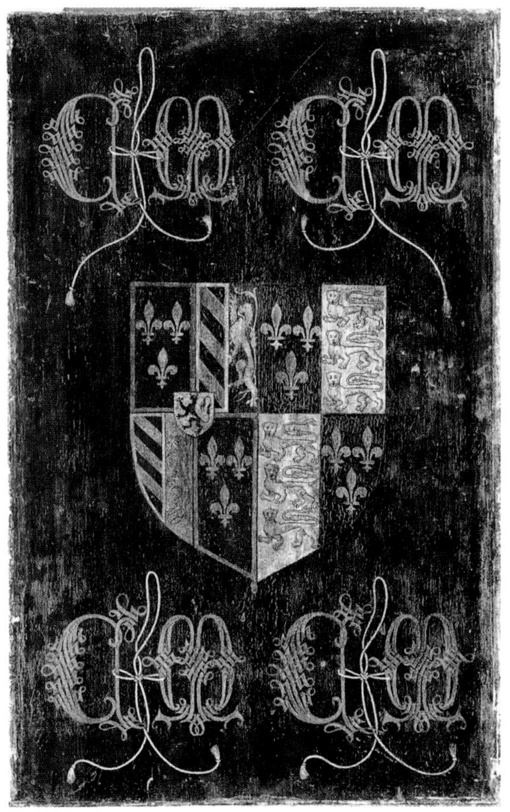

Verso, cat. no. 9

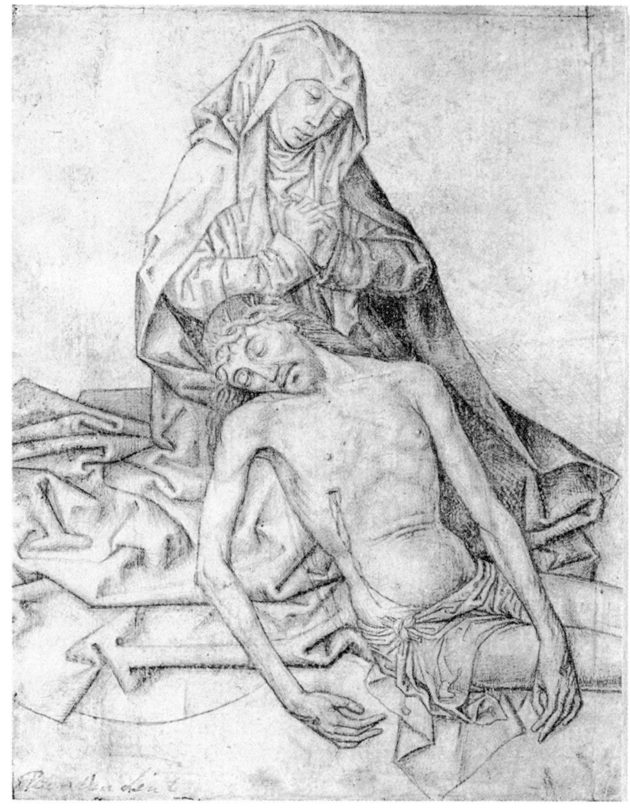

Fig. 50. Simon Marmion, *Pietà*, about 1470. Metalpoint over black chalk(?) on prepared paper. Harvard College, Harvard University Art Museums, Cambridge, Massachusetts

Provenance: Probably commissioned by Duke Charles the Bold and Margaret of York; Philip Lehman, New York; Robert Lehman, New York.

References: Friedländer 1923b, pp. 167–70; Michel 1927, pp. 142, 145; Lehman 1928, no. 91; Sterling 1941, p. 48; Ring 1949, p. 221; Heinrich 1954, p. 222; Hoffman 1958, pp. 10–11, 37, 125, 178; Lehman [1964?], p. 17; Hoffman 1969, p. 244; Szabo 1975, p. 84; Baetjer 1977, pp. 341–42; Sterling 1981, p. 12; Ainsworth 1992c, pp. 246–48; Châtelet 1996b, pp. 154, 164–65; Sterling and Ainsworth 1998, no. 1, color ill.

Christ. This subject is not based on the Gospels but is probably inspired by popular devotional narratives, such as Ludolph of Saxony's *Life of Christ*. Marmion's Virgin, Saint John, Mary Magdalene, and a female companion express grief with restraint, rather than the exaggerated pathos of traditional Netherlandish portrayals. A rare metalpoint drawing attributed to Marmion (fig. 50) served as a workshop model for this subject. In the underdrawing of the Lehman painting the pose of the Virgin more closely matches the model drawing—Mary's head is lowered and her hands are clasped in an attitude of prayer rather than crossed over her heart to express compassion.

The *Lamentation* is the only painting by Marmion other than the Saint Bertin Altarpiece (Gemäldegalerie, Berlin, and National Gallery, London), which was dedicated in 1459, that can be dated with some degree of certainty. On the verso of the present panel are the interlaced initials of Duke Charles the Bold and his wife, Margaret of York, who were married in 1468. In May of 1473 Margaret accompanied her husband to Valenciennes for a meeting of the Order of the Golden Fleece, for whose associated festivities Marmion was furnishing decorations. It may have been at this point that the duke, who had paid Marmion in 1470 for a breviary commissioned by his father, Philip the Good (fig. 11), hired the artist to paint the *Lamentation*.

A date in the early 1470s, suggested by this evidence, accords well with the style of the painting. Marmion's later works, such as the *Saint Jerome with a Donor* (Philadelphia Museum of Art), show the influence of Hugo van der Goes, in particular his *Death of the Virgin* (Groeningemuseum, Bruges). However, the isolation and psychological detachment of the figures, the stiff poses, and the general organization of the landscape in the *Lamentation* present closer affinities with earlier Netherlandish art, in particular the wings of Dieric Bouts's famous Altarpiece of the Holy Sacrament (Sint-Pieterskerk, Leuven), executed between 1464 and 1468. MWA

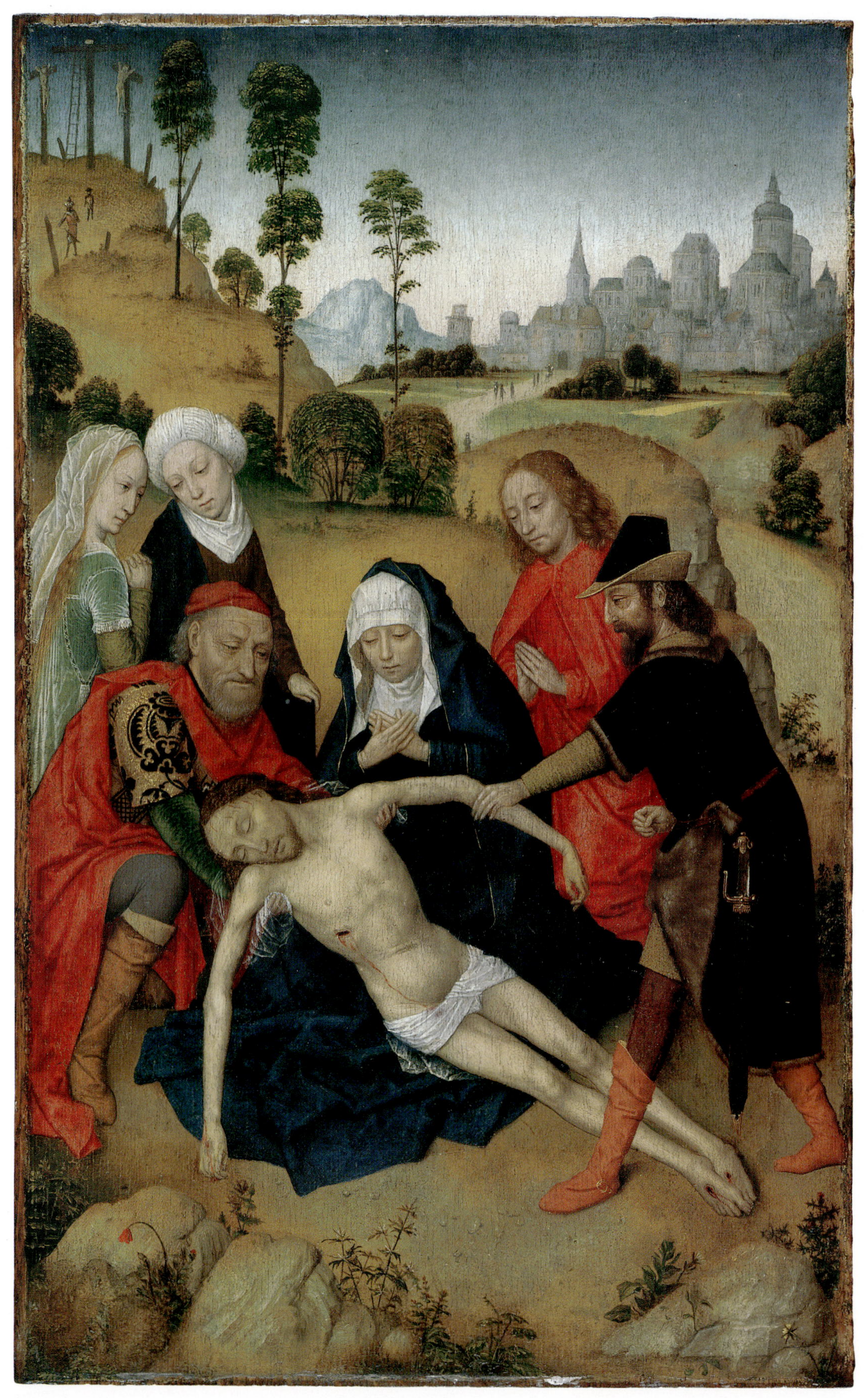

9

Workshop of Rogier van der Weyden (possibly Hans Memling)

10. The Annunciation, 1465–75

Oil on wood, 73¼ x 45¼ in. (186.1 x 114.9 cm)
Gift of J. Pierpont Morgan, 1917 17.190.7

One of the largest surviving Netherlandish Annunciations, this composition is freely adapted from the left wing of Rogier van der Weyden's Columba Altarpiece, usually dated in the mid-1450s (Alte Pinakothek, Munich). It also has features in common with an *Annunciation* probably produced in Rogier's workshop in the mid-1430s (Louvre, Paris).

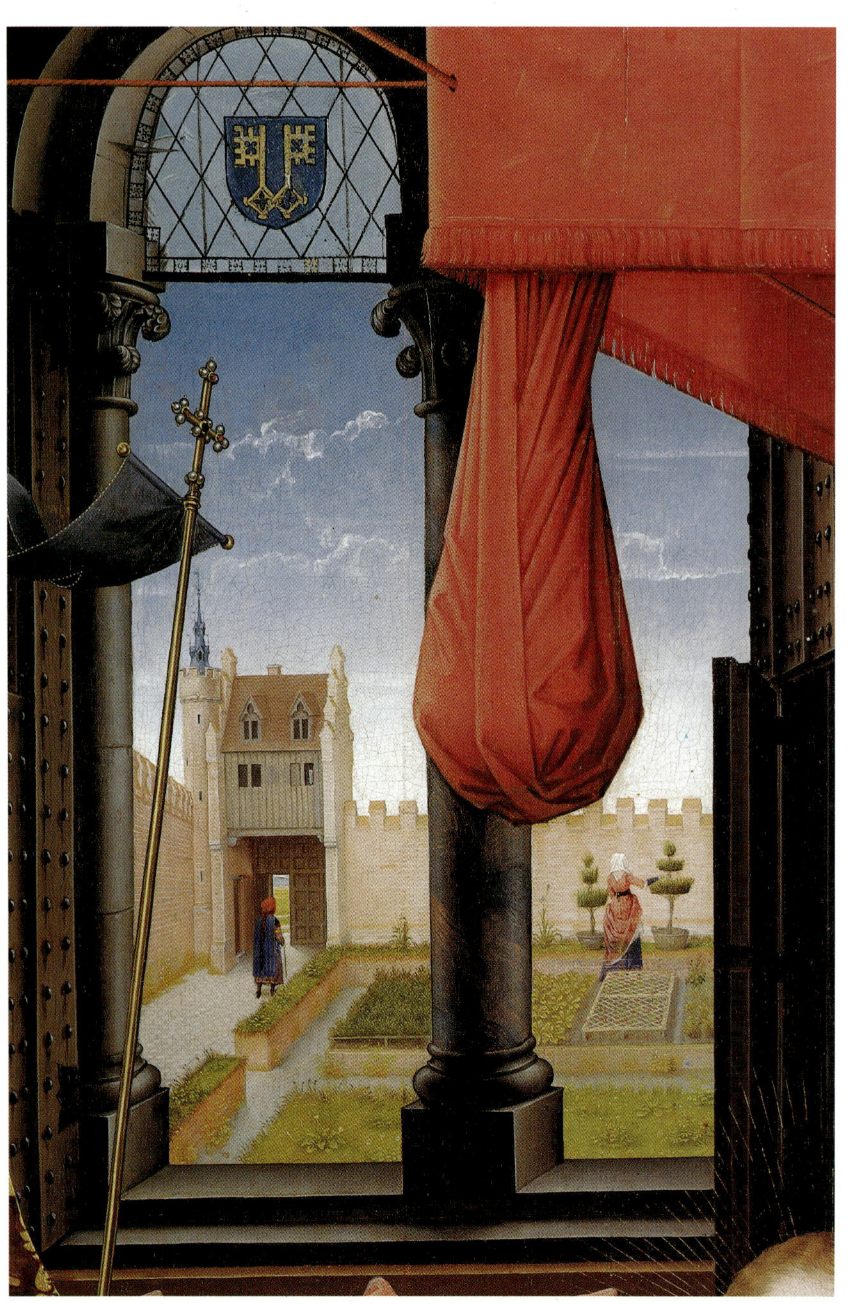

The coat of arms with the double key displayed on the window and repeated in the pattern of the rug belongs to the Clugny family. Both Ferry de Clugny (1410–1483) and his brother Willem (d. 1480)—the two family members who, based on their birth and death dates, could have commissioned the picture—played important roles at the Burgundian court; they were eminent jurists and members of the Grand Council of the Dukes, as well as ambassadors charged with sensitive negotiations. Because Ferry had a distinguished art collection, he is most often proposed as the brother who commissioned this work.

Our panel was perhaps the left wing of an altarpiece like the Columba Triptych. Such a context might account for the feeling of imbalance in the color scheme, with its abundance of intense reds along the right side, as well as the somewhat awkward effect produced by the movement of all the orthogonals toward the upper right corner of the picture. The commissioning of so large and fine an altarpiece would most likely have coincided with a key event in the life of the donor. We know of a number of such events in the careers of the Clugny brothers: in 1465 Ferry de Clugny's Chapelle Dorée at the cathedral of Autun was founded; in 1473 he was named by Charles the Bold as chancellor of the Order of the Golden Fleece; and in 1474 he was consecrated bishop of Tournai; Willem was named bishop of Poitiers in 1477. Our panel bears neither the arms of Tournai nor those of Poitiers, but one or the other could have been present on a separate panel of a larger ensemble. Dendrochronological

Detail, cat. no. 10

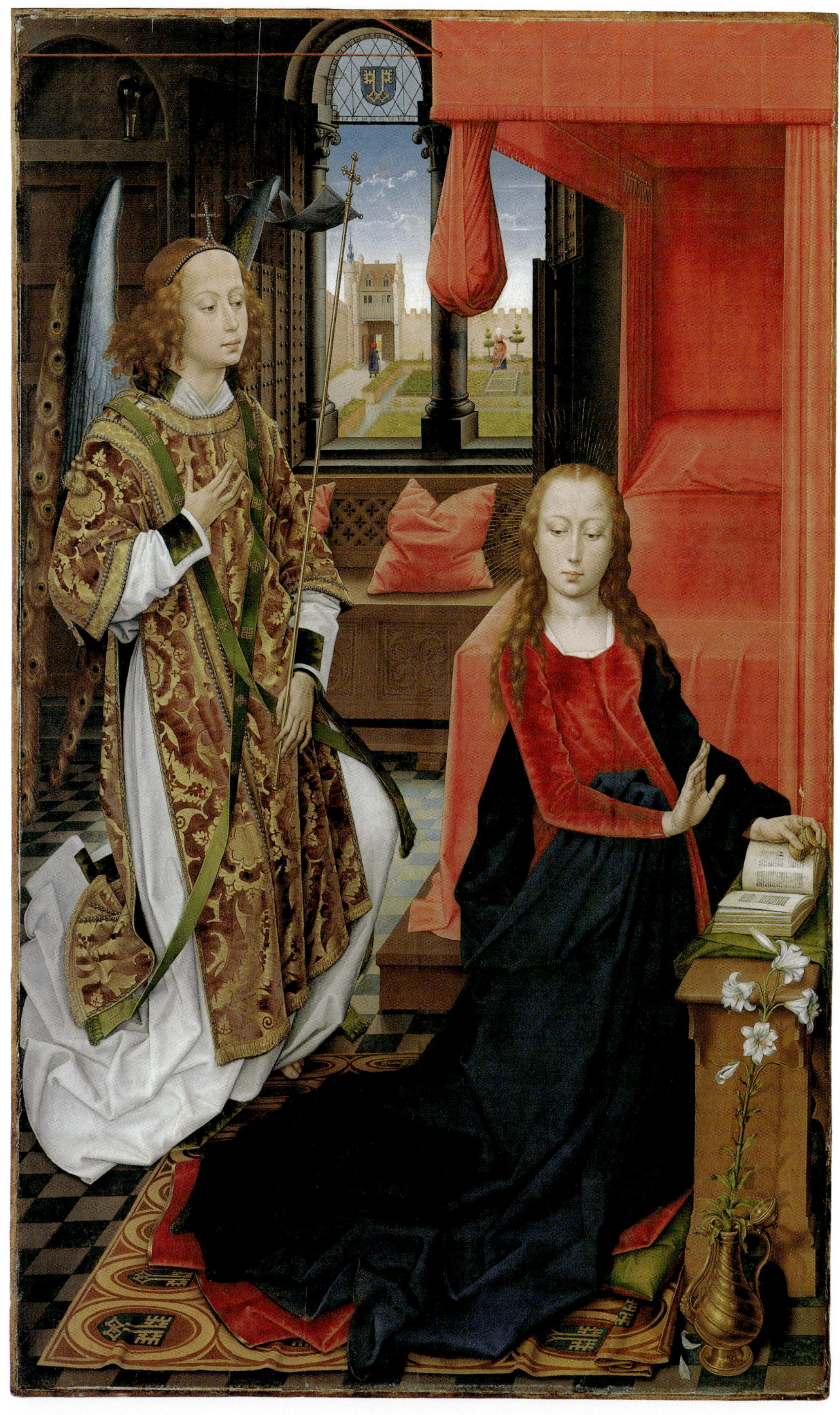

Provenance: Earls of Ashburnham, Ashburnham, Battle, Sussex (by 1878); Bertram Ashburnham, fifth earl of Ashburnham, Ashburnham (1878–1903); [Colnaghi, London (from 1903)]; Rodolphe Kann, Paris (d. 1905); estate of Rodolphe Kann, Paris (1905–7); [Duveen, Paris and New York (1907–8)]; J. Pierpont Morgan, New York (1908–17).

References: Weale 1905a, p. 141, pl. 1; Friedländer 1924–37, vol. 2 (1924), pp. 31, 106, no. 48, pl. 41; Rolland 1932, p. 44; Robb 1936, pp. 511–12, n. 86; Wehle and Salinger 1947, pp. 38–40, ill.; Panofsky 1953, p. 482 n. 1b; Held 1955, p. 227; Friedländer 1967–76, vol. 2 (1967), pp. 69, 100, n. 45, no. 48, pl. 69; Heckscher 1968, p. 64, fig. 7; Davies 1972, p. 229 (New York 3); Dykmans 1983, pp. 23–26; Blum 1992, pp. 43–44; Ainsworth 1994b, p. 80, figs. 6, 7a,b; De Vos 1994b, p. 304; Faries 1997, pp. 243–59.

examination of the *Annunciation* indicates that the picture was most likely produced after about 1470, but this does not exclude a slightly earlier date.

The Annunciation takes place in the Virgin's bedroom while she is reciting her devotions, an iconography that had developed in the Netherlands by the first quarter of the fifteenth century and was standard by midcentury; other characteristic but later examples are Hans Memling's *Annunciation* of 1480–89 (cat. no. 12), Gerard David's *Annunciation* panels of 1506 (cat. no. 79), and Joos van Cleve's *Annunciation* of about 1525 (cat. no. 97). The subject occurs frequently in altarpieces, as it served to remind the faithful of the mystery of the Incarnation, or God becoming man. As Blum has observed, to the fifteenth-century viewer the presence of the bed was a clear sign that the room represented a nuptial chamber in which the Virgin as bride and mother is joined to Christ, her bridegroom and her son, as expressed in the poetic dialogue of the Song of Solomon. The lighted rope-candle (a ball of waxed flax) held by the Virgin may indicate that the moment of her acceptance of her mission and the conception of Christ is still to come; the divine light of God has not yet overwhelmed earth's light as it has in Robert Campin's *Annunciation* (cat. no. 2), with its graphically extinguished candle. In the present picture a candlestick, a first idea discarded in favor of the rope-candle, is visible in the underdrawing just beyond the book. Gabriel wears a splendidly patterned dalmatic whose colors match those of the peacock feathers on his wings, symbolic of eternal life. This garment is the characteristic vestment of the deacon and a reminder of the Eucharist and Christ's sacrifice, reenacted through the celebration of Mass. The lilies in the foreground allude to Mary's purity, and the walled garden seen through the window refers to her chastity.

It has not been possible to firmly establish an attribution for this picture. At one time ascribed to Rogier van der Weyden late in his career, the *Annunciation* has also been attributed to Rogier's school and to a later follower. The most interesting idea, first tentatively advanced by Panofsky, is that the picture was produced by Memling. At first glance the handling, color sensibility, and general sense of design seem no closer to Memling's documented works than to Rogier's. In the past few years, however, the paintings ascribed to Memling's earliest years have been more closely studied, and we now have a different perception of the young artist. The generally held belief that Memling spent a period as a journeyman or an apprentice in Rogier's workshop in Brussels has been confirmed by stylistic evidence; indeed, he was probably active there until Rogier's death in 1464, as he is first recorded in Bruges by 1465.

Ainsworth has again brought up the possibility that our panel might be attributed to Memling, noting the similarity of its underdrawing to that found in the earliest works ascribed to him. The style of the drawing, with long brushstrokes ending in an L or a T shape and shadows formed by even, parallel, and cross-hatching, is generically similar to Rogier's, but the hand is more controlled, even schematic. There are certainly striking similarities between the underdrawing of our panel and that of Memling's altarpiece with the *Last Judgment* of 1467 (Muzeum Narodowe, Gdansk), recently published by Faries. However, in his later work, such as the *Virgin and Child with Saints Catherine of Alexandria and Barbara* (cat. no. 11), Memling employed a very different, looser black-chalk drawing.

It is possible that, as a pupil striving to follow Rogier's manner and working on a scale unfamiliar to him, Memling produced this handsome but somewhat dry painting in about 1464–65. If so, he soon thereafter developed the delicate sensibility that is so consistently present in his works as early as 1467, the year he began the *Last Judgment* (whose figures, to be sure, are considerably smaller than those in our panel). For the moment, and until the completion of further study of Memling's working techniques, it is perhaps wisest to ascribe the picture to a capable apprentice active in Rogier's workshop either during his lifetime or shortly after his death, when the establishment continued to function under the supervision of his son Pieter van der Weyden.

MSdJ

Opposite: Detail, cat. no. 10

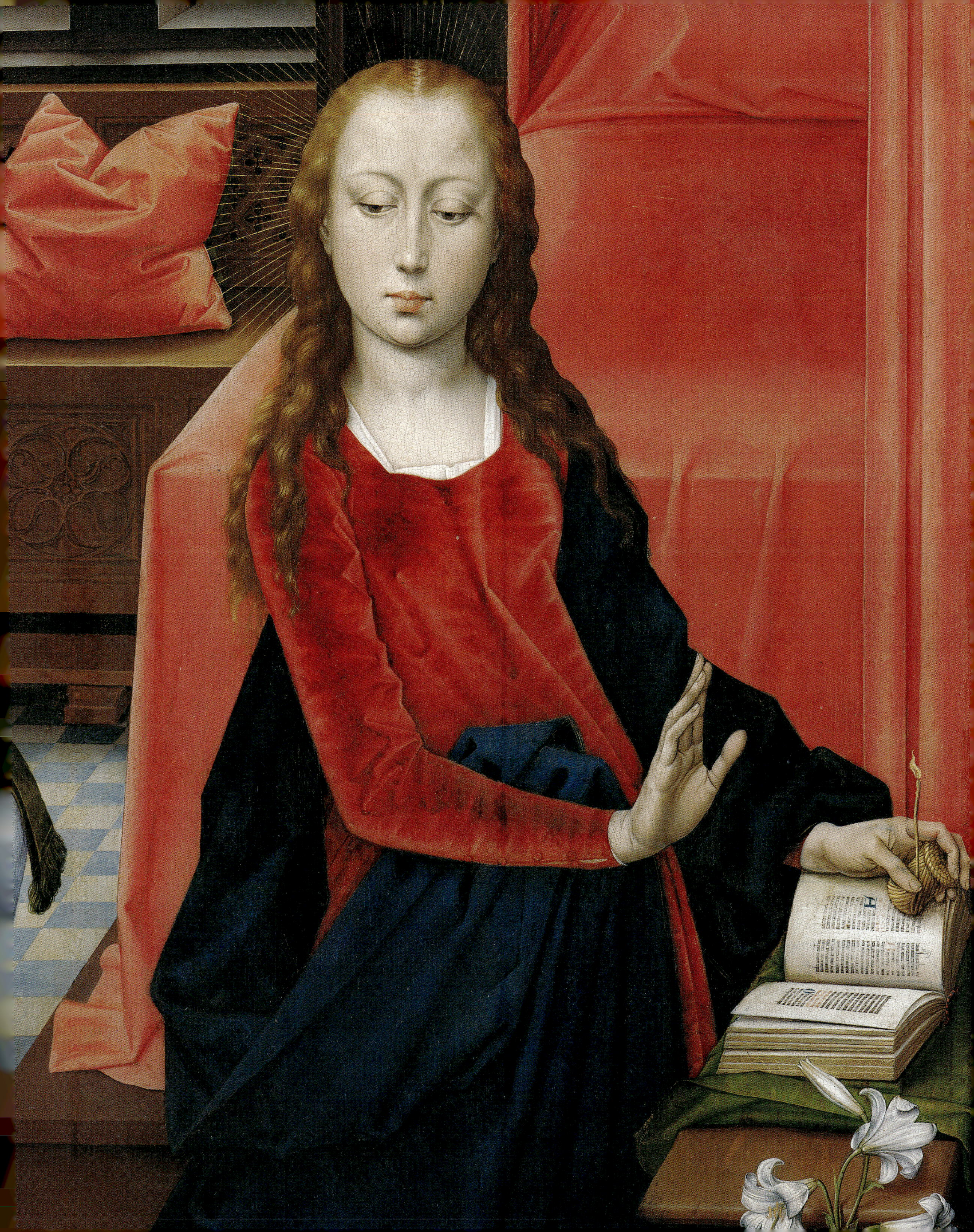

Hans Memling, active by 1465, died 1494

11. Virgin and Child with Saints Catherine of Alexandria and Barbara, early 1480s

Oil on wood; overall 26⅞ x 28⅞ in. (68.3 x 73.3 cm); painted surface 26⅜ x 28⅜ in. (67 x 72.1 cm) Bequest of Benjamin Altman, 1913 14.40.634

Provenance: ?Sir Joshua Reynolds, London; Dr. John Taylor, Ashbourne, Derbyshire; Mrs. Davenport, 2 Church Row, Hampstead, London (1884); her descendant, Mr. Davenport; Mr. G. F. Bodley, London (by 1899–1900); [Colnaghi, London (1900–1901)]; [Léopold Goldschmidt, Paris (1901–d. before 1906)]; [his daughter, Comtesse Gilberte de Sartiges, Château Louveciennes, Seine-et-Oise (by 1906–11)]; [Kleinberger, Paris and New York (1911)]; Benjamin Altman, New York (1911–13).

References: Friedländer 1900, pp. 248–49; Weale 1901, pp. 60–61, ill.; Friedländer 1924–37, vol. 6 (1928), p. 128, no. 65; Wehle and Salinger 1947, pp. 68–70, ill.; Friedländer 1967–76, vol. 6a (1971), p. 54, no. 65, pl. 108; Bauman 1986, pp. 25–26, fig. 18; Ainsworth 1989a, pp. 6, 35, n. 5; Ainsworth 1994a, p. 83, figs. 11, 13a,b; De Vos 1994a, p. 245; De Vos 1994b, pp. 41, 65–66, 154, 166–67, 234, 379–80, no. 35, fig. 27, color ill. p. 167.

In this work Memling takes up a theme familiar from Late Gothic painting—the Virgin in a Garden—updating it with an extensive landscape view. At the left, wearing a crown and dressed in rich brocade, is Saint Catherine of Alexandria, who, according to her legend, was of royal birth. Her attributes, the wheel studded with iron spikes that Emperor Maxentius devised for her martyrdom and the sword with which she was beheaded, are beside her. She extends her left hand, and Christ places a ring on her finger, symbolic of her spiritual betrothal to God. At the right Saint Barbara, another virgin martyr, is reading from a devotional book. Behind her is the tower where, legend tells, her jealous father imprisoned her to discourage suitors. It was in this tower that she was secretly baptized a Christian; the three windows may symbolize the Father, Son, and Holy Ghost. Angels in priestly robes play the harp and portable organ on either side of the Virgin; her attribute, the iris, or sword lily, grows behind her to the left. At the extreme left, in black, the youthful male donor is reciting the rosary. At the level of his hip, and barely discernible, with white details picked out against the black background, is an element that De Vos (1994b) has tentatively identified as the emblem or coat of arms of a guild but which may instead be a small purse ornamented with seed pearls and ermine.

The composition is freely adapted from Memling's large altarpiece of Saints John the Baptist and John the Evangelist, painted for the Sint-Janshospitaal in Bruges and dedicated there following its completion in 1479. The setting in that work, however, is a columned interior. Memling made a smaller, related altarpiece (National Gallery, London) for the English patron Sir John Donne, who presumably commissioned it upon seeing the 1479 picture during a visit to Bruges, and it seems likely that the Bruges model was mentioned in the contracts for both the Donne triptych and our panel. Indeed, Saints Catherine and Barbara in our painting are virtually identical in type, costume, and gesture to their counterparts in the Bruges altarpiece; however, the pattern of drapery folds differs significantly, and infrared reflectography reveals spontaneous and rather detailed underdrawing in our picture. It is probable, as De Vos (1994b) conjectures, that the Bruges altarpiece was based on preliminary studies made in the workshop and that these also served as the basis for our panel's freely sketched composition.

The grape arbor, symbol of the Eucharist, was painted over the original landscape by a later hand, presumably to satisfy the devotional requirements of an owner. The existence of an early, possibly sixteenth-century copy of the painting in the Accademia, Venice, that includes the arbor suggests that this element was added shortly after Memling's lifetime. The cult of the Eucharist was extremely popular in the early sixteenth century, and clusters of grapes appear frequently in devotional works of the period. In at least two paintings depicting the Virgin among Virgins in an Enclosed Garden (Detroit Institute of Arts and Musées Royaux des Beaux-Arts de Belgique, Brussels), the Master of the Legend of Saint Lucy, active in Bruges from about 1475 to 1505, used a grape arbor as a leafy frame that arches over the top of his composition.

This panel and the Bruges and London altarpieces are among the earliest expressions of what might be called Memling's classic phase. The artist has settled on certain successful female types: the face is a graceful oval, wider across the eyes, narrowing at the chin, and tends to reflect a state of

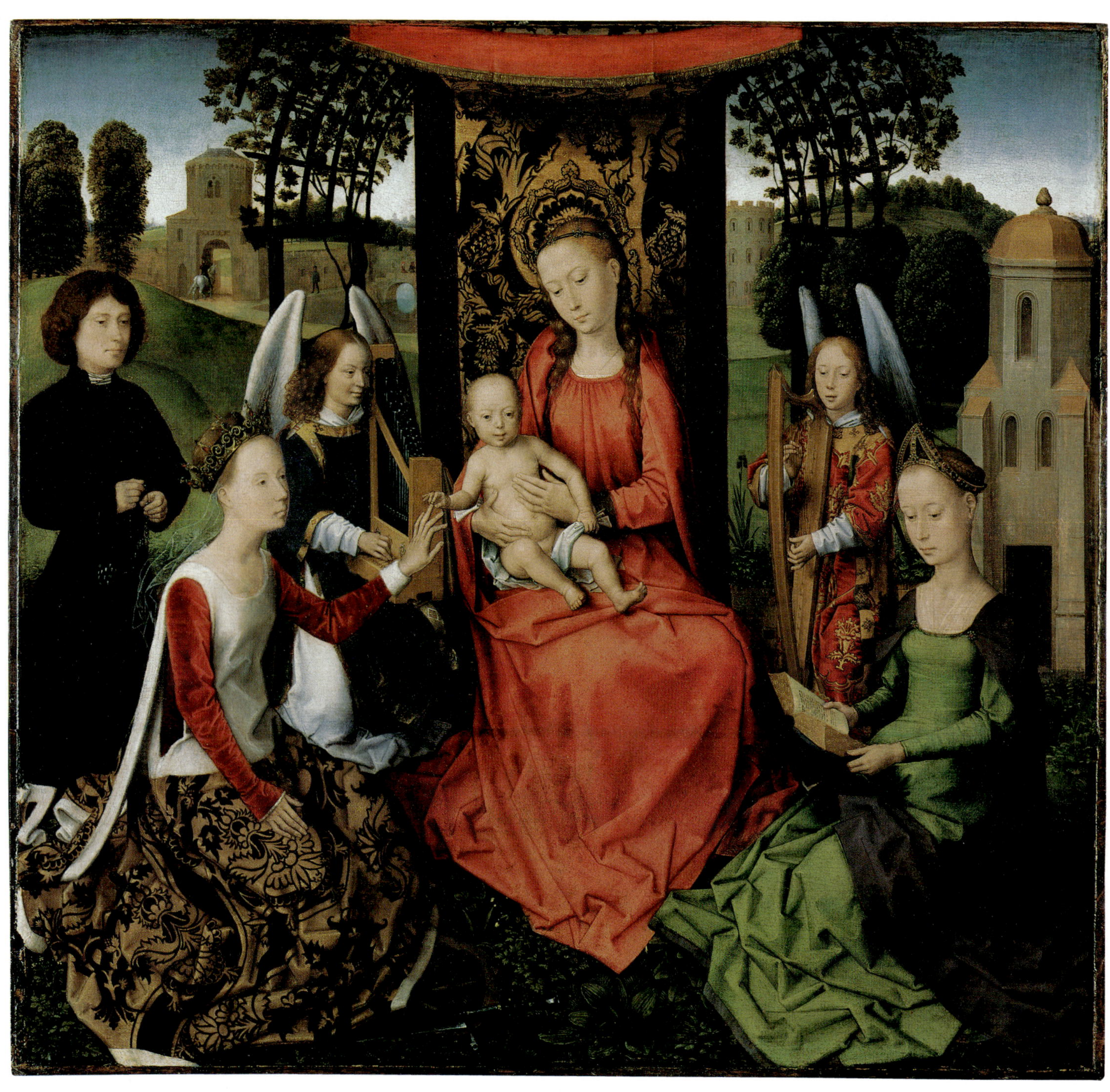

gentle, beatific acceptance. The compositions are carefully constructed, in pursuit of the greatest effect of balance and harmony. The light and color are bright and clear, and the pure air of paradise seems to circulate before, behind, and among the figures.

MSdJ

Hans Memling, active by 1465, died 1494

12. The Annunciation, 1480–89

Oil on canvas, transferred from wood, overall 30⅛ x 21½ in. (76.5 x 54.6 cm); original painted surface 30 x 21⅛ in. (76.2 x 53.6 cm)
Robert Lehman Collection, 1975 1975.1.113

Provenance: Prince Michael Radziwill (d. 1831); his son, Prince Anton Radziwill, Berlin (by 1832–d. 1833); his son, Prince William Radziwill, Berlin (d. 1870); by descent, Prince George Radziwill (d. 1904); his widow, Marie Branicka, Princess Radziwill (until 1920); sold by her to Philip Lehman, through Joseph Duveen; Philip Lehman, New York (from October 1920).

References: Boisserée (1808–54) 1978–95, vol. 2, p. 654; Waagen 1847, pp. 186–87; Förster 1860, vol. 2, p. 117; Friedländer 1903, pp. 83–84, no. 85; Weale 1903a, p. 35; Friedländer 1924–37, vol. 6 (1928), p. 121, no. 26, pl. 24; Friedländer 1967–76, vol. 6a (1971), p. 49, no. 26, pl. 79; Blum 1992, pp. 43–58, figs. 1, 4; Ainsworth 1994a, p. 87; De Vos 1994b, pp. 304–6, no. 84, ills.; Wolff 1998, no. 14, color ill.

The archangel Gabriel enters the Virgin's bedroom holding a scepter and wearing a richly ornamented cope bordered by symbols of the Evangelists; he is dressed as a priest would be for the celebration of Mass. Frequently depicted in this manner in Netherlandish art of the period, the archangel's ecclesiastical splendor is comparable in Annunciations by a follower of Rogier van der Weyden, Gerard David, and Joos van Cleve (cat. nos. 10, 79, 97).

Gabriel honors Mary by approaching her with his knees bent, and she, in response, seems at once to rise from her devotions and to swoon at his greeting. Her protruding belly and the Dove of the Holy Spirit hovering over her head confirm that the Incarnation has already taken place. While her right hand is raised in a gesture of reflection or humility, her left indicates an open prayer book (the D probably stands for *Dominus tecum* [the Lord be with you]). The Virgin is part of an unfolding drama but also an object of meditation and veneration, displayed to the viewer "as a monstrance containing the Host" (De Vos) by two angels who act as acolytes, one lifting the hem of her robe, the other soliciting our response. Mary's swooning body would have reminded a contemporary viewer of her traditional pose in representations of the Crucifixion, Deposition, and Lamentation—thus anticipating Christ's sacrifice for the salvation of mankind at the moment of his conception. Behind this group, lit from a window at the left, is an assortment of objects alluding to the qualities of the Virgin: the womb-shaped flask of clear water remains undisturbed by the light passing through it in the same way that the Virgin remains pure when her son is conceived; the unlighted rope wick and the candlestick that holds no candle symbolize the world prior to the Annunciation and birth of the Savior, herald of divine light. The lily and iris in the foreground refer to Mary's purity and her suffering through the sacrifice of Christ. The theme of the picture is doubtless set by the symbol of Saint John the Evangelist, prominently displayed on the cope over Gabriel's raised arm. John, who does not describe the Annunciation in the Gospels, articulates its theological meaning: "And the Word was made flesh."

Like the Morgan *Annunciation* (cat. no. 10), this composition takes as a starting point Rogier van der Weyden's highly influential Annunciation from the Columba Altarpiece of the mid-1450s (Alte Pinakothek, Munich) and also borrows elements from an earlier Rogierian *Annunciation* of about 1435 (Louvre, Paris). With the introduction of a swooning rather than a kneeling or standing Virgin and two attendant angels, however, Memling has created a startlingly original image, rich in connotations for the viewer or worshiper.

The painting's original frame, which was removed in the early nineteenth century, was evidently dated, and an inscribed portion of it was preserved for a time. Most early scholars, including Waagen, cite the date on this fragment as 1482. Boisserée, however, who saw the painting in 1832, records the date as 1480, and De Vos has recently suggested this was a misreading of 1489, a date that would make the picture contemporary with Memling's Greveraade Triptych (Sankt-Annen-Museum, Lübeck), which he finds it close to stylistically.

Whether this painting was an independent work or part of a larger ensemble is not clear. Its size and the sacramental nature of its subject would have been appropriate for a family chapel in a church or monastery or for the chapel of a guild corporation.

MSdJ

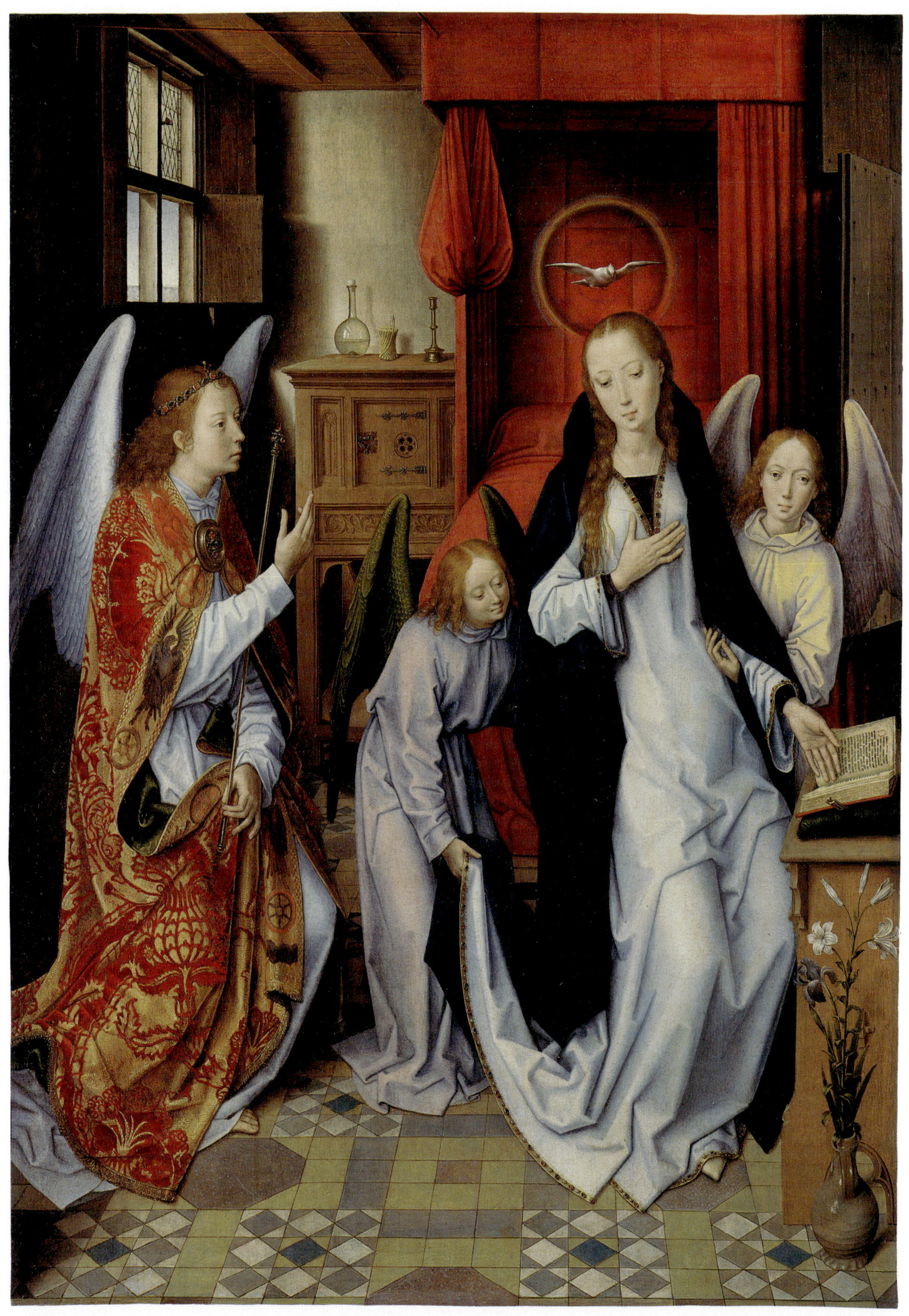

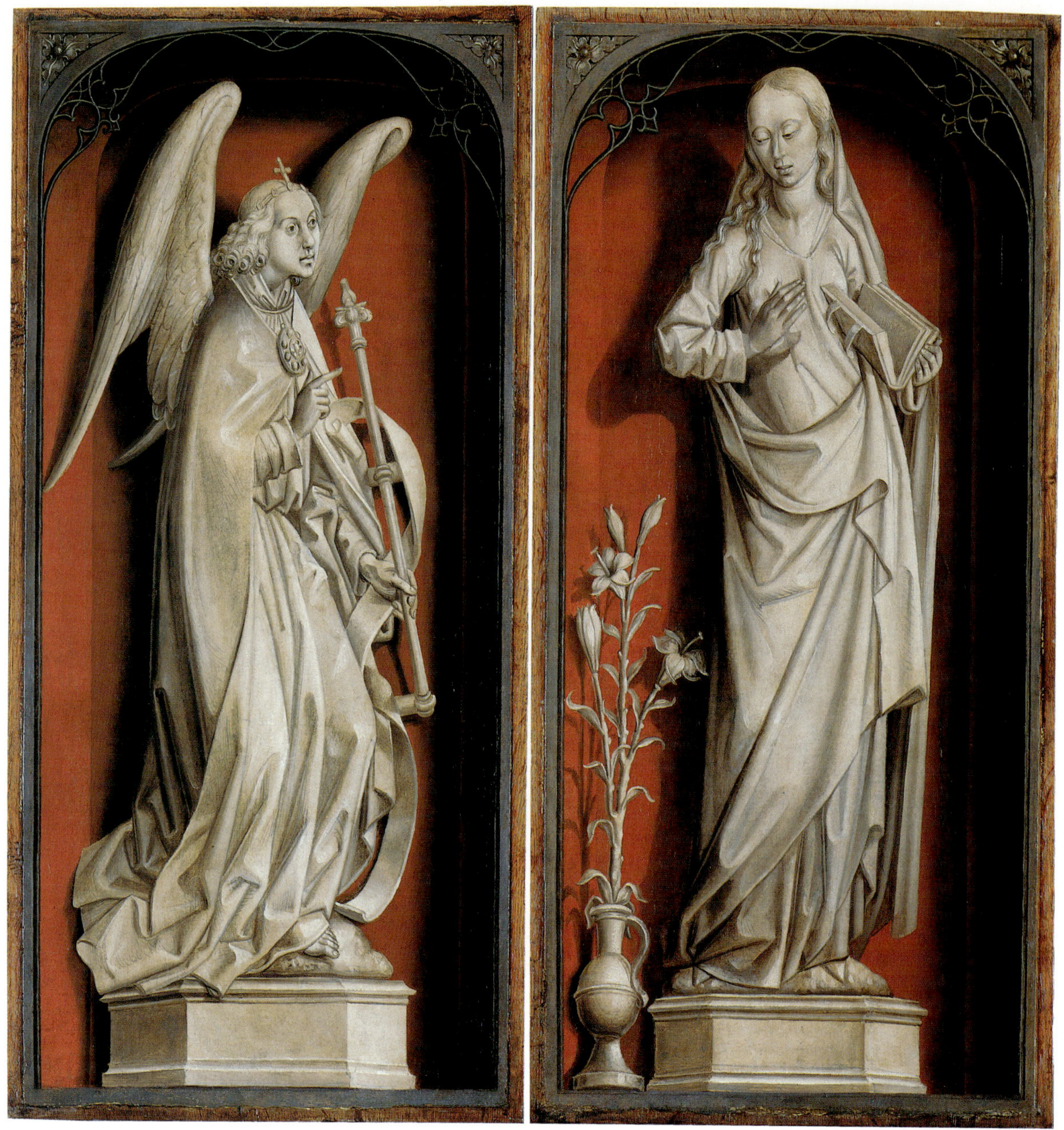

Closed

Master of the Saint Barbara Legend, active late 15th century

13. Abner's Messenger before David(?); The Queen of Sheba Bringing Gifts to Solomon; (verso) *The Annunciation,* about 1480

Oil on wood, each panel 36¾ x 17⅝ in. (93.3 x 44.8 cm)
The Friedsam Collection, Bequest of Michael Friedsam, 1931 32.100.56a-d

These panels originally formed a triptych with an *Adoration of the Magi* (fig. 51) as the central panel. The Queen of Sheba presenting gifts to Solomon (1 Kings 10:10), on the right wing, is an Old Testament prefiguration of the magi bringing gifts to the Christ Child. David, like Solomon, an Old Testament king—and an ancestor of Christ—is enthroned in the left wing, receiving a messenger who is probably one sent by Abner, ruler of the house of Saul; this messenger, the Bible tells us, was

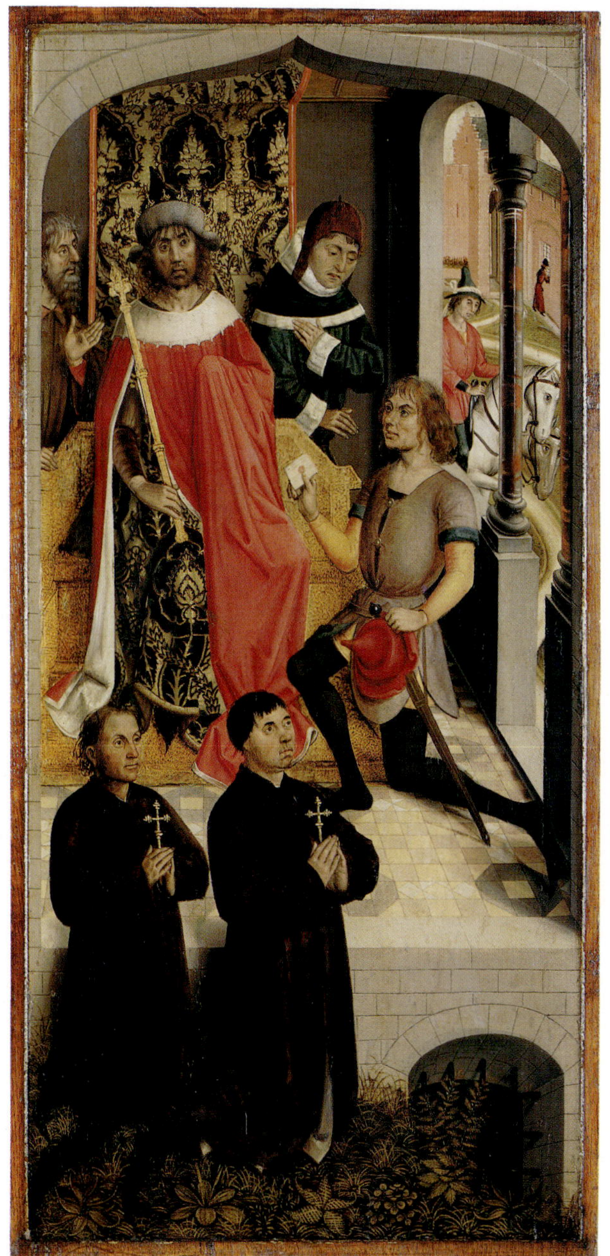

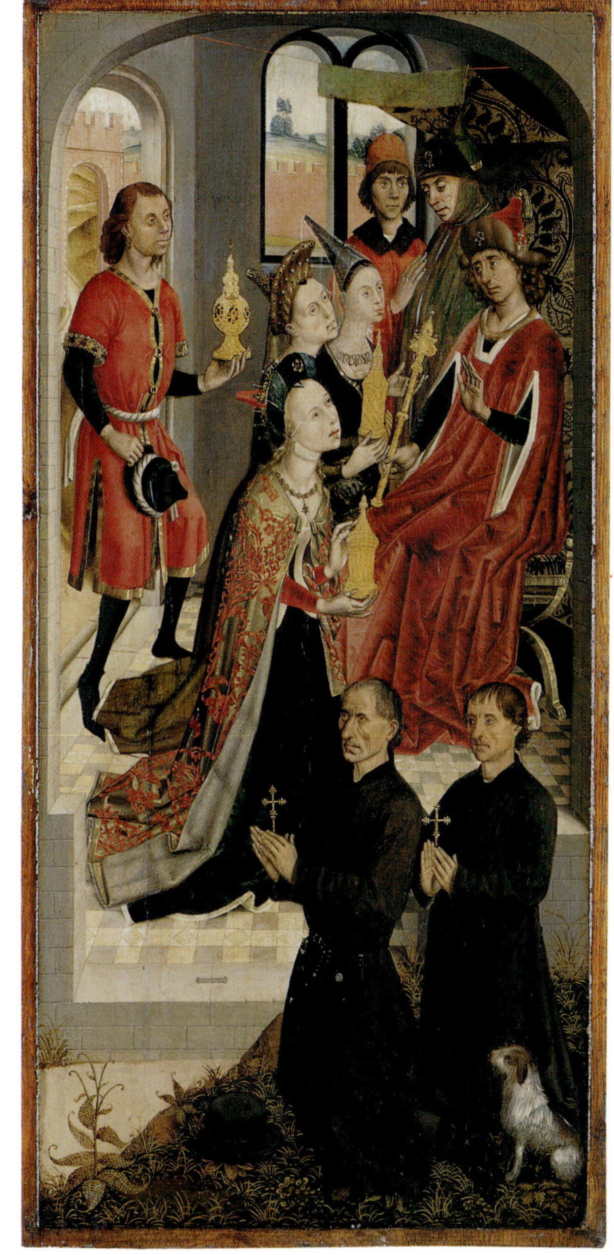

Open

dispatched to inform David that Abner will help deliver Saul's kingdom to him and thus make him ruler over all Israel (2 Samuel 3:12). Although unusual, this iconographic program also appears on the Epiphany page of an illustrated *Biblia Pauperum* published in Haarlem in the 1430s. The four similarly dressed donors kneeling in the foreground, probably members of a guild, lay confraternity, or civic group, may have died in the plague of 1489–90, which could account for the crosses above their hands, added after the picture was completed.

The rough-hewn, provincial style of our panels and of the central element is typical of the works of the Master of the Saint Barbara Legend, as are the crowded and somewhat chaotic arrangement of the figures, the variety of fanciful architectural settings, and the lively feeling for narrative. The artist, who was probably active in Brussels, was influ-

Provenance: G. Aelbrechts, Brussels (1886); Charles Léon Cardon, Brussels (1902); [Kleinberger, New York (1920)]; Michael Friedsam, New York (1920–31).

References: Brussels 1886, nos. 103, 104; Hulin de Loo 1902, p. 26, no. 110; Friedländer 1903, p. 75; Friedländer 1924–25, p. 23; Friedländer 1924–37, vol. 4 (1926), pp. 111–12, 141, no. 68; Burroughs and Wehle 1932, p. 22; Wehle and Salinger 1947, pp. 78–80; Zeri 1960, pp. 44–45, pls. 20–23; Gibson 1965, pp. 504–6, figs. 1, 2; Cuttler 1968, p. 183; Friedländer 1967–76, vol. 4 (1969), pp. 61–62, 79, 98–99, 106, n. 101, no. 68, pl. 63; Bauman 1986, pp. 26–27, ills.; Périer-d'Ieteren 1989–91, p. 169.

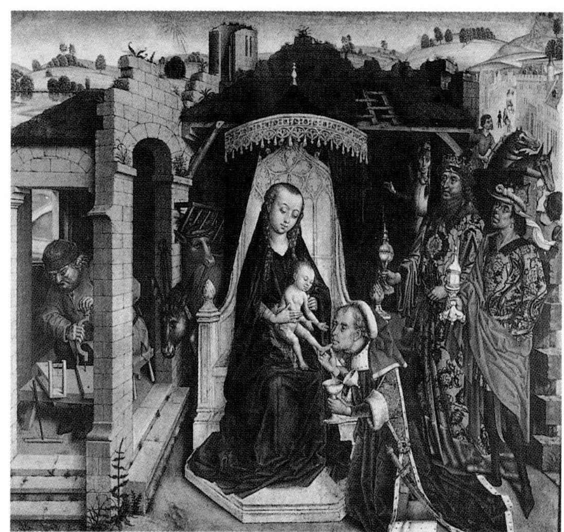

Fig. 51. Master of the Saint Barbara Legend, *The Adoration of the Magi,* central panel of a triptych, about 1480. Oil on wood. Galleria Colonna, Rome

enced by both Rogier van der Weyden and Dieric Bouts, and the composition of the right wing is clearly dependent upon Bouts's *Ordeal by Fire,* from 1471–73, a panel from the *Justice of Emperor Otto* (Musées Royaux des Beaux-Arts de Belgique, Brussels), originally installed in the Town Hall of Leuven.

Midway between craftsmen and artists, the minor masters active in the Netherlands during the late fifteenth and early sixteenth centuries depended upon help from their workshops and also collaborated with one another in order to meet the great demand for Netherlandish works in cities along the European trade routes. Périer-d'Ieteren has suggested that only the heads in our panels are by the Master of the Saint Barbara Legend, the remainder of the compositions being by a workshop assistant. There are, however, no compelling differences between the handling of the figures, draperies, and setting in these paintings and that of the master's eponymous work, *Scenes from the Legend of Saint Barbara,* divided between the Museum van het Heilig Bloed, Bruges, and the Musées Royaux des Beaux-Arts de Belgique, Brussels.

The two panels showing the Annunciation were the reverse sides of the narrative scenes and would have been visible when the wings of the altarpiece were closed. They are painted in grisaille, in imitation of stone sculpture. MSdJ

Master of the Saint Ursula Legend, active late 15th century

14. Saint Paul with Paolo Pagagnotti; Christ Appearing to His Mother, late 1480s

Oil on wood, (a) overall 37⅜ x 11⅜ in. (94.9 x 28.9 cm); (a) painted surface 36¾ x 10⅞ in. (93.4 x 27.6 cm); (b) overall 37¼ x 11¼ in. (94.6 x 28.6 cm); (b) painted surface 36¾ x 10¾ in. (93.4 x 27.3 cm)
The Friedsam Collection, Bequest of Michael Friedsam, 1931 32.100.63ab

It has recently been established by Rohlmann (1995) that these paintings are the interior wings of a folding triptych with a Virgin and Child with Angels as the central panel (fig. 53); exterior wings, which have been cut down at the top, represent the Ecce Homo in grisaille (fig. 52). Rohlmann recognized the coats of arms on the central panel as those of the Pagagnotti family of Florence and identified the patron as Paolo Pagagnotti, shown in our picture kneeling, presented to the Virgin by his patron saint, Paul. Paolo Pagagnotti was a merchant and may have commissioned the altarpiece in Bruges in the late 1480s, when he was traveling outside of Italy.

At about the same time a triptych by Hans Memling—with the Virgin and Child Enthroned (fig. 37) and Saints John the Baptist and Lawrence (National Gallery, London)—was ordered for Paolo's uncle, the learned Dominican Benedetto Pagagnotti. This work dates after 1484, when Benedetto was elected bishop of Vaison, and it may have been commissioned by Paolo or by one of the Medici agents in Bruges, as the Pagagnotti were closely allied with the Medici. Memling's triptych must have remained intact in Florence for some time, as the wings were in the hospital of Santa Maria Nuova until they were transferred to the

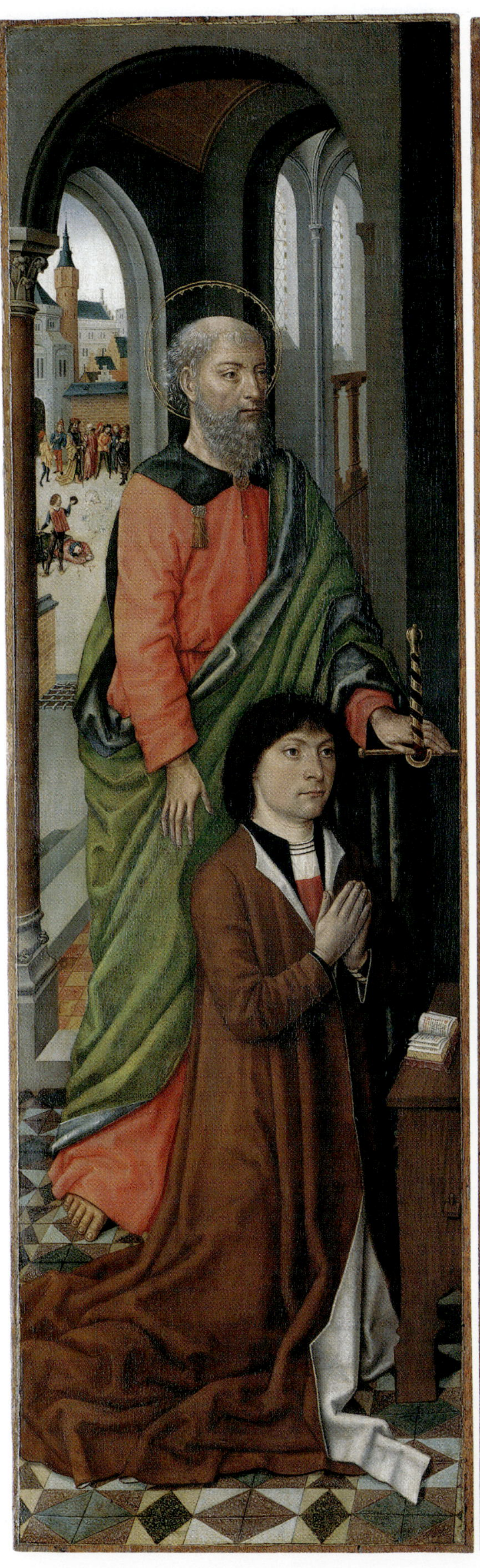

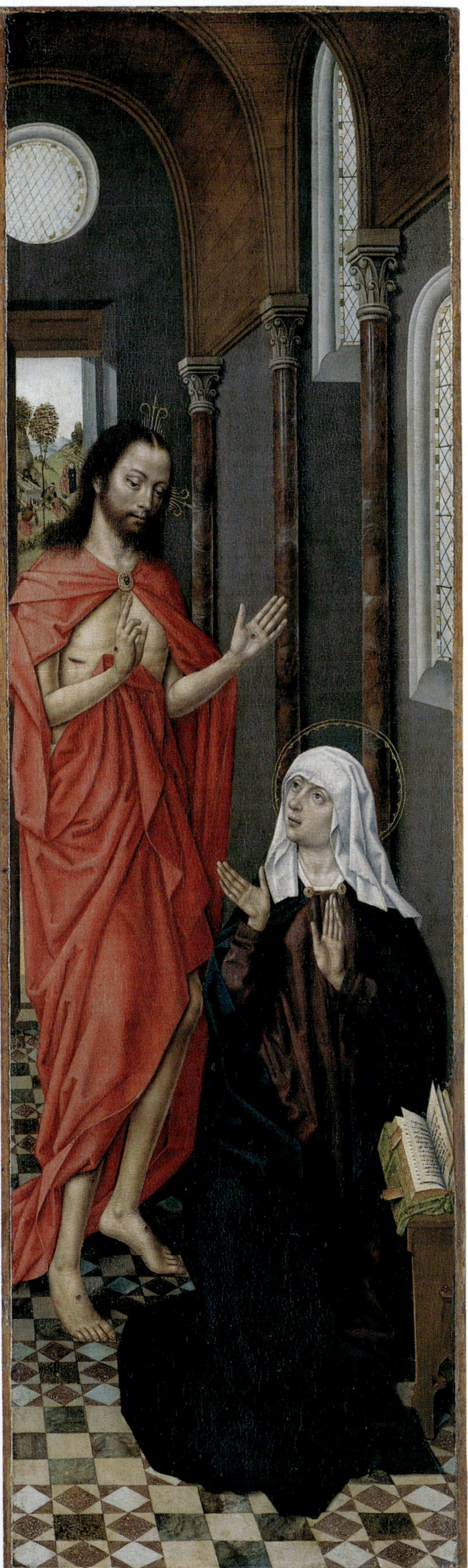

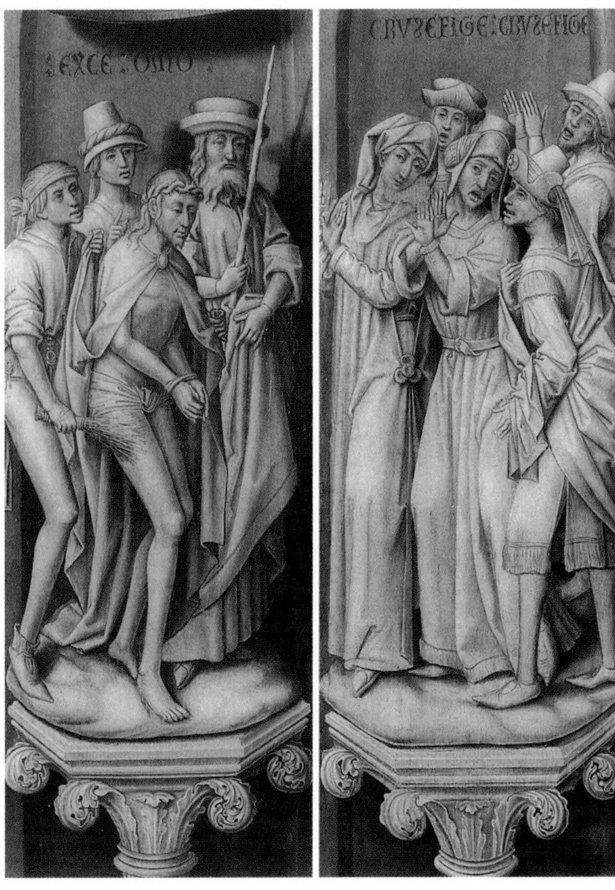

Fig. 52. Master of the Saint Ursula Legend, *Ecce Homo,* exterior wings of a triptych, late 1480s. Oil on wood. Museo Bandini, Fiesole

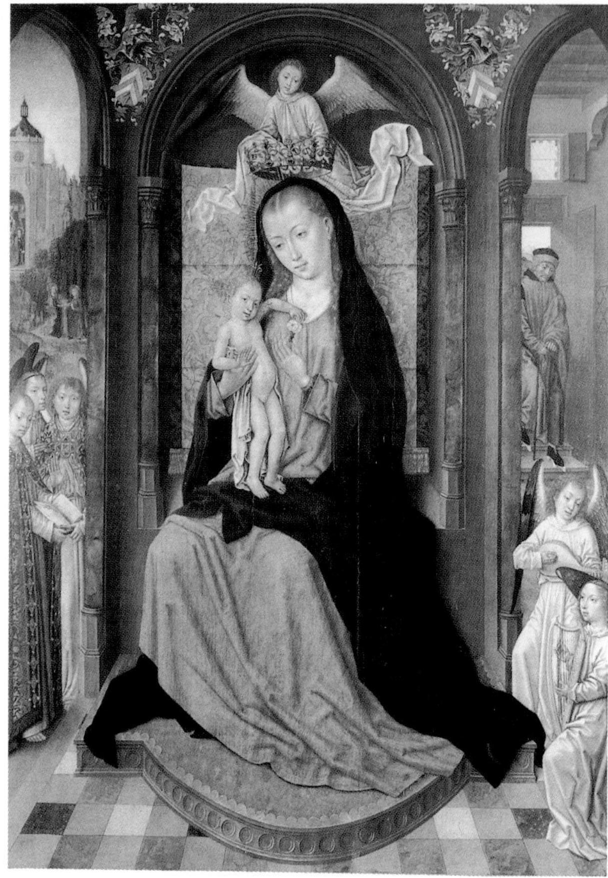

Fig. 53. Master of the Saint Ursula Legend, *Virgin and Child with Angels,* central panel of a triptych, late 1480s. Oil on wood. Musée Thomas-Henry, Cherbourg

Provenance: Marchese Ferroni, Florence; [Kleinberger, New York (1924)]; Michael Friedsam, New York (1924–31).

References: Friedländer 1924–37, vol. 6 (1928), p. 137, no. 117, pl. 52; Wehle and Salinger 1947, pp. 76–77, ill.; Marlier 1964, p. 37, no. 29; Friedländer 1967–76, vol. 6a (1971), p. 60, no. 117, pl. 143; Davies 1972, p. 215; De Vos 1986; Hand and Wolff 1986, pp. 254–56, n. 15; Levine 1989, pp. 21, 47, 53, 72, 108–12, 118 n. 77, 141, 166–71, 184; Rohlmann 1994, pp. 69–70; Rohlmann 1995, pp. 439–41.

Uffizi in 1852. The panels were studied by Fra Bartolomeo, whose Virgin and Child in the Metropolitan Museum (inv. no. 06.171) copies details of the landscape background. Although there are no known quotes by Florentine artists of the Master of the Saint Ursula Legend's triptych, it too must have been in Italy for an extended period, as our wings belonged to the Marchese Ferroni in Florence in 1924 and the exterior wings are still in Fiesole.

When open, the triptych with our pictures had the appearance of a series of interior spaces offering exterior views. In the left panel, through the open arch behind Saint Paul, is depicted the apostle's beheading in a city square. In the right panel, which shows Christ appearing to his mother—a scene taken from the Pseudo-Bonaventure's *Meditations on the Life of Christ*—we see in the distance, through the rear door of the chapel, the Virgin and Mary Magdalene approaching the tomb of Christ, which is still sealed.

Influenced primarily by Rogier van der Weyden, the Master of the Saint Ursula Legend was a contemporary of Memling's in Bruges. The long, rather stiff figures in our panels that fit narrowly into their compositions, as well as the modeling of flesh in gray tones, are characteristic of our artist, who, like the Master of the Saint Barbara Legend, was one of a group of highly productive lesser Netherlandish painters working for the mass market in the late fifteenth and early sixteenth centuries.

The composition of the right wing is loosely derived from Rogier's *Christ Appearing to His Mother*, the right wing of his Miraflores Triptych (Gemäldegalerie, Berlin; see entry for cat. no. 46). Two panels with similar compositions, both ascribed to followers of Rogier (National Gallery of Art, Washington, D.C., and National Gallery, London), suggest that there may have been an intermediate prototype.

MSdJ

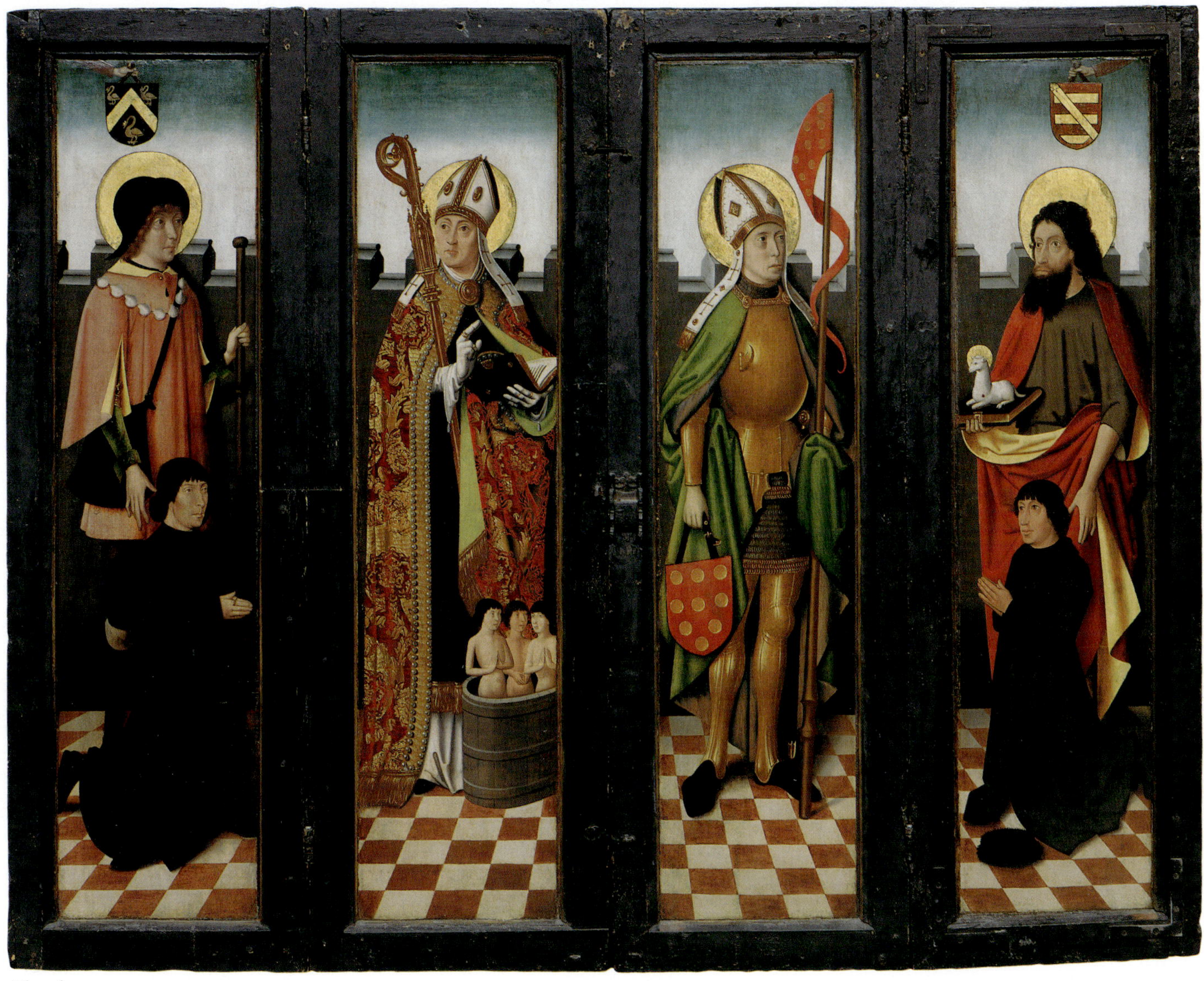

Closed

Master of the Saint Godelieve Legend,

active last quarter of 15th century

15. *The Life and Miracles of Saint Godelieve,* last quarter of 15th century

Oil on wood; open 49¼ x 126⅜ in. (125.1 x 311 cm); closed 49¼ x 63¼ in. (125.1 x 160.7 cm)
Unidentified arms (exterior)
John Stewart Kennedy Fund, 1912 12.79

The increased interest in the cult of saints in the late fifteenth century gave rise to a new form of altarpiece that portrayed the details of saints' lives in multiple episodes and in dramatic narrative style. Our altarpiece, which illustrates events in the life of Godelieve, may have been commissioned by the Guild of the Load Bearers of Onze-Lieve-Vrouw Brug (Bridge of Our Lady), whose patron saint was Godelieve, and was perhaps displayed in their chapel in the Onze-Lieve-Vrouwekerk at Bruges.

When closed, the four exterior panels depict a continuous space—a checkered floor before a crenellated wall—in which stand four saints divided into two facing pairs. The figures are, from left to right: Saint Josse, venerated in the region of Montreuil-sur-Cher, with a donor; Saint Nicholas of

Provenance: Baron Anselme de Peellaert (1795–ca. 1817); Pierre Bortier of Dixmude, chapel of abbey of Saint Godelieve, Ghistelles (ca. 1817–29); his nephew, Pierre Bortier, chapel of abbey of Saint Godelieve (ca. 1829–80); Jul. de Geyter, Antwerp (1830–ca. 1882); private collection, Germany (ca. 1882); A. Tollin, Paris (sale, Galerie Georges Petit, Paris, May 20, 1897, no. 113); Jean Dollfus, Paris ([from 1897]; sale, Galerie Georges Petit, Paris, March 2, 1912, no. 87); [Seligmann, Paris].

References: Versnaeyen 1865, p. 61; Van de Poele 1898, pp. 41–42; Burroughs 1912, pp. 126–28, ill.; Wehle and Salinger 1947, pp. 84–88, ill.; Croquez 1948; Panofsky 1953, pp. 216 n. 4, 218 n. 6, 346 n. 17; Haverkamp-Begemann 1955, pp. 194–96, ill.; Wilenski 1960, vol. 1, pp. 83, 85–88, 93, vol. 2, pls. 140–45; Madou 1970, pp. 40–43; De Vos 1979, p. 141; De Vos 1982, p. 141; Puydt 1984, pp. 163–65, ill.; Faries, Heller, and Levine 1987, p. 19, n. 14; D. Martins 1992, pp. 149–64; Cuvelier and Watrin 1989, pp. 185–89, 191; Toussaint 1994, pp. 497–99, color ill.; Kasl, verbal communication, Dec. 1997.

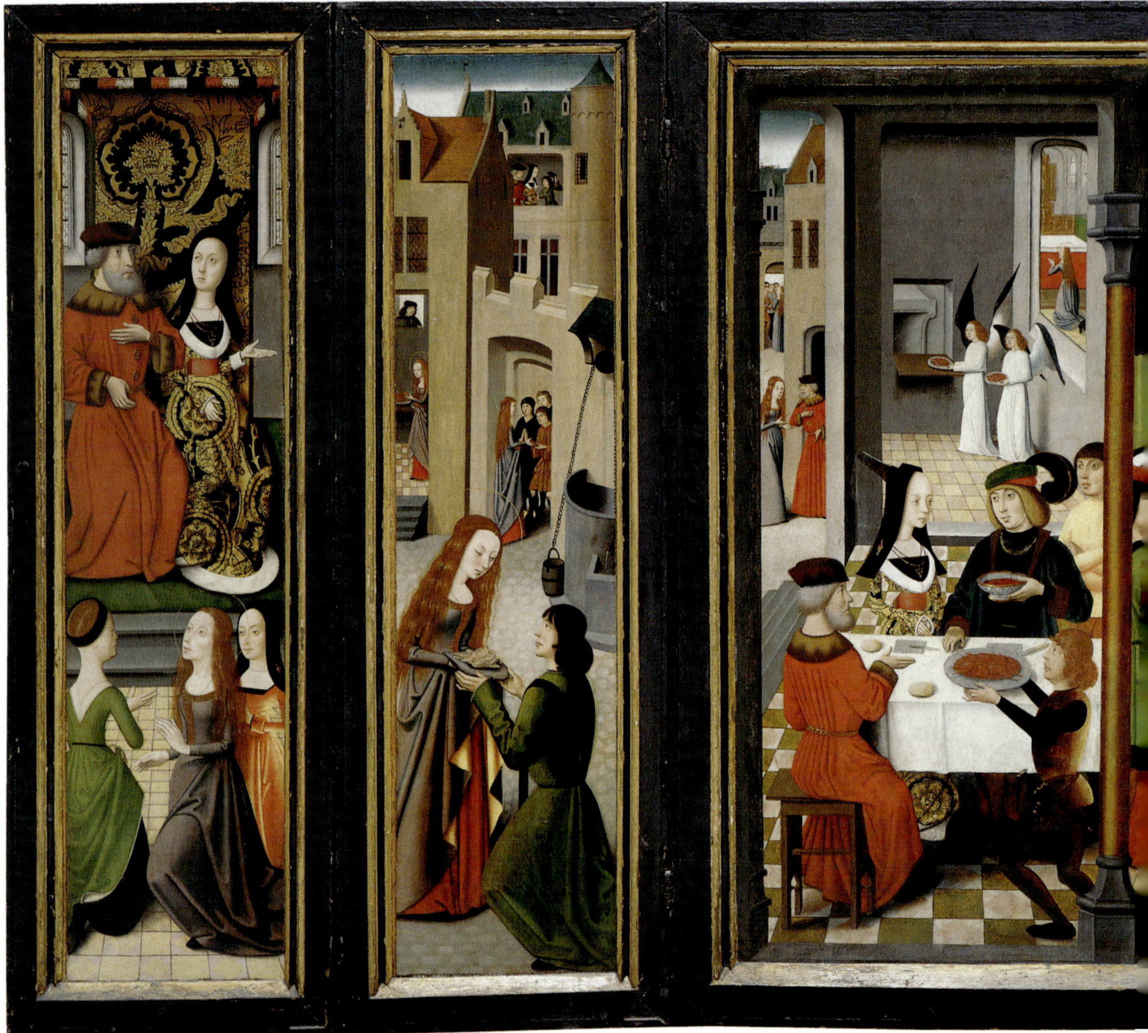

15 open

Bari; Saint Quirinus, revered in Hooglede, in Flanders; and Saint John the Baptist, with another donor. Each of the outer panels contains a coat of arms held in place by a hand and an arm, which probably served to identify the donors.

The interior of the altarpiece is the most complete existing monument to the life and miracles of Saint Godelieve, martyr of Ghistelles, near Bruges, and patroness of Flanders, whose story is told in detail in the *Acta Sanctorum* (vol. 29, Julius, part 2, pp. 359–444). Godelieve was born about 1049 in the château of Londefort, in the village of Wierre-Effroy, near Marquise, in Boulonnais, died in 1070, and was canonized in 1084. Thirty-one scenes are spread unevenly over the seven sections of the altarpiece. Godelieve appears in twenty-two episodes, in eighteen of which she is identified by her halo. The unvarying costumes of the other characters serve to identify them. Godelieve, however, appears in several types of apparel that reflect changes in her situation: she wears a plain dress as a maiden, her wedding gown, two different costumes as a married woman, and, finally, a white shift after her death.

The saint's story begins on the left and proceeds to the right. The first panel shows her as a devout daughter with her prosperous family: in the background are her parents, Heinfried and Odgive, and in front of them her two sisters, Ogena and Adèle, appear on either side of Godelieve herself. The next panel depicts Godelieve as the benefactress of the poor: the maiden distributing food from her father's larder (center right); her parents conferring with a servant about her activity (upper right); the servant following her (center left); and the food miraculously

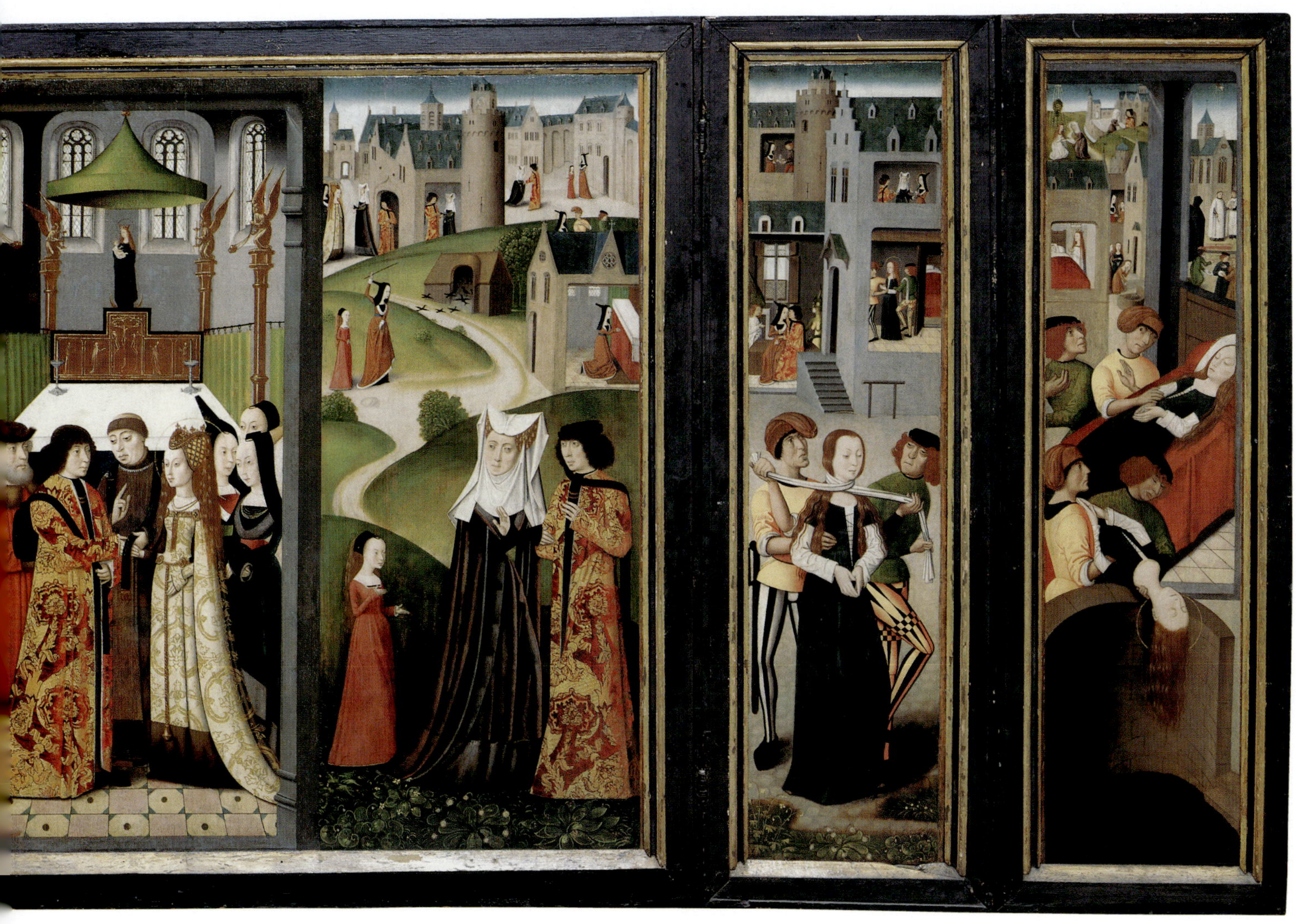

turning into wood chips when he asks to see the contents of her apron (foreground). The scenes at the left of the main panel portray Godelieve's gift to the poor of delicacies prepared for the feast her parents will give for the count of Boulogne (upper left); Godelieve's father admonishing her for her act upon her return home (center left); the young woman's second miracle, angels bearing food for the meal in answer to her prayers (upper right); and the feast itself (foreground).

The middle section of the central panel represents the wedding of Godelieve and Bertolf, a wealthy landowner from Ghistelles. In the next scenes, at the right side of the main section, Godelieve arrives at Bertolf's home and meets her nemesis, his mother, Iselinde, who hates her at first sight (upper left); Iselinde conspires with her son against Godelieve (upper center); Iselinde and Bertolf assign a maid to spy on her (upper right); the maid witnesses the crows obeying Godelieve, who has persuaded them to stay out of the fields and remain in a little hut whose door she has left open (center left) while she attends Mass (center right); the prattling maid reveals what she has seen, which she interprets as the result of witchcraft, to Iselinde and Bertolf (foreground); and Lambert and Hacca, hired by Bertolf, take Godelieve away (upper right, above the church).

In the background of the panel to the right of the central scenes, food is delivered to the room in which the young woman is imprisoned (upper left); Iselinde intercedes between Bertolf and Godelieve (upper right); husband and wife reconcile falsely, Godelieve is attended by an angel and Bertolf by a devil (center left); the victim is led from her bed by

Lambert and Hacca (center right); and in the foreground Lambert and Hacca strangle Godelieve.

The narrative in the last panel begins in the foreground, with the final acts of Lambert and Hacca, who cleanse the murdered woman's face by dipping it in a well and return her body to bed. The upper half of the panel portrays later posthumous events: Godelieve's ghost stands by the bed in which she was found dead (center left); the ground at the site of her burial is transformed into little white stones (upper right); the sight of Edith, Bertolf's daughter by his second marriage, is restored by water from the well into which Godelieve's head was plunged (center bottom); Edith reports this miracle (center top); Godelieve delivers a garment to a seamstress (upper left); and, finally, the seamstress puts the costume into the hands of Bertolf, who recognizes the distinctive stitches of his martyred wife (upper center).

This polyptych is the eponymous work of the Master of the Saint Godelieve Legend, who produced only a small group of other paintings. Among these are two other triptychs, one of the Passion in the Carthusian monastery at Miraflores, Spain, and the other a Pietà in the Onze-Lieve-Vrouwekerk in Bruges; a polyptych showing the Legend of Saint James the Great (Indianapolis Museum of Art) is a recent attribution by Kasl. The Master of the Saint Godelieve Legend appears to have come from either Ghistelles or Bruges itself, and his work may be related to that of painters from Bruges, specifically the Master of the Saint Lucy Legend and the Master of the Saint Ursula Legend. There is a copy of our altarpiece dated 1622 (Gruuthusemuseum, Bruges), which is painted on only one side of a single arched panel that is divided into five sections by fictive columns. DCS

Master of Saint Augustine, active last quarter of 15th century

16. Scenes from the Life of Saint Augustine, last quarter of 15th century

Oil and silver on wood; overall, with added strips, 54¼ x 59 in. (137.8 x 149.9 cm); painted surface 53 x 57¾ in. (134.6 x 146.7 cm)
Inscribed: (on orphreys) ihs; (on Saint Augustine's sleeve) . . . HES . . .
The Cloisters Collection, 1961 61.99

Provenance: Marquis of Exeter, Burghley House, near Stamford, Northamptonshire (by 1868–88; sale, Christie's, London, June 9, 1888, no. 295,

One of the great theologians of the early Church and author of the *Confessions* and *The City of God,* Saint Augustine (354–430) had a pagan father and a Christian mother, Saint Monica. Although he received a Christian education, he led an intemperate life as a student and professor of philosophy until his conversion and baptism in 387. This large panel is the central element of an altarpiece devoted to his life and legend of which the right wing, now in Dublin (fig. 54), and the fragment of an exterior wing, now in Aachen (fig. 55), have survived. The missing left wing must have depicted scenes from the saint's early life, including his baptism by Saint Ambrose. Five scenes are represented in the Cloisters panel: at the upper left Augustine is ordained by Bishop Valerius, and at the lower left he preaches while Valerius and Saint Monica, among others, listen; in the central image he is consecrated bishop of Hippo, in North Africa, the Roman territory of his birth; the poetic landscape at the upper right represents his best-known legend, in which he speaks with a child—understood as the Christ Child—who attempts to empty the sea in a sand hole with his hands. When the saint observes that this is impossible, the child replies that it is no more impossible than to penetrate the mystery (of the Trinity) on which Augustine meditates. At the lower right, dressed as a scholar, Augustine either teaches his disciples or argues important theological issues.

In the Dublin panel the narrative continues at the upper left, with a depiction of the apparition of Saint Jerome, who foretells Augustine's death. This is followed at the upper right by an unidentified scene in which the saint and his disciples meet in a

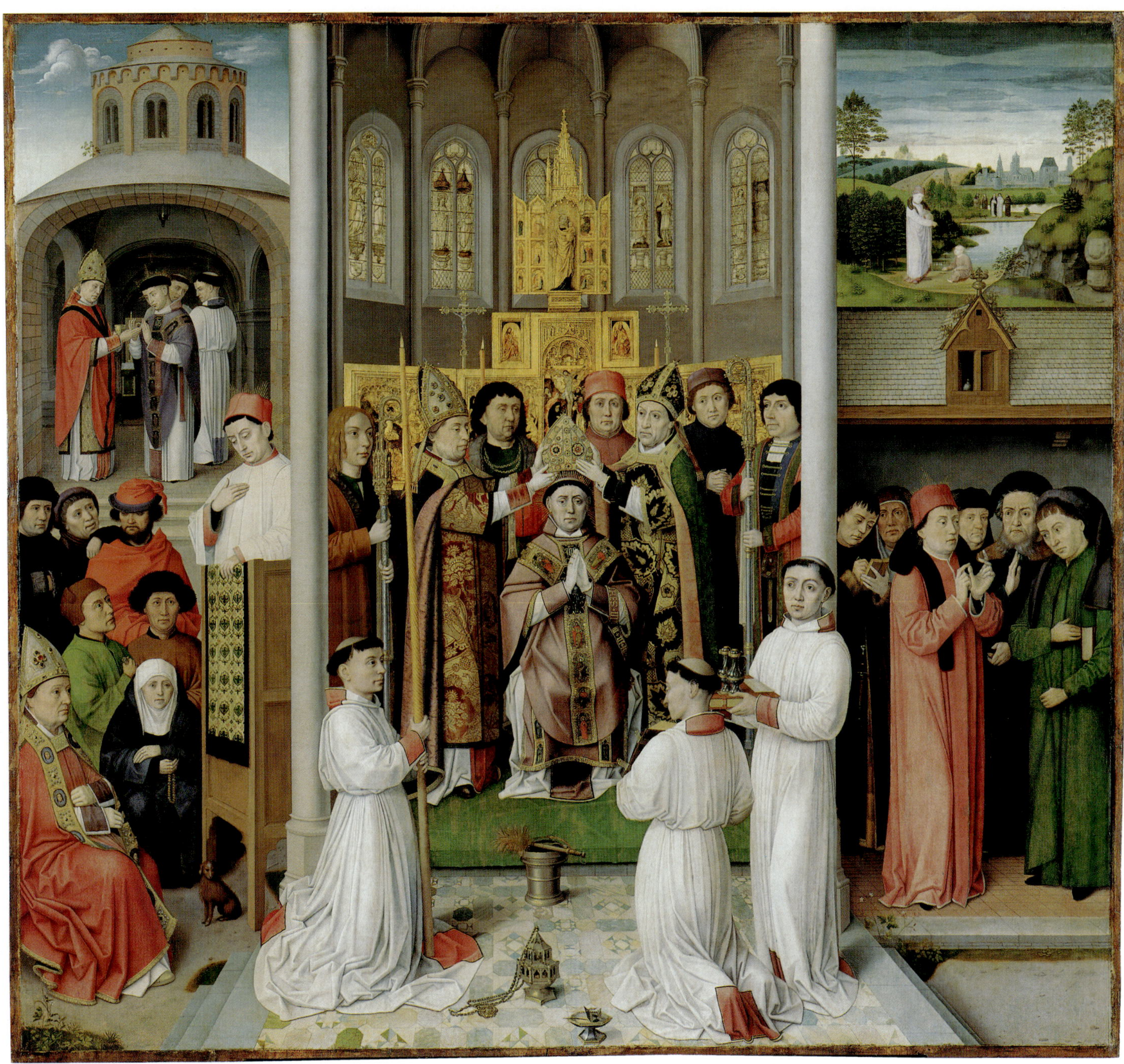

landscape outside the gates of a town or monastery. The main subject of the bottom portion of the composition is the Death of Saint Augustine. Here the saint on his deathbed receives last rites attended by members of an unidentified Augustinian community of regular canons, who must have commissioned the altarpiece. The fragment of the exterior in Aachen shows the standing Saints Augustine and Paul.

The composition is disquietingly, almost obsessively vertical, and the figures suggest a controlled, suppressed humanity. Some of the heads must be individual portraits. Friedländer (1937), with his keen eye for characterization, has described the men gathered in the central portion as "astounded or stupefied in a phlegmatic ecstasy." The altarpiece nevertheless has a stoic beauty and is of great interest, not only for its documentation of a contemporary church interior but also as an unusual stylistic hybrid reflecting a variety of disparate, yet not unrelated influences. In subject matter and composition,

as Hugo van der Goes, to Murray); Charles Butler, London (1891); anonymous sale, Hôtel Drouot, Paris, June 16, 1892, as Thierry Bouts, "La Vie de St. Austin, 'première archevêque de Cantebury [sic] *"; Comtesse de Béarn, Paris (after 1895); [Steinmeyer, Cologne (1901)]; Charles T. Yerkes, New York (1901–10; sale, American Art Association, New York, April 5–8, 1910, no. 18, as Gerard David, to J. W. Böhler); [?Fritz von Ansbach, Frankfurt-am-Main (1910)]; Fritz von Gans, Frankfurt-am-Main (before 1921); [Kurt Walter Bachstitz, The Hague (1921–24)]; Mr. and Mrs. Alfred W. Erickson, New York (1925–61; sale, Parke-Bernet, New York, November 11–14, 1961, no. 10, as Master of Saint Augustine, Bruges, 1490).*

References: Schnütgen 1902, cols. 161–66, pl. 5; Friedländer [1922], pp. 5–6; Friedländer 1937a, pp. 47–48, 53, fig. 1; Courcelle and Courcelle 1969, pp. 145–50, 153, 182–86, 190–91, pls. 102–8; Friedländer 1967–76, vol. 6a (1971), p. 44, vol. 6b (1971), p. 111, supp. 244, pl. 241; Schabacker 1972b, p. 424; Frazer 1986, pp. 24–25, ill.; Vogelaar 1987, pp. 46–49, fig. 45; Böhmer 1993, p. 164; Steinmetz 1995, pp. 85–87, TB12, pl. 5A.

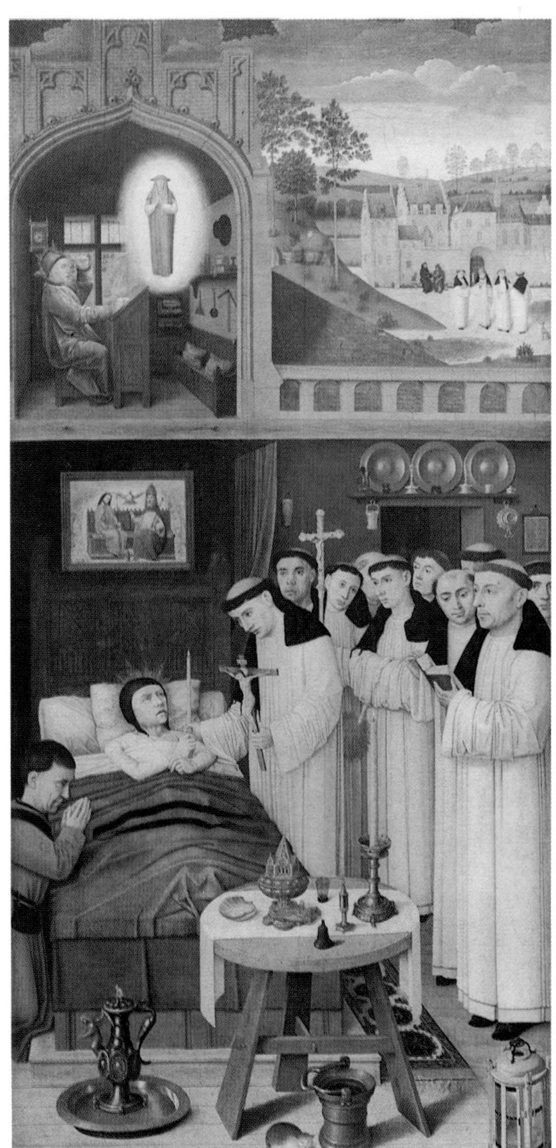

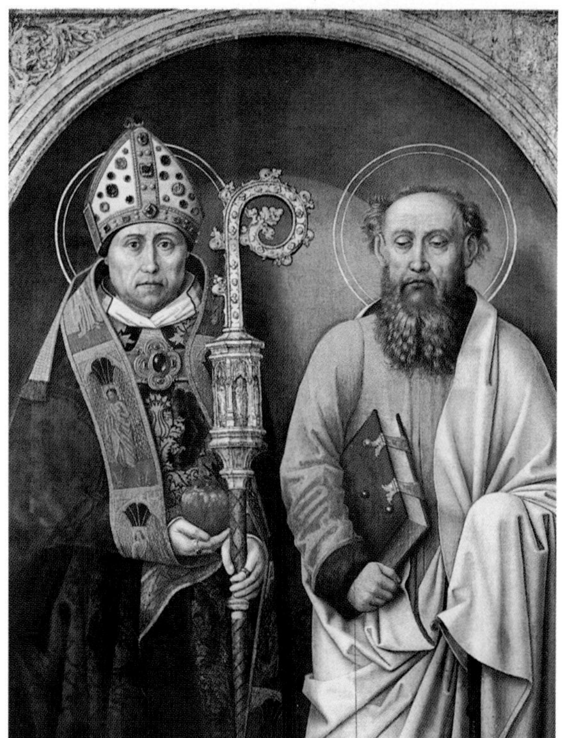

Fig. 55. Master of Saint Augustine, *Saints Augustine and Paul,* fragment, exterior wing of a triptych, last quarter of 15th century. Oil on wood. Suermondt-Ludwig-Museum, Aachen

Fig. 54. Master of Saint Augustine, *Scenes from the Life of Saint Augustine,* right wing of a triptych, last quarter of 15th century. Oil on wood. National Gallery of Ireland, Dublin

and in the use of an architectural cross section to allow a view of an interior scene, there are interesting parallels in three paintings of the mid-fifteenth century: two panels from the Brussels workshop of Rogier van der Weyden, the *Exhumation of Saint Hubert* and its pendant, the *Consecration of Saint Hubert,* of about 1440–50 (formerly Sainte Gudule, Brussels, now National Gallery, London, and J. Paul Getty Museum, Los Angeles), and the *Scenes from the Life of Saint Bertin,* from about 1455–59 (formerly abbey of Saint Bertin, Saint-Omer, France, now Gemäldegalerie, Berlin). The latter panels are by Simon Marmion, a Franco-Netherlandish artist with contacts in both Bruges and Ghent. The stiff, unfailingly upright figures of our painter, with their blocky presence, are also characteristic of Marmion's style and of much northern French art of his time. Some of the figures, particularly the Saint Paul on the right side of the exterior fragment, recall the work of Hugo van der Goes, the leading artist of the Ghent school during the second half of the fifteenth century. Finally, the unusual pastel palette of rose, white, pale gray, and acid green, with the occasional lavender, is reminiscent of the hues Marmion favored and to some extent of the eccentric, unearthly color of Hugo's late *Death of the Virgin* (Groeningemuseum, Bruges). Drawing inspiration from all these sources, most of which must predate the altarpiece by at least a quarter of a century, the Master of Saint Augustine painstakingly and literally fulfilled this commission.

The minute detail with which liturgical objects and vestments are recorded—in the Cloisters panel

Opposite: Detail, cat. no. 16

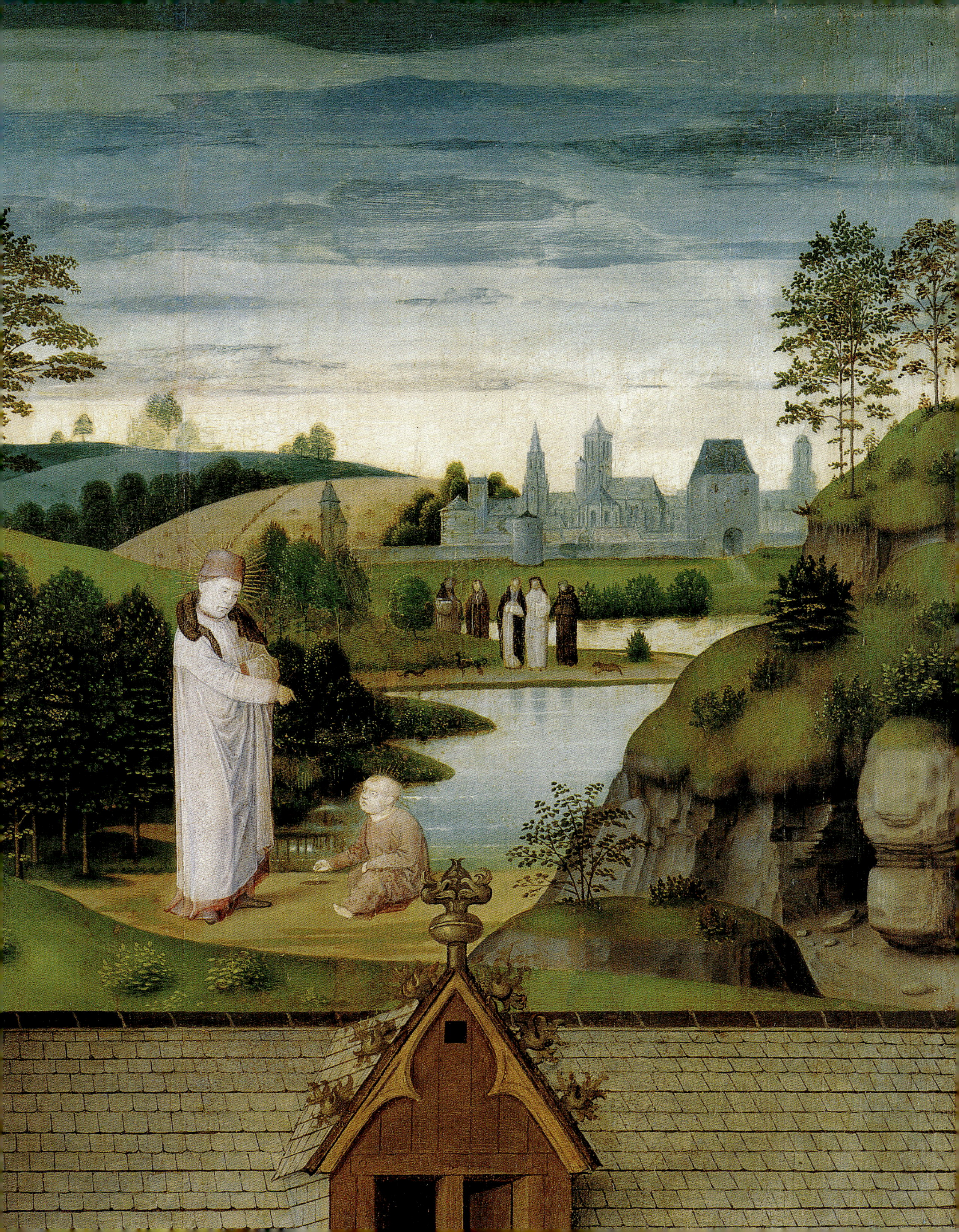

as well as in the Dublin wing—and the number that are recorded so faithfully may have been stipulated in the contract. As Schabacker has observed, a similar interest in ecclesiastical dress and rich fabrics is displayed in the Rogierian paintings with Saint Hubert, possibly also commissioned by a religious community. Some of the objects represented in our panel appear to have been individually studied and inserted into the composition with particular emphasis; the most striking example is perhaps the censer, which calls to mind Martin Schongauer's remarkable engraving of the subject from about 1480–85. Also carefully recorded are the holy-water stoup with a feathered aspergillum resting on it and the incense navette (all center foreground), as well as the cruets held by the young subdeacon at the right. The altarpieces and stained-glass windows in the church interior are described in such detail that it is possible to identify the subjects of many scenes (see Steinmetz). At the bottom of the windows at the right and left are four coats of arms, the identification of which might help pinpoint the locus of the master's activity.

The ensemble probably dates within the last quarter of the fifteenth century, when there was a proliferation in the Netherlands and northern France of altarpieces devoted to the legends and lives of saints. In striking contrast to the sober panels in New York and Dublin are three highly animated paintings of the Brussels school that belong to another series recording the Life of Saint Augustine. They are now divided among the Louvre, Paris, the Rijksmuseum, Amsterdam, and the National Gallery of Ireland, Dublin; the last two, formerly ascribed to the Master of the Saint Barbara Legend, have recently been attributed to an anonymous Brussels painter, and the Louvre picture is the eponymous work of the Master of the View of Sainte Gudule.

MSdJ

Follower of Dieric Bouts

17. Saint Christopher and the Infant Christ, about 1480 or later?

Oil on wood; overall 15¼ x 10⅛ in. (38.7 x 25.7 cm); painted surface 14⅝ x 9⅝ in. (37 x 24.5 cm)
Robert Lehman Collection, 1975 1975.1.115

According to legend, Saint Christopher, a Canaanite giant of fearful aspect, was determined to serve only the most powerful person in the land. Discovering that his first master, a king, feared Satan, and that Satan lived in fear of the cross, he decided to serve Christ. The saint devoted himself to bearing the poor and weak across a river until one night he carried a small child who grew heavier with each step he took. The child revealed that he was Christ and that he had been carrying the burden of the world on his shoulders; as a sign he turned Christopher's staff into a palm tree that blossomed and bore fruit.

Our picture represents the saint in his characteristic attitude, crossing a turbulent river, his staff in his right hand and the infant Christ on his shoulder. The figures are clearly derived from the right wing of the Adoration of the Magi Triptych (Alte Pinakothek, Munich), known as the *Pearl of Brabant.* The right and left interior wings of this triptych, which has been attributed to both Dieric Bouts and the Master of the Pearl of Brabant, show Saints John the Baptist and Christopher, respectively. The artist, however, appears also to have been familiar with Aelbert Bouts's *Saint Christopher* (Galleria Estense, Modena), in which the saint holds his staff diagonally and with both

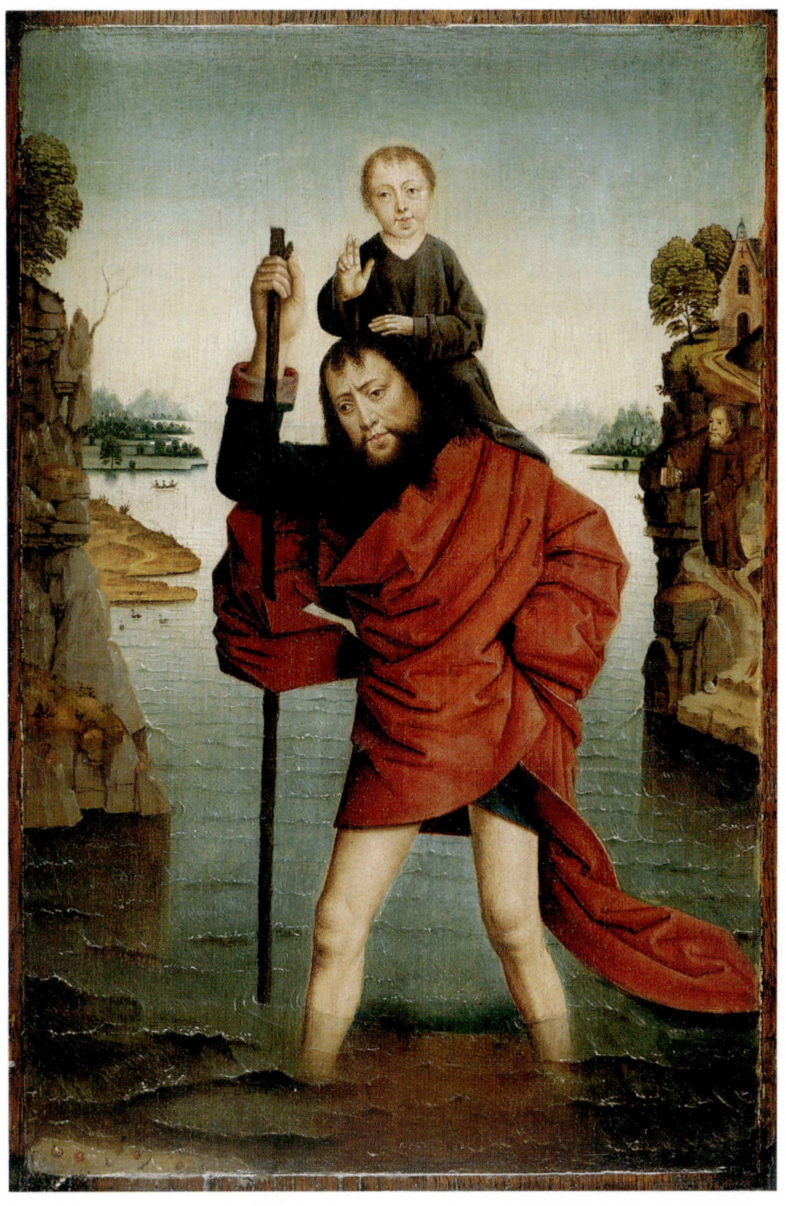

hands. The Modena and Lehman panels have in common the monk (perhaps a donor) who stands with a lantern on one of the tall rocky crags bordering the river, the small boat in a cove, and the lower-lying peninsulas along the water's edge in the background; the terrain in the Munich panel, however, is consistently mountainous. Although the Munich original, true to the nighttime setting of the saint's legend, features a hauntingly beautiful evening sky, both our panel and the painting in Modena have blue skies with wispy clouds, despite the inclusion of the lantern motif.

It is difficult to say whether this modest panel was part of a larger ensemble or simply an independent devotional work; the picture, which has not been cut down, is not as long and narrow as the Munich wings and is therefore not an obvious example of a lateral panel. Although the present painting was for many years attributed to Aelbert Bouts, it is rather stiff and provincial in feeling compared with the artist's generally accepted works and lacks the narrative elaboration that we associate with them. Dendrochronological analysis indicates a probable date of use for the panel of about 1479 or later, and Wolff reasonably ascribes the picture to a late follower of Dieric, perhaps working in association with one of the master's sons after his death in 1475. She tentatively ascribes a *Virgin and Child* in the Art Gallery of Ontario, Toronto, to the same hand.

MSdJ

Provenance: Private collection, Munich; Karl Schäfer, Munich (1927); Robert Lehman, New York (by 1942).

References: Schöne 1938, pp. 143–45, 206, nos. 27a, 124, pl. 46c; Bauman and Liedtke 1992, p. 318, no. 122, ill.; Wolff 1998, no. 17, color ill.

Jan Provost, born about 1465, died 1529

18. Virgin and Child, about 1495–1500

Oil on wood; overall 12¼ x 6¾ in. (31.1 x 17.1 cm); painted surface 11¾ x 6⅛ in. (29.8 x 15.6 cm)
Bequest of Joan Whitney Payson, 1975 1976.201.17

Provenance: Friedrich I, herzog von Anhalt, Gothisches Haus, Wörlitz (by 1863–d. 1904); Mr. and Mrs. Arthur Lehman, New York (by 1931–his d. 1936); Mrs. Arthur Lehman, New York (1936–d. 1965); [Knoedler, New York (1965–66)]; Mrs. Charles Payson, Manhasset, New York (1966–d. 1975).

References: Dülberg 1898–99, p. 275; Hulin de Loo 1902, p. 22, no. 98; Friedländer 1924–37, vol. 9 (1931), pp. 86, 149, no. 165, pl. 75; Friedländer 1935, pp. 99–104; Ring 1941, pp. 156–60; Detroit 1960, p. 168; Winkler 1964, p. 172, fig. 132; Bruges 1969, pp. 47, 53–54, 61–62, nos. 15, 20; Friedländer 1967–76, vol. 9b (1973), pp. 90–91, no. 165, pl. 177; Baetjer 1977, p. 342; De Vos 1994b, p. 314, n. 1.

This representation of the Virgin and Child in a Rose Garden is characteristic of a courtly type of Marian devotional image produced in Bruges at the end of the fifteenth century. The Virgin, represented as the Queen of Heaven, sits on a grassy brick wall in the middle of an enclosed garden, or *hortus conclusus*, carpeted with flowers. Above her, angels suspend a crown. The dense hedge of roses behind Mary not only symbolizes her virginity but also alludes to the cult of the Virgin of the Rosary, one of the most popular expressions of individual piety in Europe about 1500 (see entry for cat. no. 91).

Pictures of this kind were particularly favored in northern Italy and Germany, where the type is epitomized by Stefan Lochner's famous *Virgin and Child in a Rose Arbor* of about 1450 (Wallraf-Richartz-Museum, Cologne). According to De Vos, the theme of the Virgin in a Rose Garden was introduced to the Netherlands by Hans Memling, who popularized it in several of his late paintings, such as his *Virgin and Child with Angels* (Prado, Madrid). Indeed, our picture refers to Memling's *Virgin and Child Enthroned with Angels* of about 1490–91 (Uffizi, Florence) in the manner in which the mantle of the Virgin is draped and tucked under her right arm and the way she holds the Christ Child—with one hand on his belly and the other on his foot. The infant in our picture, represented alone with his mother, reaches out his arm somewhat awkwardly toward someone or something at the right, suggesting that our panel is the left half of a diptych.

Friedländer (1931) was the first to identify this painting as an early work by Provost. He observes that this sort of hieratic Virgin and Child motif was probably produced for export in workshops of anonymous masters, such as the Master of the Saint Lucy Legend, whose *Virgin among Virgins* of about 1480–83 (Detroit Institute of Arts) embodies the form. Ring proposes that our picture is part of an altarpiece showing the Life of the Virgin that included five scenes of approximately the same size (Friedländer 1973, vol. 9b, pl. 148). Her theory is not convincing, given the distinctly narrative treatment of the five panels she cites. She is probably correct, however, in dating our work before 1500, based on the doll-like aspect of the figures, their characteristic high foreheads and full lips, the bright colors, and the miniature size of the panel—all of which show analogies with the style of Simon Marmion, the renowned panel painter and manuscript illuminator with whom Provost apprenticed in Valenciennes. This dating places the work not long after Provost registered in Bruges in 1494, when the influence of Marmion was still very noticeable.

VS

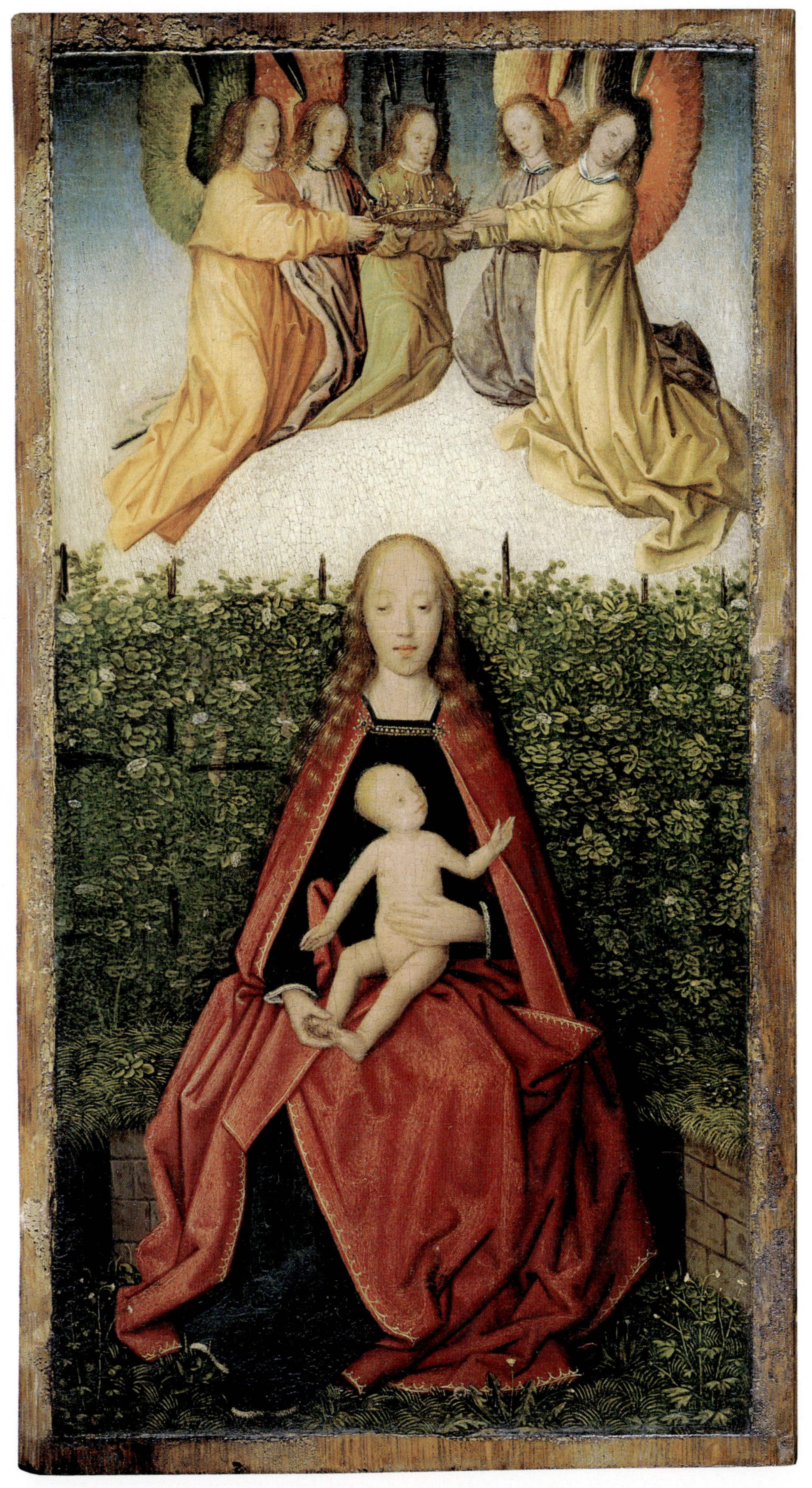

Attributed to Jan Provost, born about 1465, died 1529

19. The Crucifixion, about 1495

Oil on wood; overall 13⅛ x 10¾ in. (33.3 x 27.3 cm); painted surface 12⅝ x 10¼ in. (32.1 x 26 cm)
Inscribed (top center, on cross): INRI
The Jack and Belle Linsky Collection, 1982 1982.60.21

Provenance: Spain?; Col. Hugh Duncan Baillie; (sale Nieuwenhuys, Brussels, May 4, 1883, no. 13, as Gerard vander Meire, to Koffermans); Eugen Felix, Leipzig; [Agnew, London]; Oscar Bondy, Vienna (by 1930–51); [Newhouse Galleries, New York, 1951]; John Meyers, Ohio (1951–55); [Newhouse Galleries, New York, 1955]; Mr. and Mrs. Jack Linsky, New York (1955–80); Mrs. Belle Linsky, New York (1980–82).

References: Baldass 1930, p. 132; Pächt in Vienna 1930, p. 24, no. 32; Ring 1949, p. 225, fig. 115; Davies 1970, p. 18, no. 126, pl. 17; Schiller 1971–72, vol. 1, p. 34; Friedländer 1967–76, vol. 9 (1973), pp. 89–90, 113, no. 148, pl. 167; Russell 1978, p. 27; Bauman in Metropolitan Museum 1984, pp. 65–67, colorpl.; Frick collection 1990, n.p.; Spronk, conversation, October 1997.

This superb and exceptionally well-preserved *Crucifixion* is one of the earliest known works attributable to Provost. It exhibits northern French stylistic elements that testify to the time Provost spent in Valenciennes as an apprentice in the workshop of Simon Marmion (see entry for cat. no. 9). Provost married Marmion's widow in 1491 and moved to the Netherlands, becoming a citizen of Bruges in 1494.

The crucified Christ dominates the composition, his body turned slightly to the right, his face shadowed by the dark, cloudy sky that portends the moment of his death. On the left the Virgin collapses in the arms of Saint John, while on the right the grieving Mary Magdalene, elegantly dressed and with a rosary hanging from her belt, embraces the cross. Just beyond Mary Magdalene a figure (man or woman?) wrapped in a red mantle sits weeping, with back to the scene and face hidden by a white handkerchief. A human jawbone, one of the fragments of bones arranged like memento mori about the cross, lies in the foreground. In the middle ground, behind the cross, a caravan of soldiers with lances winds around the hills on the way back to Jerusalem. Represented in the distance on the right is the Annunciation, visible through the open portal of a Late Gothic building. The unusual pairing of this miraculous event with the Crucifixion accords with a medieval tradition that dedicates March 25 to the memory of Adam, the Annunciation, and the death of Christ, thus expressing the connection between the Fall, the conception of Christ, and the fulfillment of man's redemption through his death. It is possible that our composition belonged to a group of panels inspired by manuscript illuminations on the theme of the Life of Christ.

The dating and attribution of the picture are primarily based on its relationship to the sole documented work by Provost, the mature Last Judgment Altarpiece of 1524–25 (Groeningemuseum, Bruges). Pächt was the first to ascribe our painting to the young Provost, and his attribution was endorsed by Friedländer, who also linked it to a *Crucifixion* of about 1505 (Saint Louis Art Museum). Bauman has placed our panel close to 1495, just after the artist arrived in Bruges, a date supported by the costume of the soldier on a horse shown in profile next to the cross. Indeed, the Museum's *Crucifixion* combines stylistic idiosyncrasies and miniature-like qualities found in both northern French and Bruges painting of the late fifteenth century. The clear and bright tonality and the doll-like figures covered with heavy fabric that falls to the ground in thick folds recall Marmion's Saint Bertin Altarpiece of 1450–60 (Gemäldegalerie, Berlin, and National Gallery, London). And the anecdotal motif of the red-shrouded figure seated on the ground is reminiscent of a female figure in a panel in the Frick Collection, New York, a *Lamentation* of about 1470–80 by an anonymous French master whose work shows stylistic ties to northern painting. Moreover, the structure of the composition, with its subsidiary scene of the cavalcade used to give depth to the landscape, and the outlining of the landscape with groups of trees, as well as the particular architectural monuments, find parallels in Memling's *Scenes of the Advent and Triumph of Christ* of 1479 (Alte Pinakothek, Munich), a picture that Provost could have seen in the chapel of the Bruges tanners' guild in the Onze-Lieve-Vrouwekerk (church of Our Lady). Despite these affinities with contemporary panel painting, the present picture, like Provost's *Virgin and Child* (cat. no. 18), with its small scale, its short, blended brushstrokes, and its intense color, retains strong links to manuscript illumination, which the artist could have practiced in Marmion's shop. VS

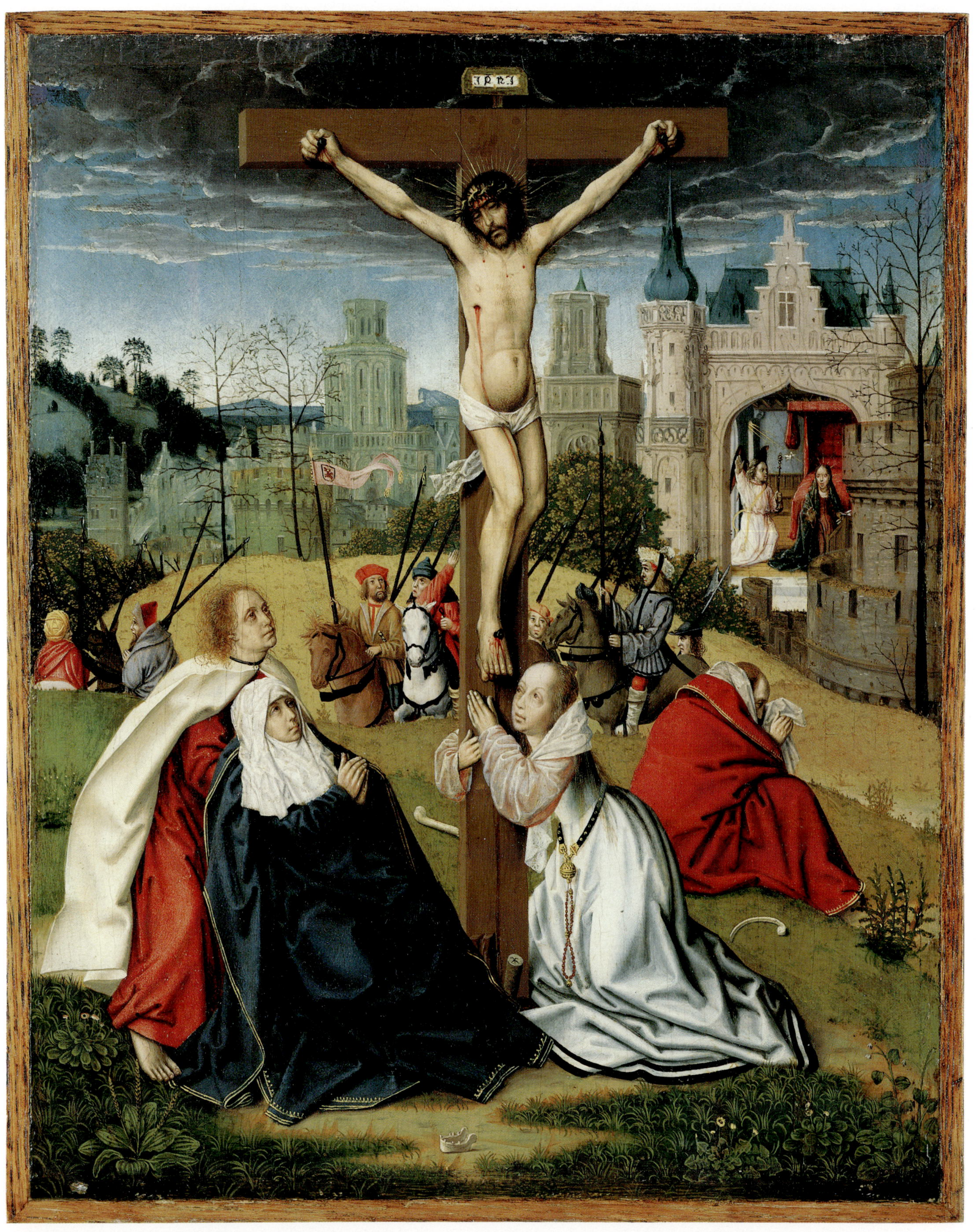

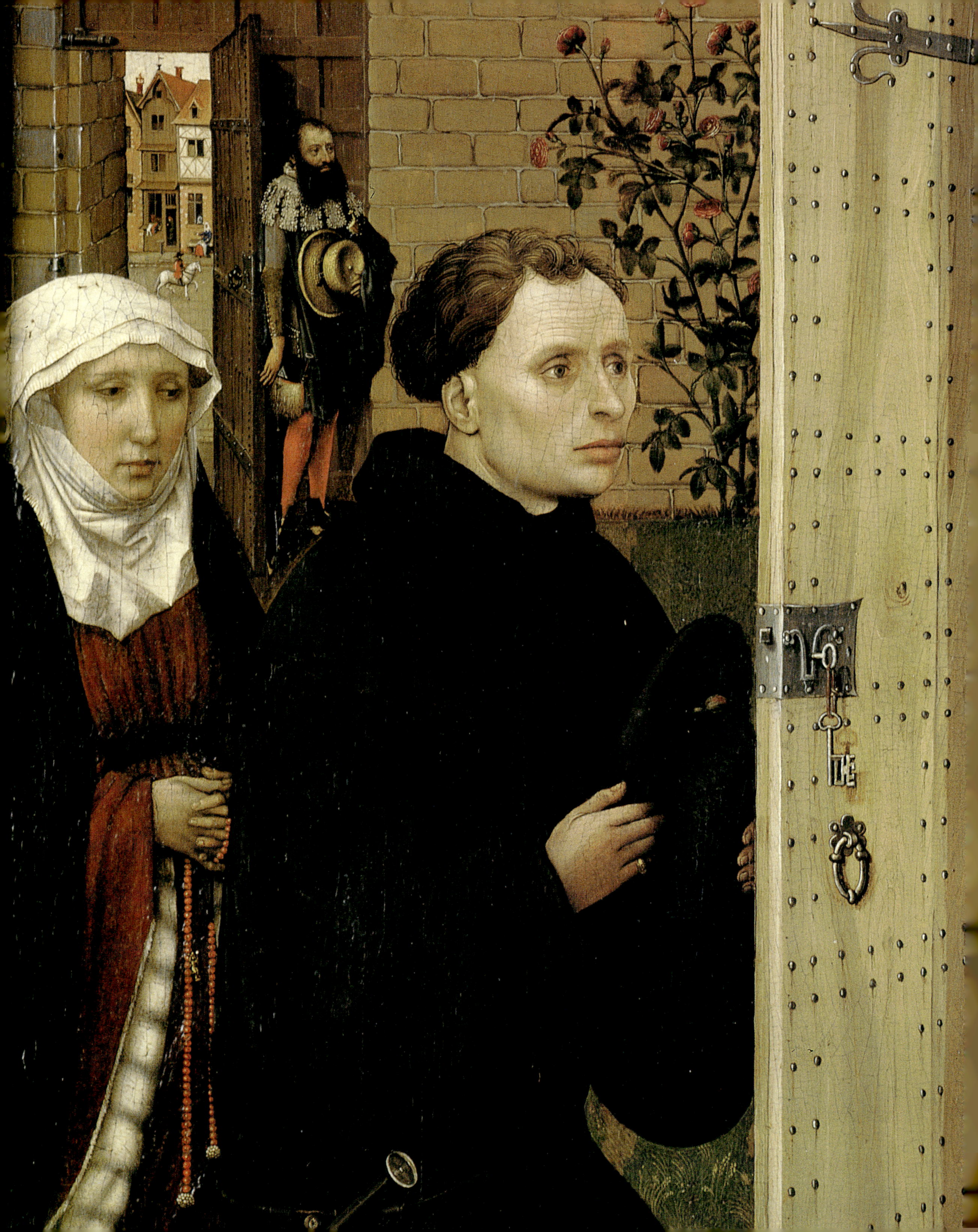

Portraiture: A Meeting of the Sacred and Secular Worlds

Opposite: Rogier van der Weyden?, detail, left wing, kneeling donors, *The Annunciation Triptych (Merode Triptych)* (cat. no. 2)

Portraiture perhaps more than any other genre of painting fulfills a chief aim of Netherlandish artists—to render precisely the tangible reality of the visible world. This aspiration came to be achieved principally through the unique qualities of the technique of oil painting. In the highly skilled handling of a master, introduced at a nearly incomparable level by Jan van Eyck, this technique allowed for the subtle blending of glazes and the meticulous attention to detail required for such advanced attempts at verisimilitude.

The purposes and functions of portraiture in the fifteenth and sixteenth centuries in the Netherlands varied considerably—they might be devotional or commemorative, or meant to impart a sense of status or position, or to accomplish certain political goals. Depending upon where the portrait was produced, by whom it was made, and whom it represented, the picture took on a unique character. The Metropolitan Museum collection of portraits of this period in northern Europe is by no means comprehensive, but it does speak eloquently to the specific interests and preoccupations of individuals of the time.

Although portraiture is generally considered secular in nature, many Netherlandish examples do not stray very far from spiritual concerns, which are oftentimes expressed either explicitly or implicitly. This confluence of the sacred and secular worlds is above all exemplified by paintings of holy figures represented as though they were living and, with increasing frequency in the sixteenth century, in pictures using the reverse device, that is, showing living beings in the guise of holy figures. Thus, in portraying the votive image of Christ, Netherlandish artists assimilated the frontal pose of Byzantine icons but transformed and humanized the figure by incorporating details of Christ's physiognomy as described in a purportedly eyewitness account sent by Publius Lentulus to the Roman Senate—as in paintings by Petrus Christus and Gerard David (cat. nos. 3, 74) that are modeled after a famous prototype by Jan van Eyck. In paintings of the Virgin Mary especially, artists strove to portray the subject's human essence. It was universally believed that Mary sat for a portrait by none other than Luke, the patron saint of painters. Certain icons, such as the Cambrai Madonna (fig. 49), brought from Rome in 1440 by Canon Fursy de Bruille and installed in the cathedral of Cambrai, were recognized as specific examples of Saint Luke's painterly skills. This particular image inspired myriad copies and versions (among them one by Dieric Bouts [cat. no. 6]), perhaps as much for the implied association with Luke as the quintessential painter as for the miraculous aura of the work of art itself.

The portraitlike aspect of paintings of Christ, the Virgin, and the multitude of saints embodies an approach that varies little from that adopted by artists for renderings of mere mortals. It is not uncommon, therefore, to encounter a certain confusion of identity in their efforts: representations of saints so highly individualized that they appear to be portraits (cat. no. 31) and portraits of contemporary men and women that have been converted into images of saints by means of the later addition of a halo (cat. nos. 21, 22) or other saintly attribute (cat. nos. 28, 80). Among our most celebrated examples of this sort of transformation are the *Portrait of a Carthusian* of 1446 (cat. no. 21) and *A Goldsmith in His Shop, Possibly Saint Eligius* of 1449 (cat. no. 22) by Christus. We know the Carthusian was a lay brother and not a saint; however, whether the goldsmith shown in his shop should still be identified with Eligius, the patron saint of goldsmiths, now that his halo, added by a later hand, has been removed, or whether he is a famous

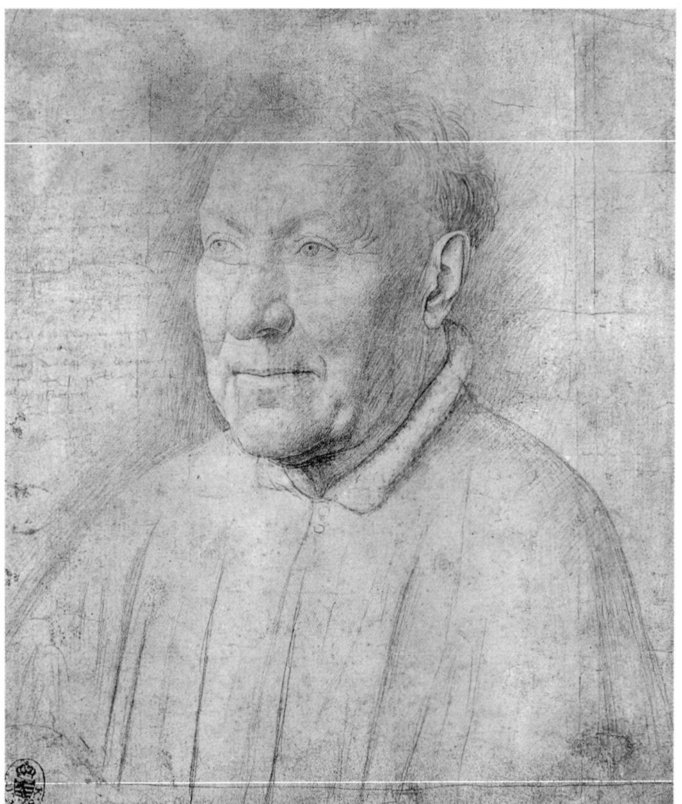

Fig. 56. Jan van Eyck, *Portrait of a Man (formerly identified as Cardinal Niccolò Albergati)*, about 1438. Silverpoint on prepared paper. Kupferstich-Kabinett, Dresden

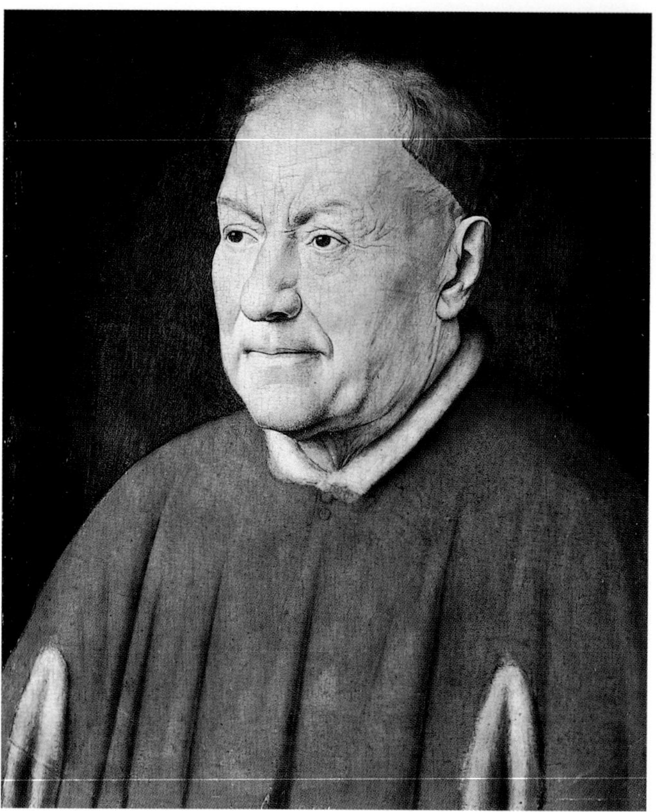

Fig. 57. Jan van Eyck, *Portrait of a Man (formerly identified as Cardinal Niccolò Albergati)*, about 1438. Oil on wood. Kunsthistorisches Museum, Vienna

craftsman carrying out his daily duties remains open to question. Perhaps Christus, who often made striking innovations to portrait conventions, here intended a new genre, a vocational portrait similar in type to Rogier van der Weyden's *Saint Luke Drawing the Virgin* (fig. 19), in which the artist featured himself as the patron saint of painters. Still rich in the symbolism that denotes both religious and secular concerns, Christus's painting may well represent the initial stages of this new form. In any event, its apparent confusions of intention had totally disappeared by the second decade of the sixteenth century, in Adriaen Isenbrant's portrait of a man weighing gold (cat. no. 41), where the sitter's identification with his occupation in the money trade (accountant or banker) is more straightforward.

In the history of early Netherlandish portraiture Jan van Eyck's descriptive talents were never surpassed (figs. 56–58). Nonetheless, in his *Portrait of a Carthusian*, Christus approaches Van Eyck's standard of excellence and goes a step further than his predecessor in representing the illusion of space around the sitter and suggesting the inhabitable, physical world of even a pious lay brother. Christus's subject is at once a corporal man and one who is sheltered within the confines of a primarily spiritual existence.

How very different were Rogier's intentions in the portrait of Francesco d'Este of about 1460 (cat. no. 23). The elegance and aristocratic refinement instantly conveyed by this likeness of an Italian who was educated alongside the young Charles the Bold at the Burgundian court are achieved by the pose of the sitter, who averts his eyes from the viewer, and by the stylized description of the forms. The components of Rogier's painting are as perfectly balanced and harmonious as those in Christus's portrait, but they are more abstract and dependent upon exquisite decorative effects of line. These linear effects draw attention to the attributes of position and achievement at court that Francesco holds in his hand as much as to his haughty demeanor.

There exist only a few examples of independent portraits by certain leading artists of the later fifteenth century, such as Dieric Bouts, Hugo van der Goes (cat. no. 30), and Gerard David, but strikingly individualized heads abound within their larger religious and historical paintings (fig. 16). Even when excised from larger compositions, they are distinguished by their detailed physiognomies (cat. nos. 26, 31).

Other early Netherlandish artists, notably Hans Memling, seem to have specialized in the portrait genre. Memling obviously was adept at satisfying the demands of his clients for images that express a sense of their devotional concerns as well as their elevated status within society. Because the object of veneration (probably a *Virgin and Child*) they once flanked is missing, his portraits of Tommaso Portinari and Maria Portinari (cat. no. 27) tend to emphasize the latter requirement. Like Francesco d'Este in Rogier's painting, each sitter is placed against a plain background so that nothing distracts from the faces. Uncompromising in the meticulous rendering of minute details, including the scar on Tommaso's chin, but idealized in a manner that constitutes a hallmark of Memling's style, these likenesses perfectly evoke the elite court society to which the sitters aspired. Indeed, Maria Portinari wears an elaborate necklace of the type shown in portraits of Margaret of York about the time of her wedding to Charles the Bold in Bruges in 1468 (Louvre, Paris, for example), an event that the Portinari couple attended.

Although he probably did not invent it, Memling popularized the convention of placing the sitter before a landscape view (cat. no. 28). This formulation was especially favored by Memling's Italian clients, and indeed the notion of an open-air portrait setting may have originated in Italy. Memling's particular innovation was to exchange a typically Italian open-air setting for a Netherlandish landscape background, which a number of Italian artists, including Verrocchio, Fra Bartolomeo (frontis., p. 38), and Lorenzo di Credi, adopted, in terms of both particular arrangements of individual natural motifs and the new portrait formula itself.

As his *Portrait of an Old Man* (cat. no. 29) and the accompanying *Portrait of an Old Woman* (fig. 63) show, Memling did not restrict himself to a clientele of wealthy foreigners and social climbers but on occasion turned his masterly skills of execution to a poignant depiction of the elderly. In the male portrait, for example, he touchingly conveyed a sense of advanced age and of the inner strength derived from years of experience by showing deeply set lines encircling the sitter's sympathetic eyes.

Portraits were routinely included in religious paintings, and changes in their positions within the composition and the way they relate to the event depicted reflect the evolution of devotional practices during the course of the fifteenth and sixteenth centuries. Whereas the donors in the *Merode Triptych* of the first half of the fifteenth century (cat. no. 2) take their place on the left wing of

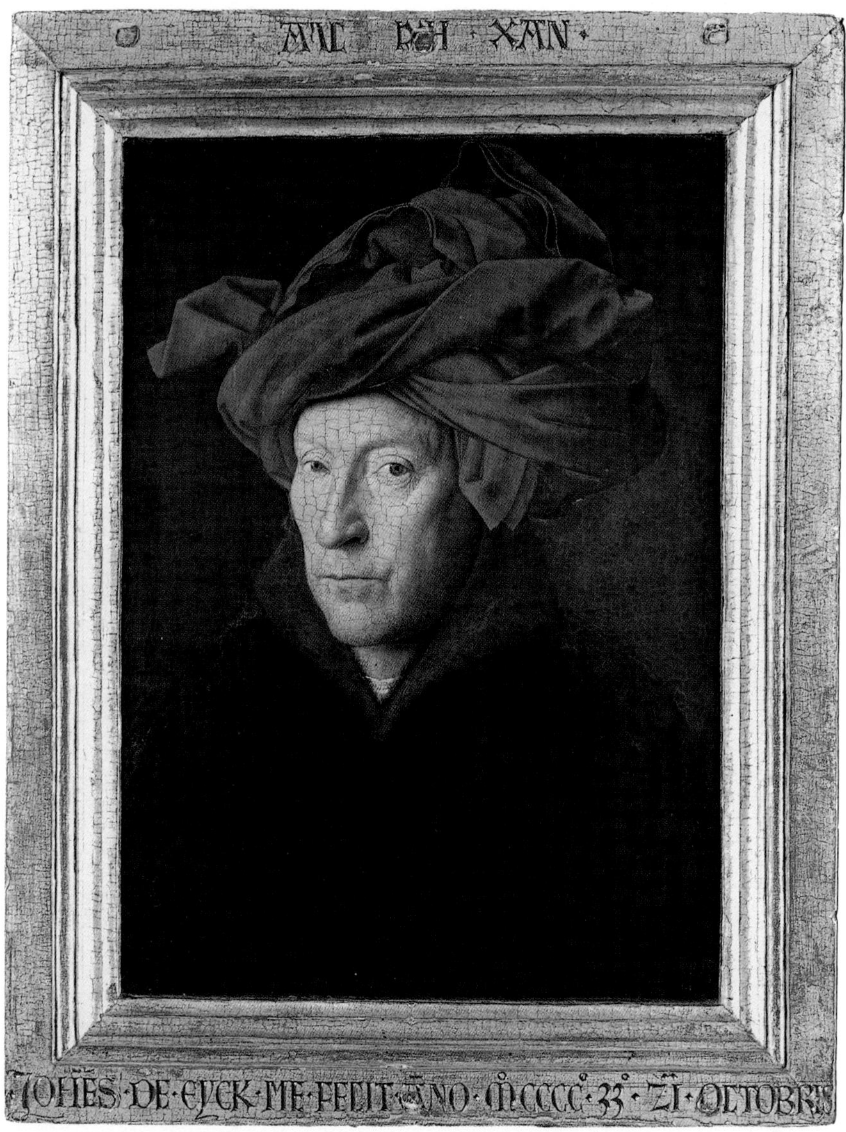

Fig. 58. Jan van Eyck, *A Man in a Turban*, 1433. Oil on wood. National Gallery, London

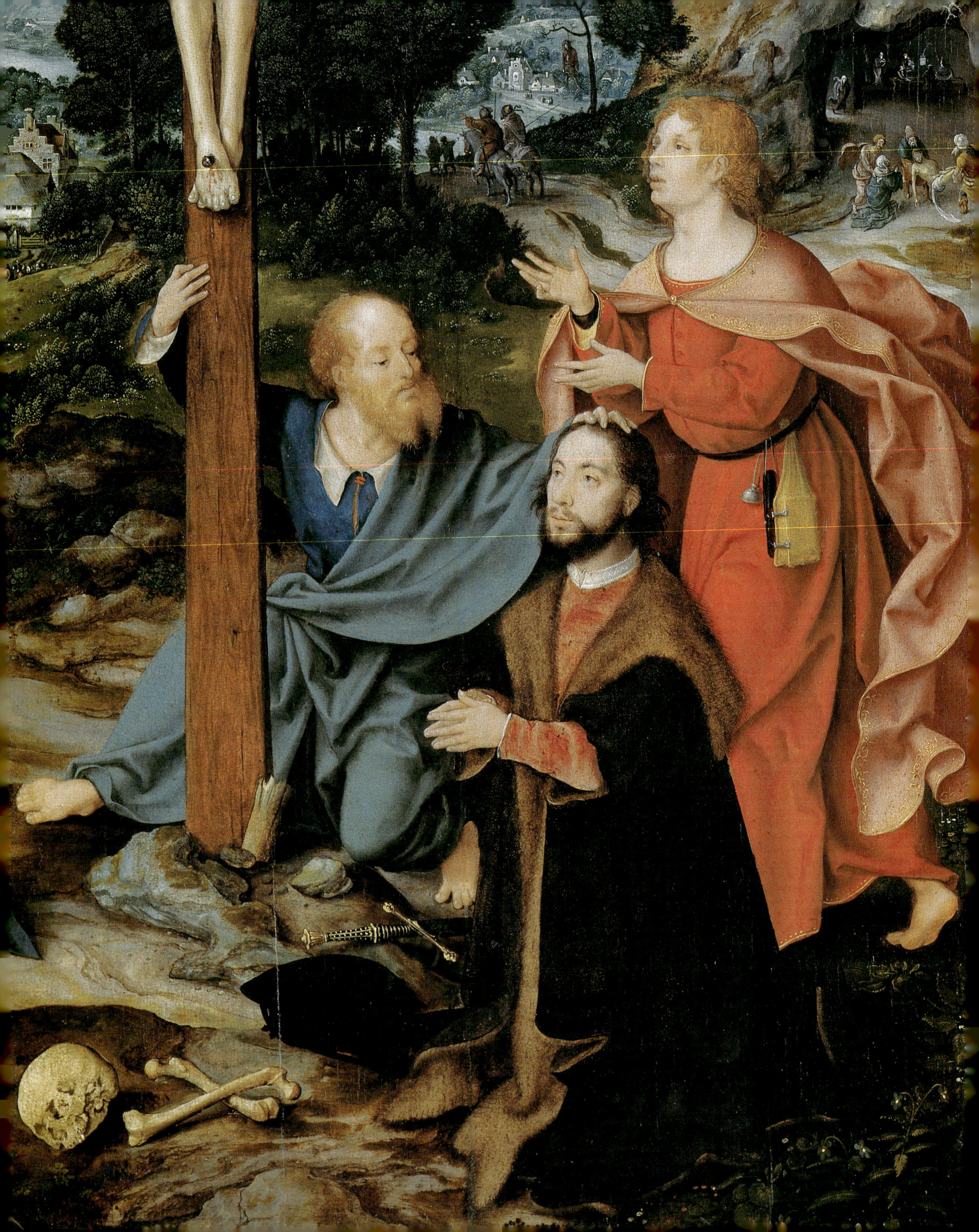

the ensemble, at a considerable distance from the *Annunciation* of the central panel, observing without being observed, in Memling's *Virgin and Child with Saints Catherine of Alexandria and Barbara* from later in the century (cat. no. 11) the donor moves closer to the holy gathering but still remains at its fringes. However, in early sixteenth-century paintings, such as Joos van Cleve's *Crucifixion with Saints and a Donor* (cat. no. 95), the donor, a certain Paul who is presented by his patron, Saint Paul, becomes more directly involved with the action, kneeling at its center, literally beneath Christ's feet (fig. 59). The desire of worshipers to identify with holy figures and to find the path to true salvation by personally taking on their trials, according to the practice of the Modern Devotion, led artists to depict donors closer and closer to their intercessory saints. The kneeling donors on the wings of certain paintings, such as David's Nativity Triptych (cat. no. 72), assume the identities of saints whose virtuous lives they hoped to emulate. This transformation is accomplished by showing the donors with the attributes of these saints—in the case of David's protagonists, the pig identifies the man with Saint Anthony, and the wheel, crown, and sword reveal the woman as Saint Catherine.

The conceit of representing living persons as holy figures emerged in individual portraits as well as in religious compositions. Such portraits for the most part depict royalty or members of the nobility, shown in the guise of saints or other divine personages. Paintings of this kind, rather than constituting sacrilege, indicate an infusion of portraiture with deeply religious feeling. Among the documented examples in the Museum's collection is Jan Gossart's *Virgin and Child* (cat. no. 40; fig. 67), which Karel van Mander explains (in his 1604 *Het Schilderboeck*) was modeled directly after Anna van Bergen, the Lady Veere, and her child, the wife and son of Adolf of Burgundy. The image follows in a tradition of pictures, exemplified by the Bouts mentioned above (cat. no. 6), in which the Virgin and Child take on the very human appearance of a contemporary mother and her child; painted some sixty years later than the Bouts, the Gossart reflects a further development of that tradition, as

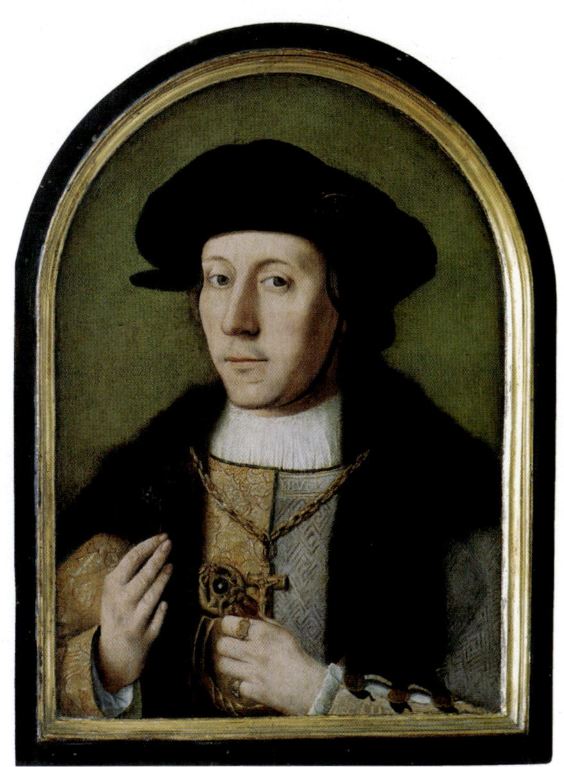

Fig. 60. Attributed to Quentin Massys, *Portrait of a Man*, about 1515–20. Oil on wood. The Metropolitan Museum of Art, New York

his Virgin and Child assume the physical traits of a particular mother, and her child, who wished to associate herself with the ideal virtues of the most revered mother of all ages.

Although some portraits reflect increasing devotional fervor, with the advent of humanism in northern Europe in the sixteenth century, others came to reveal a departure from spiritual concerns. Thus the damaged but sensitively painted *Portrait of a Man* attributed to Quentin Massys (fig. 60) reflects a new worldliness. And in Massys's *Portrait of a Woman* (cat. no. 38) and *Portrait of a Man* (fig. 66), a wife and husband are shown with the attributes of devotional practice—a prayer book and a rosary—but they are distracted from their prayers. Religion is merely one aspect of life, and not an all-consuming one, for this sophisticated man and woman whose gazes link them with the secular world beyond the picture frame. Relating the sitter to the outside world had also been the intention of Christus in the *Portrait of a Carthusian* (cat. no. 21), painted some eighty years earlier than the Massys portraits; however, Massys's subjects irreversibly

Opposite: Fig. 59. Joos van Cleve, detail, Saint John, Saint Paul, and a donor, *The Crucifixion with Saints and a Donor* (cat. no. 95)

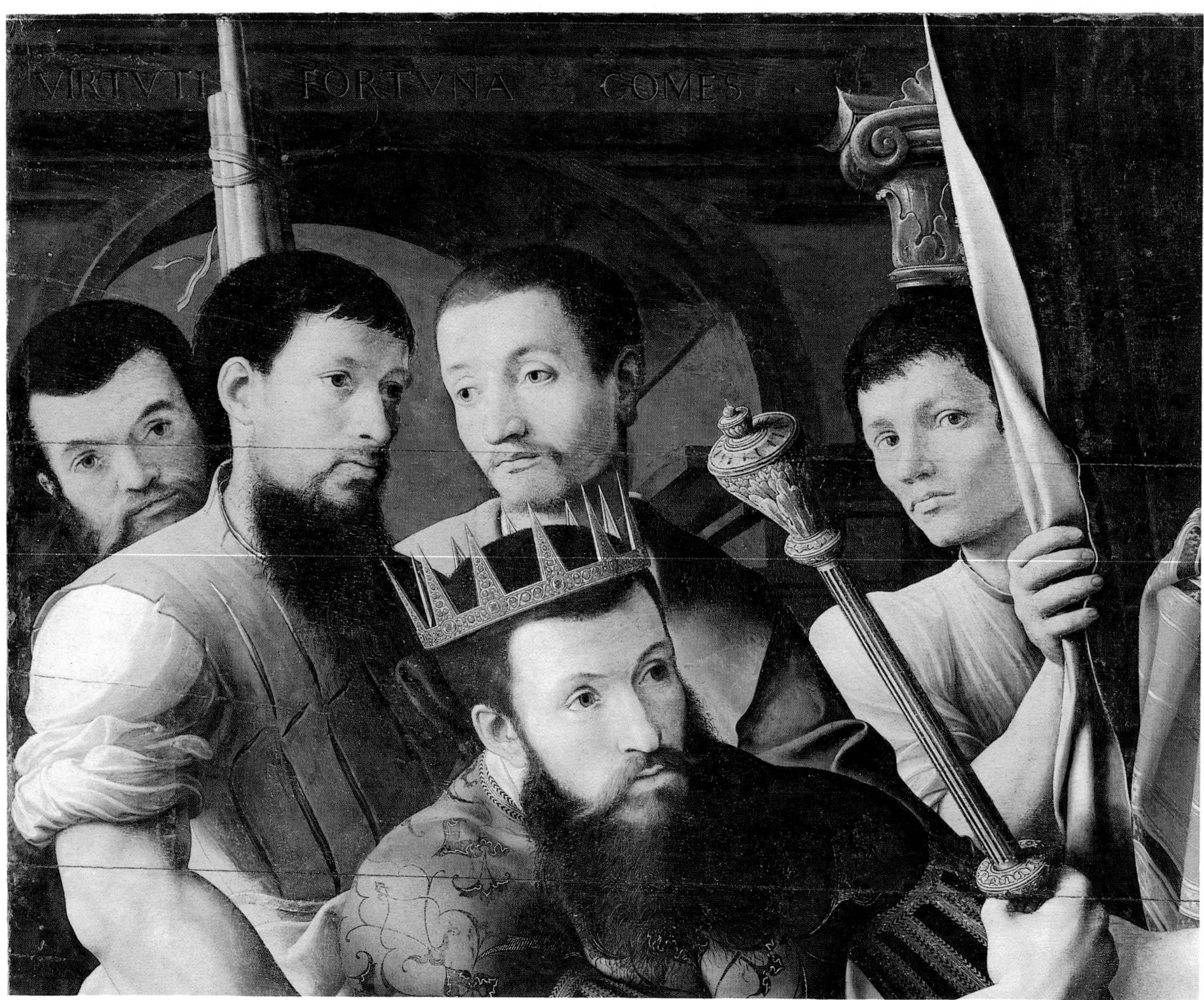

Fig. 61. Master of the Dinteville Allegory, detail, *Moses and Aaron before Pharaoh: An Allegory of the Dinteville Family* (cat. no. 43)

break the barrier of the frame, in the sense of both their ever more tangible nature and their worldly outlook, becoming more powerfully a part of the spectator's space.

The tendency toward representing an ever greater range of human expression in portraiture indicated in Massys's paintings is evolved further in Marten van Heemskerck's portrait *Jacob Willemsz. van Veen, the Artist's Father* of 1532 (cat. no. 42). This vigorous characterization is as remarkable for its larger-than-life conception as for its keenly felt emotional content. The uncompromising, stern disposition and advanced age of the artist's father are boldly characterized by the old man's fixed address of the viewer and by the poignant portrayal of his physiognomy, with its deeply set lines of age and the sagging flesh of his jowls. A sense of the difficult nature of the relationship between this father and his painter son—the father disapproved of the son's profession—is imparted by Heemskerck's highly personal rendering. The inscription at the base of the picture is factual and entirely in keeping with the father's dour outlook: "My son portrayed me here when I had lived 75 years so they say."

While the practice of casting the sitter in the guise of a hallowed being in order to suggest character evolved throughout the fifteenth and sixteenth centuries, it was in the sixteenth century that the use of allegorical portraiture to convey a strong political message was introduced. The Museum's *Moses and Aaron before Pharaoh: An Allegory of the Dinteville Family*, dated 1537 (cat. no. 43; fig. 61), is a prime example of the latter form. Here featured as players on an extremely restricted stage, whose constriction perhaps is meant to express the pressure and urgency of the protagonists' needs, are members of the noted Dinteville family appearing as Moses and Aaron and their entourage. They appeal to Pharaoh (who bears the features of Francis I) to ensure their future survival, a reference to the contemporary concerns of the Dintevilles, whose wealth and position were threatened. One of the great group portraits of the first half of the sixteenth century, this allegory once hung together with Hans Holbein's tour de force *Ambassadors* of 1533 (National Gallery, London); together they spoke eloquently to the new and diverse concerns of portraiture in the advancing sixteenth century.

MARYAN W. AINSWORTH

References: Bauman 1986; Campbell 1990; Veronée-Verhaegen 1994 (with helpful bibliography)

Workshop of Robert Campin

20. Man in Prayer, about 1430–35

Oil on wood; overall 12½ x 9⅛ in. (31.8 x 23.2 cm); painted surface 12½ x 9 in. (31.8 x 23 cm)
Bequest of Mary Stillman Harkness, 1950 50.145.35

Provenance: Ivo Francis Walter Bligh, eighth earl of Darnley, Cobham Hall, Kent (until 1925; sale, Christie's, London, May 1, no. 49, as Memling, A Man in the Attitude of Prayer, 1575, to Colnaghi); [Colnaghi, London, from 1925]; [Knoedler, New York?]; Edward S. Harkness, New York (1927–40); Mrs. Edward S. Harkness, New York (1940–50).

References: Friedländer 1924–37, vol. 3 (1925), p. 112; Hulin de Loo 1926, pp. 268–74; Destrée 1930, p. 180; Renders and Lyna 1931, pp. 289–97; De Tolnay 1939, p. 58; Beenken 1951, pp. 70, 142; Panofsky 1953, pp. 292–93, 477–78; Held 1955, pp. 227–28; Eisler 1964, pp. 99–101; Bruyn 1974, pp. 539–41; De Coo 1991; Pächt 1994, p. 77; Campbell 1996, p. 127.

This portrait poignantly conveys the sitter's introspective and reserved attitude of prayer toward a devotional object, perhaps an image of the Virgin and Child, originally placed to the left to form a diptych. The sympathetic depiction of the features of the head—particularly the nuanced rendering of the mouth, the glint in the tired eyes, the lightly etched age lines of the brow, the backlit contour of the left cheek that reveals the white stubble of the emerging beard, the softly modeled sagging jowls, and the wispy tendrils of the tousled hair—is the work of a highly accomplished artist, a fact underscored by the recent cleaning of the picture. Yet the exact placement of this portrait within the oeuvre of a known master is problematic.

Hulin de Loo pinpointed the difficulties involved in his comparison of our portrait with paintings by Campin and Rogier van der Weyden, with which, he felt, it was both consistent and inconsistent. Certain conventions known from Campin's relatively few portraits, especially the *Portrait of a Man* and *Portrait of a Woman* in the National Gallery, London, and the so-called portraits of Robert Masmines in the Gemäldegalerie, Berlin, and the Museo Thyssen-Bornemisza, Madrid, are in evidence here: the strong illumination that falls on the head, sharply defining the prominent facial features; the three-quarter profile; the tightly cropped close-up view; the psychologically mute, motionless gaze—all characteristics that led Pächt to describe Campin's portraits as "still-life[s] of the human face."

But the assertive three-dimensional form of Campin's known heads is not present in our sitter's visage, which in its flatter, more planar, and softer treatment stands closer to portraits by Rogier. Yet the head does not display Rogier's elegant, decorative quality of line. It is in the hands, even in their present damaged state, that our portrait shows the strongest similarities to this master's work: the articulation of their form, with some oddly crooked fingers and the accentuated drawing of the fingernail of the right thumb, in particular, corresponds to Rogier's mannerisms.

The *Portrait of Guillaume Fillastre* (Courtauld Institute Galleries, London) parallels our panel in terms of its conflation of Campinesque and Rogierian qualities; in fact, Panofsky illustrated them together as examples by Van der Weyden. Since Panofsky published them, they have been attributed variously to Van der Weyden and to Campin (to the latter, for example in Campbell 1996). Our portrait can perhaps best be explained as a product of the Campin workshop in Tournai when Rogier was an influential assistant there, that is, before he left for Brussels, where he established himself in 1435. This hypothesis is supported by the style of the costume, which was fashionable in the 1430s, and the dendrochronology of the panel, which is compatible with a dating of about 1430–35 for the execution of the painting.

A later copy of the portrait, made on copper and of similar size, is in the Pinacoteca Civico Tosio-Martinengo, Brescia. MWA

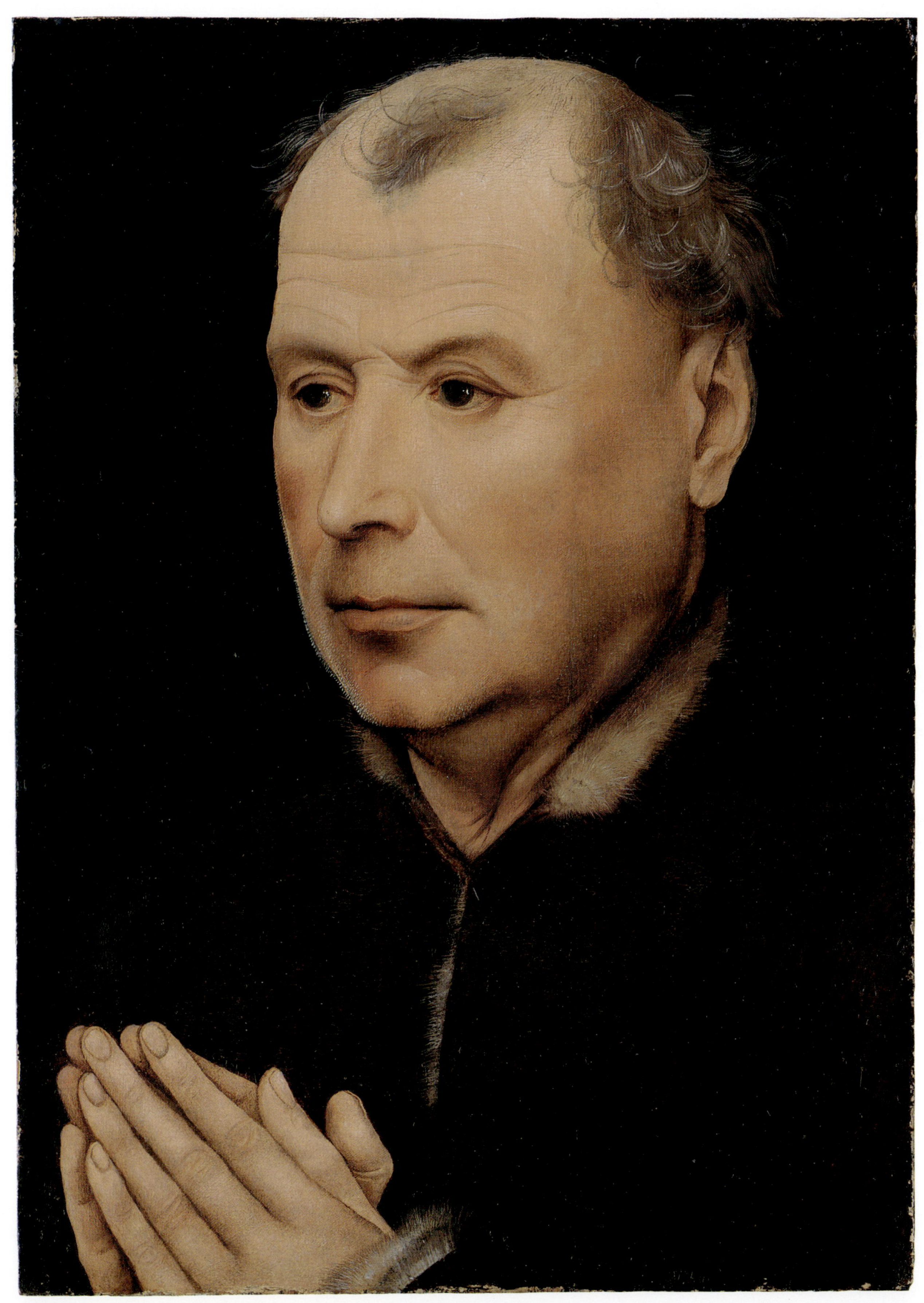

Petrus Christus, active by 1444, died 1475/76

21. *Portrait of a Carthusian*, dated 1446

Oil on wood; overall 11½ x 8½ in. (29.2 x 21.6 cm); painted surface 11½ x 7⅜ in. (29.2 x 18.7 cm)
Signed and dated (bottom, on simulated frame): ·PETRVS·XPI·ME·FECIT·A°· 1446. (Petrus Christus made me in the year 1446)
The Jules Bache Collection, 1949 49.7.19

This small, exquisitely realized painting represents an anonymous lay brother of the Carthusian order, possibly a member of the monastery at Genadedal, near Bruges. It is among the earliest individual portraits in our collection, one of the few extant independent portraits of a male cleric or a lay brother from the fifteenth century, and one of the great portraits in the history of early Netherlandish art.

In conformity with Eyckian practice, the sitter is shown in three-quarter view, behind a feigned stone molding inscribed with the artist's name and the date of the picture's execution. Despite the dependence of Christus on Eyckian portrait conventions, he dispensed with the dark, neutral background Van Eyck almost invariably used as the foil for his sitters and, instead, suggested an interior setting, posing the man against the corner space of an implied room painted a resonant red. This is one of the earliest bust-length portraits by a Netherlandish painter that explores the possibilities of an interior setting. Christus elaborated on the formulation in an exactly contemporary depiction of Edward Grimston (National Gallery, London, on loan from the earl of Verulam, Gorhambury), where the sitter is shown in a fully articulated room with a circular window on one wall, used to suggest the light source of the image. Ainsworth has noted that the underdrawings for the heads of the Carthusian and Grimston are almost identical, underscoring the close relationship of the two pictures and Christus's focus on developing a particular portrait type within a convincing interior.

The illusionistic impact of the setting of our picture is emphasized by the subtle modeling of the face and habit and by the manipulation of light—whereby the lit portion of the head is silhouetted against a dark background and the unlit portion is placed against a lighter background. It is further enhanced by the inclusion of a fly, on the implied windowsill, which may have symbolic meaning as a talisman or memento mori.

The original intention of the portrait was altered by the later addition of an incised arc and a gold halo, which was recently removed. Except for the incision and damage to the right temple from the center point of the compass used to draw the arc, the painting's surface is in superb condition. The tiny date to the extreme right of the trompe-l'oeil frame may have been added sometime after the picture was completed—it perhaps copies a date on the original frame, now lost—since it is in paint of a different color from that of the lettering, spoils the strict symmetry of the inscription, and, unlike it, is not conceived as a carving.

Two nineteenth-century copies of this portrait were made in Valencia, confirming the presence of the portrait there during that time. Both copies were formerly in Valencia, and one remains there: one with the halo (Conde de Berbedel collection, Valencia) and another, an ivory miniature without the halo, by the Valencian painter Rafael Montesinos y Ramiro (1811–1877) (Museo de Bellas Artes de Bilbao).

DCS

Provenance: Don Ramon de Oms (Don Ramon de la Cruz), viceroy of Majorca (by 1911); Marqués de Dos Aguas, Valencia (by 1916–after 1924); [Sulley, London, by 1926–27]; [Knoedler, New York, 1927]; Jules S. Bache, New York (1927–44).

References: Agrasot 1911, ill. p. 14; Friedländer 1916, p. 21, pl. 3; Friedländer 1924–37, vol. 1 (1924), pp. 145–46, pl. 50; Burroughs 1938, pp. 249–50; Panofsky 1953, pp. 188, 310, 312, 488–89 n. 5, pl. 252; Scholtens 1960, pp. 59–72; Pigler 1964, pp. 47, 51, fig. 34; Friedländer 1967–76, vol. 1 (1967), pp. 82, 95, 104,

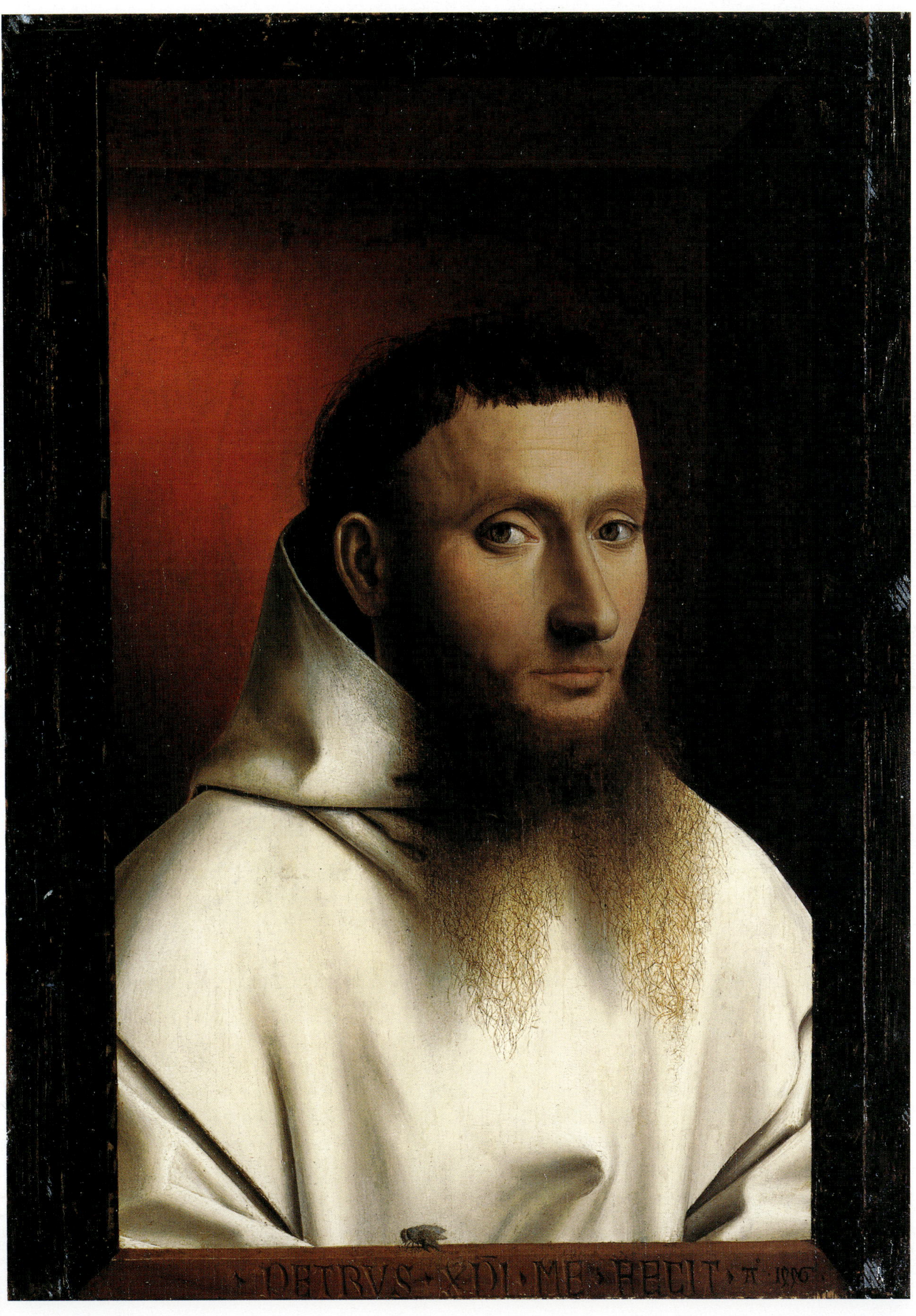

110, n. 52, pl. 74; Gellman 1970, pp. 9, 40, 49, 51–53, 64, 67, 75–80, 81, 86, 91, 271–72, 312 nn. 16, 17, 313 nn. 18, 19, 314 n. 26, 380, no. 2, fig. 6; Schabacker 1974, pp. 23–25, 33, 38, 43, 73, 81–83, 128, 130, no. 3, fig. 3; Bermejo Martinez 1980–82, vol. 1, pp. 36, 69–70; Bauman 1986, pp. 6–7, 11, 36–38, 42, 44, 51, 53, 58, figs. 6, 28; Upton 1990, pp. 22–28, 30, 32, 42, 45, 57, 67, 72, 78, 111, fig. 15; Ainsworth 1994b, pp. 15, 28–30, 32, 49–53, 89, 92–96, 100, 154, 168–69, 178–79, 186, 189–90, no. 5, colorpl. p. 92, figs. 14, 62, 63; Ainsworth 1995, pp. 53, 56–57, 60, 78, 82, 98, 143, 153, 176, 183–84, 186, 205, fig. 1.

Petrus Christus, active by 1444, died 1475/76

22. *A Goldsmith in His Shop, Possibly Saint Eligius,* dated 1449

Oil on wood; overall 39⅜ x 34¾ in. (100.1 x 85.8 cm); painted surface 38⅝ x 33½ in. (98 x 85.2 cm)
Signed and dated (bottom): m petr[vs] xpi me· ·fecit·a° 1449. (Master Petrus Christus made me in the year 1449) [with the artist's emblem, which resembles a clock escapement combined with a heart]
Robert Lehman Collection, 1975 1975.1.110

Provenance: A. Merli, Bremen (his sale, Frankfurt-am-Main, September 11, 1815, no. 144, as "ein Goldarbeiter in seinem Laden by Jan van Eyck" for fl200); bought by Silberberg for Gerhard Siebel, Elberfeld; Salomon Oppenheim the younger, Cologne (by 1825–d. 1828); his grandson, Albert, freiherr von Oppenheim, Cologne (d. 1912) (sale, Lepke, Berlin, March 19, 1918, no. 6); Busch, Mainz [Y. Perdoux, Paris]; Philip Lehman, New York, 1920; Robert Lehman, New York.

References: Brulliot 1817–20, vol. 1, cols. 874–75, no. 145; Brulliot 1832–34, vol. 3, p. 137, no. 953; Weale 1863, pp. 240–41; Woltmann 1879, pp. 298–300; Smith 1908, pp. 155–56, pl. 24; Smith 1914, pp. 326, 331–32, 335, ill. p. 333; Panofsky 1953, pp. 174, 313, 321, 340, 354, 509 n. 1 (for p. 354), fig. 407; Friedländer 1967–76, vol. 1 (1967), pp. 82–83, pl. 75;

This is among the most enigmatic as well as the most ambitious pictures by Petrus Christus, who conspicuously signed and dated it: "Master Petrus Christus made me in the year 1449." The intriguing symbol after the date appears to be a heart with the elements of a foliot escapement for a mechanical clock. Christus did not use this symbol in other works, perhaps because it relates specifically to the content of this painting.

Little beyond the authorship and date is certain about the work: its original context and the identities of the figures have long been the focus of speculation. The ostensible subject is a couple selecting a ring from a goldsmith, who is shown in his booth holding a balance, his wares displayed on the shelves behind him. A convex mirror propped against the opening of the stall reflects two passersby and a street lined with houses, at once indicating the site of the workshop and extending the space notionally in front of the picture plane. A halo on the goldsmith was discovered to be a later addition and removed in 1993. It remains unclear, nonetheless, whether the tradesman is intended to represent Saint Eligius, the patron saint of goldsmiths (halos were not commonly shown on saints in early Netherlandish painting), or whether he is an especially celebrated goldsmith of the day.

Saint Eligius brought Christianity to Flanders in the seventh century and was the bishop of Tournai and Noyon (Oise). He was particularly important in Bruges, where he was associated with the guilds of the goldsmiths, silversmiths, metalworkers, blacksmiths, and, jointly with Saint Luke, the painters and saddlemakers. Eligius also founded two churches in Bruges, Sint-Salvatorskerk (Saint Savior's) and Sint-Donaaskerk (Saint Donatian's).

Numerous interpretations of the picture have been proposed (see the summary in Ainsworth 1994b), of which the most compelling is Schabacker's. He suggests that it should be understood as a vocational painting—a depiction of a profession, in this case of a Flemish goldsmith in his workplace conducting business—and that it was commissioned to decorate a guild chapel. Whether a picture of such an apparently secular character would have been appropriate for a chapel is questionable; however, a guildhall might seem a more likely location. Indeed, a notable painting that perhaps represents an analogous type of commission is Rogier van der Weyden's *Saint Luke Drawing the Virgin* (fig. 19), which is thought by some to have been executed for the chapel of the Guild of Saint Luke in the church of Sainte Gudule in Brussels (see Eisler 1961, p. 74).

Although it seems likely that the *Goldsmith in His Shop* is a vocational painting, the possibility that its primary focus is a genre subject should not be ruled out altogether. Few fifteenth-century works of the kind survive, but inventories from the period—especially of Italian collections—leave little doubt that Netherlandish genre paintings were numerous and popular (see "The View from Italy" in this publication). In this regard it is worth noting that prior to 1543 the Italian writer and collector Marcantonio Michiel recorded a small, half-length composition in a private collection in Milan that portrayed "a gentleman settling accounts with his foreman . . . painted in 1440." The scene was ascribed to Jan van Eyck but thought by Michiel to be the work of Memling (see Morelli 1884, p. 116); according to Silver, it is the source of Quentin Massys's *Banker and His Client*, which is lost but known through two copies.

As Wolff has pointed out, Massys also painted a well-known picture of a money changer and his wife (Louvre, Paris). A seventeenth-century observer noted that its original frame, now lost, was inscribed "Let the balance be just and the weights equal"; the phrase is adapted from Leviticus 19:36 and clearly indicates the painting's moral content (see Harbison 1995a, pp. 144–45). In formal terms Massys's picture has much in common with Christus's composition, and each includes allegorical and religious content that gives a moral dimension to a genre

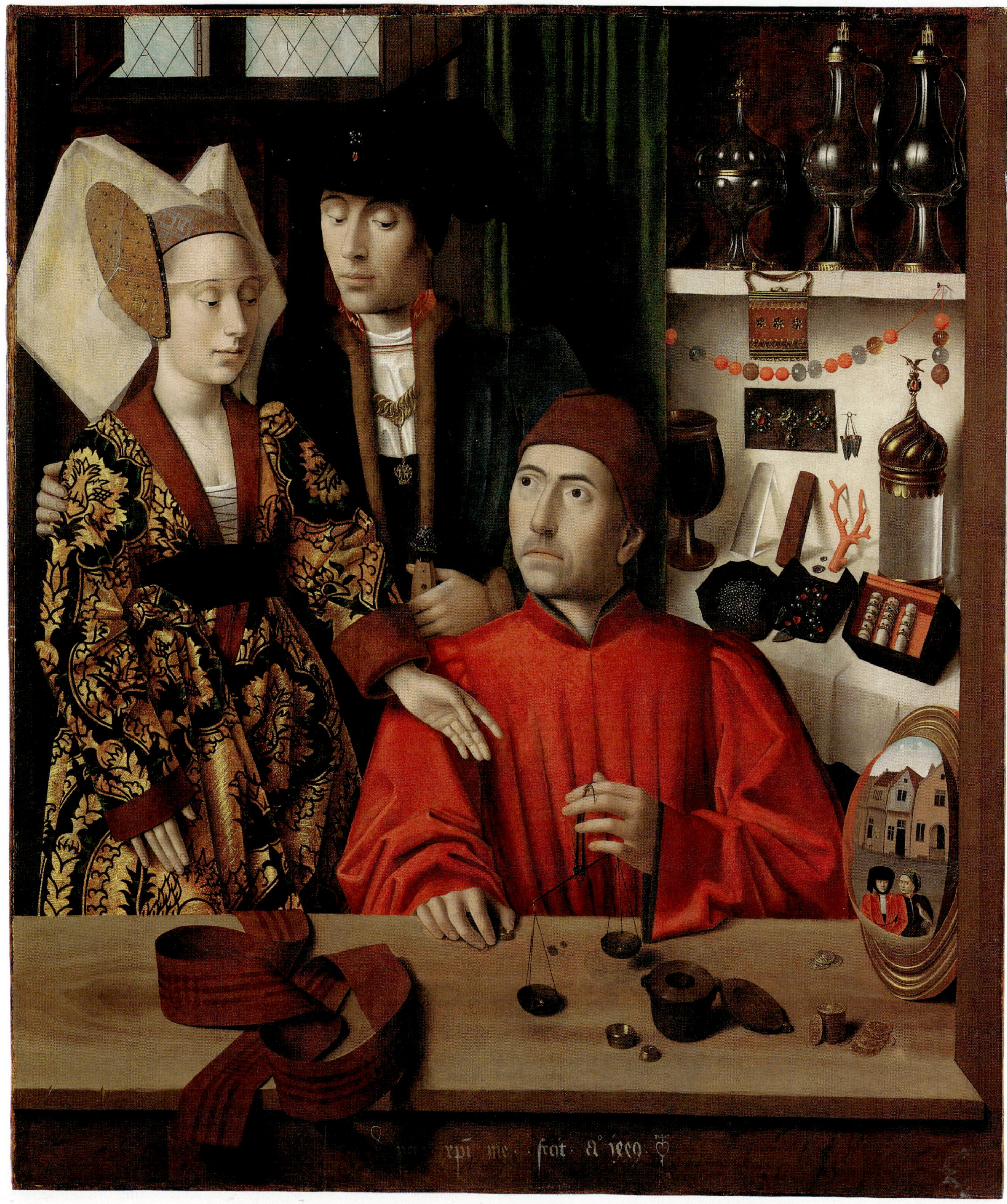
xpi me · fecit · a° 1449

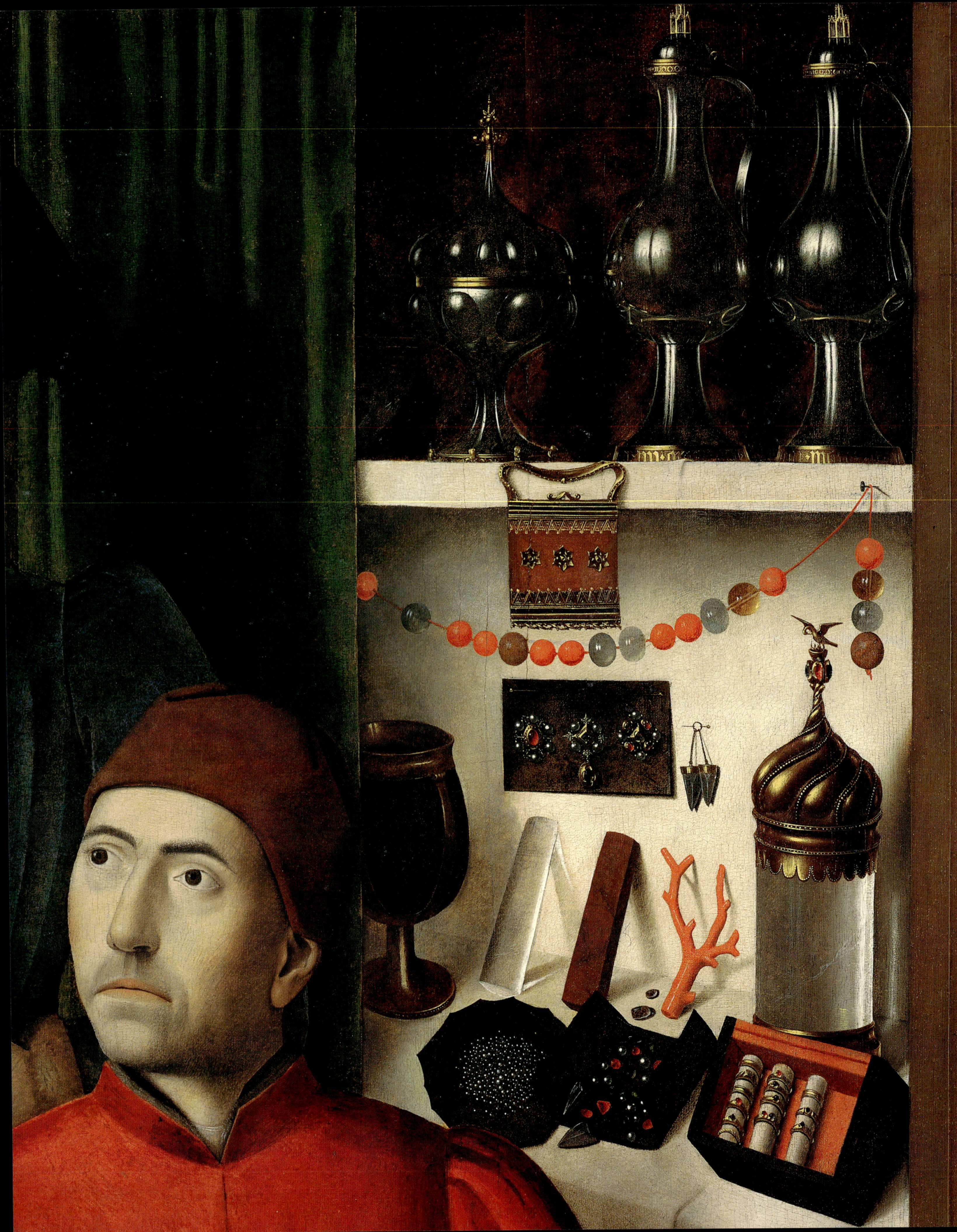

scene. At the very least, these analogies suggest the importance of the *Goldsmith in His Shop* in the history of genre painting, regardless of its original function.

The commemorative function of vocational paintings would explain our picture's extremely unusual lifesize scale; the attempt to give the goldsmith more individualized features than those displayed by his customers (his figure has the most extensive underdrawing); and the emphasis on formal gestures, which endows the image with a serious, almost hieratic quality. Indicatively, the articles shown on the shelves include the raw materials and finished products, both secular and religious, of the goldsmith's trade. The most important liturgical object is to the right on the bottom shelf, a crystal ciborium perhaps meant to house a relic or store eucharistic wafers; the top shelf holds secular wares, namely silver presentation pitchers and a hanging belt buckle, below which are exhibited beads, brooches, and rings. There are also numerous items with presumed apotropaic properties, particularly the cup made from a coconut shell, the fossilized shark's teeth, and the branch of coral.

The convex mirror is a detail that Jan van Eyck famously employed both in the portrait of the Arnolfini of 1434 (figs. 8, 9) and in his lost genre scene of a nude woman, which is known from descriptions and copies, such as the example in the Fogg Art Museum, Cambridge, Massachusetts. In our picture the mirror not only describes the site of the workshop but also may add a moralizing dimension. It perhaps signifies the imperfections of the real world, as represented by the reflection of the vast space outdoors, where one of the two standing men holds a falcon, in contrast to the small but secure and ideal space inhabited by the devoted couple and the goldsmith. The presence of a falconer on the streets of fifteenth-century Bruges would have been an anomaly, and the portrayal of one here is a discordant feature; falconers were seldom depicted by Netherlanders, occasionally appearing in hunt scenes and at official events. Ainsworth (1994b) explains that the falcon is a traditional symbol of pride and greed, a meaning reinforced by the idea of vanity associated with the mirror and played off against the sense of virtue evoked by the solemn couple in the goldsmith's shop. In the stillness of the shop's interior, the goldsmith looks out as the scales tip to his right, toward the couple and in the direction of the righteous, perhaps indicating the future fidelity of the man and woman or symbolizing the Last Judgment. DCS

Gellman 1970, pp. 96–100, 193–94, 386–95, no. 4, fig. 12; Schabacker 1972a, pp. 103–13, figs. 1, 2; Szabo 1975, pp. 79–80, colorpl. 57; Hibbard 1980, p. 188, fig. 361; Scott 1980, pp. 146–48, fig. 77; Silver 1984, pp. 9, 108, 137, fig. 119; Upton 1990, pp. 3 n. 9, 22, 32–34, 45, 47–48, 52, 56, 71–73, 76–77, 84, 89, fig. 23; Ainsworth 1994b, pp. 15, 25, 30, 37–38, 41–42, 55, 59, 96–101, 136, 189–90, 192, no. 6, colorpl. p. 97, figs. 16, 41–43, 45, 71, 77, 112–14; Ainsworth 1995, pp. 151, 153, 179, 183–84, 205; Gellman 1995, pp. 107–8; Upton 1995, pp. 57–58; Wolff 1998, no. 12, color ill.

Opposite: Detail, cat. no. 22

Rogier van der Weyden, 1399/1400–1464

23. Francesco d'Este (born about 1430, died after 1475), about 1460

Oil on wood; overall 12½ x 8¾ in. (31.8 x 22.2 cm); painted surface, each side 11¾ x 8 in. (29.8 x 20.3 cm)
Inscribed (verso): v[ost]re tout (entirely yours) / m[archio] e[stensis] (marquis of Este) [twice]/ francisque (Francesco)
Incised (verso, upper left, at slightly later date): non plus / courcelles (no longer / courcelles) [possibly referring to the village of Corcelles, near the Grandson battlefield, where the sitter may have died in 1476]
Arms and crest (verso) of the Este family, quartered with the augmentation of honor bestowed on the house of Este in 1432 by Charles VII of France
The Friedsam Collection, Bequest of Michael Friedsam, 1931 32.100.43

Provenance: Sir Audley Neeld, Grittleton House, Chippenham, Wiltshire (until 1909); Capt. R. Langton Douglas, London; [Colnaghi, London, 1910]; Sir Edgar Speyer, London and New York (1911–16); [Kleinberger, New York, 1916–18]; Michael Friedsam, New York (1918–31).

References: Fry 1910–11, pp. 198, 201–3, ills.; Kantorowicz 1939–40, pp. 165–80, pls. 32a,d; Wehle and Salinger 1947, pp. 35–38, ill.; Panofsky 1953, pp. 272–73, 291, 294, 477 n. 5 (for p. 291), pl. 225, no. 366; Davies 1972, pp. 25, 229, 244, pls. 111–12; Armstrong 1977, pp. 72, 74, ill.; Bauman 1986, pp. 38–42, ills.; Nickel 1987, pp. 144–46; Dierick 1991, pp. 182–84, pl. 103b (verso).

The sitter for this striking portrait was definitively identified by Kantorowicz as Francesco d'Este, the illegitimate son of Leonello d'Este (1407–1450), marquis of Ferrara, whose coat of arms appears on the verso. The inscription *francisque* beneath the Este arms surely refers to him. In 1444 Francesco left Ferrara for the Netherlands, where he received his military training at the court of Philip the Good, duke of Burgundy. He was educated with Philip's son, Charles de Charlerois (later Charles the Bold), and became a permanent chamberlain to Philip, acting frequently as an envoy to Italy. Engaged at the court until Philip's death in 1467 and then in service to Charles, he is last mentioned in 1475.

The picture must have been painted in the Netherlands about 1460, when Francesco was about thirty years old, and is stylistically consistent with Rogier's late work. It has the aloof, hieratic quality typical of his portraits of nobility; the liveliness of the drawing of the hands, with hammer and ring, serves as a foil to the austerity of the face against the stark white ground. This light ground is an unusual feature perhaps derived from Robert Campin, who employed it in his *Portrait of a Stout Man*, of which there are two versions (Gemäldegalerie, Berlin, and Museo Thyssen-Bornemisza, Madrid). Netherlandish portraits of the period, including Rogier's other surviving examples and Memling's somewhat later likenesses of the Portinari (cat. no. 27), more characteristically have dark backgrounds.

The hammer appears as an attribute of princes and persons of high rank in a number of male portraits of the northern Renaissance, but its meaning remains enigmatic. It was evidently used by an official of stature to ceremoniously "knock out" disqualified shields before a tournament; the ring, in this context, would be a prize for a tournament victory. The hammer has also been interpreted as a symbol of office—Francesco was, for example, captain and governor of Westerloo and LeQuesnoy.

That this is Francesco can be confirmed by comparing his features to those in a profile medallion of Francesco d'Este, painted perhaps ten years later (Biblioteca Vittorio Emmanuele, Rome; Kantorowicz, pl. 32b). However, the subject in Hans Memling's *Portrait of a Man with an Arrow* (National Gallery of Art, Washington, D.C.), which Kantorowicz tentatively identifies as Francesco in his forties, is, despite a similar aquiline nose, too different in his other features to be the same man.

The splendid coat of arms on the reverse was in all likelihood painted by workshop assistants. Apparently a dedication, the inscription *v[ost]re tout . . . francisque* suggests that the portrait was not kept by the sitter but was given by him to a friend or member of the court. MSdJ

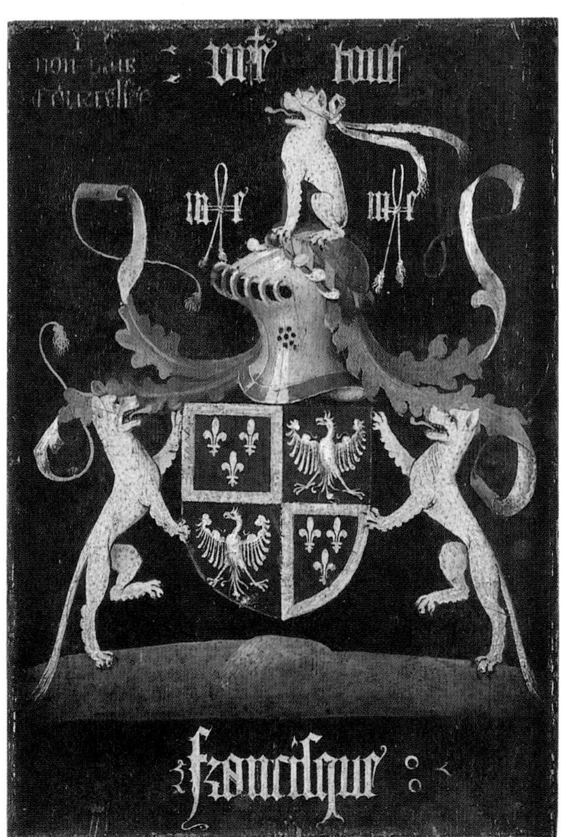

Verso, cat. no. 23

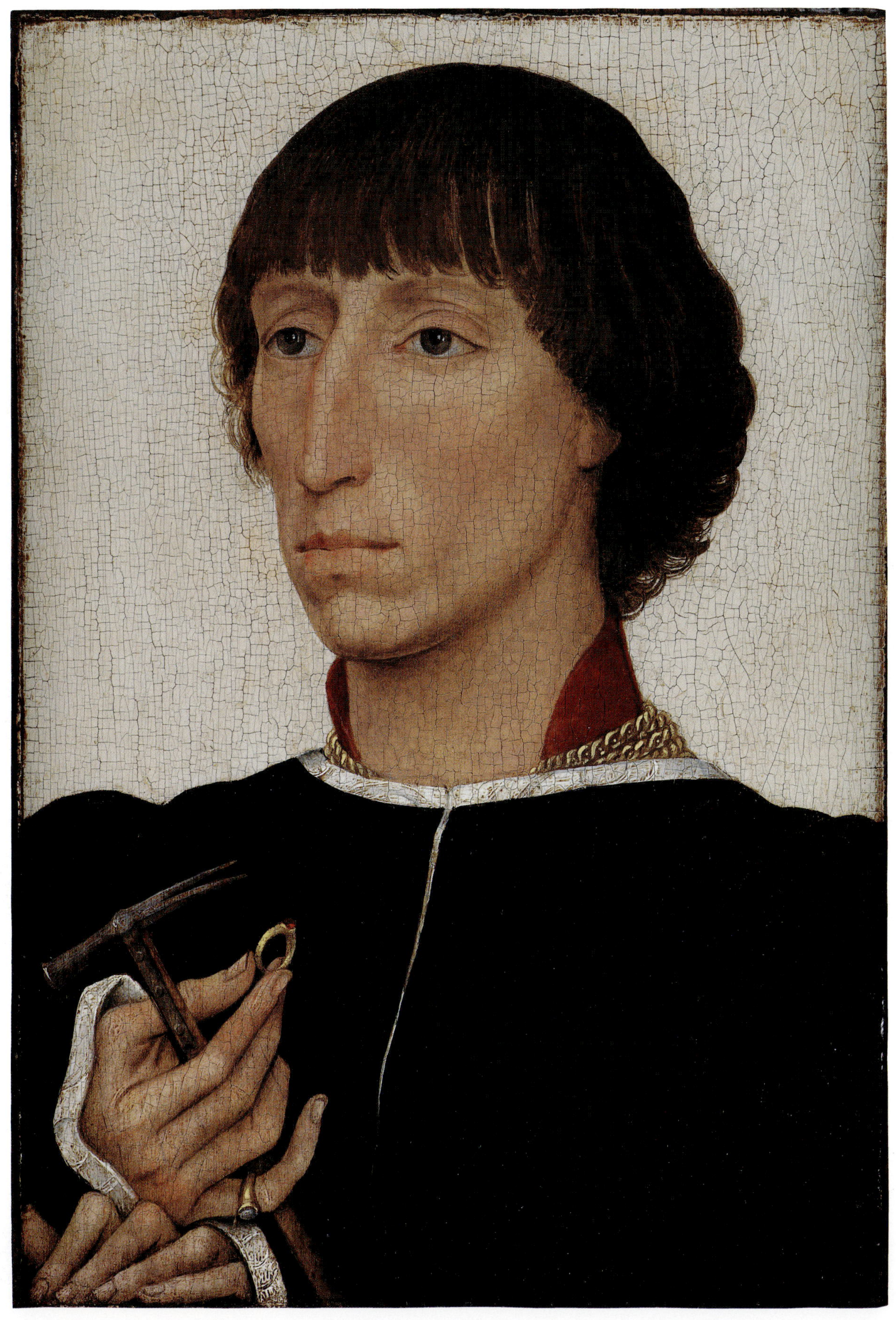

Circle of Dieric Bouts

24. *A Donor Presented by a Saint,* about 1460–65

Oil on wood, 8¾ x 7 in. (22.2 x 17.8 cm)
The Friedsam Collection, Bequest of Michael J. Friedsam, 1931 32.100.41

Provenance: Edouard Warneck, Paris (sale, Galerie Georges Petit, Paris, May 27, 1926, no. 2, as Dieric Bouts); [Kleinberger, New York (1926)]; Michael Friedsam, New York (1926–31).

References: Kervyn de Lettenhove et al. 1908, p. 80; Durand-Gréville 1910, pp. 117–18; Friedländer 1916, pp. 39–40; Conway 1921, pp. 163–64; Friedländer 1924–37, vol. 5 (1925), pp. 45, 107; Friedsam collection n.d., p. 145; Noe 1930, p. 34; Baldass 1932, pp. 100, 104, 108, 114; Burroughs and Wehle 1932, pp. 16–17; Schöne 1938, pp. 39–40, 170; Wehle and Salinger 1947, pp. 16–17; Francotte 1951, pp. 51, 183; Brussels–Delft 1957–58, pp. 40–41, no. 10; Friedländer 1967–76, vol. 3 (1968), pp. 60–61; Bauman 1986, p. 16.

When this painting was first shown in the Golden Fleece exhibition of 1907 in Bruges, the principal figure was surrounded by a dark background and appeared to represent an independent portrait. X-radiography carried out after the panel was acquired by the Metropolitan Museum, however, revealed the remains of another figure behind the sitter. In 1949 the overpaint of the background was removed, and it became clear that the panel is a fragment cut from the left wing of a triptych or from a larger devotional painting and that it depicts a kneeling donor presented by his patron saint, probably Saint John the Baptist, shown with his voluminous red cloak and bare arm.

The man's deeply pensive expression and far-away gaze imply that he is meditating upon a now-missing devotional image that once was placed at his left. His likeness is imbued with the spiritual aura of certain portraits by Jan van Eyck, for example the *Portrait of a Man (formerly identified as Cardinal Niccolò Albergati)* (fig. 57), and it is not difficult to see why the painting was at first attributed to Jan. Indeed, the rendering of the head follows the Eyckian tradition of naturalism; however, it does not show the richness of detail or the remarkable effects of verisimilitude that characterize Jan's achievements in this genre.

This donor portrait, in fact, stands closer in certain ways to the production of the next generation of north Netherlandish painters, especially Aelbert van Ouwater and Dieric Bouts, than to Jan's paintings. The pose and the special attention given to the treatment of signs of age, namely the deeply etched lines in the brow and around the eyes, nose, and mouth, as well as the pinkish tonality of the skin, are comparable to features in our donor portrait attributed to Van Ouwater (cat. no. 25). Some of these same traits and, additionally, the psychologically intense expression, are found in a *Portrait of a Donor* of about 1470–75 attributed to a follower of Bouts (National Gallery of Art, Washington, D.C.) and in the portrait heads in the Last Supper Altarpiece painted by Dieric Bouts in 1464 (Sint-Pieterskerk, Leuven); the man standing behind Saint Peter in the central panel of Bouts's work seems especially similar to the subject here. While an attribution to the young Bouts should not be ruled out, it should be noted that Bouts's heads are usually elongated, whereas our man's likeness shows squat proportions.

Although we cannot be certain of the attribution of this beautifully executed portrait, the man's costume indicates that the painting was probably made in the 1460s. MWA

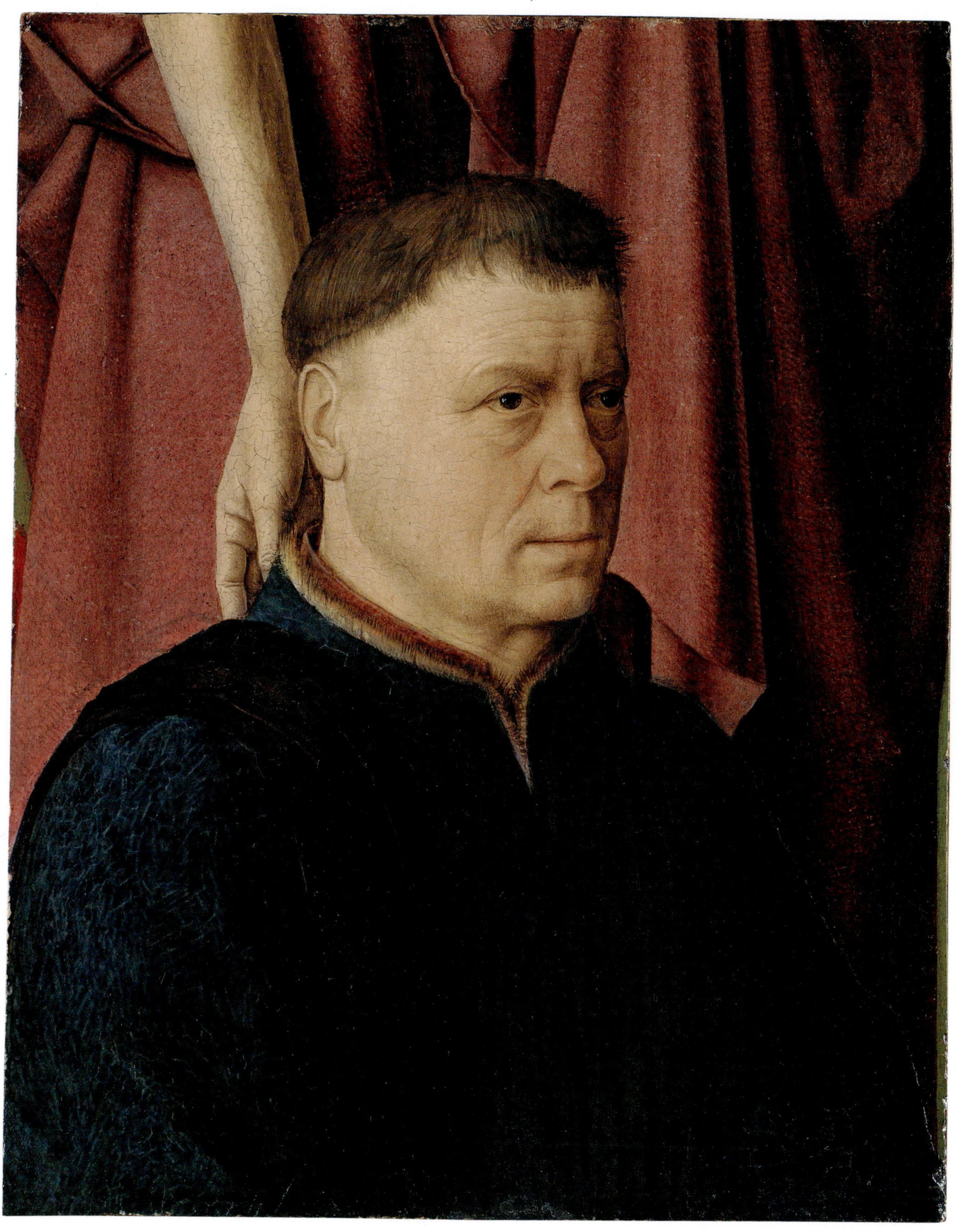

Attributed to Aelbert van Ouwater, active mid-15th century

25. *Head of a Donor,* about 1460

Oil on wood, 3⅞ x 3½ in. (9.8 x 8.9 cm)
Gift of J. Pierpont Morgan, 1917 17.190.22

Provenance: Thomas Howard, third earl of Arundel and Norfolk (d. 1652); his widow, Alethea, countess of Arundel (d. Amsterdam 1654; inventory 1655, as "Un ritratto di homo in profil, desegno de Jan van Eyck"); by descent to Henry Thomas Howard-Molyneux-Howard, Greystoke Castle, Penrith, Cumberland (d. 1824); Henry Howard, Greystoke Castle (until 1909); J. Pierpont Morgan, New York (from 1909).

References: Vertue (1741–52) 1937–38, p. 31; Scharf 1858, pp. 32–33; Weale 1904, p. 249; Weale 1908, pp. 171–72, no. 36; Friedländer 1924–37, vol. 1 (1924), p. 165, vol. 3 (1925), pp. 61, 112, no. 35, pl. 47; Schöne 1938, p. 23; Wehle and Salinger 1947, pp. 50–51, ill.; Châtelet 1960, pp. 66–67; Snyder 1960, p. 44; Friedländer 1967–76, vol. 1 (1967), p. 93, pl. 97c, vol. 3 (1968), pp. 36, 64, no. 35; Châtelet 1981a, pp. 70, 209–10, no. 43, pl. 58; Snyder 1996, p. 673.

This small painting is a fragment of a larger work, either the left wing of a devotional diptych or triptych or the left side of a single devotional panel. The donor, a priest wearing a fur-trimmed cassock and pleated surplice, must have been kneeling with his hands folded in prayer, as we see a hand at the upper left, which belonged to his patron saint, who is presenting him.

Other than the *Raising of Lazarus* (Gemäldegalerie, Berlin), a painting that documentary evidence clearly connects with Aelbert van Ouwater, our fragment is the only work that can be ascribed with some confidence to this important artist. According to Van Mander, Ouwater was the founder of the Haarlem school, and his influence can be deduced in the work of many painters who came from the northern Netherlands, including Dieric Bouts and Gerard David. The extreme attention given to folds of flesh in our painting—there are rays of little wrinkles around the eyes of the donor figure, a furrowed brow, and creases around the ear—is also found in the Berlin picture. Friedländer points out that an identically shaped ear is shared by the subject of our panel and Saint Peter, the central figure in the Berlin composition (fig. 62). The lack of animation in our man's glance, his short neck and solid round head, and the patron saint's square-nailed fingers, which do not aspire to elegance, are all consistent with what we can grasp of Ouwater's style from the *Raising of Lazarus.*

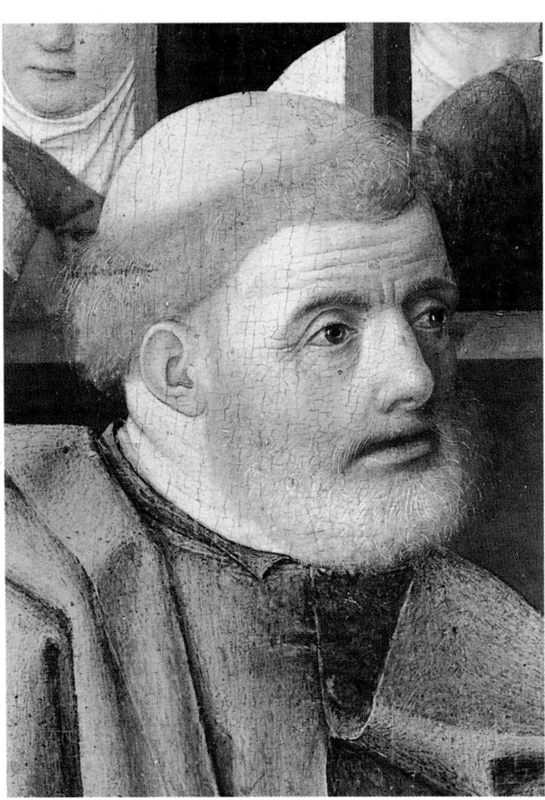

Fig. 62. Aelbert van Ouwater, detail, head of Saint Peter, *The Raising of Lazarus,* about 1450–60. Oil on wood. Gemäldegalerie, SMPK, Berlin

Two engravings of this small panel exist, both with the image in reverse. One, by Wenceslaus Hollar, omits all reference to the standing saint and shows the priest with folded hands and a sword embedded in his skull; it is dated 1647, when our fragment was in the Arundel collection, and bears an inscription declaring it to be a true likeness of Saint Thomas of Canterbury (Thomas Becket, 1118–1170) by Jan van Eyck. The second engraving, by Lucas Vorsterman, without the sword, is also identified as a likeness of this martyred English saint in its inscription. Writing in the mid-eighteenth century, Vertue does not mention any of the background elements, which most likely were overpainted before 1647 to make the panel appear to be an independent portrait. In 1905, however, when the painting was illustrated by Weale, the drapery and hand of the patron saint—perhaps John the Baptist—were again visible.

MSdJ

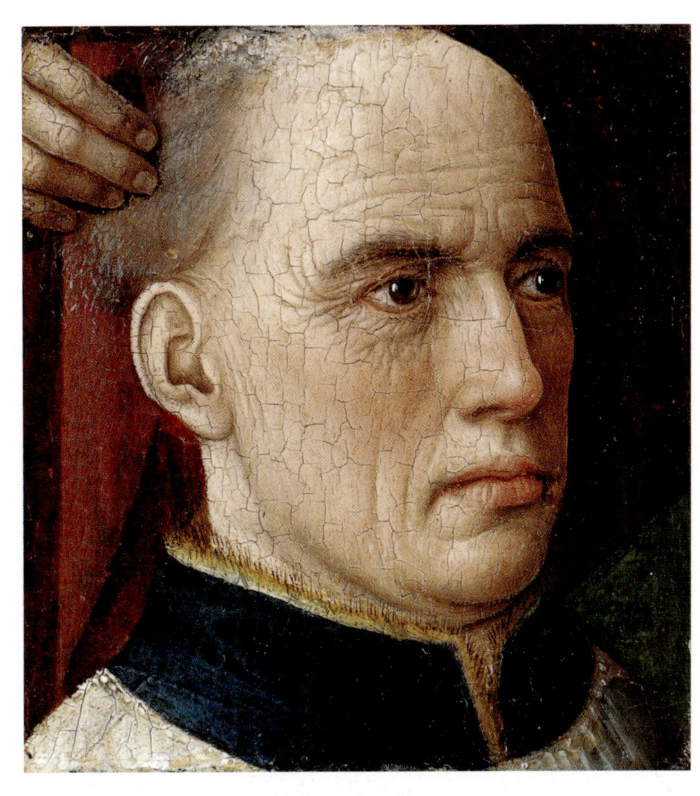

Dieric Bouts, active by 1457, died 1475

26. Portrait of a Man, about 1470

Oil on wood; overall 12 x 8½ in. (30.5 x 21.6 cm); painted surface 11⅝ x 8⅛ in. (29.5 x 20.6 cm)
Bequest of Benjamin Altman, 1913 14.40.644

Provenance: Private collection, England (until ca. 1895); Baron Albert Oppenheim, Cologne (by 1896–1912, cat. 1904, no. 3); [Kleinberger, New York (1912)]; Benjamin Altman, New York (1912–13).

References: Hulin de Loo 1902, p. 11, no. 38; Friedländer 1906a, p. 117; Friedländer 1916, p. 39; Friedländer 1924–37, vol. 3 (1925), pp. 44–45, 111, no. 32, pl. 41; Baldass 1932, pp. 100–108; Schöne 1938, pp. 7, 32, 107–8, pl. 33; Wehle and Salinger 1947, pp. 47–48, ill.; Panofsky 1953, pp. 479 n. 16 (for p. 294), 493 n. 3 (for p. 318); Friedländer 1967–76, vol. 3 (1968), pp. 27–28, 63, no. 32, pl. 51; Bauman 1986, p. 52, color ill.; Campbell 1997a.

This portrait exemplifies the austere, angular style of Bouts's mature work, in evidence after the painter settled in Leuven, where he is first recorded in 1457; as such it departs markedly from the earthy sweetness and stocky figure types of his Haarlem period. The taut drawing of the features and the firm architecture of the head, stressing horizontals and verticals, as well as the resulting expression of probity, are present as well in the portraits and some of the character heads that appear in Bouts's Holy Sacrament Altarpiece of 1467 (Sint-Pieterskerk, Leuven), a documented work of the artist's maturity. The style of our portrait is at a slight remove from the more aggressive realism of the heads depicted in *Ordeal by Fire* (Musées Royaux des Beaux-Arts de Belgique, Brussels)—a panel from Bouts's last commission, the *Justice of Emperor Otto*, which was left unfinished at his death in 1475.

The original context of this panel remains somewhat enigmatic. Trimmed on all four sides, it must be a fragment of a larger portrait or of a more extensive narrative composition. There are no technical grounds for doubting as original either the hands, which have been painted over the sitter's jacket, or the flat azurite background. Although there are few precedents in the art of this period for showing a man wearing a hat in a devotional portrait, there are later examples. The sitter in Bouts's secular *Portrait of a Man*, dated 1462 (National Gallery, London)—the artist's only other portrait that is not embedded in a larger narrative—wears a similar but shorter hat. However, the taller hat, which was in fashion in the 1470s, is ubiquitous in his altarpieces, in particular in the *Justice* panels, where they are worn by contemporary citizens, apostles, and Old Testament saints alike. The frequent use of this type of hat suggests that for Bouts it was a formal device that served to emphasize the length and verticality of his figures and portrait heads—and that for this reason he chose to represent our sitter with, rather than without, his hat.

The original panel may have been the wing of a devotional diptych or triptych (which would have included a likeness of the man's wife). Although numerous small paintings representing the Virgin and Child are attributed to Bouts and to his workshop, remarkably, no devotional diptychs or triptychs with portrait wings by him remain. The fact that there are many more surviving portraits by Rogier van der Weyden and Hans Memling, both independent and devotional (for example, cat. nos. 23, 27), suggests that Bouts was not in great demand as a portraitist by his contemporaries. They may have noticed what strikes the present-day viewer in his two surviving examples in this genre: his tendency toward abstraction, his difficulty in capturing—and animating—a likeness, and the absence of flattery. MSdJ

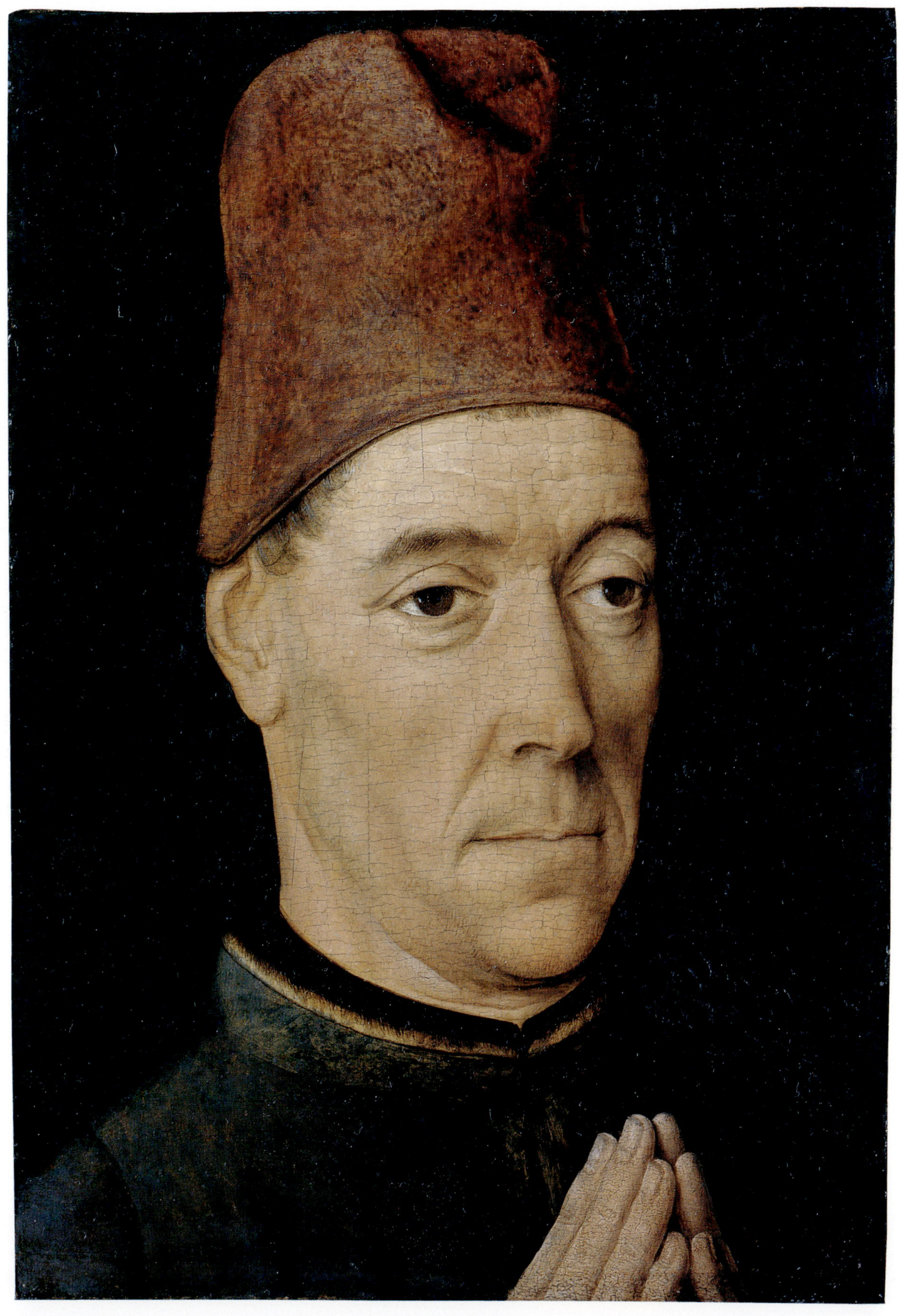

Hans Memling, active by 1465, died 1494

27. *Tommaso Portinari* (born about 1432, died 1501) *Maria Portinari* (Maria Maddalena Baroncelli, born 1456), *Wife of Tommaso Portinari,* probably 1470

Oil on wood; overall 17⅜ x 13¼ in. (44.1 x 33.7 cm); painted surface 16⅝ x 12½ in. (42.2 x 31.8 cm) Bequest of Benjamin Altman, 1913 14.40.626

Oil on wood; overall 17⅜ x 13⅜ in. (44.1 x 34 cm); painted surface 16⅝ x 12⅝ in. (42.2 x 32.1 cm) Bequest of Benjamin Altman, 1913 14.40.627

Provenance: Private collection, Italy (until 1843 or 1845); Anatole Nicolaevitch Demidov, principe di San Donato, and his wife, Princesse Mathilde Laetitia Wilhelmine Bonaparte, Paris and Florence (1843 or 1845–70) (the prince and princess separated in 1845, and the portraits were listed by Michiels in 1866 as with Mathilde in Paris, although they were sold with her husband's estate in 1870); sale, Collections de San Donato, Pillet et Petit, Paris, March 3–4, 1870, nos. 212, 213, as "Portrait d'homme" and "Portrait de Femme," by Dieric Bouts, to Huffer, for Fr. 6,000 (provenance to this point is not certain); [Huffer]; private collection, Rome (until ca. 1900); [Elia Volpi, Florence, ca. 1900]; [Agnew, London, 1901]; [Léopold Goldschmidt,

Known today for the works of art he commissioned from Hans Memling and Hugo van der Goes, Tommaso Portinari was a leading member of Bruges's large Italian mercantile community during the second half of the fifteenth century. A considerable number of Memling's surviving portraits represent members of this community, and these works—among the masterpieces of northern Renaissance art—unite an Italian taste for simplification and monumentality with a northern feeling for atmosphere and light.

Portinari was the manager of the Bruges office of the vast Medici banking empire from 1465 to 1478 and apparently rose to this position by discrediting the previous director, Angelo Tani, while Tani was away in Italy. Representing the Medici at the court of Charles the Bold, duke of Burgundy, Tommaso also served as a counselor to Charles, for whom he had the greatest admiration. He was involved in a number of risky business ventures, but his undoing was the arrangement of a loan, between 1471 and 1478, to Charles and the government of the Netherlands of the enormous sum of £9,500, only part of which was ever repaid. Charles died in battle in 1477, and in 1480 the Medici closed their Bruges office and broke their partnership contract with Tommaso. Left to take over most of the assets and liabilities of the branch, Tommaso remained in Bruges until 1497, attempting to right his financial situation. Little is known about his wife, Maria Baroncelli, beyond the fact that she came from a prominent Florentine family, some members of which were also involved in banking in Bruges.

These portraits were probably commissioned on the occasion of Tommaso and Maria's wedding in 1470, at the height of their prosperity; she was about fourteen at the time and he about thirty-eight. The sitters were first identified in 1902, presumably on the basis of their resemblance to the donor portraits of Tommaso and Maria in Hugo van der Goes's celebrated Portinari Altarpiece (fig. 29). In the altarpiece, which was painted approximately ten years later than our pictures and includes three of the couple's seven children, Maria is represented as a mature woman, but she is shown with the same intricate collar of twisted gold and jeweled enamel roses that appears in our portrait. X-radiographs reveal that the hennin, or headdress, ornamented with a V pattern and the initials T and M for Tommaso and Maria—worn by Maria in Van der Goes's right panel—was included in Memling's first idea for our portrait, but at a steeper angle; its outline is still visible to the naked eye, as is that of the part of the necklace that was originally placed higher. A considerably higher neckline for the costume, close to that of the Uffizi portrait, can also be seen in X-radiographs. Portraits of Tommaso and Maria also appear, in miniature, at the extreme left and right corners of Memling's *Scenes from the Passion of Christ* (Galleria Sabauda, Turin) and are based on their likenesses in our panels; the Turin picture is usually dated about 1470–71, before the birth of the Portinari's first child.

Our panels were no doubt the wings of a devotional triptych, with the Virgin and Child the most likely subject of the central panel. Only one complete example of a triptych of this type by Memling has survived, and it is divided between two museums: the Benedetto Portinari Triptych of 1487 (Uffizi, Florence), in which Tommaso's nephew Benedetto and his patron saint, Benedict, are portrayed on the wings that flank a central Virgin and Child (Gemäldegalerie, Berlin). This work shows the figures in a loggia overlooking an idealized landscape and exemplifies Memling's development beyond the parameters of Rogier's half-length devotional diptychs with flat, dark backgrounds—the antecedents for our own, clearly earlier, portraits. Presumably our panels, which have been thinned down and cradled, were originally painted on the reverse, like the portrait of Benedetto, whose back is decorated with what appears to be a personal emblem and motto.

The smooth volumes of the faces and the even light that plays over them are consistent with the style of a group of portraits ascribed to Memling early in his career; the closest examples are his *Portrait of Gilles Joye*, dated 1472 (Sterling and Francine Clark Art Institute, Williamstown, Massachusetts), and the *Portrait of a Man before a Landscape* (Frick Collection, New York). The latter is interesting in relation to our portraits, as its sitter is placed before a painted trompe-l'oeil frame composed of narrow gray moldings like those bordering our compositions; the moldings in the Frick picture, however, surround a view onto an extensive landscape.

De Vos (1994b) points out that in certain paintings—the portraits in particular—Memling manipulates the relation of the framing element to the figure to push the image forward. This is the case in our panels, in which the figures are positioned within, rather than behind, fictive stone moldings whose bottoms have been omitted; moreover, Maria's hennin and veil and Tommaso's right shoulder and left arm overlap these moldings. The placement of the brightly lit heads against dark backgrounds emphasizes the sense of immediacy created by these devices. As some of the paint appears to have darkened over time, it is possible that the silhouettes of the shoulders were originally more distinct, enhancing this effect.

In the powerful presence of the sitters, the Portinari portraits stand out among Memling's early efforts in the genre and offer a marked contrast to portraits by artists of the preceding generation. We have here neither the detachment and stylization of Rogier van der Weyden (cat. no. 23) nor the uncompromising realism of Van Eyck, but Memling's more humane, idealized naturalism, a feeling of living, breathing flesh that is particularly striking in the portrait of the fourteen-year-old Maria.

MSdJ

Paris, 1901–d. before 1906]; [Villeroy Goldschmidt, Paris, until 1910]; [Kleinberger, Paris and New York, 1910]; Benjamin Altman, New York, 1910–13.

References: Waagen 1847, p. 163; Michiels 1865–76, vol. 2 (1866), p. 341; Bruges 1902, pp. xxii, 26, nos. 57, 58; Warburg 1902, pp. 257–58, 260, figs. 2, 3; Friedländer 1903, p. 81, nos. 57, 58; Friedländer 1924–37, vol. 6 (1928), pp. 39–40, 129, nos. 69, 70, pls. 37, 38; Wehle and Salinger 1947, pp. 65–68, ill.; De Roover 1948, pp. 18–25; Wehle 1953, pp. 129–31, ill. p. 130, cover ill.; De Roover 1963, pp. 338–57; Hatfield Strens 1968, pp. 315–16; Friedländer 1967–76, vol. 6a (1971), pp. 26, 54, nos. 69, 70, pls. 112, 113; Ringbom 1984, p. 45; Bauman 1986, pp. 51, 53–58, color ill.; Mendes-Atanázio 1989, pp. 17–19; Lane 1991, pp. 623, 632–33; Lightbown 1992, p. 286, fig. 151; Vermeersch 1992, pp. 64, 194, 334, color ill. pp. 196–97; Ainsworth 1994a, pp. 85–86, figs. 17–18; De Vos 1994a, pp. 16, 27, 50–51, 57, 150, 156; De Vos 1994b, pp. 30–31, 34, 100–103, 108, 110, 316, 366, 370, color ills. pp. 31, 101–3; Klein 1994b, p. 103.

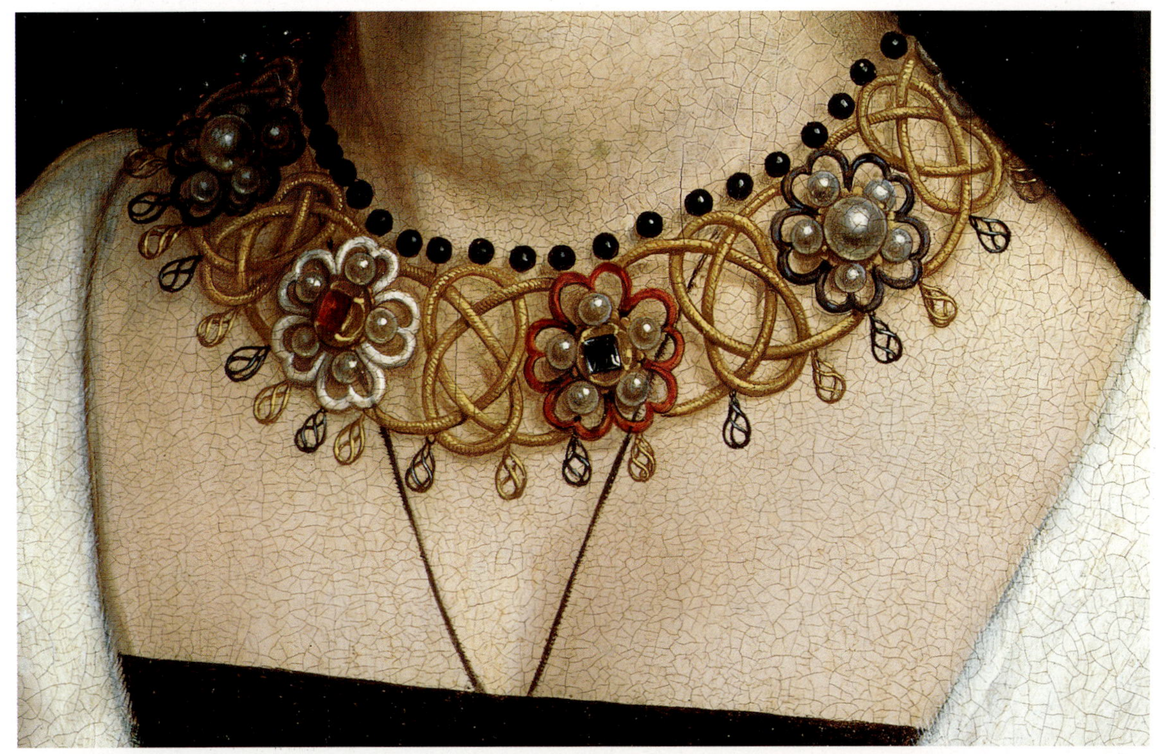

Detail, cat. no. 27

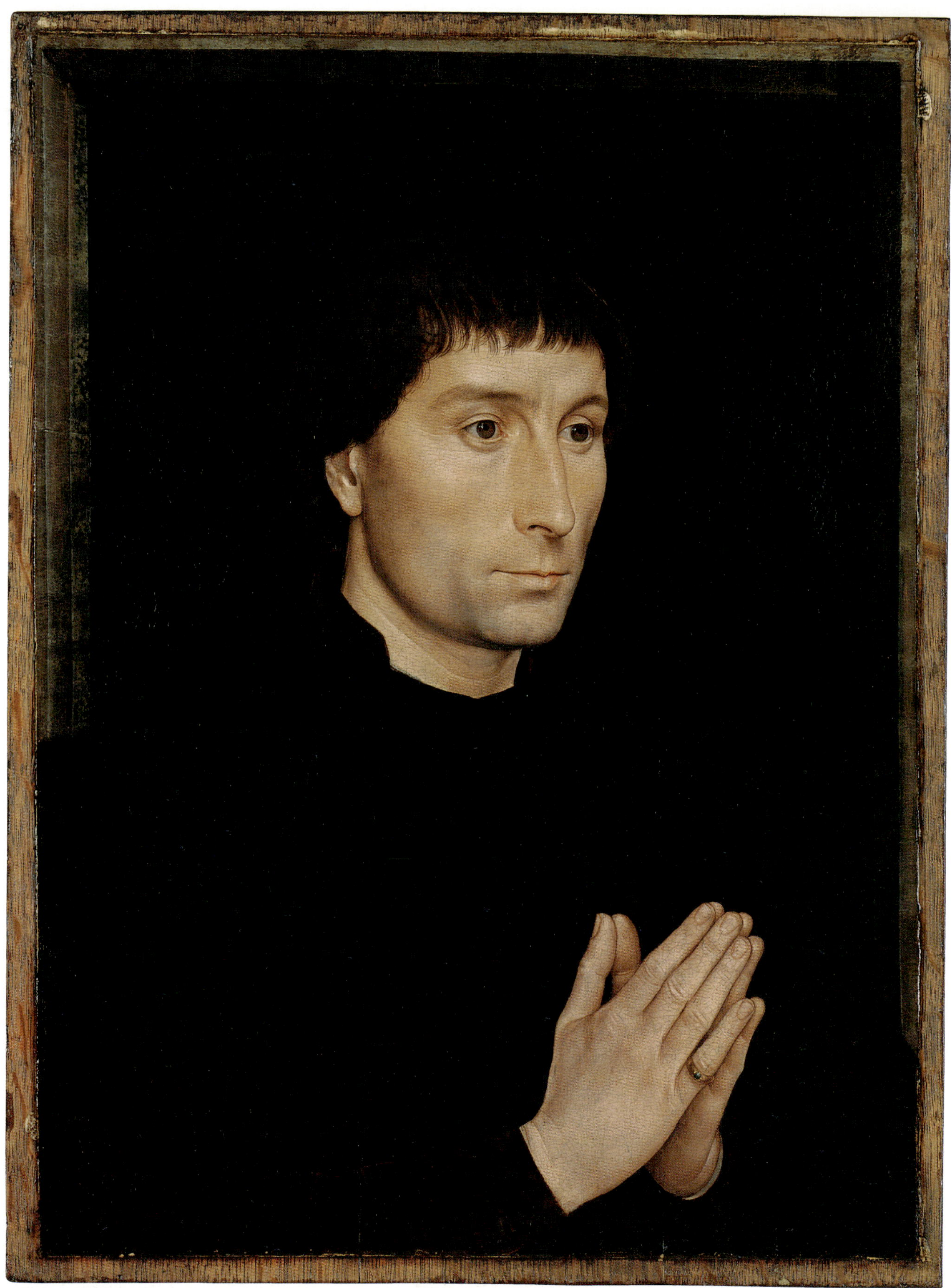

27

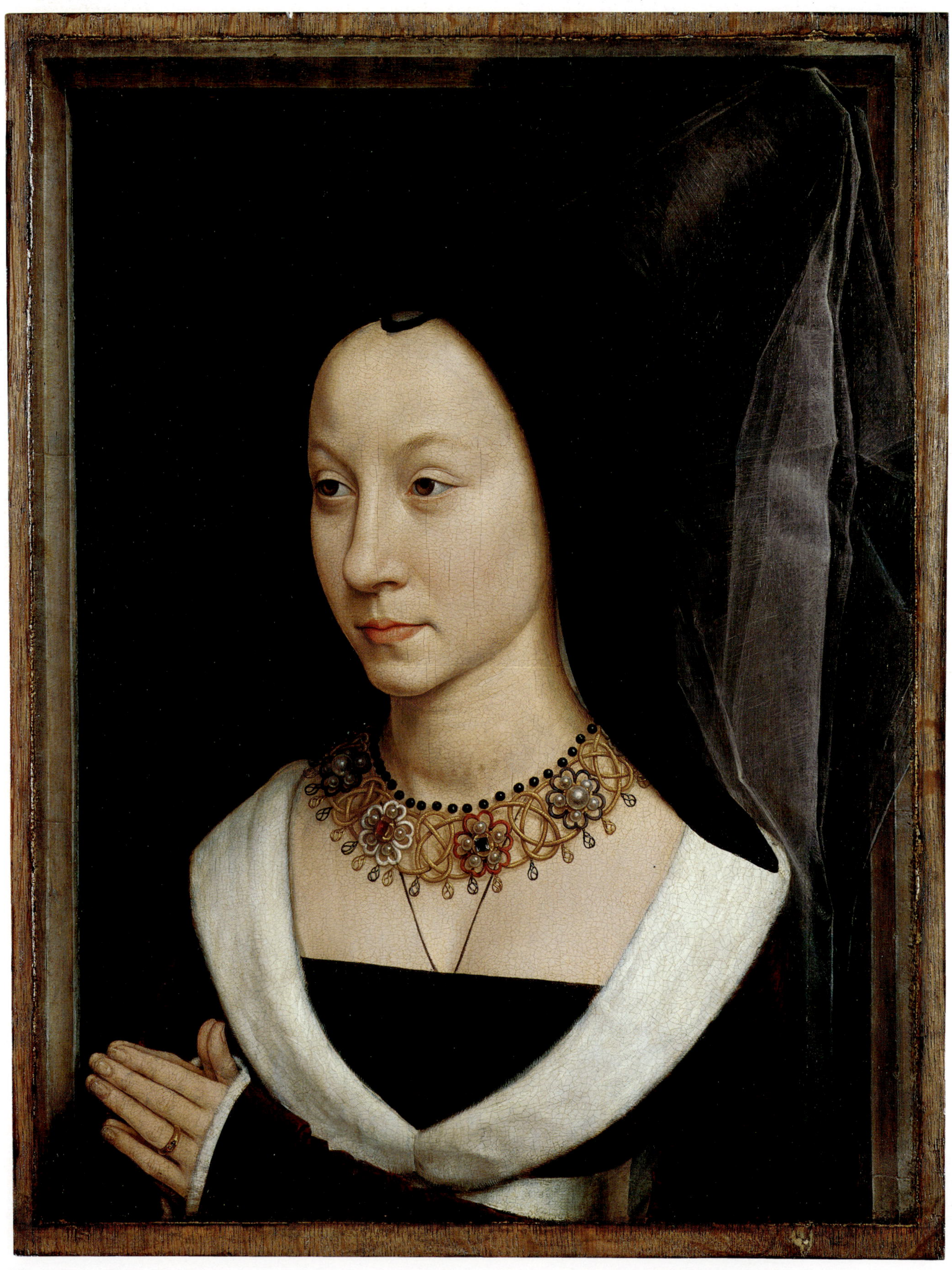

27

Hans Memling, active by 1465, died 1494

28. Portrait of a Young Man, about 1482

Oil on wood, overall 15¾ x 11⅜ in. (40 x 29 cm); painted surface 15⅛ x 10¾ in. (38.3 x 27.3 cm)
Robert Lehman Collection, 1975 1975.1.112

Provenance: Francis, ninth earl of Wemyss, Gosford House, Longniddry, Scotland (by 1857–d. 1889); his son Francis Richard, tenth earl of Wemyss, Gosford House, until 1912; R. Langton Douglas, probably as agent for tenth earl of Wemyss (1912); [Knoedler, New York (June 1912)]; J. H. Dunn, London, December 1912; [Knoedler, New York (July 1914)]; Philip Lehman, New York, December 1915; Robert Lehman, New York.

References: Waagen 1857, p. 440; Friedländer 1924–37, vol. 6 (1928), p. 130, no. 74, pl. 42; Panofksy 1953, pp. 348–49; Friedländer 1967–76, vol. 6a (1971), p. 55, no. 74, pl. 115; Campbell 1983, pp. 675–76, pls. 23–25, cover ill.; Bauman 1986, pp. 42–44, color ill.; De Vos 1994b, pp. 168, 200–201, 366, no. 48, color ill.; Klein 1994b, p. 103; Wolff 1998, no. 13, color ill.

The impassive gaze of this sitter, his appearance of immobility, and the detached recording of the details of his face, hair, hands, and costume give this portrait the character of an intensely observed still life. The young man's shoulders, head, and neck seem to be modeled in the round, chiseled more than drawn, suggesting an awareness of, or at least a strong affinity with, contemporary Italian portrait busts. The landscape, partially blocked by the elegant marble columns, creates an illusion of profound depth and serenity. As in Memling's other portraits with a full or partial landscape background, the scale and prominence of the figure in relation to the vast space and minute, distant detail of the view behind him stress the individual's dignity and endurance, and the stillness of nature implies a state of inner repose in the sitter.

The landscape was closely followed in a *Virgin and Child* ascribed to Domenico Ghirlandaio (Louvre, Paris), which, on the basis of style, cannot date much later than 1482. The probable date of our painting strongly suggests that it was sent to Florence almost immediately after its completion and, therefore, that the young man represented was an Italian, as many of Memling's sitters were. Dendrochronological evidence indicates an estimated felling date of 1476 for the tree that provided the panel. De Vos dates the picture 1480 or later, and Wolff tentatively places it about 1475–80, finding it stylistically close to earlier portraits. The extraordinary refinement of the drawing and design, however, suggests the latest possible date before Ghirlandaio's *Virgin and Child* was painted, or about 1482. In comparison with the earlier Portinari panels (cat. no. 27), where the heads are evenly lit and have the smooth, polished surfaces typical of Memling's portraits of the 1470s, the lighting here is more diffuse, lending an extraordinary sculptural presence to the head. It was doubtless the effect of atmospheric unity and the unity of subject with setting that recommended this picture to Italians at the moment Leonardo was investigating similar problems.

From the time it was first mentioned in 1857 by Waagen until about 1912, this picture was described as a representation of Saint Sebastian. However, an arrow, the saint's attribute, placed between the sitter's clasped hands, and a halo are both later addition and were removed during restoration in 1913. A faint hint of the halo is still visible against the light background of the wall. Due to the darkening of the paint film on the sitter's robe, the brocade pattern, visible in X-radiographs, is difficult to make out with the naked eye. MSdJ

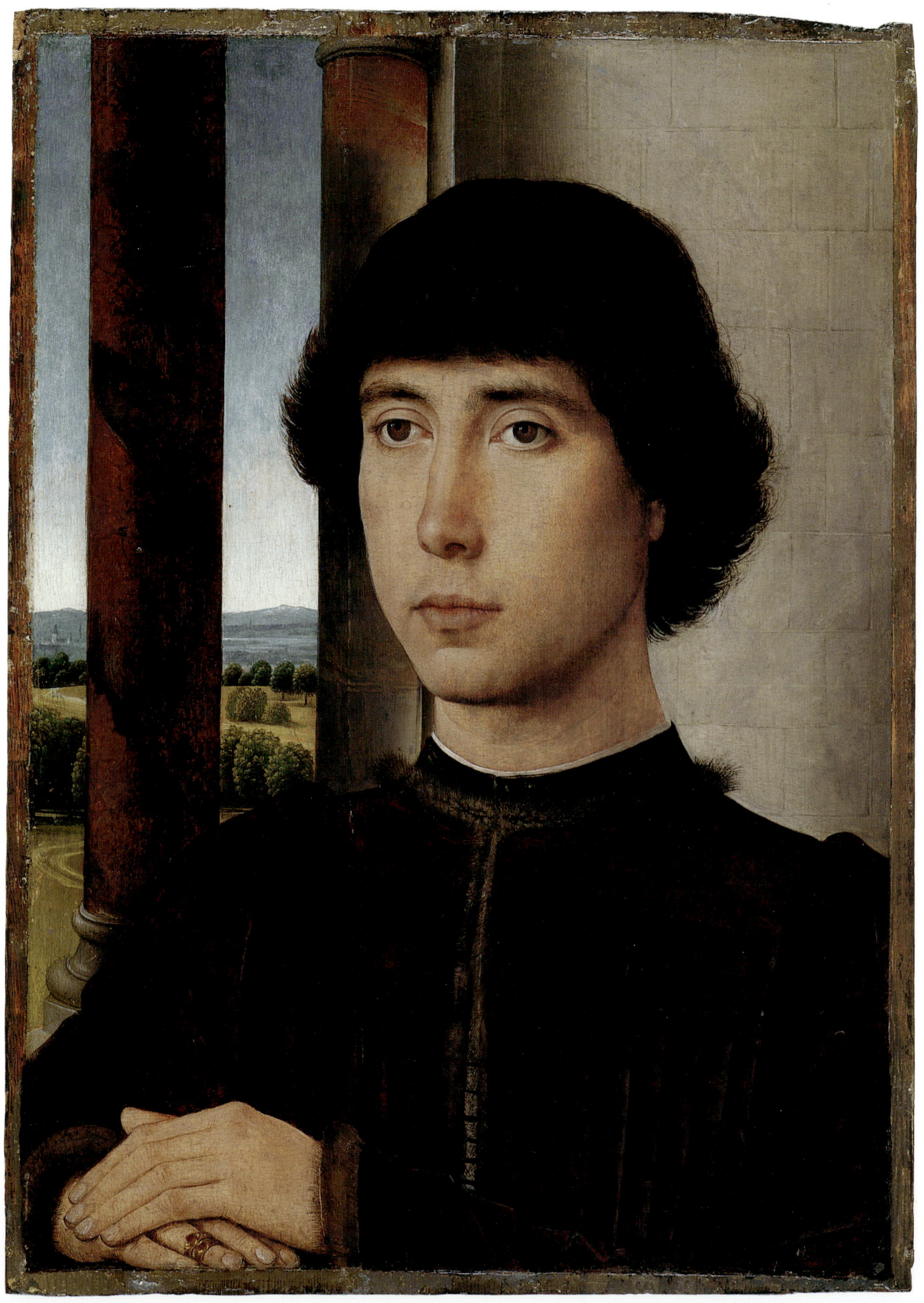

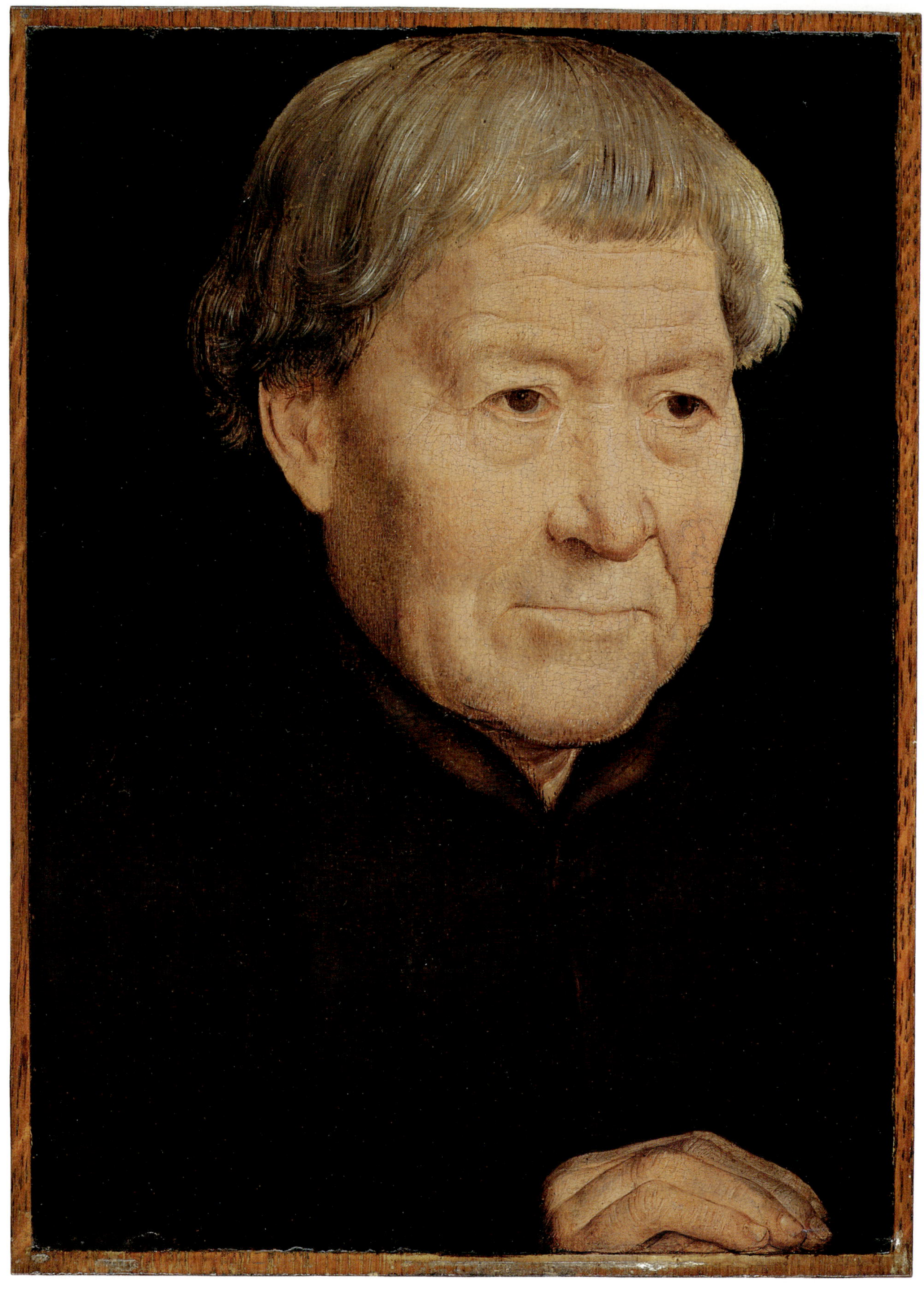

Hans Memling, active by 1465, died 1494

29. Portrait of an Old Man, 1480–90

Oil on wood; overall 10⅜ x 7⅝ in. (26.4 x 19.4 cm); painted surface 10 x 7¼ in. (25.4 x 18.4 cm)
Bequest of Benjamin Altman, 1913 14.40.648

In 1970 Schrader first associated this portrait with Memling's *Portrait of an Old Woman* in the Museum of Fine Arts, Houston (fig. 63) which is closely related in dimensions, style, and general appearance. X-radiography reveals that the Houston picture probably once showed the sitter's hands in the lower left corner of the painting in a pose similar to that of the man's hands.

It is more likely that the two paintings formed a diptych rather than the continuous double portrait that De Vos suggests. X-radiographs reveal no evidence that any of the elements—such as the man's left shoulder or the woman's white headdress—overlapped, which we would expect to find at least a hint of even if the panels had been cut down to create two independent works. Although the panels have indeed been cut on all four sides, this was probably done to fit them into frames smaller than their original ones. Further, the grain of the wood, which usually runs horizontally in horizontal panels, is vertical in these examples, and the grain of the female portrait seems to be wider than that of its companion.

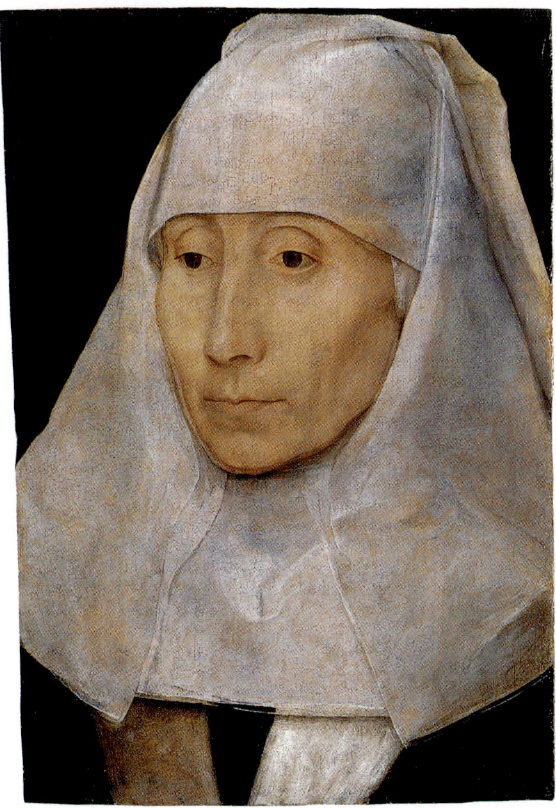

Fig. 63. Hans Memling, *Portrait of an Old Woman*, about 1480–90. Oil on wood. The Edith A. and Percy S. Straus Collection, Museum of Fine Arts, Houston

The attribution of our panel has been the subject of controversy for many years. This is perhaps due to the unprecedented realism with which the aged sitter has been portrayed and also to the cropping of the composition, which creates an image that is unusually compressed for Memling's work. Unable to place the panels chronologically in the context of Memling's more familiar idealized portraits, scholars have generally assigned the Houston and New York portraits to his earliest period of activity. Recent dendrochronological examination of the Houston picture, however, places it about 1480–90, 1480 being the earliest possible date of execution. Our panel cannot be dated by dendrochronology, as it has been trimmed and set into another panel.

Unlike Memling's Portinari portraits (cat. no. 27), which were originally part of a devotional triptych, the New York and Houston portraits are secular works created to preserve the appearance of a couple for posterity; as such they belong to a long tradition of paired portraits of bourgeois sitters, a field that would flourish in seventeenth-century Flanders and Holland. The intimate portrayal of this old man is unusual in early Netherlandish painting, and his humanity and expression of gentle forbearance seem to look ahead to certain portraits by Rembrandt.

MSdJ

Provenance: Private collection, England (until 1895); Stephan Bourgeois, Cologne (1895); Baron Albert Oppenheim, Cologne (1895–1912, cat. 1904, no. 11); [Kleinberger, Paris and New York (1912–13)]; Benjamin Altman, New York (1913).

References: Firmenich-Richartz 1896, cols. 161–64, pl. 5; Bruges 1902, no. 16; Hulin de Loo 1902, p. 4; Hymans 1902, p. 22; Friedländer 1903, pp. 80–81; Friedländer 1924–37, vol. 6 (1928), pp. 45, 131, no. 81; Wehle and Salinger 1947, pp. 62–64, ill.; Schrader 1970; Friedländer 1967–76, vol. 6a (1971), pp. 29, 55, no. 81, pl. 117; Bauman 1986, p. 34, color ill.; De Vos 1994b, pp. 28, 69, 115, 146, 230–31, 360, 370, 390, no. 60, color ill.; Klein 1994b, p. 103.

Hugo van der Goes, active by 1467, died 1482

30. Portrait of a Man, about 1475

Oil on wood, oval; overall 12½ x 10½ in. (31.8 x 26.7 cm); painted surface 12½ x 10¼ in. (31.8 x 26 cm)
H. O. Havemeyer Collection, Bequest of Mrs. H. O. Havemeyer, 1929
29.100.15

Provenance: Signol, Paris (sale, Hôtel Drouot, Paris, April 1–3, 1878, no. 10, as Antonello da Messina); Étienne Martin, Baron de Beurnonville, Paris (1878–81, sale, Pillet, Paris, May 9–16, 1881, no. 603, as Antonello da Messina); Paul Mame, Tours (1881–1904, sale, Galerie Georges Petit, Paris, April 26, 1904, lot 1, as Antonello da Messina); H. O. Havemeyer, New York (1904–29).

References: Burroughs 1923, p. 109; Burroughs 1931, pp. 71–73; Havemeyer 1930, p. 210; Mather 1930, pp. 445, 447; Havemeyer 1931, p. 34; Van Puyvelde 1935, p. 84; Friedländer 1924–37, vol. 14 (1937), *p. 93; De Tolnay 1944, pp. 183, 187–89; Lavalleye 1945, p. 23; Wehle and Salinger 1947, pp. 57–58; Panofsky 1953, pp. 479, 499, 550; Held 1955, p. 232; Larsen 1960, pp. 68, 117; Winkler 1964, pp. 57ff.; Cuttler 1968, pp. 159f.; Friedländer 1967–76, vol. 4 (1969), p. 108; Bauman 1986, p. 62; Metropolitan Museum 1987, pp. 32–33; Koch in Bauman and Liedtke 1992, p. 72; Sander 1992, pp. 127–33; Ainsworth in Frelinghuysen et al. 1993, p. 54; Belting and Kruse 1994, p. 235.*

Unlike his contemporary Hans Memling, Hugo van der Goes did not specialize in portraiture. No known independent examples from Hugo's hand have survived, and his achievements in this genre must, therefore, be evaluated from donor portraits in devotional diptychs and triptychs, notably the left wing of the Saint Hippolytus Altarpiece, whose central and right panels are by Dieric Bouts (Groeningemuseum, Bruges), the Portinari Altarpiece (fig. 29), and the Trinity Panels (National Gallery of Scotland, Edinburgh). Our *Portrait of a Man* is probably the cut-down fragment of a devotional diptych, while the *Benedictine Monk* (cat. no. 31) may be excised from an altarpiece.

Even in its fragmentary state, the present portrait asserts a bold presence and a decisive strength of character. These powerful effects are in part due to the depiction of the subject from below, as if he is in a superior position vis-à-vis the viewer. They are also the result of the setting off of the illuminated head against the dark stone wall and the introduction of a dramatic chiaroscuro that accentuates the modeling of facial features so that they appear to be chiseled out of stone. It is perhaps these characteristics, as well as the impression given by the hands and background when they were overpainted, that at first prompted scholars to assign this portrait to Antonello da Messina.

The stark realism of Hugo's approach, which depicts the swarthy tones of the man's face, his emerging beard, and his roughened hands joined in prayer, enhances the sense of fervent devotional piety conveyed by the sitter. Similar treatments appear in the donor portrait of Hippolyte de Berthoz on the left wing of the Saint Hippolytus Altarpiece and the head of Edward Bonkil on the exterior right wing of the Trinity Panels. These panels are placed about 1475 and 1473–78, respectively, and a corresponding date of about 1475 for the Museum's painting is therefore most likely.

The oval shape of our portrait is not original; it was cut down from a rectangular support, and a damaged triangular piece of the sky in the landscape view was replaced. The pose of the unknown bourgeois sitter, facing to the right in an attitude of prayer, and his concentrated gaze suggest that a devotional image, perhaps a half-length Virgin and Child, was once at the right of the portrait. A likeness of the man's wife may have been placed at the right of the object of his veneration, balancing his image and forming a conventional triptych like the one to which the Portinari portraits (cat. no. 27) presumably belonged. MWA

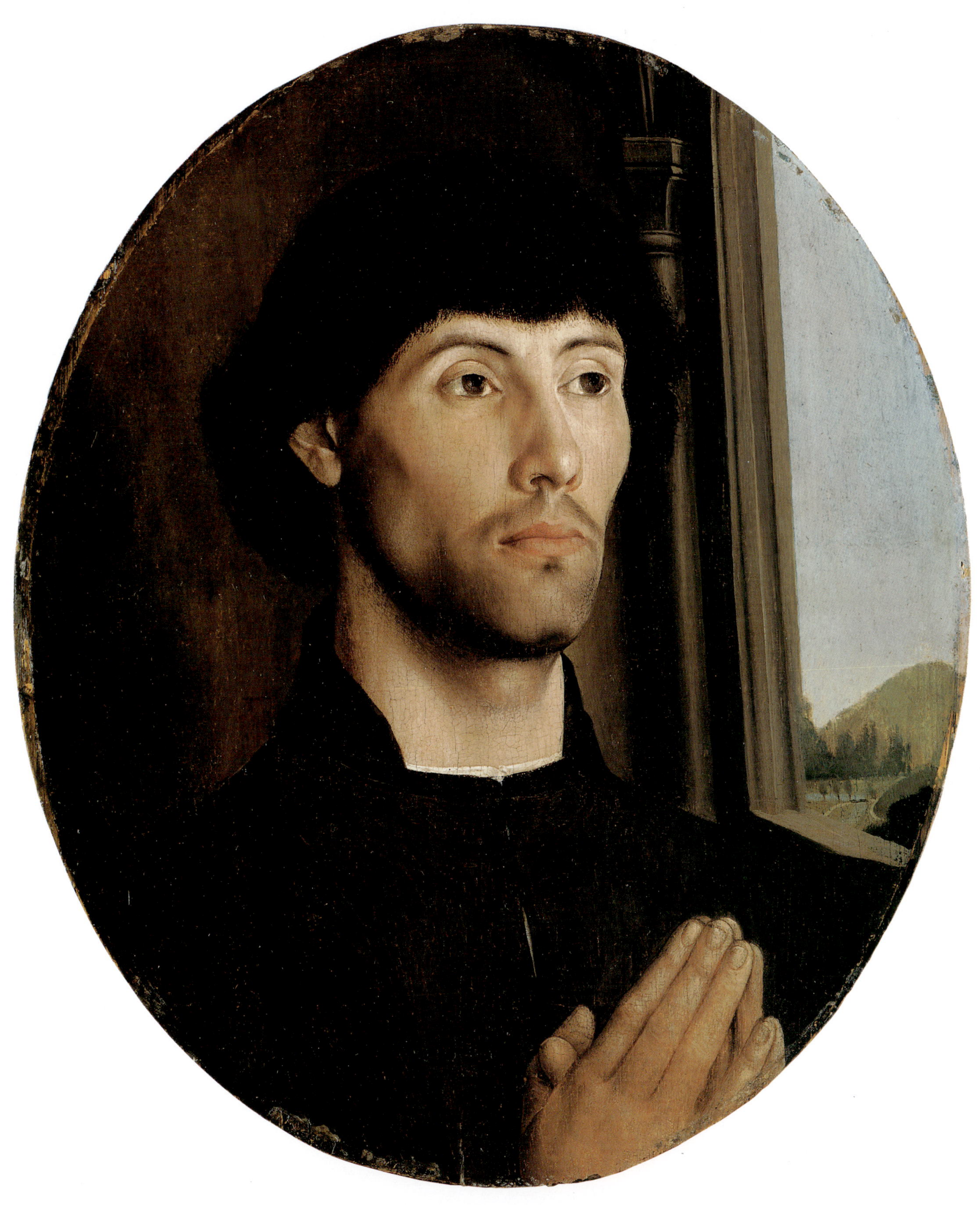

Hugo van der Goes, active by 1467, died 1482

31. A Benedictine Monk, about 1478

Oil on wood; overall 9⅞ x 7⅜ in. (25.1 x 18.7 cm), with added strip of ¾ in. (1.9 cm) at right
Bequest of Michael Dreicer, 1921 22.60.53

Provenance: Farr (sale, Christie's, London, February 26, 1813, no. 55, as Jan van Eyck); John Linnell, London (sale, Christie's, London, March 15, 1918, no. 146, as Rogier van der Weyden); [Leggatt, London]; Michael Dreicer, New York.

References: Friedländer (1916) 1921, p. 188; Wehle 1922, pp. 100, 117; Friedländer 1924–37, vol. 4 (1926), pp. 48, 126–27, 164; Dülberg 1929, p. 89; Knipping [1939], p. 43; De Tolnay 1944, pp. 188, 189; Wehle and Salinger 1947, p. 58; Panofsky 1953, pp. 499–50; Larsen 1960, pp. 68, 118; Winkler 1964, pp. 87, 91, 263–64; Friedländer 1967–76, vol. 4 (1967), pp. 30, 70; Bauman 1986, pp. 11–12; Gordon 1988, pp. 95–97; Eeckhout 1994, p. 433.

Friedländer (1967) lamented the lack of autonomous portraits by Van der Goes, noting that this master, who possessed a "keen eye for the individual and spiritual, was ordained to be a portrait painter." His appraisal fits the *Benedictine Monk,* which presents a psychologically intense image of a profoundly meditative nature. The character and fragmentary state of the painting have made it difficult to determine whether the tonsured Benedictine represented is a contemporary man or a saint. Although some scholars, following the chronicler Gaspard Ophuys's account, would like to classify this panel as a portrait of a fellow monk that Hugo painted during his final years at the Red Cloister near Brussels, this interpretation cannot be confirmed. Indeed, it is entirely possible that our picture exemplifies a convention of early Netherlandish painting wherein holy figures are represented as living portraits. Cut down on all sides and with a strip added at the right, the *Benedictine Monk* is a fragment of a larger panel, although it cannot be determined whether it came from the right wing of a triptych, in which this possible saint may have presented a donor, or represents a segment of a more substantial devotional narrative.

The near-profile view was particularly favored by Hugo, who rendered the man's physiognomy in carefully studied detail—minutely observing the softly tousled hair, the eyes set deep within heavy lids, the aquiline nose intersecting the left contour of the face, the thin, downturned lips above a strong square jaw, the sagging jowls, and the prominent, sharply defined ear. The strong illumination from the left picks out these features and accentuates the head's gaunt, elongated structure. A number of the Benedictine's traits appear in the donor head shown in another fragment, the *Saint John the Baptist and a Donor* (Walters Art Gallery, Baltimore), in which there is a nearly identical play of the meandering contour of the head against the dark background.

The individualized treatment of the subject in our picture recalls the marvelously varied heads of apostles in Hugo's greatest work, the *Death of the Virgin* (Groeningemuseum, Bruges), which, however, offer a contrast to the calm and contemplative monk in their animated unrest. Both the pose and the downcast eyes of the Benedictine are familiar from Hugo's depictions of magi and saints and other holy figures in various devotional altarpieces: for example, Saint Stephen presenting a donor on the right wing of the *Adoration of the Kings* in the Collections of the Prince of Liechtenstein, Vaduz; the head of Joseph in the *Nativity* in the Gemäldegalerie, Berlin, and two of the magi and an onlooker at the far right of the Monteforte Altarpiece in the Gemaldegälerie, Berlin. And they set our monk apart from the sitters in Hugo's donor portraits (for example, cat. no. 30), whose alert, directed gazes connect them with the objects of their devotion. The *Benedictine Monk* can be placed in the late 1470s, like the Baltimore fragment and the Vaduz and Berlin altarpieces to which they are closely connected. MWA

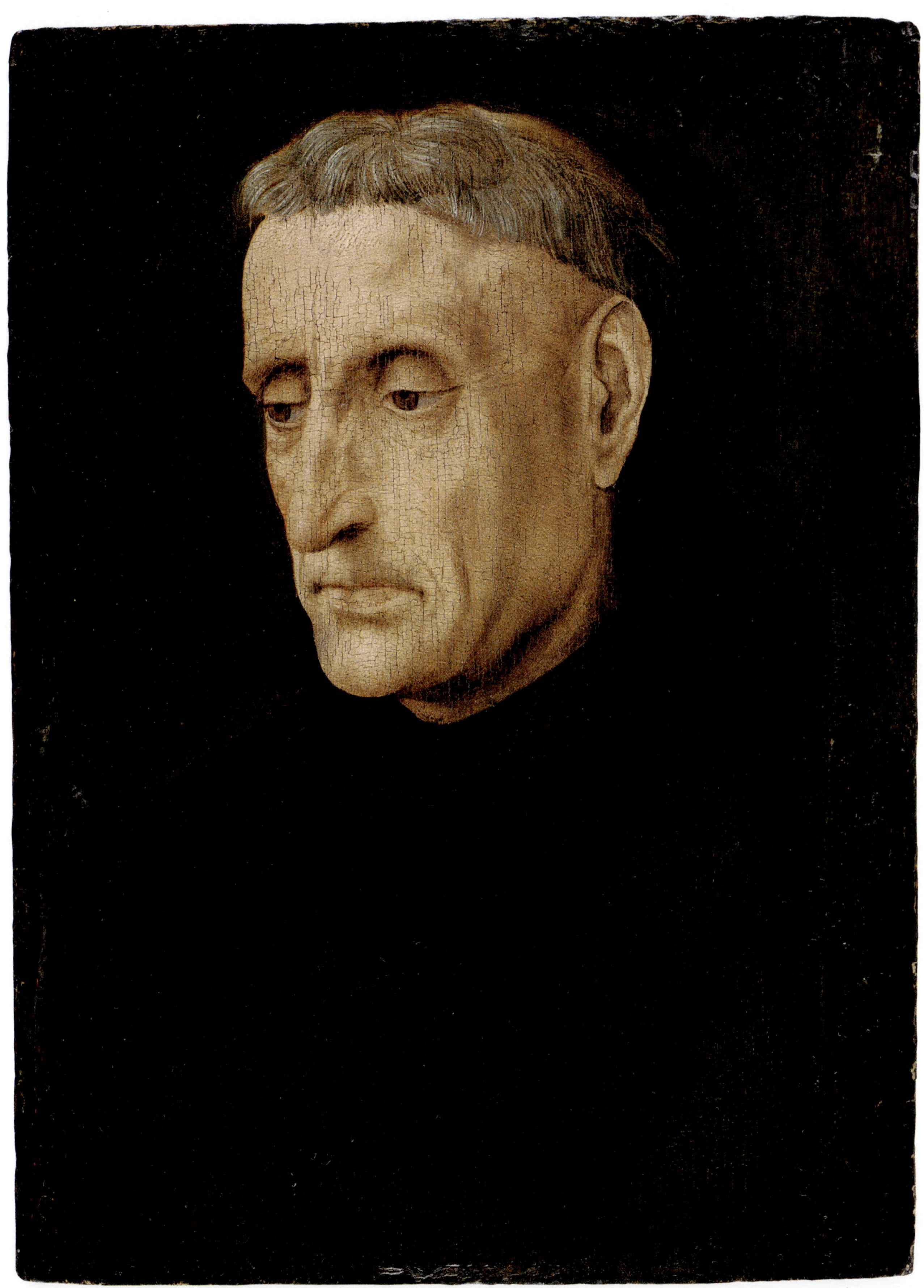

Attributed to Hans Memling, active by 1465, died 1494

32. Young Woman with a Pink, about 1485–90

Oil on wood; overall 17 x 7⅜ in. (43.2 x 18.7 cm); painted surface 17 x 6⅞ in. (43.2 x 17.5 cm)
The Jules Bache Collection, 1949 49.7.23

Provenance: Ganniba, Turin; bought by Wilhelm von Bode in Florence (early 1870s) for a good friend (presumably Vieweg); Heinrich Vieweg, Braunschweig (early 1870s–d. 1890); Vieweg family, Switzerland? and Berlin (1890–1926); [Teppelmann, Braunschweig (1926)]; [Cassirer, Berlin (1926)]; [Julius Böhler, Munich (1926)]; [Kleinberger, New York (1926)]; Jules S. Bache, New York ([1926–49], cat. 1937, no. 24, cat. 1943, no. 23).

References: Friedländer 1924–37, vol. 6 (1928), p. 119, no. 16B, pl. 19; Winkler 1928, pp. 9–12, fig. 1; Wehle and Salinger 1947, pp. 64–65, ill.; Hannema 1949, p. 39; Panofsky 1953, pp. 349, 506–7, n. 7, fig. 477; Larsen 1960, p. 7; Eisler 1964, p. 100; Friedländer 1967–76, vol. 6a (1971), p. 48, no. 16B, pl. 55; McFarlane 1971, pp. 41–42, n. 51; De Vos 1994a, pp. 27, 50, 84, 92, 114, 124–27, 148, color ill.; De Vos 1994b, pp. 107, 176, 183, 245, 264–67, 308, 391–92, no. 3, color ill.; Giltay 1994, pp. 152–53, ill.; Klein 1994b, p. 103; Campbell 1995a, pp. 253–54; Rohlmann 1995, pp. 442–44.

Long considered a portrait, this charming image of a young woman with a pink, standing behind an arched window and before a landscape, is in fact an allegorical work, a rarity in northern Renaissance art. A companion panel in Rotterdam (fig. 64) shows two horses, one brown and one white, the latter with a monkey on its back; they are viewed through a matching arched window, and the landscape behind them is continuous with that in our panel. Contemporary opinion favors the theory that the paintings were an independent diptych, either fixed or folding; dendrochronological evidence (Klein 1994b) has ruled out an earlier hypothesis that they were the front and back of one panel. It is also possible that they were the exterior wings of a triptych, which would have been juxtaposed when the ensemble was closed; such a context might help to explain the relatively weak execution of our painting and, to a lesser extent, of the Rotterdam work. The oblong proportions of the panels and the fact that their backs have been considerably planed down—suggesting that their reverses, or the interior wings, were sawed apart from them—would be consistent with this view.

Exterior wings that share the emblematic character of these pictures, showing cranes in a landscape—evidently a device conceived by the Dominican Benedetto Pagagnotti as a play on the Greek word for "bishop"—are part of Memling's Pagagnotti Triptych. This small altarpiece features a Virgin and Child Enthroned with Two Angels (fig. 37) as its central panel and Saints John the Baptist and Lawrence (National Gallery, London) on its interior wings, with the cranes on their reverses. In comparison with the three extraordinarily beautiful and refined interior panels, the paintings with the cranes are weak in execution and must be from Memling's workshop. The main panel of a triptych including the *Young Woman with a Pink* and *Two Horses in a Landscape* could conceivably have been a simple devotional subject such as a Virgin and Child, perhaps with the portraits of a donor couple on the interior wings.

Panofksy was the first to study the symbolism of our painting and its companion, noting that the pink is a familiar symbol of betrothal and that in medieval poetry the horse commonly stood for the man in love. According to Panofsky, the monkey seated on the back of the white horse is a "symbol of everything self-seeking and base in human nature"; the white horse ignores the elegant young woman and satisfies its thirst, while the brown horse, nobler in nature, gazes with selfless devotion at its beloved. De Vos (1994b) elaborates on this interpretation, seeing the crumbling bricks and parapet on the right side of the Rotterdam picture as a sign that the brown horse, like True Love, overcomes the temptations of evil. The theme, he suggests, might also be the contrast between the inveterate and the repentant or reformed sinner.

The young woman is dressed in the fashion of the Burgundian court of about 1470; her headdress and décolletage are comparable to those in our portrait of Maria Portinari (cat. no. 27). As Campbell observes, the artist has misunderstood or paid little attention to the details of the costume, omitting eyelets for the laced dress-front. A garment of this type in which every eyelet is carefully recorded appears in the anonymous portrait of Margaret of York from about 1468 in the Louvre, Paris. The ornamental cross worn as a pendant by our woman is similar to those depicted in two of Memling's male portraits from about 1480, the *Portrait of a Man at Prayer before a Landscape* (Mauritshuis, The Hague) and the *Portrait of a Young Man at Prayer* (National Gallery, London). De Vos, who places our panel and its companion about 1485–90, a dating supported by dendrochronological evidence, interprets the early costume as an intentional old-fashioned touch.

In pointing out that the physiognomy of our young woman corresponds to Memling's anonymous female type, and that the figure functions as

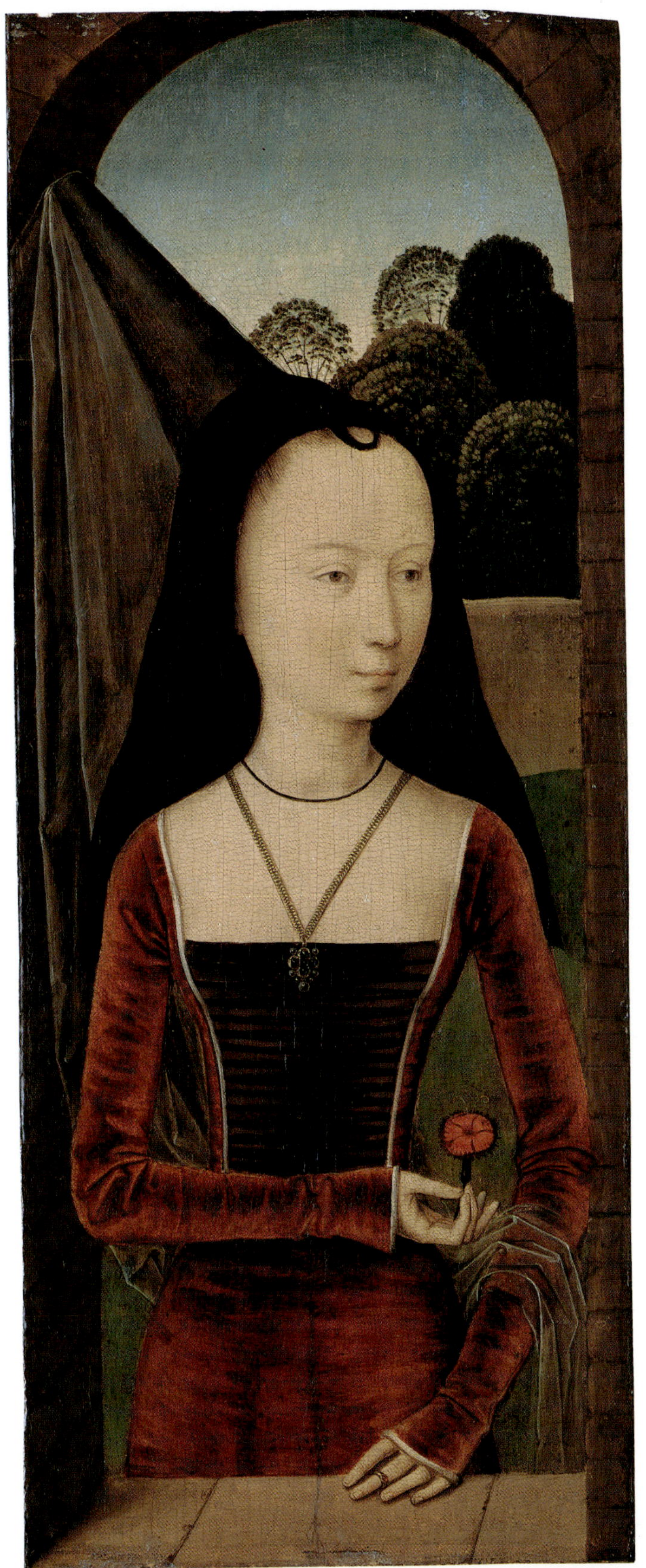

32

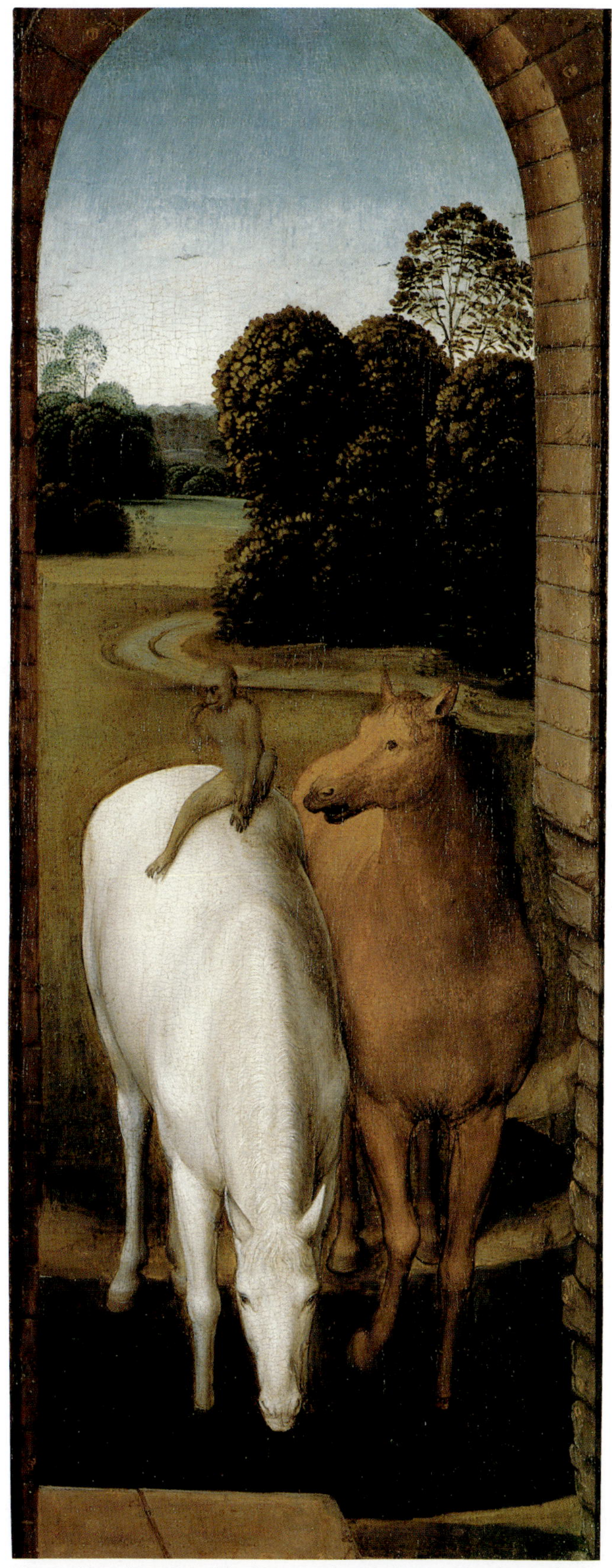

Fig. 64. Hans Memling, *Two Horses and a Monkey in a Landscape*, about 1485–90. Oil on wood. Museum Boijmans Van Beuningen, Rotterdam

part of an allegorical ensemble rather than as a portrait, De Vos has helped clarify some of the issues that cloud the panel's attribution. Experts have consistently viewed the picture as the representation of an individual and found it wanting in comparison with Memling's extraordinarily fine portraits. But if this young woman is seen instead as a profane counterpart of one of the maidens in his *Shrine of Saint Ursula* (Groeningemuseum, Bruges), it becomes easier to accept her doll-like features in the context of Memling's oeuvre. There nevertheless remains a problem of quality, reflected in the flatness of the young woman's face and, indeed, of the image as a whole, the awkward perspective of the arch, and the schematic handling of the trees and coulisses of the background. The landscape surely is not Memling's; the same hand may have been responsible for the landscape in Memling's otherwise-autograph *Portrait of a Man* (Uffizi, Florence) and perhaps also for the exterior wings of the Pagagnotti Altarpiece, in which the trees are similarly handled.

Weaknesses of this kind are less apparent in the *Two Horses in a Landscape*, which is perhaps more plausibly ascribed to Memling. The illusionism of the arch, seen from the left, is more convincing, as is the recession in space created by the winding path and judiciously placed trees. The proportions of the horses, although awkward, are typical of Memling's drawings of equine subjects. The color in general seems richer and more nuanced and convincingly suggests light, shadow, and depth. It is possible that Memling executed the *Two Horses in a Landscape* but allowed an assistant to complete our panel. Giltay, however, has observed that the apparent involvement of the workshop in our picture suggests that it also participated in the execution of the Rotterdam panel, which simply represents a better performance. Unfortunately, infrared reflectography reveals no underdrawing on either panel, and we thus have no technical evidence that might help sort out the problems of authorship here. A number of authorities, including Larsen, McFarlane, and Campbell, have doubted or rejected the attribution of these works to Memling, but De Vos strongly supports them as autograph.

The two panels are part of a small group of allegories of love and virtue attributed to Memling, including an *Allegory with a Virgin* (Musée Jacquemart-André, Paris) and the Earthly Vanity and Divine Salvation Triptych (Musée des Beaux-Arts, Strasbourg), that appear as a charming secular oasis in the midst of the artist's more familiar devotional works and formal portraits. The *Young Woman with a Pink* and *Two Horses in a Landscape* provide a fascinating glimpse of a chivalric code or sentimental ideal in relations between men and women that apparently survived well into the fifteenth century.

MSdJ

Master of the Saint Ursula Legend, active late 15th century

33. *Virgin and Child with Saint Anne Presenting Anna van Nieuwenhove,* 1479–83

Oil on wood, 19⅝ x 13½ in. (49.8 x 34.3 cm)
Inscribed (bottom): De nieuwenhoue cō[n]iunx domicella Johannis et michaelis / Obit de blasere nata Johanne Anna sub·M·C· quater/ ·X·octo·sed excipe

This modest picture with its long inscription documents the beginnings of a type of funerary or memorial art, later known as epitaph painting, that would flourish during the Protestant Reformation. Saint Anne, mother of the Virgin Mary, holds a diminutive Virgin and Child in her protection as she presents the deceased, Anna van Nieuwenhove, to the unseen object of her devotion in a lost adjacent panel. Evidence of hinging on the panel's left side is visible in X-radiographs and confirms that the painting was originally part of a diptych or triptych. Anna's dress, headdress, and shaved forehead, as well as her extreme youth, closely reflect the appearance of Maria Portinari in her

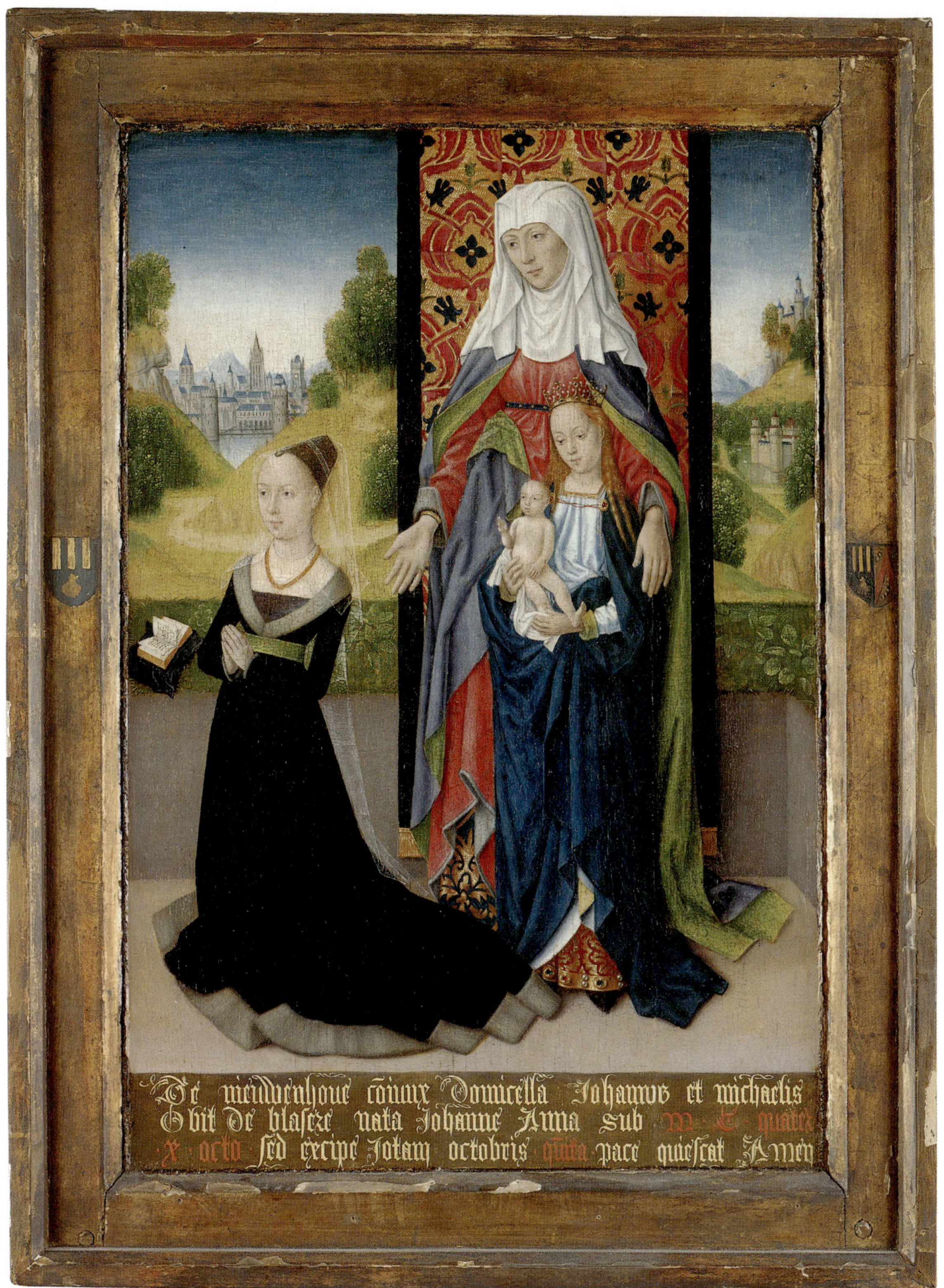

Jotam octobris·qũi[n]ta·pace quiescat Amen (The companion and wife of Jan and [sic] *Michiel van Nieuwenhove, born Anna, daughter of Johannes de Blasere, died in 1480, minus iota [1479], the 5th of October; may she rest in peace, Amen)*
Arms on frame (left) of the Van Nieuwenhove family and (right) of the Van Nieuwenhove and de Blasere
Robert Lehman Collection, 1975 1975.1.114

Provenance: Probably Onze-Lieve-Vrouwekerk, Bruges; Alliance des Arts, Paris (by 1847); Quedeville collection, Paris (by 1851); sale, Malard and François, Paris, March 29–31, 1852, no. 58, as by "Hemmeling"; R. Labordette, Amiens; [Kleinberger, New York and Paris (1912), sold to Philip Lehman]; Philip Lehman, New York, February 1912; Robert Lehman, New York.

References: Kunstblatt *1847, p. 60; Friedländer 1924–37, vol. 6 (1928), pp. 61, 137, no. 119, pl. 54; Marlier 1964, pp. 13–14, 37, no. 30; Friedländer 1967–76, vol. 6a (1971), pp. 39, 60, no. 119, pl. 142; Bauman 1986, pp. 22, 24–25, fig. 17; Levine 1989, pp. 11–12, 27, 37, 45, 51–52, 55 n. 1, 71–72, 120–21, 142, 210–13, no. 18; Martens 1992b, pp. 37–42, figs. 1–4; Harbison 1995a, pp. 26, 30, fig. 5; Martens 1995, p. 45; Wolff 1998, no. 16, color ill.*

portrait of about 1470 (cat. no. 27). Behind her, in the distance, is what Martens (1995) has described as an idealized view of Bruges, "showing the city simultaneously from different angles." At the right, closest to the foreground, is the Minnewater district with its two-towered footbridge; beyond this, at the left, is a church that seems to be Sint-Salvatorskerk (Saint Savior's), and farther back are the Onze-Lieve-Vrouwekerk (church of Our Lady) and, at the right, the Town Hall belfry. On the left side of the frame are the arms of the Van Nieuwenhove—the prominent Bruges family into which Anna married—while on its right side are the arms of the Van Nieuwenhove as well as those of Anna's own family, the de Blasere.

The inscription is somewhat garbled and resists an easy reading. Bauman has noted that Michiel van Nieuwenhove was the father of Jan, the husband of Anna, and that *domicella Johannis et michaelis*, or wife of Jan and Michiel, in the inscription must be an error for "wife of Jan, son of Michiel." Martens, who recently interpreted Anna's inscribed death date as 1479 (1480 minus 1), observes that she died just eleven days after the birth of her daughter, Catherina, probably from complications of childbirth. Anna was buried in the Onze-Lieve-Vrouwekerk in Bruges, in the chapel of the Van Nieuwenhove family, and the ensemble to which this panel belonged was probably installed there.

Jan, Anna's husband, was active in the political life of Bruges, where he served as alderman, city councillor, and *watergrave* of Flanders—the last a position that made him responsible for all the waterways in the country. He was also a counselor to Archduke Maximilian, and it was no doubt due to his connections with the court that he was tortured publicly and ultimately executed on February 29, 1488, during the revolt of Bruges against this sovereign.

Maarten van Nieuwenhove, Jan's brother, is represented on the left wing of Hans Memling's masterpiece of 1487, the Maarten van Nieuwenhove Diptych (Sint-Janshospitaal, Bruges). It is interesting that the Van Nieuwenhove family and also the Pagagnotti of Florence (see entry for cat. no. 14) commissioned works from both Memling and the Master of the Saint Ursula Legend. Apparently the conservative and relatively modest productions of this master, whose identity remains uncertain, met the needs of clients from the same levels of society and even from the same families as the extraordinarily sophisticated and refined paintings of Memling.

As is the case with a number of paintings ascribed to Bruges's minor masters who used a view of the city as a backdrop for devotional compositions, the representation of the Town Hall belfry, which was rebuilt between 1483 and 1501, helps to date the picture. The tower is shown here as it appeared before reconstruction began, and the picture can therefore be dated prior to 1483 and after October 5, 1479, the date of Anna's death; it is thus a relatively early work by the Master of the Saint Ursula Legend. MSdJ

Master of the View of Sainte Gudule, active about 1470–90

34. *Young Man Holding a Book,* about 1480

Oil on wood, arched top, overall 8¼ x 5⅛ in. (21 x 13 cm); painted surface 8⅛ x 5 in. (20.6 x 12.6 cm)
Bequest of Mary Stillman Harkness, 1950 50.145.27

In this charming but enigmatic portrait a fashionably dressed young man holding open a heart-shaped book stands at the entrance to a church, while at the left, in the background, a priest celebrates Mass in the church's interior. The view of the choir and rood screen, including the figures of priest and communicant, is freely copied from the central panel of Rogier van der Weyden's altarpiece the *Seven Sacraments* (Koninklijk Museum voor Schone Kunsten, Antwerp), whose setting is based on the interior of the church of Sainte Gudule in Brussels.

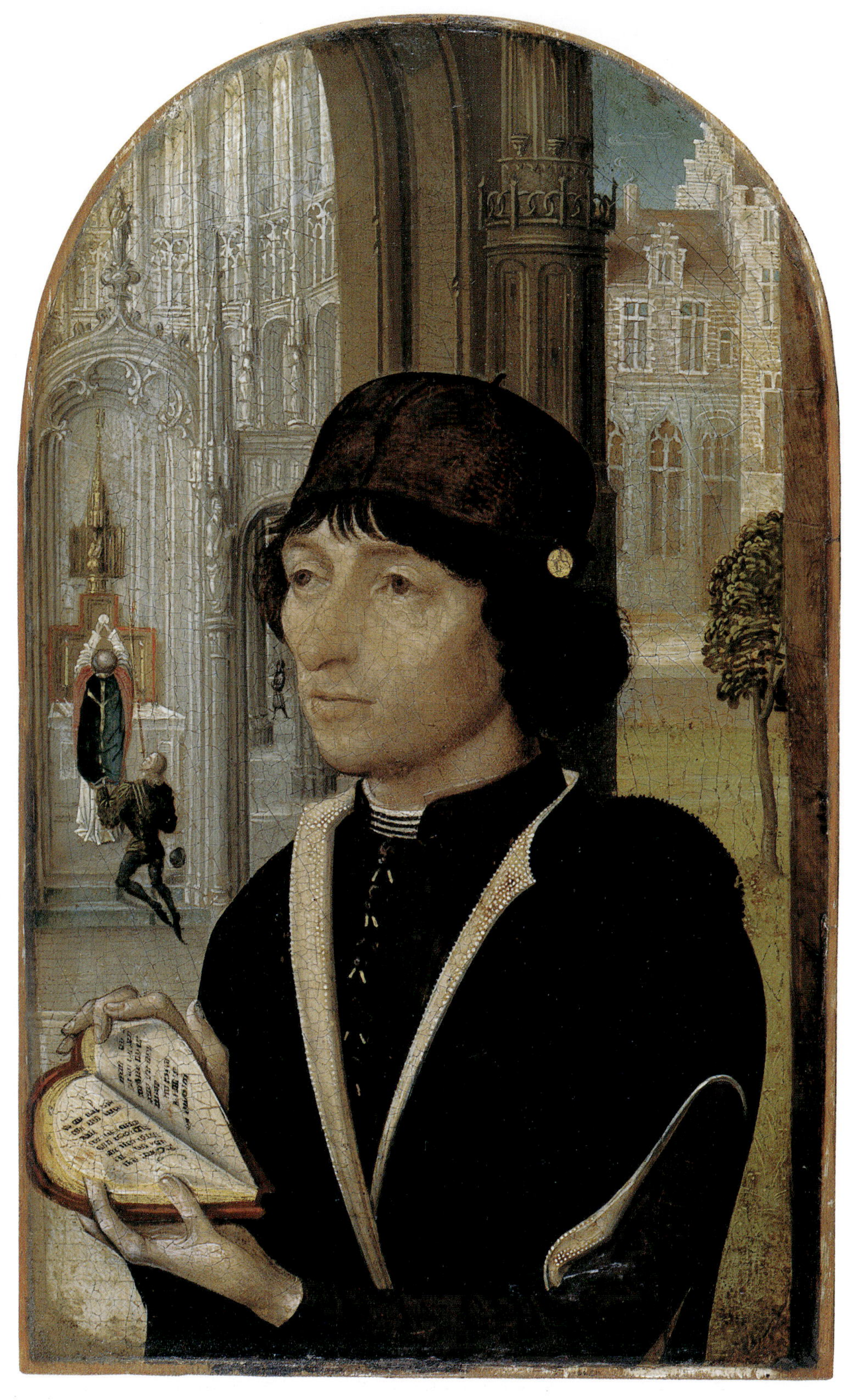

Provenance: Private collection, Lille; [inscription on reverse of picture states that it was purchased from "an aged painter at Lille"]; Leopold Friedrich Franz, duke of Anhalt, Gotisches Haus, Wörlitz (d. 1810); dukes of Anhalt, Gotisches Haus, Wörlitz, and Schloss Dessau (until at least 1902); [Knoedler, New York (by 1928)]; Edward S. Harkness, New York (1928–1950).

References: Hulin de Loo 1902, p. 36, no. 143; Friedländer 1923a, pp. 318–19, fig. 332; Van Bastelaer 1924, pp. 16–19; Friedländer 1924–37, vol. 4 (1926), p. 142, no. 77; Van de Castyne 1935, pp. 325–28; Davies 1953, pp. 203–6; Friedländer 1967–76, vol. 4 (1969), pp. 62, 80, no. 77, pl. 69; Bauman 1986, pp. 40–41, color ill.; Ainsworth 1989a, p. 11, fig. 9; Jager 1996, pp. 18–22, fig. 1; Campbell 1997b.

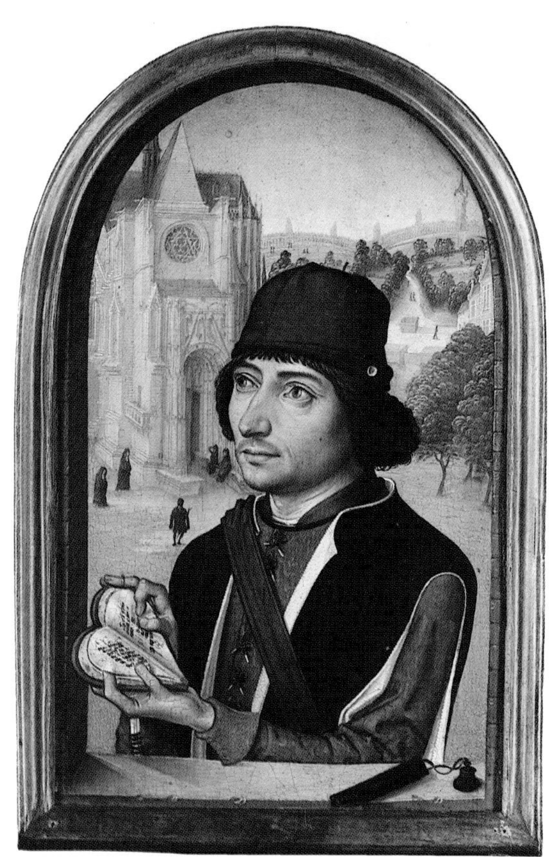

Fig. 65. Master of the View of Sainte Gudule, *Portrait of a Young Man*, about 1480. Oil on wood. National Gallery, London

A portrait that is very similar to ours (fig. 65) is in the National Gallery, London, but the exact relationship between the two works is rather ambiguous. Due to a general resemblance in the men's features, we briefly wonder if the two pictures represent the same individual, but this correspondence most likely results from the dependence on one of these paintings—or a very similar pattern—to produce the other. The settings of the two portraits, however, are dissimilar. In the London work the man is seen through a stone arch not present in our picture, and a different Brussels church, Notre Dame du Sablon, with a parklike view showing city walls at the horizon, serves as the background.

In spite of the striking contrast in their drawing and modeling, both paintings have been ascribed to the Master of the View of Sainte Gudule, whose eponymous work showing the church of Sainte Gudule is in the Louvre (known as the *Pastoral Sermon*, it has recently been identified as *Saint Augustine Preaching*). The head and hands in the London portrait are conceived in terms of simplified chiaroscuro modeling and dark outlines border most of the forms, while these parts of the Metropolitan panel show more subtle modeling and minimal outlining. Rather than evidence of the master's "broad stylistic range," as Bauman suggests, this variation in handling is more reasonably viewed as a sign of the involvement of two different hands in the workshop. The numerous surviving paintings ascribed to the Master of the View of Sainte Gudule and their disparity in quality and handling suggest that his shop was large and prolific. It is difficult, at this point, to say whether the London or the New York panel is more likely to be by the master himself; certainly the Metropolitan portrait is the more sensitive likeness.

With the exception of the blue-green sash worn over the shoulder of the London sitter (perhaps a mark of particular status), the costumes of the two men match in color as well as design, and we can therefore assume that they belonged to the same confraternity. Van Bastelaer believed they were members of the archers' guild, which was closely associated with Notre Dame du Sablon, and identified the tower at the horizon in the London picture as the Grosse-Tour, the regular site of that organization's competitions. Interestingly, three young men in the same uniform appear in the panel in the Louvre tentatively identified as *Saint Augustine Preaching*. Van de Castyne suggests that the men in the Paris narrative—two of whom hold small parchments—were students at an Augustinian seminary and that the sitters for our portrait and the one in London were scholars and aspiring canons in the churches of Sainte Gudule and Notre Dame du Sablon. She points out that a red heart surmounted by a flame was the symbolic attribute of Saint Augustine and proposes that the heart-shaped books in the paintings refer to the sitters' submission to Augustinian doctrine. The Louvre picture can be dated before 1480, as the facade of Sainte Gudule is represented in it as it appeared prior to this time, with its north tower incomplete; the London and New York panels must date from about the same period.

Although heart-shaped books are extremely rare, two survive in the Bibliothèque Nationale, Paris. One is a songbook from about 1460–76 that opens to form a double-heart shape; the other, which opens to a single-heart shape like the books in the portraits, is a fifteenth-century Book of Hours. It is certainly reasonable to assume that the sitters hold prayer books, given the representation of important churches in the panels and, in the case of our painting, a scene showing the elevation of the Host during Mass.

These portraits may originally have been right wings of devotional diptychs, as Campbell believes.

MSdJ

Jean Hey (Master of Moulins), active 1480–1500

35. *Portrait of Margaret of Austria* (1480–1530), about 1490

The sitter in this elegant portrait was convincingly identified by Hulin de Loo as Margaret of Austria (1480–1530), who as a young girl was betrothed to the dauphin Charles, the future Charles VIII, and served briefly as "queen of France," from 1483 to 1491. The initials C (backward) and M within the decoration of the left border of her collar (which would be matched by two correctly oriented letters on the right border) probably signify their union, and the chain of gold shells on her headdress may be part of the armorial insignia of the Bourbon dynasty with which she was then associated. Several other portraits show her similarly attired and with the notorious protruding lip of her Habsburg lineage.

Margaret is looking to the right, presumably toward the object of her devotion. Decorating the pendant hanging from her necklace is a white enameled pelican piercing its breast to draw blood with which to feed its young—the blood is suggested by the large ruby below the bird. These elements are mounted on a gold fleur-de-lis. The pelican is a well-known emblem of Christ's sacrifice and Resurrection and may relate to the action of Margaret, who pauses at a large gold filigree Paternoster bead while reciting her rosary.

Whether the portrait formed the left half of a diptych cannot be said definitively, but Margaret's action, pose, and gaze suggest there was a companion panel that showed a devotional image. The emphasis on sacrifice and Resurrection introduced into the portrait by the pendant and rosary indicates that such a panel might well have represented a subject from Christ's Passion instead of the more common Virgin and Child. The sacred image in diptychs of the period was usually on the sitter's right, but a reversal of this formula is not uncommon in French and Netherlandish examples showing aristocratic donors.

Since 1904 this painting has been recognized as the work of the Master of Moulins, now identified as Jean Hey. Hey spent most of his life serving the French court, but his origins were in the Netherlands, where he may have received his training in Ghent in the workshop of Hugo van der Goes. Certainly, in its precision of drawing, cool palette, and dense, opaque modeling, this portrait reflects the influence of Van der Goes, who is known to have depicted a sitter in an interior setting with a landscape view through a window on at least one occasion (cat. no. 30). In Hey's portrait the view to the exterior is rigidly bisected by a dividing wall or mullion that emphasizes the formality of the composition and enhances the regal status of the sitter.

Closest to the Lehman painting in terms of technique and execution are two other portraits by Hey, those of Madeleine of Burgundy and Pierre II of France of about 1492 (both Louvre, Paris). This date provides a likely terminus ante quem for the portrait of Margaret, who by that time was en route to the Netherlands, having been repudiated by Charles VIII in favor of Anne of Brittany. Just prior to her return, during 1490–91, Margaret of Austria and Charles VIII sojourned in Moulins, where Hey was working for Pierre II. Their visit would have provided an opportunity for Hey to paint Margaret seated before a view of the tranquil Loire valley.

MWA

Oil on wood, 12⅞ x 9⅛ in. (32.7 x 23 cm)
Robert Lehman Collection, 1975 1975.1.130

Provenance: Don Sebastián Gabriel de Beaujeu, Braganza y Borbón, infante of Spain and Portugal; his son, Prince Pierre de Bourbon et Bourbon, duc de Durcal, Paris (sale, Hôtel Drouot, Paris, February 3, 1890, no. 23); Prince Manuel de Yturbe, Paris; his granddaughter, Princess Yturbe, Paris; [Kleinberger, New York, 1926]; sold to Philip Lehman, New York, March 1926; Robert Lehman, New York.

References: De Maulde La Clavière 1896, p. 370; Benoît 1901, pp. 328–32; Buchot 1904, p. 294; Dimier 1904, p. 108; Fry 1904, p. 368; Durrieu 1911, pp. 744–45; Dimier 1925, p. 43; Hulin de Loo 1932, p. 63; Lassaigne and Argan 1955, p. 189; Huillet d'Istria 1961, pp. 80–81; Sterling 1963, pp. 65–67 n. 10; Reynaud 1968, pp. 34–37; Sterling 1968, p. 30; Sterling 1972, pp. 193–94; Szabo 1975, pp. 81–82; Baetjer 1977, pp. 343–46; Lorentz and Regond 1990, pp. 36–38; Sterling and Ainsworth 1998, no. 3, color ill.

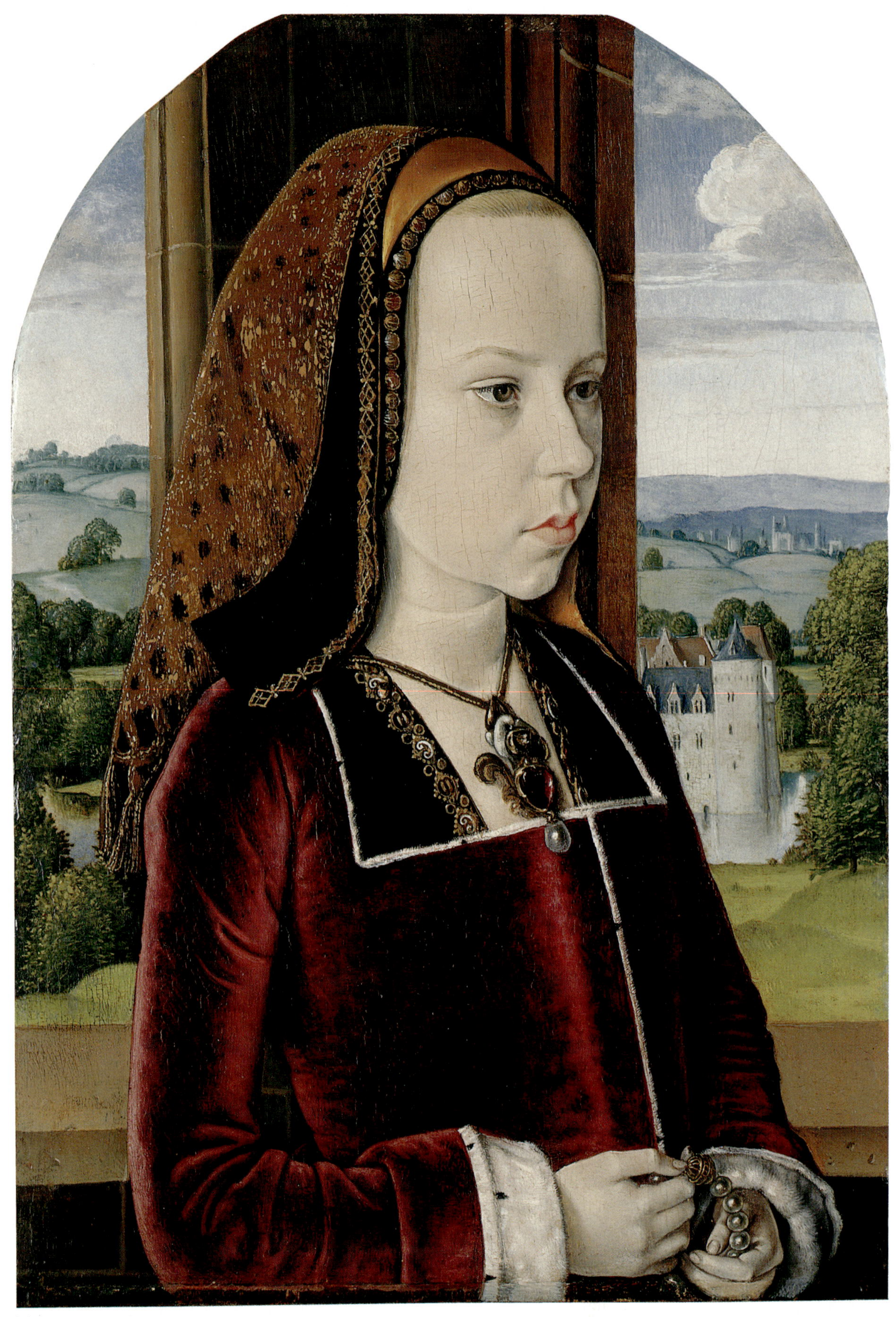

35

Opposite: Detail, cat. no. 35

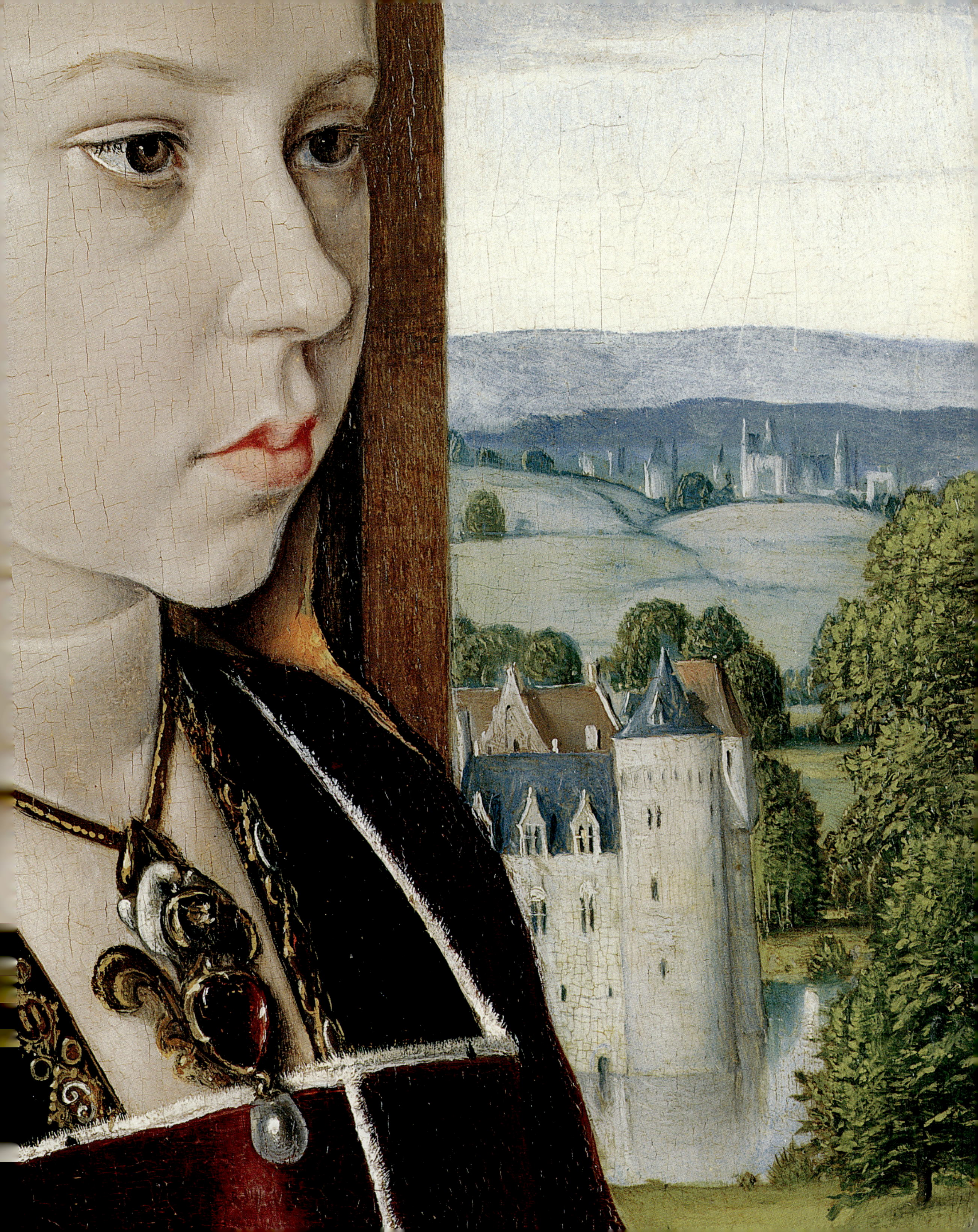

Jean Bellegambe, French, active 1504–34

36. Charles Coguin, Abbot of Anchin, about 1509–13

Oil on wood, arched top, 26¾ x 11⅜ in. (67.9 x 28.9 cm)
Arms (on prie-dieu) of Abbot Coguin
The Friedsam Collection, Bequest of Michael Friedsam, 1931 32.100.125

Provenance: A. Forgeais, Paris (ca. 1858); Jules Gréau, Paris (1890); Michael Friedsam, New York (1931).

References: Dehaines 1890, p. 125; Burroughs and Wehle 1932, p. 10; Friedländer 1924–37, vol. 12 (1935), p. 179, no. 137; Sterling 1955, pp. 20–22, ill.; Genaille 1965, p. 16; Friedländer 1967–76, vol. 12 (1975), p. 103, no. 137, pl. 66; Genaille 1976, p. 21, no. 12, ill.

Superior of the Benedictine monastery of Saint Sauveur d'Anchin, near Douai, from 1511 to 1547, Charles de Sainte-Radegonde Coguin commissioned numerous works from Bellegambe. Our portrait of the abbot is a near replica of one on the exterior of Bellegambe's Anchin Polyptych—one of the artist's principal works—formerly at Saint Sauveur and now in the Musée de la Chartreuse, Douai. The polyptych has been dated between 1509 and 1513, but both portraits certainly postdate 1508, the year Coguin was confirmed abbot by Pope Julius II and received the privilege of the miter, cross, and ring.

Abbot Coguin is represented at prayer, a Book of Hours resting on the prie-dieu in front of him. His face and outer garment—what must have been a magnificent cope—are severely abraded. Cradled in his left arm is the decorated support of an abbatial cross with a silk sudarium, or Veil of Veronica. His miter, trimmed with pearls, rests on the ground just below his coat of arms. In the background is a typically northern view with a thatched cottage, mountains, a river animated by boats, and a bridge with a man on horseback.

Our panel, no doubt the left wing of a triptych, has been cut down at the top and bottom, probably by about twenty centimeters, and separated from its reverse. A grisaille painting of Saint Barbara (87 x 28.5 cm, private collection, London) shows a coat of arms related to that of our abbot and was probably the outside right wing of the same altarpiece. The grisaille panel may have been with ours in the Gréau collection in the nineteenth century, as it was sold by the Gréau family in 1939. MSdJ

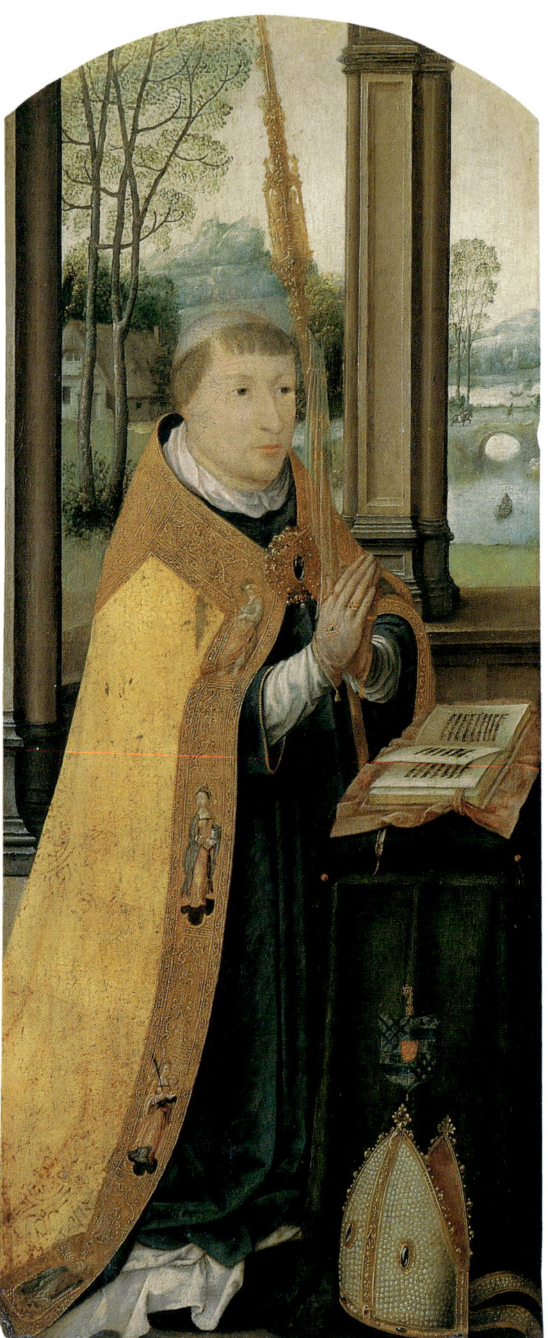

Master of Alkmaar, active by 1504

37. *Jan* (1438–1516), *First Count of Egmond*
Magdalena van Werdenburg (1464–1538), *Countess of Egmond,* about 1510

Attributed to Jacques Le Bouc, the Arras Codex (Bibliothèque Municipale, Arras) is a volume of drawn copies after fourteenth-, fifteenth-, and sixteenth-century portraits that was probably compiled during the 1560s for Alexandre Le Blancq of Lille. Drawings after our pictures in this compendium identify the sitters as "Jehan, premier Conte d'Egmond" and "Magdaleine de Wardemberghe, femme de Jehan, Conte d'Egmond" (fols. 202, 203).

Jan van Egmond, also known as Jan van Manke, holds a parchment in his hand and wears the collar of the Golden Fleece, a rare distinction granted to him in 1491 by Philip the Handsome to honor his long career in the service of the dukes of Burgundy: only twenty-four knights were admitted to the Order of the Golden Fleece, created by Philip the Good in 1430. On his return from a pilgrimage to the Holy Land in 1465, Jan had joined the archduke Maximilian and Maximilian's son, Philip, in a successful armed expedition against Jan's own father, Charles van Egmond, duke of Gelderland. Subsequently Jan became count of Goscum and later, in 1484, mayor of Holland, Zeeland, and Friesland. That same year he married Magdalena van Werdenburg, his junior by twenty-six years. In 1486 Archduke Maximilian appointed Jan first count of Egmond.

Each sitter is shown against a green background and seated in a shallow space behind a brocade or tablecloth treated as a flat surface. They are both soberly but richly garbed. The countess wears a black-and-white dress of great refinement and holds a carnation, symbol of marriage. Noteworthy is the contrast between the simplification, and perhaps idealization, of the countess's doll-like features and the sharp characterization of the elderly count, remarkable for the minute description of his wizened face.

The attribution of the portraits to the Master of Alkmaar was first proposed by Friedländer (1919), who notes that their straightforward style is comparable to that of the master's *Seven Mercies* (Rijksmuseum, Amsterdam), which is signed and dated 1504 and was commissioned by the Confraternity of the Holy Ghost in Alkmaar for the Sint-Laurenskerk.

The paintings were probably carried out a few years before Jan van Egmond's death. They represent a type of portraiture commissioned to foster a sense of a family's illustrious past or to honor the civic career of the sitter. In an anonymous portrait of about 1510 in the Rijksmuseum, Amsterdam, the count is shown with the so-called Jerusalem feather, which indicates that he belonged to the Knightly Brotherhood of the Holy Land. He is depicted as well in a posthumous portrait that casts him as a mourner on the left in a *Lamentation* of about 1535 (Centraal Museum Utrecht) that is attributed to Jan van Scorel and Cornelis Buys, who may, in fact, be the Master of Alkmaar.

The frames are original, but the portrait of the count has been transferred from wood to canvas.

VS

Oil on canvas, transferred from wood, arched top; overall 16¾ x 10¼ in. (42.5 x 26 cm); original painted surface 16¼ x 9⅝ in. (41.3 x 24.4 cm)
The Friedsam Collection, Bequest of Michael Friedsam, 1931 32.100.122

Oil on wood, arched top; overall, with engaged frame, 19¼ x 12½ in. (48.9 x 31.8 cm); painted surface 16½ x 9¾ in. (41.9 x 24.8 cm)
The Friedsam Collection, Bequest of Michael Friedsam, 1931 32.100.118

Provenance: Baron Adolphe de Rothschild, Paris; Baron Maurice de Rothschild, Paris; [Wildenstein, Paris]; [Kleinberger, New York (1920)]; Michael Friedsam, New York (1920–31).

References: Friedländer 1914, p. 50; Friedländer 1919, p. 173; Van Gelder-Schrijver 1930, pp. 105–9; Burroughs and Wehle 1932, p. 25; Hoogewerff 1936–47, vol. 2 (1937), pp. 411–15; Wehle and Salinger 1947, pp. 103–5; Dek 1958, p. 50; Cuttler 1968, pp. 448–49; Friedländer 1967–76, vol. 10 (1973), pp. 27–28, 75, no. 59, pls. 38, 39; Campbell 1977; Bauman 1986, p. 34.

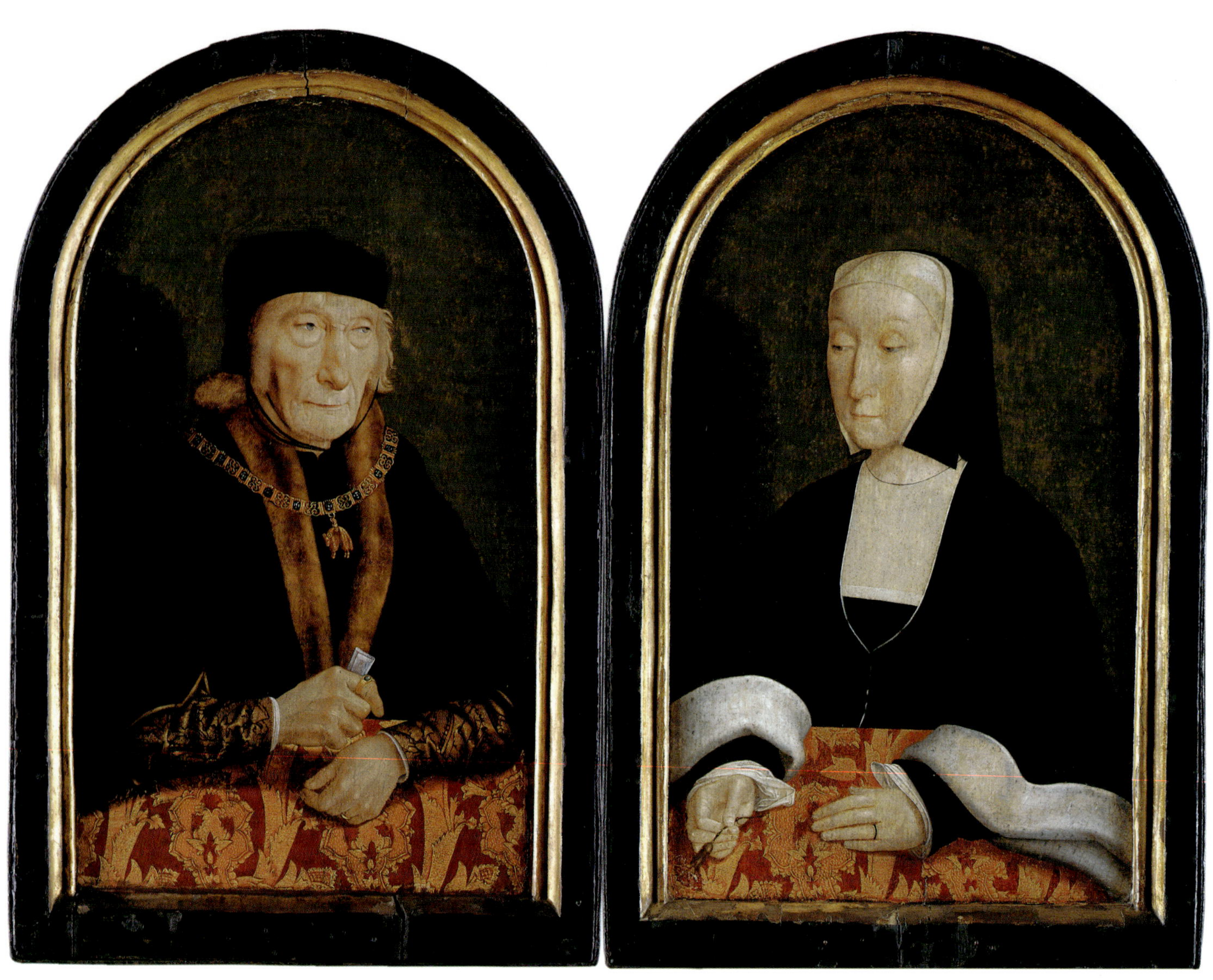

37

Quentin Massys, 1465/66–1530

38. Portrait of a Woman, about 1520

Oil on wood, 19 x 17 in. (48.3 x 43.2 cm)
The Friedsam Collection, Bequest of Michael Friedsam, 1931 32.100.47

The bust-length *Portrait of a Woman* is the right half of a portrait diptych representing a husband and wife of unknown identity. The pendant (fig. 66) is now in a private collection in Schloss Au, Switzerland. Although the man and woman depicted are dressed without ostentation, their distinctive attributes reveal that they belonged to Antwerp's literate and wealthy haute bourgeoisie. The rosary beads fingered by the man are proof of his devotion to the Virgin Mary, whose cult was especially strong in Antwerp, where she was reconsecrated annually during the Ommegang procession. The precious and expensive Book of Hours in the lady's hands is illuminated with gilded margins containing naturalistic floral decorations. They are reminiscent of the work of Simon Bening, the leading manuscript illuminator of the Bruges-Ghent school, who, like Massys, worked in Antwerp. This luxurious codex calls to mind the oft-quoted verse of Eustache Deschamps, who at the end of the fourteenth century criticized women with social pretensions:

> A Book of Hours, too, must be mine
> Where subtle workmanship will shine
> Of gold and azure, rich and smart,
> Arranged and painted with great art,
> Covered with fine brocade of gold;
> And there must be, so as to hold
> The pages closed, two golden clasps.

Each sitter is viewed behind an impressive architectural frame composed of two marble columns, a stone lintel, and an acanthus-leaf arch, examples of the Italianate motifs that were introduced into the Netherlands in the fifteenth century. The use of columns to frame sitters who inhabit a continuous loggia is a treatment used by Hans Memling in his Moreel portraits of about 1472–75 (Musées Royaux des Beaux-Arts de Belgique, Brussels). Campbell believes that our panel and its pendant may originally have formed a double portrait displayed as a single work, with the fictive frames connected visually to the actual frame.

Whereas the dark monochrome backgrounds, as well as the framing devices, are inherited from fifteenth-century models, Massys took his experiments in illusionism a step further than those of his predecessors by giving his figures assertive physical presences suggestive of their individual personalities. Placed in an almost frontal position, the woman glances to the side, away from her husband and her reading, creating the impression of suspended action: she seems caught in a moment of reflection or contemplation. The meticulous drawing and stark contrast in the modeling, compromised by abrasion, not only enhance the realism of her features but also underscore her uncompromising strength of character.

A date about 1520 for our painting is generally accepted on stylistic grounds. Silver has noted that Massys's portraits are difficult to date but points out subtle changes that occurred after he executed his Friendship Portraits of 1517, the *Erasmus*, known from a copy in the Palazzo Barberini, Rome, and *Peter Gillis* (Lord Radnor, Longford Castle): in particular the new sense of suspended activity and psychological involvement of the sitters that is apparent in our picture. The leafy marble decoration and the whitish flesh tones of the *Portrait of a Woman* link it to Massys's Rem Altarpiece of 1518–20 in the Alte Pinakothek, Munich, and his Virgin of 1520–25 in the Gemäldegalerie, Berlin, as well. Moreover, our sitter's dress and cap are typical of those worn by bourgeois women between 1515 and 1520. VS

Provenance: Private collection, England; J. Goudstikker, Amsterdam, until 1927; [Kleinberger, New York (1927–28)]; Michael Friedsam, New York (1928–31).

References: Wehle and Salinger 1947, pp. 107–8; Friedländer 1967–76, vol. 7 (1971), pp. 35, 65, 81, fig. 48; De Bosque 1975, p. 237, fig. 303; Silver 1984, pp. 123, 164–65, 185, 231–32, 237, no. 60, pl. 140; Bauman 1986, pp. 44–46, color ill.; Campbell 1990, pp. 34, 36–37, 109, 248, n. 58, fig. 44; Van Miegroet in Bauman and Liedtke 1992, pp. 100–101, ill.

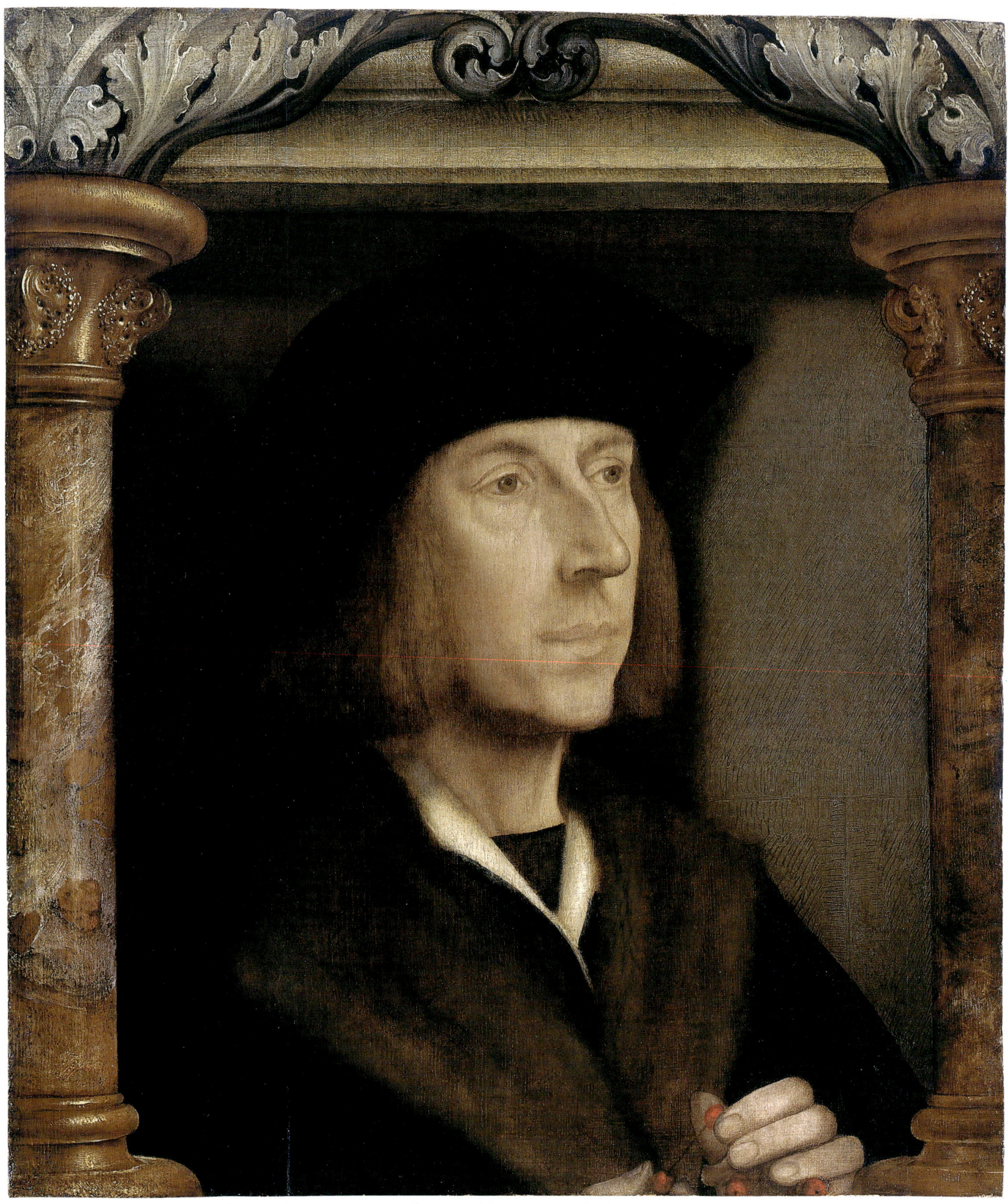

Fig. 66. Quentin Massys, *Portrait of a Man*, about 1520. Private collection, Schloss Au, Switzerland

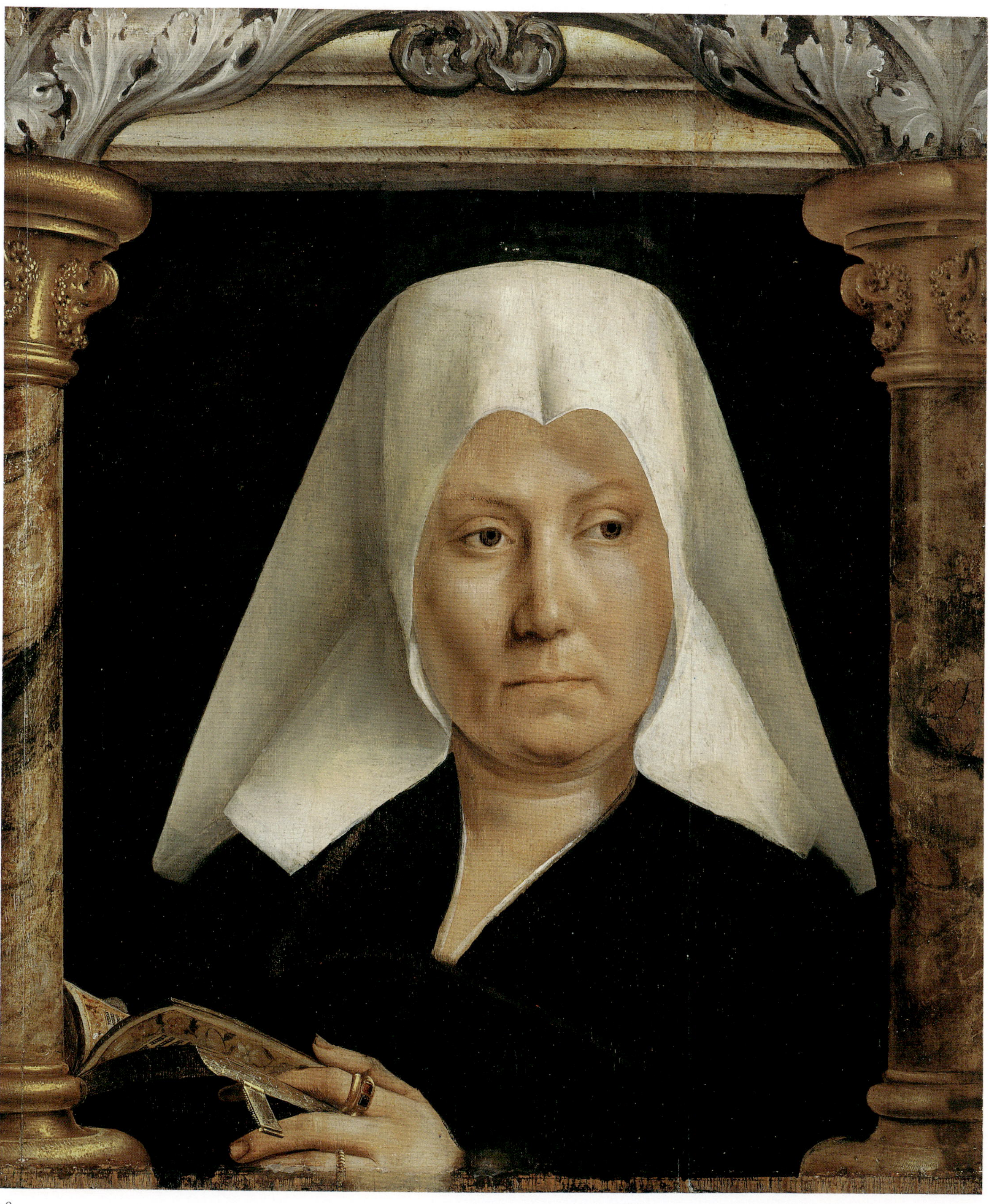

38

Jan Gossart, active by 1503, died 1532

39. Portrait of a Man, 1520–25

Oil on wood, 18½ x 13¾ in. (47 x 34.9 cm)
Signed: (on scroll) . . . om̄rpses/ J[o]annes . . . / malbodius. . . / pingeba[t]
Inscribed: (on hat ornament) IM
The Friedsam Collection, Bequest of Michael Friedsam, 1931 32.100.62

Provenance: Sir Joshua Reynolds?; [Edward Coxe, sale, Peter Coxe's, London, April 25, 1807, no. 33, as "His Own Portrait by Jan Mabuse, from the Reynolds Collection"]; Count de Quincey, Paris (sale, Hôtel Drouot, Paris, June 22, 1904, no. 35, as presumed Self-Portrait by Mabuse); Richard von Kaufmann, Berlin (sale, Cassirer and

The scroll held by the sitter in this bust-length portrait is signed with Gossart's Latinized name, Ioannes (or Joannes) Malbodius, a form that appeared for the first time in his well-known painting *Neptune and Amphitrite* of 1516 (fig. 105). The sitter wears a flat hat on which is pinned an ornament in the shape of the monogram IM, interpreted by some as Gossart's initials. On this basis the picture has sometimes been thought a self-portrait. However, the sitter bears no resemblance to the portrait of Gossart engraved by Johan Wierix for Dominicus Lampsonius's *Effigies* of 1572 (Cabinet des Estampes, Brussels) or to Gossart's presumed self-portraits, the *Portrait of a Man with a Full Beard* in the Currier Gallery of Art, Manchester, New Hampshire, and the *Portrait of a Man* in the State Pushkin Museum, Moscow. Friedländer (1906b) believed the initials stood for Ihesus Maria, a common Christian invocation, which, as Larsen contends, could be worn by an elected deacon of a guild.

This type of portraiture is rooted in the renewed interest in Van Eyck that developed in the Netherlands during the first decades of the sixteenth century, and in which Gossart played a central role. Gossart probably intended our *Portrait of a Man* as a conscious revival of Van Eyck's *Tymotheus* of 1432 (National Gallery, London). In each painting the sitter is shown in three-quarter view, staring fixedly, and with his hand holding a scroll that projects illusionistically into the spectator's space.

Gossart's sitter is richly but soberly dressed, his garments are meticulously rendered, and his brightly illuminated face is tightly framed against a neutral dark background. The features are carefully drawn, and the acutely observed details, such as the stubble of the beard, the modeling of the middle-aged cheeks and jowls, the bony protrusion of the nose, and the wrinkles on the neck, illustrate those very qualities that won the painter the praise of Albrecht Dürer and Karel van Mander. The sense of psychological detachment apparent here is found in a number of Gossart's portraits of the 1520s, such as the *Portrait of a Gentleman* of 1525–30 (Kunsthistorisches Museum, Vienna). Our painting is generally dated to the first half of the 1520s, although Herzog (1968) places it close to 1516. VS

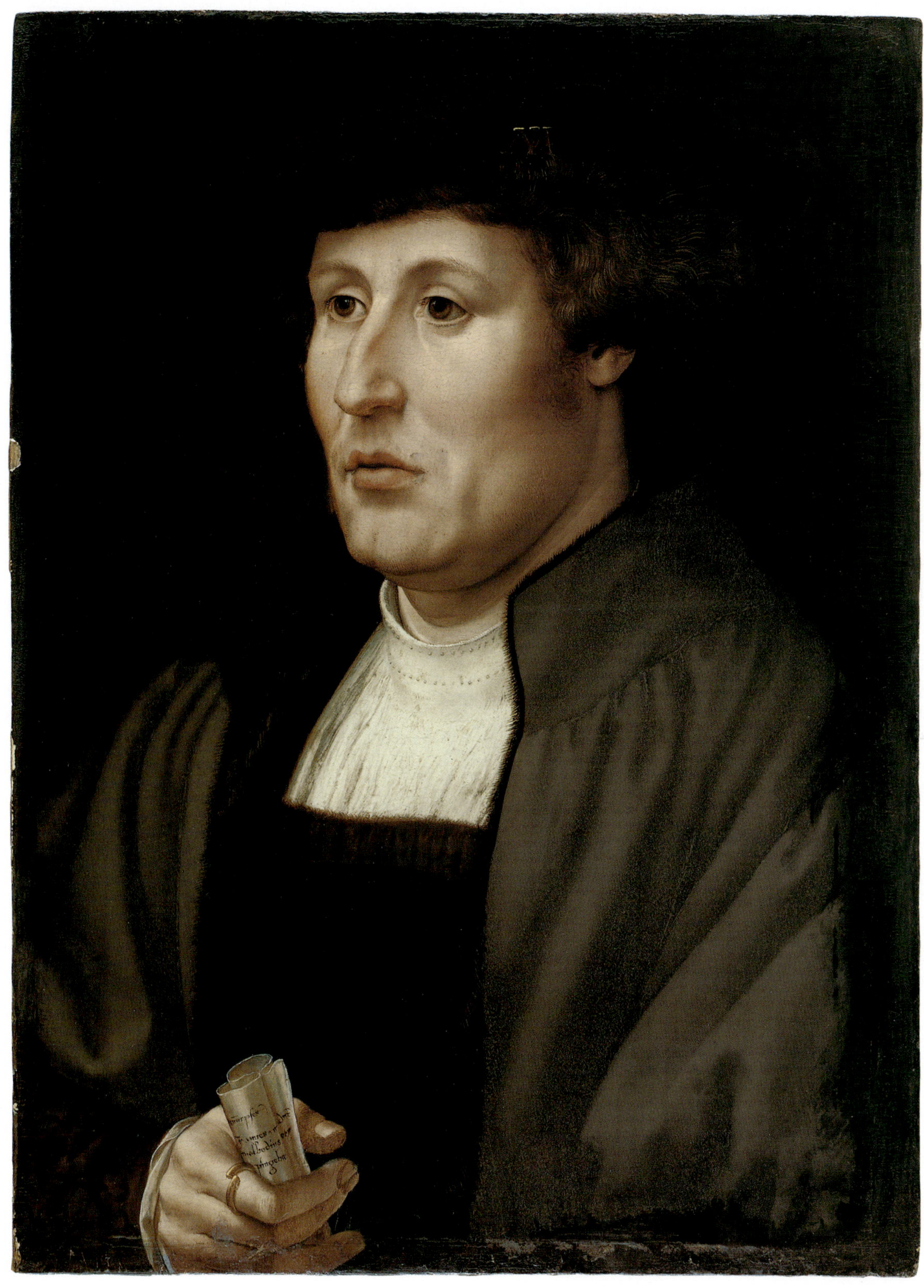

Helbing, Berlin, from December 4, 1917, no. 91, as Portrait of a Man by Jan Gossart); Camillo Castiglioni, Vienna (sale, Muller, Amsterdam, July 13–15, 1926, no. 21, as Portrait of a Man by Mabuse); [Kleinberger, New York]; Michael Friedsam, New York.

References: Friedländer 1906b, p. 34; Weisz 1913, pp. 84–85, 115 n. 66, 117, pl. 18, fig. 54; Renard 1919, passim; Burroughs and Wehle 1932, pp. 26–28, fig. 38; Wehle and Salinger 1947, pp. 141–42; Larsen 1960, pp. 88–89; Pauwels, Hoetink, and Herzog 1965, pp. 65–66, ill.; Herzog 1968, pp. 238–39, no. 14; Friedländer 1967–76, vol. 8 (1972), p. 99, no. 63; Bauman 1986, pp. 42, 48, color ill.

Jan Gossart, active by 1503, died 1532

40. Virgin and Child, about 1525

Oil on wood; overall 17 7/8 x 13 5/8 in. (45.4 x 34.6 cm); painted surface 17 1/4 x 13 in. (43.8 x 33 cm)
Gift of J. Pierpont Morgan, 1917 17.190.17

Provenance: Rodolphe Kann, Paris; J. Pierpont Morgan, New York.

References: Van Mander 1604, fols. 225–26; Ermerins 1786, p. 39; Weisz 1913, pp. 86–87; Wehle and Salinger 1947, pp. 142–43; Pauwels, Hoetink, and Herzog 1965, pp. 151–52, no. 22, ill.; Pope-Hennessy 1966, p. 257; Herzog 1968, pp. 150, 156–57, 197 n. 31, 348–49, fig. 86; Bialostocki 1970, p. 264; Friedländer 1967–76, vol. 8 (1972), pp. 35, 95–96, fig. 39a; Bauman 1986, pp. 14–16, color ill.; Campbell 1990, pp. 137, 257, n. 53.

This *Virgin and Child* is one of the finest of a dozen or so known replicas of a very popular composition by Gossart. The presumed lost original has been associated with a painting that Karel van Mander tells us in his *Schilderboeck* (1604, fols. 225–26) was made by Gossart when he worked for Adolf of Burgundy, marquis de Veere. (The artist entered the marquis's service after Philip of Burgundy's death in 1524.) According to Van Mander, the faces of Mary and the infant Jesus in this prototype were modeled after Adolf's wife, Anna van Bergen, and the couple's son. Comparison of the features of the Virgin with known depictions of Anna van Bergen—a drawing in the Arras Codex (Bibliothèque Municipale, Arras) and a likeness by Gossart (private collection) of which there are versions in the Sterling and Francine Clark Art Institute, Williamstown, Massachusetts (fig. 67), and the Isabella Stewart Gardner Museum, Boston—tends to confirm that our panel is a variant of the idealized portrait mentioned by Van Mander. The identification is further reinforced by the obvious resemblance of mother and son, who was probably Anna's youngest, Hendrik, born on September 26, 1519.

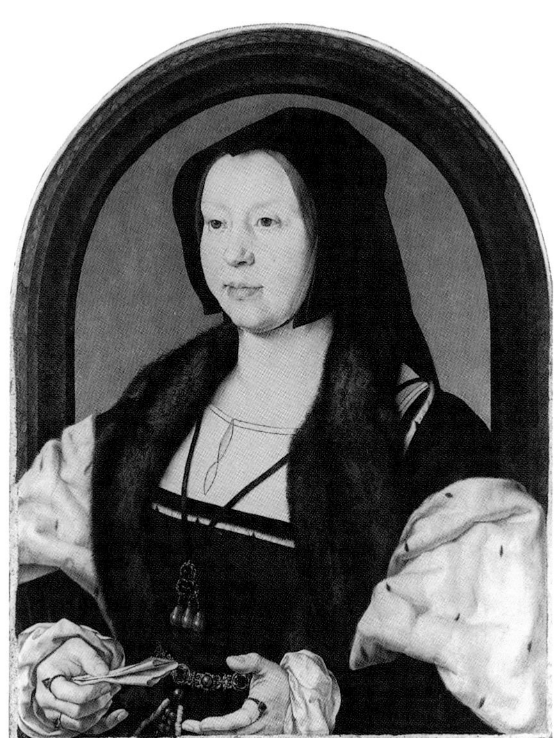

Fig. 67. Jan Gossart, *Portrait of Anna van Bergen,* about 1525. Sterling and Francine Clark Art Institute, Williamstown, Massachusetts

By showing Anna in the guise of the Virgin, Gossart would have associated the sitter with the paradigm of feminine virtue she and all women sought to emulate. Bialostocki, quoting the *Paragone* of Leonardo da Vinci, explains that the reflection of the window in the sitter's eye is emblematic of her soul: "l'occhio que se dice finestra dell'anima." This device was often used by Dürer as well.

If this Virgin and Child indeed represent Anna and her son, the picture would be an example of disguised portraiture, a type of work that appeared in the Netherlands in the first half of the fifteenth century and became increasingly popular in the early sixteenth. Among the most frequently cited disguised portraits is the figure of the saint in Rogier van der Weyden's *Saint Luke Drawing the Virgin* (fig. 19; frontis., p. 204), which is thought to be a self-portrait of the artist. Gossart himself used disguised portraiture in the wings of his Deposition Triptych of 1521 (central panel, State Hermitage Museum, Saint Petersburg; lateral panels, Toledo Museum of Art, Ohio): there he gave Saint John the Baptist his own features and Saint Peter those of the donor, Pedro de Salamanca.

In terms of the frontal postures of the mother and child, who direct their gazes at the viewer rather than interacting with each other, our devotional picture is explicitly related to Gossart's late portraits, such as the presumed likeness of one of the three daughters of Duke Adolf and Anna, *Jacqueline or Anne of Burgundy* of 1525–30 (National Gallery, London).

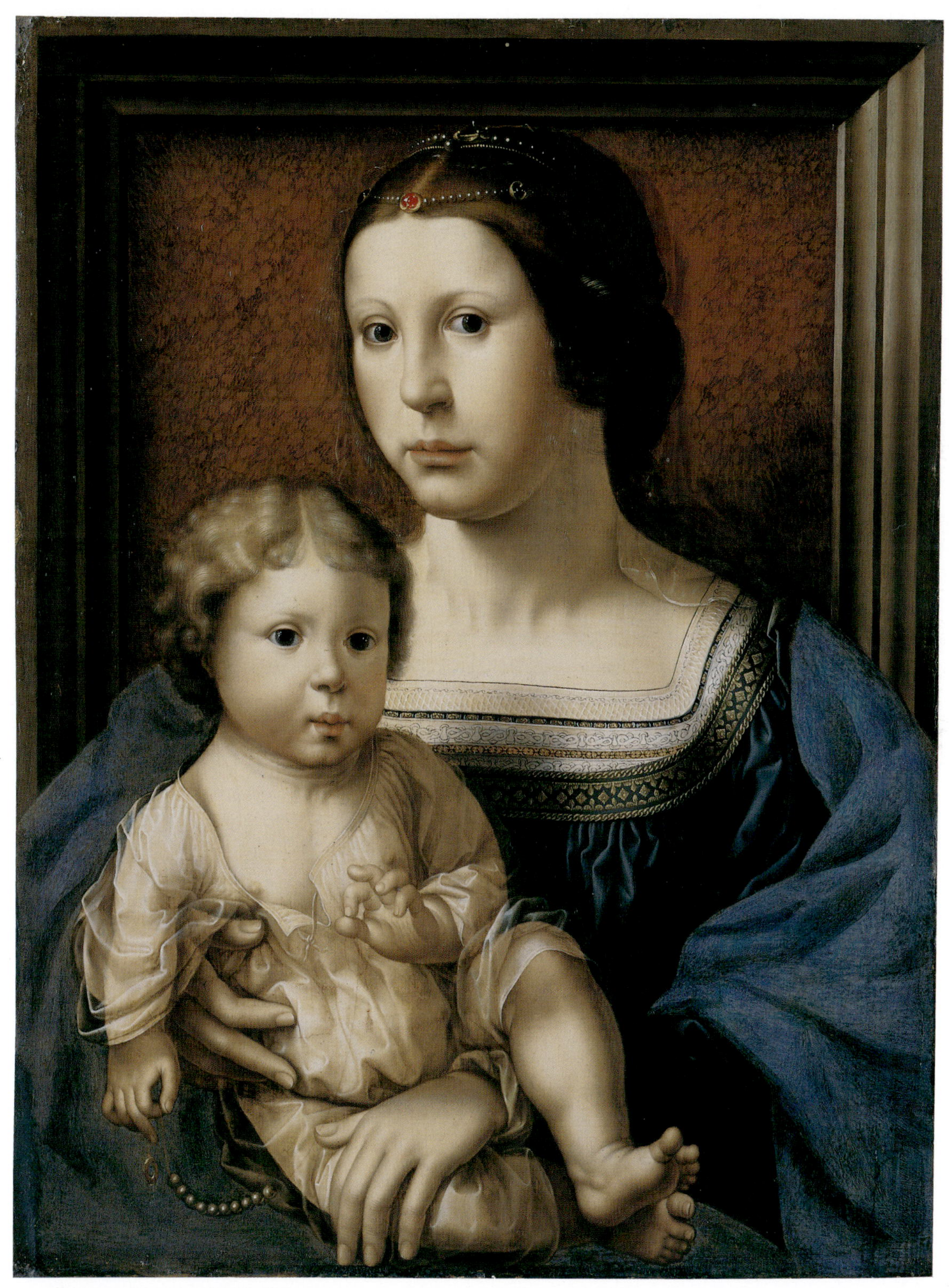

Another feature typical of Gossart is the enframed marble wall, a device he favored for devotional images of the Virgin as well as for portraits, and one that was prefigured in Memling's Portinari portraits of about 1470 (cat. no. 27). The subtle influence of Albrecht Dürer, who met Gossart during his trip to the Netherlands in 1520–21, can be detected in the type of the infant Jesus. It is visible as well in the way the Child holds the string, which calls to mind Dürer's study of a hand in a drawing of 1493, *Self-Portrait, Hand and Pillow* (Robert Lehman Collection). VS

Adriaen Isenbrant, active by 1510, died 1551

41. Man Weighing Gold, 1515–20

Oil on wood, 20 x 12 in. (50.8 x 30.5 cm) with added strips of 1¾ in. (4.5 cm) at left and right
The Friedsam Collection, Bequest of Michael Friedsam, 1931 32.100.36

Provenance: William Fuller-Maitland, Stansted Hall, Stansted, Essex (by 1818–76); William Fuller-Maitland, Stansted Hall (1876–1922); sale, Christie's, London, July 14, 1922, no. 84; [Frank T. Sabin, London, from 1922]; F. Steinmeyer, Lucerne (1923); [Kleinberger, New York, 1923]; Michael Friedsam, New York (1923–31).

References; Waagen 1854, p. 6; Friedländer 1928a, p. 4; Burroughs and Wehle 1932, p. 24; Wehle and Salinger 1947, pp. 100–101; Voet 1973, p. 330; Friedländer 1967–76, vol. 11 (1974), pp. 48, 50, 92, no. 218, pl. 150; Campbell 1981c; Bauman 1986, pp. 46–47, color ill.; Hand and Wolff 1986, p. 104; Wilson 1995, p. 6.

Our *Man Weighing Gold* is one of the earliest known examples of an occupational portrait, or a likeness in which the sitter is shown engaged in his profession. The young man holds a carefully painted balance with flat triangular trays that probably identifies him as a banker or money changer. He could, however, be one of the many early-sixteenth-century merchants who handled both commodities and money—a businessman of the type Jan Gossart explicitly depicted in his *Portrait of a Merchant* in the National Gallery of Art, Washington, D.C. Yet our sitter's thoughtful expression and the sense of arrested motion that imparts a formal quality to the image suggest that the act of weighing gold coins shown here has a symbolic as well as a realistic dimension, and may well signify the balance between worldly and spiritual values and stand as a vivid reminder of Saint Michael on Judgment Day (see entry for cat. no. 22).

Technical examination reveals that Isenbrant extensively reworked the portrait. Infrared reflectography and X-radiography show that in an earlier stage of the painting the sitter appeared almost in profile, with his left hand resting on the table and his right hand raised, as if holding an object other than the scale. The fur lapels of his coat were much wider, and the hat was slightly bigger and resembled the one depicted in Isenbrant's *Portrait of Paulus de Nigro,* dated 1515 (Groeningemuseum, Bruges). The vertical edges of the panel were cut down by an unknown amount at some point and 1¾-inch-wide strips were added later, changing the original proportions of the picture. As these additions, which are not reproduced here, have now been framed out, the panel appears very tall in relation to its width.

Rejecting the notion that the painting is an independent portrait, Bauman has suggested that it may have been paired with a likeness of a colleague or a friend to constitute a diptych like Massys's Friendship Diptych, formed by his *Erasmus,* known in a copy in the Palazzo Barberini, Rome, and *Peter Gillis* (Lord Radnor, Longford Castle). It is not surprising to find portraiture associated with money in our picture; pairings of this kind gained great popularity among such painters as Quentin Massys and Gossart and reflected the taste of their patrons, who enjoyed the extraordinary economic prosperity of the Netherlands of the early sixteenth century.

The *Man Weighing Gold,* attributed to Isenbrant on stylistic grounds, is comparable to works of about 1515–20, such as the Van de Velde Diptych (Musées Royaux des Beaux-Arts de Belgique, Brussels, and Onze-Lieve-Vrouwekerk, Bruges) and the *Adoration of the Shepherds* (National Gallery of Art, Washington, D.C.) in its warm palette, smooth surface, and slightly blurred contours of the figure against the background. VS

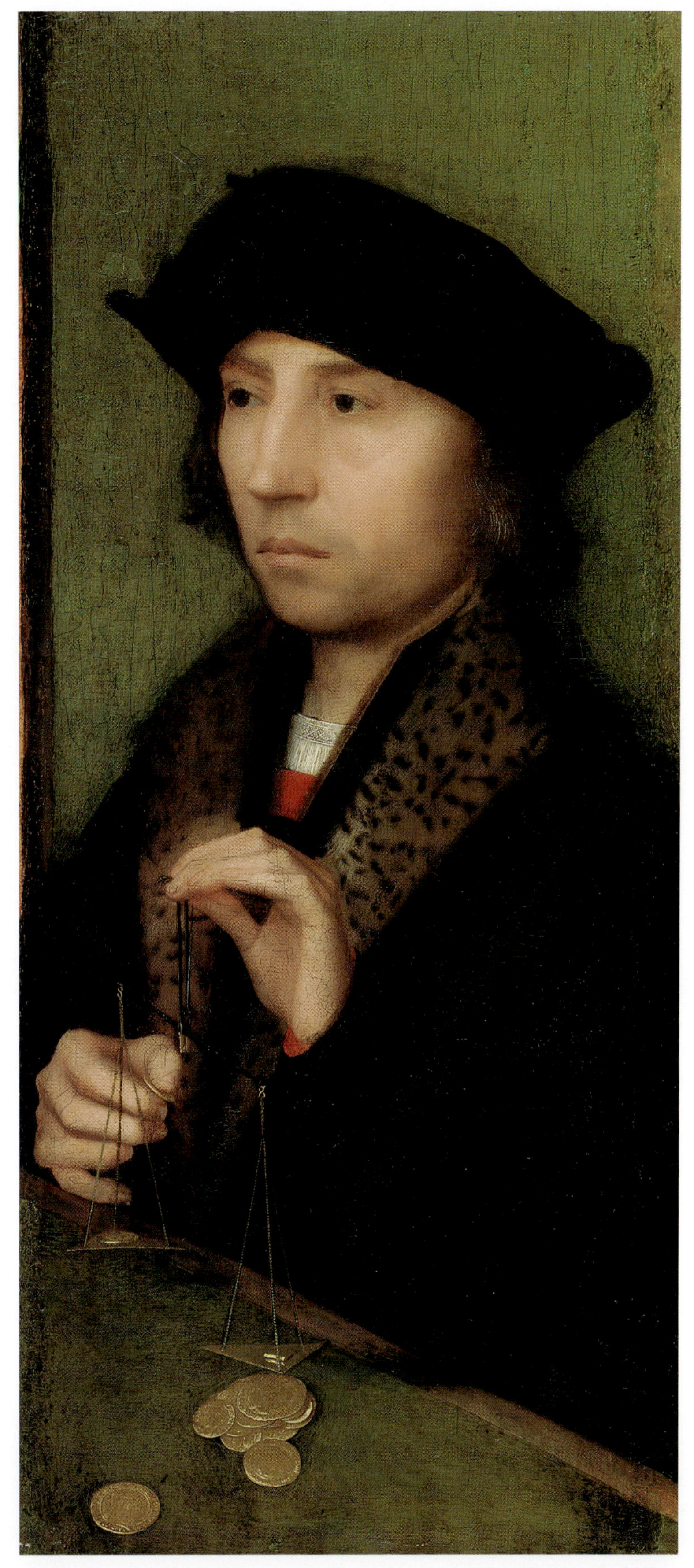

Marten van Heemskerck 1498–1574

42. Jacob Willemsz. van Veen (1456–1535), *the Artist's Father,* dated 1532

Oil on wood, 20½ x 13¾ in. (52.1 x 34.9 cm)
Signed, dated, and inscribed (bottom): mij[n] • soe[n] • heft • mij • hier • gheconterfeit • doe • ic • gheleeft • had • lxxv • iaře[n]some • seijt • (My son portrayed me here when I had lived 75 years so they say) • 1532 • MVH [monogram]
Purchase, 1871 71.36

Provenance: Johannes Enschede, Haarlem (sale, Jelgersma and van der Vinne, Harlem, May 30, 1786, no. 70); Gillis van Lichten; Count Festitis, Vienna?; [Léon Gauchez, Paris (until 1870)]; William T. Blodgett, Paris, for the Museum (1870); William T. Blodgett, Paris, and John Taylor Johnston, New York (1870–71).

References: Van Mander (1604) 1936, pp. 208–9; Van der Willigen 1870, p. 157; Preibisz 1911, pp. 8–9, 76, no. 37; Hoogewerff 1936–47, vol. 4 (1941–42), pp. 294–96, ill.; Wehle and Salinger 1947, p. 151; Bruyn 1955, pp. 32–33; Friedländer 1967–76, vol. 13 (1975), pp. 40, 44–45, 91, no. 221, pl. 113; Veldman 1977, pp. 144–45; Grosshans 1980, pp. 65, 106–7, no. 15, pl. 151; Kloek, Halsema-Kubes, and Baarsen 1986, pp. 33–35; Campbell 1990, pp. 139–40, 258 n. 7, pl. opp. p. 139.

Marten van Heemskerck signed and dated this arresting portrait the same year he traveled to Italy (he left Haarlem sometime after May 1532). It shows his father, Jacob Willemsz. van Veen, who died three years later, on September 6, 1535, at age seventy-nine, while Marten was still abroad.

In his *Schilderboeck* Van Mander describes Van Veen as a rich and stubborn farmer and recounts how the young Marten had to flee home with the help of his mother to escape his father's fury over his ambition to become a painter. There is a temptation to read these biographical details into Van Heemskerck's portrait. The elderly sitter, whose stern and uncompromising features all but fill the picture surface, stares out at the viewer from behind a stone parapet. He wears a farmer's plain black coat and a large shearling hat over a cap. The broad, firm brushstrokes enhance his sharp-featured face, represented almost lifesize, with its deep-set eyes, prominent nose, and fleshy mouth. There is an impression of immediacy and actuality that is underscored by the first-person voice of the inscription, which is written in Dutch and employs Gothic letters of great calligraphic refinement.

The plainspoken realism of this portrait strongly contrasts with the Renaissance-style, humanist-inspired memorial Van Heemskerck erected in 1570 over the grave of his father in the cemetery of the Dutch Reformed church in Heemskerk (fig. 68), only four years before his own death. By that time Van Heemskerck—a protagonist of Roman-based humanist style—had established himself as one of the most famous and erudite artists in the Netherlands and had been elected a city father of Haarlem.

The memorial includes an obelisk with a sculpted profile image of Van Veen accompanied by a Latin inscription that immortalizes his memory; beneath the inscription is a relief of a putto leaning on an upturned torch, his foot resting on a skull bearing the words *Cogita Mori*, a topos of classical imagery. The first funerary monument of the type to appear

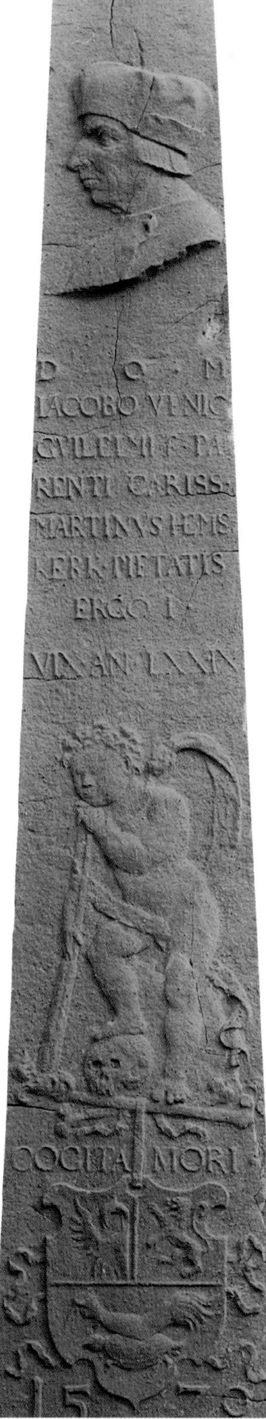

Fig. 68. Memorial to Jacob Willemsz. van Veen, 1570. Cemetery of Dutch Reformed Church, Heemskerk

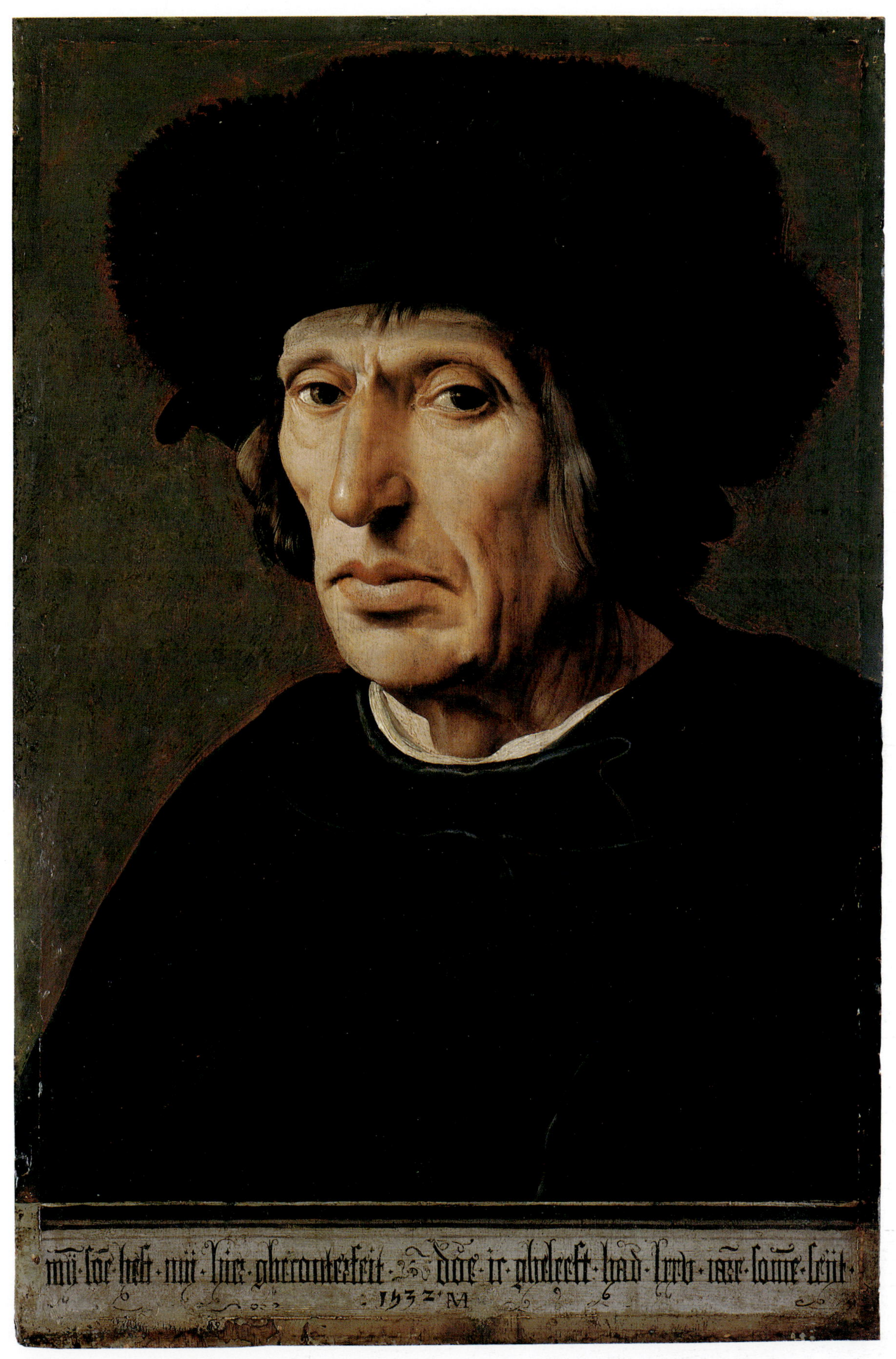
mij·soē·heft·mij·hier·ghecontersfeit· doe·ic·gheleeft·had·lxxv·iaer·somme·leit·
1532·M

in the Netherlands, the memorial has a programmatic quality that is far removed from the unadorned directness of our picture. The personal and private meaning of the painting becomes startlingly apparent when it is compared with Van Heemskerck's *Portrait of a Boy*, dated 1531 (Museum Boijmans Van Beuningen, Rotterdam). In that painting the inscription, which is borrowed from Erasmus, is written in Latin with classical letters, and the twelve-year-old sitter, shown to the waist, is depicted as though interrupted in the act of writing. The use of gesture and the boy's vivacious expression embody the humanist conceit of the speaking portrait: the picture that "lacks only voice," a topos of humanist criticism.

Van Heemskerck's portrait of his father, by contrast, draws on the strengths of a native vernacular tradition. These same strengths inform a painting by Jan van Scorel, with whom Van Heemskerck collaborated from 1527 until his departure for Italy: the *Portrait of a Man* of 1529 in the Rijksmuseum, Amsterdam, which shares with our panel the straightforward characterization of a sitter confined within a narrow frame.

Our work is one of sixty pictures purchased in Paris for the Metropolitan Museum in 1870. VS

Master of the Dinteville Allegory, Netherlandish or French, active mid-16th century

43. Moses and Aaron before Pharaoh: An Allegory of the Dinteville Family, dated 1537

Oil on wood, 69½ x 75⅞ in. (176.5 x 192.7 cm)
Dated and inscribed: (on hem of Moses' garment) •IEHAN S^{r} DE•POLISY• / •EN•AGE 33• / •BAILLY•DE•TROYES / [EN?]•1537• ; *(on hem of Gaucher's robe)* 1537 / GAVCHER•S^{r} •DE•VANLAY•/ EN AGE / 28; *(on hem of Guillaume's robe)* GVILLAVME• / DE SCHESNET[Z] / DE•DINTEVILLE •CHEV[ALIER]/ DESCV[R]IE• DE•MO[NSIEUR] *(Guillaume . . . Stable Squire to the Dauphin; last letter, O, cut by panel edge)* / EN / AGE 32; *(on Aaron's miter)* CREDIDIT. / ABRAM•DN̂O. / ETREPVTATV̂. EST•ILLI•AD.IVS / TITIAM• *(And [Abraham] believed in the Lord; and he counted it to him for righteousness [Genesis 15:6].); (respectively on lower and upper green stripes of Aaron's cape)*

This fascinating work, which presents in the guise of a biblical story a defense and justification of the Dinteville, a powerful French family, is among the largest and most compelling allegorical portraits of the sixteenth century. It hung at Polisy, the château of Jean de Dinteville, together with Hans Holbein's *Ambassadors* (National Gallery, London), and the two works remained with heirs of the Dinteville family until they were auctioned at the Beaujon sale in 1787. It has often been proposed that the Metropolitan panel, which bears the date 1537, is a pendant to Holbein's somewhat larger masterpiece, which measures 206 by 209 centimeters and is dated 1533. While this is debatable, the author of our picture may well have taken inspiration from the imposing presence and descriptive intensity of the earlier work, which pairs Jean de Dinteville, then ambassador to England, with his humanist friend Georges de Selve, bishop of Lavaur. The Museum's painting was apparently commissioned by Jean's brother François II, bishop of Auxerre, and in an unpublished inventory of 1589 recently brought to light by R. C. Famiglietti, it is described as "a large picture above the fireplace in the room called the room of the late Bishop of Auxerre, where is painted the story of Pharaoh, King of Egypt." François seems to have had a penchant for works that combined historical or religious narrative with portraiture. He commissioned the triptych *Scenes from the Legend of Saint Eugenia* of 1535, now in the church of Varzy (figs. 69, 70), in which he and his brothers appear as spectators and participants, and he is prominent as well in a *Stoning of Saint Stephen* of 1550 (cathedral of Saint Stephen, Auxerre). François may also be represented with his brothers in a second allegory, a *Judgment of Solomon* of about 1543 (art market, London, 1954), in which the figure of Solomon has been identified as the Dauphin Henri.

In the scene portrayed here, based on Exodus 7:9, contemporary court dress is juxtaposed with archaizing costumes intended to suggest Old Testament dress. Moses and Aaron plead with Pharaoh to free the Israelites; to prove they are armed with the power of the Lord, Aaron changes his rod into a serpent. Depicted in the guise of Aaron, François de Dinteville is identified by the coats of arms set into the tiles beneath his feet. His brother Jean is shown here as Moses, while the two younger brothers, Guillaume

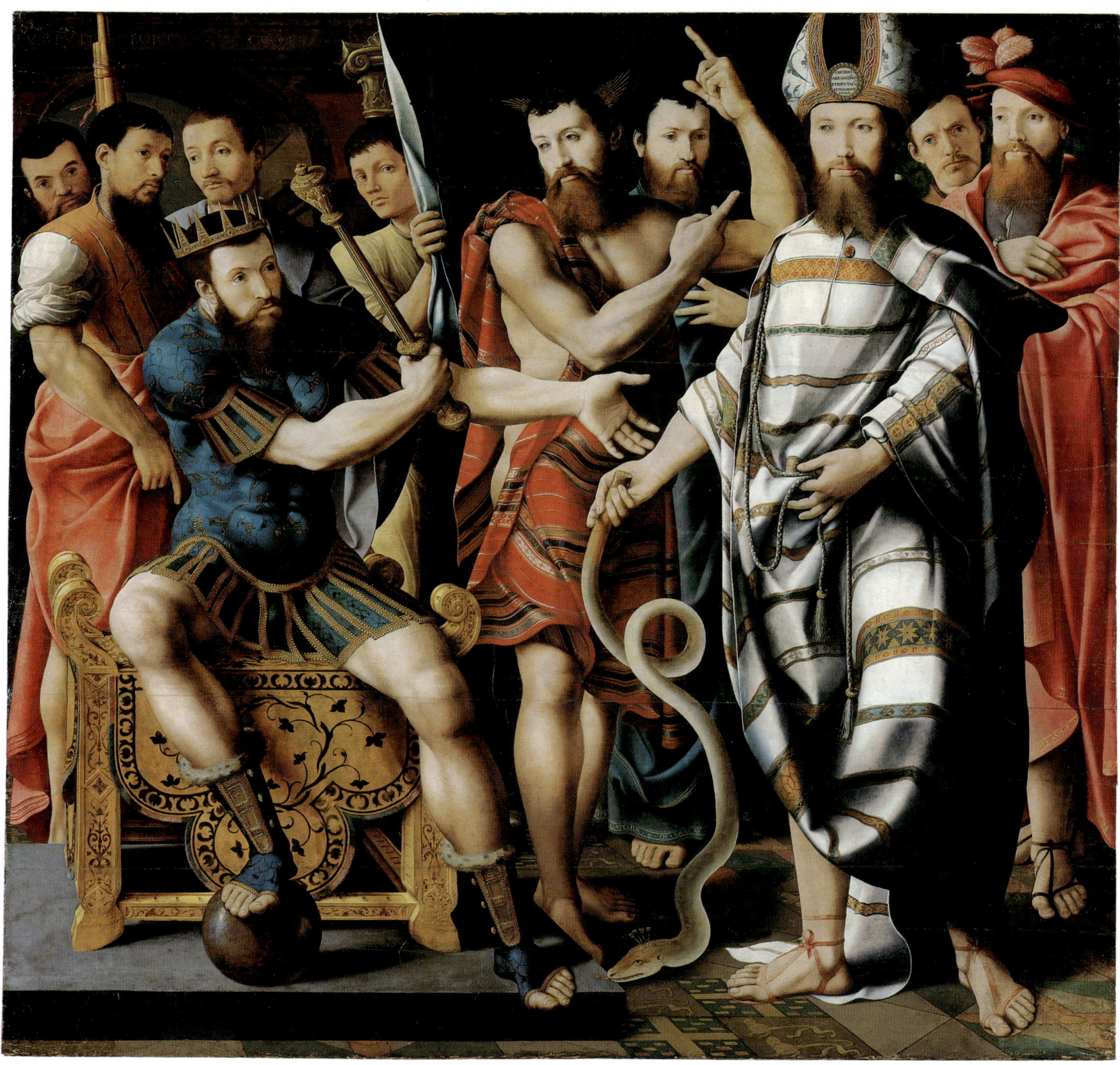

and Gaucher, stand in the background. The names of the three brothers and their ages in 1537 are inscribed on the hems of their robes. Pharaoh is clearly intended as a veiled portrait of the French king François I.

Despite the date 1537 prominently displayed in various parts of the picture, Brown argues that the panel was commissioned as the result of a family crisis that occurred in 1538: Gaucher, accused of sodomy and challenged to a duel before the king, fled to Italy, followed by Guillaume and François, and the see of Auxerre was transferred to Pierre de Mareuil, confidant of the duchesse d'Estampes, the king's mistress. Jean remained at Polisy to defend the family's honor. At least two of the brothers, François and Guillaume, were able to return to France in the spring of 1542. François was reinstated in that year as bishop of Auxerre and reconciled with the king, but it took years for the brothers to regain all they had

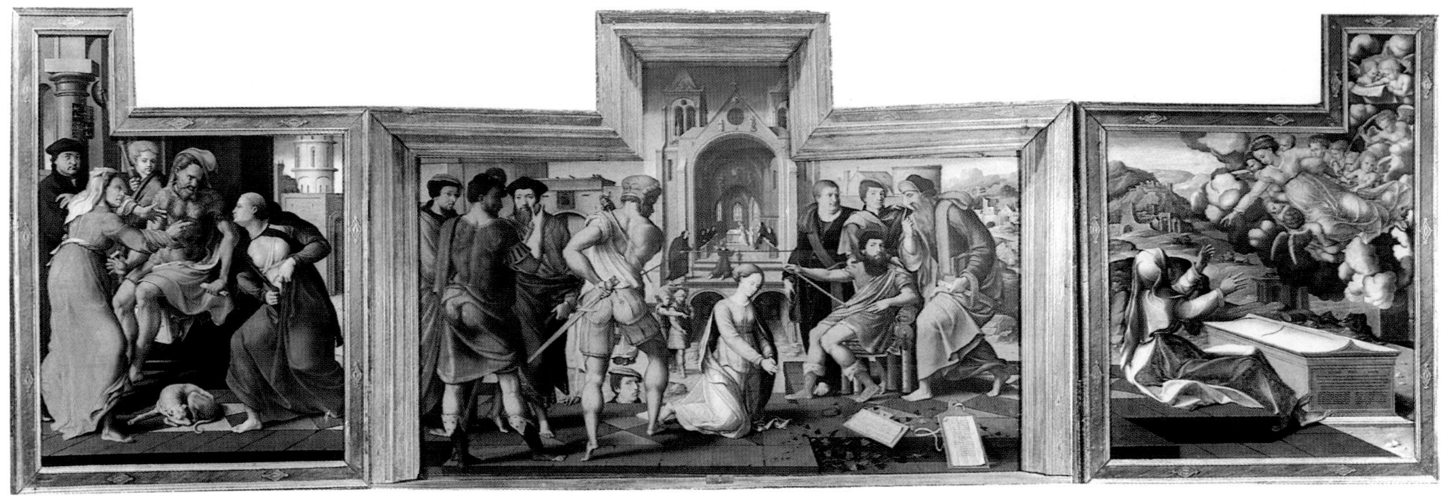

Fig. 69. Master of the Dinteville Allegory, triptych with *Scenes from the Legend of Saint Eugenia*, 1535. Oil on wood. Church of Varzy (Nièvre)

EN / 8; (upper left, on entablature) VIRTVTI FORTVNA COMES· (Fortune, the companion of merit [motto of the Dinteville family]); (lower left, falsely, on base of Pharaoh's throne) IOANNES·HOLBEIN·1537 Arms (beneath feet of François II de Dinteville) of Dinteville (left) and Duplessis (mother's family, right) Wentworth Fund, 1950 50.70

Provenance: Dinteville family, Polisy, château of Jean de Dinteville (1537–1653, inventory 1589); François de Cazillac, marquis de Cessac, descendant of Claude de Dinteville, niece of Jean, who married into the de Cazillac family in 1562, Paris (from 1653, inventory 1653); probably Marie-Renée le Genevois, granddaughter and heiress of François de Cazillac; her heir, Chrestien II de Lamoignon; his wife, Marie-Louise Gon de Bergonne, 1728 (inventory 1728); Chrétien-Guillaume de Lamoignon, son of Chrestien II de Lamoignon (from 1759, inventory 1759); his son, Chrétien-François II de Lamoignon, marquis de Basville (until 1787 [executor

forfeited during their absence. Following Brown's hypothesis, the inscription on Aaron's cape, *EN/8*, may be a cryptic record of the painting's actual date of creation, or 1538. The ubiquitous presence on the panel of the date 1537 associates the painting in a casual viewer's mind with a year in which the family's reputation was untarnished; the real subject of the allegory would thus have remained ambiguous to the uninitiated.

The composition seems to embody a carefully constructed rhetorical argument. With one arm pointing to the heavens and the other to François II as Aaron, Jean de Dinteville indicates to the king that his brother is the bishop chosen by the Lord, a truth confirmed by the sign of Aaron's serpent. The king responds by reaching out in acceptance to François. Running across the painting's upper register is a remarkable series of portrait heads, brilliantly varied in expression and physiognomy, as well as in the direction of their glances and placement in depth. These men are divided into two groups. In sight of the king and in front of the curtain are the main players—the four Dinteville brothers and an earnest-looking man with a blond mustache, his gaze fixed on the viewer. The placement of this last man, who is perhaps the artist, suggests that he sides with the brothers' cause. To the left of the curtain and behind the king are four young men—members of Pharaoh's court—who seem to witness rather than actively participate in the narrative; these may be portraits of individuals from either the Dinteville or the royal entourage.

Although the circumstances of the painting's commission have perhaps become clearer recently, the authorship of the picture remains unknown. Hervey and Martin-Holland, who first published the panel in 1911, ascribed it to Félix Chrétien, a chorister at Auxerre who, showing "delicacy of hand in penmanship and painting," became secretary to the bishop of Auxerre and accompanied him into exile. Chrétien was made a canon upon their return in 1554, the year he wrote a biography of the bishop. In 1743 Abbé Lebeuf mentioned two paintings, one at Varzy and the other at Auxerre, that included portraits of François II de Dinteville, and noted that they were "considered to be in the style of Félix Chrétien, canon" (Lebeuf 1743, vol. 1, p. 598). Influenced by these remarks, Hervey and Martin-Holland attributed to Chrétien not only the large triptych in the church of Varzy and the *Stoning of Saint Stephen* in the cathedral at Auxerre but also our panel, on the basis of its stylistic similarity to the first two works. In 1961 Thuillier doubted but did not rule out the attribution of our allegory to Chrétien, although he observed that Chrétien appeared in documents of his own time not as an artist but as a man leading "the simple and comfortable life of a canon of Auxerre." Thuillier ascribed the *Stoning of Saint Stephen* to a French artist working in the provinces, but he enlarged the oeuvre of the "Chrétien" figure to include two other pictures associated with the Dinteville family and stylistically consistent with the Metropolitan allegory and the Varzy triptych. Responding to the style of this group of paintings as well as to the discovery of a Dutch inscription on the Varzy work, he wondered whether the artist might have had a connection with the Netherlands or Germany. In 1973 Bruyn identified two coats of arms on the Varzy triptych, one of the Guild of Saint Luke (the painters' guild) and the other of the city of Haarlem, and in 1984 tentatively suggested that Bartholomeus Pons—a Haarlem painter who visited Rome and was active in Burgundy from about 1518 to 1530—was the artist responsible for the triptych, the *Stoning of Saint Stephen*, and our picture.

Although the Metropolitan allegory has stylistic affinities to the works of such Antwerp masters of the mid-sixteenth century as Jan van Scorel and Lambert Lombard, the similarities are not pronounced. The king's throne and the robed figures in our panel suggest the classical world as it is evoked in the work of Lombard and other Dutch painters of his generation, but the portrait heads, which have been compared with those of Van Scorel, are more effectively three-dimensional than his. In general the figures show a simplification and solidity of form that are more commonly found in French art than in Netherlandish painting. The artist seems to have drawn strength from provincial roots, as nothing quite like the monumentality and physical presence of our panel is seen within the main currents of Netherlandish or French painting of the period.

MSdJ

The author gratefully acknowledges the assistance of E. A. R. Brown in the preparation of this entry.

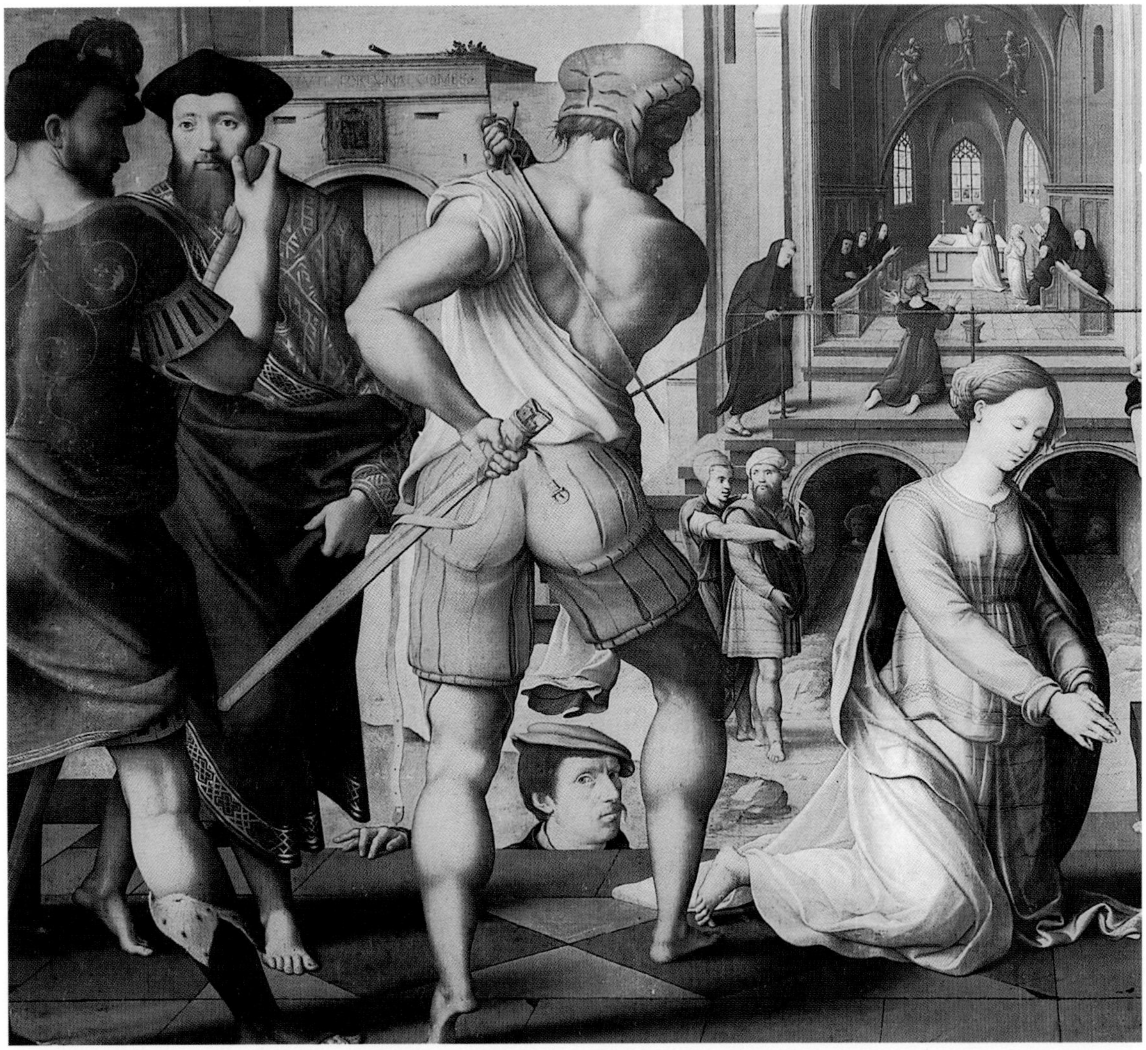

Fig. 70. Master of the Dinteville Allegory, detail, *The Martyrdom of Saint Eugenia*, central panel of triptych with *Scenes from the Legend of Saint Eugenia*, 1535. Oil on wood. Church of Varzy (Nièvre)

of estate of Nicolas Beaujon and included our panel and Holbein in sale]; sale, estate of Nicolas Beaujon, Hôtel d'Évreux, Rémy and Julliot fils, Paris, April 25–May 4, 1787, no. 16, as "La Cour de François II [sic] *. . ." by Holbein, sold with no. 16 bis, Holbein's Ambassadors, to Lebrun); Jean-Baptiste-Pierre Lebrun, Paris (1787; sale, Paris, April 11, 1791, no. 44, as "La Cour de François II* [sic] *. . ." by Holbein, to Pois); ? Comte de Cerny, château de Lisy, near Anisy-le-Château, Aisne, France; probably Capt. Stair Hathorn Stewart, Glasserton, Withorn, Scotland (d. 1865); his grandson, Stair Hathorn Johnston Stewart, Glasserton (d. 1905); his half brother, Adm. Robert Hathorn Johnston Stewart, Glasserton (by 1910–d. 1940; sale, Christie's, London, February 26, 1910, no. 106, as "Property of a Gentleman, said to represent King Henry VIII, as Pharaoh . . ." to Dale, bought in); his estate (1940–48; sale, Christie's, London, July 23, 1948, no. 58, with "one [figure] said to represent Henry VIII, as Pharaoh . . ." to Sabin); Frank T. Sabin, London (1948–50).*

References: Hervey 1900, pp. 107–38; Hervey and Martin-Holland 1911, pp. 48–55, pl. 1; Blunt 1954, pp. 68, 83, nn. 84–86, pl. 46B; Chrétien 1954, p. 193; Sterling 1955, pp. 44–47, ill.; Thuillier 1961, pp. 57–75, ill.; Châtelet and Thuillier 1963, pp. 113–15; Pope-Hennessy (1966) 1979, pp. 250–51, 324, n. 54, fig. 275; Blunt 1970, pp. 63–64, pl. 46B; Bruyn 1973; Bruyn 1984, pp. 98–110, pls. 4–5; Bonfait 1986, pp. 35–36; Guillaume et al 1990, pp. 60, 108–9, 117–19; Brown 1996, pp. 512–32; Foister 1997, pp. 23–25, 28–29, 87, fig. 15; Brown 1999.

Netherlandish Painter

44. Portrait of a Surgeon, dated 1569

Oil on wood, 8¼ x 6⅛ in. (21 x 15.6 cm)
Dated and inscribed: (left) siet om of swijcht (be cautious or keep silent); (right, on column) A.° 1[5]69 • / siet om of swijcht /ÆT^{S}• 47•
Theodore M. Davis Collection, Bequest of Theodore M. Davis, 1915
30.95.287

Provenance: Bonomi-Cereda, Milan; Theodore M. Davis, Newport, Rhode Island (1895–1915).

Reference: Wehle and Salinger 1947, p. 152.

The cryptic motto inscribed on the plain green background of this small panel gives us no information about the sitter, who has not been identified. It is clear, nevertheless, that he is an anatomist or a surgeon, portrayed with the attributes of his profession. The man's right hand rests on a skull, and the fingers of his left hand grasp a metal instrument with an eye-shaped opening that closely resembles a tool used by seventeenth-century surgeons to cauterize skulls. From his belt hang several keys and a saw. The extremely naturalistic portrayal highlights carefully observed and precisely rendered facial features and powerful hands, which attest to the physical rigors of the sitter's gory trade.

The painting belongs to a type of small cabinet portrait familiar from the production of Corneille de Lyon (1500/10–1575), a Dutch painter active in France, who specialized in small-scale paintings in which the sensitively modeled heads of sitters are invariably viewed against green backgrounds. VS

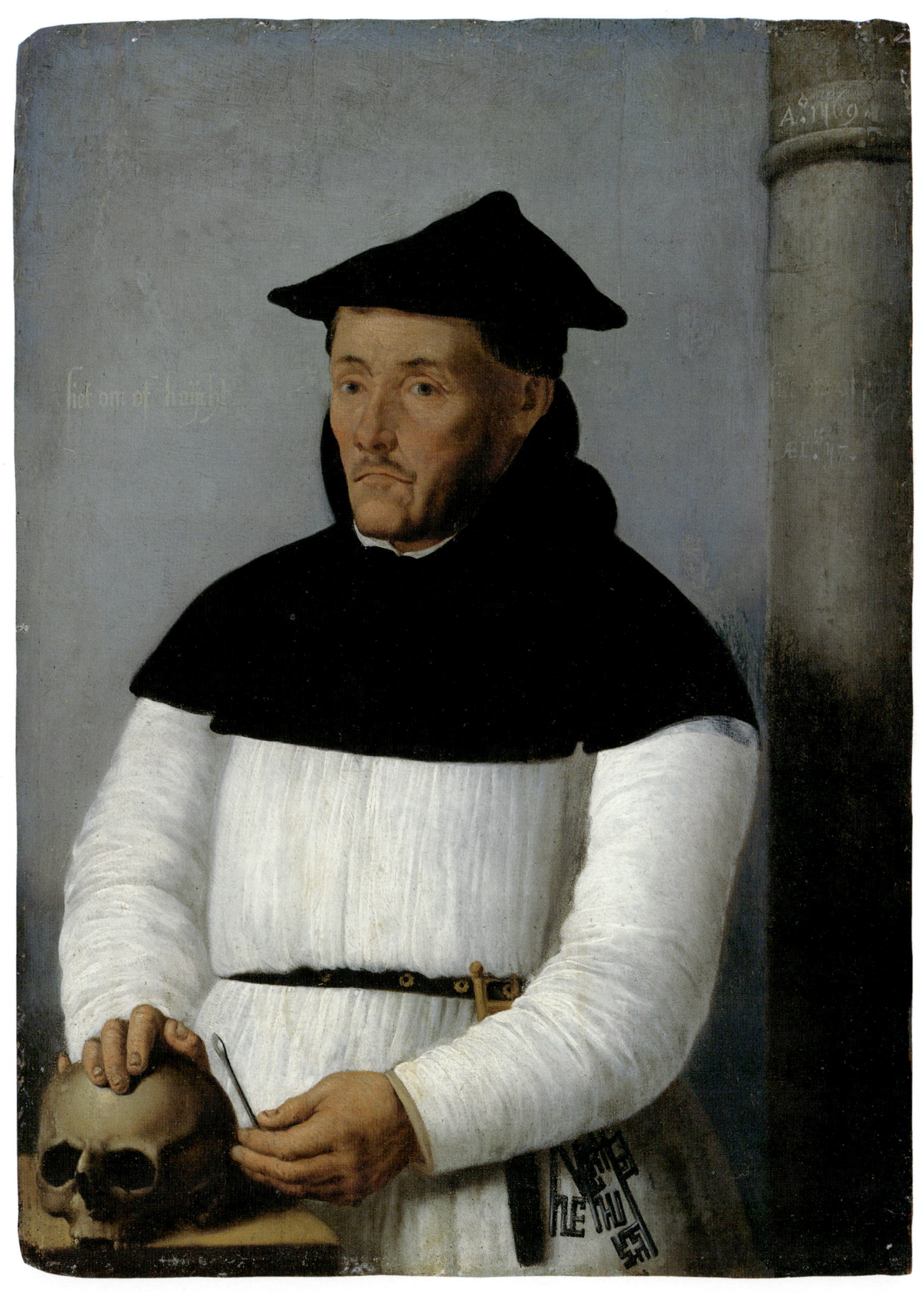

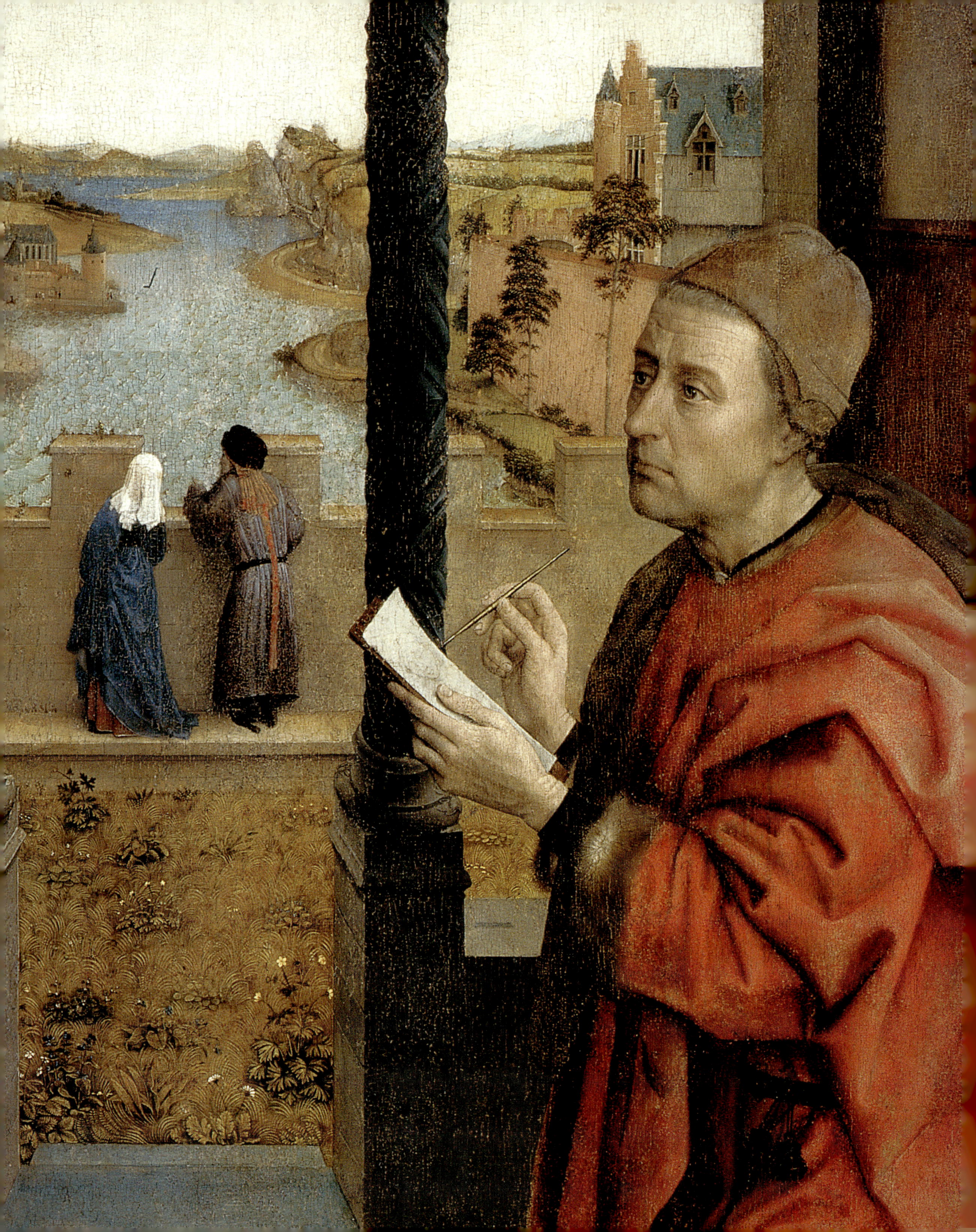

Workshop Practice in Early Netherlandish Painting: An Inside View

What exactly constituted the routine activities within the workshop of an early Netherlandish painter must be gleaned from a variety of contemporary sources—from surviving guild records, lists of guild members, legal documents, and contracts for commissions. Much of this material has been destroyed as a result of political and religious wars, accidents of nature, and indifferent record-keeping. However, relatively complete information exists for the period beginning in the fifteenth century for the painters' guilds in Tournai, Bruges, and Antwerp, where lists of members and individual organizational responsibilities have been preserved. As the strength of the Metropolitan Museum collections of Netherlandish art lies in paintings from the southern Netherlands made during the fifteenth and early sixteenth centuries, what we can learn from these records has a bearing on our holdings.

Normally an artist began as an apprentice, initially carrying out menial tasks, such as grinding pigments, in the workshop of his master. Slowly he rose through the ranks by dint of his gradually increasing competence in various stages of the painting process until he achieved the level of master. A master usually employed one or two apprentices or pupils, who sometimes shared his living quarters for a time. A *compagnon*, or journeyman, came into a master's workshop at an advanced level and stayed for a while before joining the guild or moving on to a different location. Daily assignments for the master and his assistants included not only work on formal commissions for individual paintings and altarpieces but also a variety of other jobs. These might involve making designs for sculptures or tapestries (figs. 71–73), providing polychromy for sculptures, and even supplying such ephemeral products as banners for processions, set designs for theatrical performances, and decorations for banquets at court.

Curiously, it is from descriptions of the deviations from the rules, found in records of legal battles over various issues—among them broken agreements, subcontracting, illicit use of borrowed compositional designs—that we gain insight into some of the most interesting and colorful working practices of artists. The considerable importance of the issue of ownership of workshop patterns and designs, for example, is made abundantly clear by the litigation of 1519–20 involving Gerard David and his assistant-journeyman Ambrosius Benson, an immigrant painter from Lombardy who shared the master's house for a period. According to court papers, when Benson departed David's employ, he apparently left behind two trunks filled with the paraphernalia of the workshop: projects, or *patrons*, associated with both the painter's and the illuminator's art; a small model book or sketchbook of heads and nude figures; a completed painting of the Virgin (which Benson had made for his father);

Opposite: Rogier van der Weyden, detail, *Saint Luke Drawing the Virgin*, about 1435–40. Oil on wood, Museum of Fine Arts, Boston

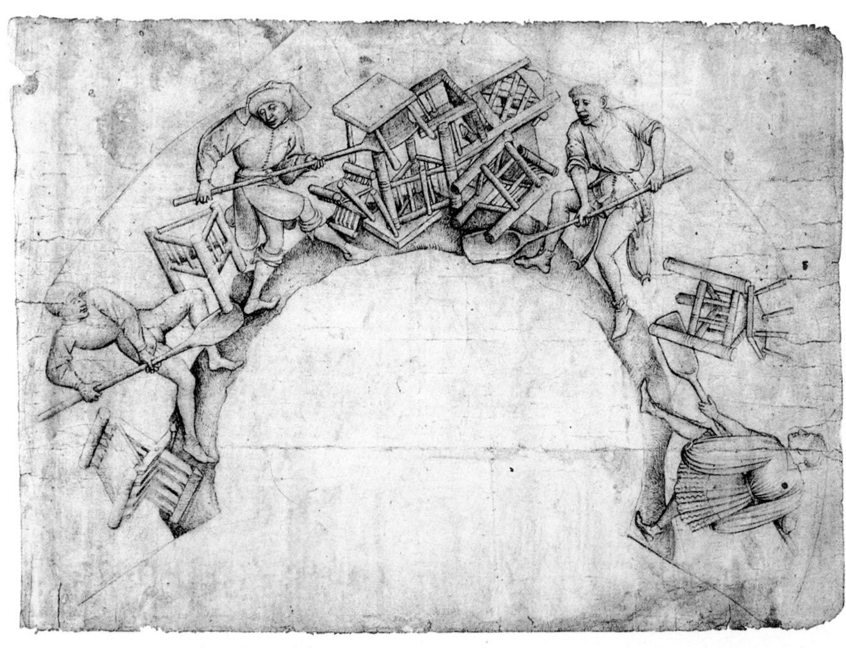

Fig. 71. Circle of Rogier van der Weyden, *Men Shoveling Chairs or "Scupstoel,"* about 1445–50. Pen and brown ink over traces of black chalk on paper. Robert Lehman Collection, The Metropolitan Museum of Art, New York

a small picture of the Pietà; a Magdalene carried out only in the underpainting stage; a box of pigments; and various patterns belonging to Benson that had been taken from the house of Adriaen Isenbrant; as well as other patterns that Benson had borrowed from Albrecht Cornelis for a fee of two florins *philippus*. The details of the legal records also reveal that David found various unfinished patterns that belonged to him among his assistant's effects. Further complicating matters was the fact that Benson owed David the considerable sum of seven *livres de gros* and had agreed to continue to serve in David's shop for three days a week until the debt was cleared. Benson, however, reneged on his promise, and David therefore retained the trunks. All that is known about the outcome of this protracted case is that David was imprisoned briefly for refusing to return workshop materials that he believed belonged to him.

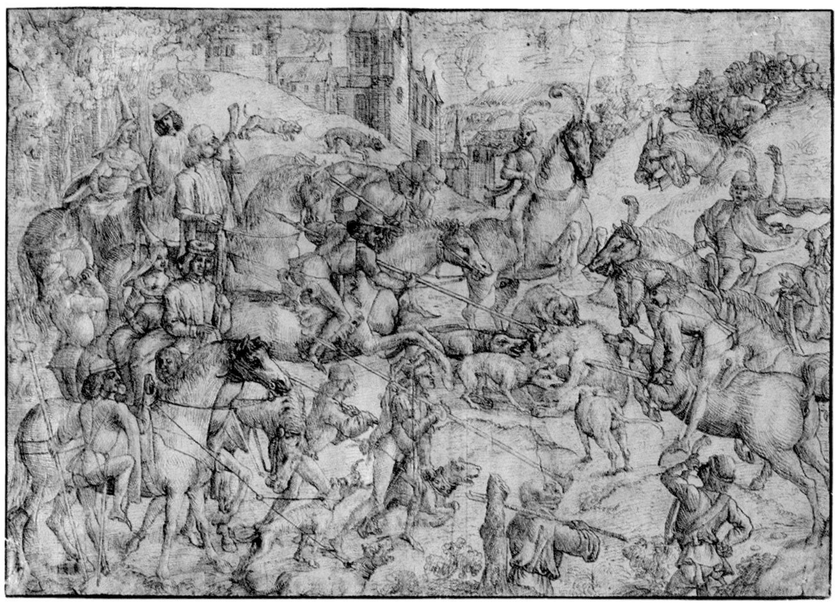

Fig. 72. Netherlandish, *Bear Hunt*, Brussels?, 1470–90. Pen and brown ink on paper. Robert Lehman Collection, The Metropolitan Museum of Art, New York

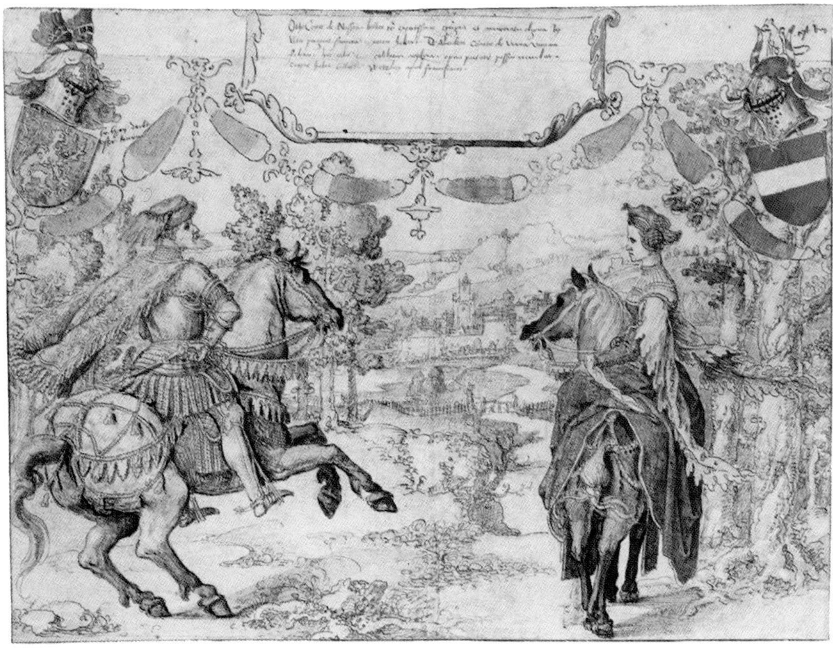

Fig. 73. Bernaert van Orley, *Nassau Genealogy: Otto, Count of Nassau, and His Wife, Adelaide Vianden*, 1528–30. Pen and brown ink, watercolor over traces of black chalk on paper. The Metropolitan Museum of Art, New York

A good deal can be learned from the details of this dispute. Perhaps most obvious, and not at all surprising, is the fact that the relationship between a master and his assistant was not always the most cordial, nor was it straightforward in terms of the artist's right—what we consider today as the copyright—to original designs. Artists apparently traded patterns or designs for projects and borrowed and rented them for a fee. This is evident from the surviving paintings of David, Isenbrant, Benson, and Cornelis, which show a high degree of imitation of standard patterns for figures, motifs, and compositions. A considerable amount of artistic exchange must have been routine, not only between panel painters but also (as the description of the items in Benson's trunks indicates) between painters and illuminators. It is no wonder that the contents of Benson's trunks were a matter of dispute—they comprised the source materials for the livelihood of the artist as well as some of his stock.

Although only a small percentage of working drawings survives, those that remain testify to the great variety of functions they served. Made on paper or parchment in metalpoint, pen or brush and various inks or dark pigments, black chalk, or charcoal, they represent initial stages in the conception of paintings. Some indicate the preliminary design for a composition; among these are *Men Shoveling Chairs* (fig. 71), made in Rogier van der Weyden's workshop for a sculpture for the Town Hall in Brussels, and an *Adoration of the Magi* (fig. 74), produced in Antwerp at the beginning of the sixteenth century as a design for a painting. Other sheets study individual figures; one such, with a standing Saint Paul (fig. 77), was perhaps used in projects for grisaille paintings meant to simulate sculpture. Certain very popular motifs, for example, the Virgin and Child or the Pietà (fig. 50), might be incorporated into a variety of settings in different paintings. Patterns of such isolated motifs or of entire compositions could be pricked and pounced for transfer to panels to facilitate the mass production of paintings for the open art market. Another kind of drawing elaborates motifs or parts of a design in greater detail, for instance the modeling of drapery folds or the detailed consideration of various textures of hair, fur, or flesh, as demonstrated by the *Studies of Saint John the Baptist* from Rogier van der Weyden's workshop (fig. 76), which was copied from a painting and kept as a workshop model. And drawings of heads recording different expressions (fig. 87) or the physiognomy of a particular sitter for a portrait—a type exemplified by the rendering of a man attributed to Dieric Bouts (fig. 75) and the study that includes detailed instructions about the depiction of a man thought to be Cardinal Albergati (fig. 56)—provided reference material for future paintings.

It is largely because they served such a utilitarian role in Netherlandish workshops of the fifteenth and early sixteenth centuries that relatively few of these drawings remain: as working drawings they were fragmentary and most unlike the highly finished designs so admired and preserved by collectors of a later age. In addition, repeated handling destroyed many sheets, which were simply replaced by new ones made as substitutes. Furthermore, northern Netherlandish artists often appear to have composed their designs directly on the grounded panel, thereby limiting the number of working drawings made in preparation for the painting. In this their practice seems to have differed from that of their Italian counterparts, whose sheets survive in far greater numbers.

The paucity of extant drawings (only one or two ascribed to the most noted artists of the day remain), very few of which are signed and dated, makes the problem of attribution particularly thorny. Also controversial is whether certain drawings were made preparatory to a painting or copied after it as a record of a motif or pattern meant for reuse. In both regards, the underdrawing beneath the painted layers on the panel, which is often executed in the artist's most personal style, provides helpful clues.

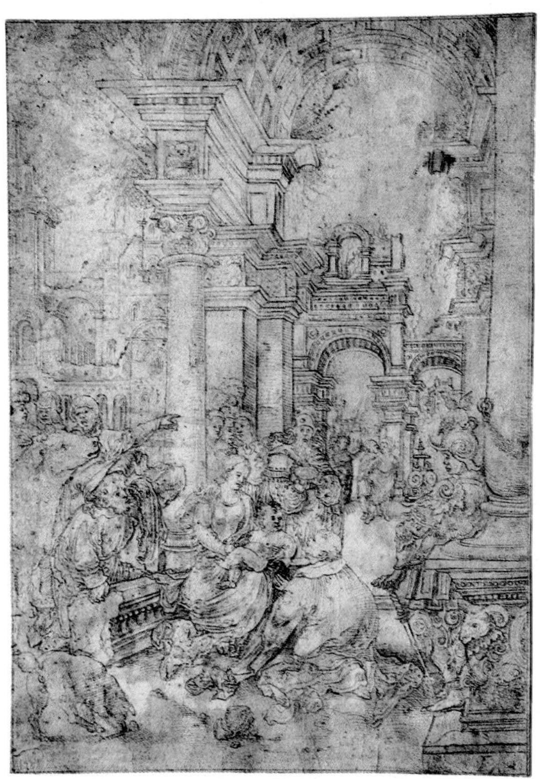

Fig. 74. Netherlandish, *Adoration of the Magi*, Antwerp, first quarter of 16th century. Pen and light brown and grayish brown ink over traces of black chalk on paper. Robert Lehman Collection, The Metropolitan Museum of Art, New York

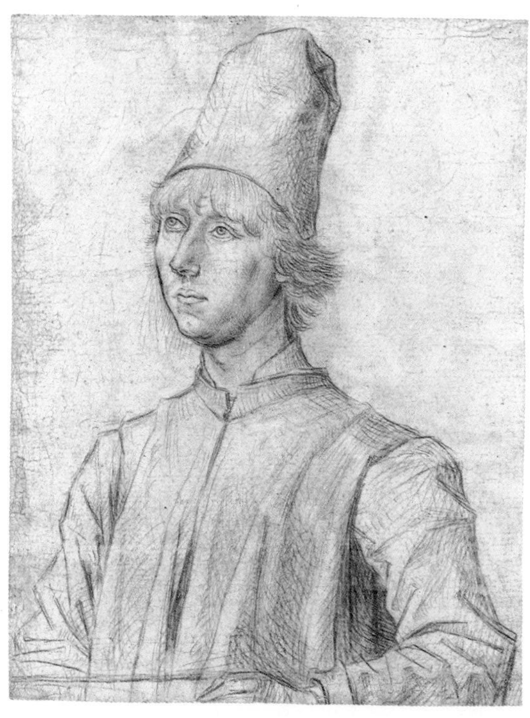

Fig. 75. Attributed to Dieric Bouts, *Portrait of a Young Man*, about 1467. Silverpoint on prepared paper. Smith College Museum of Art, Northampton, Massachusetts

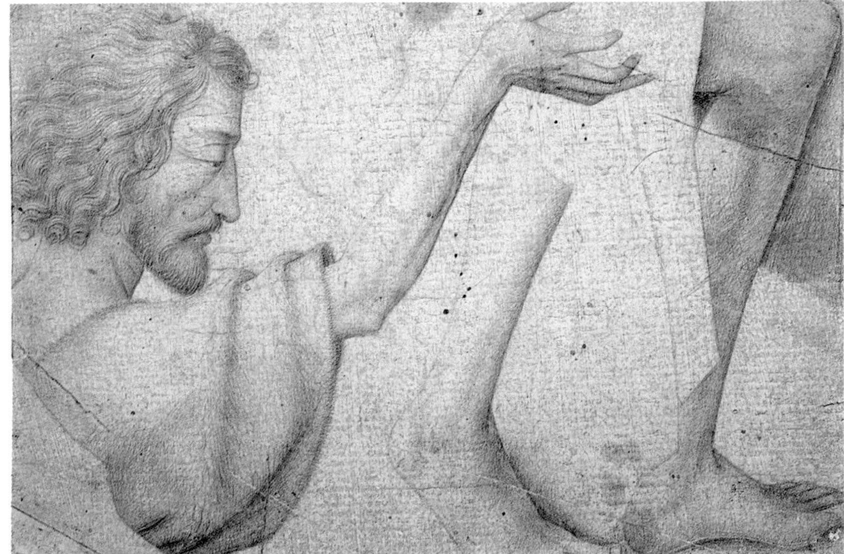

Fig. 76. Copy after Rogier van der Weyden, *Studies of Saint John the Baptist*, mid-15th century. Metalpoint on gray prepared paper. Robert Lehman Collection, The Metropolitan Museum of Art, New York

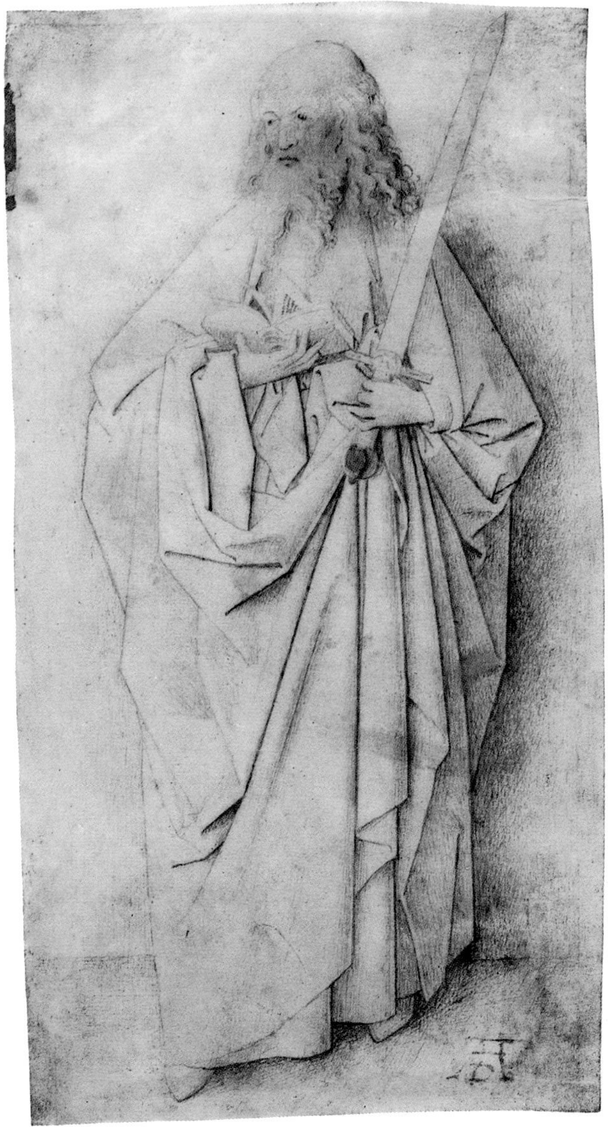

Fig. 77. Circle of Jan van Eyck, *Saint Paul*, second quarter of 15th century. Pen and brown ink, point of brush and brown ink, with purple and gold heightening in hilt of sword, on vellum. Robert Lehman Collection, The Metropolitan Museum of Art, New York

This first sketch, used as a guide for proceeding with the painted layers, can be revealed through infrared reflectography and documented for further study (compare figs. 78a and 78b). It can sometimes also be seen with the naked eye on certain paintings, such as the *Virgin and Child with Saints* (figs. 79a, 79b) and the *Arrival in Bethlehem* (cat. no. 71), attributed to the anonymous sixteenth-century Master LC. The preliminary layout of the composition that the artist sketched in black chalk directly on the grounded panel is visible in the latter picture, particularly in the village scene in the center right of the composition. At some point another artist painted out certain of the vignettes recorded in the underdrawing, changing the religious content of the work and giving it a more secular treatment.

As the changes to Master LC's panel and the evidence of other paintings demonstrate, the workshop model drawing and the underdrawing provided only the initial stage of the design, which could easily be altered according to the artist's or the patron's wishes. Thus, Simon Marmion's *Pietà* (fig. 50), a model drawing in metalpoint on prepared paper, shows the Virgin's hands joined in prayerful entreaty, a pose the artist followed in the underdrawing of his more developed *Lamentation* painting (cat. no. 9) (made visible through infrared reflectography) but altered in the final version, where her hands are crossed over her heart to express sorrowful acceptance.

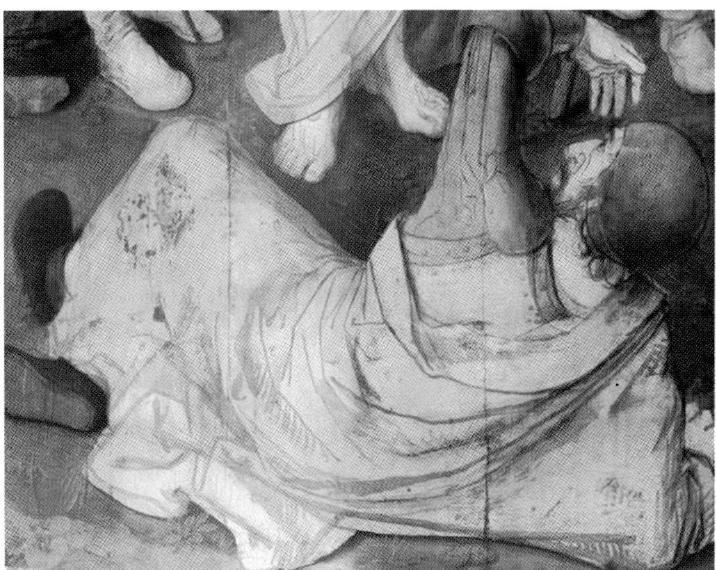

Fig. 78a. Gerard David, detail, *The Resurrection* (cat. no. 78). Infrared reflectogram computer assembly. Sherman Fairchild Paintings Conservation Department, The Metropolitan Museum of Art, New York

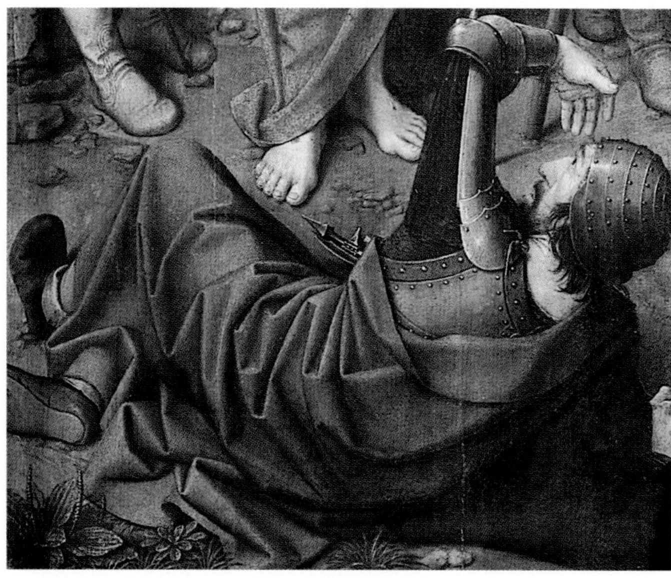

Fig. 78b. Gerard David, detail, *The Resurrection* (cat. no. 78)

Sometimes the workshop model on paper was itself used for the primary support of the painting. The *Virgin and Child with a Dragonfly* by the Master of Saint Giles (cat. no. 51), which is painted on paper pasted down on an oak panel, may well have begun as a tracing of a motif commonly found in pictures of the Virgin and Child produced by Bouts's workshop (for example, cat. no. 50). After tracing the motif onto what may have been transparent oiled paper, the artist reversed the design, glued it to his panel, and worked it up in paint, thus guaranteeing the exact transfer of the desired motif.

Although we might expect that a particular painting represents the efforts of one individual, artists often collaborated on a single work. A painting might be initiated by one artist and completed by another in the same workshop or, as happened with increasing frequency in the sixteenth century, it might be produced by specialists from various workshops, each contributing his own expertise (cat. nos. 70, 95, 96).

The most celebrated example of such cooperation is the Ghent Altarpiece (figs. 17, 18), a project jointly executed by Hubert and Jan van Eyck, as its inscription testifies—although scholarly debate continues regarding which brother completed which parts of this masterpiece. Another collaborative venture of the Eyckian workshop is the *Crucifixion* and *Last Judgment* diptych (cat. no. 1), apparently underdrawn in its entirety by Jan van Eyck but painted with the help of an assistant, who worked on the upper half of the *Last Judgment*.

Certain endeavors were planned as collaborations from the outset because of their large size or complexity. Others developed into joint ventures when the primary artist proved unable or unwilling to complete his task for any of a number of practical reasons. Thus, after Robert Campin executed the *Annunciation* centerpiece of the *Merode Triptych* (cat. no. 2), the ensemble's left wing, portraying its donors, was perhaps added by another artist, possibly Rogier when he worked in Campin's atelier in Tournai. A standard, often-repeated theme was routinely customized, at the request of the client, by just such an addition of portraits of the patron and his wife as donors.

Clients frequently ordered copies of well-known paintings, a fact that is little appreciated or understood from our twentieth-century viewpoint. Although a copy is today considered less important or valuable than an original, in the fifteenth and sixteenth centuries copies were highly regarded and were commissioned for a variety of reasons: the association of the image with a collection or collector of

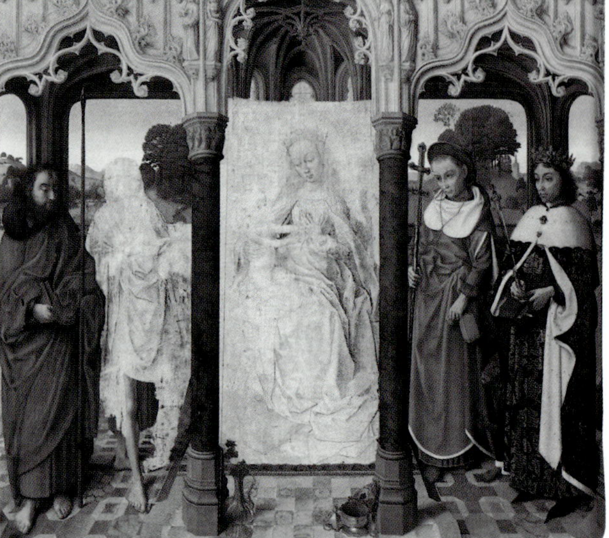

Fig. 79a. Netherlandish, possibly Ghent master, *Virgin and Child with Saints*, about 1480. Oil on wood. Private collection

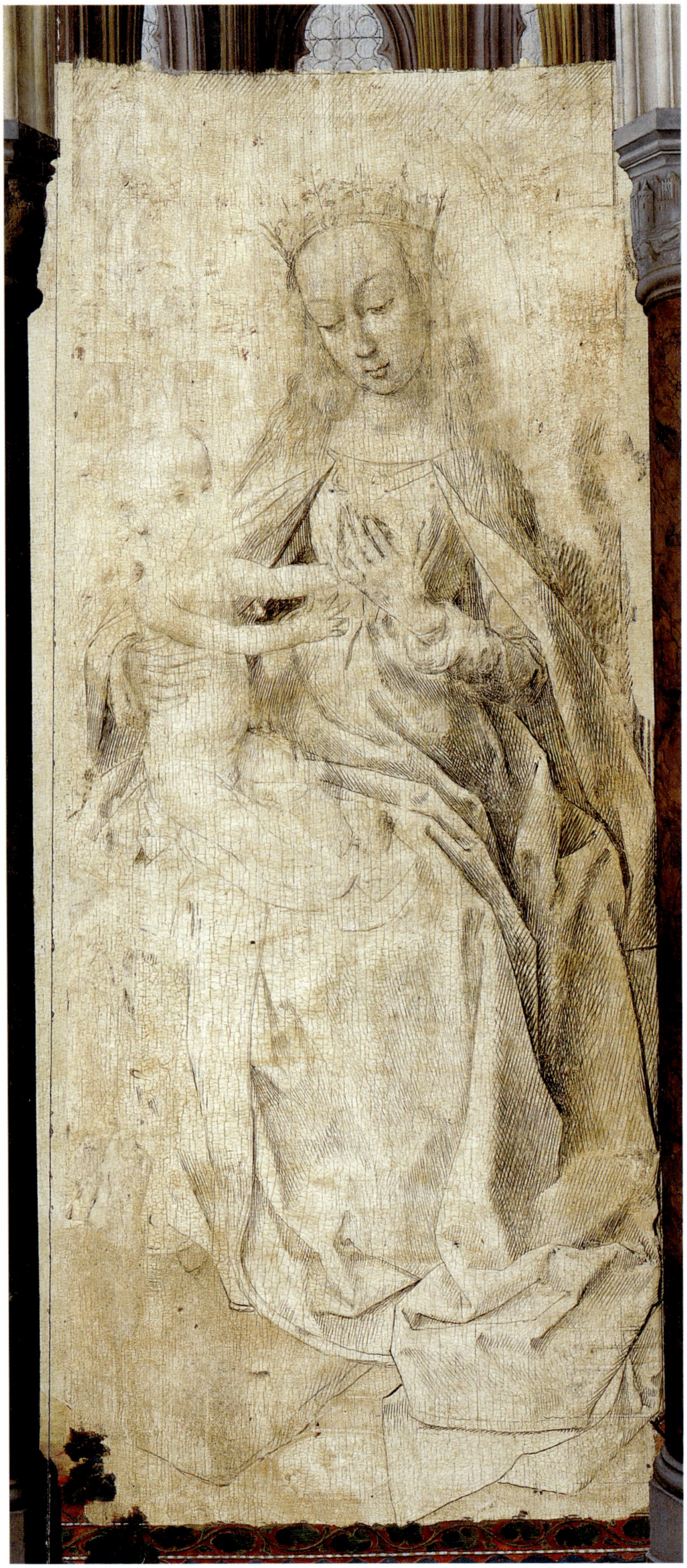

Fig. 79b. Detail, underdrawing of Virgin and Child, *Virgin and Child with Saints* (fig. 79a).

renown, its connection with a celebrated icon (such as the Cambrai Madonna), or its value as a decoration (in the form of a Head of Christ or a Virgin and Child, for example [cat. nos. 3, 55]) that lent a blessing or a certain spiritual aura to the place in which it hung.

It is in this context that not only the ready availability of workshop model drawings but also the highly skilled execution of artists trained in the rigorous craft tradition should be recognized as key factors of production. Such is the quality of execution of *Christ Appearing to His Mother* (cat. no. 46), for example, that for decades its authorship was a matter of debate. Only recently, with intense scrutiny of new information, did it become clear that it is a copy of a closely related work by Rogier van der Weyden and that it was made at the end of the fifteenth century at the request of Isabella of Castile by a talented artist working in Spain at the queen's court (quite possibly Juan de Flandes or Michel Sittow). Produced directly from the model of Rogier's original, which was displayed in the

Carthusian monastery at Miraflores, the burial site of Isabella's father, Juan II, and his first wife, Maria of Aragon, its creation was linked to both devotional and dynastic concerns.

The renown of certain icons believed to possess the power to perform miracles fostered their production in multiple versions. The many copies after the revered image in the cathedral of Cambrai, the Cambrai Madonna (fig. 49), Campin's *Virgin and Child in an Apse* (cat. no. 47), and Van Eyck's *Virgin and Child at the Fountain* (cat. no. 48) belong to this group. Exact copies in this category often were produced by common workshop methods of cartoon transfer such as pouncing or tracing, the specific evidence of which sometimes appears in the underdrawings of the paintings in question.

As the fifteenth century waned, fewer works were commissioned, and more were made for sale on the open art market. Many artists participated in the yearly art fairs known as the Pand that were held in both Antwerp and Bruges. Guild regulations allowed others to sell directly from their workshops, in whose windows they displayed available paintings that could be bought outright or customized to the client's wishes. The addition of donor portraits or armorial insignia to their traditional representations established ownership as well as the patron's devotional association with the image.

Portrayals of extremely popular themes—notably the Rest on the Flight into Egypt, the Adoration of the Magi, the Night Nativity, landscapes in the mode of Joachim Patinir or Hieronymus Bosch, the Virgin and Child with the Milk Soup, and the Holy Family—came virtually to be mass-produced by streamlined methods incorporating workshop patterns and cartoons. In this context it was not simply individual motifs but rather entire compositions that were copied, with varying levels of skill, for ready sale.

The first half of the sixteenth century saw growing specialization on the part of artists and a concomitant increase in collaborative efforts. Van Mander cites the famous example of the *Temptation of Saint Anthony*—thought to be the painting in the Prado, Madrid—in which he notes a landscape by Patinir and figures by Quentin Massys. Various Antwerp artists entered into contractual agreements to share work on individual paintings. Joos van Cleve found ready assistance in providing landscapes in the style of Patinir for his paintings, as evidenced by the Linsky Collection *Virgin and Child* (cat. no. 96) and the Crucifixion Triptych (cat. no. 95), whose landscapes a specialist produced from workshop drawings of motifs that were repeated from painting to painting. In some works the separation of tasks became exaggerated and yielded incongruities, as in the *Rest on the Flight into Egypt* attributed to a follower of Massys and a collaborator (cat. no. 70), a decidedly mannerist rendition of the theme in which the landscape and the figures appear to have gone their separate ways.

The changes in workshop structure and day-to-day operations that took place in the first half of the sixteenth century were tied to economic concerns. These concerns, the product of a thriving market involving both local and export business in Antwerp, centered on increased demand from a populous bourgeoisie and encouraged the adoption of a wider outlook, one with a worldview. Thus, the already highly organized workshop structure of Netherlandish painters evolved, fully keeping pace with economic and social developments and adjustments in the character of the buying public. The shifts that began to occur in this period are the seeds of change that matured into the grand Flemish ateliers of the seventeenth century.

MARYAN W. AINSWORTH

References: Campbell 1981a; Wilson 1983; Ainsworth 1989a; Ewing 1990; Ainsworth 1993; De Patoul and Van Schoute 1994, pp. 75–141, with essays and associated bibliographies by Campbell, Comblen-Sonkes, Mund, Sosson, and Verougstraete and Van Schoute; Ainsworth 1998; Campbell et al. 1997; Wilson 1998.

Workshop of Rogier van der Weyden

45. The Nativity, probably about 1460

Oil on wood, central panel 55⅛ x 76⅛ in. (140 x 193.4 cm); upper wings, each 18⅞ x 8⅞ in. (47.9 x 22.5 cm); lower wings, each 35 x 16⅞ in. (88.9 x 42.9 cm)
Inscribed: (on banderole of Tiburtine Sibyl) Concontritum . . . (with contrition . . .); (on banderole of Virgin and Child) . . . dixerit vobis . . . (. . . will have said to you . . .)
The Cloisters Collection, 1949 49.109

This nearly complete altarpiece was acquired by a German collector, Frasinelli, from a convent in Segovia, Spain, by 1843. The subjects are familiar, with the exception of the two scenes to the immediate left and right of the Nativity in the main panel: the Annunciation to Augustus and the Annunciation to the Magi. These derive, respectively, from the descriptions of the feasts of the Nativity and the Epiphany in Jacobus de Voragine's *Golden Legend.* According to this source, Emperor Augustus, before permitting the Roman Senate to honor him as a deity, asked the Tiburtine Sibyl if a greater man than he would someday be born. On the day of the Nativity a vision of a virgin with a child, surrounded by a golden ring, was revealed to him, and a voice proclaimed, "This woman is the altar of heaven"; Augustus was told that the child would indeed surpass him in greatness. At the left of our main panel the emperor kneels to honor the child, while three senators stand in the background, witnessing the event. The legend of the Annunciation to the Magi, depicted on the right, tells of three kings or wise men who climbed a certain mountain each year; after bathing for three days they observed the heavens, seeking the star that would announce the birth of a man to the tribe of Israel. As the magi prayed, a star in the form of a child appeared to them and they were told to seek the newborn in Jerusalem. In our panel we see the magi at two separate moments in their story, bathing in a white-capped lake or stream in the background and adoring the radiant infant in the

Provenance: Convent, Segovia, Spain; Frasinelli, Stuttgart (by 1843); John Dunn Gardner, Bottisham Hall, Cambridgeshire ([until 1854]; sale, Christie's, London, March 25, 1854, no. 65, as Memling, to Colnaghi for £200); [Colnaghi, London (1854)]; Sir James Carnegie, ninth earl of Southesk, Kinnaird Castle, Brechin, Scotland (1854–1905); Sir Charles Noel Carnegie, tenth earl of Southesk (1905–41); Charles Alexander Carnegie, eleventh earl of Southesk (sale, Christie's, London, July 23, 1948, no. 54, as Van der Weyden, to Roland for £3150); [Roland, Browse, and Delbanco, London (1948)]; [Agnew, London (1948–49)].

References: Jacobus de Voragine (ca. 1260) 1892, vol. 1, pp. 49, 85–86; Passavant 1843, p. 153; Rousseau 1951, pp. 270–83,

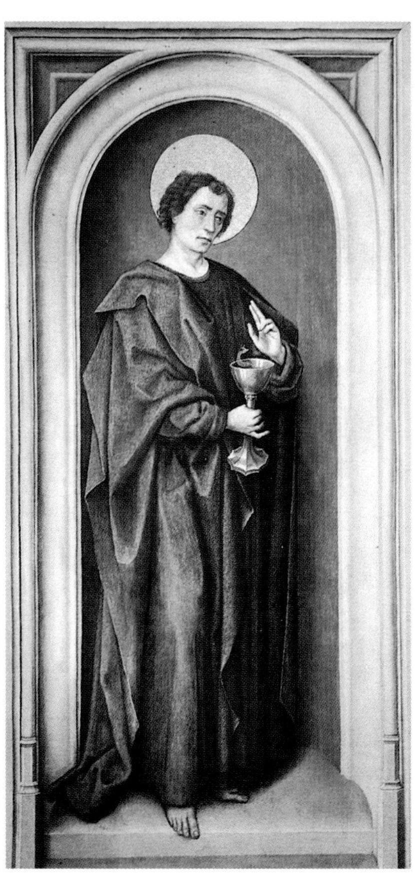

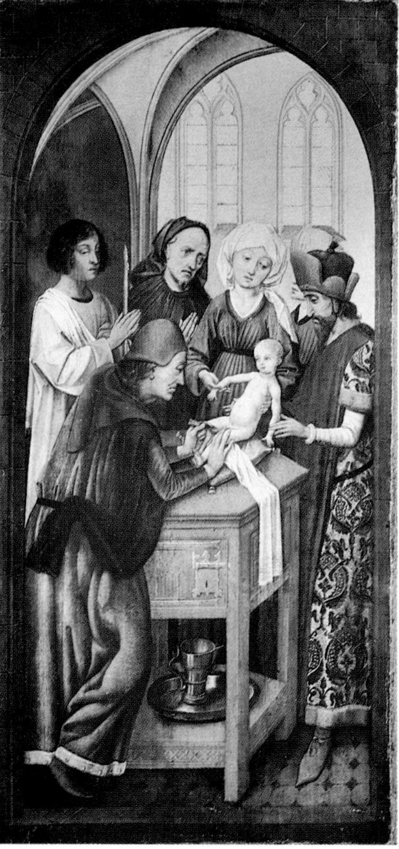

Fig. 80. Workshop of Rogier van der Weyden, *Saint John the Evangelist, The Circumcision,* exterior and interior of wing of Nativity Altarpiece (cat. no. 45), probably about 1460. Oil on wood. Private collection, Madrid

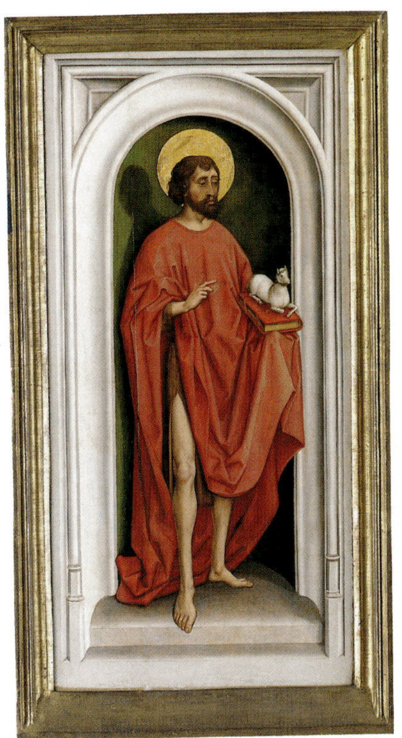

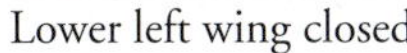
Lower left wing closed

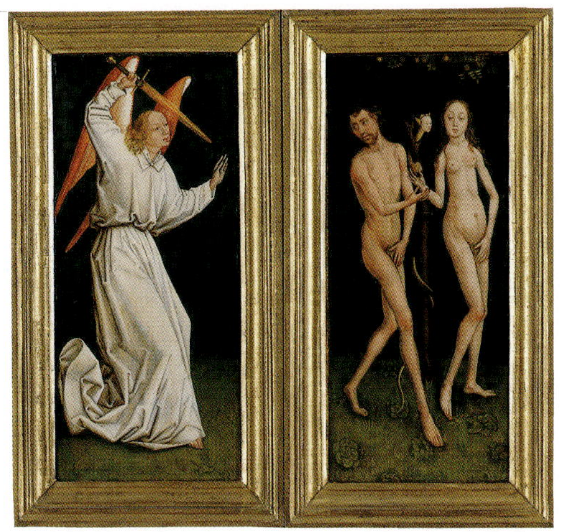
Upper wings closed

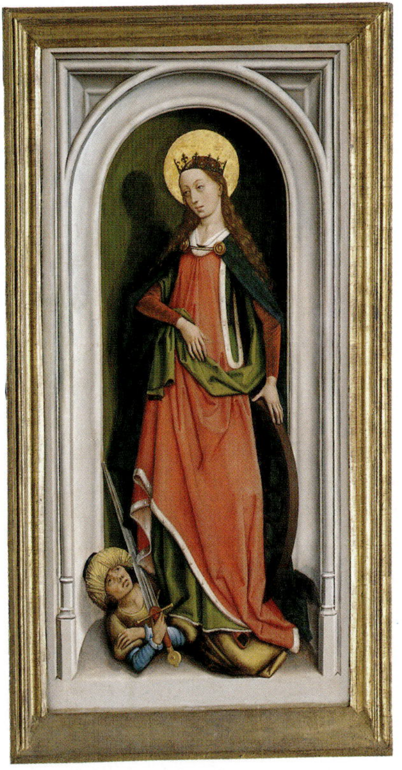
Lower right wing closed

foreground. The column with the crumbling foundation that separates this scene from the Nativity symbolizes the destruction of the old order with Christ's birth.

The lateral panels are painted on their reverses and clearly functioned as shutters. The wings on the main tier, however, do not completely cover the central panel when they are closed, and we can assume that two wings are missing from the altarpiece. An *Annunciation* in a private collection in England in 1951 (81 x 40.5 cm) has been proposed as the panel that was originally to the left of our *Visitation*. The reverse of this *Annunciation*, however, is unpainted, and from all evidence the wood has not been sawed down; the identification must therefore remain inconclusive. A panel representing the Circumcision, with Saint John the Evangelist on the exterior (fig. 80) (painted surface 87.2 x 41.6 cm, overall 88.3 x 42.6 cm), is clearly a missing element of the polyptych and has been tentatively placed between the central panel and the *Adoration of the Magi*. The young man wearing an alb and a scapular at the extreme right of the *Circumcision* may well be the donor; it is not clear to what religious order he belongs.

The influence of Rogier van der Weyden, as well as Robert Campin, is apparent in many elements of the composition: the three subjects in the central section derive, with some variations, from Rogier's Bladelin Triptych, usually dated about 1450 (Gemäldegalerie, Berlin), in which each of these scenes is depicted on a separate panel; the Visitation is closely related to two panels representing this subject that are ascribed to Rogier (Museum der Bildenden Künste, Leipzig, and Galleria Sabauda, Turin); and the figure of Saint John is close to this saint as he is shown on the left wing of the Werl Altarpiece (Prado, Madrid), which has been attributed to both Campin and Rogier. God the Father, who raises his hand in blessing above the stable, is a type that is familiar from Campin's grisaille panel of the Trinity (Städelsches Kunstinstitut, Frankfurt) or a similar work.

The presence of the banderoles in the main panel is especially interesting in relation to Rogier's Bladelin Triptych. Although neither they nor the circle around the child-star of the *Annunciation to the Magi* appear on the painted surface of Rogier's work, their outlines can be seen in the underdrawing that

ill.; Baes-Dondeyne 1969, pp. 93–108, ill.; Davies 1972, pp. 201–2, 217; Bermejo Martinez 1980–82, vol. 1, pp. 144–45; Grosshans 1982, pp. 156–76, nn. 25, 26, fig. 157; Dijkstra 1990, pp. 56–59, 227, n. 22; Campbell 1995b, p. 6.

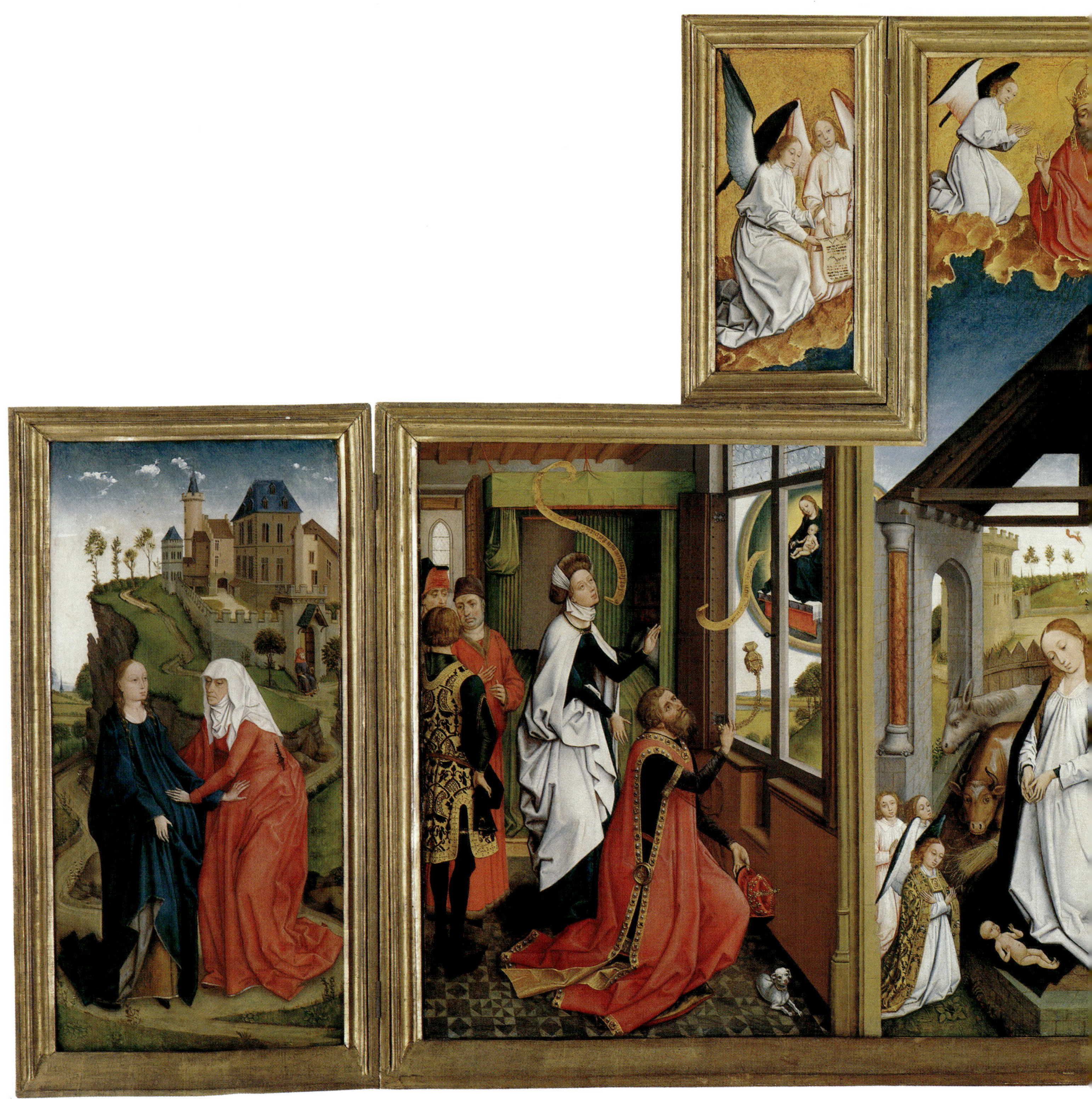

45 open

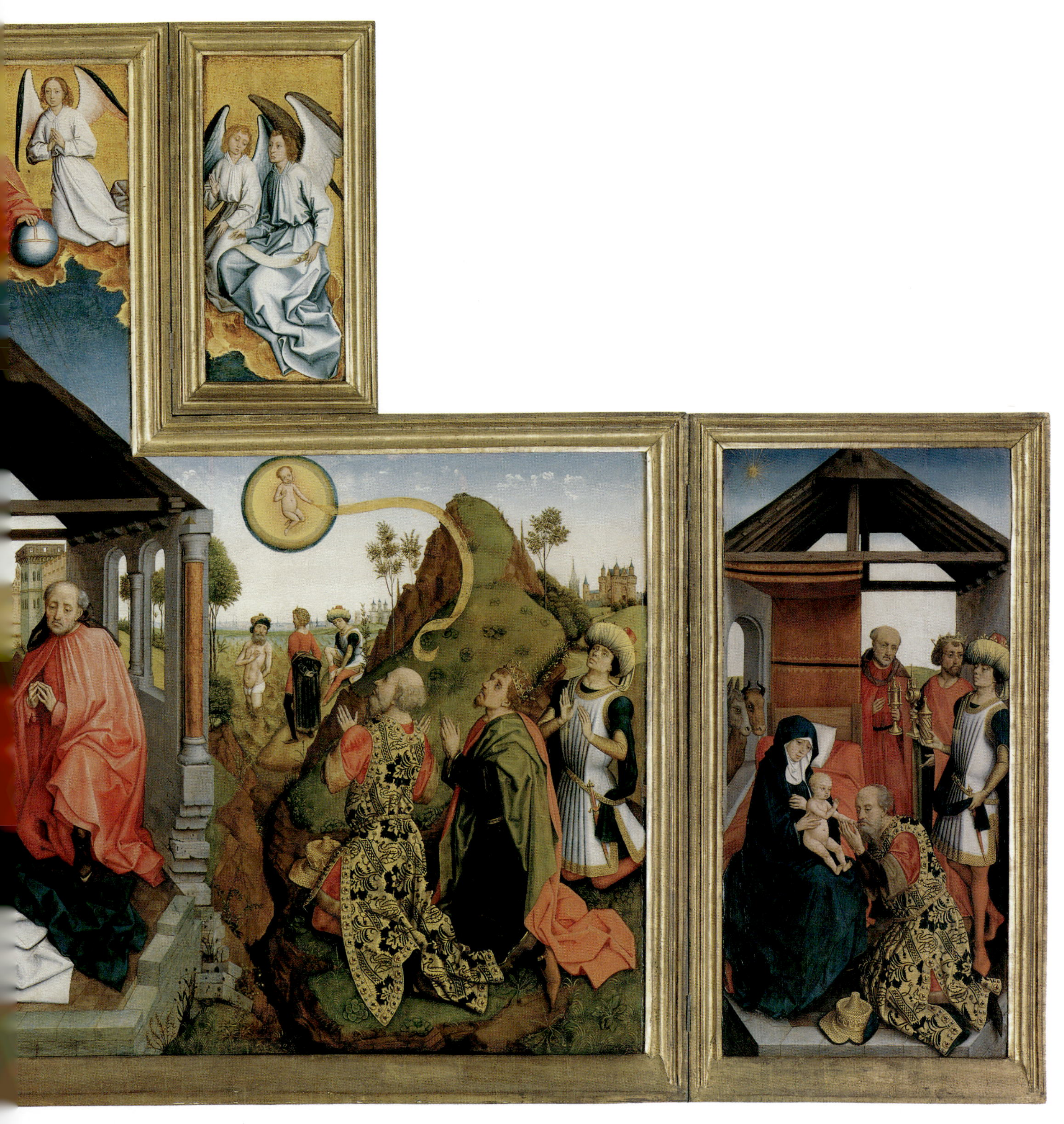

is visible through infrared reflectography. These details were taken up by the painter of our altarpiece, an indication that the original design for the Bladelin Triptych, an extremely valuable source for similar compositions, was kept for reference within the workshop and that our painter had access to it. Dendrochronological analysis gives a plausible creation time for the altarpiece of 1459 or later, and we can therefore hypothesize that it was produced within the workshop toward the end of Rogier's life (he died in 1464).

Intact, this extensive complex would have included portrayals of the important legends surrounding the infancy of Christ, reading as a continuous narrative from left to right. The scenes are clearly displayed and simply depicted, the effect of the whole being more functional than elegant. In the spirit of the *Meditations on the Life of Christ*, the altarpiece would have encouraged not only a worshiper's contemplation of the mysteries of the Christian faith but also each believer's sympathetic experience, moment by moment, of the story of the Nativity. MSdJ

Copy after Rogier van der Weyden (possibly by Juan de Flandes, active [in Spain] by 1496, died 1519, or Michel Sittow, about 1469–1525/26)

46. Christ Appearing to His Mother, about 1496

Oil on wood; overall 25 x 15 in. (63.5 x 38.1 cm); painted surface 24½ x 14⅝ in. (62.2 x 37.1 cm)
Inscribed: (on scroll held by angel) Mulier h[a]ec perseveravit vi[n]cens o[mn]ia ideo / data e [st] ei corona: ex apoc.⁻vi$^{o.}$ / $^{o.}$ (This woman persevered, conquering all; therefore a crown was given unto her [Apocalypse 6:1]); (on border of Virgin's cloak) MANGNIF[I]CAT A[NIMA MEA] DOMIN[UM] ET ET EXA[LT]AVIT [SPIRITUS] ME[US IN DEO SALUTARI MEO QUI]A RESPEXIT HUMILITATEMANCIL[A]E [SUAE] ECCE ENIM [EX HOC] BEATEM ME [DICENT] . . . AB? . . . POTENSESTE[T SANCTUM NOMINE EIUS] ([My soul] doth magnify the Lord, and my [spirit] hath rejoiced

Interrupted from her devotional reading, and with tears of joy and sorrow streaming down her cheeks, Mary is surprised by the sudden appearance of her resurrected son on Easter morning. The event is not mentioned in the Gospels, but the portrayal closely follows the mystical texts of the Pseudo-Bonaventure's *Mirror of the Blessed Life of Jesus Christ.* The iconography is augmented by Saint Ambrose's commentaries, in which Christ's unused tomb is equated with the Virgin's womb, a parallel the painter expressed in pictorial terms by casting Christ and the Virgin in the poses traditionally assumed by Gabriel and Mary in Annunciation scenes. Thus, the painting can be seen as an annunciation of eternal life. This interpretation is supported by the text on the border of the Virgin's cloak. Known as the Magnificat, it is Mary's celebration of the Incarnation and her blessed role in it, and her response to Elizabeth's recognition that she is "the mother of my Lord" (Luke 1:43).

The shallow proscenium arch that frames the figures is decorated with sculptures depicting scenes that unfold in chronological order, beginning at the upper left and proceeding counterclockwise: the holy women telling the Virgin of their visit to Christ's sepulchre (which is shown in the landscape viewed through the open door at the back of the room), the Ascension, Pentecost, the Annunciation of Mary's Impending Death, the Death of the Virgin, and the Assumption. Below, on pedestals, are figures of Saint Mark the Evangelist (left), who appears to be recording the event for his Gospel, and Saint Paul (right). On two of the capitals of the columns in the interior are Old Testament scenes that prefigure Christ's triumph over death and the Devil: David's Victory over Goliath (front left) and Samson and the Lion and Samson Carrying Away the Gates of Gaza (back right). At the apex of the arch an angel carries a crown and a banderole inscribed: *Mulier h[a]ec perseveravit vi[n]cens o[mn]ia ideo / data e[st] ei corona.* (This woman persevered, conquering all; therefore a crown was given unto her [Apocalypse 6:1]).

Together with an Adoration of the Infant Jesus and a Lamentation, this picture formed a triptych

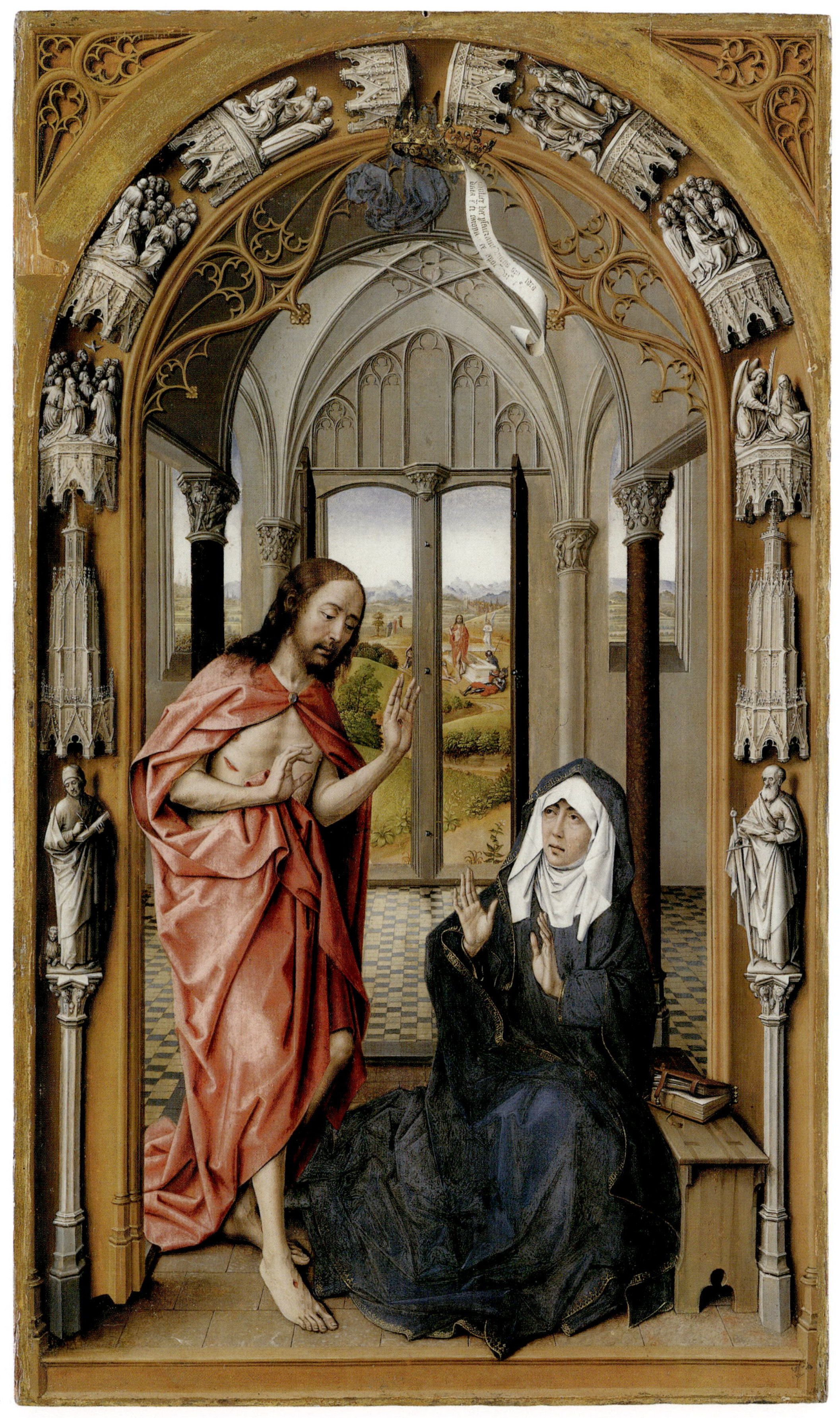

[in God my Savior. For he hath] regarded the low estate of [his] handmaiden: for, behold, [from henceforth] . . . [shall call] me blessed . . . that is mighty . . . and [holy is his name] [Luke 1:46–49].)
The Bequest of Michael Dreicer, 1921 22.60.58

Provenance: Isabella the Catholic, Queen of Castile and Léon (d. 1504); Capilla Real, Granada (1505–before 1632); Mariano, duke of Osuna, Madrid; art market, Spain?; private collection, England (from ca. 1907); [Duveen, London, by 1912–17]; Michael Dreicer, New York (1917–21).

References: Felipe de Guevara (ca. 1560) 1788, pp. 181–82; Bode 1908, cols. 29–35; Gómez-Moreno 1908, pp. 289ff.; Justi 1908, vol. 1, p. 305; Von Loga 1910, pp. 47ff.; Wauters 1912–13, pp. 75ff.; Friedländer 1916, pp. 24ff.; Mather 1917, pp. 143ff.; Conway 1921, pp. 134, 138, 140ff.; Friedländer 1924–37, vol. 2 (1924), pp. 16ff.; Smits 1933, pp. 122f.; Friedländer 1924–37, vol. 14 (1937), p. 84; Burroughs 1938, pp. 213ff., 224–34; Duveen Brothers 1941, no. 168; Wehle and Salinger 1947, pp. 30–34; Musper 1948, pp. 32, 52ff.; Sánchez Cantón 1950, pp. 177ff.; Beenken 1951, pp. 41–43, 47, 50ff.; Panofsky 1953, pp. 259, 460–61 n. 3; Breckenridge 1957, pp. 9, 22–25; Taubert 1960, pp. 67–75; Birkmeyer 1961, pp. 1–20, 99–112; Van Schoute 1963, vol. 1, pp. 101ff., vol. 6, pp. 87–109; Sonkes 1971–72, p. 167; Davies

that in 1504 was bequeathed by Queen Isabella the Catholic to the Capilla Real in the cathedral at Granada, the burial site of Spanish royalty. We know that the triptych is listed in the 1505 inventory of the queen's effects and that sometime before 1632 the Metropolitan panel was separated from the other two, which were cut down to fit the doors of a reliquary for Philip IV in the Capilla Real, where they remain today.

Another version of the complete work, known as the Miraflores Triptych, is in the Gemäldegalerie, Berlin. Although the New York–Granada paintings were long ascribed to Rogier van der Weyden and considered the prototype, there is now conclusive technical evidence that pride of place belongs to the Berlin triptych and that the slightly smaller New York–Granada panels are a later variant by a very talented copyist. The Berlin *Christ Appearing to His Mother* (fig. 81) exhibits Rogier's typical hooked strokes in a brush underdrawing that is full of details that have been changed in the painting (in the preliminary design the Virgin's dress spilled out over the lower step, the background showed a crenellated wall instead of the open double doors, and Christ's right hand and head were in different positions); our picture, however, presents a fixed underdrawing that closely follows the solutions of the final composition of the Berlin panel. In addition, the Berlin example employs empirical perspective, while the components of the Metropolitan painting are adjusted slightly to conform to a one-point perspective scheme. Discrepancies of painting technique are also telling: the Berlin panel shows multiple glazes applied to achieve modeling of drapery forms in rich reds and blues, but in our version the handling is abbreviated, with, for example, mixed colors tending toward a pinkish red for Christ's garment. Incidental details, such as the shrubbery in the background landscape, are also painted differently, revealing Rogier's characteristic execution only in the Berlin example. Finally, definitive information is supplied by the dendrochronological analysis of the panels, which suggests that the Berlin painting is from about 1435 (confirming the dating indicated by art-historical study) and that the New York panel dates closer to the mid-1490s—some thirty years after Rogier's death.

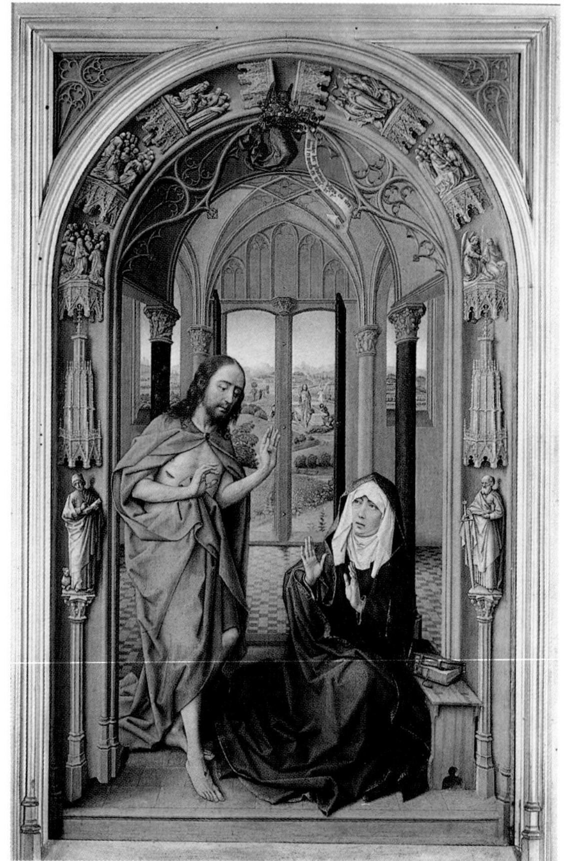

Fig. 81. Rogier van der Weyden, *Christ Appearing to His Mother*, about 1435. Oil on wood. Gemäldegalerie, SMPK, Berlin

The Miraflores Triptych, also known as the Mary Altarpiece, belonged to Queen Isabella's father, Juan II, king of Castile. Ponz, who first described the triptych after a visit to Miraflores in 1783, reported the monastery's traditional account that the work had been given to Juan II by Pope Martin V (d. 1431). However, the dating of the altarpiece accords more with the term of Martin's successor, Eugenius IV. Justi therefore suggested that the ensemble may have been given to the king by the later pope, whose views Juan had strongly supported at the Council of Basel in 1436. In a document of 1438 Eugenius IV granted to Juan II the privilege of owning a portable altar and hearing Mass in a private house before dawn, and the Miraflores Triptych is certainly a likely candidate for the decoration of a temporary oratory of this kind. Juan II gave the triptych to the Carthusian monastery at Miraflores, near Burgos, in 1445, perhaps, as Kasl (in conversation, December

1997) suggests, on the occasion of the death of his first wife, Marìa of Aragon. The triptych's emphasis on birth, death, and the promise of eternal life through the Resurrection of Christ is an appropriate commemoration for a burial site, and suitable for a monastery that is dedicated to the Virgin as the Church.

Given the high esteem in which the Miraflores Triptych doubtless was held, it is not surprising that Isabella would have commissioned an exact, portable copy to accompany her on her frequent travels throughout her far-flung territories. (That the Metropolitan's copy was made in Spain, quite likely in front of the original, is indicated by the material of its ground preparation, which is calcium sulfate, or gypsum, used south of the Alps, rather than the calcium carbonate, or chalk, of northern grounds.) If the original was indeed a gift from the pope, the replica could have been a constant reminder of Juan's close affiliation with the head of the Church, a link that possibly served some personal religious or political agenda of Isabella's. Its use perhaps also allowed Isabella to feel that she was continuing the tradition of her family's devotional practices and may, therefore, have helped her in offering perpetual prayers for the souls of her father and his first wife. In this regard, it may be significant that the copy was probably commissioned about the time her mother, Isabella of Portugal (Juan's second wife), died, in 1496. Following her father's example, she bequeathed her own Mary Altarpiece to her own burial site upon her death.

Because the artist responsible for our panel so closely imitated not only the composition but also the details of the style of Rogier's work, attempts to solve the riddle of its attribution have been confounded. Among the most likely authors of the New York–Granada panels are Michel Sittow and Juan de Flandes, two prominent Netherlandish artists Isabella had lured to Spain to serve as court painters. Sittow's work as a copyist is documented in Isabella's inventory of 1505, which lists replicas he made of devotional pictures belonging to the archbishop of Granada, Hernando de Talavera. Another relevant, but considerably less reliable, notice is provided by Felipe de Guevara in his *Comentarios de la pintura* of about 1560, in which he refers to two portraits of his father, Diego de Guevara, one painted by "Rugier" and another by "Michel," whom he calls a "discípulo de dicho Rugier." Guevara's account testifies to the popularity of Rogier in Spain and the tendency to attribute Netherlandish paintings to him. In point of fact, Sittow lived too late to know Rogier and probably was the "disciple" of Memling. Still more intriguing in regard to the attribution of our panel are certain details about the whereabouts and production of Juan de Flandes. He is documented in Burgos, painting a now-dismembered altarpiece on the theme of Saint John the Baptist for the monastery of Miraflores between 1496 and 1499, precisely the years during which the New York–Granada paintings were most likely to have been produced. Two of the surviving paintings from the John the Baptist altarpiece, the *Beheading of John the Baptist* (Musée d'Art et d'Histoire, Geneva) and the *Banquet of Herodias* (Museum Mayer van den Bergh, Antwerp), are executed on panels that come from the same tree as those used for the New York–Granada pictures (Klein and Vynckier). At the very least this suggests that the wood supports for both sets of paintings could have been used at the same time in the same workshop in the service of Queen Isabella. Further study of Sittow's and particularly Juan's painting techniques may help resolve the intriguing mystery of our picture's authorship.

MWA

1972, pp. 16–18, 200, 213–16, 230; Fuchs 1977, pp. 39–82; Hall and Uhr 1978, pp. 249, 254, 258–62, 264ff.; Lane 1978, pp. 655, 672; Grosshans 1981, pp. 49–112; Grosshans 1982, pp. 140, 150–52, 175; Snyder 1985a, p. 178; Dijkstra 1990, pp. 82–97, 100–109; Ainsworth 1992b, pp. 59–68; Van Asperen de Boer et al. 1992, pp. 244–49; Klein 1992; Périer–d'Ieteren, Rinuy, Vynckier, and Kockaert 1993, pp. 89–97; Weniger 1997, pp. 121–31.

Copy after Robert Campin

47. Virgin and Child in an Apse, about 1480

Oil on canvas, transferred from wood, 17¾ x 13½ in. (45.1 x 34.3 cm)
Rogers Fund, 1905 05.39.2

Provenance: Spain (Salamanca?); Sir John Charles Robinson, Newton Manor, Swanage, Dorset.

References: Robinson 1905, pp. 238, 387–93; Winkler 1913c, pp. 7–9, 44; Conway 1921, p. 115; Friedländer 1924–37, vol. 2 (1924), pp. 75, 114–16; Winkler 1924, p. 70; Schmarsow 1928, pp. 38–40; Destrée 1928–29, p. 114; Bazin 1931, p. 495; Renders 1931, pp. 66–68; Friedländer 1938, p. 22; De Tolnay 1939, p. 59; Denis 1944, pp. 97–99; Wehle and Salinger 1947, pp. 26–28; Baldass 1952, p. 16, n. 1; Davies 1953, pp. 60–65; Panofsky 1953 (1971), pp. 175, 352, 426 n. 2; Shorr 1954, pp. 58–82; McNamee 1963, pp. 142–43; Frinta 1966, p. 41; Friedländer 1967–76, vol. 2 (1967), pp. 43, 74–75, n. 74; Davies 1972, p. 253; Vandura 1988, pp. 114–16; Klein 1991, pp. 32–33; Lievens-de Waegh 1991, p. 112; Van Asperen de Boer et al. 1992, p. 126; Ainsworth 1996, pp. 149–58.

Of the many versions of this composition—over sixty are known—the Metropolitan's is among the earliest. None can be dated within the lifetime of Campin (about 1425–d. 1444), who is generally credited with the invention of the image, but one in Zagreb is monogrammed *VIE*? and inscribed *1420*, which may refer to the date of the prototype. Later variations, dating from between about 1480 and 1530, enlarge the space for the figures and view the scene straight on rather than from above. They also introduce genre elements such as flowers, animals, and landscapes, altering the strictly iconic presentation of the early works.

The popularity of the image was a consequence of the burgeoning of the cult of the Virgin during the fifteenth and sixteenth centuries, especially in the southern Netherlands, where several of her relics, including her hair, milk, veil, and girdle, were housed and venerated. The significant demand for this devotional image suggests that the type was highly regarded for its spiritual value, perhaps because miracles or indulgences were associated with it.

The composition alludes to several themes. The motif of the suckling Child reclining in his mother's arms derives from the Byzantine type known as the *galactotrophousa*. Standing in a shallow apse, the Virgin symbolizes the Church and the *Ara Coeli*, or the tabernacle holding the body and blood of Christ. The subject of Christ's sacrifice is emphasized by the resigned expression of the Virgin and the position of her arms, which are crossed in adoration, as well as by the cloth beneath the Child, suggesting both the shroud that covered Christ's body at his burial and the altar cloth beneath the Host at the celebration of the Eucharist. Supporting the reference to the Mass is the angel at the right, who wears the vestments appropriate for this occasion, a cope fastened by a morse decorated with figures of the Virgin and Child and an angel.

Music-making angels such as those shown here were often included in representations of the Virgin and Child to evoke the joyful choirs of the heavenly realm (see also cat. nos. 11, 59, 60). The lute and the harp played by the angels in this panel are *bas* instruments, which possess a soft, silvery timbre and were used to accompany liturgy as well as mystery plays and tableaux vivants. In this setting the angels call to mind the numerous popular hymns sung to the Virgin that extol her virtues of mercy, charity, and kindness and refer to her as a shrine or the vessel of Christ. MWA

Netherlandish Painter

48. Virgin and Child in a Niche, about 1500

Oil on wood, 23 x 12⅛ in. (58.4 x 30.8 cm)
Inscribed: (on canopy) DOMVS. DEI. EST. ET. PORTA. C[O]ELI ([This is

Like a piece of sculpture miraculously come to life, the Virgin appears in a shallow, flamboyant Gothic niche, lovingly embracing the Christ Child. Mary stands before a throne decorated with a magnificent brocade cloth of honor and a canopy embellished with a text from Genesis (28:17): "[This is none other than] the house of God, and [this is] the gate of heaven." On the upright of the step below, another excerpt from Genesis (24:44) reads: "Let the same be [the woman] whom the Lord hath

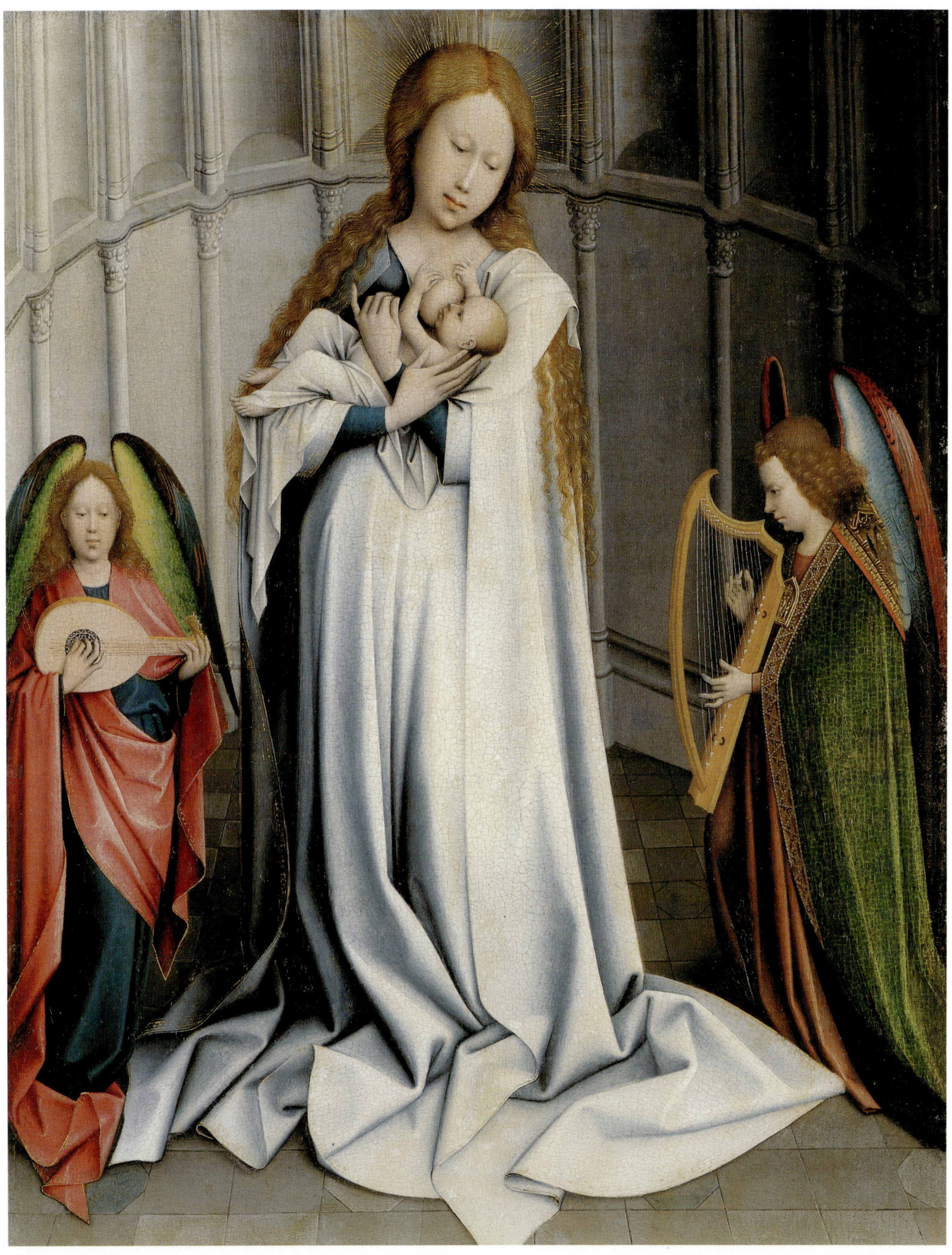
47

none other than] the house of God, and [this is] the gate of heaven [Genesis 28:17].); (on step) IPSA EST [MVLIER] QVAM PR[A]EPARAVIT DOM[INV] FILIO D[OMI]NI MEI *(Let the same be [the woman] whom the Lord hath appointed out for my master's son [Genesis 24:44].)* *Gift of Henry G. Marquand, 1889 89.15.24*

Provenance: "An old monk in Ghent" (Nieuwenhuys); acquired by Nieuwenhuys (April 20, 1823); King William II of the Netherlands; sale, The Hague, 1850, to Nieuwenhuys, London; A. J. Beresford Hope, London; sale, Christie's, London, May 15, 1886, no. 30, as Jan van Eyck; [Lesser?]; [Sedelmeyer, Paris, cat. 1898, no. 32]; Henry G. Marquand, New York.

References: Nieuwenhuys 1843, no. 3; Conway 1887, pp. 144–45; Weale 1908, pp. 160–61; Durand-Gréville 1910, pp. 100–101; Durand-Gréville 1911, pp. 142, 203, 206; Vaughn 1928, pp. 27, 31; Wehle and Salinger 1947, pp. 20–23 (with earlier bibliography); Bazin 1952, p. 199; Panofsky 1953, pp. 146, 416 n. 5; Bruyn 1957, pp. 43, 104 n. 2, 123–28, 132, 134, 150; Quarré 1957, pp. 59–64, esp. pp. 62–63; Larsen 1960, pp. 38–39, 109; Gellman 1970, pp. 497–99; Upton 1972, pp. 420–21; Cavalcaselle 1973, p. 73; Urbach 1974, pp. 349–51; Silver 1983, pp. 95–96; Hinterding and Horsch 1989, p. 56; Klein 1991; Heck 1996.

appointed out for my master's son." The tiny niches in the buttresses are adorned with statuettes of the Old Testament figures Moses and Isaiah (above left and right) and of personifications of the Church and the Synagogue (below left and right).

The biblical passages are from the story of Rebekah and her son, Jacob. Both refer to the Lord's chosen ones: Genesis 24:44 to God's selection of Rebekah as the wife of Isaac (signaling the line of succession from the patriarch of Israel, Abraham, through Isaac to Jacob) and Genesis 28:17 to his appointment of Jacob as head of the tribes of Israel. These Old Testament texts prefigure God's designation of the Virgin as the Mother and Bride of Christ (as interpreted in contemporary exegesis of the Song of Solomon and signified by the ring she wears on her left hand) and as the intercessor for mankind at the gate of heaven. The account of Jacob's dream in Genesis, which describes a ladder that rises from earth to heaven and supports the angels of God who descend and ascend on it, is related in medieval exegetical literature to the vision of the Virgin as the ladder on which God went down to earth. As Heck has pointed out, in his sermon *De beata Maria Virgine* Saint Bernard writes: "She is the ladder . . . the door. . . . She is Jacob's ladder. . . . By these rungs the angels go up, and men ascend" (*Patrologia latina*, vol. 184, col. 1016).

The intimate embrace of mother and child shown here is familiar from other early Netherlandish paintings in the Metropolitan Museum (cat. nos. 6, 47), and the specific type of the standing Virgin with Christ, except for the position of the Child's left arm, is identical to Jan van Eyck's model in the *Virgin and Child at the Fountain* (fig. 10) as well as to the image that inspired Gerard David's *Virgin and Child with Four Angels* (cat. no. 81). In 1843 Nieuwenhuys attributed our painting to Jan because of its close connection with the Antwerp example, and earlier in this century it was given to Petrus Christus. In the last twenty years, however, the latter attribution has been questioned, and in 1991 Klein's dendrochronological investigation demonstrated that the painting dates from about 1500. Yet the Late Gothic style of the architecture shown, with tracery similar to that found in the *Christ Appearing to His Mother* (cat. no. 46), and the representation of sculptures come to life, seen, for example, in Rogier van der Weyden's paintings of the Virgin and Child in the Kunsthistorisches Museum, Vienna, and the Museo Thyssen-Bornemisza, Madrid, are typical of mid-fifteenth-century practices. Clearly, then, the painter of our much later example emulated these features, either because he was adopting an archaizing mode or because he was making a copy of a well-known and highly revered devotional image.

Quarré has related our picture to a portion of a considerably larger painting known only in a fragmentary state and showing similar but not identical architecture (Musée des Arts Décoratifs, Paris), which he believes is connected to a lost Eyckian work from the Carthusian monastery of Champmol, the burial site of the dukes of Burgundy. He speculated that the architecture of the fragment surrounded a standing Virgin and Child of the type shown in the Metropolitan painting. If this is the case, our relatively small picture (which is itself cut down at the top but intact at all other edges) would have provided a replica of an important ducal commission. Further investigation concerning the dukes' gifts to the monastery of Champmol and to the chapel attached to the ducal palace in Dijon may reveal additional information about this hypothetical connection. MWA

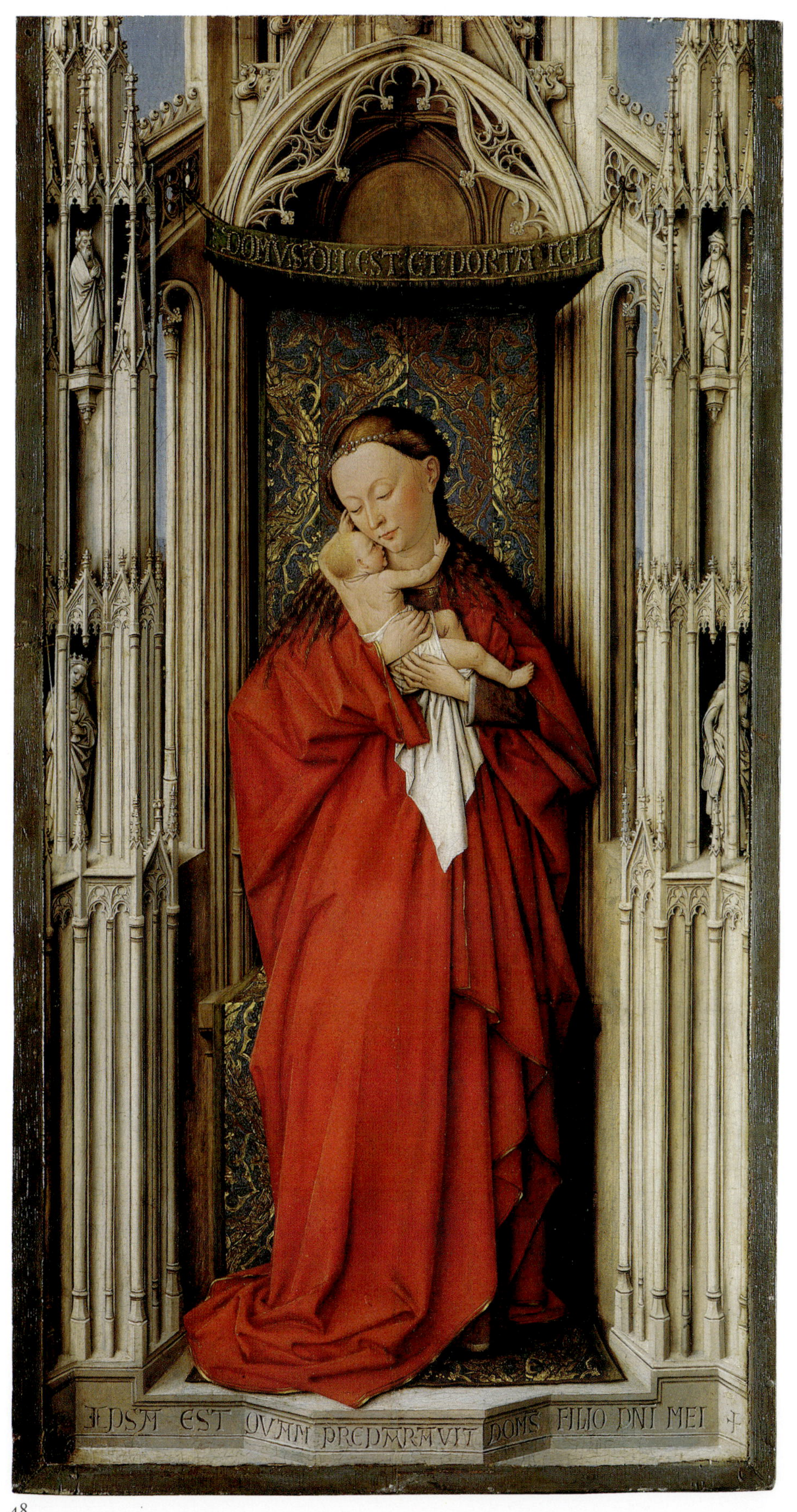

48

Master of the Saint Ursula Legend, active late 15th century

49. Virgin and Child, last quarter of 15th century

Oil on wood, arched top, 22⅛ x 13½ in. (56.2 x 34.3 cm)
Gift of J. Pierpont Morgan, 1917 17.190.16

Provenance: [Horace Buttery, London, 1898]; Stanley Mortimer II, New York (until 1909); [Kleinberger, New York, 1909]; J. Pierpont Morgan, New York (1909–d. 1913); his estate, New York (1913–17).

References: Burroughs 1909a, p. 154; Valentiner 1914, p. 164; Friedländer 1924–37, vol. 2 (1924), p. 129, vol. 6 (1928), pp. 62, 137, no. 107g; Wehle and Salinger 1947, pp. 75–76; Larsen 1960, p. 121; Marlier 1964, pp. 17, 37; Friedländer 1967–76, vol. 2 (1967), pp. 83, 101 n. 99, no. 107g, pl. 102; Carandente 1968, p. 20; De Vos 1971, pp. 126–30; Friedländer 1967–76, vol. 6a (1971), pp. 39, 60, no. 120, pl. 142; Faries, Heller, and Levine 1987, p. 17, n. 21; Levine 1989, pp. 12 n. 28, 76–77, 98–101, 143, 261–63, no. N4; Dijkstra 1990, pp. 129, 244 n. 401, 250 n. 457; Ishikawa 1990, p. 59, n. 26; Stroo and Syfer-d'Olne 1996, p. 171, fig. 120; D'Olne 1997.

This devotional painting, in its original engaged frame, may once have been the center panel of a triptych, as plugs in hinge holes (two on each outside frame edge) appear to indicate. The presumed wings could have shown music-making angels, saints, or—less likely—donors. Our picture shows the seated Virgin surrounded by raised gold beams of light and nursing the Christ Child, her fingers pressed to her breast. The figures are set against a gold background modeled with black cross-hatching that, in combination with the frame, suggests an effect of precious gilt metalwork.

The purported remains of the Virgin's milk were worshiped as a relic in Bruges at Sint-Donaaskerk (the church of Saint Donatian), among other places in the Netherlands, where the theme of the Virgin Suckling the Christ Child, or *Maria lactans*, enjoyed widespread popularity in the fifteenth century. Memling's *Virgin and Child* (cat. no. 55) is an earlier example of the subject. This theme is particularly appropriate for a private devotional panel, since it presents the Virgin in her most human aspect and expresses her special role as intercessor between humankind and God.

The composition of our picture ultimately derives from the motif of the Virgin and Child in Rogier van der Weyden's influential *Saint Luke Drawing the Virgin* (fig. 19). Rogier painted a number of half-length images of the *Maria lactans* on the wings of his late devotional diptychs, such as those in the Renders collection, Bruges, and the Musée des Beaux-Arts de Tournai. However, it was his workshop assistants and his followers who capitalized on the prestige of the *Saint Luke* and adapted two of its principal figures to the format seen in our picture, which is one of numerous nearly identical compositions.

Of the other extant examples, those in the Musées Royaux des Beaux-Arts de Belgique, Brussels, and the Fogg Art Museum, Cambridge, Massachusetts, are particularly noteworthy. Both are important because, as Stroo and Syfer-d'Olne have pointed out, they are nearly identical in size, suggesting that they derive from the same pattern. Examination of their underdrawings reveals evidence of pouncing, which indicates that a pricked cartoon was used to facilitate the transfer of a specific motif. Although our painting does not show pouncing, the close correspondence between the Metropolitan and the Brussels versions—revealed by the placement of a tracing of the contours of the former over the latter painting (d'Olne 1997)—indicates that they likely came from a common model. Three other versions of this painting also appear to have been made from the same pattern; these are in the Gemäldegalerie Alte Meister, Kassel; Museo Nacional de Escultura, Valladolid; and the J. G. Nyssen-Wiegand collection, Barcelona. All five pictures most likely originated in the same workshop, which presumably was in Bruges, since the patrons of the Brussels and Cambridge versions lived in that city.

The style of the master of this workshop is close to that of Rogier and must have influenced the Master of the Saint Ursula Legend, the probable author of our painting. A number of characteristics, such as the Virgin's dark eyes and broadly parted hair with deep curves on both sides, seen in the five works cited above are comparable to features of the Virgin in our panel. The Christ Child in our painting in particular resembles the infant in other works by the Master of the Saint Ursula Legend.

The arched top and gold background of the present *Virgin and Child* differ from the rectangular formats and interior settings of the workshop versions. In these respects our panel bears a closer relation to Rogier's own half-length diptychs, in which the figures are placed against plain backgrounds and often highlighted by radiating lines of light. An example of a diptych with an arched top by the Master of the Saint Ursula Legend is his only dated painting, the *Virgin and Child and Three Donors* of 1486, in the Koninklijk Museum voor Schone Kunsten, Antwerp. DCS

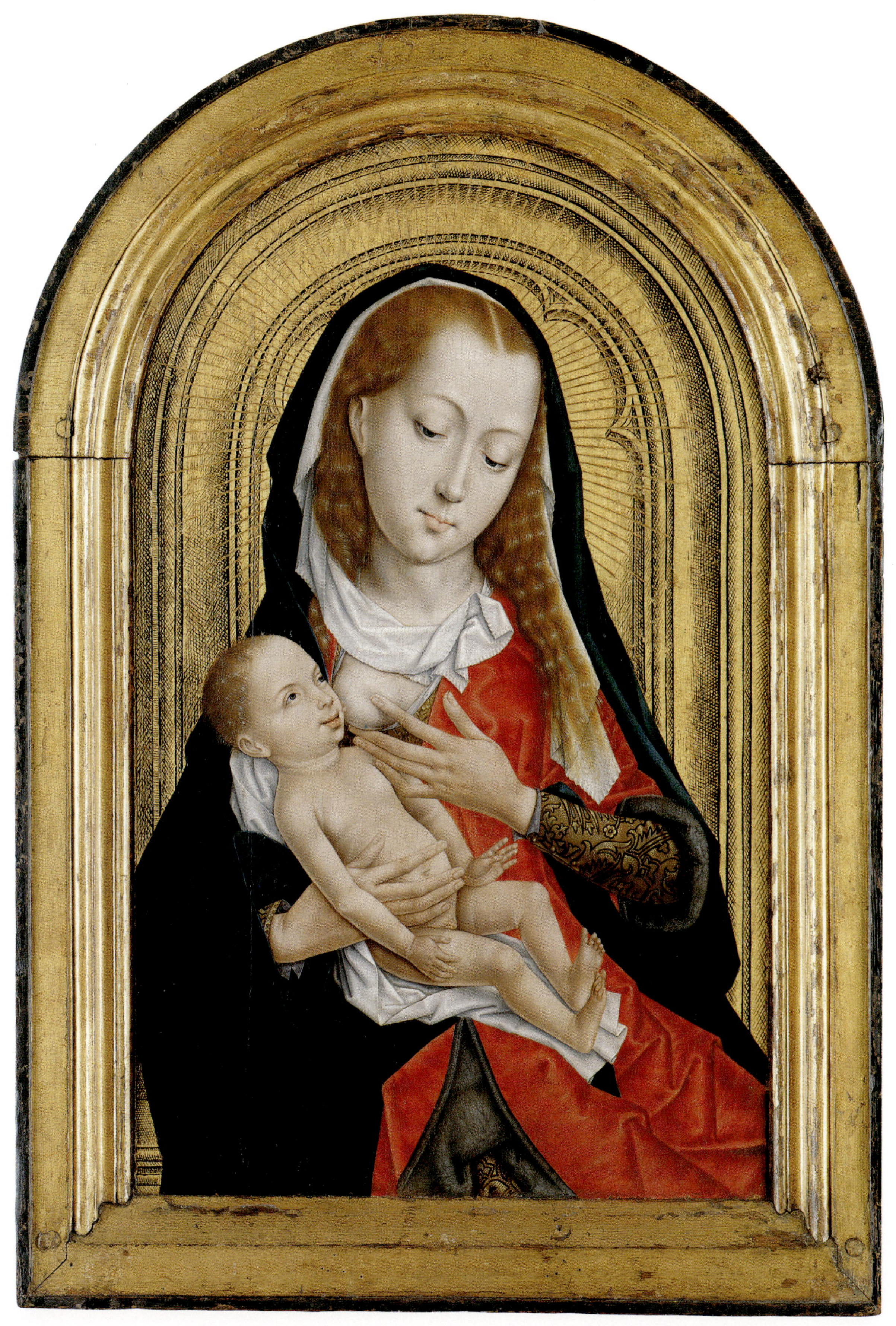

Workshop of Dieric Bouts

50. Virgin and Child, last quarter of 15th century

Oil on wood; overall 11½ x 8¼ in. (29.2 x 21 cm); painted surface 11¼ x 7¾ in. (28.6 x 19.7 cm)
The Jack and Belle Linsky Collection, 1982 1982.60.16

Provenance: Bricken, Cologne; bought by A. Müller for prince of Hohenzollern Sigmaringen; Prince Karl Anton von Hohenzollern Sigmaringen (by 1868–85); princes of Hohenzollern, Fürstlich Hohenzollern'sches Museum, Sigmaringen (from 1885); [A. S. Drey, Munich and New York (by 1928–29)]; Ernst Rosenfeld, New York (1929–37); his estate (1937–43); Mr. and Mrs. Jack Linsky, New York (1980–82).

References: Lehner 1868, no. 34; Bode 1898, p. 38; Friedländer 1924–37, vol. 3 (1925), pp. 47–48, 126, no. 93a; Schöne 1938, pp. 214–15, no. 145; Adhémar 1962, pp. 63–64; Friedländer 1967–76, vol. 3 (1968), pp. 29, 72, no. 93a, pl. 97; Bauman in Metropolitan Museum 1984, pp. 51–53, ill.

This charming *Virgin and Child* is the finest surviving workshop copy of a lost original by Dieric Bouts. At least fifteen copies of this popular devotional image remain; not all are from Bouts's workshop, and both the setting and the attribute of the Christ Child vary from panel to panel. A second copy of high quality (Gemäldegalerie, Berlin), also with a landscape background, is very similar to ours; the landscape, however, is curiously gridlike and flat in comparison with the felicitous and variegated countryside depicted here. The representation of a half-length Virgin and Child before an idealized landscape view was a development of the last quarter of the fifteenth century, popularized by the devotional triptychs of Hans Memling; in them, the figures are often portrayed in front of an open landscape or within a loggia overlooking the countryside (cat. nos. 54, 55). In the present work the Virgin stands not in a loggia but before a stone wall that appears to border a raised and enclosed garden, permitting a slightly elevated perspective.

With his right hand the Child plays with a toe, a motif that also appears in our Memling workshop *Virgin and Child* (cat. no. 54) and may ultimately derive from a prototype by Rogier van der Weyden. In his left hand Christ holds a pink. Since the Greek name for this flower, *dianthose*, means "flower of God," it is frequently placed beside the Virgin or in the Child's hand. However, as Bauman has pointed out, in medieval Flemish the pink "was called *nagelbloem* . . . because of its spikelike petals," and it therefore also alludes to the nailing of Christ to the cross and his death there for man's salvation. Yet the mood of the painting—set by the proud maternal glance of the Virgin, the playful, smiling Child, and a landscape that is both serene and animated—is hardly foreboding.

Bouts's original composition must have been painted within the last years of his life, or close to 1475, and this panel was probably produced shortly thereafter, within the last two decades of the fifteenth century. The picture is in an unusually good state of preservation. MSdJ

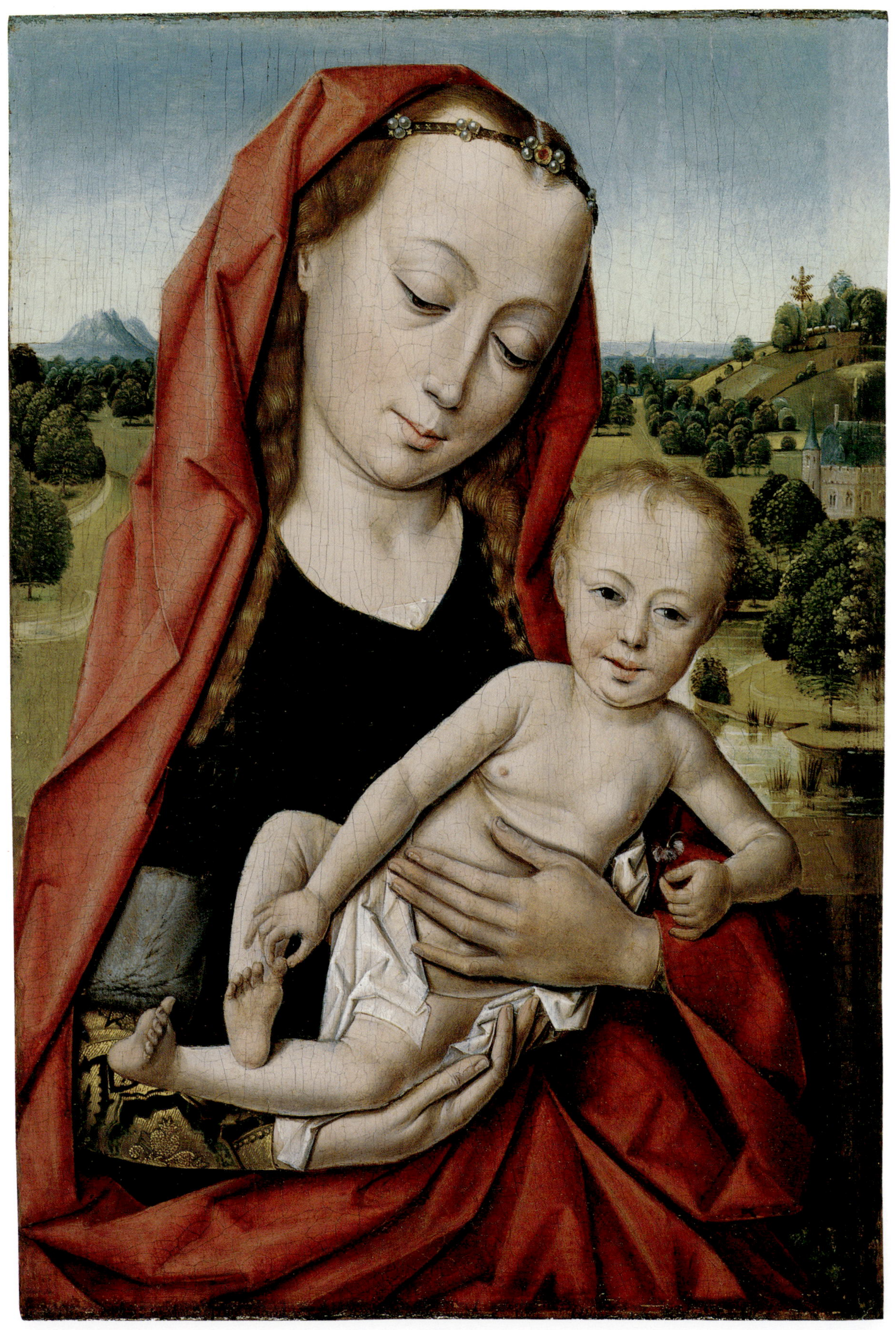

Master of Saint Giles, active about 1490–1510

51. Virgin and Child with a Dragonfly, about 1500

Oil and tempera? on paper laid down on wood, 10½ x 7⅛ in. (26.6 x 18.2 cm) Robert Lehman Collection, 1975 1975.1.131

Provenance: Martin Le Roi, Paris; [Kleinberger, Paris]; sold to Philip Lehman, New York (November 1911); Robert Lehman, New York.

References: Lehman 1928, no. 89; Mayer 1930b, p. 116; Friedländer 1937b, pp. 222, 230, no. 5, fig. 11; Ring 1949, p. 231, no. 245; Heinrich 1954, p. 222; Sterling 1957, no. 37; Lehman [1964?] p. 18; Szabo 1975, p. 89, pl. 68; Heffner 1987, pp. 55–56; Sterling 1990, pp. 300–302, no. 31, fig. 267; Sterling and Ainsworth 1998, no. 4, color ill.

Among the eponymous masters of northern Renaissance painting is one whose name derives from two remarkable panels in the National Gallery, London, that represent scenes from the Life of Saint Giles. Although certain stylistic features of his work, most notably the manner of rendering light and texture, suggest a Netherlandish background for the artist, his portrayal of sites in Paris points to a livelihood made in that city. Indeed, the oeuvre of the Master of Saint Giles indicates that he was an itinerant artist, who perhaps trained in the Netherlands and was subsequently active in Paris.

Several panels of about 1490–95 showing the Virgin and Child readily demonstrate that the Master of Saint Giles was initially influenced by the work of Rogier van der Weyden, but for the Lehman painting he turned to Dieric Bouts. Infrared reflectography and X-radiography reveal that the Metropolitan Museum panel was carried out in two stages. At first the general pose of the Virgin and the position of the legs of the Christ Child followed, although in reverse, a popular Boutsian design exemplified in the Linsky *Virgin and Child* (cat. no. 50); here the Christ Child was shown with his right arm hanging down at his side, his left arm positioned farther to the right than in the final version, and his left leg pulled up tightly to his body at a sharp angle. The Virgin of this stage held a piece of fruit in her right hand.

In revising his original composition, the Master of Saint Giles repainted the Christ Child to match another model from Bouts's workshop, one found in replicas such as the *Virgin and Child* in the Statens Museum for Kunst, Copenhagen. Instead of grasping the rosary of the Bouts versions, however, the Lehman Christ Child restrains a dragonfly, holding it by the tail with his left hand and at the end of a tether with his right. The background cloth of honor is not original, having been overpainted with viridian green sometime after the mid-nineteenth century.

Unusual, but not unique, is the use of paper laid down on an oak panel as the support of the *Virgin and Child.* Given the evolution of the painting from one Boutsian type to another, it is possible that it began as a workshop drawing after one Bouts composition and was subsequently developed into a painting with elements inspired by knowledge of another. In the broad application of rather opaque paint and the sculptural solidity of the forms, the Lehman panel most closely resembles the paintings on the Life of Saint Giles located in London, which were executed about 1500.

A rare variation on the iconography of the Boutsian models is the substitution of a dragonfly for the coral beads the Christ Child ordinarily holds to ward off evil. The dragonfly is symbolic of the Devil, here subdued by Christ, who through the Incarnation, Crucifixion, and Resurrection triumphed over Satan. The Christ Child's action is a visually potent response to the common prayer of supplication inscribed on paintings of the Virgin by Gerard David and Bernaert van Orley in the Metropolitan's collection (cat. nos. 79, 89): "Ave Maria Mater Graciae, Mater Misericordiae, tu nos abhoste protege" (Hail Mary, Mother of Grace, Mother of Mercy, protect us from the enemy). MWA

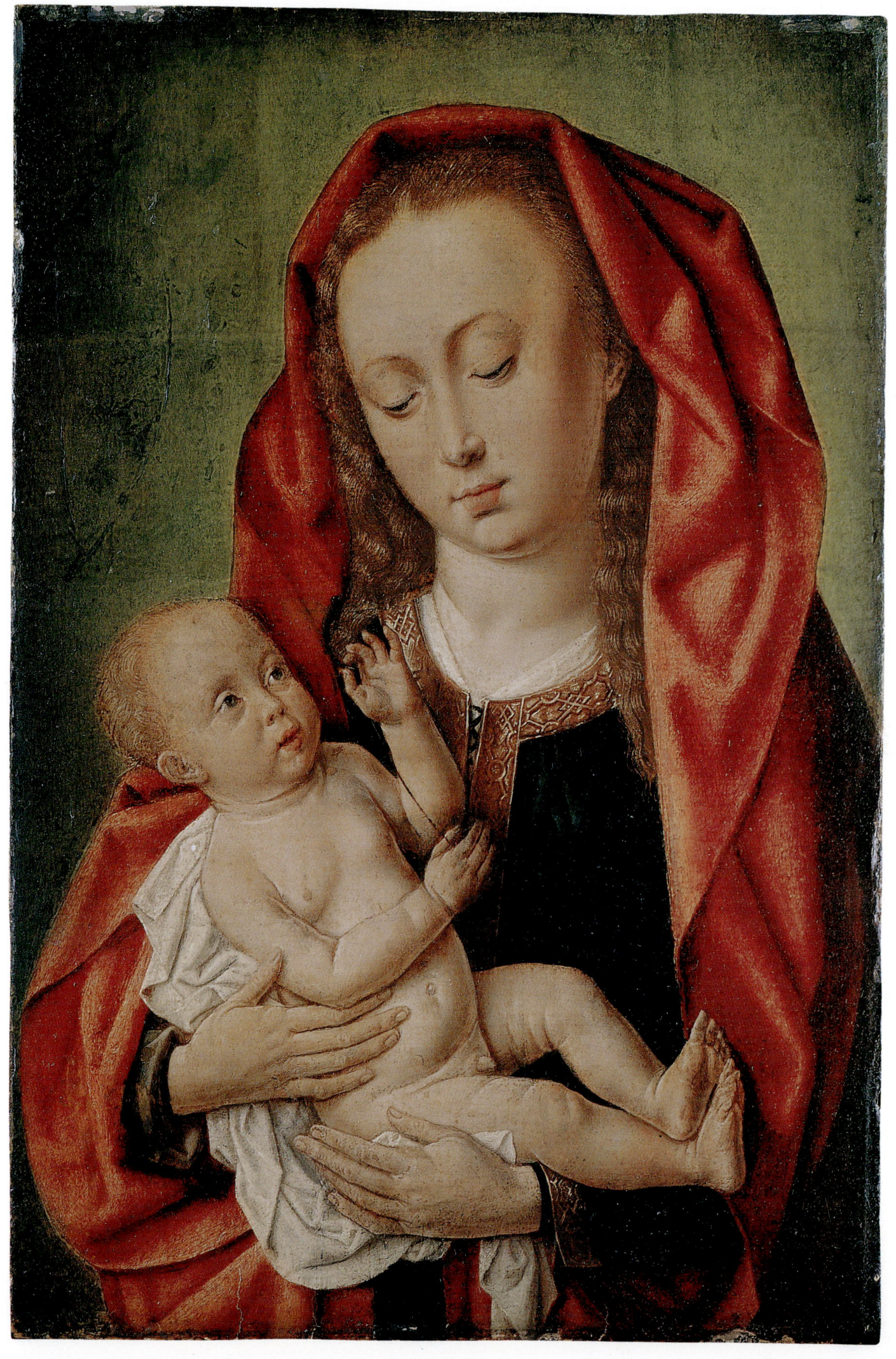

Workshop of Dieric Bouts

52. *Virgin and Child,* last quarter of 15th century

Oil on wood, 11½ x 8¼ in. (29.2 x 21 cm)
The Jules Bache Collection, 1949 49.7.18

Provenance: Gabriel Johann Peter Weyer, Cologne (1852); Prince Karl Anton von Hohenzollern Sigmaringen; princes of Hohenzollern, Königliches Museum, Sigmaringen; [A. S. Drey, Munich and New York (1928)]; [Duveen, New York (1928)]; Jules Bache, New York (1928–49).

References: Weyer 1852, p. 56, no. 180; Lehner 1871, p. 9, no. 29; Friedländer 1924–37, vol. 3 (1925), p. 127, no. 94a, vol. 14 (1937), p. 91; Schöne 1938, p. 215, no. 146; Wehle and Salinger 1947, pp. 45–47, ill.; Eisler 1964, p. 102; Friedländer 1967–76, vol. 3 (1973), no. 95a, pl. 98.

Probably made in Bouts's workshop after his death, this small panel is based on the master's larger *Virgin and Child* from about 1465, in the National Gallery, London; the prototype, however, includes a landscape view as well as a patterned backdrop. Our painting is at a considerable remove from its model in quality and feeling for form, and, as in a second replica formerly in the Albenas collection, Montpellier (Florence Gould sale, Sotheby's, New York, April 25, 1985), the Virgin's head has been schematized into a heart shape with little three-dimensional presence. Mary's hair, which falls in soft waves around her neck in the London panel, has been covered with a cape, and the long-fingered hands, which lack Bouts's nuanced modeling, are somewhat wooden in appearance. The Child in the London model sits on a ledge with a brocade-covered cushion that has not been included in our picture or the Albenas panel, leaving his legs in a curious, unsupported position. The placement of the Child's body, which is higher in these compositions than in the original, forced the draftsman in both cases to raise the Virgin's breast to an unnatural position just below her collarbone in order to place it opposite Christ's mouth. As no doubt happened in Netherlandish workshops throughout the late fifteenth and early sixteenth centuries, many adjustments were made here to simplify a sophisticated, detail-filled composition so that an artist of lesser ability could quickly turn out a product. The underdrawing shows the rigid contour lines of a pattern transfer, with some freehand parallel hatching in brush to indicate the modeling of individual forms.

The Christ Child in our panel wears a coral necklace as a talisman. MSdJ

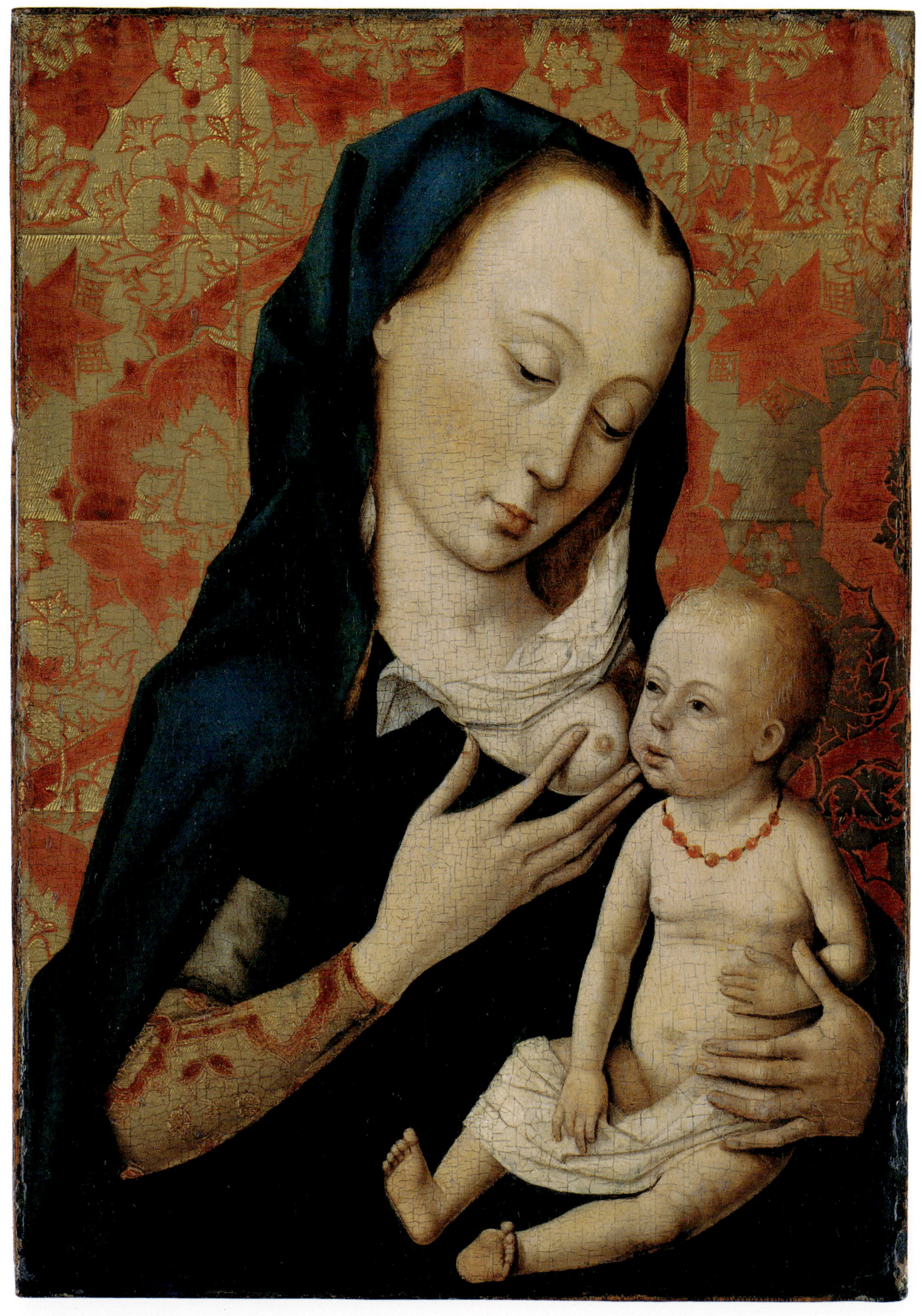

Follower of Dieric Bouts, German

53. *Virgin and Child,* about 1500

Oil on wood, 15⅝ x 12⅛ in. (39.7 x 30.8 cm)
Purchase, Joseph Pulitzer Bequest, 1922 22.96

Provenance: James Broughton, Hillary Place, Leeds (d. ca. 1887); Grosvenor Thomas, London (until 1922); [Durlacher, New York (1922)].

References: Conway 1922, p. 120, ill. opp. p. 107 (as Ouwater); Friedländer 1924–37, vol. 3 (1925), pp. 61, 112, no. 36, pl. 49 (as neither an original of Bouts or Ouwater); Baldass 1932, pp. 80–81, 114; Schöne 1938, pp. 6–7, 23, 25, 30, 136–38, no. 22a, pl. 50b; Wehle and Salinger 1947, pp. 52–53, ill.; Snyder 1960, pp. 43–44; Friedländer 1967–76, vol. 3 (1968), pp. 36, 64, no. 36, pl. 53; Talbot 1979; Châtelet 1981a, pp. 78, 212, no. 54; Jennings 1993, p. 242, pl. 99.

Netherlandish painting was a major influence on German art in the second half of the fifteenth century, and Dieric Bouts's compositions and figure types were among the most widely copied. Our artist has taken the Virgin from the scene of the Visitation and the Child from the Adoration of Bouts's early Infancy Altarpiece (Prado, Madrid) and adapted the compositional type from his later *Virgin and Child* (National Gallery, London). The distinctly un-Netherlandish landscape seen through the window is characteristic of those represented in the same context in German portraits and depictions of the Virgin of about 1500, as is the emphatic pattern of the brocade. The Virgin's abundant hair recalls neither precedents by Bouts, whose Virgin and Child paintings usually show Mary's hair tucked modestly into her robe (cat. no. 6), nor contemporary Netherlandish pictures of this subject; such thick, wavy hair, however, is not uncommon in German representations of the Virgin from the late fifteenth and early sixteenth centuries. As the painting is made on pearwood (not oak) with a gesso (or calcium sulfate, not chalk, or calcium carbonate) ground, it cannot have been produced in Bouts's workshop. More likely it was made in Germany after Boutsian designs circulated there, or perhaps by a German artist working in Spain, where the Infancy Altarpiece and the London *Virgin and Child* could once be seen in the Escorial.

Talbot has commented on the "draftsman's or engraver's conventions" in the picture—which include the linear accentuation of the highlighted strands of hair and the cross-hatching on the drapery in the lower left—finding them more typical of the work of Swabian and Upper Rhenish painters about 1500 than of Bouts's practice. The even, rigid underdrawing restricted to the contours of the Child and of the Virgin's head, visible through infrared reflectography, indicates that these parts of the composition were copied from a standard pattern using some form of mechanical transfer. The Virgin's drapery, awkwardly drawn hands, sunlit hair, and presumably also the landscape are original elements added by our unknown artist.

A rosary with flat, lozenge-shaped beads is attached to the Virgin's girdle. Its inclusion testifies to the importance in private devotion of the late fifteenth and early sixteenth centuries of the ritualized Ave Maria and Paternoster prayers, which were recited with the rosary's aid. MSdJ

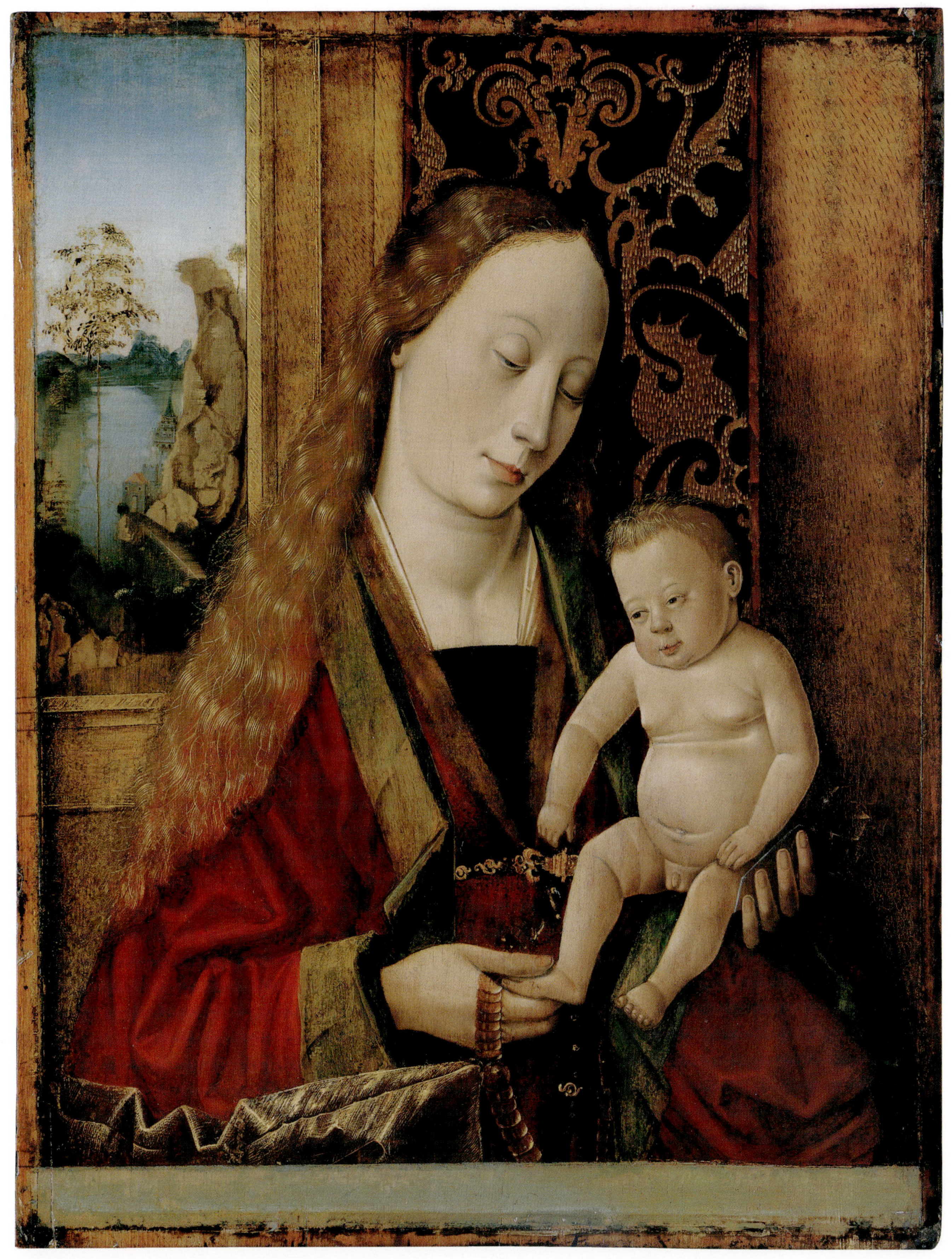

Workshop of Hans Memling

54. Virgin and Child, about 1490

Oil on wood; overall 10¾ x 8¼ in. (27.3 x 21 cm); painted surface 9 x 6⅝ in. (22.9 x 16.8 cm)
The Jules Bache Collection, 1949 49.7.22

Provenance: Dr. Carvallo, Paris; René della Faille de Waerloos, Antwerp (sale, Muller, Amsterdam, July 7, 1903, no. 3); Caspar Bourgeois, Cologne (sale, Heberle, Cologne, October 27–29, 1904, no. 53, as by the Master of the Ursula Legend); [Julius Böhler, Munich]; Richard von Kaufmann, Berlin (sale, Cassirer and Helbing, Berlin, November 25–December 2, 1917, no. 70, as Memling); [Duveen, New York]; Jules S. Bache, New York (cat. 1943, no. 22).

References: Firmenich-Richartz 1904, pp. 68–69; Friedländer 1906b, p. 31; Friedländer 1924–37, vol. 6 (1928), p. 126, no. 53; Wehle and Salinger 1947, pp. 71–72, ill.; Friedländer 1967–76, vol. 6a (1971), pp. 52–53, no. 53; Urbach 1971, under no. 16; Ainsworth 1994a, pp. 84, 85, nn. 19–20; De Vos 1994a, pp. 162–65, 224, no. 42, color ill.; De Vos 1994b, pp. 344, 395–96, 400, n. 12, no. A11, ill.

One of many standard devotional works produced for the mass market in Memling's workshop, this *Virgin and Child* is usually described as a reprise in reverse of the left wing of Memling's Maarten van Nieuwenhove Diptych, dated 1487 (Sint-Janshospitaal, Bruges). It may be closer, however, to his *Virgin and Child* of about the same date in the Museu Nacional de Arte Antigua, Lisbon. A more direct prototype by Memling must once have existed, as in our panel and its variants the Child reaches for his foot with one hand, a gesture not present in either the Bruges or Lisbon pictures. A version in the Szépmüvészeti Múzeum, Budapest, has been ascribed to both Jan Provost and Michel Sittow (probably an apprentice in Memling's shop in the mid-1480s), and another, by Juan de Flandes, with the Child on the left, is in a private collection.

Attempts to connect this painting with other works by the same hand have not been entirely successful. Two panels from Memling's workshop showing the Virgin and Child (Metropolitan Museum, inv. nos. 32.100.58, 1975.5.111) that De Vos associates with our painter are not as accomplished as the present picture, in which the volume of the figures is convincingly rendered, the types of the Virgin and Child are close to Memling's, and the landscape and the decorative details of fur and brocade on the Virgin's costume are handled with some skill, if not inspiration.

Although various mechanical means such as tracing or pouncing were frequently used in workshop settings to copy compositions literally, no evidence of these procedures is present here, and the motif appears to have been freely drawn after a workshop design. Ainsworth notes, however, that the underdrawing in this panel is mostly confined to the contours of forms, as is typical of copies, with some adjustments made on the painted surface.

The apple that the Virgin offers to the Child in this picture and in many of Memling's other Virgin and Child compositions is the forbidden fruit of the tree of knowledge and alludes to Christ as the future Redeemer of mankind from Original Sin.

The painting probably dates from the last decade of the fifteenth century. MSdJ

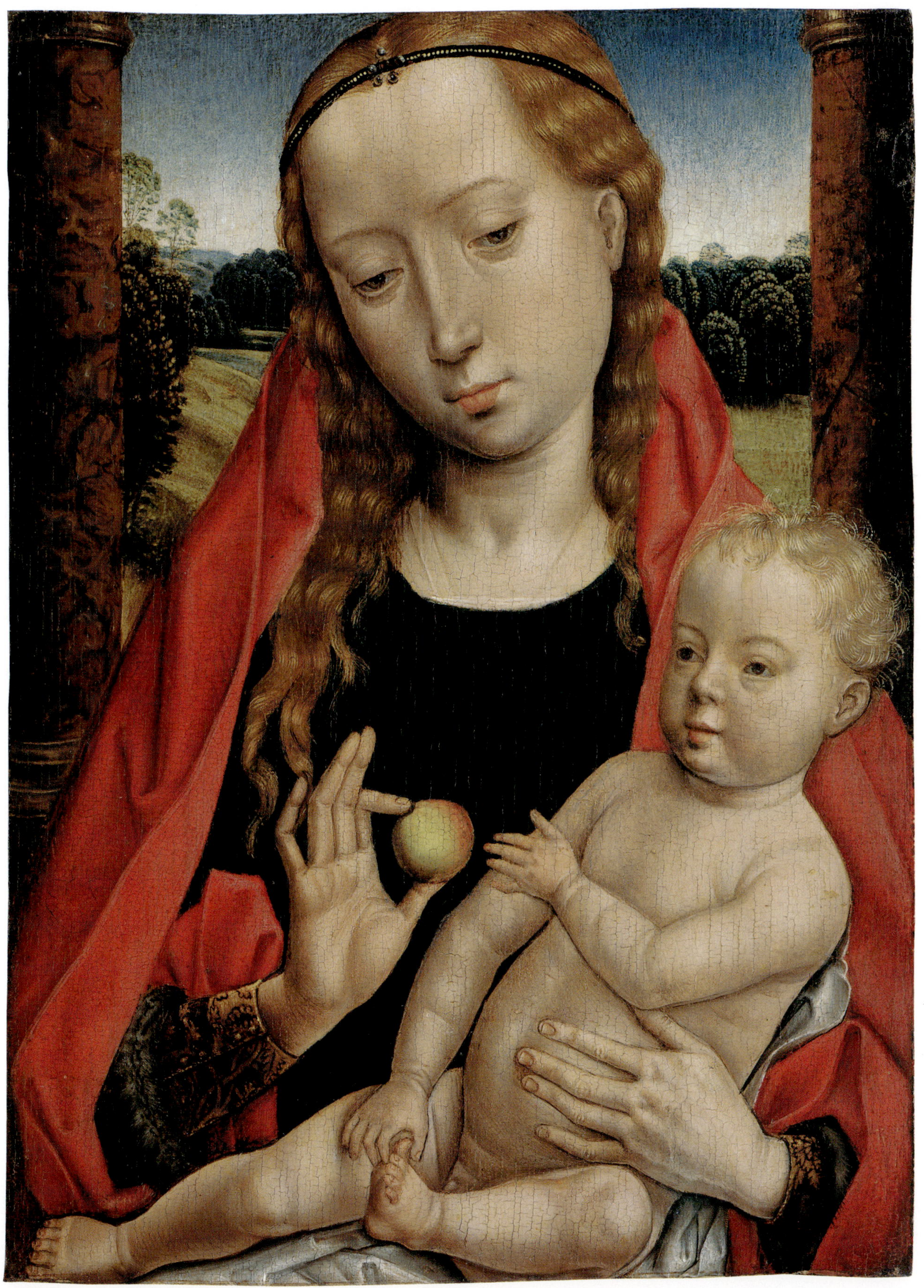

Hans Memling, active by 1465, died 1494

55. *Virgin and Child,* about 1475–80

Oil on wood; overall, with integral frame, d. 9¾ in. (24.8 cm); painted surface d. 6⅞ in. (17.5 cm)
The Friedsam Collection, Bequest of Michael Friedsam, 1931 32.100.59

Provenance: Lord Northwick, Northwick Park, Blockley, Worcestershire (sale, Christie's, London, May 26, 1838, no. 117, as by Van Eyck); Sir William Hart Dyke, Lullingstone Castle, Dartford, Kent (by 1865); Sir Charles Dilke, London (until 1912); Percy Moore Turner, Paris (1912); [Kleinberger, Paris and New York (1912–15)]; Michael Dreicer, New York (1915–16); [Kleinberger, New York (1916)]; Michael Friedsam, New York (1916–31).

References: American Art News *1916, p. 1, ill.; Friedländer 1924–37, vol. 2 (1924), p. 113, vol. 6 (1928), pp. 27, 126, no. 52; Wehle and Salinger 1947, pp. 61–62, ill.; Held 1952, p. 234; Bialostocki 1966, p. 39; Friedländer 1967–76, vol. 2 (1967), p. 73, no. 70a, pl. 98, vol. 6a (1971), pp. 19, 52, no. 52, pl. 99; Johnson collection 1972, pp. 21–22; De Vos 1994a, pp. 16, 136; De Vos 1994b, pp. 80–81, 294, no. 3, color ill.*

A mild, tender icon with a landscape setting, this charming panel belongs to a group of similar roundels of the Virgin Suckling the Child, all of which derive from the composition of Robert Campin's lifesize painting of a standing Virgin and Child (Städelsches Kunstinstitut, Frankfurt). An intermediate work, representing a bust-length Virgin and Child, may once have existed. De Vos (1994a) has observed that the large number of Virgin and Child tondos of roughly the same type and format that exist, as well as the fact that the Child is sometimes on the left and sometimes on the right in these works, suggests that the composition was widely disseminated through model drawings and workshop cartoons.

Only two of the surviving roundels are attributed to Memling: the present picture and one of approximately the same size in a private collection (De Vos 1994b, no. 82). Although the latter has been placed later in Memling's career than our panel, it is actually closer in composition and feeling to the other, more Campinesque variants of the subject. In this later example the Child's body is held parallel to the Virgin's, and she inclines her head only slightly toward him; the picture's gold background invests it with the formality of an icon. In contrast, the relationship of the Virgin and Child in our panel has greater warmth and informality, and the drawing is freer, the prototype being only a point of departure for Memling's design. The landscape background is unique among the extant Virgin and Child roundels and is similar to the setting of the *Salvator Mundi* (cat. no. 56), a slightly larger tondo from Memling's workshop.

Usually considered an early work, the picture has been dated shortly after Memling left the workshop of Rogier van der Weyden, or between about 1465 and 1470; the type of the Virgin and Child, however, seems more characteristic of the mature Memling, and a later date, possibly as late as 1480, cannot be ruled out.

Roundels depicting a variety of simple devotional subjects have survived and seem to have had a precise function. Held notes that small circular painted and sculpted images are shown hanging above the heads of beds in a number of Netherlandish Annunciations. In a Rogierian *Annunciation* in the Louvre, Paris, for example, such a panel is represented in a well-appointed bedroom of the time. These roundels may have had a dual purpose: to serve as a blessing for a marriage and to encourage virtuous conduct in its partners.

The painting and frame are a single piece of wood.

MSdJ

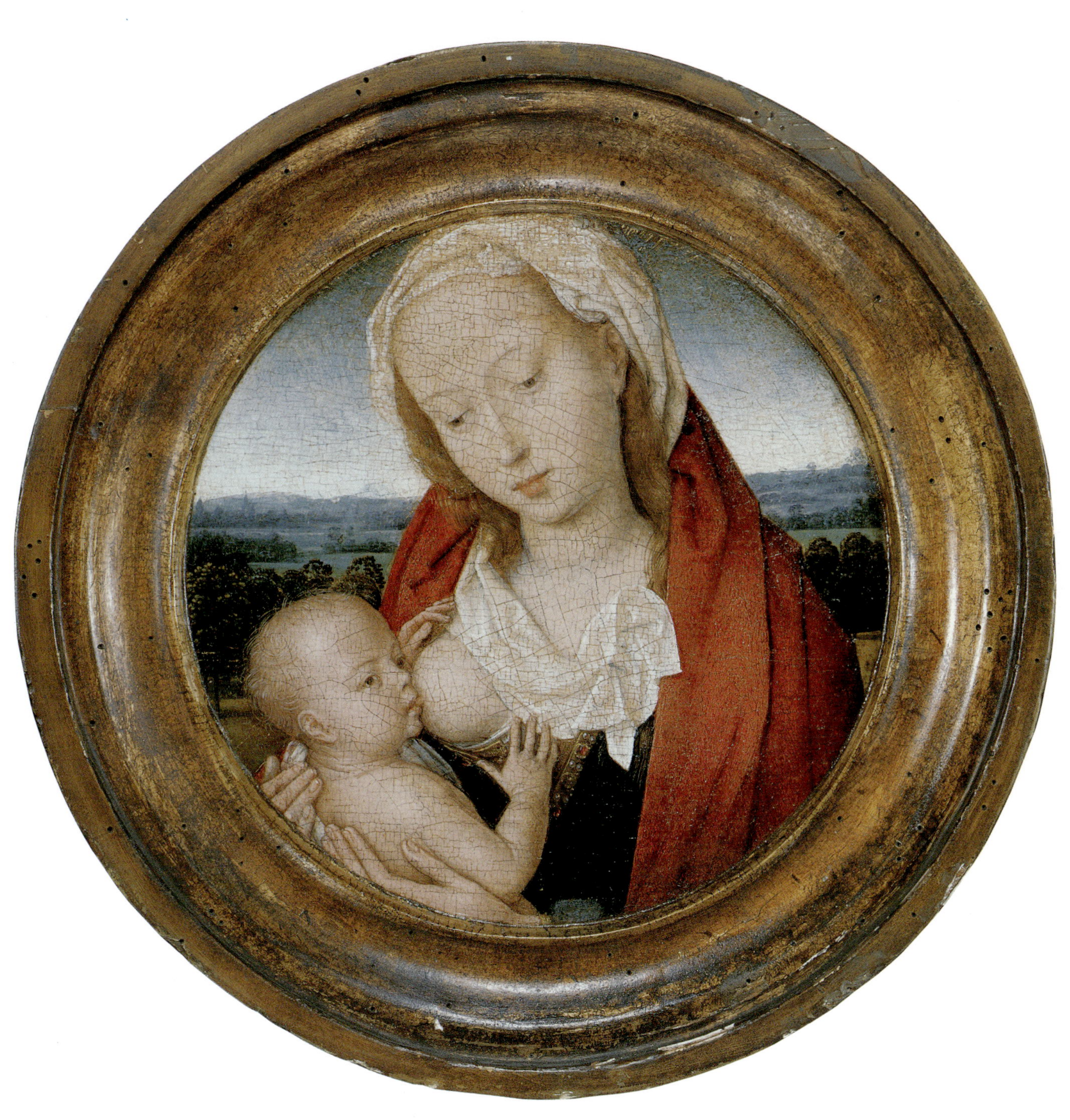

Workshop of Hans Memling

56. Salvator Mundi, last quarter of 15th century

Oil on wood; overall, with integral frame, d. 10¾ in. (27.3 cm); painted surface d. 8 in. (20.3 cm)
The Friedsam Collection, Bequest of Michael Friedsam, 1931 32.100.54

Provenance: Von Arnim, Schwedt, Germany (until 1904); Richard von Kaufmann, Berlin ([d. 1908]; his sale, Cassirer and Helbing, Berlin, December 4, 1917, no. 69, for DM 72,000); [Kleinberger, New York (1921)]; Michael Friedsam, New York (1921–31).

References: Friedländer 1906b, pp. 30–31, ill.; Huisman 1923, p. 123; Friedländer 1924–37, vol. 6 (1928), p. 123, no. 38; Wehle and Salinger 1947, p. 70, ill.; Held 1952, p. 234; Gottlieb 1960, p. 330, n. 12; Friedländer 1967–76, vol. 6a (1971), p. 51, no. 38, pl. 90; De Vos 1994b, pp. 142, 232, 344, no. A12, ill.

The iconographic type of Christ as Salvator Mundi, or Savior of the World, merging the themes of the Holy Face (see cat. nos. 3, 74) and Christ in Majesty, became extremely popular in the Netherlands in the last quarter of the fifteenth century. Perhaps the earliest and most influential example of the subject is the half-length Christ at the center of Rogier van der Weyden's Braque Triptych from about 1452 (Louvre, Paris). In the Louvre panel Christ holds in his left hand a globe representing the earth, surmounted by a Greek cross; his right hand is raised in blessing. The cross refers to the Crucifixion, the means of Christendom's salvation. The curious reflected light on the globe in our picture derives from Rogier's prototype, in which the reflection of a large light-filled window appears on the globe; this light and window, symbols of salvation, became a convention in representations of the orb held by Christ as Salvator Mundi.

The conception of this small picture, a holy image before an open landscape in a round format, is very similar to that of Memling's *Virgin and Child* (cat. no. 55). But the handling of the *Salvator Mundi* is dry and mechanical in comparison, and it must have been produced by an assistant from a pattern readily available within the workshop. The head of Christ is quite different from the type found in Memling's two images of the Blessing Christ of 1478 and 1481 (Norton Simon Museum, Pasadena, and Museum of Fine Arts, Boston) and in the large Salvator Mundi that is the central figure of his Nájera Altarpiece of about 1487–90 (Koninklijk Museum voor Schone Kunsten, Antwerp). It is, however, relatively close to the head in his only other surviving panel showing Christ as Savior, part of the triptych *Earthly Vanity and Divine Salvation* (Musée des Beaux-Arts, Strasbourg). Christ does not hold the orb in Memling's Salvator Mundi images as he does in Rogier's Braque Triptych but rests his hand on it as in our tondo; moreover, a cross very like the one in our panel, and tilting at the same angle, surmounts the orb in each of these works.

There was a great demand for roundels of this kind, which were hung over the heads of beds as talismans (see entry for cat. no. 55). Most likely this small panel was painted in the last quarter of the fifteenth century.

The painting and frame are a single piece of wood.

MSdJ

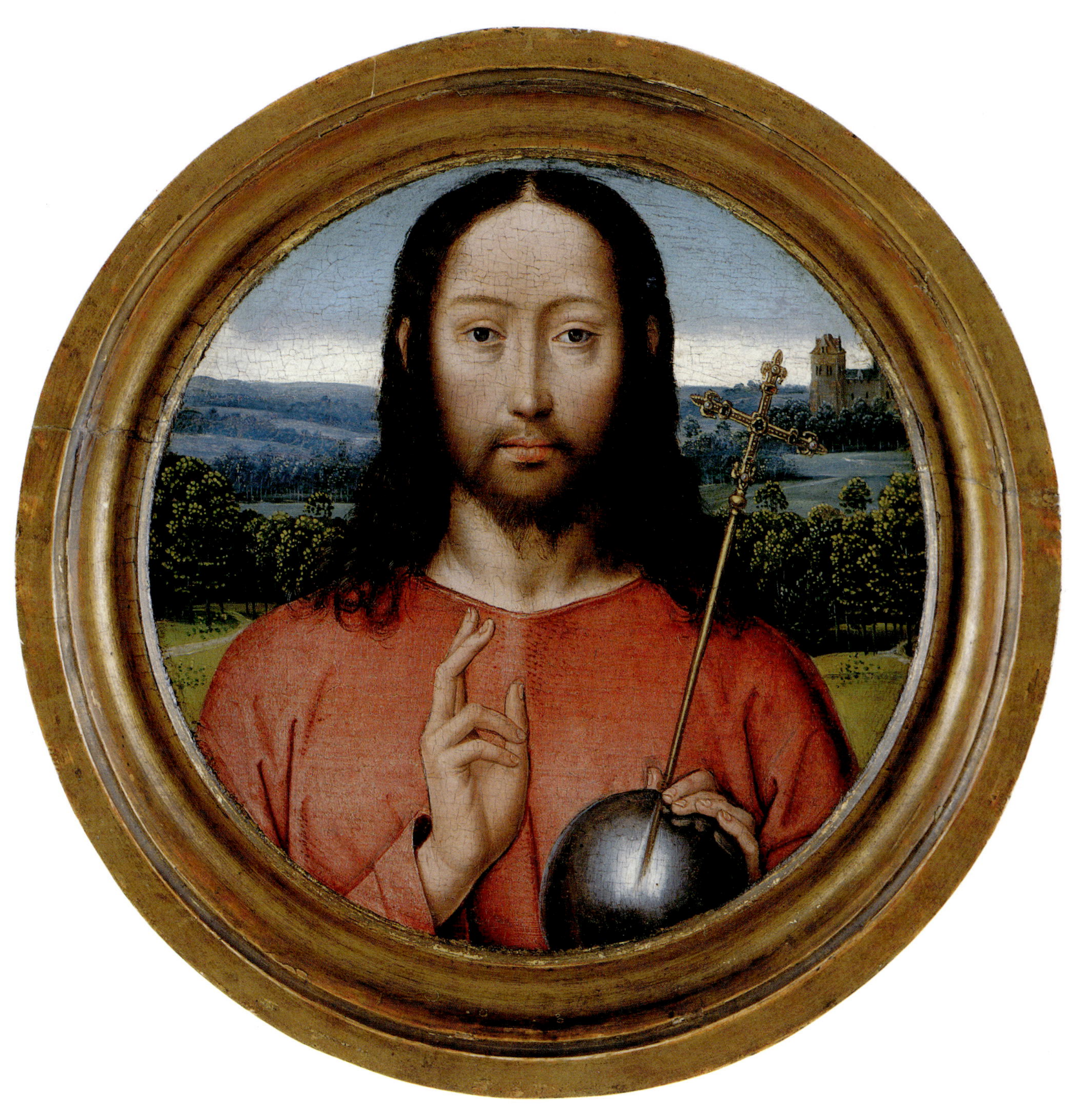

Aelbert Bouts, born about 1451/54, died 1549

57. *Head of Saint John the Baptist on a Charger,* first quarter of 16th century

Oil on wood, d. 11⅛ in. (28.3 cm)
Bequest of Rupert L. Joseph, 1959 60.55.2

Provenance: Count Wallmoden, Hanover (until 1819; sold to prince of Schaumburg-Lippe); Prince Georg Wilhelm zu Schaumburg-Lippe, Bückenburg (1819–60, inv. no. 667); by descent to Prince Adolf zu Schaumburg-Lippe (1911–29; sold to Rosenbaum); [Rosenbaum, Frankfurt, and Böhler, Munich (1929–at least 1931)]; Sir Robert Abdy, Newton Ferrers, Callington, Cornwall (until 1936; sale, Sotheby's, London, May 28, 1936, no. 56, to Joseph for £120); Rupert L. Joseph, New York (1936–59).

References: Schöne 1938, pp. 140–42, no. 25k; Bialostocki 1966, p. 24; Stuebe 1969, pp. 1–16; Hollanders-Favart, Van Schoute, and Verougstraete-Marcq 1975, pp. 66–81.

John the Baptist was imprisoned by King Herod after the saint shamed him for marrying Herodias, wife of the king's own brother. When Herodias's daughter, Salome, enchanted the king with her dancing during a banquet, he promised the young woman whatever she wished. At her mother's urging, she asked for the head of the Baptist on a platter; the act accomplished, Salome presented Herodias with the trophy.

According to early sources, in 1206, following the Fourth Crusade, the relic of Saint John's head was brought to Amiens, where the city's great cathedral was gradually built around it like a giant reliquary. Housed in a jeweled silver mask on a silver charger, the relic, which was reputed to have miraculous healing and protective powers, attracted large numbers of pilgrims. As many as thirteen relics of the saint's head were subsequently claimed by churches throughout Europe. A sculptural tradition that showed a fully three-dimensional head, often polychromed, on a charger preceded images such as this picture, in which the illusionistic properties of painting are exploited to counterfeit a severed head on a gilt platter.

Like the *Mourning Virgin* and *Man of Sorrows* (cat. no. 58), this panel is one of a large number of similar representations of the saint's head, all of which were produced through some form of mechanical transfer. They probably derive from a prototype by Dieric Bouts and are generally viewed as works from the circles of Dieric and his son Aelbert; some, however, may have been painted considerably after Aelbert's lifetime. The physiognomy of the saint seems to have been adapted from the head of the Baptist held by the executioner in the right wing of Rogier van der Weyden's Saint John the Baptist Triptych (Gemäldegalerie, Berlin).

The composition can be understood as a hybrid of the miracle-working Amiens relic and a literal icon representing the head of the saint as it was presented by Salome to her mother. Since John the Baptist was viewed as Christ's forerunner and herald, events in his life were often interpreted as metaphors for similar occurrences in the life of Christ. Just as John's birth was related to the Nativity, his beheading by Salome was linked to the Crucifixion. Thus, sculpted and painted images of this subject not only assumed the healing powers of the relics but also brought with them associations with Christ's sacrifice and the Eucharist. A text on the Feast of the Decollation of Saint John the Baptist in the York Breviary, printed in 1493, makes this clear: "Saint John's head on the dish signifies the body of Christ, which feeds us on the holy altar."

The fact that many of the painted images of the saint's head have neither an unpainted edge nor an engaged frame suggests that the panels were exhibited unframed, in a specific context. (The frame on the Metropolitan Museum's example is modern.) In these roundels the idea of painting as a window onto a fictive world has been inverted, and the head is depicted as a projection into the viewer's space. Such a realistic effect enhanced the function of the work as an object of devotion.

It is difficult to date the present panel or even to be entirely confident of its traditional attribution to Aelbert Bouts. The composition was extremely popular by at least the end of the fifteenth century and through the early seventeenth century, and the replicas are so close to one another that to some extent they seem interchangeable. This is not to deny their hypnotic power as icons and the strange poetry they possess as extreme still lifes.

MSdJ

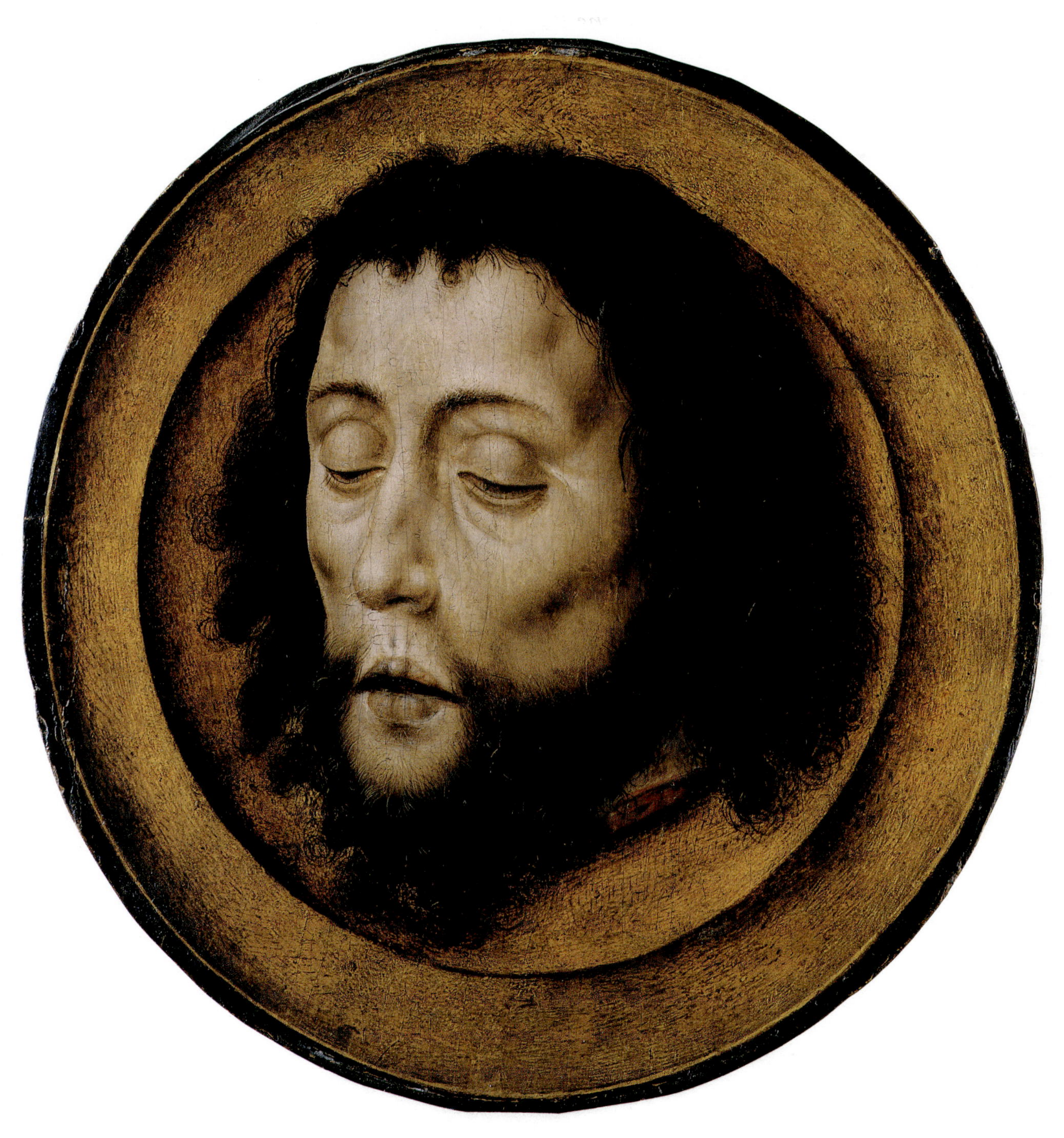

Copy after Dieric Bouts

58. The Mourning Virgin; The Man of Sorrows, about 1525

Oil on wood, each 16 x 12½ in. (40.6 x 31.8 cm)
Purchase, 1871 71.156–157

Provenance: Count Cornet de Ways Ruart de Vanêche, near Brussels (1870); [Étienne Le Roy, Brussels, and Leon Gauchez, Paris]; William T. Blodgett, Paris (1870, for the Museum); William T. Blodgett, Paris, and John Taylor Johnston, New York (1870–71).

References: Harck 1888, p. 74; Schöne 1938, pp. 129–30 [for versions]; Wehle and Salinger 1947, pp. 49–50; Eisler 1961, pp. 59–60; Ringbom 1984, pp. 36, 37, 142–43 [for iconography and versions]; Ainsworth 1989a, pp. 11, 36, n. 22; Wolff 1989, p. 122, fig. 14; Schuler 1992, pp. 14–15; Klein 1995, p. 157.

One of numerous copies of a lost original by Bouts, this diptych was produced through the transfer of a workshop drawing by pouncing perhaps fifty years after the master's death—an indication of the highly conservative taste and requirements of the patrons of Netherlandish devotional art. Christ wears the scarlet mantle and crown of thorns in which he was dressed by Pilate's soldiers as a prelude to his mocking (Matthew 27: 27–31), while beside him his grief-stricken mother is engaged in timeless prayer on behalf of mankind. During the late fifteenth and early sixteenth centuries the Modern Devotion encouraged a growing emphasis on the cult of the Virgin and identification with her sorrows (see entry for cat. no. 101). Consequently, there was great demand for images of this kind, by means of which the devout—as they empathized with the Virgin's suffering as well as Christ's—might anticipate Mary's support for eternal salvation through her powers as an intercessor.

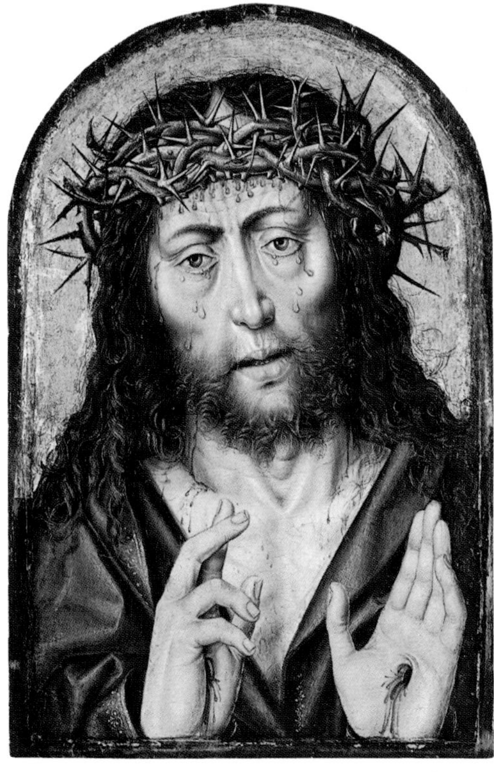

Fig. 82. Aelbert Bouts, *The Man of Sorrows*, about 1525. Oil on wood. The Friedsam Collection, Bequest of Michael Friedsam, 1931, The Metropolitan Museum of Art, New York

Copies of Bouts's lost painting vary in quality and in their apparent date of production, and single panels of either the Virgin or Christ are also extant. One of these, representing the Sorrowing Virgin (Art Institute of Chicago), previously considered Bouts's prototype, has recently been dated through dendrochronological analysis to between about 1480 and 1495, or shortly after the master's death. The Chicago panel, nevertheless, is closest in handling and style to Bouts's autograph works. The lost original is difficult to place chronologically but can be tentatively dated between about 1460 and 1475.

The gold background and iconic presentation of the many panels showing this subject suggest that the composition ultimately derives from an Italo-Byzantine model. The earliest surviving Netherlandish example is Robert Campin's *Praying Virgin and Blessing Christ* (John G. Johnson Collection, Philadelphia Museum of Art), where the two heads are arranged in a continuous space rather than in a diptych format. A setting of this kind was, in fact, intended in the present pair, which shares a lighting source and a continuous internal painted framing device. Iconographically close to our panels and perhaps contemporaneous with them is Adriaen Isenbrant's monumental *Christ Crowned with Thorns and the Mourning Virgin* (cat. no. 101), a more complex and innovative composition.

From about the same period is a *Man of Sorrows* (fig. 82) attributed to Aelbert Bouts, son of Dieric. Aelbert is known particularly for the mass production of exaggerated versions of his father's devotional compositions. It was just such aggressive icons and the indulgences associated with prayers to them that were criticized by leaders of the Reformation.

The thickness and opacity of flesh tones in the present diptych result from a dense buildup of lead white. This surface, found in many sixteenth-century Netherlandish works, offers a marked contrast to the transparent and delicate effects of fifteenth-century technique. MSdJ

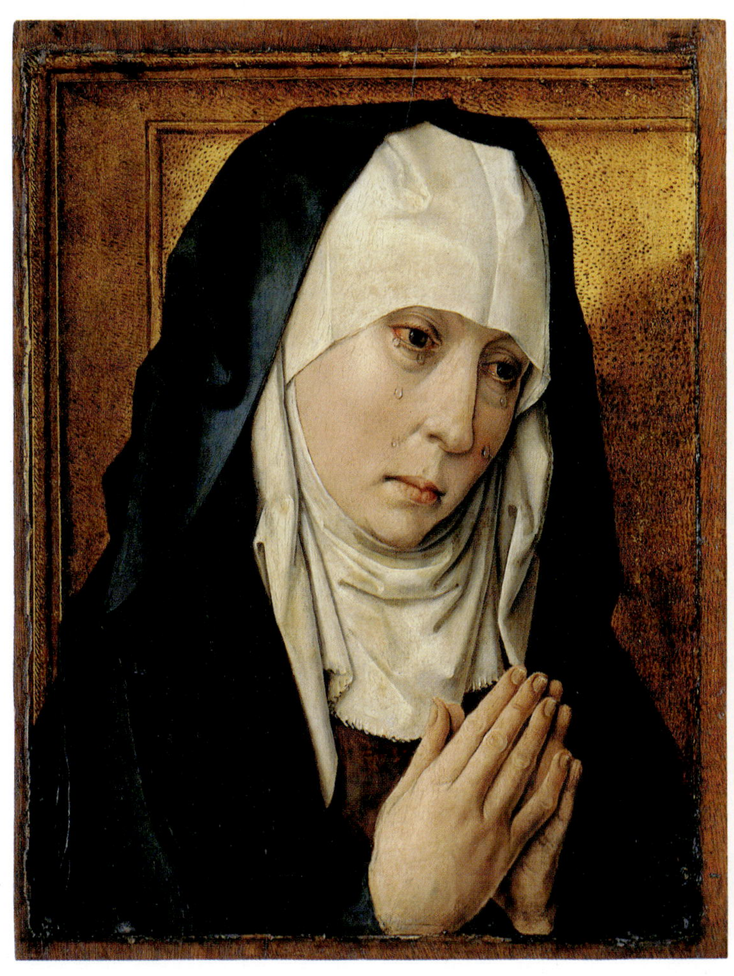

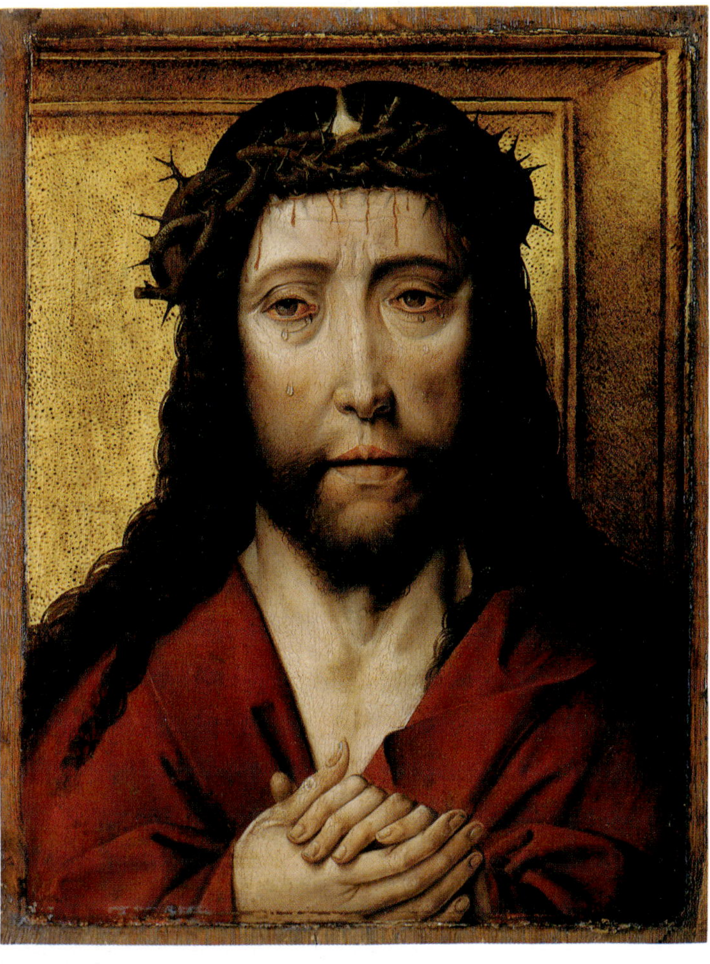

Follower of Jan Joest of Kalkar

59. The Adoration of the Christ Child, about 1515

Oil on wood; overall 41 x 28¼ in. (104.1 x 71.8 cm); painted surface 41 x 27⅝ in. (104.1 x 70.2 cm)
The Jack and Belle Linsky Collection, 1982 1982.60.22

Provenance: Richard von Kaufmann, Berlin (until 1917; sale Paul Cassirer, Berlin, from December 4, 1917, no. 110); F. Haniel, Düsseldorf (1917–after 1964); Herbert Ritter, Munich, for Mrs. Lieven (until 1967; sale Christie's, London, June 23, 1967, no. 73); Mr. and Mrs. Jack Linsky, New York (1967–80); The Jack and Belle Linsky Foundation, New York (1980–82).

References: Baldass 1920–21, p. 46; Rosenberg 1925, p. 377; Friedländer 1924–37, vol. 9 (1931), pp. 17–18, 126, no. 4a; Hoogewerff 1936–47, vol. 2 (1937), pp. 447–48; Baudisch 1940, pp. 144–48; Friedländer 1940, p. 162; Stange 1934–61, vol. 6 (1954), pp. 64, 67; Friedländer 1956, pp. 108–9; Winkler 1964, p. 153; Friedländer 1967–76, vol. 9a (1972), pp. 15, 52, no. 4a; Goddard 1983, pp. 146–47; Bauman in Metropolitan Museum 1984, pp. 67–70; Goddard 1985, pp. 409, 416; Sutton 1990, p. 297; Wolff-Thomsen 1997, pp. 354–63; Wolff 1998, under no. 18.

One of the most influential accounts of the Nativity was provided by Saint Bridget of Sweden, who recorded specific details of the event as she witnessed it in a vision experienced during a pilgrimage to Bethlehem in August of 1372. Although Netherlandish artists did not always follow Bridget's text exactly, certain of its features became part of their pictorial tradition: the young Virgin with long, flowing hair, the naked Christ Child, the angels who provided what Bridget called "wonderfully sweet and most dulcet songs." But perhaps the most important element of the saint's story for painters was the illumination she described as the "great and ineffable light" emanating from the Christ Child to which "the sun could not be compared" and the "divine splendor [that] totally annihilated the material splendor of the candle" shielded in Joseph's hands. The portrayal of the spiritual light, which encouraged artists to introduce dramatic chiaroscuro effects in their paintings, conveyed the mystical aura of the event. Winkler supposed that there was a prototype of the Night Nativity by Hugo van der Goes, now lost but thought to survive in versions by Gerard David and Michel Sittow (both Kunsthistorisches Museum, Vienna). However, an adaptation of the composition, which Friedländer suggested was invented by Jan Joest, became an especially popular model in early-sixteenth-century Antwerp painting.

Joest's autograph work has not survived, but several paintings, most notably the present one and a panel in the Dunedin Public Art Gallery, New Zealand, are executed in a manner that resembles his style as it is known from his polyptych for the high altar of the Stadtpfarrkirche Sankt Nicolai in Kalkar, Germany. The Virgin, with her delicate features, and especially the frizzy-haired angels in our picture are similar to Joest's Virgin and Gabriel in the Kalkar altarpiece. But the faces of Joseph, the shepherds, and the angels at the manger deviate from Joest's types, indicating that the Linsky panel can more likely be assigned to a follower working in Antwerp than to the master himself.

Two surviving drawings of this subject, one attributed to Joest in the State Hermitage Museum, Saint Petersburg, and the other ascribed to Dirk Vellert in the Szépmüvészeti Múzeum, Budapest, share some features with our painting. There are as well at least ten paintings, including the Lehman panel from the workshop of the Master of Frankfurt (cat. no. 60), that repeat the basic composition and figures of the Linsky painting. That so many works of the kind survive attests to the wide circulation of this popular composition in Antwerp workshops. Although our picture largely conforms to the prototype, the spirited group of angels overhead singing from the text on a banderole decorated with calligraphic swirls is an inventive addition to the standard pattern that greatly enhances the euphoric mood of the joyous event depicted.

MWA

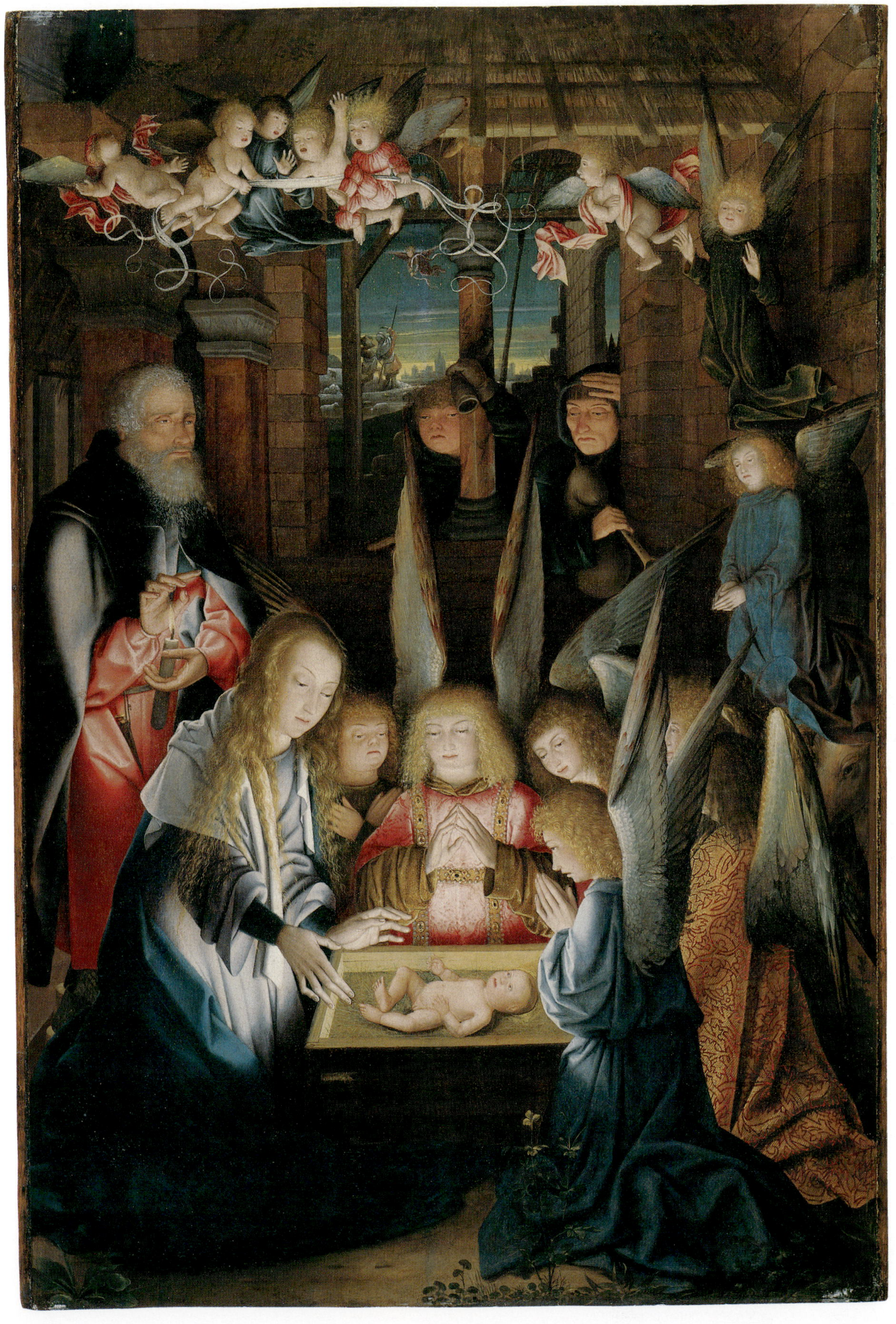

Workshop of the Master of Frankfurt

60. The Adoration of the Christ Child, about 1510–20

Oil on wood; overall 23⅛ x 16¼ in. (58.7 x 41.3 cm); painted surface 22⅞ x 16 in. (58.1 x 40.1 cm)
Robert Lehman Collection, 1975 1975.1.116

Provenance: Russian collection?; [Paul Bottenwieser, Berlin and New York]; sold to Robert Lehman, New York (December 1930).

References: Friedländer 1924–37, vol. 9 (1931), pp. 17–18, 126, no. 4d; Valentiner 1945, p. 212; Winkler 1964, p. 153; Friedländer 1967–76, vol. 7 (1971), p. 85, no. add. 204, pl. 131, vol. 9 (1972), pp. 15, 52, 133, n. 24, no. 4d; Bauman in Metropolitan Museum 1984, p. 68; Goddard 1984, pp. 90–91, 93–94, 111, 113, 116, 134–35; Goddard 1985, pp. 409, 416; Sutton 1990, p. 297; Wolff-Thomsen 1997, p. 359; Wolff 1998, no. 18, color ill.

Variations of this sort of crowded scene of adoration, ultimately derived from the works of Hugo van der Goes and copies by Gerard David and Michel Sittow, became widely popular in Antwerp in the early sixteenth century. Their dissemination in that city was mainly effected by the thriving workshop of the Master of Frankfurt, which was responsible for our picture. The traditional rendition of the theme shows a night scene, as exemplified by a panel in the Linsky collection (cat. no. 59), but the author of the Lehman painting presented an evenly lit daytime event, thus significantly diminishing the sense of mystery attached to the more standard variations.

A large number of panels with this Nativity composition survive, suggesting that pattern drawings for it circulated among various workshops in Antwerp. No doubt some of these drawings were cartoons pricked for transfer or employed for tracings, although the Lehman painting reveals no clear evidence of the use of these common workshop aids. Goddard (1985) has shown that certain brocade designs on the garments of the angels in our picture appear frequently in paintings associated with the shop of the Master of Frankfurt and must, therefore, have been among the atelier's stock patterns. The workshop model of the Adoration of the Christ Child could have been adjusted according to the client's personal requirements; moreover, such prototypes were available in different sizes, as comparison of the Linsky and Lehman examples demonstrates. Since neither painting shows any indication of customized additions made for an individual buyer, it is likely that they were produced for the open market, perhaps to be sold at the Pand in Antwerp along with representations of other popular subjects.

MWA

Joos van Cleve, active by 1507, died 1540/41

61. The Holy Family, about 1512–13

Oil on wood, 16¾ x 12½ in. (42.5 x 31.8 cm)
Inscribed (on scroll): . . . et benedictus / fructus ventris tui / . . . / . . . / Magnificat [a]N̄[im]A / mea dominum / Et exultavit Sp[iritu]s me / us in deo salutari meo / Quia respexit humi / litatem ancillae suae / [ecce enim ex hoc] b[ea]tam / [me dicent

Joos van Cleve was the artist primarily responsible for popularizing the theme of the Holy Family, a subject that gained new prominence in early-sixteenth-century Netherlandish painting. For this tender depiction of the Virgin nursing the Christ Child while Joseph looks on, Joos quoted the Virgin and Child from Jan van Eyck's Lucca Madonna of nearly eighty years earlier (fig. 26). But he removed Jan's Virgin from the exalted setting of a throne room, where her regal status as Queen of Heaven is emphasized, and placed her in the shallow and tightly cropped space of a domestic interior.

In this rendition of the subject, which was intended for private devotional use, Joos gave traditional representations new interpretations. Joseph is no longer banished to the background, reduced to playing a marginal role, but now takes his place as Mary's equal partner in the upbringing of the Christ Child.

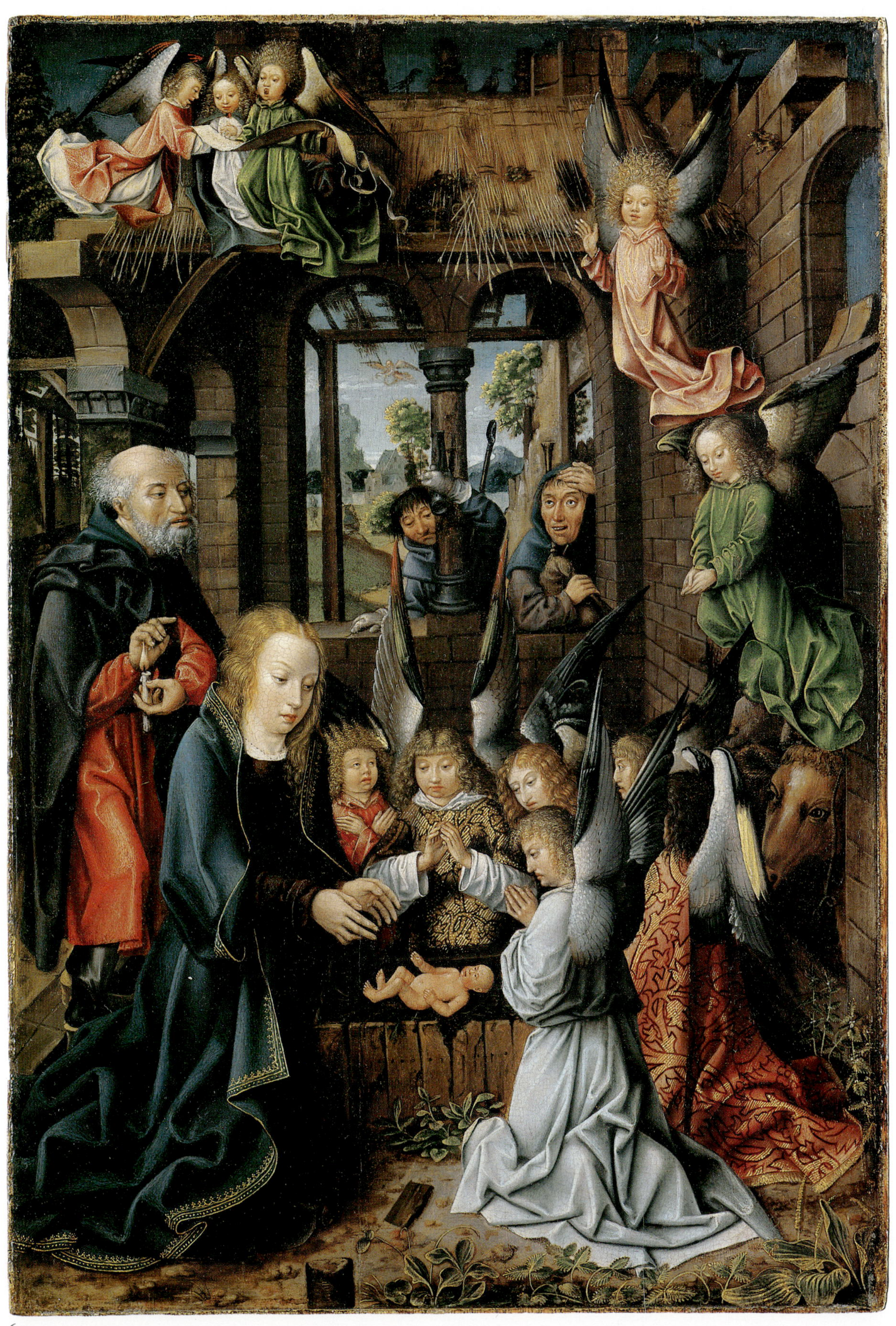

60

omnes] generat / [iones. Quia] fecit mihi [magna] / qui potens est et / [sanctum nomen] ejus Et / [misericordia] ejus a / [progenie in progenies timentibus eum.] (. . . and blessed is the fruit of thy womb. . . . My soul doth magnify the Lord, and my spirit hath rejoiced in God my Saviour. For he hath regarded the low estate of his handmaiden: [for, behold, from henceforth all] generations [shall call me] blessed. For he that is mighty hath done to me [great things]; and [holy is his name]. And his [mercy is on them that fear him from generation to generation] [Luke 1:42, 46–50, including the first five lines of the Magnificat])
The Friedsam Collection, Bequest of Michael Friedsam, 1931 32.100.57

Provenance: E. Sécrétan, Paris (until 1885); Joseph Spiridon, Paris (from 1885; sale, Cassirer and Helbing, Berlin, May 31, 1929, no. 73); [Kleinberger, New York]; sold to Michael Friedsam, New York (March 11, 1930).

References: Winkler 1924, p. 249; Baldass 1925, p. 18, no. 18; Lotthé 1947, vol. 1, pp. 124–25, vol. 2, p. 331, no. 280; Wehle and Salinger 1947, pp. 132–33; Van Puyvelde 1953, p. 335; Bergström 1955, pp. 304, 346; Larsen 1960, pp. 91–92, 130–31; Friedländer 1967–76, vol. 9a (1972), pp. 28–29, 64, no. 65; De Jongh 1974, p. 185; Hand 1978, pp. 155–58, 299, no. 32; Mundy 1981–82, p. 221; Silver 1984, p. 177; Snyder 1985, p. 417; Metropolitan Museum 1987, pp. 12, 53; Hand 1989, pp. 10–13; Belting and Kruse 1994, pp. 474–75.

In depicting him this way, Joos was reflecting contemporary attitudes that were in part inspired by the writings of Jean Gerson, chancellor of the University of Paris and dean of Sint-Donaaskerk (Saint Donatian's) in Bruges during the fourteenth century. Gerson championed Joseph and saw the Holy Family as the equivalent of an earthly trinity in which the saint played a featured part. In the fifteenth century Joseph was elevated to a new position as the earthly father, chaste husband, and protector of Christ and the Virgin. By 1479 Pope Sixtus IV had introduced The Feast of Saint Joseph into the liturgical calendar, and about 1490 the Brothers of the Common Life issued the first account of Joseph's life printed in the Netherlands, *Historie van den heiligen Joseph*; this was followed in 1522 by the earliest scholarly treatise on the saint, the *Summa de donis S. Josephi*, by the Dominican Isidro Isolani.

Often, Joseph serves as an exemplar of humility and devotion, and it is as such that Joos presented him in our painting. Having just removed his glasses, the beardless old man looks up from the scroll he has been reading to witness the fulfillment of its text, which begins with the enthusiastic greeting of Elizabeth to Mary, the pregnant mother of the Lord: "et benedictus fructus ventris tui" (and blessed is the fruit of thy womb) (Luke 1:42). It continues with five lines from the Magnificat that constitute Mary's response to Elizabeth, a hymn of praise uttered by the Virgin in celebration of Christ's Incarnation and God's omnipotence and vision of mankind's future (Luke 1:46–50). Here the words of the Magnificat serve to tie together the symbolic meanings of the objects shown at the upper right and on the parapet below the figures.

On a shelf on the back wall and hanging on a hook beneath it are a small wooden box, a tightly sealed carafe, and a whisk broom—all traditional symbols of the Virgin's purity. Spilling out into the viewer's space on the foreground ledge is an arrangement of objects that refer to Christ's Incarnation and the redemption of man: the wine in the beaker and the grapes on the pewter platter signify the Eucharist; the pomegranate, with its many parts in one whole and its blood red color, may symbolize the Church as well as Christ's Passion; and the cherries stand for paradise. The meat of the open walnut suggests Christ's divine nature, while the shell represents the wood of the cross, or *lignum crucis*. The Christ Child as Redeemer in the guise of the New Adam holds an apple in his left hand, and with his right hand he gently touches the wrist of his mother, the New Eve, his co-Redemptrix.

Joos blurs the distinction between objects presented as symbols and those presented as part of everyday life. Prominently placed in the foreground, the glass of wine, knife, and plate of fruit are, in fact, an early embodiment of the genre of still life, which by the seventeenth century would develop into an independent art form. It must have been the depiction of the still life and also the charming sense of intimacy conveyed by the vignette of family life that appealed to contemporary viewers, who especially favored the image. Our picture, which dates to about 1512–13, is one of the earliest of many widely popular variations on this subject that were produced in Joos's Antwerp workshop for sale both locally and abroad. The extremely delicate modeling (in the Virgin's face), subtle passages of transparent materials (in the veil, for example), reflected light (in the still life), and a reliance upon decorative, sinuous line to describe forms mark it as a work that precedes Joos's panels with more robust figures and stronger chiaroscuro effects derived from Italian models.

Friedländer lists at least four variants of this composition, only one of which has been located. This is a modified replica in the Art Museum of the Ateneum, Helsinki, by a follower of Joos, which repeats the figures of the Virgin, Child, and Saint Joseph but places them in an elaborate Renaissance architectural setting. MWA

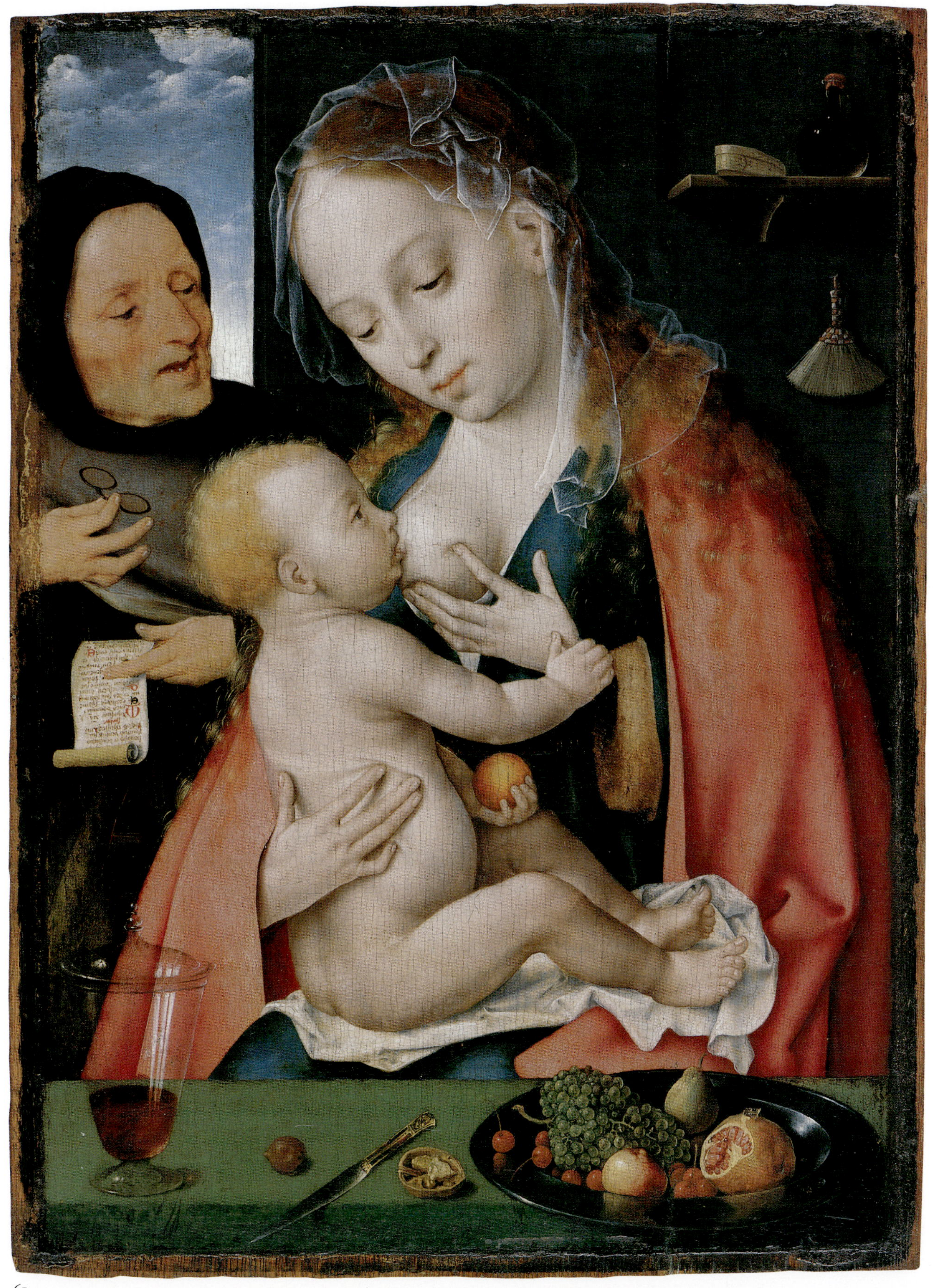

61

Workshop of Joos van Cleve

62. The Holy Family, about 1515

Oil on wood, 20⅜ x 14⅝ in. (51.8 x 37.1 cm)
Bequest of George Blumenthal, 1941 41.190.19

Provenance: George and Florence Blumenthal, New York.

References: Friedländer 1916, p. 185; Rubinstein 1916, pp. 343ff.; Conway 1921, p. 407; Baldass 1925, p. 35, no. 107; Friedländer 1924–37, vol. 9 (1931), pp. 39ff.; Wehle and Salinger 1947, p. 135; Friedländer 1967–76, vol. 11a (1972), p. 65, no. 66m.

As Joos van Cleve's early depictions of the Holy Family (cat. no. 61) gained popularity, the artist developed methods to standardize production so that multiple versions of them could efficiently be turned out for sale on the open market. This *Holy Family* is one of many variations on a pattern developed in Joos's shop and carried out by assistants, who used a pricked cartoon to transfer exactly the master's design to numerous panels. The standard pattern apparently provided the starting point for these works, in which changes of various types were made during the painting process.

The prototype of the present composition appears to be a *Holy Family* by Joos in the National Gallery, London. Apart from showing the Christ Child standing (with a strategically placed rosary across his groin) and the Virgin's left hand in a slightly different pose, the model is nearly identical to our painting. Infrared reflectography of the London panel indicates that the Christ Child originally reclined as he does in our version and that his posture was altered as the picture was developed. Another variant, in the Art Institute of Chicago, is closely allied to our painting in terms of the poses of the figures but substitutes a vase with columbine and a pink for the vase of lilies and the cherries our Virgin holds. In a third variation, in the Lehman Collection (fig. 83), an especially self-assured Christ Child stands facing the spectator, and, instead of a plain background, a brocade hangs from a marble column and there is a view to a landscape behind the figures.

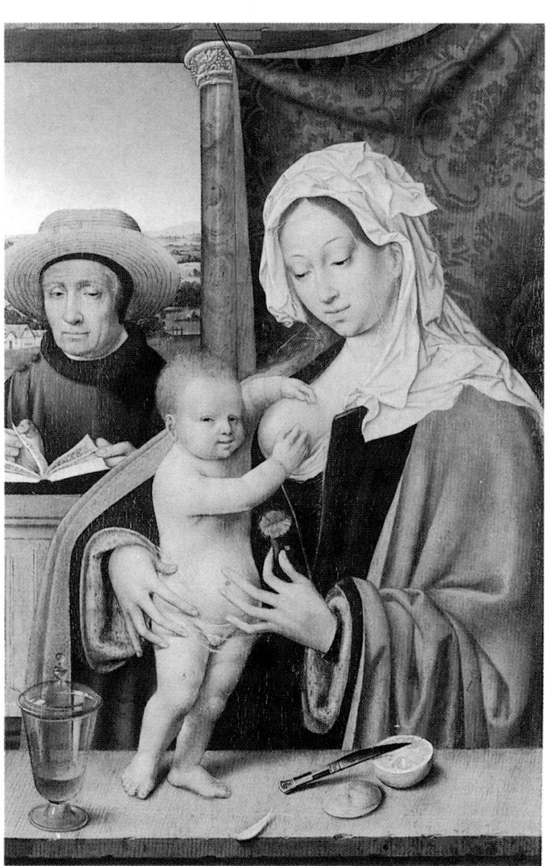

Fig. 83. Workshop of Joos van Cleve, *The Holy Family,* about 1530. Oil on wood. Robert Lehman Collection, The Metropolitan Museum of Art, New York

This *Holy Family* is as tightly cropped but not as densely packed with objects as the related Friedsam *Holy Family* (cat. no. 61). Here the three figures are presented before a bright green background and behind a stone parapet, in the tradition of contemporary portraiture. Joseph is not distracted by the Virgin nursing the Child as he is in the Friedsam picture but, with his spectacles on and wearing the straw hat of a traveler (a motif perhaps borrowed from representations of the Flight into Egypt), is engrossed in an unidentifiable text. The formal still life of the Friedsam example is considerably reduced in the present painting: a glass contains a stalk of lilies (*Lilium candidum*) denoting the Virgin's purity; nearby are half a lemon (expressing the bitterness of Christ's Passion) supporting a knife blade, and a stem of three cherries, the fruit of paradise, which the Virgin holds.

In a somewhat less than successful adaptation of the design of the London prototype, the Christ Child appears to float on his white cloth, supported only by the Virgin's right hand at his back. With both hands he grasps the Virgin's breast to nurse from it. Like the Christ in Gerard David's *Rest on the Flight into Egypt* (cat. no. 82), this Child looks out of the picture and engages the viewer, implying that even as he derives his physical nourishment from the

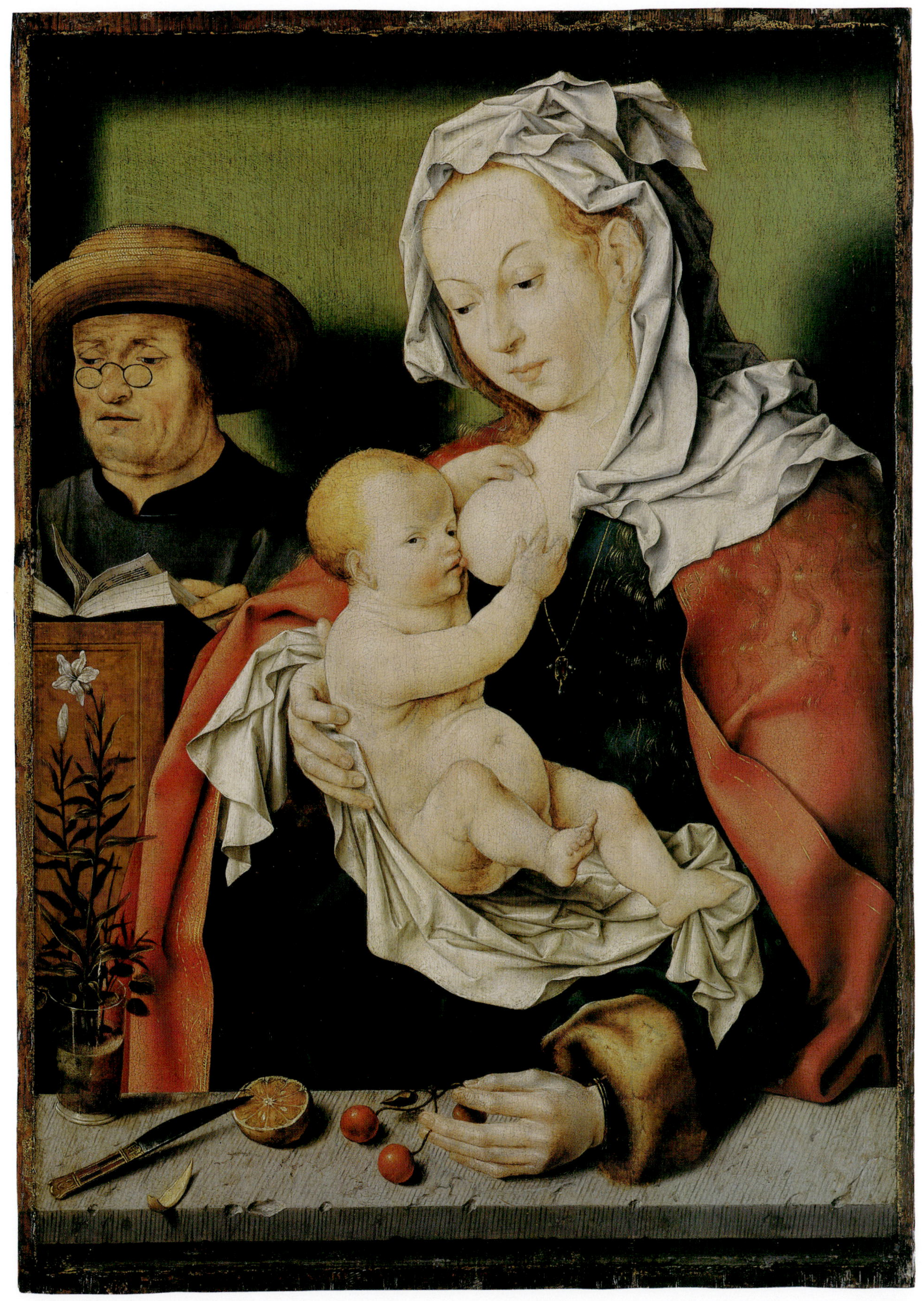

Virgin's milk, so too will the devout find spiritual food in the blood he sheds for their redemption.

The figures do not exhibit Joos's subtle modeling of forms, and there is a certain insensitivity in the facial expressions of Joseph, Mary, and the Christ Child, indicating that the panel is a product of Joos's workshop rather than from the master's own hand. Its robust figures, however, reflect the development of Joos's style, suggesting a date later than that of the Friedsam painting, probably about 1515. This date would be in keeping with Friedländer's assignment of the London prototype to the same period.

MWA

Netherlandish (Antwerp) Painter

63. Virgin Suckling the Child, about 1520

Tempera and gold on linen, 15⅝ x 11⅞ in. (39.7 x 30.2 cm)
Inscribed (on simulated frame): (sides and top) Ave • regina • celorum • ave • domina • angelorum • salve • radix sancta • ex • qua • mundo • lux • [est] • orta (Hail [Mary], Queen of Heaven, Hail, Mistress of angels, Hail Root [of Jesse], Whence the world's true light was born.); (base) Beata • es • maria • qu[ae] • omniu[m] • p[o]rtasti / creatorem • genuisti • eum qui • te fecit / et • in aeternum • permane[s] Virgo (Blessed art thou, O Virgin Mary, who didst bear the creator of all things, thou didst bring forth him who made thee, and remainest forever a virgin.)
Gift of Robert Lehman, 1945
45.170.1

At least eight surviving paintings on linen and three in oil on panel show this tender Virgin, her eyes modestly downcast, looking at the Christ Child, who eagerly grasps her breast to nurse. This *Maria lactans*, or the Virgin suckling the infant Jesus, may ultimately derive from the Campin-inspired *Virgin and Child in an Apse* (cat. no. 47), and its proliferation in the early sixteenth century could well have been tied to the veneration of a particular image that was believed to have miraculous powers. Friedländer (in Cust 1907, p. 232) suggested that the relatively inexpensive paintings on linen could have been sold to pilgrims as souvenirs of visits to such a revered icon and as reminders of indulgences received upon reciting the associated prayers.

In view of the inscriptions on these paintings, it is possible that they were connected with a devotion of a particular kind. Beginning at the lower left and proceeding around the top and right side of the picture is the first stanza of an anthem recited in the evening at Compline, the last of the Hours of the Virgin (a devotional text found in both breviaries and Books of Hours): "Hail [Mary], Queen of Heaven, Hail, Mistress of angels, Hail Root [of Jesse], Whence the world's true light was born." At the base of the image is a response found in the Hours of the Virgin after the second lesson at Matins: "Blessed art thou, O Virgin Mary, who didst bear the creator of all things, thou didst bring forth him who made thee, and remainest forever a virgin."

The *radix sancta*, or Root of Jesse, mentioned in the first inscription indicates the earthly genealogy of Christ and is sometimes connected with the Immaculate Conception; the second text is more specifically related to that doctrine. The image of the Virgin portrayed here, nursing, behind a window (to heaven), and surrounded with radiating flames as the Virgin of the Sun, is consistent with representations of the Virgin of the Immaculate Conception.

The doctrine of the Immaculate Conception, which holds that Mary was conceived without sin, was debated throughout the fifteenth century and was ultimately accepted: Pope Sixtus IV introduced offices for the Feast of the Immaculate Conception in 1476 and 1480 and guaranteed indulgences to those who celebrated this office in bulls of 1476 and 1477. The movement to honor the principle of the Immaculate Conception was especially strong in France, Germany, and Spain—particularly at the courts of the Habsburgs and the *reyes católicos.* The dogma gained considerable popularity under King Ferdinand and Queen Isabella, and a number of convents and monasteries featuring special devotions

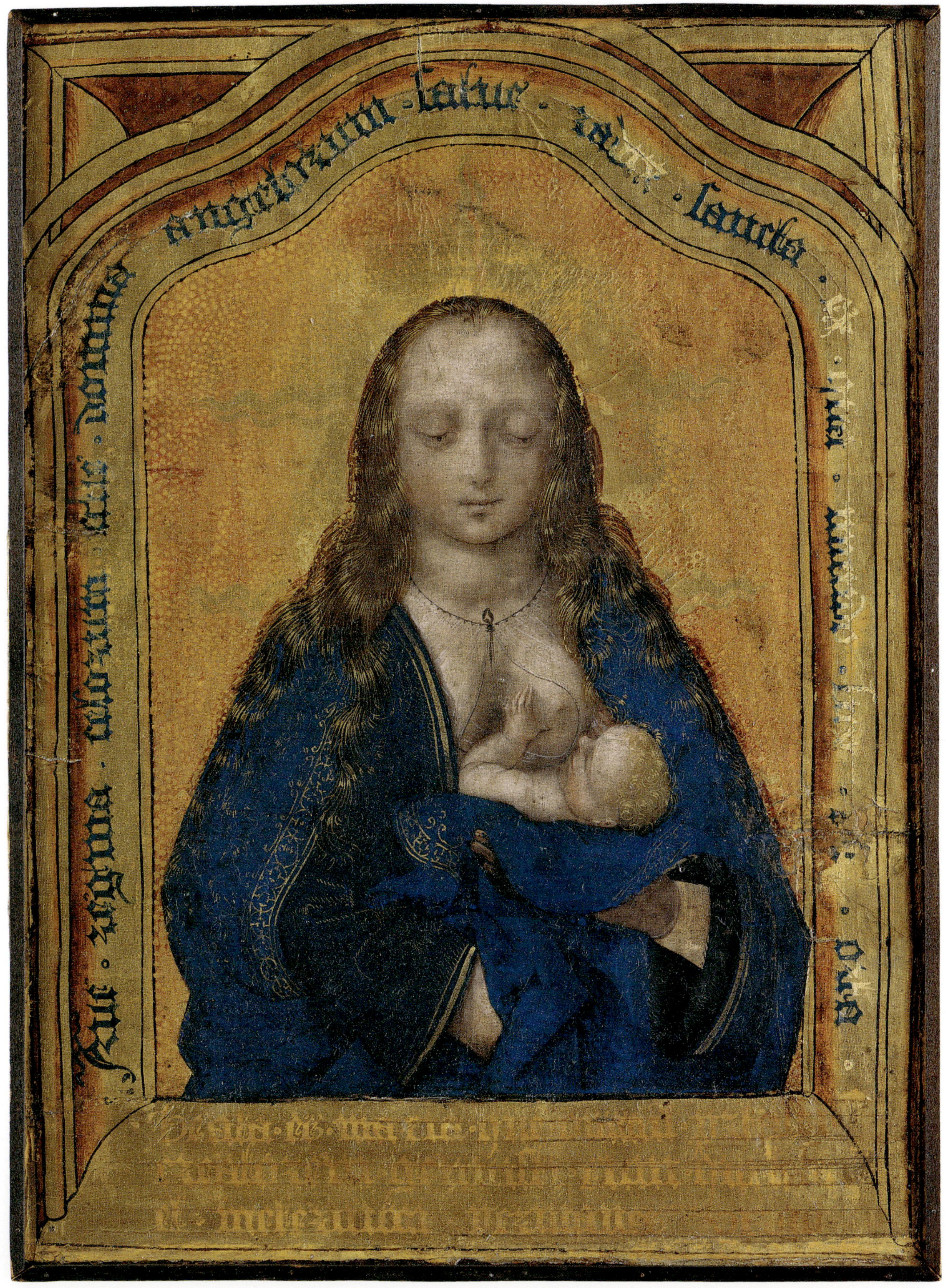
Aue · regina · celorum · aue · domina
angelorum · salue

Provenance: Robert Lehman, New York.

References: Cust 1907, pp. 231–32; Baldass 1931; Wehle and Salinger 1947, p. 113; Levi-d'Ancona 1957, pp. 13, 55, 56, 62, 65; Ringbom 1962, pp. 326–30; Martens 1986; Eisler 1989, pp. 236–39; Wolfthal 1989, pp. 80–85, esp. p. 81; Mayberry 1991; Stratton 1994, pp. 12–20, 35–39.

connected with it were founded in Spain. It is against this background that the function of our painting and others of its type can perhaps best be evaluated. Indeed, Martens submits that the two prayers inscribed on our picture and its relatives were said by members of religious orders dedicated to the Immaculate Conception, and it is therefore possible that these small paintings on linen were mass-produced to aid them in their observances.

The frontal, moon-faced Virgin and the pudgy Christ Child seen here are types made popular by Quentin Massys and his followers in Antwerp (examples are in the Musées Royaux des Beaux-Arts de Belgique, Brussels, and the Newhouse Gallery, New York). Martens has identified eight paintings on linen showing two close variations of this image, which he attributes to the Master of the Louvre Madonna. Although all appear to have been made in the same workshop, differences among them suggest that they were produced by several artists.

MWA

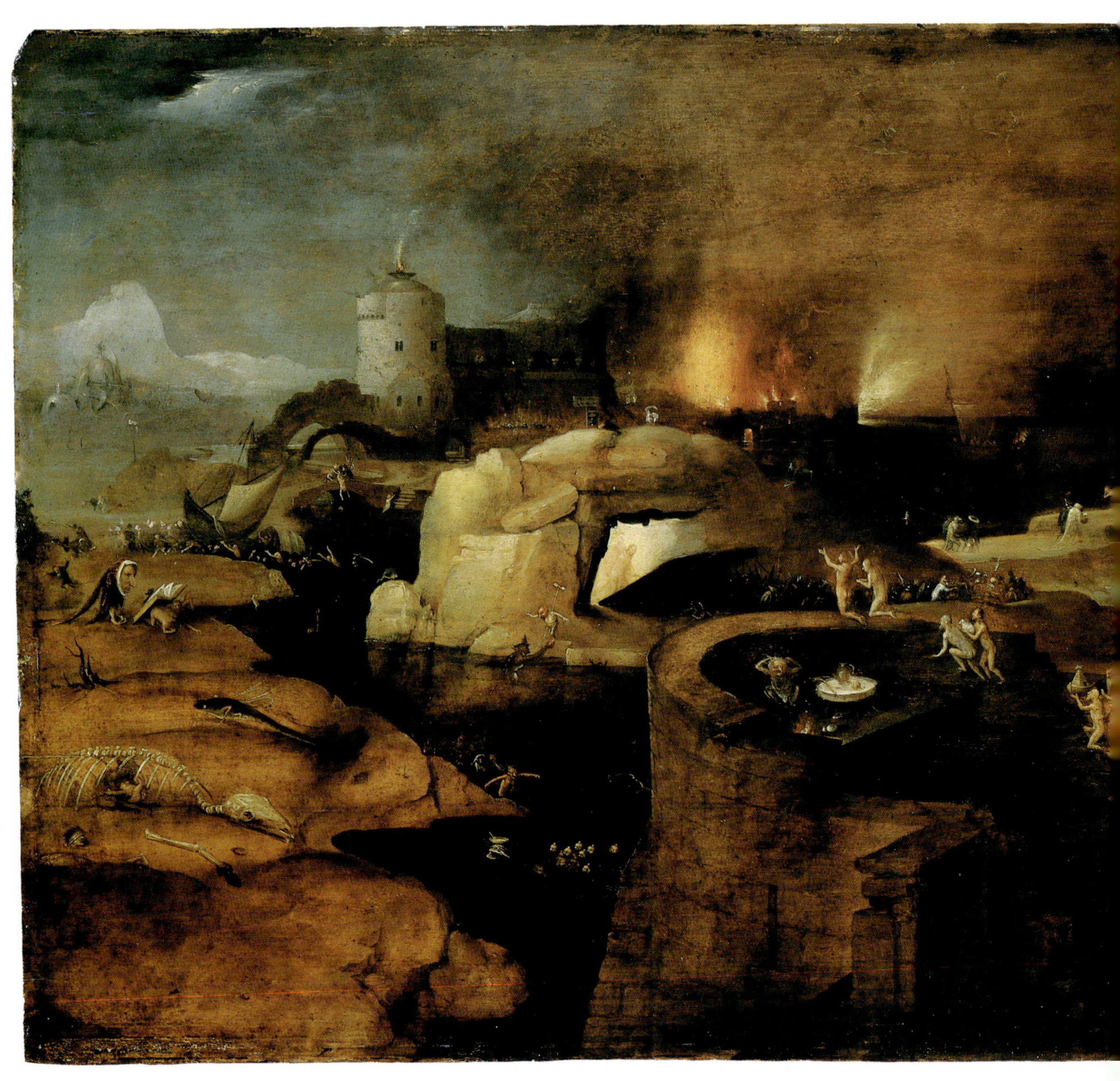

Style of Hieronymus Bosch

64. Christ's Descent into Hell, 1530–60

Our picture illustrates a passage in the Gospel of Nicodemus in the Apocryphal New Testament (16:1–13) that recounts how Christ descended to the gates of hell after the Crucifixion. There, in a voice like the sound of thunder and the rushing of winds, he demanded, "Lift up your gates, Princes [of Hell] . . . and the King of Glory shall come in," and proceeded to rescue the souls of the just, the patriarchs, and the prophets.

Christ, miraculously illuminated in the light of glory, breaks down the gates of hell at the side of a rocky tunnel. Opposite him are Adam and Eve, with arms outstretched and kneeling at the top of a circular tower in ruins. Behind them, mounting the

Oil on wood, 21 x 46 in. (53.3 x 116.8 cm)
Harris Brisbane Dick Fund, 1926 26.244

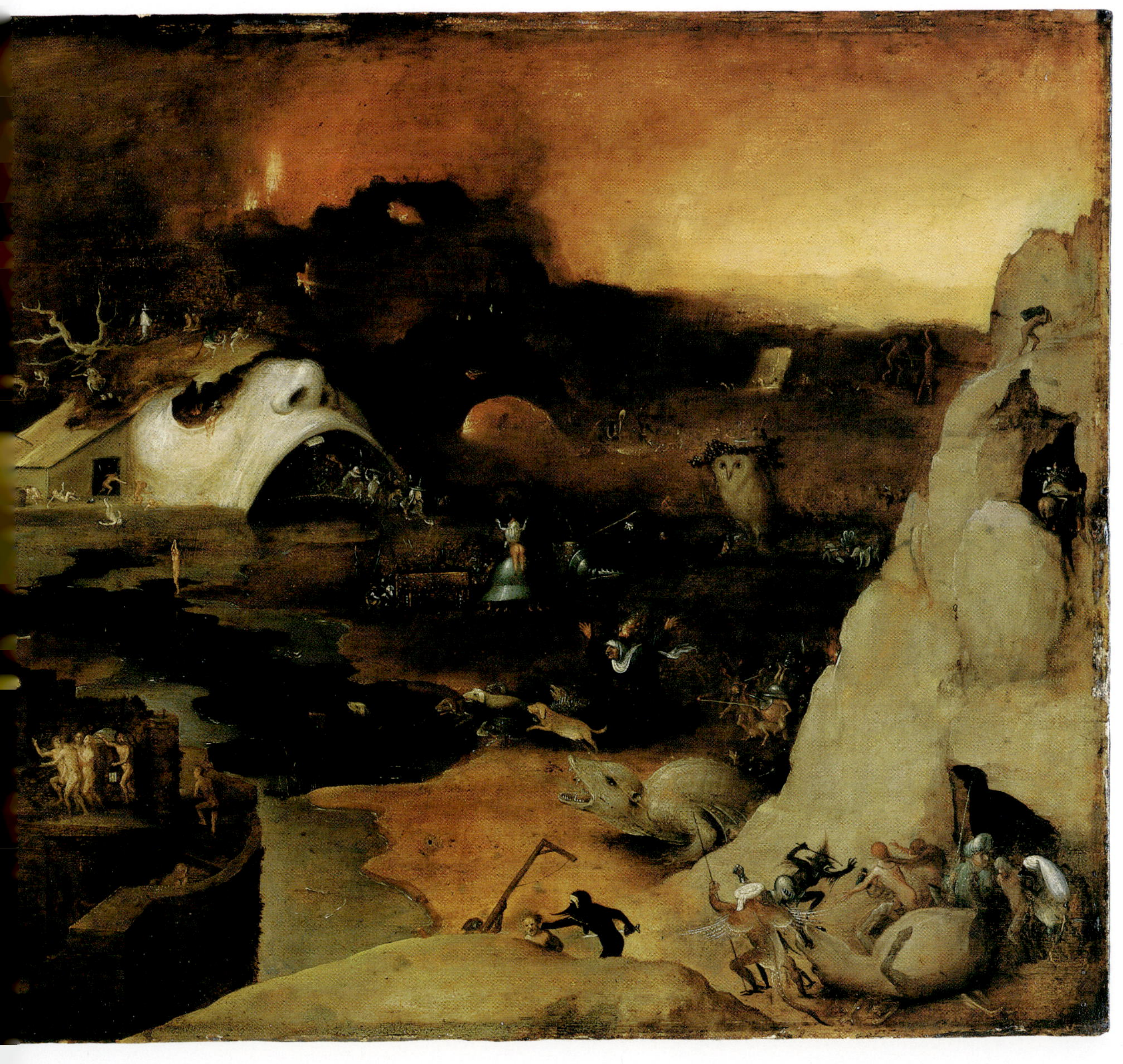

Provenance: Philipp, count of Saint Genois, Vienna (before 1895); [Kominik, Prague, after 1895]; František Kominik, Prague (until 1926); [Hugo Feigl, Prague, 1926].

References: James 1926, p. 139; Burroughs 1927, pp. 272–74; Wehle and Salinger 1947, pp. 123–24; Bergmans in Brussels 1963, pp. 136–37; De Tolnay 1966, p. 385; Friedländer 1967–76, vol. 5 (1969), p. 85, no. 88; Corwin 1976, pp. 127–30, 406–8, 483–84, 521–23; Unverfehrt 1980, pp. 201–2, 289, no. 158.

winding staircase from the depths of hell, come Old Testament figures carrying their attributes: Abraham and Isaac with the sacrificial ram, Noah bearing a model of the ark, Moses with the tablets, David with his harp, the repentant thief and the cross, Lot and his daughters. The last man may be the lantern-bearing Diogenes.

Portrayed as hell on earth and seen from above, the landscape, illuminated by the city on fire in the background, is a vast, murky, and desolate place with details—such as the river Styx at the left, the owl near center, and fire at the right—associated with evil and calamity. Its fantastic features are directly derived from the vocabulary of Hieronymus Bosch, whose work continued to influence landscapes of hell throughout the sixteenth century; the skeletons, man-eating reptiles, nightmarish mutants, and figures with machines of war recall details in Bosch's *Garden of Earthly Delights* (Prado, Madrid) and *Temptation of Saint Anthony* (Museu Nacional de Arte Antigua, Lisbon). Our panel juxtaposes such bizarre imaginary motifs with a realistic depiction of a city with burning buildings, towers, bridges, and ruins: a combination characteristically used in the second third of the sixteenth century, which saw a revival of interest in Bosch.

Fiery landscapes and hell scenes, used with such subjects as the Last Judgment, the Temptation of Saint Anthony, Saint Christopher, and Lot and His Daughters, were extremely popular during the sixteenth century; moreover, subjects such as death, the afterlife, and the fear of hell and its terrible punishments were vividly described in contemporary writings. This trend can best be explained by the belief generally held in northern Europe that the end of the world was imminent. However, a new taste for dramatic representation of light with vivid dark contrasts and eruptions of devouring flame may also have inspired the mass production in the Netherlands and particularly in Antwerp of a new genre of cabinet picture centered on such scenes.

There is great diversity of opinion regarding the date of our picture, which has sometimes been considered to have been produced during the lifetime of Bosch (1450–1516). De Tolnay, however, has proposed a date of about 1530–50. Corwin classifies our composition among the Bosch Revival group of paintings of the 1560s that do not have a direct source in the works of Bosch—who does not seem to have painted this subject himself—but copy his style. Bergmans attributes a nearly identical version (formerly Mangilli-Valmarana collection, Venice) to Gillis Mostaert (1528–1560) and observes that the figure of Diogenes holding the lantern does not appear in the north before 1559, when Vascosan published a French translation of Plutarch's *Lives*. Another detail found in our picture that may argue for a date in the 1550s or later is the conspicuous sinking house in the form of a gigantic head, a motif that appears in Bruegel's drawing the *Temptation of Saint Anthony*, which is dated 1559 (Ashmolean Museum of Art and Archaeology, Oxford). VS

Workshop of Herri met de Bles

65. The Temptation of Saint Anthony, about 1550–60

Oil on wood; overall 8⅞ x 13¾ in. (22.5 x 34.9 cm); painted surface 8½ x 13⅜ in. (21.6 x 34 cm)
Bequest of Harry G. Sperling, 1971 1976.100.1

In a doomsday landscape filled with monsters, a frail and diminutive Saint Anthony kneels, praying, in a ruined chapel. He is situated in the center of the space between the gaping mouth of hell and a triptych of the Crucifixion on the altar. The saint extends his arms, imploring the painted image of the cross to protect him, for a grotesque demon has hold of his cloak and is trying to drag him down into the inferno. A spectacular conflagration fills the entire upper left side.

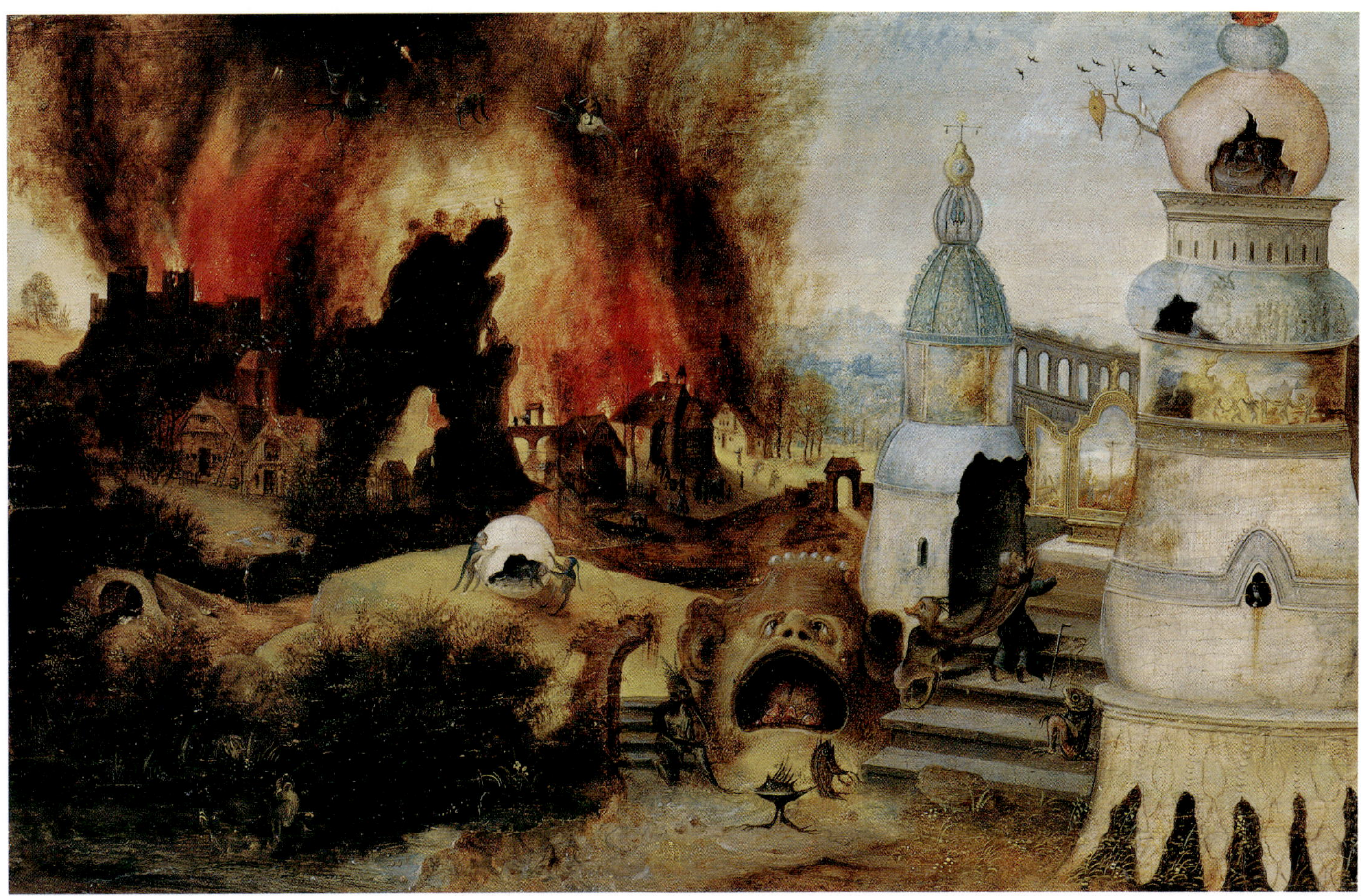

65

The Temptation of Saint Anthony, as inspired by Voragine's account in the *Golden Legend*, was one of the most popular subjects in sixteenth-century landscape painting (see entry for cat. no. 88). According to Corwin, the representation of the theme was bound up with the mission of the Antonine order, which treated patients suffering from venereal diseases, known collectively as "Saint Anthony's Fire." This reference may be intended by the burning hospital shown at the left, as well as by the flock of black birds, symbolizing the sin of lust, that survey the scene from above. In the fantastic structure at the right is an owl, traditionally a sign of calamity and doom and also a motif used as a signature by Herri met de Bles, who, along with Joachim Patinir, was one of the earliest practitioners of pure landscape painting in the southern Netherlands.

This picture exhibits the miniature-like quality of Herri met de Bles's own small-scale panels and is typical of paintings produced in great numbers in his shop by collaborators who worked under his supervision. Corwin notes that in these workshop productions there is a tendency to exaggerate the characteristics of Bles's autograph panels; she dates our painting about 1550–60.

VS

Provenance: Heinz Kisters, Kreuslingen; [Julius Böhler, Munich (until 1969)]; [Kleinberger, New York, 1969–75].

References: Corwin 1976, pp. 101–3, 290, no. 79, pl. 86; Unverfehrt 1980, p. 279, no. 120; Serck 1990, vol. 4, pp. 938, 941, 943, no. 73; Serck 1991.

Style of Hieronymus Bosch

66. The Adoration of the Magi, about 1550

Oil and gold on wood, 28 x 22¼ in. (71.1 x 56.5 cm)
John Stewart Kennedy Fund, 1913 13.26

Provenance: Friedrich Lippmann, Berlin ([d. 1903]; sale, Lepke, Berlin, November 26–27, 1912, no. 38).

References: Glück 1904, p. 182; Burroughs 1913, pp. 130–33, ill.; Friedländer 1916, p. 74; Schürmeyer 1923, pp. 34–36, 38, pl. 2; Friedländer 1924–37, vol. 5 (1927), pp. 88–89, 91, 143, no. 66, fig. 66; De Tolnay 1937, pp. 103, 128, no. 47, fig. 114a; Held 1947, pp. 139–40; Wehle and Salinger 1947, pp. 121–23, ill.; Bax 1949, pp. 248–50, 253 n. 50, 254 n. 87, 264, 272, 274 n. 15, 323; Friedländer 1956, pp. 56–58, colorpl. 6; Larsen 1960, pp. 98, 132–33, fig. 37; Eisler 1964, p. 104; De Tolnay 1966, p. 383, no. 47, fig. 36; Friedländer 1967–76, vol. 5 (1967), pp. 49, 81, no. 66, pl. 45; Lemmens and Taverne 1967, p. 77; Bax 1979, pp. 328 n. 50, 329–30, 349, 357, 401; Unverfehrt 1980, pp. 123–25, 127, 147, 150, 249–50, no. 23, fig. 66; Metropolitan Museum 1987, pp. 12, 45, color ills. pp. 44–45; Garrido 1990, p. 1; Van Schoute 1990b, p. 1; Ainsworth 1992b, pp. 59, 68–71, 75, nn. 18, 20, 28, 30, figs. 12, 17–19.

The paintings of Hieronymus Bosch enjoyed enormous popularity in the Netherlands and abroad, particularly in Italy and Spain. This *Adoration of the Magi*, probably made after workshop patterns, was obviously created to satisfy the great demand for pictures in his style. Although dendrochronological evidence suggests a felling date of about 1472 for the tree that furnished the support, our panel was most likely painted much later, about the middle of the sixteenth century.

The attribution of the present picture to Bosch was unquestioned until 1937, when De Tolnay listed it with contested works. In 1964 Eisler called it "a charming but inconsequential Boschian pastiche." Since then the sources of elements in our painting have been noted in a chronologically diverse group of autograph paintings by Bosch: the *Garden of Earthly Delights* (Prado, Madrid) for the figure of the Virgin; the central panel of the Epiphany Triptych (Prado, Madrid) for the landscape; and the *Adoration of the Magi* (John G. Johnson Collection, Philadelphia Museum of Art) for the two standing kings, particularly for the exaggerated facial features of the black magus. Moreover, an investigation of the underdrawings on the panel has revealed the hand of a follower rather than the characteristics of Bosch's own execution (Ainsworth 1992b).

In our composition the oldest magus kneels before the Christ Child offering gold, in homage to his kingship; the black magus carries frankincense, symbolizing his divinity; and the youngest king brings myrrh, foreshadowing his death. The vessels held by the magi are described with considerable care. The one carried by the black magus has a pelican piercing its breast with its beak, signifying Christ's sacrifice for humankind. A similar object appears in the hands of the black magus in the central panel of Bosch's Epiphany Triptych, and Schürmeyer suggests that containers of this kind may have been used as props in mystery plays in Bosch's hometown of 's-Hertogenbosch.

The carefully observed costumes reflect sixteenth-century fashions worn by men and women of high birth. Characteristic details include wide collars, the particular lengths of garments, the fur trim at cuffs and hems, and the distinctive shape of the costume of the dark-bearded magus. The highly decorated gold arms of the black magus were typical in Europe until late in the century. His fist shield, or buckler, hangs from the left side of the scabbard of his scimitar, and both fist shield and scimitar are suspended from his sword belt. The curve of his scimitar is an iconographic sign for the Orient, as is the Asian pattern on the costume worn by the magus behind him. Hanging from the mouth of the animal-headed pommel is a loop that probably secured a chain, which likely served as a knuckle guard, to the handle of the sword. An example of a chain of this type appears on the sword handle in the right foreground of Quentin Massys's *Adoration of the Magi* (cat. no. 99).

Our composition is set apart from Bosch's autograph work by the emphasis on the tunneling perspective of the ruined castle, with the Virgin aligned along the central axis, as well as by the diffident fashion in which the figures occupy the resulting space: the kneeling magus in the foreground, for example, is quite distant from the Child, toward whom his gaze is presumably directed. There are incidental details of haunting charm—the single egg in a window of the tower, the figures peering in through windows of the shelter (one leans in to warm his hand at a fire in the back of the enclosure)—but these do not really counterbalance the disturbing sense of emptiness. The picture is a testament to both the enduring appeal of Boschian figure types and their basic incompatibility with the space of a Renaissance painting.

A copy after our painting, attributed to the Studio of Hieronymus Bosch, in the Museum Boijmans Van Beuningen in Rotterdam, was also made about 1550. DCS

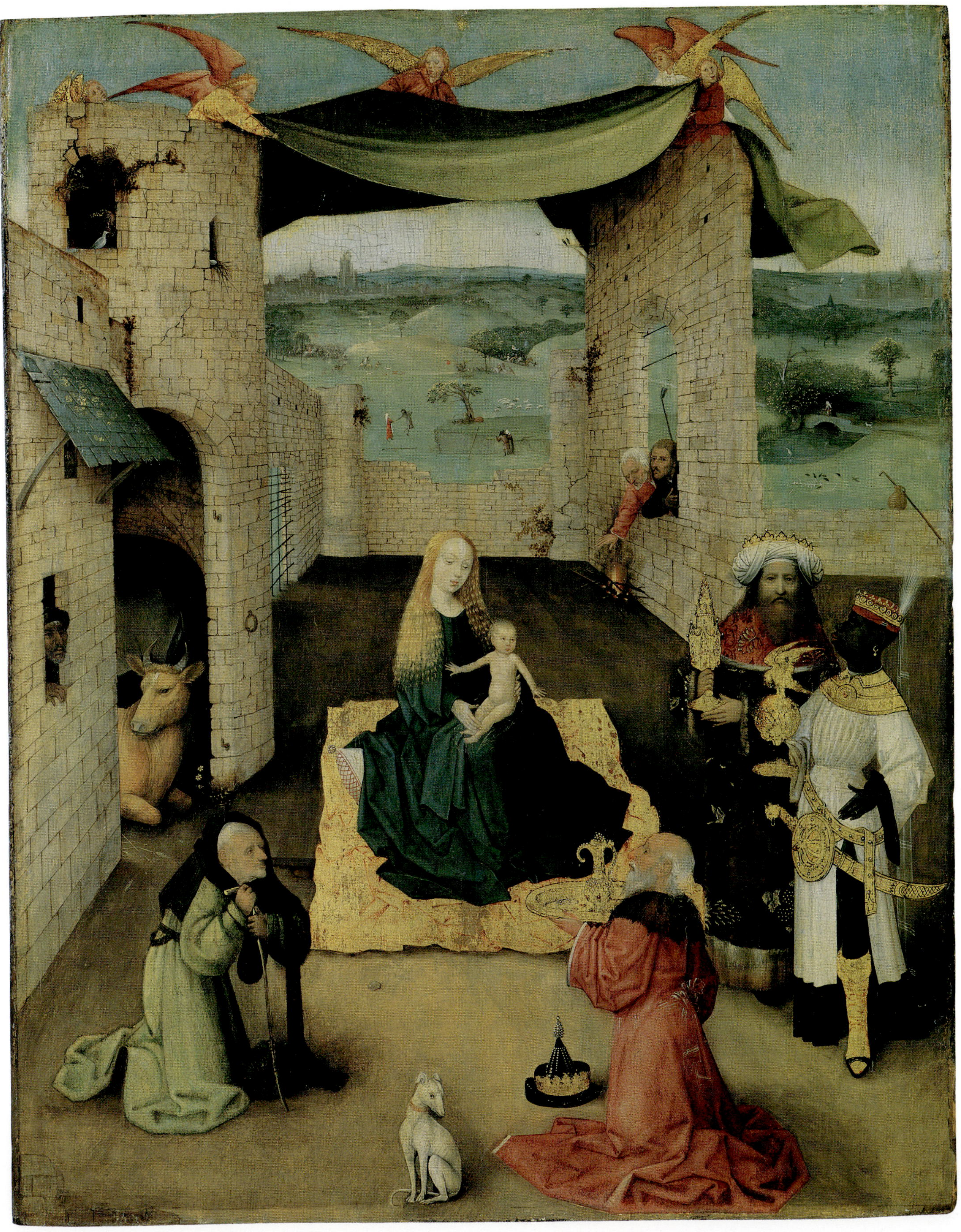

Netherlandish (Antwerp Mannerist) Painter

67. The Adoration of the Magi, about 1520

Oil on wood, 27⅛ x 21½ in. (68.9 x 54.6 cm)
Signed (on right pilaster): [e a] [monogram]
Bequest of Helen L. Bullard, in memory of Harold C. Bullard, 1921 21.132.2

Provenance: Helen Lister Bullard, New York (by 1916–21).

References: Friedländer 1915, pp. 65–91; Kernodle 1943, pp. 26–27; Wehle and Salinger 1947, p. 127; Bruges 1969, no. 90, pp. 162, 291–92; Jacobus de Voragine 1969, pp. 84–88; Johnson collection 1972, p. 55; Friedländer 1967–76, vol. 11 (1974), p. 70, pl. 29b; Newton 1975, pp. 226–27; Ewing 1978, pp. 21–22, 26, 118–21; Szmodis-Eszlary and Urbach 1990, pp. 21–22; Urbach 1991, p. 81.

The Adoration of the Magi was by far the favorite theme of the Antwerp Mannerists, whose workshops mass-produced images such as the present picture for the Antwerp market and for export, making exact replicas of entire compositions or parts of compositions. Antwerp Mannerist painting is characterized by flamboyant style with depictions of fantastic architecture and exotic costumes painted with elegant chromatic effects; however, the anonymous author of our *Adoration of the Magi,* who signed himself with the monogram [e a] on the pilaster at the right, exercised considerable restraint. An identical composition, without the monogram, in the Szépmüvészeti Múzeum, Budapest, shows variations in handling that suggest it was executed by another artist working in the same shop as our painter.

Ewing argues that the composition of our picture derives from a late work, now lost, by Jan de Beer (about 1475–1536), one of the few leading Antwerp Mannerists recorded in the city's archives. And indeed the architectural setting, with its central arch through which a distinctive landscape is viewed, and the motif of the draped curtain in the present work are very similar to details in De Beer's Nativity Altarpiece (Wallraf-Richartz-Museum, Cologne). Friedländer (1915), however, identified the prototype of our painting as an *Adoration of the Magi* in the Philadelphia Museum of Art now attributed to an anonymous master active in Antwerp during the first quarter of the sixteenth century. The composition and figures of our picture are certainly based on the pattern used in the Philadelphia model, but in the latter the architectural setting is limited to the central arch and the draped curtain has been left out. An anonymous *Adoration of the Magi* in the Staatliche Kunsthalle, Karlsruhe, similar in composition to the Philadelphia example but much more theatrical and exuberant in its handling, is dated 1519.

Our artist's treatment of rich satins, brocades, and velvets echoes the technique of *couleur changeante* that is applied with such mastery in the Philadelphia and Karlsruhe versions. The elaborate costumes he has given the magi are unrelated to contemporary fashion and recall theater. A connection to theater is evoked as well by the staged-looking arrangement of the magi and Saint Joseph around the Virgin and the formal postures of the figures, which create the effect of a tableau vivant of the kind presented in religious dramas performed in churches and processions. In this context, it is worth pointing out that in 1515 Jan de Beer is reported to have been "greatly occupied with the making of stages and pictures for the plays" commissioned on the occasion of the Joyous Entry of Charles V to Antwerp and Mechelen. VS

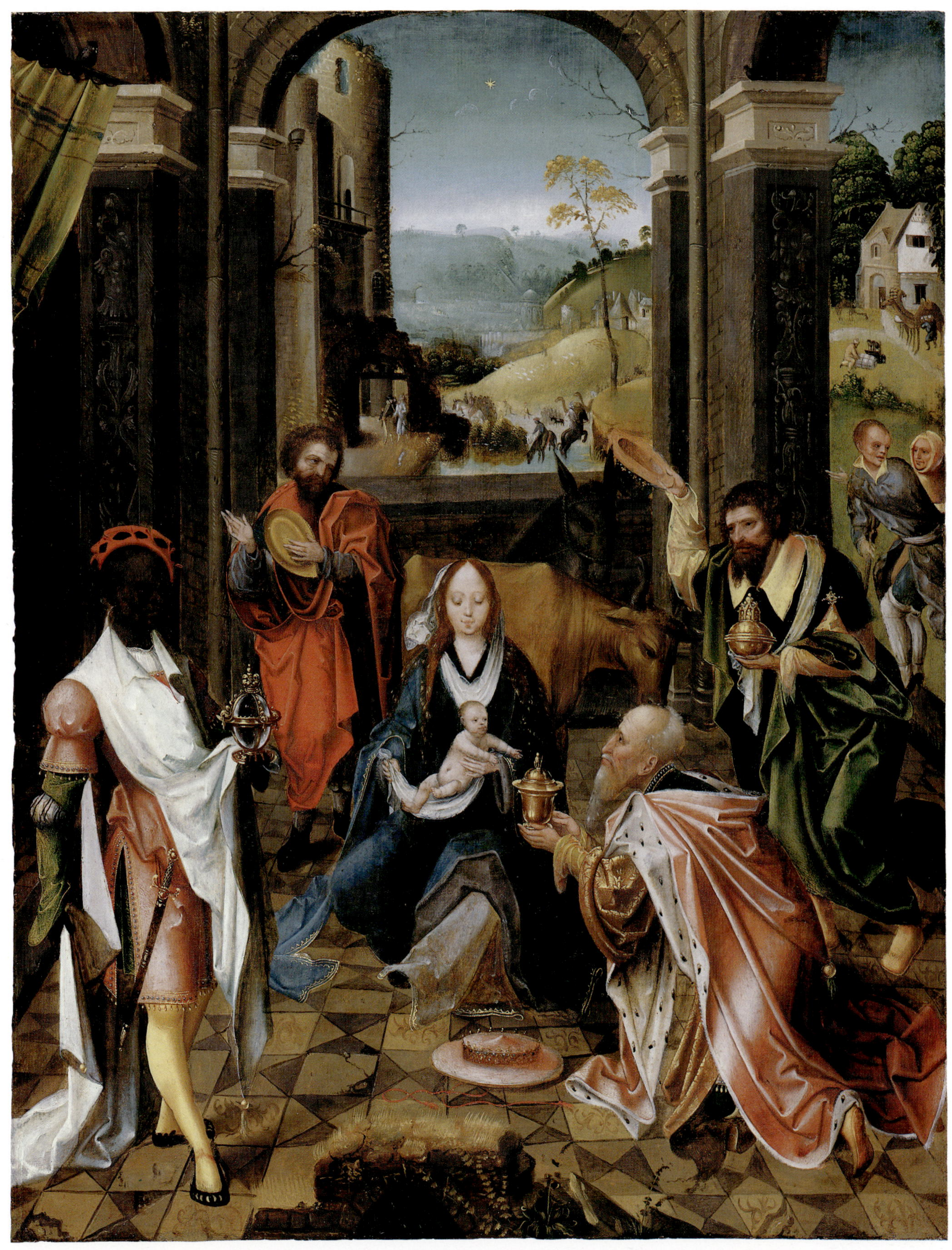

Netherlandish (Antwerp Mannerist) Painters, first quarter of 16th century

68. The Last Supper, 1515–20

Oil on wood, shaped top; central panel, overall, with engaged frame, 47 x 33¾ in. (119.4 x 85.7 cm); left wing, overall, with engaged frame, 47 x 16⅞ in. (119.4 x 42.9 cm); right wing, overall, with engaged frame, 47⅛ x 17 in. (119.7 x 43.2 cm)
Inscribed (on frame): (under left wing) CENANTIBVSILLIS, ACZEPIT; *(under central panel)* IESVS PANEM BENEDIXIT, [AC]FREJIT DEDITQV[E]; *(under right wing)* DISCIPVLIS, SVIS, DICENS *(And as they were eating, Jesus took bread, and blessed it, and brake it, and gave it to the disciples, and said . . . [Matthew 26:26]); (right wing, on tent in background)* AVE MARIA . . .
Gift of J. Pierpont Morgan, 1917 17.190.18a–c

Provenance: Comte de Montebello, Paris (until 1909); [Kleinberger, Paris and New York (1909)]; J. Pierpont Morgan, New York (1909–13).

References: Burroughs 1909a, pp. 154–55; Friedländer 1915, p. 81, no. 42; Vloberg 1946, pp. 34–37; Wehle and Salinger 1947, pp. 129–30; Marlier 1966, p. 106; Schiller (1968) 1971–72, vol. 2, pp. 37–38; Bruges 1969, pp. 65–67, no. 91; Friedländer 1967–76, vol. 11 (1974), pp. 25, 71, no. 43; Welzel 1991, pp. 108–9, 158, no. 9; Van Suchtelen, Bruijnen, and Buijsen 1997, pp. 66–67.

During the first half of the sixteenth century the Last Supper, like the Adoration of the Magi, was one of the most popular subjects portrayed by Antwerp Mannerists. This exceptionally well preserved altarpiece, which is still in its original, although regilt, frame shows Adam and Eve, or the Fall of Man, on its exterior as a prelude to the interior scenes that represent man's redemption through Christ's sacrifice.

The central panel depicts the Last Supper in a fantastic setting of Renaissance architectural motifs. Christ, Saint John, and Saint Peter are seated in front of a brocade cloth of honor that hangs across an arched opening, the central column of which is surmounted by a statue of Moses holding the Ten Commandments. The beloved apostle John leans on the shoulder of Christ, who directs his blessing at Peter and an apostle drinking wine from a pitcher at the end of the table. Judas, identified by his racially stereotyped features as well as by the purse on his belt, is poised to flee the sacramental meal. While the apostles are easily recognizable types in conventional dress, the figure holding a pitcher in the left foreground bears highly individualized facial features and is dressed in the fashion of the times, suggesting that he may be the patron of the altarpiece.

According to Marlier, this panel owes its conception of enclosed space and certain details—such as the chair at the right, the dog gnawing a bone, the basket of bread, and the exaggeratedly Semitic features of Judas—to an engraving of the Last Supper by the monogrammist IAM of Zwolle, who was active during the last quarter of the fifteenth century in the northern Netherlands and Gouda in particular. The composition also recalls many other scenes of the Last Supper produced in Antwerp Mannerist workshops, for example the Last Supper Triptych (Musées Royaux des Beaux-Arts de Belgique, Brussels) and the painted shutters from the carved wooden altarpiece of the cathedral of Vasteras, Sweden, a type of ensemble made for export, especially to Scandinavia and the Rhineland.

On the interior lateral panels are two scenes from the Old Testament traditionally considered prefigurations of the Eucharist. The left section, drawing from Genesis (14:18), shows the king and high priest Melchizedek outside the gates of Salem giving bread and wine to the patriarch Abraham, who is returning triumphantly from the expedition that saved his brother Lot. The right wing depicts Moses and the Israelites in the Desert fed by the manna falling from heaven as described in Exodus (16:11–36) and Numbers (11:7–9). A woman in the center of this scene holds up a large plate to catch the wafers, which fall like snowflakes, while Moses witnesses the miracle. This iconographic program can be traced back to a precedent in Dieric Bouts's well-documented Last Supper Altarpiece of 1464–67, commissioned by the Brotherhood of Corpus Christi for Sint-Pieterskerk, Leuven, where it remains today. Bouts's model, however, includes not only the Last Supper and the same Old Testament scenes shown in our work but also two others, the Jewish Passover and Elijah's Dream—a program that, according to the contract for the altarpiece, was chosen with the help of two theologians at the time the project was commissioned.

Our own altarpiece is the product of a collaboration among anonymous artists, a typical example of the many works that resulted from the division of labor practiced in busy Antwerp Mannerist workshops in the 1520s. One painter, particularly adept at representing nudes, executed the idealized Adam and Eve of the exterior after Dürer's 1504 engraving the *Fall of Man*; another produced the highly stereotyped figures on the interior, which are characterized by stiff postures and wooden faces and seem to

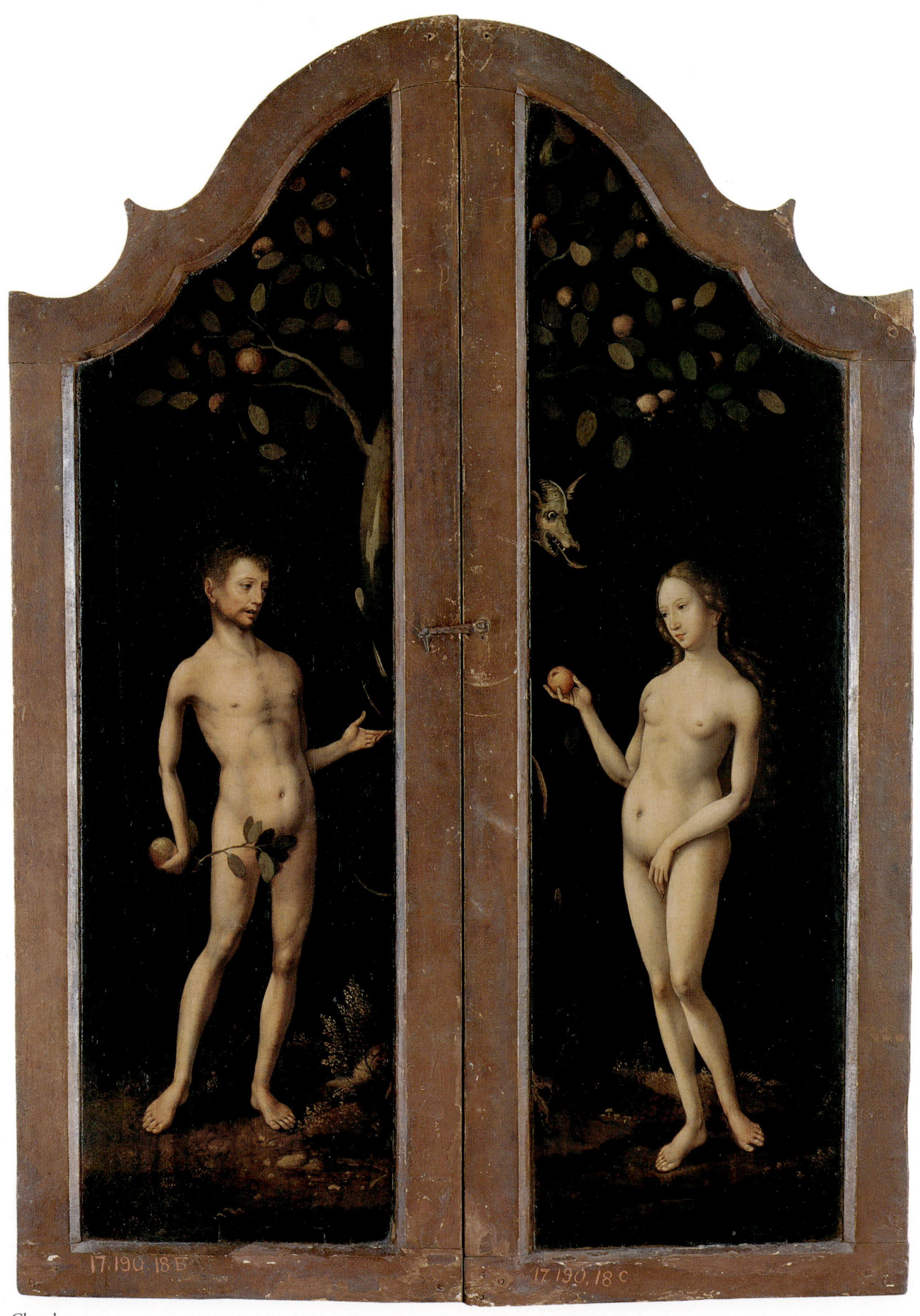

Closed

come to life only through the nervous gesticulation of hands with long expressive fingers; and a third, who specialized in portraiture, may have contributed the far more individualized hypothetical donor portrait. VS

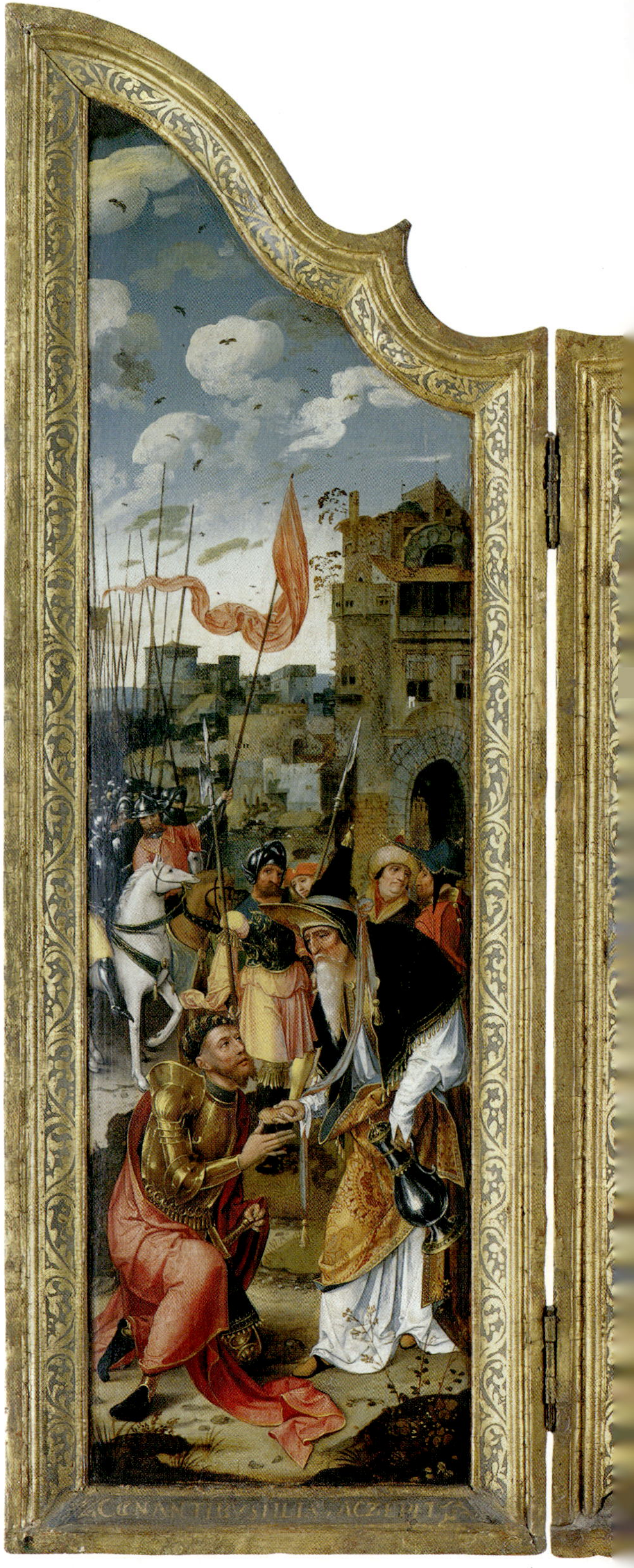

68 open

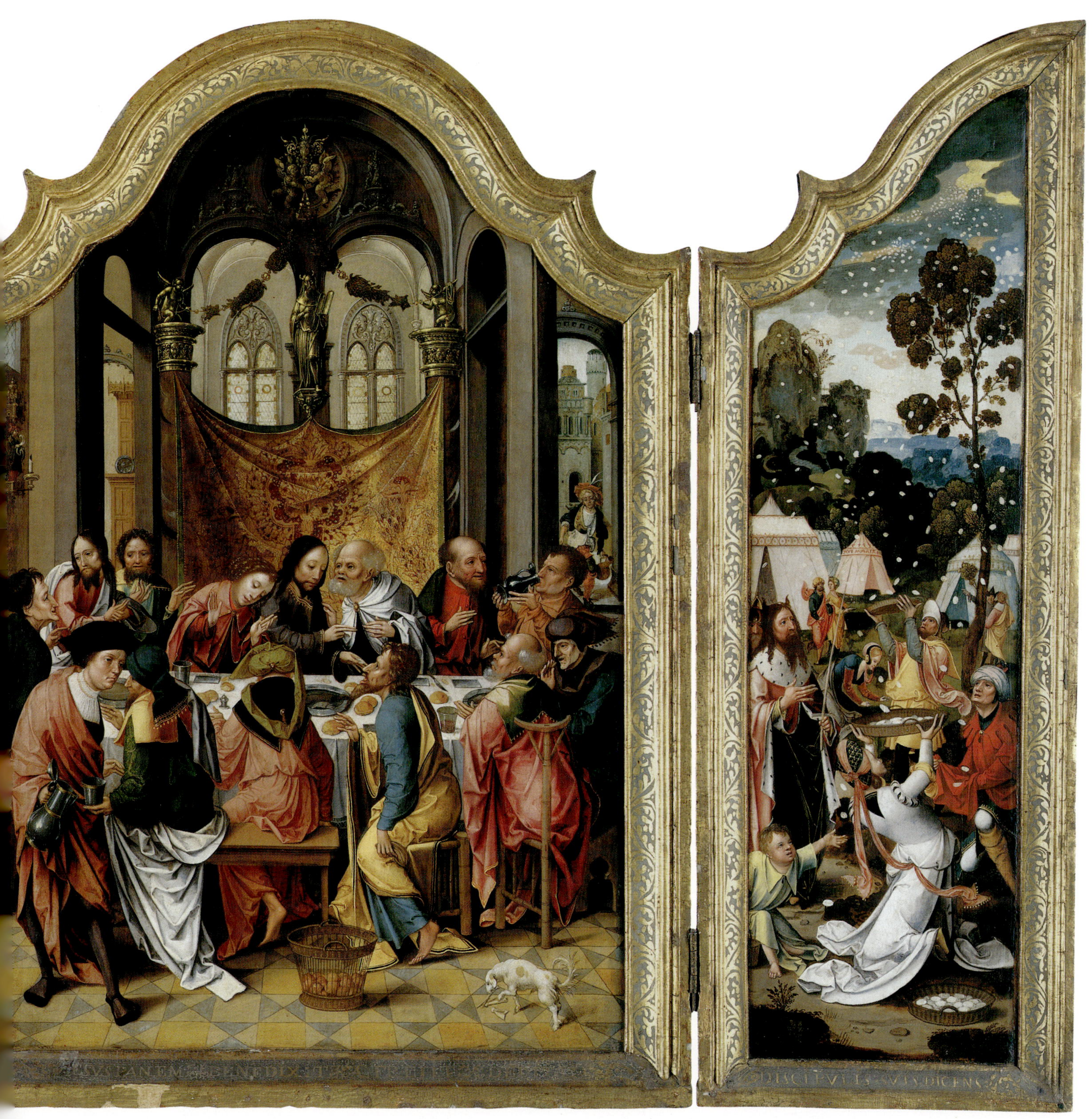
PANEM BENEDIXIT
DISCIPVLIS SVIS DICENS

Attributed to the Master of the Female Half-Lengths and Collaborator, active first half of 16th century

69. The Rest on the Flight into Egypt, about 1525

Oil on wood, 23⅜ x 28 in. (59.4 x 71.1 cm)
H. O. Havemeyer Collection, Bequest of Mrs. H. O. Havemeyer, 1929
29.100.599

Provenance: Bought in Spain by Mr. and Mrs. H. O. Havemeyer, New York (1901–7); Mrs. H. O. Havemeyer, New York (1907–29).

References: Havemeyer 1961, pp. 160–62; Falkenburg 1988; Havemeyer 1993, pp. 160–62, 326, n. 221; Stein and Wold 1993, pp. 229, 286, 341.

Although the Bruges painter Gerard David produced a number of vertical paintings of this subject with the Virgin and Child dominating the composition (see cat. no. 82), the artist here has adopted the horizontal format popularized by David's contemporary in Antwerp, Joachim Patinir. As in Patinir's surviving interpretations of the theme in the Prado, Madrid, and the Gemäldegalerie, Berlin, the scale of the Virgin and Child is reduced in relation to the landscape, which takes on a new prominence. In our panel the subject of the Rest on the Flight into Egypt, which at first glance seems to be merely the pretext for the creation of a charming fantasy landscape, is, in fact, discreetly referred to in motifs and scenes scattered in the foreground and background. We can therefore assume that the painting was conceived as an augmented *Andachtsbild,* in which a worshiper might follow the story from scene to scene during private devotion, traveling the various paths of the landscape. Falkenburg has suggested that in landscapes of this type, where Patinir's horizontal, narrative treatment of the subject is followed, the Holy Family's journey was understood by contemporary viewers as a metaphor for pilgrimage, in particular the pilgrimage of every human life, confronting at each step along the way the choice between the easy path of a sinful existence and the more difficult one of virtue and godliness.

In this panel we see the members of the Holy Family as they rest briefly on their journey, fleeing the soldiers sent by Herod to kill the Christ Child. The story of their flight, mentioned only by Matthew among the apostles, and by him in passing (2:13–18), is elaborated on by the Pseudo-Matthew in the Apocrypha (chaps. 16–24). Mary is seated on the ground surrounded by flowering plantain, a lowly plant that symbolizes not only her humility but also the well-worn path of the faithful who seek Christ. The fountain at the left indirectly suggests the refreshment provided at one point in the family's journey by a miraculous spring of water, "very clear, fresh, and completely bright" (Pseudo-Matthew). However, the broken figure that surmounts the fountain must refer to the idols that toppled from their pedestals as the Holy Family arrived in Heliopolis. In the foreground are a traveler's basket and saddlebags wrapped around a pilgrim's staff; directly behind these the ass is grazing, while at the far right Joseph gathers food for the family. The charming vignette on the hillside in the left background refers to the legend of the miraculous wheat field, according to which the infant Christ made wheat ripen overnight after he had passed it with his family; the farmer who appears here was able to tell Herod's soldiers, who are also shown, that the group passed his field when it was newly sown, causing the troops to give up their pursuit in discouragement.

The most prominent feature of the middle distance is the architectural fantasy, a small castle that is surrounded by water and approached over a footbridge by an elegant woman in a long pink robe. So similar in conception is this castle to one in the *Arrival in Bethlehem* by Master LC (cat. no. 71) that we can assume it was a stock motif in the sixteenth-century landscapist's repertoire, which, like the scattered scenes of peasant life in the present work, appealed to the increasingly secularized middle class.

Our panel appears to have been a collaborative effort. Although the worn condition of the Virgin and Child precludes any certainty on this point, they are similar to Virgin and Child types from the workshop of Quentin Massys and seem stylistically inconsistent with the rest of the painting. The landscape, which is well preserved and of high quality, however, can be most closely associated with works of the Master of the Female Half-Lengths, a painter

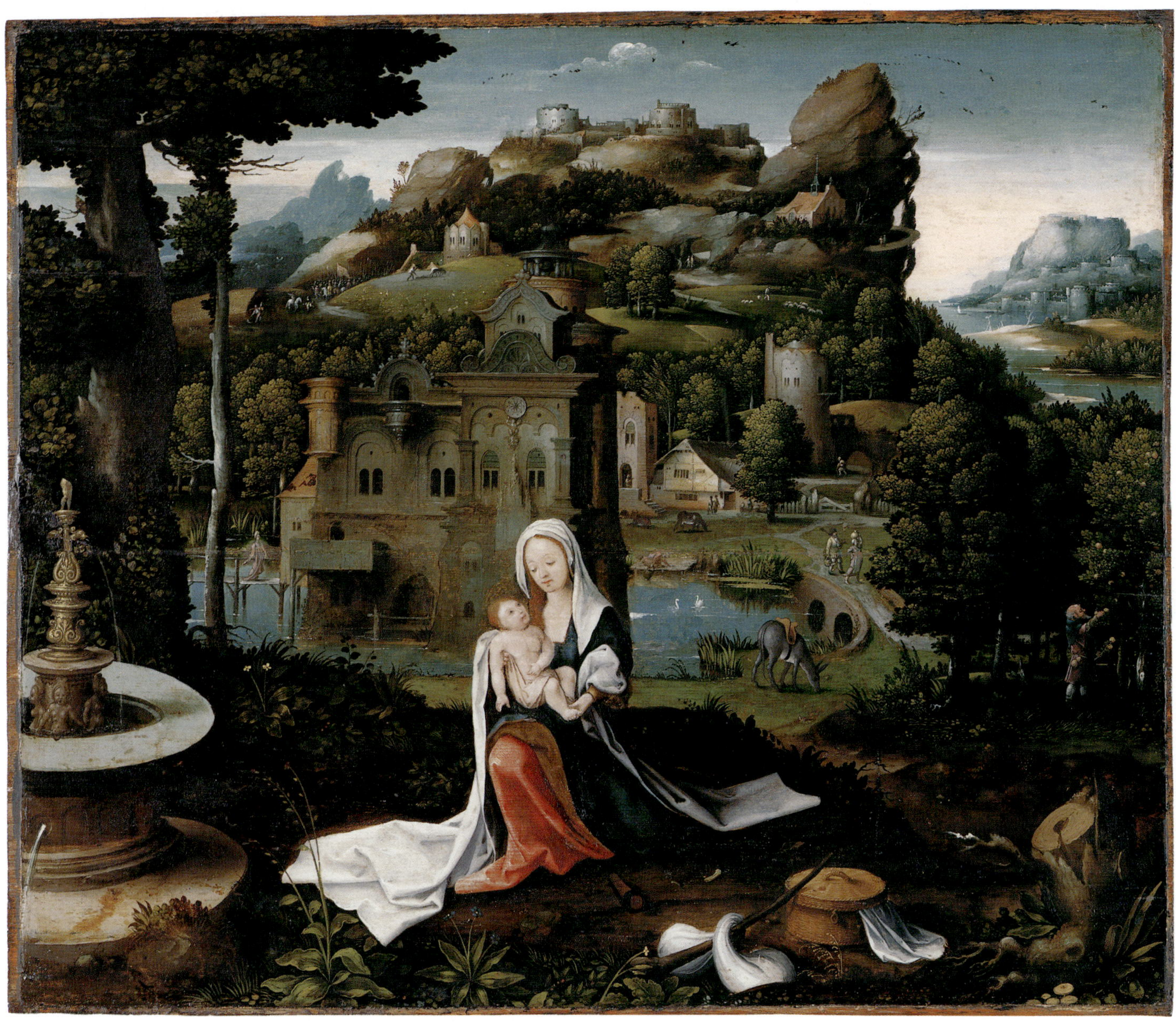

(or group of painters) apparently trained in Patinir's shop. His landscapes are more conventionally balanced in their design compared with the epic breadth of Patinir's compositions and present a more comfortable, picturesque nature with lively subordinate scenes. Typical of works attributed to him, and present in our panel, are the tree with a wide trunk that serves as an anchor along one side of the composition and the pattern of light and shade that has the dense, textured appearance of a tapestry. MSdJ

Follower of Quentin Massys and Master of the Liège Disciples at Emmaus, active mid-16th century

70. The Rest on the Flight into Egypt, about 1540

Oil on wood, 37½ x 30¼ in. (95.3 x 76.8 cm)
The Friedsam Collection, Bequest of Michael Friedsam, 1931 32.100.52

Provenance: Spanish collection?; Rev. Montague Taylor (estate sale, Christie, Manson, and Woods, London, May 19, 1897, no. 152, to Colnaghi); [Colnaghi, London (from 1897)]; Baron Albert Oppenheim, Cologne ([by 1902]; sale, Lepke, Berlin, March 19, 1918, no. 24); [Kleinberger, New York (1921)]; Michael Friedsam, New York (1921–31).

References: Hulin de Loo 1902, pp. 74–75, no. 278; Bosschère 1907, p. 125; Friedländer 1924–37, vol. 7 (1929), p. 125, nos. 66, 125, pl. 53; Burroughs and Wehle 1932, p. 28, no. 41, ill. p. 27; Wehle and Salinger 1947, pp. 111–12, ill.; Faggin 1968, p. 41, n. 34; Friedländer 1967–76, vol. 7 (1971), p. 67, no. 66, pl. 62; De Bosque 1975, p. 225, fig. 277; Franz 1982, pp. 167–77; Gibson 1989, p. 33; Serck 1990, vol. 5, p. 1234, no. A.10.

As in Joos van Cleve's highly refined *Virgin and Child* of about 1525 (cat. no. 96), one artist has painted the figures in this panel and a second provided the landscape. The influence of Leonardo da Vinci, which was so profound in the Netherlands in the first half of the sixteenth century, is present in both of these paintings, and the compositional type in which a Virgin and Child of classical weight and simplicity dominate the foreground, while a remarkably detailed landscape creates a visual foil in the background, can be traced to him. The two works also share the eucharistic symbolism of grapes in their still lifes and motifs from the story of the Rest on the Flight in their backgrounds.

The present panel is a clear example of the division of labor between figure painter and landscape artist as it was practiced in the Netherlands during the first half of the sixteenth century. The Virgin and Child, along with the still life of grapes and apples, are the work of an anonymous follower of Quentin Massys, a master who in his late career was strongly influenced by Italian painting, in particular by the style of Leonardo. The landscape has been associated with a group of works whose backgrounds can be ascribed to a single artist; the figures in the foreground or middle ground of these paintings, which provide their ostensible subjects, are the work of various collaborators. The landscapist was christened the Master of the Lille Sermon by Faggin, after a panel entitled *Sermon of Saint John* in the Musée des Beaux-Arts, Lille. However, Franz later pointed out that the work of the figure painter is predominant in the Lille *Sermon* and proposed a new name: the Master of the Liège Disciples at Emmaus, after the *Journey to Emmaus* in the Musée d'Art Religieux et d'Art Mosan, Liège. Our panel was first ascribed to this master by Gibson in 1989.

Informal, nonheroic, and meandering, the sparsely wooded countryside the artist described here is similar in its loose organization to the setting of the *Arrival in Bethlehem* by his contemporary Master LC (cat. no. 71). The landscapes in our *Rest on the Flight* and in other compositions attributed to the Master of the Liège Disciples at Emmaus not only help us to understand the artistic environment from which Pieter Bruegel emerged but also seem to presage works by later sixteenth-century Flemish painters, such as Gillis van Coninxloo and Joos de Momper the Younger.

MSdJ

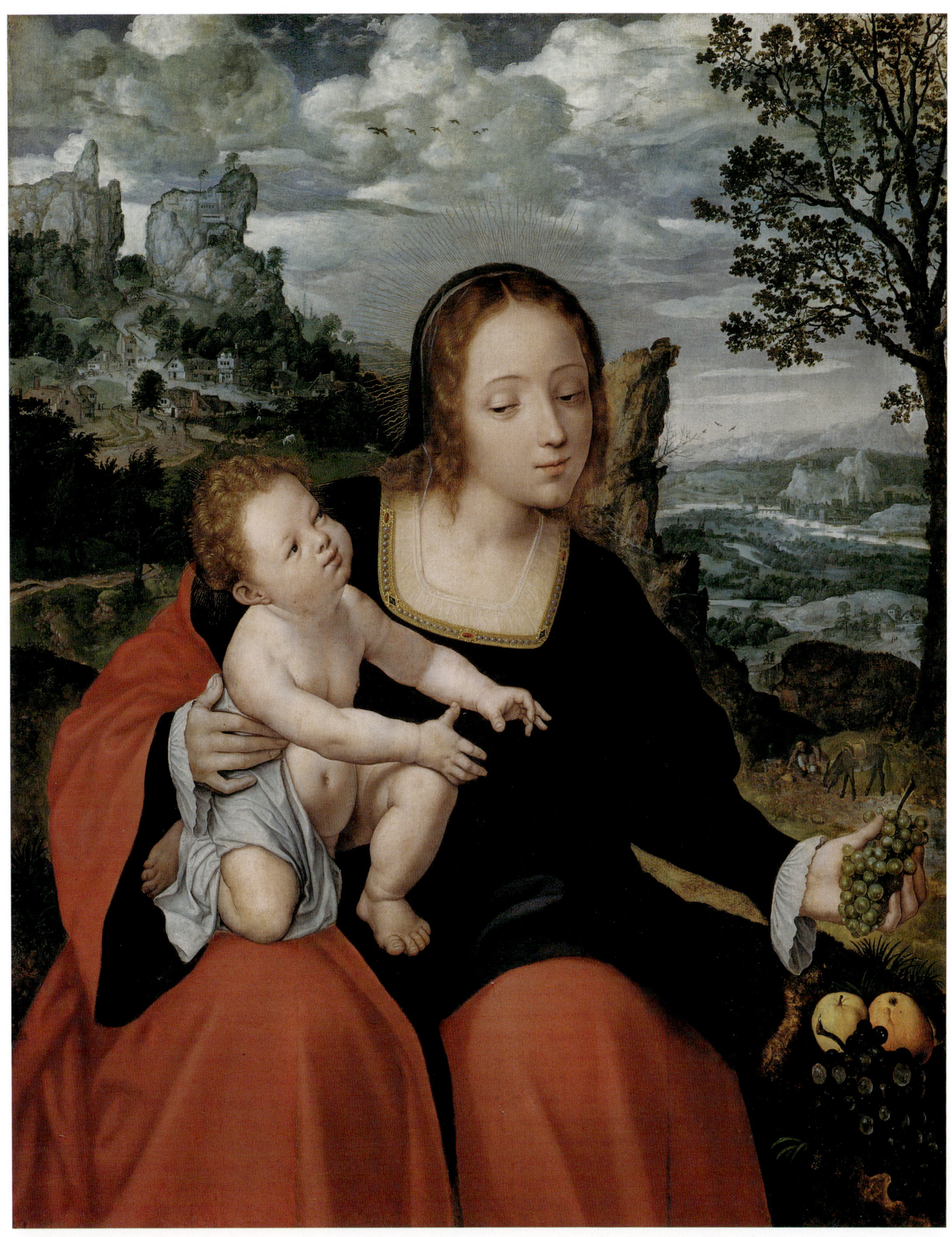

Attributed to Master LC, active second quarter of 16th century

71. The Arrival in Bethlehem, about 1540

Oil on wood, 26½ x 36⅞ in. (67.3 x 93.7 cm)
Rogers Fund, 1916 16.69

Provenance: Count A. Golenistcheff-Koutousoff, Saint Petersburg (acquired in Vienna as Abraham Hassler); Nicholas Riabouchinsky, Moscow (sale, American Art Association, Plaza Hotel, New York, April 26, 1916, no. 29, as Patinir).

References: Schmidt et al. 1910, pp. 59ff.; Burroughs 1916; Clark 1918, pp. 43–48; Wilcox 1920; Frankfurter 1931, p. 27; Friedländer 1924–37, vol. 13 (1936), p. 35; Wehle and Salinger 1947, pp. 118–19; Faggin 1968, p. 39, n. 18; Bergmans 1969, p. 21; Dunbar 1972, vol. 2, pp. 252–54; Dunbar 1980, pp. 116–18; Gibson 1989, pp. 20–21; Serck 1990, vol. 6, pp. 1252–58; Ainsworth 1998b.

The art of landscape painting was developed as an independent genre in the sixteenth century by such artists as Joachim Patinir, Cornelis Massys, and Lucas Gassel, each of whom has at some point been identified as the author of the *Arrival in Bethlehem*. This panel, however, is unquestionably by the artist responsible for another painting with a biblical subject, the *Calling of Saint Matthew* (Musées Royaux des Beaux-Arts de Belgique, Brussels), which appears to be signed with the initials LC. The works of this anonymous master are most closely related to those of Gassel in their compositional conventions, individual landscape motifs, and subtle matte tones. It is likely that the artist responsible for our painting was a member of Gassel's workshop in Antwerp or Brussels toward the middle of the sixteenth century.

The *Arrival* shows a development beyond the compositions of Patinir, in which the most important figures are prominently displayed in the foreground, with the landscape serving as extended backdrop scenery (cat. no. 88). Here, however, the episodes of the narrative are more fully integrated into the landscape, inviting the viewer to travel along with the main characters and experience their journey. In a contemporary setting, featuring a castle surrounded by a moat, Joseph and the Virgin Mary accompanied by the ox and the ass set out at the lower left. We encounter them farther along the way, in the middle distance, as they are refused a night's lodging at the inn, and again, at the far right, as they kneel with other figures in adoration before the newborn Christ Child.

The unfinished state of this work provides an uncommon opportunity to view various stages of the painting process, especially the underdrawing, which is easily seen with the naked eye in the village in the middle distance and in the rocky mountains beyond it. Additional information provided by infrared reflectography indicates that the narrative was originally more ambitious and was to have included scenes of the Nativity and the Annunciation to the Shepherds that are now hidden beneath the pink tent in the village in the middle ground and under the verdant hillside to the upper right.

At a certain point the painting process was interrupted for unknown reasons; somewhat later it was taken up again, probably by a second artist, who suppressed the religious narrative in favor of genre motifs, which he sprinkled throughout the landscape. These elements—the couple heading toward the open gate in the foreground, the two characters passing beneath the archway at the lower right, the figures at the riverbank where the wash is laid out to dry—were not planned in the underdrawing but merely painted freehand. The de-emphasis of religious content signals a transitional phase in Netherlandish landscape painting, when the focus on narrative concerns was giving way and the form was about to achieve a new status as an independent genre. MWA

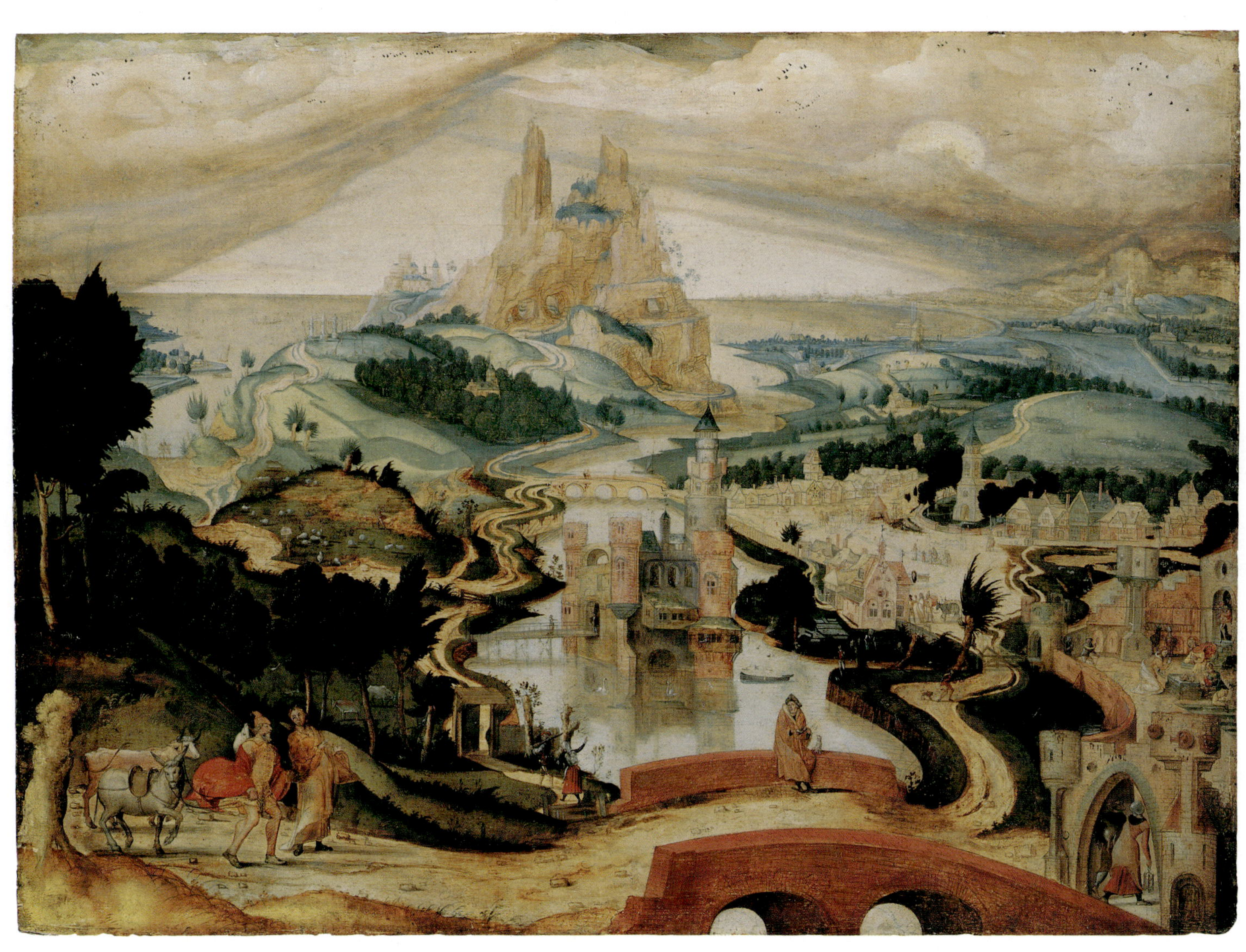

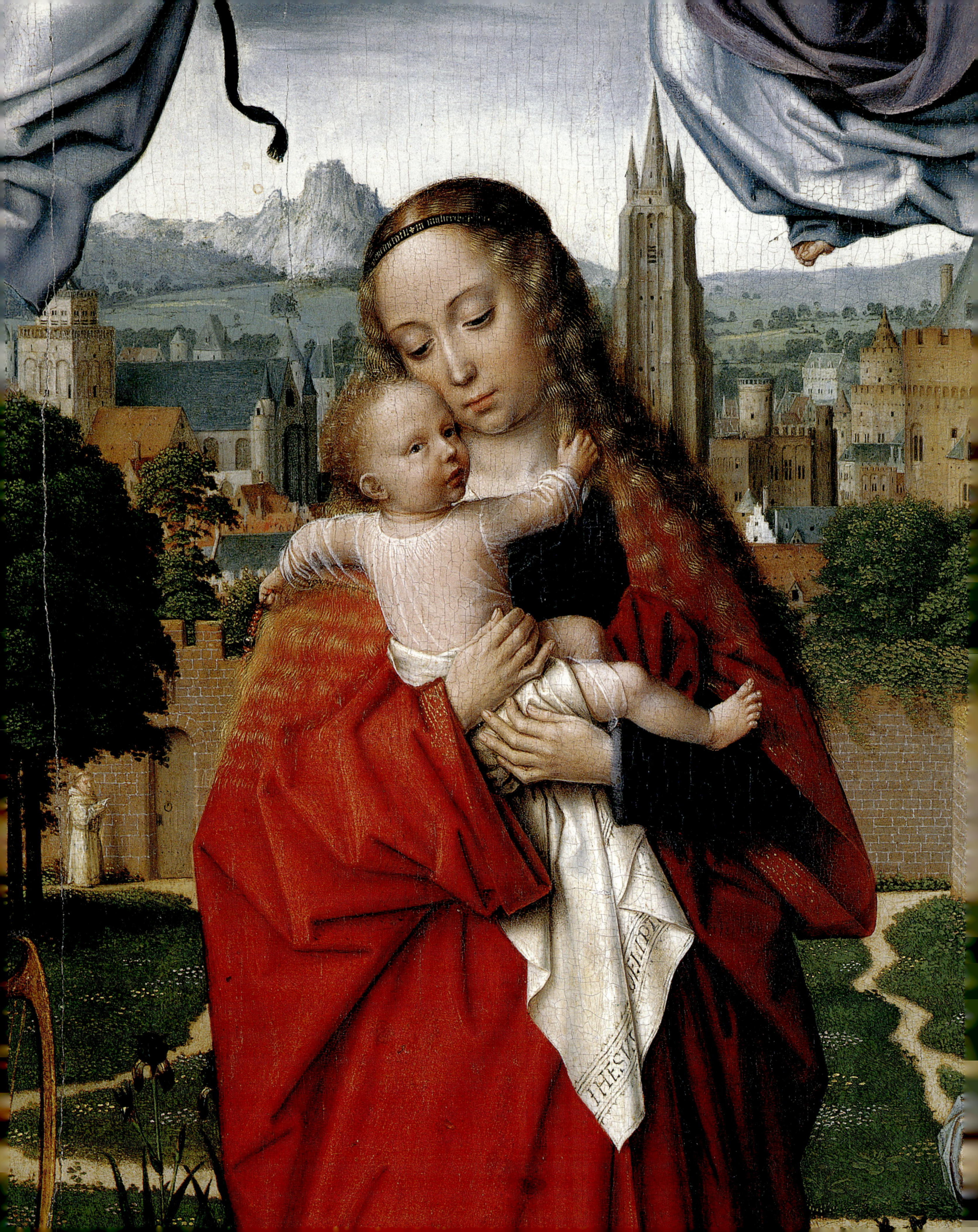

Gerard David: Purity of Vision in an Age of Transition

Opposite: Gerard David, detail, *Virgin and Child with Four Angels*, (cat. no. 81)

With its prime location not far from the western coast of what is today Belgium and its easy access to the Atlantic Ocean through the Zwin River, fifteenth-century Bruges became the chief economic hub of western Europe and an important international center with especially strong trade links to Italy and Spain, as well as to England and the German territories. In addition, the Prinsenhof there was the favored residence of the dukes of Burgundy, whose regular visits with full entourage, occasional triumphal entries, ducal weddings, and official meetings of state lent a festive atmosphere to the city.

The concentration of wealth, power, and prestige in Bruges attracted artists and craftsmen, guaranteeing them unequaled opportunities to pursue their livelihoods. It is not surprising, therefore, that an unbroken succession of highly skilled immigrant painters recognized the advantage of settling in Bruges to practice their craft: Jan van Eyck came from Maaseik in the Mosan region; Petrus Christus from Baerle, near the present Dutch-Belgian border; Hans Memling from the more distant German territories; and Gerard David from Oudewater, in the northern Netherlands, near Gouda.

The details of the lives of these painters were lost over time and were rediscovered only in the nineteenth century, largely due to the painstaking research carried out by the Englishman James Weale in the Bruges archives. It was pure serendipity that some of the paintings identified in the archival records as the work of Gerard David have survived. These paintings, among them the *Justice of Cambyses* of 1498 (fig. 16) and the *Virgin among Virgins* of 1509 (fig. 84), provide a small core group of examples to which others may be linked through

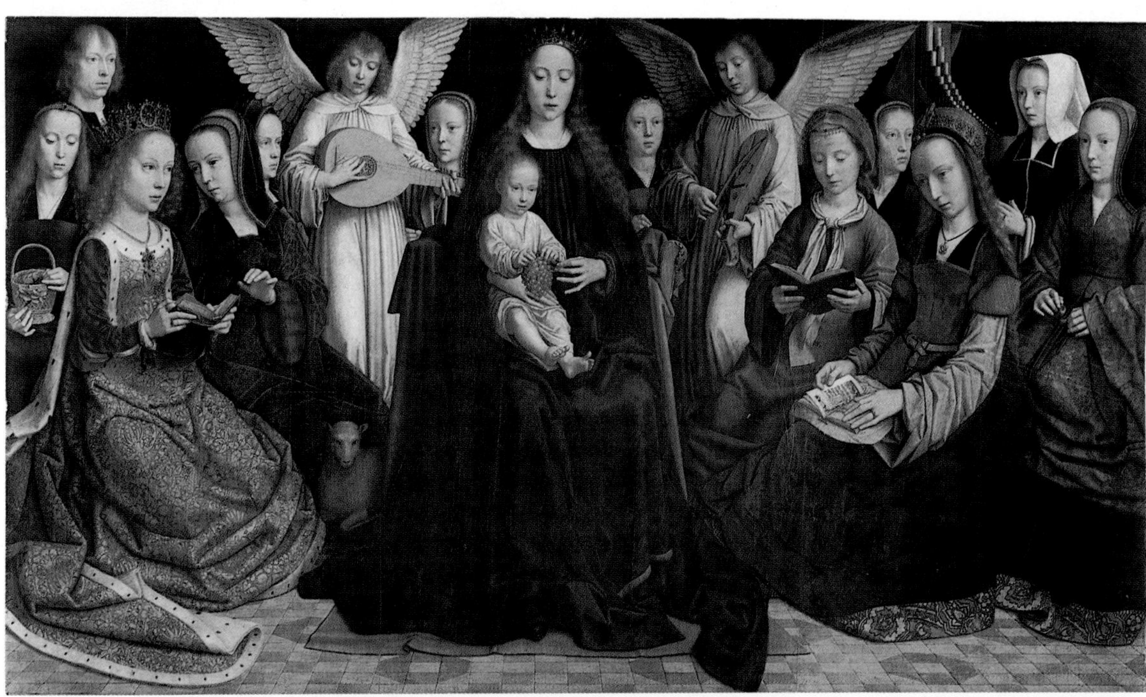

Fig. 84. Gerard David, *Virgin among Virgins*, 1509. Oil on wood. Musée des Beaux-Arts, Rouen

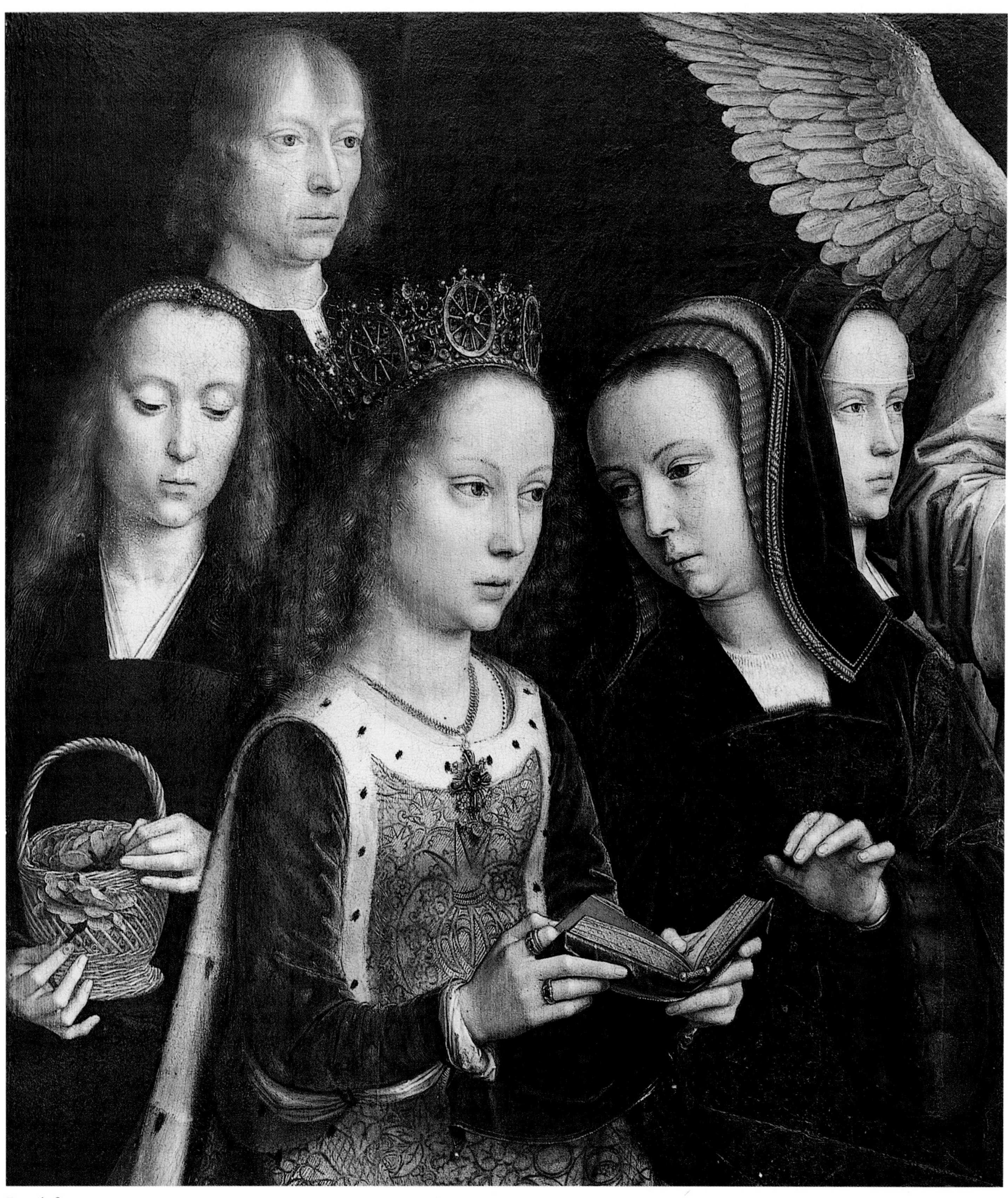

Detail, fig. 84

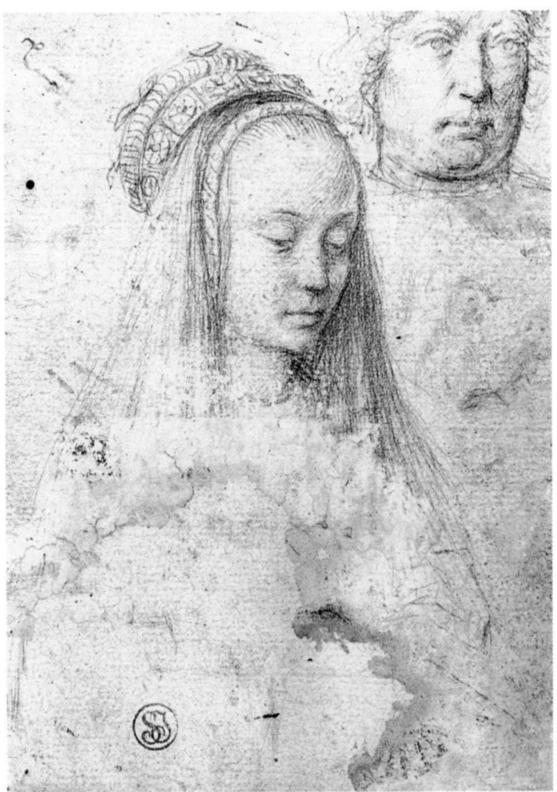

Fig. 85. Gerard David, *Four Heads*, about 1495 (recto of fig. 86). Metalpoint over traces of black chalk on prepared paper. Städelsches Kunstinstitut, Frankfurt

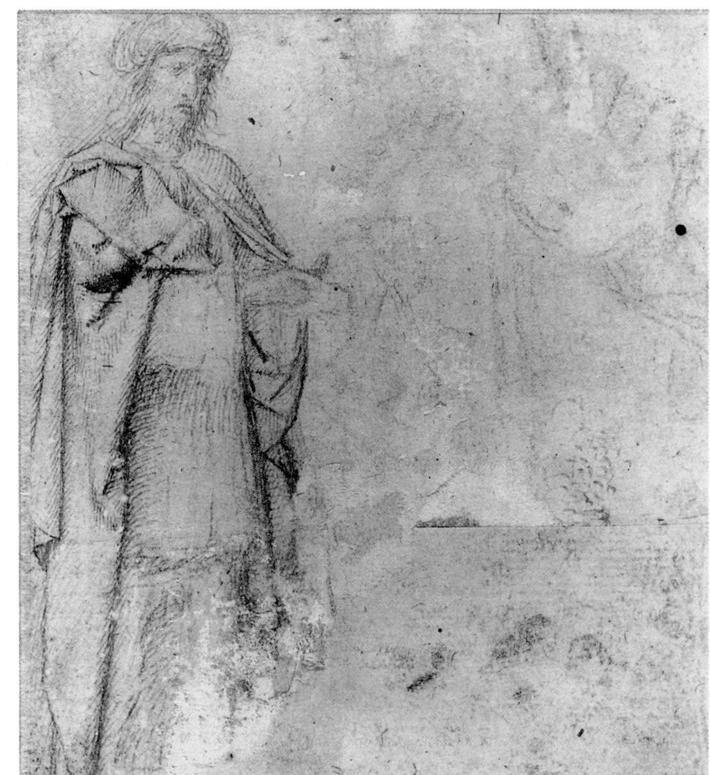

Fig. 86. Gerard David, *Study for King Cambyses*, about 1495 (verso of fig. 85). Pen and ink over black chalk on paper. Städelsches Kunstinstitut, Frankfurt

their close similarities of style and execution. Because David did not leave a single signed painting (except indirectly, by inserting in some compositions his self-portrait peering out at the viewer from a crowd of figures), documented works must provide a starting point for reconstructing the artist's oeuvre of both paintings and drawings. This is an ongoing process. Mundy recognized that a double-sided sheet of heads and a standing male figure showed preparatory drawings for David's *Justice of Cambyses* panels (compare figs. 16 and 85 and 86). This sheet was originally part of a sketchbook, long disassembled, most of whose pages were studies of heads and hands. The extant drawings are now in several collections; one (fig. 87) spontaneously captures from life numerous heads shown in different views and with a variety of expressions that provided David with a stock of material for use in his paintings. Quite recently it became possible to attribute a previously unknown fragment of the *Mocking of Christ* (fig. 88) to David partly on the basis of the close connection between two of the heads in this drawing and two in the painting (Ainsworth 1997a). Such connections between drawings and paintings allow not only for the occasional new attribution but also for a greater understanding of an artist's working methods.

Although the Metropolitan Museum does not own any complete triptychs by David, its collections include the most numerous holdings of his individual paintings in this country or abroad. These range from his earliest to his late works and exemplify his innovative approach to landscape, his novel depictions of traditional themes, and his original effects of color and light, which had considerable influence on successive generations of artists. Indeed these paintings reveal that far from being the artist Panofsky characterized as representing the "last flowering" of late medieval art, David worked in a progressive, even enterprising, mode, casting off his late medieval heritage and proceeding with a certain purity of vision in an age of transition.

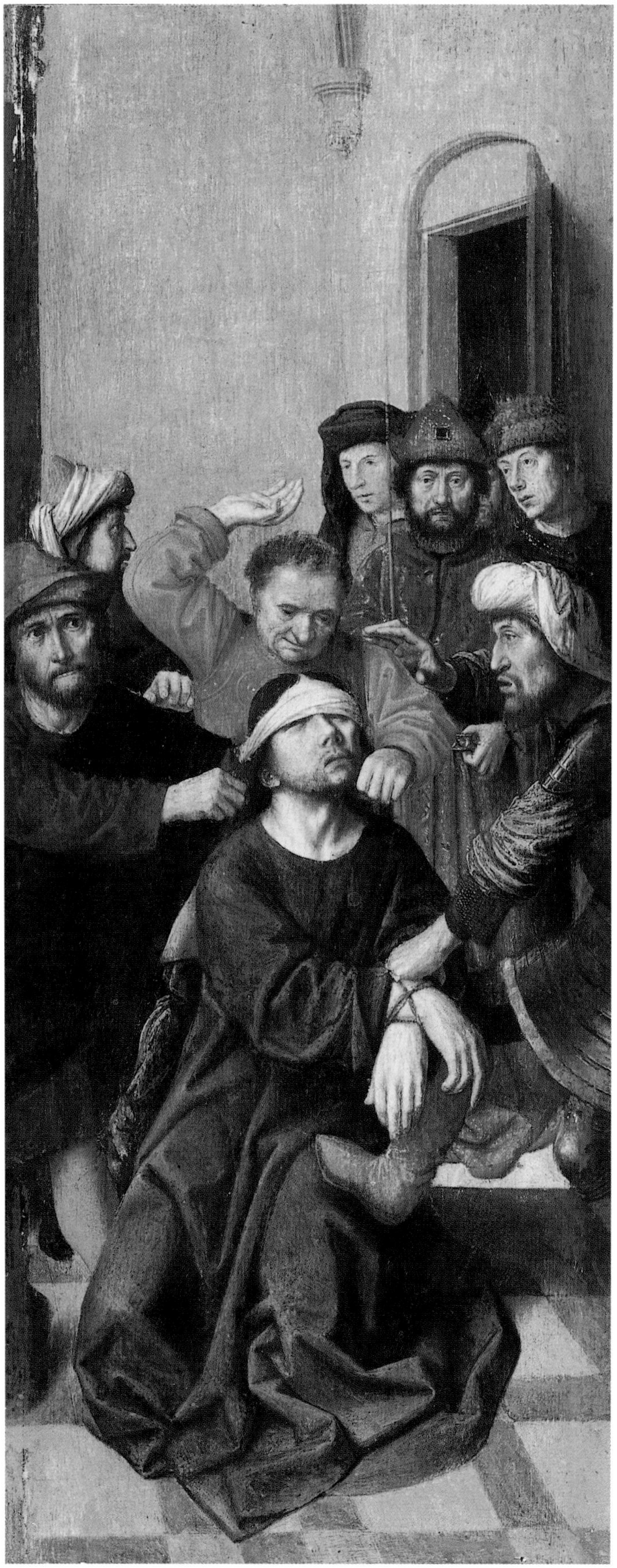

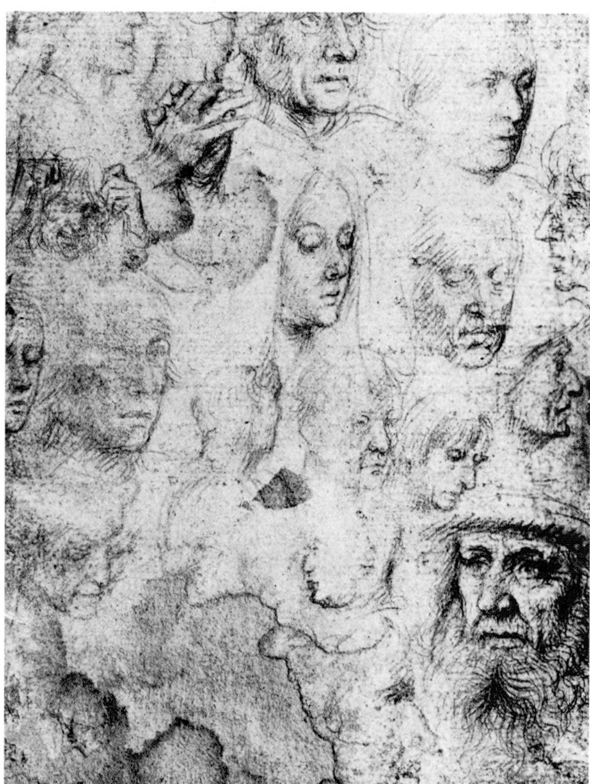

Fig. 87. Gerard David, *Study of Heads and Hands*, about 1490. Metalpoint on prepared paper. Location unknown

Fig. 88. Gerard David, fragment, *The Mocking of Christ*, about 1490. Oil on wood. Private collection

It is from the epitaph on his tomb in the Onze-Lieve-Vrouwekerk (church of Our Lady) in Bruges that we learn that David came from Oudewater, but exactly when he was born (the date was probably about 1455) and where he received his early training are matters of speculation. The route he traveled from the northern Netherlands before reaching Bruges in 1484, the year he was inducted as a free master into the Corporation of Imagemakers and Saddlers (which included panel painters), is to some extent disclosed in his paintings. The naive charm of the doll-like figures in the early *Nativity* (cat. no. 72) links this panel with David's north Netherlandish origins and with works of the Haarlem painter Geertgen tot Sint Jans. And the spatial construction of the scene is influenced by the art of another Haarlem painter, Dieric Bouts, who himself immigrated to the south Netherlands, settling permanently in Leuven by 1457. It is likely that before going to Bruges, David was drawn to the workshop of Bouts, which was continued by his sons Dieric the Younger and Aelbert after their father's death in 1475. He must have spent some time there, for the mark of Bouts's style pervades David's paintings of the last two decades of the fifteenth century and beyond (cat. nos. 72, 78).

Whether David already worked as a manuscript illuminator as well as a panel painter early in his career remains a somewhat controversial issue. However, evidence that he did so is provided by a tiny illumination in the Lehman Collection, a *Holy Face* (cat. no. 74), recently attributed to him. Long ago cut out of a book, it may be the missing image that originally accompanied the Holy Face prayer in a 1486 Book of Hours in the Escorial near Madrid. David is also thought to have contributed a few illuminations to a Book of Hours presented to Queen Isabella of Castile in 1496, among which is a *Nativity* (fig. 89) that, despite its considerably later date and more advanced construction of space, is modeled on a reverse image of the early *Nativity* panel in the Metropolitan Museum. No document attests to David's membership in the guild of illuminators or to his authorship of any specific illumination; however, certain examples, especially the *Virgin among Virgins* of about 1505–10 (fig. 90), so nearly approximate the style, handling, and execution of David's panels and preparatory drawings (fig. 91) that they must be by him. In this regard, it is interesting to note that in the first decade of the sixteenth century the Corporation of Image-makers attempted to exert control over the Guild of the Book Trades (Librariërsgild), also known as the Guild of Saint John and Saint Luke, which included illuminators; although only partly successful, these attempts brought manuscript illumination and panel painting into a particularly close alliance. It was during this time that David advanced to the position of dean of the corporation. By 1519–20, when there was litigation between David and his assistant Ambrosius Benson (see "Workshop Practice in Early Netherlandish Painting" in this publication), the interrelationship of panel painters and manuscript illuminators may well

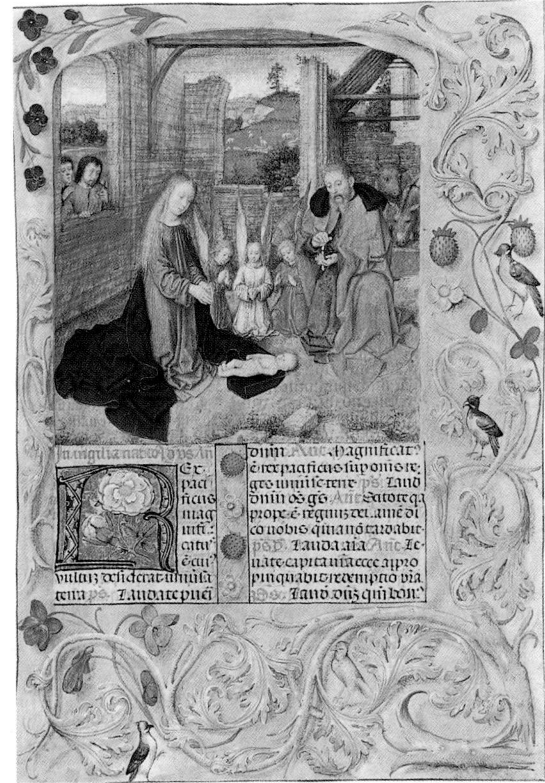

Fig. 89. Gerard David, *The Nativity*, from *Breviary of Queen Isabella of Castile*, before 1497. Tempera on vellum. The British Library, London (Add. MS 18851, fol. 29)

have been established: patterns for both paintings and illuminations whose ownership was disputed by the two artists were found among the workshop paraphernalia in trunks in the master's shop.

The international and courtly environment of Bruges as well as the elegant art of the city's preeminent painter, Hans Memling, must have motivated David to adopt a more refined style in his paintings upon his arrival there. This new approach is evident in the more graceful poses and attitudes of his figures and the more subtle modeling of their faces; these particular changes, not yet visible in the *Saint John the Baptist* wing of a triptych of about 1485–90 (cat. no. 73), have already taken place in the *Saint Francis* from the same ensemble and are even more marked in the *Crucifixion* of the late 1490s (cat. no. 75). In some respects David moved beyond his predecessor Memling. Thus, a heightened sensitivity to nature and a specific interest in the depiction of landscape (whose individual

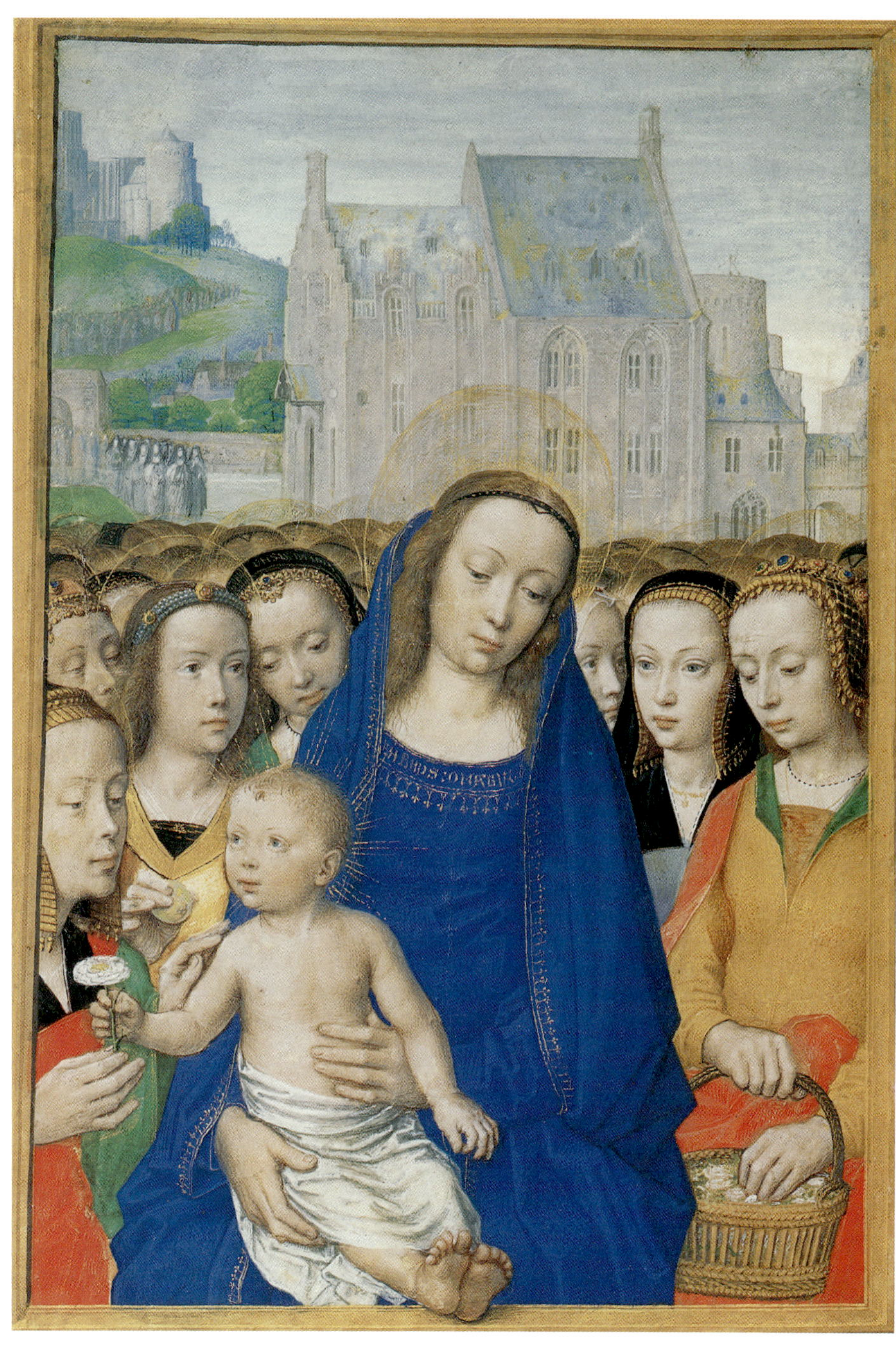

Fig. 90. Gerard David, *Virgin among Virgins*, about 1505–10. Tempera on vellum. The Pierpont Morgan Library, New York

forms the artist studied in silverpoint and pen and ink in sketchbook drawings [figs. 92, 93]) are apparent also in these earlier paintings, where he deliberately matched the type of natural setting to the theme depicted. Saint John the Baptist, for instance, inhabits an enclosed wilderness of cypress and magnolia trees, while Saint Francis receives the stigmata in a remote field, at a distance from his monastery in the background. And the *Crucifixion* shows subtle tonal shifts from the browns of the foreground to the greens and blues near the far horizon of an integrated and naturalistic scheme of hills, valleys, towns, and forests—features that demonstrate a dramatic departure from the formulaic depictions of Memling (cat. no. 11), who had little interest in the landscape genre.

David's greatest achievement in the portrayal of landscape and in its integration with the theme set within it occurs in the Nativity Triptych of about 1510–15 (cat. no. 80). The exterior wings show a forest scene devoid of human presence, a startling innovation for its time and, indeed, a precursor of the highly developed independent landscape genre of seventeenth-century Dutch and Flemish painting. Influenced by the Modern Devotion and the popularity of contemporary pilgrimages undertaken by believers hoping to earn salvation by literally following in the path of Christ, David encouraged viewers to participate in the scene by presenting an unpopulated landscape; we are invited to wander, like the Holy Family, through the isolated forest of the exterior wings and share with its members the jubilant and hallowed Nativity that is revealed when the wings are opened.

The requirements imposed for commissions did not always allow David free reign in his expression. The *retardataire* landscape of the Passion wings of about 1505 (cat. no. 78), for example, with their vertically stacked hills that obscure the distant view to the horizon, probably respond to the strictures of the commission. David may have adopted this solution to suit the formal characteristics of the missing centerpiece, which possibly was not a painting but rather a series of sculpted scenes from Christ's Passion—the sort of work that in contemporary examples is typically arranged as a vertical stacking of vignettes. The mode of the *Annunciation* on the reverse of the Passion wings—the only example of grisaille, or simulated sculpture, on a triptych exterior in David's surviving oeuvre—would also have been appropriate for a sculpted centerpiece.

David's obvious talent for sensing and fulfilling the specific nature of the individual requirements of his clients in terms not only of theme but also of expression guaranteed him a considerable business. The thriving economic relationship between Italy, especially Genoa, and Bruges involved trade in luxury goods, including paintings. In response to the great popularity of Netherlandish paintings in Italy, wealthy Italian merchants and bankers living in Bruges sought out Netherlandish painters to provide altarpieces for their chapels and churches at home and abroad, thereby paying homage to the artists of their adopted homeland and garnering status and prestige in their native cities.

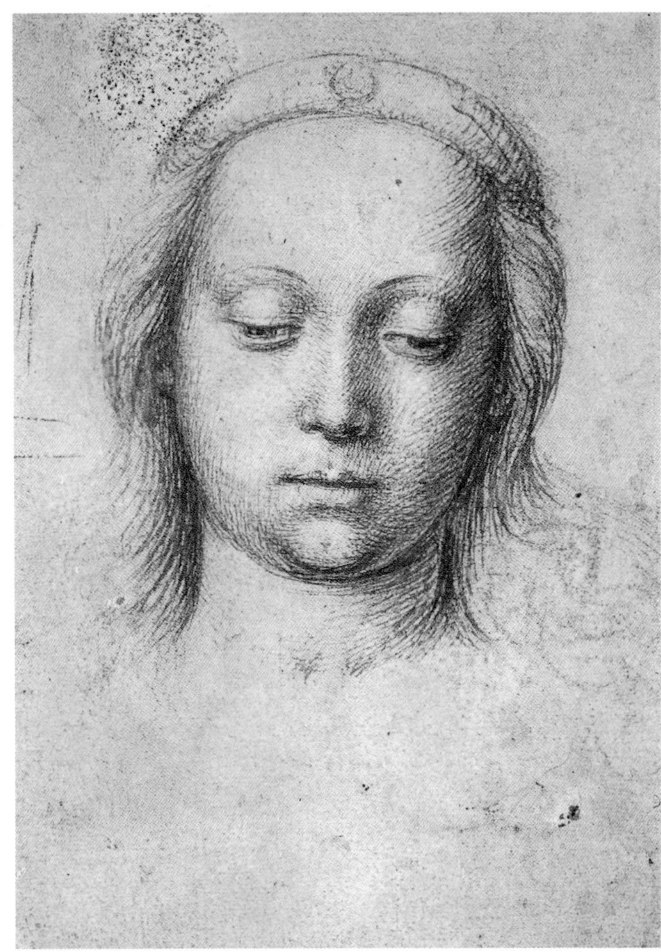

Fig. 91. Gerard David, *Head of a Girl*, about 1505–10 (recto of fig. 92). Brush and ink over traces of black chalk on paper. Hamburger Kunsthalle

Several Italians became patrons of David's, among them the diplomat and banker Vincenzo Sauli. Near the peak of his career, in 1506, David received the prestigious commission for a large altarpiece comprising seven paintings in Italian polyptych form (see cat. no. 79) directly from Sauli or from intermediaries, possibly his relatives in Bruges. Meeting the challenge of producing this monumental work (it is one of the largest known Netherlandish altarpieces) for the high altar of the abbey church of San Gerolamo della Cervara, a Benedictine monastery in Liguria, not far from Genoa, must have been his sovereign achievement. No expense was spared, and the commission included

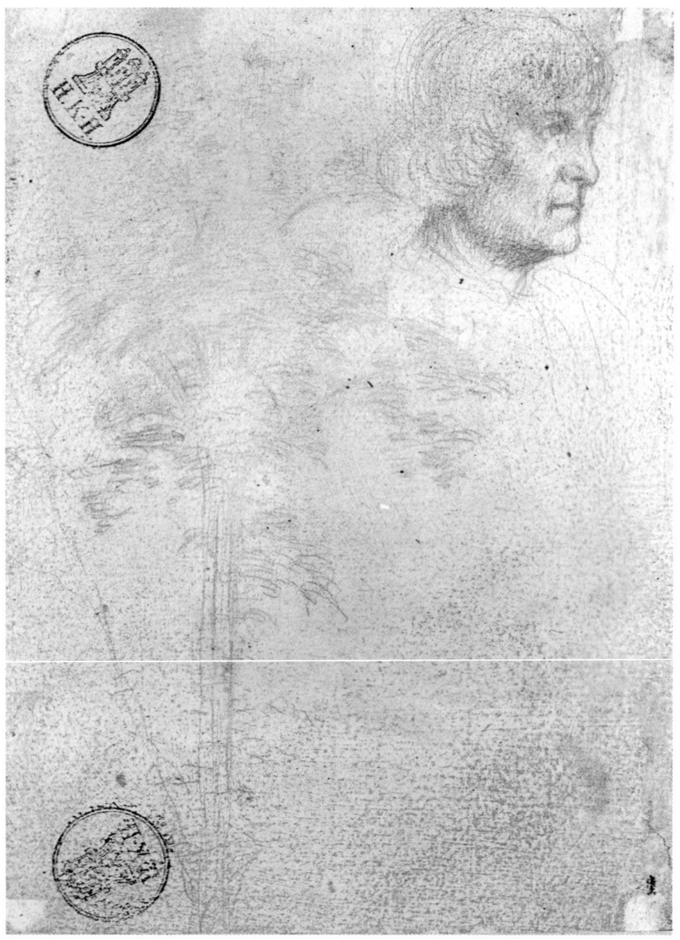

Fig. 92. Gerard David, *Study of a Head and Tree*, about 1505–10 (verso of fig. 91). Silverpoint on prepared paper. Hamburger Kunsthalle

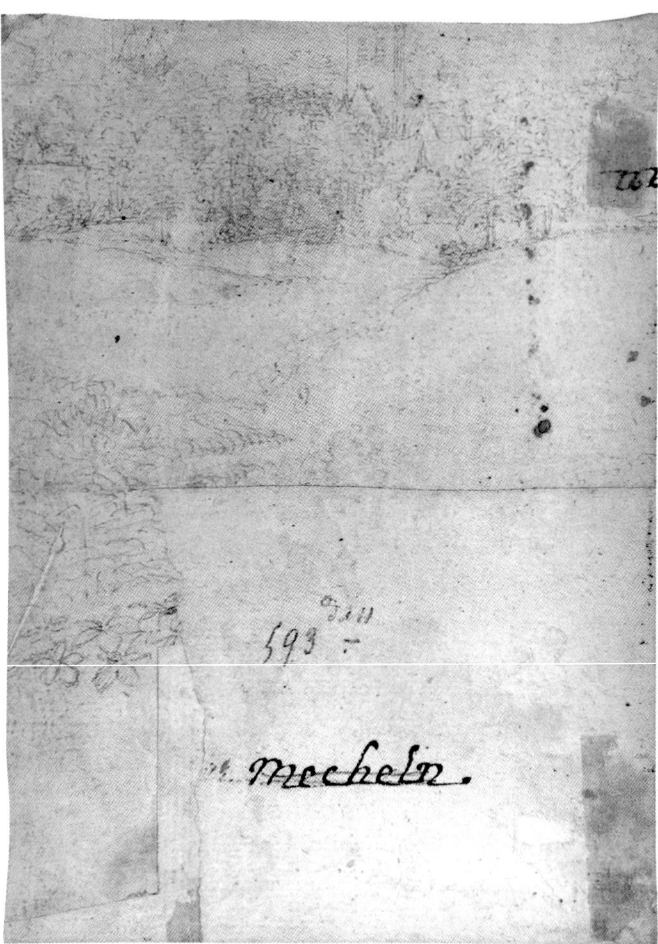

Fig. 93. Gerard David, *Landscape*, about 1505–10. Pen and ink on paper. Collection Edmond de Rothschild, Musée du Louvre, Paris

a large gilt frame, a predella, and curtain hangings in addition to the main panels.

By the second decade of the sixteenth century, toward the end of David's career, Italian artists, who had been assimilating northern style, began to influence their Netherlandish counterparts. David's production of the Cervara Altarpiece, the acquaintance with the art of Lombardy and Liguria he likely gained through that experience, as well as his employment of a Lombard assistant by 1519, placed him at the forefront of this reverse trend, in an ideal position to convey the Italian mode to his northern colleagues.

Although hints of David's shift in style are clearly visible in the *Virgin and Child with Four Angels* (cat. no. 81), the contemporary *Rest on the Flight into Egypt* (cat. no. 82) is the more telling manifestation of the new manner. Here the lessons of Italian art are most keenly felt: the chiaroscuro effects, the setting of the central figures against the nichelike foil of trees, the subtle sfumato modeling of the faces, the sophisticated balance of light, and the deeply saturated hues of blue and green function together to ensure the convincing and natural placement of the great pyramidal form of the Virgin and Child within, and not simply before, the landscape.

In treatment of subject matter, as well as in style, David broke new ground in the *Rest on the Flight into Egypt*. The Virgin is no longer an icon but rather a human and accessible mother tenderly caring for her child. Slowly evolving changes in the nature of religious practice, in the view of family life, in the social role of women, even in the concept of nurturing, are reflected here, providing an ideal of motherhood that would be treated as a new, independent genre in seventeenth-century Dutch painting. David's innovations—in particular the assimilation of Italian art and the shifting focus from the traditional iconic image of the Virgin and Child to their portrayal as human presences—were quickly absorbed by his contemporaries Quentin Massys and Joos van Cleve in Antwerp, which had become the center of Netherlandish artistic production by the close of David's career.

MARYAN W. AINSWORTH

References: Weale 1895; Bodenhausen 1905; Boon [1946]; Van Miegroet 1989; Ainsworth 1998a.

Gerard David, about 1455–1523

72. The Nativity, early 1480s

Oil on wood; overall 18¾ x 13½ in. (47.6 x 34.3 cm); painted surface 18½ x 13⅜ in. (47 x 34 cm)
The Friedsam Collection, Bequest of Michael Friedsam, 1931 32.100.40a

Provenance: Count de Galliera (by 1874); Mr. Gore, London; Steinmeyer, Lucerne (1923); [Kleinberger, New York (1923)]; Michael Friedsam, New York (1923–31).

References: Wehle and Salinger 1947, pp. 89–91 (with earlier bibliography); Cuttler 1968, p. 191; Friedländer 1967–76, vol. 6b (1971), p. 100; Urbach 1971, pp. 10, 28; Fahy and Watson 1973, p. 53; Cleveland Museum 1974, p. 151; Scillia 1975, pp. 113, 127, 129–31, 133, 137, 174, 193; Morse 1979, p. 92; Ainsworth 1985, p. 59; Snyder 1985, p. 188; De Vos 1987, col. 215; Périer-d'Ieteren 1987, pp. 95–106; Urbach 1987, pp. 83–94; Van Miegroet 1989, pp. 273–74 (with additional earlier bibliography); Ainsworth 1994c, p. 484; Ainsworth 1998a.

Although the *Nativity* has been displayed with two wings (cat. no. 73), as if the painting is part of a portable triptych, it was probably intended as a single, private devotional panel. The wings were cut down in their vertical dimensions prior to 1905 and the three panels assembled only in 1923, when all were owned by F. Kleinberger and Co. Similar, larger pictures by David, of a slightly later date, are in the Szépmüvészeti Múzeum, Budapest, and the Cleveland Museum of Art.

The *Nativity* probably dates from the early 1480s, before David established himself in Bruges. Indeed, the simple geometry of the composition and the homely figure types recall features in the work of his north Netherlandish compatriots, some of whom had resettled in the southern territories before this time. The type of the Virgin, with her oval face and flowing red hair, for example, occurs in the paintings of Geertgen tot Sint Jans and Jacob Jansz, while the figure of Joseph and the setting with a brick wall pierced by double-arched windows, used to divide foreground from background, derive from a composition by Dieric Bouts, known only from fragments (Gemäldegalerie, Berlin, and Louvre, Paris) and copies of the lost painting.

This intimate scene of the Nativity depends on both biblical and mystical literature. Luke 2:1–20 gives a general description of the circumstances of the birth of Christ as well as the angel's annunciation of the event to the shepherds and the peasants' subsequent adoration of the newborn infant. Specific details of the depiction here—namely, the kneeling Virgin with loose, flowing hair, the Christ Child lying on the ground on her extended drapery, and Joseph shielding the flame of his candle—are based on a vision of the Swedish mystic Saint Bridget as recorded in her very popular *Revelations*. According the ass more prominence than the ox is an unusual reversal of traditional representations showing that "The ox knoweth his owner, and the ass his master's crib" (Isaiah 1:3).

Closely related to the Friedsam painting is an illumination in a breviary produced in Bruges about 1496 (fig. 89), presented by the Spanish ambassador Francisco de Rojas to Queen Isabella of Castile. Possibly one of three illuminations made for this book by David himself, it is almost a mirror image of our *Nativity* but shows a more developed spatial conception and the Virgin type of the artist's later works. The exchange of models and compositional patterns between panel painters and manuscript illuminators was common in Bruges, where David was a key practitioner of both arts.

MWA

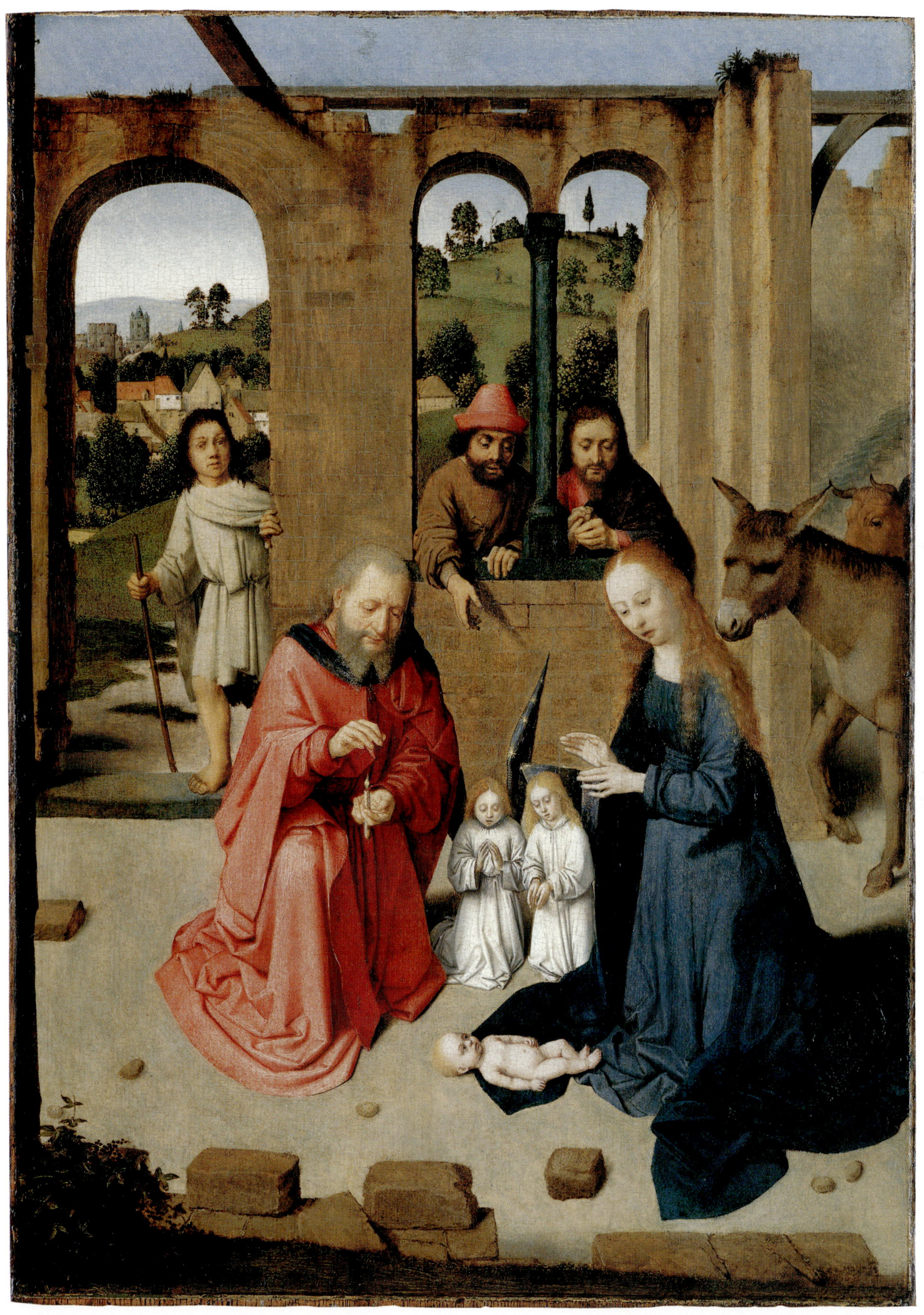

Gerard David, about 1455–1523

73. Saint John the Baptist; Saint Francis Receiving the Stigmata, about 1485–90

Wings of a triptych
Oil on wood; left wing, overall 18 x 6⅝ in. (45.7 x 16.8 cm); left wing, original painted surface 17⅝ x 5⅞ in. (44.8 x 14.9 cm); right wing, overall 17⅞ x 6½ in. (45.4 x 16.5 cm); right wing, original painted surface 17⅝ x 5¾ in. (44.8 x 14.6 cm)
The Friedsam Collection, Bequest of Michael Friedsam, 1931 32.100.40bc

Provenance: Private collection, Genoa; Richard Kaufmann, Berlin (1898–1917); sale, Cassirer and Helbing, Berlin, December 7, 1917, no. 76–77; Omnes van Nijenrode, Breukelen (1917–23); sale, Muller, Amsterdam, July 10, 1923, no. 7; Paul Bottenweiser, Berlin (1923); [Kleinberger, New York (1923)]; Michael Friedsam, New York (1923–31).

References: Wehle and Salinger 1947, pp. 89–92 (with earlier bibliography); Friedländer 1967–76, vol. 6b (1971), p. 100; Urbach 1971, pp. 10, 28; Fahy and Watson 1973, p. 53; Cleveland Museum 1974, p. 151; Scillia 1975, pp. 113, 127, 129–31, 133, 137, 174, 193; Morse 1979, p. 92; Ainsworth 1985, p. 59; Snyder 1985, p. 188; De Vos 1987, col. 215; Périer-d'Ieteren 1987, p. 95–106; Urbach 1987, p. 83–94; Van Miegroet 1989, pp. 273–74 (with additional earlier bibliography); Ainsworth 1994c, p. 484; Ainsworth 1998a.

When these two small paintings were bequeathed to the Museum by Michael Friedsam in 1931, they formed a triptych with the *Nativity* (cat. no. 72). Close physical examination of these works and new research, however, have revealed that before 1905 the panels with the saints were cut down somewhat at their lower edges and overpainted on the bare wood margins at their tops and sides to alter the dimensions of their painted surfaces. Although they were placed together with the *Nativity* in 1923 by the dealer Kleinberger, they did not originally belong with it.

John the Baptist was often represented in Netherlandish painting and was particularly popular in Bruges, but his pairing with Saint Francis, who was more universally venerated in Italy and Spain, is rare in the north. Instead of traditional gray, Saint Francis wears the brown habit of the reformed branch of the Franciscans (the Friars Observants), which had a cloister near the Ezelspoort in Bruges. Perhaps one of the prominent Italian merchants associated with the Franciscans there ordered an altarpiece with these wings, for the two panels were once in a collection in Genoa, to which they may well have been exported.

Only a few clues remain for a hypothetical reconstruction of the small altarpiece to which these wings once belonged. Both paintings share the theme of Christ's sacrifice and Crucifixion. Saint John points to a familiar metaphor for Christ, the "Lamb of God, which taketh away the sin of the world" (John 1:29–30); and Saint Francis miraculously receives the stigmata of Christ's Crucifixion from a winged seraph, while praying on Mount Alverna on the Feast of the Exultation of the Cross in 1224. The symbolism the paintings have in common indicates a Crucifixion, or possibly a Lamentation, as the most likely subject of the lost central panel. Indeed, paintings from David's workshop, namely a panel in the Chrysler Museum, Norfolk, Virginia, and a triptych in the Escorial, Spain, show the same two saints flanking a Crucifixion and a Lamentation, respectively.

Both *Saint John the Baptist* and *Saint Francis* reveal the influence of Bruges's most famous painter, Jan van Eyck, particularly of the renowned Ghent Altarpiece (figs. 17, 18), completed for Sint-Baafs church (Saint Bavo's) in Ghent in 1432. The frontal stance and massive bulk of the figure of Saint John, with its rhythmic and deeply cut drapery folds, recall the simulated sculpture, or grisaille, of the Saint John on the exterior of Jan's altarpiece as well as model drawings for a series of saints and apostles from Jan's workshop. The backdrop of carefully described exotic magnolia and cypress trees that cut off the view to the horizon likewise reflects the setting of one of Jan's interior panels portraying the hermit saints. In just the same way, the landscape construction of the *Saint Francis* imitates that of the *Saint Christopher with the Pilgrim Saints*, another interior wing of Jan's altarpiece. The figure of Francis, however, which is marked by a less rigid pose, more naturally arranged draperies, and a more refined facial type, looks forward to the developments in David's somewhat later works, namely the *Crucifixion* (cat. no. 75). The panels of the two saints may be dated after the *Nativity*, to David's early years in Bruges, about 1485–90.

MWA

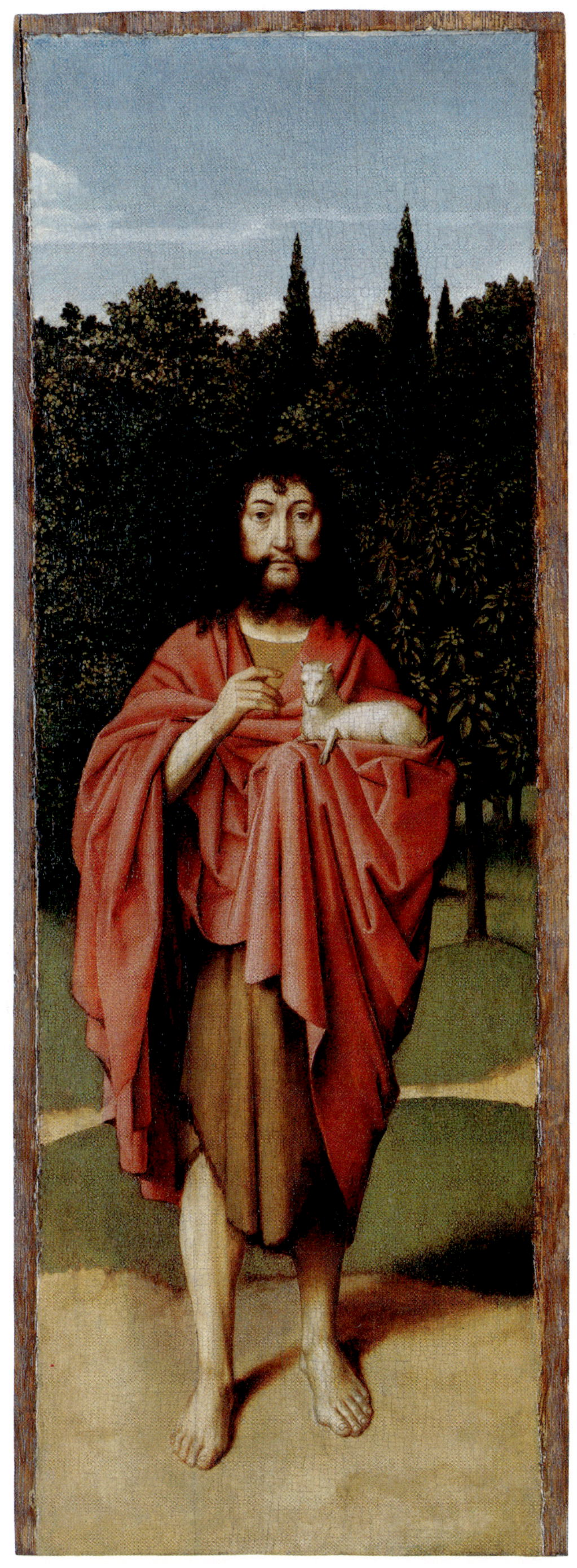

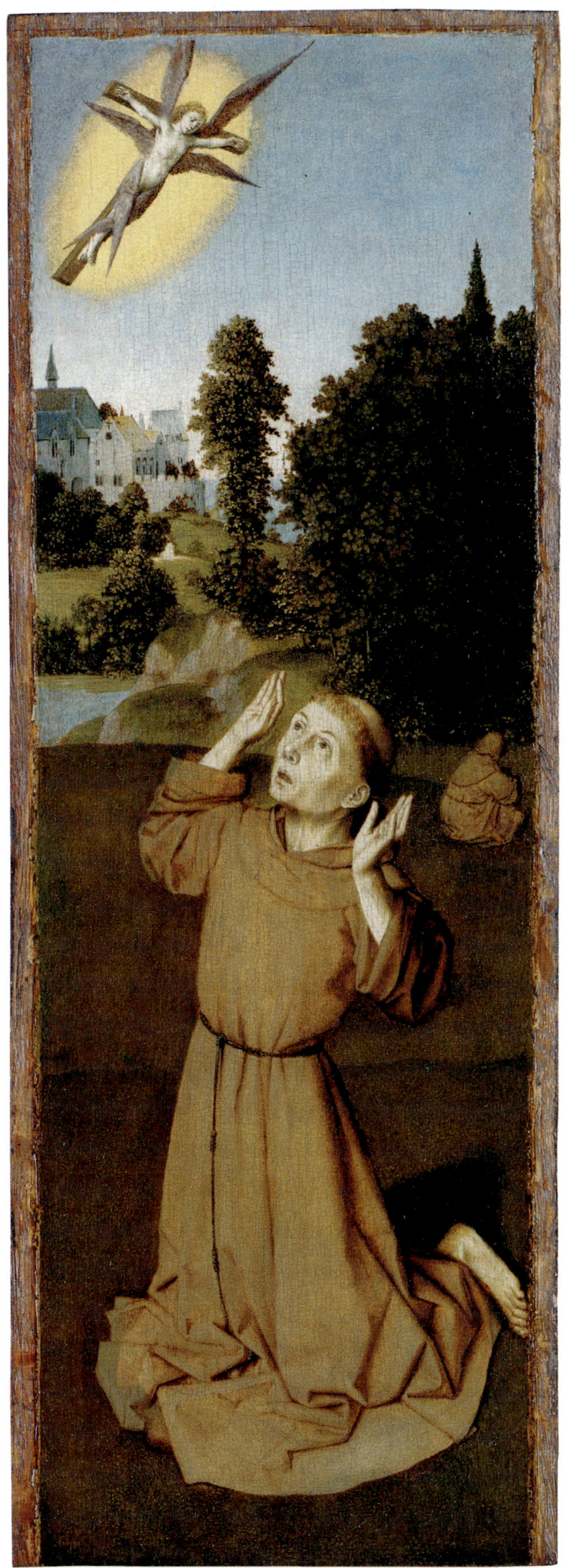

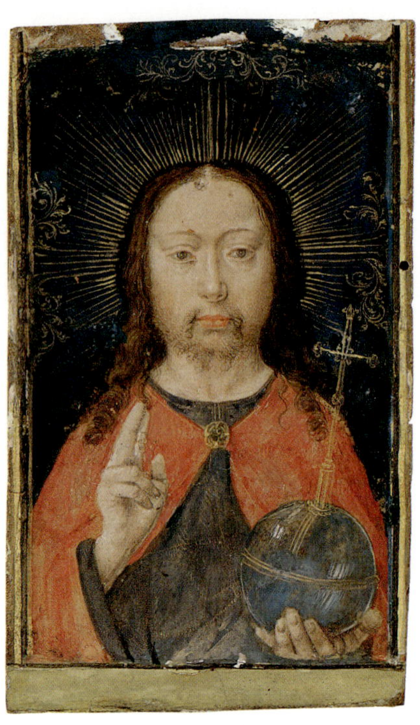

Gerard David, about 1455–1523

74. Holy Face, about 1485

Leaf from a Book of Hours
Tempera and gold leaf on parchment, trimmed and laid down on wood, 3½ x 2⅛ in. (90 x 54 mm)
Robert Lehman Collection, 1975 1975.1.2486

Provenance: Luigi Grassi, Florence?; [M. and R. Stora, Paris?]; Robert Lehman, New York, 1926.

References: Dobschütz 1899, pp. 197–262, 306–9; Hulin de Loo 1931, p. 42; De Ricci 1935–40, vol. 2, p. 1716; Schöne 1937, pp. 170–74; Van de Walle de Ghelcke 1952, pp. 402–6; Réau

This poignant, diminutive image presents not the stern judge of the Last Judgment but a portrait of Christ in all his humanity. Like the *Head of Christ* by Petrus Christus (cat. no. 3), it derives from a group of images believed to have been created miraculously. Known as *acheiropoetoi,* these included both the *vera icon* and the Holy Face. Most fifteenth-century versions of the Holy Face were based on one of two literary descriptions: an account purportedly written to the Roman Senate by Publius Lentulus but actually composed about the thirteenth century, and the fourteenth-century *Life of Christ* of Ludolph of Saxony. Publius Lentulus described Christ as "having a reverend countenance which they that look upon may love and fear; having hair of the hue of an unripe hazelnut . . . parting at the middle of the head according to the fashion of the Nazareans . . . ; having a full beard of the colour of his hair, not long, but a little forked at the chin."

Jan van Eyck followed this description for his frontal, hieratic portraits of Christ; two of the many extant copies of these paintings (Gemäldegalerie, Berlin, and Alte Pinakothek, Munich) are dated 1438 and carry the appellation *Rex Regnum* on the neckline of Christ's robe. This is the type that directly influenced the depiction in the Lehman illumination—David, however, added the right hand blessing and the left hand holding the orb, transforming the *Rex Regnum* into a *Salvator Mundi.*

This *Holy Face* was originally one of the many illuminations accompanying a text in a Book of Hours, but it has been trimmed on all sides and mounted and framed as an independent painting. *Holy Face/Salvator Mundi* miniatures were particularly popular in Books of Hours made in Bruges toward the end of the fifteenth century and into the beginning of the sixteenth; in these the image most often accompanied the prayer or hymn "Salve sancta facies" near the front of the book. One in particular, a *Holy Face* from the Croy Book of Hours (Österreichische Nationalbibliothek, Vienna, Codex 1858, fol. 14v), is very similar to the Lehman illumination, although there are variations in the gesture of the left hand and in the orb as well as in a number of other details. With its almond-shaped eyes and dense modeling, the Croy head recalls David's later paintings, such as the *Virgin among Virgins* of 1509 (fig. 84), which is extremely close to the illumination showing the same subject in the Morgan Library, New York (fig. 90). The Lehman example, with its rounder face, less severe expression, and rather stocky fingers, however, is more readily associated with David's early works.

There is a possibility that this miniature was excised from a Book of Hours dated 1486 that contains illuminations by several artists, including some attributed to David. The volume, which is in the Escorial, Spain (ciii 2, fol. 14v), is missing a number of miniatures that were cut out at an unknown early date, among them an image that accompanies the "Salve sancta facies" hymn near the beginning of the book. The dimensions, proportions, and even the traces of the arched top (most of which is cut off but whose lower remnants are visible at the right and left edges) of the Lehman illumination match the corresponding features of the few miniatures in the Escorial volume that have been attributed to David. If the Lehman *Holy Face* does indeed come from the Escorial Book of Hours, it should be dated about 1485; moreover, as a miniature from his hand it would provide evidence that David was active both as a panel painter and as a manuscript illuminator.

MWA

1955–59, vol. 2, part 2, pp. 17–19; Schiller 1971–72, vol. 2, pp. 78–79; Scillia 1975, pp. 165–73, 282, 286–87, figs. 31–33; Thoss 1986, pp. 131–45; Dogaer 1987, p. 166; Thoss 1987, pp. 117–18, no. 77; Van Miegroet 1989, pp. 77–79, 326–27, no. 84; Hand 1992, p. 10; Hindman 1997, pp. 84–92, no. 11, color ill.; Ainsworth 1998a.

Gerard David, about 1455–1523

75. The Crucifixion, about 1495–1500

Among Gerard David's most poignant images, this *Crucifixion* is presented as an enactment of the written word. Saint Jerome, one of the four fathers of the Church, is shown in his cardinal's robes, psychologically detached from the event at hand but reading about it from the Bible that he translated from Hebrew and Greek into Latin in the fourth century. True to the account of the Gospels, David has provided an appropriate sense of time and place. The sky is darkened, as it suddenly came to be at the death of Christ; bones are strewn on the ground, indicating the Crucifixion site of Golgotha; and the octagonal building in the background signifies the church of the Dome of the Rock in the holy city of Jerusalem. These token biblical references, however, are well integrated with a verdant hilly landscape of more local than foreign character. The scene epitomizes an early stage of David's interest in landscape, but one in which he had already mastered the subtle tonal transitions from foreground browns, to intermediate greens, to distant blue hues that achieve a convincing progression of space from the front of the picture plane to the far horizon. Jerome's lion casually wanders in the middle distance as a living part of nature rather than as an inanimate attribute of the saint.

This work was intended for private devotion, the figures of Saint John, the Virgin Mary, and Mary Magdalene assuming the poses and gestures of the viewer's own appropriate responses to Christ's ultimate sacrifice. As in the *Lamentation* by Petrus Christus (cat. no. 4), the Virgin collapses in John's

Oil on wood; overall 21 x 15 in. (53.3 x 38.1 cm); painted surface 20⅝ x 14¾ in. (52.5 x 37.5 cm)
Inscribed (on cross): ·Î N̂ R̂ Î
Rogers Fund, 1909 09.157

Provenance: Matteo Sarasqueta (by 1892); Robert Dell, London (until 1909).

References: Madrid 1892–93, no. 148; Bodenhausen and Valentiner 1911, p. 186; Conway 1921, p. 291;

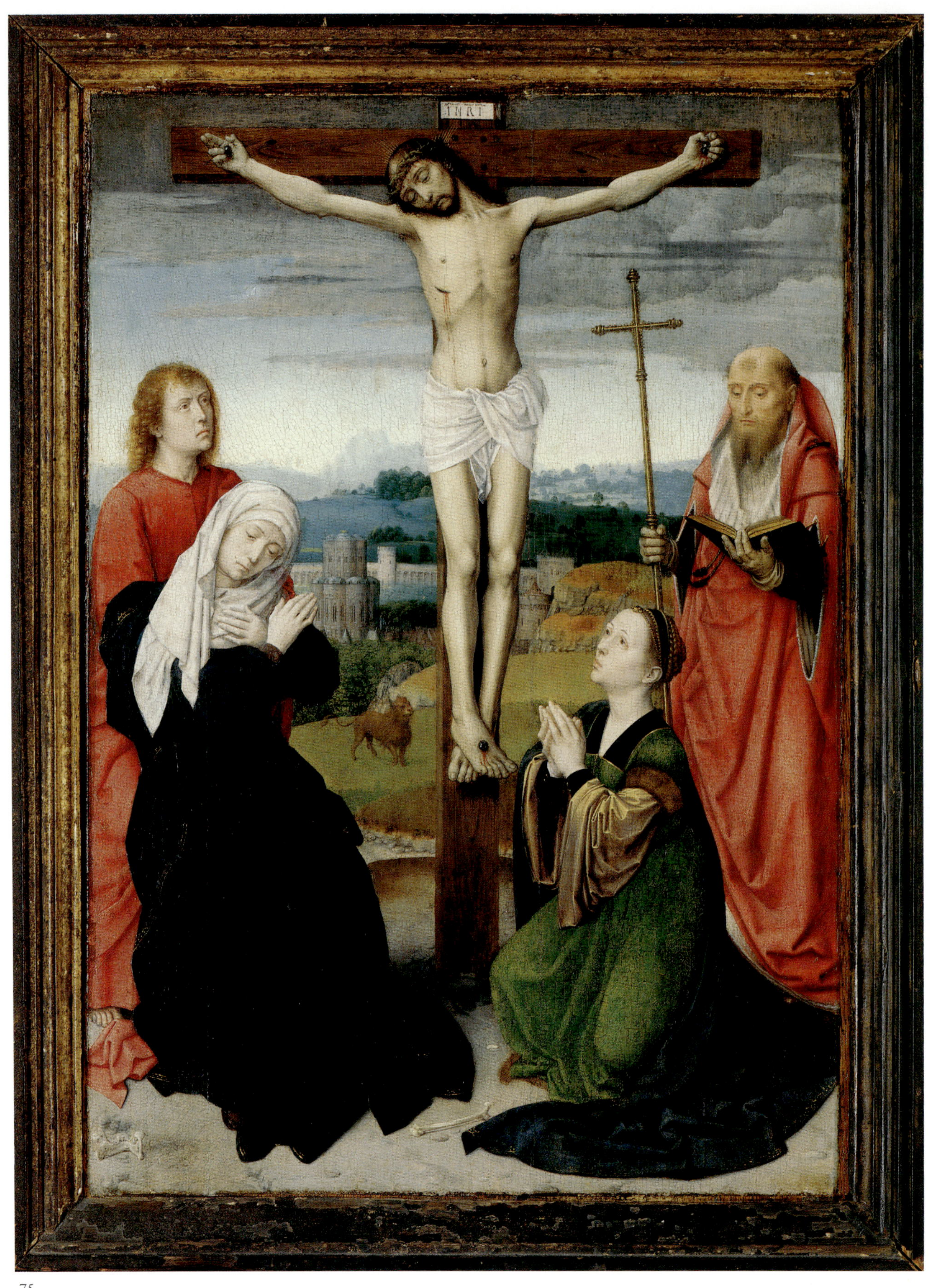

75

arms, dramatically exemplifying the themes of *compassio* and *co-redemptio*, or her empathic accord with the suffering and redemptive power of Christ. In a gesture of blessing with his right hand, Christ acknowledges the new relationship between his mother and the disciple John, who would henceforth take care of her, articulated in his declarations to her, "Woman, behold thy son!" and to John, "Behold thy mother!" (John 19:26–27). The lavishly attired and bejeweled Mary Magdalene, a repentant sinner, serves as an exemplum for the viewer in her prayerful appeal to Christ for salvation.

Although still favoring the palette of orange reds, olive greens, and gray blues for draperies, David abandoned the harsher brown hues of his earlier works for more subtle modulations in the flesh tones. Sweeter, softer facial types emerge here, perhaps as a response to the considerable influence that Hans Memling's art exerted in Bruges.

David's *Crucifixion*, in turn, inspired other versions of the subject attributed to artists who worked in his style, namely Adriaen Isenbrant (cathedral, Cuenca, Spain, and Collection of Her Majesty the Queen of England) and Ambrosius Benson (private collection, Wassenaar, the Netherlands).

Except for a replacement piece at the right, the frame is old and quite possibly original to the picture. Remnants of hinges at the left side, however, appear to be of more modern manufacture and most likely belong to a component for another painting that was added at a later date. MWA

Friedländer 1924–37, vol. 6 (1928), p. 145, no. 190; Wehle and Salinger 1947, p. 96; d'Otrange 1952, pp. 206, 210; Larsen 1960, p. 126; Friedländer 1967–76, vol. 6b (1971), p. 104, no. 190, pl. 198; New York 1972; Morse 1979, p. 92; Ainsworth 1985, pp. 54, 58, n. 3; Van Miegroet 1989, pp. 51, 280, no. 7; Ainsworth 1998a.

Gerard David, about 1455–1523

76. Christ Taking Leave of His Mother, about 1500

Devotional diptychs fashioned to close like books provided a convenience for travelers, who could easily display the small paintings at any stop during a journey. *Christ Taking Leave of His Mother* originally formed the right half of such a portable diptych, but at an unknown date it was separated from its pendant and cut at the top to fit a new frame.

The likely candidate for the left half is a *Virgin and Child with Angels*, also elaborately reframed, now in the Bearstead Collection, Upton House, Warwickshire (fig. 94). The two tiny panels are the same size and have matching gilt backgrounds decorated with remnants of stippling and feathered strokes emanating from the holy figures. The reverse of each panel is painted to simulate marble or porphyry, creating a decorative effect that enhances the precious quality of the diptych when it is closed. This pair is part of a series of similar diptychs produced by Gerard David (Kunstmuseum, Basel, and Alte Pinakothek, Munich) that show slight variations in the treatment of the two subjects. In the Metropolitan–Upton House diptych the *Virgin and Child* follows a standard pattern that has been transferred to the panel by pouncing; for the *Christ Taking Leave of His Mother* David made a rough underdrawn sketch in black chalk, adding the figures of the weeping Mary Magdalene and Martha to the more commonly depicted image limited to the Virgin and Christ.

Portable diptychs of this sort developed from Eastern icon painting and were produced in the fourteenth century in Italy and Bohemia. Taken together, the two panels focus on the human nature of Christ and the period of his presence on earth to achieve man's redemption. Neither theme comes directly from the Gospels but instead is linked to the *Meditations on the Life of Christ*, attributed to a

Oil on wood, arched top, 6⅛ x 4¾ in. (15.6 x 12.1 cm)
Bequest of Benjamin Altman, 1913 14.40.636

Provenance: Spain; Otto H. Kahn, New York; [Duveen, New York]; Benjamin Altman, New York.

References: Bodenhausen and Valentiner 1911, pp. 185, 188, no. 11; Conway 1916; Conway 1921; Friedländer 1924–37, vol. 6 (1928), p. 146; Boon [1946], p. 49; Wehle and Salinger 1947, pp. 92–93; Bruges 1949, p. 16; d'Otrange 1952, p. 211;

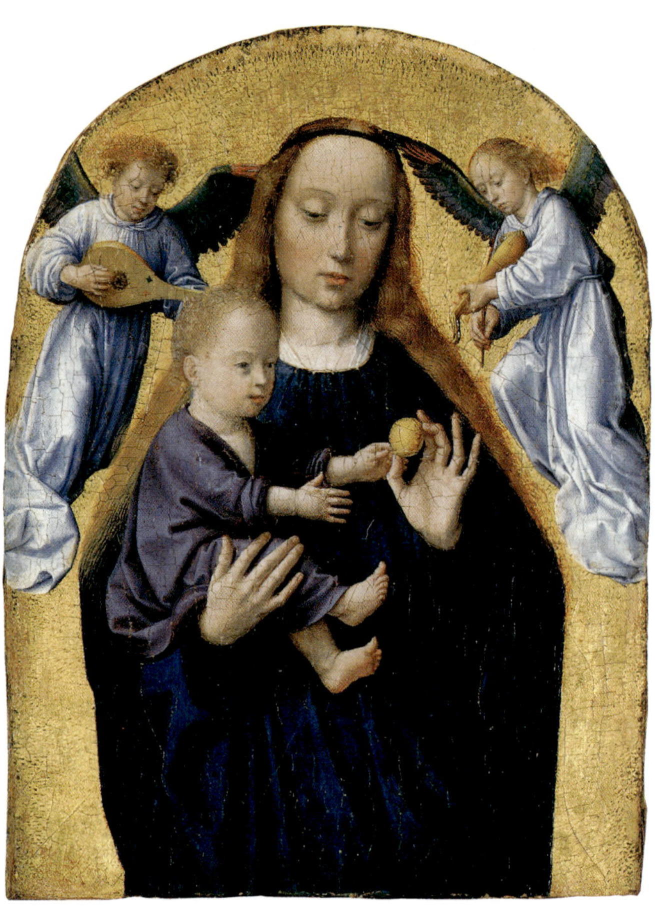

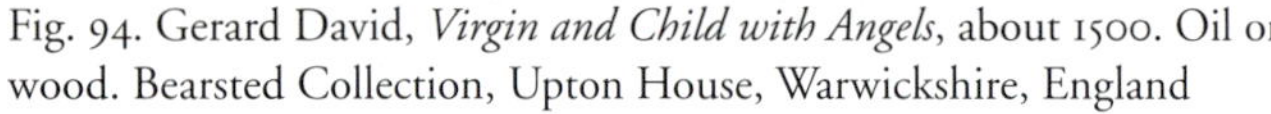

Fig. 94. Gerard David, *Virgin and Child with Angels*, about 1500. Oil on wood. Bearsted Collection, Upton House, Warwickshire, England

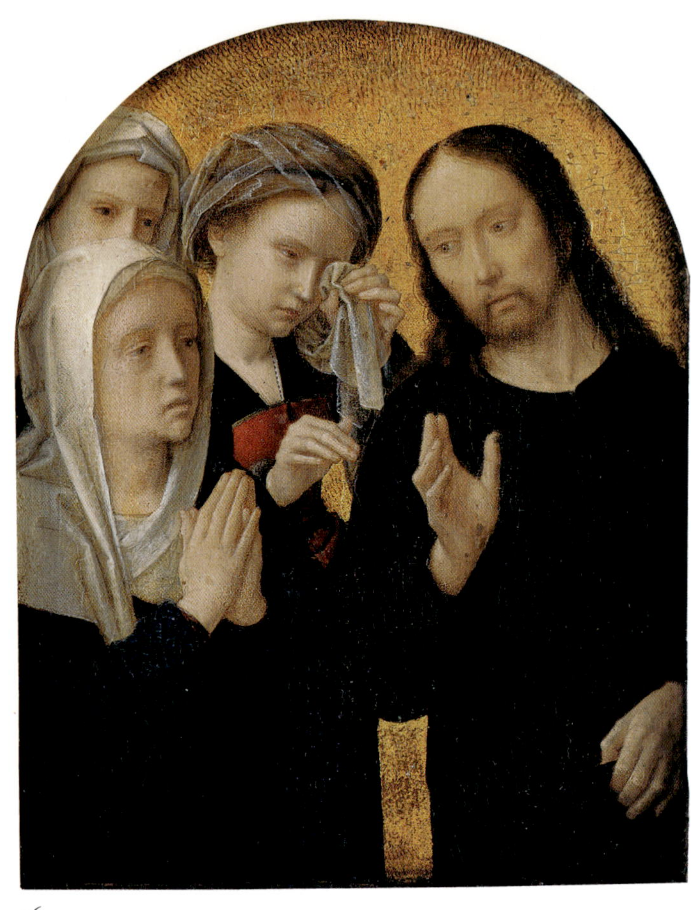

76

Mallet 1964, pp. 46–47; Friedländer 1967–76, vol. 6b (1971), p. 102, nos. 167–69, pls. 184, 185; Scillia 1975, p. 185; Mundy 1980a, p. 34, n. 56; Ringbom 1983, p. 175, n. 13; Vogelaar 1984, pp. 22–23; Woudhuysen-Keller 1987, pp. 112–13; Van Miegroet 1989, pp. 282–83, no. 11b, ill. pp. 102–3; Ainsworth 1998a.

Franciscan friar called the Pseudo-Bonaventure, which urges the reader to review the various stages of Christ's life. Thus, the Upton House panel examines one phase, emphasizing the sweet and tender nurturing of the Christ Child by the Virgin, while the Metropolitan painting depicts the drama of the mature Christ's departure for Jerusalem and his ultimate sacrifice. Chapter 72 of the *Meditations* tells of Christ's visit with his mother and Mary Magdalene to the house of Mary and Martha, where he dined with his disciples. There, although he is begged to stay, he utters, "Most beloved mother . . . the time of redemption is coming. Now all things said of me will be fulfilled, and they will do to me what they wish" (Ragusa and Green 1961, pp. 308–9). The diptych thus recalls Simeon's prophecy to the Virgin at the Presentation in the Temple: "This child is destined to be a sign which men reject; and you too will be pierced to the heart" (Luke 2:34–35). The Virgin in these two panels is a model for the compassionate response of the viewer to the joys and sorrows of her life and that of Christ.

The types of the Virgin, Mary Magdalene, and Christ are familiar from their appearances, albeit on a far grander scale, in David's *Deposition* in the Frick Collection, New York, and his Bruges *Transfiguration* and *Baptism of Christ*, respectively. The parallels suggest a date of about 1500 for *Christ Taking Leave of His Mother*, which corresponds to the date of the larger pictures. MWA

Workshop of Gerard David

77. Virgin and Child, about 1510

In the last half of the fifteenth and well into the sixteenth century in the Netherlands, individual pictures of the Virgin and Child were much in demand. Often they were hung on the walls of bedchambers or placed on sideboards to provide inspiration for private moments of prayer.

Renewed interest in this particular type of image, showing the tender embrace between mother and child, which is ultimately derived from Byzantine icons of the *glykophilousa* or *elousa* type, was stimulated by famous fourteenth-century Italian paintings, such as the Cambrai Madonna (fig. 49). In the Lehman variation the sorrowful expression of the Virgin betrays her prescience of the sad events to come and calls to mind another common type, known in numerous replicas from Gerard David's workshop, which portrays the Virgin with her cheek pressed against that of the dead Christ.

The specific pose in this *Virgin and Child,* in which the Child stands on the Virgin's lap as the two figures share an embrace, may have been developed by Rogier van der Weyden, as copies of a larger-format composition (a painting in the Ministry of National Education and Culture, Brussels, and a drawing in the Kupferstich-Kabinett, Dresden) by that master indicate. Our painting, however, does not show the full image presented in these copies—the left hand of the Virgin and the torso of the Child are oddly truncated, but the panel is not cut down. Several contemporary versions—in particular, two in reverse that are attributed to Adriaen Isenbrant (Aurora Trust, New York, and Museo Provincial, Saragossa)—give an idea of the more complete composition.

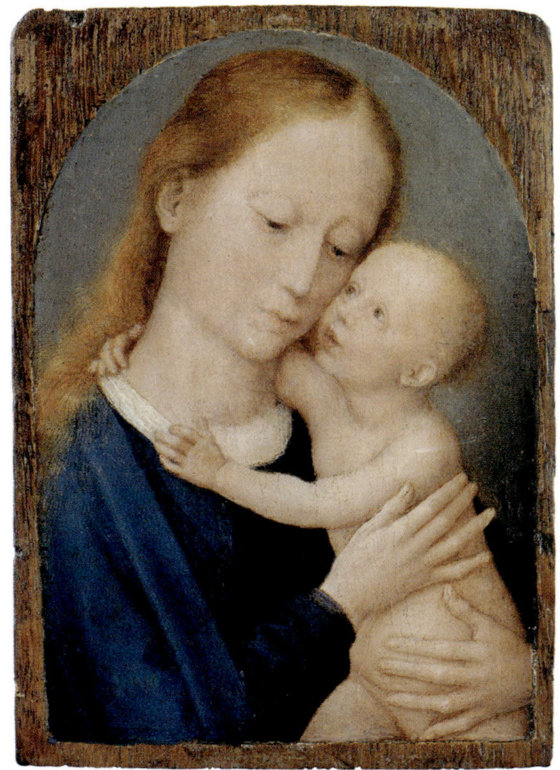

Oil on wood; overall 6⅛ x 4½ in. (15.6 x 11.4 cm); painted surface 5¾ x 4⅛ in. (14.6 x 10.5 cm)
Robert Lehman Collection, 1975 1975.1.118

Provenance: Sale, Sotheby's, London, November 3, 1965, no. 111, as Flemish School, 16th century, to Agnew, London; sold to Robert Lehman, New York, 1966.

References: De Vos 1971, pp. 146–48; Bermejo 1975, pp. 259–61, fig. 1; Ainsworth 1990, p. 654; Ainsworth 1993; Ainsworth 1998a; Wolff 1998, no. 22 color ill.

The wide dissemination of this motif suggests that the artist depended on a standard workshop pattern that was used repeatedly, and the underdrawing reveals a summary sketch for the Child's shirt and possibly a veil for the Virgin, features that appear in other painted replicas. The Lehman painting exhibits elements that indicate that it is the product of a workshop assistant: a tentative quality evident in the relatively weak drawing and also in the underdrawing of the Virgin's hands and facial features, as well as an awkward elongation of Christ's body in comparison with David's handling and execution.

MWA

Gerard David, about 1455–1523

78. The Annunciation; Christ Bearing the Cross and the Crucifixion; The Resurrection and the Pilgrims at Emmaus, about 1505

Exterior and interior wings of a triptych
Oil on wood; left wing, overall 34⅝ x 11⅝ in. (87.7 x 29.5 cm); painted surface 34 x 11 in. (86.2 x 27.9 cm); right wing, overall 34½ x 11⅞ in. (87.6 x 30 cm); painted surface 34 x 11⅛ in. (86.3 x 28.2 cm)
Robert Lehman Collection, 1975 1975.1.119, 1975.1.120

Provenance: Fourth earl of Ashburnham, Ashburnham, Battle, Sussex; Henry Willett, Brighton (by 1897); sold to Rodolphe Kann, Paris (d. 1905, cat. 1907, nos. 99, 100); sold by executors of the Kann estate to Duveen, New York (by 1908); sold to Philip Lehman, New York, March 1912; Robert Lehman, New York.

References: Weale 1903b, cols. 276–79, pl. 7; Bodenhausen 1905, pp. 108–11, fig. 11; Weale 1905c; Kann 1907, pp. 5–6, nos. 99, 100, pl. 100; Bodenhausen and Valentiner 1911, p. 189; Johnson collection 1913–14, p. 10; Friedländer 1916, p. 181; Conway 1921, pp. 282–83; Friedländer 1921, p. 191; Friedländer 1924–37, vol. 6 (1928), pp. 95, 144, no. 163, pls. 71, 72; Lehman 1928, nos. 86, 87, ill.; Siple 1929, p. 332; Mayer 1930b, p. 116, ill. p. 112; Tietze 1935, p. 334; Baldass 1936, pp. 92–93; Worcester–

The *Annunciation* originally formed the outside of wings that flanked the central panel of a folding triptych, and the two scenes from the Passion of Christ constituted the interior wings. When the altarpiece was closed, the *Annunciation* introduced the theme to be revealed on the interior, namely the redemption of mankind through Christ's sacrificial death and Resurrection.

The angel Gabriel and the Virgin Mary are painted in grisaille, to simulate stone sculptures. However, in an advance over earlier grisaille figures, by the Master of the Saint Barbara Legend, for example (cat. no. 13), David has discarded the socle bases and introduced natural coloring to the heads and hands, creating an ambiguous form of living sculpture. Further allusions to reality include the dove hovering without a connecting wall strut, draperies spilling out naturally over the edge of the niche, and nicks in the stone ledge indicating the effects of time and wear.

The interior wings show episodes from the Passion of Christ in a simultaneous narrative: *Christ Bearing the Cross* appears with the *Crucifixion* in its upper background, and the *Resurrection* is also depicted in front of and below events that took place later, namely Christ meeting two disciples on the road to Emmaus and revealing his true identity as he breaks bread with them in a small room above that scene. The likely theme for the centerpiece would be an event that occurred in the chronological interval between those portrayed on the wings, that is, a Descent from the Cross or a Lamentation. No Descent from the Cross by David of comparable dimensions remains, but Valentiner's proposal that the missing panel is the *Lamentation* in the John G. Johnson Collection at the Philadelphia Museum of Art has received general acceptance, mainly because the three paintings share compatible subject matter, similar dimensions, and a supposedly continuous landscape.

The reconstruction of these panels as an ensemble (fig. 95), however, shows an awkward juncture with disjointed spatial schemes and figures of different scales. Close examination of the *Lamentation* (by the author with Mark Tucker of the Philadelphia Museum of Art) indicates that early on it was cut down at its lower edge and repainted in the area of the rock masses at the far left and over the tomb opening at the right and in portions of the foreground, including the skull, bones, and plants, as well as in the dark streaks in the sky, in order to make it better match the wings. The draperies of Mary Magdalene and Saint John were also substantially repainted.

The *Annunciation* panels are David's only known grisailles on exterior altarpiece wings. Also anomalous is the vertical arrangement of narrative scenes and landscape on the interiors, which is *retardataire* and antithetical to the artist's contemporaneous innovations in landscape. The simulated stone figures, the vertical stacking of scenes, and the high horizon line are, however, consistent with the format of contemporary sculpted centerpieces. It is quite likely, then, that the missing centerpiece was originally intended to be a sculpted corpus presenting a Lamentation or Deposition as a main scene surrounded by subsidiary episodes of the Passion of Christ. Plans for the presumed sculpted centerpiece must have been altered at some point, and the Philadelphia *Lamentation* was apparently substituted for it. This necessitated adjustments to the *Lamentation* to suit the wings.

Despite questions about the original form of the Passion triptych to which they belonged, the attribution of the wings to Gerard David has not been questioned since their first publication by Weale in 1903. In particular, the attention to the details of individual figures—the varied and sensitive expressions of the faces, the studied hand gestures (especially those of the sleeping guard with opposing

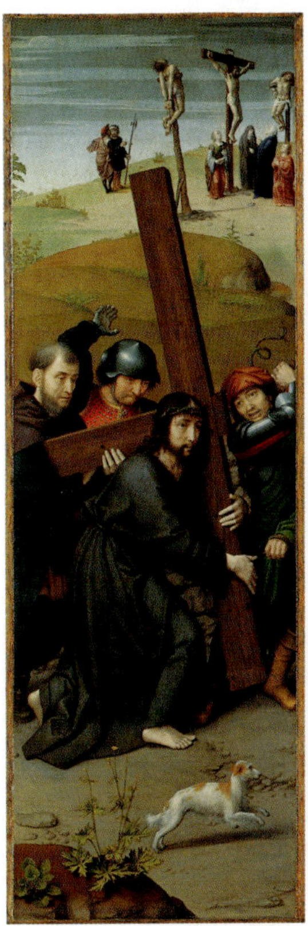
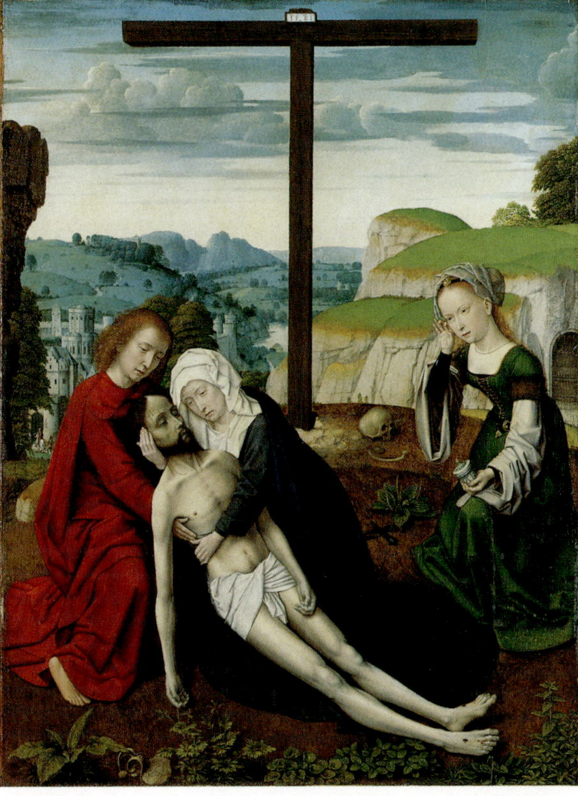
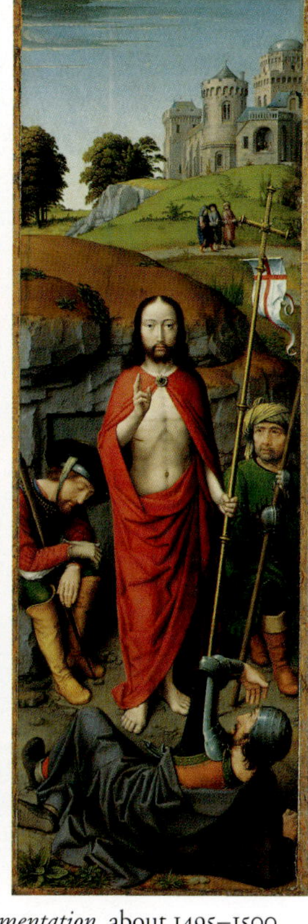

Fig. 95. Reconstruction of Gerard David, Lamentation Triptych, including central panel, *The Lamentation*, about 1495–1500. Oil on wood. John G. Johnson Collection, Philadelphia Museum of Art, and cat. no. 78, lateral internal wings,

Philadelphia 1939, p. 30; Heinrich 1954, p. 220; Larsen 1954, p. 103; Sterling 1957b, p. 136; Friedländer 1967–76, vol. 6a (1971), pp. 89, 101, no. 163, pl. 172; Johnson collection 1972, p. 28; Scillia 1975, pp. 238–39, 247, 297; Szabo 1975, pp. 88–89, figs. 62–64; Rutherford 1982, p. 178; Janssens de Bisthoven, Baes-Dondeyne, and De Vos 1983, p. 147; Ainsworth 1985, p. 58; De Vos 1987, col. 216; Metropolitan Museum 1987, p. 46, pl. 22; Van Miegroet 1989, pp. 48, 51, 278–79, no. 6, pls. 90, 91; Ainsworth 1990, pp. 649, 653; Bauman and Liedtke 1992, p. 326, no. 173, ill.; Ainsworth 1998a; Wolff 1998, no. 21, color ill.

gloved and bare hands), the specific description of costume (including reflections in the armor), the palette of reds, greens, and slate-gray blues—is characteristic of David's work in a phase that reveals his formative experiences with the art of Dieric Bouts.

The dating of the wings, however, is somewhat problematic, given the contradictory evidence of the rather outmoded composition and David's progressive tendencies. Certain facial types and rich color effects recall David's *Justice of Cambyses* paintings of 1498 (fig. 16), but the draperies, which are less sculptural and more supple than the ones in those works, indicate a later date. As Wolff has noted, the similarity of the present figure of Gabriel to the one featured in the *Annunciation* of the Cervara Altarpiece of 1506 (cat. no. 79) is significant. Furthermore, in its combination of a summary sketch in black chalk and a brush underdrawing that not only corrects but models the forms (compare figs. 78a and 78b), the underdrawing in the panels is comparable to that of David's Baptism of Christ Triptych of about 1502–8 (Groeningemuseum, Bruges). Dendrochronological analysis, indicating a time of creation after 1496, is consistent with a dating about 1505, which all of these factors suggest. MWA

The author gratefully acknowledges extremely helpful discussions regarding the Lehman and Philadelphia paintings with Mark Tucker (Conservator, Philadelphia Museum of Art).

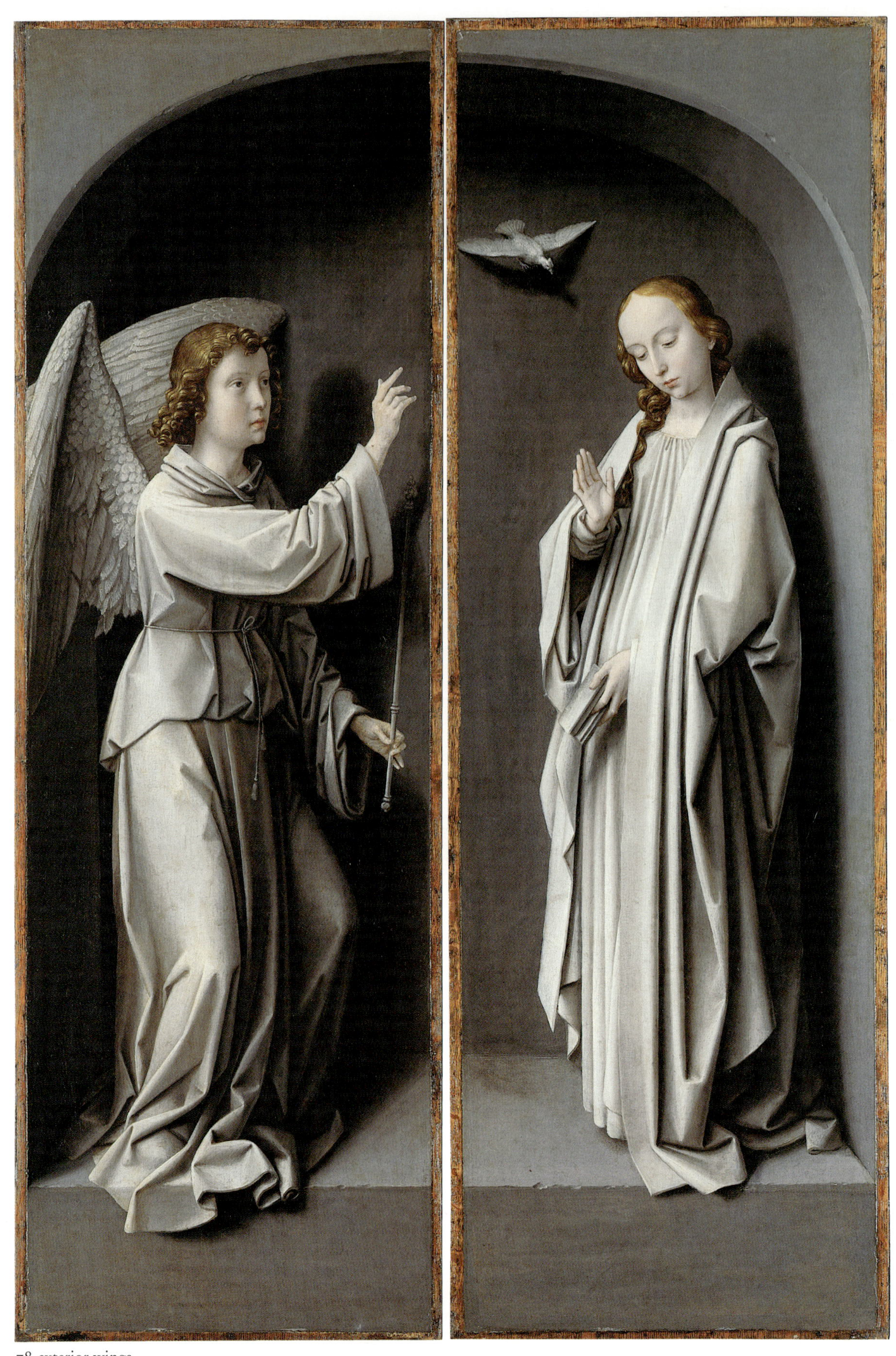

78 exterior wings

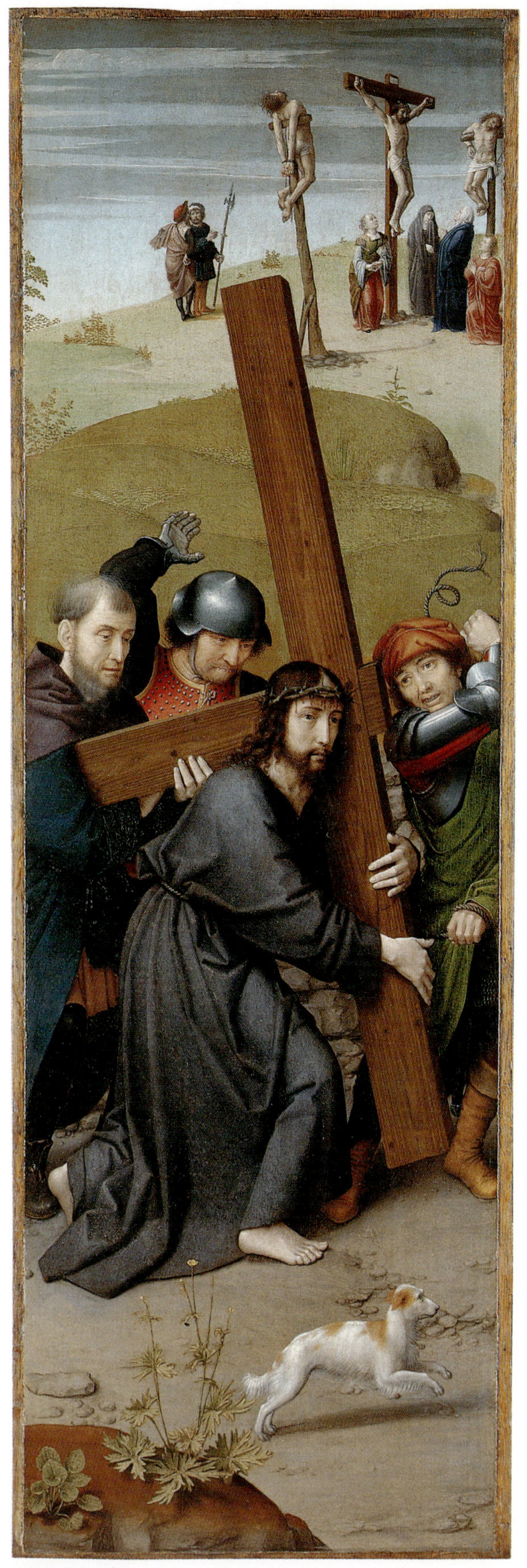

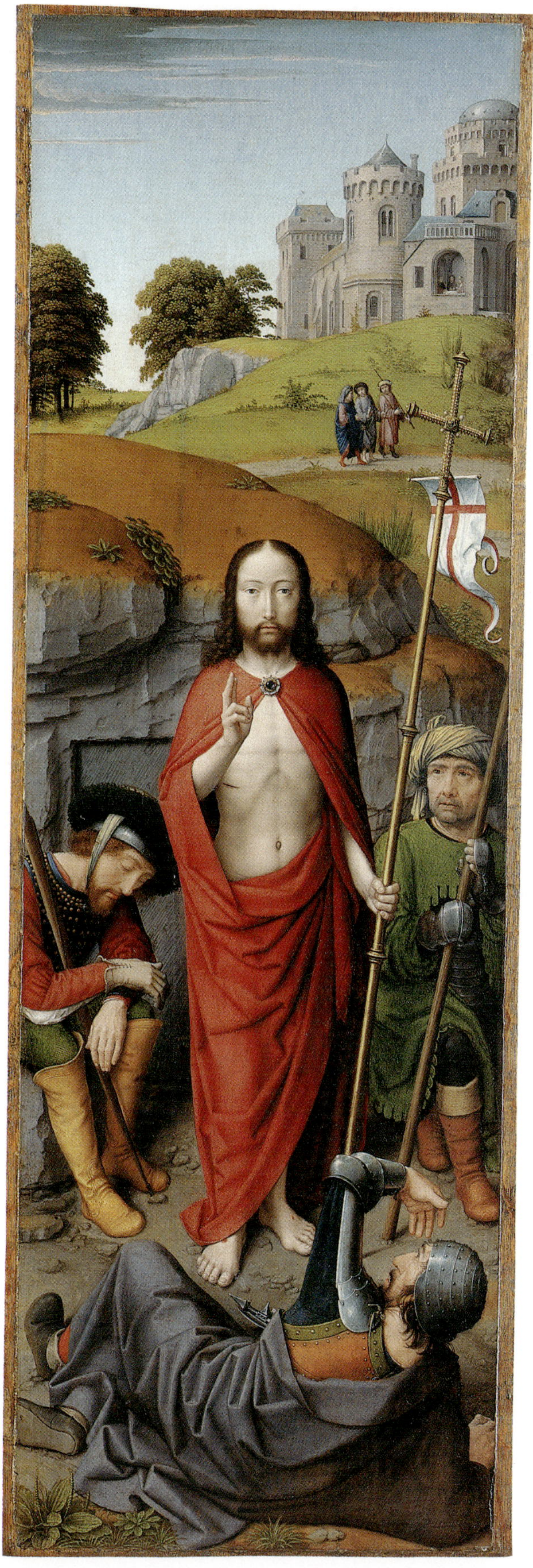

78 interior wings

Gerard David, about 1455–1523

79. The Annunciation: The Archangel Gabriel and the Virgin, 1506

Oil on wood; angel, overall 31⅛ x 25 in. (79.1 x 63.5 cm); painted surface 30¼ x 24⅜ in. (76.8 x 61.9 cm); Virgin, overall 31⅛ x 25¼ in. (79.1 x 64.1 cm); Virgin, painted surface 30½ x 24¾ in. (77.5 x 61.9 cm)
Inscribed: (on angel's cope) [VIRTUS AL]TISSIMI OBOMBRABIT T[IBI] ([The power of the] Highest shall overshadow thee [Luke 1:35].) and ALPHA ET OM[EGA] (I am Alpha and Om[ega], the beginning and the ending [Revelation 1:8]); (on Virgin's robe) MOEDER ONS HER[N] / AVE • MARIA MATER GRACI[A]E • M[ATER] / MISERICORDI[A]E • TV • NOS:ABHOS[TE] • [PROTEGE] (Mother of our Lord / Hail Mary, Mother of Grace, Mother of Mercy, protect us from the enemy [and at the hour of death take us] [from a hymn, the Salve Regina, and its response])
Bequest of Mary Stillman Harkness, 1950 50.145.9ab

Provenance: Benedictine abbey of San Gerolamo della Cervara, Liguria; Gabriel J. P. Weyer, Cologne (1862); Heberle sale, Cologne, August 25, 1862, no. 217–18, as Van Eyck; Prof. Dr. A. Muller; Prince Karl Anton von Hohenzollern Sigmaringen, Sigmaringen (1885–1929); [A. S. Drey, Munich and New York]; Mr. and Mrs. Edward S. Harkness, New York (1929); Mary S. Harkness, New York (1940).

Gerard David's most important foreign commission was for a large retable comprising seven separate panels to be installed on the high altar of the former Benedictine abbey of San Gerolamo della Cervara, situated on the coast of Italy near Genoa, midway between Portofino and Santa Margherita Ligure. The now-lost inscription on the base of the altarpiece read: "Vincenzo Sauli had this work made in 1506 on the seventh day of September." In 1799, during the Napoleonic suppressions, the Benedictine monks had to abandon the abbey, and the polyptych was dispersed.

Giuseppe Spinola mentioned six panels in the description of the altarpiece he penned in his 1790 history of the monastery; Castelnovi later suggested a hypothetical reconstruction with six pictures: a lunette, *God the Father* (Louvre, Paris); the Metropolitan's two *Annunciation* panels below the lunette; and, on the lowest level, the *Virgin and Child* flanked by *Saint Jerome* and *Saint Benedict* (Palazzo Bianco, Genoa). Recent research by Hyde into the provenance of the individual panels, as well as our consideration of stylistic and iconographic factors, now allows for a revised reconstruction (fig. 96) that also includes a *Crucifixion* (Palazzo Bianco, Genoa) placed between our two panels on the second tier of the polyptych in a configuration typical for Ligurian altarpieces. Although originally attributed to Frans Floris, Luca d'Olanda (Lucas van Leyden), and Albrecht Dürer, all seven of these paintings have been indisputably ascribed to David since 1895.

Vincenzo Sauli, the wealthy banker and diplomat who commissioned the altarpiece, was a member of a prominent Genoese family that had connections with Bruges. Whether the commission was carried out in Genoa or in Bruges, where Sauli family members worked as bankers by 1506, cannot be determined. However, the detailed nature of the iconography and the style of the paintings make clear that David had specific information about the location for which they were destined and suggest that he may even have visited the abbey before embarking on the project.

The seven panels constitute an ensemble that is not only David's most ambitious surviving work but also one of his most beautifully conceived and executed designs (see fig. 96). The majestic symmetrical arrangement of the panels provides the overall composition with flanking figures accompanying the Virgin and Child and the Crucifixion—the key iconographic components of the first two tiers—and the climax in the lunette of God the Father with two seraphim at the apex. The altarpiece employs a unified one-point perspective scheme for the first and second levels with focal points that are intentionally off-center to the left, probably devised to somewhat soften the severity of the mood. An internal system of sight lines that move through carefully positioned motifs continually directs the viewer's eye through the figures on the central axis.

In the *Annunciation* and the *Crucifixion* David took the position of the viewer and the placement of the panels within the altarpiece into account, adjusting the perspective scheme and scale of the figures. Thus, the rapidly receding perspective of the floor tiles in the *Annunciation*, the odd proportions of the figures in the paintings—for example, Gabriel's foreshortened lower legs and elongated upper legs and torso and the elongated bodies in the *Crucifixion*—and the low horizon line of the *Crucifixion* were adopted because these panels occupied the second register and were meant to be seen from below. By the same token, the figures in both the *Annunciation* and the *Crucifixion* are smaller than those in the paintings on the first level, since they are seen from farther away.

Much of the subject matter and presentation of David's polyptych was dictated by the nature of the abbey church for which it was commissioned and by the fact that it was meant for the high altar (see Ainsworth 1998). In its depiction of the Virgin and Saints Jerome and Benedict the lower tier honors

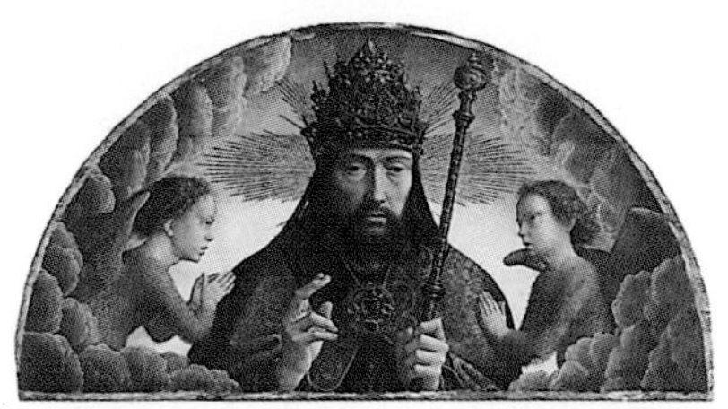

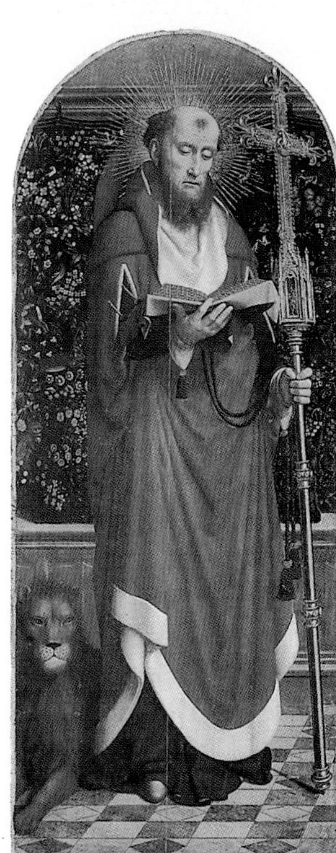

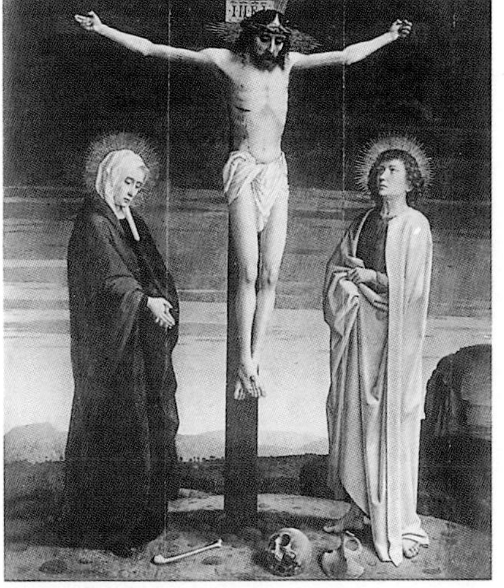

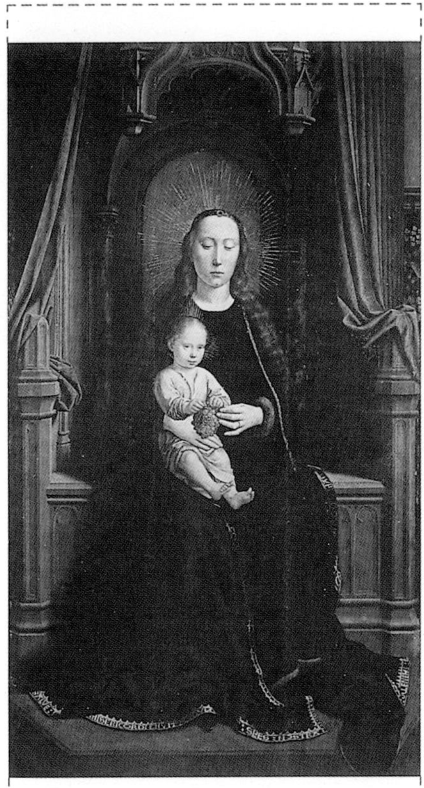

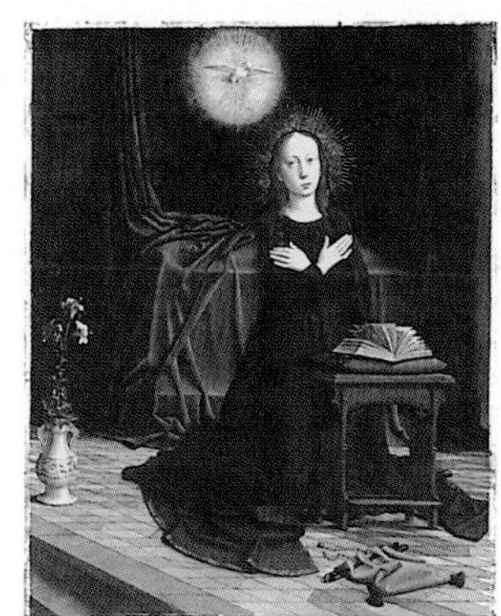

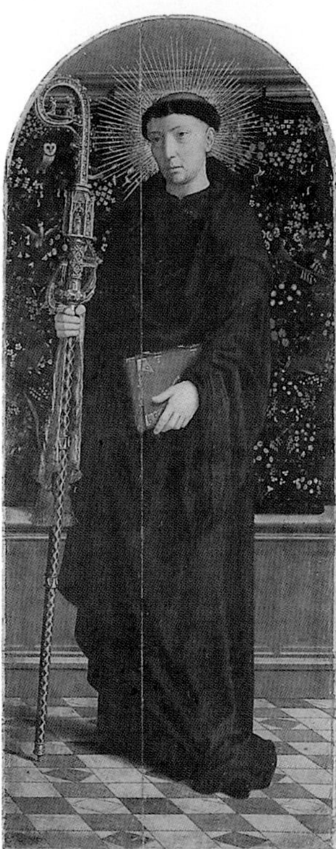

Fig. 96. Reconstruction of Gerard David, Cervara Altarpiece, 1506

References: Bodenhausen 1905, pp. 157–58, 164–65, 173–75, 178–79; Vitale 1934, pp. 4, 48, 134–35; Castelnovi 1952, pp. 22–27; Hoogewerff 1953, pp. 72–73; Röthel 1956, pp. 361–65; Adhémar 1962, pp. 135–44; Friedländer 1967–76, vol. 6b (1972), pp. 107, 127; Klein 1986; Van Miegroet 1989, pp. 212–17, 294–95, no. 25; Ainsworth 1990, p. 652; Ainsworth in Bauman and Liedtke 1992, pp. 88–89; Tagliaferro and Di Fabio 1992, p. 40; Hyde 1994, pp. 246–60; Di Fabio 1997; Hyde 1997; Ainsworth 1998a.

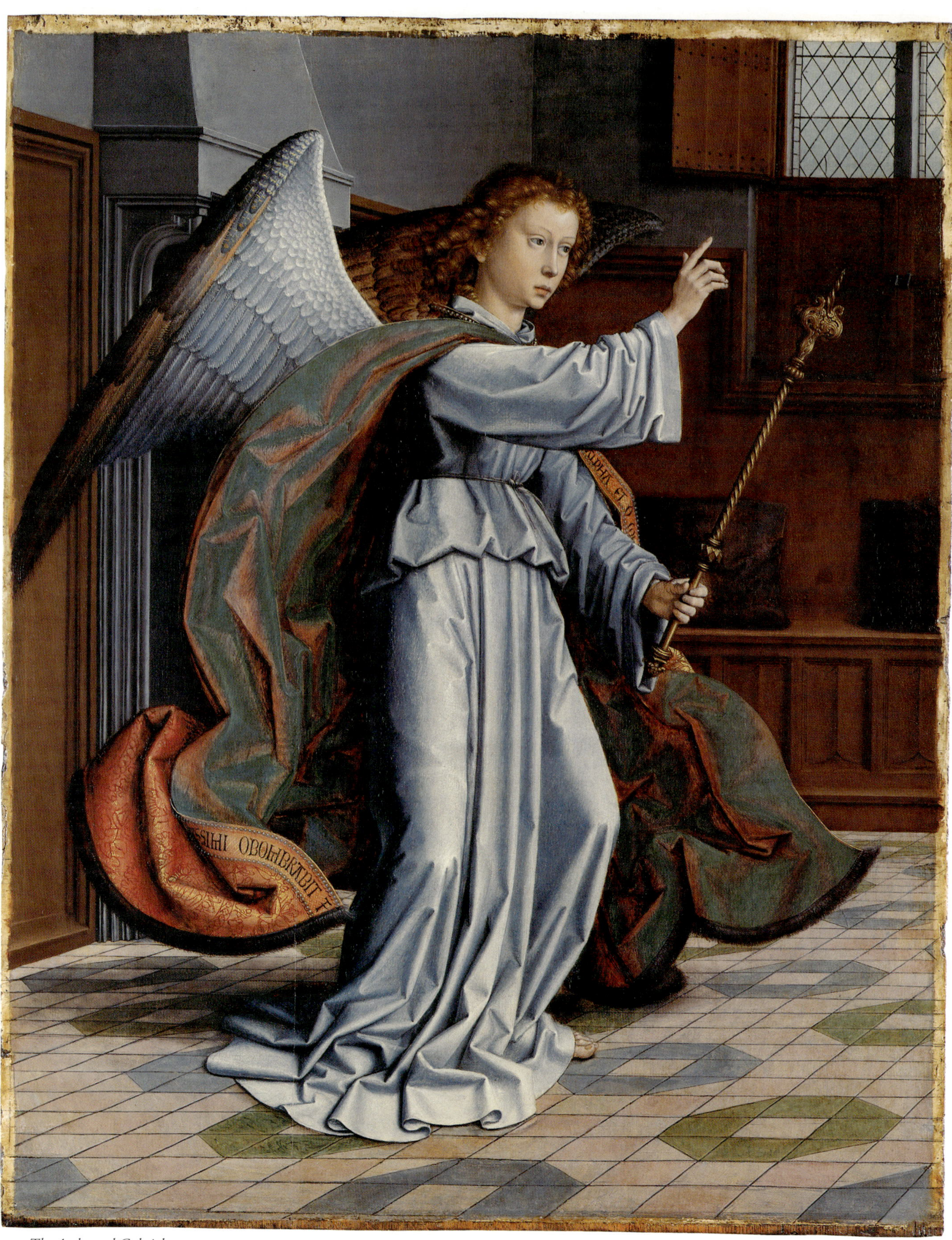

79, *The Archangel Gabriel*

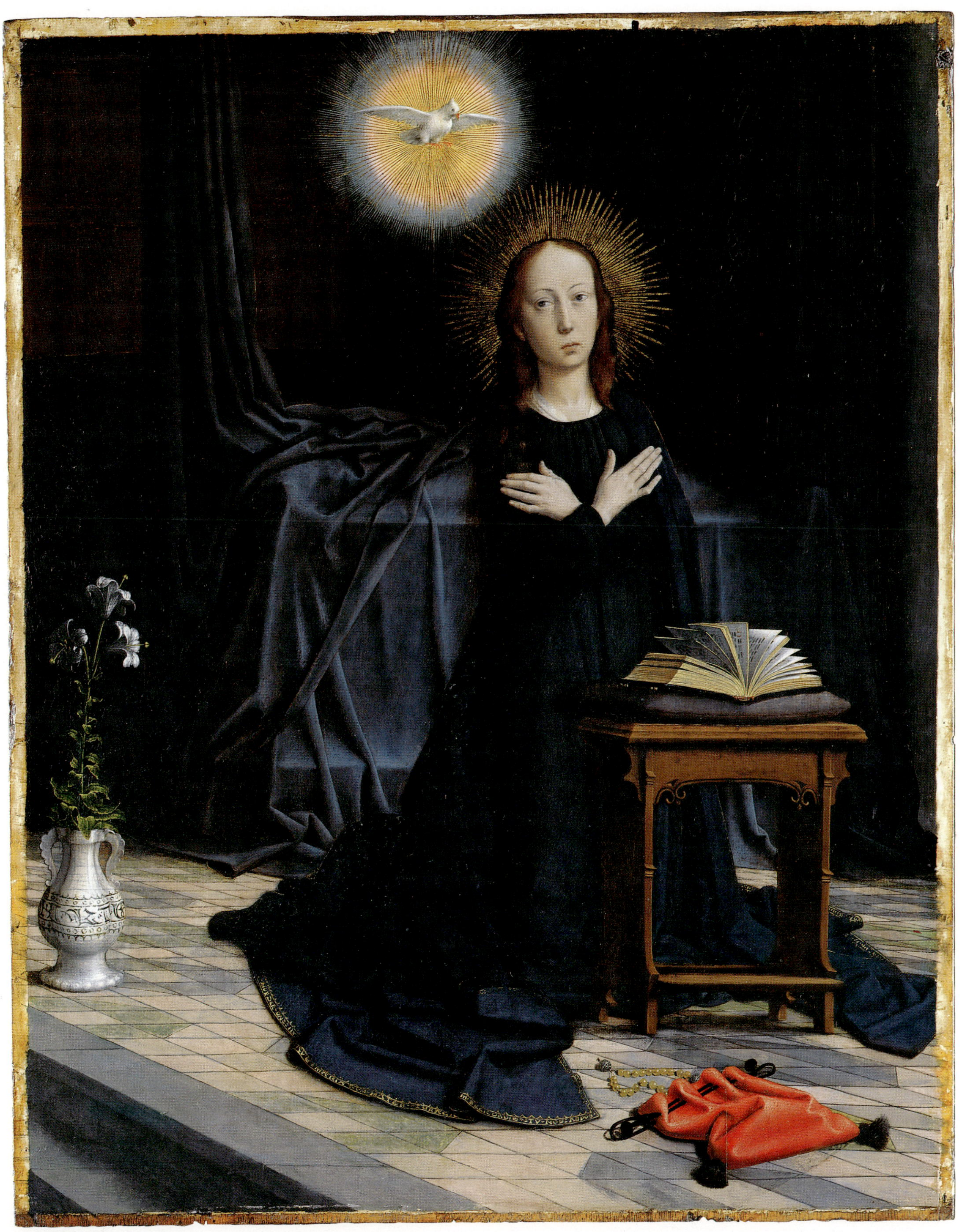

79, *The Virgin*

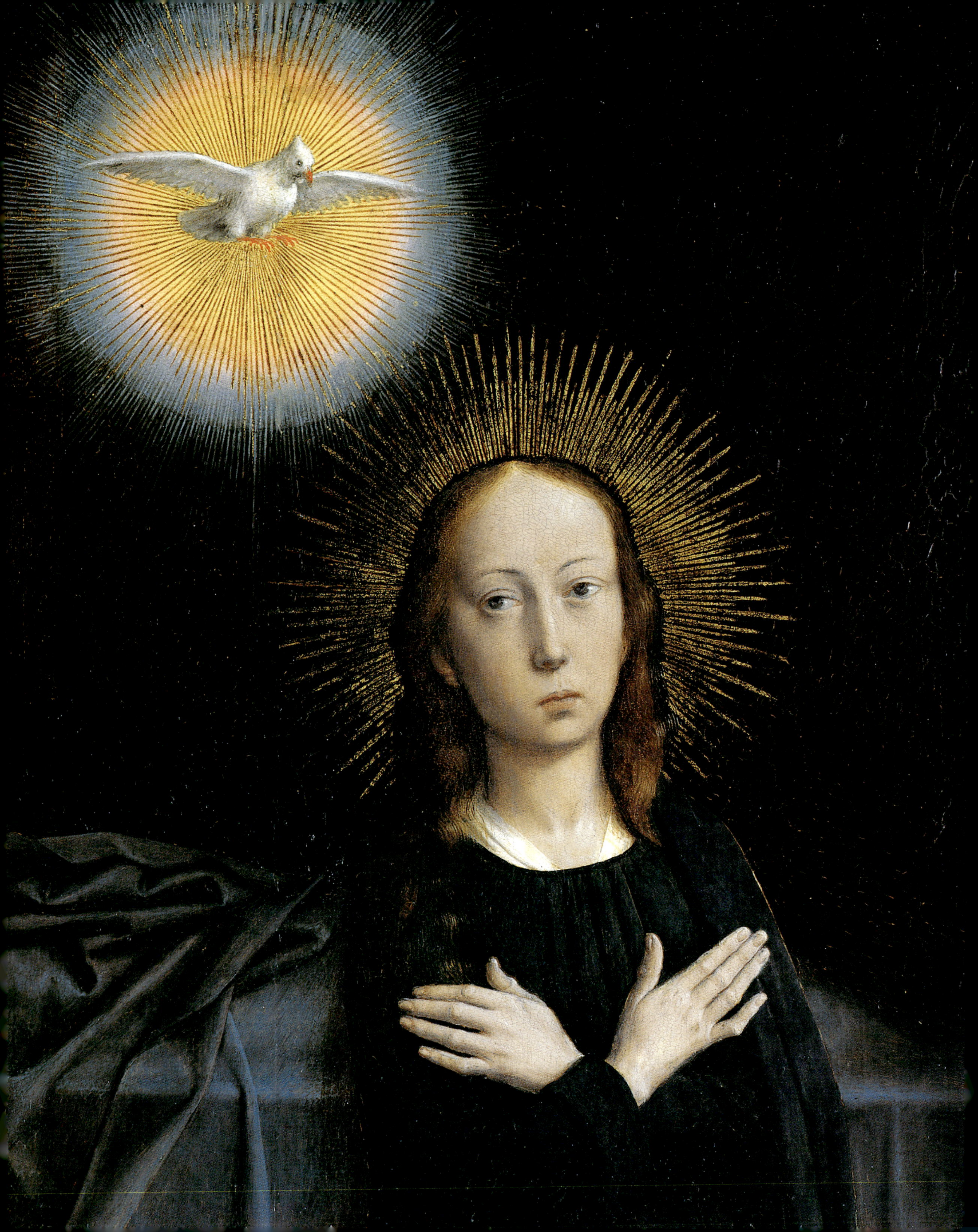

the devotion of the church and its monastery to Mary and the veneration of Jerome (for whom the abbey is named) and Benedict (founder of the Benedictine order of its monks). On the second level the two Annunciation panels signal the Incarnation of Christ, shown sacrificed on the cross in the painting positioned between them. In the top register God the Father, all knowing and all seeing, carries out his will from the heavens above. The words of the Lord from Luke 1:35 and Revelation 1:8 that adorn Gabriel's cope unite the second and uppermost tiers: "[The power of the] Highest shall overshadow thee. . . . I am Alpha and Om[ega], the beginning and the ending." A special emphasis on the Eucharist, which was celebrated at the high altar, is established by motifs along the main vertical axis of the ensemble, beginning at the bottom with the Christ Child holding the grapes (signifying the blood of Christ), proceeding to the actual act of sacrifice—the Crucifixion—and culminating at the top in God the Father, who brings judgment and redemption. Inscriptions refer to liturgical practice that would have been carried out regularly: on the hem of the Annunciate Virgin's dress are the words "Mother of our Lord / Hail Mary, Mother of Grace, Mother of Mercy, protect us from the enemy [and at the hour of death take us]" from a hymn sung at vespers and lauds in the office of the Virgin and the commendation of the soul; and on the hem of the garment of the Virgin on the first tier is the text of an extremely popular antiphon, the Salve Regina, and its response.

There can be no mistaking the altarpiece's Italianate organization, which is modeled after that of Ligurian retables of the late fifteenth and early sixteenth centuries. In its style, however, the ensemble reveals a synthesis of northern and Italian modes that perhaps reflect the Sauli family's personal and professional ties to both regions. The monumentality and solemnity of the Virgin, the exclusion of all anecdotal detail from the Crucifixion, and the division of the Annunciation into two separate panels are among the Italianate features. Moreover, in a departure from David's habitual manner, light is shown issuing from the right in every panel, in conformity with the convention of north Italian altarpieces that are placed on the high altar. Also in accordance with Italian practice, halos adorn the principal figures: those of Christ and God the Father are of one type—a tripartite nimbus—while those of the Virgin and saints are a general golden radiance. And the figure of Gabriel, imbued with a new grace and urgency of movement and wearing a classical, peploslike robe and a cope with a red-and-green *couleur changeante* interior, suggests a particular Italian model. This may have been the Gabriel in Vincenzo Foppa's 1468 fresco of the Annunciation in the Portinari chapel of Sant'Eustorgio in Milan, which David could have seen on a trip to Lombardy and Liguria. Coexisting with these elements of Italian derivation are others firmly rooted in northern tradition: the figures of God the Father and the Annunciate Virgin, inspired by the Van Eyck brothers' Ghent Altarpiece, and details of typical Bruges manufacture, such as the millefleur tapestry that hangs behind the figures on the first level.

The extent of David's accommodation of his foreign client in the Cervara Altarpiece is readily apparent when the Metropolitan's *Annunciation* is compared to another version of the same subject by the artist, the *Annunciation* in the Städelsches Kunstinstitut, Frankfurt. The two interpretations treat the theme in terms of similar poses and compositions, and they also share the same date (indeed, according to Klein, both are made on panels from the same tree); yet the Gabriel of the Frankfurt work is the pure northern counterpart of the Italianate angel in our panel. MWA

Opposite: Detail, cat. no. 79

Gerard David, about 1455–1523

80. The Nativity with Donors and Saints Jerome and Leonard, about 1510–15

Oil on canvas, transferred from wood; central panel 35½ x 28 in. (90.2 x 71.1 cm); each wing 35½ x 12⅜ in. (90.2 x 31.4 cm)
The Jules Bache Collection, 1949 49.7.20a–c

Provenance: Urrutia family, Navarra; Ramon F. Urrutia, Madrid (by 1920); [Duveen, Paris and New York (by 1928)]; sold to Jules S. Bache, New York (1928); exterior wings detached from triptych (1930–32), sold to Rijksmuseum, Amsterdam (1932), and placed on long-term loan to Mauritshuis, The Hague (1948).

References: Wehle and Salinger 1947, pp. 95–96 (with earlier bibliography); Bruges 1949, p. 15; d'Otrange 1952, pp. 207–9; Panofsky 1953, pp. 278, 470 n. 1; Mauritshuis 1956, pp. 16–17, no. 12; Marlier 1957, pp. 88, 124; Van Braam 1958, p. 105, no. 1170; Larsen 1960, pp. 125–26, figs. XXVa–c; Winkler 1964, p. 152, n. 4; Cuttler 1968, p. 197, fig. 247; Koch 1968, p. 66; Mauritshuis 1968, p. 22, no. 843; Van Puyvelde 1968, p. 211; Von der Osten and Vey 1969, p. 307; Van Miegroet 1989, pp. 230–32, 298, no. 30 (with additional earlier bibliography); Cleven 1990; Devisscher 1992, p. 191; Harbison 1995d, pp. 137–38; Härting 1995; Ridderbos 1995a, pp. 123–24; Bruijnen 1997; Buijsen 1997; Ainsworth 1998a.

One of Gerard David's major contributions to the development of early Netherlandish painting was his naturalistic portrayal of landscape, and the outside wings of this Nativity Triptych (fig. 97) are his greatest achievement in this realm. These lush forest scenes of oak, silver walnut, and beech trees, plantain, and yellow iris are inhabited by an ox, two asses, and a great tit perched on a foreground branch, but they are devoid of human presence. As such, these landscapes were unique for their time; they heralded a genre that would become commonplace only later, in seventeenth-century Dutch and Flemish painting.

Perhaps because of their complete novelty as well as a "picturesque" overpainting (since removed) of the building on the left wing, the landscapes were not thought to be by David and were removed from the triptych in the 1930s and sold to the Rijksmuseum, Amsterdam. (They are now on long-term loan to Mauritshuis, The Hague.)

The frequent designation of the Mauritshuis panels as the first independent landscapes in Netherlandish painting disregards their function, which is to introduce the Nativity on the triptych's interior. Among the various theories that have been proposed concerning the enigmatic meaning of the forest views, one of the most plausible links them with Old Testament passages from the Book of Job (39:5–9) or from Isaiah (32:11–20). In the former the wild asses and the wild ox (seen in the left and right foreground of each panel) are described wandering in the free state they enjoyed before finding their true master in Jesus Christ (near whom they kneel in the triptych's interior scene). The latter text also features the ox and the ass, as well as other details of the forest scene—the "thorns and briers," the "waters," the deserted "houses of joy"—that prefigure the birth of Christ.

Although these references may provide the biblical context for this portrayal, David's specific representation of the forest elicits the viewer's perception of and participation in the scene, as a familiar, contemporary local site. In accordance with the text of Ludolph of Saxony's *Life of Christ,* which encourages the reader to experience the sufferings and joys of the Holy Family event by event, the viewer visually wanders through the forest as Joseph and Mary physically wandered, seeking a place for the birth of Christ. Passing by the house at the left (the inn where Joseph and Mary were refused a night's stay?) and out of the forest (shown again with a similar house at the upper right of the open triptych) onto the broad grassy plain, the viewer suddenly encounters the magnificent Nativity scene on the interior of the altarpiece. The notion of the journey to this site and its later continuation is underscored by Joseph's uncommon appearance. Instead of the conventional old man in long robe, cloak, and pattens (cat. nos. 7, 45, 72), a youthful Joseph (conforming to the descriptions in tracts by the Bruges theologian Jean Gerson) appears, wearing the traveling costume more usual in depictions of the subsequent Flight into Egypt (cat. nos. 69, 82), that is, a short robe, long hose, and soft boots, with his walking stick placed nearby on the sheaf of wheat.

The setting here is no mere hovel, but a dilapidated palace often identified as the former residence of the Old Testament King David, an ancestor of Christ. Despite the joyful moment depicted, the expressions and gestures of the figures strike a somber tone, in recognition of the fact that this birth will culminate in Christ's sacrifice for the redemption of mankind. This meaning is reinforced by the dandelion—a flower that blooms at Easter time—prominently displayed on the wall above the ox and the ass, the eucharistic symbolism of the sheaf of wheat ("I am the bread of life"), and the basket with

Opposite: Fig. 97. Gerard David, *Forest Scenes* (exterior wings, Nativity Triptych), about 1510–15. Oil on wood. Mauritshuis, The Hague, on loan from Rijksmuseum, Amsterdam

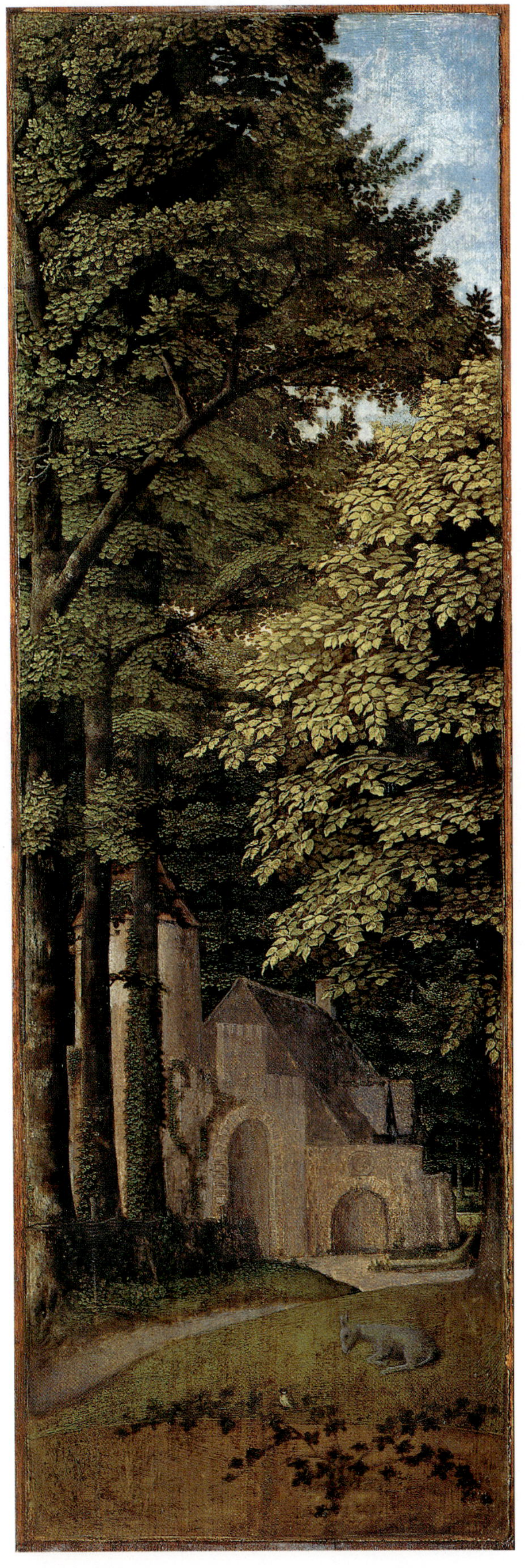
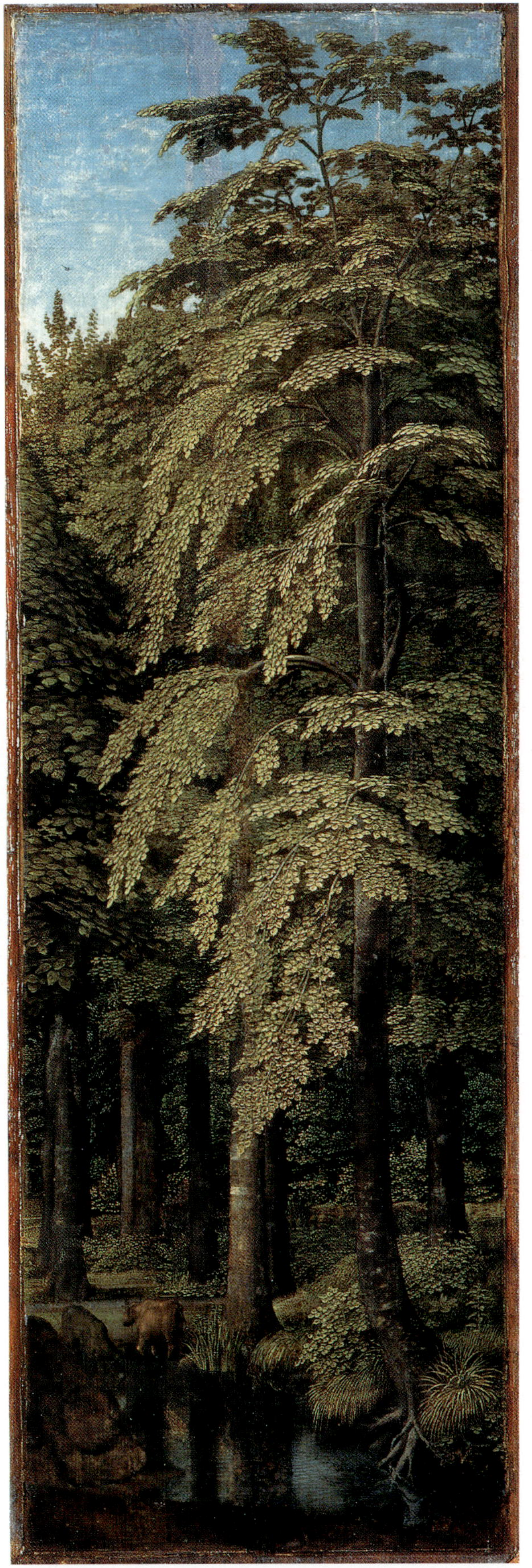

the swaddling cloth, which suggests the winding cloth used to prepare the dead Christ for burial.

Such an innovative altarpiece must have been an important commission. Its provenance can be traced to the Urrutia family, which originally came from Navarra in Spain. The female donor portrayed on the right wing and her husband, shown on the left wing, however, have remained unidentified. They may be a Catherine and an Anthony because they are represented in the guise of saints of those names, together with their accompanying attributes: Saint Catherine, richly garbed, with her crown, sword, and wheel, and Saint Anthony Abbot, identified by the pig at his feet. (Technical examination reveals these attributes to have been planned at the outset, not added at a later time, as previously supposed.) The two donors are presented by Saint Leonard, a deacon, holding a devotional book and shackles, and Saint Jerome, in cardinal's attire, with his lion resting nearby.

Certain details of the composition, specifically the imagery of the manger and the young Joseph and Mary in adoration of the Christ Child, and the placement of the sheaf of wheat in the foreground, owe a debt to the paintings of Hugo van der Goes, especially his *Nativity* in the Gemäldegalerie, Berlin. David has, however, reformulated these features for his own grand concept, in which the figures are now fully integrated into a naturalistically arranged space where landscape assumes a new prominence. These innovations are characteristic of David's later phase, even surpassing his achievement in the Baptism of Christ Altarpiece of 1502–8 (Groeningemuseum, Bruges). The Nativity Triptych, therefore, can be dated about 1510–15.

The triptych inspired a number of later paintings produced by David's workshop and close followers: a *Rest on the Flight into Egypt*, which takes place before a landscape modeled on the *Forest Scenes* (private collection, Genoa), two Nativities attributed to Ambrosius Benson (The State Hermitage Museum, Saint Petersburg, and Yale University Art Gallery, New Haven), and several Nativity panels by members of the group associated with Adriaen Isenbrant (Museum Mayer van den Bergh, Antwerp, and Öffentliche Kunstsammlung, Basel, among others).

MWA

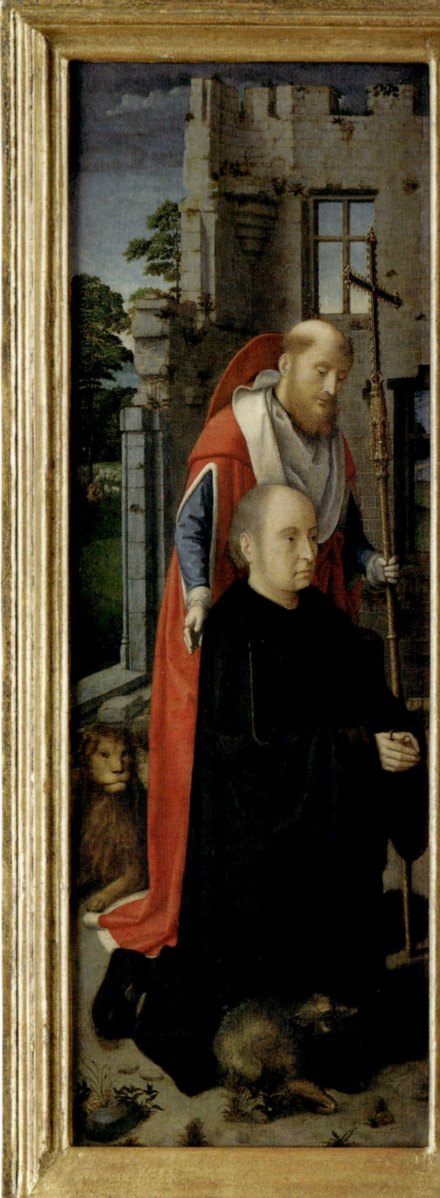

80

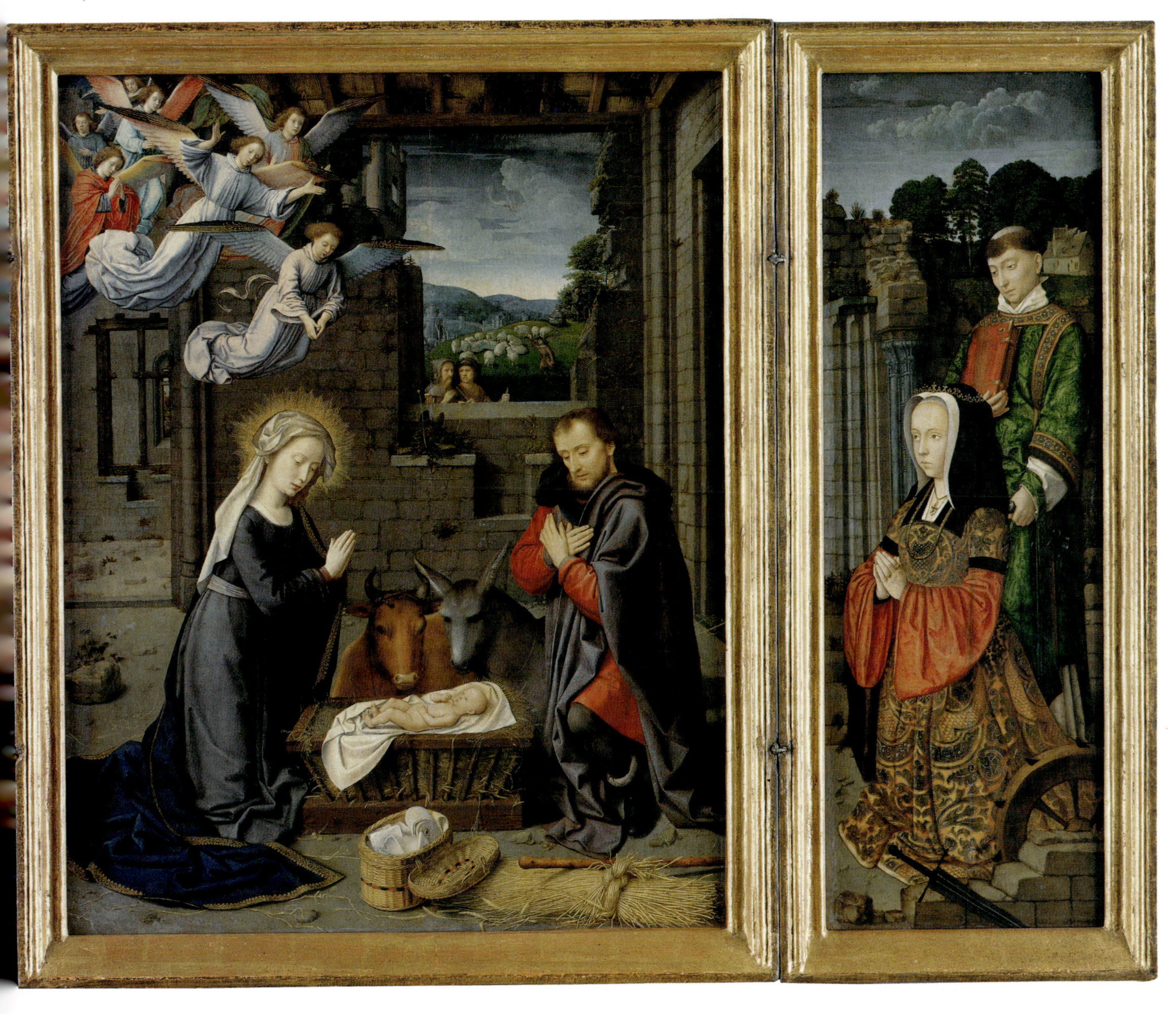

Gerard David, about 1455–1523

81. Virgin and Child with Four Angels, about 1510–15

Oil on wood, 24⅞ x 15⅜ in. (63.2 x 39.1 cm)
Inscribed (on cloth): IHESVS [RE]DEMPT[OR] (Jesus Redeemer)
Gift of Mr. and Mrs. Charles Wrightsman, 1977 1977.1.1

Provenance: Private collection, Madrid; Abelardo Linares S.A., Madrid (ca. 1940); Charles B. Wrightsman, New York (1962–77).

References: Scholtens 1938, pp. 49–62; Fahy 1969, pp. 190–95; Thyssen-Bornemisza collection 1969, p. 207; Fahy and Watson 1973, pp. 53–61; Silver 1983, p. 101; Ainsworth 1985, pp. 53–60; Van Miegroet 1989, pp. 305–6, no. 38; Martens 1995, pp. 29–55; Ainsworth 1998a.

Resplendent in her red cloak with gold trim, the Virgin holding the Christ Child is crowned Queen of Heaven by two angels to the accompaniment of strains from the lute and the harp played by two additional angels. The Coronation of the Virgin refers not only to Mary's Assumption and triumph over death but also to her particular relationship with Christ as it is discussed in the contemporary exegeses of the love poetry of the Song of Solomon. In this context the rosary beads held by the Christ Child in his left hand allude to the prayer recited with the rosary, the Ave Maria.

The presentation of the theme is conventional in its iconography, but David has transformed and modernized it by indicating a setting in contemporary Bruges. The Virgin stands as the personification of the Church at the *Porta Coeli* (Gate of Heaven) in a grand arched porch whose columns are decorated with ornate Italianate capitals. The traditional *hortus conclusus*, signifying the Virgin's purity, is converted into a naturalistic garden where a Carthusian monk casually strolls while reading. The Carthusian monastery at Genadedal, outside the city walls of Bruges, may be intended here, as the local churches of Sint-Jakobs (Saint James) and Onze-Lieve-Vrouw (Our Lady) (its tower as it appeared before alterations were made in 1519) are visible beyond the wall in the background, at the left and right of the Virgin's head.

Beyond the Coronation theme, the painting is specifically concerned with the redemption of man and the Virgin's participatory role as co-Redemptrix with Christ, a concept developed extensively by Carthusian writers. The flowers of the garden—columbine (for melancholy or sorrow) and iris (or sword lily, representing the prophecy of Simeon that the rejection of Christ by man will pierce the Virgin through her heart), here accompanied by the strawberry (symbol of perfect righteousness)—are those associated with the Seven Sorrows of the Virgin, whereby Mary showed her compassion in connection with specific events of Christ's suffering. The words "IHESVS [RE]DEMPT[OR]" on the cloth below the Child underscore this meaning, as do the headbands with crosses worn by the angels and the red of the Virgin's cloak (the color of Christ's Passion). By sharing Mary's compassion through meditation on the suffering of Christ, the devout sought her intercessory powers for their own salvation.

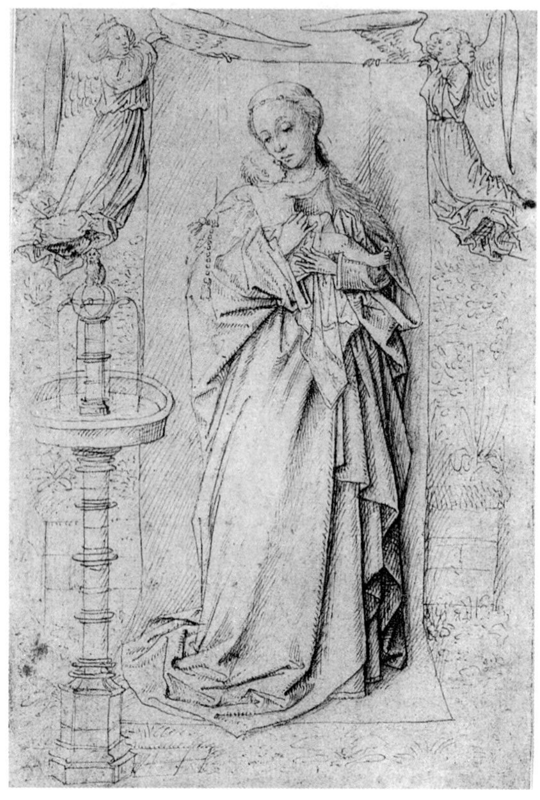

Fig. 98. Gerard David, copy after Jan van Eyck, *Virgin and Child at the Fountain*, about 1505–10. Pen and ink on paper. Kupferstichkabinett, SMPK, Berlin

The model of the Virgin and Child in David's picture appears in no fewer than six paintings and at least one manuscript illumination by various artists, most of which were made in Bruges. This fact suggests that the prototype was a venerated icon, probably located in Bruges. In this connection, it is intriguing to recall that three paintings described as

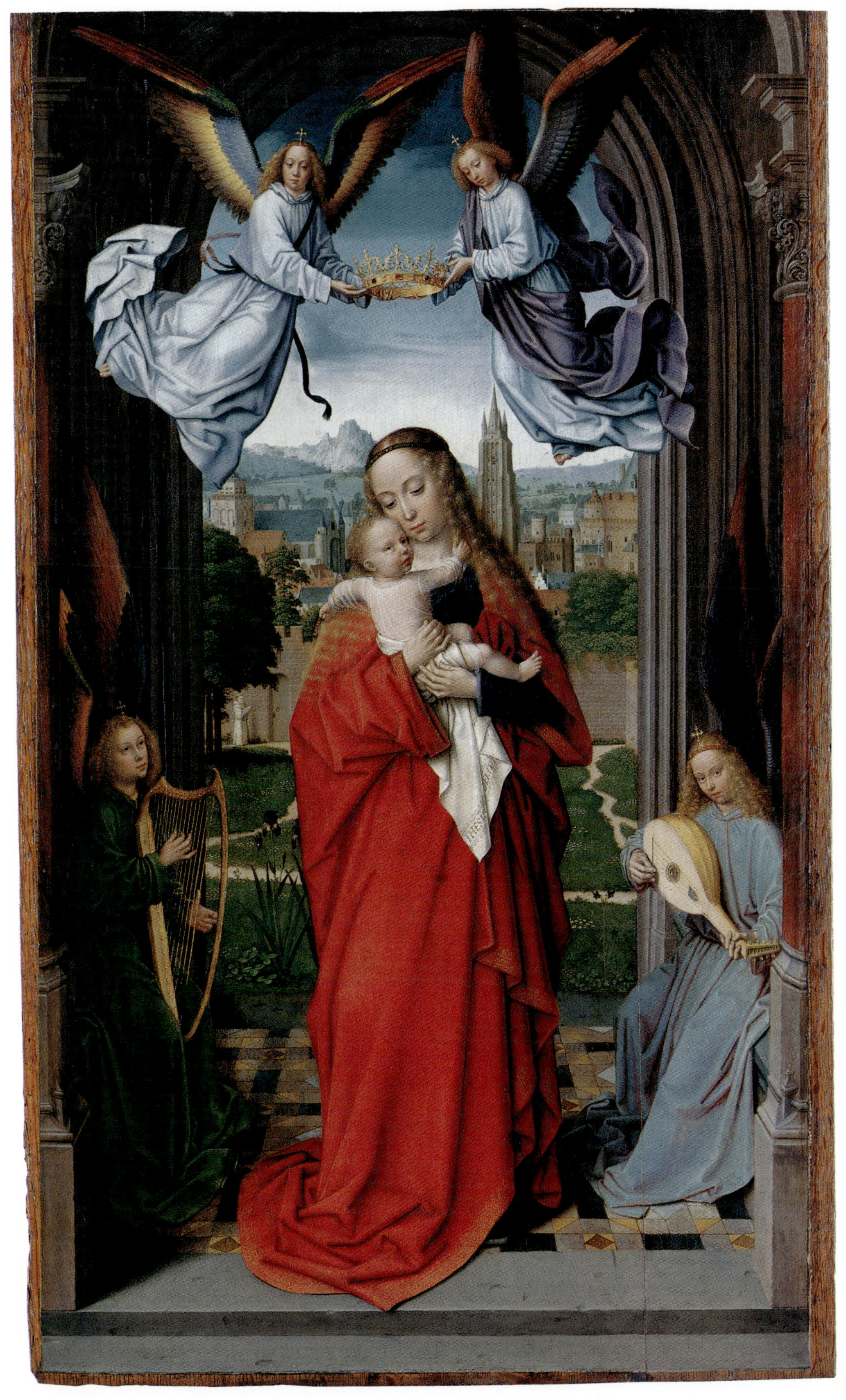

variants of a Virgin and Child, among them the *Virgin and Child with Saints Barbara and Elizabeth and Jan Vos* from Van Eyck's workshop (fig. 14), were consecrated with indulgences associated with them by Bishop Martinus of Mayo on his visit to the Carthusian monastery of Genadedal in 1443. Through fervent prayer before such an image, viewers hoped to realize their most deeply desired experience, a vision of the Holy Virgin come alive—as embodied in David's painting.

David's specific inspiration for his *Virgin and Child* was Jan van Eyck's *Virgin and Child at the Fountain* (fig. 10)—a painting to which he undoubtedly had access, for he made an exact copy of it in pen and ink on paper (fig. 98). Here, as in the *Rest on the Flight into Egypt* (cat. no. 82), the artist demonstrated an advanced understanding of the balance of color and light, evident in the chiaroscuro treatment of the music-making angels and the sfumato effects of the modeling of the heads of the Virgin and Child, that achieves a convincing placement of the figures within their space. He lavished attention on the details—the gold strings of the harp, the *couleur changeante* effects of the robe of the lute-playing angel, the sumptuous tile floor of the porch—but integrated them into a grand concept that includes the city of Bruges and the mountainous landscape of the world beyond the intimate foreground space that encloses the figures. Doubtless an important commission from a client who was probably associated with the Carthusian monastery at Genadedal, this painting shows David at the peak of his career and must date about 1510–15.

MWA

Gerard David, about 1455–1523

82. *The Rest on the Flight into Egypt,* about 1510–15

Oil on wood, 20 x 17 in. (50.8 x 43.2 cm)
The Jules Bache Collection, 1949 49.7.21

Provenance: W. Mansell MacCulloch, Touillets, Guernsey (until 1902); sale, Christie's, London, May 31, 1902, no. 70, as Flemish School; [Dowdeswell and Dowdeswell, London]; Frank Stoop, London (by 1906); [Duveen, New York (1928)]; Jules S. Bache, New York (1928–49).

References: Wehle and Salinger 1947, p. 93 (with

The Flight into Egypt is barely mentioned in the Gospels (Matthew 2:13–14), but the subject is considerably embellished in the *Life of Christ* of Ludolph of Saxony and the *Meditations on the Life of Christ* by the Pseudo-Bonaventure, both late-medieval works of literature. David took his inspiration from those texts, which describe the arduous journey of the aged Joseph and the young Virgin Mary carrying the Christ Child, clearly heeding Ludolph's telling of the family's travels "through dark and uninhabited forests, and by very long routes past rough and deserted places to Egypt." Popular expanded versions of the *Life of Christ* contemporary with David's painting present the Flight in terms of a pilgrimage on which the reader should accompany the Holy Family.

In a sense continuing the journey from the forests of the Bache *Nativity* (cat. no. 80), a tiny scene in the right middle ground of the *Rest on the Flight into Egypt* shows the Holy Family emerging from the woods to the broad open plain where the Virgin nurses the Christ Child. In the central image as in the forest scene, David has recalled the mood and description of Ludolph of Saxony's tract: "The eye of devotion observes the little Jesus who sweetly drinks at the breast of the glorious Virgin his Mother. . . . What could be more pleasant or delightful to see?" At the left a spring has opened near Mary's feet to quench the thirst of the members of the Holy Family, who, as fugitives, were refused water along their route by the inhabitants of "Materca" (according to Jan van Coudenberghe's 1482 *Devotion of the Seven Sorrows of the Virgin*).

David's interpretation here may also allude to accounts by female mystics in the Low Countries wherein holy food (or the Eucharist) is equated with

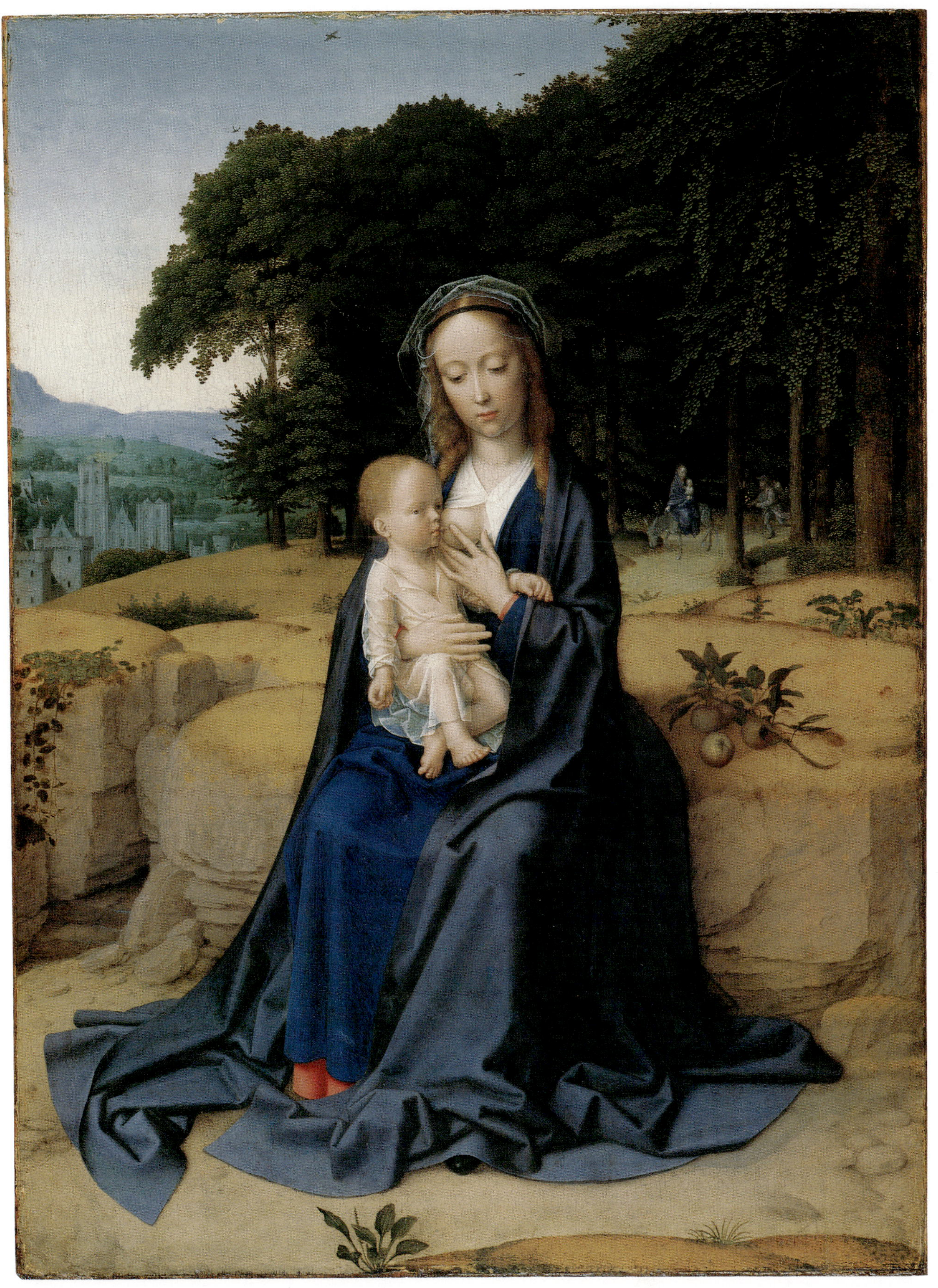

earlier bibliography); d'Otrange 1952, p. 211; Marlier 1957, pp. 103–4, 109, 122, 127; Larsen 1960, pp. 80, 124; Wilenski 1960, p. 104; Cuttler 1968, p. 195; Whinney 1968, p. 114; Friedländer 1967–76, vol. 6b (1971), p. 107, no. 212a; Dufey-Haeck 1979, pp. 54–55; Mundy 1981–82, p. 219; Silver 1984, pp. 58, 177; Ainsworth 1985, pp. 54, 56; Vandenbroeck 1985, p. 73; Genaille 1986, p. 68; Hand and Wolff 1986, p. 64; Bynum 1987, pp. 117, 270–71; Falkenburg 1988, pp. 27–28, 47–50; Van Miegroet 1989, pp. 301–4; Ainsworth 1994c, pp. 489, 491; Ainsworth 1998a; Wilson 1998, pp. 93–110.

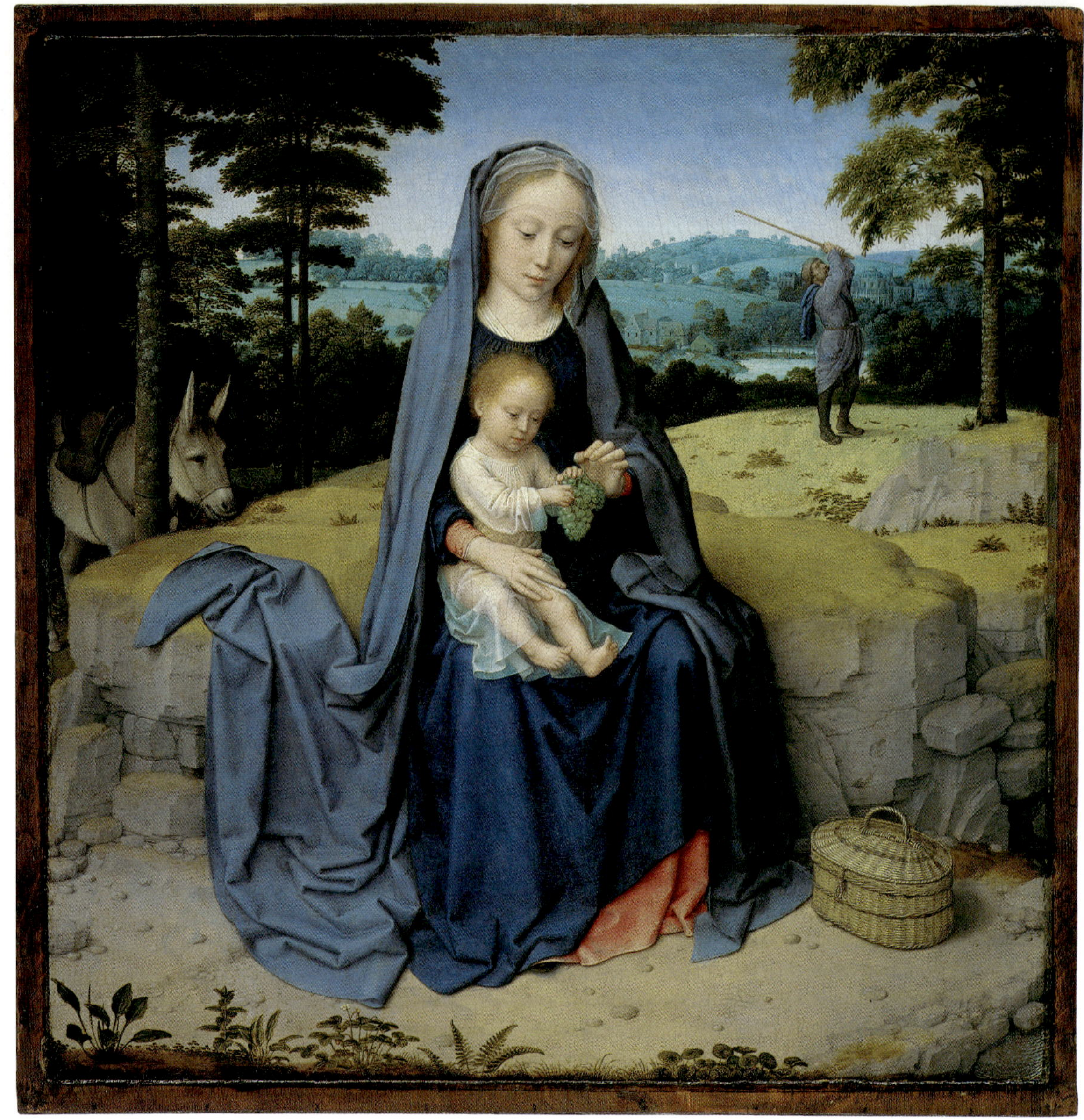

Fig. 99. Gerard David, *The Rest on the Flight into Egypt*, about 1500–1505. Oil on wood. Andrew W. Mellon Collection, National Gallery of Art, Washington, D.C.

ordinary eating. Just as the Virgin provides the child with her milk, so, in turn, Christ nourishes the faithful with his own sacrificed body and blood. This message is indicated by the posture of the Christ Child, who turns toward the viewer, as if extending an invitation to partake in this nourishment; it is emphasized in details shown directly below the Child: the glimpse of the Virgin's underdress, which is red (the color of Christ's Passion), and the broadleaf plantain, popularly known for its medicinal value as a stancher of blood. That Christ's act will redeem mankind's transgressions is made clear by the ivy at the left, a symbol of salvation, and the bough with apples to the right of the Virgin, a reminder of the Original Sin of Adam and Eve.

This is one of David's most poetic images—a symphony of blues and greens handled with striking clarity in the foreground, featuring the deeply saturated hues of the Virgin's dress and cloak, and in the area behind the figures, with its rich green nichelike foil of trees. The remarkably subtle modulations of color in the left background achieve a sense of light and atmosphere and a unity of the heavens and the earth that David realized only in his most mature works. David's successful integration of three-dimensional figures within a landscape here depended on his understanding of lessons introduced in the north, especially in Antwerp, not long before he undertook the painting; these were Italian, especially Leonardesque, lessons of geometric form and the importance of shadow in creating perspective. True to Italian prototypes, his Virgin with Child sits like a great pyramid on the rocky ledge and is modeled with broad zones of shadow in her face and draperies at the right to create rich chiaroscuro effects.

David's treatment of the figures and landscape in this *Rest on the Flight* distinguishes it from a version of the theme in the National Gallery of Art, Washington, D.C. (fig. 99), which is often considered to be of the same date as the Metropolitan panel. In the Washington example, however, David placed a fully frontal Virgin and Child in a landscape in which he achieved an effect of spatial recession by breaking it into a series of overlapping parallel planes of wedges of different colors in alternating dark and light zones, an organization similar to that of the landscape in the *Crucifixion* (cat. no. 75). The planar conception of the forms and the lack of chiaroscuro effects in their modeling suggest a date about 1500–1505, while the slightly turned postures of the figures and the other Italian-inspired features of the Metropolitan painting typify David's works of 1510–15. Both paintings inspired numerous replicas and versions by close followers and imitators. A copy of the Metropolitan *Flight into Egypt*, considerably weaker than the original, is in the Prado, Madrid.

MWA

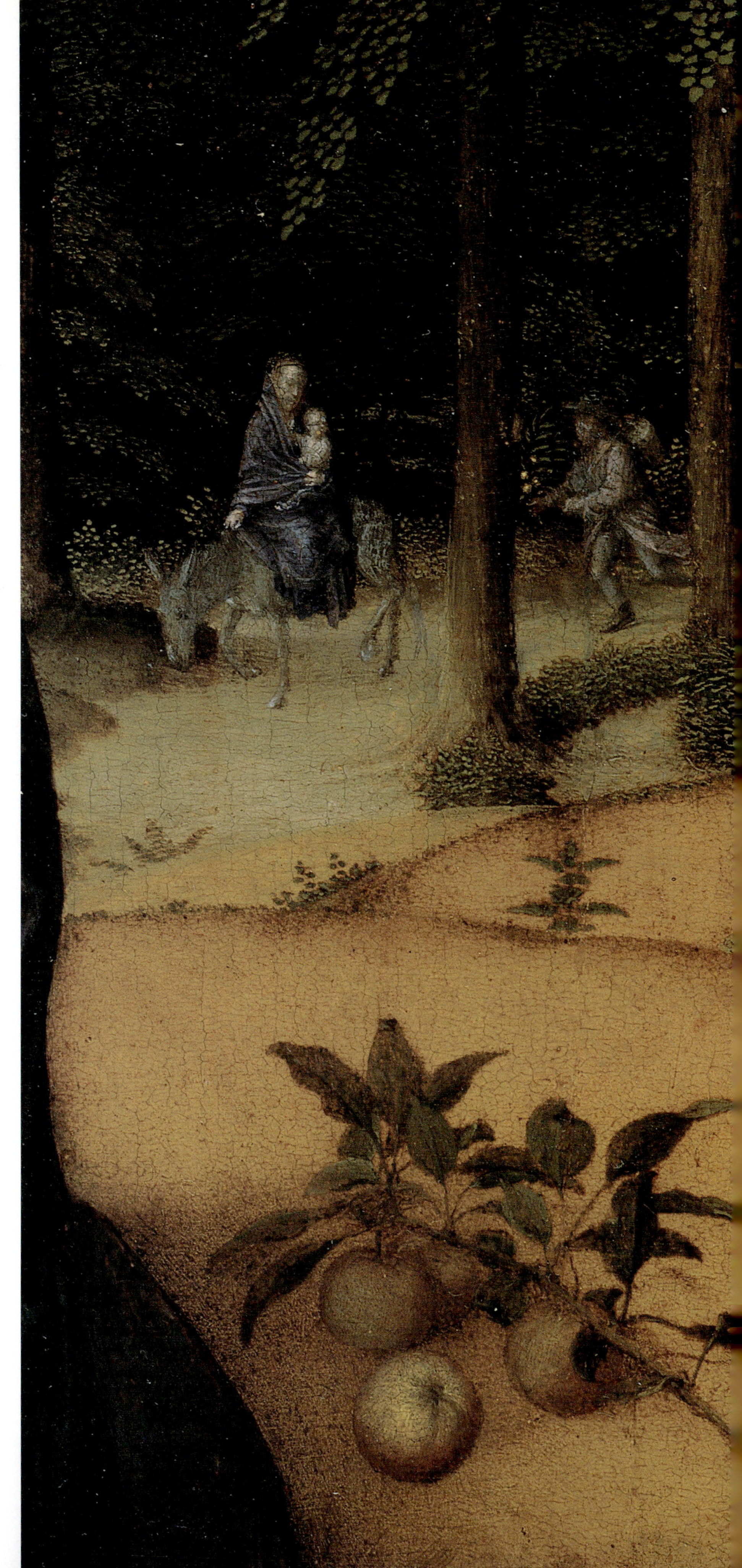

Detail, cat. no. 82

Attributed to Simon Bening, about 1483/84–1561

83. Virgin and Child, about 1520

Oil on wood; overall 10 x 8¼ in. (25.4 x 21 cm), with added strip of ⅜ in. (1 cm) at top; painted surface 9⅝ x 8¼ in. (24.4 x 21 cm)
The Friedsam Collection, Bequest of Michael Friedsam, 1931 32.100.53

Provenance: Claramonte family, counts of La Bisbal, Madrid; R. Traumann, Madrid (until 1914); [Agnew, London (1914–16)]; [Duveen, New York (1916–18)]; Michael Friedsam, New York (1918–31).

References: Friedländer (1916) 1921, p. 191; Conway 1921, p. 286; Burroughs and Wehle 1932, p. 24; Friedländer 1924–37, vol. 4 (1934), p. 154, no. 212c; Wehle and Salinger 1947, pp. 97–98; Bologna 1956, p. 29, n. 18; Marlier 1957, p. 109; Larsen 1960, p. 7; Eisler 1964, p. 100; Friedländer 1967–76, vol. 6b (1971), p. 107, no. 212c; Mundy 1980a, p. 33; Kren 1987–88, pp. 203–23; Verougstraete, De Schryver, and Marijnissen 1995, pp. 95–105; Ainsworth 1998a.

An embodiment of the early-sixteenth-century tendency to suppress overtly religious content in favor of more secular treatments, this painting presents the Virgin as the very model of a nurturing mother, rather than as an expression of Church doctrine. Surrounded by attributes denoting her character, she sits on the wall of an enclosed garden, which indicates her purity; at her left and right is mint, a plant with healing and cleansing properties symbolic of her virtue; and below the mint are violets, a sign of her humility. A stream of milk flows from the Virgin's breast to the lips of the Child, who turns to the viewer, spoon in hand, to directly communicate the notion of physical and spiritual nourishment.

The motif of the Virgin and Child is excerpted from the full-length figures in David's *Rest on the Flight into Egypt* (cat. no. 82) or perhaps from its replica in the Prado, Madrid, where the Child holds a spoon, but here the Joseph of the model is absent, and there is no reference to the journey. Whether contemporary viewers made any connections between the themes of various paintings that employed the same motif is difficult to say. The reuse of patterns, rather than involving the associative value of a motif, was more likely a practical issue in workshops where it was necessary to streamline production in order to meet the considerable market demand for images of particular types.

Most scholars consider this painting the product of a workshop assistant, based on aspects of the execution that differ from David's handling: the extremely glossy and smooth treatment of the faces, which are built up in rather dense applications of paint; the stylized, rounded facial features (crescent-shaped slits for eyes, a prominent spherical chin, short, thin eyebrows); the formulaic brushwork in the highlights of the Virgin's hair; the more generalized depiction of the hands. Above all, the landscape is uncharacteristic for David. It is, however, typical for Simon Bening, the great innovator in landscape depiction in contemporary Ghent-Bruges book illumination. Bening favored just the approach seen in this panel: compositions with a patternlike treatment of foreground plants that push the figures forward in front of a landscape that recedes into the far distance—devices that create an unresolved compositional tension; large trees rendered with discrete round clusters of branches uniformly dotted with highlights; and, frequently, the inclusion of a vignette of a small house surrounded by trees near the edge of a pond. Moreover, some of the full-page illuminations attributed to Bening show the Virgin type and a number of details of execution that appear in the Metropolitan painting.

During the first decades of the sixteenth century the arts of manuscript illumination and panel painting were particularly closely allied; at this time Bening often integrated David's popular figural motifs into landscapes of his own conception. A *Virgin and Child* panel in the Prado, Madrid (cat. no. 1537, called Follower of Gerard David), appears to be by the same hand as the Metropolitan's painting.

MWA

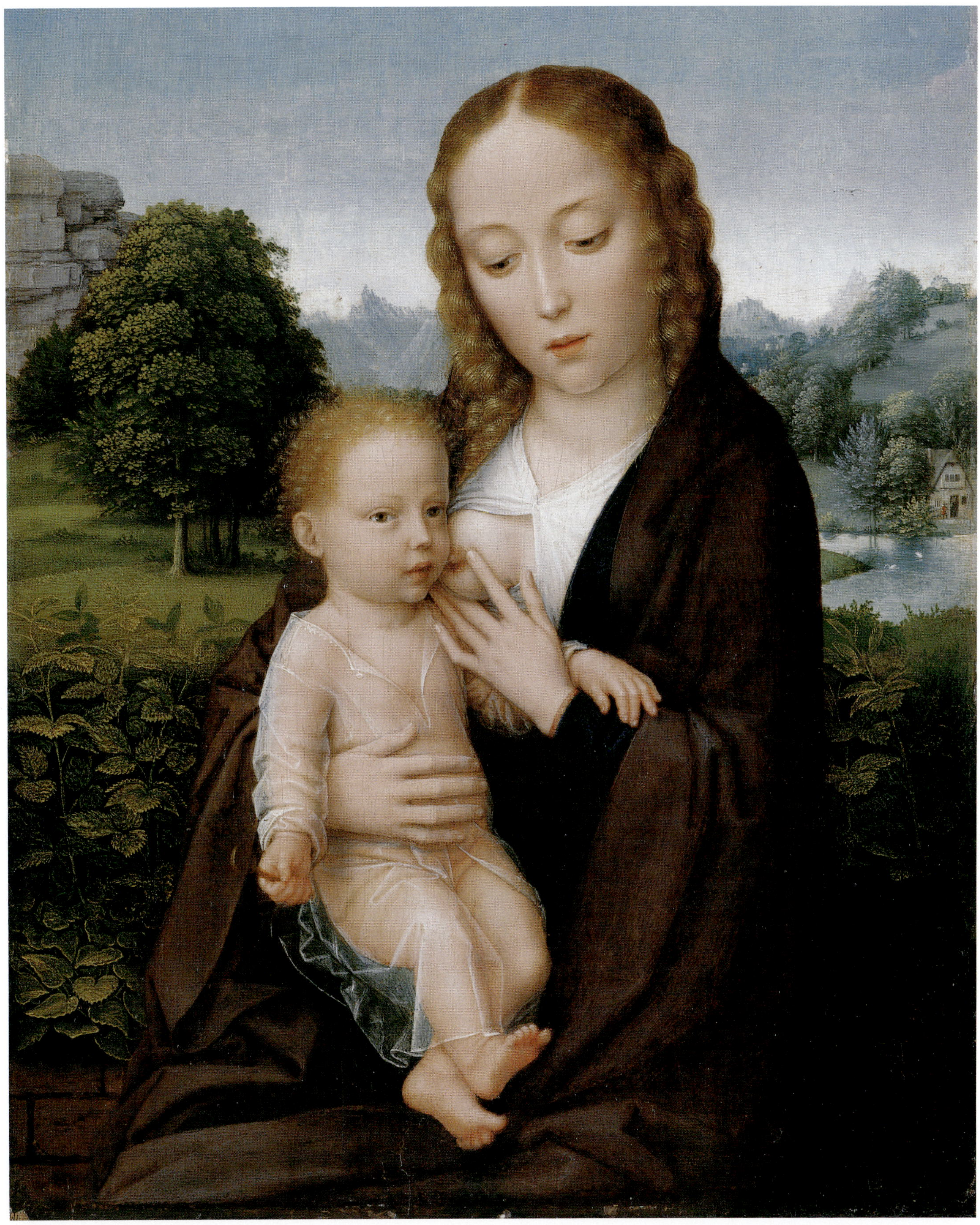

Workshop of Gerard David

84. The Adoration of the Magi, about 1520

Oil on wood; overall 27¾ x 27⅞ in. (70.5 x 73.3 cm); painted surface 27½ x 28⅜ in. (69.2 x 72.1 cm)
The Jack and Belle Linsky Collection, 1982 1982.60.17

Provenance: John Rushout, second Lord Northwick, Thirlestane House, Cheltenham (by 1854–59; sale, Phillips, London, July 27, 1859, no. 172, as Van Eyck, to John W. Brett, Esq.); probably John Watkins Brett, London (1859–64; sale, Christie's, London, April 9, 1864, no. 858, as J. Hemmelinck); George Rushout Bowles, third Lord Northwick, Northwick Park, Gloucestershire (until 1887); his widow, Elizabeth Augusta Bowles, Lady Northwick, Northwick Park (1887–1912); her grandson, Capt. E. G. Spencer-Churchill, Northwick Park (1912–64; sale, Christie's, London, May 28, 1965, no. 41, as Gerard David); [Julius Weitaner, New York, 1965]; Mr. and Mrs. Jack Linsky, New York (1965–80); The Jack and Belle Linsky Foundation, New York (1980–82).

References: Crowe and Cavalcaselle 1872, p. 298; Northwick collection 1921, p. 58; Waterhouse 1937, p. 45; Grossmann 1957, p. 4; Van Puyvelde 1962, p. 365; Lindsay in Cooper 1963, p. 43; Friedländer 1967–76, vol. 7 (1971), p. 73; Bauman in Metropolitan Museum 1984, pp. 54–57; Scailliérez 1992, p. 22; Ewing 1994.

This beautifully composed *Adoration of the Magi* ultimately derives from the Monteforte Altarpiece by Hugo van der Goes in the Gemäldegalerie, Berlin, but is most closely associated with Gerard David's *Adoration of the Magi* in the National Gallery, London. The group at the left adopts from David's painting a quiet, intimate mood and a sense of reverence, which is conveyed here by two of the kings as they pay homage to the tiny, seemingly self-possessed Christ Child. By contrast, the right side of the painting is livelier, with its lavishly dressed and elegantly posed Moorish king, who stands patiently at the forefront of a motley group engaged in animated discourse. These figures appear to have just arrived after wandering through the captivating landscape that is featured like a separately framed vignette at the center of the picture.

The recent discovery of the wings of the panel by De Vos strengthens the link with David. Now in a private collection in Europe, these wings (fig. 100) show the Annunciation on the exterior and a Night Nativity and a Presentation in the Temple on the interior. The Virgin of the *Annunciation* is modeled after David's Annunciate Virgin from the Cervara Altarpiece (cat. no. 79), and the *Night Nativity* is a version of a painting by David in the Kunsthistorisches Museum, Vienna. The Presentation in the Temple is not a subject known in David's extant works.

The author of the Linsky panel and its wings was familiar not only with David's compositions but also with his figure types (especially the Virgin and Child) and even the incidental details he favored: for example, the curious, sniffing dog and the careful botanical description and foreground placement of plant life. But he could not equal the refinement of David's mature handling and execution, and he departed considerably from the master in the way he organized space.

Features of the reconstructed triptych that have no basis in David's art reflect contemporary Antwerp painting. The themes themselves are among those favored in Antwerp, for representations of the Adoration of the Magi were very much in vogue there, especially in combination with the Nativity and the Presentation in the Temple—as found, for example, in the work of the Master of Hoogstraten. Also typical of Antwerp painting, indeed one of its recurrent themes, is the expansive space, with its prominent landscape view (see cat. no. 67), featured in the *Adoration*. Open views of this kind provided ample room for the other leitmotiv of Antwerp painting—the depiction of travelers, often transporting goods by camel (as in the far background here). The popularity of this subject can surely be connected with Antwerp's status as the economic hub of northern Europe and as a major center of export-import business. As such, the magi and their retinue are reminders not only of an exemplary pilgrimage undertaken on behalf of the Christ Child but also of themes very much associated with everyday life. MWA

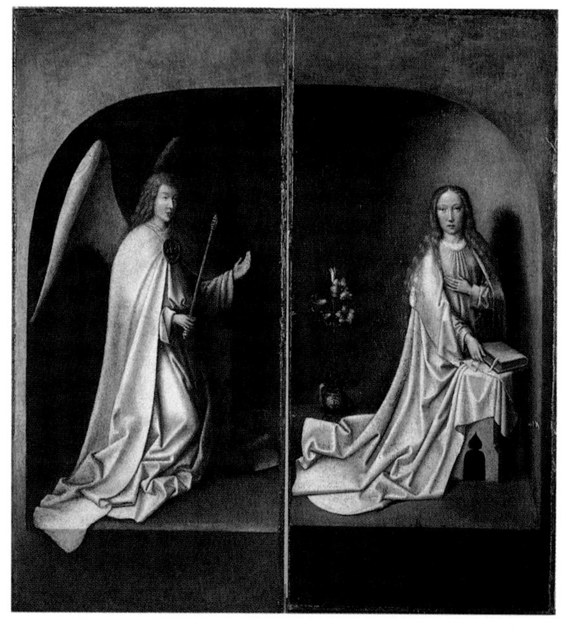

Fig. 100. Follower of Gerard David, *Annunciation*, exterior wings, *Nativity*, *Presentation in the Temple*, left and right interior wings of Adoration of the Magi Triptych (cat. no. 84), about 1520. Oil on wood. Private collection

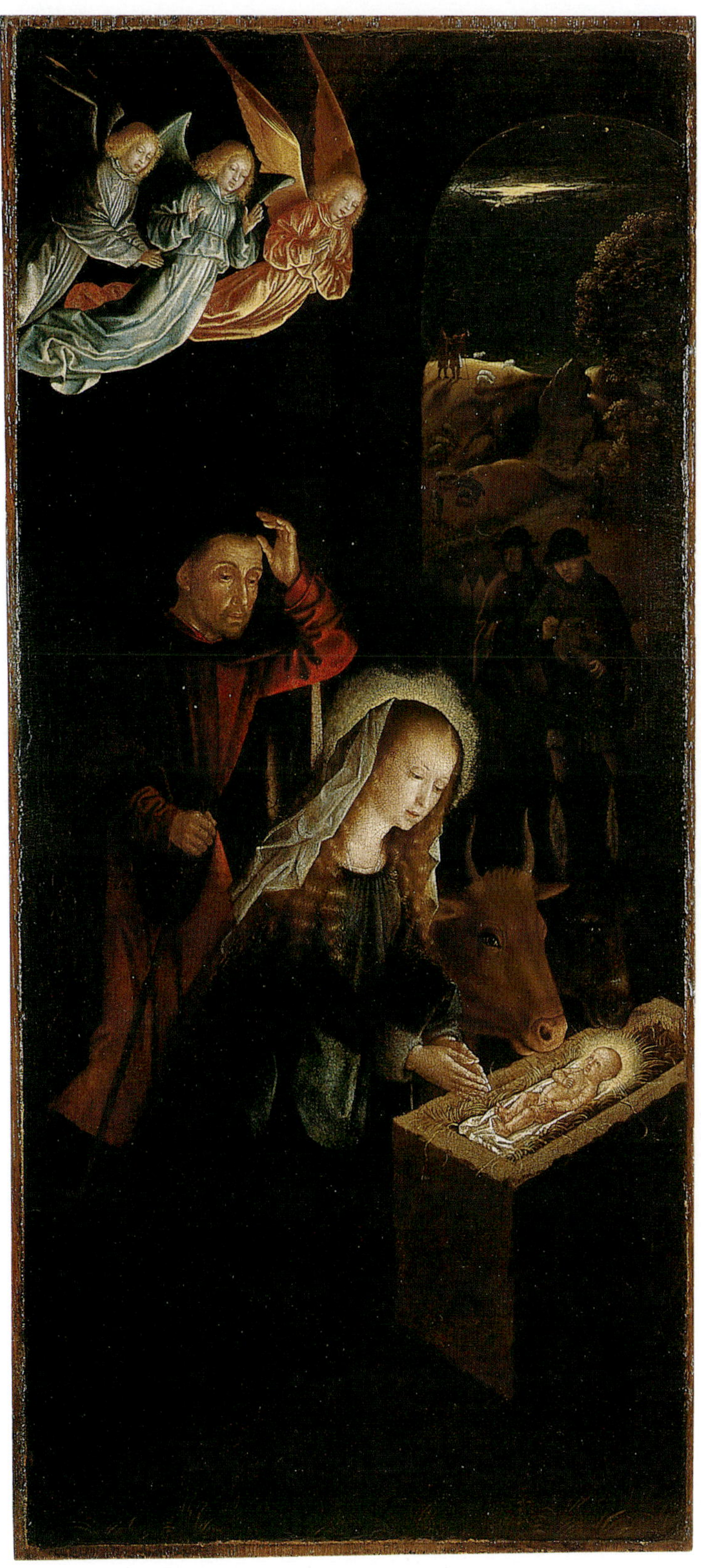

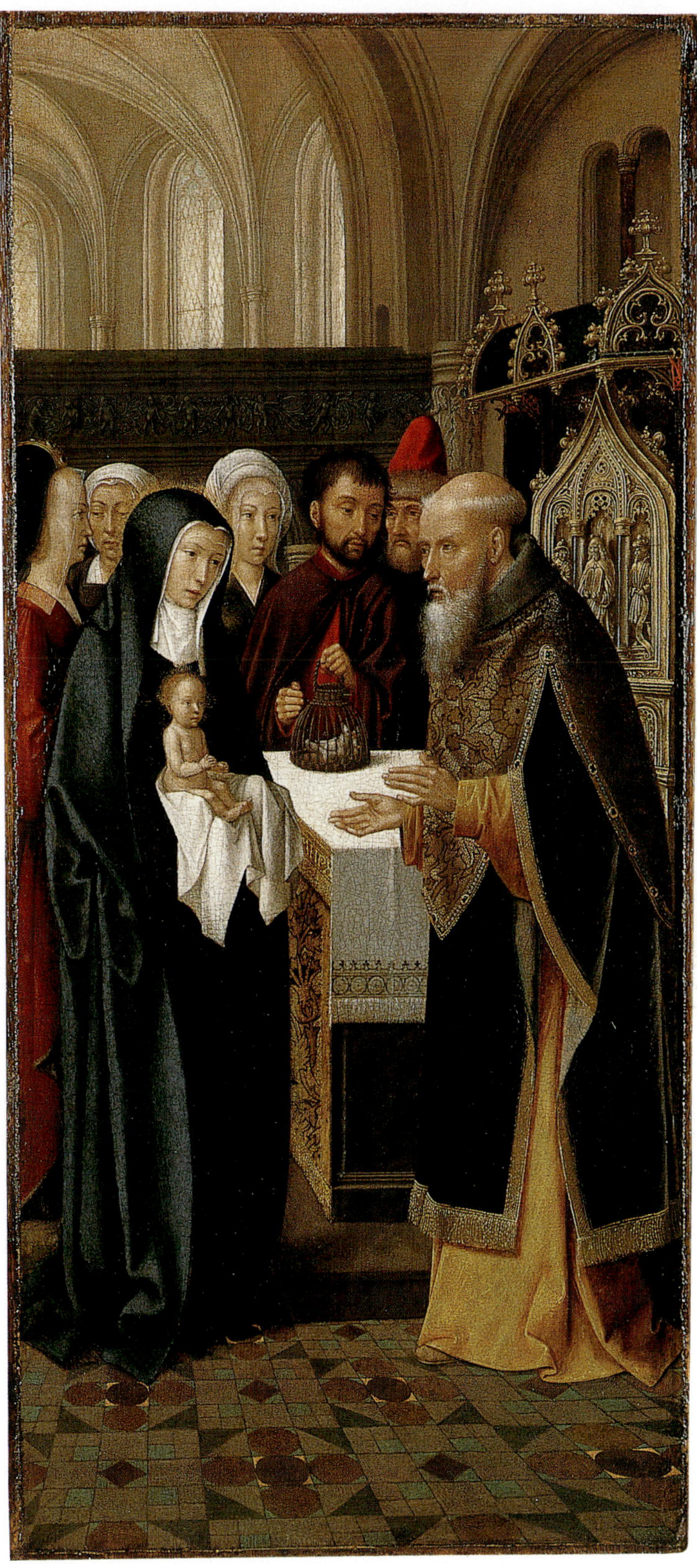

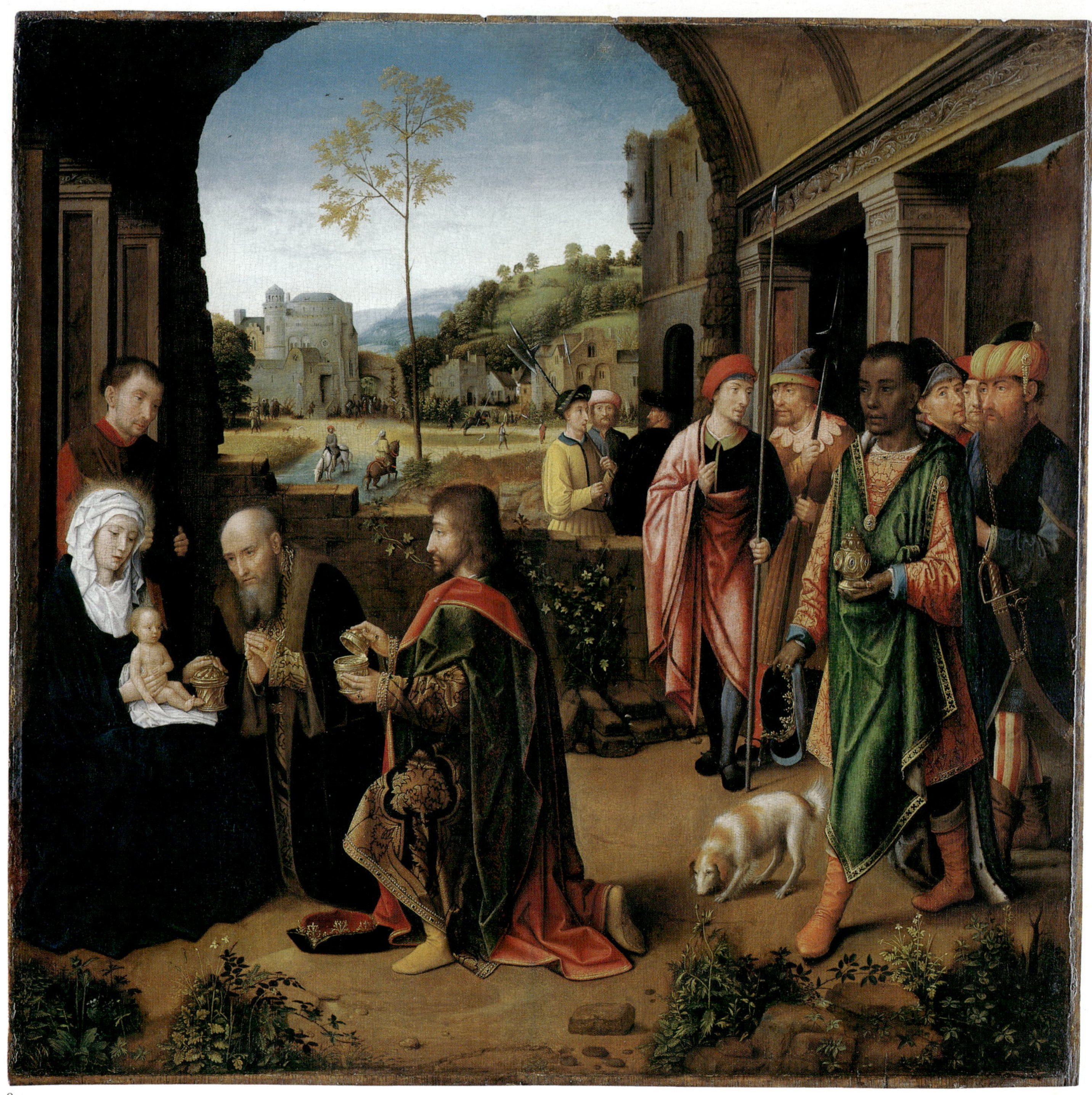

84

Opposite: Detail, cat. no. 84

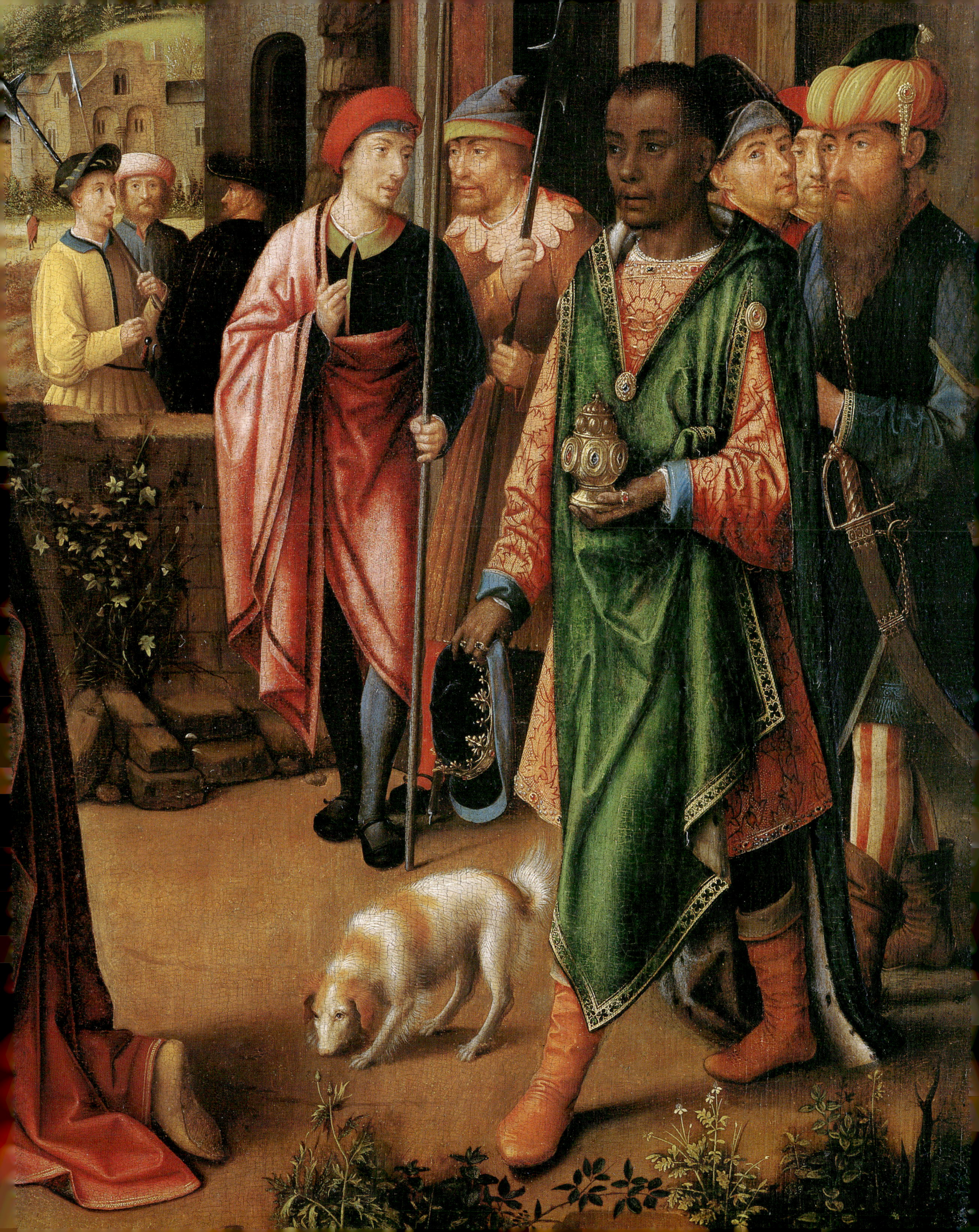

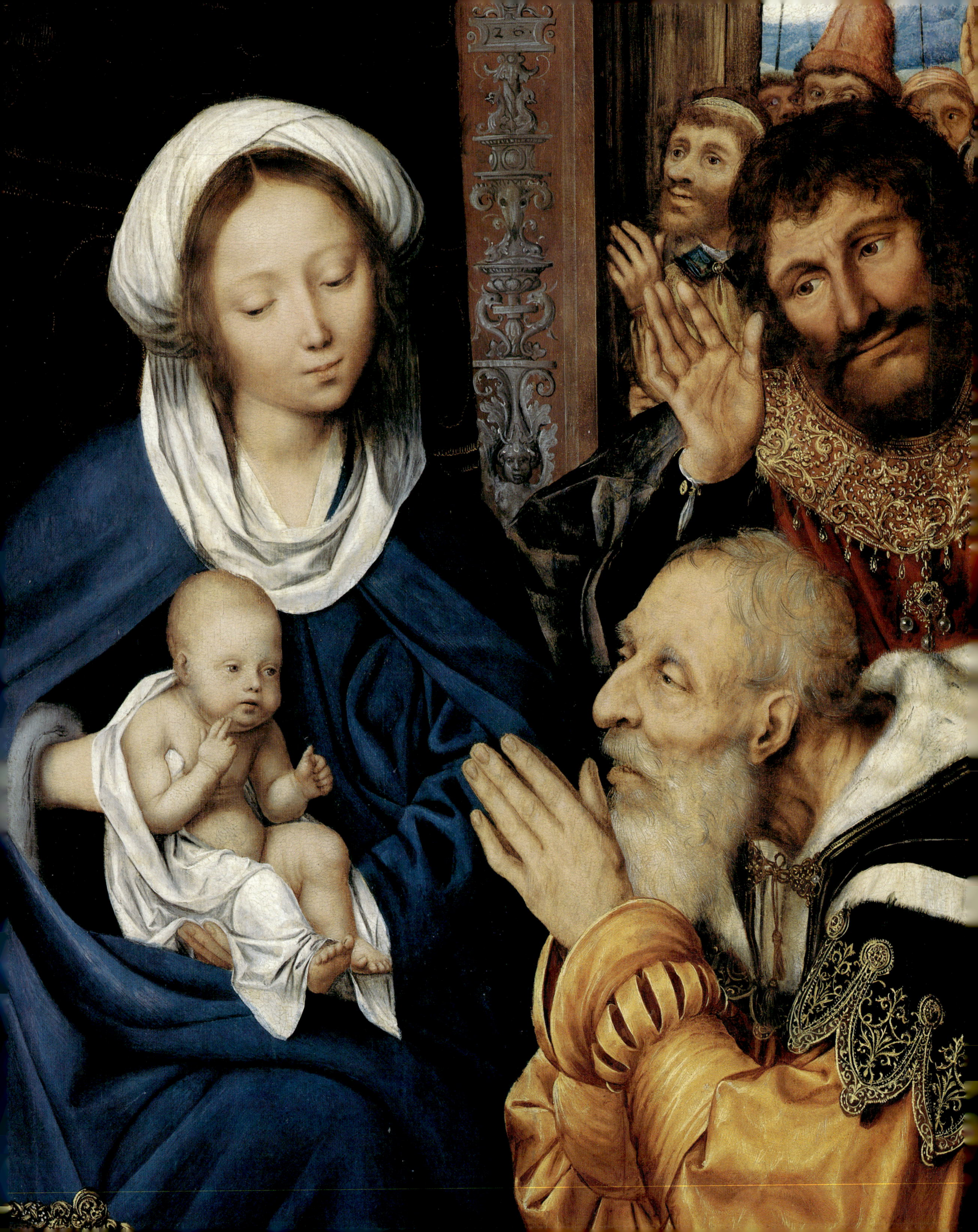

Religious Painting from 1500 to 1550: Continuity and Innovation on the Eve of the Iconoclasm

Opposite: Quentin Massys, detail, *The Adoration of the Magi* (cat. no. 99)

The evolution of devotional painting during the sixteenth century took place against the backdrop of the Reformation. As early as 1525 reformers called into question the use of images for religious practice, and in the first two decades of the century both in Germany and Switzerland there had been isolated outbursts of iconoclasm. In the Netherlands matters came to a head in 1566. Few were prepared for the full-scale destruction of the cathedral in Antwerp on August 20 of that year—one day after the annual procession of the Virgin; altarpieces and lavish church vestments were destroyed, and even the Blessed Sacraments were desecrated. The following day the churches of Tournai were sacked, and the iconoclasts moved on to Douai, where the splendid altarpieces of Jan van Scorel had been spirited away barely in advance of the marauding hordes. There was less havoc in Bruges and Ghent, but much was destroyed, so much, in fact, that our ability to reconstruct a complete picture of Netherlandish devotional art of this period has inevitably been affected. What has survived reveals startlingly different approaches to religious images and their use, marked, on the one hand, by continuity with the past and, on the other, by new directions that ultimately led to a secularization of religious painting.

Some sixteenth-century artists worked in a deeply entrenched traditional mode—either at their clients' request or by their own volition—deliberately emulating early-fifteenth-century models. This archaistic trend is evident in Jan Gossart's faithful copy (Galleria Doria Pamphili, Rome) after Jan van Eyck's *Madonna in the Church* (Gemäldegalerie, Berlin) and in his close rendition of Jan's Deesis group—Christ, the Virgin, and Saint John the Baptist—(fig. 101) from the Ghent Altarpiece (compare fig. 18). In the same vein, Joos van Cleve placed the figures of Rogier van der Weyden's Prado *Deposition* within a landscape (Philadelphia Museum of Art) and recast Van Eyck's Lucca Madonna (fig. 26) as a half-length *Holy Family* (cat. no. 61) by adding a figure of Saint Joseph.

The cult status of the Virgin reached new heights, and contemporary mystical movements devised special devotions that featured particular aspects of her life and being. These were precisely the sorts of developments the Protestant reformers railed against. The veneration of the rosary, which had been championed most insistently by the Dominicans (especially Alanus de Rupe, 1428–1475), became widely popular. The first Confraternity of the Rosary had been established in 1470 in Douai, and in 1479 Pope Sixtus IV granted an indulgence to all who recited the prayers associated with the rosary. Soon afterward, in 1483, there appeared an inspirational handbook whose precepts became the basis for the standardization of the iconography used in pictures on the theme of the cult. By the early sixteenth century paintings such as the *Fifteen Mysteries and the Virgin of the Rosary* (cat. no. 91), which portrays the five Joyful Mysteries, the five Sorrowful Mysteries, and the five Glorious Mysteries in detailed individual scenes, provided the viewer with step-by-step guides for worship.

The intimate relationship between the object and the individual was enhanced by rosaries of many types and materials that were mass-produced to meet the demand for their use in daily worship. Among these are a group of quite extraordinary Paternoster beads made of boxwood, which when opened reveal intricately carved scenes for contemplation (fig. 102). Worn hanging from the belt or attached to a series of rosary beads, these remarkable artifacts served to accentuate the religious

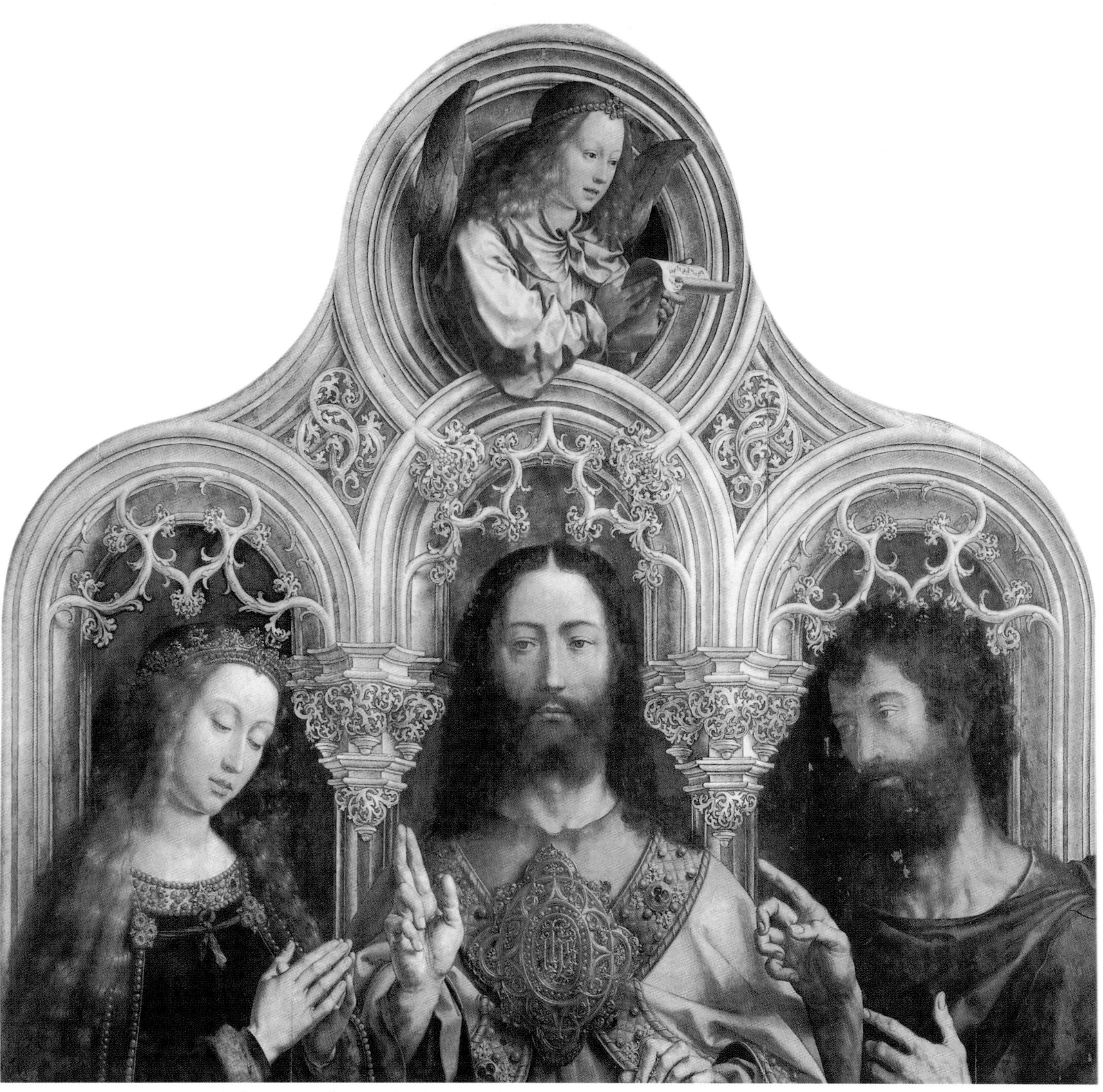

Fig. 101. Jan Gossart, *Christ with the Virgin and Saint John the Baptist*, about 1520. Heads, oil on parchment or vellum on wood; remainder, oil on wood. Museo del Prado, Madrid

experience, both visually and tactilely. Alone or in combination with other rosary beads, they facilitated a superior form of piety in devotions that united an empathy with the Passion of Christ as well as with the sufferings of the Virgin Mary.

About the same time the veneration of the rosary was intensifying, in 1482, the priest Jan van Coudenberghe initiated the devotion to Our Lady of the Seven Sorrows. This became extremely popular, especially in the southern Netherlands, after a confraternity centered on the cult was formed in 1492, and over time its content evolved: the seven specfic incidents that originally constituted the Virgin's sorrows—three from Christ's childhood and four

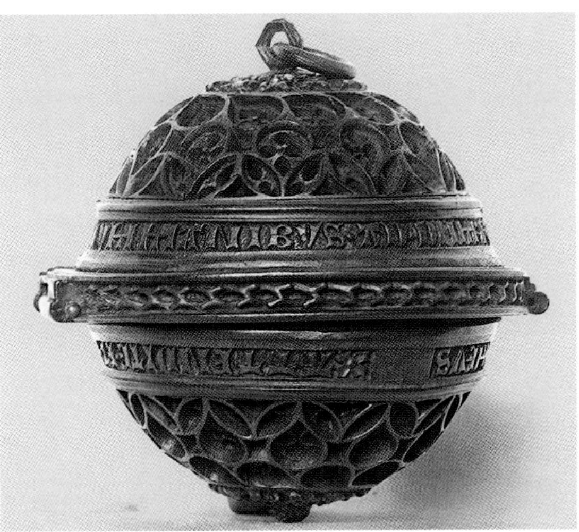

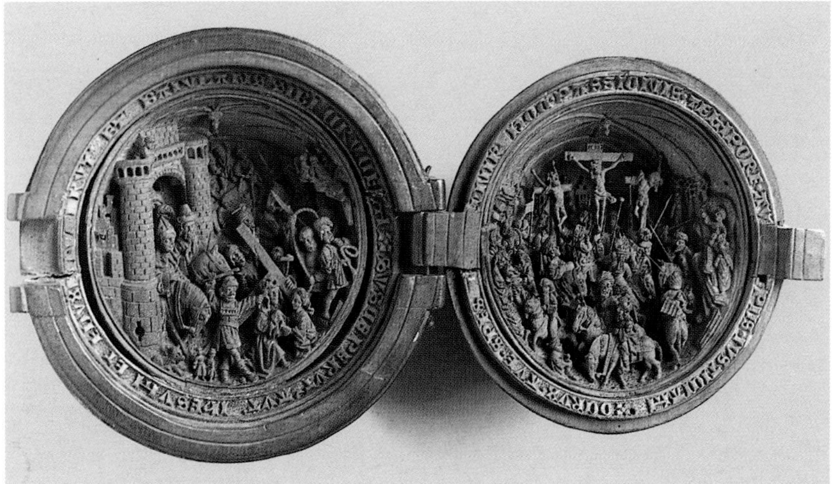

Fig. 102. Netherlandish, Rosary Bead, actual size, closed and open, with *Road to Calvary and the Crucifixion*, early 16th century. Boxwood. The Metropolitan Museum of Art, New York

from the Passion—were expanded by some authors to include as many as 150 separate events. A tract published in Antwerp in 1494, *Of the Passion and Bitter Suffering of Our Lord Jesus Christ*, describes events of particular suffering for the Virgin, divided over the seven hours of the Divine Office: Christ's Imprisonment, his Trial, the Scourging, the Carrying of the Cross, the Crucifixion, the Deposition, and the Entombment. Such a text may well have influenced Adriaen Isenbrant's *Christ Crowned with Thorns and the Mourning Virgin* (cat. no. 101), in which the artist captured the essence of the Virgin's compassion as co-Redemptrix, while Christ faces the viewer, who becomes part of the crowd assembled before him, gathered to pass public judgment.

The impact of such writings notwithstanding, popular religious movements of the time in general stressed methods of personal prayer and meditation more than the introduction of new and unusual religious themes. Devotional manuals placed increasing emphasis on impassioned empathy with the details of the lives of Christ and the Virgin, which prompted artists to transform traditional themes into emotionally gripping invitations to meditation and spiritual visions. Such attempts are evidenced in alterations of standard compositional and figural formulas. For example, Quentin Massys enlivened the traditional theme of his *Adoration of the Magi* (cat. no. 99) by tight cropping of the image and dramatic close-up placement of figures; moreover, he introduced a certain urgency (as well as artistic modernity) to the normally staid scene through the use of menacing, caricature-like faces from newly imported Italian models—specifically those of Leonardo da Vinci. A similar Italianate strategy was initiated in Brussels by Bernaert van Orley, whose Job Altarpiece of 1521 (fig. 103) portrayed figures influenced by Raphael's cartoons for the *Acts of the Apostles* tapestries, which had been sent to the city in 1516. Not only Van Orley but also numerous other Netherlanders of the time were affected by Raphael's work: the wide dissemination of Raphaelesque models through reproductive prints had a decisive impact on devotional painting, as witnessed by our *Last Judgment* by Joos van Cleve (cat. no. 98), among many other examples. A journey to Italy provided the inspiration for change for some artists. For Gossart, for instance, a trip to Rome in 1508 was the catalyst for transforming his Gothic style into a mannerist one in which the sacred and the profane often merge. In such pictures as Gossart's *Virgin and Child* in the National Gallery, London, the Child looks like a baby Hercules who is barely restrained by the mother; and the line between the biblical and mythological worlds is further blurred in his figures of Adam and Eve and Neptune and Amphitrite, whose treatment is remarkably similar (figs. 104, 105).

Artists elicited responses to the joys and sorrows of the lives of Christ and the Virgin not only with impassioned reinterpretations of themes in individual panels but also through a very different means: elaborate narrative cycles that followed the Pseudo-Bonaventure's *Meditations on the Life of Christ* and Ludolph of Saxony's *Life of Christ* and encouraged step-by-step identification with their histories. The Oratorio of Queen Isabella the Catholic, of which our *Marriage Feast at Cana* by Juan de Flandes (cat. no. 85) was part, and the small panel that includes the four scenes of the Passion of Christ (cat. no. 90) exemplify this mode. So does our portable triptych by Isenbrant (cat. no. 100), which shows the Annunciation and the Visitation on the exterior and the Nativity, the Adoration of the Magi, and the Flight into Egypt on the interior, thus encompassing the Virgin's participation in the main events of Christ's infancy. Similar cycles devoted to the Life of the Virgin are also found in contemporary tapestries (fig. 106). Diptychs that portrayed episodes from narratives, such as those produced in multiple versions by Gerard David and his workshop (cat. no. 76), increasingly emphasized the human nature of Christ rather than his divine character, which was the standard in medieval art. By emblematically showing excerpts from the beginning and the end of Christ's earthly existence (for example, the Virgin and Child with Angels and Christ Taking Leave of His Mother), the diptych form encouraged the viewer to imagine and contemplate the intervening events, and to experience with heightened emotional awareness the drama of the departure of Christ for his ultimate sacrifice for mankind.

A more direct method of emulating the life of Christ and sharing in the joys and sorrows of the Virgin involved pilgrimages—both real and imaginary—to the Holy Land undertaken in an effort to retrace their steps. In the fifteenth century renowned artists (Jan van Eyck, Robert Campin, and Rogier van der Weyden among them), aristocrats (notably Philip the Good), and quite ordinary people made pilgrimages to holy sites near and far. Various generations of the Adornes family of Bruges traveled to the Holy Land and kept diaries that provide vivid accounts of their adventures; they even brought back architectural plans of the Holy Sepulchre in Jerusalem and had a version of it constructed and attached to

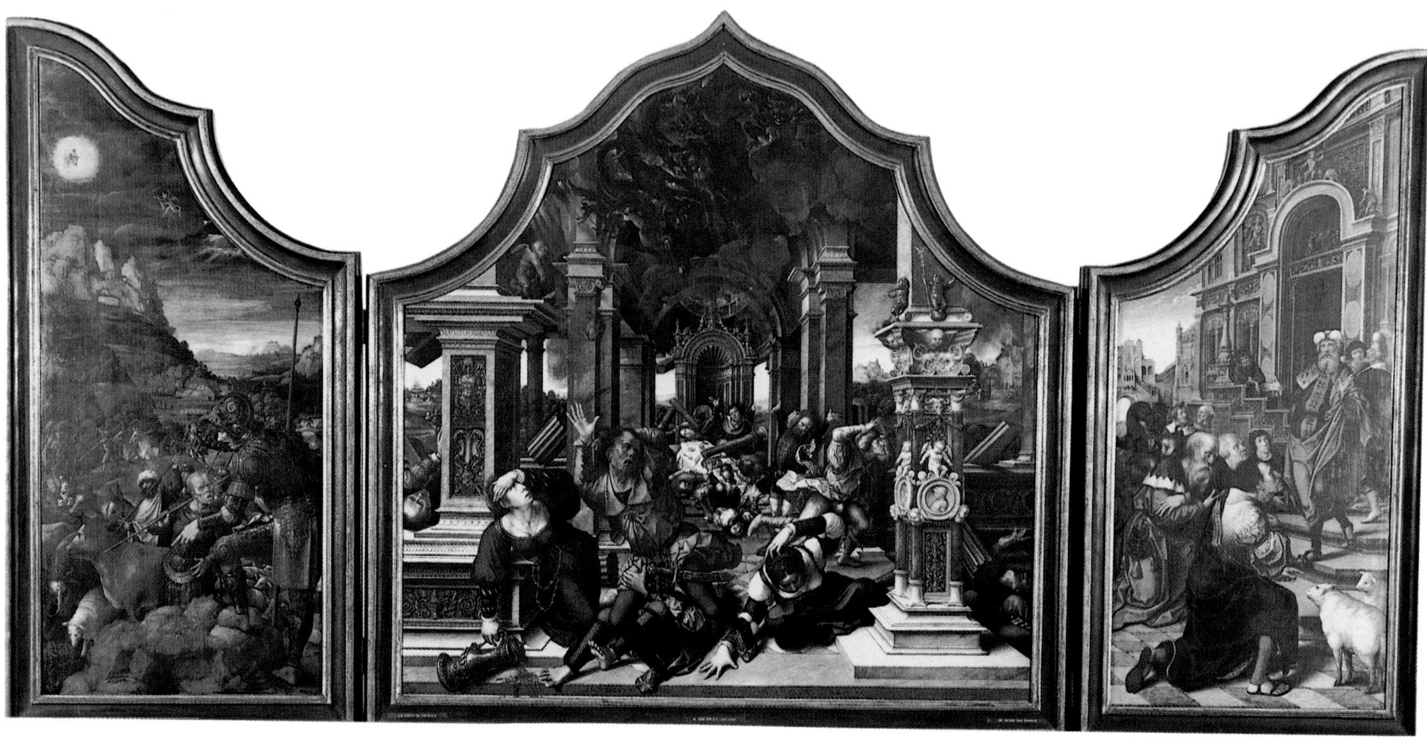

Fig. 103. Bernaert van Orley, Job Altarpiece, 1521. Oil on wood. Musées Royaux des Beaux-Arts de Belgique, Brussels

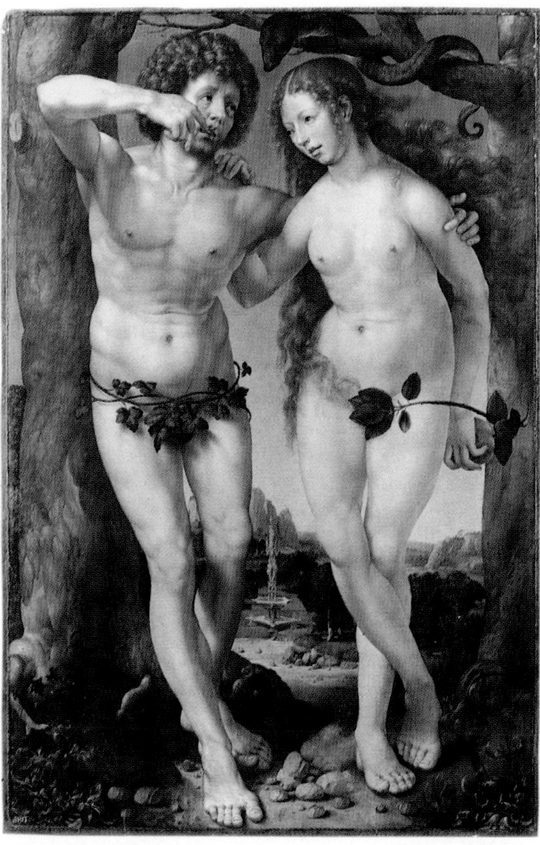

Fig. 104. Jan Gossart, *Adam and Eve*, about 1520. Oil on wood. The Royal Collection, Her Majesty Queen Elizabeth II, Hampton Court, Surrey

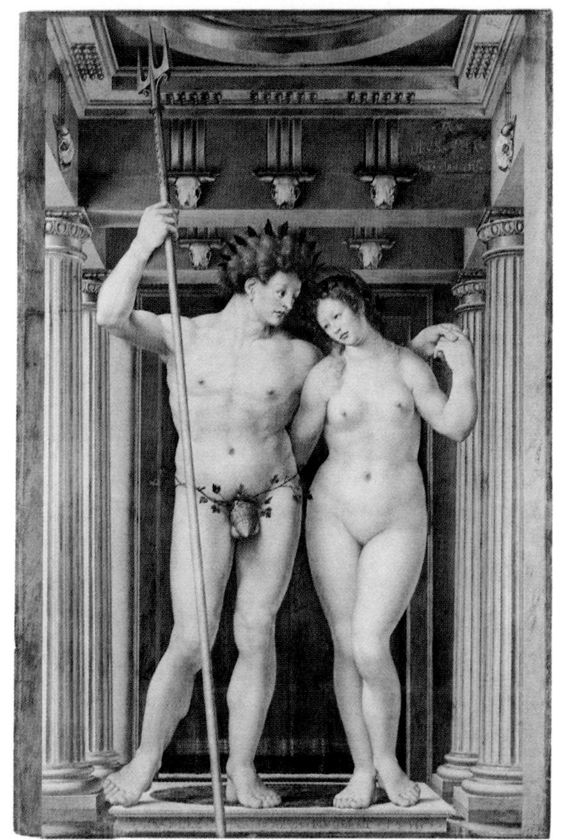

Fig. 105. Jan Gossart, *Neptune and Amphitrite*, 1516. Oil on wood. Gemäldegalerie, SMPK, Berlin

their living quarters in Bruges for family religious services, which allowed them to relive their pilgrimages.

Paintings provided mental pilgrimages for those who could not afford an actual journey to the Holy Land. An example of a picture that offered a substitute for a real pilgrimage is Hans Memling's *Scenes from the Advent and Triumph of Christ (Seven Joys of the Virgin Mary)* of about 1480 (fig. 107), where the holy sites are distributed in a landscape through which the viewer is meant to travel in the mind's eye. Other works of this kind, such as the *Passion of Christ in the Panorama of Jerusalem* (Museu Nacional do Azulejo, Lisbon), made for Eleanor of Portugal about 1500, label the sites depicted and include inscriptions that detail the dialogue taking place between the figures portrayed at each stop along the way.

In the early sixteenth century artists developed new strategies for more effectively involving the viewer in the experience. Thus, the outside wings of Gerard David's Nativity Triptych (cat. no. 80) show a landscape without human presence, leaving a void that is meant to be filled by the viewer's participation in the scene. Traveling through the dark forest, like the Holy Family in search of a hospitable inn, the viewer, like Mary and Joseph, is rejected. When the triptych is opened, the interior reveals the glorious scene of the Nativity, which the viewer has reached. The notion of journeying to this hallowed site is reinforced by the portrayal of Joseph in his traveling attire—a short robe, cloak, stockings, and soft boots—and the appearance of his walking staff prominently placed near him on the sheaf of wheat. Similar imagined pilgrimages are intended in paintings by Joachim Patinir (cat. no. 88) and one of his many followers, the so-called Master of the Female Half-Lengths (cat. no. 69), who habitually included travelers along the well-worn routes of their vast landscapes,

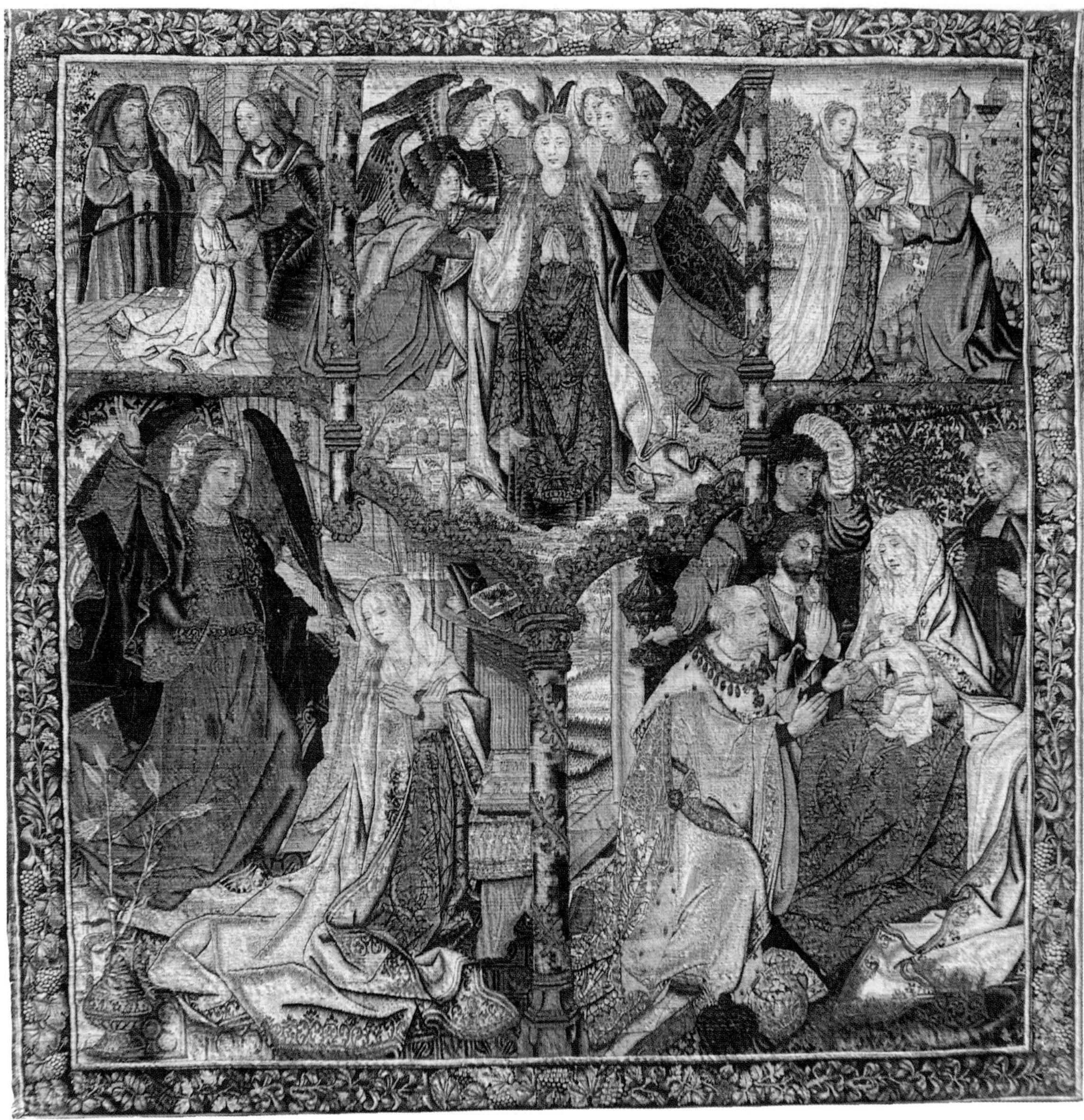

Fig. 106. South Netherlandish, *Scenes from the Life of the Virgin*, 1490–1510. Tapestry. The Metropolitan Museum of Art, New York

sometimes with the baggage, walking staffs, and typical costumes of pilgrims.

The pilgrimages represented by Netherlandish artists were connected with cults of the Virgin and the saints and with the veneration of their relics; they were bound up as well with the fervent desire on the part of the devout to experience a miraculous vision before the cult object at the completion of the journey portrayed. Such a vision takes shape in David's *Virgin and Child with Four Angels* (cat. no. 81), for example, where the cult image, which was perhaps housed at the Carthusian monastery of Genadedal near Bruges, comes alive through the believer's fervent prayers. The Christ Child turns his head to engage the devotee, forging a lasting bond between holy image and worshiper. This kind of conflation of visionary experience with painted images provoked anxiety among Protestant reformers, who deemed the function of pictures to be purely didactic.

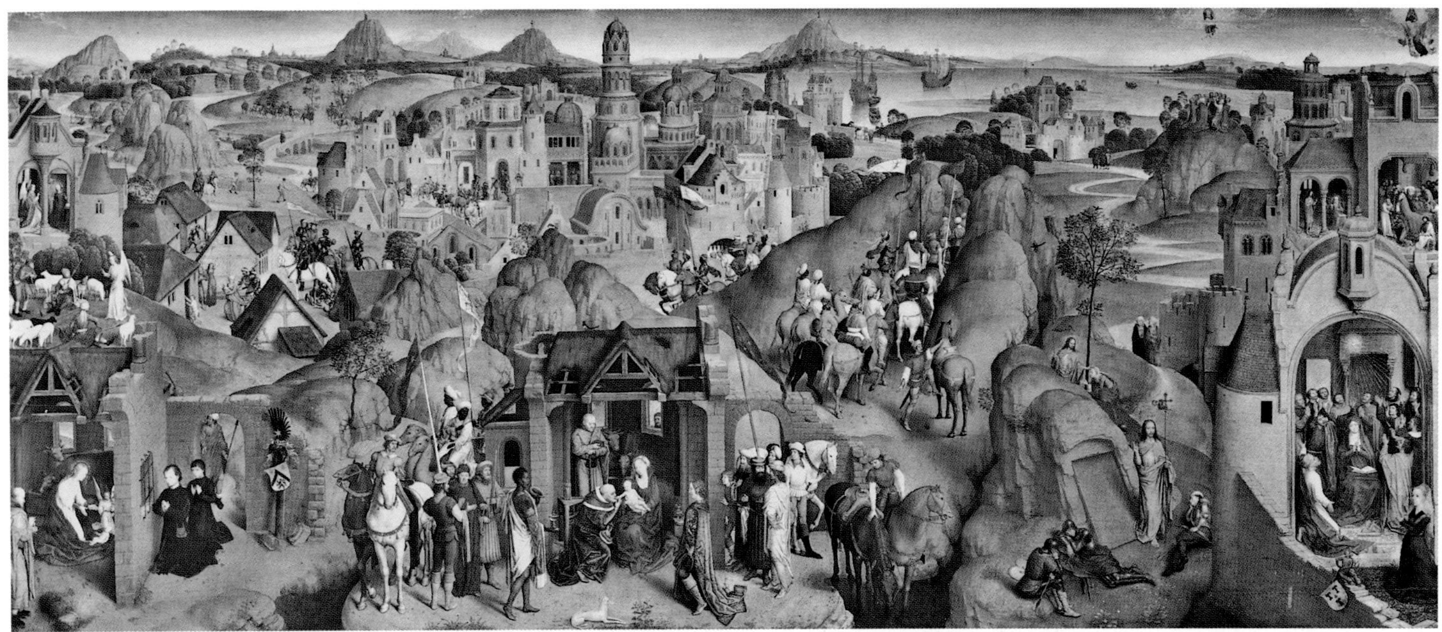

Fig. 107. Hans Memling, *Seven Joys of the Virgin Mary*, about 1480. Oil on wood. Alte Pinakothek, Munich

Although the Museum's collections are not rich in paintings inspired by the reform movements of the sixteenth century, a few in our holdings hint at the changing emphases that were taking place in certain religious circles. A panel often thought to illustrate events from the Life of Saint Anthony (cat. no. 94) may express the tenets of Biblical Humanism, a short-lived movement dedicated to social reform. The group focused on acts of charity, and the portrayal in our picture of the distribution of wealth to the poor and downtrodden possibly reflects its teachings. Other movements saw Christ in a new light, stressing his human aspect, a point of view conveyed in Van Cleve's *Last Judgment* (cat. no. 98); here, in a break from tradition, the Christ appears without the Virgin and Saint John as intercessors and is thus presented as a directly approachable figure. The changes embodied in these examples foreshadow far more dramatic transformations to come.

Fifteenth-century devotional painting had successfully merged real and symbolic worlds, but in the art of the sixteenth century a tension developed between sacred and secular elements, wherein details from each realm competed for attention. This tension is manifested in various ways in pictures made during the course of what was clearly an evolutionary, rather than a revolutionary, artistic process. Paintings created for the mass market in Antwerp sometimes reveal fascinating ambiguities that express changing social as well as religious values. Joos van Cleve's many depictions of the Holy Family (cat. nos. 61, 62, fig. 83), for example, mark a striking departure from most fifteenth-century images by introducing Joseph as an active parent alongside the Virgin. Joseph's new role doubtless reflects the precepts of the Catholic reformers, including Erasmus and Thomas More, who esteemed marriage, motherhood, and the family rather than honoring only Mary's absolute female virtue of virginity. Joos's paintings of this type would thus appear to represent the model family of the reform movement—the educated father reading the Scriptures as his wife nurses their hungry child—in the guise of a Holy Family, thereby subverting the narrowly devotional function of the works. In keeping with the more secular emphasis of the figures, the still life invariably

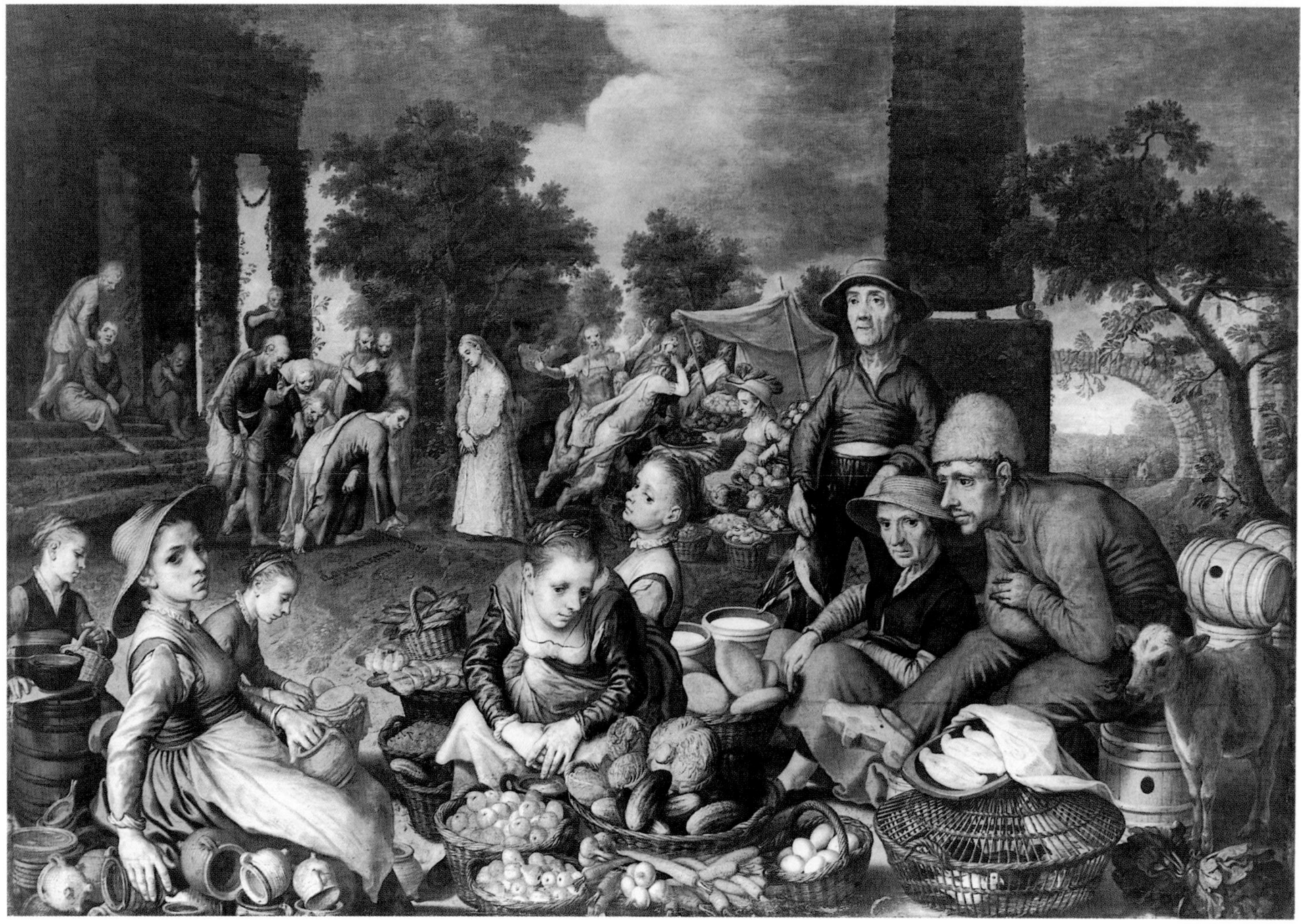

Fig. 108. Pieter Aertsen, *Christ and the Woman Taken in Adultery*, 1559. Oil on wood. Städelsches Kunstinstitut, Frankfurt

included in the foreground of such a picture seems more a fragment of everyday life than a eucharistic symbol. In the Museum's splendid *Virgin and Child* (cat. no. 96) and other examples, the still life appears to be almost as important as the primary subject.

Secular imagery overtook sacred content most emphatically in landscape painting—one of the most popular genres that developed in the sixteenth century. We begin to see this secularization in Joachim Patinir's grand landscapes, in which the holy figures become ever more marginalized, as if the role of religion is diminishing within the sweeping expanse of the world. A unique opportunity to witness the process of change from sacred to more secular concerns is afforded by the *Arrival in Bethlehem* attributed to Master LC (cat. no. 71). In this unfinished painting the original and the revised conceptions are literally laid bare. The initial version by the first artist, visible in the underdrawing, shows several episodes from the narrative of the Birth of Christ. However, a second artist edited some of these out in a subsequent painted stage and replaced them with a variety of motifs from everyday life, to achieve a transformation that reflects not merely the painter's personal whim but also the shifting priorities of an increasingly worldly society.

The total inversion of the premise of devotional painting occurs in the work of Pieter Aertsen and his pupil Joachim Beuckelaer (neither of whom is represented in the Museum's collection). In the

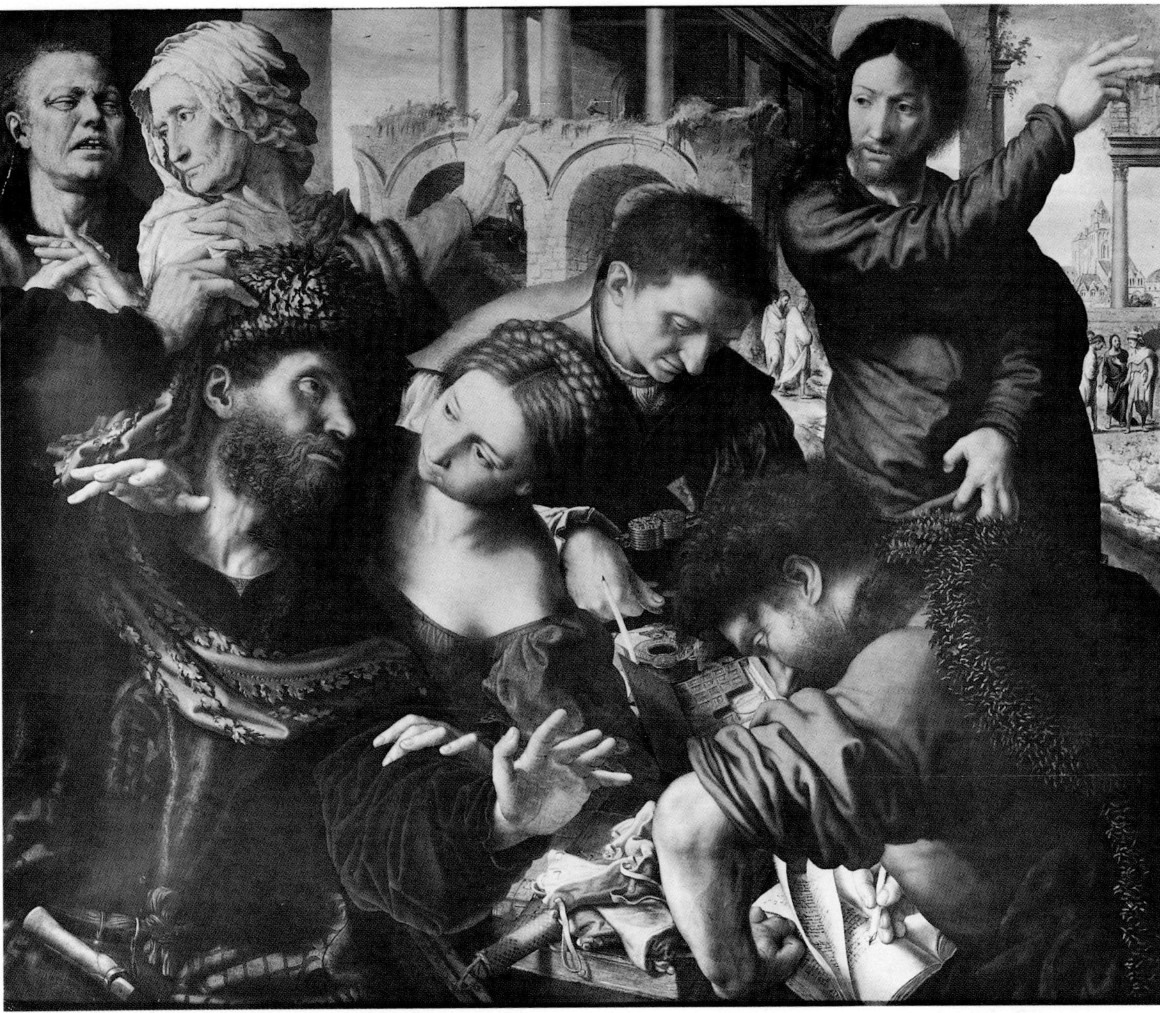

Fig. 109. Jan Sanders van Hemessen, *The Calling of Matthew*, about 1540. Oil on wood. Kunsthistoriches Museum, Vienna

1550s Aertsen produced a series of remarkable pictures in which a bold still life or kitchen scene fills the foreground and the religious subject is relegated to the background as a small vignette, serving merely to signal an allegorical meaning (fig. 108). Here the religious or devotional purpose is supplanted by a moralizing and didactic function, following a precedent set by Jan van Hemessen's large narrative compositions painted for the Antwerp market. While they retain overtly religious themes, Van Hemessen's pictures clearly tend toward moralizing content: the exaggerated poses and gestures of the figures in his *Calling of Matthew* (fig. 109; see also a workshop copy in the Metropolitan's collection [Additional Works in this publication]), for example, force the viewer to confront the vice and greed of the money changer and his customers. This is a theme that was also treated by Quentin Massys and may ultimately have had its roots in a much earlier, innovative precursor by Jan van Eyck (see entry for cat. no. 22). Their possible inspiration in fifteenth-century precedents notwithstanding, these late works with a Protestant, didactic bent are far removed from the mainstream of devotional panels created by the founders of Netherlandish painting—Jan van Eyck, Robert Campin, and Rogier van der Weyden. In subject matter as well as in formal presentation they vividly evoke the troubled times on the eve of the Iconoclasm.

MARYAN W. AINSWORTH

References: Van der Osten and Vey 1969; Ringbom 1984; Kloek, Halsema-Kubes, and Baarsen 1986 (with helpful bibliography); Parshall and Parshall 1986; Falkenburg 1988; Gibson 1989; Van der Stock 1993; Falkenburg 1994.

Juan de Flandes, active (in Spain) by 1496, died 1519

85. The Marriage Feast at Cana, about 1500–1504

Oil on wood, 8¼ x 6¼ in. (21 x 15.9 cm)
The Jack and Belle Linsky Collection, 1982 1982.60.20

Provenance: Isabella, queen of Castile, Castle of Toro, province of Zamora (until 1504); Diego Flores, probably as agent for Margaret of Austria (1505); Margaret of Austria, regent of the Netherlands, Mechelen (by 1516–30); her nephew, Charles V, Holy Roman Emperor and (as Charles I) king of Spain (1530–58); his son, Philip II, king of Spain, Palacio Real, Madrid (1558–98); Oderisio di Sangro, prince of Fondi, Naples ([until 1895]; his sale, Galerie Sangiorgi, Palazzo Borghese, Rome, May 1, 1895, no. 738 bis, as "école Bolonaise du XVIIe siècle"); [Bardini, Florence (until 1899)]; Vernon J. Watney, Cornbury Park, Charlbury, Oxfordshire (1899–1928); his son, Oliver Vernon Watney, Cornbury Park ([1928–67]; his sale, Christie's, London, June 23, 1967, no. 33, to Mr. and Mrs. Jack Linsky, New York [1967–80]); The Jack and Belle Linsky Foundation, New York (1980–82).

The feast takes place within an airy, classically inspired loggia, in the courtyard of which stands a man, possibly representing a portrait of the artist or a court functionary. The bride and groom are at the head of the table, their gestures echoing those of Christ and his mother, who are seated at the left. Christ holds his right hand in a gesture of blessing, as the Virgin looks toward him and presses her hands together in prayer. A convex mirror, hanging in front of a cloth of honor that frames the bride and groom, reflects the backs of their heads and the table, as well as a colonnade parallel to the picture plane, which is notionally in our space.

According to the biblical text (John 2:1–11), Christ performed his first miracle at the feast at Cana, which prefigures the Last Supper; in response to a plea of the Virgin, who had noticed that there was no more wine, he instructed that jars be filled with water, which turned into wine of the finest quality. Our picture shows the moment before the miracle, when the wine steward, in the right foreground, pours water from a pitcher into a jar. Behind him stands the master of the feast holding a covered cup that will contain the wine he will taste before asking the bridegroom why he saved the best until last.

This exquisite panel is one of a group of forty-seven paintings made for Queen Isabella the Catholic, of Castile and León. It is not clear whether the series, which was carried out by no fewer than three artists, among whom was Michel Sittow, was ever completed: the inventory of Isabella's estate, drawn up in 1505, describes the panels as stored "in a cupboard"—perhaps because the entire sequence had not been finished. The pictures illustrate episodes from the lives of Christ and the Virgin and are of the same size, suggesting that the original intention was to arrange and incorporate them into a framework.

Following Isabella's death, thirty-two of the works, including ours, were acquired for Margaret of Austria and brought to Mechelen, near Brussels, where they were recorded in 1516. It was there that Albrecht Dürer encountered them, writing in his journal on June 7, 1521, "On Friday Lady Margaret showed me all her beautiful things. Among them I saw about forty small panels painted in oil, the likes of which I have never seen for purity [*reinigkeith*] and quality [*güth*]." By 1524 only twenty-two panels remained at Mechelen. Twenty of these were sent by Margaret's nephew, Charles V, to Spain, where eighteen were mounted in a silver-gilt diptych surmounted by the *Temptation of Christ* (National Gallery of Art, Washington, D.C.) and the *Marriage Feast at Cana.*

In the arrangement of the colonnade and its placement to the left, the positions of some of the figures, and the inclusion of what may be a portrait outside the loggia, our painting resembles Gerard David's *Marriage Feast at Cana* of about 1501 (Louvre, Paris). The similarities suggest the possibility that Juan de Flandes used as a model an earlier version of David's composition that he could have seen during his apprenticeship in Flanders. It is also conceivable that another, common model inspired both artists. However, Juan made an extraordinarily refined, vertical composition, depicting only the essential characters disposed within a richly articulated space. DCS

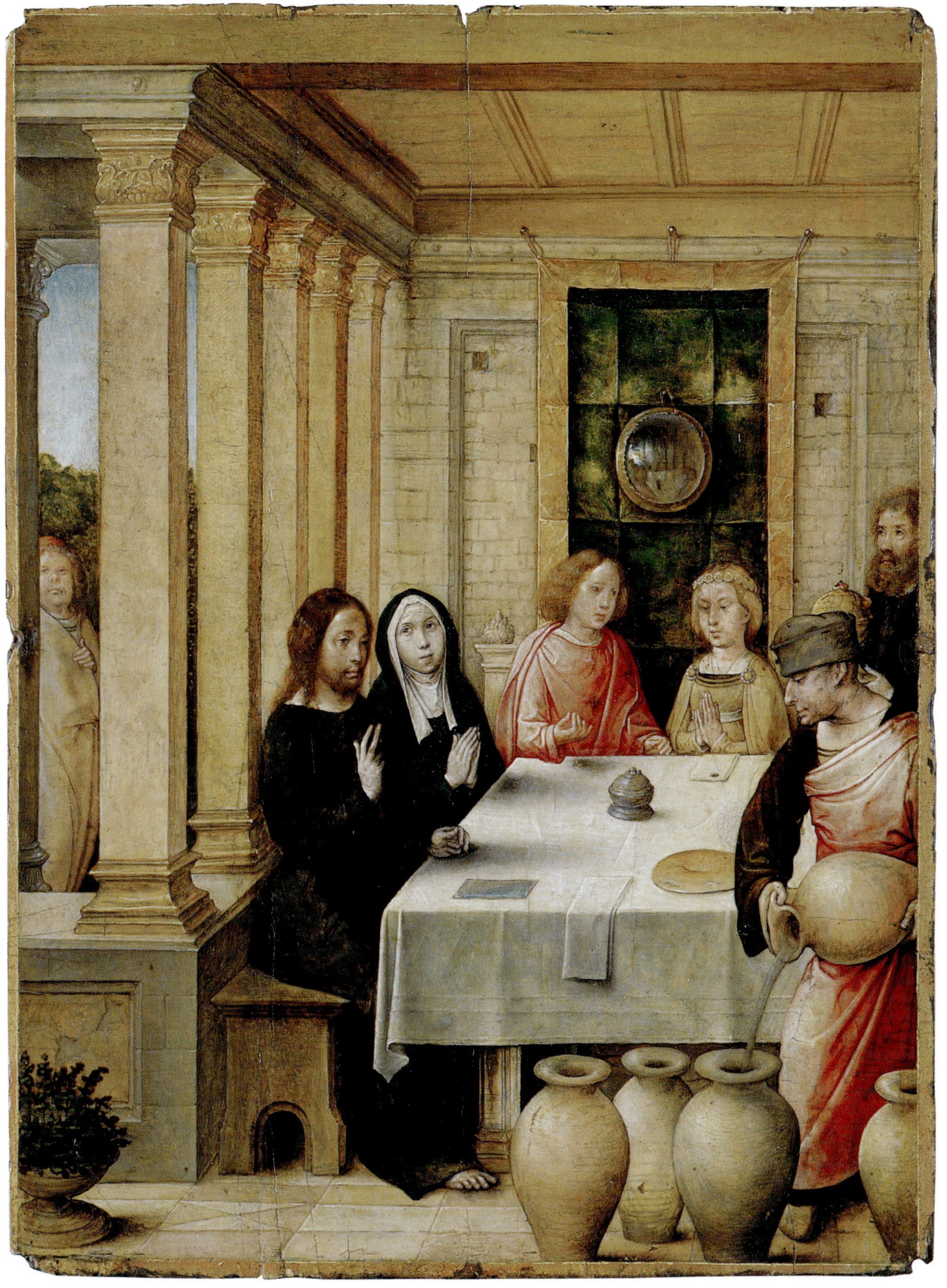

References: Justi 1887, p. 159; Justi 1908, vol. 1, pp. 318–19, no. 10; Veth and Muller 1918, p. 84; Friedländer 1930, pp. 2–3; Sánchez Cantón 1930, pp. 100, 109, 120, no. 25, pl. 1; Sánchez Cantón 1931, pp. 149, 150, pl. 1; Davies 1970, p. 15, no. 25; Bauman in Metropolitan Museum 1984, pp. 59–64, no. 20, color ill.; Bauman 1986, p. 15, colorpl. 10; Metropolitan Museum 1987, p. 43, color ill.; Ishikawa 1989, pp. 26 no. 25, 45–46, 61, 91–92, 151–58, no. 2, figs. 3–5; Wolff 1992, pp. 27, 98–99, no. 25b, color ill.

Juan de Flandes, active (in Spain) by 1496, died 1519

86. Saints Michael and Francis, about 1505–9

Oil on wood, gold ground; overall, with added strips at right and bottom, 36⅞ x 34¼ in. (93.7 x 87 cm); painted surface 35⅜ x 32¾ in. (89.9 x 83.2 cm)
Inscribed (below figures): SANT:MIGVEL; Sant:franciscó:
Purchase, Mary Wetmore Shively Bequest, in memory of her husband, Henry L. Shively, M.D., 1958 58.132

Provenance: Sir Frederick Lucas Cook, Doughty House, Richmond, Surrey (by 1908–20); Sir Herbert Frederick Cook, Doughty House (1920–39); Sir Francis F. M. Cook, Doughty House (1939–54); [Rosenberg and Stiebel, New York, 1954–58].

References: Tormo y Monzó 1909, p. 240; Bertaux 1914, p. 252; Brockwell 1915, pp. 124, 126, no. 490, ill.; Moreno Villa 1917, pp. 276, 278–80, ill.; Friedländer 1930, pp. 2, 4, ill.; Sánchez Cantón 1930, p. 113; Post 1933, pp. 41, 48; Eisler 1959, pp. 128–37, ills.; Bermejo 1962, pp. 31, 144, no. 44, fig. 44; Vandevivere 1967, pp. 44, 46, 51.

The flamboyant archangel Michael, at the left, who extends beyond his niche in every direction, contrasts with the frontal, ascetic image of Saint Francis of Assisi, so visibly contained within his shallow space. The outspread wings of Michael appear to be momentarily stilled as he looks earthward and impales the dragon with his cruciform lance. Much like a convex mirror, the shield reflects what seems to be a walled, smoking city viewed through a series of bars and marked by fissures—a truly apocalyptic vision in keeping with the subject. Michael's resplendent wings, his blue alb, and the jewels on his forehead, shield, and lance frame his smooth young face and softly draped figure. Saint Francis, wearing the brownish gray habit and the tonsure of his order, looks heavenward, his stigmata-marked hands raised in the ancient gesture of prayer (orans).

Juan probably introduced a gold background and large, broadly painted figures in an effort to adapt his style to Spanish taste. He applied glazes over the gold ground to create the illusion of niches and affixed trompe-l'oeil depictions of vellum scrolls identifying the saints to the wall below them. The bluish green border, which now surrounds the gold, is not original and would have been covered with framing elements (on the right and bottom it is painted on modern additions to the panel).

Bertaux was the first to attribute this panel to Juan de Flandes. It was perhaps part of a large retablo, or altarpiece, which was commissioned in 1505 for the chapel of the University of Salamanca; the altarpiece included polychrome sculpture by Felipe de Borgoña that still belongs to the university (Gómez-Moreno 1914, ill. after p. 324). Our panel could have belonged to a colonnade of saints in niches surrounding a narrative scene. In 1505 Juan de Flandes contracted to paint eight scenes and three sacred figures for the altarpiece, and in 1507 he further agreed to create ten images designated for the *banco*, or lowermost register. Two extant images from the *banco*—fragmentary, half-length grisaille representations of Saints Apollonia and Mary Magdalene in niches (fig. 110)—were linked with Juan de Flandes and this altarpiece by Gómez-Moreno (1914, p. 326). On the basis of comparison with these panels, our picture has also been associated with the altarpiece (Haverkamp-Begemann in Eisler 1959, pp. 134–35), which Juan is thought to have worked on until 1509. DCS

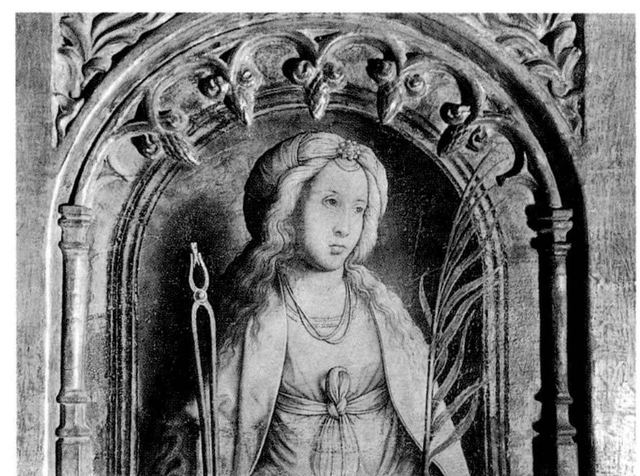
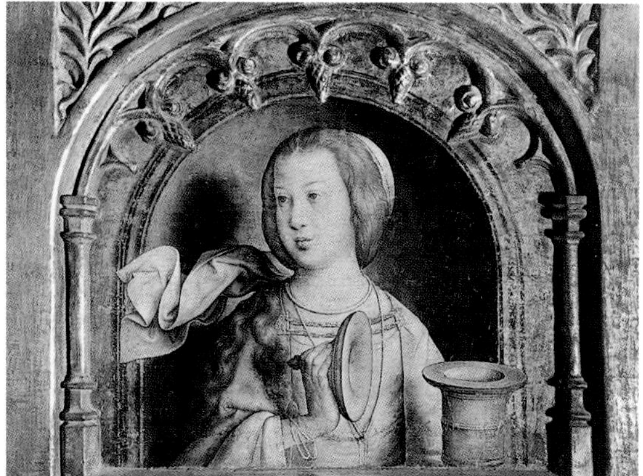

Fig. 110. Juan de Flandes, *Saints Apollonia and Magdalene,* about 1507. Oil on wood. University of Salamanca

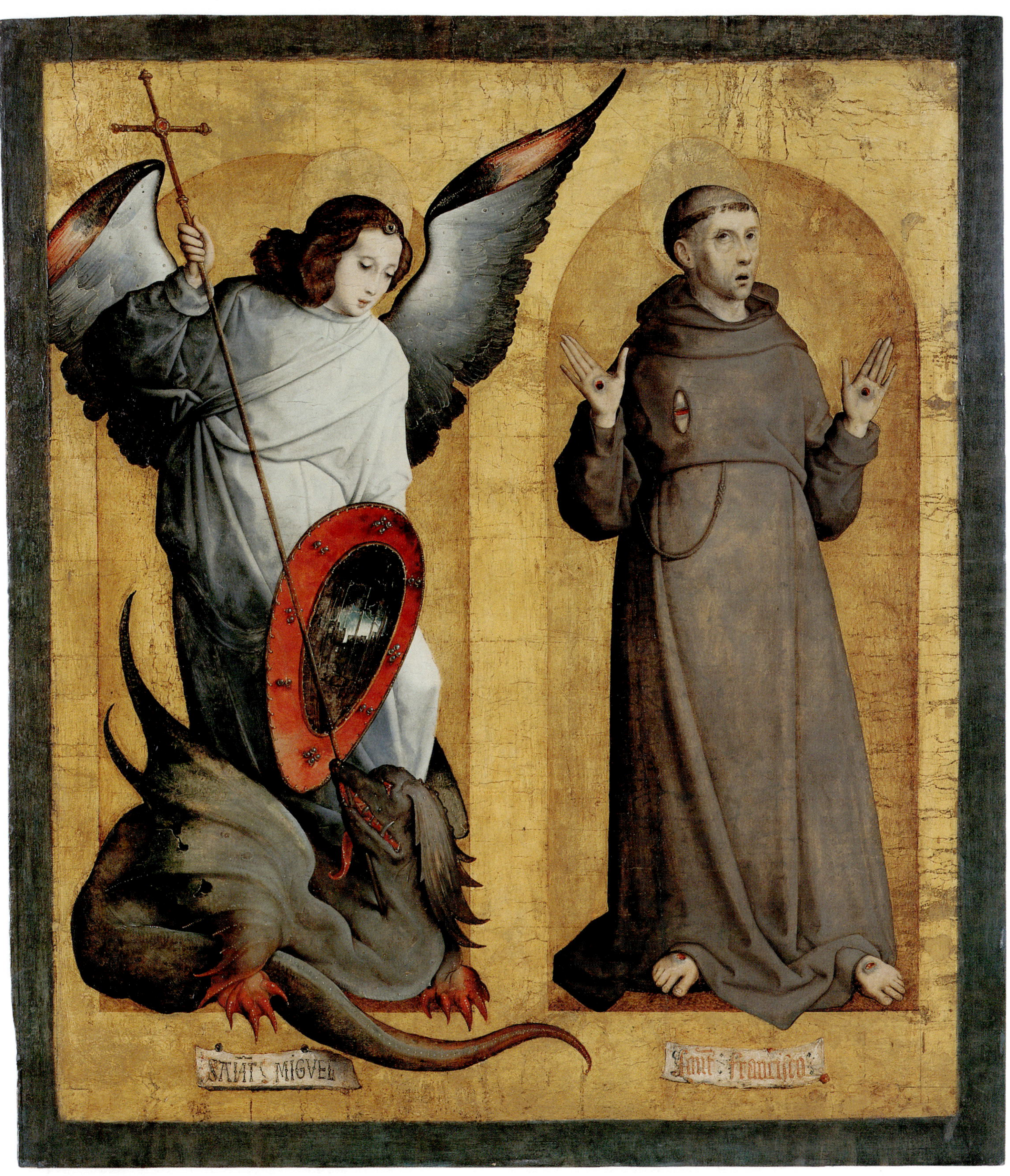
SANT MIGVEL
Sant francisco

Jean Bellegambe, French, active 1504–34

87. The Le Cellier Altarpiece, 1509

Oil on wood, shaped top; central panel 40 x 24 in. (101.6 x 61 cm); left wing 37¾ x 10 in. (95.9 x 25.4 cm); right wing 37½ x 9½ in. (95.3 x 24.1 cm)
Arms (interior of left wing, top) of the family of Saint Bernard, used by the Cistercian order, and (interior of right wing, top) of Jeanne de Boubais, abbess of the Cistercian convent of Flines
The Friedsam Collection, Bequest of Michael Friedsam, 1931 32.100.102

Provenance: Found in chapel of Le Cellier, former granary or cellar of abbey of Clairvaux, Colombe-le-Sec, Champagne (1861); Baron Antoine de Tavernost, Paris (by 1906); Baronne de Tavernost, Savigny-les-Beaune, Côte d'Or (until 1922); [Wildenstein, Paris and New York, from 1922]; Michael Friedsam, New York (by 1927–31).

References: Arbois de Joubainville 1861, pp. 36f.; Mély 1908, pp. 97–108, ill. opp. p. 100; Sperling 1927, pp. 98–100, no. 40, ills.; Friedländer 1924–37, vol. 12 (1935), pp. 36–38, 177, no. 119, pls. 14–15; Genaille 1952, pp. 99–108, figs. 1–3; Sterling 1955, pp. 18–21, ill.; Friedländer 1967–76, vol. 12 (1975), pp. 23–24, 101, no. 119, pls. 56, 57; Genaille 1976, pp. 17–18, fig. 5; Will 1981, pp. 124–25.

Working in the Franco-Netherlandish border town of Douai and a witness to art currents of northern France as well as to trends in the thriving commercial center of Antwerp, Bellegambe developed an independent style, the sources of which are difficult to pinpoint. His graceful, solidly grounded figures appear French in spirit but are placed before landscapes that are similar in atmosphere and invention to those of Joachim Patinir and Jan Provost; the decorative impulse in the architecture is clearly derived from Antwerp.

Since its discovery in 1861 in the Le Cellier chapel, the former granary or cellar of the Cistercian abbey of Clairvaux, this triptych has been referred to as the *Le Cellier Altarpiece.* Genaille (1952) plausibly identified it with a work mentioned in contemporary documents as commissioned from Bellegambe by Jeanne de Boubais, abbess of Flines, and completed in 1509; indeed the style and relatively sober design of our painting are consistent with this early date. Genaille, furthermore, identified the theme as Saint Bernard, assisted by Saint Malachy, presenting his family to the Virgin. This was largely confirmed in 1981 when Will published an engraving of the subject—possibly an inspiration for the design of our altarpiece—as the frontispiece to an edition of the sermons of Saint Bernard, published in Paris in 1508.

The devout and richly dressed couple represented closest to the Virgin are Bernard's parents, Tescelin and Aleth, nobles from the Dijon region. His mother, a woman of exemplary faith, was said to have committed each of her children to the service of God at the moment of birth. Indeed, after Bernard chose to enter the Cistercian monastery of Cîteaux, founded by Saint Benedict, and became a key figure in the movement to reform Benedictine rule, he enlisted the aid of his five pious brothers, drawing them as well into the Cistercian order. The brothers are depicted in the lower register of figures with their more worldly sister, Humbeline, who eventually became a Benedictine nun. She is shown behind her mother in the habit of her order but with the features of Jeanne de Boubais, known to us from Bellegambe's portrait of her in the Frick Art Museum, Pittsburgh. In the Frick panel, however, Jeanne is shown in the habit of a Cistercian abbess with her ornate abbatial cross beside her, while here she has the modest appearance appropriate to her role. Jeanne's coat of arms, somewhat altered in restoration, is held by an angel in the uppermost corner of the right wing. Saint Bernard stands in our left wing beneath the arms of his family; in the landscape behind him is a view of Douai with the abbey of Flines and, beyond it, the four bell towers of the abbey of Anchin. The imposing figure on the right wing may be Saint Malachy, archbishop of Armagh—another reformer and a close friend of Bernard's—who appears as Bernard's counterpart in the 1508 engraving.

Perhaps the most directly appealing elements of the composition are the wonderfully childlike music-making angels who fill every spare nook around the throne and animate the landscape behind it. Such cherubs are also present in certain works of the contemporary Antwerp painter Jan Gossart. The throne itself, with its exaggerated spatial recession and the refined detail of its ornament, reflects the Antwerp school's decorative enthusiasm, seen elsewhere, for example, in Quentin Massys's *Adoration of the Magi* (cat. no. 99). The entire scene is witnessed by God the Father from a golden nimbus above the throne.

The grisaille exterior wings depict the best-known legend associated with Saint Bernard, the miracle of lactation: milk spurts from the Virgin's breast and moistens the saint's lips, an occurrence that emphasizes the Virgin's role not only as Christ's mother but also as mother of—and intercessor for—all mankind.

The altarpiece may have served a particular purpose. At the moment of Jeanne de Boubais's election as abbess of Flines, toward the end of 1507, Guillaume de Bruxelles, her superior at the abbey

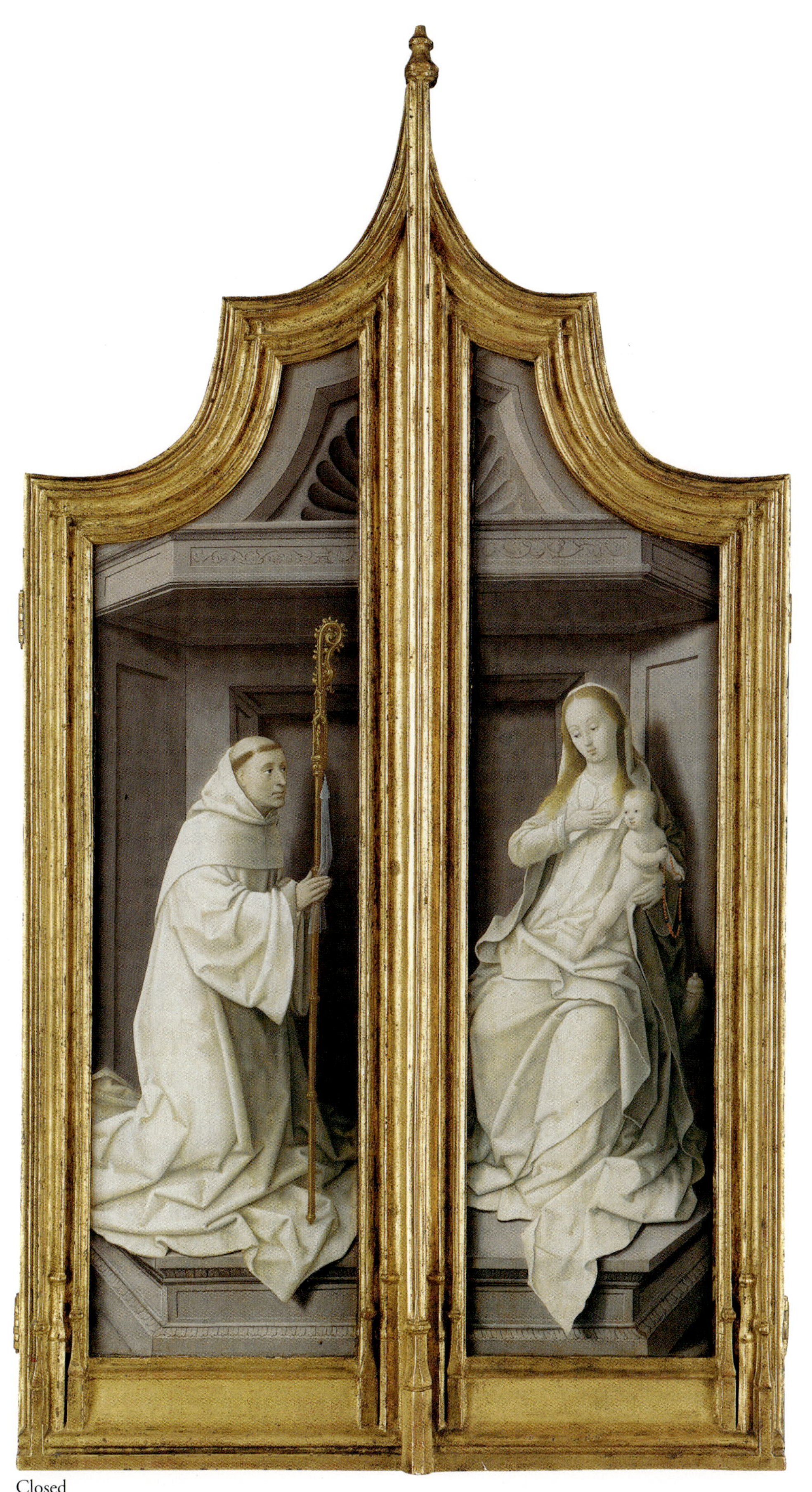

Closed

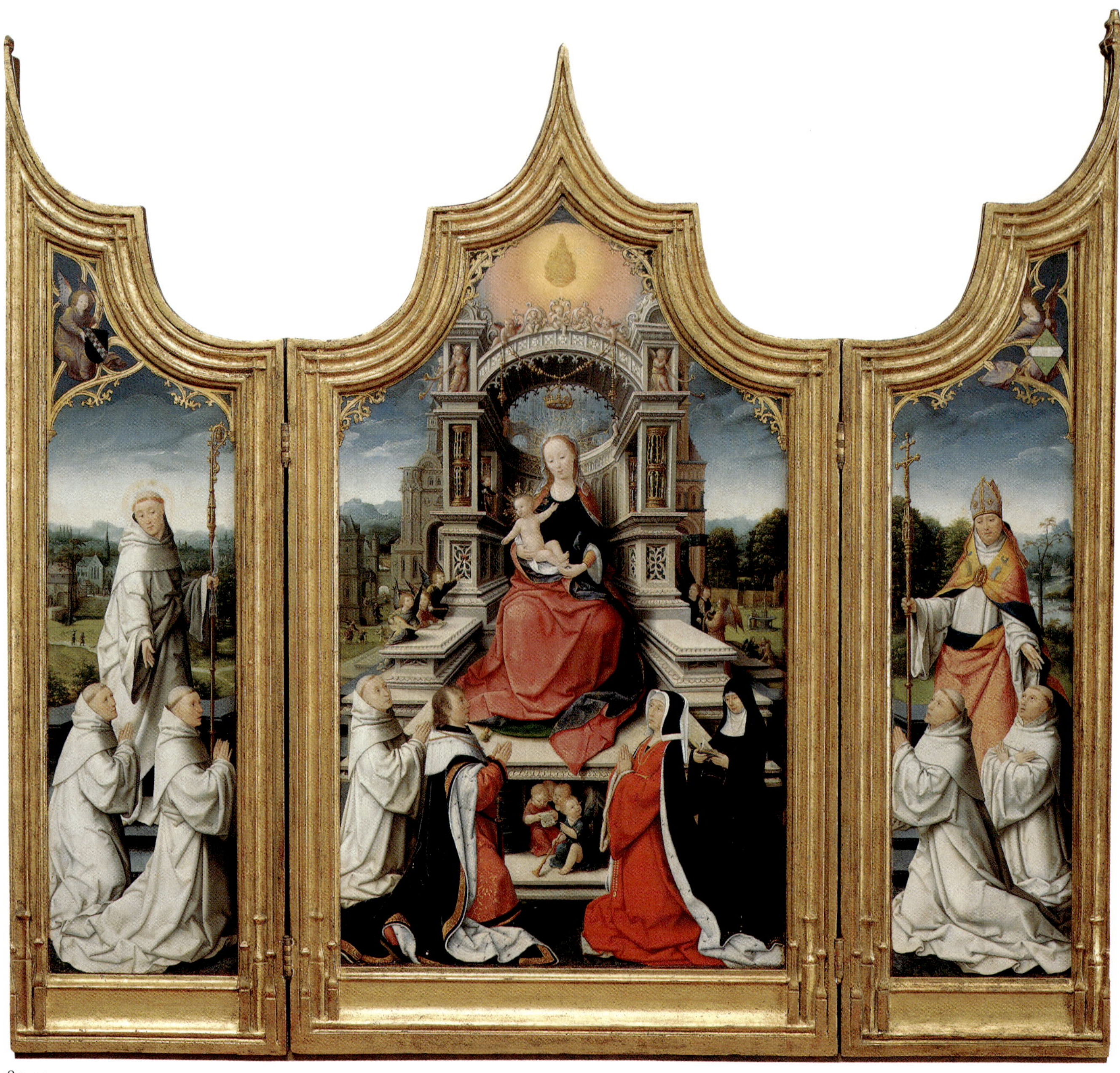

87 open

of Clairvaux—which Saint Bernard had founded—called for a return to stricter Benedictine rule. The subject of our triptych would have been particularly appropriate under these circumstances, as it was Saint Bernard who so energetically carried out the first Cistercian reform of Benedictine rule. Genaille (1952) suggests that the *Le Cellier Altarpiece* was commissioned by Jeanne de Boubais to present to Guillaume, at Clairvaux, as an expression of her commitment to reform.

In a later discussion of the altarpiece, Genaille (1976) observes that, rather than Malachy, the presenting saint on the right wing could be Guillaume de Bourges, patron saint of Guillaume de Bruxelles.

MSdJ

Joachim Patinir, active by 1515, died 1524

88. The Penitence of Saint Jerome, about 1518

Our splendid and complete altarpiece, which is in an exceptional state of preservation, is one of Patinir's finest and most complex works. The three saints shown are all but overwhelmed by a continuous panoramic landscape, of the sort Dürer must have admired during his trip to the Netherlands in 1520–21. It was at this time that he referred to Patinir as the "good landscape painter"—a remark

Oil on wood, shaped top; central panel, overall with engaged frame, 46¼ x 32 in. (117.5 x 81.3 cm); each wing, overall, with engaged frame, 47½ x 14 in. (120.7 x 35.6 cm)
Fletcher Fund, 1936 36.14a–c

Provenance: Emperor Leopold I of Austria (until 1674); monastery of Kremsmünster, Austria (1674–1935); [Knoedler, New York (1935)].

References: Werner 1929, p. 54; Wehle 1936, pp. 80–84; Wehle and Salinger 1947, pp. 115–17; Koch 1968, pp. 11–12, 16–18, 23, 34–36, 77, no. 14, figs. 35, 37, 38; Cuttler and Dunbar 1969, p. 432; Friedländer 1967–76, vol. 9b (1973), pp. 125–26, supp. 226, figs. 250, 251; Falkenburg 1985, pp. 10, 73–74, 84, fig. 8; Falkenburg 1988, pp. 52–53, 55, 62–63, fig. 8; Gibson 1989, pp. 4, 7–8, 10, figs. 1.8, 1.9; Koch 1992, pp. 108–10, colorpl. opp. p. 110.

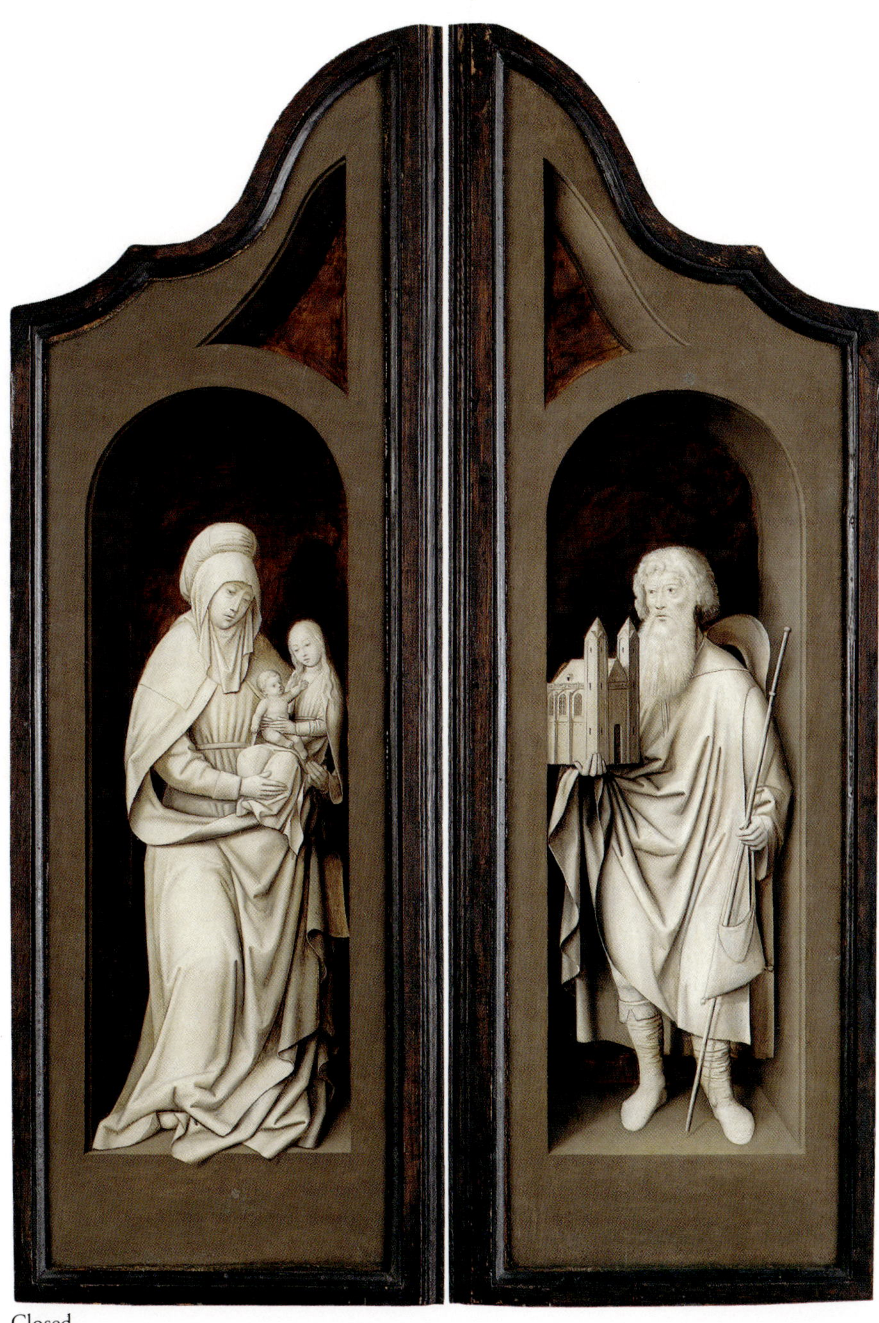

Closed

that constitutes the first known use of the word "landscape" to indicate a separate genre of painting.

The triptych was very likely commissioned by south German patrons, since the grisaille exterior wings show Saint Sebald, the patron saint of Nuremberg, and the *Anna Selbdritt*—the Virgin and Child with Saint Anne—one of the most popular themes in German art at the end of the fifteenth century. Later owned by the Habsburgs, in 1674 the ensemble was given by Emperor Leopold I to the Benedictine monastery of Kremsmünster near Linz in Austria, where it remained until shortly before the Metropolitan purchased it in 1936. Although the altarpiece's curved frame, including its hinges, is original, at some point the gesso and gilding were removed, somewhat altering its original appearance.

In the center panel is Saint Jerome, kneeling on a rocky ledge dotted with ivy, between a dead tree sending forth a flourishing branch and a small stream springing from a rock. He is described in the *Vaderboec* as "slight and withered of body through great fasting" (Gouda 1480, fol. 7). The scene is based on Jerome's famous letter to Eustochium in which the saint describes his life in the desert of Chalcis, Syria, between 374–75 and 376–77, after he fled from Rome. Mortifying the flesh of his bare chest with a stone, he is imploring Christ, whom he visualizes alive on the small cross in front of him. Another instrument of self-punishment, the scourge, is nearby. The flora and fauna, painted with remarkable verisimilitude, are the disguised natural symbols of the saint's struggle with good and evil, specifically the sinful desires and impure thoughts that afflicted him during his self-imposed exile. The wild vegetation—dandelions, strawberries, and ferns—emphasizes the hermit's humility, while the coral wards off the devil, and the salamander stands for temptation. Small anecdotal vignettes illustrating the legend of Jerome's lion as told in Jacobus de Voragine's *Golden Legend* are shown in the landscape behind him and to the right of the saint. The monastery that Jerome founded near Bethlehem is nestled on a high plateau in the middle ground.

The left wing features the Baptism of Christ, which marks the beginning of Christ's public ministry, undertaken after he retired to the desert for forty days. The three members of the Trinity are

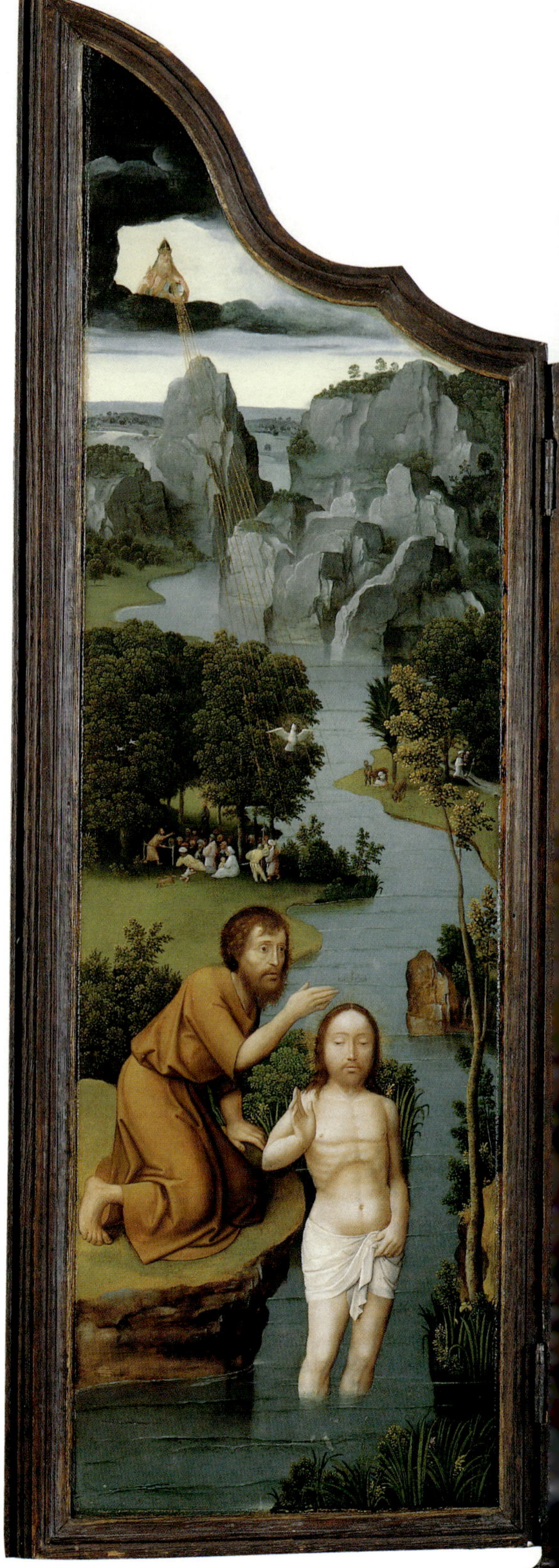

88 open

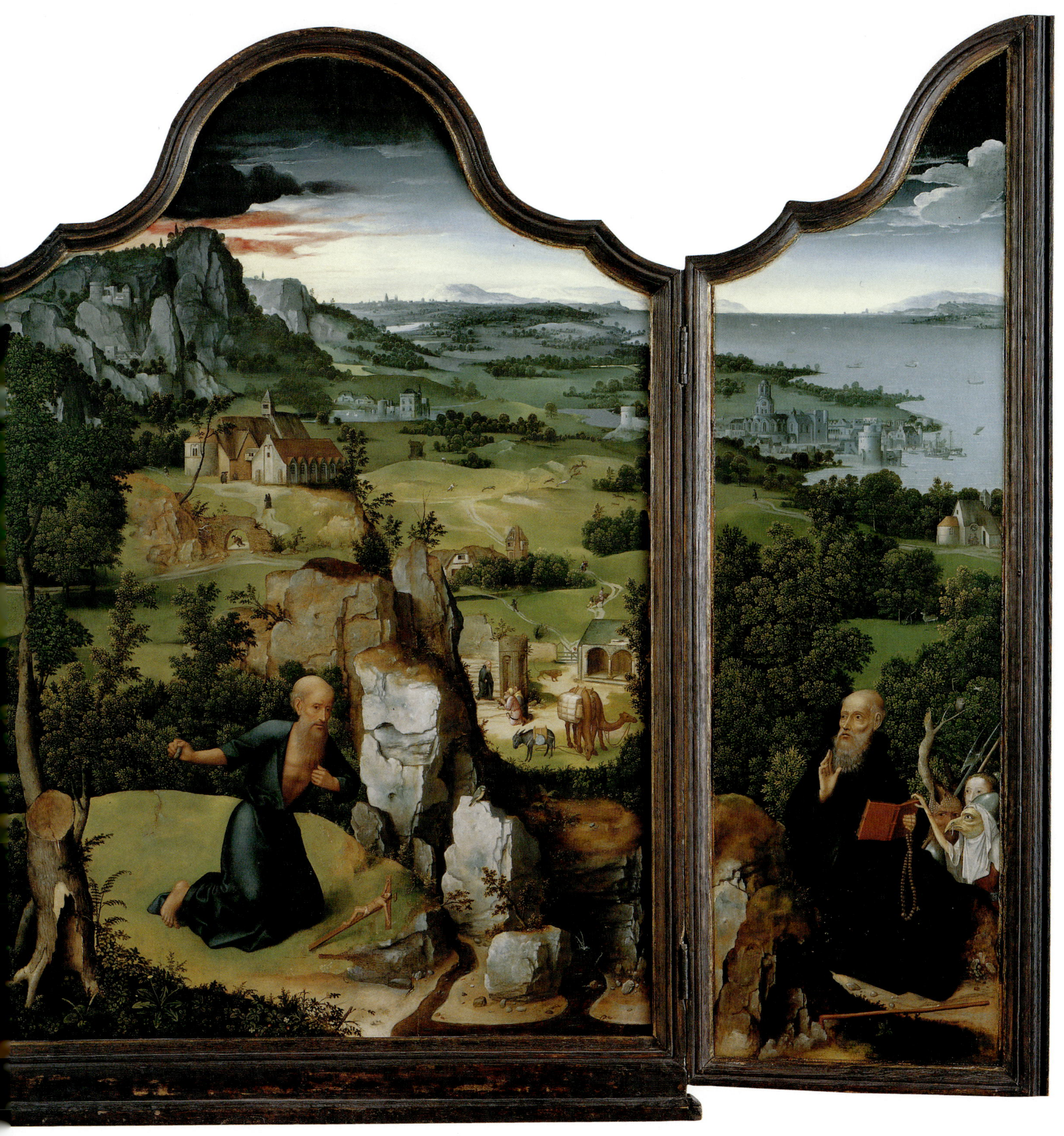

Following pages: Details, cat. no. 88

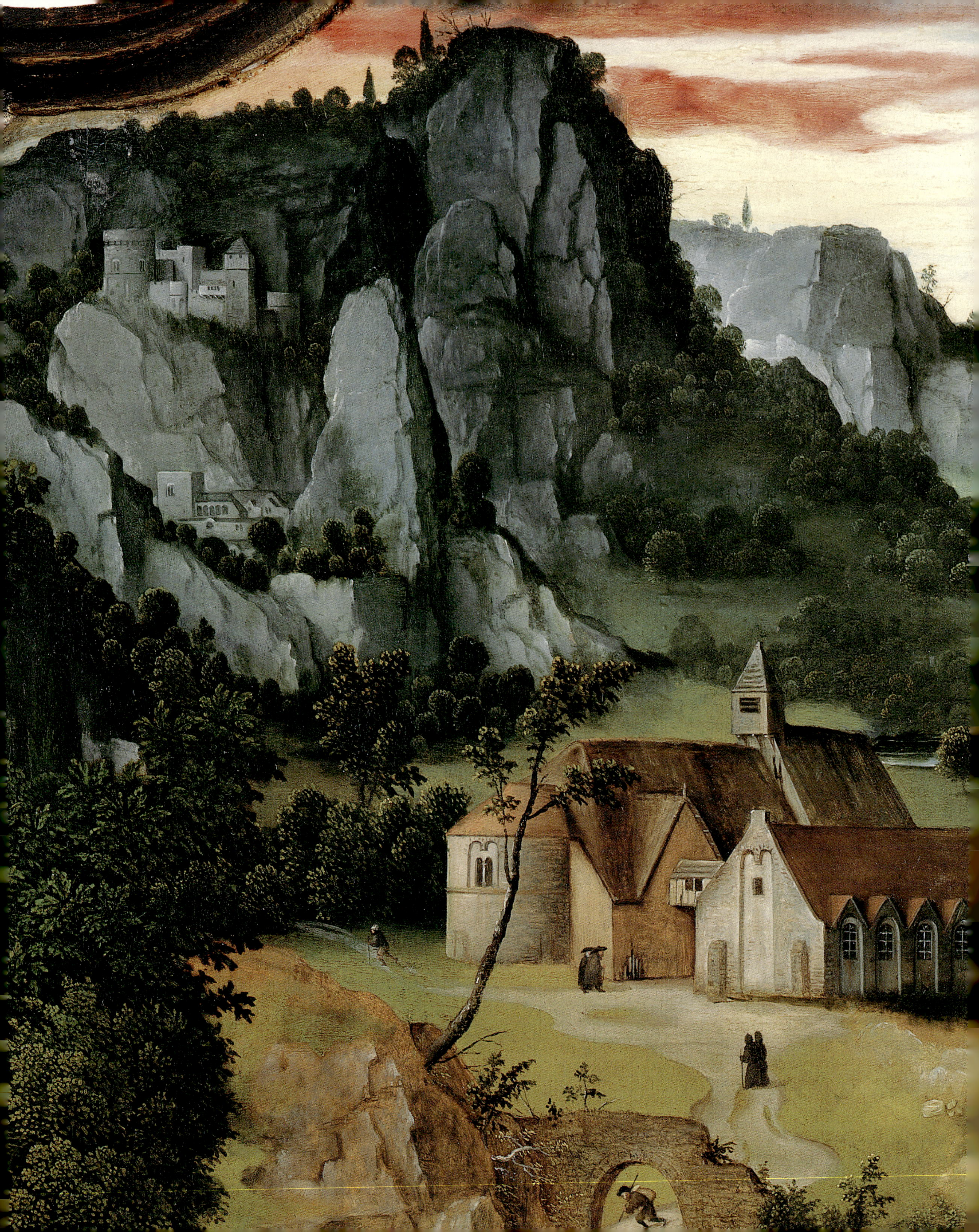

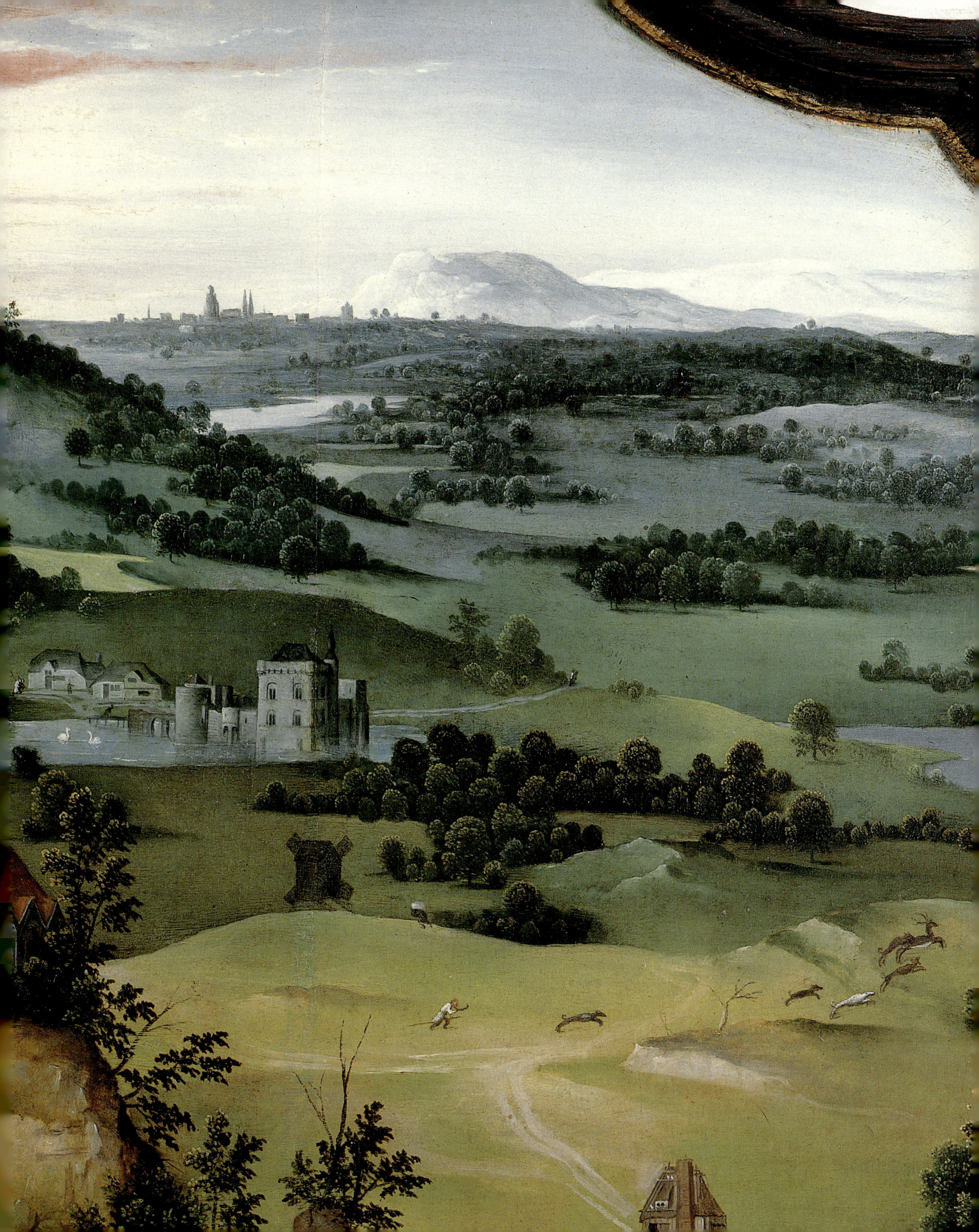

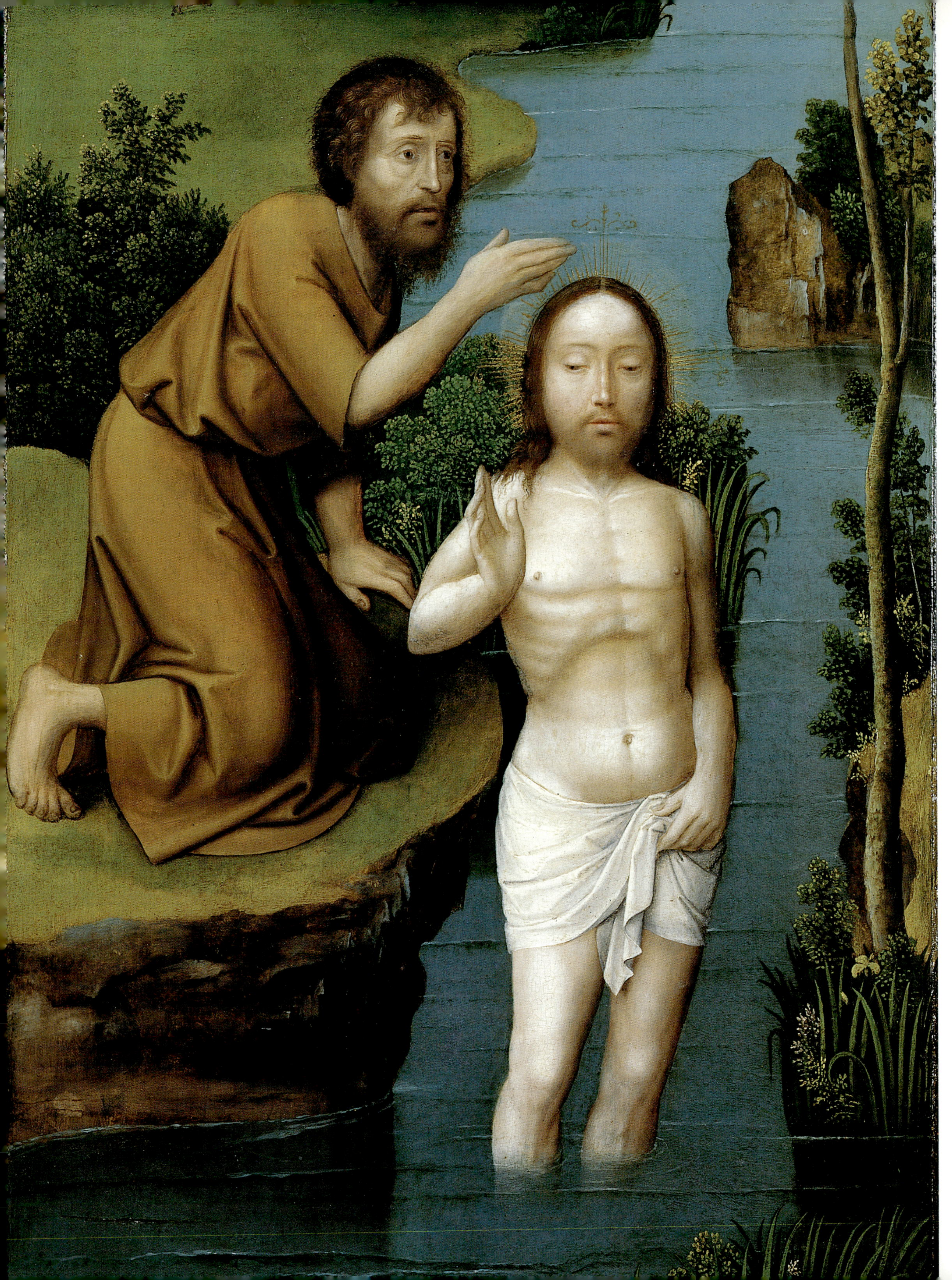

linked by the golden rays emanating from God the Father, who sends the Holy Spirit forth in the form of a dove. In the middle distance Saint John is preaching in the wilderness. As in the painter's signed *Baptism of Christ* of about 1515–19 (Kunsthistorisches Museum, Vienna), the figures of Saint John and Christ are adapted from Gerard David's *Baptism of Christ* of about 1503–8 (Groeningemuseum, Bruges). However, here John appears to be blessing Christ, and Christ, in turn, blesses the beholder, whereas in the David *Baptism* Christ's hands are joined in prayer.

The right wing shows Saint Anthony the Hermit, the legendary founder of the *vita contemplativa*, set in the foreground of a landscape where the far distance and the sky fuse, recalling the open spaces in paintings by Hieronymus Bosch, such as the Bronchorst-Bosschuyze Triptych (Prado, Madrid). In his left hand Saint Anthony holds a book and a rosary, an attribute that was particularly important for the Antonines, who used it in their hospitals to alleviate pain and fight disease, especially the plague. The Boschian monsters and the owl sitting on a branch allude to the saint's own struggle against temptation by Satan.

Although the figures of the hermit saints in the foreground of the altarpiece are arresting, it is the magnificent landscape, with its uninterrupted horizon sweeping across the three panels, that most captures attention. The distant and craggy mountains linking the central panel to the left wing are reminiscent of Patinir's birthplace in the Meuse Valley. The forbidding peaks gradually evolve into bright yellow-green rolling hills and a broad expanse of water evoking the lush estuary of the Schelde in Antwerp, which stretches out into the right wing. Scenes of country life, anticipating those in Flemish and Dutch landscapes of the later sixteenth and seventeenth centuries, are scattered in the middle ground: a couple milking a cow, people roaming the countryside around a windmill, peasants coming back from the fields, hounds pursuing a stag. The painter's palette, although limited, is incredibly varied in its nuances and succeeds in creating a perspective that recedes in fluent transition from warm brown and warm green to cool blue: the reddish brown of the foreground, green of the middle distance, and blue in the far distance fuse at the borders of their zones to produce a naturalistic rendering of the landscape's silhouette. All is revealed in the evenly distributed light of the sun shining through an overcast sky.

Falkenburg (1988) interprets Patinir's landscape, especially with regard to the Penitence of Saint Jerome, as a complex of related metaphors of the two paths through life described in Saint Augustine's *De civitate Dei* (413–27), pointing out that the artist contrasts the prosperous *civitas terrena*, or the world of sin, to the arduous *civitas dei*, or the world of salvation. The landscape is, in fact, divided into two zones, one soft and lush, the other harsh, and the saints appear to be integral parts of the deserted rocky mountains in the left background, inviting the beholder to follow the arduous path of penitence.

Patinir further developed the compositional devices inherited from his fifteenth-century predecessors, such as the depiction of the landscape in minute detail and the use of atmospheric perspective, the bird's-eye view, and the high horizon. He repeated the open panoramas of Bosch's background landscapes, and he embraced a much vaster space than the normal vantage point of the spectator would allow. Using multiple viewpoints borrowed from contemporary mapmaking and topography, Patinir mixed broad horizontal segments of the earth seen from above with vertical elements—buildings, trees, mountains, animals, and figures—all painted with tiny details, as if they were observed at eye level.

Comparison of the figures of Christ and Saint John with their counterparts in Patinir's signed *Baptism of Christ* in Vienna underscores the difficulty in establishing a chronology of the artist's work. According to Koch (1968), our picture represents an early phase of Patinir's maturity. He dates it after the Vienna panel, even though the drawing and the modeling of the figures in our altarpiece reflect a less advanced understanding of the human body. The disparity between the two works could be explained by the fact that the figures in some of Patinir's landscapes are painted by other artists, as in the *Temptation of Saint Anthony* of about 1520–24 (Prado, Madrid), for example, where they are by Quentin

Massys. The landscape in that picture shares the open spaces and panoramic views of our altarpiece, and in each work compact groups of trimly rounded trees, highlighted with dots, are used in the middle ground to separate large pockets of land. The structure of our landscape is also related to that in Patinir's *Rest on the Flight into Egypt* of 1518–20 (Gemäldegalerie, Berlin). However, the somewhat stiff figures that characterize our painting are closer to the figures in his earlier *Assumption of the Virgin* (John G. Johnson Collection, Philadelphia Museum of Art), commissioned from the artist by Lukas Rem in Antwerp about 1516–17.

VS

Bernaert van Orley, active by 1515, died 1541/42

89. Virgin and Child with Angels, about 1515

Oil on wood, 33⅝ x 27½ in. (85.4 x 69.9 cm)
Inscribed: (on Virgin's robe) MARIA MATER GRASIA MA . . . *(Mary, Mother of Grace, mo[ther] . . .); (falsely, lower left, with date and initials of Albrecht Dürer) 1505/*AD *[monogram]*
Bequest of Benjamin Altman, 1913 14.40.632

Provenance: Count von Sierstorpff, Driburg (sale, Lepke, Berlin, April 19–20, 1887, no. 4, as by Mabuse); Riedel, anonymous collector (sale, Rudolf Bangel, Frankfurt, February 12, 1901, no. 17, as by Dürer); Jakob Emden, Hamburg; Herman Emden, Hamburg (sale, Lepke, Berlin, May 3, 1910, no. 89); Benjamin Altman, New York.

References: Parthey 1863–64, vol. 1, p. 362, no. 27; Friedländer 1909, pp. 9–10, ill.;

A courtly, Italianate Madonna of Humility, the Virgin wears a luxurious fur-trimmed dress and is seated on the ground surrounded by flowering strawberry and plantain. Her allegorical role as Bride of Christ, following Saint Bernard's interpretation of the love poetry of the Song of Solomon, is alluded to in the setting of the enclosed garden and the fountain, or "well of living waters," at the left. As Ainsworth has pointed out, the intense physical interaction of the Virgin and Child underscores the importance of this biblical source as the inspiration for the picture.

To a degree rarely seen in early Netherlandish painting, the body of the Child is truly animated and plastic; muscled as a small man, his right leg is raised to reveal his genitals, a focus of the composition. He holds the Virgin's head in the chin-chuck, a convention going back to ancient art and present as well in medieval Christian works. The current of sexual tenderness in the gestures of mother and child and, as Steinberg points out, the chin-chuck in particular emphasize Christ's role as the Heavenly Bridegroom, who has chosen Mary for his mother and as his eternal consort in heaven. Furthermore, the explicit evidence of Christ's manhood and the protective gesture of the Virgin's left hand draw our attention to his humanity and thus his vulnerability.

In this moment when forward-looking Netherlandish artists seemed to flaunt the progressive influence of the Italian Renaissance, there remained a strong tendency to repeat earlier models. Van Orley, like Dieric Bouts in his *Virgin and Child* (cat. no. 6), adopted the profile-to-profile intimacy of mother and child from the Italo-Byzantine Cambrai Madonna (fig. 49); the chin-chuck as well was present in this iconic type. The general pose of the Virgin may ultimately derive from Robert Campin, whose workshop produced numerous images of the Virgin and Child seated in an interior. In all of these paintings, as in Van Orley's panel, the sculptural folds of the drapery create a solid pyramidal base for the holy pair, and Mary's hair falls in loose waves around her shoulders. A particularly close example, the *Virgin and Child in an Interior* recently ascribed to Campin's pupil Jacques Daret (National Gallery, London), shares with our panel the juxtaposed profiles of the Virgin and Christ, a modified chin-chuck, and a decided emphasis on the Child's genitals. This suggests that we are dealing in these pictures with a specific and long-standing iconographic type.

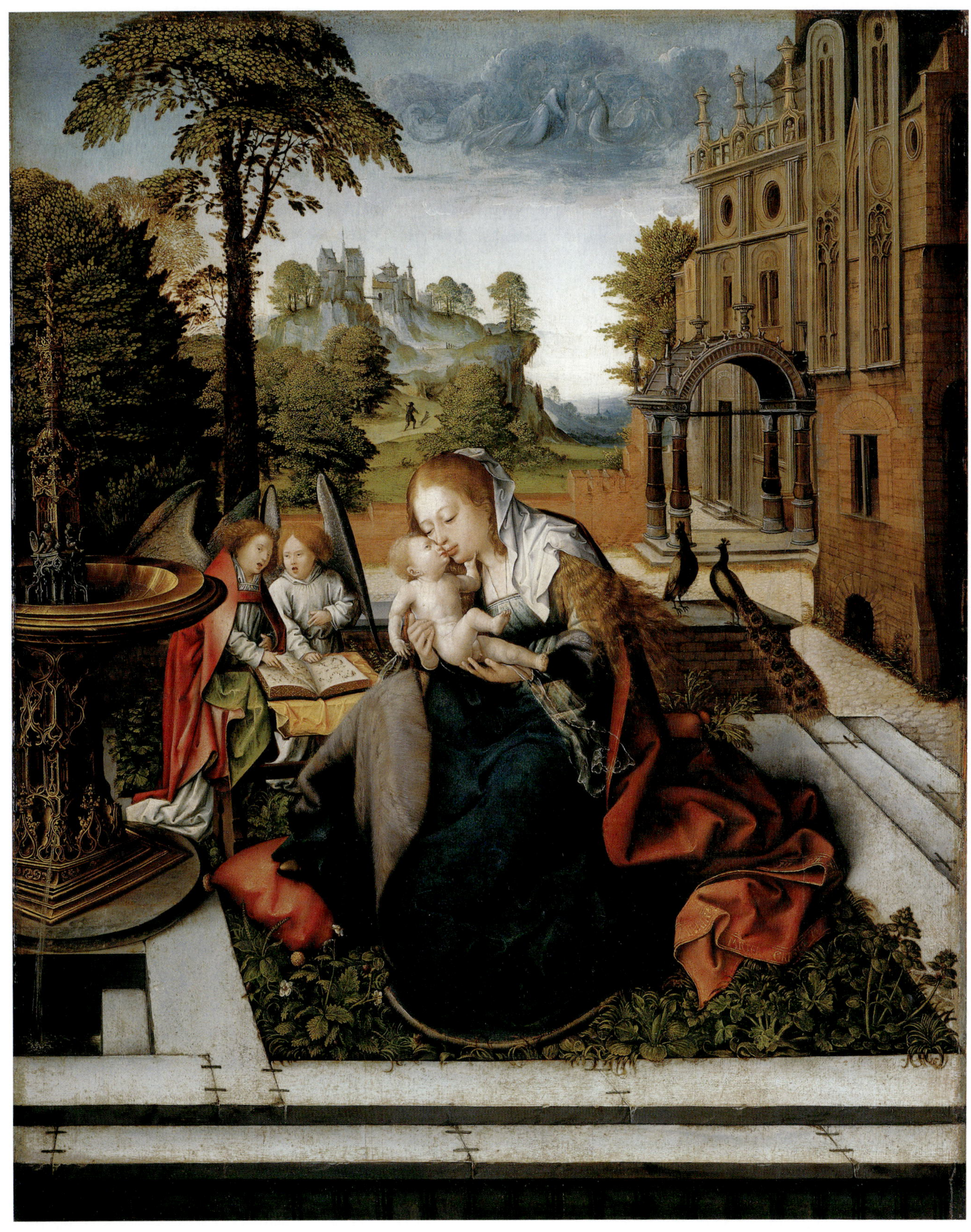

Friedländer 1924–37, vol. 8 (1930), pp. 88–89, 173, no. 124, pl. 87; Wehle and Salinger 1947, pp. 144–45, ill.; Friedländer 1967–76, vol. 8 (1972), pp. 56, 107, no. 124, pl. 110; Farmer 1981, pp. 70–74, 87, n. 65; Silver 1983, pp. 101–2, fig. 15; Ainsworth 1992a, pp. 126–28, colorpl. 36; Steinberg 1996, pp. 3, 5, fig. 11.

Referring to a now-illegible text in their choir book, two angels sing what must have been a hymn to the Virgin; opposite them are two peacocks on the garden wall, symbols of immortality and thus of Christ's Resurrection. Grisaille angels in the clouds echo the two angels who sing the Virgin's praises in the garden below. Other elements of the composition call to mind the *Rest on the Flight into Egypt* attributed to the Master of the Female Half-Lengths (cat. no. 69) and suggest that certain motifs, for example the fountain, the palace, and the single tall tree—already popular conventions in contemporary sacred landscapes—were adopted by the artist in an effort to bring the narrative interest of such works to the traditionally static theme of the Virgin in an Enclosed Garden. The meandering path in the background landscape, the engaging detail of a man walking beside a leaping dog, and the picturesque hilltop, all of which draw the eye into the distance, further indicate Van Orley's awareness of the developing genre of landscape painting.

Generally recognized as a masterpiece of the artist's early period, and remarkable in his oeuvre for its simplicity, our panel was probably painted shortly after his signed Saints Thomas and Matthew Altarpiece of about 1512–15 (Kunsthistorisches Museum, Vienna, and Musées Royaux des Beaux-Arts de Belgique, Brussels). The picture's courtly refinement and the richly dressed Virgin suggest that it was made about the time of Van Orley's appointment in 1518 as painter in ordinary to Margaret of Austria, regent of the Netherlands. MSdJ

Follower of Bernaert van Orley

90. Four Scenes from the Passion, about 1520

Oil on wood, 11¾ x 11⅜ in. (29.8 x 28.9 cm)
Bequest of George Blumenthal, 1941 41.190.14

Provenance: Don Ramon Gil de la Cuadra, Madrid; Benito Carriga, Madrid (sale, Paris Hôtel Drouot, March 24, 1890, no. 18, as a primitive); Léon de Somzée, Brussels (sale, J. Fievez, Brussels, May 26, 1904, no. 549, as School of Antwerp); George and Florence Blumenthal, New York (from 1912).

Texts such as the Pseudo-Bonaventure's *Meditations on the Life of Christ* recommended pious contemplation of the individual events of the Savior's life as an effective form of devotional practice, and artists produced extended narrative cycles in panel paintings and manuscript illumination in response to the popularity of this form of piety. Whether they comprised a relatively small grouping of scenes, like the present work, or a large number, as in the Stein Quadriptych by Simon Bening (Walters Art Gallery, Baltimore), which shows sixty-four separate vignettes on vellum mounted on four panels, or the multiscene Oratorio of Queen Isabella the Catholic (see entry for cat. no. 85), these cycles all had the same objective: to encourage the viewer's empathic participation in events depicted as if they were taking place in contemporary life.

The four delicately painted miniature scenes on this panel represent pivotal events of Christ's Passion: the Agony in the Garden of Gethsemane, Christ Bearing the Cross, the Crucifixion, and the Lamentation. The episodes are divided by an intricate trompe-l'oeil frame, which includes a column and a plinth supporting two statuettes of Old Testament prophets that stand beneath elaborate Gothic canopies, as well as a triad of delicate foliate motifs above each scene. These elements must have been part of a larger ensemble and may have included a *Noli Me Tangere* in a private collection in Switzerland that retains parts of an identical decorative framing and shows a setting and figures similar to those of our work. This diminutive fragment is the same height as each of the Metropolitan scenes, but it is narrower, suggesting, as Farmer notes, that it

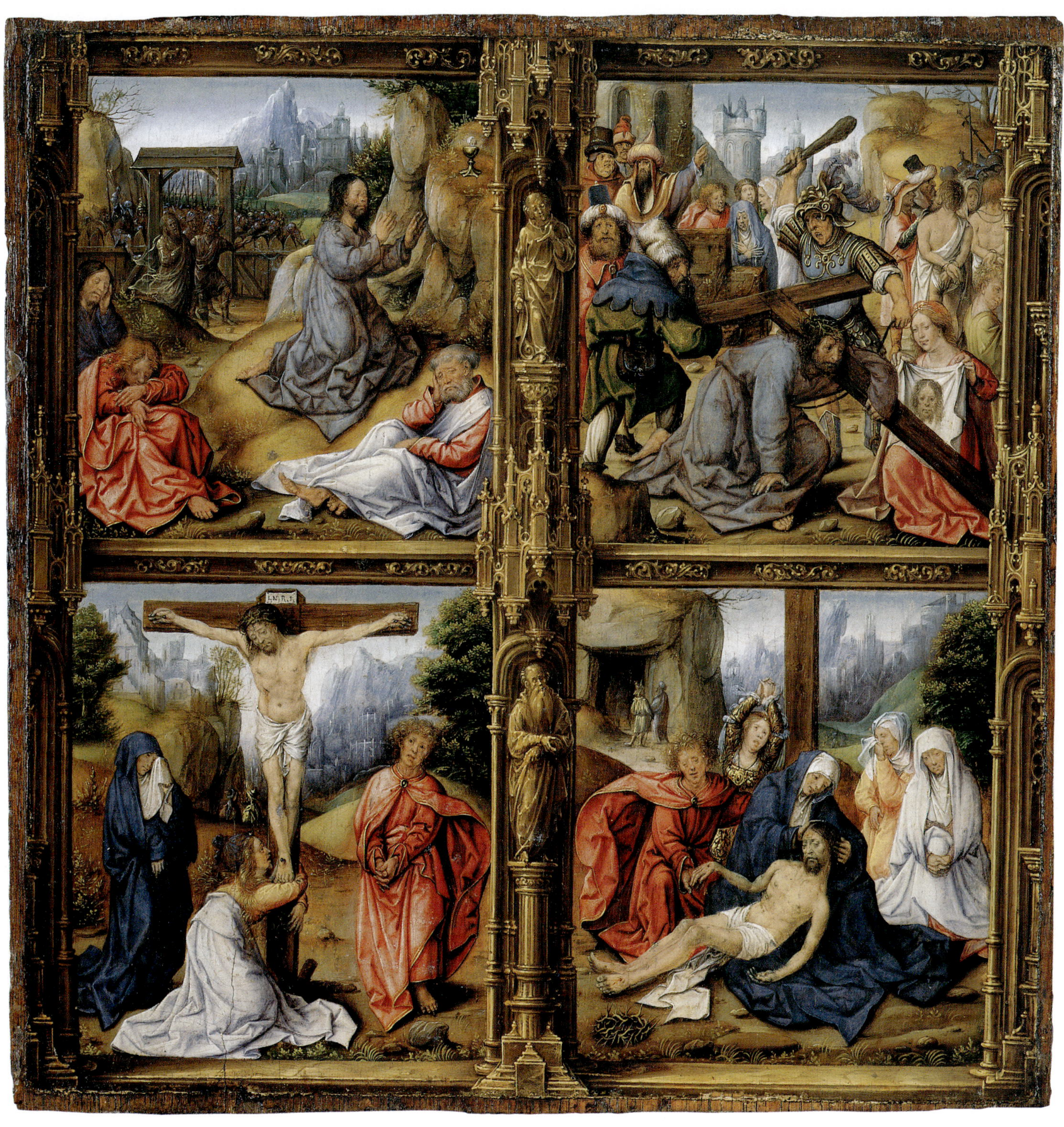

References: Armstrong 1892, p. 14; Friedländer 1900, pp. 255–56; Rubinstein-Bloch 1926, pl. 47; Wehle and Salinger 1947, pp. 145–46; Eisler 1964, p. 104; Farmer 1981, pp. 226–32, 242.

may have formed the upper part of one of the lateral wings, each of which displayed two scenes and a framing device wider than our panel's. In such a triptych the missing episodes could well have been a Resurrection, an Ascension, and a Christ Appearing to His Mother, assuming that the wings followed the Gospels as closely as our panel does. A Passion Altarpiece attributed to a Bruges artist (Collection Robert Smeets, Milan) has lateral scenes whose dimensions are different from those of the central panel. Another panel (De Boer collection, Amsterdam, in 1971), which shows three of the Passion scenes that appear in the Metropolitan painting but includes a Resurrection instead of a Bearing of the Cross, seems to have come from the same workshop as our painting, although it is not by the same artist.

Both our panel and the De Boer painting are strongly influenced by the compositions and figure types found in Bernaert van Orley's paintings of the 1520s, particularly works most likely produced in his workshop. The miniature-like scenes of the Seven Sorrows that surround the Virgin in pictures by the master in the Galleria Colonna, Rome, and the Koninklijk Museum voor Schone Kunsten, Antwerp, are especially relevant. Our diminutive Passion scenes also reflect an acquaintance with figure motifs in certain of Albrecht Dürer's prints; they are, in fact, loosely based on Dürer's *Engraved Passion* of 1507–12. This derivation may indicate that the painting was executed in the early 1520s, after Dürer made his trip to the Netherlands in 1520–21, the period in which his prints, in particular the *Engraved Passion*, were most widely disseminated in the region.

An animated rhythm conveyed by the poses and gestures of the figures in all four scenes boldly articulates the subjects. Although the female types appear somewhat bland and homogeneous, their male counterparts are individualized almost to the point of caricature. The palette of light tonalities (rose reds, yellows, and a variety of blues) imbues these paintings with an ethereal quality and a lighter feeling than that conveyed by Van Orley's more usual range of deeply saturated primary colors. The gentle colors, as well as the attention to detail in these diminutive scenes, call to mind the handling and refined sensibility of a manuscript illuminator, in particular the production of Gerard Horenbout, who was a court painter and illuminator for Margaret of Austria. But the differences outweigh the similarities when the Metropolitan painting is compared to Horenbout's work. In their overall conception and details our artist's forms, however, are close to those in the *Parents of the Virgin* by Cornelis van Coninxloo, a follower of Van Orley's (Musées Royaux des Beaux-Arts de Belgique, Brussels), as Farmer has noted. For now, while we await discoveries about the master's close followers, our panel must be assigned to an anonymous artist in the orbit of Van Orley. MWA

Netherlandish Painter (possibly Goswijn van der Weyden, active by 1491, died after 1538)

91. The Fifteen Mysteries and the Virgin of the Rosary, about 1515–20

This multiscene picture highlights the popularity of the cult of the Virgin of the Rosary as an expression of individual piety. A Carthusian monk, Dominik of Prussia (died 1461), was the first to propose that this worship take the form of the contemplation of fifty different events, or mysteries, from the lives of Christ and the Virgin, one for each Ave Maria in a chaplet (one third of a full rosary). However, a Dominican, Alanus de Rupe, who founded the Confraternity of the Psalter of the Glorious Mary at Douai about 1475, was responsible for the cult's widespread dissemination. After Alanus's death in 1475, his mission was carried on by his disciples, and the Fifteen Mysteries of the Rosary appeared for the first time in a popular devotional handbook, the *Unser Lieben Frawen Psalter*, published in Ulm in 1483.

Divided into three registers, the small scenes in our painting depict those fifteen events: the five Joyful Mysteries (the Annunciation, the Visitation, the Nativity, the Presentation of Christ in the Temple, and the Finding of the Child in the Temple); the five Sorrowful Mysteries (the Agony in the Garden, the Scourging of Christ, the Mocking of Christ, Christ Carrying the Cross, and the Crucifixion); and the five Glorious Mysteries (the Resurrection, the Ascension, the Descent of the Holy Spirit, and the Death and Coronation of the Virgin).

In the center of the scene on the larger panel below these registers, the Virgin of the Rosary, crowned as Queen of Heaven, stands on a tiled dais beneath a red-canopied baldachin. The Christ Child holds in his left hand the end of an oversized chaplet shown as a garland of white roses separated into sections of ten blossoms by five larger red roses representing the Paternosters. With his right hand Christ blesses a kneeling man, from whose mouth a stem of roses issues and who is being attacked by three armor-clad assailants. Illustrated here is a miracle widely associated with the origin of the cult of the Rosary, one version of which, showing a knightly gentleman saved from death by the intervention of the Virgin of the Rosary, is depicted in a woodblock print published in Strasbourg about 1480 (British Library, London). The four kneeling figures at the left of the Virgin are Saint Dominic, followed by a pope, an emperor, and a king, representing the Christian Estates. The artist made little attempt to portray anything beyond generic types, but if these men are meant to represent contemporary individuals, Leo X, Maximilian I, and the youthful Charles V would be likely candidates.

A little-known woodblock, signed and dated Francisco Domenech 1488, resembles the design of our picture to a remarkable degree. According to Bauman, this print is the only known work whose iconography might have served as a model for our painter. The engraving (a modern impression of which is in the Metropolitan Museum collection) shows the fifteen mysteries arranged exactly as they are in our painting, above a large horizontal compartment that illustrates the Virgin of the Rosary surrounded by the Christian Estates and a more elaborate version of the same early miracle of the rosary. Bands with inscriptions identify the figures.

The background landscape of the present painting portrays, with surprising accuracy, the park and the palace of the dukes of Brabant in Brussels known as the Coudenberg. The church of Sainte Gudule in the upper left corner is clearly recognizable as well. The old twelfth-century town wall, the body of water called the Clutinck, the stone gate giving access to the steep hillside, and the pleasure grounds are depicted as they appeared in the early sixteenth century. Although seen from a different vantage point, the topography agrees in every detail with that in a sketch in brown ink drawn by Albrecht Dürer during his visit to the Netherlands in 1520–21 (Kupferstichkabinett, Vienna).

Oil on wood; (a) 9⅞ x 21 in. (25.1 x 53.3 cm); (b–p) each 5 x 4⅛ in. (12.7 x 10.5 cm)
Anonymous Bequest, 1984
1987.290.3a–p

Provenance: Zacharie Astruc, Paris ([until 1878]; sale, Hôtel Drouot, Paris, April 11–12, 1878, no. 1, as Hans Memling); (Haro, Paris [until 1892]; sale, Galerie Sedelmeyer, Paris, May 30–31, 1892, no. 30, as School of Memling); Claude Lafontaine, Paris; [Seligman, New York (1924)]; V. Everit Macy, New York ([1924–38]; sale, American Art Association–Anderson Galleries, New York, January 6–8, 1938, no. 325, as School of Antwerp, early 16th century); [Schnittjer, New York (until 1943)]; sale, Parke-Bernet, New York, January 14–16, 1943, no. 71, as School of Antwerp, early 16th century; Maurice Dekker, New York (from 1943); Waldemar von Zedtwitz, Honolulu (by 1956).

References: Biographie nationale [de Belgique], *vol. 4 (1873), cols. 152–53; Thurston 1900, pp. 403–18, 513–27, 620–37; Thurston 1901, pp. 67–79; Hulin de Loo 1913, pp. 86–87, fig. 10; Held 1943; Valentiner 1943; Hollstein 1949, vol. 5, p. 265; Anzelewsky 1957, pp. 87–107;*

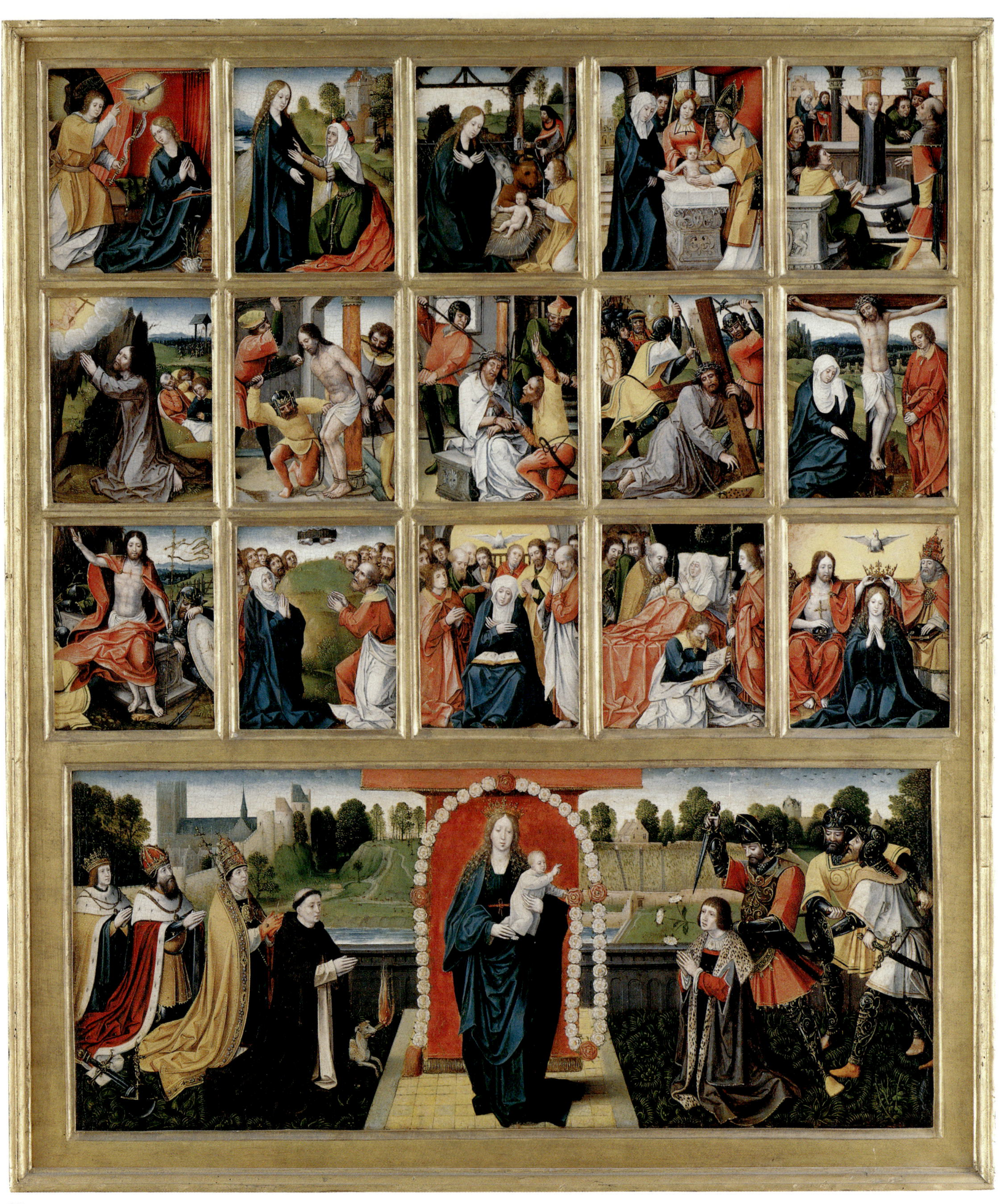

91

It is clear from the setting that the picture was commissioned by someone in Brussels who was closely connected to the Habsburg court and also associated with the Dominicans and the cult of the Rosary. Circumstantial evidence favors identifying the patrons as the lords of Ravensteyn, members of one of the most illustrious patrician families of Brussels, who had ceded to the Dominicans the part of their *hôtel* that was contiguous with the Dominican convent and church, established in 1464 not far from the northwest side of the Coudenberg. Adolph de Cleves (1425–1492), a lord of Ravensteyn, grandson of Duke John the Fearless, and nephew of Philip the Good, whose second wife was Philip's illegitimate daughter, paid for stained-glass windows in the Dominican church. Adolph's son, Philip de Cleves (about 1459–1527), erected a chapel in the same church to serve as a mausoleum for himself and his wife.

The attribution to Goswijn van der Weyden and the identification of the iconography were not made until 1943, when they were suggested by Held. His attribution is based on the fact that the characteristic *retardataire* style of our panel and the type of millefleur ground cover in its lower section are also displayed in the artist's well-documented Antonius Tsgrooten Triptych (Koninklijk Museum voor Schone Kunsten, Antwerp), painted in 1507 for the abbot of the monastery of Tongerloo. According to Bauman, it is the strong stylistic and chromatic analogies between our painting and Goswijn's Crucifixion Triptych, datable shortly after 1517 (Museum of Fine Arts, Springfield, Massachusetts), that allows this attribution. Bauman agrees with Held's proposed dating of the present picture to between 1515 and 1520 because of its connections to Dürer's work—not only the landscape sketch of 1520 but also his *Small Passion*, published in 1511, from which Goswijn's Annunciation scene is derived. He notes that if the suggested date is correct, the Museum's picture must have preceded the drawing that Dürer made during his stay in Brussels from August 28 to September 1, 1520. VS

Robinson 1959, no. 3; Strauss 1980, pp. 342, 408–9, no. 139; Bauman 1989, pp. 135–51; Winston-Allen 1997, pp. 57, 66–68.

Jan Mostaert, active by 1498, died 1555/56

92. Christ Shown to the People, 1510–15

Oil on wood; overall 12 x 8⅞ in. (30.5 x 22.5 cm); painted surface 11½ x 8¼ in. (29.2 x 21 cm)
The Jack and Belle Linsky Collection, 1982 1982.60.25

Provenance: Probably sale, Phillips, London, July 27, 1832, no. 4, as Cornelius Engebrechtszen, to Lord Northwick; probably John Rushout, second lord Northwick, Thirlestane House, Cheltenham (1832–59; sale, Phillips, London, August 18, 1859, possibly no. 1466, as Quentin Matsys, to Rev. Boyd); George Rushout Bowles, third lord Northwick, Northwick Park, Blockley, Gloucestershire (by 1864–87); his widow, Elizabeth Augusta Bowles, Lady Northwick, Northwick Park (1887–1912); her grandson, Capt. E. G. Spencer-Churchill, Northwick Park (1912–64); sale, Christie's, London, May 28, 1965, no. 59, as Jan Mostaert, to Mr. and Mrs. Jack Linsky, New York (1965–80); The Jack and Belle Linsky Foundation, New York (1980–82).

References: Northwick collection (1864) 1908, p. 25; Friedländer 1916, p. 148; Northwick collection 1921, p. 89, no. 203; Friedländer 1924–37, vol. 10 (1932), p. 120, no. 12; Romanov 1934, p. 47; Van Mander 1936, pp. 129–30; Hoogewerff 1936–47, vol. 2 (1937), pp. 491–93; Friedländer 1956, p. 116; Friedländer 1967–76, vol. 10 (1973), p. 69, no. 12, pl. 11; Bauman in Metropolitan Museum 1984, pp. 77–80.

The Ecce Homo, or Christ Shown to the People, was a particularly popular theme in the Netherlands in the early sixteenth century, when it was frequently portrayed in dramatic close-up views, as if the observer were part of the judgmental crowd (see cat. no. 101). This small panel, which is in an excellent state of preservation, exemplifies such scenes and is typical of Jan Mostaert's small private devotional paintings.

The scene, set in a contemporary Netherlandish cobblestoned city square, presents details as they are described in the Gospel of John (19:4–15): Christ is shown three-quarter length, crowned with thorns, with his hands tied at the wrists. The column behind Christ refers to the one at which he has just been flogged. A bearded Pilate, wearing a red robe trimmed with fur, a gold chain, and a large hat, stands behind and slightly above Christ on a vaulted balcony. With one hand he lifts a corner of Christ's cloak, exposing his wounds, and with the other he gestures eloquently as he utters the words "Behold the man!," appealing to the compassion of the three richly dressed individuals at the right, who are no less demonstrative. In the middle ground are the swooning Virgin, collapsing in Saint John's arms, Mary Magdalene, and the two other Marys. These small figures occupy the center of a contemporary town square beyond which lie the turreted gatehouse with three windows and, in the background, the verdant countryside.

In 1916 Friedländer ascribed our painting to Mostaert, an attribution that has not been questioned, and in 1932 he associated it with the half-length *Christ Shown to the People* in the Museum of Fine Arts, Moscow. According to Hoogewerff, the Moscow picture is the Ecce Homo by Mostaert that Karel van Mander saw at the house of the artist's grandson in Haarlem in 1604 and described in the *Schilderboeck*. Many variants of the Moscow composition exist; the Metropolitan panel, however, seems to be unique, and its style very much remains in the tradition of Geertgen tot Sint Jans, Mostaert's predecessor in Haarlem. Bauman dates our painting about 1510–15, after Mostaert's *Christ before Pilate* of about 1510 (Saint Louis Art Museum) but before his Adrichem Triptych of the 1520s (Musées Royaux des Beaux-Arts de Belgique, Brussels), in which Christ before Pilate is represented on the right interior wing. These two key works share with our picture the same treatment of the cobblestone pavement, the inclusion of diminutive figure scenes in the middle ground, and the use of similar mushroomlike trees. The conception of the background space and its relation to the foreground figures are similar to formulations in Mostaert's *Portrait of the Knight Abel van de Coulster, Counselor to the Court of Holland* (Musées Royaux des Beaux-Arts de Belgique, Brussels).

VS

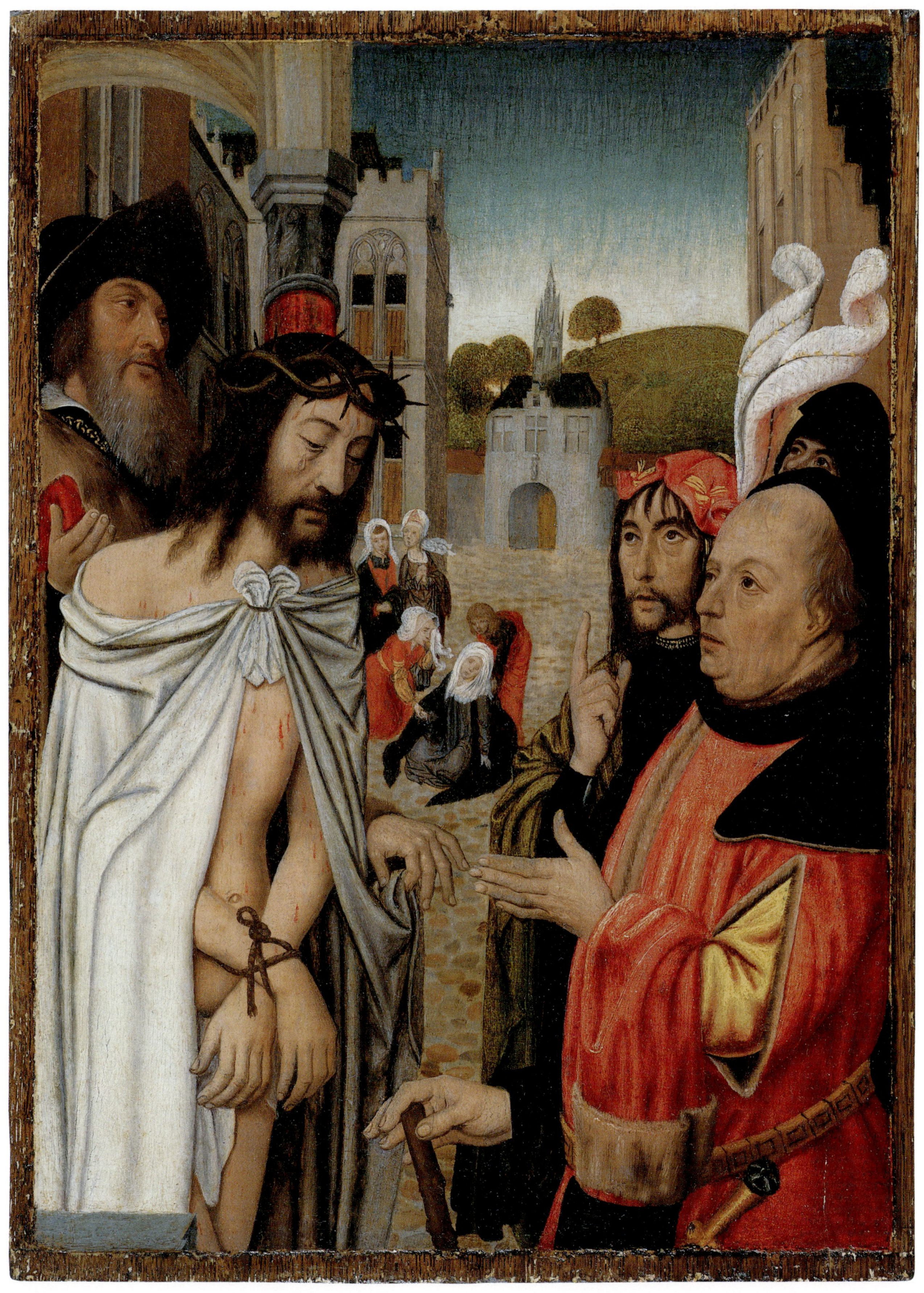

Cornelis Engebrechtsz, 1468–1527

93. The Crucifixion with Donors and Saints Peter and Margaret, about 1525–27

Oil on wood, 24¼ x 35¼ in. (61.5 x 89.5 cm)
*Inscribed (on cross): ^I^N^R^I^*
Gift of Coudert Brothers, 1888 88.3.88

Provenance: Mme d'Oliveira, Florence (until 1887); Coudert Brothers, New York (1887–88).

References: Conway 1921, p. 453; Wescher 1924, p. 100; Winkler 1924, p. 226; Dülberg 1929, p. 166; Friedländer 1924–37, vol. 10 (1932), pp. 68, 131, no. 90; Hoogewerff 1936–47, vol. 3, pp. 199–201, vol. 5, p. 132; Wehle and Salinger 1947, pp. 125–26; Pelinck 1949, p. 61; Friedländer 1967–76, vol. 10 (1973), pp. 41, 77, no. 90; Van Asperen de Boer and Wheelock 1973, pp. 61–94; Gibson 1977b, pp. 151–53, 160, 227, 240, no. 15; Bangs 1979, pp. 37–38.

Clearly isolated against the sky, the crucified Christ occupies the very center of this dramatic, strikingly symmetrical composition. Christ's suffering is represented with particular poignancy: his lifeless body is stretched out and his head pitched forward pathetically. On either side of him are the crucified thieves, whose contorted bodies hang from their crosses. While the grieving Virgin emulates the posture of her son, suggesting her empathic suffering, Saint John grimaces in pain at the vision of the dead Christ. Mary and John are the immediate intercessors between Christ and the donors, who face each other, kneeling in prayer at their prie-dieux in the foreground. Nothing is known about these richly but austerely dressed donors, who were probably husband and wife and may have been named after Peter and Margaret of Antioch, the patron saints who stand behind them and present them to the holy figures. In a direct reference to the Eucharist, three angels, painted in a gray-blue monochrome that almost blends into the background, fill their chalices with the blood of Christ.

Generally considered a late work, our picture, which was probably an altarpiece made for a private chapel, indeed summarizes many of the major influences Engebrechtsz absorbed during his lifetime. The rather stiff Late Gothic manner of the artist's youthful years, exemplified in his *Crucifixion with the Virgin and Saints* in the Rijksmuseum, Amsterdam, has been abandoned for sustained energy of drawing and figures in twisted postures that reveal his affinity for Antwerp Mannerism. In its expressivity and emotional effect the present painting is closely related to Engebrechtsz's earlier Crucifixion Altarpiece (Stedelijk Museum De Lakenhal, Leiden), a complex and crowded work filled with subsidiary narrative scenes. Painted about 1517–22, the Leiden altarpiece, which marked a turning point in the artist's career and is the basis for the attribution and chronology of his oeuvre, displays a vivid focus on dramatically foreshortened muscular bodies, especially striking in the figures of Christ and the thieves, that clearly is echoed in the Metropolitan panel. Saint Margaret's graceful serpentine posture and richly decorated gown in our painting illustrate another aspect of Engebrechtsz's virtuoso drawing and his mannered style and recall the figure of Helena in his *Emperor Constantine and Saint Helena* of sometime after 1517 (Alte Pinakothek, Munich). However, the simplicity of our composition is exceptional among the artist's biblical narratives and serves to emphasize the monumentality and spiritual expressiveness of the figures, which are projected against a low horizon in an evenly spaced friezelike formation.

The palette is restrained, and the paint applied in thin layers with broad brushstrokes. The spontaneous and loose underdrawing is visible through the painted layers, especially in the figures of Christ, the thieves, and the angels. Both in style and technique our picture anticipates the work of Lucas van Leyden, Engebrechtsz's pupil, who became one of the most important and prolific artists of the northern Netherlandish Renaissance. VS

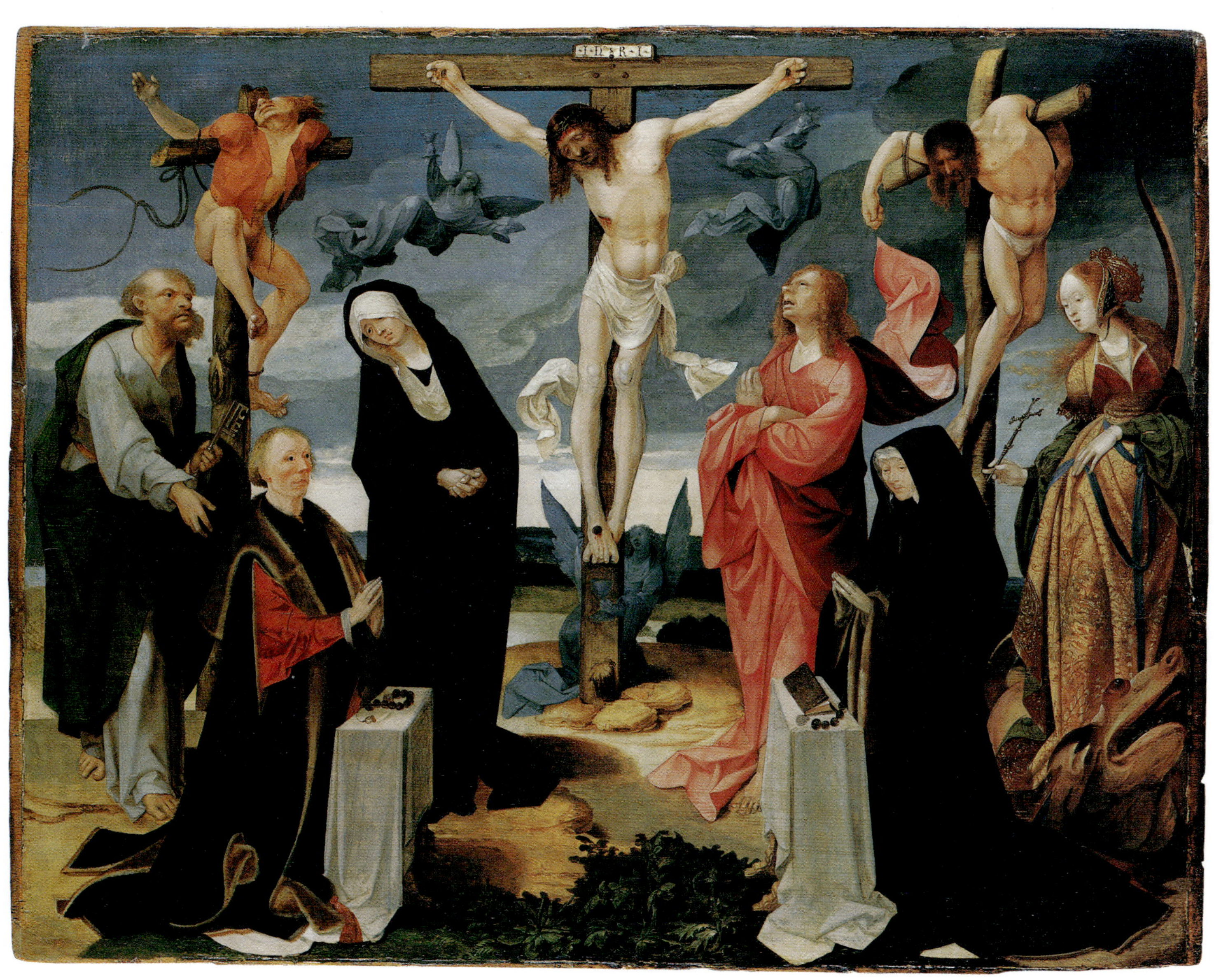

Netherlandish (Antwerp Mannerist) Painter

94. A Sermon on Charity (possibly the Conversion of Saint Anthony), about 1520–25

Oil on wood, 33½ x 23 in. (85.1 x 58.4 cm)
Rogers Fund, 1908 08.183.2

Provenance: [Georges Sortais, Paris]; [Kleinberger, New York].

References: Breck 1909, p. 293; Fry 1909, pp. 25–27; Friedländer 1915, p. 68; Baldass 1937, p. 132; Van Gelder 1946, p. 102; Wehle and Salinger 1947, pp. 127–29; Bruyn 1960, pp. 41–42; Friedländer 1967–76, vol. 11 (1974), pp. 20, 67, 104, 122; Bangs 1979, pp. 129–30; Muller 1985, pp. 64, 258; Kloek, Halsema-Kubes, and Baarsen 1986, pp. 161–62, no. 44; Steinmetz 1995, pp. 79–80.

In a church under construction, a young man, elegantly dressed in the fashion of the time, his hat in one hand and a prayer book in the other, approaches the altar, where three priests, one of whom is at a lectern, read from the Holy Scriptures. The same layman is seen to the right outside the church, dispensing alms from a chest of coins to a group of cripples, orphans, and mendicant women with children; to his right a gnomelike figure with the shell of a pilgrim on his hood tugs at his cloak. The scene illustrates the biblical ideal of compassion and Jesus' teaching in the parable of the rich man in Matthew (19:21): "If thou wilt be perfect, go and sell that thou hast, and give to the poor, and thou shalt have treasure in heaven."

The young man has often been identified as Saint Anthony, whose conversion occurred when he heard this verse from Matthew during Mass. Anthony sold his possessions, distributed his worldly wealth, and retired to the desert, where he lived as a hermit. However, given the absence of scenes showing other events from Anthony's life, the picture might have been intended as a visual sermon on charity not strictly connected to the saint. (To be sure, the right side of our panel has been cut, and we do not know if it formed part of a larger altarpiece that could have included additional scenes.) The theme of charity was a particular focus during the early sixteenth century in humanist circles in the Netherlands, where assistance to the poor and needy was considered an essential moral obligation and a prerequisite for lasting happiness. The Gospel according to Matthew, published in a vernacular translation after Erasmus in 1522, was especially favored by the Biblical Humanists, a reform group concerned with contemporary social problems, which, from 1520, were intensifying due to deepening economic crisis. Advocating acts of charity, they maintained that a life lived in conformity with Christianity was more important than participation in Church ritual. This doctrine may explain the central position in our painting of the unfinished brick wall that clearly divides the composition in two parts, one showing ritual, the other active intervention in terms of offering charity. The statue of Moses holding the Ten Commandments, placed on the column separating the two choirs, signifies the reaffirmation of the fundamental laws of Christianity, while Cain and Abel, sculpted in the tondo high on the church facade, prefigure the sacrifice of Christ. The eclectic nature of the architectural elements of the existing church contrasts with the contemporary flavor of the minutely described new construction. The building tools and the evidence of the making of mortar and moldings probably allude to the concept of a renewed and reformed faith. Further underscoring the theme of contrasting types of Christian dedication, the sacred architecture is set off against secular buildings that include towers embellished by battle scenes.

Because of its subject and composition, our picture has often been compared to a later panel by an anonymous artist sometimes identified as Aertgen van Leyden, the *Calling of Saint Anthony* of about 1530–35 (Rijksmuseum, Amsterdam). The main figure in the latter work is dressed in a fur-lined coat, holds a hat, and wears a tau cross, suggesting that he is a member of the Confraternity of Saint Anthony, the guild that administered the Sint-Antonius Hospitaal on the outskirts of Leiden. The Amsterdam picture recalls a group of woodcut pamphlets, including the *Inhalt Zweierlei Predig* of 1529 by Georg Pencz, which promoted the preaching of the message of the Lord's Prayer (Matthew 6:11) and its plea "Give us this day our daily bread."

In his pioneering article of 1915 Friedländer wrote that he recognized the hand of an Antwerp Mannerist of the 1520s in our picture, and his later

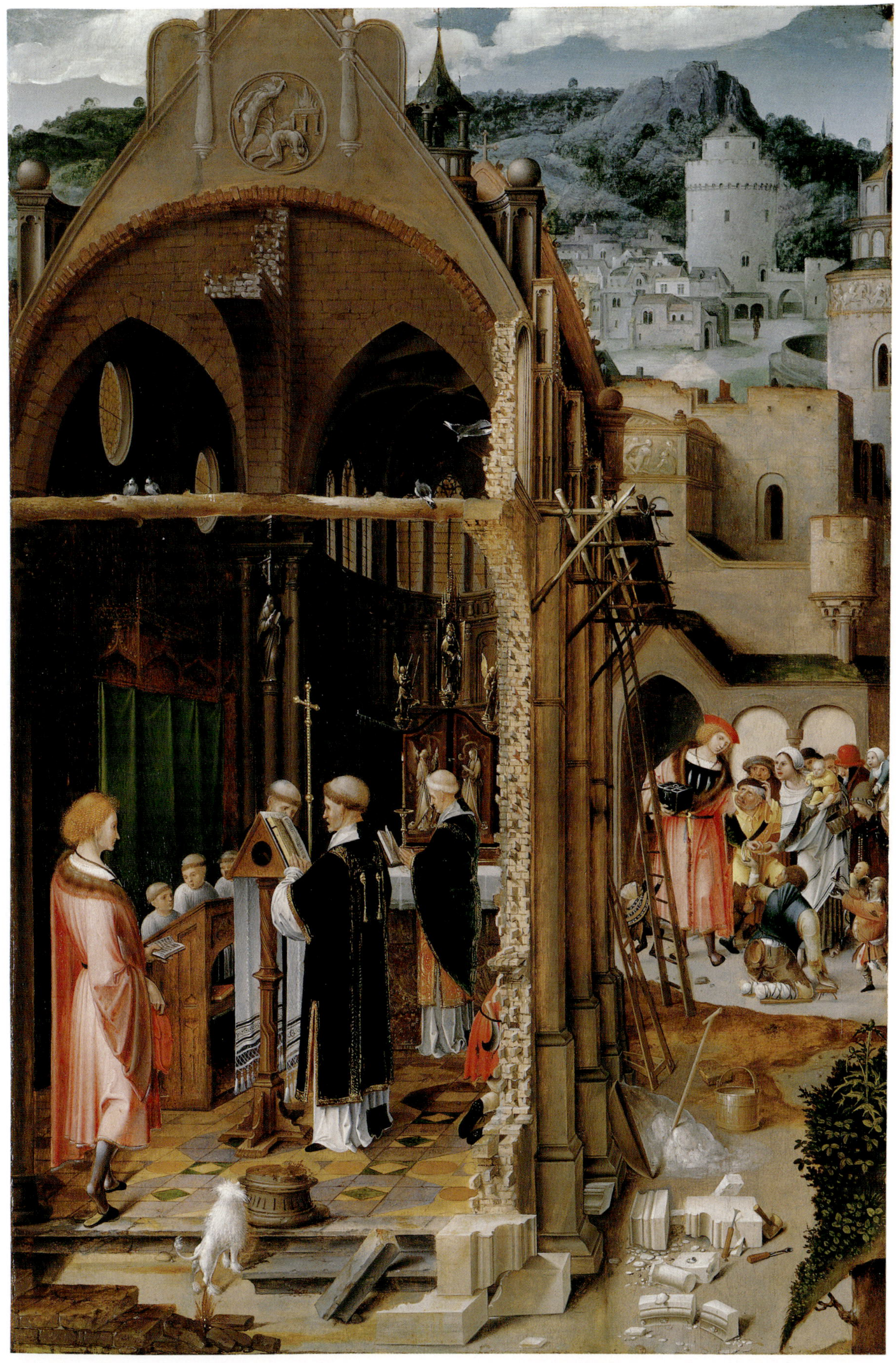

ascription of it to an artist working in the circle of the Pseudo-Blesius and Jan de Beer in Antwerp was published in 1974. Indeed, the fantastic architectural details, the style of the triptych shown on the altar in the choir of the church, the elongated figures, and the cool palette conform to elements in Mannerist paintings produced in the northern Netherlands during the 1520s. VS

Joos van Cleve, active by 1507, died 1540/41, and Collaborator

95. The Crucifixion with Saints and a Donor, about 1520

Oil on wood, shaped top; central panel, painted surface 38¾ x 29¼ in. (98.4 x 74.3 cm); each wing, painted surface 39¾ x 12⅞ in. (101 x 32.7 cm)
Inscribed (on cross): •INRI•
Bequest of George Blumenthal, 1941
41.190.20a–c

Provenance: Del Vecchio, Genoa; Adolf Thiem, San Remo; George and Florence Blumenthal, New York (1926).

References: Bode 1889, p. 75; Firmenich-Richartz 1909, p. 217; Friedländer 1916, p. 186; Rubinstein 1916, pp. 343ff.; Conway 1921, pp. 403, 407; Baldass 1925, pp. 34–35; Friedländer 1924–37, vol. 9 (1931), p. 128, no. 12; Krönig 1936, p. 100; Wehle and Salinger 1947, pp. 133–35; Larsen 1960, p. 91; Hoogewerff 1961, pp. 176–94; Doehard 1963, p. 100; Koch 1968, pp. 52–55; Friedländer 1967–76, vol. 9a

Christ's head droops to one side, his open mouth gasping with his last breath, while the heavens above are suddenly darkened—it is the very moment of death on the cross. Although a rosary dangles from the girdle of the Virgin Mary, and Saint John has a devotional book in its protective covering suspended from his belt, these two holy figures do not use their devotional aids but respond directly to the event. The Virgin prays in quiet acceptance of her son's death while John gestures in grief toward the cross. Between them Saint Paul, in his role as intercessor for the kneeling donor, embraces the cross while laying his left hand in blessing on the head of his namesake, linking him physically to the cross and spiritually with Christ's supreme sacrifice for the redemption of man. On the left wing are Saints John the Baptist and Catherine of Alexandria and on the right Saints Anthony of Padua and Nicholas of Tolentino, the figures in each pair turning toward each other, apparently in conversation. The paintings of the exterior wings are no longer extant; the frame is original to the triptych but regilt.

Displaying the full maturity of his Antwerp style, Joos enlivened the customarily sober presentation of the Crucifixion through the contrapposto stances, animated gestures, and swirling draperies of the figures. These devices and juxtapositions of rich color harmonies, mostly of reds and blues, unite the protagonists. The individual parts of the triptych are unified by a continuous landscape.

The concept of uniting the three interior panels of an altarpiece by a continuous landscape was developed early in the history of Netherlandish painting, as Rogier van der Weyden's Crucifixion Triptych of about 1440 (Kunsthistorisches Museum, Vienna), for example, demonstrates. But it was the Antwerp artists of the first decades of the sixteenth century, among them Joos, who focused on these landscapes and enlarged them, expanding a conventional motif and thereby conveying an expanded sense of the world and a feeling for man's place in it. Thus, in the present work the figures occupy only a shallow foreground strip of a vast panoramic landscape filled with multifarious details, some related to the Crucifixion and a great many others of merely incidental nature. Just to the right of the cross in the middle ground is the dead body of the traitor Judas hanging from a tree; farther to the right Christ's body is being carried into a cave for the Entombment. Behind the saints on the left wing are tiny depictions of the Baptism of Christ and Saint John Preaching in the Wilderness. Interspersed with these biblical subjects are scenes of daily life—travelers crowding the roads, ships docked at the river port for the transfer of goods, and shepherds and cowherds tending to their livestock.

The landscape, whose style is indebted to Joachim Patinir, was probably executed by a follower of Patinir's who collaborated with Joos. The landscapist painted with looser brushwork than Joos

Opposite: Detail, cat. no. 95

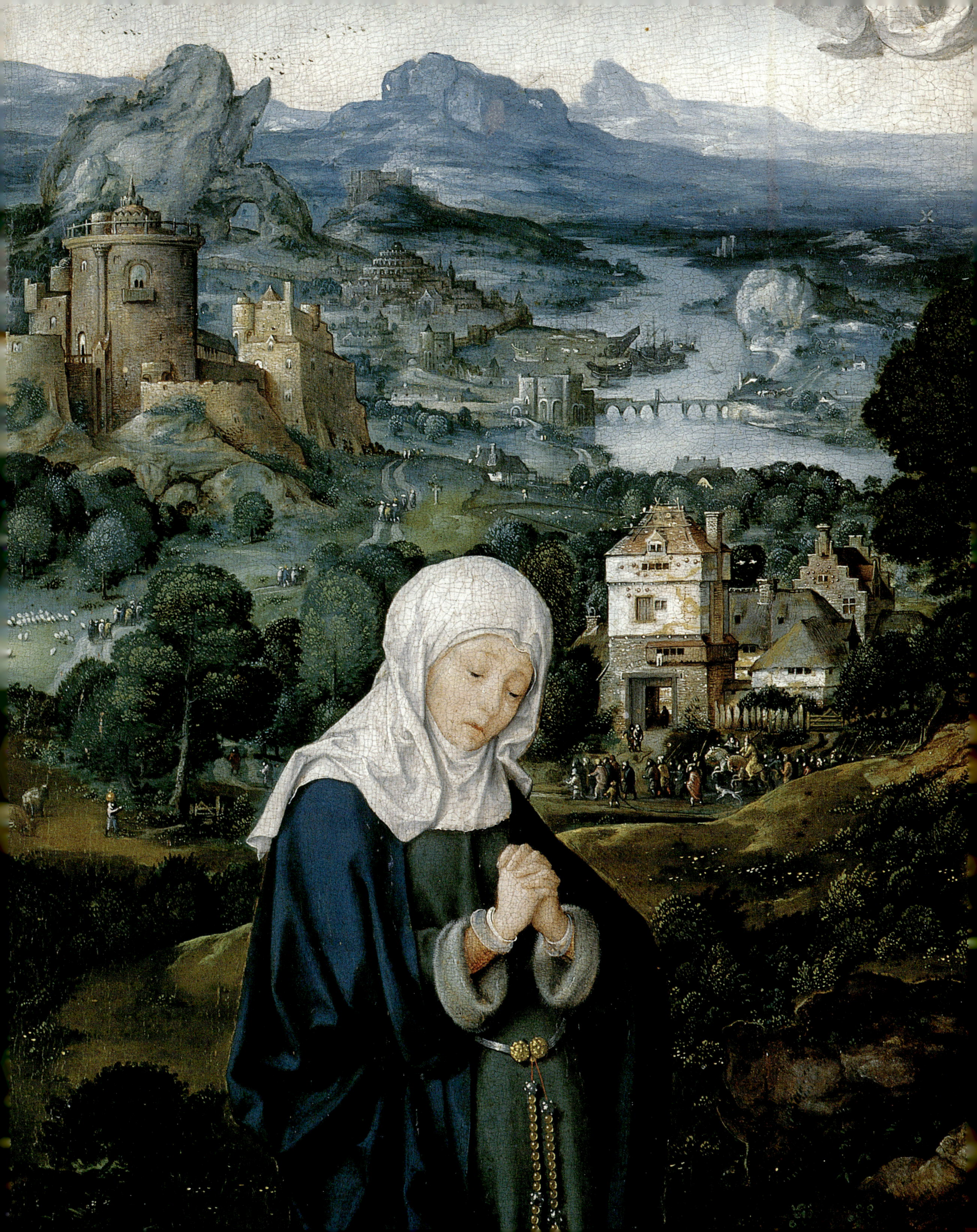

(1972), no. 12; Heller 1976, p. 181; Hand 1978, pp. 174–76, 178–79; Scaillierez 1991, pp. 80, 83; Ainsworth in Bauman and Liedtke 1992, pp. 112–14.

employed for the meticulously rendered figures. X-radiographs show reserve areas left for the figures and the broadly brushed-in landscape features abutting but not overlapping their contours. Joos made underdrawings for the entire composition of his *Crucifixion* in the Museum of Fine Arts, Boston, and some of his other paintings, but only the figures in our work are underdrawn in his typical style. The landscape shows no perceptible preliminary sketch, indicating that the painter who executed it perhaps worked directly on the panel, using model drawings for motifs, which he arranged to suggest a convincing recession in space from the middle ground to the distant horizon. Castles, farmhouses, ships, and waterways similar to those seen here are found in other landscapes in paintings attributed to Joos, supporting the notion that his collaborators used patterns. Moreover, the vignette of Christ Carried to His Entombment is identically rendered in Joos's Schmitgen Triptych of 1524 (Städelsches Kunstinstitut, Frankfurt), implying that workshop models for these diminutive subsidiary scenes were also available for repeated use.

The Metropolitan triptych is a variant on Joos's Crucifixion Triptych in the Capodimonte, Naples: the poses of several figures correspond and the landscape forms are similar in both pictures. The Naples triptych is generally dated about 1515, while our example can probably be placed about five years later.

Because our ensemble has a Genoese provenance and represents Anthony of Padua and Nicholas of Tolentino—saints rarely encountered in the art of Flanders but commonly depicted in southern Europe—it is thought to have been made for an Italian client. This cannot be confirmed, for our painting is not mentioned in early guides to Genoa, and the identity of the patron cannot be established. However, given the strong trade relationships between Genoa and the thriving international port city of Antwerp and the influx of large numbers of Genoese to the city between 1488 and 1513, it is quite likely that the present panels were among the early works Joos produced for a foreign, specifically Genoese, clientele—with whom he developed a prosperous export business in the 1520s and 1530s.

MWA

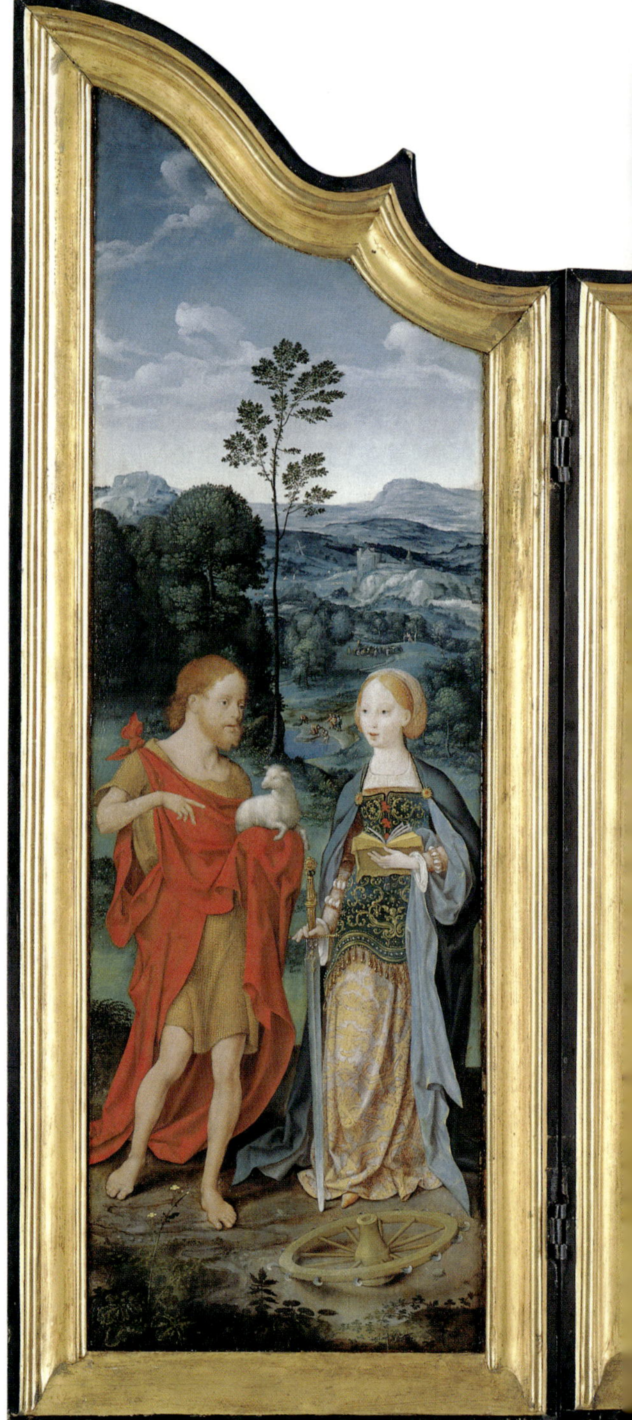

95

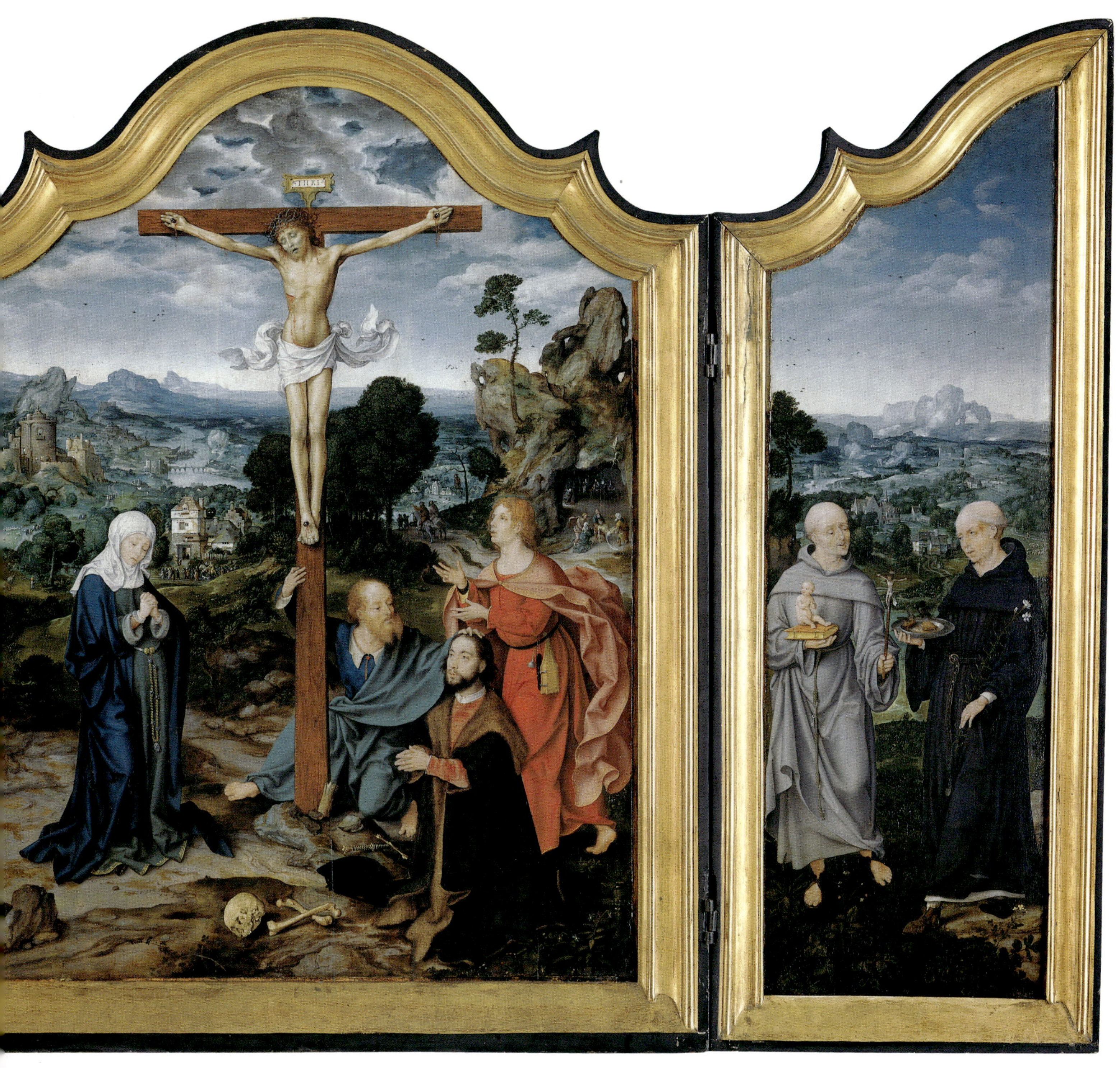

Joos van Cleve, active by 1507, died 1540/41, and Collaborator

96. Virgin and Child, about 1525

Oil on wood; overall 28⅜ x 21¼ in. (72.1 x 54 cm); painted surface 27¾ x 20¾ in. (70.5 x 52.7 cm)
Inscribed (on prayer book pages): . . . / recordatus misericordiae suae / Sicut loctus•est ad / patres nostras Abra / ham et=semini eius i[n] / saecula Gloria patri et / filio et spir[ito] / sancto S[icut erat in] / principi[o et nunc et semper] / et in saecu[la saeculorum] / De profundis clamavi / [ad te] domine : domine ex / [audi v]ocem : meam / [Fiant aures tua]e intenden / [tes in vocem depraca]tiones / [meae.] / . . . misericordia et co / [piosa] (. . . in remembrance of his mercy; As he spake to our fathers, to Abraham, and to his seed for ever. Glory to the Father and to the Son and to the Holy Spirit, [as it was in the] beginning, [is now, and shall be for ever.] Out of the depths have I cried [unto thee,] O Lord. Lord, [hear] my voice: [let thine ears] be attentive [to the voice of my] supplications [Luke 1:54–55, the Gloria patri, and Psalms 130:1–2 and possibly 7].)
The Jack and Belle Linsky Collection, 1982 1982.60.47

Provenance: Louis Apollinaire Sicard, Lyons (ca. 1848–before 1853); ?Georges Dupré, Lyons (d. 1853); Dr. Stanislas Gilibert, Lyons (by 1853–d. 1870; sale, Lyons, from March 11, 1872); Calamard, Lyons

This panel, which is in astonishingly fine condition, retains the qualities for which Netherlandish painting is justly praised: jewel-like, deeply saturated colors and extraordinary verisimilitude, with minute observation of surface detail. Here tour-de-force execution of varied textures—transparent glass, translucent grapes, the fur of an inner sleeve, the vellum of a prayer book—is accompanied by extremely subtle tonal transitions, particularly in the flesh areas of the Virgin and Child, to produce remarkably lifelike effects.

The notable stylistic changes that took place in Joos van Cleve's work between his early years as a free master in the Antwerp painters' guild and the time of his full-fledged maturity in the mid-1520s are immediately made clear by a comparison of the artist's *Holy Family* of about 1512–13 (cat. no. 61) and this *Virgin and Child*, which was executed about 1525. Although the images of the Virgin in these panels share a resemblance, especially in the pose of the head and the physiognomy, and both pictures show Mary and the Christ Child behind a stone balustrade with a still life, the earlier work looks back to Jan van Eyck for its inspiration, while the later one shows a new monumentality and volumetric treatment of form, probably influenced by Italian painting. Moreover, the figures in the earlier example are shown in an interior, while the present Virgin and Child are placed before the requisite Patinir-inspired landscape so popular from the mid-1520s. In addition to the familiar craggy rock formations and villages nestled in the gently rolling hills of this setting, there is a large port in a bay like that of Genoa, the destination of a number of Joos's panels of this period.

Tiny biblical scenes are integrated into a landscape filled with villagers, herdsmen, and farmers going about their daily activities. At the left the Miracle of the Wheat Field and the Massacre of the Innocents appear, and at the right the Holy Family is shown on its journey, implying the association of this Virgin and Child with the Rest on the Flight into Egypt. However, the figures, sitting on a balcony high above the landscape, are relatively detached from the setting. In fact, the landscape itself is somewhat disjunctive, for, like the background of the *Crucifixion with Saints and a Donor* (cat. no. 95), it appears not to be by Joos but to have been added by a specialist: the forms are not underdrawn and are more loosely painted than the Virgin and Child, which have underdrawings in a style close to that of the preliminary designs for the figures in Joos's *Crucifixion* and his *Annunciation* (cat. no. 97). Further testifying to the presence of two separate hands at work here, the landscape carefully circumscribes a reserve area left for the figures.

This ostensibly casual depiction of a mother contemplating her devotional readings as she holds her innocent sleeping child is actually pregnant with symbolic meaning. The sleeping infant is traditionally understood as a prefiguration of events of the Passion, specifically of the dead Christ embraced by the Virgin, or the Pietà. In view of various motifs presented here, the painting may well allude to the Song of Solomon, which was extremely popular in the Netherlands in Joos's time and which, according to contemporary exegesis, identifies the Virgin and Christ as bride and bridegroom: "May your breasts be like clusters of the vine, and the scent of your breath like apples; and your kisses like the best wine that goes down smoothly, gliding over lips and teeth [of sleepers]" (7:8–9). Christ wears a necklace of coral, noted for its apotropaic function, and holds an apple, referring to his identity as the New Adam and recalling Original Sin. This fruit echoes the shape of the bare breast of the Virgin, the New Eve, who nourished Christ with her body, just as he fed the faithful with his own blood. The still life displayed below the figures, nearly identical to the one shown in the *Holy Family*, underscores the eucharistic meaning of the central symbolism.

The Virgin points to her open prayer book, in which two pages of text are visible: on the first are

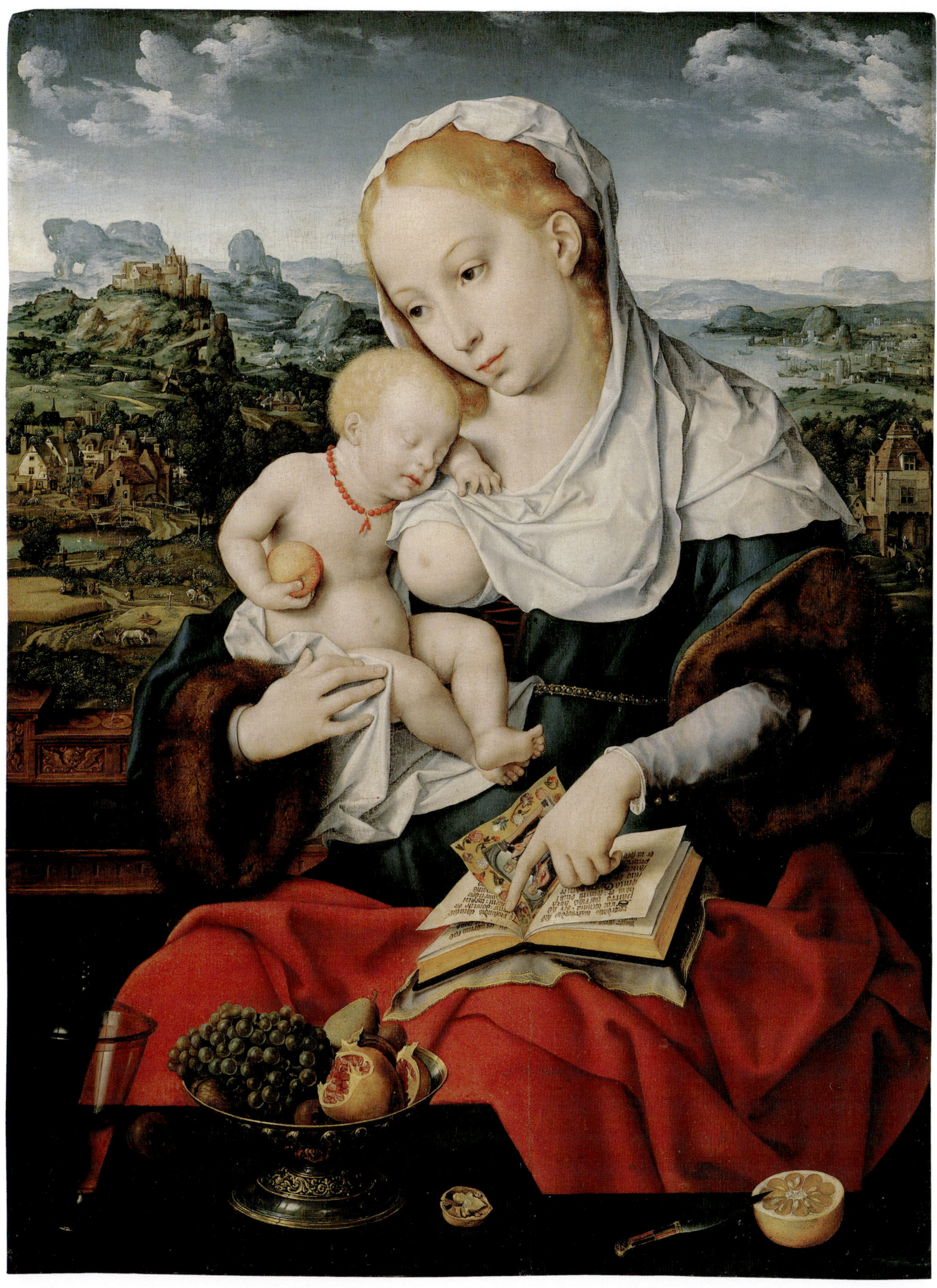

(from 1872); [Spiridon, Rome and Paris (until 1877–78)]; Ernest Odiot, Paris (1877/78–89); sale, Hôtel Drouot, Paris, April 26–27, 1889, lot 6, as Mabuse [Gossart]; Mme Angèle de Miranda (1889–after 1925); Edward Julius Berwind, The Elms, Newport, Rhode Island (d. 1936); Julia A. Berwind, The Elms (1936–61); sale, The Elms, by Parke-Bernet, June 27–28, 1962, lot 222, to Frederick P. Victoria for Linsky; Mr. and Mrs. Jack Linsky, New York (1962–80); The Jack and Belle Linsky Foundation, New York (1980–82).

References: De Cazenove 1883, pp. 28–30; Darcel 1889, pp. 257–58; Firmenich-Richartz 1909, p. 217; Wurzbach 1906–10, vol. 2, p. 609; Conway 1921, p. 402; Winkler 1924, pp. 249–50; Baldass 1925, pp. 26, 31; Friedländer 1924–37, vol. 11 (1931), p. 136, no. 57; Neugass 1962, p. 13; Friedländer 1967–76, vol. 9a (1972), p. 62, no. 57; Hand 1978, p. 310, no. 83; Campbell 1985, p. 32; Bauman in Baetjer et al. 1986, pp. 154–59; Bermejo 1991, pp. 349–53; Falkenburg 1994, pp. 15, 84–85, no. 56.

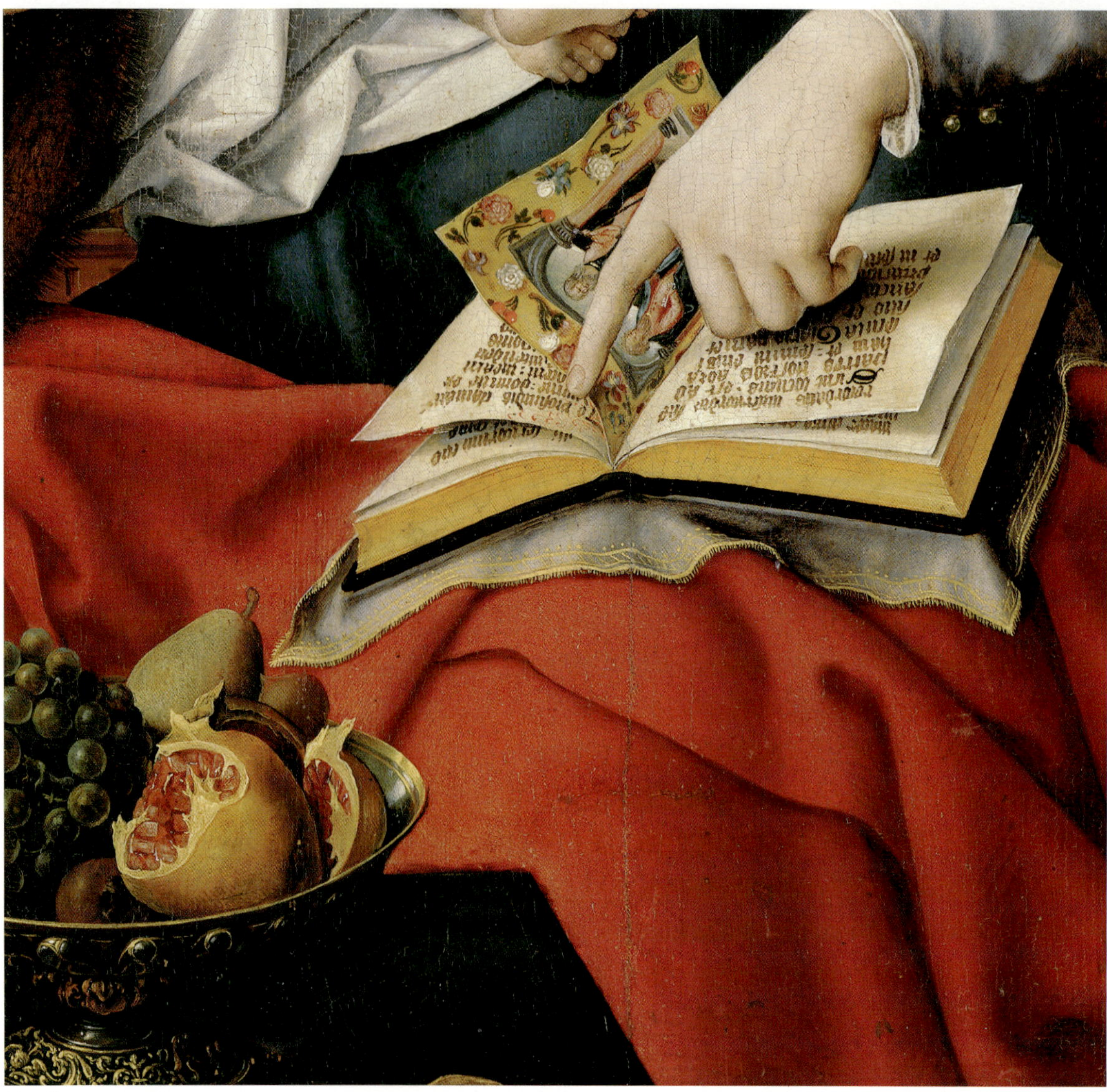

Detail, cat. no. 96

the last two lines of the Magnificat, "in remembrance of his mercy: As he spake to our fathers" (Luke 1:54–55), and on the second we see the opening words of the De Profundis, "Out of the depths have I cried unto thee, O Lord" (Psalm 130:1–2). The two passages, one from a hymn of praise and rejoicing, the other words of anguish, express the conflicting emotions of the Virgin. In this context the pensive, even sorrowful expression of Mary suggests that she foresees her son's destiny, which inspires both joy and grief. Dividing the two texts is an illuminated page showing Saints Paul and Peter, the founders of the Church, indicating the eventual outcome of Christ's sacrifice.

The Linsky panel is one of at least three known variants of this composition. Two others, which are in private collections (one in Spain, the other sold at Sotheby's, London, July 19, 1980, no. 43), place the Virgin and Child before a cloth of honor and only a partial view of an open landscape and show the still life on a tablecloth draped over the balustrade. Bermejo has identified a lowercase d and a capital B on the plate in the still life of the version in the Spanish private collection; she maintains that these are the initials of Joos's pseudonym, van der Beke, and that the picture is, therefore, the artist's only monogrammed work. Apparent deficiencies in the work's quality suggest, however, that these initials merely identify Joos as the head of the workshop that produced the painting rather than as its specific author.

MWA

Opposite: Detail, cat. no. 96

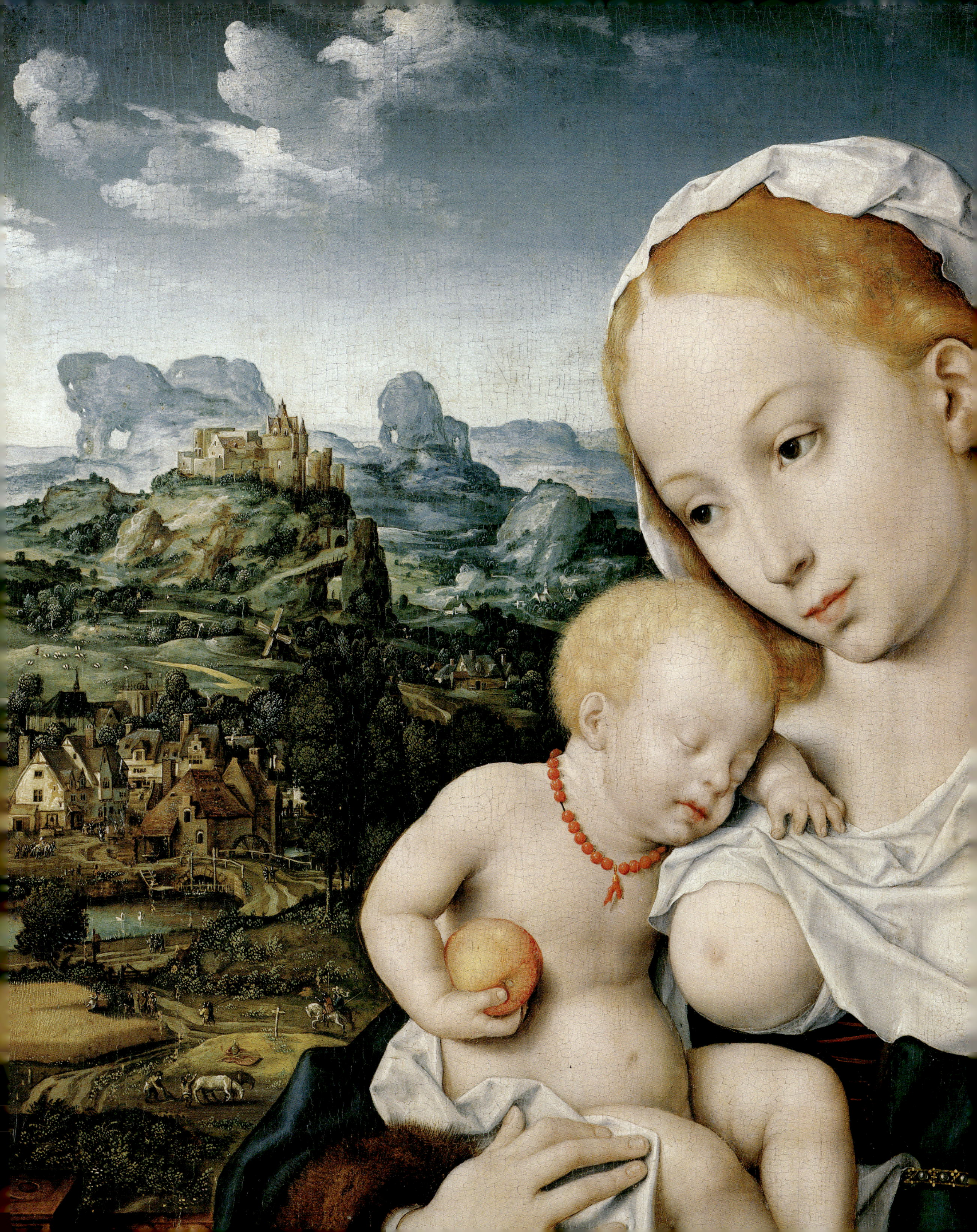

Joos van Cleve, active by 1507, died 1540/41

97. The Annunciation, about 1525

Oil on wood, 34 x 31½ in. (86.4 x 80 cm)
Inscribed (background, on predella of altarpiece): ABRAHAM; MELCHICED [Melchizedek]
The Friedsam Collection, Bequest of Michael Friedsam, 1931 32.100.60

Provenance: Francis Douce, London (d. 1834); Sir Samuel Rush Meyrick, Goodrich Court, Herefordshire (d. 1848); Lt. Col. Augustus Meyrick, Goodrich Court (sold ca. 1871); W. Twopenny, Woodstock Park, Sittingbourne; B. M. Twopenny (sale, Christie's, London, June 20, 1896, no. 71, as Martin Schongauer); [Dowdeswell and Dowdeswell, London]; Jules Porgès, Paris; [Kleinberger, New York]; Michael Friedsam, New York.

References: Hulin de Loo 1902, pp. xxvii, 74, no. 276; Friedländer 1903, no. 276; Friedländer 1916, p. 186; Conway 1921, p. 403; Winkler 1924, p. 249; Baldass 1925, p. 25, no. 48; Friedsam collection n.d., p. 126; Burroughs and Wehle 1932, pp. 24ff.; Panofsky 1935, p. 452 n. 32; Wehle and Salinger 1947, pp. 135–37; Larsen 1960, pp. 92–93, 131; Hand 1978, pp. 196–98; Koslow 1986, p. 32.

Here objects with symbolic meaning are not prominently placed to demand attention and interpretation as they are in the Annunciation panel of the *Merode Triptych* (cat. no. 2); rather they are disposed unobtrusively within the domestic interior in much the same way sixteenth-century viewers of the painting might have arranged them in their own homes. Thus Joos emphasizes how these objects would have been used as part of daily devotional practice. The Virgin kneels at a prie-dieu with a sumptuously decorated Book of Hours to guide her prayers, although she might also have worshiped before the house altar showing Abraham and Melchizedek—Old Testament prefigurations of the Eucharist—that is placed on the cabinet. Indifferently tacked to the wall is a cheap devotional image (probably a colored woodcut) of Moses, an antetype of Christ and an indication of the era *sub Lege*, or the time before the advent of Christ. Symbols of the Virgin's purity—the basin, ewer, and towel beneath the triptych on a lower shelf of the cabinet, and the vase of lilies on the floor—are informally placed; and the *thalamus virginis*, or nuptial bed, with its embroidered and tasseled canopy, the gold-framed mirror, and the casually fluffed pillow are as much a part of the trappings of a wealthy Antwerp household as they are of the traditional setting for an Annunciation. Familiarity with these objects, which are arranged in a more convincing perspectival space than in earlier Netherlandish pictures, invited the contemporary viewer into the scene to share in the mystery of the Incarnation.

The robust, fully rounded forms of the Virgin and Gabriel, similar to those found in the Linsky *Virgin and Child* by Joos (cat. no. 96), as well as the accomplished depiction of space, signal the artist's mature phase in Antwerp. Only weak hints of his origins in Kalkar under the tutelage of Jan Joest are apparent in the relationship between the Virgin and Gabriel in the present picture and its counterpart in Joest's *Annunciation* on the high altar of the Stadtpfarrkirche Sankt Nicolai at Kalkar. But there is ample evidence that Joos knew paintings made in Bruges, especially Gerard David's *Annunciation* panels for the Cervara Altarpiece of 1506 (cat. no. 79). Following David's lead, Joos appropriated a new Italianate canon of beauty, a new repertory of rhetorical gesture, and a striking grace of movement, particularly in his figure of Gabriel. Joos must have known David's example, so similar are the compositions of the two Annunciations, which share the positions of the figures and the dove, the placement of the bed and the prie-dieu with open Book of Hours, the banquette by the open windows at the back left, and even the design of the tile floor. But to David's stripped-down painting made to fit into a large-scale Italianate retable Joos added the customary Flemish motifs of everyday life, introducing an anecdotal aspect to his work that would have spoken most directly to his Antwerp clients. The domestic nature of his *Annunciation* suggests that it was made for private devotional use and perhaps served as a house altar of the type depicted in the painting.

MWA

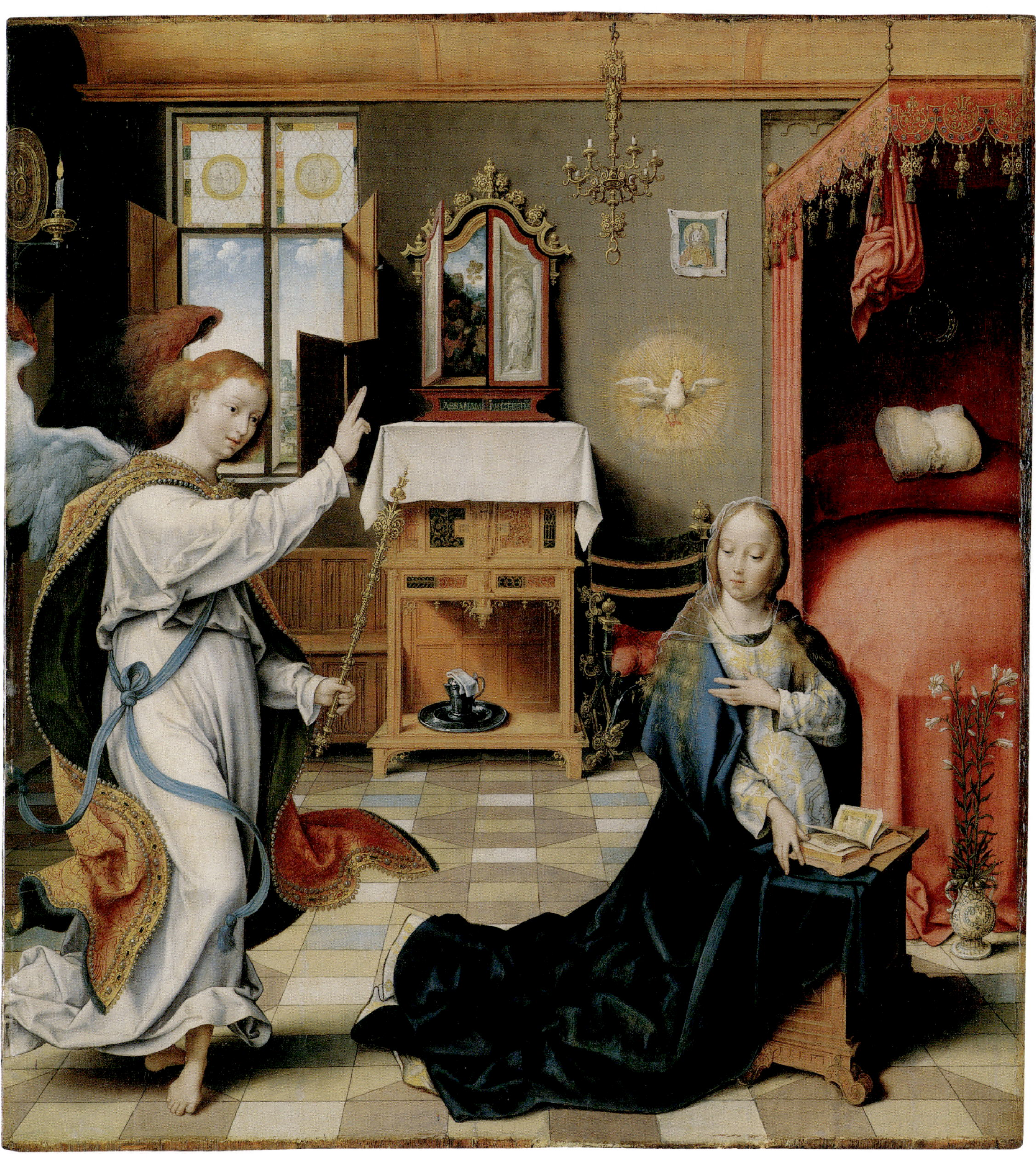
ABRAHAM

Joos van Cleve, active by 1507, died 1540/41

98. The Last Judgment, about 1520–25

Oil on wood, 48¾ x 34 in. (123.8 x 86.4 cm)
Bequest of Mr. and Mrs. Graham F. Blandy, 1940
40.174.1

Provenance: Monastery near Douai (presented ca. 1764 as a work of Bellegambe by parents of a member of the order); [Delehaye, Antwerp (1909)]; Mr. and Mrs. Graham F. Blandy (from 1909).

References: Salinger 1941, pp. 109–11; Wehle and Salinger 1947, pp. 137–38; Larsen 1960, p. 93; Harbison 1976, pp. 27–30, 146; Farmer 1981, pp. 153–54.

Portrayals of the Last Judgment were suitable not only for churches but also for city halls, where they functioned as religious counterparts to secular judgment scenes. Such paintings served a didactic purpose, admonishing judges to administer justice impartially.

In this beautiful and ambitious composition, the upper and lower zones are linked by two angels with fantastic multicolored wings and swirling mauve and yellow-orange garments who are blowing lily-shaped trumpets, their cheeks swelling with their considerable efforts. Christ appears at the moment of judgment in a burst of light and color, surrounded by voluminous clouds, apostles, and a host of angels and putti with rainbow-hued wings. The sunburst may have been inspired by the artist's close reading of Saint Augustine's *City of God* (Book 20: chap. 27), in which the author speaks of "that sun of righteousness" who brings "the brightness of eternal life" and quotes Matthew (13:43) describing the time of the Last Judgment when "the righteous [shall] shine forth as the sun in the kingdom of heaven" (Book 20: chap. 1). The effect of this blinding radiance and variegated color in the upper part of the composition is in sharp contrast to the subdued tones in the area of the mass of humanity pictured below. Christ blesses the saved, shown at the left, and, with the assistance of Saint Michael in the lower register, he banishes the damned to the hell burning in the distance at the right.

Although the apostles populate the heavenly realm on either side of the Lord, the traditional intercessors—the Virgin Mary and Saint John the Baptist—do not appear, signaling a change in the hierarchical arrangement of the scene customary since the Middle Ages. As Harbison notes, the absence of the Virgin and John may signify a Protestant interpretation, but painters expressing the Catholic viewpoint occasionally also reduced the number of figures shown in heaven in order to focus on the image of Christ. It is not possible to determine the original location and, hence, the specific religious intent of our work, because its earliest provenance is unknown.

The attribution of the painting is somewhat problematic. The closest parallel for the composition is seen in Bernaert van Orley's altarpiece showing the Last Judgment and the Seven Acts of Mercy (Koninklijk Museum voor Schone Kunsten, Antwerp), commissioned by the Almoners in 1518–19 and completed in 1525. Our work shares with Van Orley's center panel earthly and heavenly realms of equal size arranged in two grand semicircles modeled on Raphael's *Disputa* for the Stanza della Signatura in the Vatican. Both paintings also follow Raphaelesque models in their renditions of poses and gestures that emphasize elegance and eloquence. The Italianate nudes in the foreground of our picture need not have been encountered firsthand in Raphael's originals but most likely were assimilated from drawings and prints made after works by Raphael and his followers. They were probably derived above all from the Italian's cartoons for a series of tapestries portraying the Acts of the Apostles to be woven for Pope Leo X; these were brought to Brussels by 1516, when Raphaelesque and other Italian, primarily Roman, models were entering the north, particularly through Brussels, and infusing the art of the region. One such prototype, a print attributed to Amico Aspertini, the *Expulsion of Adam and Eve from Paradise* (Davis 1988, p. 42, no. 3), shows figures viewed from the front and back and disposed across a foreground plane in a manner that is imitated in our *Last Judgment.*

Despite the affinities the Metropolitan panel shares with the work of Van Orley, the Christ and especially the angels in our work are softer and sweeter than his types and closer in some ways to the figures encountered in the work of Joos van Cleve, to whom the painting has been attributed. Joos's Italianate manner, however, was not usually inspired by Raphael's example but by Leonardo's

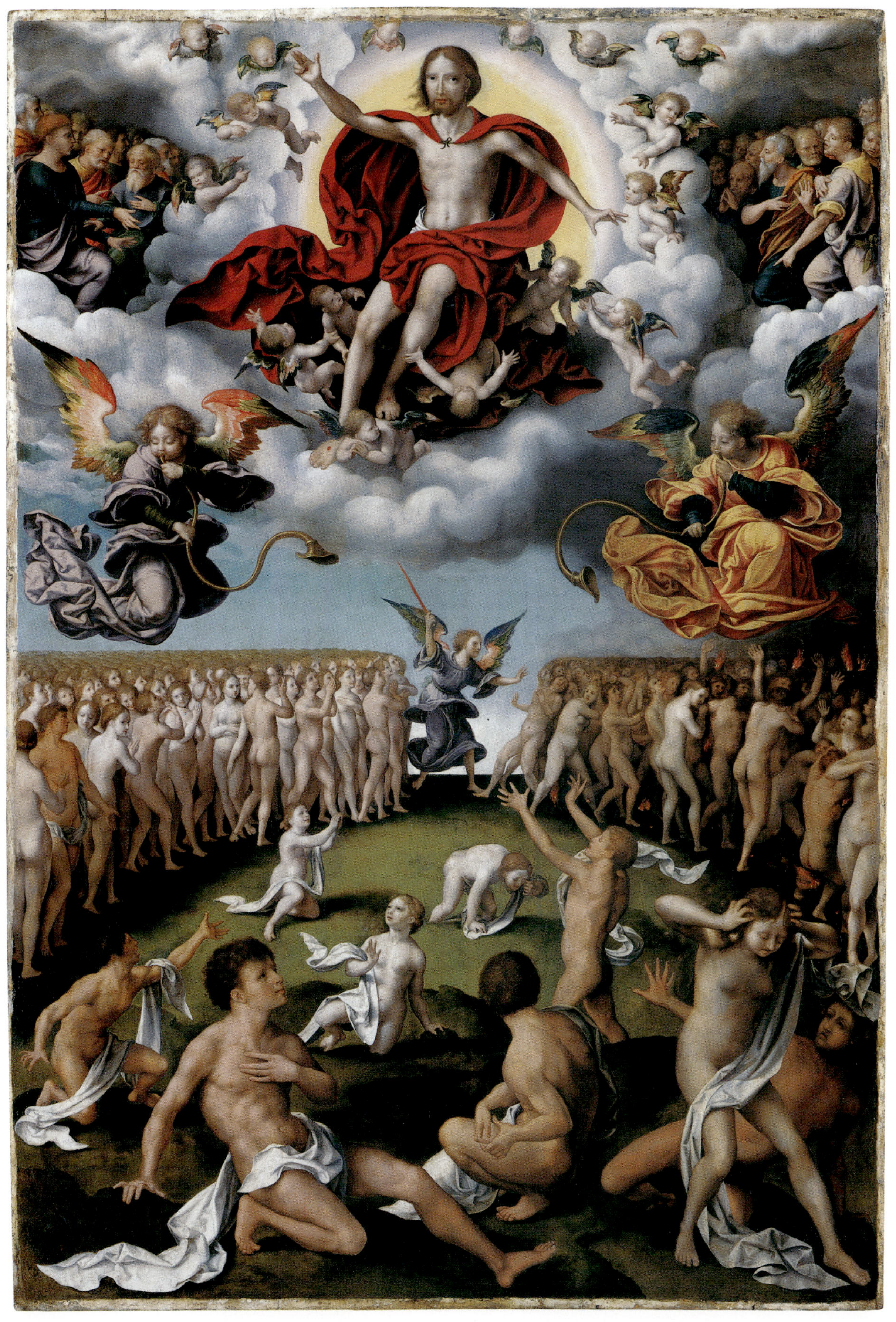

works, in particular those he saw while at the court of Francis I, where Leonardo spent his last years. Oddly enough, the type of angel found in our picture is seldom seen in Joos's paintings—only his *Crucifixion* in the Capodimonte, Naples, shows a few of these impish creatures—and the Christ type is known in just two works attributed to him—*Christ the Gardener with the Magdalene* (Suermondt-Ludwig-Museum, Aachen) and *Christ Giving the Blessing* (Louvre, Paris). However, we find Joos's characteristic types in the heads of the apostles and the sprawling man in the left foreground of our panel (that is, in the well-preserved parts of the painting and not in the area of the saved and the damned, which has been heavily restored). It is likely that a brief, passing encounter with Raphaelesque models spurred Joos to depart from his habitual manner; indeed, it could be that a commission for a Last Judgment, a subject not otherwise treated by Joos, prompted him to investigate unaccustomed Italianate models shortly after they arrived in the north. This splendid example probably dates about 1520–25.

MWA

Quentin Massys, 1465/66–1530

99. The Adoration of the Magi, 1526

Oil on wood, 40½ x 31½ in. (102.9 x 80 cm)
Dated (on pilaster): [15]26
John Stewart Kennedy Fund, 1911 11.143

With its clear spatial divisions, varied figure types, and emphasis on Italianate decorative motifs, this compelling picture is a key late work by Quentin Massys and a paradigm of the ambitions of the first generation of Renaissance artists in Antwerp. An inscription in the ornamentation of the pilaster in the background dates it [15]26.

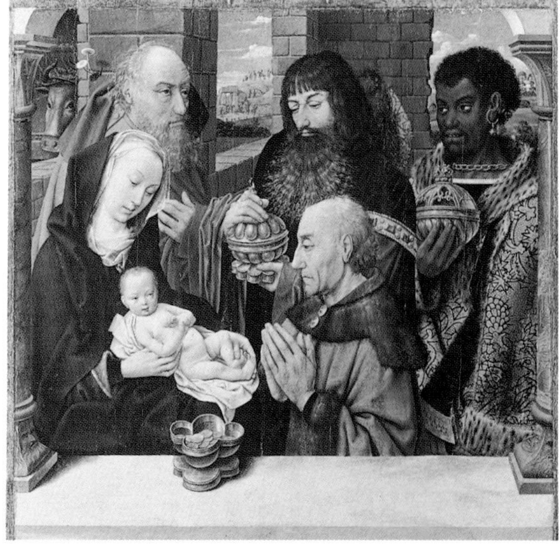

Fig. 111. Copy after Hugo van der Goes, *The Adoration of the Magi*, about 1500. Oil on wood. The Metropolitan Museum of Art, New York

The scene is compressed into a narrow foreground space defined by portions of ruined architecture, by a patterned curtain that serves as a cloth of honor for the Virgin, and by a foreground ledge, upon which the oldest magus has placed his finely wrought scepter and vessel. Behind him and the two other magi a group of followers, shown on a smaller scale and crowded tightly together, partly obstructs the far-distant view. In the extreme upper right the three kings on horseback are barely visible. The setting and the sumptuous gold-embroidered silk and velvet attire of the magi may well have been inspired by the kind of contemporary theatrical practice recorded by the miniaturist Robert Cailleau in his illustration of the Passion play held in Valenciennes in 1547 (Collection G. de Rothschild, Bibliothèque Nationale, Paris). The exotic neckpieces worn by the magi and their vessels inlaid with precious stones and decorated with gold filigree are a reminder of the opulent taste of the wealthy cosmopolitan community in Antwerp—which included Portuguese who inspired a vogue for rich Oriental jewels and objects imported from their eastern colonies. Coifs, or nets, of gold wire such as the one worn by the black

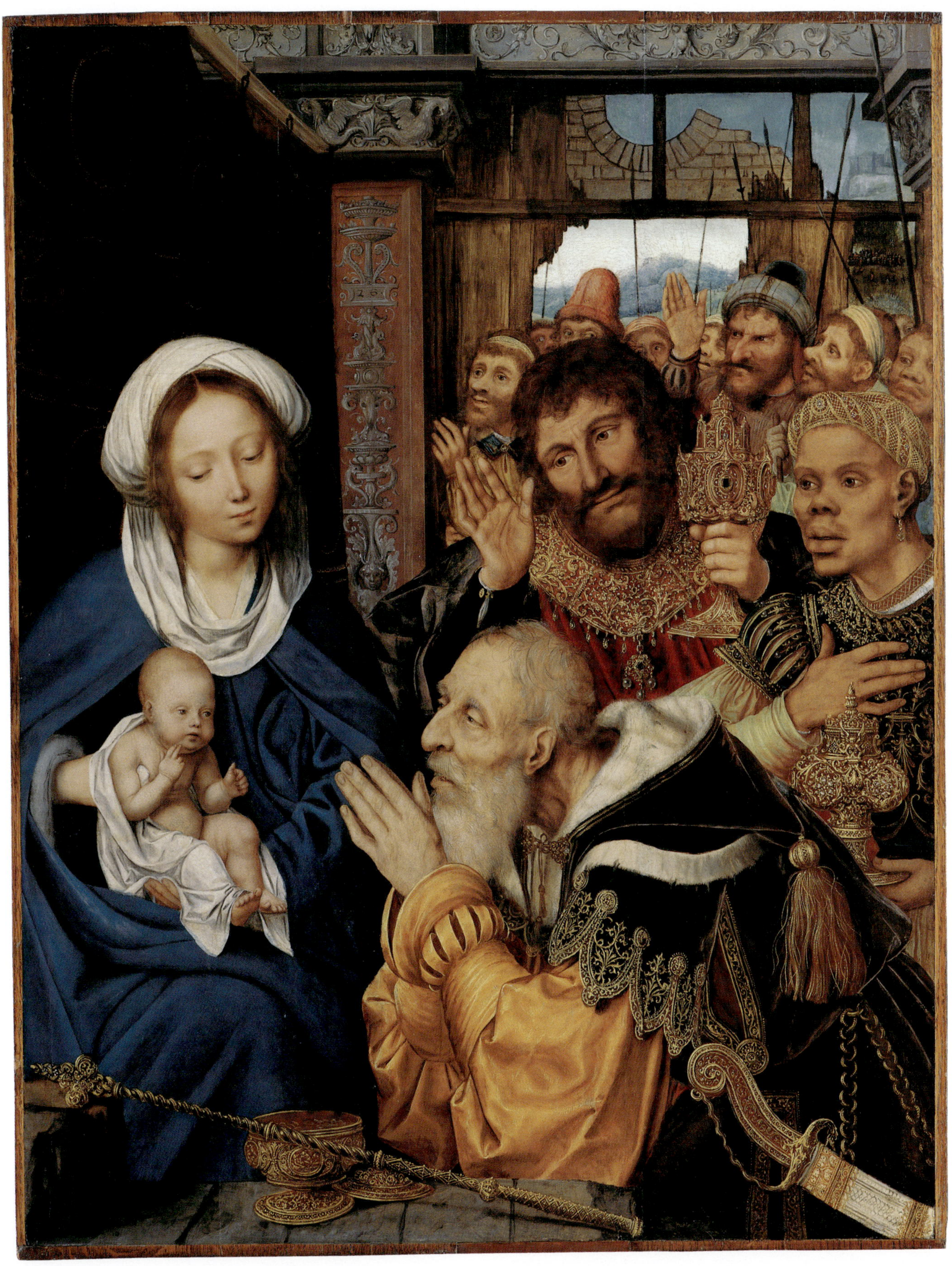

99

Provenance: Hugh Robert Hughes, Kinmel, Abergele, North Wales; Rodolphe Kann, Paris; [Duveen, London]; [Dowdeswell and Dowdeswell, London].

References: Wehle and Salinger 1947, pp. 108–10; Konigson 1969, pl. 3; Friedländer 1967–76, vol. 7 (1971), pp. 26–27, 61, no. 8; Voet 1973, p. 301; De Bosque 1975, pp. 218, 220, 225–26, fig. 278; Ringbom 1983, pp. 90–91; Silver 1984, pp. 47, 82, 91–95, 121, 127, 180, 184, 191, 222–23, 226, no. 40, fig. 79; Meijer 1988, pp. 407–8; Dacos-Grifo 1991, pp. 152–58; Kwakkelstein 1991, p. 135, n. 44; Hand in Bauman and Liedtke 1992, pp. 102–3; Koch in Bauman and Liedtke 1992, pp. 104–5, color ill.; Lightbown 1992, p. 365; Silva 1992, pp. 54–61.

magus were sold by mercers at the open markets and fairs in Antwerp. The black magus himself may be modeled after African servants Massys observed in the city's Portuguese households.

The most salient element of the picture is the contrast between the sweet countenance of the Virgin, the almost grotesque features of the magi, and the individuals in the crowd pressing in behind them, who communicate as much through gestures as through facial expressions: the juxtaposition of the magi's grimacing followers, with their swarthy complexions, and the beautiful pale, smooth-skinned Virgin and her sweet child creates an almost comic effect. In showing such a variety of physiognomies, devised to express character, Massys was one of the first Netherlandish painters to apply an idea presented by Leonardo da Vinci in his *Paragone* asserting that paintings, like poetry, should reveal moral habits; in so doing Massys was also among the earliest Netherlanders to react against the depiction of uniform facial types.

The head of the old king is adopted directly from Leonardo's *Head of an Old Man* of 1492–97 (Royal Library, Windsor), and the caricatured faces of some of the followers reflect close study of the same artist's *Physiognomics* (Royal Library, Windsor). We do not know how the *Physiognomics* reached Antwerp, but they must have been available by the time Massys painted his Saint John Altarpiece of 1508–11 (Koninklijk Museum voor Schone Kunsten, Antwerp), for their influence is already apparent in the distorted and evil faces of Saint John's tormentors in that work.

The basic composition of the present picture derives from a lost *Adoration of the Magi* by Hugo van der Goes, known through a later copy in the Metropolitan Museum (fig. 111). Following the lead of his predecessor Hugo, Massys invested his own late half-length composition with a new grandeur and monumentality meant to stimulate the emotional involvement of the beholder. Silver observes that Joos van Cleve exercised a notable influence on the late work of Massys, who adapted some of Cleve's pictorial vocabulary here: for example, the ruined pagan setting and the type of the black magus, which appear in Cleve's *Epiphany* (Detroit Institute of Arts).

Despite damage in the blue mantle of the Virgin, the faces in the crowd, and the landscape at the upper right corner, Massys's detailed observation, dazzling virtuosity of handling, and extraordinary palette of unusual colors—a rainbow of gold, purple, green, and orange—remain compelling.

VS

Adriaen Isenbrant, active by 1510, died 1551

100. Scenes from the Life of the Virgin, after 1521

Oil on wood; central panel, overall, with engaged frame, 12⅜ x 10⅛ in. (31.4 x 25.7 cm); central panel, painted surface 9⅛ x 6⅞ in. (23.2 x 17.5 cm); each wing, overall, with engaged frame, 12⅜ x 5 in. (31.4 x 12.7 cm); each wing, painted surface 10¾ x 3½ in. (27.3 x 8.9 cm)
Frederick C. Hewitt Fund, 1913 13.32a–c

A portable altarpiece notable for its precious, miniature-like qualities, this small triptych is one of the earliest works attributed to Adriaen Isenbrant. His oeuvre is remarkable for its size (over five hundred pictures are given to him and his workshop); it is notable as well for its dependence on models by other artists, particularly those of Gerard David, the leading painter in early-sixteenth-century Bruges, who, according to Sanderus (*Flandria illustrata*, 1924), was Isenbrant's teacher. Our triptych repeats popular scenes of the Life of the Virgin, borrowed from well-known, standardized compositional models that circulated among contemporary workshops in Bruges and Antwerp. These conventional images served the spiritual needs of a broad middle-class audience, which, following the tenets of the Modern Devotion, sought empathic contemplation of the Virgin and Christ as a basis of religious experience and salvation.

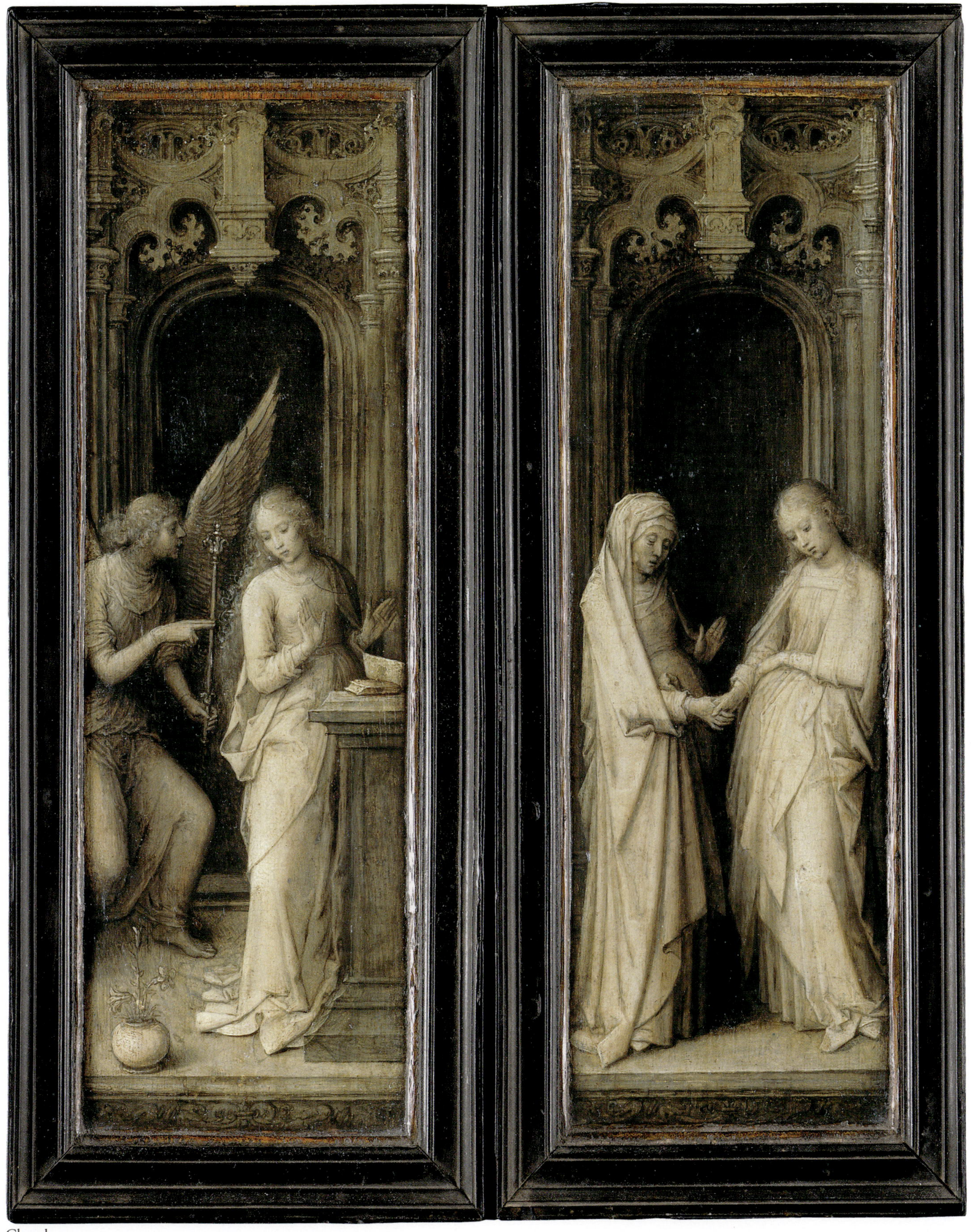

Closed

Provenance: Friedrich Lippmann, Berlin ([by 1898–1912]; sale, Lepke, Berlin, November 26, 1912, no. 42, to Seligmann); [Seligmann, Paris (1912–13)].

References: Bodenhausen 1905, p. 214; Burroughs 1913a, pp. 67–69; Conway 1921, p. 303; Wehle and Salinger 1947, pp. 99–100; Panofsky 1953, p. 448 n. 6; Philippot 1966, pp. 238–39; Herzog 1968, p. 230; Friedländer 1967–76, vol. 9b (1973), p. 111, no. 122, pls. 140–41, vol. 11 (1974), p. 80, no. 124, pls. 101, 102; Hand and Wolff 1986, p. 121; Dülberg 1990, p. 230, no. 174, pls. 112–14; Wilson 1990, p. 525; Wilson 1995, pp. 2, 4, 5.

The portrayals of the Virgin and her infant son on the interior of the altarpiece are introduced by grisailles on the exterior that depict the Annunciation and the Visitation. Their presentation in two separate scenes instead of one on the outer wings is unusual and signals the focus of this triptych on the Virgin. Each of these scenes, which are executed in a lively mannerist style, is placed under a richly carved canopy, a type of fanciful architectural decoration that became very fashionable among artists in the southern Netherlands during the first third of the sixteenth century. The conception of the Virgin reading at a lectern and the exceptionally animated figure of the archangel Gabriel in the Annunciation scene derive directly from Dürer's *Annunciation*, a woodcut from his *Life of the Virgin*, published in 1511 (an impression is in the Metropolitan Museum collection). These popular woodcuts by Dürer were probably already available in Bruges before the German artist visited the Netherlands in 1520–21 and gave an entire set of his prints to Margaret of Austria.

The more traditional interior scenes are linked to one another by a beautiful and distinctive continuous landscape. The Nativity scene is loosely derived from Gerard David's *Nativity with Donors and Saints Jerome and Leonard* triptych (cat. no. 80) and replicates its motif of the tiny body of the infant Christ—the *corpus verum*—lying naked on a white cloth on top of an overturned basket transformed into an altar. The image prefigures the tragic destiny of Christ and alludes to the sacrament of the Eucharist. The Adoration of the Magi scene is a condensed version of David's early *Adoration of the Magi* in the Musées Royaux des Beaux-Arts de Belgique, Brussels. The Flight into Egypt, often represented by Isenbrant, was an especially popular theme in the early sixteenth century: encouraged by the Modern Devotion, viewers embraced the notion of traveling with the Holy Family and experiencing its day-to-day travails. The high horizon of the landscape, seen through the Italianate architectural setting, allows ample room for the distinctively represented human figures, animals, buildings, textured trees, and winding paths, which are rendered in a manner that recalls the work of David as well as of Patinir.

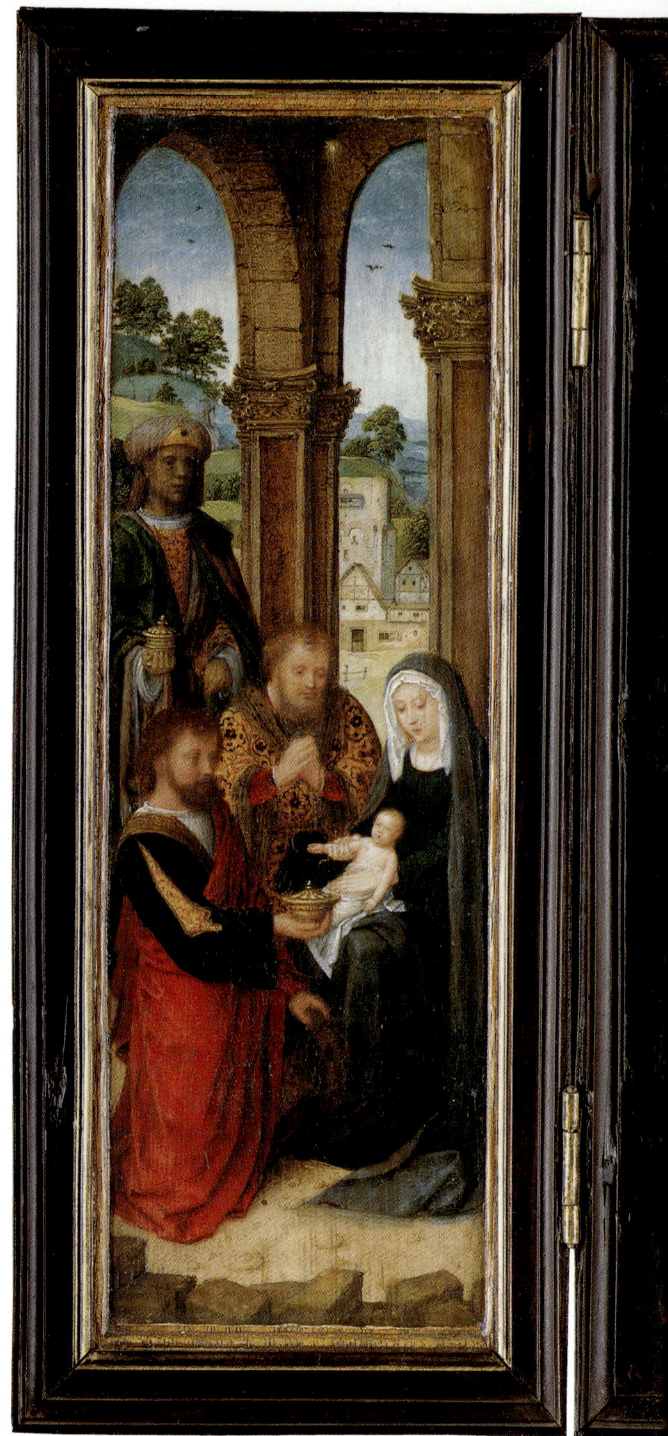

100 open

Isenbrant's use here of the fashionable mannerist style in the grisaille exterior wings in combination with more conventional models on the interior panels typifies his practice, which, while rooted in tradition, kept pace with popular stylistic developments and the new interest on the part of Netherlanders in Italian motifs. The wings are painted in a brownish

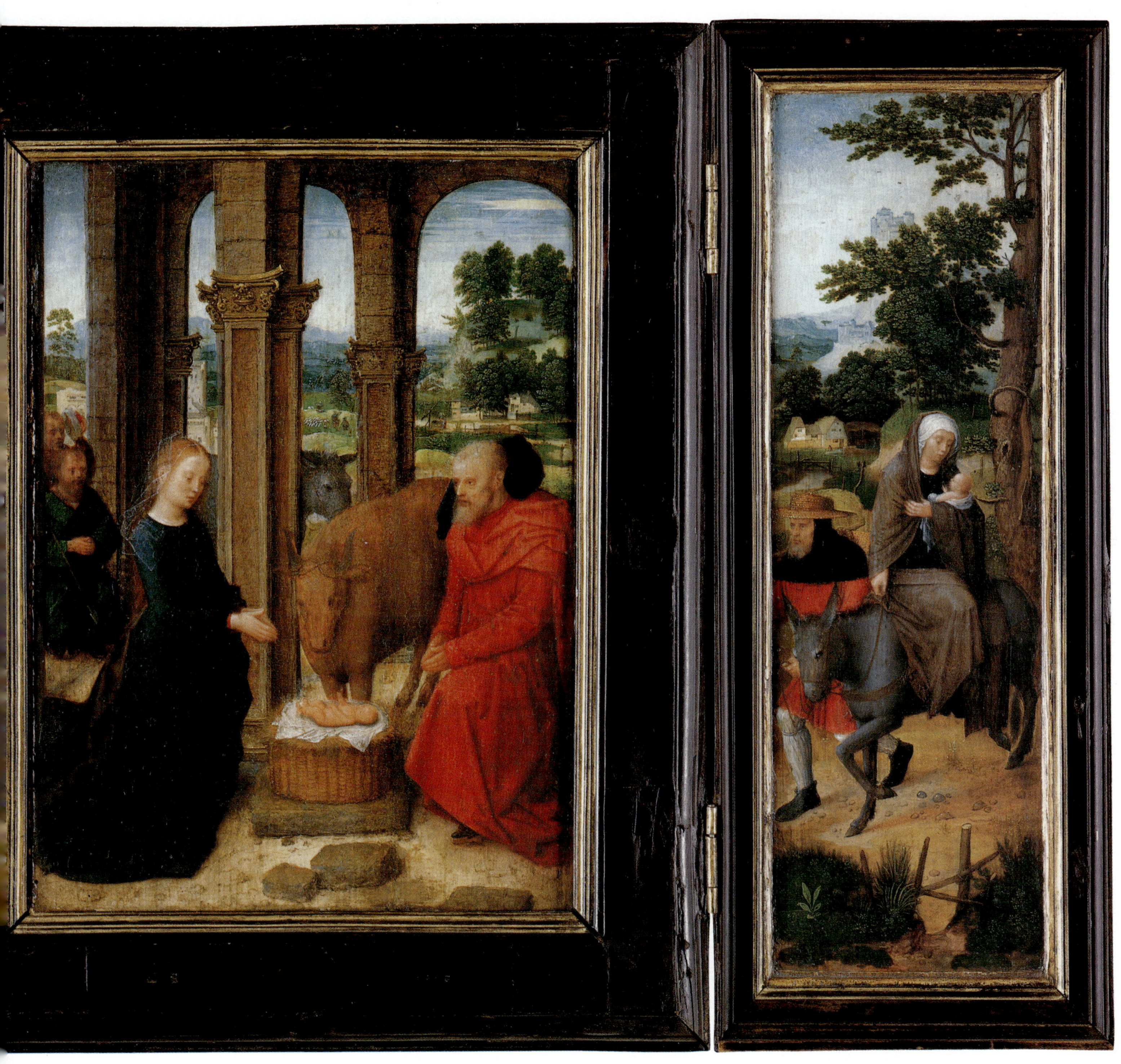

monochrome palette rather than the gray of more traditional grisaille imitations of autonomous sculptural images, a feature Philippot sees as the mark of a transition beyond Late Gothic style. His concern with new trends is exemplified not only in the style of the exterior wings but also in the shape of the triptych: the wings are noticeably taller than the central panel, constituting a format that was adopted with increasing frequency during the early sixteenth century.

The exceptionally fine condition of this altarpiece suggests that it was probably kept in a protective case similar to a rare surviving one made for the Roi René and Jeanne de Laval Diptych (Louvre, Paris), attributed to Nicolas Froment. VS

Adriaen Isenbrant, active by 1510, died 1551

101. Christ Crowned with Thorns and the Mourning Virgin (Ecce Homo), about 1530–40

Oil on canvas, transferred from wood, 41½ x 36½ in. (105.4 x 92.7 cm)
Rogers Fund, 1904 04.32

Provenance: Dr. Friedrich Lippmann (until 1903); [Dowdeswell and Dowdeswell, London (1903–4)].

References: FitzGerald 1905, p. 9; Wehle and Salinger 1947, pp. 101–2; Panofsky 1956, pp. 106, 108, 110, 112–16, fig. 22; Gottlieb 1971, p. 184; Friedländer 1967–76, vol. 11 (1974), p. 90, no. 198; Ringbom 1984, pp. 42–45, 142–43, n. 6.

Richly descriptive in its treatment of detail, yet restrained, even solemn in its emotion, this haunting *Christ Crowned with Thorns and the Mourning Virgin* ranks among Isenbrant's finest paintings. The image of Christ, in the form of an Ecce Homo, represents him as he was shown by Pilate to the chief priests and assembled Jews to judge whether he should be saved or crucified (John 19:4–6). Christ wears the regal cloak and crown of thorns in which the soldiers dressed him to mock the claim that he was King of the Jews (John 19:2). His hands are crossed and bound, the right one holding a reed substituted for a royal scepter (Matthew 27:29). And his exposed body shows the bloody wounds from the Flagellation; behind him, tied to the central column, are the scourge and bundle of twigs with which he was thrashed. The subsidiary figures that would normally accompany him in a narrative treatment of the Ecce Homo (see cat. no. 92) have been eliminated, and Christ is shown with his mother, whose hands are crossed on her breast in a gesture of silent compassion. Although the narrative is alluded to in the background, where several figures approach the entrance to a palace (Pilate's, where the crowning with thorns took place?), Christ and the Virgin have been isolated for devotional contemplation by the viewer-worshiper.

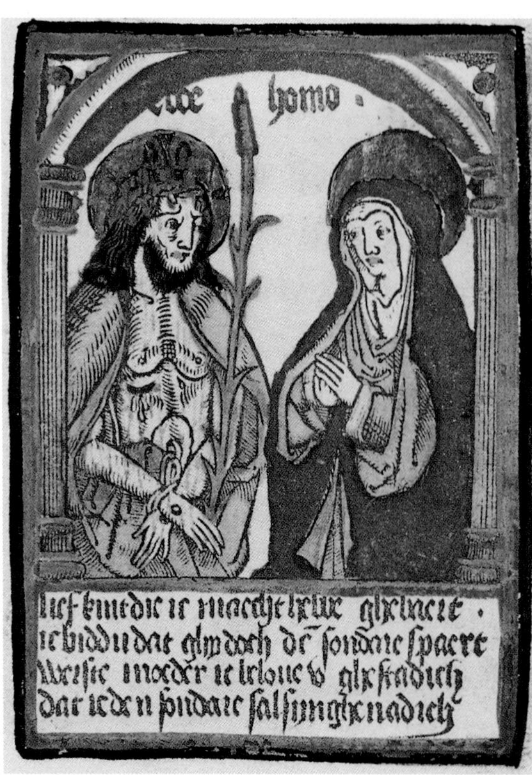

Fig. 112. Netherlandish, *The Man of Sorrows and His Mother*, about 1500. Multicolored woodcut. The National Gallery of Art, Washington, D.C.

The composition of this *Salvator Coronatus and Virgo Doloris*, which evolved from the iconography of the Ecce Homo as well as that of the *Salvator Mundi*, or Christ as Savior of the World, is based in part on a bust-length devotional diptych of the subject produced in the workshop of Dieric Bouts that remained very popular in the Netherlands well into the sixteenth century (cat. no. 58). In a variant by Hugo van der Goes (Museo de Santa Cruz, Toledo) and a version by an anonymous Hispano-Flemish painter (San Diego Museum of Art) the diptych is merged into one continuous scene in which the holy figures face each other behind a double-arched window.

Our painting not only reflects the pictorial tradition of these devotional panels but also recalls the popular woodcuts of the *Ecce Homo and Mater Doloris* that illustrated prayer books and indulgences produced in the Netherlands during the early sixteenth century. In one such print whose composition is very close to that of our painting (fig. 112), Christ and the Virgin Mary turn toward each other, apparently engaged in conversation; it is inscribed *Ecce Homo*, and the accompanying Dutch text, elucidating the Virgin's intercessory role on behalf of the suppliant, reads:

> Dear child that I, the Virgin, have borne
> I ask that you save the sinners /
> Wisest Mother, I promise you always
> that I shall be merciful to the sinner.

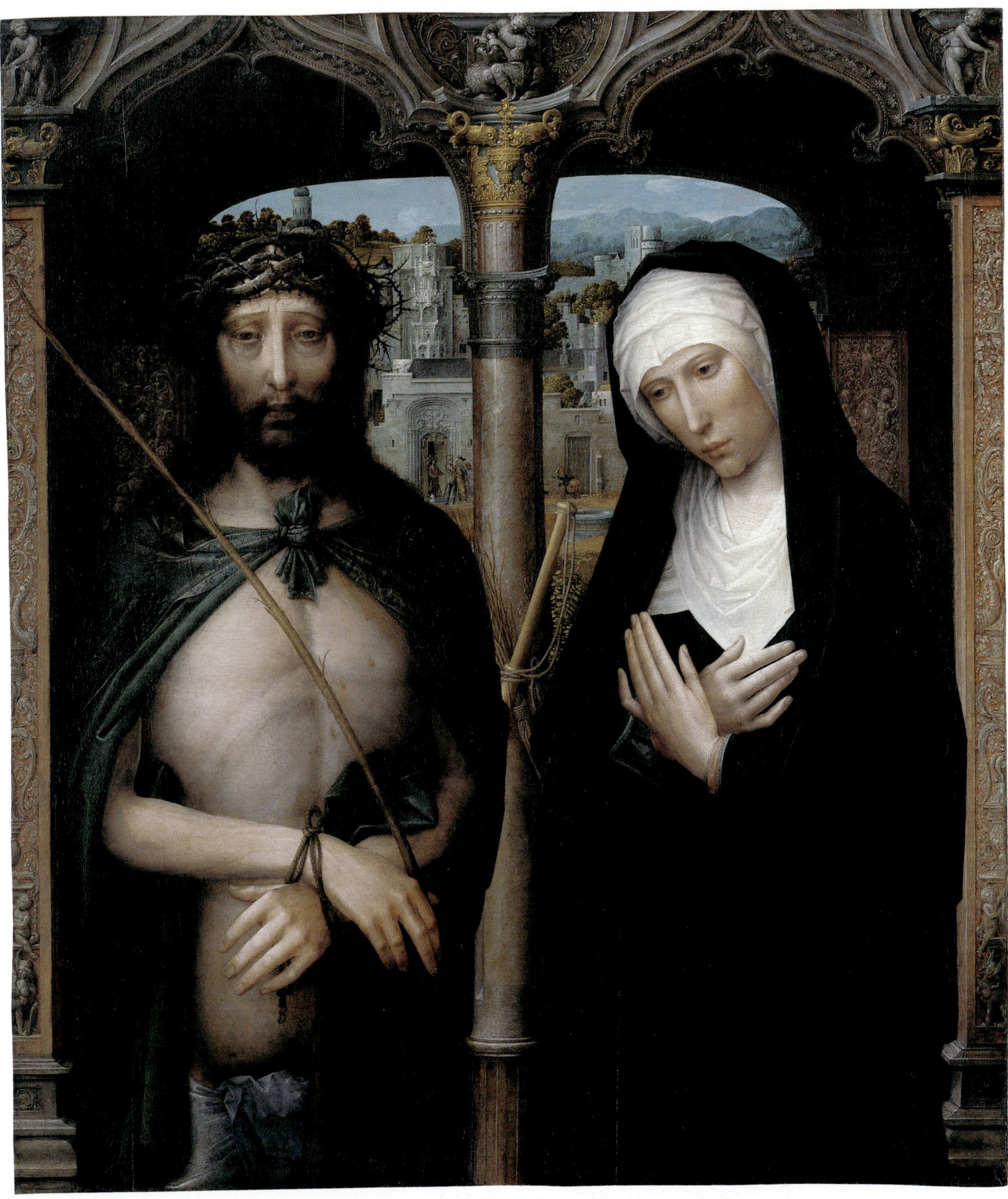

Study of our painting with infrared reflectography and X-radiography reveals that in its initial stages Christ turned toward his mother as in the print, and there was an arrow or sword piercing the Virgin's heart from the left. The latter detail refers to Mary as the Virgin of the Seven Sorrows, whose cult became increasingly popular after 1492, when Jan van Coudenberghe founded a Confraternity of the Seven Sorrows of the Virgin in Sint-Salvator in Bruges and two other Netherlandish churches. Some of the devotional manuals associated with this cult (for example, *Of the Passion and Bitter Suffering of Our Lord Jesus Christ*, published in Antwerp in 1494) focused specifically on the episodes of Christ's Passion, during which the Virgin is thought to have suffered most grievously, and both woodcut illustrations and cycles of panel paintings showed these sorrows. Our picture may originally have been meant to be one element in a continuous narrative program of this sort, as the initial painted stages of the Virgin with a pierced heart suggest. However, any such intention was abandoned in favor of an *Andachtsbild*. In this context, Isenbrant's alteration of the three-quarter view of Christ into a frontal one can be understood as an adjustment that gives greater consideration to the relationship between the image and the viewer, as is appropriate to the *Andachtsbild*. The transformed Christ of our painting directly confronts the devotee with the anguish of the moment when the crowd condemns him to death on the cross, and the effect is all the more powerful because his figure and Mary's are nearly lifesize, standing in a space that appears continuous with our own. It was through the empathic response encouraged by such works that the pious believed they would find the path to salvation, whose promise is indicated here by the scene sculpted on the column between Christ and the Virgin—which represents Daniel and the Lion, an Old Testament prefiguration of the Resurrection of Christ.

In contrast to the austere figures, the Renaissance-style balcony is sumptuously decorated with Italianate stucco pillars, gilded bronze capitals with acanthus leaves and dolphins, and sculpted putti—all inspired by ornament prints of the second quarter of the sixteenth century. The incorporation of these features represents a concession to fashion made to please a wealthy middle-class clientele and is characteristic of Isenbrant's practice. A stylistic maturity not evident in the artist's earlier *Scenes from the Life of the Virgin* (cat. no. 100) is exhibited here; in particular the bold modeling of the figures and the warm palette mark it as a work of Isenbrant's late phase. The present panel must have been produced somewhat after the Van de Velde Diptych of 1517–28 (Onze-Lieve-Vrouwekerk, Bruges, and Musées Royaux des Beaux-Arts de Belgique, Brussels), which treats the Seven Sorrows of the Virgin and shows similar qualities.

MWA and VS

Opposite: Detail, cat. no. 101

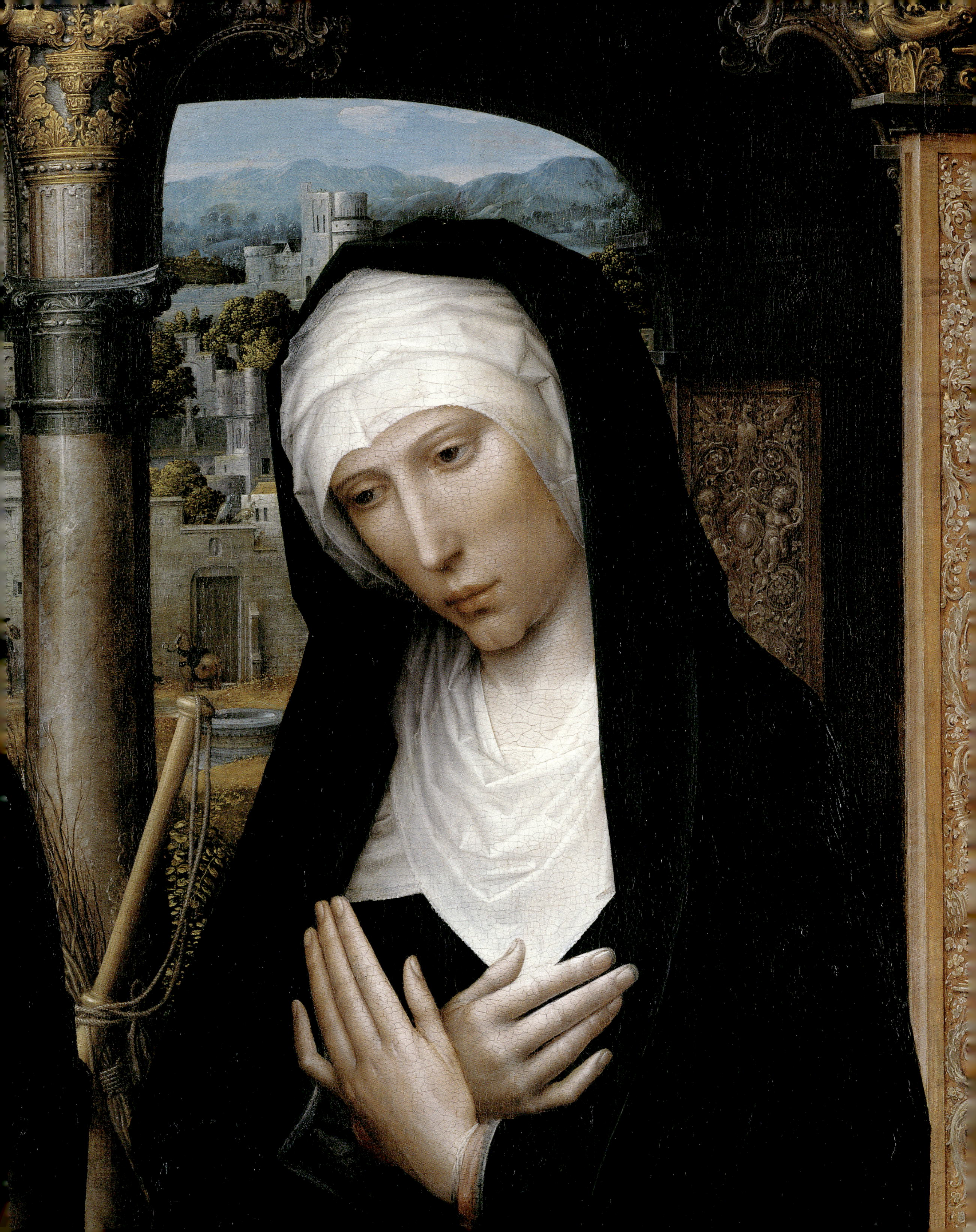

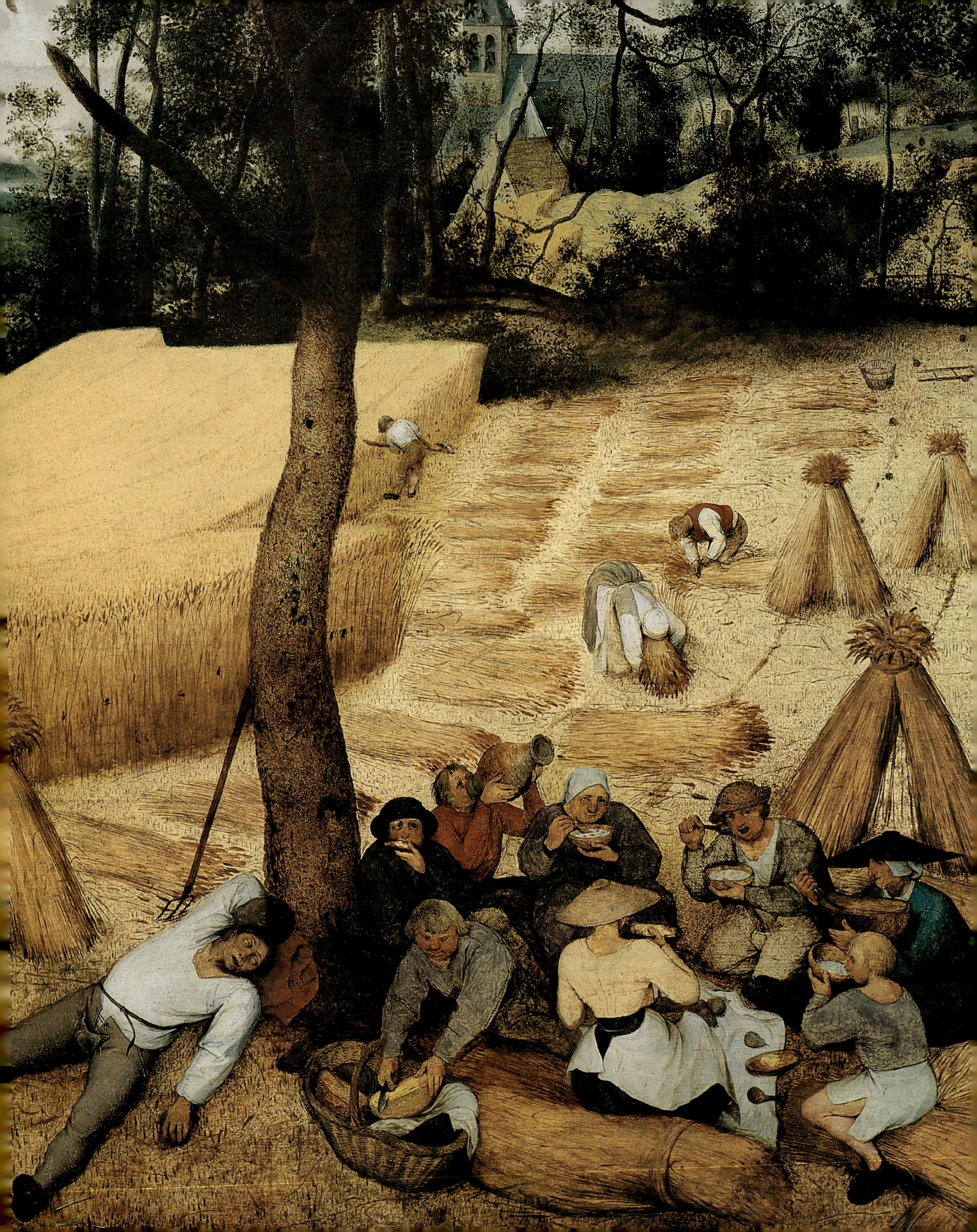

Bruegel, the Land, and the Peasants

Opposite: Pieter Bruegel the Elder, detail, *The Harvesters* (cat. no. 102)

Bruegel was singled out and praised during his own time and long after for his mastery of nature. The artist's friend, the humanist cartographer Abraham Ortelius, wrote in an epitaph for him that his death may have been caused by Nature, "who feared that she would be held up in contempt because of his artistic and talented skills at imitation." Karel van Mander, author of the first biography of Bruegel, published in 1604 as part of his *Lives of the Illustrious Netherlandish and German Painters*, vividly put it this way: "On his travels he drew many views from life so that it is said that when he was in the Alps he swallowed all those mountains and rocks which, upon returning home, he spat out again onto canvases and panels, so faithfully was he able, in this respect and others, to follow Nature."

Bruegel's first influential contribution to the depiction of landscape was not made in the medium of painting but in the form of prints. Shortly after his return to Antwerp about 1555, following a two-year stay in Italy, Bruegel produced drawn designs for a series of twelve prints known as the Large Landscapes, which were engraved by Jan and Lucas van Doetecum (figs. 113–15). They combine diverse landscape types and subject matter of different kinds, but their uniform format and size suggest that they were meant to constitute a single series. While most present expansive mountainous vistas, the group also includes views of the waterfall at Tivoli and a wooded area outside a Flemish village. Although the compositions vary, Bruegel anchored almost all of them with small pieces of land in the foregrounds that serve as scenic overlooks from which to peer into the valleys that precipitously plunge into the distance. The subjects shown, underscored by the inscriptions provided below the images, range from the biblical—the *Flight into Egypt* and the *Way to Emmaus*—to the secular—*Soldiers at Rest* (fig. 113) and the *Crafty Bird-Catcher*. The stories, however, merely accompany the views, serving as convenient pretexts for the magnificent mountainscapes that unfold behind them; the figures are tucked away into corners, almost as afterthoughts. Rarely had landscape been given such pride of place as subject matter.

The dramatic impact of these prints can best be appreciated by considering the typical style of Netherlandish landscapes of the time. The most common form had been established by Joachim Patinir some forty years before Bruegel executed the Large Landscapes. In Patinir's splendid *Penitence of Saint Jerome* (cat. no. 88) the main figures, placed at the very front of the composition, are emphasized. Behind them a wide and varied landscape, rather fanciful and stylized, tilts dramatically upward, each element distinct and receiving equal treatment. By contrast, in Bruegel's *Saint Jerome in the Wilderness* (fig. 114) the minute figure of the saint in the lower right corner almost merges with the setting. The horizon is lower, the progression of forms into the distance more believable, and the rock formations are truer to nature. Bruegel based these naturalistic views on sketches he made during his trips through the Alps, and, indeed, he gave similarly majestic and realistic treatment to his native Netherlands in the engraving entitled *Wooded Region* (fig. 115).

Bruegel was not the first artist to produce expansive and realistic interpretations of Netherlandish or Alpine scenery. Cornelis Massys drew rather intimate depictions of the Flemish countryside in the 1530s and 1540s, and earlier artists active in German lands rendered Alpine vistas in ink-and-wash drawings with equal breadth and naturalism; Albrecht Dürer, for example, created colorful landscape sketches on his trip to Italy in 1495 and incorporated some of these views into the backgrounds of his prints. In the 1520s Albrecht Altdorfer even etched nine small examples of pure landscape for a limited audience. But these works were personal or intended for a rather small group of connoisseurs.

Fig. 113. Jan and Lucas van Doetecum after Pieter Bruegel the Elder, *Soldiers at Rest*, about 1555–56. Etching and engraving. The Metropolitan Museum of Art, New York

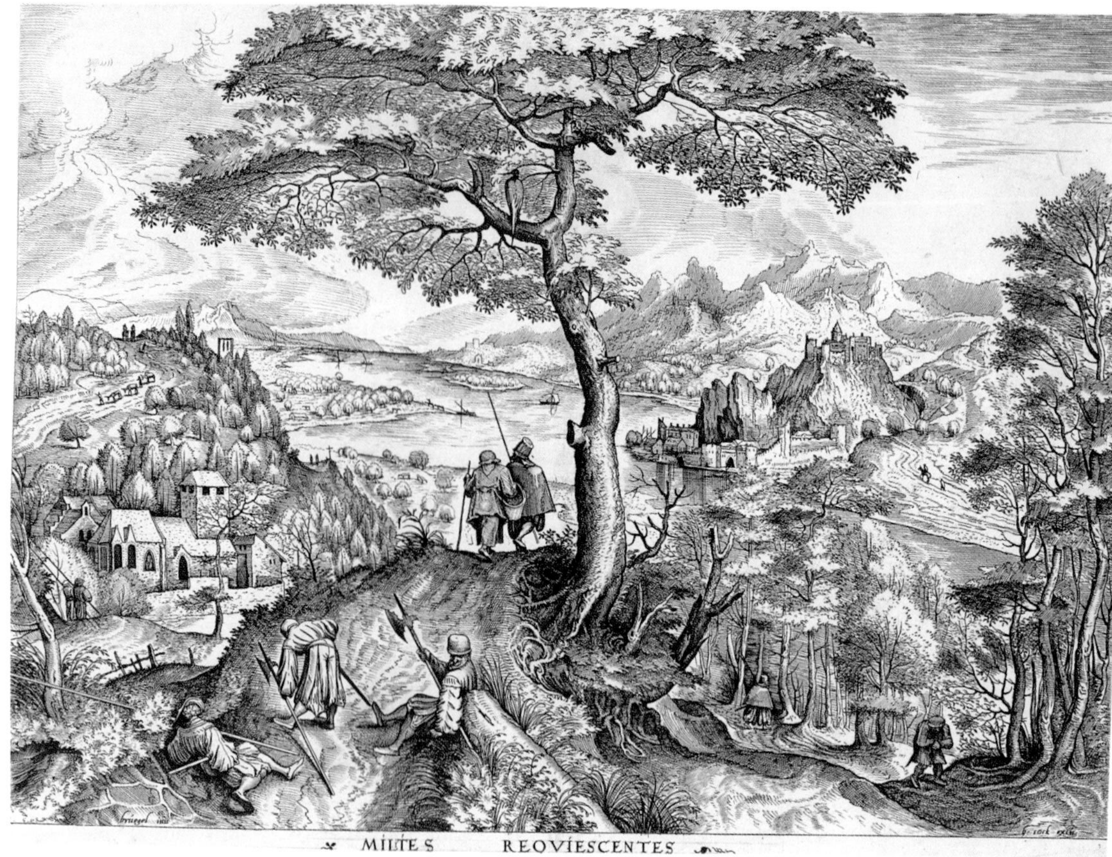

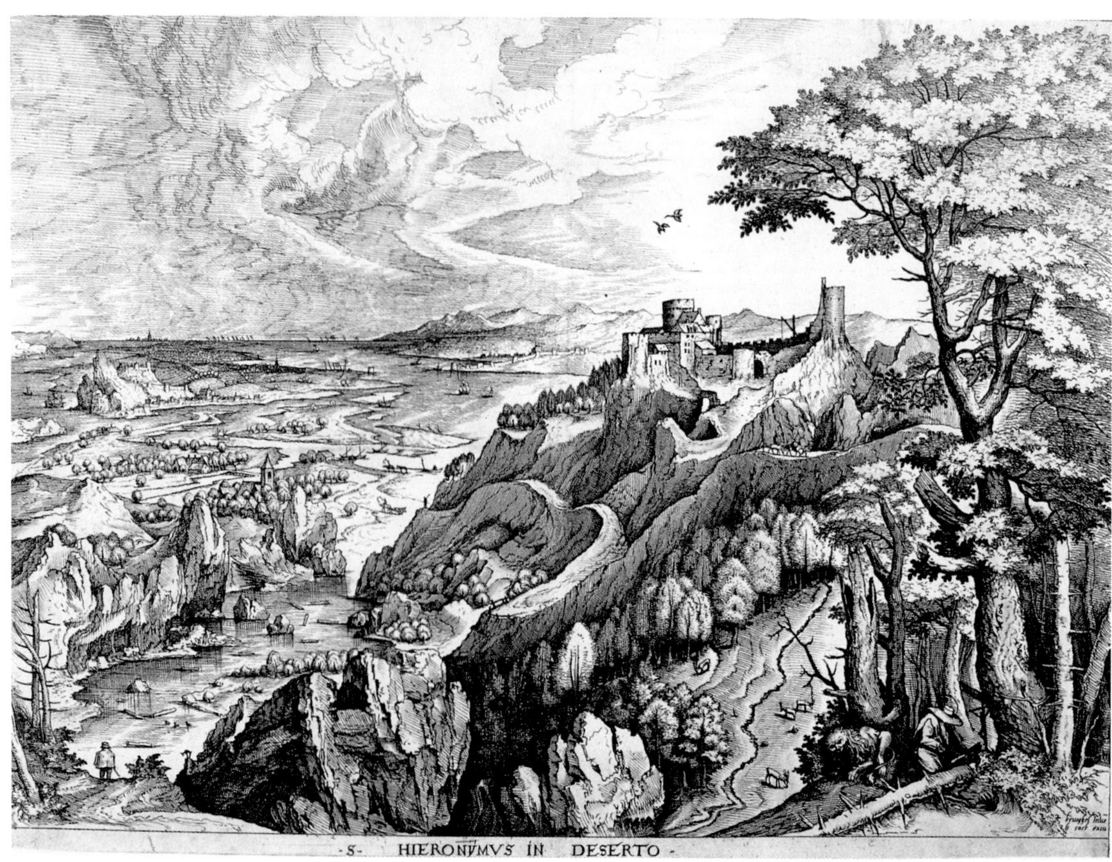

Fig. 114. Jan and Lucas van Doetecum after Pieter Bruegel the Elder, *Saint Jerome in the Wilderness*, about 1555–56. Etching and engraving. The Metropolitan Museum of Art, New York

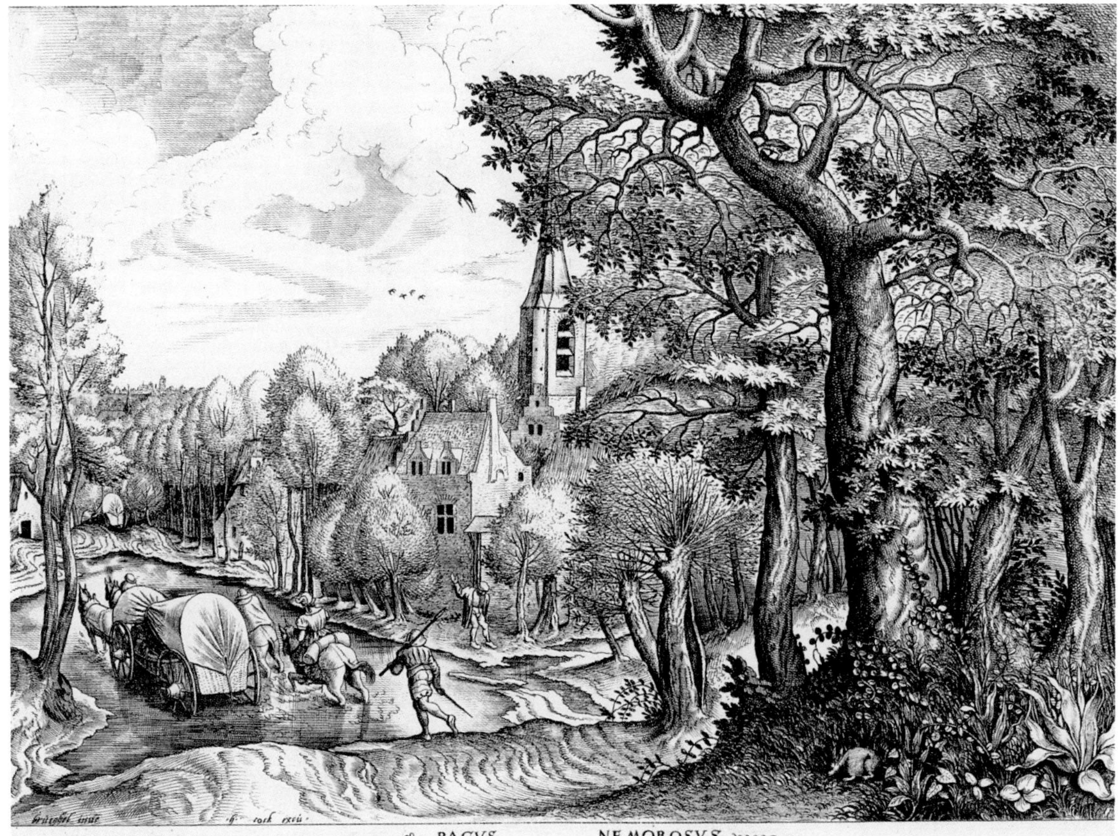

Fig. 115. Jan and Lucas van Doetecum after Pieter Bruegel the Elder, *Wooded Region*, about 1555–56. Etching and engraving. The Metropolitan Museum of Art, New York

The purpose of Bruegel's landscape drawings and the prints based on them was quite different. Hieronymus Cock, the main publisher of his prints, distributed them throughout most of Europe, and judging from the number of impressions that have survived, he had them produced in relatively large quantities. Thus, Bruegel was the first to conceive of naturalistic landscape as something major, a form to be appreciated as a subject in itself and circulated to a wide audience.

Bruegel made the etching *Rabbit Hunters*, published by Hieronymus Cock in 1560 (fig. 116), a few years after he created the designs for the Large Landscapes. As in that series, a small section of land in the foreground anchors the broad and varied landscape that lies beyond, here made up of mountains, hills, and a river valley. At the lower right a hunter aims his crossbow at some small rabbits on the hillside, while a second man, with a spear, circles around the tree behind him. It is a subject with the sort of ambiguity common to Bruegel's work: What is the second man's purpose? Is the hunter himself being hunted? Although not a professional engraver, Bruegel worked on the etching plate himself to produce the only print he ever took beyond the design stage. He almost completely eliminated outlines in favor of spirited dots and dashes that echo the graphic vocabulary of his drawings and create a sense of atmosphere and light.

A few years later he made this sense of atmosphere a defining characteristic of the Months, the series of six paintings to which the *Harvesters* (cat. no. 102) belongs. Painting, a medium in which he was more at home than in prints, provided a greater range of possibilities for color and tone than the dots and dashes of the etched line. In the Months, Bruegel captured not just the most obvious aspects of weather, such as snow and sun, but also the specific type of light and atmospheric quality particular to different times of the year. The somber skies and the rough waters of the *Gloomy Day* (Kunsthistorisches Museum, Vienna), for example, summon up the damp days and penetrating winds of February and March. The compositional structure

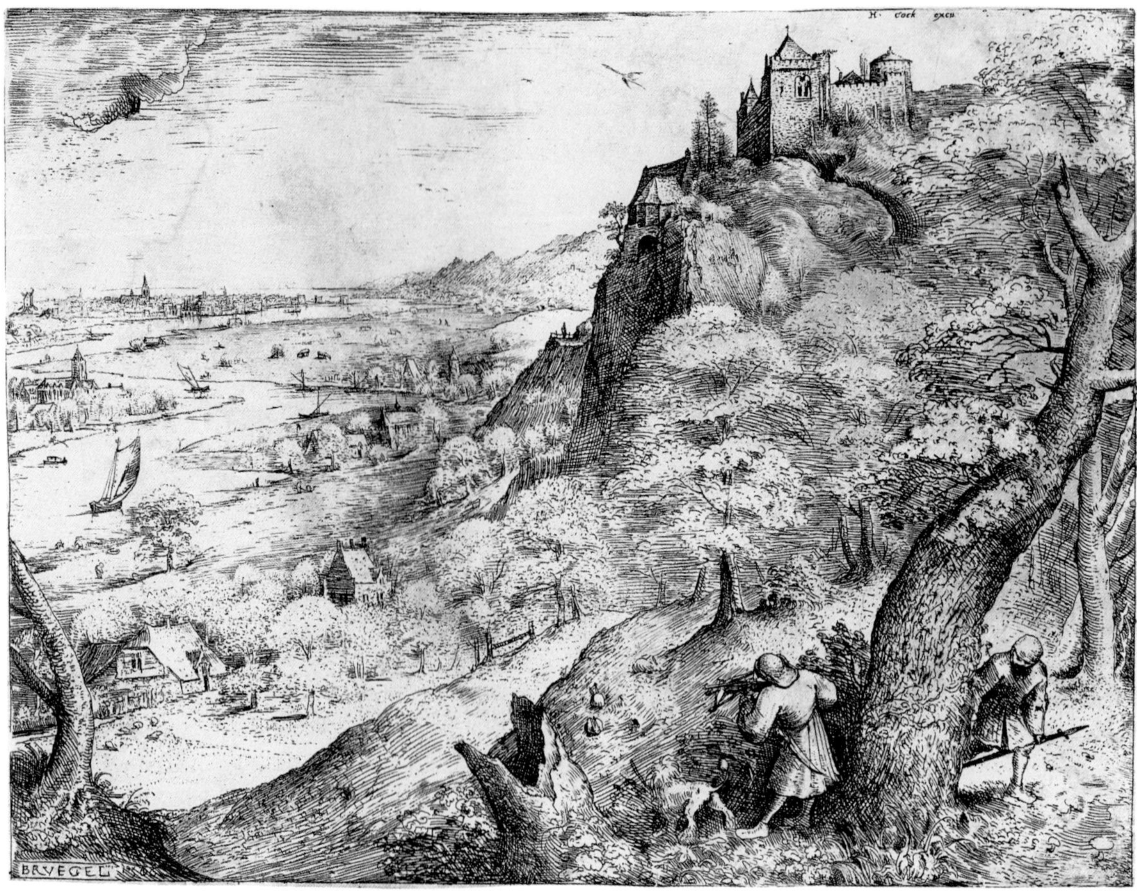

Fig. 116. Pieter Bruegel the Elder, *The Rabbit Hunters*, 1560. Etching. The Metropolitan Museum of Art, New York

is more sophisticated in the Months than in the prints. Instead of pitching the viewer abruptly down into the valleys from his little scenic overlooks, Bruegel eased the transitions into the distance with large foreground plateaus that gently descend to the low-lying areas beyond.

The Months had been a favored subject since the Middle Ages, but in illumination rather than in painting. Bruegel's source was illuminated calendar pages in contemporary manuscripts. Here, as in so many other works, Bruegel elevated scenes commonly found in small formats by endowing them with the large scale, subtle handling, and greater intricacy and complexity he could bring to bear through painting.

In his own time as today, Bruegel was most famous for his peasant subjects. Images of industrious figures working the land and amorous peasant couples embracing, by turn serious or satirical, allegorical or moralizing, had a long tradition. Hieronymus Bosch's paintings of proverbs and more immediate models by such contemporaries as Pieter Aertsen and Jan van Amstel were influential for Bruegel. But Bruegel's biblical references and moralistic intent, unlike those of his contemporaries, are often subtly presented and enigmatic. His faceless figures and unusual twists on traditional imagery seem to have been created expressly to prompt discussion and personal interpretation.

According to Van Mander, Bruegel and the Nuremberg merchant Hans Franckert on occasion disguised themselves in peasant clothes and attended country fairs and weddings: "Here Bruegel entertained himself observing the nature of the peasants—in eating, drinking, dancing, leaping, lovemaking and other amusements—which he then most animatedly and subtly imitated with paint. . . ." Whether or not Van Mander's account is factual, the story underscores the quality of observation Bruegel brought to the treatment of rustic subjects.

Some of his peasant scenes had their sources in contemporary theater. His lively drawing the

Wedding of Mopsus and Nisa (fig. 117), for example, represents a coarse, bedraggled bride led from the nuptial tent by a prancing groom and surrounded by a motley band of figures. The drawing, executed on a woodblock, was meant to serve as a design for a woodcut; for some reason the carving of the block was carried out only in the upper left corner and then was abandoned for an engraving plate. The story of Mopsus and Nisa derives from the eighth *Eclogue* of the Roman poet Virgil, which by Bruegel's day had been corrupted into humorous popular plays for Flemish fairs and carnivals. The ludicrous scene, in which Virgil's mythical lovers have been transformed into coarse Flemish peasants, appears to represent performers at such festivals; the man on the left even sports a false nose.

Certain of his country scenes present peasants in a more laudatory light. The Months series, for instance, with its hardworking laborers who, heads bowed, go about their tasks in all manner of weather, honors their industrious toil. This noble view of the peasant, like the comic one, can be traced to Virgil, who praised labor on the land in his *Georgics*. By Bruegel's time portrayals of working peasants had also come to be associated with diligence and virtue. But the figures harvesting, herding, and hunting in the Months would have evoked for some contemporary spectators related themes as well, namely the seasonal agricultural routine and the bountifulness of the land. Others, most notably the wealthy urbanite Niclaes Jongelinck, the Antwerp merchant who commissioned the series, might have been reminded of the prosperous local industries that had enriched them.

The figure of the man resting with legs splayed in the foreground of the *Harvesters* was repeated by Bruegel in the *Land of Cockaigne* of 1567 (Alte Pinakothek, Munich), a painting that represents characters who are the antithesis of the diligent farmer. According to folktale, the land was an overeater's delight and could be reached only by eating one's way through three miles of porridge. An engraving by Pieter van der Heyden that reproduces *Land of Cockaigne* in reverse (fig. 118) is accompanied by a Flemish inscription that reinforces the moralistic aspect of this depiction of a land of pure sloth and gluttony: "The lazy and gluttonous farmers, soldiers, and clerks get and taste all without working. The gardens are sausages, the houses are made of tarts. The fowl fly by already roasted."

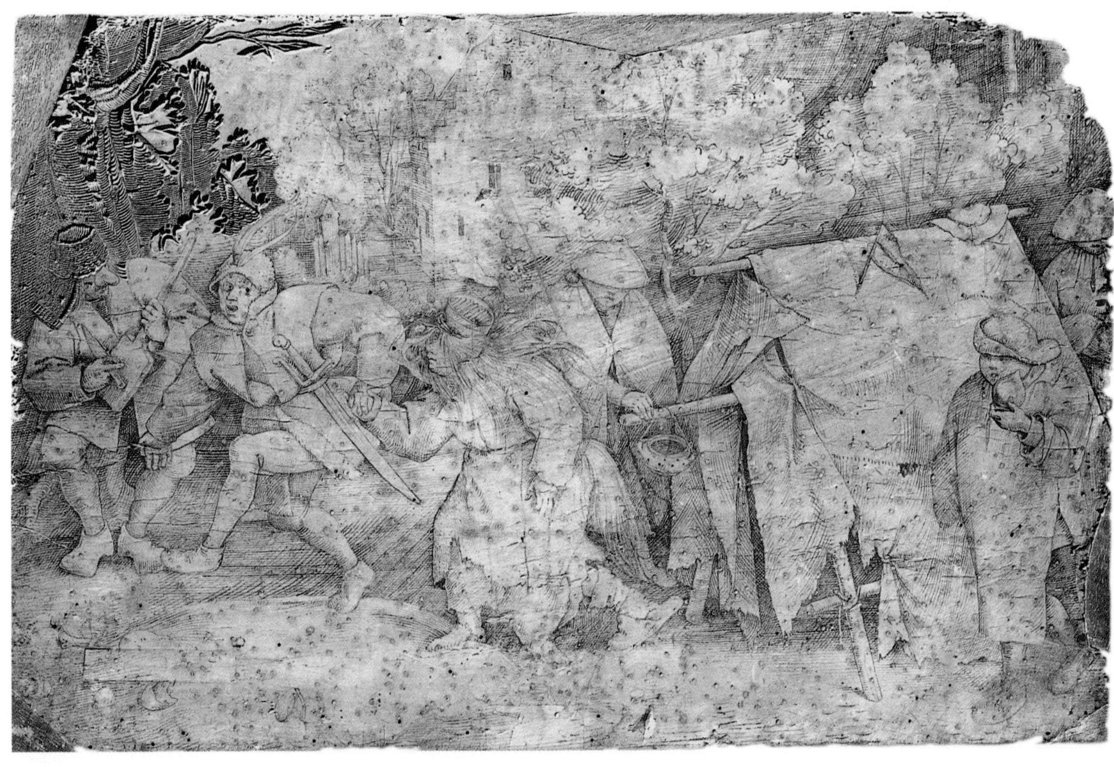

Fig. 117. Pieter Bruegel the Elder, *The Wedding of Mopsus and Nisa*, 1566. Pen and ink on partially carved woodblock. The Metropolitan Museum of Art, New York

Fig. 118. Pieter van der Heyden after Pieter Bruegel the Elder, *Land of Cockaigne*, about 1567. Engraving. The Metropolitan Museum of Art, New York

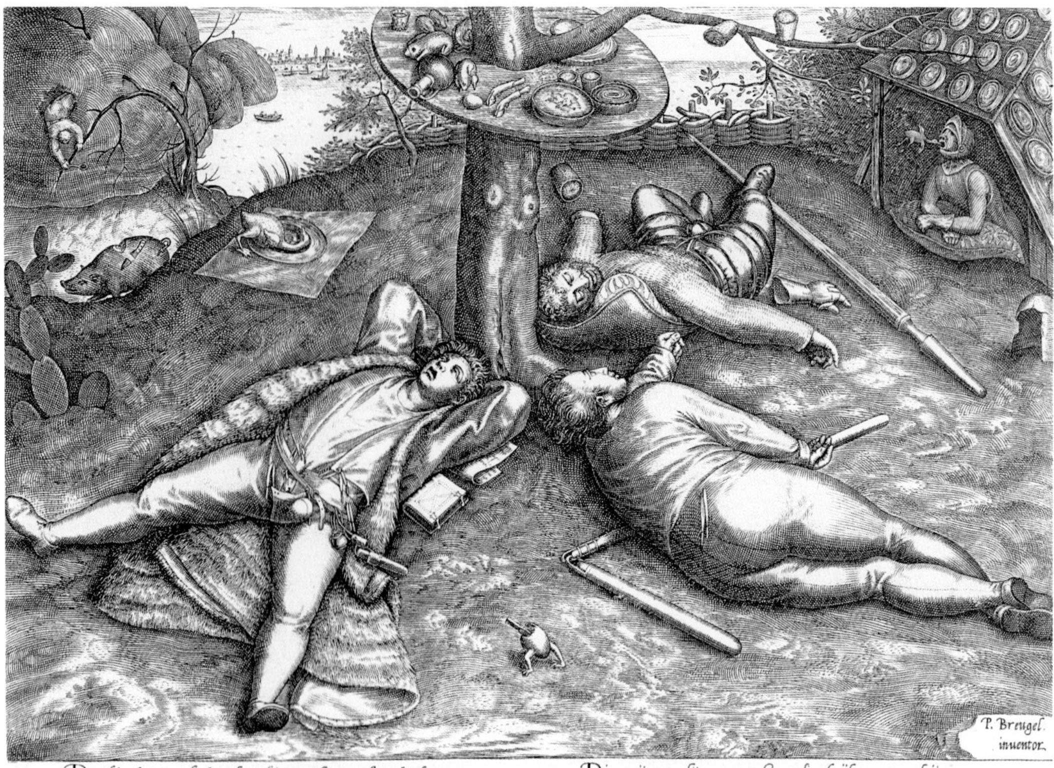

Fig. 119. Pieter van der Heyden after Pieter Bruegel the Elder, *Summer*, 1570. Engraving. The Metropolitan Museum of Art, New York

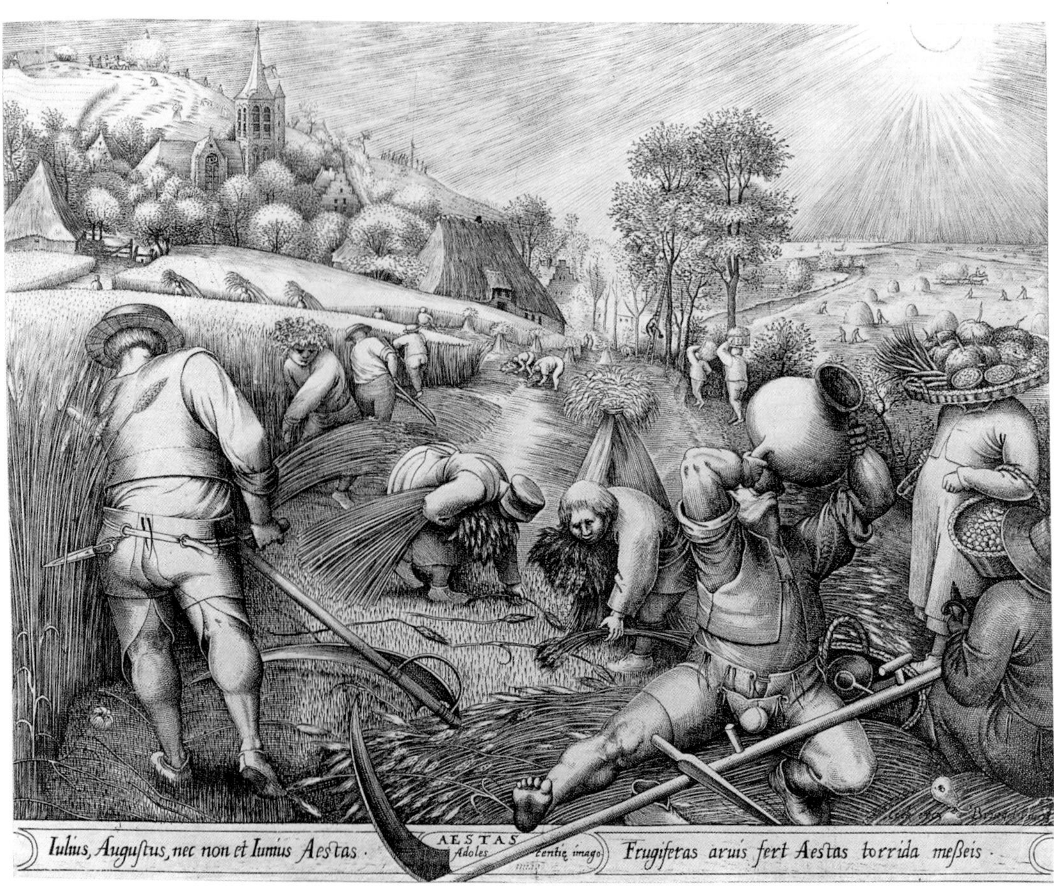

At about the same time he painted the *Harvesters*, Bruegel designed the print *Summer* (fig. 119), also a scene of harvesters but one that he gave a somewhat different treatment. The peasants in *Summer* are hard at work, except for one man in the foreground who has laid aside his scythe, which overshoots the border of the image, as he drinks from a large jar. The workers are anonymous, their backs turned to the viewer, their heads bowed or obscured by their headdresses. Some even fuse with their equipment. On the right, for instance, a woman carrying a basket of vegetables hardly appears to have a head, for her basket has become her head; she has literally turned into the fruits of the land. Bruegel endowed the figures with a certain nobility through the use of forms inspired by his study of classical sculpture, yet at the same time he subverted their grandeur by abstracting their forms and giving them a comical twist. Like many of Bruegel's works, this image can be appreciated on several levels. Not only a celebration of the labors of particular months and the diligence of the peasants, it is as well a picture that no doubt was meant to amuse.

Many have searched for possible clues to the meanings of Bruegel's work in the attitudes and beliefs that the artist and his patrons might have held—but these views offer few sure explanations. The picture that can be compiled of Bruegel's patrons is a partial one, since most cannot be identified. However, the available evidence seems to indicate that, in general, they were wealthy, well-educated residents of the prosperous cities of Antwerp and Brussels, men who would certainly have considered peasants a lower social class. But whether they would have condemned the often raucous country fairs and weddings that Bruegel interpreted is a matter of disagreement among scholars. It is clear that these patrons represent a range of religious and political viewpoints. The Spanish rulers of the southern Netherlands faced opposition from various factions, in particular the Calvinists, and turmoil erupted in 1566, dividing the citizenry. Among Bruegel's patrons can be counted Antoine Perrenot de Granvelle, archbishop of Mechelen and counselor to Margaret, duchesse de Parma and regent of the Netherlands, who acquired several paintings by Bruegel, including a *Flight into Egypt*. He would have held religious beliefs and, no doubt, political opinions quite different from those of the humanist Abraham Ortelius, the owner of a *Death of the Virgin* painted by Bruegel and member of a clandestine sect, the Family of Love, that rejected all religious ceremony and hierarchy. That Bruegel also belonged to the Family of Love has generally been thought unlikely, but the possibility has remained a matter of conjecture. Indeed, the relative paucity of documents concerning the artist's life and, more important, his beliefs has left the nature of his intentions open to interpretation. Van Mander's admittedly questionable biography of Bruegel intriguingly asserts that, as the artist lay dying, he had his wife burn some of the drawings that "were too caustic or derisory, either because he was sorry or that he was afraid that on their account she would get into trouble or she might have to answer for them."

Did Bruegel produce imagery that disparaged the Spanish government and the Catholic religion? Was he trumpeting his national pride in his land and its people when he depicted Flemish peasants? Did he sympathize with them, admire their steady working of the land, and identify with their values? Or did he, rather, make fun of their foolishness and immoral behavior and look down on them? Or was he perhaps using them to parody the foolish behavior of urban residents or to allegorize contemporary historical and religious events? Unfortunately, there are no certain answers.

Bruegel's depictions of peasants and the land possess a naturalism, a humanist perspective, and a spirited graphic rendering that endow them with a profoundly modern appearance absent from portrayals of the subjects by his predecessors. They were copied time and time again by his prolific offspring and by his contemporaries, and they set the course for the development of both landscape and genre scenes in the southern and northern Netherlands in the seventeenth century.

NADINE M. ORENSTEIN

References: Gibson 1977a; Freedberg et al. 1989; Van Mander 1994, 233 recto–234 recto; Butts and Koerner 1995; Meadow et al. 1996; Mielke 1996.

Pieter Bruegel the Elder, active by 1551, died 1569

102. The Harvesters, dated 1565

Oil on wood; overall, including added strips at top, bottom, and right, 46⅞ x 63¾ in. (119 x 162 cm); original painted surface 45⅞ x 62⅞ in. (116.5 x 159.5 cm)
Signed and dated (lower right): BRVEGEL / [MD]LXV [now largely illegible]
Rogers Fund, 1919 19.164

Provenance: Niclaes Jongelinck, Antwerp ([by 1566]; the paintings are cited as surety for a debt in a document of 1566 and may have been returned to him, although they are not mentioned in the inventory of his estate [d. 1570]); [Hane van Wijke, Antwerp (1594), sold to Antwerp City Council for fl 1,400 as a gift for Archduke Ernst on the occasion of his triumphal entry into Antwerp in July 1594]; Archduke Ernst, governor of the Netherlands, Brussels ([1594–d. 1595]; inventory July 17, 1595, nos. 7–12, as "Sechs taffell, von 12 Monathenn des Jars von Bruegel"); Emperor Rudolf II (d. 1612), Prague; Archduke Leopold Wilhelm, governor of the Netherlands, Brussels and Vienna ([b. 1614] d. 1662; inventory 1659, nos. 582–86, as "Fünff grosse Stuckh einer Grossen, warin die Zeithen desz Jahrs von Öhlfarb auf Holz . . . Original vom alten Brögel"); Emperor Leopold I, Vienna (1662–d. 1705); Imperial collection, Vienna (until 1809); Count Antoine-François Andréossy, Vienna and Paris (1809–16; his sale, Pérignon, Paris, March

It is fair to say that no more satisfying image of a wheat field, the labor of harvesting, or the atmosphere of late summer has ever been painted. Moving well beyond the panoramic landscapes of Joachim Patinir (cat. no. 88), in which sacred figures and picturesque vignettes—all competing for our attention—recede in neat horizontal rows, Bruegel created here a brilliantly integrated and harmonious secular universe featuring peasant labors within a nature of arresting realism. Blanketing the hillside, a ripe field of wheat has been partially cut and stacked, while in the foreground a group of peasants, pausing in their work, picnic in the relative shade of a pear tree. Behind them and to their left we see that work continues: a couple gather wheat into bundles and tie them; three men cut the stalks with scythes; and women, making their way through a corridor in the field, carry stacks of grain over their shoulders. In the valley a wagon heaped with wheat is pulled by oxen along the main road, villagers play a game of cock throwing in one field, while monks swim in a pond. Beyond this valley is another wheat-covered hillside, and in the haze near the horizon we can make out a bay with the traffic of several ships. A church is visible at the upper right, and at the far right a man shakes the branches of an apple tree as two small figures gather the fallen fruit. In all of this there is an intoxicating sense of elapsed time and of continuity.

The focus of the picture is the group of peasants picnicking in the foreground, absorbed by appetite and the pleasure of a shared meal. They have used stacks of grain as benches and consume—in addition to pears from the tree—bread and bowlfuls of milk into which bits of bread have been broken. Perhaps their milk is kept cool in the large earthenware pitcher sheltered in the grain at the far left. Opposite them a man sleeps in a position of complete abandon; perhaps he is not exhausted from honest labor but rather, as Sullivan suggests, may have had too much to drink and illustrates Proverbs 10:5: "He that gathereth in summer is a wise son; he that sleepeth in harvest is a son that causeth shame." (The figure of the sleeping man is repeated in Bruegel's *Land of Cockaigne*, a painting in the Alte Pinakothek, Munich.)

Typical of the artist's wry humor, two peasants glance out at us curiously as they eat, leaving us to wonder who is the viewer and who the subject. Elsewhere mankind and nature appear inextricably bound together: a woman gathering wheat in the background, with grain growing out of her headdress, has taken on the form of one of her haystacks, while the heads of two women crossing the field with grain stacks over their shoulders seem from a distance to have undergone a similar metamorphosis.

The panel is part of a series commissioned from Bruegel by the wealthy Antwerp merchant Niclaes Jongelinck, apparently as part of an extensive decorative scheme for his suburban home, Ter Beken. Of Bruegel's pictures, five are extant: our *Harvesters*; the *Gloomy Day*, *Hunters in the Snow*, and the *Return of the Herd* (all Kunsthistorisches Museum, Vienna); and *Haymaking* (Roudnice Lobkowicz collection, Nelahozeves, Czech Republic). Jongelinck was an avid patron of Bruegel's and in the 1566 inventory of his collection "16 pieces" by the artist are listed; of these only two independent works and the "Twelff maenden" (twelve months) are mentioned by name, suggesting that the series may originally have included twelve panels. However, by 1595 the panels, purchased by the city of Antwerp and presented as a gift to Archduke Ernst, are described as six paintings representing the twelve months. De Tolnay, relating the pictures to the tradition of calendar illustration in illuminated manuscripts, noted that each combines labors and pastimes that would normally have been allotted two separate months, and argued on this account that the original number of panels was six. He suggested—again based on analysis of the motifs included in each panel—

Opposite: Detail, cat. no. 102

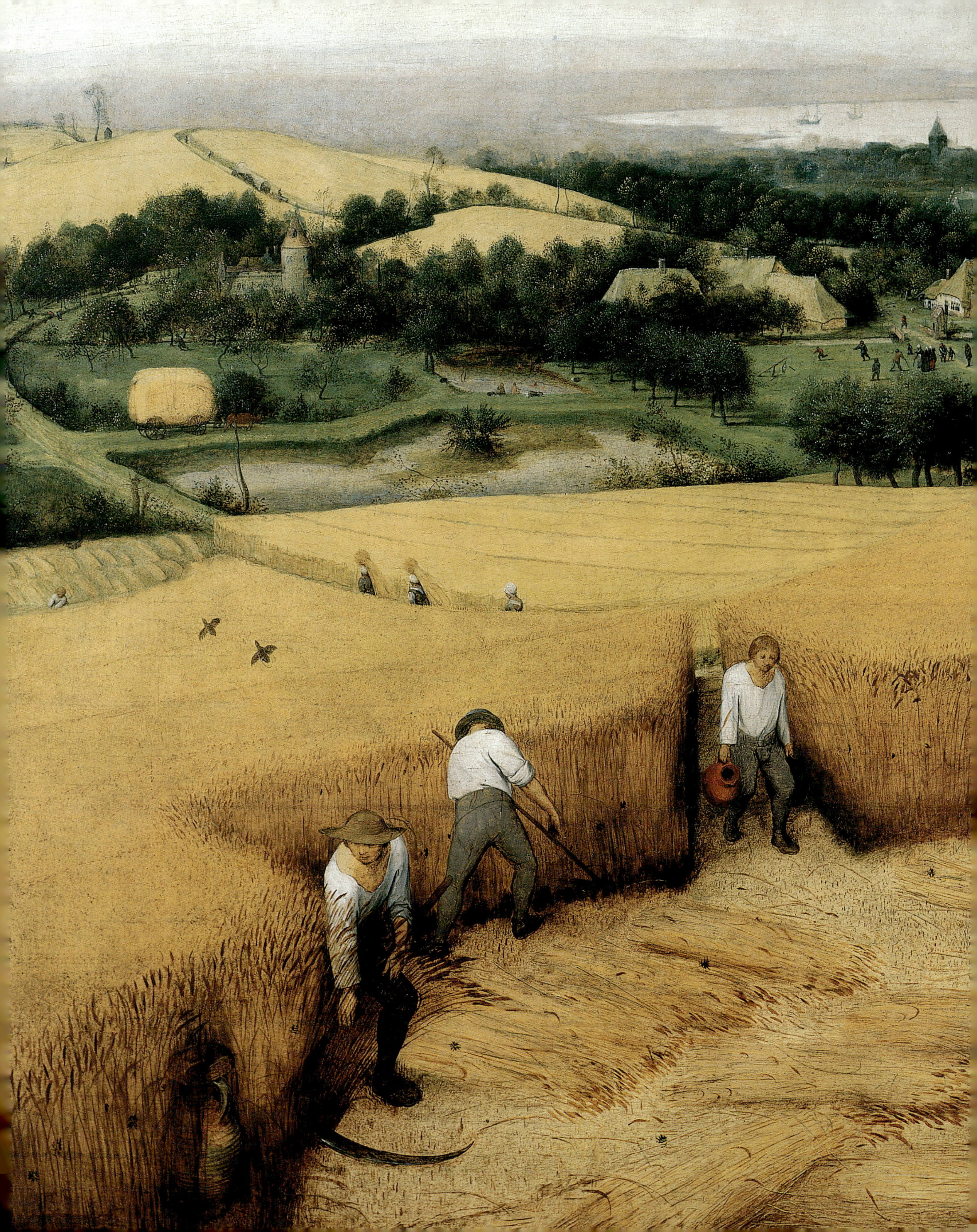

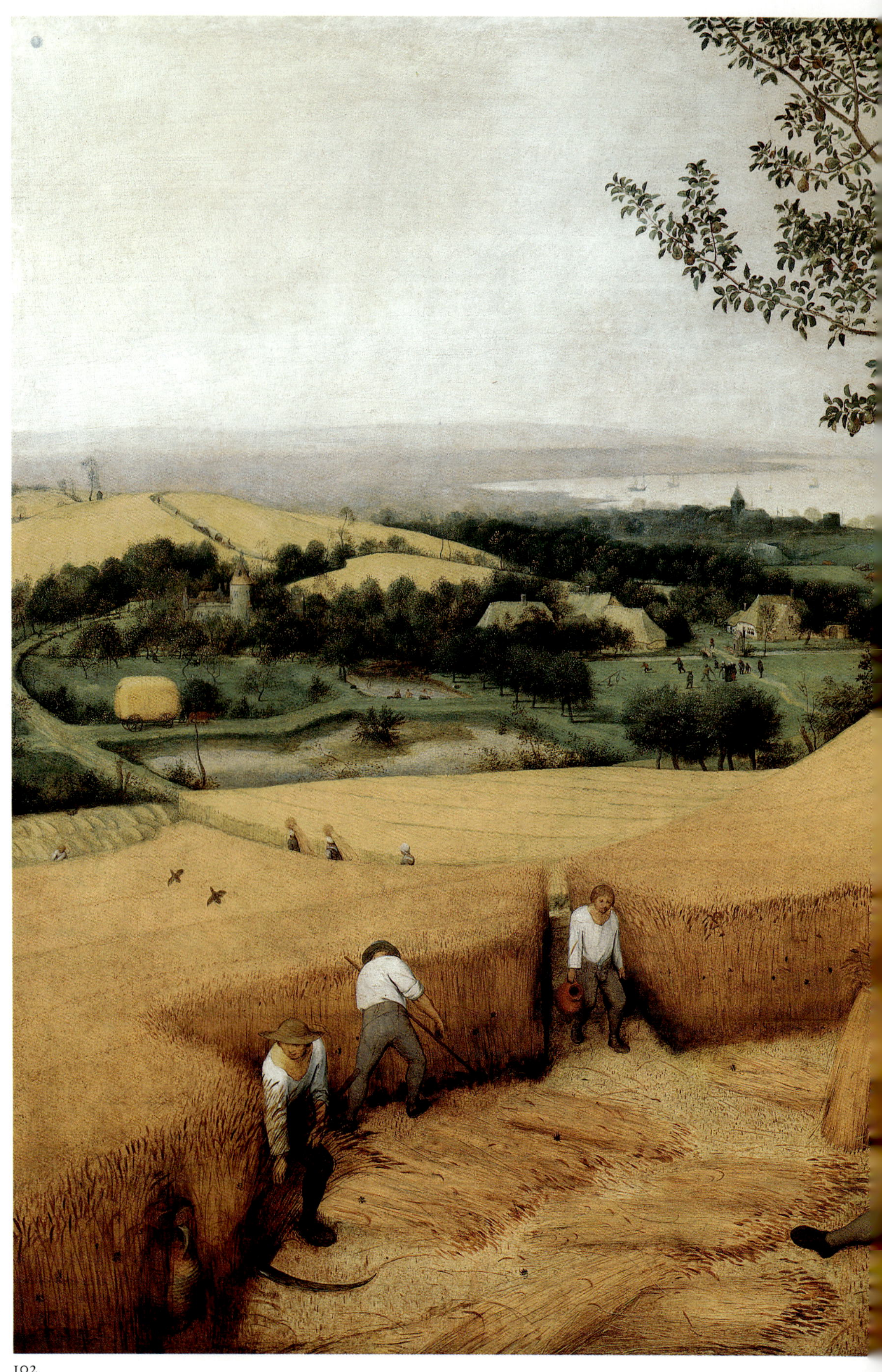

102

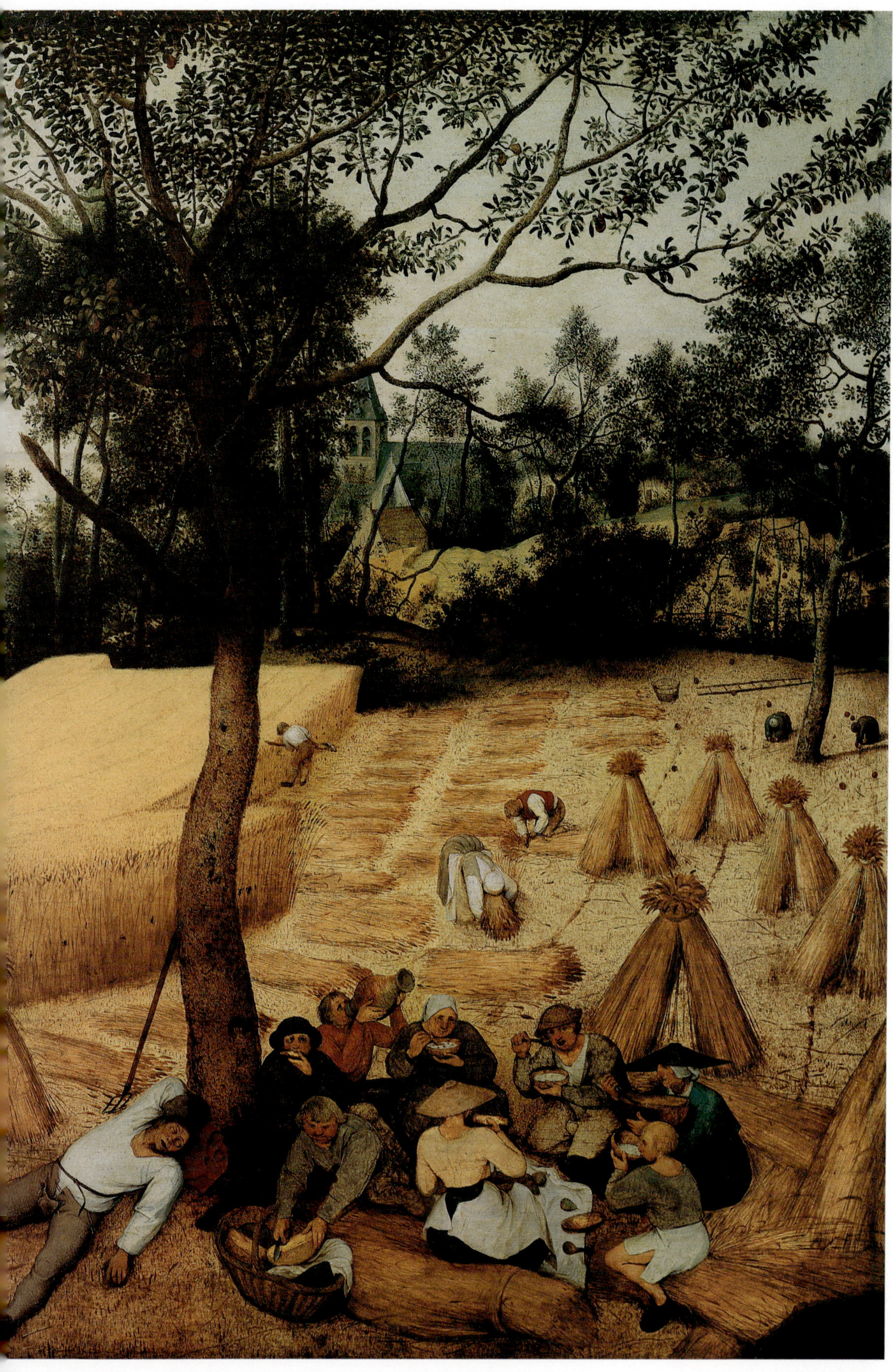

11, 1816, no. 1, as "Par un maître de l'ancienne . . . École allemande . . . Avec la date de 1546," for Fr 90.11); Jacques Antoine Doucet, Paris (until shortly before 1912; sold to Cels); Paul Jean Cels, Brussels (shortly before 1912–1919).

References: Teniers 1660, unpaginated, [p. 2] of text; Mechel 1784, p. 184, no. 162; Coremans 1847, pp. 101, 141; Berger 1883, p. cxliii; Engerth 1884, pp. 156–57; Hulin de Loo 1907, pp. 302, 304, 343–44, no. B.34; Burroughs 1921, pp. 96–99, 102–3, ill.; Denucé 1932, p. 5; Glück 1932, pp. 40–42, 60, 66–69, colorpl. 22; Tolnai 1934, pp. 125–28; De Tolnay 1935, pp. 37–38, 40, 55, 69–70 nn. 85d–e, 84, no. 19, figs. 79–81 on pls. 48, 49; Glück 1936, pp. 22–23, 43, no. 29, colorpls. 29, 29a–c; Michel 1936, pp. 105–7, fig. 1; Friedländer 1924–37, vol. 14 (1937), pp. 27–29, 60, pl. 28, no. 28; Wehle and Salinger 1947, pp. 156–59, ill.; Novotny 1948, pp. 1–41, no. 3, pls. 21–27; Held 1949, pp. 142–43; Grossmann [1955], pp. 19, 30–31, 36, 197–99, pls. 99–103; Bialostocki 1956, pp. 23–24, 27–30, 34, 36, 39, 46, 48; Grossmann 1959, p. 342; Menzel 1966, pp. 31, 43, 70–76, 96, colorpl. 56; Gibson 1977a, pp. 147–48, 154, 156–58, pls. 110, 128; Demus 1981, pp. 86–94; Van Miegroet 1986, pp. 29–35, ill.; Demus 1987, pp. 82, 84, 86; Gibson 1989, pp. 70–75, 125, nn. 97–99, fig. 5.30; Buchanan 1990a, pp. 102, 106, 112; Buchanan 1990b, pp. 541–50, figs. 18, 27; Sullivan 1994, pp. 43–44; Wied 1994, pp. 25–27, 94, 103, 160, color ill. p. 103, pl. 160, no. 30; Wied 1996, pp. 900, 902.

that the series begins with December rather than with January. *Hunters in the Snow* would thus represent December–January; the *Gloomy Day*, February–March; the missing painting, April–May; *Haymaking*, June–July; our *Harvesters*, August–September; and the *Return of the Herd*, October–November. Van Miegroet has recently published a drawing by Pieter Stevens comparable to the *Gloomy Day* and bearing the inscriptions *februarius* and *mert*, lending support to De Tolnay's thesis.

Although most contemporary scholars tend to accept De Tolnay's view, Gibson and others maintain that there must initially have been twelve panels. No doubt the original number of works in the series and the month or months represented in each picture will remain points of contention. Many of the activities shown in our panel—harvesting wheat, picking apples, and peasants eating and drinking—appear as Labors for the month of August in contemporary calendar cycles, and none are traditionally associated with September; those scholars, therefore, who believe there were originally twelve works in the series generally view our panel as August, but it has also been identified as July and July–August. Novotny, Demus, and others reasonably suggest that Bruegel may have had in mind a cycle of extended seasons of the year that depicted the changing moods of land, sky, and atmosphere. This position is supported by evidence of a Netherlandish tradition dividing the year into six parts, with early spring and late autumn augmenting the four main seasons. The surviving panels from Bruegel's series are identified by most of these authors as early spring (the *Gloomy Day*), early summer (*Haymaking*), late summer (the *Harvesters*), fall (the *Return of the Herd*), and deep winter (*Hunters in the Snow*); the missing panel would have represented late spring.

As Buchanan (1990a, 1990b) has pointed out, Jongelinck owned four series of works made by contemporary Netherlandish artists for his home: Bruegel's Months; the Seven Liberal Arts and the twelve Labors of Hercules, both commissioned from Frans Floris; and the Seven Planets, a sculpture series by Jongelinck's brother Jacques. It is not surprising that he chose to show these subjects together at Ter Beken, for astrological themes, as Buchanan notes, were often combined in decorative schemes—as they were in early calendar illustrations—where planets appear as ruling deities who govern the months and the labors of men. We know that a room was devoted to each of Floris's series, and it can reasonably be assumed that the Months and the Seven Planets were also displayed in their own rooms. Buchanan suggests that Bruegel's paintings were installed in Jongelinck's dining room, where their subject matter would have been especially appropriate; here they could offer the merchant a pastoral respite from the bustling commercial life of Antwerp. Side by side the panels would, no doubt, have been breathtaking, and the artist appears to have orchestrated the contrasting color harmonies and effects of atmosphere and light, each keyed to the time of year portrayed, among and between the paintings as carefully as he did the elements within them.

This remarkable series of pictures is a watershed in the history of Western art. The religious pretext for landscape painting—so strictly adhered to by artists of both the northern and southern Renaissance—has been abandoned, and we have in its place a new humanism, at once pastoral and vernacular. Although the panels are often compared in spirit to Virgil's *Georgics*, widely read and admired by cultivated Europeans of the sixteenth century, Bruegel was hardly a propagandist for peasant virtue or the joys of the yeoman's life celebrated by the poet; rather he was a passionate observer of nature in all its forms, including human nature, with a genius for narrative and the defining gesture. His unidealized scenes of peasant life, in the Months and elsewhere in his oeuvre, anticipate the development in Flanders and Holland of genre and peasant scenes as subjects in their own right—a flourishing area of artistic endeavor in the next century. In our painting in particular, and in others of the series perhaps to a lesser extent, the artist created scenes that can be read with pleasure as narratives but which are also timeless. The extraordinary variety of seasonal motifs and vignettes of peasant life gathered into a single work does not seem contrived; on the contrary, there is conveyed a vivid sense that Bruegel has actually been in this place and witnessed this entirely believable range of activity. Indeed, Novotny has called the five paintings of the series "Mischlandschaften," partly invented and partly inspired by landscape studies Bruegel brought back from an Italian journey, and Michel and others have observed that the setting of our painting bears a remarkable resemblance to views of Geneva seen from surrounding villages.

Bruegel's drawing *Summer* (Kunsthalle, Hamburg) is a harvest scene with some elements in common with our *Harvesters* but is, nonetheless, quite different from it in composition. His *Spring* (Albertina, Vienna), from the same series of drawings, is inscribed by the artist *De Lenten Meert April Meij*, and may resemble in subject the missing panel of the Months that presumably represented April–May or early spring. The *Autumn* and *Winter* of the drawings sequence were completed by Hans Bol, and the four designs were published as an engraved set by Hieronymus Cock in 1570. MSdJ

Biographies of the Artists

JEAN BELLEGAMBE, *active 1504–34*

Bellegambe was the most sought-after painter of Douai and produced numerous works for the churches and religious communities of the surrounding region, which was under the rule of the Burgundian-Habsburg dynasty. As Friedländer remarked, the artist worked "on the outer fringes of both Netherlandish and French culture." Bellegambe may have trained in nearby Valenciennes in the workshop of Marmion, which Provost inherited before 1491. The agitation of Bellegambe's later compositions and the prevalence in them of Romanist architectural detail suggest familiarity with the work of the Antwerp Mannerists.

SIMON BENING, *about 1483/84–1561*

Born in Ghent and one of the most successful illuminators of the day, Simon probably apprenticed with his father, Alexander Bening. Although he registered his illuminator's mark in Bruges in 1500 and joined the illuminators' Guild of Saint John and Saint Luke there in 1508, he continued to live in Ghent until 1519, when he permanently resettled in Bruges. Bening's first major commission, painted about 1515, for the Da Costa Hours (Pierpont Morgan Library, New York), shows his debt to the patterns and designs of the Master of the First Prayer Book of Maximilian (probably Bening's father). Shortly thereafter he contributed several full-page miniatures to the Grimani Breviary (Biblioteca Marciana, Venice), perhaps the most splendid of all sixteenth-century Flemish manuscripts, which was in the collection of Cardinal Grimani by 1520. Bening's figure style was greatly influenced by that of Gerard David, and he explored new territory in the genre of landscape, expressed above all in his calendar illustrations for Books of Hours.

HERRI MET DE BLES, *about 1510–died after 1550*

According to Van Mander and Lampsonius, Bles was born in Bouvignes, near Dinant, about 1510; he is probably the Herri de Patinir recorded in Antwerp as a master painter in 1535. Thought by some to be the nephew of Joachim Patinir, Bles shares with that artist the distinction of being among the earliest landscape painters in the southern Netherlands. Like Patinir, he preferred high viewpoints and dramatic rocky masses that divide space. However, Bles's landscapes are more atmospheric and naturalistic than Patinir's, and his figures, which usually occupy a broad area in the foreground, are harmoniously integrated with the landscape. In addition to religious themes, he painted secular scenes, showing forges and mines as well as fiery landscapes. After Patinir's death, Bles became the most widely acclaimed landscape painter in Europe. He was especially favored in Italy, where he was nicknamed Civetta (owlet) because a small owl, which Van Mander regarded as the artist's signature, often appears in his pictures.

HIERONYMUS BOSCH, *1450–1516*

Best known for his fantastic creatures, weird landscapes, and moralizing subjects, Bosch was an enormously popular and idiosyncratic painter. Born in s'Hertogenbosch in the northern Netherlands, he came from a family of painters. In 1481 he married the daughter of a well-to-do patrician and no longer had to paint for a living. He enjoyed social prominence and through the Brotherhood of Our Lady had wide social contacts that included several Spaniards. Philip the Fair ordered at least one work from him, and Queen Isabella the Catholic also owned a number of his pictures. Bosch's paintings were in great demand throughout the sixteenth century, particularly in Italy and Spain, and inspired both imitations and pastiches.

AELBERT BOUTS, *born about 1451/54, died 1549*

Aelbert was one of the two sons of Dieric Bouts who inherited the paternal workshop in Leuven. Whereas Dieric's paintings can be described as classic and austere, Aelbert's are more narrative and descriptive, with broad, somewhat coarse, physical types, showing the influence of the contemporary Antwerp Mannerists. Under his direction the workshop produced a number of large altarpieces, but it seems to have specialized in the mass production of pictures of the Man of Sorrows, the Mourning Virgin, the Head of Saint John the Baptist, and other such pre-Reformation devotional images sometimes associated with indulgences. In these works it is extremely difficult to tell where Aelbert's involvement ends and a workshop assistant's begins.

Dieric Bouts, *active by 1457, died 1475*

Along with Aelbert van Ouwater and Geertgen tot Sint Jans, Bouts is mentioned by Van Mander as one of the founders of the Haarlem school of painting, and his north Netherlandish origins are confirmed by the eloquent reserve and naïveté that persist in his mature works. We do not know when he left Haarlem or the year he first established himself in Leuven, where he became the official city painter in 1468, but he is mentioned several times in the Leuven archives, starting in 1457. His only documented works are from the middle and end of his career: the Holy Sacrament Altarpiece of 1467–68 (Sint-Pieterskerk, Leuven) and two panels from the *Justice of Emperor Otto III* (Musées Royaux des Beaux-Arts de Belgique, Brussels), one of which was installed in the Town Hall in 1473 and the other finished by assistants after the artist's death in 1475. The attributions of paintings to Bouts made prior to his arrival in Leuven are somewhat controversial: the Infancy Triptych (Prado, Madrid), which is generally accepted as his, has also been attributed to Ouwater and, at one time, to Petrus Christus.

Pieter Bruegel the Elder, *active by 1551, died 1569*

Perhaps from Breda, as Lodovico Guicciardini reports, Bruegel was trained in the workshop of the Antwerp Mannerist Pieter Coeck van Aelst but was also influenced by Coeck's brother-in-law Jan van Amstel (the Brunswick Monogrammist). After leaving Coeck's workshop, Bruegel worked for the Antwerp-based publisher Hieronymus Cock, who would later issue sixty-four of the artist's drawings as etchings. Bruegel became a master in the Guild of Saint Luke in Antwerp in 1551 and left for Italy soon afterward. The journey seems to have stimulated Bruegel's interest in landscape subjects and to have provided him with a lifetime's store of imagery.

He returned to Antwerp by 1555, the year his important series of twelve prints known as the Large Landscapes was published by Cock; his first dated paintings are from the late 1550s. The *Netherlandish Proverbs* (Gemäldegalerie, Berlin) and the *Battle between Carnival and Lent* of 1550 and *Children's Games* of 1560 (both Kunsthistorisches Museum, Vienna) are the artist's first truly characteristic works, revealing his satiric wit and keenly observant eye. Two-thirds of Bruegel's surviving output (about thirty paintings), including many of his most impressive compositions, possibly date from the last four years of his life.

Robert Campin, *about 1375–1444*

Three works by this artist—a *Standing Virgin and Child, Saint Veronica,* and *Holy Trinity* (all now in the Städelsches Kunstinstitut, Frankfurt)—were wrongly thought to have come from a nonexistent abbey at Flémalle, near Liège, giving rise to the creation of an anonymous Master of Flémalle. It is now generally agreed that this painter is identical with Robert Campin.

Campin's origins and exact date of birth remain obscure. In 1410 he acquired his citizenship in Tournai, where he was already working as a painter by 1405–6. He was dean of the Guild of Saint Luke between 1425 and 1427 and was elected to the town council. Probably the head of a large workshop, Campin accepted commissions from city officials, churches, and the bourgeoisie, made designs for banners, coats of arms, and costumes, and sometimes produced manuscript illuminations. He had two famous pupils, Rogelet de la Pasture (Rogier van der Weyden) and Jacques Daret, both of whom worked for him until 1432. The early works of Rogier and those of his master are sometimes confused.

A triptych with the Lamentation (Courtauld Institute Galleries, London) is considered the earliest of his works; among the latest is the Von Werl Altarpiece, dated 1438 (Prado, Madrid), sometimes ascribed to Rogier. While the *Annunciation Triptych* at The Cloisters (cat. no. 2) has traditionally been viewed as a key painting by the master, its attribution, as well as that of a number of other works within the Campin group, is a matter of controversy. Campin's influence was widespread, and some of his compositions were frequently copied well into the sixteenth century.

Petrus Christus, *active by 1444, died 1475/76*

Christus probably came from Baerle, a village in the duchy of Brabant, near the present Dutch-Belgian border. In July 1444 he purchased citizenship in Bruges to become a master. Nine of his works are signed and dated between 1446 and 14[5]7, the earliest being the *Portrait of a Carthusian* (cat. no. 21). That both Christus and his wife, Gaudicine, belonged to the illustrious Bruges Confraternity of Our Lady of the Dry Tree suggests not only that they enjoyed high social status but also that Christus was well positioned to attract important commissions.

Little is known about Christus's training. He had a talent for assimilating motifs as well as methods of execution and was, above all, influenced by the art of Jan van Eyck. Christus's meticulous technique is related to that of manuscript illumination; he was most assured and accomplished working on a diminutive scale, but he became increasingly adept at describing the volume of figures in large works. His attempts to convincingly render one-point perspective in his paintings culminated in the *Virgin and Child with Saints Jerome and Francis,* dated 14[5]7 (Städelsches Kunstinstitut, Frankfurt).

Gerard David, *about 1455–1523*

David was probably born in Oudewater; exactly when he emigrated from this north Netherlandish town near Haarlem to the southern Netherlands is not known. He may have spent a period of time in Dieric Bouts's Leuven workshop, which continued under Bouts's sons, Aelbert and Dieric the Younger. In 1484 David registered in the Bruges painters' guild, and he subsequently held several official posts in that organization. Although in 1515 he also registered in the Antwerp painters' guild, David continued to live in Bruges until his death.

Two documented works, the *Justice of Cambyses* of 1498 (fig. 16) and the *Virgin among Virgins* of 1509 (fig. 84), form the linchpins of David's oeuvre, around which many other paintings with similar characteristics have been grouped. David enjoyed a thriving business serving both local and foreign clients, and he was at the forefront of artists who standardized working procedures in order to facilitate production of paintings for sale on the open market.

Although David perpetuated the stylistic traditions of other north Netherlandish artists who had settled in the southern provinces (particularly Jan van Eyck and Dieric Bouts), he was also influenced to some degree by the works of Hugo van der Goes and Hans Memling and was open to Italian ideas as well.

Cornelis Engebrechtsz, *1468–1527*

In 1482 Engebrechtsz apparently received a partial payment from the monastery of Hieronymusdal, near Leiden, for a painting. From 1487 his name appeared regularly in the tax and militia-company records of Leiden, where he was trained, rose to prominence, and secured commissions from the council (a map of the city in 1522 and banners for the city trumpeters in 1525).

Engebrechtsz's early works are painted in a style close to that of Geertgen tot Sint Jans, but he established contact with the artistic centers in the southern Netherlands and in his two most important altarpieces, the *Lamentation* of about 1508 and the *Crucifixion* of 1517–22 (both Stedelijk Museum De Lakenhal, Leiden), he embraced the expressive power of the Antwerp Mannerists. These paintings form the basis for attributions to him. His later paintings display a variety of influences that probably reflect the participation of pupils, sometimes making it difficult to isolate his work from that of his collaborators, one of whom was Lucas van Leyden.

Jan van Eyck, *active by 1422, died 1441*

Van Eyck probably came from Maaseik, near Maastricht. A document dated 1422 mentions him in The Hague, where he was employed as *varlet de chambre* by John of Bavaria, count of Holland. In 1425 he moved to Bruges, serving Duke Philip the Good of Burgundy in the same capacity. Jan also was entrusted with various diplomatic missions, including an unsuccessful one to Spain in 1427 to negotiate a marriage between the duke and Isabella of Aragon and one to Lisbon in 1428–29 to secure the marriage contract between the duke and Isabella of Portugal. Thereafter, Jan remained in Bruges as court painter to Philip, but he also carried out a number of commissions for the city and for local clerics and burghers until his death.

The most famous painter of his time in Europe, Jan is considered the founder of early Netherlandish painting and its most exemplary practitioner. He was the first Netherlandish artist known to have signed and/or dated his works, in which he often included his motto "Als ich kan" (As best I can). The magnificent Ghent Altarpiece (figs. 17, 18), dated 1432 and described in an inscription as a collaboration between Jan and his brother, Hubert, marks a watershed in Western painting. Nine other paintings, dating between 1432 and 1439, are signed by Jan. Several unsigned panels, as well as one silverpoint drawing, the *Portrait of a Man (formerly identified as Cardinal Niccolò Albergati)* (fig. 56), and a few illuminations in the Turin-Milan Hours (Museo Civico, Turin), can be attributed to him.

Hugo van der Goes, *active by 1467, died 1482*

Hugo was born about 1440 in Ghent, where he enrolled in the painters' guild in 1467. Between 1468 and 1474 Hugo was regularly charged with producing decorations for civic pageants and celebrations. As one of the most notable painters of the day, he was called to Bruges to help with the decorations for the marriage of Margaret of York to Charles the Bold in 1468, and to Leuven in 1475 to evaluate the paintings left unfinished by Dieric Bouts, who had died earlier that year. He became a lay brother in the Red Cloister, near Brussels, about 1475, remaining there until his death.

His most important work is the Portinari Altarpiece (fig. 29), painted between 1473 and 1478 for the hospital church of Sant Egidio in Florence. With his *Adoration of the Shepherds* and *Adoration of the Magi* (both Gemäldegalerie, Berlin) and *Death of the Virgin* (Groeningemuseum, Bruges), it forms the core group of his oeuvre. Hugo's first paintings combine an Eyckian description of detail with an interest in spatial effects and single-point perspective. His later works, notably the *Death of the Virgin*, emphasize expressive distortion of space and figures and employ novel color harmonies.

Jan Gossart (called Mabuse), *active by 1503, died 1532*

Signatures on a number of Gossart's paintings indicate that the artist was born in or near Maubeuge (in present-day northern France). It is possible that he trained in the workshop of Gerard David in Bruges before enrolling in the Guild of Saint Luke in Antwerp in 1503. In 1508–9 Gossart accompanied Philip of Burgundy on a diplomatic mission to Italy. He made drawings of Roman antiquities and introduced classical models to the Netherlands, among which are the lifesize nude figures of Neptune and Amphitrite (fig. 105), part of the surviving decorations the artist painted in 1516 for the castle of Philip of Burgundy in Souburg (Zeeland). But Gossart also pursued an archaizing mode, copying the work of fifteenth-century Netherlandish painters such as Jan van Eyck (fig. 101). After the death of his patron in 1524, Gossart settled in Middelburg (Zeeland), where he worked for Adolf of Burgundy (see cat. no. 40). The large number of existing copies of Gossart's smaller panels—those on the theme of the Virgin and Child, for example—suggest he was the head of a lively workshop that produced paintings for the open market.

Goswijn van der Weyden, *active by 1491, died after 1538*

Goswijn, grandson of Rogier van der Weyden, settled about 1500 in Antwerp, where he directed a large and flourishing workshop. The group of relatively pedestrian works attributed to him reveals his roots in the Brussels school as well as the influence of the Antwerp painter Quentin Massys. The inconsistency in style and quality of these paintings can best be explained as the result of the participation of the workshop in their production.

Marten van Heemskerck, *1498–1574*

Born in Heemskerk (between Haarlem and Alkmaar), this north Netherlandish artist was the son of a wealthy farmer. A draftsman and print designer, he also produced more than one hundred paintings ranging from large altarpieces to portraits and small works with religious and mythological themes. Heemskerck's first dated pictures reflect the influence of Jan van Scorel, with whom he collaborated in Haarlem, beginning in 1527. In 1532, before he departed for Italy, he presented his famous *Saint Luke Painting the Virgin* (Frans Hals Museum, Haarlem) to the Guild of Saint Luke. Two sketchbooks with studies of antique ruins and statuary (Kupferstichkabinett, Berlin) have survived from his Italian sojourn, which lasted until 1536/37 and exposed him to the powerful influence of Michelangelo and Giulio Romano. These sketchbooks provided source material for many of his paintings. After his return home, Heemskerck produced work in an intensely mannerist style. The mythological and allegorical scenes that the artist conceived during his mature years in Haarlem reflect his acquaintance with Dutch humanists and engravers such as Dirck Volkertsz. Coornhert, who engraved and widely disseminated his drawings.

Jean Hey (Master of Moulins), *active 1480–1500*

The Master of Moulins was named after the French city where, about 1498–1500, the Bourbon dukes donated the artist's Virgin in Glory Triptych to the cathedral. It is now generally agreed that this master is the Jean Hey whom the contemporary writer Jean Lemaire called *pictor egregius* (outstanding painter) and who in 1494 produced an *Ecce Homo* (Musées Royaux des Beaux-Arts de Belgique, Brussels) for Jean Cueillette, treasurer of the Bourbons. Hey's earliest works, especially the *Nativity of Cardinal Jean Rolin* (Musée Rolin, Autun), painted about 1480, indicate his artistic origins in the Netherlands and his debt to the work of Hugo van der Goes. In addition to the Lehman Collection *Portrait of Margaret of Austria* (cat. no. 35) there is a series of splendid portrait fragments of members of the Bourbon dynasty (Louvre, Paris), painted by Hey toward the end of the fifteenth century, that shows a highly personal style combining Netherlandish and French traits. Hey was essentially a panel painter but on occasion worked as an illuminator.

Adriaen Isenbrant, *active by 1510, died 1551*

Isenbrant occupied a prominent position in Bruges, where he became a master in the painters' guild in 1510; he served nine times as *vinder* (juror) between 1518 and 1538 and as *gouverneur* (treasurer) in 1526–27 and 1537–38. Like Jan Provost, he helped create the decorations for the triumphal entry of Emperor Charles V into Bruges in 1520.

Although no picture is signed, more than five hundred paintings are attributed to Isenbrant, who ran a busy shop that produced works for the local market as well as the export trade. His pictures usually reflect the influence of his celebrated fifteenth-century predecessors Jan van Eyck, Rogier van der Weyden, Hans Memling, and especially Gerard David. Sanderus claimed that Isenbrant was David's pupil, but since Isenbrant was already a master on his arrival in Bruges in 1510, it is more likely that he collaborated in David's workshop. Only two of the works attributed to Isenbrant are known to have been dated: the *Portrait of Paulus Denigro* of 1518 (Groeningemuseum, Bruges) and the now-destroyed Adoration Triptych of 1517 (formerly Marienkirche, Lübeck). The attribution and chronology of his oeuvre are chiefly based on the documented Van de Velde Diptych (Musées Royaux des Beaux-Arts de Belgique, Brussels, and Onze-Lieve-Vrouwekerk, Bruges).

Jan Joest of Kalkar, *German, about 1455/60–1519*

Joest was born in the lower Rhine region, in the city of Wesel, where he was probably trained by Derick Baegert. He also worked in the Netherlands and in Spain. His two most important commissions were for a series of twenty panels of 1505–8 on the Life of Christ for the Stadtpfarrkirche Sankt Nicolai in Kalkar and an altarpiece of 1505 for Palencia cathedral comprising eight panels showing the Sorrows of the Virgin. Many other religious paintings and portraits have been attributed to Jan, who worked for the Benedictine abbey of Saint Luidger in Werden in 1512 and for the Sint-Bavokerk (Saint Bavo's) in Haarlem in 1515. Jan's influence spread widely: in Antwerp through his pupils Joos van Cleve and the Master of Frankfurt, in Cologne through Bartholomaeus Bruyn, and in Spain by the example of the works he painted there.

Joos van Cleve, *active by 1507, died 1540/41*

As his name indicates, Joos van Cleve probably came from Kleve, a city located in the lower Rhine region. Although his birthdate is unknown, in the first decade of the sixteenth century Joos was a member of the workshop of Jan Joest, preparing paintings for the high altar of the Stadtpfarrkirche Sankt Nicolai in Kalkar. By 1511 Joos was a resident of Antwerp, where he became a free master in the Guild of Saint

Luke, subsequently serving as its codeacon in 1519, 1520, and 1525.

Joos's earliest works, which include an *Adam and Eve* of 1507 in the Louvre, reveal the influence of his early training in Kalkar and a knowledge of the Bruges school of painting. He is best known, however, for his keen interest in Patinir-like landscapes as the setting for his figures, hints of the lively color schemes of the Antwerp Mannerists, and a predilection for newly imported Italian motifs and the sfumato effects of the art of Leonardo da Vinci. Joos and his workshop apparently specialized in portrayals of the Virgin and Child and of the Holy Family, which were mass-produced to accommodate a significant market demand. Reported by Lodovico Guicciardini to have been an acclaimed portraitist, Joos was called to the French court of Francis I to paint the likenesses of the king and his queen, Eleanor of Austria, which survive in examples in the Philadelphia Museum of Art and in the Queen's Collection in Hampton Court, as well as in numerous copies.

Joos van Gent (Joos van Wassenhove), *active by 1460, died about 1480*

Although only a small number of works can be confidently attributed to him, Van Gent is an important figure in the generation following Jan van Eyck and the only artist of his stature among his contemporaries who worked in Italy. Usually identified with Joos van Wassenhove, who is said to have left the Netherlands for Rome between about 1469 and 1475, he is surely the Netherlandish painter called to Urbino by Federigo da Montefeltro to paint a portrait series of twenty-eight Famous Men in the *studiolo* of the Palazzo Ducale in Urbino (Palazzo Ducale, Urbino, and Louvre, Paris); these were apparently completed by the Spanish painter Pedro Berruguete after Joos's presumed premature death, and there is continued uncertainty about the role of each artist in these remarkable but heavily damaged works. Joos's sole documented painting is the Communion of the Apostles Altarpiece, painted in 1473 for the Confraternity of Corpus Domini in Urbino, and it is on the basis of the style of this picture that two other paintings, executed in Ghent before the artist's departure for Italy, have been attributed to him: the *Adoration of the Magi* in the Metropolitan Museum (cat. no. 7) and the large Calvary Triptych in Sint-Baafs (Saint Bavo's) in Ghent. These early works reveal the influence of Hugo van der Goes, as well as that of Dieric Bouts, in whose workshop Joos may have been briefly engaged.

Juan de Flandes, *active (in Spain) by 1496, died 1519*

The name Juan de Flandes indicates that this artist came from Flanders, but he is first documented in Spain in 1496 as painter to Queen Isabella the Catholic, a position he held until her death in 1504. His early paintings for her Oratorio (private chapel), such as the *Marriage Feast at Cana* (cat. no. 85), suggest that he was trained in the south Netherlandish tradition.

From 1505 until 1509 Juan was in Salamanca, painting portions of a large altarpiece commissioned by the university for its chapel (see *Saints Michael and Francis* [cat. no. 86]). He spent the last part of his life in Palencia, where he received a commission to enlarge the altarpiece for the high altar of the cathedral. The scenes he painted for it are his most important works that survive in situ.

Simon Marmion, *active by 1449, died 1489*

Hailed as the "prince of illumination, " the Franco-Netherlandish Marmion was celebrated by the contemporary writers Jean Molinet and Jean Lemaire de Belges. Although he left no signed or dated work, Marmion's oeuvre can be reconstructed by relating a stylistically cohesive group of miniatures and panel paintings to the details of his life. His major work is the painted portion of the Saint Bertin Altarpiece (Gemäldegalerie, Berlin, and National Gallery, London), ordered by Bishop Guillaume Fillastre for the abbey of Saint Bertin at Saint-Omer and dedicated in 1459.

Marmion was born in Amiens about 1425 and is mentioned in that city's records for decorative work executed between 1449 and 1451. In 1454 he was paid for a *Calvary* for the chambers of justice in the Town Hall. Marmion's name began to appear in the archives of Valenciennes in 1458; he also worked for the cathedral of Cambrai and became a master in Tournai in 1468. He was employed intermittently by the dukes of Burgundy, providing decorations for official events, illuminations for a sumptuous breviary for Charles the Bold in 1470 (fig. 11) and at least one panel painting (cat. no. 9).

QUENTIN MASSYS (also Matsys or Metsys), *1465/66–1530*

Born in Leuven and possibly trained there in the workshop of Aelbert Bouts, Massys moved to Antwerp and became a member of the Guild of Saint Luke in 1491. Between 1495 and 1510 he accepted four apprentices, suggesting that he ran a busy workshop to accommodate a growing demand for paintings on the open market. The Saint Anne Triptych (Musées Royaux des Beaux-Arts de Belgique, Brussels), commissioned in 1507 by the Confraternity of Saint Anne for its chapel in Sint-Pieterskerk in Leuven, and the Saint John Altarpiece of 1508–11 for the chapel of the guild of joiners in the Antwerp cathedral are his most monumental public commissions and offer a basis for understanding Massys's chronology and stylistic development. Although there is no evidence that he ever went to Italy, in his mature works he experimented with Italianate ornament and an atmospheric lighting that recalls Leonardo da Vinci's sfumato effects. Leonardo's taste for the grotesque is evident in satiric paintings by Massys such as the *Ill-Matched Lovers* (National Gallery of Art, Washington, D.C.). The *Banker and His Wife*, signed and dated 1514 (Louvre, Paris), is, by contrast, an example of Massys's archaizing secular work with a moral message. Massys's portraits draw upon the pictorial formulas of Hans Memling. Massys was renowned throughout Europe at his death.

MASTER OF ALKMAAR, *active by 1504*

This north Netherlandish painter is generally believed to be Cornelis Buys the Elder, who was active in Alkmaar between 1490 and 1524. His key work is an altarpiece commissioned for the Sint-Laurenskerk (Saint Lawrence's) in Alkmaar and representing the Seven Acts of Mercy (Rijksmuseum, Amsterdam) that is dated 1504 and signed with a monogram. The monogram—the letter *V* crossing two *A*s—is very similar to the one used by Jakob Cornelisz. van Oostsanen, who, according to Van Mander, was the brother of Cornelis Buys. The Master of Alkmaar's style and particularly his feeling for atmospheric effects of light and color suggest that he may have been trained in Haarlem, in the milieu of Jan Mostaert.

MASTER OF THE DINTEVILLE ALLEGORY, *Netherlandish or French, active mid-16th century*

At least two paintings have been consistently ascribed to this anonymous artist: the Metropolitan Museum's *Moses and Aaron before Pharaoh: An Allegory of the Dinteville Family*, dated 1537 (cat. no. 43), and *Scenes from the Legend of Saint Eugenia* (Church of Varzy [Nièvre], France), a triptych dated 1535 and bearing an illegible Dutch inscription and the arms of the Haarlem painters' guild. Both works include portraits of the four Dinteville brothers, courtiers of François I, king of France, and they are generally believed to have been commissioned by François II de Dinteville, bishop of Auxerre. The painter was at one time identified with Félix Chrétien, the bishop's secretary, based on a reference in an early ecclesiastical history of Auxerre; however, no confirming evidence of activity by Chrétien as a painter exists in contemporary documents. The style of the two Dinteville paintings is at once Netherlandish and French (a hybrid of international influences that was not unusual in sixteenth-century France), and some authors have also commented on their Germanic appearance. This last characteristic may have come by way of the German Hans Holbein, from whom Jean de Dinteville commissioned the *Ambassadors* (National Gallery, London), which was clearly an inspiration to the artist who produced the Dinteville allegory.

MASTER OF THE FEMALE HALF-LENGTHS, *active first half of 16th century*

This name has been attached to a group of stylistically similar half-length paintings of fashionably dressed young women in interior settings, surrounded by such attributes as songbooks, musical instruments, and ointment jars (the last refer to Mary Magdalene). Although originally viewed as the works of a single artist, these small panels are now generally thought to have come from a workshop that produced paintings of this kind for an international market in the first half of the sixteenth century; many of these pictures found their way into private collections in Spain. Also ascribed to the workshop are paintings of devotional subjects, such as the Holy Family or the Rest on the Flight into Egypt, with charmingly conceived landscape backgrounds. The clear influence of Joachim Patinir on these landscapes suggests that this shop was active in Antwerp, a hub of the export market during these years.

Master of Frankfurt, *active 1490–early 16th century*

According to an inscription on the frame of the *Portrait of the Artist and His Wife* (Koninklijk Museum voor Schone Kunsten, Antwerp) indicating that the artist was thirty-six in 1496, this anonymous master must have been born about 1460. His conventional name is taken from two altarpieces produced for Frankfurt patrons: the Humbracht Triptych of 1504 (Städelsches Kunstinstitut, Frankfurt) and the Holy Kinship Altarpiece (Historisches Museum, Frankfurt). That these altarpieces are related stylistically to two earlier works with Antwerp connections, the *Portrait of the Artist and His Wife* and the *Festival of the Archers' Guild* (also Koninklijk Museum voor Schone Kunsten, Antwerp), suggests that the artist worked mainly in that city.

Nothing is known about the early training of the Master of Frankfurt, although he may have studied with Jan Joest of Kalkar. He apparently managed an active workshop that produced works on commission as well as for the open market. Delen's suggestion that the Master of Frankfurt is identical with the painter Hendrik van Wueluwe, an active guild member who worked in Antwerp from 1483 to 1533, cannot be proven, as there are no surviving works securely attributed to that master.

Master LC, *active second quarter of 16th century*

This artist was so named because a key painting in his oeuvre, the *Calling of Saint Matthew* (Musées Royaux des Beaux-Arts de Belgique, Brussels), appears to show the letters *L* and *C* on a tree trunk in the foreground. About a dozen works can now be attributed to the same master. They all show characteristics of landscape paintings by Lucas Gassel, who worked in Antwerp in the mid-sixteenth century. Master LC seems to have trained with Gassel or at least to have been greatly influenced by his painting style.

Master of the Liège Disciples at Emmaus, *active mid-16th century*

One of several landscape specialists active in the Netherlands before the appearance of Pieter Bruegel the Elder, this artist was responsible for the landscape backgrounds of a number of paintings with biblical subjects. Various hands produced the foreground figures in these works. This painter was initially christened the Master of the Lille Sermon after the *Sermon of Saint John* in the Musée des Beaux-Arts, Lille. However, the figures are the focus of the Lille work and a new name was therefore proposed for him—the Master of the Liège Disciples at Emmaus, after the *Journey to Emmaus* in the Musée d'Art Réligieux et d'Art Mosan, Liège, in which the landscape is more central. The master is related stylistically to Lucas Gassel and Jan van Amstel.

Master of Saint Augustine, *active last quarter of 15th century*

The artist was named by Friedländer for an incomplete altarpiece with scenes from the legend of Saint Augustine (see cat. no. 16). Friedländer also ascribed a number of portraits to the same hand; in addition he gave him a *Saint Nicholas Enthroned* (Groeningemuseum, Bruges), which has since been reattributed to the Master of the Saint Lucy Legend. The artist's apparent familiarity with paintings from the workshop of Rogier van der Weyden that hung in the church of Sainte Gudule, Brussels, during his lifetime—namely the *Exhumation of Saint Hubert* (National Gallery, London) and the *Dream of Pope Sergius* (J. Paul Getty Museum, Los Angeles)—suggests that he may have been active in or near that city. Since his paintings have stylistic affinities, as well, with works by the Franco-Netherlandish artist Simon Marmion, the Master of Saint Augustine may be among the numerous painters of the Netherlandish school with roots in what is today France.

Master of the Saint Barbara Legend, *active late 15th century*

Named for a panel representing the legend of Saint Barbara, now divided between the Museum van het Heilig Bloed, Bruges, and the Musées Royaux des Beaux-Arts de Belgique, Brussels, this artist collaborated on an altarpiece with the Master of the Saint Catherine Legend, suggesting that he was active in

Brussels. His animated and brightly colored narrative compositions, frequently representing the legends of saints, are set in fanciful open architecture, and his elegant and fair-complexioned women with high foreheads and oval faces are juxtaposed with swarthy men with unkempt beards and hair. Works ascribed to the Master of Crispin and Crispinian may have been painted by this same artist at a different point in his career.

Master of Saint Giles, *Netherlandish or French, active about 1490–1510*

The artist's eponymous works are from an altarpiece featuring the legend of Saint Giles, whose cult flourished at Saint-Gilles, near Arles. Two panels from this ensemble, in the National Gallery, London, and other works by the same hand, including panels from the same altarpiece in the National Gallery of Art, Washington, D.C., have been grouped together to form the small oeuvre of this apparently itinerant master. The artist's visual references in his paintings of the Virgin and Child to compositions by Rogier van der Weyden and Dieric Bouts, as well as his handling of details of light and costume, suggest a training in the Netherlands. The paintings in London and Washington, however, depict sites in Paris, indicating that he was active there about 1500. Although it cannot be determined unequivocally whether he was of Netherlandish or French origin, this anonymous artist was partially responsible for the international dissemination of the style of Netherlandish painting.

Master of the Saint Godelieve Legend, *active fourth quarter of 15th century*

The artist's eponymous work is an altarpiece that is the most complete extant monument to the life and miracles of Saint Godelieve, martyr of Ghistelles, near Bruges, and patroness of Flanders (cat. no. 15). The style of this master resembles those of two other painters from Bruges, the Master of the Saint Ursula Legend and the Master of the Saint Lucy Legend. Six other works by the Master of the Saint Godelieve Legend are known.

Master of the Saint Ursula Legend, *active late 15th century*

The artist is named after an altarpiece illustrating the legend of Saint Ursula (Groeningemuseum, Bruges), formerly in the convent of the Augustinian Black Sisters, Bruges. He is closely associated with Bruges: several of his paintings include depictions of the city and can be dated by the state of completion of the belfry on the Town Hall. His only dated painting is the *Virgin and Child and Three Donors* of 1486 (Koninklijk Museum voor Schone Kunsten, Antwerp). A contemporary of Memling's, the Master of the Saint Ursula Legend was influenced primarily by Rogier van der Weyden. He was one of the productive lesser Netherlandish painters working for the art market in Bruges during the late fifteenth and early sixteenth centuries.

Master of the View of Sainte Gudule, *active about 1470–90*

This artist was named by Friedländer for the view of the Brussels church of Sainte Gudule in the background of a painting in the Louvre (formerly called *Pastoral Sermon*) that shows the Preaching of Saint Augustine. This work can be tentatively dated before 1480 on the basis of the unfinished construction on the church's north tower. Sainte Gudule is featured as well in the background of cat. no. 34, and another Brussels church, Notre Dame du Sablon, appears in a portrait in the National Gallery, London, indicating that the master was active in that city. The large number of surviving paintings in the style of the Master of the View of Sainte Gudule and their uneven quality suggest that he had a large and active workshop whose various members produced these pictures.

Hans Memling, *active by 1465, died 1494*

Born between about 1430 and 1446 in Seligenstadt, on the Main River in Germany, Memling must have arrived in Brussels by at least 1460. There, it is now generally assumed, he was an apprentice or journeyman in the workshop of Rogier van der Weyden. Rogier died in 1464, and Memling is first mentioned in the records of Bruges in January 1465, when he registered as a citizen. Although his name does not appear on the list of members of the painters' guild and he was not a court appointee, he was that city's leading painter during his lifetime. His commissions came largely from wealthy burghers and the Italian banking community of Bruges, which included the Tani and Portinari families. Memling's earliest documented work is the impressive Last Judgment Triptych (Muzeum Narodowe, Gdansk) commissioned by Angelo Tani and dating between 1466 and 1471. Although his style does not show a great deal of change over time, Memling's works of the 1470s and 1480s move toward an ideal of balance and harmony, an inclination that sets this artist apart in the world of Netherlandish painting and allies him with Italian taste.

JAN MOSTAERT, *active by 1498, died 1555/56*

Van Mander tells us that Mostaert learned his craft in Haarlem from Jacob Jansz. van Haarlem; his youthful works emulate the delicate style and bright colors of the Haarlem painter Geertgen tot Sint Jans. A resident of Haarlem for most of his life, Mostaert was regularly mentioned in the records of the painters' guild of that city until 1544.

His most ambitious religious works include the Deposition Altarpiece (Musées Royaux des Beaux-Arts de Belgique, Brussels) and the Last Judgment Altarpiece (Rheinisches Landesmuseum, Bonn). The latter work reflects his interest in such Antwerp artists as Joachim Patinir and Herri met de Bles. Born into a noble family and enjoying steady patronage from the local aristocracy, Mostaert is perhaps best known as a portrait painter. In 1519 and 1521 he was recorded at the court of Margaret of Austria, regent of the Netherlands, for whom he painted the likenesses of Philibert II of Savoy, the young Charles V, and Philip the Fair.

BERNAERT VAN ORLEY, *active by 1515, died 1541/42*

The artist came from a family of Brussels painters and was probably apprenticed to his father, Valentin van Orley. Although Bernaert was a leading advocate of the Romanist style practiced in Brussels and Antwerp, there is no evidence that he traveled to Italy. He clearly studied Raphael's tapestry designs for the Acts of the Apostles, which could be seen in Brussels beginning in 1516.

Van Orley is first documented at the time of his marriage to Agnes Seghers in 1512, and his earliest important work, the Apostles Thomas and Matthew Altarpiece (Kunsthistorisches Museum, Vienna, and Musées Royaux des Beaux-Arts de Belgique, Brussels), commissioned by the Brussels guild of masons and joiners, must date from about this time. By 1515 Van Orley was painting portraits of the Habsburg family; in this way he came to the attention of Margaret of Austria, regent of the Netherlands, who appointed him court painter in 1518. At Margaret's death, in 1530, Van Orley became court artist to her niece, the new regent, Mary of Hungary. From 1525 onward he increasingly devoted his time to designing for tapestries and stained glass, and the quality of his paintings, most of which involve workshop participation, declined.

AELBERT VAN OUWATER, *active mid-15th century*

Ouwater was the founder of the Haarlem school of painting and Jan van Eyck's contemporary. A *Raising of Lazarus* in the Gemäldegalerie, Berlin, is the sole work that can be attributed to him with certainty, and it is the cornerstone of any effort to distinguish north Netherlandish from south Netherlandish sensibility. Similarities exist between the styles of Ouwater and Dieric Bouts, who was perhaps active in Ouwater's shop, and consequently works such as the Infancy Triptych (Prado, Madrid) which have been attributed to both artists.

JOACHIM PATINIR, *active by 1515, died 1524*

A native of the southern Netherlands, Patinir was probably born in the vicinity of Bouvignes, near Dinant. He settled in Antwerp, where he is mentioned as a master in the painters' guild in 1515. Patinir enjoyed considerable fame during his lifetime, yet his oeuvre is remarkably small, comprising only nineteen generally accepted works, none dated, and only five signed. Dürer, who met Patinir during a visit in Antwerp in 1520–21, praised him as "the good landscape painter," and his panoramic vistas must have impressed Bruegel as well. Although his known paintings illustrate biblical subjects, Patinir always subordinated the figures to the landscape, establishing an approach followed by such artists as the Master of the Female Half-Lengths, Lucas Gassel, and Herri met de Bles. In the *Temptation of Saint Anthony* (Prado, Madrid), acquired by Philip II of Spain, the figures are by Massys and the landscape is by Patinir. On October 5, 1524, his second wife was described as a widow and the artist Quentin Massys was recorded as the guardian of his children.

JAN PROVOST, *born about 1465, died 1532*

Provost was born in Bergen in Henegouwen and

probably first trained with his father, Jan Provost the Elder. Early in his career he must have met Simon Marmion, with whom he subsequently worked in Valenciennes and whose widow he married. In 1493 he moved to Antwerp, where he joined the Guild of Saint Luke. The following year he settled in Bruges, where he purchased his citizenship in order to join that city's painters' guild; he was dean of the guild in 1519 and 1525. For the town council and church authorities he carried out several decorative projects, including a stage set for the festivities that marked the triumphal entry of Charles V into Bruges in 1520.

Provost's artistic personality is defined by two documented works, the *Last Judgment* (Groeningemuseum, Bruges), commissioned for the council chamber of the Bruges Town Hall in 1525, and the *Virgin in Majesty* (The State Hermitage Museum, Saint Petersburg), installed in 1524 for the Sint-Donaaskerk (Saint Donatian's) in Bruges. An artist of transition, Provost favored subjects with complicated theological content.

Rogier van der Weyden, *1399/1400–1464*

Born in Tournai, Rogier is assumed to be the Rogelet de la Pasture who is mentioned in the Tournai guild records and who, by 1427, was in the workshop of Robert Campin. In 1432 he became a master in the Guild of Saint Luke and soon thereafter, in 1435, permanently relocated to Brussels, where, a year later, he assumed the prestigious post of official city painter.

Like Campin, Rogier became the head of a busy workshop, undertaking commissions from churches, monasteries, various brotherhoods, and also the ducal court of Philip the Good, serving the nobility above all in a thriving business as a portrait painter. Rogier had well-developed international connections and received requests for works from Italy, Spain, France, and Germany. He made a pilgrimage to Rome in 1450, the year of a papal jubilee, and thereafter his fame spread even more widely in Italy. So renowned was Rogier that foreign artists—among them Zanetto Bugatto, court painter to Francesco Sforza, duke of Milan—came to Brussels to study with him.

None of Rogier's works is signed or dated, but three are documented in contemporary or near-contemporary accounts: the *Descent from the Cross* (Prado, Madrid), made for the crossbowmen's guild in Leuven; the Miraflores Altarpiece (see cat. no. 46); and a *Crucifixion* (Escorial, Spain), originally from the Carthusian monastery at Scheut.

The expressive intensity of Rogier's altarpieces is unparalleled in the works of his contemporaries. His influence was at least as great as Jan van Eyck's, and his paintings were widely copied.

Michel Sittow, *about 1468–1525/26*

The son of a painter in Reval (now Tallinn), Estonia, Sittow was apprenticed in Bruges about 1484, possibly with Hans Memling. He was in service to Queen Isabella the Catholic in Spain by 1492 and remained in her employ, working alongside Juan de Flandes, until her death in 1504. Sittow returned to Reval, where he settled, in 1506 and joined the artists' guild within the next year. Thereafter, he traveled intermittently, visiting England and Denmark; later in his career he worked for the Habsburg court in the Netherlands. His two securely documented paintings, the *Ascension* (private collection, England) and the *Assumption of the Virgin* (National Gallery of Art, Washington, D.C.), are mentioned in the 1516 inventory of Margaret of Austria. Marked by an international, courtly flavor, Sittow's style reveals in particular his familiarity with the work of Memling,Gerard David, and Juan de Flandes.

Additional Works in the Collection

RELIGIOUS PAINTINGS

Netherlandish Painter, second half of 15th century
Saint Michael; The Mystic Mass of Saint Gregory; Saint Jerome
Oil on wood; central panel 6⅛ x 3¾ in. (15.6 x 9.5 cm); left panel 6¼ x 3⅞ in. (15.9 x 9.8 cm); right panel 6¼ x 3¾ in. (15.9 x 9.5 cm)
Bequest of William H. Herriman, 1920
21.134.3a–c

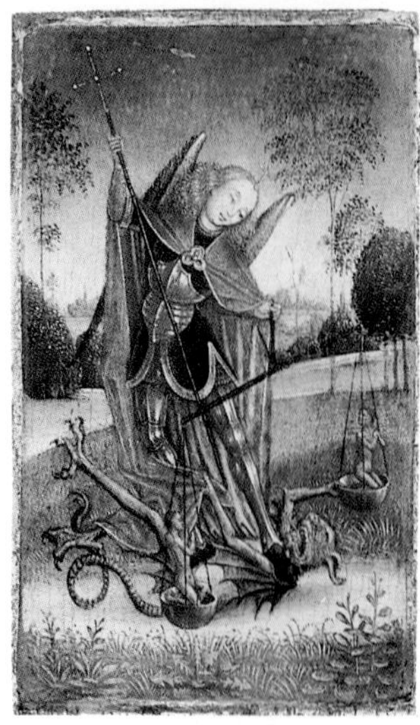
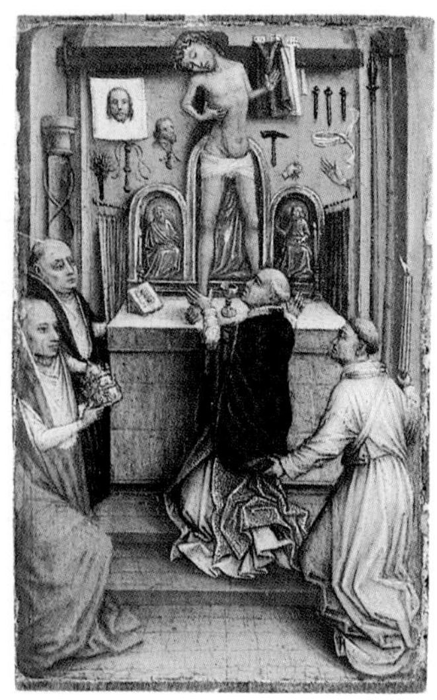
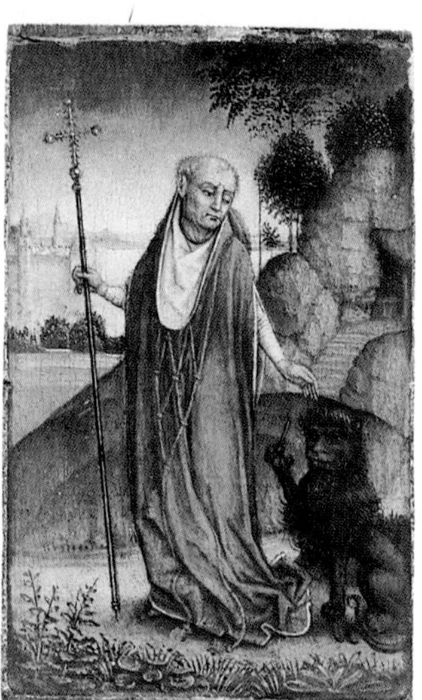
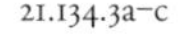

21.134.3a–c

Style of Rogier van der Weyden, mid-15th century
The Holy Family with Saint Paul and a Donor
Oil on wood; overall, with added strip, 22⅝ x 19 in. (57.5 x 48.3 cm); painted surface 22 x 18⅛ in. (55.9 x 46 cm)
The Friedsam Collection, Bequest of Michael Friedsam, 1931 32.100.44

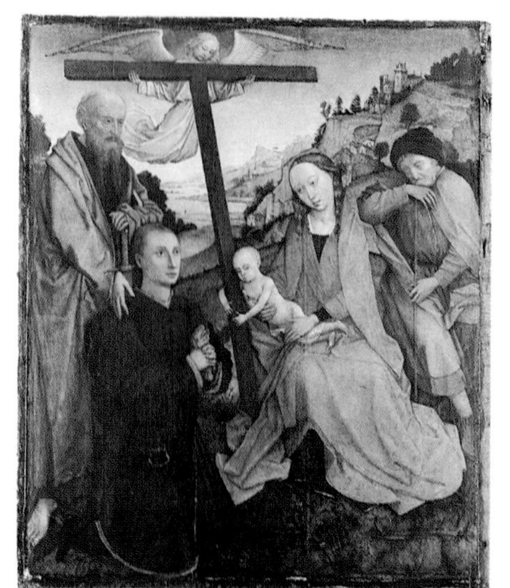
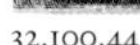

32.100.44

Follower of Hans Memling, late 15th–early 16th century
Virgin and Child
Oil on wood; overall 12½ x 8 in. (31.8 x 20.3 cm); painted surface 12 7/16 x 7 15/16 (31.5 x 20.2 cm)
Robert Lehman Collection, 1975 1975.1.111

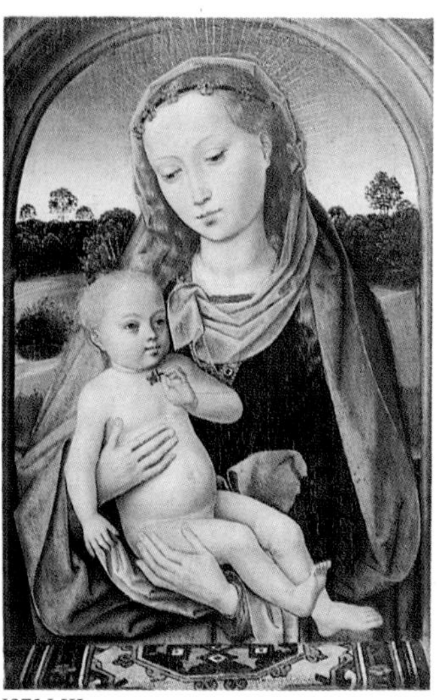
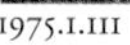

1975.1.111

Style of Hans Memling, late 15th century
Virgin and Child
Oil on wood; overall 14⅛ x 10¼ in. (35.9 x 26 cm); painted surface 13⅜ x 9½ in. (34 x 24.1 cm)
The Friedsam Collection, Bequest of Michael Friedsam, 1931 32.100.58

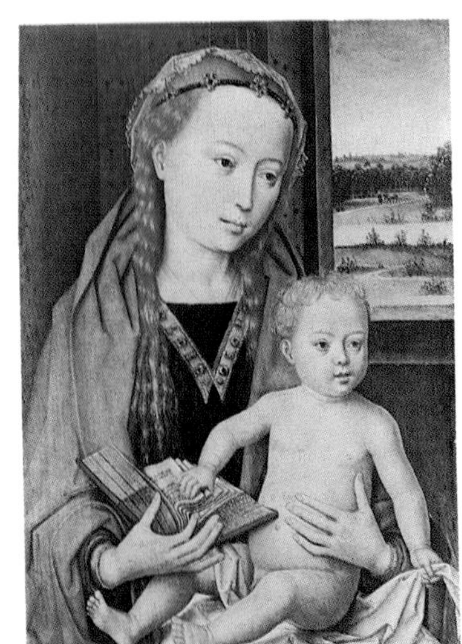
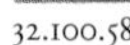

32.100.58

Copy after Hugo van der Goes, late 15th century
The Adoration of the Magi
Oil on wood, 29⅛ x 25⅝ in. (74 x 65.1 cm)
Purchase, 1871 71.100

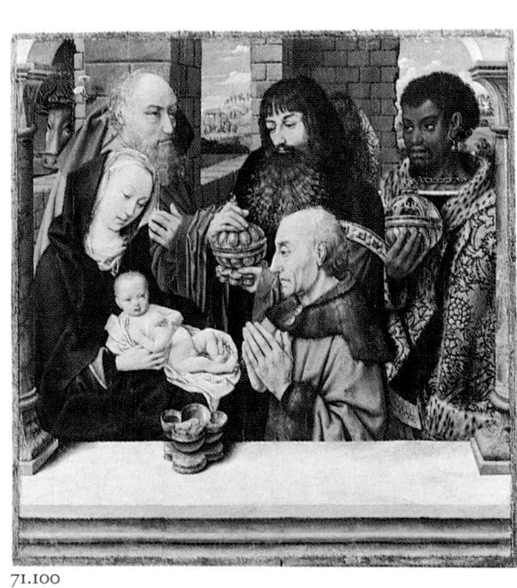

71.100

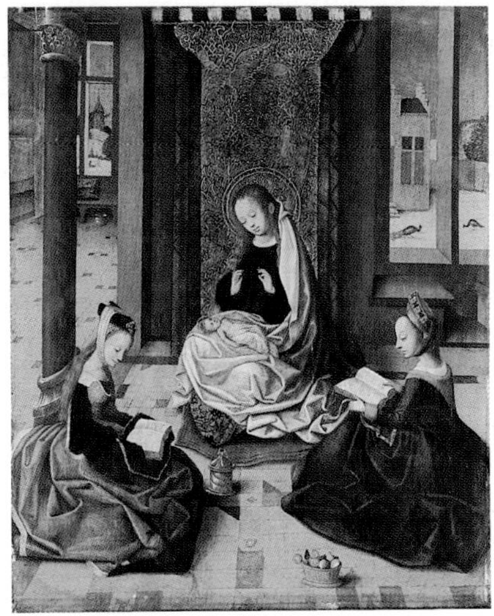
60.18

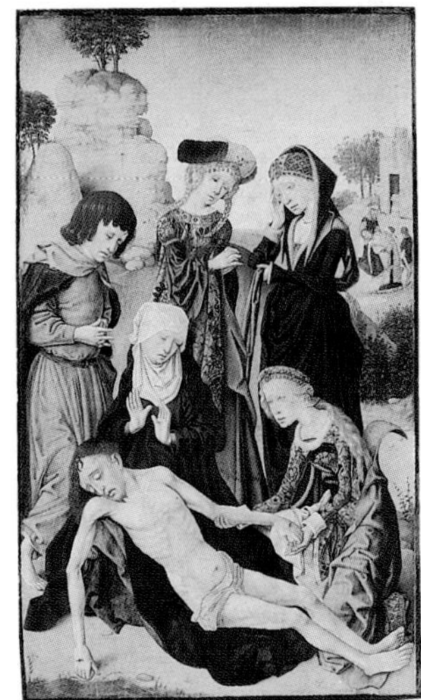
26.26

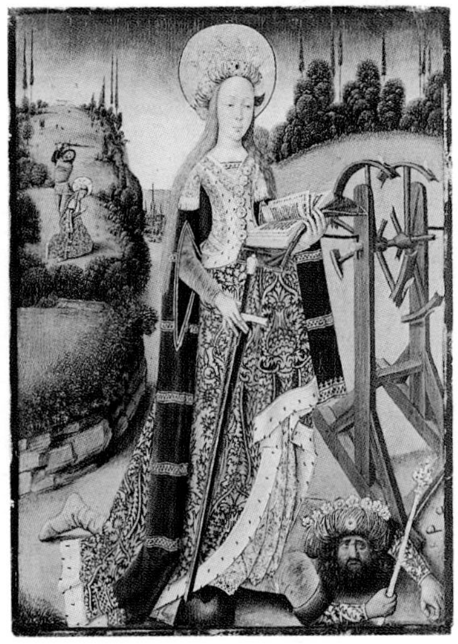
44.105.2

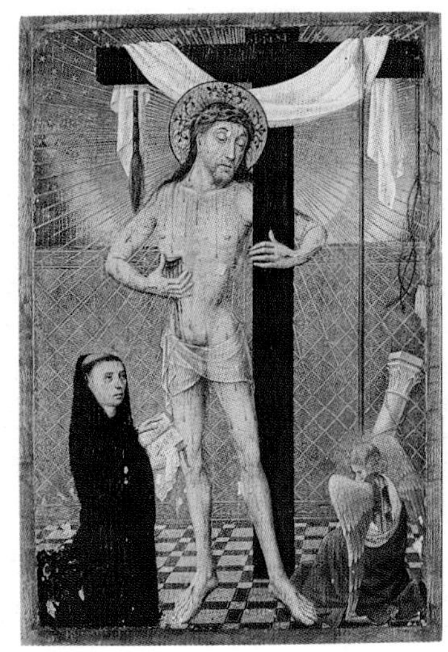
1974.392

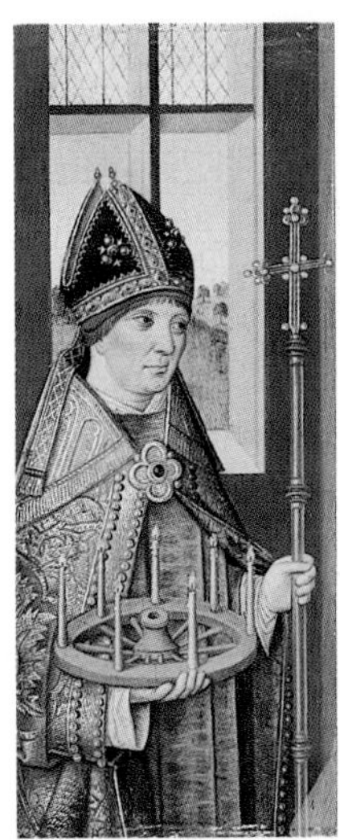
1982.60.18

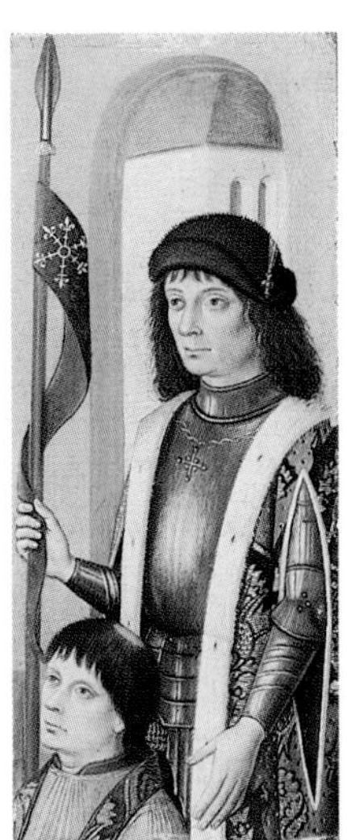
1982.60.19

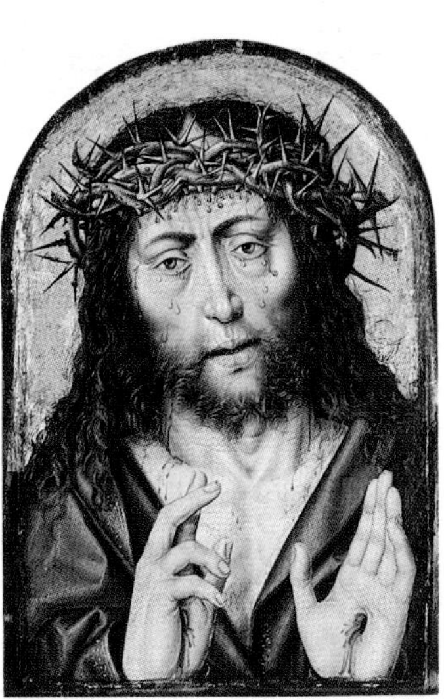
32.100.55

Master of the Brunswick Diptych, active late 15th century
Virgin and Child with Saints
Oil on wood, 19¼ x 15¼ in. (48.9 x 38.7 cm)
Gift of Dr. and Mrs. Max A. Goldzieher, 1960
60.18

Follower of the Master of the Virgin among Virgins, active late 15th century
The Lamentation
Oil on wood, 34⅞ x 20¼ in. (88.6 x 51.4 cm)
Rogers Fund, 1926 26.26

Netherlandish Painter, fourth quarter of 15th century
Saint Catherine of Alexandria
Oil on wood, 16⅛ x 11¾ in. (41 x 29.8 cm)
Bequest of George D. Pratt, 1935 44.105.2

Netherlandish Painter, fourth quarter of 15th century
Man of Sorrows with Kneeling Donor
Oil on wood, 18 x 12½ in. (45.7 x 31.8 cm)
The Cloisters Collection, 1974 1974.392

Netherlandish Painter, about 1490
Saint Donatian; A Warrior Saint, Probably Victor, Presenting a Donor
Oil on wood, (18) 9½ x 3⅞ in. (24.1 x 9.8 cm); (19) 9½ x 4 in. (24.1 x 10.2 cm)
The Jack and Belle Linsky Collection, 1982
1982.60.18–19

Aelbert Bouts, born about 1451/54, died 1549
The Man of Sorrows
Oil on wood, arched top, 17½ x 11¼ in. (44.5 x 28.6 cm)
The Friedsam Collection, Bequest of Michael Friedsam, 1931 32.100.55

Master of the Story of Joseph, about 1500
Joseph Interpreting the Dreams of His Fellow Prisoners
Oil on wood, d. 61½ in. (156.2 cm)
Harris Brisbane Dick Fund, 1953 53.168

Master of the Female Half-Lengths, active about 1525–50
Virgin and Child
Oil on wood; painted surface 3½ x 2 11/16 in. (8.9 x 6.8 cm)
Robert Lehman Collection, 1975 1975.1.123

Flemish Painter, second half of 16th century
Virgin and Child with Saint Joseph
Oil on wood, 8¾ x 8⅝ in. (22.3 x 22 cm)
Robert Lehman Collection, 1975 1975.1.121

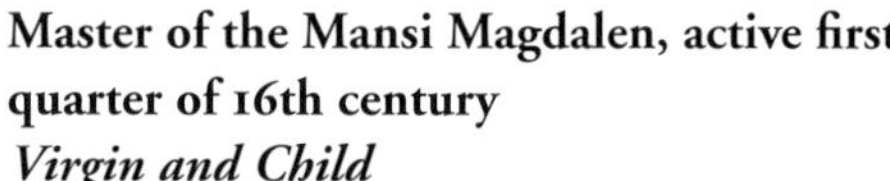

Master of the Mansi Magdalen, active first quarter of 16th century
Virgin and Child
Oil on wood, 19⅛ x 15¼ in. (48.6 x 38.7 cm)
Bequest of William H. Herriman, 1920 21.134.2

Flemish Painter, second quarter of 16th century
Virgin and Child
Oil on wood, 5⅛ x 4 in. (13 x 10.2 cm)
Robert Lehman Collection, 1975 1975.1.124

Master of the Holy Blood, about 1520
The Descent from the Cross
Oil on wood; central panel, overall 36 x 28½ in. (91.4 x 72.4 cm), painted surface 35⅝ x 28½ in. (90.5 x 72.4 cm); left panel, overall 36 x 12⅜ in. (91.4 x 31.4 cm), painted surface 35½ x 12⅜ in. (90.2 x 31.4 cm); right panel, overall 35⅞ x 12⅝ in. (91.1 x 32.1 cm), painted surface 35⅜ x 12½ in. (89.9 x 31.8 cm)
Gift of Clyde Fitch and Ferdinand Gottschalk, 1917 17.187a–c

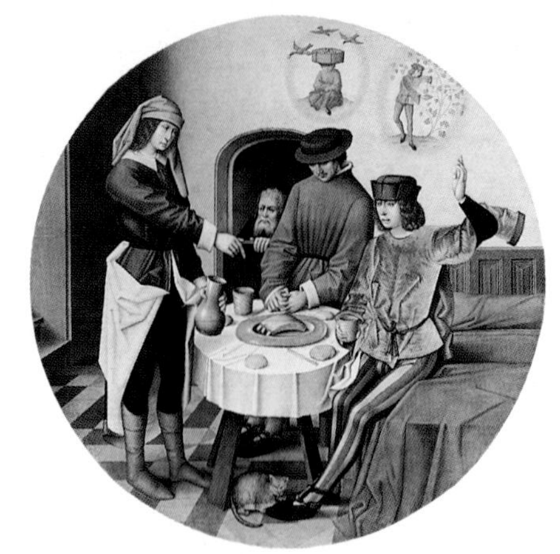

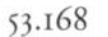

53.168

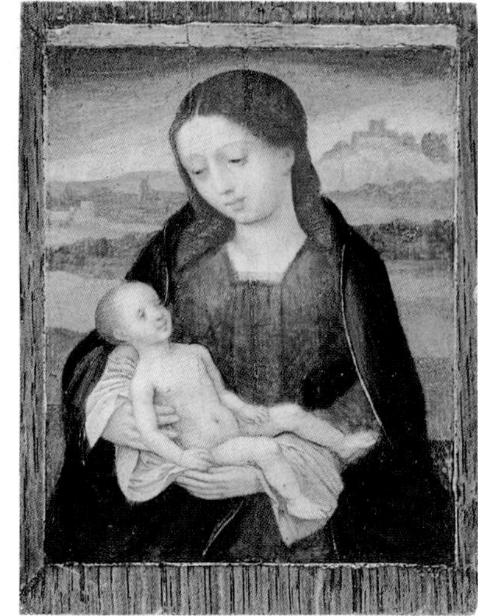

1975.1.123

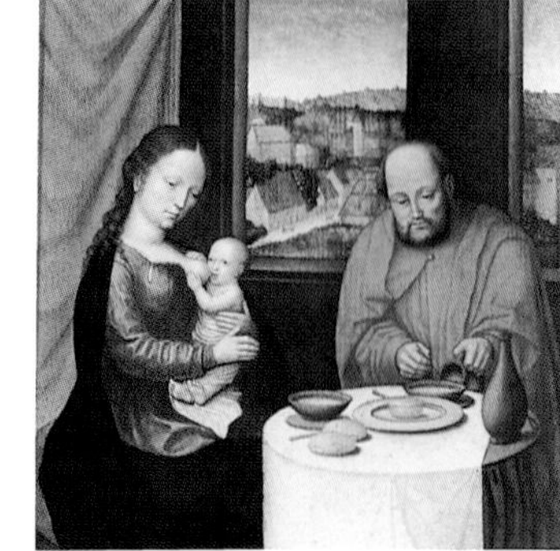

1975.1.121

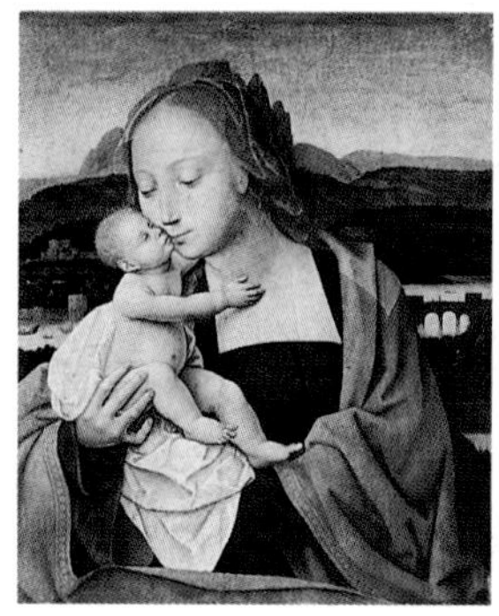

21.134.2

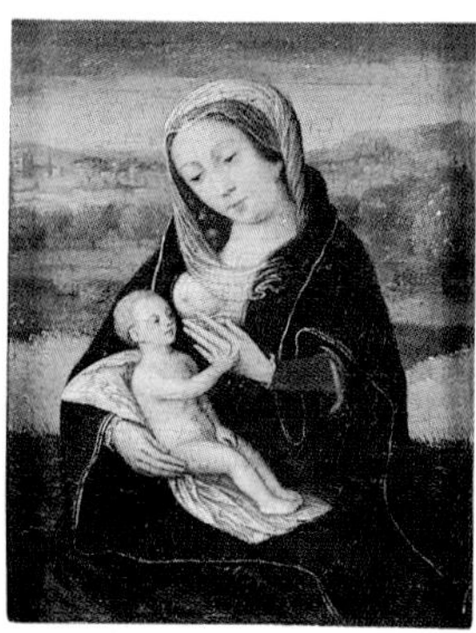

1975.1.124

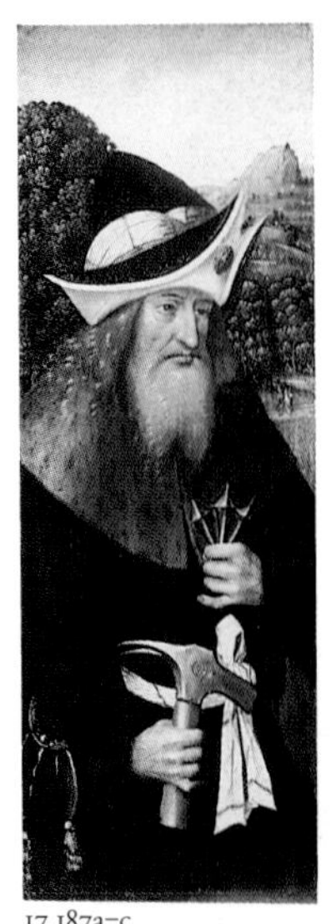

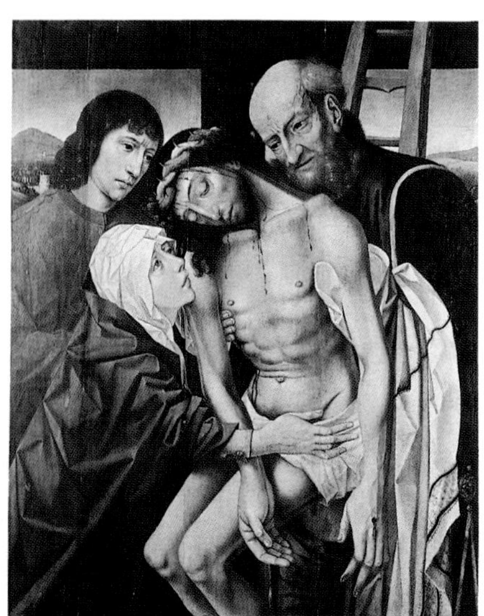

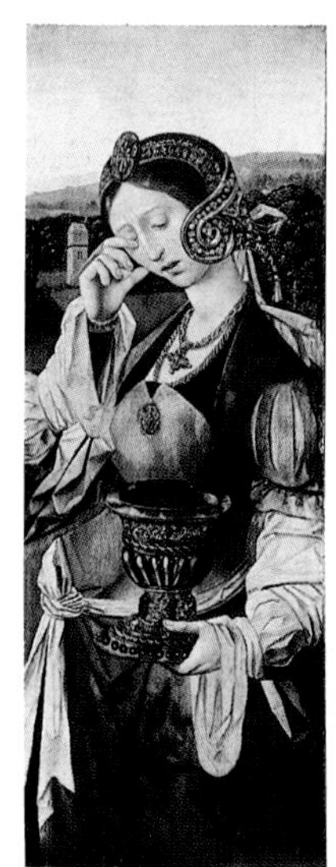

17.187a–c

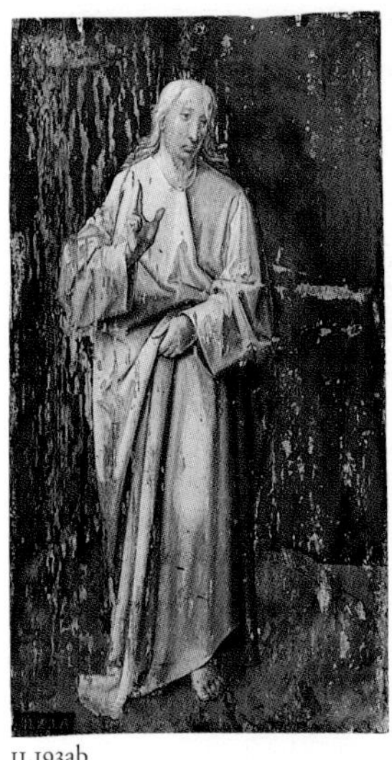
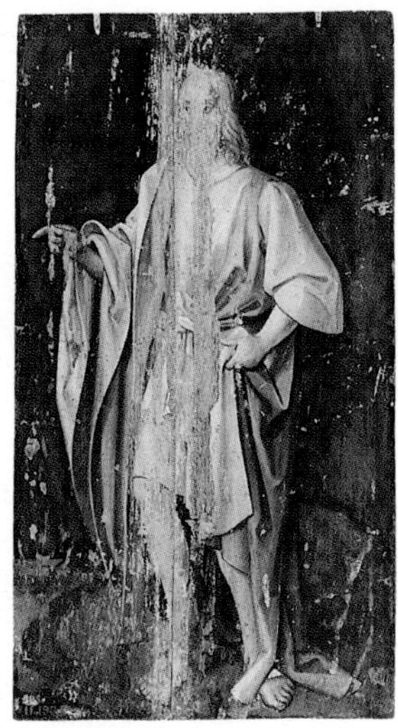
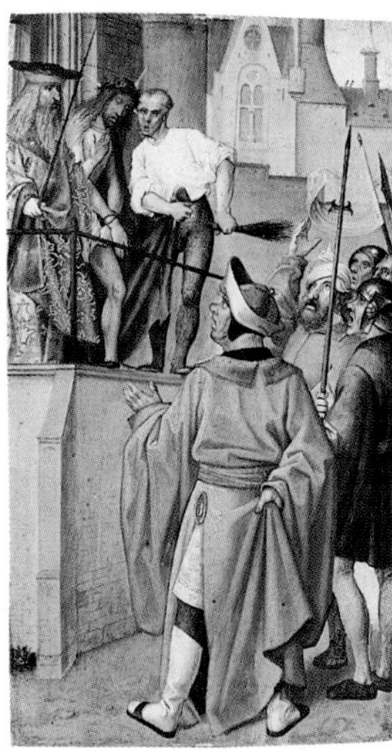
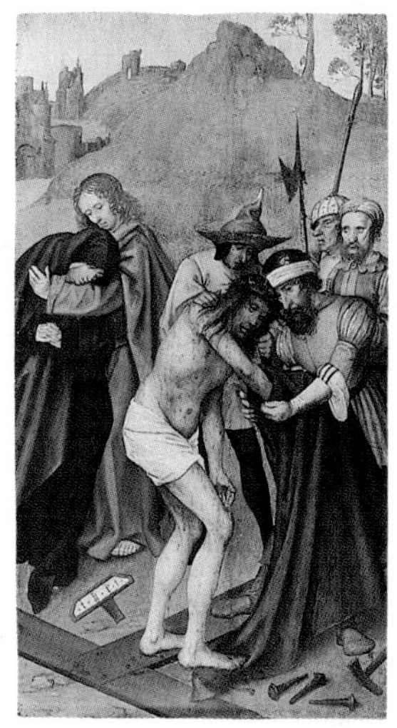

11.193ab

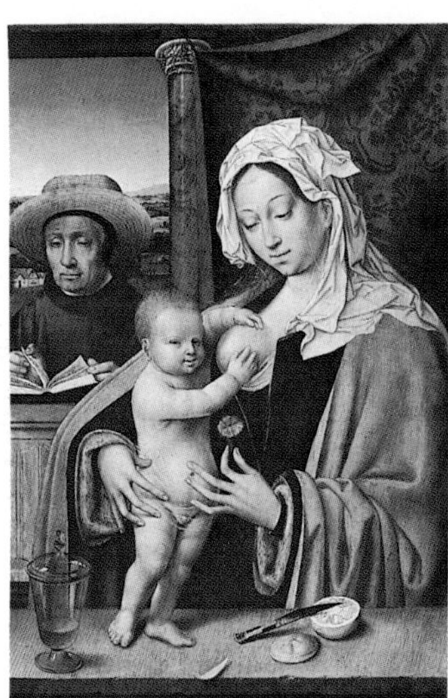

1975.1.117

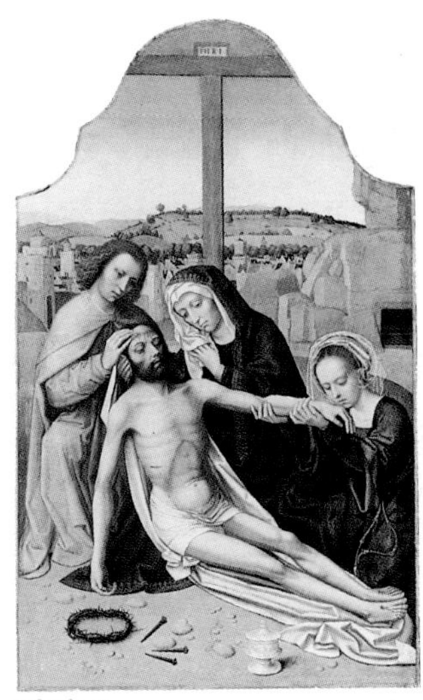

1982.60.23

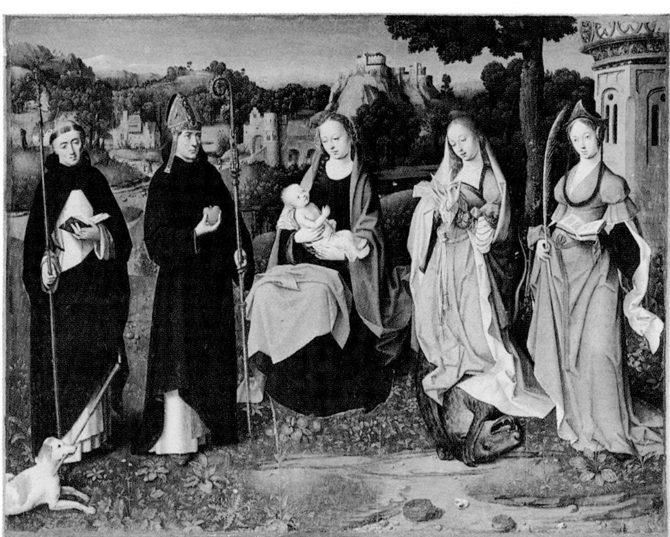

41.190.18

Workshop of Cornelis Engebrechtsz, 1468–1527
***Christ Blessing* (recto), *Saint John the Baptist* (recto), *Ecce Homo* (verso), *The Disrobing of Christ* (verso)**
Oil on wood, each 16½ x 8¾ in. (41.9 x 22.2 cm)
Inscribed (Disrobing of Christ, on plaque):
·ī·n̄·r̄·ī·
Gift of Ferdinand Hermann, 1911 11.193ab

Workshop of Joos van Cleve, active by 1507, died 1540/41
The Holy Family
Oil on wood, 21 13/16 x 14 9/16 in. (55.4 x 37 cm)
Robert Lehman Collection, 1975 1975.1.117

Ambrosius Benson, active by 1519, died 1550
The Lamentation
Oil on canvas, transferred from wood, shaped top, 36 x 22⅛ in. (91.4 x 56.2 cm)
Inscribed (top center, on cross): INRI
The Jack and Belle Linsky Collection, 1982
1982.60.23

Netherlandish (Antwerp) Painter, about 1510
Virgin and Child with Saints Dominic, Augustine, Margaret, and Barbara
Oil on canvas, transferred from wood, 38¾ x 51 in. (98.4 x 129.5 cm)
Bequest of George Blumenthal, 1941 41.190.18

Copy after Lucas van Leyden, Netherlandish or German, possibly late 16th century
Christ Presented to the People
Oil on wood, 10⅞ x 18 in. (27.6 x 45.7 cm)
Marquand Collection, Gift of Henry G. Marquand, 1889 89.15.13

Workshop of Jan Sanders van Hemessen, active by about 1524, died about 1564
The Calling of Matthew
Oil on wood, 43⅞ x 59½ in. (111.4 x 151.1 cm)
Purchase, 1871 71.155

Pieter Huys, active by 1545, died 1584
The Temptation of Saint Anthony
Oil on wood, 43 x 59 in. (109.2 x 149.9 cm)
Inscribed (lower left, falsely): V. Breughel
Anonymous Gift, 1915 15.133

Marcellus Coffermans, active 1549–70
The Adoration of the Shepherds
Oil on wood, 8⅛ x 5½ in. (20.6 x 14 cm)
Signed (lower right): MARCEL.HELMON.FE[CIT]
Gift of J. Pierpont Morgan, 1917 17.190.3

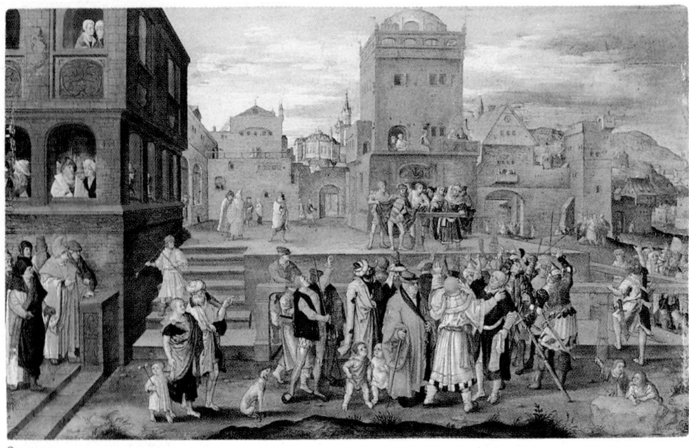

89.15.13

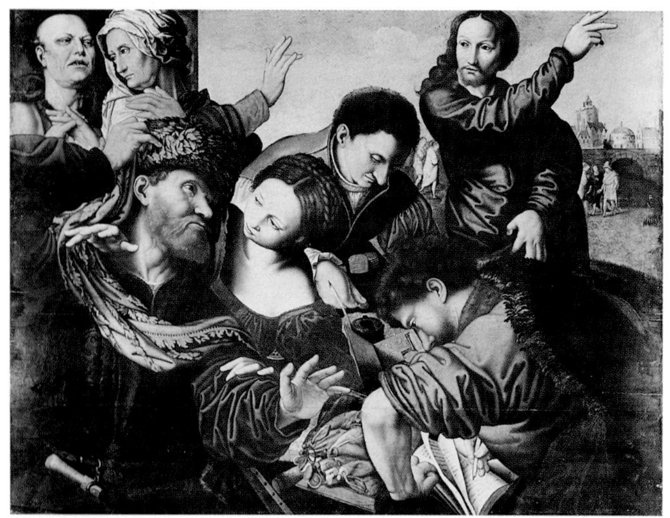

71.155

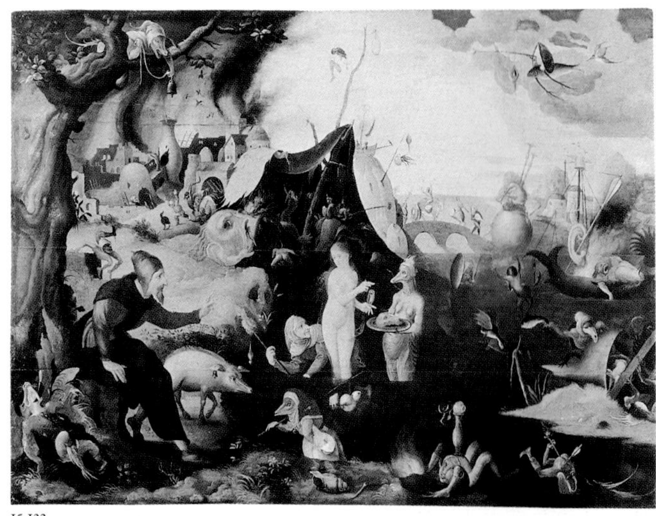

15.133

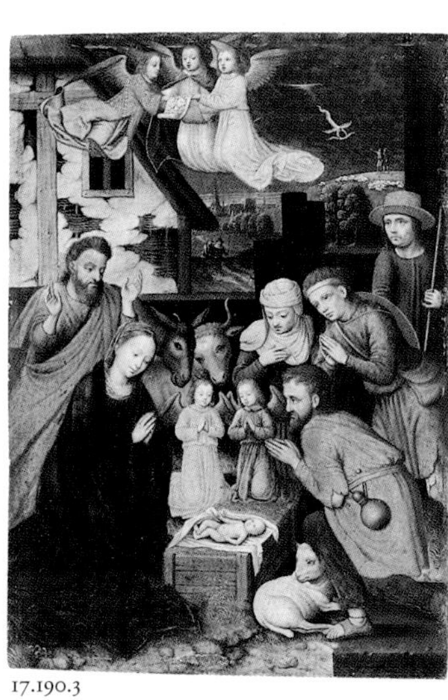

17.190.3

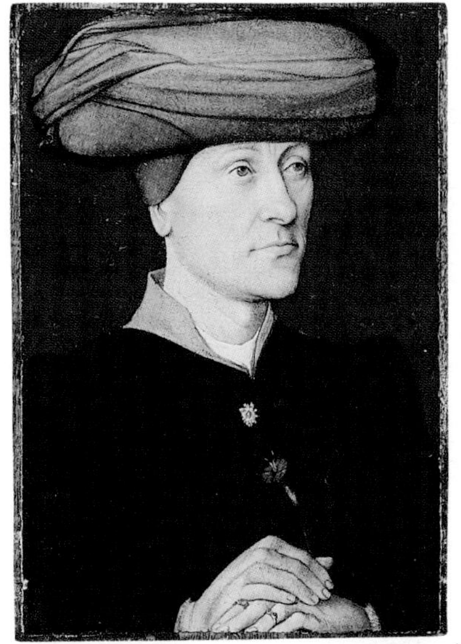
49.7.24

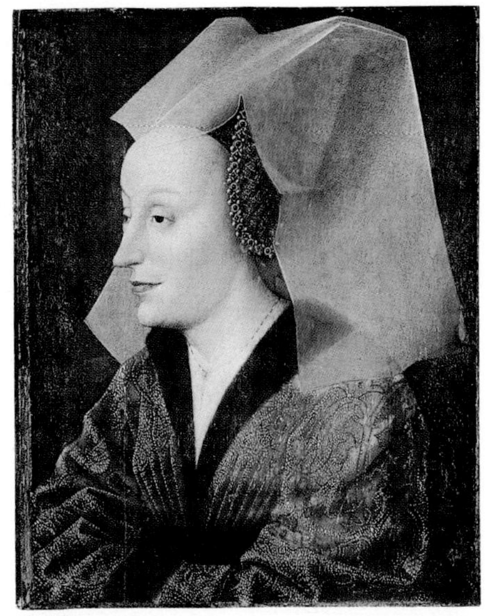
50.145.15

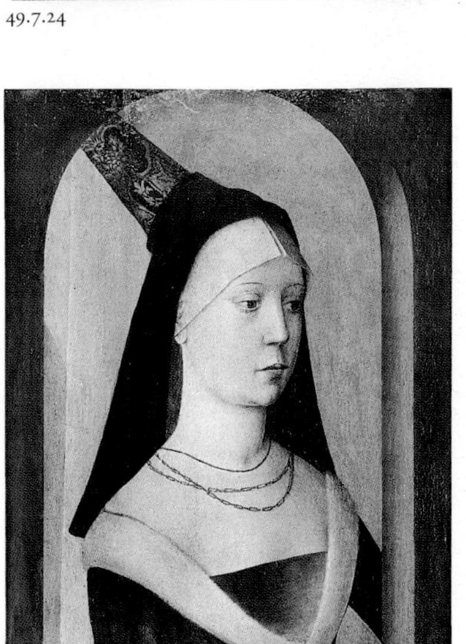
1975.1.129

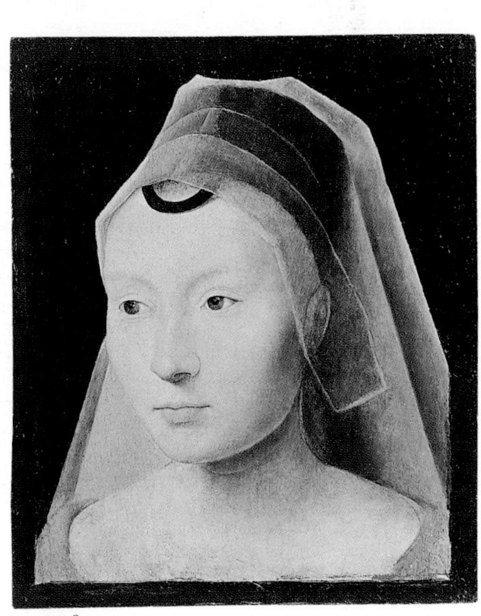
50.145.28

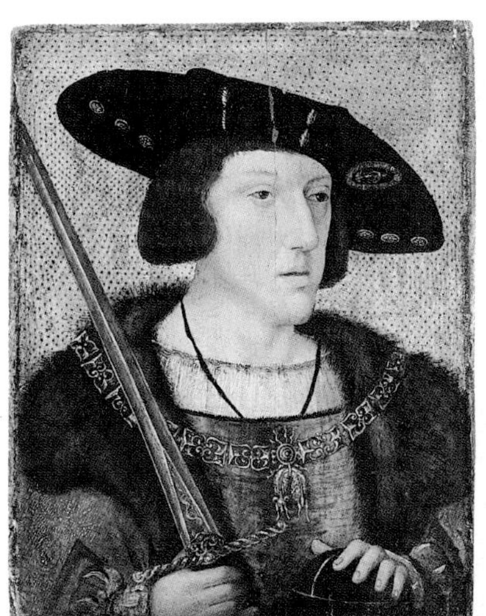
32.100.46

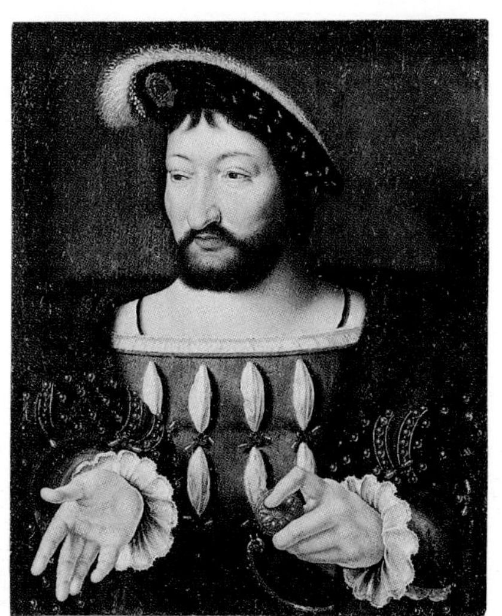
32.100.120

PORTRAITS

Attributed to Rogier van der Weyden, 1399/1400–1464
Portrait of a Man in a Turban
Oil on wood; overall 11 x 7¾ in. (27.9 x 19.7 cm); painted surface 10⅝ x 7¼ in. (27 x 18.4 cm)
The Jules Bache Collection, 1949 49.7.24

Netherlandish Painter, mid-15th century
***Portrait of a Noblewoman, Probably Isabella of Portugal* (1397–1472)**
Oil on wood; overall 13⅝ x 10⅝ in. (34.6 x 27 cm), with added strips of ⅛ in. (.3 cm) at each side
Bequest of Mary Stillman Harkness, 1950 50.145.15

Franco-Flemish Painter, about 1470
Portrait of a Lady
Oil on wood, 22⅝ x 16⅜ in. (57.5 x 41.6 cm)
Robert Lehman Collection, 1975 1975.1.129

Attributed to Hans Memling, active by 1465, died 1494
Portrait of a Young Woman
Oil on wood; overall 10¼ x 8¼ in. (26 x 21 cm); painted surface 9⅛ x 7¼ in. (23.2 x 18.4 cm)
Bequest of Mary Stillman Harkness, 1950 50.145.28

Netherlandish Painter, about 1520
Charles V* (1500–1558), *Holy Roman Emperor
Oil on wood, 11⅝ x 8⅞ in. (29.5 x 22.5 cm)
The Friedsam Collection, Bequest of Michael Friedsam, 1931 32.100.46

Workshop of Joos van Cleve, active by 1507, died 1540/41
Francis I* (1494–1547), *King of France
Oil on canvas, transferred from wood, 16 x 12⅞ in. (40.6 x 32.7 cm)
The Friedsam Collection, Bequest of Michael Friedsam, 1931 32.100.120

Netherlandish Painter, first quarter of 16th century
Portrait of a Young Man of the Van Steynoert Family
Oil on wood, with arched top; overall, with engaged frame, 16⅛ x 12¾ in. (41 x 32.4 cm); painted surface 13⅝ x 10⅛ in. (34.6 x 25.7 cm)
Arms (upper left) of the Van Steynoert family
The Friedsam Collection, Bequest of Michael Friedsam, 1931 32.100.45

Attributed to Quentin Massys (also Matsys or Metsys), 1465/66–1530
Portrait of a Man
Oil on wood, arched top; overall, with engaged frame, 18⅛ x 13½ in. (46 x 34.3 cm); painted surface 15⅝ x 11¼ in. (39.7 x 28.6 cm)
Inscribed (on collar): LEVER
The Friedsam Collection, Bequest of Michael Friedsam, 1931 32.100.49

Netherlandish Painter, first half of 16th century
Portrait of a Man
Oil on wood, arched top; overall 8¼ x 6½ in. (21 x 16.5 cm); painted surface 8⅛ x 6⅛ in. (20.6 x 15.6 cm)
The Jack and Belle Linsky Collection, 1982 1982.60.28

Attributed to Jan Cornelisz. Vermeyen, 1500–1559
Portrait of a Man with a Rosary
Oil on wood, 20 x 16¼ in. (50.8 x 41.3 cm)
Dated and inscribed: (left of sitter's head) ·1545·; (right of sitter's head) ·63·
The Jack and Belle Linsky Collection, 1982 1982.60.27

Attributed to Jan Cornelisz. Vermeyen, 1500–1559
***Queen Mary of Hungary* (1505–1558)**
Oil on wood, 21½ x 18 in. (54.6 x 45.7 cm)
The Jack and Belle Linsky Collection, 1982 1982.60.26

Netherlandish Painter, about 1535
Portrait of a Young Woman
Oil on wood, 10½ x 8¼ in. (26.7 x 21 cm)
The Jules Bache Collection, 1949 49.7.32

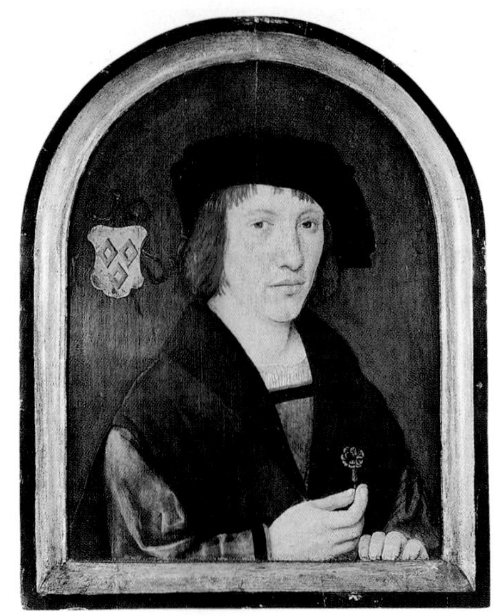
32.100.45

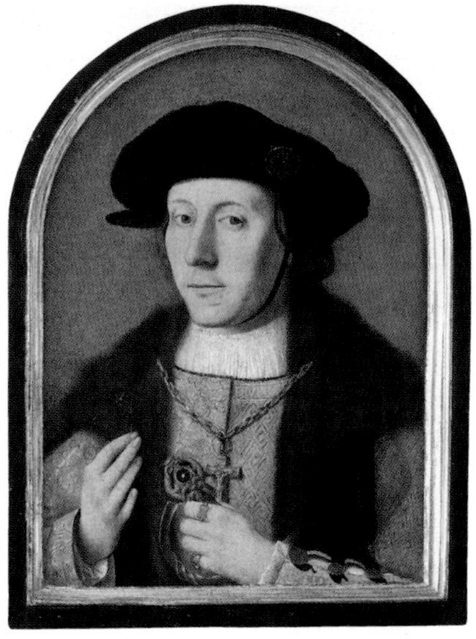
32.100.49

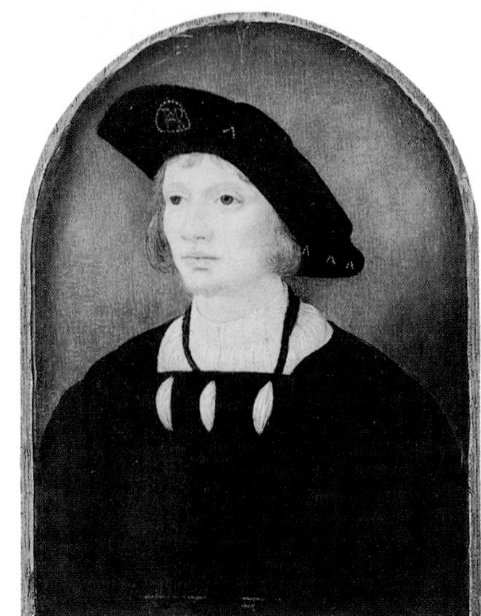
1982.60.28

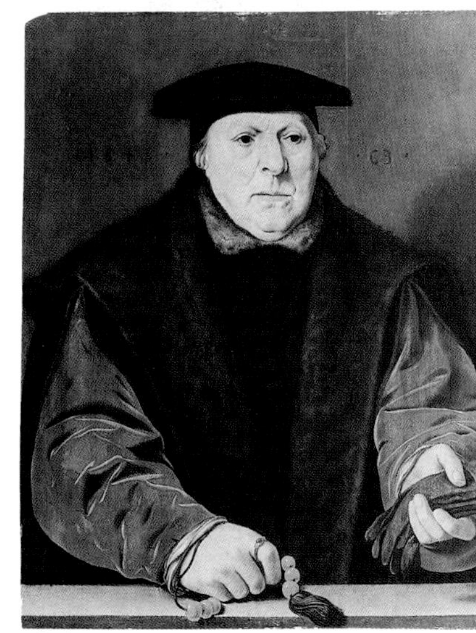
1982.60.27

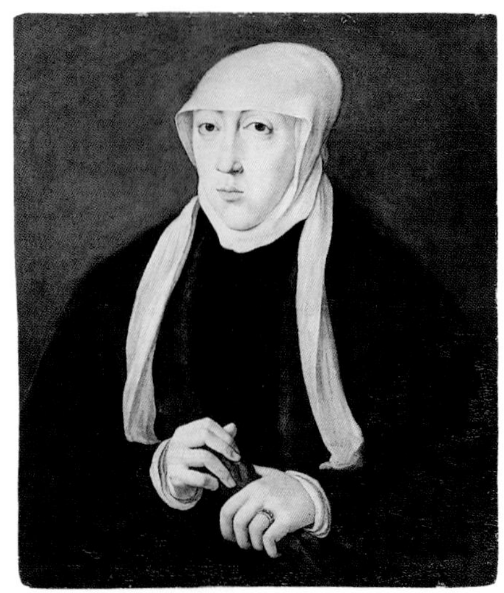
1982.60.26

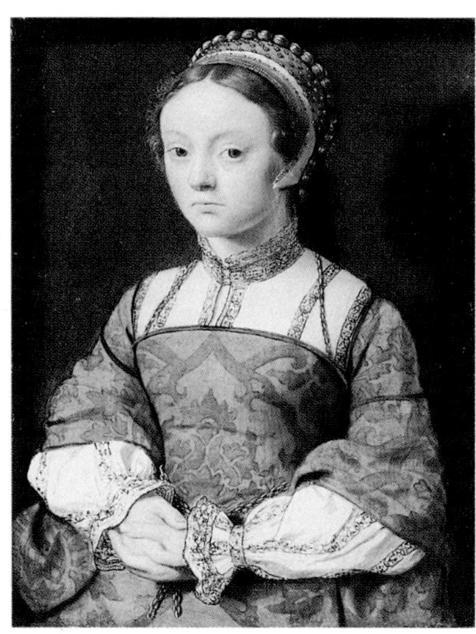
49.7.32

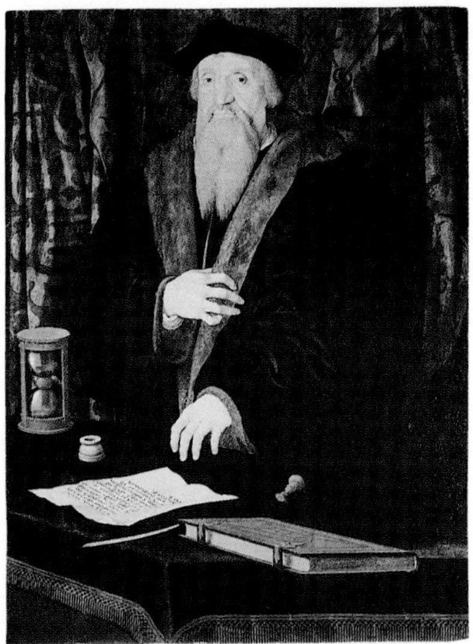
91.26.3

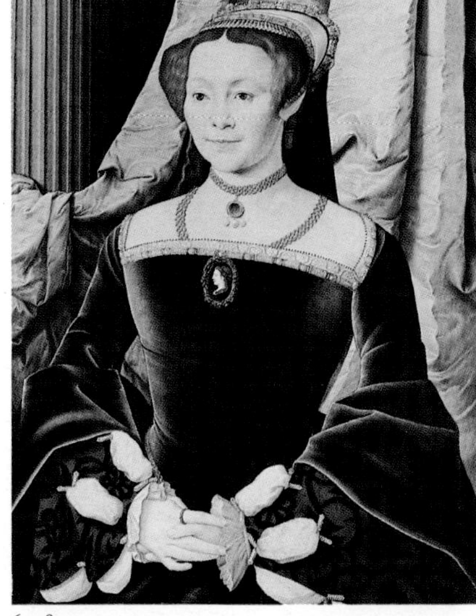
69.282

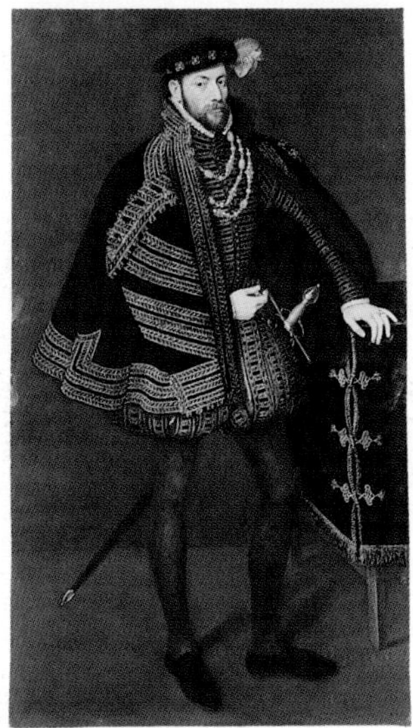
51.5

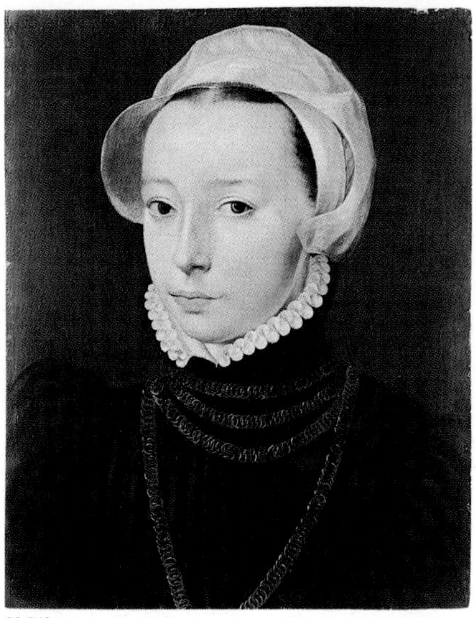
39.143

Netherlandish Painter, dated 1539
Portrait of a Man, Possibly Jean de Langeac* (died 1541), *Bishop of Limoges
Oil on wood, 47¼ x 34½ in. (120 x 87.6 cm)
Dated and inscribed: (lower left) A° D. 1539; (on paper) SCĪAMVS ENIM QVONĪA[M] / TERRESTRIS DOMVS N[OST]R̄A / HVIVS HABITATIO[N]ĪS DIS SOVLET̄[VR] ET Q[VOD] [A]EDIFICATIO[N]Ē[M] / EX DEO HABEM'[VS] DOMV̄[M] NO[N] / MANVFACTA[M] [A]ETERNA[M] IN / C[O]ELIS NĀ[M] ET INhOC Ī[N]GEMISCIM'[VS] / HABITATIO[N]Ē[M] N[OST]R̄A[M] Q[VAE] DE / C[O]ELO Ē[ST] SVP[ER]Ī[N]DVI CVPIĒ[N]TES / SI T[AME]N̄ VESTITI ET NŌ[N] / [N]VDI INVENIAMVR / AD. COR.2 / CAP.5. (For we know that, if our earthly house of this tabernacle were dissolved, we have a building of God, a house not made with hands, eternal in the heavens. For in this we groan, earnestly desiring to be clothed upon with our house which is from heaven: If so be that being clothed we shall not be found naked [2 Corinthians 5:1–3].)
Marquand Collection, Gift of Henry G. Marquand, 1890 91.26.3

Netherlandish Painter, about 1540–50
Portrait of a Woman
Oil on wood, 29¼ x 22⅝ in. (74.3 x 57.5 cm)
Gift of Winston F. C. Guest, 1969 69.282

Anthonis Mor van Dashorst, 1519–1575
Portrait of a Man, Possibly Ottavio Farnese* (1524–1586), *Duke of Parma and Piacenza
Oil on canvas, 82¼ x 46¾ in. (208.9 x 118.7 cm)
Dated (left center): 1563
Gift of Mr. and Mrs. Nate B. Spingold, 1951 51.5

Pieter Jansz. Pourbus, 1524–1584
Portrait of a Young Woman
Oil on wood, 15½ x 12½ in. (39.4 x 31.8 cm)
Charles B. Curtis Fund, 1939 39.143

Glossary

acheiropoetoi: images not made by human hands; thought to have been miraculously created, such as the *vera icon,* or the Holy Face; associated with devotional practices in the Eastern Church

alb: a full-length white linen tunic or vestment gathered by a rope or belt at the waist that is worn by the clergy during Mass

Andachtsbild: German for "devotional image"; used to signify an image extracted from a larger, often narrative context as an aid in private prayer

Antwerp Mannerists: artists who worked during the first half of the sixteenth century producing paintings for the Antwerp art market directed at an international clientele; their work synthesized Italian ideals and native traditions, emphasizing demonstrative gestures, elaborate costumes, architectural settings with both Gothic and Renaissance motifs, and decorative and figurative elements derived from prints

Ara Coeli: Latin for "Altar of Heaven"; a reference to the vision of Emperor Augustus of a virgin on an altar and holding a child and, by extension, to Mary and Christ

Ark of the Covenant: the gilt box containing the Tablets of the Law, which by analogy came to signify the Virgin bearing Christ, the heir of the Law, in her womb

aspergillum: a brush for the sprinkling of holy water

Benedictine order: founded by Saint Benedict (about 480–547) and the oldest Western monastic order; its rule became the standard for subsequent monastic law and includes vows of poverty, chastity, and obedience, stressing both worldly and religious education

Biblia Pauperum: literally "Bible of the Poor"; the text is accompanied by images that draw parallels between Old and New Testament themes; used to instruct poor clergy and the laity

Saint Bonaventure (about 1217–1274): the Franciscan author of *The Mind's Road to God,* a treatise designed to guide the individual along a sacred journey, during which the spiritual self unites with God; religious texts of this kind were extremely popular during the fifteenth and sixteenth centuries and inspired devotional art emphasizing Christ's suffering and humanity

book of hours: an often lavishly illustrated book used by the laity for private devotions, consisting of prayers organized according to the eight specified times (canonical hours) of the Church day

breviary: a book of texts, often illustrated, used by the clergy and members of monastic orders for the daily recitation of the Divine Office

canonical hours: see Divine Office

Carthusian order: established by the hermit saint Bruno (about 1030–1101) at the monastery of Chartreuse, France, in 1084; the most austere of Western monastic orders, it cultivates a solitary and contemplative life

cartoon: a full-scale pattern drawing used to transfer a motif or composition to the prepared ground of a panel by means of pouncing or by tracing outlines with a stylus

censer: a container for incense suspended from chains and swung at designated times during Mass

chiaroscuro: an Italian term used to describe pronounced effects of light and dark in painting

ciborium: a container for the consecrated wafer, or Host, offered during Communion; also a canopy over the altar

cloth of honor: a cloth of brocade or other sumptuous material that is usually shown hanging behind the Virgin to signify her status as Queen of Heaven

compassio* and *co-redemptio: the doctrine that Mary, through her empathic suffering (*compassio*) with Christ at the Crucifixion, shares her son's power to redeem mankind (*co-redemptio*)

corpus verum: Latin for "true body"; the Eucharist; with its liturgical associations, the *corpus verum* can also apply to Christ worshiped by Mary and Joseph at the Nativity

couleur changeante: literally "changing color" in French; refers to shot, or iridescent, woven fabrics, and in painting to a style of modeling draperies of one color with another of lower value; especially favored by the Antwerp Mannerists

dendrochronology: a method of dating the wood of panel paintings; by measuring the annual hardwood rings at the edge of a panel and comparing them to a master chronology based on securely dated wood, a terminus post quem can be established for the painting

Devotio moderna: see Modern Devotion

diptych: two panel paintings of equal size joined together by hinges at their inner edges; the diptych can be closed like a book and is usually small and portable

Divine Office: the ritual of daily prayer of Catholic

nuns, monks, and clerics; it includes psalms and lessons and is divided into the canonical hours, the eight services of Matins, Lauds, Prime, Terce, Sext, None, Vespers, and Compline

Dominican order: founded by Saint Dominic (1170–1221) in 1216 and dedicated to preaching and study; prominent in medieval universities and often the order of official theologians, such as Thomas Aquinas; it was a strong proponent of the rosary

Ecce Homo: "Behold the Man," the words uttered by Pilate when, finding no crime had been committed, he presented Jesus to the assembled crowd of chief priests and other Jews who would decide Christ's fate (John 19:4–16)

***elousa* icon:** a compassionate type; an image of the Virgin and the Christ Child (see *glykophilousa*)

engaged frame: a frame that is attached to the panel before it is painted; also a frame carved from the panel that supports the painting, with which it forms a single unit

Eucharist: the sacrament in which consecrated bread (the Host) and wine are offered to communicants as the body and blood of Christ; whether Christ is literally or symbolically present in the Eucharist was debated during the Reformation

Franciscan order: founded in 1208 by Saint Francis of Assisi (about 1182–1226); also known as the Friars Minor, its vows include poverty, chastity, and obedience

galactotrophousa* or *Virgo lactans: a Byzantine-derived image in which Mary nurses the Child while he sits or reclines on her lap

glykophilousa: an affectionate type; Byzantine-derived image in which the Child turns toward Mary, presses his cheek to hers, looks up to her face, and embraces her with both arms

The Golden Legend: see Jacobus de Voragine

grisaille: derived from *gris,* French for "gray"; painting in shades of gray intended to simulate sculpture

ground: the priming applied to the panel support as the initial layer of a painting; during the period under consideration, it was composed of chalk (calcium carbonate) and rabbit-skin glue in northern Europe and gypsum (calcium sulfate) in southern Europe

Holy Face: the image said to have been miraculously imprinted upon Veronica's veil when she wiped the sweat from Christ's face as he carried the cross to Golgotha; Veronica, whose name means "true image," or *vera icon,* was a particularly popular subject in fifteenth-century devotional images

hortus conclusus: an enclosed garden, referred to in the Song of Solomon (4:12), and used in painting as a metaphor for Mary's virginity

icon: Greek for "image"; an image of a sacred person for veneration

iconography: the study and interpretation of images and symbols as they relate to the meaning of a work of art

Imago Pietatis: Latin for "image of pity"; often Christ as the Man of Sorrows and sometimes showing the crucified Christ before the cross with his hands folded in front of his chest; the type was based on an icon brought from Constantinople to Santa Croce in Gerusalemme, Rome, about 1380

indulgence: a remission of temporal punishment for the commission of sins or shortening of time to be spent in purgatory before admission to heaven; gained by reciting prayers, undertaking of pilgrimages, donating money, or performing good works

infrared reflectography: an imaging technique used to study underdrawings and underlayers of paint invisible to the naked eye, whereby an infrared vidicon sensitive to infrared radiation in a wavelength up to approximately 2,000 nanometers penetrates paint layers to varying degrees; in use with early Netherlandish painting, the vidicon camera detects the underdrawing (usually executed in black chalk, charcoal, or dark inks or pigments), which absorbs infrared radiation, while the white ground reflects it; the resulting image is visible on a monitor and can be documented photographically or digitally and stored for further processing on a computer

laity: practicing Christians who are not members of the clergy and have not taken religious vows

The Life of Christ: see Ludolph of Saxony

liturgy: the religious ceremony or ceremonies conducted in church; also the texts for such ceremonies

Ludolph of Saxony (about 1295–1377): the Carthusian who wrote *The Life of Christ;* drawn from the Gospels, the volume was the most widely read life of Christ in the Middle Ages and became an influential force in late medieval piety

Magnificat: a song of praise recited by the Virgin Mary during the Visitation, as she responded to her cousin Elizabeth's recognition of her as the Mother of God; recorded in the Gospel of Luke (1:46–55)

Man of Sorrows: see *Imago Pietatis*

Maria lactans* or *Virgo lactans: a representation of the Virgin suckling the Christ Child; a popular subject in mystical literature of the late Middle Ages

Meditations on the Life of Christ: see Pseudo-Bonaventure

The Mind's Road to God: see Saint Bonaventure

miniature: a picture on vellum or parchment framed by decorative motifs, which can be part of a book or an independent work

Modern Devotion: in Latin, *Devotio moderna;* a reform movement started in the late fourteenth century by the north Netherlander Geert Grote; it held that the individual must imitate Christ by identifying with his life and sufferings, renounce the world, and embrace virtue; first practiced by the Brothers of the Common Life, it became more popular and widespread in the fifteenth century

Nicholas of Cusa (1401–1464): wrote *The Vision of God* in 1453 while he was bishop of Brixen (today Bressanone); the treatise, delivered to the monks at the abbey of Tegernsee with a now-lost icon, sanctions the use of icons for devotional contemplation

Ommegang: a procession, often of members of local confraternities and guilds, that includes tableaux vivants and reenactments of sacred themes and celebrates a religious event and/or venerated icon

orans: Latin for "praying"; a position of the hands raised in prayer toward heaven and beseeching God

parchment: animal skin, usually from a sheep or goat, prepared to receive writing and illuminations (see vellum)

Passion of Christ: the events surrounding the Crucifixion of Christ; a popular subject for religious drama and painting, it often begins with the Entry into Jerusalem and ends with the Ascension or Descent of the Holy Ghost; single subjects or entire cycles of consecutive scenes can be represented

pastiche: elements from a variety of paintings by a single artist or several different artists combined and reconfigured to make a new work

paten: a flat, round plate, often of gold or silver, used to hold the wafer or bread of the Eucharist

paternoster beads: the large rosary beads that divide groups of ten small beads, or aves; the Paternoster, or Lord's, prayer begins "Our Father who art in heaven" and is recited while pausing at this bead (see rosary)

polyptych: an ensemble of four or more painted panels; in early Netherlandish practice they are usually hinged together to form a folding altarpiece; southern European polyptychs are more commonly placed in fixed architectural frames

Porta Coeli: "Gate of Heaven"; Latin epithet for the Virgin, who at the Incarnation provided access to heaven for humanity

pouncing: a technique of transferring a design from a cartoon to the grounded surface of a painting, whereby holes are pricked along the contours of the drawing in a design that is placed on top of the panel to be painted; a loose-weave bag holding powdered charcoal or chalk dust is then daubed onto the drawing, whose holes allow the dust to filter through to the panel, leaving a series of dots conforming to the outlines of the pattern

Pseudo-Bonaventure: the thirteenth-century author of *Meditations on the Life of Christ*, a popular devotional text that guides the reader through the major events of Christ's life, such as the Passion; the extremely graphic descriptions—elaborations of accounts in the Gospels—are intended to evoke intense emotional responses; it also elicits identification with the Virgin Mary and her compassion for Christ's suffering

retable: an architectural structure, organized in horizontal tiers or vertical bands and usually of carved and polychromed wood, placed behind the altar to frame paintings, sculptures, reliefs, or reliquaries; typically used in Spain and Portugal

Rex Regnum: Latin for "King of Kings"; refers to Christ as Lord of all humankind

rosary: devotional aid with set prayers to the Virgin; divided into five decades of small ave, or Hail Mary, prayer beads, separated by large paternoster, or Our Father, prayer beads; the practice of saying the rosary originated in the second half of the fifteenth century and was especially promoted by the Dominicans

Salvator Mundi: Latin for "Savior of the World"; a bust-length, frontal devotional image of Christ in a decorated red robe, blessing with his right hand and holding an orb surmounted by a cross in his left hand

sfumato: the soft blending of shadows

Speculum Humanae Salvationis: a typological text by an anonymous early-fourteenth-century author; each page is divided into four equal rectangular fields, each containing an illustration above a column of text; the illustrations and the text draw parallels between a scene from the Life of Christ or the Life of the Virgin and three prefigurations from the Old Testament

stigmata: five marks corresponding to the wounds Christ sustained at the Crucifixion as his hands and feet were nailed to the cross and his side was pierced by Longinus's spear; these miraculously appeared on the body of Saint Francis as he meditated upon the crucified Christ

tabernacle: a receptacle used to house the consecrated Host (see Eucharist)

tableau vivant: French for "living picture"; a scene from a sacred or secular text portrayed by motionless and usually silent costumed actors on a temporary stage during a religious or secular procession, entry into a city by an official, or court celebration

thalamus virginis: Latin for "bed of the Virgin"; refers to the Virgin Mary's conjugal bed

triptych: three painted panels, in the Netherlands usually hinged together; the centerpiece is commonly twice the width of the lateral wings, which can be folded over the central panel to close the ensemble and protect it

trompe l'oeil: French for "fool the eye"; a style of painting intended to trick the viewer into believing that the minutely observed objects shown are real

underdrawing: the preliminary sketch, either summary or detailed, on the grounded panel or canvas by which the artist works out the design to be represented in the upper, painted layers; although hidden by the painted layers, the underdrawing can be made visible through infrared reflectography

Vaderboec: a fifteenth-century text on the lives of the saints, published by Gerard Lecu, that was a source for popular motifs in devotional paintings

veil of Veronica: see Holy Face

vellum: calfskin prepared to receive writing and illuminations (see parchment)

vera icon: see Holy Face

The Vision of God: see Nicholas of Cusa

Jacobus de Voragine (1228 or 1230–1298): a Dominican friar and archbishop of Genoa; author of the immensely popular *Golden Legend* (1255–66), a chronicle of the lives of the saints that combines fact and fiction and includes legends of the Virgin as well as narratives related to feast days of the Church

X-radiograph: an image produced by passing low-voltage X-rays through paintings and overlying sensitive film simultaneously; because X-rays penetrate pigments of different densities in different degrees, they leave light film images of the areas of greatest density, particularly those with lead white, and dark ones of the less dense areas; radiographs show details of brushwork and often reveal losses or changes made during the painting process that are not visible to the naked eye

Bibliography

SELECTED READINGS

The reader is directed to this brief selection of general books on the history, culture, and art of the Netherlands during the fifteenth and sixteenth centuries, particularly as these topics relate to the Metropolitan Museum's collection:

Benesch, Otto. *The Art of the Renaissance in Northern Europe: Its Relation to the Contemporary Spiritual and Intellectual Movements.* London, 1965.

Blum, Shirley Neilsen. *Early Netherlandish Triptychs: A Study in Patronage.* Berkeley, 1969.

Cuttler, Charles D. *Northern Painting from Pucelle to Bruegel: Fourteenth, Fifteenth, and Sixteenth Centuries.* New York, 1968. Reprint ed., New York, 1973.

Friedländer, Max J. *Early Netherlandish Painting.* Translated by Heinz Norden. Comments and notes by Nicole Veronée-Verhaegen. 14 vols. in 16. New York, 1967–76.

Harbison, Craig. *The Mirror of the Artist: Northern Renaissance Art in Its Historical Context.* London, 1995.

Huizinga, Johan. *The Autumn of the Middle Ages.* Translated by R. J. Payton and U. Mammitzsch. Chicago, 1996.

Lane, Barbara G. *Flemish Painting outside Bruges, 1400–1500: An Annotated Bibliography.* Boston, 1986.

Mundy, E. James. *Painting in Bruges, 1470–1550: An Annotated Bibliography.* Boston, 1985.

von der Osten, Gert, and Horst Vey. *Painting and Sculpture in Germany and the Netherlands, 1500–1600.* Translated from German by Mary Hottinger. Harmondsworth, 1969.

Panofsky, Erwin. *Early Netherlandish Painting: Its Origins and Character.* Cambridge, Mass., 1953. Reprinted, New York, 1971.

Parshall, Linda B., and Peter W. Parshall. *Art and the Reformation: An Annotated Bibliography.* Boston, 1986.

de Patoul, Brigitte, and Roger van Schoute. *Les Primitifs flamands et leurs temps.* Louvain-la-Neuve, 1994.

Prevenier, Walter, and Wim Blockmans. *The Burgundian Netherlands.* Translated by P. Kin and Y. Mead. Cambridge, 1986.

Ringbom, Sixten. *Icon to Narrative: The Rise of the Dramatic Close-up in Fifteenth-Century Devotional Painting.* 2d ed. Doornspijk, 1984.

Snyder, James. *Northern Renaissance Art: Painting, Sculpture, and the Graphic Arts from 1350 to 1575.* New York, 1985.

van der Stock, Jan, ed. *Antwerp, Story of a Metropolis, 16th–17th Century.* Exh. cat. Antwerp: Hessenhuis, 1993.

Vermeersch, Valentin, ed. *Bruges and Europe.* Antwerp, 1992.

REFERENCES

Acres, Al

n.d. "The Columba Altarpiece and the Time of the World." *Art Bulletin.* Forthcoming.

Acta Sanctorum

1863–1931 *Acta Sanctorum,* by Conrado Ianningo, Ioanne Bapt. Sollerio, Ioanne Pinio, and Societate Iesu Presbyteris Theologis. New ed., revised by Joanne Carnandet. 67 vols. in 69 parts. Paris.

Adhémar, Hélène

1962 *Le Musée National du Louvre, Paris.* Les primitifs flamands, I: Corpus de la peinture des anciens Pays-Bas mériodionaux au quinzième siècle, 5. Brussels.

Agrasot, R.

1911 "La civilización actual y las artes." *Museum: Revista mensual de arte español* 1, pp. 9–20.

Ainsworth, Maryan W.

1985 "Gerard David's Working Methods: Some Preliminary Observations." In *Le dessin sous-jacent dans la peinture: Colloque V, 1982,* edited by R. van Schoute and D. Hollanders-Favart, pp. 53–60. Louvain-la-Neuve.

1988 "Gerard David's Drawings for the *Justice of Cambyses* Once Again." *Burlington Magazine* 130, pp. 528–30.

1989a "Northern Renaissance Drawings and Underdrawings: A Proposed Method of Study." *Master Drawings* 27 (spring), pp. 5–38.

1989b "Reassessing the Form and Function of Gerard David's Drawings and Underdrawings." In *Le dessin sous-jacent dans la peinture: Colloque VII, 1984,* edited by R. van Schoute and D. Hollanders-Favart, pp. 131–36. Louvain-la-Neuve.

1990 Review of *Gerard David,* by Hans J. van Miegroet. *Art Bulletin* 72, pp. 649–54.

1992a Entries on Bernaert van Orley, Gerard David, Joos van Cleve, and Hans Memling. In Bauman and Liedtke 1992.

1992b "Implications of Revised Attributions in Netherlandish Painting." *Metropolitan Museum Journal* 27, pp. 59–76.

1992c "New Observations on the Working Technique in Simon Marmion's Panel Paintings." In *Margaret of York, Simon Marmion, and "The Visions of Tondal,"* edited by Thomas Kren, pp. 243–55. Malibu.

1993 "Gerard David's Workshop Practice—an Overview." In *Le dessin sous-jacent dans la peinture: Colloque IX, 1991*, edited by R. van Schoute and H. Verougstraete-Marcq, pp. 11–33. Louvain-la-Neuve.

1993–95 *Facsimile in Early Netherlandish Painting: Dieric Bouts's "Virgin and Child."* Exh. cat. New York: The Metropolitan Museum of Art.

1994a "Hans Memling as a Draughtsman." In De Vos 1994a, vol. 2, pp. 78–87.

1994b *Petrus Christus, Renaissance Master of Bruges.* Contributions by Maximiliaan P. J. Martens. Exh. cat. New York: The Metropolitan Museum of Art.

1994c "Gerard David." In De Patoul and Van Schoute 1994, pp. 482–93.

1995 [as editor]. *Petrus Christus in Renaissance Bruges: An Interdisciplinary Approach.* New York and Turnhout.

1996 "The *Virgin and Child in an Apse*: Reconsidering a Campin Workshop Design." In Foister and Nash 1996, pp. 147–58.

1997a "The *Mocking of Christ*: A Hitherto Unknown Painting by Gerard David." *Städel-Jahrbuch*, n.s., 16, pp. 159–70.

1997b "Old Assumptions Reconsidered Through Revised Methodologies." In *Le dessin sous-jacent dans la peinture: Colloque XI, 1995*, edited by R. van Schoute and H. Verougstraete-Marcq. Louvain-la-Neuve.

1998a *Gerard David—Purity of Vision in an Age of Transition: Paintings in The Metropolitan Museum of Art and Other New York Collections.* New York. Forthcoming.

1998b "An Unfinished Landscape Painting Attributed to the Master LC and Sixteenth-Century Workshop Practice." In *Herri Met de Bles: Studies and Explorations of the World Landscape Tradition*, edited by James Marrow, Betsy Rosasco, and Norman Muller, pp. 117–27. Turnhout.

Alberti, Leon Battista

1966 *On Painting.* Rev. ed. Translated by John R. Spencer. New Haven.

1972 On Painting *and* On Sculpture*: The Latin Texts of* De pictura *and* De statua. Edited and translated by Cecil Grayson. London.

1988 *On the Art of Building in Ten Books.* Translated by Joseph Rykwert, Neil Leach, and Robert Tavernor. Cambridge, Mass.

Ames-Lewis, Francis

1979 "Fra Filippo Lippi and Flanders." *Zeitschrift für Kunstgeschichte* 42, pp. 253–73.

1993a "Painters in Padua and Netherlandish Art, 1435–1455." In *Italienische Frührenaissance und nordeuropäisches Spätmittelalter*, edited by Joachim Poeschke, pp. 179–93. Munich.

1993b "Princes, Court Painters, and Netherlandish Art." In *Mantegna and 15th-Century Court Culture*, edited by Francis Ames-Lewis and Anka Bednarek, pp. 103–14. London: Birkbeck College.

Angelantoni Malfatti, Giuseppina

1997 "Hans Memling à Milan: Une hypothèse." In *Memling Studies* 1997, pp. 105–14.

Anzelewsky, Fedja

1957 "À propos de la topographie du pard de Bruxelles et du quai de l'Escaut à Anvers de Durer." *Bulletin des Musées royaux des Beaux-Arts de Belgique* 6, pp. 87–107.

Arasse, Daniel

1976 "À propos de l'article de Meyer Schapiro, *Muscipula Diaboli*: Le 'réseau figuratif' du retable de Mérode." In *Symboles de la Renaissance*, pp. 47–56. Paris.

Arbois de Joubainville, H. d'

1861 *Répertoire archéologique de l'Aube.* Paris.

Armstrong, C. A. J.

1977 "The Golden Age of Burgundy: Dukes That Outdid Kings." In *The Courts of Europe: Politics, Patronage, and Royalty, 1400–1800*, edited by A. G. Dickens, pp. 55–75. London.

Armstrong, Walter

1892 *Exhibition of Pictures by Masters of the Netherlandish and Allied Schools of XV and Early XVI Centuries.* Exh. cat. London: Burlington Fine Arts Club.

van Asperen de Boer, J. R. J.

1970 "Infrared Reflectography: A Contribution to the Examination of Earlier European Painting." Dissertation, Amsterdam University.

van Asperen de Boer, J. R. J., Bernhard Ridderbos, and Manja Zeldenrust

1991 "*Portret van een man met een ring* door Jan van Eyck / *Portrait of a Man with a Ring* by Jan van Eyck." *Bulletin van het Rijksmuseum* 39, pp. 8–35.

van Asperen de Boer, J. R. J., and Arthur K. Wheelock

1973 "Underdrawing in Some Paintings by Cornelis Engebrechtsz." *Oud Holland* 87, pp. 61–94.

van Asperen de Boer, J. R. J., et al.

1992 "Underdrawing in Paintings of the Rogier van der Weyden and Master of Flémalle Groups," by J. R. J. van Asperen de Boer, Jellie Dijkstra, and Roger van Schoute, with the collaboration of C. M. A. Dalderup and J. P. Filedt Kok. *Nederlands Kunsthistorisch Jaarboek* 41 (1990).

Bache, Jules Semon

1937 *A Catalogue of Paintings in the Bache Collection.* New York.

1943 *A Catalogue of Paintings in the Bache Collection.* Rev. ed. Exh. cat. New York: The Metropolitan Museum of Art.

Baes-Dondeyne, Marguerite

1969 "Een teruggevonden luik van het Brussels geboorteretabel uit 'The Cloisters' te New York." *Bulletin van het Koninklijk Instituut voor het Kunstpatrimonium* 11, pp. 93–108.

Baetjer, Katharine

1977 "Pleasures and Problems of Early French Painting." *Apollo* 106, pp. 340–49.

1980 *European Paintings in The Metropolitan Museum of Art by Artists Born in or before 1865: A Summary Catalogue.* 3 vols. New York.

1995 *European Paintings in The Metropolitan Museum of Art by Artists Born before 1865: A Summary Catalogue.* New York.

Baetjer, Katharine, et al.

1986 "The Jack and Belle Linsky Collection in The Metropolitan Museum of Art: Addenda to the Catalogue." *Metropolitan Museum Journal* 21, pp. 153–84.

Baldass, Ludwig von

1920–21 "Mabuses 'Heilige Nacht,' eine freie Kopie nach Hugo van der Goes." *Jahrbuch der Kunsthistorischen Sammlungen in Wien* 35, pp. 34–48.

1920–21a "Ein Frühwerk des Geertgen tot Sint Jans und die holländische Malerei des XV. Jahrhunderts." *Jahrbuch der Kunsthistorischen Sammlungen in Wien* 35, pp. 1–33.
1925 *Joos van Cleve, der Meister des Todes Mariä.* Vienna.
1927 "Die Niederländer des 15. und 16. Jahrhunderts auf der Ausstellung flämischer Kunst in London 1927." *Belvedere,* 11, pp. 109–11.
1930 "Drei Jahrhunderte flämische Malerei." *Pantheon* 5 (January–June), pp. 130–36.
1931 "Ein Madonnentüchlein aus der Nähe des Quinten Massys." In *Mélanges Hulin de Loo,* pp. 1–9. Brussels and Paris.
1932 "Die Entwicklung des Dirk Bouts." *Jahrbuch der Kunsthistorischen Sammlungen in Wien,* n.s., 6, pp. 77–114.
1936 "Gerard David als Landschaftsmaler." *Jahrbuch der Kunsthistorischen Sammlungen in Wien,* n.s., 10, pp. 89–96.
1937 "Die niederländischen Maler des spätgotischen Stiles." *Jahrbuch der Kunsthistorischen Sammlungen in Wien,* n.s., 11, pp. 117–38.
1952 *Jan van Eyck.* London.

Bangs, Jeremy D.
1979 *Cornelis Engebrechtsz.'s Leiden: Studies in Cultural History.* Assen.

Barocchi, Paola, ed.
1971–77 *Scritti d'arte del cinquecento.* 3 vols. Milan and Naples.

van Bastelaer, René
1924 "Notes sur quelques peintures du maître anonyme dit 'de Sainte-Gudule.'" *Bulletin de la Classe des Beaux-Arts . . .* 6, no. 1–3, pp. 16ff.

Baudisch, Carl
1940 *Jan Joest von Kalkar: Ein Beitrag zur Kunstgeschichte des Niederrheins.* Bonn.

Bauman, Guy C.
1986 "Early Flemish Portraits, 1425–1525." *Metropolitan Museum of Art Bulletin* 43, no. 4 (spring).
1989 "A Rosary Picture with a View of the Park of the Ducal Palace in Brussels, Possibly by Goswijn van der Weyden." *Metropolitan Museum Journal* 24, pp. 135–51.

Bauman, Guy C., and Walter A. Liedtke, eds.
1992 *Flemish Paintings in America: A Survey of Early Netherlandish and Flemish Paintings in the Public Collections of North America.* Antwerp.

Bax, Dirk
1949 *Ontcijfering van Jeroen Bosch.* The Hague.
1979 *Hieronymus Bosch: His Picture-Writing Deciphered.* Translated by N. A. Bax-Botha. Rotterdam.

Baxandall, Michael
1971 *Giotto and the Orators: Humanist Observers of Painting in Italy and the Discovery of Pictorial Composition, 1350–1450.* Oxford.
1986 *Giotto and the Orators: Humanist Observers of Painting in Italy and the Discovery of Pictorial Composition, 1350–1450.* Revised ed. Oxford.

Bazin, Germain
1931 "L'Esprit d'imitation dans l'art flamand: Le thème de la Madone dans une abside." *L'amour de l'art* 12.
1952 "Petrus Christus et les rapports entre l'Italie et la Flandre au milieu du XVe siècle." *Revue des arts,* December, pp. 194–208.

Beenken, Hermann
1937 "The Annunciation of Petrus Christus in the Metropolitan Museum and the Problem of Hubert van Eyck." *Art Bulletin* 19, pp. 220–41.
1951 *Rogier van der Weyden.* Munich.

Belting, Hans
1981 *Das Bild und sein Publikum im Mittelalter.* Berlin.

Belting, Hans, and Dagmar Eichberger
1983 *Jan van Eyck als Erzähler: Frühe Tafelbilder im Umkreis der New Yorker Doppeltafel.* Worms.

Belting, Hans, and Christiane Kruse
1994 *Die Erfindung des Gemäldes: Das erste Jahrhundert der niederländischen Malerei.* Munich.

Benesch, Otto
1965 *The Art of the Renaissance in Northern Europe: Its Relation to the Contemporary Spiritual and Intellectual Movements.* London.

Benoît, Camille
1901 "La peinture française à la fin du XVe siècle (1480–1501)." *Gazette des Beaux-Arts,* ser. 3, 26, pp. 89–101, 318–32, 368–80.

Berger, Adolf, ed.
1883 "Inventar der Kunstsammlung des Erzherzogs Leopold Wilhelm von Österreich." *Jahrbuch der Kunsthistorischen Sammlungen des Allerhöchsten Kaiserhauses* 1, pp. LXXIX–CLXXVII.

Bergmans, S.
1969 "Cornelis Massys (Antwerpen um 1510–nach 1562)." In Galerie Friederike Pallamar, *Katalog der 22. Austellung in Wien,* p. 21. Vienna.

Bergström, Ingvar
1955 "Disguised Symbolism in 'Madonna' Pictures and Still Life." *Burlington Magazine* 97, pp. 303–8, 342–49.

Bermejo, Elisa
1962 *Juan de Flandes.* Madrid.
1975 "Gerard David y Ambrosius Benson, autores de dos pinturas ineditas de la Virgen con el Niño." *Archivo español de arte* 3, pp. 259–63.
1991 "Una Virgen con el Niño de Joos van Cleve monogramada y noticias sobre una adoración." *Archivo español de arte* 64, pp. 349–53.

Bermejo Martinez, Elisa
1980–82 *La pintura de los primitivos flamencos en España.* 2 vols. Madrid.

Bertaux, Emile
1914 "Correspondance d'Angleterre: L'Exposition espagnole de Londres." *Gazette des Beaux-Arts,* ser. 3, 56, pp. 250–64.

Bialostocki, Jan
1956 *Bruegel–Pejzażysta.* Poznań.
1966 *Les musées de Pologne: (Gdansk, Krakow, Warszawa).* Les primitifs flamands, I: Corpus de la peinture des anciens Pays-Bas mériodionaux au quinzième siècle, 9. Brussels.
1970 "The Eye and the Window." In *Festschrift für Gert von der Osten.* Cologne.

van Biervliet, Lori
1991 *Leven en werk van W. H. James Weale: Een Engels kunsthistoricus in Vlaanderen in de 19de eeuw.* Verhandelingen van de Koninklijke Academie voor Wetenschappen, Letteren, en Schone Kunsten van België 53, no. 55. Brussels.

Birkmeyer, Karl M.
1961 "The Arch Motif in Netherlandish Painting of the Fifteenth Century," parts 1, 2. *Art Bulletin* 43, pp. 1–20, 99–112.

Blanc, Charles
1857–58 *Le trésor de la curiosité tiré des catalogues de vente. . . .* 2 vols. Paris.

Blockmans, Wim
1992 "Bruges, a European Trading Center." In Vermeersch 1992, pp. 41–55.

Blum, Shirley Neilsen
1969 *Early Netherlandish Triptychs: A Study in Patronage.* Berkeley.
1992 "Hans Memling's *Annunciation* with Angelic Attendants." *Metropolitan Museum Journal* 27, pp. 43–58.

Blunt, Anthony
1954 *Art and Architecture in France, 1500 to 1700.* Baltimore.
1970 *Art and Architecture in France, 1500 to 1700.* 2d ed. Baltimore.

Bode, Wilhelm von
1887 "La Renaissance au Musée de Berlin." *Gazette des Beaux-Arts* 35, pp. 204–20.
1889 Review of *Jan van Scorel und die Geheimnisse der Stilkritik,* by H. Toman. *Repertorium für Kunstwissenschaft* 12, pp. 72–77.
1895 "Alte Kunstwerke in den Sammlungen der Vereinigten Staaten." *Zeitschrift für bildende Kunst* 6, pp. 13–19.
1898 *Beschreibendes Verzeichnis der Gemälde.* Berlin: Königliche Museen zu Berlin.
1908 "Roger van der Weydens sogen. Reisealtar Kaiser Karls V. im Kaiser-Friedrich-Museum und der Altar mit den gleichen Darstellungen in der Capilla Real des Doms zu Granada." *Amtliche Berichte aus den Königlichen Kunstsammlungen* 30, cols. 29–35.
1997 *Mein Leben.* Edited by Thomas Gaethgens and Barbara Paul. 2 vols. Berlin.

Bodenhausen, Eberhard Freiherr von
1905 *Gerard David und seine Schule.* Munich.

Bodenhausen, Eberhard Freiherr von, and Wilhelm R. Valentiner
1911 "Zum Werk Gerard Davids." *Zeitschrift für bildende Kunst,* n.s., 22, pp. 183–89.

Böhmer, Sylvia, ed.
1993 *Von der Erde zum Himmel: Heiligendarstellungen des Spätmittelalters aus dem Suermondt-Ludwig-Museum.* Exh. cat. Aachen: Suermondt-Ludwig-Museum.

Boisserée, Sulpiz
1978–95 *Tagebücher: 1808–1854.* Edited by Hans-J. Weitz. 6 vols. Darmstadt.

Bologna, Ferdinando
1956 "Nuove attribuzioni a Jan Provost." *Musées Royaux des Beaux-Arts, Bulletin* 5, pp. 13–31.

Bomford, David, Lorne Campbell, et al.
1996 "The *Virgin and Child before a Firescreen*: History, Examination, and Treatment." In Foister and Nash 1996, pp. 37–54.

Bonenfant-Feytmans, A.-M.
1991 "Aert van den Bossche, peintre du polyptych des saints Crépin et Crépinien." *Université Libre de Bruxelles, Annales d'histoire de l'art et d'archéologie* 13, pp. 43–58.

Bonfait, Olivier
1986 "Les collections des parlementaires parisiens du XVIIIe siècle." *Revue de l'art,* no. 73, pp. 28–42.

Boon, Karel G.
[1946] *Gerard David.* Amsterdam, n.d.

Borchert, Till-Holger
1993 "Untersuchungen zum Frühwerk des Malers Hans Memling." M. A. thesis, Universität Bonn.
1995 "De geschiedenis van het verzamelen van de Oudnederlandse schilderkunst in de negentiende eeuw." In *"Om iets te weten van de oude meesters": De Vlaamse primitieven—herontdekking, waardering, en onderzoek,* edited by Bernhard Ridderbos and Henk van Veen, pp. 140–88. Nijmegen.
1998 "Rogier's St. Luke: The Case for Corporate Identification." In *Rogier van der Weyden: Saint Luke Drawing the Virgin and Child; Selected Essays in Context,* edited by Carol Purtle, pp. 61–86. Turnhout.

de Bosque, Andrée
1975 *Quentin Metsys.* Brussels.

Bosschère, Jean de
1907 *Quinten Metsys.* Brussels.

Botvinick, M.
1992 "The Painting as Pilgrimage: Traces of a Subtext in the Work of Campin and His Contemporaries." *Art History* 15, pp. 1–18.

Bouchot, Henri
1904 *Les primitifs français, 1292–1500: Complément documentaire au catalogue officiel de l'exposition.* Paris.

van Braam, Frederik A., comp.
1958 *Art Treasures in the Benelux Countries.* Vol. 1, *The Netherlands.* With the assistance of Hans Klinkenberg. N.p.

Breck, Joseph
1909 "Sammlungen die neuerwerbungen des Metropolitan Museum in New York." *Der Cicerone* 1, pp. 291–94.

Breckenridge, J.
1957 "Et prima vidit: The Iconography of the Appearance of Christ to His Mother." *Art Bulletin* 39, pp. 9–32.

Brockwell, Maurice W.
1915 *A Catalogue of the Paintings at Doughty House Richmond and Elsewhere in the Collection of Sir Frederick Cook, Bt.* Vol. 3, *English, French, Early Flemish, German, and Spanish Schools, and Addenda.* Edited by Herbert Cook. London.

Brown, Elizabeth A. R.
1996 "Sodomy, Honor, Treason, and Exile: Four Documents Concerning the Dinteville Affair (1538–1539)." In *Sociétés et idéologies des temps modernes: Hommage à Arlette Jouanna,* pp. 511–32. Montpellier.
1999 "The Dinteville Family and the Allegory of *Moses and Aaron before Pharaoh.*" *Metropolitan Museum Journal.* Forthcoming.

Bruges
1902 *Exposition des Primitifs flamands et d'art ancien,* by W. H. James Weale. Exh. cat. Bruges: Palais du Gouvernement.
1949 *Gerard David.* Exh. cat. Bruges: Groeningemuseum.
1969 *Primitifs flamands anonymes: Maîtres aux noms d'emprunt des Pays-Bas méridionaux du 15eme et du debut du 16eme siècle. Catalogue avec supplement scientifique.* Exh. cat. Bruges: Groeningemuseum.

Bruijnen, Yvette
1997 "Celebrating the Reunification of Gerard David's Triptych." In Van Suchtelen, Bruijnen, and Buijsen 1997, pp. 11–23.

Bruin, T. L. de
1966 "Le Maître de Flémalle et sa crypto-signature." *Gazette des Beaux-Arts*, ser. 6, 67, pp. 5–6.

Brulliot, François
1817–20 *Dictionnaire des monogrammes, chiffres, lettres initiales, et marques figurées sous lesquels les plus célèbres peintres, dessinateurs, et graveurs ont designé leurs noms.* 2 vols. Munich.
1832–34 *Dictionnaire des monogrammes, marques figurées, letters initiales, noms abrégés, etc., avec lesquels les peintres, dessinateurs, graveurs et sculpteurs ont designé leurs noms.* Rev. ed. 3 vols. Munich.

Brusati, Celeste
1990–91 "Stilled Lives: Self-Portraiture and Self-Reflection in Seventeenth-Century Netherlandish Still-Life Painting." *Simiolus* 20, pp. 168–82.

Brussels
1886 *Exposition de tableaux de maîtres anciens.* Exh. cat. Brussels: Académie Royale de Belgique.
1963 *Le siècle de Bruegel: La peinture en Belgique au XVIe siècle.* Brussels: Musées Royaux des Beaux-Arts de Belgique.

Brussels–Delft
1957–58 *Dieric Bouts.* Exh. cat. Brussels: Palais des Beaux-Arts; Delft: Museum Prinsenhof.

Bruyn, Josua
1955 "Vroege portretten van Maerten van Heemskerck." *Bulletin van het Rijksmuseum* 3, pp. 27–35.
1957 *Van Eyck Problemen: De Levensbron het werk van een leerling van Jan Van Eyck.* Utrecht.
1960 "Twee Sint Antonius-panelen en andere werken van Aertgen van Leyden." *Nederlands Kunsthistorisch Jaarboek* 11, pp. 37–119.
1973 Letter regarding the Varzy Triptych and the Dinteville Allegory, February 14. Archives, Department of European Paintings, Metropolitan Museum.
1974 "A New Monograph on Rogier" [review of Davies 1972]. *Burlington Magazine* 116, pp. 539–41.
1984 "Over de betekenis van het werk van Jan van Scorel omstreeks 1530 voor oudere en jongere tijdgenoten, IV. De Pseudo-Félix Chrétien: Een Haarlemse schilder (Bartholomeus Pons?) bij de bischop van Auxerre." *Oud Holland* 98, pp. 98–110.

Buchanan, Iain
1990a "The Collection of Niclaes Jongelinck, I: 'Bacchus and the Planets' by Jacques Jongelinck." *Burlington Magazine* 132, pp. 102–13.
1990b "The Collection of Niclaes Jongelinck, II: The 'Months' by Pieter Bruegel the Elder." *Burlington Magazine* 132, pp. 541–50.

Buck, Stephanie
1995 "Petrus Christus's Berlin Wings and the Metropolitan Museum's Eyckian Diptych." In Ainsworth 1995, pp. 65–83.

Buijsen, Edwin
1997 "Considering the Ox and the Ass in Search of an Interpretation for Gerard David's *Forest Scene.*" In Van Suchtelen, Bruijnen, and Buijsen 1997, pp. 24–38.

Burroughs, Alan
1938 *Art Criticism from a Laboratory.* Boston.

Burroughs, Bryson
1909a "Recent Loans." *Bulletin of The Metropolitan Museum of Art* 4 (September), pp. 154–55.
1909b "Recent Loans." *Bulletin of The Metropolitan Museum of Art* 4 (January–December), pp. 154–56.
1912 "A Polyptych Representing the Life of Saint Godelieve." *Bulletin of The Metropolitan Museum of Art* 7 (July), pp. 126–28.
1913 "A Picture by Hieronymous Bosch." *Bulletin of The Metropolitan Museum of Art* 8 (June), pp. 130–33.
1913a "A Triptych by Adriaen Isenbrant." *Bulletin of The Metropolitan Museum of Art* 8 (April), pp. 67–68.
1916 "An Imaginary Landscape." *Bulletin of The Metropolitan Museum of Art* 11 (June), p. 129.
1921 "*The Harvesters* by Pieter Bruegel the Elder." *Bulletin of The Metropolitan Museum of Art* 16 (May), pp. 96–99, 102–3.
1923 "Loan Exhibition of the Arts of the Italian Renaissance: Paintings." *Bulletin of The Metropolitan Museum of Art* 18 (May), pp. 108–9.
1927 "The *Descent of Christ into Hell* by Hieronymus Bosch." *Bulletin of The Metropolitan Museum of Art* 22, pp. 272–74.
1931 "Un portrait inédit attribué à Van der Goes." In *Mélanges Hulin de Loo*, pp. 71–73. Brussels.

Burroughs, Bryson, and Harry B. Wehle
1932 "The Michael Friedsam Collection." *Bulletin of The Metropolitan Museum of Art* 27 (November), pp. 3–72.

Burrows, Carlyle
1930 "Letter from New York." *Apollo* 11, pp. 449–52.

Butts, Barbara, and Joseph Leo Koerner
1995 *The Printed World of Pieter Bruegel the Elder.* Exh. cat. Saint Louis: Saint Louis Art Museum; Cambridge, Mass.: Arthur M. Sackler Museum, Harvard University.

Bynum, Caroline Walker
1987 *Holy Feast and Holy Fast: The Religious Significance of Food to Medieval Women.* Berkeley.

Callmann, Ellen
1982 "Campin's Maiolica Pitcher." *Art Bulletin* 64, pp. 629–31.

Campbell, Lorne
1974 "Robert Campin, the Master of Flémalle and the Master of Mérode." *Burlington Magazine* 116, pp. 634–46.
1976 "The Art Market in the Southern Netherlands in the Fifteenth Century." *Burlington Magazine* 118, pp. 188–98.
1977 "The Authorship of the 'Recueil d'Arras.'" *Journal of the Warburg and Courtauld Institutes* 40, pp. 301–13.
1981a "Early Netherlandish Painters and Their Workshops." In *Le dessin sous-jacent dans la peinture: Colloque III, 1979*, edited by D. Hollanders-Favart and R. van Schoute, pp. 43–61. Louvain-la-Neuve.
1981b "Notes on Netherlandish Pictures in the Veneto in the Fifteenth and Sixteenth Centuries." *Burlington Magazine* 123, pp. 467–73.
1981c "Netherlandish Portraits." Typescript. Archives, Department of European Paintings, Metropolitan Museum.
1983 "Memlinc and the Followers of Verrocchio." *Burlington Magazine* 125, pp. 674–76.
1985 *The Early Flemish Pictures in the Collection of Her Majesty the Queen.* Cambridge.

1990 *Renaissance Portraits: European Portrait Painting in the 14th, 15th, and 16th Centuries.* New Haven.
1993 "Rogier van der Weyden and His Workshop." *Proceedings of the British Academy* 84, pp. 1–24.
1994 "L'organisation de l'atelier." In De Patoul and Van Schoute 1994, pp. 89–100.
1995a Review of De Vos 1994b. *Burlington Magazine* 137, pp. 253–54.
1995b "Approaches to Petrus Christus." In Ainsworth 1995, pp. 1–10.
1996 "Campin's Portraits." In Foister and Nash 1996, pp. 123–35.
1997a Letter regarding Dieric Bouts's *Portrait of a Man.* Archives, Department of European Paintings, Metropolitan Museum.
1997b Letter regarding Praying Men in Hats, August 28. Archives, Department of European Paintings, Metropolitan Museum.

Campbell, Lorne, et al., eds.
1997 "The Methods and Materials of Northern European Painting, 1400–1550." *National Gallery Technical Bulletin* 18, pp. 6–55.

Carandente, Giovanni
1968 *Collections d'Italie.* Vol. 1, *Sicile.* Translated by A. Uyttebrouck. Les primitifs flamands, II: Repertoire des peintures flamandes du quinzième siècle, vol. 3. Brussels.

Carter, D. G.
1962 "The Providence Crucifixion, Its Place and Meaning for Dutch Fifteenth-Century Painting." *Bulletin of Rhode Island School of Design* 48, no. 4 (May), pp. 1–39.

Castelfranchi, Liana
1997 "Firenze e la ritrattistica di Memling." In *Scritti per l'Istituto Germanico di Storia dell'Arte di Firenze,* edited by Cristina Acidini Luchinat et al., pp. 151–55. Florence.

Castelnovi, G. V.
1952 "Il Polittico di Gerard David nell'Abbazia della Cervara." *Commentari* 3, pp. 22–27.

Castelnuovo, Enrico
1987 "Presenze straniere: Viaggi di opere, itinerari di artisti." In *La pittura in Italia: Il quattrocento,* edited by Federico Zeri, pp. 514–23. Milan.

van de Castyne, Oda
1935 "Autour de *L'instruction pastorale* du Louvre." *Revue belge d'archéologie et d'histoire de l'art* 5 (October–December), pp. 319–28.

Cavalcaselle, Giovanni Battista
1973 *Disegni da antichi maestri.* Venice and Verona.

de Cazenove, Raoul
1883 *Les tableaux d'Albert Dürer au Musée de Lyon.* Lyons.

Chapon, François
1996 *Jacques Doucet; ou, L'art du mécénat, 1853–1929.* New ed. Paris.

Chastel, André
1984 *Musca depicta.* Milan.

Châtelet, Albert
1960 "Albert van Ouwater." *Gazette des Beaux-Arts,* ser. 6, 55 (February), pp. 65–78.
1981a *Early Dutch Painting.* Translated by Christopher Brown and Anthony Turner. New York.
1981b "Fenêtre et fontaine dans l'Annonciation." In *Études d'art médiévale offertes à Louis Grodecki,* pp. 317–23. Paris and Strasbourg.
1996a *Robert Campin: Le Maître de Flémalle.* Antwerp.
1996b "Simon Marmion." In *Valenciennes aux XIVe et XVe siècles,* edited by L. Nys and d'A. Salamagne, pp. 151–67. Valenciennes.

Châtelet, Albert, and Jacques Thuillier
1963 *French Painting from Fouquet to Poussin.* Translated by Stuart Gilbert. Geneva.

Chrétien, Félix
1954 "The Dintevilles before the Dauphin Henri (circa 1543): In 'The Judgement of Solomon.'" *Connoisseur* 133 (May), pp. 146, 193.

Christiansen, Keith
1990 "Masaccio and the 'pittura di luce.'" *Burlington Magazine* 132, pp. 736–39.
1992 "Paintings in Grisaille." In *Andrea Mantegna,* edited by Jane Martineau, pp. 394–400. Exh. cat. London: Royal Academy of Arts; New York: The Metropolitan Museum of Art.

Clark, E.
1918 "On a Picture by Patinir." *Art in America* 7, pp. 43–48.

Cleveland Museum
1974 *The Cleveland Museum of Art: European Paintings before 1500.* Catalogue of the Paintings, vol. 1. Cleveland.

Cleven, E.
1990 "'Ach, was ist der Wald schön grün': Gerard David, das 'bosgezicht' und sein (Miss-)Verständnis." *Akt* 46, pp. 2–14.

Comblen-Sonkes, Micheline
1994 "Le dessin." In De Patoul and Van Schoute 1994, pp. 117–23.
1996 *The Collegiate Church of Saint Peter Louvain.* 2 vols. Translated by John Cairns. Corpus of Fifteenth-Century Painting in the Southern Netherlands and the Principality of Liège, 18. Brussels.

Conway, William Martin
1887 *Early Flemish Artists and Predecessors on the Lower Rhine.* London.
1916 "Gerard David's *Descent from the Cross.*" *Burlington Magazine* 29, pp. 309–10.
1921 *The Van Eycks and Their Followers.* London.
1922 "Albert van Ouwater." *Burlington Magazine* 40, p. 120, ill. opp. p. 107, pl. 2.

Cooper, Douglas, ed.
1963 *Great Private Collections.* New York.

Coremans, [A.]
1847 "L'Archiduc Ernest, sa cour, ses dépenses, 1593–1595. D'après les comptes de Blaise Hütter, son secrétaire intime et premier valet de chambre." *Compte-rendu des séances de la Commission Royale d'Histoire* 13.

Coremans, Paul, et al.
1953 *L'Agneau Mystique au laboratoire: Examen et traitement.* Les primitifs flamands, 3: Contributions à l'étude des primitifs flamands, 2. Antwerp.

Cortissoz, Royal
1930 "The Jules S. Bache Collection." *American Magazine of Art* 31, pp. 243–59.

Corwin, Nancy

1976 "The Fire Landscape: Its Sources and Its Development from Bosch through Jan Bruegel I, with Special Emphasis on the Mid-Sixteenth Century Bosch 'Revival.'" Ph.D. dissertation, University of Washington, Seattle.

Courcelle, Jeanne, and Pierre Courcelle

1969 *Iconographie de Saint Augustin: Les cycles du XVe siècle.* Paris.

Croquez, Albert

1948 Letter to Elizabeth Gardner, December 9. Archives, Department of European Paintings, Metropolitan Museum.

Crowe, Joseph Archer, and Giovanni Battista Cavalcaselle

1872 *The Early Flemish Painters: Notices of Their Lives and Works.* 2d ed. London.

Cust, L.

1907 "Franco-Flemish School: 'Divine Mother.'" *Burlington Magazine* 11, pp. 231–32.

Cuttler, Charles D.

1968 *Northern Painting from Pucelle to Bruegel: Fourteenth, Fifteenth, and Sixteenth Centuries.* New York. Reprint ed., New York, 1973.

Cuttler, Charles D., and Burton L. Dunbar

1969 Review of *Joachim Patinir,* by Robert Koch. *Art Quarterly* 32, pp. 431–33.

Cuvelier, Therese, and Janine Watrin

1989 *Godeleine de Wierre/Godelieve de Flandre.* Étaples.

Dacos-Grifo, Nicole

1991 "Les artistes flamands et leur influence au Portugal." In *Flandre et Portugal: Au confluent de deux cultures.* Europalia Portugal 1991. Antwerp.

Darcel, A.

1889 "La collection de M. Ernest Odiot." *Gazette des Beaux-Arts,* ser. 3, 1, pp. 257–58.

Davies, Martin

1953 *The National Gallery London.* 2 vols. De Vlaamse primitiven I: Corpus van de viftiende-eeuwse schilderkunst in de zuidelijke Nederlanden, 3. Antwerp.

1970 *The National Gallery, London, Volume III.* Les primitifs flamands, I: Corpus de la peinture des anciens Pays-Bas méridionaux au quinzième siècle, vol. 11. Brussels.

1972 *Rogier van der Weyden: An Essay with a Critical Catalogue of Paintings Assigned to Him and to Robert Campin.* London.

Davis, Bruce

1988 *Mannerist Prints: International Style in the Sixteenth Century.* Exh. cat. Los Angeles: Los Angeles County Museum of Art.

Deam, Lisa

1998 "Flemish Versus Netherlandish: A Discourse of Nationalism." *Renaissance Quarterly* 51, pp. 1–33.

De Coo, Jozef

1981 "A Medieval Look at the Merode Annunciation." *Zeitschrift für Kunstgeschichte* 44, pp. 114–32.

1991 "Robert Campin, weitere vernachlässigte Aspekte." *Wiener Jahrbuch für Kunstgeschichte* 44, pp. 79–105, 241–56.

Dehaisnes, Chrétien C. A.

1890 *La vie et l'oeuvre de Jean Bellegambe.* Lille.

Dek, A. W. E.

1958 *Genealogie der Heren en Graven van Egmond.* The Hague.

De Marchi, Andrea

1994 "Diversità di Antonio da Fabriano." In *Un testamento pittorico di fine '400.* Fabriano.

Demonts, Louis

1925 "Essai sur Juste de Gand: A propos d'une 'Adoration des Mages' et d'une 'Morte de la Vièrge.'" *Revue d'art* 25, pp. 56–74.

Dempsey, Charles

1987 "The Carracci and the Devout Style in Emilia." In *Emilian Painting of the 16th and 17th Centuries: A Symposium,* edited by Henry A. Millon, pp. 75–88. Bologna.

Demus, Klaus

1981 In *Flämische Malerei von Jan van Eyck bis Pieter Bruegel d. Ä.* Vienna.

1987 Entries for "Pierre Bruegel l'Ancien." In *La peinture flamande au Kunsthistorisches Museum de Vienne: Flandria Extra Muros,* pp. 66–101. Antwerp.

Denis, Valentin

1944 *De Muziekinstrumenten in de Nederlanden en Italie.* Vol. 1, *Hun Vorm en Ontwikkeling.* Leuven.

Denucé, Jean

1932 *The Antwerp Art-Galleries: Inventories of the Art-Collections in Antwerp in the 16th and 17th Centuries.* The Hague.

De Ricci, Seymour

1935–40 *Census of Medieval and Renaissance Manuscripts in the United States and Canada.* With the assistance of William J. Wilson. 3 vols. New York.

De Roover, Raymond

1948 *The Medici Bank: Its Organization, Management, Operations, and Decline.* New York.

1963 *The Rise and Decline of the Medici Bank, 1397–1494.* Cambridge, Mass.

Destrée, Jules

1928–29 "Le Maître dit de Flémalle: Robert Campin." *Revue de l'art ancien et moderne* 53, pp. 3–14, 81–92, 137–52; 54, pp. 113–24, 169–80; 56, pp. 117–36.

1930 *Roger de la Pasture van der Weyden.* 2 vols. Paris and Brussels.

Detroit

1960 *Flanders in the Fifteenth Century: Art and Civilization. Catalogue of the Exhibition Masterpieces of Flemish Art: Van Eyck to Bosch.* Exh. cat. Detroit Institute of Arts, October–December.

Devisscher, Hans

1992 "Die Entstehung der Waldlandschaft in den Niederlanden." In *Von Bruegel bis Rubens: Das goldene Jahrhundert der flämischen Malerei,* pp. 191–202. Cologne: Wallraf-Richartz-Museum.

De Vos, Dirk

1971 "De Madonna-en-Kindtypologie bij Rogier van der Weyden en enkele minder gekende Flemalleske voorlopers." *Jahrbuch der Berliner Museen* 13, pp. 60–161.

1979 *Stedelijke Musea Brugge: Catalogus schilderijen 15de en 16de eeuw.* Bruges.

1982 *Bruges Musées Communaux: Catalogue des tableaux du 15e et du 16e siècle.* Translated by J. Lebbe. Bruges.

1986 Letter reconstructing the Master of the Saint Ursula Legend altarpiece, November 4. Archives, Department of European Paintings, Metropolitan Museum.

1987 "David, Gerard, schilder." In *Nationaal Biografisch Woordenboek*, vol. 12, cols. 208–20. Brussels: Koninklijke Academiën van België.

1994a *Hans Memling.* 2 vols. Exh. cat. Bruges: Groeningemuseum.

1994b *Hans Memling: The Complete Works.* Antwerp and Ghent.

Dierick, Alfons Lieven

1991 "La lecture des textes." In *Le dessin sous-jacent dans la peinture: Colloque VIII, 1989*, edited by R. van Schoute and H. Verougstraete-Marcq, pp. 181–84, pl. 103. Louvain-la-Neuve.

Di Fabio, Clario

1997 "Gerard David e il Polittico di San Gerolamo della Cervara." In *Pittura fiamminga in Liguria, secoli XIV–XVII*, edited by Piero Boccardo and Clario Di Fabio, pp. 59–81. Genoa.

Dijkstra, Jeltje

1990 "Origineel en kopie: Een onderzoek naar de navolging van de Meester van Flémalle en Rogier van der Weyden." Doctoral thesis, Universiteit van Amsterdam.

1994 "Le Maître de Flémalle, Jacques Daret, et Rogier van der Weyden." In De Patoul and Van Schoute 1994, pp. 311–61.

1995 "Het materieel-technisch onderzoek." In *"Om iets te weten van de oude meesters": De Vlaamse primitieven—herontdekking, waardering, en onderzoek*, edited by Bernhard Ridderbos and Henk van Veen, pp. 290–331. Nijmegen.

Dimier, Louis

1904 *Les Primitifs français, 1292–1500: Le portrait du XVIe siècle.* Paris.

1925 *Histoire de la peinture française, des origines au retour de Vouet, 1300 à 1627.* Paris.

Dobschütz, Ernst von

1899 *Christusbilder: Untersuchungen zur christlichen Legende.* Leipzig.

Doehard, R.

1963 *Études anversoises: Documents sur le commerce international à Anvers, 1488–1514.* 3 vols. Paris.

Dogaer, Georges

1987 *Flemish Miniature Painting in the 15th and 16th Centuries.* Translated by Anna E. C. Simoni et al. Amsterdam. Updated version and supplement to Winkler 1978.

Duchesne-Guillemin, J.

1976 "On the Cityscape of the Merode Altarpiece." *Metropolitan Museum of Art Journal* 2, pp. 129–31.

Dufey-Haeck, M.-L.

1979 "Le thème du repos pendant la fuite en Egypte dans la peinture flamande de la seconde moitié du XVe au milieu du XVIe siècle." *Revue belge d'archéologie et d'histoire d'art* 48, pp. 45–76.

Dülberg, Angelica

1990 *Privatporträts: Geschichte und Ikonologie einer Gattung im 15. und 16. Jahrhundert.* Berlin.

Dülberg, Franz

1898–99 "Altholland in Wörlitz." *Zeitschrift für bildenden Kunst*, n.s., 10, pp. 273–80.

1929 *Die niederländische Malerei der Spätgotik und Renaissance.* Wildpark-Potsdam.

Dunbar, Burton L.

1972 "The Landscape Art of Cornelis Massys." 2 vols. Ph.D. dissertation, University of Iowa, Iowa City.

1980 "The Landscape Paintings of Cornelis Massys." *Bulletin Bruxelles* 23–29 (1974–80), pp. 97–126.

Durand-Gréville, Émile

1906 *Les arts anciens de Flandre.* Vol. 2. Brussels.

1910 *Hubert et Jean van Eyck.* Brussels.

1911 "Les deux Petrus Christus," parts 1–3. *Reuve de l'art ancien et moderne* 30, pp. 43–54, 129–42, 195–208.

Durrieu, Paul

1911 *Histoire de l'art depuis les premiers temps chrétiens jusqu'à nos jours*, edited by André Michel. Vol. 4, part 2, *La Renaissance.* Paris.

1920 "Les Van Eyck et le Duc de Berry." *Gazette des Beaux-Arts*, ser. 5, 1, pp. 77–105.

Duveen Brothers

1941 *Duveen Pictures in Public Collections in America.* New York.

Dykmans, Marc

1983 "Les sceaux et les armoiries du Cardinal Ferry de Clugny, Évêque de Tournai." *Revue belge d'archéologie et d'histoire de l'art* 52, pp. 23–42.

Eeckhout, Paul

1994 "Hugo van der Goes." In De Patoul and Van Schoute 1994, pp. 415–35.

Eichberger, Dagmar

1987 *Bildkonzeption und Weltdeutung im New Yorker Diptychon des Jan van Eyck.* Wiesbaden.

Eisler, Colin

1959 "Juan de Flandes's Saint Michael and Saint Francis." *Bulletin of The Metropolitan Museum of Art* 18 (December), pp. 128–37.

1961 *New England Museums.* Les primitifs flamands, I: Corpus de la peinture des anciens Pays-Bas méridionaux au quinzième siècle, 4. Brussels.

1964 Review of Larsen 1960. *Art Bulletin* 46, pp. 99–106.

1989 *Early Netherlandish Painting: The Thyssen-Bornemisza Collection.* London.

Engerth, Eduard Ritter von

1884 "Über die im Kunsthistorischen Museum neu zur Aufstellung gelangenden Gemälde, III: Niederländische Schulen." *Jahrbuch der Kunsthistorischen Sammlungen des Allerhöchsten Kaiserhauses* 2, pp. 145–66.

Ermerins, Jacobus

1786 *Eenige Zeeuwsche oudheden.* Vol. 3, part 2. Middelburg.

Everaert, John, and Eddy Stols, eds.

1991 *Flandre et Portugal: Au confluent de deux cultures.* Antwerp.

Ewing, Dan

1978 "The Paintings and Drawings of Jan de Beer." 2 vols. Ph.D. dissertation, University of Michigan, Ann Arbor.

1990 "Marketing Art in Antwerp, 1460–1560: Our Lady's *Pand.*" *Art Bulletin* 72, pp. 558–84.

1994 "An Antwerp Triptych: Three Examples of the Artistic and Economic Impact of the Early Antwerp Art Market." In *Antwerp: Artworks and Audiences, Smith College, November 11–12, 1994.* Forthcoming.

Faggin, Giorgio T.

1968 *La pittura ad anversa nel cinquecento.* Florence.

Fahy, Everett

1969 "A Madonna by Gerard David." *Apollo* 90, pp. 190–95.

Fahy, Everett, and Francis Watson

1973 *The Wrightsman Collection.* Vol. 5, *Paintings, Drawings, Sculpture.* New York.

Falkenburg, Reindert L.

1985 "Joachim Patinir: Het landschap als beeld van de levenspelgrimage." Thesis, Universiteit van Amsterdam.

1988 *Joachim Patinir: Landscape as an Image of the Pilgrimage of Life.* Translated by Michael Hoyle. Amsterdam and Philadelphia.

1991 "Het huis-houden van de ziel: Burgerlijk decor in het Mérode-altaarstuk." In *Op belofte van profijt,* by H. Pleij et al., pp. 244–61, 404–10. Amsterdam.

1994 *The Fruit of Devotion: Mysticism and the Imagery of Love in Flemish Paintings of the Virgin and Child, 1450–1550.* Amsterdam and Philadelphia.

Faries, Molly

1993 "Master and Pupil: A North-Netherlandish Example." In *Le dessin sous-jacent dans la peinture: Colloque IX, 1991,* edited by R. van Schoute and H. Verougstraete-Marcq, pp. 101–11. Louvain-la-Neuve.

1997 "The Underdrawing of Memling's Last Judgment Altarpiece in Gdansk." In *Memling Studies* 1997, pp. 243–59.

1998 *Discovering Underdrawings: A Guide to Method and Interpretation.* Turnhout. Forthcoming.

Faries, Molly, Barbara Heller, and Daniel Levine

1987 "The Recently Discovered Underdrawings of the Master of the Saint Ursula Legend's *Triptych of the Nativity.*" *Bulletin of the Detroit Institute of Arts* 62, no. 4, pp. 4–19.

Farmer, John David

1981 "Bernard van Orley of Brussels." Ph.D. dissertation, Princeton University.

Felipe de Guevara

1788 *Comentarios de la pintura* (ca. 1560). Madrid.

Fierens-Gevaert, Hippolyte

1908 *Histoire de la peinture flamand des origines à la fin du XVe siècle.* Vol. 1, *Les créateurs de l'art flamand.* Paris and Brussels.

1908–12 *La peinture en Belgique; musées, églises, collections, etc.: Les primitifs flamands.* 4 vols. Brussels.

1927–29 *Histoire de la peinture flamand des origines à la fin du XVe siècle.* Vol. 3, *La maturité de l'art flamand.* Edited by Paul Fierens from his father's notes. Paris.

Firmenich-Richartz, Eduard

1896 "Die altniederländischen Gemälde der Sammlung des Freiherrn A. v. Oppenheim zu Köln: I. Männliches Porträt von Jan van Eyck." *Zeitschrift für christliche Kunst* 9.

1899 "Rogier van der Weyden, der Meister von Flémalle: Ein Beitrag zur Geschichte der vlämischen Malerschule." *Zeitschrift für bildenden Künste,* n.s., 10, pp. 1–12, 129–44.

1904 *Kunsthistorische Ausstellung Düsseldorf 1904, Katalog.* Düsseldorf.

1909 "Beke, Joos van der, gen. van Cleve." In *Allgemeines Lexikon der bildenden Künstler von der Antike bis zur Gegenwart,* edited by Ulrich Thieme and Felix Becker, vol. 3, pp. 212–17.

1916 *Sulpiz und Melchior Boisserée als Kunstsammler.* Jena.

[FitzGerald, C. M.]

1905 "Accessions: How They Will Be Treated in the Bulletin." *Bulletin of The Metropolitan Museum of Art* 1, p. 9.

Fletcher, Jennifer

1981a "Marcantonio Michiel: His Friends and Collection." *Burlington Magazine* 123, pp. 453–67.

1981b "Marcantonio Michiel, 'che ha veduto assai.'" *Burlington Magazine* 123, pp. 602–8.

Foister, Susan

1997 "Jean de Dinteville and the Château of Polisy." In *Making and Meaning: Holbein's Ambassadors,* pp. 21–29, 87. Exh. cat. London: National Gallery.

Foister, Susan, and Susie Nash, eds.

1996 *Robert Campin: New Directions in Scholarship.* Papers delivered at the Robert Campin Symposium, March 12–13, National Gallery, London. Turnhout, Belgium.

Förster, Ernst

1860 *Geschichte der deutschen Kunst.* 2d ed. 5 vols. Leipzig.

Fourcaud, Louis de

1911 "La fin de l'art primitif à Bruges: Gerard David." *Revue de l'art ancien et moderne* 30, pp. 337–52, 421–34.

Fowles, Edward

1976 *Memoirs of Duveen Brothers: Seventy Years in the Art World.* London.

Francis, H. S.

1958 "*The Nativity* by Gerard David." *Bulletin of the Cleveland Museum of Art* 6, no. 10, pp. 227–36.

Francotte, Jan

1951 *Dieric Bouts, zijn kunst, zijn Laatste Avondmaal.* Leuven.

Frankfurter, A. M.

1931 "Masterpieces of Landscape Painting in American Collections." *Fine Arts* 18, pp. 22–32.

Franz, Heinrich Gerhard

1982 "Landschaftsbilder als kollektive Werkstattschöpfungen in der flämischen Malerei des 16. und frühen 17. Jahrhunderts." *Jahrbuch Graz* 18, pp. 165–81.

Frazer, Margaret English

1986 "Medieval Church Treasuries." *Metropolitan Museum of Art Bulletin* 43, no. 3.

Freedberg, David

1986 "Art and Iconoclasm, 1525–1580: The Case of the Northern Netherlands." In *Kunst voor de beeldenstorm: Noordnederlandse kunst, 1525–1580,* edited by J. P. Filedt Kok, W. Halsema-Kubes, and W. Th. Kloek, pp. 69–84. Exh. cat. Amsterdam: Rijksmuseum.

Freedberg, David, et al.

1989 *The Prints of Pieter Bruegel the Elder.* Exh. cat. Tokyo: Bridgestone Museum of Art.

Freeman, M.

1957 "The Iconography of the Merode Altarpiece." *Bulletin of The Metropolitan Museum of Art* 16, pp. 130–39.

Frelinghuysen, Alice Cooney, et al.

1993 *Splendid Legacy: The Havemeyer Collection.* Exh. cat. New York: The Metropolitan Museum of Art.

Frick collection

1990 *Paintings from the Frick Collection.* Texts by Bernice Davidson, Edgar Munhall, and Nadia Tscherny. New York.

Friedländer, Max J.

[1899] "Malerei Niederländer und Deutsche." In *Ausstellung von Kunstwerken des Mittelalters und der Renaissance aus Berliner Privatbesitz veranstaltet von der Kunstgeschichtlichen Gesellschaft 20 Mai bis 3 Juli 1898,* pp. 12–14. Berlin.

1900 "Die Leihausstellung der New Gallery in London, Januar–März 1900.—Hauptsächlich niederländische Gemälde des XV. und XVI. Jahrhunderts." *Repertorium für Kunstwissenschaft* 23, pp. 245–58.
1903 "Die Brügger Leihausstellung von 1902." *Repertorium für Kunstwissenschaft* 26, pp. 66–91, 147–75.
1906a *Die altniederländische Malerei von Jan van Eyck bis Memling.* Leipzig.
1906b "De verzameling von Kaufmann te Berlijn." *Onze Kunst* 10, pp. 29–40.
1909 "Bernaert van Orley, II: Orleys Tätigkeit zwischen 1515 und 1520." *Jahrbuch der Königlich Preuszischen Kunstsammlungen* 30, pp. 9–34.
1914 "Kleine Studienergebnisse." *Kunstchronik, no. 4* (October), p. 50.
1915 "Die Antwerpener Manieristen von 1520." *Jahrbuch der Königlich Preuszischen Kunstsammlungen* 36, pp. 65–91.
1916 *Von Eyck bis Bruegel: Studien zur Geschichte der niederländischen Malerei.* Berlin. 2d ed., 1921. English trans. London, 1956.
1919 "Der Meister von Alkmaar." *Monatshefte für Kunstwissenschaft* 12, pp. 173–74.
[1922] Letter to Mr. [Kurt] Bachstitz. In *Bachstitz Gallery, The Hague: Exhibition of Primitiv* [sic] *Masters*, pp. 5–9. The Hague, n.d.
1923a "Die Brüsseler Tafelmalerei gegen den Ausgang des 15. Jahrhunderts." In *Belgische Kunstdenkmaler*, vol. 1, pp. 309–20. Munich.
1923b "Einige Tafelbilder Simon Marmions." *Jahrbuch für Kunstwissenschaft*, 1923, pp. 167–70.
1924–25 "Der Meister der Barbara-Legende." *Jahrbuch für Kunstwissenschaft*, pp. 20–25.
1924–37 *Die altniederländische Malerei.* 14 vols. Berlin and Leiden.
1928 "Petrus Christus, *The Annunciation.*" In Friedsam collection n.d., no. B-119.
1928a "Adriaen Ysenbrant als Porträtmaler." *Pantheon* 1, pp. 1–7.
1930 "Juan de Flandes." *Der Cicerone* 22, pp. 1–4.
1935 "Eine Zeichnung von Hugo van der Goes." *Pantheon* 15, pp. 99–104.
1937a "The Bruges Master of St. Augustine." *Art in America* 25 (April), pp. 47–54.
1937b "Le Maître de Saint Gilles." *Gazette des Beaux-Arts* 17, pp. 221–31.
1938 "Über den Zwang der ikonographischen Tradition in der vlämischen Kunst." *Art Quarterly* 1, pp. 19–23.
1940 "Eine Zeichnung von Jan Joest von Kalkar." *Oud-Holland* 57, pp. 161–67.
1956 *From Van Eyck to Bruegel.* Edited by F. Grossman; translated by Marguerite Kay. London.
1967–76 *Early Netherlandish Painting.* Translated by Heinz Norden. Comments and notes by Nicole Veronée-Verhaegen. 14 vols. in 16. New York.

Friedsam collection
n.d. "The Michael Friedsam Collection." Italian section by Bernard Berenson; Dutch section by W. R. Valentiner; Flemish and German section by Max Friedländer. Unpublished catalogue [1928?]. Thomas J. Watson Library, Metropolitan Museum.

Frinta, Mojmir S.
1966 *The Genius of Robert Campin.* The Hague.
1968 "The Authorship of the Merode Altarpiece." *Art Quarterly* 31, pp. 246–51.

Frizzoni, Gustavo
1884 *Notizia d'opere di disegno*, by D. Jacopo Morelli. 2d ed. Revised by Gustavo Frizzoni. Bologna.

Fronek, Joe
1995 "Painting Techniques, Their Effects and Changes in the Los Angeles *Portrait of a Man* by Christus." In Ainsworth 1995, pp. 175–80.

Fry, Roger E.
1904 "The Exhibition of French Primitives." *Burlington Magazine* 5, p. 368.
1909 "The Story of the Conversion of a Saint." *Bulletin of The Metropolitan Museum of Art* 4, no. 2 (February), pp. 25–27.
1910–11 "A Portrait of Leonello d'Este by Roger van der Weyden." *Burlington Magazine* 28, pp. 198, 200–203.

Fuchs, Anne Simonson
1977 "The Netherlands and Iberia: Studies in Netherlandish Painting for Spain, 1427–55." Ph.D. dissertation, University of California at Los Angeles.

Galassi, Maria Clelia
1997 "A Technical Approach to a Presumed Memling Diptych: Original Work and Some Italian Copies." In *Memling Studies* 1997, pp. 339–50.

Garas, Klara
1954 "Some Problems of Early Dutch and Flemish Painting." *Acta Historiae Artium Academiae Scientiarum Hungaricae* 1, no. 3–4, pp. 237–62.

Garrido, Carmen
1990 Record of conversation with Maryan Ainsworth, September 26. Archives, Department of European Paintings, Metropolitan Museum.

Geismeier, Irene
1990 "Ein Kunstwerk von Weltrang als Streitobjekt in zwei Weltkriegen." *Staatliche Museen zu Berlin: Forschungen und Berichte* 28, pp. 231–35.

van Gelder, J. G.
1946 "De kerkprediking van Lucas van Leyden." *Oud Holland* 61, pp. 101–6.

van Gelder-Schrijver, N. F.
1930 "De Meester van Alkmaar: Eene bijdrage tot de kennis van de Haarlemsche schilderkunst." *Oud Holland* 47, pp. 97–121.

Gellman, Lola B. Malkis
1970 "Petrus Christus." Ph.D. dissertation, Johns Hopkins University, Baltimore.
1995 "Two Lost Portraits by Petrus Christus." In Ainsworth 1995, pp. 101–14.

Gemäldegalerie
1975 *Gemäldegalerie Staatliche Museen Preussischer Kulturbesitz Berlin: Katalog der ausgestellten Gemälde des 13.–18. Jahrhunderts.* Berlin.

Genaille, Robert
1952 "Recherches sur de Jean Bellegambe: L'énigme du Retable du Cellier." *Revue des arts* 2 (June), pp. 99–108.
1965 "Le vrai sujet du polyptyque d'Anchin." *Bulletin de la Société de l'Histoire de l'Art Français,* 1964, pp. 7–24.

1976 "L'oeuvre de Jean Bellegambe." *Gazette des Beaux-Arts,* ser. 6, 87 (January), pp. 7–28.
1986 "La paysage flamand et wallon au XVIe siècle." *Jaarboek Koninklijk Museum voor Schone Künsten Antwerpen,* 1986, pp. 59–82.
Gibson, Walter S.
1965 "A New Identification for a Panel by the St. Barbara Master." *Art Bulletin* 47, pp. 504–6.
1977a *Bruegel.* New York.
1977b *The Paintings of Cornelis Engebrechtsz.* Outstanding Dissertations in the Fine Arts. New York.
1989 *"Mirror of the Earth": The World Landscape in Sixteenth-Century Flemish Painting.* Princeton.
1990 *Hieronymus Bosch and the Vision of Hell in the Late Middle Ages.* Meiji University International Exchange Programs, Guest Lecture Series, no. 8. Cleveland.
Gilbert, Creighton
1992 *Italian Art, 1400–1500: Sources and Documents.* Evanston.
Giltay, Jeroen
1994 In *Van Eyck to Bruegel, 1400–1550: Dutch and Flemish Painting in the Collection of the Museum Boymans-van Beuningen.* Rotterdam.
Glavimans, A.
1946 "Notities bij de primitieven in het Mauritshuis: Nederlandsche kunst van de 15[e] en 16[e] eeuw." *Phoenix* 1, pp. 46–57.
Glück, Gustav
1904 "Zu einem Bilde von Hieronymus Bosch in der Figdorschen Sammlung in Wein." *Jahrbuch der Königlich Preuszischen Kunstsammlungen* 25, pp. 174–84.
1932 *Bruegels Gemälde.* Vienna.
1936 *Peter Brueghel, the Elder.* New York.
Goddard, Stephen H.
1984 *The Master of Frankfurt and His Shop.* Verhandelingen van de Koninklijke Academie voor Wetenschappen, Letteren, en Schone Kunsten van België. Klasse der Schone Kunsten 46, no. 38. Brussels. Originally the author's Ph.D. dissertation, University of Iowa, 1983.
1985 "Brocade Patterns in the Shop of the Master of Frankfurt: An Accessory to Stylistic Analysis." *Art Bulletin* 67, pp. 401–17.
Gómez-Moreno, M.
1908 "Un trésor de peintures inédites du XVe siècle à Grenade." *Gazette des Beaux-Arts,* ser. 3, 40, pp. 289–314.
1914 "La Capilla de la Universidad de Salamanca." *Boletin de la Sociedad Castellana de Excursiones* 6, pp. 321–29.
Gordon, E. A.
1988 "The Conservation of Hugo van der Goes's *Portrait of a Donor with St. John the Baptist* in the Walters Art Gallery." *Journal of the Walters Art Gallery* 46, pp. 95–97.
Gottlieb, Carla
1960 "The Mystical Window in Paintings of the Salvator Mundi." *Gazette des Beaux-Arts,* ser. 6, 56 (December), pp. 313–32.
1970 "Respiciens per Fenestras: The Symbolism of the Merode Altarpiece." *Oud Holland* 85, pp. 65–84.
1971 "The Living Host." *Konsthistorisk tidskrift* 40 (May), pp. 30–46.
Grayson, Marion Spears
1976 "The Northern Origin of Nicolas Froment's Resurrection of Lazarus Altarpiece in the Uffizi Gallery." *Art Bulletin* 58, pp. 350–56.
Grisebach, August
1912 "Architekturen auf niederländischen und französischen Gemälden des 15. Jahrhunderts," parts 1, 2. *Monatshefte für Kunstwissenschaft* 5, pp. 207–15, 254–72.
Grosshans, Rainald
1980 *Maerten van Heemskerck: Die Gemälde.* Berlin.
1981 "Rogier van der Weyden: Der Marienaltar aus des Kartause Miraflores." *Jahrbuch der Berliner Museen* 23, pp. 49–112.
1982 "Infrarotuntersuchungen zum Studium der Unterzeichnung auf den Berliner Altären von Rogier van der Weyden." *Jahrbuch preussischer Kulturbesitz* 19, pp. 137–77.
Grossmann, F.
[1955] *Bruegel: The Paintings.* London.
1957 "Flemish Paintings at Bruges." *Burlington Magazine* 99, pp. 3–9.
1959 "New Light on Bruegel, I: Documents and Additions to the Oeuvre; Problems of Form." *Burlington Magazine* 101 (September/October), pp. 341–46.
Guillaume, Marguerite, et al.
1990 *La peinture en Bourgogne au XVIe siècle.* Exh. cat. Dijon: Musée des Beaux-Arts de Dijon.
Hahn, Cynthia
1986 "Joseph Will Perfect, Mary Enlighten, and Jesus Save Thee: The Holy Family as Marriage Model in the Mérode Triptych." *Art Bulletin* 68, pp. 54–66.
Hall, Edwin
1994 *The Arnolfini Betrothal: Medieval Marriage and the Enigma of Van Eyck's Double Portrait.* Berkeley and Los Angeles.
Hall, Edwin, and Horst Uhr
1978 "*Aureola* and *Fructus*: Distinctions of Beatitude in Scholastic Thought and the Meaning of Some Crowns in Early Flemish Painting." *Art Bulletin* 60, pp. 249–70.
Hand, John Oliver
1978 "Joos van Cleve: The Early and Mature Paintings." 2 vols. Ph.D. dissertation, Princeton University.
1989 "Joos van Cleve's *Holy Family.*" *Currier Museum of Art Bulletin,* pp. 4–25.
1992 "*Salve sancta facies*: Some Thoughts on the Iconography of the *Head of Christ* by Petrus Christus." *Metropolitan Museum Journal* 27, pp. 7–18.
Hand, John Oliver, and Martha Wolff
1986 *Early Netherlandish Painting.* Collections of the National Gallery of Art: Systematic Catalogue. Washington, D.C.
Hannema, Dirk
1949 *Catalogue of the D. G. Van Beuningen Collection.* Rotterdam.
Harbison, Craig
1976 *The Last Judgment in Sixteenth Century Northern Europe: A Study of the Relation Between Art and the Reformation.* Outstanding Dissertations in the Fine Arts. New York.
1985 "Visions and Meditations in Early Flemish Painting." *Simiolus* 15, pp. 87–118.

1991 *Jan Van Eyck: The Play of Realism.* London.
1995a *The Art of the Northern Renaissance.* London.
1995b "Fact, Symbol, Ideal: Roles for Realism in Early Netherlandish Painting." In Ainsworth 1995, pp. 21–34.
1995c "De iconologische benadering." In *"Om iets te weten van de oude meesters": De Vlaamse primitieven—herontdekking, waardering, en onderzoek,* edited by Bernhard Ridderbos and Henk van Veen, pp. 394–428. Nijmegen.
1995d *The Mirror of the Artist: Northern Renaissance Art in Its Historical Context.* New York.

Harck, F.
1888 "Berichte und Mittheilungen aus Sammlungen und Museen, über staatliche Kunstpflege und Restaurationen, neue Funde. Aus amerikanischen Galerien." *Repertorium für Kunstwissenschaft* 11, pp. 72–81.

Härting, Ursula
1995 "Bilder der Bibel: Gerard Davids 'Waldlandschaften mit Ochsen und Esel' (um 1509) und Pieter Bruegels 'Landschaft mit wilden Tieren.'" *Niederdeutsche Beiträge zur Kunstgeschichte* 34, pp. 81–105.

Haskell, Francis
1993 *History and Its Images: Art and the Interpretation of the Past.* New Haven.

Hatfield Strens, Bianca.
1968 "L'arrivo del trittico Portinari a Firenze." *Commentari* 19, pp. 315–19.

van den Haute, Charles
1913 *La corporation des peintres à Bruges.* Bruges.

Havemeyer, Henry Osborne
1930 "Die Sammlung Havemeyer im Metropolitan Museum." *Pantheon* 5, pp. 210–13.
1931 *H. O. Havemeyer Collection: Catalogue of Paintings, Prints, Sculpture, and Objects of Art.* Portland, Me.

Havemeyer, Louisine W.
1961 *Sixteen to Sixty: Memoirs of a Collector.* New York.
1993 *Sixteen to Sixty: Memoirs of a Collector.* 2d annotated ed. Edited by Susan Alyson Stein. New York.

Haverkamp-Begemann, Egbert
1952 "Juan de Flandes y los Reyes Católicos." *Archivo español de arte* 25, pp. 237–47.
1955 "De Meester van de Godelieve-Legende, een Brugs schilder uit het einde van de XVe eeuw." *Musées Royaux des Beaux-Arts Bulletin: Miscellanea, Erwin Panofsky* 4, pp. 185–98.

Heck, Christian
1996 Letter to Maryan W. Ainsworth, April 17.

Heckscher, William S.
1968 "The Annunciation of the Mérode Altarpiece: An Iconographic Study." In *Miscellanea Jozef Duverger,* pp. 37–65. Ghent.

Heffner, D.
1987 "A Memento Diaboli in Dürer's 'The Virgin with the Dragonfly.'" *Print Collector's Newsletter,* 1987, pp. 55–56.

Heil, W.
1929 "The Jules Bache Collection." *Art News* 27, pp. 4–7.

Heinrich, Theodore Allen
1954 "The Lehman Collection." *Bulletin of The Metropolitan Museum of Art* 12 (April), pp. 217–32.

Held, Julius S.
1943 Letter to Maurice Dekker, with an attached study on his Flemish panels, March 23, 1943. Archives, Department of European Paintings, Metropolitan Museum.
1949 Review of Wehle and Salinger 1947. *Art Bulletin* 31 (June), pp. 139–43.
1952 "A Tondo by Cornelis Engebrechtsz." *Oud-Holland* 67, pp. 233–37.
1955 Review of Panofsky 1953. *Art Bulletin* 37, pp. 205–34.

Heller, Elisabeth
1976 *Das altniederländische Stifterbild.* Tuduv-Studien: Reihe Kulturwissenschaften, vol. 6. Munich.

Henne, Alexandre, and Alphonse Wauters
1845 *Histoire de la ville de Bruxelles.* 3 vols. Brussels.

Hervey, Mary F. S.
1900 *Holbein's "Ambassadors": The Picture and the Men.* London.

Hervey, Mary F. S., and Robert Martin-Holland
1911 "A Forgotten French Painter: Félix Chrétien." *Burlington Magazine* 19, pp. 48–55.

Herzog, Sadja Jacob
1968 "Jan Gossart, Called Mabuse: A Study of His Chronology with a Catalogue of His Works." Ph.D. Dissertation, Bryn Mawr College.

Hibbard, Howard
1980 *The Metropolitan Museum of Art.* New York.

Hills, Paul
1980 "Leonardo and Flemish Painting." *Burlington Magazine* 122, pp. 609–15.

Hindman, Sandra
1992 "Two Leaves from an Unknown Breviary: The Case for Simon Marmion." In Kren 1992, pp. 223–32.
1997 "Northern Europe." In *The Robert Lehman Collection,* vol. 4, *Illuminations,* by Sandra Hindman, Mirella Levi D'Ancona, Pia Palladino, and Maria Francesca Saffiotti, pp. 1–119. New York.

Hinterding, Eric, and Femy Horsch
1989 "Reconstruction of the Collection of Old Master Paintings of King Willem II." *Simiolus* 19, no. 1–2, pp. 55–122.

Hocquet, A.
1925 "Le Maître de Flémalle, quelques documents." *Annales de l'Académie Royale d'Archéologie de Belgique* 73, ser. 7, 3, pp. 5–17. Antwerp.

Hoffman, Edith W.
1958 "Simon Marmion." Ph.D. dissertation, Courtauld Institute of Art, London.
1969 "Simon Marmion Reconsidered." *Scriptorium* 23, pp. 243–71.

Hollanders-Favart, Dominique, Roger van Schoute, and Hélène Verougstraete-Marcq
1975 "Les 'Chefs de Saint Jean-Baptiste' attribués a l'entourage de Bouts: Considérations sur la datation à partir de l'étude de l'état matériel." *Arca Lovaniensis* 4, pp. 66–81.

Hollstein, F. W. H.
1949– *Dutch and Flemish Etchings, Engravings and Woodcuts, ca. 1450–1700.* 43 vols. Amsterdam.

Holly, Michael Ann
1984 *Panofsky and the Foundations of Art History.* Ithaca.

Holroyd, Charles
1903 *Michael Angelo Buonarroti.* London.

Hoogewerff, G. J.
1936–47 *De noord-Nederlandische schilderkunst.* 5 vols. The Hague.
1953 "A proposito del polittico di Gerard David nell'Abbazia della Cervara." *Commentari* 4, pp. 72–73.
1961 "Pittori fiamminghi in Liguria nel secolo XVI (Gherardo David, Giovanni Provost, Joos van der Beke, Giovanni Massys)." *Commentari* 12, pp. 176–94.
Hoyt, Edwin P., Jr.
1966 *The House of Morgan.* New York.
Huillet d'Istria, Madeleine
1961 *La peinture française de la fin du Moyen Âge.* Vol. 1, *Le Maître de Moulins.* Paris.
Huisman, Georges
1923 *Memlinc.* Paris.
Huizinga, Johan
1927 *The Waning of the Middle Ages: A Study of the Forms of Life, Thought, and Art in France and the Netherlands in the XIVth and XVth Centuries.* London.
1996 *The Autumn of the Middle Ages.* Translated by R. J. Payton and U. Mammitzsch. Chicago.
Hulin de Loo, Georges
1902 *Exposition de tableaux flamands des XIVe, XVe, et XVIe siècles: Catalogue critique, précédé d'une introduction sur l'identité de certains maîtres anonymes.* Ghent.
1907 "Une catalogue raisonné de son oeuvre peint." In *Peter Bruegel l'Ancien, son oeuvre et son temps,* by René van Batelaer. Brussels.
1913 "Ein authentisches Werk von Goossen van der Weyden im Kaiser-Friedrich-Museum, I." *Jahrbuch der Koninglich Preuszischen Kunstsammlungen* 34, pp. 59–88.
1924 "A Mysterious *Our Lady* by Dieric Bouts." *Burlington Magazine* 45, pp. 56–60.
1926 "Robert Campin or Rogier van der Weyden?: Some Portraits Painted between 1432 and 1444." *Burlington Magazine* 49, pp. 268–74.
1931 "Quelques oeuvres d'art rencontrées en Espagne." *Bulletin van de Koninklijke Academie voor Wetenschappen, Letteren, en Schone Kunsten van België, Klasse der Schone Kunsten* 13, pp. 39–43.
1932 *L'exposition de l'art français à Londres.* Extracted from *Bulletin de l'Académie Royale de Belgique.*
Hunter, John
1993 "Who Is Jan van Eyck's 'Cardinal Nicolo Albergati?'" *Art Bulletin* 75, pp. 207–18.
Hyde, H. M.
1994 "Early Cinquecento 'Popolare' Art Patronage in Genoa, 1500–1528." 2 vols. Ph.D. dissertation, Birkbeck College, University of London.
1997 "Gerard David's Cervara Altarpiece—An Examination of the Commission for the Monastery of San Girolamo della Cervara." *Arte Cristiana* 85, no. 781 (July–August), pp. 245–54.
Hymans, Henri
1902 *L'exposition des primitifs flamands à Bruges.* Paris.
1907 "L'exposition de la Toison d'Or à Bruges." *Gazette des Beaux-Arts,* ser. 3, 38, pp. 199–217, 296–314.
Illies, Florian
1997 "Gustav Friedrich Waagen und England." M.A. thesis, Universität Bonn.
Installé, Henri
1992 "Le triptych Merode: Evocation mnémonique d'une famille de marchands colonais, réfugiée à Malines." *Handelingen van de Koninklijke Kring voor Oudheidkunde, Letteren, en Kunst van Mechelen* 96, pp. 55–154.
Ishikawa, Chiyo L.
1989 "The *Retablo de la Reina Católica* by Juan de Flandes and Michel Sittow." Ph.D. dissertation, Bryn Mawr College, Bryn Mawr, Pennsylvania.
1990 "Rogier van der Weyden's *Saint Luke Drawing the Virgin* Reexamined." *Journal of the Museum of Fine Arts* (Boston) 2, pp. 49–64.
Jacobus de Voragine (ca. 1229–98)
1892 *The Golden Legend* (ca. 1260). Edited by Frederick S. Ellis. 3 vols., London, 1892.
1969 *The Golden Legend.* Translated and adapted from the Latin by Granger Ryan and Helmut Ripperger. New York.
1993 *The Golden Legend: Readings on the Saints.* Translated by William G. Ryan. 2 vols. Princeton.
Jager, Eric
1996 "The Book of the Heart: Reading and Writing the Medieval Subject." *Speculum* 71, pp. 1–26.
James, Montague Rhodes, trans.
1926 *The Apocryphal New Testament, Being the Apocryphal Gospels, Acts, Epistles, and Apocalypses, with Other Narratives and Fragments.* Oxford.
Janssens de Bisthoven, Aquilin, M. Baes-Dondeyne, and Dirk De Vos
1983 *Musée Communal des Beaux-Arts (Musée Groeninge) Bruges.* 3d ed. Les primitifs flamands, I: Corpus de la peinture des anciens Pays-Bas méridionaux au quinzième siècle, vol. 1. Brussels.
Jennings, Jeffrey
1993 "Infrared Visibility of Underdrawing Techniques and Media." In *Le dessin sous-jacent dans la peinture: Colloque IX, 1991,* edited by R. van Schoute and H. Verougstraete-Marcq. Louvain-la-Neuve.
Johnson collection
1913–14 *Catalogue of a Collection* [John G. Johnson] *of Paintings and Some Art Objects.* 3 vols. Philadelphia.
1972 *Catalogue of Flemish and Dutch Paintings.* Preface by Barbara Sweeny. Philadelphia. Revised ed. of *Catalogue of a Collection* [John G. Johnson] *of Paintings and Some Art Objects,* vol. 2, *Flemish and Dutch Paintings,* by W. R. Valentiner, Philadelphia, 1914.
de Jongh, E.
1974 "Grape Symbolism in Paintings of the 16th and 17th Centuries." *Simiolus* 7, pp. 182–99.
Justi, Carl
1887 "Juan de Flandes, ein Niederländerischer Hofmaler Isabella der Katholischen." *Jahrbuch der Königlich Preussischen Kunstsammlungen* 8, pp. 157–69.
1908 *Miscellaneen aus Drei Jahrhunderten spanischen Kunstlebens.* 2 vols. Berlin.
Kann, Rodolphe
1907 *Catalogue of the Rodolphe Kann Collection.* 2 vols. Paris.
Kantorowicz, Ernst
1939–40 "The Este Portrait by Roger van der Weyden." *Journal of the Warburg and Courtauld Institutes* 3, nos. 3–4, pp. 165–80.

Kaplan, Paul H. D.
1985 *The Rise of the Black Magus in Western Art.* Studies in the Fine Arts: Iconography, edited by Linda Seidel, no. 9. Ann Arbor.
Kemperdick, Stephan
1997 *Der Meister von Flémalle: Die Werkstatt Robert Campins und Rogier van der Weyden.* Turnhout.
Kern, G. J.
1927 *Die Verschollene "Kreuztragung" des Hubert oder Jan Van Eyck.* Berlin.
Kernodle, George R.
1943 "Renaissance Artists in the Service of the People: Political Tableaux and Street Theaters in France, Flanders, and England." *Art Bulletin* 25, pp. 59–64.
Kervyn de Lettenhove, H., et al.
1908 *Les chefs-d'oeuvre d'art ancien à l'exposition de la Toison d'Or à Bruges en 1907.* Brussels.
Klein, Peter
1986 Letter to Maryan W. Ainsworth, November 11.
1991 "The Differentiation of Originals and Copies of Netherlandish Panel Paintings by Dendrochronology." In *Le dessin sous-jacent dans la peinture: Colloque VIII, 1989,* edited by H. Verougstraete-Marcq and R. van Schoute, pp. 29–42. Louvain-la-Neuve.
1991a Letter to Maryan W. Ainsworth, May 15.
1991b Letter to Maryan W. Ainsworth, May 6.
1992 Letter to Maryan W. Ainsworth, December 22.
1994a "Dendrochronological Analysis of Panels Attributed to Petrus Christus." In Ainsworth 1994b, pp. 213–15.
1994b "Dendrochronological Analysis of Panels of Hans Memling." In De Vos 1994a, vol. 1, pp. 101–3.
1995 "Dendrochronological Findings of the Van Eyck–Christus–Bouts Group." In Ainsworth 1995, pp. 149–66.
Kloek, W. Th., W. Halsema-Kubes, and R. J. Baarsen
1986 *Art before the Iconoclasm: Northern Netherlandish Art, 1525–1580.* Translated by Patricia Wardle. 2 vols. Exh. cat. Amsterdam: Rijksmuseum.
Knipping, John B.
[1939] In *Palet-serie: Een recks monografieen over Hollandse en Vlaamse schilders.* Vol. 1, *Vijftiende en zestiende eeuw.* Amsterdam, n.d.
Koch, Robert A.
1968 *Joachim Patinir.* Princeton.
1992 "Joachim Patinir (ca. 1485–1524)." In Bauman and Liedtke 1992, pp. 108–10.
König, Eberhard
1982 *Französische Buchmalerei um 1450: Der Jouvenel-Maler, der Maler des Genfer Boccaccio, und die Anfänge Jean Fouquets.* Berlin.
1996 *Das Liebentbrannte Herz: Der Wiener Codex und der Maler Barthelemy d'Eyck.* Graz.
Konigson, Elie
1969 *La représentation d'un Mystère de la Passion à Valenciennes en 1547.* Paris.
Konody, P. G.
1911 "Reviews and Notices: 'A Forgotten French Painter: Félix Chrétien.'" *Burlington Magazine* 19, p. 106.
Koslow, Susan
1986 "The Curtain-Sack: A Newly Discovered Incarnation Motif in Roger van der Weyden's Columba Annunciation." *Artibus et historiae,* no. 13, pp. 9–34.
Kren, Thomas
1987–88 *Flämischer Kalender / Flemish Calendar / Simon Bening.* Facsimile ed. 2 vols. Lucerne.
1992 [as editor]. *Margaret of York, Simon Marmion, and* The Visions of Tondal*: Papers Delivered at a Symposium Organized by the Department of Manuscripts of the J. Paul Getty Museum in Collaboration with the Huntington Library and Art Collections, June 21–24, 1990.* Malibu.
Kren, Thomas, and J. Rathofer
1987–88 Commentary. In Kren 1987–88, pp. 203–73.
Krönig, Wolfgang
1936 *Der italienische Einfluss in der flämischen Malerei im ersten Drittel des 16. Jahrhundert: Beitrage zum Beginn der Renaissance in der Malerei der Niederlände.* Würzburg.
Krul, W. E.
1995 "Realisme, Renaissance, en nationalism: Cultuurhistorische opvattinen over de Oudnederlandse schilderkunst tussen 1860 en 1920." In *"Om iets te weten van de oude meesters": De Vlaamse primitieven—herontdekking, waardering, en onderzoek,* edited by Bernhard Ridderbos and Henk van Veen, pp. 236–284. Nijmegen.
Kwakkelstein, Michael W.
1991 "Leonardo da Vinci's Grotesque Heads and the Breaking of the Physiognomic Mould." *Journal of the Warburg and Courtauld Institutes* 54, pp. 127–36.
Labuda, Adam S.
1993 "Jan van Eyck, Realist and Narrator: On the Structure and Artistic Sources of the New York *Crucifixion.*" *Artibus et Historiae* 14, no. 27, pp. 9–30.
Lambotte, Paul
1927 *Flemish Painting before the Eighteenth Century.* Edited by Geoffrey Holme; translated by Herbert Grimsditch. London.
Lane, Barbara G.
1975 "Ecce Panis Angelorum: The Manger as Altar in Hugo's Berlin *Nativity.*" *Art Bulletin* 57, pp. 477–86.
1978 "Rogier's Saint John and Miraflores Altarpieces Reconsidered." *Art Bulletin* 60, pp. 655–72.
1984 *The Altar and the Altarpiece: Sacramental Themes in Early Netherlandish Painting.* New York.
1986 *Flemish Painting outside Bruges, 1400–1500: An Annotated Bibliography.* Boston.
1988 "Sacred and Profane in Early Netherlandish Painting." *Simiolus* 18, pp. 107–15.
1991 "The Patron and the Pirate: The Mystery of Memling's Gdansk *Last Judgment.*" *Art Bulletin* 73, pp. 623–39.
Larsen, Erik
1954 "Views and News of Art in America." *Apollo* 59, p. 103.
1960 *Les primitifs flamands au Musée Metropolitan de New York.* Utrecht.
Lavalleye, Jacques
1936 *Juste de Gand, peintre de Frédéric de Montefeltre.* Leuven.
1945 *Le portrait au XVme siècle.* 2d ed. Brussels.

Lebeuf, Abbé
1743 *Mémoires concernant l'histoire ecclésiastique et civile d'Auxerre (Recueil de monumens, chartes, titres, et autres pièces concernant l'église et la ville d'Auxerre).* 2 vols. Paris.
Lehman, Robert
1928 *The Philip Lehman Collection, New York: Paintings.* Paris.
[1964?] *The Lehman Collection.* [New York, n.d.]
Lehner, F. A. von, ed.
1868 *Fünfzig der bedeutenderen Gemälde zu Sigmaringen.* Stuttgart.
1871 *Fürstlich Hohenzollern'sches Museum zu Sigmaringen: Verzeichniss der Gemälde.* Sigmaringen.
Lemmens, G., and E. Taverne
1967 In *Jheronimus Bosch,* edited by Karel G. Boon et al. Exh. cat. 's Hertogenbosch: Noordbrabants Museum.
Levi-D'Ancona, Mirella
1957 *The Iconography of the Immaculate Conception in the Middle Ages and Early Renaissance.* New York.
Levine, Daniel M.
1989 "The Bruges Master of the St. Ursula Legend Reconsidered." Ph.D. dissertation, Indiana University, Bloomington.
Lievens-de Waegh, M.-L.
1991 *Le Musée National des Carreaux de Faience de Lisbonne.* 2 vols. Les primitifs flamands, I: Corpus de la peinture des anciens Pays-Bas méridionaux au quinzième siècle, 16. Brussels.
1994 "Les sujets des oeuvres." In De Patoul and Van Schoute 1994, pp. 183–215, 634–35.
Lightbown, Ronald W.
1992 *Medieval European Jewellery, with a Catalogue of the Collection of the Victoria & Albert Museum.* London.
von Loga, Valerian
1910 "Zum Altar von Miraflores." *Jahrbuch der Königlich Preussischen Kunstsammlungen* 31, pp. 47–56.
Lomazzo, Gian Paolo
1584 *Trattato dell'arte della pittura.* Milan.
London
1892 *Exhibition of Pictures by Masters of the Netherlandish and Allied Schools of the XV and Early XVI Centuries.* Introduction by Walter Armstrong. Exh. cat. London: Burlington Fine Arts Club.
Lorentz, Philippe
1995 *Hans Memling au Louvre.* Exh. cat. Paris: Musée du Louvre.
Lorentz, Philippe, and Annie Regond
1990 *Jean Hey: Le Maître de Moulins.* Exh. cat. N.p.
Lotthé, Ernest
1947 *La pensée chrétiene dans la peinture flamande et hollandaise de Van Eyck à Rembrandt, 1432–1669.* 2 vols. Lille.
Lugt, Fritz
1968 *Inventaire général des dessins des écoles du nord: Maîtres des anciens Pays-Bas nés avant 1550.* Paris: Musée du Louvre.
Luzio, Alessandro
1913 *La Galleria dei Gonzaga: Venduta all'Inghilterra nel 1627–28.* 2d ed. Rome.
[Madou, Hildegardis]
1970 *Sinte Godelieve, 1070–1970.* Exh. cat. Ghistelles: Onze-Lieve-Vrouwekerk.
Madou, M. J. H.
1988 "Het gebruik van de spiegel in de Middeleeuwen." In *Oog in oog met de spiegel,* pp. 48–65. Amsterdam.
Madrid
1892–93 *Exposición histórico-Europea: Las joyas de la exposición.* Madrid.
Mallet, John
1964 *Upton House: The Bearsted Collection, Pictures.* London. This is a revision of the 1950 catalogue compiled by the second Lord Bearsted.
van Mander, Karel
1604 *Het Schilder-Boeck waerin voor eerst de leerlustighe lueght den grondt der edel vry schilderconst in verscheyden deelen wort voorghedraghen. . . .* Haarlem.
1936 *Dutch and Flemish Painters.* Translation and introduction by Constant van de Wall. New York.
1969 *Het Schilder-Boeck waerin voor eerst de leerlustighe lueght den grondt der edel vry schilderconst in verscheyden deelen wort voorghedraghen. . . .* Utrecht. First published Haarlem, 1604.
1994 *The Lives of the Illustrious Netherlandish and German Painters, from the First Edition of the* Schilder-Boeck *(1603–1604), Preceded by the Lineage, Circumstances and Place of Birth, Life and Works of Karel van Mander, Painter and Poet and Likewise His Death and Burial, from the Second Edition of the* Schilder-Boeck *(1616–1618).* Introduction and translation, edited by Hessel Miedema. 4 vols. Doornspijk.
Mantz, Paul
1872 "Exposition rétrospective de Milan." *Gazette des Beaux-Arts,* ser. 2, 6, pp. 449–63.
Marlier, Georges
1954 *Erasme et la peinture flamande de son temps.* Damme.
1955 "Beweinung Ysenbrants nach Petrus Christus." *Weltkunst* 25, no. 5 (March 1), p. 12.
1957 *Ambrosius Benson et la peinture à Bruges au temps de Charles-Quint.* Damme.
1964 "Le Maître de la Legende de Sainte Ursule." *Koninklijk Museum voor Schone Kunsten, Jaarboek,* pp. 5–42.
1966 *La renaissance flamande: Pierre Coeck d'Alost.* Brussels.
Marrow, James
1979 *Passion Iconography in Northern European Art of the Late Middle Ages and Early Renaissance.* Kortrijk.
1983 "*In desen spiegell*: A New Form of *Memento Mori* in Fifteenth-Century Netherlandish Art." In *Essays in Northern European Art Presented to Egbert Haverkamp-Begemann on His Sixtieth Birthday,* pp. 154–63. Doornspijk.
1986 "Symbol and Meaning in Northern European Art of the Late Middle Ages and Early Renaissance." *Simiolus* 16, pp. 150–69.
Martens, Didier
1986 "À propos d'un 'Tüchlein' flamand du XVIe siècle conservé au Louvre." *La revue du Louvre* 36, pp. 394–402.
1992 "Le triptyque de Bientina: Motifs et sources." *Gazette des Beaux-Arts,* ser. 6, 134 (November), pp. 149–64.
1994 "L'illusion du réel." In De Patoul and Van Schoute 1994, pp. 255–77.
1995 "Identification de deux 'portraits' d'église dans la peinture brugeoise de la fin du Moyen Âge." *Jaarboek van het Koninklijk Museum voor Schone Kunsten (van) Antwerpen,* 1995, pp. 29–55.

Martens, Maximiliaan P. J.

1992a "Artistic Patronage in Bruges Institutions, c. 1440–1482." Ph.D. dissertation, University of California at Santa Barbara.

1992b "The Epitaph of Anna van Nieuwenhove." *Metropolitan Museum Journal* 27, pp. 37–42.

1994a "La clientèle de peintre." In De Patoul and Van Schoute 1994, pp. 142–47, 632–33.

1994b "De opdrachtgevers van Hans Memling." In De Vos 1994a, pp. 14–29.

1995 "Discussion: Response to Craig Harbison." In Ainsworth 1995, pp. 44–47.

1997 "Hans Memling and His Patrons: A Cliometrical Approach." In *Memling Studies* 1997, pp. 35–41.

Mather, Frank J.

1917 "*Christ Appearing to His Mother*, by Rogier de la Pasture." *Art in America* 5, pp. 143–49.

1930 *The Havemeyer Pictures.* London.

de Maulde la Clavière, R.

1896 "Jean Perréal, dit Jean de Paris—sa vie et son oeuvre," part 4. *Gazette des Beaux-Arts,* ser. 3, 15, pp. 367–81.

Mauritshuis

1956 *Mauritshuis La Haye: Guide illustré.* The Hague.

1968 *Koninklijk Kabinet van Schilderijen [Mauritshuis]: Schilderijen en beeldhouwwerken 15de en 16de eeuw.* The Hague.

1977 *Mauritshuis. The Royal Cabinet of Paintings: Illustrated General Catalogue.* Vol. 1. The Hague.

1985 *The Royal Picture Gallery, Mauritshuis.* Edited by Hendrik R. Hoetink; with contributions by A. Blankert et al. Translated by Michael Hoyle. Amsterdam and New York.

Mayberry, N.

1991 "The Controversy over the Immaculate Conception in Medieval and Renaissance Art, Literature, and Society." *Journal of Medieval and Renaissance Studies* 21, no. 2 (fall), pp. 207–24.

Mayer, August L.

1920 "Ein unbekanntes Triptychon von Gerard David." *Zeitschrift für bildende Kunst* 31, p. 97.

1930a "Die Sammlung Jules Bache in New York." *Pantheon* 6, pp. 537–42.

1930b "Die Sammlung Philip Lehman." *Pantheon* 5, pp. 111–18.

McClellan, Andrew

1994 *Inventing the Louvre: Art, Politics, and the Origins of the Modern Museum in Eighteenth-Century Paris.* Cambridge.

McFarlane, K. B.

1971 *Hans Memling.* Oxford.

McNamee, M. B.

1963 "Further Symbolism in the Portinari Altarpiece." *Art Bulletin* 45, pp. 142–43.

1976 "An Additional Eucharistic Allusion in Van der Weyden's Columba Triptych." *Studies in Iconography* 2, pp. 107–13.

Meadow, Mark, et al., eds.

1996 "Pieter Bruegel." *Nederlands Kunsthistorisch Jaarboek* 47.

Mechel, Chrétien de

1784 *Catalogue des tableaux de la Galerie Impériale et Royale de Vienne.* Basel.

Meijer, Bert W.

1988 "From Leonardo to Bruegel: Comic Art in Sixteenth-Century Europe." *Word and Image* 4, no. 1 (January–March), pp. 405–11.

Meiss, Millard

1956 "Jan van Eyck and the Italian Renaissance." In *Atti del XVIII Congresso Internazionale di Storia dell'Arte—Venezia e l'Europa,* pp. 58ff. Venice.

Mély, F. de

1908 "Le Retable du Cellier et la signature de Jean Bellegambe." *Revue de l'art* 24 (August), pp. 97–108.

Memling Studies

1997 *Memling Studies: Proceedings of the International Colloquium, Bruges, 10–12 November 1994,* edited by Hélène Verougstraete-Marcq, Roger van Schoute, and Maurits Smeyers. Leuven.

Mendes-Atanázio, M. C.

1989 "Il trittico Portinari." *Revue des archéologues et historiens d'art de Louvain* 22, pp. 17–27.

Menzel, Gerhard W.

1966 *Pieter Bruegel der Ältere.* Leipzig.

Metropolitan Museum

1984 *The Jack and Belle Linsky Collection at The Metropolitan Museum of Art.* New York.

1987 *The Metropolitan Museum of Art: The Renaissance in the North.* New York.

Michel, Édouard

1927 "À propos de Simon Marmion." *Gazette des Beaux-Arts,* ser. 5, 16, pp. 141–54.

1936 "Bruegel le Vieux a-t-il passé à Genève?" *Gazette des Beaux-Arts,* ser. 6, 15, pp. 105–7.

Michiels, Alfred

1865–76 *Histoire de la peinture flamande depuis ses débuts jusqu'en 1864.* 2d ed. 10 vols. Paris.

van Miegroet, Hans J.

1986 "The Twelve Months Reconsidered: How a Drawing by Pieter Stevens Clarifies a Bruegel Enigma." *Simiolus* 16, pp. 29–35.

1989 *Gerard David.* Antwerp.

Mielke, Hans

1996 *Pieter Bruegel: Die Zeichnungen.* Turnhout.

Minott, C. I.

1969 "The Theme of the Merode Altarpiece." *Art Bulletin* 51, pp. 267–71.

Montias, J. M.

1990 "Socio-Economic Aspects of Netherlandish Art from the Fifteenth to the Seventeenth Century: A Survey." *Art Bulletin* 73, pp. 358–73.

Morand, Kathleen

1991 *Claus Sluter: Artist at the Court of Burgundy.* Austin.

Morelli, D. Jacopo

1884 *See* Frizzoni 1884.

Moreno Villa, D. José

1917 "Un pintor de la Reina Católica." *Boletin de la Sociedad Española de Excursiones* 25, pp. 276–81.

Morse, John D.

1979 *Old Master Paintings in North America: Over 3000 Masterpieces by 50 Great Artists.* New York.

Mottola Molfino, Alessandra, and Mauro Natale
1991 *Le Muse e il Principe: Arte di corte nel Rinascimento padano.* 2 vols. Exh. cat. Milan: Museo Poldi Pezzoli.

Mulazzani, Germano
1971 "Observations on the Sforza Triptych in the Brussels Museum." *Burlington Magazine* 113, pp. 252–53.

Muller, Sheila D'moch
1985 *Charity in the Dutch Republic: Pictures of Rich and Poor for Charitable Institutions.* Ann Arbor.

Mund, H.
1994 "La copie." In De Patoul and Van Schoute 1994, pp. 125–41.

Mundy, E. James
1980a "Gerard David Studies." Ph.D. dissertation, Princeton University.
1980b "A Preparatory Sketch for Gerard David's *Justice of Cambyses* Panels in Bruges." *Burlington Magazine* 122, pp. 122–25.
1981–82 "Gerard David's *Rest on the Flight into Egypt*: Further Additions to Grape Symbolism." *Simiolus* 12, pp. 211–22.
1985 *Painting in Bruges, 1470–1550: An Annotated Bibliography.* Boston.

Musper, H. Theodor
1948 *Untersuchungen zu Rogier van der Weyden und Jan van Eyck.* Stuttgart.

Neugass, Fritz
1962 "Abschluß einer Epoche: Versteigerung der Sammlung Berwind." *Weltkunst* 32, no. 15 (August 1), p. 13.

New York
1954 *Works of Art from the Collection of Robert Lehman.* Exh. cat. New York: The Metropolitan Museum of Art.
1972 *Gerard David: Flanders' Last Medieval Master.* New York: The Metropolitan Museum of Art.

Newton, Stella Mary
1975 *Renaissance Theatre Costume and the Sense of the Historic Past.* New York.

Nicholas, Lynn H.
1994 *The Rape of Europa: The Fate of Europe's Treasures in the Third Reich and the Second World War.* New York.

Nickel, Helmut
1966 "The Man Beside the Gate." *Bulletin of The Metropolitan Museum of Art* 25, pp. 237–44.
1987 "A Heraldic Note About the Portrait of Ladislaus, Count of Haag, by Hans Mielich." *Metropolitan Museum Journal* 22, pp. 141–47.

Nieburg, P.
1946 "Twee boschgezichten van Gerard David." *Constghesellen* 1, pp. 16–17.

Nieuwenhuys, C. J.
1843 *Description de la Galerie des tableaux de S. M. le roi des Pays-Bas, avec quelques remarques sur l'histoire des peintres et sur le progrès de l'art.* Brussels.

Nilgen, Ursula
1967 "The Epiphany and the Eucharist: On the Interpretation of Eucharistic Motifs in Mediaeval Epiphany Scenes." *Art Bulletin* 99, pp. 311–16.

Noe, S. P.
1930 "Flemish Primitives in New York." *American Magazine of Art* 21, pp. 30–38.

Northwick collection
1908 *A Catalogue of the Pictures, Works of Art, Etc., at Northwick Park.* Reprint ed., with additions. [London]. First published 1864.
1921 *Catalogue of the Collection of Pictures at Northwick Park*, by Tancred Borenius. London.

Novotny, Fritz
1948 *Die Monatsbilder Pieter Bruegels d. Ä.* Vienna.

Nuttall, Paula
1992 "Decorum, Devotion, and Dramatic Expression: Early Netherlandish Painting in Renaissance Italy." In *Decorum in Renaissance Narrative Art*, edited by Francis Ames-Lewis and Anka Bednarek, pp. 70–77. Paper delivered at annual conference of the Association of Art Historians, London, April 1991. London: Birkbeck College.
1993 "'Fecero al Cardinale di Portogallo una tavola a olio': Netherlandish Influence in Antonio and Piero Pollaiuolo's San Miniato Altarpiece." *Nederlands Kunsthistorsh Jaarboek* 44, pp. 111–24.
1995 "The Medici and Netherlandish Painting." In *The Early Medici and Their Artists*, edited by Francis Ames-Lewis, pp. 135–52. London: Birkbeck College.

d'Olne, Pascale
1997 Letter to Lisa Murphy, November 17. Archives, Department of European Paintings, Metropolitan Museum.

O'Meara, Cara Ferguson
1981 "'In the Hearth of the Virginal Womb': The Iconography of the Holocaust in Late Medieval Art." *Art Bulletin* 67, pp. 75–88.

van Os, Henk, et al.
1994 *The Art of Devotion in the Late Middle Ages in Europe, 1300–1500*, by Henk van Os, with contributions by Eugene Honee, Hans Nieuwdorp, and Bernhard Ridderbos; translated by Michael Hoyle. Exh. cat. Amsterdam: Rijksmuseum.

von der Osten, Gert, and Horst Vey
1969 *Painting and Sculpture in Germany and the Netherlands, 1500–1600.* Translated from German by Mary Hottinger. Harmondsworth.

d'Otrange, M. L.
1952 "Gerard David at the Metropolitan, New York." *Connoisseur* 128 (January), pp. 206–11.

Ozment, Steven
1980 *The Age of Reform, 1250–1550: An Intellectual and Religious History of Late Medieval and Reformation Europe.* New Haven.

Pächt, Otto
1926 "Die Datierung der Brüsseler Beweinung des Petrus Christus." *Belvedere* 10, pp. 155–66.
1933 "Gestaltungsprinzipien der westlichen Malerei des 15. Jahrhunderts." *Kunstwissenschaftliche Forschungen* 2, pp. 75–100.
1994 *Van Eyck and the Founders of Early Netherlandish Painting.* Edited by Maria Schmidt-Dengler; translated by David Britt. London.
1997 *Early Netherlandish Painting: From Rogier van der Weyden to Gerard David.* Edited by Monika Rosenauer; translated by David Britt. London.

Panhans, Günter
1974 "Florentiner Maler verarbeiten ein Eyckisches Bild." *Wiener Jahrbuch für Kunstgeschichte* 27, pp. 188–98.

Panhans-Bühler, Ursula
1978 *Eklektizismus und Originalität im Werk des Petrus Christus.* Wiener kunstgeschichtliche Forschungen, no. 5. Vienna.
Panofsky, Erwin
1927 "'Imago Pietatis': Ein Beitrag zur Typengeschichte des 'Schmerzensmannes' und der 'Maria Mediatrix.'" In *Festschrift für Max J. Friedländer zum 60. Geburtstage,* pp. 261–308. Leipzig.
1934 "Jan van Eyck's *Arnolfini* Portrait." *Burlington Magazine* 64, pp. 117–27.
1935 "The Friedsam Annunciation and the Problem of the Ghent Altarpiece." *Art Bulletin* 17, pp. 433–73.
1938 "Once More 'The Friedsam Annunciation and the Problem of the Ghent Altarpiece.'" *Art Bulletin* 20, pp. 419–42.
1953 *Early Netherlandish Painting: Its Origins and Character.* Cambridge, Mass. Reprinted 1971.
1956 "Jean Hey's 'Ecce Homo': Speculations about Its Author, Its Donor, and Its Iconography." *Musées Royaux des Beaux-Arts, Bulletin,* September–December, pp. 106, 108, 110, 112–16.
Parshall, Linda B., and Peter W. Parshall
1986 *Art and the Reformation: An Annotated Bibliography.* Boston.
Parthey, Gustav
1863–64 *Deutscher Bildersaal.* 2 vols. Berlin.
Passavant, Johann David
1841 In *Kunstblatt,* January 12, p. 9.
1843 "Beiträge zur Kenntniß der alt-niederländischen Malerschulen bis zur Mitte des sechszehnten Jahrhunderts." *Kunstblatt* 61 (August 1), p. 253.
Passoni, Riccardo
1988 "Opere fiamminghe a Chieri." In *Arte del Quattrocento a Chiere: Per I restauri nel Battistero,* edited by Michela Di Macco and Giovanni Romano, pp. 67–97. Turin.
de Patoul, Brigitte, and Roger van Schoute
1994 *Les primitifs flamands et leurs temps.* Louvain-la-Neuve.
Pauwels, Henri, Hendrik R. Hoetink, and Sadja Jacob Herzog
1965 *Jean Gossaert dit Mabuse: Catalogue.* Exh. cat. Rotterdam: Museum Boymans-van Beuningen; Bruges: Groeningemuseum.
Paviot, Jacques
1990 "La vie de Jan van Eyck selon les documents écrits." *Revue des archéologues et historiens d'art de Louvain* 23, pp. 83–93.
Pelinck, E.
1949 "Cornelis Engebrechtsz: De herkomst van zijn kunst." *Nederlandsch Kunsthistorisch Jaarboek,* 1948–49, pp. 40–74.
Périer-d'Ieteren, Catheline
1987 "Précisions sur le dessin sous-jacent et la technique d'exécution de la Nativité de Gérard David du musée de Budapest." *Annales d'histoire d'art et d'archéologie* 60, pp. 95–106.
1989–91 "Le 'Retable du Martyre des Saints Crépin et Crépinien' et le Maître de la Légende de Sainte Barbe." *Bulletin des Musées Royaux des Beaux-Arts de Belgique,* nos. 1–3, pp. 157–73.
Périer-d'Ieteren, Catheline, A. Rinuy, J. Vynckier, and L. Kockaert
1993 "Apport des méthodes d'investigation scientifique à l'étude de deux peintures attribuées à Juan de Flandes." *Genava,* n.s., 41, pp. 107–18.
Peters, H.
1968 "Zum New Yorker 'Diptychon' der 'Hand G.'" In *Minuscula Discipulorum: Festschrift H. Kauffmann,* pp. 235ff. Berlin.
Philip, Lotte Brand
1971 *The Ghent Altarpiece and the Art of Jan van Eyck.* Princeton.
Philippot, Paul
1966 "Les grisailles et les 'degrès de réalité' de l'image dans la peinture flamande des 15ème et 16ème siècles." *Bulletin des Musées Royaux des Beaux-Arts de Belgique* 4, pp. 225–46.
1994 *La peinture dans les anciens Pays-Bas, XVe–XVIe siècles.* Paris.
Pigler, André
1964 "La mouche peinte: Un talisman." *Bulletin du Musée Hongrois des Beaux-Arts,* no. 24, pp. 47–64.
Pliny, the Elder
1938–62 *Natural History.* Translated by H. Rackham. Loeb Classical Library. 10 vols. Cambridge, Mass., and London.
Podro, Michael
1982 *The Critical Historians of Art.* New Haven.
van de Poele, C.
1898 "Eene merkwaardige Schilderij." *Kunst, Tijdschrift voor Kunst & Letteren* 2, no. 6 (March 24), pp. 41–42.
Ponz, Antonio
1783 *Viage de España.* Vol. 12. Madrid.
Pope-Hennessy, John
1966 *The Portrait in the Renaissance.* A. W. Mellon Lectures in the Fine Arts, 1963. Washington, D.C. Paperback ed., Princeton, 1979.
Post, Chandler Rathfon
1933 *A History of Spanish Painting.* Vol. 4, part 1, *The Hispano-Flemish Style in North-Western Spain.* Cambridge, Mass.
Poulot, Dominique
1997 *Musée, nation, patrimoine, 1789–1815.* Paris.
Preibisz, Leon
1911 *Martin van Heemskerck: Ein Beitrag zur Geschichte des Romanismus in der niederländischen Malerei des XVI-Jahrhunderts.* Leipzig.
Preimesberger, Rudolf
1991 "Zu Jan van Eycks Diptychon der Sammlung Thyssen-Bornemisza." *Zeitschrift für Kunstgeschichte* 54, pp. 459–89.
Prevenier, Walter, and Wim Blockmans
1986 *The Burgundian Netherlands.* Translated by P. Kin and Y. Mead. Cambridge.
Previtali, Giovanni
1964 *La fortuna dei primitivi dal Vasari ai neoclassici.* Turin.
1994 *La fortune des primitifs: De Vasari aux neoclassiques.* Translated by Nadia Di Mascio. Paris.
Priest, A.
1940 "Loans from the Collection of George D. Pratt." *Bulletin of The Metropolitan Museum of Art* 35 (December), pp. 237–38.

Puydt, Raoul Maria de
1984 "De H. Godelieve in de plastische kunsten." *Godeliph, 1084–1984. Vlaanderen* 33, no. 200 (May–June), pp. 161–81.
van Puyvelde, Leo
1935 "Two Exhibitions at Brussels." *Burlington Magazine* 67, pp. 83–84.
1947 [as editor]. *Les primitifs flamands: Catalogue.* 2d ed. Paris. First published 1941.
1953 *La peinture flamande au siècle des Van Eyck.* Brussels.
1962 *La peinture flamande au siècle de Bosch et Brueghel.* Paris.
1968 *La peinture flamande des Van Eyck à Metsys.* Brussels.
Quarré, Pierre
1957 "Fragment d'un primitif de la chartreuse de Champmol." *Revue des arts* 7 (March–April), pp. 59–64.
Ragusa, Isa, and Rosalie B. Green, trans. and eds.
1961 *Meditations on the Life of Christ: An Illustrated Manuscript of the Fourteenth Century, by Saint Bonaventure.* Princeton.
Réau, Louis
1955–59 *Iconographie de l'art chrétien.* 3 vols. in 6 parts. Paris.
Reinach, Salomon
1905–23 *Répertoire de peintures du Moyen Âge et de la Renaissance (1280–1580).* 6 vols. Paris.
Renard, Georges F.
1919 *Guilds in the Middle Ages.* London.
Renders, Émile
1931 *La solution du problème Van der Weyden-Flémalle-Campin.* With contributions by Jos. De Smet and Louis Beyaert-Carlier. 2 vols. Bruges.
Renders, Émile, and F. Lyna
1931 "Le Maître de Flémalle, Robert Campin, et la prétendue école de Tournai." *Gazette des Beaux-Arts,* ser. 6, 6, pp. 289–97.
Reynaud, Nicole
1968 "Jean Hey, peintre de Moulins et son client Jean Cueillette." *Revue de l'art* 1, no. 2, pp. 33–37.
1970 "Primitifs flamands anonymes," exhibition review. *Revue de l'art* 8, pp. 67–71.
1975 "Une allégorie sacrée de Jan Provost." *La revue du Louvre* 25, pp. 7–16.
Ridderbos, Bernhard
1995a "Objecten en vragen." In *"Om iets te weten van de oude meesters": De Vlaamse primitieven—herontdekking, waardering, en onderzoek,* edited by Bernhard Ridderbos and Henk van Veen, pp. 15–133. Nijmegen.
1995b "Van Waagen tot Friedländer: Het kunsthistorisch onderzoek naar de Oudnederlandse schilderkunst gedurende de negentiende en het begin van de twintigste eeuw." In *"Om iets te weten van de oude meesters": De Vlaamse primitieven—herontdekking, waardering, en onderzoek,* edited by Bernhard Ridderbos and Henk van Veen, pp. 189–235. Nijmegen.
Rietstap, Johannes Baptist
1972 *Armorial General de Belgique. . . .* Baltimore.
Rijksmuseum
1976 *All the Paintings of the Rijksmuseum in Amsterdam: A Completely Illustrated Catalogue,* by J. J. van Thiel, C. J. de Bruyn, J. Cleveringa, W. Kloek, and A. Vels Heijn. Amsterdam.
Ring, Grete
1941 "Additions to the Work of Jan Provost and Quentin Massys, I." *Burlington Magazine* 79, pp. 156–60.
1949 *A Century of French Painting, 1400–1500.* London. Reprint, New York, 1979.
Ringbom, Sixten
1962 "Maria in Sole and the Virgin of the Rosary." *Journal of the Warburg and Courtauld Institutes* 25, nos. 3–4, pp. 326–30.
1965 *Icon to Narrative: The Rise of the Dramatic Close-up in Fifteenth-Century Devotional Painting.* Acta Academiae Aboensis, ser. A., Humaniora, vol. 31, no. 2. Åbo.
1969 "Devotional Images and Imaginative Devotions: Notes on the Place of Art in Late Medieval Piety." *Gazette des Beaux-Arts,* ser. 6, 73, pp. 159–70.
1984 *Icon to Narrative: The Rise of the Dramatic Close-up in Fifteenth-Century Devotional Painting.* 2d ed. Doornspijk. First published 1965.
Robb, David M.
1936 "The Iconography of the Annunciation in the Fourteenth and Fifteenth Centuries." *Art Bulletin* 18, pp. 480–526.
Robinson, Frederick B.
1959 "An Early Flemish Triptych." *Museum of Fine Arts Bulletin* (Springfield, Mass.) 25, no. 3.
Robinson, J. C.
1905 "The *Virgin of Salamanca* by the Maître de Flémalle" and "The Maître de Flémalle and the Painters of the School of Salamanca." *Burlington Magazine* 7, pp. 238, 387–93.
Rohlmann, Michael
1992 "Ein flämisches Vorbild für Ghirlandaios 'Prime Pitture.'" *Mitteilungen des Kunsthistorischen Institutes in Florenz* 36, pp. 388–96.
1993a "Flämische Tafelmalerei im Kreis des Piero de'Medici." In *Piero de'Medici "il Gottoso" (1416–1469): Kunst im Dienste der Mediceer,* edited by Andreas Beyer and Bruce Boucher, pp. 181–87. Berlin.
1993b "Zitate flämischer Landschaftsmotive in Florentiner Quattrocentomalerei." In *Italienische Frührenaissance und nordeuropäisches Spätmittelalter: Kunst der frühen Neuzeit im europaischen Zusammenhang,* edited by Joachim Poeschke, pp. 235–47. Munich.
1994 "Auftragskunst und Sammlerbild: Altniederländische Tafelmalerei im Florenz des Quattrocento." Ph.D. dissertation, Universität zu Köln.
1995 "Memling's 'Pagagnotti Triptych.'" *Burlington Magazine* 137, pp. 438–45.
Rolland, Paul
1932 *Les primitifs tournaisiens, peintres et sculpteurs.* Brussels and Paris.
Romanov, Nikolai Ilich
1934 "Jan Mostaert's Great *Ecce Homo.*" *Art in America* 22 (March), pp. 40–48.
Rorimer, James J.
1957 "The Merode Altarpiece." *Bulletin of The Metropolitan Museum of Art* 16, no. 4, p. 116.
Rosell y Torres, Isidoro
1873 "Estampa española del siglo XV grabada por Fray Francisco Domenec." *Museo Español de Antigüedades* (Madrid) 2, pp. 445–64.

Rosenberg, Jacob
1925 "Jan Joest." In *Allgemeines Lexikon der bildenden Künstler von der Antike bis zur Gegenwart,* edited by Ulrich Thieme and Felix Becker, vol. 18, pp. 376–77.

Röthel, H. K.
1956 "Ein Paliotto Gerard Davids aus der Abtei von Cervara." *Die Kunst und das schöne Heim* 54, pp. 361–65.

Rousseau, Theodore, Jr.
1951 "A Flemish Altarpiece from Spain." *Bulletin of The Metropolitan Museum of Art* 9 (June), pp. 270–83.
1957 "The Merode Altarpiece." *Bulletin of The Metropolitan Museum of Art* 16, pp. 117–29.

Rubinstein, Stella
1916 "Two Pictures by Joos van Cleve (Master of the Death of the Virgin)." *Art in America* 4, pp. 343–52.
1922 "An Annunciation Group in the Michael Dreicer Collection." *Art in America* 10, pp. 56–63.

Rubinstein-Bloch, Stella
1926 *Catalogue of the Collection of George and Florence Blumenthal, New York.* Vol. 1. Paris.

Ruda, Jeffrey
1993 *Fra Filippo Lippi: Life and Work with a Complete Catalogue.* London.

Russell, John Malcolm
1978 "The Iconography of the Friedsam *Annunciation.*" *Art Bulletin* 58, pp. 23–27.

Rutherford, Jessica
1982 "Henry Willett As a Collector." *Apollo* 115, pp. 176–81.

Salinger, Margaretta
1941 "Two New Flemish Paintings." *Bulletin of The Metropolitan Museum of Art* 36 (May), pp. 109–11.

Samuels, Ernest
1979 *Bernard Berenson: The Making of a Connoisseur.* Cambridge, Mass.

Sánchez Cantón, Francisco Javier
1930 "El retablo de la Reina Católica." *Archivo español de arte y arqueología* 6, pp. 97–133.
1931 "El retablo de la Reina Católica." *Archivo español de arte y arqueología* 7, pp. 149–52.
1950 *Libros, tapices, y cuadros que coleccionó Isabel la Católica.* Madrid.

Sander, Jochen
1992 *Hugo van der Goes: Stilentwicklung und Chronologie.* Mainz.
1993 *Kataloge der Gemälde im Stadelschen Kunstinstitut Frankfurt am Main.* Vol. 2, *Niederländische Gemälde im Städel, 1400–1550.* Mainz.

Scailliérez, Cécile
1991 *Joos van Cleve au Louvre.* Exh. cat. Paris: Musée du Louvre.
1992 "Entre enluminure et peinture: À propos d'un *Paysage avec Saint Jérôme Pénitent* de l'École Ganto-Brugeoise récemment acquis par le Louvre." *Revue du Louvre,* no. 2, pp. 16–31.

Schabacker, Peter H.
1972a "Petrus Christus' *Saint Eloy*: Problems of Provenance, Sources and Meaning." *Art Quarterly* 35, no. 2, pp. 103–20.
1972b "*Rogier van der Weyden,* by Martin Davies." *Art Quarterly* 35, no. 4, pp. 422–25.
1974 *Petrus Christus.* Utrecht.

Schapiro, Meyer
1945 "'Muscipula Diaboli,' the Symbolism of the Merode Altarpiece." *Art Bulletin* 27, pp. 182–87.
1959 "A Note on the Mérode Altarpiece." *Art Bulletin* 41, pp. 327–28.

Scharf, George
1858 *Artistic and Descriptive Notes of the Most Remarkable Pictures in the British Institution: Exhibition of the Old Masters, Pall Mall.* Exh. cat. London.

Schiller, Gertrud
1971–72 *Iconography of Christian Art.* 2d ed. 2 vols. Translated by Janet Seligman. New York.

Schmarsow, August
1928 *Robert van der Kampine und Roger van der Weyden: Kompositionsgesetze des Mittelalters in der Nordeuropäischen Renaissance.* Abhandlungen der Philologisch-historischen Klasse der Königl. sächsischen Akademie der Wissenschaften, 39, no. 2. Leipzig.

Schmidt, James, et al.
1910 *Les anciennes écoles de peinture dans les palais et collections privées russes représentées à l'exposition organisée à St.-Petersbourg en 1909 par la Revue d'art ancien, "Staryé Gody."* Brussels.

Schnütgen, Alexander
1902 "Altniederländisches Gemälde mit Szenen aus dem Leben des hl. Augustinus." *Zeitschrift für christliche Kunst* 14 (1901), cols. 161–66.

Scholtens, H. J. J.
1938 "Jan van Eyck's 'H. Maagd met den Kartuizer' en de Exeter-Madonna te Berlijn." *Oud Holland* 55, pp. 49–62.
1960 "Petrus Christus en zijn portret van een kartuizer." *Oud-Holland* 75, pp. 59–72.

Schöne, Wolfgang
1937 "Über einige altniederländische Bilder vor allem in Spanien." *Jahrbuch der Preuszischen Kunstsammlungen* 58, pp. 153–81.
1938 *Dieric Bouts und seine Schule.* Berlin.

Schopenhauer, Johanna
1822 *Johann van Eyck und seine Nachfolger.* 2 vols. Frankfurt am Main.

van Schoute, Roger
1963 *La Chapelle Royale de Grenade.* Les primitifs flamandes, I: Corpus de la peinture des anciens Pays-Bas méridionaux au quinzième siècle, 6. Brussels.
1990a Record of conversation with and letter to Maryan W. Ainsworth, April 24. Archives, Paintings Conservation Department, Metropolitan Museum.
1990b Record of conversation with Maryan W. Ainsworth, September 19. Archives, Paintings Conservation Department, Metropolitan Museum.

Schrader, Jack
1970 Letter regarding Memling's *Portrait of an Old Man,* Archives, Department of European Paintings, Metropolitan Museum.

Schuler, Carol M.
1992 "The Seven Sorrows of the Virgin: Popular Culture and Cultic Imagery in Pre-Reformation Europe." *Simiolus* 21, pp. 5–28.

Schürmeyer, Walter
1923 *Hieronymous Bosch.* Munich.

Scillia, Diane Graybowski
1975 "Gerard David and Manuscript Illumination in the Low Countries, 1480–1509." Ph.D. dissertation, Case Western Reserve University, Cleveland.
Scott, Margaret
1980 *Late Gothic Europe, 1400–1500: The History of Dress.* London.
Seligman, Germain
1961 *Merchants of Art, 1880–1960: Eighty Years of Professional Collecting.* New York.
Serck, Luc
1990 "Henri Bles et la peinture de paysage dans les Pays-Bas méridionaux avant Bruegel." 6 vols. Ph.D. dissertation, Université Catholique de Louvain.
1991 Letter to Véronique Sintoben regarding the *Temptation of Saint Anthony.* Archives, Department of European Paintings, Metropolitan Museum.
Shorr, Dorothy C.
1954 *The Christ Child in Devotional Images in Italy During the XIV Century.* New York.
Silva, Nuno Vassallo e
1992 "O Ouro de Quilos." *Oceanos* (Lisbon), no. 10, pp. 54–61.
Silver, Larry
1983 "Fountain and Source: A Rediscovered Eyckian Icon." *Pantheon* 41, pp. 95–104.
1984 *The Paintings of Quentin Massys with Catalogue Raisonné.* Montclair, N.J.
Siple, Ella S.
1929 "Art in America—Messrs. Knoedler's Exhibition." *Burlington Magazine* 55, pp. 331–32.
Smeyers, Maurits, and Bert Cardon
1991 "Utrecht and Bruges—South and North 'Boundless' Relations in the 15th Century." In *Masters and Miniatures: Proceedings of the Congress on Medieval Manuscript Illumination in the Northern Netherlands (Utrecht, 10–13 December 1989)*, pp. 89–108. Doornspijk.
Smith, H. Clifford
1908 *Jewellery.* New York.
1914 "The Legend of St. Eloy and St. Godeberta, by Petrus Christus." *Burlington Magazine* 25, pp. 326–35.
1915 *The Goldsmith and the Young Couple of the Legend of S. Eloy and S. Godeberta by Petrus Christus.* N.p.: Privately printed.
Smits, K.
1933 *De iconografie van de Nederlandsche primitieven.* Amsterdam.
Snyder, James
1960 "The Early Haarlem School of Painting, I: Ouwater and the Master of the Tiburtine Sibyl." *Art Bulletin* 42, pp. 39–56.
1985 *Northern Renaissance Art: Painting, Sculpture, and the Graphic Arts from 1350 to 1575.* New York.
1985a "'The Joyous Appearance of Christ with a Multitude of Angels and Holy Fathers to His Dearest Mother': A Mystical Devotional Diptych by Jan Mostaert." In *Tribute to Lotte Brand Philip, Art Historian and Detective*, pp. 175–84. New York.
1987 Introduction. In Metropolitan Museum 1987, pp. 6–17.
1996 "Ouwater, Albert van." In *The Dictionary of Art*, edited by Jane Turner, vol. 23, pp. 671–72. New York.
Sonkes, Micheline
1971–72 "Le dessin sous-jacent chez Rogier van der Weyden et le problème de la personnalité du Maître du Flémalle." *Institut Royal du Patrimoine Artistique, Koninklijk Instituut voor het Kunst Patrimonium, bulletin* 13, pp. 161–203.
Sosson, J.-P.
1994 "Le statut du peintre." In De Patoul and Van Schoute 1994, pp. 75–87.
Spantigati, Carlenrica, and Joseph J. Rishel
1997 *Jan van Eyck, 1390–c. 1441: Opere a confronto.* Exh. cat. Turin: Galleria Sabauda.
Sperling, E. M.
1927 *Catalogue of a Loan Exhibition of French Primitives and Objects of Art in Aid of the French Hospital in New York.* New York: Kleinberger Galleries.
Sricchia Santoro, Fiorella
1986 *Antonello e l'Europa.* Milan.
Stange, Alfred
1934–61 *Deutsche Malerei der Gotik.* 11 vols. Berlin.
Stechow, Wolfgang
1966 *Northern Renaissance Art, 1400–1600: Sources and Documents.* Evanston, Illinois.
Stein, Susan Alyson, and Gretchen Wold
1993 In Frelinghuysen et al. 1993.
Steinberg, Leo
1996 *The Sexuality of Christ in Renaissance Art and in Modern Oblivion.* 2d ed., revised and expanded. Chicago. Originally published 1983.
Steinmetz, Anja Sibylle
1995 *Das Altarretabel in der altniederländischen Malerei: Untersuchung zur Darstellung eines sakralen Requisits vom frühen 15. bis zum späten 16. Jahrhundert.* Weimar.
Sterling, Charles
1941 [as Charles Jacques (pseud.)]. *La peinture française: Les peintres du Moyen Âge.* Paris.
1955 *The Metropolitan Museum of Art: A Catalogue of French Paintings.* Vol. 1. Cambridge, Mass.
1957a In *La collection Lehman de New York.* Exh. cat. Paris: Musée de l'Orangerie. Catalogue by Charles Sterling, Olga Raggio, Michel Laclotte, and Sylvie Béguin.
1957b "Expositions: Musée de l'Orangerie—La collection Lehman." *Revue des arts* 7 (May–June), pp. 133–42.
1963 "Du nouveau sur le Maître de Moulins." *L'oeil* 107, pp. 2–15, 55–68.
1968 "Jean Hey, le Maître de Moulins." *Revue de l'art,* no. 1, pp. 27–33.
1971 "Observations on Petrus Christus." *Art Bulletin* 53, pp. 1–26.
1972 "Jean Hey." *Propyläen Kunstgeschichte* 7, pp. 193–94.
1976 "Jan van Eyck avant 1432." *Revue de l'art* 33, pp. 7–82.
1981 "Un nouveau tableau de Simon Marmion." *Revue d'art canadienne/Canadian Art Review* 8, p. 12.
1990 *La peinture médiévale à Paris, 1300–1500.* Vol. 2. Paris.
Sterling, Charles, and Maryan W. Ainsworth
1998 "France." In *The Robert Lehman Collection, II: Fifteenth- to Eighteenth-Century European Paintings, France, Central Europe, Flanders, the Netherlands, Spain, and Great Britain*, by Charles Sterling et al., nos. 1–5. New York.

Sterne, Margaret
1980 *The Passionate Eye: The Life of William R. Valentiner.* Detroit.
van der Stock, Jan, ed.
1993 *Antwerp, Story of a Metropolis, 16th–17th Century.* Exh. cat. Antwerp: Hessenhuis.
Stoichita, Victor
1993 *L'instauration du tableau: Métapeinture à l'aube des temps modernes.* Paris.
Stratton, Suzanne L.
1994 *The Immaculate Conception in Spanish Art.* Cambridge.
Strauss, Walter L.
1980 *Albrecht Dürer: Woodcuts and Wood Blocks.* New York.
Stroo, Cyriel, and Pascale Syfer-d'Olne
1996 *The Flemish Primitives: Catalogue of Early Netherlandish Painting in the Royal Museums of Fine Arts of Belgium.* Vol. 1, *The Master of Flémalle and Rogier van der Weyden Groups.* Edited by Elizabeth Moodey and Stanton Thomas; translated by Katy Kist and Jennifer Kilian. Brussels.
Stuebe, Isabel Combs
1969 "The *Johannisschüssel*: From Narrative to Reliquary to *Andachtsbild.*" *Marsyas* 14 (1968–69), pp. 1–16.
van Suchtelen, Ariane, Yvette Bruijnen, and Edwin Buijsen
1997 *Art on Wings: Celebrating the Reunification of a Triptych by Gerard David.* Exh. cat. The Hague: Mauritshuis.
Suhr, William
1957 "The Restoration of the Merode Altarpiece." *Bulletin of The Metropolitan Museum of Art* 16, no. 4 (December), pp. 140–44.
Sullivan, Margaret A.
1994 *Bruegel's Peasants: Art and Audience in the Northern Renaissance.* Cambridge.
Sutton, Denys, ed.
1972 *Letters of Roger Fry.* 2 vols. London and New York.
Sutton, Peter C.
1990 *Northern European Paintings in the Philadelphia Museum of Art from the Sixteenth through the Nineteenth Century.* Philadelphia.
Szabo, George
1975 *The Robert Lehman Collection: A Guide.* New York.
Szmodis-Eszlary, Eva, and Susan Urbach
1990 *Middeleeuwse Nederlandse kunst uit Hongarije: Een keuze uit de collecties van het Museum voor Schone Kunsten, Boedapest, en het Museum voor Christelijke Kunst, Esztergom.* Utrecht.
Tagliaferro, Laura, and Clario Di Fabio
1992 *La Galleria di Palazzo Bianco: Guida.* Milan.
Talbot, Charles
1979 Letter regarding the *Virgin and Child*, by a follower of Dieric Bouts. Archives, Department of European Paintings, Metropolitan Museum.
Taubert, Johannes
1956 "Zur kunstwissenschaftlichen Auswertung von naturwissenschaftlichen Gemäldeuntersuchungen." Dissertation, Universität Marburg.
1960 "Die Beiden Marienaltäre des Rogier van der Weyden." *Pantheon* 18, pp. 67–75.
1975 "Beobachtungen zum schöpferischen Arbeitsprozess bei einigen altniederländischen Malern." *Nederlands kunsthistorisch jaarboek* 26, pp. 41–71.
Teniers, David
1660 *Theatrum Pictorium. . . .* Brussels.
Thoss, Dagmar
1986 "Die Bebilderten Handschriften der Bibliothek des Prinzen Eugen von Savoyen." In *Bibliotheca Eugeniana: Die Sammlungen des Prinzen Eugen von Savoyen,* pp. 131–45. Exh. cat. Vienna: Österreichische Nationalbibliothek and Graphische Sammlung Albertina.
1987 *Flämische Buchmalerei: Handschriftenschätze aus dem Burgunderreich.* Exh. cat. Vienna: Österreichische Nationalbibliothek.
Thuillier, Jacques
1961 "Études sur le cercle des Dinteville: L'énigme de Félix Chrestien." *Art de France*, no. 1, pp. 57–75.
Thürlemann, Felix
1995 *Robert Campin—der Meister von Flémalle: Das Mérode Triptychon. Ein Hochzeitsbild für Peter Engebrecht und Gretchen Schrinemechers.* Frankfurt am Main.
1997 *Robert Campin, das Mérode Triptychon: Ein Hochzeitsbild für Peter Engelbrecht und Gretchen Schrinmechers aus Köln.* Frankfurt am Main.
Thurston, Herbert
1900 "Our Popular Devotions, II: The Rosary." *Month: A Catholic Magazine* 96, pp. 403–18, 513–27, 620–37.
1901 "Our Popular Devotions, II: The Rosary." *Month: A Catholic Magazine* 97, pp. 67–79, 172–88, 286–304, 383–404.
Thyssen-Bornemisza collection
1969 *The Thyssen-Bornemisza Collection, Castagnola.* Catalogue prepared by Johann C. Ebbinge-Wubben, Christian Salm, Charles Sterling, and Rudolf Heinemann. Castagnola-Ticino.
Tietze, Hans
1930 "Exhibition of Flemish Art at Vienna." *Formes* (Paris), no. 4 (April), pp. 15–16.
1935 [as editor]. *Meisterwerke europäischer Malerei in Amerika.* Vienna.
1939 [as editor]. *Masterpieces of European Painting in America.* New York.
Tolnai, Karl von [Charles de Tolnay]
1934 "Studien zu den Gemälden Pieter Bruegels d. Ä." *Jahrbuch der Kunsthistorischen Sammlungen in Wien,* n.s., 8, pp. 105–35.
de Tolnay, Charles
1935 *Pierre Bruegel l'Ancien.* Brussels.
1937 *Hieronymus Bosch.* Basel.
1939 *Le Maître de Flémalle et les frères Van Eyck.* Brussels.
1944 "Hugo van der Goes as Portrait Painter." *Art Quarterly* 7, pp. 183, 187–89.
1959 "L'autel Mérode du Maître de Flémalle." *Gazette des Beaux-Arts*, ser. 6, 53, pp. 65–78.
1960 "Supplément concernant l'autel Mérode du Maître de Flémalle." *Gazette des Beaux-Arts*, ser. 6, 55, pp. 177–78.
1966 *Hieronymus Bosch.* Reprint of 1965 ed. New York.
Tormo y Monzó, Elias
1909 "La pintura aragonesa cuatrocentista y la retrospectiva de la exposición de Zaragoza en general," part 3. *Boletín de la Sociedad Española de Excursiones* 17, pp. 234–43.

Torresan, Paolo
1981 *Il dipingere di Fiandra: La pittura neerlandese nella letteratura artistica italiana del quattro e cinquecento.* Modena.
Toussaert, Jacques
1963 *Le sentiment religieux en Flandre à la fin du Moyen Âge.* Paris.
Toussaint, Nathalie
1994 "Les petits maîtres de la fin du XVe siècle à Bruges." In De Patoul and Van Schoute 1994.
Trexler, Richard C.
1997 *The Journey of the Magi: Meanings in History of a Christian Story.* Princeton.
Tschudi, Hugo von
1893 "Berichte und Mitteilungen aus Sammlungen und Museen über staatliche Kunstpflege und Restaurationen. London: Die Ausstellung altniederländische Gemälde Burlington Fine Arts Club." *Repertorium für Kunstwissenschaft* 16, pp. 100–116.
1898 "Der Meister von Flémalle." *Jahrbuch der Königlich Preussischen Kunstsammlungen* 19, pp. 8–34, 89–116.
Turner, Richard
1966 *The Vision of Landscape in Renaissance Italy.* Princeton.
Unverfehrt, Gerd
1980 *Hieronymus Bosch: Die Rezeption seiner Kunst im frühen 16. Jahrhundert.* Berlin.
Upton, Joel M.
1972 "Petrus Christus." Ph.D. dissertation, Bryn Mawr College, Bryn Mawr, Pennsylvania.
1990 *Petrus Christus: His Place in Fifteenth-Century Flemish Painting.* University Park, Pennsylvania.
1995 "PETRVS.XPI.ME.FECIT: The Transformation of a Legacy." In Ainsworth 1995, pp. 53–64.
Urbach, Susan
1971 *Early Netherlandish Painting.* Translated by Mari Kuttna. New York. Originally published as *Korai nemetalfoldi tablakepek.*
1974 "Domus Dei Est et Porta Coeli: Megjegyzések Petrus Christus Madonna-Képének Ikonográfiájához." *Építés-építészettudomány* 3–4, pp. 341–53.
1987 "Contribution à l'étude de la Nativité de Gérard David à Budapest." *Annales d'histoire d'art et d'archéologie* 60, pp. 83–94.
1991 "Research Report on Examinations of Underdrawings in Some Early Netherlandish and German Panels in the Budapest Museum of Fine Arts, II." In *Le dessin sous-jacent dans la peinture: Colloque VIII, 1989,* edited by H. Verougstraete-Marcq and R. van Schoute , pp. 77–93. Louvain-la-Neuve.
Valentiner, Wilhelm R.
1914 "Two Paintings Acquired for the Minneapolis Institute of Fine Arts." *Art in America* 2, pp. 163–64.
1943 "Flemish Primitives—16 Panels." Certificate of September 26. Archives, Department of European Paintings, Metropolitan Museum.
1945 "Jan de Vos, The Master of Frankfort." *Art Quarterly* 8, pp. 197–215.
Vandenbroeck, Paul
1985 *Catalogus schilderijen 14de en 15de eeuw.* Antwerp: Koninklijk Museum voor Schone Kunsten.
Vandevivere, Ignace
1967 *La Cathédrale de Palencia et l'Église Paroissiale de Cervera de Pisuerga.* Brussels.
Vandura, Duro
1988 *Nizozemske Slikarske Skole u Strossmayerovoj Galerij, Starih Majstora Jugoslavenske Akademije Zanosti i Umjetnosti.* Zagreb.
Vaughn, Malcolm
1928 "Paintings by Petrus Christus in America." *International Studio* 89 (January), pp. 27–31.
Veldman, Ilja M.
1977 *Maarten van Heemskerck and Dutch Humanism in the Sixteenth Century.* Maarsen.
Verlant, Ernest
1924 *La peinture ancienne à l'exposition de l'art belge à Paris en 1923.* Brussels and Paris.
Vermeersch, Valentin, ed.
1992 *Bruges and Europe.* Antwerp.
Veronée-Verhaegen, Nicole
1968 "*La vierge embrassant l'Enfant Jésus,* par Dieric Bouts." *Musées Royaux des Beaux-Arts de Belgique, Bulletin* 17, pp. 5–10.
1994 "Le portrait." In De Patoul and Van Schoute 1994, pp. 217–39, 635.
Verougstraete, Hélène, and Roger van Schoute
1994 "La réalisation matérielle du tableau." In De Patoul and Van Schoute 1994, pp. 101–15.
1995 "La *Lamentation* de Petrus Christus." In Ainsworth 1995, pp. 193–203.
Verougstraete, Hélène, Antoine de Schryver, and Roger H. Marijnissen
1995 "Peintures sur papier et parchemin marouflés aux XVe et XVIe siècles: L'exemple d'une *Vierge et Enfant* de la suite de Gerard David." In *Le dessin sous-jacent dans la peinture: Colloque X, 1993,* edited by H. Verougstraete and R. van Schoute, pp. 94–105. Louvain-la-Neuve.
Versnaeyen, M. K.
1865 "Commission royale des monuments: Province de Flandre Occidentale." *Bulletin des Commissions Royales d'Art et d'Archéologie* 4, pp. 31–185.
Vertue, George
1937–38 *Notebooks, 1741–52.* Vol. 5. Walpole Society, vol. 26. London.
Vespasiano da Bisticci
1926 *The Vespasiano Memoirs: Lives of Illustrious Men of the XVth Century.* Translated by William George and Emily Waters. London and New York.
1997 *The Vespasiano Memoirs: Lives of Illustrious Men of the XVth Century.* Translated by William George and Emily Waters. Toronto. Reprint of the 1963 ed.
Veth, Jan, and Samuel Muller
1918 *Albrecht Dürers niederländische Reise.* Vol. 1, *Die Urkunden über die Reise.* Berlin.
Vienna
1930 *CX. Ausstellung der Vereinigung Bildender Künstler Wiener Secession: Drei Jahrhunderte vlämische Kunst, 1400–1700.* Frühwerk: Otto Pächt. Exh. cat. Vienna: Veranstaltet vom Verein der Museums-Freunde in Wien.

Virch, Claus
1969 "The Story of Bruegel's Harvesters: A Curator's Coup." *Connoisseur* 172, no. 693 (November), pp. 221–27.
Vitale, V.
1934 "Diplomatici e consoli della Republica di Genova." *Atti della Società Ligure di Storia Patria* 63, pp. 4, 48, 134–35.
Vloberg, Maurice
1946 *L'Eucharistie dans l'art.* 2 vols. Grenoble and Paris.
Voet, Leon
1973 *Antwerp, the Golden Age: The Rise and Glory of the Metropolis in the Sixteenth Century.* Antwerp.
Vogelaar, Christiaan
1987 *Netherlandish 15th and 16th-Century Paintings in the National Gallery of Ireland: A Complete Catalogue.* Dublin: National Gallery of Ireland.
Waagen, Gustav Friedrich
1822 *Ueber Hubert und Johann van Eyck.* Breslau.
1847 "Nachträge zur Kenntniß der altniederländische Malerschulen des 15ten und 16ten Jahrhunderts." *Kunstblatt,* no. 41 (August 24), p. 163, no. 47 (September 25), pp. 185–87.
1854 *Treasures–Great Britain.* Vol. 3. London.
1857 *Galleries and Cabinets of Art in Great Britain.* London.
Walker, John
1969 *Self-Portrait with Donors: Confessions of an Art Collector.* Boston and Toronto.
van de Walle de Ghelcke, Thierry
1952 "Y a-t-il un Gérard David miniaturiste?" In *Studies over de kerkelijke en kunstgeschiedenis van West-Vlaanderen,* pp. 399–422. Bruges.
Warburg, Aby
1902 "Flandrische Kunst und florentinische Frührenaissance Studien." *Jahrbuch der Königlich Preussischen Kunstsammlungen* 23, pp. 247–66.
1932 *Gesammelte Schriften.* 2 vols. Leipzig.
Ward, John L.
1968 "A New Look at the Friedsam Annunciation." *Art Bulletin* 50, pp. 184–87.
Waterhouse, E.
1937 "The Winter Exhibition at the Burlington Fine Arts Club." *Burlington Magazine* 70, p. 45.
Wauters, A. J.
1912–13 "Roger van der Weyden," parts 1, 2. *Burlington Magazine* 22, pp. 75–82, 230–32.
Weale, W. H. James
1861 *Catalogue: Notices et descriptions avec monogrammes, etc.* Bruges: Groeningemuseum.
1863 "Pierre & Sebastien Cristus." *Le Beffroi* 1.
1864–65 "Gerard David" and "Documents inédits sur les enlumineurs de Bruges." *Le Beffroi* 2, pp. 288–317.
1895 *Gerard David: Painter and Illuminator.* London.
1901 *Hans Memling.* London.
1903a "The Early Painters of the Netherlands as Illustrated by the Bruges Exhibition of 1902, Article IV." *Burlington Magazine* 2, pp. 35–41.
1903b "Les peintures des maîtres inconnus." *Revue de l'art chrétien,* ser. 4, 14, cols. 276–79.
1904 "Paintings by John van Eyck and Albert Dürer Formerly in the Arundel Collection." *Burlington Magazine* 6, pp. 244–49.
1905a "The Annunciation by Roger de la Pasture." *Burlington Magazine* 7, p. 141.
1905b "Painting by Gerard David in the Collection of Don Pablo Bosch at Madrid." *Burlington Magazine* 7, pp. 469–70.
1905c "The Shutters of a Triptych by Gerard David." *Burlington Magazine* 7, pp. 234–37.
1908 *Hubert and John van Eyck: Their Life and Work.* London.
1911 "Peintres brugeois: Les Claeissins." *Annales de la Société d'Emulation de Bruges* 61, pp. 26–76.
Wehle, Harry B.
1922 "The Michael Dreicer Collection, Part I: Paintings." *Bulletin of The Metropolitan Museum of Art* 17 (May), pp. 100–106.
1936 "A Triptych by Patinir." *Bulletin of The Metropolitan Museum of Art* 31 (April), pp. 80–84.
1943 "A Painting by Joos van Gent." *Bulletin of The Metropolitan Museum of Art,* n.s., 2 (December), pp. 133–39.
1953 "Maria Portinari." *Bulletin of The Metropolitan Museum of Art,* n.s., 11 (January), pp. 129–31, cover ill.
Wehle, Harry B., and Margaretta Salinger
1947 *A Catalogue of Early Flemish, Dutch, and German Paintings.* New York: The Metropolitan Museum of Art.
Weiss, Roberto
1956–57 "Jan van Eyck and the Italians," parts 1, 2. *Italian Studies* 11, pp. 1–15; 12, pp. 7–21.
Weisz, Ernst
1913 *Jan Gossart gen. Mabuse: Sein Leben und Seine Werke.* Parchim.
Welzel, Barbara
1991 *Abendmahlsaltäre vor der Reformation.* Berlin.
Weniger, Matthias
1997 "*Bynnen Brugge in Flandern*: The Apprenticeships of Michel Sittow and Juan de Flandes." In *Memling Studies* 1997, pp. 115–31.
Werner, Konstantin
1929 *Kremsmunster in Wort und Bild.* Steyr.
Wescher, Paul
1924 "Zur Chronologie der Gemälde des Cornelis Engebrechtsen." *Zeitschrift für bildende Kunst* 58, pp. 96–103.
Weyer, G. J. P.
1852 *Beschreibung des Inhaltes der Sammlung von Gemälden älterer Meister des Heern Johann Peter Weyer in Coeln.* Cologne.
Whinney, Margaret
1968 *Early Flemish Painting.* London.
Wied, Alexander
1994 *Bruegel.* Milan.
1996 "Pieter Bruegel I." In *The Dictionary of Art,* edited by Jane Turner, vol. 4, pp. 894–910. New York.
Wilcox, M.
1920 "Joachim Patinir." *Art and Life* 11, p. 472.
Wilenski, Reginald H.
1960 *Flemish Painters, 1430–1830.* 2 vols. New York.
Will, Robert
1981 "Une peinture murale, datée de 1504, se trouvant jadis en l'église Saint-Guillaume de Strasbourg: Contribution à l'iconographie de saint Bernard." *Cahiers alsaciens d'archéologie d'art et d'histoire* 24, pp. 121–26.

Williams, Robert C.
1980 *Russian Art and American Money, 1900–1940.* Cambridge, Mass.
Williamson, J. H.
1986 "The Meaning of the Mérode Altarpiece." Ph.D. dissertation, Michigan State University, East Lansing.
van der Willigen, A.
1870 *Les artistes de Haarlem: Notices historiques avec un précis sur la gilde de St. Luc.* Haarlem and The Hague.
Wilson, Jean
1983 "The Participation of Painters in the Bruges 'Pandt' Market, 1512–1550." *Burlington Magazine* 125, pp. 476–79.
1986 "Marketing Paintings in Late Medieval Belgium." In *Artistes, artisans, et production artistique au Moyen Âge: Rapports provisoires,* vol. 2, pp. 1759–66. Paris.
1990 "Workshop Patterns and the Production of Paintings in 16th Century Bruges." *Burlington Magazine* 132, pp. 523–27.
1995 "Adriaen Isenbrant and the Problem of His Work." *Oud Holland* 109, pp. 1–17.
1998 *Painting in Bruges at the Close of the Middle Ages: Studies in Society and Visual Culture.* University Park, Pa.
Winkler, Friedrich
1913a "David, Gerard." In *Allgemeines Lexikon der bildenden Künstler von der Antike bis Gegenwart,* edited by Ulrich Thieme and Felix Becker, vol. 8, pp. 452–55. Leipzig.
1913b "Gerard David und die brügger Miniaturmalerei seiner Zeit." *Monatshefte für Kunstwissenschaft* 6, pp. 271–80.
1913c *Der Meister von Flémalle und Rogier van der Weyden: Studien zu ihren Werken und zur Kunst ihrer Zeit mit mehreren Katalogen zu Rogier.* Strasbourg.
1916 "Über verschollene Bilder der Brüder Van Eyck." *Jahrbuch der Königlich Preuszischen Kunstsammlungen* 37, pp. 287–301.
1924 *Die altniederländische Malerei: Die Malerei in Belgien und Holland von 1400–1600.* Berlin.
1928 "An Unknown Portrait of a Woman by Memling." *Apollo* 7 (January), pp. 9–12.
1964 *Das Werk des Hugo van der Goes.* Berlin.
Winston-Allen, Anne
1997 *Stories of the Rose: The Making of the Rosary in the Middle Ages.* University Park: Pennsylvania State University.
Wohl, Hellmut
1980 *The Paintings of Domenico Veneziano, ca. 1410–1461: A Study in Florentine Art of the Early Renaissance.* New York.
Wolff, Martha
1989 "An Image of Compassion: Dieric Bouts's *Sorrowing Madonna.*" *Museum Studies* 15, no. 2, pp. 113–25.
1992 "Juan de Flandes." In *Flemish Paintings in America: A Survey of Early Netherlandish and Flemish Paintings in the Public Collections of North America,* edited by Arnout Balis, Carl Van de Velde, and Hans Vlieghe. Flandria extra muros. Antwerp.
1998 "Flanders." In *The Robert Lehman Collection, II: Fifteenth- to Eighteenth-Century European Paintings, France, Central Europe, Flanders, the Netherlands, Spain, and Great Britain,* by Charles Sterling et al., nos. 12–27. New York.
Wolff-Thomsen, Ulrike
1997 *Jan Joest von Kalkar: Ein niederländischer Maler um 1500.* Schriften der Heresbach-Stiftung Kalkar, 3. Bielefeld.
Wolfthal, Diane
1987 "The Technique of Early Netherlandish Canvases." In *Le dessin sous-jacent dans la peinture: Colloque VI, 1985,* edited by H. Verougstraete-Marcq and R. van Schoute. Louvain-la-Neuve.
1989 *The Beginnings of Netherlandish Canvas Painting, 1400–1530.* Cambridge.
Woltmann, Alfred
1879 "Der heilige Eligius von Petrus Christus." *Repertorium für Kunstwissenschaft* 2, pp. 298–300.
Worcester–Philadelphia
1939 *The Worcester–Philadelphia Exhibition of Flemish Painting.* Exh. cat. Worcester Art Museum; John G. Johnson Collection, Philadelphia Museum of Art. Catalogue by Mr. Marceau, Barbara Sweeny, Perry B. Cott, and Alice Mundt.
Woudhuysen-Keller, Renate
1988 "Gerard David." *Hamilton Kerr Institute Bulletin* 1, pp. 112–13.
Wurzbach, Alfred von
1906–10 *Niederländisches Künstler-Lexikon.* 2 vols. Vienna and Leipzig.
Zeri, Federico
1960 "Un trittico del Maestro della Leggenda di Santa Barbara." *Paragone* 9, no. 125, pp. 41–45.
Zimmermann, Heinrich
1917 "Über eine frühholländische Kreuztragung." *Amtliche Berichte aus den Königlichen Kunstsammlungen* 39 (October), cols. 15–24.

Index of Artists and Works

Note: Pages in italics indicate illustrations.

Index of Former Owners*

*Index refers to catalogued paintings.

Photograph Credits

Most photographs were provided by the owners of the works and are published by their permission. The following are additional credits.

New photography of Metropolitan Museum of Art works by the Photograph Studio, The Metropolitan Museum of Art, New York, Bruce Schwarz, Juan Trujillo, and Susanne Cardone

Alinari/Art Resource, New York: figs. 16, 25, 29
© Jörg P. Anders: figs. 62, 81, 105
Jörg P. Anders/copyright Kupferstichkabinett, SMPK, Berlin: fig. 98
Archivio Fotografico del Comune di Genova-Settore Musei, Genoa: fig. 96
Copyright Bibliothèque Royale Albert Ier, Brussels: frontis., p.22; fig. 41
Copyright © The British Museum: fig. 38
All rights reserved Sterling and Francine Clark Art Insitute/copyright Sterling and Francine Clark Art Insititute: fig. 67
© Ursula Edelmann: fig. 26
Photo Ursula Edelmann: figs. 85, 86
Fotographia Lensini: fig. 30
Copyright The Frick Collection, New York: fig. 14
Copyright Kunsthistorisches Museum, Vienna: fig. 57
Gabinetto Fotografica Nazionale: fig. 27
Giraudon/Art Resource, New York: fig. 84
Giraudon/Art Resource, New York, and Scala/Art Resource, New York: fig. 2
Copyright Anne Gold, Aachen: fig. 55
© President and Fellows, Harvard College, Harvard University Art Museums, Cambridge, Massachusetts: fig. 50
© IRPA-KIK, Brussels: figs. 3, 4, 8, 9, 13, 15, 17
Murray K. Keyes/ © 1998 Board of Trustees, National Gallery of Art, Washington, D.C.: fig. 33
Mas, Barcelona: fig. 110
© Mauritshuis, The Hague: fig. 97
© National Gallery, London: figs. 32, 34, 36, 58, 65
© 1998 Board of Trustees, National Gallery of Art, Washington, D.C.: figs. 22, 44, 99, 112
National Trust Photographic Library/ Upton House (Bearsted Collection)/Angelo Hornak
Rijksdienst voor de Monumentenzorg, Zeist, the Netherlands: fig. 68
© Photo RMN: figs. 39, 69, 93
The Royal Collection © 1998 Her Majesty Queen Elizabeth II: figs. 35, 104
Scala/Art Resource, New York: fig. 18
© Photo Ph. Sebert: fig. 100
Photo Speltdoorn: fig. 103
Walter Steinkopf; composite photo courtesy Musée du Louvre, Paris: fig. 24
Walter Wachter: fig. 40
© Elke Walford: figs. 91, 92